Stephen A. Ross, Mentor

Influence through Generations

Stephen A. Ross, Mentor

Influence through Generations

Edited by Mark Grinblatt

McGraw-Hill Irwin

Boston Burr Ridge, IL Dubuque, IA New York San Francisco St. Louis
Bangkok Bogotá Caracas Kuala Lumpur Lisbon London Madrid Mexico City
Milan Montreal New Delhi Santiago Seoul Singapore Sydney Taipei Toronto

STEPHEN A. ROSS, MENTOR: INFLUENCE THROUGH GENERATIONS

Published by McGraw-Hill/Irwin, a business unit of The McGraw-Hill Companies, Inc., 1221 Avenue of the Americas, New York, NY, 10020.

This book is printed on acid-free paper.

1 2 3 4 5 6 7 8 9 0 QPD/QPD 0 9 8 7

ISBN 978-0-07-336537-4
MHID 0-07-336537-8

Executive editor: *Michele Janicek*
Editorial assistant: *Katherine Mau*
Marketing manager: *Ashley Smith*
Lead project manager: *Christine A. Vaughan*
Production supervisor: *Gina Hangos*
Design manager: *Kami Carter*
Cover image: *© Illustration Works*
Typeface: *10/12 Times Roman*
Compositor: *Aptara*
Printer: *Quebecor World Dubuque Inc.*

www.mhhe.com

The McGraw-Hill/Irwin Series in Finance, Insurance and Real Estate

Stephen A. Ross
Franco Modigliani Professor of Finance and Economics
Sloan School of Management
Massachusetts Institute of Technology
Consulting Editor

FINANCIAL MANAGEMENT

Adair
Excel Applications for Corporate Finance
First Edition

Benninga and Sarig
Corporate Finance: A Valuation Approach

Block and Hirt
Foundations of Financial Management
Twelfth Edition

Brealey, Myers, and Allen
Principles of Corporate Finance
Eighth Edition

Brealey, Myers, and Marcus
Fundamentals of Corporate Finance
Fifth Edition

Brooks
FinGame Online 5.0

Bruner
Case Studies in Finance: Managing for Corporate Value Creation
Fifth Edition

Chew
The New Corporate Finance: Where Theory Meets Practice
Third Edition

Chew and Gillan
Corporate Governance at the Crossroads: A Book of Readings
First Edition

DeMello
Cases in Finance
Second Edition

Grinblatt (editor)
Stephen A. Ross, Mentor: Influence through Generations

Grinblatt and Titman
Financial Markets and Corporate Strategy
Second Edition

Helfert
Techniques of Financial Analysis: A Guide to Value Creation
Eleventh Edition

Higgins
Analysis for Financial Management
Eighth Edition

Kester, Ruback, and Tufano
Case Problems in Finance
Twelfth Edition

Ross, Westerfield, and Jaffe
Corporate Finance
Eighth Edition

Ross, Westerfield, Jaffe, and Jordan
Corporate Finance: Core Principles and Applications
First Edition

Ross, Westerfield, and Jordan
Essentials of Corporate Finance
Fifth Edition

Ross, Westerfield, and Jordan
Fundamentals of Corporate Finance
Eighth Edition

Shefrin
Behavioral Corporate Finance: Decisions That Create Value
First Edition

White
Financial Analysis with an Electronic Calculator
Sixth Edition

INVESTMENTS

Adair
Excel Applications for Investments
First Edition

Bodie, Kane, and Marcus
Essentials of Investments
Sixth Edition

Bodie, Kane, and Marcus
Investments
Seventh Edition

Hirschey and Nofsinger
Investments: Analysis and Behavior
First Edition

Hirt and Block
Fundamentals of Investment Management
Eighth Edition

Jordan and Miller
Fundamentals of Investments: Valuation and Management
Fourth Edition

FINANCIAL INSTITUTIONS AND MARKETS

Rose and Hudgins
Bank Management and Financial Services
Seventh Edition

Rose and Marquis
Money and Capital Markets: Financial Institutions and Instruments in a Global Marketplace
Ninth Edition

Saunders and Cornett
Financial Institutions Management: A Risk Management Approach
Fifth Edition

Saunders and Cornett
Financial Markets and Institutions: An Introduction to the Risk Management Approach
Third Edition

INTERNATIONAL FINANCE

Eun and Resnick
International Financial Management
Fourth Edition

Kuemmerle
Case Studies in International Entrepreneurship: Managing and Financing Ventures in the Global Economy
First Edition

REAL ESTATE

Brueggeman and Fisher
Real Estate Finance and Investments
Thirteenth Edition

Corgel, Ling, and Smith
Real Estate Perspectives: An Introduction to Real Estate
Fourth Edition

Ling and Archer
Real Estate Principles: A Value Approach
Second Edition

FINANCIAL PLANNING AND INSURANCE

Allen, Melone, Rosenbloom, and Mahoney
Retirement Plans: 401(k)s, IRAs, and Other Deferred Compensation Approaches
Tenth Edition

Altfest
Personal Financial Planning
First Edition

Harrington and Niehaus
Risk Management and Insurance
Second Edition

Kapoor, Dlabay, and Hughes
Focus on Personal Finance: An Active Approach to Help You Develop Successful Financial Skills
First Edition

Kapoor, Dlabay, and Hughes
Personal Finance
Eighth Edition

Dedication

Dedicated to Stephen A. Ross, "The Mentor," by all of the contributors to this volume. We are truly grateful for how you have changed our lives.

Gregory Connor

Chester Spatt

Yasushi Hamao

Douglas W. Diamond

[illegible] Huang

Leonid Kogan

Thomas E Copeland

David J. Teece

[illegible]

Mark Grinblatt

Philip H. Dybvig

Guy Huberman

S. Kandel

[illegible]

Anat Admati

Nancy L. Stokey

Foreword

It always begins with a phone call. "Mark, it's Steve Ross. Are you going to the AFA meetings? Are you free for dinner tonight? I'll make reservations..."

If there is any way you can make it, you always do. After all, this is Steve Ross. He has done this for 25 years, dozens of times, grabbing a few hours out of a jet setter's schedule to keep in touch—with you. He always makes the time to stay in touch with former students. Sometimes it is just a simple lunch, or a glass of wine. If wine is involved, it typically is great wine. Occasionally, it is the greatest meal you ever ate.

You always know you are in for a treat. Steve is larger than life. He is part of your intellectual make-up—about who you are and how you think about things. Spending an hour or two with Steve is like reconnecting with a part of yourself. It often is an intellectual discussion about a research project, or some confusion you have about what someone else wrote about a subject that interests you. A couple of sentences from Steve are usually sufficient to straighten out your brain wiring. But the topic of conversation could just as easily be a life lesson about raising your kids or some key decision about your career. It always matters and it almost always changes your life in some small way.

He'll find you, whatever city you are in. Sometimes he'll pick you up in a Porsche he rents or owns. Other times, he'll just drop in to your office for a cafeteria meal. Sometimes it is at a conference in a location like Paris. If a long time has passed, he'll find a way to just make a telephone call—to congratulate you on a book or a paper you wrote, a student you mentored, or an award you received. It always is great wherever the location, whatever the circumstances.

That is Steve. Always positive and encouraging. Always energetic. Always interested in the well-being of former students. It is his attempt to have an impact on a small part of a very large world. But boy does it work. Whenever I have a tough problem, I think of how Steve would attack it, from multiple angles in new and unorthodox ways. When I supervise a grad student, I try to treat him (or her) the way Steve treated me. When I think of the principles that determine good research, Steve's principles, which are always clear and always make sense, are what I turn to for guidance.

I know he does the same thing to connect with others in the field, including a number of colleagues who are contributing to this volume. Irrespective of how that connection was made, these contributors all know he made a difference in their lives and that he still cares about them. Partly for that reason, 27 authors who were influenced by Steve Ross jumped at the opportunity to contribute to this volume. Each chapter contains a reprint of that author's best or most influential article, or one that was particularly influenced by Steve. The articles are organized by institution at which the student made contact with Steve. Each article also is accompanied by a few paragraphs of tribute to the man. Some of these are personal recollections of interactions with Steve. Others use part of the brief essay as an opportunity to trace their article to Steve's intellectual legacy.

Obviously, constraints prevent us from including many deserving articles. Among these are other pieces of enormous influence, written not just by the contributing authors of this volume, but by other well-known academics and practitioners who rightly and proudly claim the same debt to Steve for their success. The debt all of us feel, contributors and noncontributors alike, clearly comes through in the essays. And it is amazing how intimately familiar I was with the emotions and experiences expressed in these essays on reading them for the first time. That is Steve's gift—making everyone feel special and unique during the precious moments we get to spend with him.

The debt of these scholars is also evident from the reprinted articles in this volume, which run the gamut of topics in finance and economics. There are papers on stock market anomalies, market microstructure, performance evaluation, asymmetric information, trading volume, asset pricing theory, banking theory, and corporate finance, to name a few. There are theory articles and empirical articles. Some of the most widely cited and most seminal articles in finance and economics are contained in this volume. Some have won awards, naming them among the most influential articles ever in their field. Also included are articles that some authors felt might ultimately be regarded as their best. Most have already appeared in the very best journals in economics and finance: *The American Economic Review*, *Econometrica*, *Journal of Political Economy*, *Journal of Economic Theory*, *The Review of Economic Studies*, *The Journal of Finance*, *Journal of Financial Economics*, and *The Review of Financial Studies*, among others. Despite this diversity, the papers share one common thread: Steve Ross's hand, thought process, and creativity show in the research philosophy and maturity of the authors in the craft of these articles.

It is clear from the articles and the accompanying commentary that Steve Ross's legacy is more than intellectual. The legacy of Steve Ross also lies in the creation of a community. For some of us, it was apparent that we belonged to that community the moment we started that teacher–student relationship. I, for one, "discovered" Steve Ross thanks to Doug Diamond. "There is a pretty good young professor who has an office at SOM. You should take his course," said Doug. Thanks to Doug, I learned finance from Steve Ross. But I also learned finance from many of the great minds who were influenced by Steve Ross. Students living in New Haven in the late 70s and early 80s included Doug, Paul Pfleiderer, Greg Connor, Anat Admati, Gur Huberman, Chester Spatt, Phil Dybvig, Shmuel Kandel, and John Campbell.

We supported each other back then and maintained a mutual support network throughout the decades. Steve has this legacy and the more permanent legacy that students who came into contact with him tended to foster a love of learning in their students the way Steve fostered a love of learning in them. There are literally hundreds of former students—in academia and business—who can trace their intellectual heritage to Steve.

As a community, no matter what the generation, we are saddened by the passing on of the best and brightest among us. Shmuel Kandel knew he had terminal brain cancer at the time he contributed his essay to this volume. He also knew that he would not live to see its publication. Raymond Chiang never had an opportunity to learn about this volume. Our community knows how much he would have wanted to contribute to this volume and include a piece that he wrote with another Ross student.

One thing that is clearly missing from this volume is any piece co-authored with Stephen Ross. Steve wrote with many of his former students, but it seems appropriate to leave these pieces to a volume of collected works. That volume will clearly demonstrate what most everyone knows about Stephen A. Ross from his writings: that he is an intellectual giant in the field of financial economics and one of the most creative minds of the 20th and 21st centuries.

His incredible intellectual legacy, however, is multiplied many times over by his pedagogy and mentorship. The Ross influence on the field continues with the contributions of three generations of students. Among them are two former presidents of the American Finance Association, five presidents of the Western Finance Association, a former president of the Society for Financial Studies, a Fischer Black Prize Winner, numerous editors, co-editors, and associate editors of major scholarly journals as well as a sizable number of chaired professors and enormously successful finance practitioners.

On behalf of all of us who have had such great fortune in our lives, thank you, Steve, for your generosity, wisdom, and friendship. May your influence continue for many more generations.

Mark Grinblatt
Yale 1982

Contents

Stephen A. Ross, Mentor

Influence through Generations

The University of Pennsylvania Generation

One

Stephen F. LeRoy

Stephen F. LeRoy received a Ph.D. from the University of Pennsylvania in 1971. He started out at the Federal Reserve Bank of Kansas City and now works at the University of California, Santa Barbara. •

Steve Ross's first job was as an assistant professor in the economics department at the University of Pennsylvania, where I was a graduate student. At that time he was interested mostly in international trade, whereas I was interested in finance and macroeconomics, so I didn't see any need then to pay much attention to him. About that decision, the less said the better. Also, I had decided at that time that I had more to learn from the senior faculty than the junior faculty. This attitude is usually a mistake, and it was a spectacular mistake at Penn in those years. Besides Steve, the junior faculty included Tom Sargent, Ed Burmeister, Ed Prescott, Karl Shell, Bob Pollak, and several others of comparable stature. I still remember Tom Cooley telling me about spending hours with Ed Prescott in Smokey Joe's drinking beer, eating peanuts, and talking economics. I never did anything like that.

Some weeks before my defense, my dissertation supervisor asked Steve to serve as the third member of my committee. I don't remember anything about my defense except that I was passed, which was pretty much the only thing I was interested in. I assumed then that my dissertation would be buried in the mists of time, and so it turned out for five years or so. However, some economists came across my dissertation paper and cited it favorably. Steve was aware of this, and he apologized to me for not having read my dissertation more carefully prior to my defense.

I had a very mixed reaction to this: Steve was a junior member of my committee, and he had been added at the last minute. It was clear to me that he had nothing to apologize about. I have been guilty myself of not reading dissertations as carefully as I might have; had I ever apologized to the student in question? I began to realize then that Steve stands out from the crowd at least as much by virtue of his personal qualities as by his intellectual abilities.

After leaving Penn I never worked in the same place as Steve, so I didn't get to know him personally as well as most of those who are writing these reminiscences. His influence on me came more from my reading his papers than from personal contact. More than anything, I learned from Steve's papers to take economic theory completely seriously as a means for learning about the world. Like many younger economists, I started out much more cynical about neoclassical theory than I became subsequently, partly because of spending a lot of time with Steve's papers. These days, when so many scholars are ready to jettison theoretical economics, the lessons one learns from Steve's papers are more important than ever.

I would like to think that Steve's influence on me is most evident in the monograph-text that I wrote with Jan Werner on financial economics. Steve was kind enough to write an introduction for this book, from which I conclude that he shares my estimate of the importance of looking at asset prices from the vantage of equilibrium theory. Like everyone else whose papers appear in this volume, I owe Steve an immense debt of gratitude.

The Present-Value Relation: Tests Based on Implied Variance Bounds[1]

By *Stephen F. LeRoy and Richard D. Porter*[2]

This paper investigates the implications for asset price dispersion of conventional security valuation models. Successively sharper variance bounds on asset prices are derived. Large-sample tests of the bounds are determined and applied to aggregated and disaggregated price and earnings data of U.S. corporations. •

1. Introduction and Summary of Conclusions

Consider a scalar time series $\{x_t\}$ which is generated jointly with a vector time series $\{\underline{z}_t\}$ as a stationary multivariate linear stochastic process. We then may define $\{y_t\}$ as another scalar time series related to $\{x_t\}$ and $\{\underline{z}_t\}$ by

$$y_t = \sum_{j=0}^{n} \beta^j x_t^e(j), \tag{1}$$

where $x_t^e(j)$ denotes $E(x_{t+j}|I_t)$, I_t is the realization of $\{x_t\}$ and $\{\underline{z}_t\}$ up to and including time t, and $\beta < 1$. The multivariate time series $\{x_t, \underline{z}_t\}$ may be labeled the independent-variable series, its distribution being taken as exogenous, and $\{y_t\}$ the dependent-variable series. Equation (1) is the present-value relation. It states that the distribution of the dependent-variable process is related to that of the independent-variable process in such a way that the current realization of the dependent-variable process equals the present discounted expected value of one element of the independent-variable process, $\{x_t\}$, where the expectation is conditional on all information currently available.

The present-value relation is repeatedly encountered in economic theory. The most familiar application is to the theory of stock prices, where $\{x_t\}$ refers to some corporation's earnings, $\{\underline{z}_t\}$ to any variables other than past earnings which are used to predict its future earnings, $\{y_t\}$ to the price of stock, and β to the discount factor.[3] In expectations theories of the term structure of interest rates, the present-value relation also appears (with a finite upper limit in the summation in (1)), although its validity in such applications is based on a linear approximation (Shiller [**15**]). Finally, the permanent income hypothesis of Friedman [**2**] may also be cast in the framework of equation (1).

In Section 2 of the present paper we state and prove three theorems about the variance of the dependent-variable process as it relates to that of the independent-variable process.

---

[1]The analyses and conclusions set forth are those of the authors and do not necessarily indicate concurrence by other members of the research staffs, by the Board of Governors, or by the Federal Reserve Banks.

[2]We wish to thank Evelyn Flynn, Gregory Connor, Juan Perea, and Birch Lee for able assistance and William Barnett, Fischer Black, Christopher Sims, Michael Dooley, Donald Hester, Agustin Maravall, Bennett McCallum, Darrel Parke, David Pierce, William Poole, Jack Rutner, and especially Robert Shiller, and two anonymous referees for helpful criticism. Thanks are also due to Susan Fay Eubank for typing innumerable drafts.

[3]As is well known in the finance literature, the representation of stock prices as the present value of discounted earnings involves double counting if any earnings are retained, since in that case both retained earnings and the revenues generated subsequently by these retentions are counted. However, in our model the maintained hypothesis that earnings are stationary implicitly presumes no retention. In the empirical work examined below an adjustment to the data to correct for earnings retention will be required.

Reprinted with permission:
LeRoy, Stephen F. and Richard Porter. "The Present-Value Relation: Tests Based on Implied Variance Bounds." *Econometrica* 49 (1981): 555–574.

The theorems embody successively sharper restrictions on the parameters of the independent and dependent variable processes. Theorem I asserts that the coefficient of dispersion (i.e., the ratio of the standard deviation to the mean) of $\{y_t\}$ is less than that of $\{x_t\}$. The second theorem involves two new time series $\{\hat{y}_t\}$ and $\{y_t^*\}$ which are generated by altering the amount of information assumed available about the future innovations of $\{x_t\}$ from that implicit in the specified joint distribution of $\{x_t\}$ and $\{\underline{z}_t\}$. If it is assumed that there is no information about the future innovations in $\{x_t\}$, the derived present value series is defined to be $\{\hat{y}_t\}$. On the other hand, if the future innovations in $\{x_t\}$ are taken as known, the derived present value series is labeled $\{y_t^*\}$. The dependent-variable series of primary interest, $\{y_t\}$, is in a sense an intermediate case since the realizations of $\{\underline{z}_t\}$ may be viewed as in general providing some information about the innovations in the univariate process for $\{x_t\}$, but not complete information. Theorem 2 exploits this fact, asserting that the variances of $\{\hat{y}_t\}$ and $\{y_t^*\}$ constitute lower and upper bounds, respectively, on the variance of $\{y_t\}$. Theorem 3, unlike Theorems 1 and 2 which state that the variance of $\{y_t\}$ lies within an interval, is the basis for an asymptotic point test of the null hypothesis defined by the present-value relation. If $\{\pi_t\}$ is defined as the present value of the forecast errors for $\{x_t\}$, we show that $\text{var}(y_t) + \text{var}(\pi_t) = \text{var}(y_t^*)$. Theorem 3 asserts that the three terms of this variance decomposition can all be estimated from observations on x_t and y_t and, therefore, forms the basis for a large-sample test of the present-value equation.

These theorems furnish a basis for constructing tests of the validity of the present-value relation. Such theorems are necessary because the present-value relation cannot be tested directly without also specifying the variables $\underline{z}_t$ used to predict x_t and then determining the joint distribution of $\{x_t, \underline{z}_t\}$, since in the absence of such a procedure the $x_t^e(j)$ are not measurable. Consequently, direct tests of the present-value relation are always conditional on the specification of the set of variables used to predict x_t, and the difficulty of specifying these variables exhaustively greatly weakens the plausibility of any conclusions based on such direct tests. By contrast, our three theorems are valid for general specifications of the joint distribution of $\{x_t, \underline{z}_t\}$, and do not require identification of the distribution of $\{x_t, \underline{z}_t\}$, or even specification of what the variables $\underline{z}_t$ are. Thus even though we do not measure the expectations $x_t^e(j)$ or the discounted forecast errors π_t, our theorems constitute testable implications of the present-value relation. The fact that the maintained assumptions required for our indirect tests are so much weaker than those required for the direct tests adds to the appeal of our results. Statistical tests of the three theorems are derived in Section 3.

In Section 4 we consider the application of our results to the theory of stock prices. First it is shown that the efficient capital markets hypothesis as conventionally formulated implies (and is implied by) the present-value relation between earnings and stock prices. Consequently, the hypothesis of capital market efficiency implies the validity of the theorems, and the latter may therefore be used to construct tests of market efficiency. That capital market efficiency implies restrictions on the volatility of stock prices is at first surprising because the most commonly-cited implication of market efficiency is that stock prices should move instantaneously rather than gradually in response to news. However, the result that if markets are efficient the coefficient of dispersion of stock prices should be less than that of earnings (Theorem 1) makes sense if it is observed that the present-value equation defines stock prices as a kind of weighted average of earnings, and an average is generally less volatile than its components. Another consideration strengthens this conclusion. Since stock prices are an average of expected rather than actual earnings, and since expected earnings can plausibly be assumed to regress toward a mean (correcting for trend) in the increasingly distant future, it follows that expected earnings should show less dispersion than actual earnings, further reducing the anticipated dispersion of stock prices.

Our first data set is based on Standard & Poor's Composite Index of stock prices and the related earnings and dividends series. The observations are quarterly over the interval 1955 to 1973, and the data are corrected for trend.[4] The estimated coefficients of dispersion of earnings and stock prices are 0.172 and 0.452, indicating that the inequality of Theorem 1 is contradicted (Table III). The point estimates on which the tests of Theorems 2 and 3 are based imply an even more flagrant violation of the model; for example, the estimated variance of y_t is 4.89, whereas the estimated variance of y_t^*, which theoretically should exceed that of y_t, is 0.255. These results, while dramatic, are difficult to interpret in the absence of any indication of the reliability of the test statistics. To provide such an indication, we calculated formal tests based on the asymptotic distribution of the parameter estimates, as described in Section 3. Because the test statistics measuring departures from the null hypothesis are all insignificant, the derived confidence intervals suggest that our statistical tests may have very little power.

The outcome of these tests may reflect the fact that they are based on aggregate data, whereas the theory applies to individual firms; a simple argument (presented in detail in Section 2) demonstrates the possible existence of bias in our tests due to aggregation error across firms. If the earnings of each firm consist of a common factor and an individual uncorrelated term, and if the common factor is forecastable whereas the individual term is not, then our tests will be biased in favor of rejection of market efficiency. In the reverse case, our tests will be biased in favor of acceptance. We do not know which case, if either, is more plausible than the intermediate case under which these biases approximately cancel, but the example provides strong motivation to examine data for individual firms. We collected quarterly earnings and price data for three large corporations—American Telephone & Telegraph, General Electric, and General Motors—then adjusted them for trend in the same way as the aggregate data, and calculated the test statistics for the three theorems.

The empirical results for the firm data show, as might be expected, that sharper hypotheses are more often rejected than blunt hypotheses. The point estimates for the tests of Theorem 1 were somewhat closer to being consistent with the null hypothesis of market efficiency for the individual firms than for the aggregate data. For one firm (GM) the coefficient of dispersion of earnings exceeded that of stock prices, as implied by the theory, while for another (GE) the two were virtually identical. Only AT&T was similar to the aggregate data in that earnings were considerably less volatile than stock prices, although for AT&T as with the aggregate data the test statistic did not allow rejection of the null hypothesis of Theorem 1 at the usual significance levels. Contrary to the implication of Theorem 2, however, the variance of y_t exceeded that of y_t^* by a wide margin for each of the three firms as with the aggregate data. Further, the relevant test statistic was significant for one firm (GE) and of borderline significance for another (GM), although it was insignificant for the third (AT&T). Finally, the test statistics for the more restrictive Theorem 3 all indicated rejection of the null hypothesis at the one per cent level.

Comparison of the results for the three firms with those for the Standard & Poor's series gives no clear reason to suspect that aggregation over firms biases aggregate tests either way, although, of course, this conclusion is not unequivocal since the Standard & Poor's series cannot be viewed as a simple aggregate of the three firms alone. As with the aggregate data, the point estimates for the firms are not consistent with the efficient markets model, although they are somewhat closer to those expected from theory than those

[4]For a detailed description of the data, the complete derivation of the statistical tests, and for the data themselves, see LeRoy and Porter [**9**]; this paper is available upon request from the authors.

for the aggregate data. However, the confidence intervals for the firms are more prone to indicate rejection of the null hypothesis; the smaller confidence regions for the firm data suggest that tests based on firm data may be somewhat more powerful than those for aggregate data.

We see that based on both aggregated and disaggregated data, stock prices appear to be more volatile than is consistent with the efficient capital markets model. This conclusion differs from that of most studies of market efficiency, such as that of Fama [**1**]. In many studies of market efficiency, it is observed that the martingale assumption requires that measured rates of return be serially uncorrelated; consequently, the efficient capital markets model may be tested by determining whether it is possible to reject the joint hypothesis that all the autocorrelations of rates of return are zero. Typically this null hypothesis cannot be rejected at the usual significance levels; we show this to be the case also for the rates of return earned on the stock of our three firms. Since these tests of the nonautocorrelatedness of rates of return are derivable consequences of the same model used to generate our variance restrictions, we are led to inquire why the nonautocorrelatedness implication is apparently satisfied, whereas the variance implications are not. Although it is possible that the difference in the outcomes of the dispersion and autocorrelation tests is due to differing sensitivity to specification or measurement error, an explanation that appears more attractive to us is that the dispersion tests have greater power than the autocorrelation tests against the hypothesis of market efficiency, given that alternative hypothesis which actually generated the data. This argument suggests that a promising way to investigate the stock market would be to ascertain what kinds of structures in earnings and prices would lead to deviations from market efficiency that would be more readily detected by a dispersion test than by an autocorrelation test. We have not yet pursued this line, however.

It is not clear how to interpret our rejection of the hypothesis we have characterized as "market efficiency." It should be recognized that our theorems are actually tests of a joint hypothesis, some elements of which have only tenuous support. The most important elements in our joint hypothesis are (i) the present-value relation (or, in the stock market application, the equivalent martingale assumption), (ii) the assumption that the real conditional expected rate of return on stock is constant over time, and (iii) the assumption of rational expectations. If our tests are not subject to econometric or measurement difficulties, then our rejection of the theorems implies that one or more of these elements of the joint hypothesis must be rejected. There is no reason to doubt that with further work it will be possible to distinguish which of the components of the rejected joint hypothesis must be revised.

In an important recent paper, Shiller [**16**] has independently derived and conducted tests of expectations models of the term structure of interest rates based on implied restrictions on the admissible dispersion of long rates relative to short. These restrictions are similar to our Theorems 1 and 2; in addition, Shiller obtained some important frequency-domain implications of the model. Although Shiller's tests, unlike ours, are based on point estimates rather than confidence intervals, implying that there is no way to determine statistical significance, he finds that the expectations model of the term structure appears to be violated, long rates being too volatile relative to short rates. The fact that Shiller's results on interest rates so closely parallel ours on stock prices suggests that neither set of results can be dismissed as a statistical accident. Rather, in our view, the fact that asset prices appear to fluctuate more than is consistent with most financial models in current use should be regarded as a major challenge to those models. As yet, however, it is impossible to determine what changes in financial theory may turn out to be necessary to accommodate our results and those of Shiller.

2. Three Theorems on the Variance of the Dependent-Variable Process[5]

It is assumed that the $p \times 1$ vector $\{x_t, \underline{z}_t\}$ follows a multivariate linearly regular stationary stochastic process:

$$\begin{bmatrix} x_t \\ \underline{z}_t \end{bmatrix} = \underline{c} + \underline{\epsilon}_t + D_1\underline{\epsilon}_{t-1} + D_2\underline{\epsilon}_{t-2} + \cdots = \underline{c} + D(B)\underline{\epsilon}_t, \tag{2}$$

where the innovations sequence $\{\underline{\epsilon}_t\}$ is a set of serially uncorrelated vector random variables with zero mean and positive definite covariance matrix Σ, where $\underline{c}$ is a $p \times 1$ vector, the D_t are square matrices of order p, and where B is the lag operator, defined by $B^j\underline{\epsilon}_t = \underline{\epsilon}_{t-j}$.[6] If we delete all but the first element of the vector equation (2), we obtain

$$x_t = c + \underline{\delta}'_0\,\underline{\epsilon}_t + \underline{\delta}'_1\,\underline{\epsilon}_{t-1} + \cdots = c + \underline{\delta}'(B)\underline{\epsilon}_i, \tag{3}$$

where c is the first element of $\underline{c}$ and $\underline{\delta}'_i$ is the first row of D_t.[7] We incur no loss of generality by ignoring the distribution of $\underline{z}$ since the information content of current and past values of $\underline{z}$ is contained in the current and past values of $\underline{\epsilon}$, which are known. The conditional expected future values of x are given by

$$x^e_t(j) = c + \underline{\delta}'_j\underline{\epsilon}_t + \underline{\delta}'_{j+1}\underline{\epsilon}_{t-1} + \cdots. \tag{4}$$

In general, the forecasts $x^e_t(j)$ depend on the $\underline{z}_t$ as well as the x_t, since both are needed to construct the lagged $\underline{\epsilon}_t$. In this case the series $\{\underline{z}_t\}$ is said to be a leading indicator of $\{x_t\}$, in Pierce's [**11**] usage; see also Granger [**3**]. In the special case in which all the elements of $\underline{\delta}_j$ are zero except the first, efficient forecasts of $\{x_t\}$ can be constructed from past realizations of $\{x_t\}$ alone since in that case $\{\underline{z}_t\}$ is not a leading indicator of $\{x_t\}$. In this special case $\underline{\epsilon}_t$ and $\underline{\delta}_j$ can be taken as scalars without loss of generality. More generally, when $\underline{z}_t$ is a leading indicator of x_t, we can express the dependent-variable series in terms of the (vector) innovations in the independent-variable series. By substituting (4) into (1), it is easily verified that we have

$$y_t = \frac{c}{1-\beta} + \sum_{j=0}^{\infty}\left[\sum_{k=j}^{\infty}\beta^{k-j}\,\underline{\delta}'_k\right]\underline{\epsilon}_{t-j} \equiv \frac{c}{1-\beta} + \underline{a}'(B)\underline{\epsilon}_t, \tag{5}$$

where $\underline{a}'_j = \sum_{k=j}^{\infty}\beta^{k-j}\underline{\delta}'_k$.

We now state and prove the three theorems restricting the variance of $\{y_t\}$.

THEOREM 1: *The coefficient of dispersion of $\{y_t\}$ is less than that of $\{x_t\}$ for any distribution obeying* (2).

The proof of Theorem 1 is most conveniently presented later. At this point, it is useful to consider a special case in order to render Theorem 1 as intuitive as possible. Suppose that $\{\underline{z}_t\}$ is not a leading indicator of $\{x_t\}$ and that $\{x_t\}$ is distributed by a first-order autoregressive process,

$$x_t - c = \phi(x_{t-1} - c) + \epsilon_t, \qquad |\phi| < 1,$$

which has the moving-average representation

$$x_t = c + \epsilon_t + \phi\epsilon_{t-1} + \phi^2\epsilon_{t-2} + \cdots.$$

[5]In the remainder of this paper we let the upper limit (n) in the summation in (1) be infinite, as is appropriate for application to the stock market.

[6]$D(B) = D_0 + D_1B + D_2B^2 + \cdots$, with $D_0 = I$.

[7]That is, $\delta(B) = \underline{\delta}_0 + \underline{\delta}_1B + \underline{\delta}_2B^2 + \cdots$ where $\underline{\delta}'_0 = (1,0,0,\ldots,0)$. See Rozanov [**12**] or Hannan [**4**] for a general discussion of the statistical properties of (2).

It is easily verified that the ratio of the coefficients of dispersion takes the simple form

$$\frac{CD(y_t)}{CD(x_t)} = \frac{1 - \beta}{1 - \beta\phi}, \tag{6}$$

which is always less than one since β is bounded by zero and one. Equation (6) shows that the lower ϕ is and the higher β is, the lower will be the ratio of the coefficients of dispersion. The reason is that if ϕ is near zero, expected x_t regresses rapidly toward the trend value c, which means that y_t is approximately equal to current x_t plus the discounted value of a series of constants. The addition of constants to x_t raises the mean of y_t without increasing its standard deviation, thereby lowering its coefficient of dispersion. Similarly, if β is near 1, relatively more weight is given to future expected x_t than to current x_t, compared to the case when β is near zero. Since for any value of ϕ expected future x_t has less dispersion than current x_t, the effect of larger values of β is to lower the ratio of the coefficients of dispersion.

Depending on the actual distribution of $\{x_t\}$, the test implied by Theorem 1 may not be very powerful statistically. Thus, if β is near one in the population and the distribution of $\{x_t\}$ incorporates strong damping, the efficient markets model might imply that the coefficient of dispersion of $\{y_t\}$ is a small fraction of that of $\{x_t\}$, say, one-quarter. In that case, the test implied by Theorem 1 that the ratio of coefficients of dispersion is less than unity would with high probability indicate acceptance of the null hypothesis even when it should be rejected (for example, if in the population the ratio of coefficients of dispersion were 1/2 or 3/4). Again, it is impossible to test this conjecture directly without knowledge of the joint distribution of $\{x_t\}$ and $\{\underline{z}_t\}$. We seek to derive restrictions on the dispersion of $\{y_t\}$ stronger than those implied by Theorem 1, but still without specifying the distribution of $\{\underline{z}_t\}$.

To do so we observe that so far we have used only one function of the parameters of the marginal distribution of $\{x_t\}$: its coefficient of dispersion. It might be expected that stronger restrictions on the behavior of $\{y_t\}$ could be derived if all the parameters of the distribution of $\{x_t\}$ were employed. To show that this is in fact possible we consider once again the general leading indicator case under which there exist variables $\underline{z}_t$ which figure in the forecasts of future x_t, but which do not predict x_t perfectly. Now fix the marginal distribution of $\{x_t\}$ and consider two polar cases: one under which there exist variables $\underline{z}_t$ which in addition to past x_t allow perfect forecasting of x_t, and the other in which $\{\underline{z}_t\}$ is not a leading indicator of $\{x_t\}$ (i.e., in which there are no variables other than lagged x_t which assist in the forecasting of future x_t). Define $\{y_t^*\}$ and $\{\hat{y}_t\}$ as the series generated when the present-value relation operates on $\{x_t\}$ in each of these cases, and note that the distributions of these hypothetical price variables, unlike that of $\{y_t\}$, are completely determined by the marginal distribution of $\{x_t\}$.

THEOREM 2: *When $\underline{z}_t$ is a leading indicator of $\{x_t\}$ the coefficient of dispersion of $\{y_t\}$ is greater than or equal to that of $\{\hat{y}_t\}$, and less than that of $\{y_t^*\}$.*[8]

Theorem 2 gives bounds on the variance of any series $\{y_t\}$ that is generated by some joint distribution of x_t and $\underline{z}_t$, and these bounds can be calculated from the marginal distribution of

[8] As Singleton [**18**] observed, the proof to follow applies without modification in the case when y_t is given by

$$\sum_{k=1}^{k} \sum_{J=0}^{\infty} \beta_k^j x_{kt}^e(j), \tag{1'}$$

that is, when y_t is the sum of K terms of the form of (1). Since this vector extension is immediate, our proof is restricted to the case $K = 1$. Note also that in economic applications of the present-value relation discussed in this paper, equation (1) is sufficiently general.

$\{x_t\}$ alone, implying that, as required, the general leading indicator case be tested without actually estimating the joint distribution of $\{x_t\}$ and $\{\underline{z}_t\}$.

The proof of Theorem 2 is direct. By definition, y_t^* is expressible as

$$y_t^* = x_t + \beta x_{t+1} + \beta^2 x_{t+2} + \cdots. \tag{7}$$

Now define π_t, the discounted value of forecast errors, as

$$\pi_t = \sum_{j=1}^{\infty} \beta^j (x_{t+j} - x_t^e(j)), \tag{8}$$

where the $x_t^e(j)$ are the forecasts made under the general leading indicator model, as before. Then we have

$$y_t^* = y_t + \pi_t.$$

Now y_t depends only on the innovations in x_t and $\underline{z}_t$ up to and including period t, while π_t depends only on the innovations occurring after period t. Accordingly, they are statistically independent, and we have

$$\text{var}(y_t^*) = \text{var}(y_t) + \text{var}(\pi_t). \tag{9}$$

Equation (9) shows that the higher the variance of the discounted sum of forecast errors, the lower the variance of $\{y_t\}$. Consequently, the variance of $\{y_t^*\}$ provides an upper bound for the variance of $\{y_t\}$. Also, assuming as throughout that the information set always contains at least the past history of $\{x_t\}$, the variance of $\{\hat{y}_t\}$ furnishes a lower bound for the variance of $\{y_t\}$, since the presence of forecasting variables $\underline{z}_t$ in the information set can never increase the variance of discounted forecasting errors. Stating this conclusion in terms of coefficients of dispersion, we have

$$CD(\hat{y}_t) \leqslant CD(y_t) < CD(y_t^*).$$

Note that the right-hand side strict inequality follows from the fact that the model is one in which uncertainty cannot be entirely eliminated.

We are now in a position to prove Theorem 1. By virtue of Theorem 2, it is sufficient to show that the coefficient of dispersion of $\{y_t^*\}$ is less than that of $\{x_t\}$. But that result may be developed directly from equation (7). We have

$$\text{var}(y_t^*) = E[(x_t - c) + \beta(x_{t+1} - c) + \beta^2(x_{t+2} - c) + \cdots]^2$$

or

$$\text{var}(y_t^*) = \frac{1}{1-\beta^2}[\gamma_x(0) + 2\beta\gamma_x(1) + 2\beta^2\gamma_x(2) + \cdots], \tag{10}$$

where $y_x(i) \equiv$ covariance (x_t, x_{t-i}) for all t. From the Cauchy-Schwartz inequality and stationarity, $\gamma_x(i) < \gamma_x(0)$ if $i > 0$, so

$$\text{var}(y_t^*) < \gamma_x(0)\left[\frac{1}{1-\beta^2} + \frac{2\beta}{(1-\beta)(1-\beta^2)}\right] = \frac{\gamma_x(0)}{(1-\beta)^2}. \tag{11}$$

From (11) it follows immediately that

$$\frac{\sqrt{\gamma_y^*(0)}}{c/(1-\beta)} < \frac{\sqrt{\gamma_x(0)}}{c}.$$

THEOREM 3: *When $\{\underline{z}_t\}$ is a leading indicator of $\{x_t\}$, the variance of $\{y_t^*\}$ is equal to the variance of $\{y_t\}$ plus the variance of $\{\pi_t\}$, the discounted forecast error. Further, all these variances may be estimated directly using only measurements on $\{x_t\}$ and $\{y_t\}$.*[9]

We have already proved the first part of Theorem 3 (see equation (9)). Thus the significant assertion of Theorem 3 is that equation (9) may be used to construct a point test of the efficient markets model which can be applied without specifying the variables $\underline{z}_t$ and estimating their joint distribution with x_t. This is not obvious since the forecasts $x_t^e(j)$ which are used to calculate the π_t are not directly observable, nor can they be calculated without knowledge of the joint distribution of $\{\underline{z}_t\}$ and $\{x_t\}$. However, it happens that even though π_t is not directly observable, its variance can be calculated from the distribution of $\{x_t\}$ and $\{y_t\}$ alone, and this is the content of Theorem 3.

To show this, substitute (3) and (4) into (8) to obtain

$$\pi_t = \beta\underline{\delta}_0'\underline{\epsilon}_{t+1} + \beta^2(\underline{\delta}_0'\underline{\epsilon}_{t+2} + \underline{\delta}_1'\underline{\epsilon}_{t+1}) + \beta^3(\underline{\delta}_0'\underline{\epsilon}_{t+3} + \underline{\delta}_1'\underline{\epsilon}_{t+2} + \underline{\delta}_2'\underline{\epsilon}_{t+1}) + \cdots.$$

Collecting terms, squaring, and taking expectations gives

$$\text{var}(\pi_t) = \frac{\beta^2\underline{a}_0'\Sigma\underline{a}_0}{1-\beta^2}, \tag{12}$$

where $\underline{a}_0$ is as defined in (5). Although $\underline{a}_0$ is not directly estimable, its weighted length is. Equation (5) may be used to derive

$$\underline{a}_0'\underline{\epsilon}_{t+1} = y_{t+1} + \frac{x_t - y_t}{\beta}, \tag{13}$$

from which we calculate an expression for $\underline{a}_0'\Sigma\underline{a}_0$:

$$\underline{a}_0'\Sigma\underline{a}_0 = \text{var}[y_{t+1} + 1/\beta(x_t - y_t)]. \tag{14}$$

Since Σ is positive definite, $\text{var}(\pi_t) > 0$. Combining equations (12) and (14), we have

$$\text{var}(\pi_t) = \frac{\text{var}(\beta y_{t+1} + x_t - y_t)}{1-\beta^2} \tag{15}$$

which is directly measurable. Since the variances of $\{\hat{y}_t\}$ and $\{y_t^*\}$ are functions of β and a univariate representation for $\{x_t\}$, they are, of course, directly estimable from observations on x_t and y_t.[10]

The theorems just proved apply to individual firms; can they be tested on cross-section averages? A simple example[11] shows that aggregation bias may be a problem, depending on the covariance of x_{it} among firms and on the assumption made about the forecastability of x_{it}. Suppose that x_{it} depends linearly on a common factor z_t, which is perfectly forecastable, and a white noise term w_{it}:

$$x_{it} = \alpha(z_t + w_{it}).$$

---

[9]Singleton [**18**] also obtained a vector extension of Theorem 3; see footnote 8 supra. His extension, however, assumes that the $\beta_k(k = 1, 2, \ldots K)$ are known, whereas in our model β is estimable.

[10]Observe that $E(x_t) = c$ and $E(y_t) = c/(1-\beta)$ so that β may be readily estimated from the means of the two observed processes.

[11]We are indebted to a referee for this example.

Further, suppose that w_{it} is independent across firms, is independent of z_t, has common variance across firms, and is not forecastable. Since the forecastable component of each x_{it} is identical across firms, we have $CD(y_t) = CD(y_{it})$ for all i, as is readily verified. However, upon aggregation, the cancellation of the white noise terms, w_{it}, implies that $CD(y_t^*) < CD(y_{it}^*)$ for all i. If $CD(y_t^*)$ were viewed as an estimate of $CD(y_{it}^*)$, it would be biased toward zero, and a test of the null hypothesis, $CD(y_{it}) < CD(y_{it}^*)$ based on the inequality $CD(y_t) < CD(y_t^*)$ would be biased toward rejection. More generally, the example suggests that our tests will be biased toward rejection if the common component of x_{it} is more forecastable than the independent components. We do not know if this assumption is more reasonable than its opposite, in which case our tests are biased toward acceptance. However, since we do not wish to prejudge the question by presuming that the two components are equally forecastable, as must be implicitly assumed under tests based on aggregated data, we are motivated to conduct our tests on both disaggregated and aggregated data, and thereby to avoid the issue of aggregation error.

3. Test Statistics

The three theorems developed in Section 2 impose nonlinear restrictions on the expected value and autocovariance function of the bivariate process for x_t and y_t. To restate these restrictions in a way that is convenient for testing, we first define

$$\gamma_{xy}(k) = E[(x_t - c)(y_{t-k} - c/(1-\beta))] \tag{16}$$

for $k = 0, \pm 1, \pm 2$, and so forth. Theorem 1 states that

$$f_1 > 0, \tag{17}$$

where

$$f_1 = \frac{[\gamma_x(0)]^{1/2}}{c} - \frac{[\gamma_y(0)]^{1/2}}{c/(1-\beta)}. \tag{18}$$

Theorem 3 imposes the restriction

$$f_3 = 0, \tag{19}$$

where

$$\begin{aligned} f_3 &= \gamma_y^*(0) - \gamma_y(0) - \gamma_\pi(0) \\ &= \frac{1}{1-\beta^2}\left[\gamma_x(0) + 2\sum_{j=l}^{\infty}\beta^j\gamma_x(j)\right] - \gamma_y(0) \\ &\quad - \frac{1}{1-\beta^2}[(1+\beta^2)\gamma_y(0) + \gamma_x(0) + 2\beta\gamma_{xy}(-1) - 2\beta\gamma_y(1) - 2\gamma_{xy}(0)], \end{aligned} \tag{20}$$

in view of (10) and (15). The upper bound in Theorem 2 may be written as

$$f_2^u > 0, \tag{21}$$

where

$$\begin{aligned} f_2^u &= \frac{[\gamma_{y^*}(0)]^{1/2}}{c/(1-\beta)} - \frac{[\gamma_y(0)]^{1/2}}{c/(1-\beta)} \\ &= \frac{(1-\beta)}{c(1-\beta^2)^{1/2}}\left[\gamma_x(0) + \sum_{k=1}^{\infty} 2\beta^k\gamma_x(k)\right]^{1/2} - \frac{[\gamma_y(0)]^{1/2}}{c/(1-\beta)}. \end{aligned} \tag{22}$$

Finally, the lower bound restriction in Theorem 2 is

(23) $$f_2^l \geqslant 0,$$

where

(24) $$f_2^l = \frac{[\gamma_y(0)]^{1/2}}{c/(1-\beta)} - \frac{[\gamma_{\hat{y}}(0)]^{1/2}}{c/(1-\beta)}$$

and

$$\gamma_{\hat{y}}(0) = \sum_{j=0}^{\infty}\left[\sum_{k=j}^{\infty}\beta^{k-j}b_k\right]^2\sigma_v^2$$

where σ_v^2 and $b(B)(= 1 + b_1B + b_2B^2 + \cdots)$ may be obtained by factoring the autocovariance generating function of $\{x_t\}$.[12]

Large-sample tests of the nonlinear restrictions in (17), (19), (21), and (23) on the functions in (18), (20), (22), and (24), respectively, may be constructed in a straightforward manner. First, a bivariate stationary and invertible ARMA representation for x and y is specified.[13] To estimate the ARMA model parameters, Wilson's **[20]** quasi-maximum likelihood algorithm is used except that the means are estimated first and then treated as if they are known.[14] The form of the estimated model is thus

$$\begin{bmatrix}\phi_{11}(B) & \phi_{12}(B)\\ \phi_{21}(B) & \phi_{22}(B)\end{bmatrix}\begin{bmatrix}x_t - \bar{x}\\ y_t - \bar{y}\end{bmatrix} = \begin{bmatrix}\theta_{11}(B) & \theta_{12}(B)\\ \theta_{21}(B) & \theta_{22}(B)\end{bmatrix}\underline{\zeta}_t,$$

where $\phi_{ij}(B)$ and $\theta_{ij}(B)$ are polynomials of order p_{ij} and q_{ij}, respectively,

$$\phi_{ij}(B) = k_{ij} - \sum_{s=1}^{p_{ij}}\phi_{ij,s}B^s,$$

$$\theta_{ij}(B) = k_{ij} - \sum_{s=1}^{q_{ij}}\theta_{ij,s}B^s,$$

$k_{ij} = 1$ if $i = j$ and is 0 otherwise, and $\{\underline{\zeta}_t\}$ is a set of serially uncorrelated bivariate random variables with zero mean and covariance matrix V. Let $\underline{\omega}$ be the vector of ARMA parameters (including intercepts and distinct elements of V) with $\hat{\underline{\omega}}$ denoting the estimate of $\underline{\omega}$. Under general conditions $\hat{\underline{\omega}}$ is asymptotically normally distributed with mean $\underline{\omega}$ and covariance matrix Ω.[15] Next, given $\hat{\underline{\omega}}$ and an estimate of Ω, the associated function $f_i(\underline{\omega})$, i.e., the functions in (18), (20), (22), and (24), and its asymptotic standard error may be evaluated. Since each of the test functions, f_i, is continuous, the ratio of $f_i(\hat{\underline{\omega}})$ to its

[12]That is, σ_v^2 and $b(B)$ are solutions to

$$\sigma_v^2 b(B)b(B^{-1}) = \sum_{j=-\infty}^{\infty}\gamma_x(j)B^j.$$

[13]See Wilson [**19** and **20**] for a description of multiple ARMA models. From (3) and (5) it will be seen that the bivariate process for y and x is a linear regular stationary process so that there exists an infinite order moving average representation (Wold decomposition). We assume that this representation can be approximated by a finite parameter bivariate ARMA representation; see Sims [**17**] for a proof that rational functions provide a mean square approximation to such linear regular processes. We also assume that under the alternative hypothesis, x and y are generated by a linear regular process which can be approximated as under the null hypothesis by a finite parameter ARMA model.

[14]Wilson's procedure maximizes the logarithm of the likelihood function under a normality assumption concerning the error, neglecting effects of initial conditions. The sample means x and y are used to estimate the population means c and $c/(1 - \beta)$, respectively.

[15]See LeRoy and Porter [**9**] for a detailed examination of the conditions and our estimate of the Ω based on $\hat{\omega}$. We assume that the fourth cumulants of ζ_t are zero in estimating the covariance matrix of V.

estimated asymptotic standard error will have a $N(0, 1)$ distribution under the null hypothesis. That is,

$$\sqrt{T}\,(f_i(\hat{\underline{\omega}}) - f_i(\underline{\omega})) \rightarrow N\,(0, \underline{j}_i^{\prime}\Omega\,\underline{j}_i),$$

where

$$\underline{j}_i = \frac{\partial f_i(\underline{\omega})}{\partial \underline{\omega}}$$

and T denotes the sample size.

4. Application to the Efficient Markets Model of Stock Prices

The efficient markets model may be characterized by the restriction that the (real) rate of return on stock $\{r_t\}$ is a time series obeying the relation

$$E(r_t \mid I_t) = \rho \tag{25}$$

for all I_t, where ρ is a positive constant. This relation is the basis for most empirical tests of market efficiency, since it implies that no information contained in I_t is of any assistance in predicting future expected rates of return.[16] The analytical justification for identifying such a restriction with some economic notion of market efficiency, such as Pareto-optimal resource allocation or costless dissemination of information, is not immediate. This point is not pursued here; see, however, LeRoy [**6, 7, 8**], Lucas [**10**], Rubinstein [**13**], and Woodward [**21**] for discussion. If all (real) earnings on stock x_t are paid out in dividends and the payout is assumed to occur at the beginning of the period, the rate of return is

$$r_t = \frac{y_{t+1}}{y_t - x_t} - 1, \tag{26}$$

where y_t is the (real) price of stock. Taking expectations conditional on I_t and using (25), this becomes

$$y_t = x_t + \frac{y_t^e(1)}{1 + \rho}.$$

Repeating this procedure and assuming convergence, we obtain the present-value relation (1), with $\beta = (1 + \rho)^{-1}$.[17]

[16] In Fama's review article on the efficient capital markets theory [**1**], the efficient markets model when $\{\underline{z}_t\}$ is a leading indicator of x_t is termed the semi-strong-form constant-return model, while the case in which $\underline{z}_t$ is the empty set is called the weak-form constant return model. In his context, the terminology is appropriate since it appears to be natural to view a model in which the expected return is constant conditional on the broader set of information as involving a stronger restriction on reality. Here, however, these usages would be misleading since in fact neither model is generally a special case of the other. Further, we will derive results that apply over all multivariate stationary earnings distributions, and therefore a fortiori over all distributions in which $\underline{z}_t$ is not a leading indicator. Thus in Fama's terminology, some of our weak-form results follow as a special case of the strong-form results. We see that Fama's definition, while analytically equivalent to our usage, would be misleading in the present context.

[17] This argument, of course, does no more than motivate the connection between equation (25) defining an efficient capital market and the present-value relation. A formal derivation is found in Samuelson [**14**]. Note that even though under certainty the present-value relation is an immediate consequence of the definition of the rate of return, under uncertainty the strong restriction (25) on the distribution of rates of return is required in order to derive the present-value relation from the definition of the rate of return. Under general conditions of uncertainty (i.e., without assuming (25)), the present-value relation does not obtain.

The fact that stock prices are expressible as the present value of expected earnings means that the theorems derived in Section 2 are consequences of capital market efficiency as defined by (25). These results provide insights into the functions of capital markets that are interesting and not altogether obvious. For example, Theorem 1 says that the coefficient of dispersion of stock prices is necessarily less than that of earnings; this fact was noted and interpreted in the introduction. Additionally, equations (9), (13), and (15) show that the greater the accuracy with which individuals are able to forecast earnings, the higher the variance of stock prices, but the lower the variance of the rate of return on stock. These results are surprisingly powerful considering the generality with which the distribution of earnings has been specified. However, our primary interest is in constructing statistical tests of market efficiency, and not in providing extended interpretation of the properties of efficient markets, so we turn now to the empirical implementation.

Earnings and price data for Standard & Poor's Composite Index, AT&T, GE, and GM were assembled, and an attempt was made to correct for trends induced by inflation and earnings retention.[18] The question remains whether the resulting series can be assumed to obey the stationarity requirement. There appears to be some evidence of downward trends, although they are not clearly significant. We have decided to neglect such evidence and simply assume that the series are stationary since otherwise it is necessary to address such difficult questions as ascertaining to what degree stockholders can be assumed to have foreseen the assumed trend in earnings. It seems preferable to assume instead that there exist long cycles in the earnings series, implying that a sample of only a few decades may well appear nonstationary. On this interpretation, no correction for nonstationarity is indicated, but we must expect that, as with any statistical test based on a small sample, high Type II error will occur. We do not argue that this treatment is entirely adequate, nor do we in any way minimize the problem of nonstationarity; the dependence of our results on the assumption of stationarity is probably their single most severe limitation.

Table I presents the bivariate ARMA estimates for the four different data sets as well as the large-sample standard errors.[19] Table II shows the chi-square statistics $C(i, j)$ for the overall adequacy of the bivariate model.[20] The results in Table II suggest that the overall specification is adequate. The lefthand panel of Table III displays estimates of the four

---

[18]To correct for inflation, we divided all variables by the GNP deflator. The correction for retained earnings was somewhat more involved. First, we calculated a new variable, k_t, which may be viewed as a quantity index of the physical capital to which corporate equity is title. This index was assumed to equal unity at the initial time period and was augmented in proportion to the amount of retained corporate earnings in each quarter:

$$k_t = \begin{cases} 1, & t = 1 \\ k_{t-1} + \dfrac{E_t - D_t}{P_0}, & t = 2, 3, \ldots, \end{cases}$$

where E_t is real earnings, D_t is real dividends, and P_t is real stock value. Finally, the adjusted earnings and equity value series, x_t and y_t, were calculated by dividing the actual earnings and equity value series by k_t:

$$x_t = E_t/k_t, \quad y_t = P_t/k_t.$$

See LeRoy and Porter [**9**] for the original data and adjusted series.

[19]As indicated earlier, a circumflex over a parameter denotes an estimate. Only the nonzero lags are reported in Table I. Selection of the nonzero lags followed the identification procedures suggested by Haugh [**5**].

[20]See Wilson [**19, 20**].

TABLE 1 | Parameter Estimates of the Bivariate ARMA Process

Firm or Aggregate	$\bar{x}$	$\bar{y}$	$\hat{\beta}$	$\hat{v}_{11}$	$\hat{v}_{12}$	$\hat{v}_{22}$	$\hat{\phi}_{11}$		$\hat{\theta}_{11}$		$\hat{\theta}_{12}$		$\hat{\theta}_{21}$		$\hat{\phi}_{22}$		$\hat{\theta}_{22}$	
Standard and Poor							**Lag**	**Coeff.**	**Lag**	**Coeff.**	**Lag**	**Coeff.**	**Lag**	**Coeff.**	**Lag**	**Coeff.**	**Lag**	**Coeff.**
Estimate	.285	4.89	.942	$.542 \times 10^{-3}$	$.990 \times 10^{-2}$	.280	1	.814	4	−.182					1	.761	3	.158
Standard Error	.0343	3.79	.0456					.072		.082						.068		.062
Estimate							4	.099	5	.338					4	.240	4	.082
Standard Error								.068		.082						.072		.080
Estimate									12	−.237							5	.447
Standard Error										.072								.075
									17	.268							12	−.306
										.076								.079
																	17	.246
																		.086
American Telephone and Telegraph							**Lag**	**Coeff.**	**Lag**	**Coeff.**	**Lag**	**Coeff.**	**Lag**	**Coeff.**	**Lag**	**Coeff.**	**Lag**	**Coeff.**
Estimate	.783	46.8	.983	3.21×10^{-3}	-3.28×10^{-2}	1.09×10^{-2}	1	.988	7	.231			3	-4.85×10^{-2}	1	.966	1	−.298
Standard Error	.095	13.7	5.29×10^{-3}					.022		.086				1.64×10^{-2}		.032		.102
Estimate									13	−.179			14	-3.06×10^{-2}			3	−.265
Standard Error										.087				1.58×10^{-2}				.103
Estimate													16	3.67×10^{-2}				
Standard Error														1.61×10^{-2}				
General Electric							**Lag**	**Coeff.**	**Lag**	**Coeff.**	**Lag**	**Coeff.**	**Lag**	**Coeff.**	**Lag**	**Coeff.**	**Lag**	**Coeff.**
Estimate	.497	44.7	.989	.0139	.0416	18.1	1	.273	9	.288	8	−.008	3	12.16	1	.944	12	−.290
Standard Error	.00173	6.91	.00169					.090		.095		.002		3.63		.048		.100
Estimate									11	.194			5	5.37			13	.359
Standard Error										.100				3.48				.102
Estimate									12	−.451			10	5.04				
Standard Error										.094				3.36				
Estimate													11	9.75				
Standard Error														3.41				
General Motors							**Lag**	**Coeff.**	**Lag**	**Coeff.**	**Lag**	**Coeff.**	**Lag**	**Coeff.**	**Lag**	**Coeff.**	**Lag**	**Coeff.**
Estimate	1.37	69.5	.980	.217	.590	41.5	4	.632	1	−.144	2	−.0209			1	.965	6	−.147
Standard Error	.104	18.2	4.86×10^{-3}					.082		.114		.0082				.029		.105
Estimate									9	.262	3	−.0181					9	.066
Standard Error										.118		.0083						.102
Estimate									10	.178	16	−.0158						
Standard Error										.121		.0082						

TABLE II | "Chi-Square" Statistics for Overall Adequacy of Bivariate Specification

Firm or	Chi-Square Statistics			
Aggregate	**C(1,1)**	**C(1,2)**	**C(2,1)**	**C(2,2)**
Standard & Poor	49.3	32.2	28.7	20.7
	(38)	(38)	(38)	(38)
AT&T	30.2	27.2	28.4	22.2
	(46)	(46)	(46)	(46)
GE	35.2	35.8	27.1	21.8
	(47)	(47)	(47)	(47)
GM	22.0	41.2	21.0	32.8
	(44)	(44)	(44)	(44)

Note:
$C(i,j) = T\left(\sum_{k=1}^{df} r_{ij}^2(k)\right)$

where

$r_{ij}(k) = \frac{1}{T}\left(\sum_{t=i}^{T-k} \hat{\zeta}_{ij}\hat{\zeta}_{ij+k}\right)$

and df, the degress of freedom, is reported in parentheses beneath each "chi-square" statistic.

statistics f_1, f_2^l, f_2^u and f_3, and of the asymptotic standardized normal ratios (z ratios) for f_1, f_2^u and f_3, namely:

$$z_1 = f_1 / \left(\hat{\underline{j}}_1'\left(\frac{1}{T}\right)\hat{\Omega}\,\hat{\underline{j}}_1\right)^{1/2}, \qquad z_2^u = f_2^u / \left(\hat{\underline{j}}_2^{u\prime}\left(\frac{1}{T}\right)\hat{\Omega}\,\hat{\underline{j}}_2^u\right)^{1/2},$$

$$z_3 = f_3 / \left(\hat{\underline{j}}_3'\left(\frac{1}{T}\right)\hat{\Omega}\,\hat{\underline{j}}_3\right)^{1/2}.[21]$$

The middle and right panels of Table III present estimates of the variance and coefficients of dispersion, respectively, of y_t, $\hat{y}_t$, y_t^*, and π_t. For GM the coefficient of dispersion of earnings exceeds that of prices, as required by Theorem 1. However, for GE the two statistics are virtually identical, while for AT&T and the Standard & Poor's Index the coefficients of dispersion of prices are several times higher that those of earnings. Despite these apparently pronounced inequalities, none of the three z-statistics for the associated test $H_0 : f_1 = 0$ are even nearly significant, so we can conclude that at the 5 percent level the data are consistent with Theorem 1. These results indicate that, as reported in the introduction, our tests have very wide confidence intervals. As expected, the hypothesis $H_0 : f^l > 0$ that stock price variance exceeds its theoretical lower bound is accepted; since the point estimate indicates acceptance, it is unnecessary to calculate the z statistics associated with f^l.

On the basis of point estimates, the Theorem 2 upper bound test, $\gamma_y(0) < \gamma_y^*(0)$, or, equivalently, $f_2^u > 0$, is flagrantly violated for all four data sets. However, as before, the asymptotic variances of the test statistics are very high—only for GE is rejection of the null hypothesis clearly called for. GM is a borderline case at the 5 per cent level, while for AT&T and the Standard & Poor's Index acceptance is indicated. Finally, for the more restrictive Theorem 3 test that $\gamma_y^*(0) = \gamma_y(0) + \gamma_\pi(0)$, the z statistic for the hypothesis H_0: $f_3 = 0$

[21] To conserve space we have listed the estimates of $\underline{j}_i$ and Ω in LeRoy and Porter **[9]**. The sample periods for the four data sets were 1955:1 to 1973:4 (Standard & Poor), 1955:1 to 1977:4 (AT&T); 1955:1 to 1978:2 (GE); and 1955:4 to 1977:4 (GM). To let starting transients damp out, the first ten observations in each sample were used to provide initial conditions; see Wilson **[19]**. The sample means $\bar{x}$ and $\bar{y}$ were also based on this truncated sample.

TABLE III | Test Statistics, Variances, and Coefficients of Dispersion

	Test Statistics				Variances				Coefficients of Dispersion			
Firm or Aggregate												
Index	f_1	f_2^l	f_2^u	f_3	$\gamma_y(0)$	$\gamma_{\hat{y}}(0)$	$\gamma_y^*(0)$	$\gamma_\pi(0)$	$CD(x)$	$CD(\hat{y})$	$CD(y)$	$CD(y^*)$
Standard & Poor	−.280	.396	−.348	−8.63	4.89	1.64×10^{-1}	.255	3.99	.172	8.28×10^{-2}	.452	.052
z Statistic	−.193	—	−.242	−.254								
AT&T	−.281	.420	−.314	−828.7	385.7	9.77×10^{-6}	24.6	467.6	.139	6.68×10^{-5}	.420	.106
z Statistic	−1.096	—	−1.223	−2.006								
GE	-6.84×10^{-4}	.288	−.264	−1478.4	165.9	3.81×10^{-4}	1.12	1313.6	.287	4.36×10^{-4}	.288	.024
z Statistic	−.0056	—	−2.57	−4.41								
GM	.103	.375	−.314	−1773.9	690.5	3.37×10^{-2}	19.90	1103.3	.481	2.64×10^{-3}	.378	.064
z Statistic	.596	—	−1.84	−2.76								

TABLE IV | Tests of Overall Market Efficiency

	Chi-Square Statistics for Rates of Return	
Firm or Aggregate	$\chi^2(12)$	$\chi^2(24)$
Standard & Poor	88.0	155.4
American Telephone and Telegraph	9.4	15.2
General Electric	10.2	17.0
General Motors	10.8	14.4

indicates clear rejection of market efficiency for the three firms; for the aggregate index the test statistic was not significantly different from zero.

Our results may be summarized as follows: the point estimates corresponding to our three theorems all indicate that the bounds on price dispersion implied by the efficient markets model are dramatically violated empirically, although the confidence intervals on our tests are so wide that the departures are not always statistically significant. This conclusion differs from that of most tests of restriction (25), which generally indicate acceptance of the null hypothesis (Fama [**1**]).[22]

In order to interpret this discrepancy, we computed the standard autocorrelation test of the sort that has led to the acceptance of market efficiency (Table IV). The statistic appropriate for testing the joint hypothesis that the population autocorrelation of the rate of return up to lag k equal zero is

$$\chi^2(k) = T\sum_{i=1}^{k}[\hat{\gamma}_r(i)/\hat{\gamma}_r(0)]^2, \tag{27}$$

where the term in brackets is the sample autocorrelation of rates of return, equation (26), at lag i. Under the null hypothesis of market efficiency, (27) is distributed as a chi-square statistic with k degrees of freedom. We calculated $\chi^2(k)$ for $k = 12$ and $k = 24$; for $k = 12$ ($k = 24$) the critical value of the chi-square statistic at the twenty-five per cent level is 14.8 (28.2), while at the one per cent level the critical value is 26.2 (43.0). Comparison of the sample statistics with the critical values indicates that the hypotheses that all lagged autocorrelations in rates of return are zero is accepted at the 25 per cent level for either $k = 12$ or $k = 24$ for the firm data, although it is rejected at the one per cent level for the Standard & Poor's Index for either $k = 12$ or $k = 24$.

As indicated earlier in Section 1, we are not able to resolve this difference between our results in which market efficiency is rejected with the standard results in which the opposite conclusion is reached. As suggested in the introduction, one possibility is that our test has greater power than the standard test for the particular dispersion restriction embodied in Theorem 3.[23]

University of California, Santa Barbara and Federal Reserve Board

Manuscript received March, 1978; revision received January, 1980.

[22]It should be noted that we have tested the model in real terms in contrast to most work in which nominal magnitudes are examined.

[23]Both our test and the standard test may be derived from (13). Theorem 3 tests only one of the restrictions contained in (13), while the standard test is a simultaneous test of all the restrictions. The situation is analogous to a multivariate test that all the coefficients in a linear model are simultaneously zero versus a t test on an individual coefficient. If one particular coefficient is nonzero, the t test for that coefficient would have greater power than the multivariate test.

References

1. Fama, Eugene F.: "Efficient Capital Markets: A Review of Theory and Empirical Work," *Journal of Finance*, 25 (1970), 383–416.
2. Friedman, Milton: *A Theory of the Consumption Function.* Princeton: Princeton University Press, 1957.
3. Granger, C. W. J.: "Investigating Causal Relations by Econometric Models and Cross-Spectral Methods," *Econometrica*, 37 (1969), 424–438.
4. Hannan, E. J.: *Multiple Time Series*. New York: John Wiley and Sons, 1970.
5. Haugh, Larry D.: *The Identification of Time Series Interrelationships with Special Reference to Dynamic Regression Models*, Ph.D. Dissertation, Department of Statistics, University of Wisconsin, 1972.
6. LeRoy, Stephen F.: "Risk Aversion and the Martingale Property of Stock Prices," *International Economic Review*, 14 (1973), 436–446.
7. ___: "Efficient Capital Markets: Comment," *Journal of Finance*, 31 (1976), 139–141.
8. ___: "Securities Prices Under Risk-Neutrality and Near Risk-Neutrality," reproduced, University of Chicago, 1979.
9. LeRoy, Stephen F., and Richard D. Porter: "The Present-Value Relation: Test Based on Implied Variance Bounds," Federal Reserve Board Special Studies Paper, 1980.
10. Lucas, Robert E., Jr.: "Asset Prices in an Exchange Economy," *Econometrica*, 46 (1978), 1426–1446.
11. Pierce, David A.: "Forecasting Dynamic Models with Stochastic Regressors," *Journal of Econometrics*, 3 (1975), 349–374.
12. Rozanov, Yu. A.: *Stationary Random Processes*, Tr. by A. Feinstein. San Francisco: Holden-Day, 1963.
13. Rubinstein, Mark: "Securities Market Efficiency in an Arrow-Debreu Economy," *American Economic Review*, 65 (1975), 812–824.
14. Samuelson, Paul A.: "Proof that Properly Anticipated Prices Fluctuate Randomly," *Industrial Management Review*, 6 (1965), 41–49.
15. Shiller, Robert J.: *Rational Expectations and the Structure of Interest Rates*, unpublished Ph.D. dissertation, Department of Economics, M.I.T., 1972.
16. ____: "The Volatility of Long-Term Interest Rates and Expectations of the Term Structure," *Journal of Political Economy*, 87 (1979), 1190–1219.
17. Sims, Christopher A.: "Approximate Price Restrictions in Distributed Lag Estimation," *Journal of the American Statistical Association*, 67 (1972), 169–175.
18. Singleton, Kenneth J.: "Expectations Models of the Term Structure and Implied Variance Bounds," *Journal of Political Economy*, 88 (1980), 1159–1176.
19. Wilson, G. Tunnicliffe: Unpublished Ph.D. dissertation, Lancaster University, 1970.
20. ____: "The Estimation of Parameters in Multivariate Time Series Models," *Journal of the Royal Statistical Society*, Series B, 35 (1973), 76–85.
21. Woodward, S. E.: "Properly Anticipated Prices Do Not, In General, Fluctuate Randomly," reproduced, University of California, Santa Barbara, 1979.

Two

Thomas E. Copeland

Thomas E. Copeland received a Ph.D. from the University of Pennsylvania in 1973. His academic career started at UCLA, where he became a full professor of Finance before resigning in 1987 to be co-leader of McKinsey's global financial consulting practice until 1998. Currently, he is senior lecturer in finance at MIT and CEO of CFM, a hedge fund. •

I did some quick research among my friends when Hans Stoll began to insist that a new assistant professor at the University of Pennsylvania—Steve Ross—be assigned to my thesis committee. The message was that I would find him brilliant and tough. Being risk averse, I tried, unsuccessfully, to keep him off my committee. It is my privilege to have known him as a mentor and friend over the following 33 years.

Others have their Steve Ross anecdotes and I would like to share two of my own. The first explains why he chose economics as a profession. It goes back to the day of his first college-level class in mathematics as an undergraduate at Cal Tech. He was proud of his score in the AP math test—which I recall was second in the state of California. He was curious too and asked the person seated to his left, "What was your rank on the AP math test?" The reply was "First in California." Somewhat humbled, Steve turned to his right and asked the same question. The answer was "First in the nation." It seems that it was at that very moment that he decided to abandon mathematics and opt for economics as his profession. At least that is the way the story has been told.

Years later, I visited Steve at his office in New Haven and we went to the best French restaurant in town for lunch. After a great meal and extraordinary bottle of wine, the waiter handed the check to Steve. Even he seemed surprised at the total. With a gleam in his eye he turned to me and said he would make a bet. If I could answer an economics question correctly, he would pay for lunch, but if I failed I would pay. He cautioned me that under similar circumstances Ken Arrow had paid last week. Having no deficit of hubris and feeling the effect of the wine, I agreed to the wager. Once again Steve cautioned me—"Remember," he said, "this is a bet and not an option!" Then he asked his question. "Suppose you are offered ownership of a Black box that guarantees to return $1.05 to you exactly one year after you put $1.00 into it—and you may do so at any time for up to a year. Alternatively, you can put your $1.00 into a bank today and receive $1.10 at the end of the year with absolute certainty. How much would you pay for the Black box?" I thought about it and answered, "I know about opportunity cost and given the bank offer with certainty the box is worth nothing." I also paid for lunch, because as Steve articulated, I had assumed that market rates of interest would stay at 10 percent throughout the year, but if there was any chance at all that they would fall to less than 5 percent, then the Black box was an option on interest rates and worth a positive amount.

These two anecdotes illustrate Steve's mastery of mathematics and the modeling of difficult problems in economics, his ability to simplify and clarify complex concepts, and his uncanny ability to explain difficult concepts in plain English. But there is also his passion for ideas, his joie de vivre, and his sincerity that make it a pleasure to spend time with him. I am forever grateful to call him friend and mentor.

Information Effects on the Bid-Ask Spread

Thomas E. Copeland and Dan Galai[*]

Abstract

An individual who chooses to serve as a market-maker is assumed to optimize his position by setting a bid-ask spread which maximizes the difference between expected revenues received from liquidity-motivated traders and expected losses to information-motivated traders. By characterizing the cost of supplying quotes, as writing a put and a call option to an information-motivated trader, it is shown that the bid-ask spread is a positive function of the price level and return variance, a negative function of measures of market activity, depth, and continuity, and negatively correlated with the degree of competition. Thus, the theory of information effects on the bid-ask spread proposed in this paper is consistent with the empirical literature. •

This paper is concerned with the determination of bid-ask spreads in organized financial markets, where the trading is done through economic agents who specialize in market-making for a limited set of securities. The commitment made by dealers to buy or sell at the bid and ask prices, respectively, is analyzed as a combination of put and call options, and empirical results published in previous works are shown to be consistent with the model.

While there have been several papers concerned with the bid-ask spread, no entirely satisfactory theory has yet emerged. Demsetz [10] was the first to formalize the problem. He treated the bid-ask spread as a (transaction) cost to the trader for immediacy, and analyzed it in a static supply and demand framework.

Since Demsetz's seminal paper there have been two main lines of thought about the theory of the bid-ask spread and they are not necessarily antithetical. Several papers focus primarily on the relationship between the bid-ask spread and dealer inventory costs. However, with the exception of Ho and Stoll [19], none of them explains the bid-ask spread with competitive dealers.[1] Some of the studies[2] are based on the assumption that risk-averse specialists are not well diversified, although this is inconsistent with the dealers' common practice of sharing their risks through partnerships and pooling agreements.

The second line of thought follows Bagehot [2].[3] The dealer is assumed to face (at least) two different types of traders, namely those possessing special information and liquidity-motivated traders. Informed traders possess nonpublic information which allows them to have a better estimate of the future security price than either the dealer or liquidity traders. The dealer and liquidity traders are equally well informed vis-à-vis each other but uninformed relative to information-motivated traders. Because traders with special information have the option

---

[*]Copeland is Associate Professor of Finance at UCLA and Galai is Associate Professor of Finance at the Hebrew University of Jerusalem and Visting Professor of Finance at UCLA. We wish to express our gratitude to Yakov Amihud, Harold Demsetz, Ken French, Robert Geske, Ron Masulis, Steve Lippman, and Richard Roll and to the referee, Thomas Ho. We are also indebted to the Finance workshops at Columbia, New York University, Wharton, and Berkeley/Stanford for their comments on earlier versions of this paper. Any errors are, of course, our responsibility.

[1]For example, see Stoll [27], Ho and Stoll [18], Garman [16], Cohen et al. [7, 8], Bradfield [6], and Amihud and Mendelson [1].

[2]For example, see Stoll [27], and Ho and Stoll [18, 19].

[3]See Bagehot [2], Logue [21], and Jaffe and Winkler [20].

Reprinted with permission:
Copeland, Thomas E. and Dan Galai. "Information Effects on the Bid-Ask Spread." *The Journal of Finance* 38 (1983): 1457–1469.

of not trading with the dealer, he will never gain from them. He can only lose. On the other hand the dealer gains in his transactions with liquidity-motivated traders. They are willing to pay a "fee" in order to obtain immediacy. This paper models the dealer's bid-ask spread as a tradeoff between expected losses to informed traders and expected gains from liquidity traders. The theory will be applied to both monopoly and perfect competition in dealer markets.

Section I of the paper details the assumptions which provide the framework for our analysis of the bid-ask spread. Section II develops a bid-ask model and analyzes the comparative statics of the bid-ask spread for the case of dealer monopoly and for perfect competition. Section III shows how the cost of the dealer's bid-ask spread may be characterized as a combination of a put and a call option (a straddle). Section IV shows via numerical examples that the empirical results of previous studies, namely the positive correlation of the bid-ask spread with the security's price level and its residual risk and the negative correlation with various measures of market activity, depth, and continuity, are consistent with the model proposed. Section V discusses the limitations of the model and some extensions. Section VI concludes the paper.

I. A Simplified Framework for Analyzing the Bid-Ask Spread

We will define S_0 as the current "true" price of the security as perceived by the dealer.[4] The dealer makes a commitment to buy a fixed quantity (for example 100 shares) at the bid price, K_B, or to sell at the ask price, K_A. The commitment is usually very short-lived as it can be terminated with the next transaction or with the arrival of new information.[5]

The assumptions which determine the exogenously given framework for our analysis are listed below and discussed in the paragraphs which follow:

a) There are no taxes and short-selling is unconstrained.
b) The instantaneous risk-free borrowing and lending rate, $r_f \geq 0$, is constant. The "true" underlying asset value, S, follows a stochastic process, $f(S)$, which is known (ex ante) to all market participants.[6]
c) Information about the realizations of S is generated by exogenous events (e.g., the weather) and informed traders convey it to the marketplace. Dealers or liquidity traders are uninformed as to the realizations of $f(S)$ until after an informed trade takes place. Liquidity trading is also motivated by exogeneous independent events (e.g., immediate consumption needs), hence all traders arrive at the market trading post (not necessarily a physical location) according to a stationary stochastic process, $g(\tau)$, which is known to all participants and which has calendar time arrival $\tau > 0$ and finite mean $E(\tau)$.[7] The trader arrival process, being exogenously determined, is independent of the price change process, but not necessarily vice versa.

[4]In accordance with Demsetz [10, p. 36] we define the "true" price as the equilibrium price which would exist in a world without any demand for immediacy and where all market participants are equally well informed. Also, Beja and Goldman [3, p. 599] distinguish between the equilibrium prices which are free of market "imperfections" and follow a "random walk" and the observed prices which are affected by the bid-ask spread, for example.

[5]For example, in the dealer market for the U.S. government securities (the Garban market), the bid-ask quotes are firm for at least two minutes, but may be revised when "hit." The market is organized for broker interdealer trading in currently listed U.S. Treasury issues by providing videoscreen listings of the best bid and offer prices for each issue. For a more complete description of the Garban market see Garbade [14, pp. 433–34].

[6]Examples of stochastic processes are: 1) Brownian motion (continuous price movements), and 2) jump processes (discrete movements), see Cox and Ross [9].

[7]For example, think of information events and liquidity needs as being generated by independent Poisson processes. Their convolution is also a Poisson process which can be represented by $g(\tau)$.

d) $p_I (0 < p_I < 1)$ is the probability, determined exogenously, that the next request for a quote is motivated by superior information regarding the next price realization, and $p_L = 1 - p_I$ is the probability that the quote request is liquidity-motivated.

e) Asset markets are anonymous in the sense that the dealer does not know, ex ante, whether or not the other side of the transaction possesses superior information.

f) The dealer(s) gives a quote limited to a fixed number of shares, *n,* and only to the first trader to arrive at the trading post. (There may be different quotes for *2n, 3n* shares, etc.)

g) The dealer is risk neutral, and hence is an expected profit maximizer.

h) Once at the trading post, the consummation of trades is a function of the bid-ask spread, i.e., both liquidity and information traders have price-elastic demand.[8]

The dealer's objective is to choose a bid-ask spread which maximizes his profits. If he sets the bid-ask spread too wide, he loses expected revenues from liquidity traders but reduces potential losses to informed traders. On the other hand, if he establishes a spread which is too narrow, the probability of losses incurring to informed traders increases, but is offset by potential revenues from liquidity trading. His optimal bid-ask spread is determined by a tradeoff between expected gains from liquidity trading and expected losses to informed trading.

Some of the above assumptions require no further discussion, but others do; for example, a sufficient condition for information to have private value is the anonymity of asset markets. If markets were personal, then traders known to possess superior knowledge could easily be identified and no one would agree to trade with them. One of the services of a broker is to maintain the anonymity of the client who initiates a trade.

The information arrival process, and the dealer's reaction to it, can be characterized as follows. An exogenously determined event (e.g., a thunderstorm over Kansas wheat crops) is revealed to an informed trader who is the first to come to the marketplace. The dealer limits the size of his commitment on each quote in order to limit his potential loss to a better-informed trader. After each trade any private information becomes public, and the dealer may then revise his estimate of the "true" price. The rate of trader arrival (in this one-period model) is independent of the stochastic process which generates price changes.

The stochastic process which generates information arrival (e.g., see Merton [23]) may follow either a continuous stochastic process, a discontinuous jump process, or some mixture of the two. We will examine the dealer's choice of a bid-ask spread for both types of stochastic process, starting with the jump process. As might be expected, the implications of our model will be the same, regardless of the process chosen.

The dealer knows, ex ante, that p_I is the probability that the next trader is informed. If all traders were better informed than the dealer ($p_I = 1.0$), the dealer could only lose. Therefore, we assume that p_I is strictly less than unity. Moreover, if there were no informed traders ($p_I = 0$), the marginal cost to the dealer would be zero and the competitive bid-ask spread would be driven to zero,[9] which is unrealistic. Consequently, we assume that p_I is strictly positive.

If the dealer knows the stochastic process which generates prices, knows the probability that the next trader is informed, and knows the elasticity of demand for liquidity traders, he can establish his equilibrium bid-ask spread by trading off potential losses to information traders against potential gains from liquidity traders. A formal model is discussed in the next section.

[8]The nature of the demand elasticity is specified in the next section of the paper.

[9]If the dealer were a monopolist, the bid-ask spread would be positive even though all market participants had homogeneous expectations. This was the case studied by Demsetz [10].

II. Bid-Ask Valuation Models

There are two scenarios which capture the mechanics of the trading process and they have very similar implications for the bid-ask spread. The simpler scenario is an instantaneous quote model. It posits that the dealer waits before offering his quote until a trader reaches the trading post. The quote is offered with knowledge that in the next instant the "true" price may jump to a new level (a jump process) if the trader is informed or remain unchanged if the trader is liquidity motivated. No time interval passes between a quote, the trade, and the revelation of a new price (if any). The second scenario, discussed later on, examines an open quote interval. The dealer offers his quote immediately and waits during some open time interval (either fixed in length or stochastic) until either the next trader reaches the market or new information is received via alternate means (whereupon he changes his quote).

A. Instantaneous Quotes

Given that the dealer withholds his quote until requested, we can model the bid-ask spread by first considering the dealer's expected costs and then his expected revenues. His expected losses to informed traders (his expected costs) will depend on p_I, the probability that the next trader is informed; the dealer's knowledge of the stochastic process governing price changes, $f(S)$; and on his choice of ask and bid prices, K_B [sic] and K_B. Recall that the quantity traded on any quote is fixed. Without loss of generality, assume it is one share. Then the expected dealer loss to an informed trader is,[10]

$$p_I\left\{\int_{K_A}^{\infty}(S - K_A)f(S)\,dS + \int_0^{K_B}(K_B - S)f(S)\,dS\right\} \tag{1}$$

We have used S to designate the post-trade "true" price of the asset. Not all informed traders who arrive at the marketplace will consummate a trade. Nontraders are informed individuals who believe the post-trade price will fall between K_A and K_B, the ask and bid prices, respectively. Hence, the elasticity of demand by informed traders with respect to the bid-ask interval is implicit in the limits of integration of Equation (1). The dealer's expected cost (i.e., expected losses to informed traders) is graphed as line WX in Figure 1. Note that for convenience we have chosen to graph only the ask spread (only one part of the bid-ask spread) along the horizontal axis. As the ask spread increases, dealer expected losses to better informed traders will decline.

The dealer's revenues come from those liquidity traders who are willing to pay $K_A - S_0$ or $S_0 - K_B$ as a price for immediacy. In order to express the price elasticity of the liquidity trader's demand for immediacy, we partition the fraction of traders who are liquidity motivated, $p_L = (1 - p_I)$, into two parts. Let p_{TL} and p_{NL} be the probabilities of trading and nontrading, given that a trader is a liquidity trader. In addition, decompose p_{TL} into two parts, p_{BL} and p_{SL} (such that $p_{BL} + p_{SL} = p_{TL}$), which give the probability of buying and selling by a liquidity trader.[11] It is assumed that, given S_0, the probability, p_{TL}, that a liquidity trader will transact falls as the dealer spread increases.[12] p_{TL} as a function of the bid-ask spread

---

[10]We have previously defined p_I as the probability that the next quote request is information-motivated and $p_L = 1 - p_I$ as the fraction who are liquidity traders. These fractions are exogeneously determined and are not a function of the bid-ask spread (assumption d).

[11]Recall that $p_L = 1 - p_I$ is exogenously determined (assumption d), and that K_A and S_0 are known parameters at the time the liquidity trader makes his trading decision: Consequently, the partial derivative in Equation (2) contains no stochastic elements. If p_{BL} were a function of a stochastic parameter, e.g., S, then the problem would be much more complicated.

[12]Because liquidity traders are uninformed, they perceive no price change in the interval between quotes.

FIGURE 1. | The Competitive and Monopoly Spreads. For each transaction the expected cost (line WX) and expected revenue (line OV) functions are shown as a function of the ask spread, $K_A - S_0$. The competitive ask spread, $(K_A - S_0)^*$, occurs where expected revenue equals expected cost, and the monopoly ask spread, $(K_A - S_0)^{**}$, occurs where expected profit is maximized.

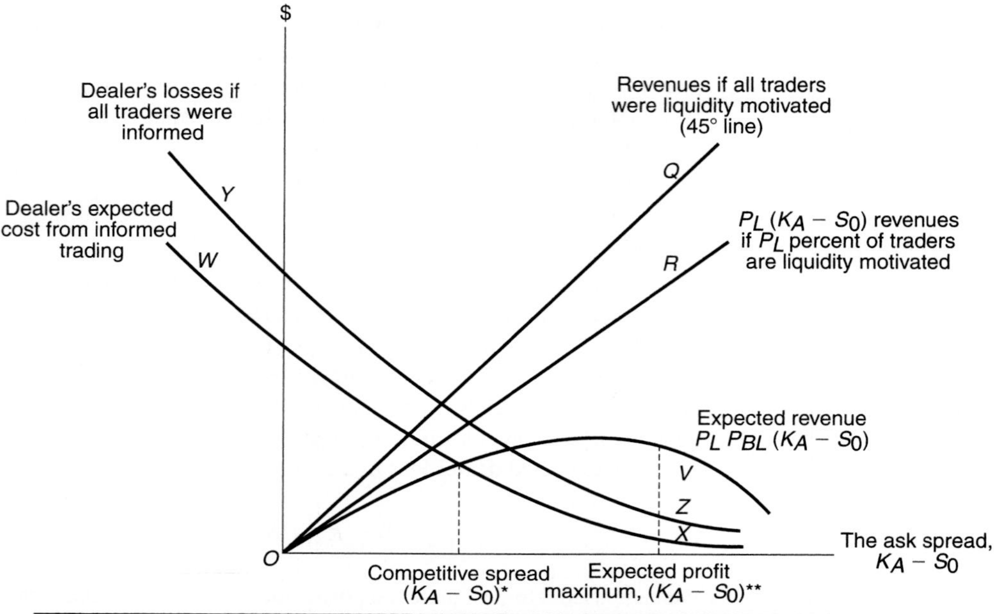

could have been expressed directly; we have decomposed it into buying and selling components so that the bid and ask spread can be analyzed separately later in the paper,

$$\left.\frac{\partial p_{BL}}{\partial K_A}\right|_{S_0} < 0 \quad \text{and} \quad \left.\frac{\partial p_{SL}}{\partial K_B}\right|_{S_0} > 0 \tag{2}$$

The dealer's expected revenue per transaction from liquidity traders is

$$(1 - p_I)\{p_{BL}(K_A - S_0) + p_{SL}(S_0 - K_B) + p_{NL} \cdot 0\} \tag{3}$$

In Figure 1, the dealer's expected revenue curve is obtained by first multiplying the unconditional gain per transaction (the 45° line OQ) by the percentage of liquidity traders, p_L. The result is line OR. Next, this is multiplied by p_{BL}, the probability of a liquidity trader buying the asset given an ask spread. Elastic demand (Equation (2)) implies that the likelihood that a liquidity trader will consummate a trade declines as the ask spread increases. The resulting expected revenue curve (line OV) will be concave if p_{BL} decreases monotonically as a function of K_A.

The objective of a risk neutral dealer is to choose the bid-ask spread which maximizes his expected profit. Mathematically, this may be expressed as

$$\max_{K_A,K_B}\Big\{(1 - p_I)[p_{BL}(K_A - S_0) + p_{SL}(S_0 - K_B)] - p_I\left[\int_{K_A}^{\infty}(S - K_A)f(S)\,dS + \int_0^{K_B}(K_B - S)f(S)\,dS\right]\Big\} \geq 0 \tag{4}$$

If the dealer is a monopolist, he will maximize the difference between the expected revenue and cost functions (in Figure 1) by setting the ask price, K_A^{**}.[13] If there is free entry, then the long-run competitive equilibrium will be established where the expected costs and revenues are equal at an asking price of K_A^*. At this point expected long-run profit is zero. If the percentage of informed traders increases, then expected dealer costs increase relative to revenues and the ask price increases.

Although it is difficult to analyze the differences between the monopoly and competitive results without knowing more about the demand for immediacy, at least three things can be said. First, the bid-ask spread decreases as we shift from the monopoly to the competitive case (in Figure 1). This result is consistent with the empirical work of Tinic and West [29]. Second, if the percentage of informed traders increases, the difference between the monopoly and competitive spreads expressed as a percentage of the security price, $(K_A^{**} - K_A^*)/S_0$, will decrease; i.e., the monopoly and competitive solutions look more alike as the market becomes "flooded" with informed traders.[14] Third, if the elasticity of demand for liquidity trading decreases, ceteris paribus, then the dealer's expected revenue curve will shift to the left thereby causing the ask price to decrease.

Admittedly, the above model is a simplification, especially in the assumption of dealer risk neutrality. However, an important result is that even with risk neutral dealer behavior the bid-ask spread will be positive so long as there are informed traders. Dealer risk aversion is not necessary in order to explain the existence and behavior of the bid-ask spread. In addition, the above model has intuitively appealing implications regarding the comparative static results which it predicts, mainly the role of the specific risk of the stock as measured by the standard deviation of the rate of return. In Figure 1, as the variance of the stock rate of return increases, ceteris paribus, the dealer expected total cost function (line WX) shifts to the right and the competitive equilibrium ask price is raised (unless there is an offsetting effect on p_{BL}). Another prediction of the model is that an increase in the percentage of traders who are informed will result in an increase in the bid-ask spread. If large price changes result from informed trading, then transactions data should show a positive contemporaneous relationship between large price changes and bid-ask spreads.

The relationship between the bid-ask spread and trading volume may take two forms. First, p_I may be higher for thinly traded stocks (perhaps because they are, on average, more closely held). This implies a negative correlation between the bid-ask spread (or the percentage bid-ask spread) and trading volume *holding the size of the transaction constant.* Second, p_I may increase if more information is associated with the size of the transaction. In this case, there will be a positive correlation between volume and the bid-ask spread (or percentage bid-ask spread) *holding the number of transactions (per unit time) constant.*

B. Open Quote Interval

The instantaneous quote scenario is useful because it provides unambiguous comparative statics results. No discounting is involved. Although more complicated, an open quote interval provides similar comparative static results and provides additional insight into the relationship between the bid-ask spread, information arrival, and trading volume. With an open quote interval, the dealer provides his quote before requested and waits for the next

[13]By differentiating Equation (4), the necessary condition for maximization in terms of the expected marginal cost and marginal revenue can be presented.

[14]This result can be seen in Figure 1. With a higher p_I the WX curve, i.e., the expected cost from informed trading, will shift upward and to the right thereby increasing both K_A^* and K_A^{**}. Usually, K_A^* will increase by more than K_A^{**} due to the elasticity of the expected revenue function, however even if the difference between K_A^{**} and K_A^* remains constant, the ratio $(K_A^{**} - K_A^*)/S_0$ will decline.

trader to arrive at the trading post. Neither the dealer nor the liquidity traders receive any information during the interval between quotes, hence both expect the price will be $S_0 e^{r_t \tau}$ at the trade. All participants know the stochastic process which generates trader arrival (assumption c) and know that it is independent of past price changes.

The open quote bid-ask model is complicated by the fact that the dealer's effective quote interval, τ may be established for a fixed interval or it may be stochastic. The general expression for the dealer's expected losses to informed traders (Equation (1)) must be modified to discount his expected end-of-period losses as follows:

$$p_I \left\{ \int_0^\infty e^{-r_t \tau} \left[\int_{K_A}^\infty (S - K_A) f(S \mid \tau)\, dS + \int_0^{K_B} (K_B - S) f(S \mid \tau)\, dS \right] g(\tau)\, d\tau \right\} \quad (5)$$

If τ is of fixed length, then it is unnecessary to integrate across arrival times, $g(\tau)$.[15] If τ is stochastic, the comparative statics analysis of the dealer's expected cost for any given time of arrival τ, will also hold for the unconditional expectations across all arrival times. This is true because[16]

$$E_\tau[E_s(S \mid \tau)] = E_\epsilon(S) \quad (6)$$

The open quote model provides additional insight into the relationship between the expected time between quotes, the bid-ask spread, and trading volume. Empirical evidence indicates that smaller companies have less frequent trading (e.g., see Scholes and Williams [24] or Dimson [11]), i.e., $E(\tau)$ is high. This observation is consistent with other empirical evidence (Demsetz [10], Tinic and West [29], Benston and Hagerman [4], and Hamilton [17]) which has shown the bid-ask spread to be inversely correlated with the volume of trading. Since low trading volume usually means less frequent trading, the open quote model is consistent with this result because the present value of the dealer's expected cost increases with the expected duration of the quote, but the present value of his expected revenue does not.

III. The Cost of the Bid-Ask Spread as a Combination of a Call and a Put Option

Another way of looking at the dealer's problem is to consider the cost of the bid-ask spread as a "free" straddle option.[17] The dealer gives a prospective trader a call option to buy at the asking price, $K_A > S_0$, and also a put option to sell the security at the bid price, $K_B < S_0$. Note that both options are issued out-of-the-money (at least from the dealer's perspective). A liquidity trader will be willing to suffer a certain loss by exercising the out-of-the-money option. His loss is the price he is willing to pay for immediacy. The informed trader, on the other hand, will be trading for a gain by using updated information on future states of nature. He trades when $S > K_A$ or when $S < K_B$.

Equation (1), the dealer's expected loss to informed traders, can be transformed into an option-pricing framework if we assume that the quote interval, τ, is of length zero (a jump

[15]For an example of a market with fixed quote intervals see footnote 5. In the next section the case of fixed time intervals will be discussed and used for illustrative purposes.

[16]For proof see Feller [12, pp. 222–23].

[17]An American call option is the right to by the underlying asset at a predetermined price (the exercise price) during a certain time period. The American put is the right to sell the underlying asset at a predetermined price during a certain time period. A straddle is a combination of a put and a call on the same underlying security. Usually a straddle has a single exercise price for both put and call. However, our straddle has two different exercise prices. For a characterization of options, see Galai [13].

process). Alternatively, the quote interval may be of fixed length or a random variable, as in Equation (5).[18] The comparative statics results are unchanged because what is true for any time of arrival, τ, will also be true for the unconditional expectation across all intervals (see Equation (5) and the following discussion). Defining $C(K_A)$ as the present value of the call option and $P(K_A)$ as the present value of the put option and given a fixed quote interval, we can rewrite the dealer's expected loss to informed traders as

$$p_I[C(K_A) + P(K_B)] \tag{7}$$

The values of both put and call options increase with the riskiness of the underlying asset. The call, $C(K_A)$, increases in value with the risk free rate, r_f, and with the ratio S_0/K_A. Similarly, the value of the put $P(K_B)$, decreases with an increase in the ratio S_0/K_B.

It is interesting to note, however, that for the above framework, the specific risk of the underlying asset is an important factor which affects the bid-ask spread. This result is consistent with the empirical findings of Benston and Hagerman [4] and eliminates the need to assume costly diversification. It does not require a positive coefficient of risk aversion as in Stoll [27] or Ho and Stoll [18, 19].

Note also that $C(K_A)$ and $P(K_B)$ are homogeneous functions of degree one with respect to S_0 and K. Multiplying both S_0 and K by a constant proportion, λ, affects the cost of the quote by exactly the same proportion. However, if p_{BL} is a declining function of the *difference* between K_A and S_0, then the proportional change in S_0 and K_A will cause the benefit from potential liquidity trading to increase at a slower rate than λ.[19] Hence we can expect that a share with a price of \$100 will have a relatively narrower percentage bid-ask spread than a share whose price is \$50, ceteris paribus.[20]

IV. A Numerical Analysis of the Cost of the Competitive Bid-Ask Spread as a Straddle

A natural question is whether or not the option prices implied by very short-lived dealer quotes can result in realistic estimates of the bid-ask spread. In order to illustrate the potential magnitude, several examples are given below.

Using a risk neutral valuation model to price the options and assuming that for short intervals the risk free rate is approximately zero, the call and put values become[21]

$$C(K_A) = S_0 N(d_1) - K_A N(d_2)$$

$$d_1 = \frac{\ln(S_0/K_A) + \theta^2/2}{\theta}, \quad d_2 = d_1 - \theta, \quad \theta^2 = \sigma^2\tau \tag{8}$$

[18] Limitations of the option-pricing analogy are discussed in Section V of the paper. An open quote interval is one of them.

[19] Implicit in the assumption that p_{BL} (or p_{SL}) is a decreasing function of the absolute difference $K_A - S_0$ (or $S_0 - K_B$) is that the liquidity trader may have an alternative which requires a fixed cost of transacting. In other words, it is consistent with the assumption of increasing economies of scale in transacting various financial assets.

[20] However, if p_{BL} is a declining function of the ratio K_A/S_0, a proportional change in S_0 and K_A would not affect p_{BL}, and the equilibrium percentage spread will be constant for mere scale changes.

[21] The risk neutral model (which is equivalent to the Black and Scholes model) is used only for illustrative purposes. No claim is made that it is the ideal closed-form solution for the problem at hand. Other models such as the jump process of the binomal [sic] model would serve equally well because they have the same comparative static results. In fact, the jump process yields the same results with no time interval at all.

and

$$P(K_B) = -S_0N(-d_3) + K_BN(-d_4)$$

$$d_3 = \frac{\ln(S_0/K_B) + \theta^2/2}{\theta}, \quad d_4 = d_3 - \theta \tag{9}$$

where $N(\cdot)$ is the cumulative standard normal distribution, and σ is the instantaneous standard deviation of rates of return.

A simplified approach assumes that the quote interval is 2, 5, or 10 minutes and the annual standard deviation is 0.2, 0.4, or 0.6. Table I, Part A, shows estimates of $\theta = \sigma\sqrt{\tau}$, the standard deviation given the quote interval length, τ, and the estimated put and call values for various bid and ask prices for a \$100 stock.[22] Table I, Part B illustrates values of the call and put options for a \$100 stock as a function of the various bid and ask prices, given the time between trades, τ, and the standard deviation, σ.[23]

The following numerical example illustrates the computation of a bid-ask spread. Let

$$p_L = 0.5, \quad p_I = 0.5, \quad p_{BL} = 0.5, \quad \text{and} \quad K_A - S_0 = 0.125$$

For these numbers, the per transaction expected revenue from a liquidity trader is \$0.03125 [i.e., $p_L p_{BL}$ $(K_A - S_0)$]. Hence the call value at the competitive spread[24] should be $C(100.125) =$ \$0.0625. From Table I, Part B, we can see that such a call value is consistent with $\tau = 2$ minutes and $\sigma = 0.6$ or with $\tau = 5$ minutes and $\sigma = 0.4$. Actually it is consistent with all combinations of σ and τ where $\theta = 0.4/\sqrt{82500/5} = 0.003$. If for example, $K_A - S_0 = 0.0625$, the resulting call value should be \$0.0313 (given that $p_L p_{BL} = 0.25$), and it will be consistent with $\tau = 5$ and $\sigma = 0.2$.

Although these estimates are crude, they serve to demonstrate that the bid-ask spread represented by a short-lived option is of the same order of magnitude as bid-ask spreads observed on a stock exchange.[25] To further illustrate this point, we employed an estimation of the transaction's standard deviation, $\theta = \sigma\sqrt{\tau}$, measured by Garbade and Lieber [15] for Potlatch, Inc. They estimated θ to be equal to 0.002, which is consistent with an annualized standard deviation of 0.4 and a time interval of 2 minutes per transaction. If we assume that $p_{BL} = 0.5$ and $p_I = 1 - p_L = 0.5$, then the implied ratio of the ask price to the "true" value, K_A/S_0, is 1.00085. This ratio implies a bid-ask spread of approximately 1⁄16 for the stock, which had a price of around \$37 on December 2, 1980.[26] However, the observed spread for the stock was 3⁄8, which is higher than the competitive spread under the assumed set of parameters.

[22]We assume that σ is annualized on the basis of trading days not calendar days. There were 250 trading days per year, 5.5 trading hours per day, and 60 minutes per hour. This gives 82,500 trading minutes per year. A five minute θ for $\sigma = 0.2$ is $\theta = 0.2/\sqrt{82{,}500/5}$.

[23]Note that short quote intervals, τ, were paired with high standard deviations of return. This was arbitrary. Other values are available from the authors.

[24]If $p_I = 1 - p_L$, S_0 and p_{BL} as function of K_A are given, the value of K_A/S_0 can be found for the competitive spread using one equation of one unknown by means of trial and error in order to get the equality $p_L p_{BL}(K_A - S_0) = p_I C(K_A)$ (See Figure 1).

[25]Some of the difference in magnitude might be attributed to clerical costs, clearing costs, etc.

[26]For $S_0 =$ \$37 the ask price, K_A, should be $1.00085 \cdot S_0$ or \$37.031. In a similar way $S_0 - K_A = 0.031$ for a total spread of \$0.062 or 1⁄16.

V. Limitations and Extensions

Throughout the paper we have maintained the assumption that the stochastic process governing price changes is either discrete or continuous but not mixed. The dealer's response to a mixed stochastic process will depend on what information he has. For example, if public information generates the Brownian motion component of price changes, the dealer can continuously adjust his quote. The only cost he bears is related to price jumps which come

TABLE I Call and Put Values for Various Bid and Ask Prices in Dollars for S_0 =$100

Part A: Estimates of θ

Annual σ	2 min	5 min	10 min
0.2	0.0009847	0.0015569	0.0022019
0.4	0.0019694	0.0031139	0.0044038
0.6	0.0029541	0.0046709	0.0066057

Part B: Estimated Option Values

European Call Values

Ask Price	2 min, σ = 0.6	5 min, σ = 0.4	10 min, σ = 0.2
$100.00	$0.117355	$0.123459	$0.086899
100.05	0.094177	0.100952	0.065002
100.10	0.074570	0.081024	0.046646
100.15	0.058029	0.063568	0.032715
100.20	0.044250	0.049164	0.021744
100.25	0.033020	0.037811	0.014411
100.30	0.024059	0.027985	0.008563
100.35	0.017067	0.020449	0.005337
100.40	0.012185	0.014852	0.003026
100.50	0.008233	0.007310	0.001705
100.60	0.005430	0.003359	0.000895
100.70	0.003620	0.001367	0.000466

European Put Values

Bid Price	2 min, σ = 0.6	5 min, σ = 0.4	10 min, σ = 0.2
$100.00	$0.117355	$0.123458	$0.086899
99.95	0.095398	0.100861	0.064926
99.90	0.074326	0.080902	0.047028
99.85	0.057114	0.062927	0.032227
99.80	0.043304	0.048462	0.021882
99.75	0.032303	0.037094	0.014023
99.70	0.023398	0.027756	0.008607
99.65	0.017083	0.020391	0.005210
99.60	0.011967	0.014464	0.002953
99.50	0.008121	0.006987	0.001635
99.40	0.005523	0.003105	0.000859
99.30	0.003598	0.001291	0.000423

as surprises to him. If the Brownian motion component contains nonpublic information, an open quote interval is an undesirable assumption because competitive dealers could reduce their costs by shortening their quote interval. Ultimately, the quote duration would diminish to zero in a competitive equilibrium.

A logical extension of the model is to make the quote interval an endogenous variable which is determined simultaneously with the bid-ask spread. This may be done by introducing transaction costs which are associated with revising a quote. More frequent revisions will reduce the cost associated with giving a combination of options, but also may result in higher transaction costs per unit time. An equilibrium quote interval can be found for a given bid-ask quote and a specific transaction cost function. It can be expected that higher volatility of the stock's return will lead to a shorter quote interval, ceteris paribus.

VI. Summary and Conclusions

Given the behavior of liquidity traders and informed traders, the dealer is assumed to offer an out-of-the-money straddle option for a fixed number of shares during a fixed time interval. The exercise prices of the straddle determine the bid-ask spread. The dealer establishes his profit maximizing spread by balancing the expected total revenues from liquidity trading against the expected total losses from informed trading. A monopolistic dealer will establish a wider bid-ask spread than will perfectly competitive dealers.

The positive implications of the model are consistent with empirically observed phenomena. The bid-ask spread increases with greater price volatility in the asset being traded, with a higher asset price level, and with lower volume. These predictions are verified by the empirical work of Demsetz [10], Tinic and West [29], Tinic [28], Benston and Hagerman [4], and Hamilton [17]. In addition, Stoll [26] finds that NASDAQ dealers tend to acquire shares when prices fall and sell when prices rise; also that dealer inventories tend to increase on days prior to price declines and decrease prior to price rises. This type of dealer behavior is consistent with our supposition that dealers suffer losses to informed traders. Within the context of our model a rational dealer will always set an ask price higher and a bid price lower than what he believes the "true" market price to be.

References

1. Yakov Amihud and Haim Mendelson. "Dealership market: Market-making with Inventory." *Journal of Financial Economics* (March 1980), 31–53.
2. Walter Bagehot (pseud). "The Only Game in Town." *Financial Analysts Journal* (March/April 1971).
3. Avraham Beja and M. Barry Goldman. "On the Dynamic Behavior of Prices in Disequilibrium." *The Journal of Finance* 35 (May 1980), 235–48.
4. George J. Benston and Robert L. Hagerman. "Determinants of Bid-Ask Spreads in the Over-the-Counter Market." *Journal of Financial Economics* (January–February 1974), 353–64.

5. Fischer Black and Myron Scholes. "The Pricing of Options and Corporate Liabilities." *Journal of Political Economy* (May/June 1973), 637–59.

6. James Bradfield. "A Formal Dynamic Model of Marketing Making." *Journal of Financial and Quantitative Analysis* (June 1979), 275–91.

7. Kalman J. Cohen, Steven Maier, Robert Schwartz, and David Whitcomb. "Limit Orders, Market Structure and the Returns Generation Process." *Journal of Finance* 33 (June 1978), 723–36.

8. _______. "The Determinants of the Bid-Ask Spread; A Simulation Study," Working Paper No. 162, Salomon Brothers Center, New York University, 1979a.

9. John Cox and Steven Ross. "The Valuation of Options for Alternative Stochastic Processes." *The Journal of Financial Economics* (January/March 1976), 145–66.

10. Harold Demsetz. "The Cost of Transacting." *Quarterly Journal of Economics* (February 1968), 33–53.

11. Elroy Dimson. "Risk Measurement When Shares are Subject to Infrequent Trading." *The Journal of Financial Economics* (June 1979), 197–226.

12. William Feller. *An Introduction to Probability Theory and Its Applications*, Volume I, third edition. New York, John Wiley and Sons, (1968).

13. Dan Galai. "Characterization of Options." *Journal of Banking and Finance* (December 1977). 373–85.

14. Kenneth Garbade. *Securities Markets.* New York, McGraw Hill Book Co., (1982).

15. _______ and Zvi Lieber, "On the Independence of Transactions on the New York Stock Exchange." *Journal of Banking and Finance* (March 1977), 151–72.

16. Mark Garman. "Market Microstructure." *The Journal of Financial Economics* (June 1976), 257–75.

17. James Hamilton. "Marketplace Organization and Marketability: NASDAQ, the Stock Exchange, and the National Market System." *The Journal of Finance* 33 (March 1978), 487–503.

18. Thomas Ho and Hans Stoll. "Optimal Dealer Pricing under Transactions and Return Uncertainty." *The Journal of Financial Economics* (March 1981), 47–74.

19. _____. "On Dealer Markets under Competition." *Journal of Finance* (May 1980), 259–68.

20. Jeff Jaffee and Robert Winkler, "Optimal Speculation against an Efficient Market." *The Journal of Finance* 31 (March 1976), 49–61.

21. Dennis Logue "Market-Making and the Assessment of Market Efficiency." *The Journal of Finance* 30 (March 1975), 115–23.

22. Robert Merton. "The Theory of Rational Option Pricing." *The Bell Journal of Economics and Management Science* (Spring 1973), 93–121.

23. _____. "Theory of Finance from the Perspective of Continuous Time." *Journal of Financial and Quantitative Analysis* (November 1975), 659–74.

24. Myron Scholes and Joseph Williams. "Estimating Betas from Nonsynchronous Data," *The Journal of Financial Economics* (December 1977), 359–80.

25. Seymour Smidt. U. S. Securities and Exchange Commission, Institutional Investor Study Report of the SEC (IIS), Volume 4, Chapter 12, (1969).

26. Hans Stoll. "Dealer Inventory Behavior: An Empirical Investigation of NASDAQ Stocks." *The Journal of Financial and Quantitative Analysis* (September 1976), 350–80.

27. _____. "The Supply of Dealer Services in Securities Markets." *The Journal of Finance* 33 (September 1978), 1133–51.

28. Seha Tinic. "The Economics of Liquidity Services." *Quarterly Journal of Economics* (February 1972), 79–93.

29. _____ and Richard West, "Competition and the Pricing of Dealer Services in the Over-the-Counter Stock Market." *Journal of Financial and Quantitative Analysis* (June 1972), 1707–28.

Three

David J. Teece

David J. Teece received a Ph.D. from the University of Pennsylvania in 1975. He started out at Stanford University, and now is a chaired faculty member and Institute director at the University of California at Berkeley. •

As a graduate student at Penn, in the early 70s, I had the great fortune of being taught macroeconomics by Steve Ross. The text was Don Patinkin's book *Money, Interest, and Prices.* Steve struck me right off as a genius, not only in his ability to understand and analyze, but also in the clarity of his teaching. I was awestruck. My interests at the time were in welfare economics and applied micro, particularly the economics of innovation. Despite the fact that my interests were not precisely aligned with his, Steve continued as a mentor, opened his home, and shared his delightful family with myself and other graduate students almost every Sunday morning. We admired his rusty old Volkswagen, which was semi-permanently parked on the street. Carol's and Steve's warmth and kindness, coupled with their intelligence and enthusiasm for life and good living, were simply unparalleled.

Steve also has helped countless graduate students find jobs and get started in their careers. If Steve thought you were a good student, he broadcast it to everyone, much like a proud father might talk up his own kids. I never felt—and still don't feel—that I deserved Steve's superlatives. He undoubtedly helped jump-start my career; I am extremely grateful to him for doing so.

In short, Steve Ross has demonstrated all the hallmarks of a great man—a brilliant intellect, a great teacher, a compassionate person, and a loyal and generous friend. There may be other great scholars, but there are so few who can so confidently embrace theory and practice while displaying warmth and humility. I am happy to join a chorus of former students to raise my voice in unqualified admiration for someone who touched my life and turbocharged my career. Thank you, Steve, and thank you, Carol; and thank you, Penn, for capturing Steve for a few brilliant years. Steve continues to inspire us to be the best we can on all fronts all the time.

Vertical Integration and Risk Reduction

Constance E. Helfat
University of California at Davis

David J. Teece
University of California at Berkeley

1. Introduction

In this paper we propose an indirect test of the "new institutional economics" (Williamson, 1975, 1981, 1985) by exploring the relationship between vertical integration and uncertainty. We present evidence that suggests that vertical integration, executed by merger, may reduce a firm's systematic or undiversifiable risk. That is, vertical mergers reduce risk by more than the simple portfolio effects that arise from combining business units in which returns are not perfectly correlated, suggesting that internal organization does have distinctive properties which cannot be easily replicated by stockholders taking separate asset positions in specialized companies operating at each stage of an industry.

Uncertainty creates several kinds of problems for the organization of production. One is that it complicates decisionmaking. Because of uncertainty and bounded rationality, comprehensive contingent planning on how to deploy resources in the future is impossible. Not only are there too many contingencies, but many contingencies are simply unknown—the "event set" simply cannot be fully specified.[1] Decisionmakers accordingly find advantage in being able to adapt to unanticipated contingencies as they are revealed over time. In fact, a firm that is able to do so quickly is likely to be considered well managed. Putting it differently, "uncertainty appears as the fundamental problem for complex organization and coping with uncertainty is the essence of the administrative process" (Thompson: 159).

Several sources of uncertainty can be recognized. One approach adopted by Koopmans involves separating primary from secondary uncertainty (Koopmans: 162). Primary uncertainty is of the state contingent kind and results from future natural events, discoveries, and changes in preferences. Secondary uncertainty arises "from the lack of communication, that is from one decisionmaker having no way of finding out the concurrent decisions and plans made by others" (163). According to Koopmans, this kind of uncertainty is "quantitatively at least as important as the primary uncertainty arising from random acts of nature and unpredictable changes in consumers' preferences" (162–63).

The secondary uncertainty which Koopmans has in mind appears to be of a rather passive kind. But as Williamson (1975, 1979, 1981) has frequently pointed out, economic agents may sometimes fail to disclose information and may in fact disguise and distort it. They may also adopt business strategies designed to create additional business uncertainty for their rivals.

We are indebted to Richard Castanias, Pablo Spiller, an anonymous referee, and the editor for their many useful suggestions, and to Amy Abramson for her research assistance. We wish to thank Henry Armour and Garth Saloner for extensive help on an earlier version which was widely circulated in 1980. The earlier version (Teece et al., 1980) outlined the methodology employed here but contained several technical errors. This paper refines that methodology and reports new results computed on a different and more satisfactory sample. The technical errors brought to our attention have been corrected. John Cox, Jeffrey Pfeffer, Steven Ross, and Robert Wilson also provided useful comments on the earlier draft.

[1]See, for example, Hadley (16–17).

Reprinted with permission:
Helfat, Constance E. and David J. Teece. "Vertical Integration and Risk Reduction."
Journal of Law, Economics, and Organization 3 (1987): 47–67.

In addition, therefore, to the problems of "nonconvergent expectations" to which Koopmans (and later Malmgren) referred, it is necessary to make provision also for what has subsequently been referred to as "behavioral uncertainty" (Williamson, 1985: 58–59).[2]

Both kinds of uncertainty are relevant to vertical supplier–buyer relationships. Suppose a downstream firm requires components or raw materials from an upstream source. Suppose further that the two firms bear a bilateral dependency relation (by reason of asset specificity) to one another. Both secondary and behavioral uncertainties thereby result. Thus whereas vertical integration has no impact on primary uncertainty, it is hypothesized here to reduce both secondary and behavioral uncertainties as compared to the unintegrated alternative.

The reasoning is quite straightforward. Internal organization facilitates information flows between separable stages since there are no proprietary boundaries encountered, and furthermore, communication codes and routines commonly emerge within organizations, which minimize the cost of identifying and disclosing information to the relevant parties (Armour and Teece, 1978, 1980; Arrow; Williamson, 1975; Nelson and Winter; Monteverde and Teece). More important for our purposes here, incentives for strategic distortion and nondisclosure are attenuated, since such behavior has a zero-sum impact on profits at the corporate level. Agents can place greater reliance on information communicated between vertically related divisions of the firm than on that communicated between vertically related firms.

If vertical integration can reduce a firm's exposure to uncertainty, and the risks investors face in holding its securities, then there are theoretical and empirical reasons for believing that its cost of capital and its costs of production will be lower than otherwise. In a competitive market, these savings will tend to be translated into lower product prices and will also render entry by firms that are not vertically integrated difficult because their capital costs will be higher. Lower risk also implies lower expected rates of return to investors in vertically integrated firms if capital markets are efficient. However, lower returns need not leave investors worse off since there is an offsetting reduction in the riskiness of the investor's portfolio. Thus, if risk is reduced by vertical integration, and lower risks mean lower capital costs and rates of return, vertical integration will benefit the consumers of the firm's output while leaving investors no worse off.

2. The Capital Asset Pricing Model and Systematic Risk

We have hypothesized that vertical integration may enable a firm to produce a de facto reduction in the uncertainty of its environment. In order to translate this hypothesis into a form that will enable it to be tested, we first trace the implications of the hypothesis through to its impact on the riskiness to investors holding the firm's securities.

Various measures of investor risk have been proposed. One is the variance of a security's total return, and another is the coefficient of variation, which is the standard deviation divided by the mean or expected return. But neither of these measures takes into account that investors hold assets not in isolation but jointly with other assets, so that the riskiness of an asset can be influenced by the interaction of the pattern of its return with the patterns of returns of the other assets with which it is combined in an investor's portfolio. Thus the riskiness of assets held in portfolios can be measured by their contribution to portfolio risk. The relationship can be measured by the covariance of the assets' return with the return on the market as a whole, commonly known as beta (β). The Capital Asset Pricing Model (CAPM) of Sharpe (1964), Lintner, and Mossin sets forth a theory of the relationship

[2]Subsequent to our earlier discussion (Teece et al., 1980) of secondary uncertainty, Williamson has coined the term *behavioral uncertainty* to describe the phenomenon we identified. The label is most helpful, and we adopt it hereafter.

between the risk of an asset and the required risk adjustment factor. The relationship is expressed in the security market line (Sharpe, 1964). In short, the total risk involved in holding an asset can be decomposed into two parts:

$$\text{total risk} = \underset{\text{(nondiversifiable)}}{\text{systematic risk}} + \underset{\text{(diversifiable)}}{\text{unsystematic risk.}}$$

Unsystematic risk, such as wildcat strikes or a technological breakthrough that makes obsolete a firm's products but has minimal repercusions [sic] elsewhere, is unique to the particular company. Systematic risk such as a congressional tax initiative or an oil shock, on the other hand, affects securities overall. It cannot be diversified away. If one assumes that investors as a whole are efficiently diversified, unsystematic risk becomes quantitatively unimportant and systematic risk emerges as the relevant measure of a firm's risk.[3]

3. Vertical Integration and Systematic Risk (Beta)

While systematic risk cannot be reduced through the use of capital market instruments, the arguments in section 1 above suggest that internal organization, and in particular vertical integration, can be an instrument for reducing systematic risk. To understand why, we must explore beneath the surface of the CAPM market model.[4]

In the CAPM, it is not the expected market return (in excess of the risk-free rate) which generates the expected asset return. Rather, anticipated economic events are the causal factors behind both R_m and R_F. If one looks forward in time one can see that the market will be significantly affected by changes in the expected rate of inflation, interest rates, regulation, the growth rate of real GNP, and many other factors. There are also a number of less general events, related to these, that deserve greater attention: movements in crude oil and other raw material prices, developments in alternative domestic energy supplies, changes in public attitudes toward regulation, and possible changes in the tax law, among others. Each of these events is important in contributing to the uncertainty of future market returns; and for each, one can anticipate the effect upon any particular security.

Consider, for example, a domestic oil stock. Oil shocks will have a proportionally greater effect upon such a stock, and inflation-related events probably a proportionally smaller effect, than for the market as a whole. As a result, if one foresees that the major

---

[3]Roll specifically criticized beta as a risk measure on two grounds: first, that it will always be (significantly) positively related to observed average individual returns if the market index is on (not significantly off) the positive sloped section of the ex-post efficient frontier, regardless of investors' attitudes toward risk; and second, that it depends, nonmonotonically, on the particular market proxy used. These criticisms are theoretically valid and imply, as suggested above, that estimated betas may be unreliable measures of diversifiable risk.

[4]We wish to warn that the test presented, since it assumes the validity of the CAPM, is exposed to some of the criticisms of this particular theoretical construct, the most serious of which questions the empirical usefulness of the model. Roll has pointed out that while the underlying theory of the CAPM suggests a relationship between an asset's returns and the covariability of these returns with the returns of all other assets (including human capital), empirical application of the market model, by necessity, restricts examination and estimation of covariability to a much smaller population of assets, typically publicly traded securities. Thus an estimate of the systematic risk (covariability) associated with an asset may differ from the "true" theoretical risk. Further, two individual investors holding different efficient portfolios, neither containing a complete representation of all assets, may obtain different systematic risk estimates for the same asset due to differing covariability with the returns associated with the other assets in their portfolios. Ross has questioned the empirical appeal of two alternative assumptions required to derive the basic model, that of quadratic preferences or, alternatively, that asset returns are multivariate normally distributed. The implication of these limitations to the present study lie in making the results conditionally applicable to the population of assets utilized. That is, the comparison of pre- and post-merger systematic risk estimates is strictly relevant only to those investors holding the portfolio used to generate the risk estimates.

source of uncertainty in future returns is from developments in energy markets, one will anticipate an unusually high beta, but if one foresees that the major source of uncertainty lies in inflation-related events, one will anticipate an unusually low beta (Rosenberg and Guy: 3). Notice from the example that two types of parameters determine the level of systematic risk (beta): the degree of uncertainty associated with potential economic events, and the responses of security returns to those events. If vertical integration enables the firm to adapt to uncertainty/complexity in a fashion which cannot be replicated as efficiently by long-term contracts and spot trading, then vertical integration should reduce the response of the security relative to the market response to an event. If vertical integration reduces the relative response of security returns to economic events outside of the firm, it will reduce beta.

4. The Data and Statistical Design

We wish to establish a quasi-controlled experiment to examine the effects of vertical integration on a firm's beta. Hypothesis testing using vertically integrated firms that have become vertically integrated via internal expansion is rendered difficult by the fact that the firms in this category have maintained a fairly constant level of vertical integration over the time period for which data is available. Accordingly, it is extremely difficult, if not impossible, to execute a controlled experiment by analyzing firms that have become vertically integrated by internal growth.

By focusing on vertical mergers, we are able to observe the effects of vertical integration on beta over a much more compressed timespan. This reduces the data and statistical problems to manageable proportions. However, to the extent that vertical integration by merger renders vertical communication and administrative control more difficult than it is when the vertical integration is achieved by internal growth, a statistical design based on vertical mergers will bias the results against our hypothesis. Spiller, using a different approach to that employed here, has also used vertical mergers in his examination of the gains to merger and risk reduction.[5]

The general design employed here involves forming an "experimental" group of U.S. firms that have participated in vertical mergers. Each pair of experimental firms is then matched against a pair of control firms similar in most important respects save that of merger activity. There is sometimes a presumption, based on studies such as Blume (1971), that betas do not change greatly over time. Other studies have showed, however, that individual firm betas may be nonstationary and do tend to regress to the grand mean of all betas, equal to 1.00 (Blume, 1977).[6] Over time, the betas that are less than 1.00 tend to rise, and vice versa. In addition, changes in the economic environment and other variables may also affect post-merger betas. Therefore, a straightforward calculation of pre- and post-merger betas might not permit the effect of vertical integration on risk to be effectively isolated.

In their study of the microeconomic consequences of all types of mergers, Lev and Mandelker use a paired sample technique similar to the one employed here. They note that merging firms may differ systematically from nonmerging firms and suggest that a pairing system that accounts for the major sources of differences between the two groups may

[5] In an excellent recent study, Pablo Spiller explored market power versus efficiency explanations of the risk reduction associated with vertical mergers and found that latter more compelling. In particular, he found that vertical mergers amongst firms with geographically proximate vertically related facilities (his proxy for specialized assets) showed largest gains from merging as well as a larger reduction in their systematic risk.

[6] Estimated beta coefficients tend to regress toward the grand mean of all betas over time. According to Blume (1977), part of this observed regression tendency represents real nonstationarities in the betas of individual securities. In other words, companies of extreme risk—either high or low—tend to have less extreme risk characteristics over time. See Blume (1977:31) for possible explanations.

reduce some of this systematic bias. Lev and Mandelker controlled for industry, firm size, and chronological time period. There is some evidence that industry betas vary over time; for example, in the oil industry, firm betas exhibited similar patterns of change throughout the 1970s.[7] Additionally, if factors other than covariance with the market return affect individual stock returns (as suggested by King), pairing may control for some of these factors. In order to net out such influences we use a procedure described below to select two firms as comparable as possible to the merging firms; using the same estimation procedures and chronological periods, we calculate the pre- and post-merger betas.

U.S. firms involved in vertical mergers between 1948 and 1979 inclusive, as reported by the Federal Trade Commission,[8] formed the sample from which the companies in this study were chosen. The analysis was performed using monthly security returns from the Center for Research in Security Prices (CRSP) tapes. Companies were included in the monthly sample provided that:

1. their shares were publicly traded for at least fifty months before the end of the seventh month prior to the announcement of the merger;[9]
2. the merged firm was publicly traded for at least fifty months following the merger;[10]
3. market data was contained on the CRSP tapes of monthly New York Stock Exchange security returns;
4. firms involved in other nonvertical mergers, with either the acquiring or acquired company (as reported by the FTC),[11] were also listed on the monthly CRSP tapes during the time periods described in 1 and 2 above.

Because other nonvertical mergers may change the value of the merged firm's stock market beta, the nonvertically acquired companies must be included in the analysis.[12]

Of the companies involved in vertical mergers listed by the FTC, over forty pairs of firms were listed on the CRSP tapes. The other criteria, however, caused numerous firms in the original sample to be excluded from our analysis. The firms involved in the fourteen mergers using monthly data that satisfy these criteria are listed in table 1.[13] The vertical nature of each of these mergers was double-checked using the type of business descriptions in Moody's *Industrial Manual.*

Pre-merger betas were estimated using OLS and fifty months of data for the monthly sample. Betas were estimated in the standard way from the relationship:

$$R_{jt} = \alpha_j + \beta_j R_{Mt} + \bar{e}_{jt} \tag{1}$$

[7]This information is based on unpublished work by Richard Castanias.

[8]In its 1981 *Statistical Report on Mergers and Acquisitions.*

[9]Studies have shown that the stock market anticipates mergers well before their announcement dates. We rely on Halpern's results showing abnormal returns as early as the end of the seventh month prior to the announcement date. The announcement date is the first public announcement of possible intentions to merger appearing in the *Wall Street Journal* or in the *New York Times* where *Wall Street Journal* information is not readily available.

[10]The merger date is taken as the last month when the acquired company's stock was traded or a return recorded on CRSP.

[11]Many firms were involved in smaller mergers of less than $10 million not listed by the FTC. We expect that mergers involving relatively small firms will not greatly affect the computed values of the betas.

[12]In his work on vertical mergers, Spiller uses similar criteria to select a sample of firms using monthly CRSP data, with the omission of criterion number 4. Because we incorporate the impact of other nonvertical mergers on the estimates of beta, our sample of vertical mergers is smaller than Spiller's.

[13]This sample provides a strong test of our hypothesis in that we do not attempt to screen out those vertical mergers for which transactional considerations are unimportant, or for which transactional economies were not realized because of managerial ineptitude or failure to implement the organizational linkages necessary to improve scheduling and coordination advantages and the like. To the extent that firms with these characteristics are in our sample, the data will be biased against our hypothesis.

TABLE 1 | Sample Firms Involved in Vertical Mergers, 1948–79 Monthly Return Data (Acquired firms listed first)

Case no.	Firm name	Market value ($MM)* (equity and debt)	Merger date**
1	Hinde & Dauche	27.4	Nov. 1953
	W. Va. Pulp & Paper	109.9	
2	Lion Oil	252.0	Nov. 1955
	Monsanto	862.1	
3	National Container	156.2	Nov. 1956
	Owens Illinois	447.3	
4	Visking	109.2	Jan. 1957
	Union Carbide	3,902.7	
5	Superior Steel[a]	8.1	Dec. 1958
	Copperweld Steel[a]	29.9	
6	Philco	154.8	Dec.1961
	Ford Motor Co.	6,571.6	
7	Columbian Carbon[b]	91.4	Feb. 1962
	(Miami Copper)[b]	36.9	June 1960
	(Tennessee Corp.)[b]	163.4	June 1963
	Cities Service[b]	1,087.5	
8	Haveg[c]	57.4	Aug. 1964
	Hercules Powder[c]	813.2	
9	Sealrite Oswego	42.0	Oct. 1964
	Phillips Petroleum	2,006.3	
10	American Potash	146.4	Jan. 1968
	Kerr-McGee	1,015.3	
11	Amerada Petroleum	1,582.5	June 1969
	Hess Oil	644.1	
12	Kelsey Hayes	151.3	Nov. 1973
	Fruehauf	367.4	
13	Latrobe Steel	28.1	Apr. 1975
	Timken	342.1	
14	Sprague Electric[d]	134.9	Dec. 1976
	(Automation Inds.)[d]	110.3	May 1978
	General Cable Corp.[d]	411.4	

*Debt includes long-term debt plus preferred stock. Stock market equity is valued as of the last trade date on CRSP of the acquired company. Debt is valued at year-end prior to the merger.

**Merger date is that of last CRSP record for the acquired company.

[a]The post-merger sample has only 40 observations.

[b]Cities Service acquired Tennessee Corp. in a nonvertical merger. Tennessee Corp. had previously acquired Miami Copper in a nonvertical merger.

[c]The pre-merger sample has only 42 observations due to lack of CRSP data for another nonvertical merger at the beginning of the pre-merger period.

[d]General Cable acquired Automation Inds. in a nonvertical merger. The post-merger sample has only 35 observation[s] because General Cable (then called GK Technologies) was acquired by another firm and delisted.

where

R_{jt} = the ex-post return for security j for month t[14]

R_{Mt} = the ex-post return of the value-weighted market index,

[14]More specifically, $R_{jt} = (P_{jt} + \text{DIV}_{jt} - P_{j,t-1})/P_{j,t-1}$ where P_{jt} is the price of security j in period t, and DIV_{jt} is the dividend associated with security j in period t.

and

$$E(e_{jt}) = 0, E(e_{it}e_{jt}) = 0, i \neq j.$$

These estimated betas reflect the systematic risk associated with the firm's stock market equity, rather than with the entire value of the firm. Therefore, firm asset betas are derived from the estimated stock market betas as follows:

$$\hat{\beta}_A = \hat{\beta}_{\text{debt}}\left(\frac{\text{debt}}{\text{debt} + \text{equity}}\right) + \hat{\beta}_{\text{equity}}\left(\frac{\text{equity}}{\text{debt} + \text{equity}}\right) \tag{2}$$

where

$\hat{\beta}_A$ = estimated asset systematic risk

$\hat{\beta}_{\text{debt}}$ = estimated debt systematic risk, assumed to equal zero[15]

$\hat{\beta}_{\text{equity}}$ = estimated beta from (1) above

equity = CRSP stock market value of common stock

debt = par or liquidating value of preferred stock plus book value of debt at year-end.[16]

For the pre-merger asset betas, the debt and equity values are those as of the last date in the pre-merger sample. A predicted post-merger beta for the merged firms which reflects diversification effects was then computed as follows:[17]

$$\hat{\beta}_p = W_1\hat{\beta}_1 + W_2\hat{\beta}_2 \tag{3}$$

where

$\hat{\beta}_p$ = the predicted post-merger systematic risk

$\hat{\beta}_i$ = the estimated pre-merger systematic risk of firm i

W_i = the market value (debt + stock market equity) of firm i as a proportion of the total value of the surviving firm $(W_1 + W_2 = 1)$.[18]

In cases where one of the firms had other nonvertical mergers during the pre-merger period, the asset betas for the acquired firms were estimated; each was weighted by its market value as a share of the market value of the surviving firm (computed subsequent to all mergers) and included in the predicted post-merger beta.

The actual post-merger beta, $\hat{\beta}_a$, for each of the merged firms was then estimated with the same regression model using the fifty monthly return observations subsequent to the merger date. The betas from the OLS regression were transformed into asset $\hat{\beta}_a$'s using debt and equity values just subsequent to the merger. These asset betas adjust for the possible impact on stock market betas of an increase in debt to finance the merger. In the absence of

[15]See Brealey and Myers (chap. 9). Although the beta for debt may not in fact be zero, this approximation is often used.

[16]Due to the difficulty of estimating the market values of firm debt, we have used book values, a common procedure in computing firm asset betas. This may introduce some bias in the net risk reduction calculations. For hypothetically perfect controls, which have the same relation of market to book values of debt and the same pre-merger betas as do the merging firms, the use of a book value greater than the true market value yields a lower absolute net risk reduction than is actually the case. The reverse occurs if book value is less than the true market value of debt.

[17]See Sharpe (1970: chap. 7) for the derivation of this algorithm.

[18]The market value is computed as of the merger date.

risk reduction and confounding effects, one would expect $\hat{\beta}_p - \hat{\beta}_a = 0$ on average. If, however, risk reduction effects are present and confounding effects are absent, then $\hat{\beta}_p - \hat{\beta}_a > 0$.

To handle confounding effects, a control group was chosen by searching the CRSP and COMPUSTAT tapes and Moody's *Industrial Manual* in each case to find firms which matched the merging firms as closely as possible on the criteria of industry group, market value, and listing on the CRSP tapes for the pre- and post-merger sample periods. In order to control for effects of regression toward the mean, firms qualifying on the above criteria were selected on the basis of closeness of pre-merger estimated beta to that of the matched merging firms. More specifically, the industry group occupied by each of the merging firms was first identified. This was followed by a search for firms of approximately the same asset size who were not involved in vertical mergers during the period in which they would serve as controls. For the six firms (or fewer, depending on the availability of firms on CRSP in the same industry group in the sample period) closest in market value (including debt), asset betas were calculated and the firm selected which had the closest value of beta.[19] The resulting betas were reasonably close. To be precise, the average absolute difference in pre-merger betas between the monthly sample and control firms was .124 for the acquiring firms and .236 for the acquired firms. The selected control firms for the monthly sample are listed in table 2, and the asset betas for the original and control companies are displayed in tables 3 and 4.[20]

The risk effect of vertical integration can be isolated by the following measure:

$$D = (\hat{\beta}_p - \hat{\beta}_a) - (\hat{\beta}_{cp} - \hat{\beta}_{ca}) \tag{4}$$

where

$\hat{\beta}_{cp}$ = the predicted post-merger weighted asset beta for the control group

$\hat{\beta}_{ca}$ = the actual post-merger weighted asset beta for this group.[21]

D thus measures the additional reduction in systematic risk in the vertically merging firms over that in the control group and is therefore the effect that can be attributed to vertical integration. Under the null hypothesis D is not significantly different from zero. If the null hypothesis can be rejected on a one-dimensional test, this will confirm that vertical integration is associated with risk-reduction.

Formally, the null hypothesis is

$$H_0: D = 0 \tag{5}$$

while the alternative hypothesis is

$$H_A: D > 0.$$

Rather than resorting to distributional assumptions about D, we use the Wilcoxon Matched Pairs Signed Ranks Test to test the null hypothesis.[22] This test ranks D according to the magnitude of the difference in the pre- and post-merger risk reduction of the merging firms

---

[19] Debt/equity ratios for the control firms were assumed to stay the same during both the pre- and post-merger sample periods; the ratios used to compute asset betas for the controls are those at the start of the post-merger period. We do not attempt to adjust for changes in these ratios for reasons other than merger.

[20] Note that firms in the original sample could also serve as control companies for other firms providing the original firms had no vertical mergers during the time period for which they serve as a control.

[21] The weights used to compute $\hat{\beta}_{cp}$ and $\hat{\beta}_{ca}$ are those that existed at the start of the post-merger period.

[22] The power-efficiency of the Wilcoxon test for small samples is near 95 percent. Its asymptotic efficiency compared with the parametric t-test is $3/\pi = 95.5$ percent (Mood). This means that $3/\pi$ is the limiting ratio of sample sizes necessary for Wilcoxon test and t-test to attain the same power.

TABLE 2 | Control Group—Monthly Sample (Firm-matched, with acquired firm listed first)

Case no.	Firm name	Market value ($MM)* (equity and debt)
1	Chesapeake Corp.	14.6
	KVP Paper	31.5
2	Champlin Oil	144.3
	Koppers	111.7
3	United Board & Carton	6.7
	Corning Glass	436.1
4	National Vulcanized Fibre	7.7
	Diamond Alkali	180.0
5	Lukens	64.2
	Revere Copper & Brass	89.3
6	Magnavox	300.7
	General Motors	16,704.2
7	Atlas Chemical	75.3
	(Granby Mining)	9.5
	(Olin Corp.)	847.6
	Shell Oil	2,903.0
8	Dayco	45.4
	Reichhold Chemicals	82.0
9	Chesapeake Corp.	68.1
	Shell Oil	4,072.4
10	Publicker	46.5
	Quaker State Oil	87.2
11	General American Oil Co., Texas	278.9
	Apco Oil	123.9
12	Smith (A.O.) Co.	129.2
	Chrysler Corp.	1,771.2
13	Florida Steel	40.5
	Federal Mogul Corp.	173.9
14	International Rectifier	26.1
	(Simmonds Precision Products)	49.9
	Asarco	780.0

*Long-term debt plus preferred stock plus market value of common stock as of the first month following the merger.

and that of the firms in the control group. The highest number is assigned to the *D* with the highest absolute value. The ranks are then signed so that where the merging firms had a greater risk-reduction than the control firms, the rank receives a positive sign. If the null hypothesis is correct the summation of the positively signed ranks and that of the negatively signed ranks summed separately should be approximately equal. The smaller sum of the like-signed ranks, *T*, is approximately normally distributed for large sample sizes, while for smaller sample sizes approximations exist.[23]

5. Results

The methodology described above is, in many ways, biased against a finding that vertical mergers reduce risk. The generally small sizes of the acquired companies compared to that of the acquiring companies makes it more difficult to discern an impact of a

[23]Critical values were obtained from *Biometrika Tables for Statisticians,* volume 2 (1976).

given merger on the estimated post-merger betas. This is due to the lower weights which smaller firms have in the weighted beta calculations. In addition, the merger sample size is small.

Table 3 shows the calculations of the measured risk reduction in the merging firms. Because the impact of vertical mergers on risk in the absence of controls may be of interest, the extreme right-hand column displays the results of a Wilcoxon test for the merging firms only. The sum of the negative ranks (the less frequent sign) is 18; the null hypothesis of no change in risk can be rejected in favor of a positive risk reduction (without controls) at the 98.5 percent level of significance.[24]

Table 4 displays the calculation of the measured risk reduction for the control groups. In table 5, the risk reduction figures for both the merging and the control firms are displayed and the result of the Wilcoxon test for the two groups is shown in the extreme righthand column. The sum of the negative signed ranks (the less frequent sign) is 14; we are able to reject the null hypothesis that $D = 0$ in favor of the alternate hypothesis that $D > 0$ at the 99.3 percent level of significance.

This very high level of significance is encouraging; however, it does occur in part because some of the control firms experienced risk increases. These risk increases are not anomalous. In two of the cases, numbers 8 and 14, virtually all of the possible control companies for the acquiring (and larger) firm had an increase in risk. For case 4, betas increased for two-thirds of the possible controls for both the acquired and the acquiring companies. The risk increase to the acquiring firm's control in case 5 accounts for almost all of the rise in the weighted beta; here again, two-thirds of the possible controls had increased risk. The rise in the betas for both control companies in case 11 most likely occurs for a different reason—regression toward the mean. The merging companies in case 11 also had estimated pre-merger betas well below 1.00, but their risk decreased following the merger. In summary, for those controls whose risk increased, much of the rise appears to be explained by industry effects or regression toward the mean, factors which the controls were designed to capture.

The results of the Wilcoxon test for the risk changes in the samples with and without controls are also highly robust. To test robustness, we progressively drop the observation with the highest rank from the sample and recompute the significance level. Table 6 shows the results of this procedure for the samples with and without controls. Where controls are used, the deletion of the top four net risk changes, over one quarter of the sample, still produces a significance level of over 90 percent; similarly, for the sample without controls, the deletion of the top three net risk changes produces a significance level of approximately 90 percent.

To provide yet another check on our results, we have calculated the net risk reductions using an alternative control group—industry indexes. Each merging firm is assigned a value-weighted industry index, composed of all firms in the industry who were listed on CRSP during the entire pre- and post-merger periods and were not involved in mergers during that time. The asset beta for each firm in the index is weighted by the share of the firm's asset value relative to the industry total.[25] For each merger in the sample, the

[24]Since it is possible that the assumption that $\hat{\beta}_{\text{debt}} = 0$ may be incorrect, we also performed this test under the extreme assumption that $\hat{\beta}_{\text{debt}} = \hat{\beta}_{\text{equity}}$. Under this assumption, the null hypothesis of no risk change for the merging firms can be rejected at the 91.4 percent level of significance.

[25]Firm debt figures are only available on an annual basis, rather than on a monthly basis as are the CRSP stock market returns and stock market equity values. Furthermore, the debt figures are not available on COMPUSTAT prior to 1966 and must be obtained from Moody's. Due to these data availability problems, the betas in the industry indexes are weighted by firm values at the time of the merger.

TABLE 3 | Risk Reduction in Merging Firms

(1) Case no.	(2) Pre-merger $\hat{\beta}$ of acquired co.	(3) Pre-merger $\hat{\beta}$ of acquiring co.	(4) Weighted average of pre-merger $\hat{\beta}$'s	(5) Post-merger $\hat{\beta}$ of integrated firm	(6) Risk reduction (4)–(5)	(7) Rank of absolute magnitude of column 6	T
1	1.017445	.5992289	.6826984	.8331071	−.1504087	6	6
2	.9772209	1.0036458	.9976681	.9318527	.0658154	3	
3	.5718657	.9578601	.8579764	.6526582	.2053182	10	
4	.7078524	.9792752	.9718876	.7968439	.1750437	9	
5	1.2684521	.9606079	1.0262742	.6775343	.3487399	13	
6	1.0099688	.9722603	.9731282	1.0654082	−.09228	4	4
7	1.1527121[a] (1.536450)[b] (1.218366)[c]	.8042226	.8959696	.2508674	.6451022	14	
8	2.5441532	1.0486786	1.1473104	1.2857318	−.1384214	5	5
9	.6596737	.814925	.8117442	.847195	−.0354508	2	2
10	.845915	.9848874	.9673769	.7955002	.1718767	8	
11	.558048	.678802	.5929784	.2467771	.3462013	12	
12	.5731739	.9215254	.819901	.4845268	.3353742	11	
13	.7182735	1.124393	1.093533	1.0995292	−.0059962	1	1
14	.7872474[d] (1.2605765)[e]	.7808936	.8627669	.7053954	.1573715	7	

[a] $\hat{\beta}$ for Columbian Carbon.
[b] $\hat{\beta}$ for Miami Copper.
[c] $\hat{\beta}$ for Tennessee Corp.
[d] $\hat{\beta}$ for Sprague Electric.
[e] $\hat{\beta}$ for Automation Inds.

TABLE 4 | Risk Reduction in Control Group

(1) Case no.	(2) Pre-merger $\hat{\beta}$ of firm matched with acquired firm	(3) Pre-merger $\hat{\beta}$ of firm matched with acquiring firm	(4) Weighted average of pre-merger $\hat{\beta}$'s	(5) Post-merger $\hat{\beta}$ of firm matched with acquired firm	(6) Post-merger $\hat{\beta}$ of firm matched with acquiring firm	(7) Weighted average of post-merger $\hat{\beta}$'s	(8) Risk reduction (4)–(7)
1	1.296059	.7242077	.9052537	1.286096	.8504807	.9883949	.0831412
2	.918111	.9680148	.9434507	1.1037528	.82962566	.9645558	−.0211051
3	.4580774	.9650575	.9573405	.7809048	1.5090916	1.4980075	−.540667
4	.6493176	.976841	.9633996	1.2986353	1.0870248	1.0957091	−.1323095
5	1.3816054	1.0636639	1.1966767	1.7164166	1.8052947	1.768112	−.5714353
6	.1308006	1.0919257	1.0857463	1.5327794	.843351	.855541	.2402053
7	1.0171632[a] (1.4917961)[b] (1.087984)[c]	1.0494717	1.0584573	.6621023[a] (1.912625)[b] (1.0443062)[c]	.8601623	.8995811	.1588762
8	.8408465	.995641	.9405225	1.0171964	1.3728347	1.2462008	−.3056783
9	.7489922	.7016597	.702437	.347047	.6981332	.6861659	.0162711
10	.9473385	.9645965	.9585976	1.6274997	.9971185	1.216273	−.2576754
11	.546873	.7772373	.6177254	1.353818	.9955759	1.2436345	−.6259091
12	.4713638	.7019615	.6862806	.4990933	.4941231	.494461	.1918196
13	.8109566	.42445	.4975121	.6130173	.4611883	.4898888	.0076233
14	.8331745[d] (.9734299)[e]	.5773559	.6145383	1.070555[d] (1.2930393)[e]	1.2522501	1.2546624	−.6377118

[a] $\hat{\beta}$ for Atlas Chemical.
[b] $\hat{\beta}$ for Granby Mining.
[c] $\hat{\beta}$ for Olin Corp.
[d] $\hat{\beta}$ for International Rectifier.
[e] $\hat{\beta}$ for Simmunds Precision Products.

TABLE 5 | Wilcoxon Signed Rank Test of the Risk-Reduction Hypothesis

(1) Case no.	(2) Risk reduction of merging firms (from table 3)	(3) Risk reduction of firms in control group (from table 4)	(4) Net risk reduction (2)–(3)	(5) Rank of absolute magnitude of col. (4)	(6) T
1	−.1504087	−.0831412	−.0672675	3	3
2	.0658154	−.0211051	+.0869205	4	
3	.2053182	−.540667	+.7459852	11	
4	.1750437	−.1323095	+.3073532	7	
5	.3487399	−.5714353	+.9201752	13	
6	−.09228	.2402053	−.3324853	8	8
7	.6451022	.1588762	+.486226	10	
8	−.1384214	−.3056783	+.1672569	6	
9	−.0354508	.0162711	−.0517219	2	2
10	.1718767	−.2576754	+.4295521	9	
11	.3462013	−.6259091	+.9721104	14	
12	.3353742	.1918196	+.1435546	5	
13	−.0059962	.0076233	−.0136195	1	1
14	.1573715	−.6377118	+.7950833	12	

predicted and actual post-merger industry betas are computed using the weights assigned to the merging firms themselves to weight the matched industry index for each firm. Table 7 displays the computed risk changes for the industry index controls.

An industry index provides a much less precise control for a merging company than does a single matched company. Neither regression toward the mean nor firm size differences are taken into account. One or more relatively large companies within the industry may disproportionately affect the beta for the index. Therefore, although one might expect the industry controls to show risk changes between the pre- and post-merger periods of close to zero, in fact the numbers on table 7 show some relatively large positive and negative risk reductions for the indusry index controls. As in the case of the matched company

TABLE 6 | Tests for Robustness

Sample size	Wilcoxon test results using matched pairs Cases deleted	Significance level (%)
14	None	99.3
13	11	98.7
12	11, 15	97.4
11	11, 5, 14	94.9
10	11, 5, 14, 3	90.3
Sample size	**Wilcoxon test results without controls Cases deleted**	**Significance level (%)**
14	None	98.5
13	7	97.1
12	7, 5	94.5
11	7, 5, 11	89.7

TABLE 7 | Risk Reduction in the Industry Index Control Group

(1) Case no.	(2) Pre-merger $\hat{\beta}$ of industry index matched with acquired firm	(3) Pre-merger $\hat{\beta}$ of industry index matched with acquiring firm	(4) Weighted average of pre-merger $\hat{\beta}$'s	(5) Post-merger $\hat{\beta}$ of industry index matched with acquired firm	(6) Post-merger $\hat{\beta}$ of industry index matched with acquiring firm	(7) Weighted average of post-merger $\hat{\beta}$'s	(8) Risk Reduction (4)–(7)
1	.7016437	1.0092889	.9478876	.6333556	.7289348	.7098586	.238029
2	1.1059951	.9504503	.9856365	1.0585817	.7269082	.8019371	.1836994
3	.9354547	1.0719177	1.0366052	.4858373	.9290353	.814349	.2222562
4	.646298	.9835204	.9743419	.8179408	.963752	.9597833	.0145586
5	1.288932	1.2234688	1.2374328	1.0313338	1.31907	1.2576927	−.0202599
6	1.3362581	1.0690792	1.075229	1.3224691	.8487366	.8596407	.2155883
7	.7462736[a] (1.1217788)[b] (.9384292)[c]	.9974425	.9771353	1.0040381[a] (1.2580779)[b] (1.0792388)[c]	.735879	.8082978	.1688275
8	.7941593	.9255073	.9168444	1.0264571	1.0284881	1.0283541	−.1115097
9	1.0509585	.6692943	.6771138	1.1481767	.7117748	.7207157	−.0436019
10	.9231105	.7036367	.7312903	.5578946	.7811225	.7529958	−.0217055
11	.9598239	.5415657	.8388346	.9663155	.6735198	.8816186	−.042784
12	.8285786	.7388191	.7650045	2.3242701	.610835	1.1106944	−.3456899
13	.666581	.42445[d]	.4428489	.6726809	.4611883[d]	.477259	−.0344101
14	1.2277426[e] (1.285288)[f]	.5051038	.7845767	1.4878796[e] (1.2509527)[f]	1.0013182	1.1431882	−.3586115

[a]Industry index match for Columbian Carbon.
[b]Industry index match for Miami Copper.
[c]Industry index match for Tennessee Corp.
[d]The industry match here consists of only one company because the company in the original sample, Timken, manufactures a very specialized product.
[e]Industry index match for Sprague Electric.
[f]Industry index match for Automation Inds.

TABLE 8 | Wilcoxon Signed Rank Test Using Industry Index Controls

(1) Case no.	(2) Risk reduction of merging firms (from table 3)	(3) Risk reduction of industry index control group (from table 7)	(4) Net risk reduction (2)−(3)	(5) Rank of absolute magnitude of col. (4)	(6) T
1	−.1504087	.2262132	−.3884377	10	10
2	.0658154	.1836994	−.117884	5	5
3	.2053182	.2222562	−.016938	2	2
4	.1750437	.0145586	.1604851	6	
5	.3487399	−.0202599	.3689998	9	
6	−.09228	.2155883	−.3078683	8	8
7	.6451022	.1688375	.4762647	12	
8	−.1384214	−.1115097	−.0269117	3	3
9	−.0354508	−.0436019	.0081511	1	
10	.1718767	−.0217055	.1935822	7	
11	.3462013	−.042784	.3889853	11	
12	.3353742	−.3456899	.6810641	14	
13	−.0059962	−.0344101	.0284139	4	
14	.1573715	−.3586115	.515983	13	

controls, many of the industry controls (eight in this case) show risk increases. Table 8 presents the results of the Wilcoxon test using the industry index controls. The sum of the negative signed ranks (the less frequent sign) is 28; we are able to reject the null hypothesis that $D = 0$ in favor of the alternate hypothesis that $D > 0$ at the 93.2 percent level of significance. Again, the test rejects the null hypothesis; given the less precise nature of the industry index controls, it is not surprising that this occurs at a somewhat lower level of significance.

6. Conclusion

The results, both with and without controls, suggest that vertical integration, at least when executed via vertical mergers, may be associated with a reduction in systematic risk. Although further work is needed to affirm the generality of these findings, the results are encouraging and appear to be robust. The statistical findings were sustained using "matched pairs" as controls, using industry indexes as controls, and using no controls at all. Most important, using control firms which were similar in many important ways, we obtained statistical significance of greater than 99 percent.

It is interesting to note that evidence elsewhere suggests that this phenomenon is not associated with horizontal or conglomerate mergers. A study that did not differentiate between the various generic classes of mergers found that mergers had no clear directional effect on the riskiness of acquiring firms, as measured by beta (Lev and Mandelker). The results here suggest that vertically integrated firms may have cost advantages in raising equity capital (Bicksler), which has important implications for assessing whether vertical integration might create "barriers" to entry (Williamson, 1975: 110–13; Bork: 148). To order vertical divestiture in circumstances where secondary and behavioral uncertainties are believed to be important, moreover, could raise the cost of capital for the firms involved (Mitchell). Clearly, more research is needed before the welfare implications of this organizational model can be accurately assessed. Nevertheless, it appears that vertical integration involves more than a portfolio effect with respect to risk reduction. Specifically, the results indicate that enterprise managers can reduce an investment's exposure to risk in ways which portfolio managers cannot.

There appear to be important implications for both the theory of the firm and investment theory. In particular, vertical integration appears to have a wider set of performance ramifications than is commonly supposed.

References

Armour, Henry, and David J. Teece. 1978. "Organizational Structure and Economic Performance: A Test of the M-Form Hypothesis," 9 *Bell Journal of Economics* 106–22.

______. 1980. "Vertical Integration and Technological Innovation," 62 *Review of Economics and Statistics* 470–74.

Arrow, Kenneth J. 1975. "Vertical Integration and Communication," 6 *Bell Journal of Economics* 173–83.

Bicksler, James. 1977. "The Usefulness of Beta Risk for Estimating the Cost of Capital," in I. Friend and J. Bicksler, eds., *Risk and Return in Finance.* Cambridge: Ballinger.

Black, Fisher, Michael Jensen, and Myron Scholes. 1972. "The Capital Asset Pricing Model: Some Empirical Tests," in M. Jensen, ed., *Studies in the Theory of Capital Markets.* New York: Praeger.

Blume, Marshall. 1971. "On the Assessment of Risk," 26 *Journal of Finance* 1–10.

______. 1977. "Betas and Their Regression Tendencies," in I. Friend and J. Bicksler, eds., *Risk and Return in Finance.* Cambridge: Ballinger.

Bork, Robert H. 1969. "Vertical Integration and Competitive Processes," in J. F. Weston and S. Peltzman, eds., *Public Policy towards Mergers.* Pacific Palisades: Goodyear Publishing.

Brealey, Richard, and Stewart Myers. 1984. *Principles of Corporate Finance.* New York: McGraw-Hill.

Carlton, Dennis W. 1978. "Market Behavior with Demand Uncertainty and Price Inflexibility," 68 *American Economic Review* 571–87.

Federal Trade Commission. 1981. *Statistical Report on Mergers and Acquisitions.* Washington, DC: Bureau of Economics.

Foster, George. 1978. *Financial Statement Analysis.* Englewood Cliffs: Prentice Hall.

Hadley, G. 1967. *Introduction to Probability and Statistical Decision Theory.* San Francisco: Holden Day.

Halpern, Paul. 1973. "Empirical Estimates of the Amount and Distribution of Gains to Companies in Mergers," 46 *Journal of Business* 554–75.

King, Benjamin. 1966. "Market and Industry Factors in Stock Price Behavior," 39 *Journal of Business* 139–90.

Klein, Benjamin, Robert G. Crawford, and Armen A. Alchian. 1978. "Vertical Integration, Appropriable Rents and the Competitive Contracting Process," 21 *Journal of Law and Economics* 297–326.

Koopmans, Tjalling C. 1957. *Three Essays on the State of Economic Science.* New York: McGraw-Hill.

Lev, Baruch, and Gershon Mandelker. 1972. "The Microeconomic Consequences of Corporate Mergers," 45 *Journal of Business* 85–104.

Lintner, John. 1965. "Security of Prices, Risk and Maximal Gains from Diversification," 20 *Journal of Finance* 587–616.

Malmgren, H. B. 1961. "Information, Expectations and the Theory of the Firm," 75 *Quarterly Journal of Economics* 399–421.

Mitchell, Edward. 1976. "Capital Cost Savings of Vertical Integration," in E. Mitchell, ed., *Vertical Integration in the Oil Industry.* Washington, DC: American Enterprise Institute.

Monteverde, Kirk, and David J. Teece. 1982. "Supplier Switching Costs and Vertical Integration in the Automobile Industry," 13 *Bell Journal of Economics* 206–13.

Mood, Alexander M. 1954. "On the Asymptotic Efficiency of Certain Non-Parametric Two-Sample Tests," 25 *Annals of Mathematical Statistics* 514–22.

Mossin, Jan. 1966. "Equilibrium in a Capital Asset Market," 34 *Econometrica* 768–83.

Nelson, Richard R., and Sidney E. Winter. 1982. *An Evolutionary Theory of Economic Change.* Cambridge: Harvard University Press.

Rohlf, F. James, and Robert R. Sokal. 1969. *Statistical Tables.* San Francisco: W. H. Freeman.

Roll, Richard. 1977. "A Critique of the Asset Pricing Theory Test," 4 *Journal of Financial Economics* 129–76.

Rosenberg, Barr, and James Guy. 1975. *The Prediction of Systematic Risk.* Working paper no. 33. Berkeley: Institute of Business and Economic Research, University of California.

Ross, Steven A. 1977. "Risk, Return, and Arbitrage," in I. Friend and J. Bicksler, eds., *Risk and Return in Finance.* Cambridge: Ballinger.

Sharpe, William F. 1964. "Capital Asset Prices: A Theory of Market Equilibrium under Conditions of Risk," 19 *Journal of Finance* 425–42.

———. 1970. *Portfolio Theory and Capital Markets.* New York: McGraw-Hill.

———. 1978. *Investments.* New Jersey: Prentice-Hall.

Spiller, Pablo. 1985. "On Vertical Mergers," 1 *Journal of Law, Economics, and Organization* 285–312.

Teece, David J. 1976. *Vertical Integration and Vertical Divestiture in the U.S. Oil Industry.* Stanford: Institute for Energy Studies.

———. 1981. "Internal Organization and Economic Performance: An Empirical Analysis of the Profitability of Principal Firms," 30 *Journal of Industrial Economics* 173–90.

———, Henry Armour, and Garth Saloner. 1980. "Vertical Integration and Risk Reduction," Research paper no. 563, revised May 1983. Graduate School of Business, Stanford University.

Thompson, James D. 1967. *Organizations in Action.* New York: McGraw-Hill.

Williamson, Oliver E. 1975. *Markets and Hierarchies: Analysis and Antitrust Implications.* New York: Free Press.

———. 1979. "Transactions-Cost Economics: The Governance of Contractual Relations," 22 *Journal of Law and Economics* 233–61.

———. 1981. "The Modern Corporation: Origins, Evolution, Attributes," 19 *Journal of Economic Literature* 1537–68.

———. 1985. *The Economic Institutions of Capitalism.* New York: Free Press.

Four

Laurence J. Kotlikoff

Laurence J. Kotlikoff first met Steve Ross as an undergraduate at the University of Pennsylvania. He received a Ph.D. from Harvard University in 1977. He started out at UCLA, and now works at Boston University. •

When I went to college at Penn, I wanted to be a doctor. But after performing open heart surgery on a defenseless frog, whose name I forget, I figured maybe a career in law. Then I took first-year economics and lucked out. I had an unbelievable teacher—Steve's good buddy Bob Pollak. I did okay in Bob's class, and he took me under his wing, suggesting I attend a seminar he, Steve, and Penn law professor Bruce Ackerman were running on social choice.

Well, it was just the most exciting and infectious intellectual experience—listening to Steve, Bob, and Bruce passionately discuss Arrow's impossibility theorem and related topics and drawing me, my sidekick Larry Weiss, Nancy Stokey, and our other classmates into the adventure.

Then, as now, Steve was red hot—bursting with insights, intellectually fearless, thinking at warp speed, and talking far faster than the mind can travel. I quickly realized I was in the presence of an economic superman. It made me nervous. I knew Steve would catch me saying something stupid even before it was out of my mouth. And he sure did (and still does).

But Steve is one of God's gifts when it comes to teaching. He knows how to sort out your ego as well as your brain. His warm smile, friendship, laughter, and enthusiasm were just what I needed to let myself learn and to find the courage to apply to graduate school. I'm so glad I did.

Once I got to know Steve, I realized that he was a sweetheart, but tough as nails when it came to intellectual rigor and truth. I also realized that Steve could not tolerate intellectual arrogance or sloth and was going to break some china along his path to the top. I was right.

My paper with Jerry Green, which we are so honored to have in this volume, breaks some china too. It argues that there is no economic basis for distinguishing private and public property. What we call private and public is simply what we call private and public. If we take the same assets and call more of them private and less of them public or vice versa and appropriately relabel future income flows between the public and the government, we've just changed words, not economic reality.

This proposition, that fiscal labeling conventions are, economically speaking, content-free, has important implications for empirical research in finance. Household A may seem to have a very safe portfolio because it's full of "government bonds." But what it really has is state-specific net flows from the government, which can just as well be labeled future transfer payments. So the same "data" on household A can be read as entailing large holdings of government bonds or zero holdings. Indeed, with the right words, household A can be said to hold any amount (positive or negative) of government bonds you'd like.

The message here is that we can't do empirical finance on the cheap. We need to consider household A's stochastic, remaining lifetime budget constraint in its full glory (and gory) to assess the risks it's taking. Doing so is no picnic. Doing otherwise is sophistry, something neither Steve Ross nor any of his devoted students will ever learn to tolerate.

On the General Relativity of Fiscal Language

Jerry Green
Laurence J. Kotlikoff

Abstract

A century ago, everyone thought time and distance were well defined physical concepts. But neither proved absolute. Instead, measures/reports of time and distance were found to depend on one's reference point, specifically one's direction and speed of travel, making our apparent physical reality, in Einstein's words, "merely an illusion."

Like time and distance, standard fiscal measures, including deficits, taxes, and transfer payments, depend on one's reference point/reporting procedure/language/labels. As such, they too represent numbers in search of concepts that provide the illusion of meaning where none exists.

This paper, dedicated to our dear friend, David Bradford, provides a general proof that standard and routinely used fiscal measures, including the deficit, taxes, and transfer payments, are economically ill-defined. Instead these measures reflect the arbitrary labeling of underlying fiscal conditions. Analyses based on these and derivative measures, such as disposable income, private assets, and personal saving, represent exercises in linguistics, not economics. •

I. Introduction

This paper provides a general proof that standard fiscal measures, including the deficit, taxes, and transfer payments, are economically ill-defined. Instead these measures reflect the arbitrary labeling of underlying fiscal conditions. Analyses based on these and derivative measures, such as disposable income, private assets, and personal saving, constitute the perusal of nomenclature, not the application of economics.

The argument that any underlying fiscal policy can be reported as entailing any time path of deficit, taxes, and transfer payments and that these measures are, economically speaking, content-free was originally advanced by Kotlikoff (1986). Auerbach and Kotlikoff (1987) and Kotlikoff (2002) provide formal treatments of the point, but neither provide a general proof of the proposition. This paper fills this gap. It posits a competitive, contingent claims economy that can accommodate uncertainty, information asymmetries, distortions, externalities, public goods, time inconsistent policy, imperfect credit markets, and incomplete/segmented markets.

II. The Model

In what follows, there are K agents, N states, M goods, V firms, and H endowments. Goods include leisure. Endowments include time, various types of physical capital, and natural resources. As in Arrow (1964), a state of the world is defined by a particular date, a particular resolution of uncertainty, and a specification of all economically relevant variables. The terms p_s and q_s reference pre-policy producer and endowment price vectors in state s.

Reprinted with permission:
"On the General Relativity of Fiscal Language" by Jerry Green and Laurence J. Kotlikoff reprinted by permission of the publishers from the forthcoming 2008 title, *Key Issues in Public Finance*, edited by Alan Auerbach and Daniel Shaviro, Cambridge, MA: Harvard University Press,

Profit Maximization

There are V firms, which may be operated by private agents, the government, or both. Firm j's profit is

$$\text{(1)} \qquad \pi_j \equiv \max_{y_{js}}\left(\sum_s p_s y_{js} - \sum_s q_s \varphi_{js} + m_j \right),$$

where y_{js} is firm j's $1 \times M$ vector of net goods supply in state s, φ_{js} is firm j's $1 \times H$ vector of endowment demands, and m_j is a function determining the government's net payment to firm j. Producers are atomistic and take producer prices, endowment prices, and their net payment functions as given.

Firm j's constant returns production function is given by

$$\text{(2)} \qquad f_j(y_{j1}, \ldots, y_{jN}, \varphi_{j1}, \ldots, \varphi_{jN}; Y_{-j1}, \ldots, Y_{-jN}, \varphi_{-j1}, \ldots, \varphi_{-jN}, X_1, \ldots, X_N, Z_1, \ldots, Z_N, \omega_1, \ldots, \omega_N) = 0$$

where Y_{-js} is a $1 \times M \times (V-1)$ vector of net supplies of firms other than j in state s, φ_{-js} is a $1 \times H \times (V-1)$ vector of state-s endowment demands of firms other than j, X_s references the $1 \times M \times K$ vector of goods demanded by agents 1 through K in state s, Z_s references the $1 \times M$ vector of goods demanded by the government in state s, and ω_s references the $1 \times H$ vector of economy-wide endowments in state s. For future reference we denote by Y_s the $1 \times M \times V$ vector of net supplies of firms 1 through V in state s and by φ_s the $1 \times H \times V$ vector of endowment demands of firms 1 through V.

Including the Y_{-js}'s, φ_{-js}'s, X_s's, Z_s's, φ_s's, and ω_s's in (2) entertains the possibility of production externalities, consumption externalities, externalities from the use of economy-wide endowments, as well as externalities arising from the levels of economy-wide endowments.

Firm j's net payment function, m_j, may depend on its own state-specific net supplies of goods and demands for endowments. But it may also depend on the state-specific net supplies and demands of other firms, the constellation of agents' state-specific demands, the constellation of government state-specific demands for goods and endowments, and the economy's overall endowments. In other words, the firm's net payment function may depend on any real variable in the economy. This potential dependency, which may be highly non-linear, is expressed in

$$\text{(3)} \quad m_j = m_j(y_{j1}, \ldots, y_{jN}, \varphi_{j1}, \ldots, \varphi_{jN}; Y_{-j1}, \ldots, Y_{-jN}, \varphi_{-j1}, \ldots, \varphi_{-jN}, X_1, \ldots, X_N, Z_1, \ldots, Z_N, \omega_1, \ldots, \omega_N)$$

Preferences

Let x_{is} reference the $1 \times M$ vector of goods demanded by agent i in state s, X_{-is} reference the $1 \times M \times (K-1)$ vector of goods consumed by agents other than i in state s, and Z_s reference the $1 \times M$ vector of goods consumed by the government in state s. The utility of agent i is given by

$$\text{(4)} \quad U_i = U(x_{i1}, \ldots, x_{iN}; X_{-i1}, \ldots, X_{-iN}, Z_1, \ldots, Z_N, Y_1, \ldots, Y_N, \varphi_1, \ldots, \varphi_N, \omega_1, \ldots, \omega_N)$$

The arguments of these preferences accommodate consumer and producer externalities as well as externalities/public goods generated by producers' and government demands. These arguments can also determine commodity characteristics, like average quality, that can be important determinants of demand and welfare in economies characterized by asymmetric information.

Private Budgets

The budget constraint of agent i is given by

(5) $$\sum_s p_s x_{is} = e_i,$$

where e_i is the net resource function of agent i. The net resource function references the amount of resources the government arranges for agent i to be able to spend on state-specific claims. As indicated in (6), this function may depend not only on the agent's own demand for claims in states of nature, but also on the claims of other agents, the production of each firm, the government's state-specific goods demands, and the economy's state-specific overall endowments. This dependency may also be highly non-linear.

(6) $$e_i = e_i(x_{i1}, x_{i2}, \dots, x_{iN}; X_{-i1,} X_{-i2}, \dots, X_{-iN}, Z_1, Z_2, \dots, Z_N, Y_1\, Y_2, \dots, Y_N, \omega_1, \omega_2, \dots, \omega_N).$$

In addition to (5), agent i's demands are constrained by

(7) $$x_{is} \in \Psi(X_1, X_2, \dots, X_N, Z_1, Z_2, \dots, Z_N, Y_1, Y_2, \dots, Y_N, \omega_1, \omega_2, \dots, \omega_N).$$

Equation (7) can accommodate a variety of important restrictions on trade, including those arising because of incomplete/segmented markets and borrowing constraints.

Market Clearing

In equilibrium firms' supplies of goods in each state s must cover agents' and government demands and the economy-wide supplies of endowments must cover firms' endowment demands.

(8) $$\sum_j y_{js} = \sum_i x_{is} + Z_s.$$

(9) $$\omega_s = \sum_j \varphi_{js}.$$

The Government's Budget

Equations (1), (5), (8), and (9) imply

(10) $$\sum_s p_s Z_s = \sum_s q_s \omega_s + \sum_j \pi_j - \sum_i e_i - \sum_j m_j.$$

The economy's overall resources consist of the value of its overall endowments plus the value of pure profits. These overall resources less the amount of net resources that the government provides to agents and firms must finance the government's demand for goods.

Government Policy

Government policy consists of a set of $e_i()$ and $m_j()$ functions as well as state-specific government product demand functions given by

(11) $$Z_s = Z_s(X_1, X_2, \dots, X_N, Z_1, Z_2, \dots, Z_N, Y_1, Y_2, \dots, Y_N, \omega_1, \omega_2, \dots, \omega_N).$$

As (10) indicates, these four sets of policy functions are not mutually independent.

Equilibrium

In equilibrium households maximize (4) subject to (5) and (7), firms maximize (1) subject to (2), the government jointly chooses its $m_j(\,)$, $e_i(\,)$, and $Z_s(\,)$ functions consistent with (10), and the market clearing conditions (8) and (9) are satisfied.

Reporting Policy

Agent *i*'s net resources, e_i, can be reported as reflecting the market value of a *1 x H* vector of state-specific private endowments, a_{is}, proportionate holdings of firm *j* of θ_{ij}, less a *1 x K* vector of state- and good-specific net tax functions, τ_{is}, i.e.,

$$(12) \qquad e_i = \sum_s q_s a_{is} + \sum_i \theta_{ij}\pi_j - \sum_s p_s \tau_{is}.$$

Since the elements a_{is} and agent *i's* reported share of firm profits will be described as constants, the τ_{is} functions must contain the same arguments as the e_i function,

$$(13) \qquad \tau_{is} = \tau_{is}(x_{i1}, x_{i2}, \ldots, x_{iN}; X_{-i1}, X_{-i2}, \ldots, X_{-iN}, Z_1, Z_{2.}, \ldots, Z_N, Y_1, Y_2, \ldots, Y_N, \omega_1, \omega_2, \ldots, \omega_N).$$

Note that in equilibrium endowment and producer price vectors depend on the same arguments as τ_{is}, namely $X_1, \ldots, X_N, Z_1, \ldots, Z_N, Y_1, \ldots, Y_N, \omega_1, \ldots, \omega_1$, so there is no need to list them in (13) as separate arguments.

Let Ω_s reference a *1 x H* vector of reported government endowments in state *s*. Since endowments are held either by agents or the government, reporting, for agent *i*, endowments of a_{is} in state *s* also requires, for consistency, announcing a government net endowment vector Ω_s satisfying

$$(14) \qquad \Omega_s = \omega_s - \sum_i a_{is}.$$

Combining (10), (12), and (14) yields the more conventional expression for the government's budget, namely

$$(15) \qquad \sum_s p_s Z_s + \sum_s \sum_j m_{js} = \sum_s q_s \Omega_s + \sum_j \theta_{gj}\pi_j + \sum_s \sum_i p_s \tau_{is},$$

where

$$(16) \qquad \theta_{gj} = 1 - \sum_i \theta_{ij}$$

references the government's reported ownership share of firm *j*. Equation (15) can be described as the government financing its goods and its net subsidies payments to firms from its net worth (the sum of the first two terms on the right-hand side of (15)) plus its net taxation of agents.

Given an equilibrium, any party, be it a private agent or government official, is free to report any constellation of private endowments and corresponding government endowments she wants. Assume, for example, that there is a single endowment, namely capital and that agent *k* reports private asset values of $\hat{a}_{is}$ for $i = 1, \ldots, K$ and $s = 1, \ldots, N$ and private firm ownership shares $\hat{\theta}_{ij}$. Her corresponding announcement of government net tax payments by agent *i* in state *s*—denoted by $\hat{\tau}_{is}$, and government assets in state *s*, $\hat{\Omega}_s$, must satisfy (17) and (18).

$$(17) \qquad e_i = \sum_s q_s \hat{a}_{is} + \sum_i \hat{\theta}_{ij}\pi_j - \sum_s p_s \hat{\tau}_{is}.$$

$$(18) \qquad \hat{\Omega}_s = \omega_s - \sum_i \hat{a}_{is}.$$

If agent k is a fiscal conservative (liberal) and is reassured by contemplating a large government surplus (debt) and low (high) taxes, she can simply declare very low (high) values of private assets, $\hat{a}_{is}$, which will lead, according to (17) and (18) to high reported values of $\hat{\Omega}_s$, and low reported values of $\Sigma_s p_s \hat{\tau}_{is}$. Thus the reported levels of these fiscal variables are completely undetermined as individual magnitudes, but they are linked to each other by (17) and (18). In this sense these variables are mutually determined, but not individually determined. As we discuss below, however, many economic analyses in macroeconomics and public finance have used the levels of taxes or deficits as measurable, identifiable variables, as if these levels had an unambiguous, independent meaning.

Deficits

Time is one of many characteristics of our model's states of nature. If we consider two states, s' and s'' that differ with respect to their measure of time, the difference in government net debt (the negative of government assets) between the two states constitutes their intervening deficit. Since one can report any size debt or surplus for states s' and s'', one is free to report any size deficit (reduction in debt) across those two states and, indeed, across any two states that one wants. Hence, each agent is free to concoct whatever deficit and associated net tax payment times series, past or present, that she wants.

Tax and Transfer Payments

Net taxes are defined as gross taxes minus transfer payments. Given one's reported level of net taxes, one can report any level of gross taxes minus a corresponding level of transfer payment. Hence, gross taxes and transfer payments are just as ill defined as net taxes. The same holds for any measures that rely on gross taxes and gross transfer payments such as average tax rates or the unfunded liabilities of transfer programs.

Intuition

There's an old joke in which a husband claims to be in charge of his household. As he puts it to his friends, "I make the important decisions—I determine our household's foreign policy and let my wife handle everything else." Knowing who's really in charge in a marriage is tough business, and determining who owns what can be even harder. Indeed, if the household resides in a community property state, it's impossible to allocate ownership. The husband and wife may have "separate" bank and other accounts, but neither can withhold the corpus of "their" accounts from the other. Indeed, a variant of the quoted joke is "I own the money and my wife spends it."

The private sector and the government are no different from a couple living under community property law. They jointly own everything and jointly determine how to spend it. Whether the government says a) "It's all mine, but I'll let you (the private sector) have some." b) "It's all yours, but I'll take whatever I'd like." or c) "It's partly mine and partly yours, but I'll determine how much of mine to give you and how much of yours to keep." does not make an iota of economic difference.

III. Illustrating the Model

The canonical model of government "debt" is Diamond's (1965) two period life-cycle formulation. We now show how the above general formulation accommodates this model.

Agents are assumed to consume a single good and leisure when young and old. Labor supplied by young and old is homogeneous. Output of the good, call it corn, is produced under constant returns with capital and labor. There is neither population nor productivity growth. We normalize each cohort's population to unity. The endowment of time that can be used for work or leisure is 1 per generation per period. For simplicity, we assume the government makes no net payments to firms, but does have a demand for consumption of the economy's single good.

Let c_{yt}, l_{yt}, c_{ot+1}, and l_{ot+1} stand, respectively, for consumption and leisure when young and old of the generation born at time t.

The lifetime utility of the generation born at time t is given by

$$u_t = u_t(c_{y,t}, l_{yt}, c_{ot+1}, l_{ot+1}) \tag{19}$$

Consider the economy as of time $t = 0$. The budget constraint facing the old at time 0 is given by

$$c_{o0} + w_0 l_{o0} = e_{o0}. \tag{20}$$

For generations born at time $t \geq 0$, the budget constraint is given by

$$c_{yt} + \frac{c_{ot+1}}{1 + r_{t+1}} + w_t l_{yt} + \frac{w_{t+1} l_{ot+1}}{1 + r_{t+1}} = e_t. \tag{21}$$

In (20) and (21) $e_{o,0}$ stands for the remaining lifetime net resource function of the old at time 0, and e_t is the lifetime net resource function of the generation born at time t. Each generation's net resource function can depend freely and in a highly non-linear way on its consumption and leisure decisions. And since each generation will consider how its consumption and leisure decisions affect its net resources both infra-marginally and at the margin, this formulation fully accommodates distortionary policy.

The production function is

$$Y_t = F(K_t, L_t) \tag{22}$$

The government's demand for corn at time t is g_t. The economy's endowment of capital evolves according to

$$K_{t+1} - K_t = Y_t - c_{yt} - c_{ot} - g_t. \tag{23}$$

Labor supply is determined by

$$L_t = 2 - l_{yt} - l_{ot}. \tag{24}$$

Using (22) and (24), rewrite (22) as

$$K_{t+1} - K_t = F(K_t, 2 - l_{yt} - l_{ot}) - c_{yt} - c_{ot} - g_t. \tag{24}$$

In hiring capital and labor, firms equate marginal factor products to pre-policy factor prices; i.e.,

$$F_K(K_t, 2 - l_{yt} - l_{ot}) = r_t \tag{25}$$

$$F_L(K_t, 2 - l_{yt} - l_{ot}) = w_t$$

Policy

In equilibrium the government announces a time-path of net resource functions—the terms e_{o0} and e_t—and a time path of corn demand, gt, that satisfy (24) in each period given utility maximization subject to (19) and (20), and given the determination via (25) of pre-policy factor prices.

Labeling

Suppose the economy is in dynamic equilibrium given government policy as determined by its net resource and spending functions. Denote by an upper bar this equilibrium's variables. Now consider announcing/reporting any time-path of official debt, $\hat{D}_t$ starting at time *0*. If one reports $\hat{D}_0$ as the amount of government debt prevailing at time *0*, the corresponding report of private assets at time *0*, $\hat{a}_0$, is determined by (26) for $t = 0$. The consistent report of net taxes facing the elderly at time *0*, $\hat{\tau}_{o0}$ is determined by (27). The reported debt for time $t > 0$ determines $\hat{a}_t$ from (26). This determines $\hat{\tau}_{yt}$ from (28), and, given $\hat{\tau}_{yt}$, the reported value of $\hat{\tau}_{ot+1}$ is determined by (29).

(26) $$\hat{a}_t = \hat{D}_t + \overline{K}_t.$$

(27) $$\overline{e}_{o0} = \hat{a}_0(1 + \overline{r}_0) + \overline{w}_0 - \hat{\tau}_{o0}.$$

(28) $$\hat{a}_{t+1} = \overline{w}_t(1 - \bar{l}_{yt}) - \overline{c}_{yt} - \hat{\tau}_{yt}.$$

(29) $$\overline{e}_t = \overline{w}_t + \frac{\overline{w}_{t+1}}{1 + \overline{r}_{t+1}} - \hat{\tau}_{yt} - \frac{\hat{\tau}_{ot+1}}{1 + \overline{r}_{t+1}}.$$

Relationship to the General Formulation

In the above example, (20) and (21) are specific cases of (5), (24) is a specific case of (8), and the equation of economy-wide capital and time endowments with firm demands for these endowments in (25) is a specific case of (9).

Although we've presented this example assuming that all cohort members are identical, the example can readily be modified to include cohort-specific heterogeneity. One need simply apply an individual-specific subscript to each of the cohort-specific variables. Doing so does not rule out anonymous net resource functions. Subscripting net resources by an agent's identity does not imply that the function determining those resources (as opposed to the arguments of the function) is agent-specific. Hence, Mirrlees' (1971) optimal income "tax" can be relabeled as freely as any other "tax," with no alteration in his underlying optimal net resource function.

A Second Illustration with Adverse Selection, and Credit Constraints

Our second example, informed by Jaffee and Russel (1976) and Hayashi (1987), shows that the relativity of fiscal language is compromised neither by incomplete information, adverse selection, nor credit constraints.

Agents again live for two periods. But each cohort now features two types of agents—*A* and *B*. An agent's type is private information. Type *B* agents are honest. They always repay what they owe, whether they owe payments to private parties or the government. In contrast, type *A* agents are dishonest.

Define c^*_{Ay} by

(30) $$V_A = u(c^*_{yA}, 0),$$

where for $i = A, B$,

(31) $$V_i \equiv \max_{c_{iy}, c_{io}} u_i(c_{iy}, c_{io}) \text{ s.t. } c_{iy} + \frac{c_{io}}{1 + r} = e_i.$$

Note that for standard concave utility functions, $c^*_{Ay} > e_A$.

If type-A agents are permitted to consume more than c^*_{Ay} when young, the present value of their consumption will exceed their lifetime net resources.

Denote by ^ the utility maximizing value of c_{iy} and c_{io}. Consider a separating equilibrium in which

$$\hat{c}_{By} > c^*_{Ay} \tag{32}$$

and "financial" and "fiscal" institutions permit agents to set their consumption when young as high as c^*_{yA}, but no higher. Since type A agents are indifferent between consuming c^*_{yA} and consuming less than this amount, we assume they consume less. In contrast, given (32), the consumption of type B agents is given by

$$c_{Byt} = c^*_{Ayt} \text{ and } c_{Bo} = (e_B - c^*_{Ay})(1 + r). \tag{33}$$

The consumption of type A agents is given by $\hat{c}_{Ay}$ and $\hat{c}_{Ao}$.

Note that we have described this economy with no reference to "borrowing," "taxes," or "transfer payments." The budget constraint in (31) is a specific case of (5), and the constraint on agent B's consumption when young and old in (33) is a specific case of (7).

If we want, we can describe type-B agents as "facing high taxes when young, but being able to borrow large amounts" or as "facing low taxes, but being able to borrow small amounts." A "policy" of "raising current taxes" and "cutting future taxes" that leaves lifetime net resources unchanged can be described as engendering an increase in "private lending" that leaves type-B agents with the same first and second period consumption values.

IV. Research and Policy Implications

The fact that one can construct an infinite number of equally meaningless time series of government debt, deficits, taxes, transfer payments, private assets, private saving, and disposable income vitiates a vast number of economic analyses predicated on these measures. Recent examples include Gale and Orsag's (2004) and Engen and Hubbard's (2005) studies of the effects of budget deficits on interest rates, Bell and Bosworth's (2005) study of the decline in personal saving, Banks, Blundell, Smith's (2001) study of financial wealth inequality, Slemrod's (1994) study of tax progressivity and income inequality, the OECD's (1997) analysis of inequality in disposable income, the IMF's study of fiscal policy and financial development (Hauner 2006), and the World Bank's study of fiscal sustainability (Burnside, 2005).

The failure to distinguish economics from linguistics also undermines theoretical research. Consider, for example, Barsky, Mankiw, and Zeldes' (1986) paper on Keynesian tax cuts. Their policy entails a short-run across-the-board "tax cut" coupled with a long-run progressive "tax hike," which is present value neutral in terms of the government's net receipts. The policy provides earnings insurance, which leads to more current consumption. The authors suggest that this provides a neoclassical basis for the Keynesian view that tax cuts expand aggregate demand.

In fact, it does no such thing since the policy could equally well be run/described/labeled as entailing a tax hike. No doubt someone will someday write a paper arguing, from the perspective of this model, that a tax hike policy and a tax cut policy are equivalent. This projected paper will add to the long list of papers purporting to identify "equivalent policies"—policies that can be run/implemented differently, but that generate the same economic outcomes. Such papers miss a central point. There are no equivalent policies in neoclassical economics. Policies are unique. What's different is simply the words we use to describe the same underlying policy.

Fischer's (1980) famous paper on the time inconsistency provides yet another example of the confusion of economics and language. In Fischer's two-period model agents fail to save out of fear of ex-post efficient, but ex-ante inefficient capital levies. But from the perspective of the second period, Fischer's capital levy is no different, apart from labeling, from a second-period infra-marginal labor income tax. Were Fischer's agents to adopt such a non-distortionary labor tax in their second period and also in their first, they'd achieve a first-best equilibrium.

So why does Fischer conclude that his economy ends up in a third best equilibrium in which no one saves for fear of a capital levy? The answer is his assumption that only proportional labor income taxes may be levied/announced. But this assumption is not based on any economic feature of his model. Instead it boils down to a non-economic restriction on language since, from the perspective of the second period, a "capital levy" could just as well be called "an infra-marginal labor income tax." Fischer's rational agents will surely realize this and also realize that if they can infra-marginally tax labor in the second period, they can do so in the first. Having figured this out, they'll end up in the first best.[1]

A third example of theoretical confusion over real policy and labels is the ubiquitous invocation of transversality conditions requiring that government debt grow, in the long run, no faster than the economy's return on capital[2] and the presumption that economies that violate such conditions are dynamically inefficient. As indicated here, there is no limit to the growth in reported debt time nor is there any economic association between the growth rate of reported debt and what matters for dynamic efficiency, namely the deviation between the growth rate of the economy and its return to capital.

To see this in a less abstract framework, consider a dynamically efficient two period life-cycle model with a zero intrinsic growth rate. Assume the economy is sitting in a stationary state with a positive return to capital of r. Also assume the economy's government consumes nothing and takes, on net, nothing from any generation either when it's young or when it's old. Now, starting at time 1, let's label this policy as the government's "borrowing $m^t h$ from each agent born at time t, making infra-marginal transfer payments of $m^t h$ to each agent born at time t, repaying principal plus interest of $m^t h(1 + r)$ at time $t + 1$ to each agent born at time t, and infra-marginally taxing at time $t + 1$ each agent born at time t in the amount $m^t h(1 + r)$." This economy's reported debt at the beginning of time $t + 1$ is $m^t h$. If $m > 1$, the economy's debt and deficit will head to infinity with no affect [sic] whatsoever on the economy or any agent in the economy.[3]

Turning to actual policy, one need only consider the Maastricht Treaty limiting members of the EURO to 3 percent deficits, the Stability and Growth Pact that sanctions EU members with deficits above 3 percent, the IMF's enduring use of the deficit to assess fiscal prudence, the Gramm-Rudman-Hollings Act to limit U.S. deficits, or the ongoing movement for a U.S. balanced budget amendment to realize that official reports of deficits are a) dramatically influencing policy decisions and b) diverting attention from fundamental and meaningful measures of fiscal policy.

[1] Kotlikoff (2002) discusses both Barsky, Mankiw, and Zeldes (1986) and Fischer (1980).

[2] See, for example, Blanchard (1985).

[3] If $m < -1$, the government's surplus heads to infinity. If $-1 < m < 1$, the government's [sic] reports a declining debt or surplus through time.

V. Conclusion

A century ago, everyone thought that time and distance were well defined physical concepts. But neither proved to be absolute. Instead, measures/reports of time and distance were found to depend on one's direction and speed of travel making our apparent physical reality, in the words of Einstein, "merely an illusion."

Like time and distance, standard fiscal measures, including deficits, taxes, and transfer payments, depend on one's reference point/reporting procedure/language/labels. As such, they too represent numbers in search of concepts that provide the illusion of meaning where none exists. Economists must accept this fact and acknowledge that much of what they have been writing and saying about fiscal policy has been an exercise in linguistics, not economics.

References

Arrow, Kenneth J., "The Role of Securities in the Optimal Allocation of Risk-Bearing," *Review of Economic Studies*, 31, 1964, 91–6.

Auerbach, Alan J. and Laurence J. Kotlikoff, *Dynamic Fiscal Policy*, Cambridge, England: Cambridge University Press, 1987.

Banks, James, Richard Blundell, and James P. Smith, *Financial Wealth Inequality in the United States and Britian*, The Rand Institute, 2001.

Barsky, Robert B., Gregory Mankiw, and Steven P. Zeldes, "Richardian Consumers with Keynesian Propensities," *The American Econonomic Review*, 76 (4), 1986, 676–91.

Bell, Linda and Barry Bosworth, "The Decline in Household Saving: What Can We Learn from Survey Data," mimeo, *The Brookings Institution*, August 2005.

Blanchard, Olivier, "Debts, Deficits, and Finite Horizons," *Journal of Political Economy*, 93 (2), April 1985, 223–47.

Burnside, Craig, ed., *Fiscal Sustainability in Theory and Practice*, Washington, D.C.: The World Bank, 2005.

Engen, Eric M. and R. Glenn Hubbard, "Federal Government Debt and Interest Rates," in *NBER Macroeconomics Annual 2004*, Mark Gertler and Ken Rogoff, eds., 2005, 83–138.

Fischer, Stanley, "Dynamic Inconsistency, Cooperation, and the Benevolent Dissembling Government," *Journal of Economic Dynamics and Control*, 2, 1980, 93–107.

Gale, William and Peter R. Orsag, "Budget Deficits, National Saving, and Interest Rates," *Brookings Papers on Economic Activity*, 2, 2004, 101–210.

Hauner, David, "Fiscal Policy and Financial Development," IMF Working Paper, WP/06/26, January 2006.

Hayashi, Fumio, "Tests for Liquidity Constraints: A Critical Survey," invited paper, 5th World Congress of the Econometric Society, Cambridge, Mass., in T. Bewley. ed., *Advances in Econometrics II: Fifth World Congress*, Cambridge University Press, 1987, 91–120.

Hubbard, Glenn, and Eric Engen, "Government Debt and Interest Rates," in M. Gertler and K. Rogoff, *NBER Macroeconomics Annual 2004,* Cambridge: MIT Press, 2005.

Jaffee, D. M. and T. Russel, "Imperfect Information, Uncertainty, and Credit Rationing," *Quarterly Journal of Economics*, 90, 651–66.

Kotlikoff, Laurence J., "Deficit Delusion," *The Public Interest*, Summer 1986.

Kotlikoff, Laurence J., *Generational Policy*, Cambridge, MA: MIT Press, 2002.

Mirrlees, James A., "An Exploration in the Theory of Optimal Income Taxation," *Review of Economic Studies*, 38, 175–208.

OECD, "Income Distribution and Poverty in Selected OECD Countries," *OECD Economic Outlook*, December 1997.

Slemrod, Joel, ed., *Tax Progressivity and Income Inequality*, Cambridge, England: Cambridge University Press, 1994.

Tabellini, Guido, "The Politics of Intergenerational Redistribution," *Journal of Political Economy*, 99 (2), 1991, 335–57.

Five

Laurence Weiss

Lawrence Weiss first met Steve Ross as an undergraduate at the University of Pennsylvania. He received a Ph.D. from Harvard University in 1977. He started out at Yale University. He's taught at the University of Chicago and the University of California, San Diego. He was a partner at Goldman Sachs. He now is a private investor. •

My first meeting with Steve Ross was humbling and life changing. It was my first week as a freshman at Penn, where the newly minted Assistant Professor Ross informed me that my SATs were not high enough for admittance to his math-intensive freshman micro class. Rejection! I was shocked but intrigued. What subtle, esoteric, and vital knowledge would now be denied me because I was not one of the elite? The fact that Steve was obviously smooth and smart, and from Harvard yet, only added to my pain at being excluded. All during my freshman economics class I wondered what they were holding back from my prosaic mind and what was going on in Professor Ross's class with the smart kids. I vowed to find out.

Shortly later, Steve substituted for the regular teacher. The topic for that day was the then current New York City drought of '69 and the economics of water metering. Steve's class was a transformation. He gave the impression that he only prepared for the class on the walk over, that he didn't do any of the required reading, which was probably wrong, anyway. Nevertheless, he could attack the issues head on and seemed to spontaneously develop the correct analysis right before our very eyes! Here was the power of first principles and a rapier-like intellect that appeared invincible. And it looked easy and cool and I dare say sexy. Steve hinted that there were great financial rewards to be had with mastering this knowledge, which sealed the deal. I wanted to be just like Steve. I still do.

I went on to take three undergraduate courses with Steve, enjoying every minute. After that I modeled my career on Steve's example and had the great privilege of being Steve's colleague. Those were the years of the "cruel dilemma" of galloping inflation and rising unemployment, and I was seduced by the topicality of macroeconomics. Steve thought macro was a sinkhole best left to grey-haired luminaries, but humored me anyway. I have fond memories of Steve in the Cowles Foundation coffee room, where Jim Tobin would turn bright red as he glared disapprovingly at Steve for advocating some politically incorrect position. Steve was on the side of the angels, but could be the devil when confronted with pomposity. When I came around to Steve's view of macro and decided to sample the real world, Steve gave me good advice.

The paper that I include in this volume is "Borrowing Constraints and Aggregate Economic Activity," co-authored with Jose Scheinkman, my delightful and wide-ranging colleague at the University of Chicago. The importance of borrowing constraints was a general theme at Yale and was often served up as a rebuttal to market advocates. My interest was also motivated by a question often raised by Steve, which has continued to vex me. Why do asset prices move? Steve often cited Dick Roll's important study of orange juice futures, which showed that observed weather patterns could explain only a tiny fraction of observed price movements. What generated the rest? Were we missing something? This paper presented a novel channel by which variations in wealth between different sectors can give rise to movement in aggregate asset prices (and also output, which was included because I was a macro economist). I'm not sure how important this effect is, but I am most proud of the paper for coming closest to meeting the exacting standards of economic theory set by Steve. It builds on first principles, particularly asymmetric information that precludes complete markets, a point developed by Steve. It uses the notion of economic equilibrium in a stochastic setting and, thanks chiefly to my co-author, is shown to be logically complete and consistent. Most importantly, I think there is some distance between assumptions and conclusions, a term I associate with Steve. This is ultimately an aesthetic issue. I like to think Steve trained my eye.

Borrowing Constraints and Aggregate Economic Activity[1]

By *Jose A. Scheinkman and Laurence Weiss*[2]

A model of aggregate economic activity is formulated which emphasizes the effects of borrowing constraints in the presence of uninsurable risk. An important determinant of current income level is shown to be the cross-sectional distribution of wealth. As this distribution evolves endogenously, the model is capable of producing rich dynamics from a simple specification of exogenous shocks. The model shows that this phenomena can contribute to observed asset price volatility. •

1. Introduction

It is commonly thought that individuals have only limited opportunities to borrow against future labor income and cannot totally insure all types of risk. It has also been suggested that such departures from the presumptive norm of frictionless, complete information capital markets may have implications for aggregate economic activity. Although there has been some work analyzing the implications of borrowing constraints for individual savings behavior [**18, 2, 8**], there has been no systematic analysis of how such borrowing constraints will affect the time series properties of output, prices, and interest rates.

In this paper, we present a completely specified infinitely lived two agent equilibrium model which emphasizes the roles of borrowing constraint and uninsured risk for affecting aggregate outcomes. Specifically we assume that agents are prohibited from ever having negative nonhuman wealth. The model has the central feature that there is no aggregate uncertainty, but each agent's own productive opportunities are stochastic. If there were a full set of Arrow-Debreu contingent claim markets each agent could attain a certain consumption stream and the resulting allocation and (implicit) relative prices would be constant through time. However, we assume that such markets do not exist. Rather, we assume that at each point in time agents may trade only the single durable "asset" for the single perishable consumption good. This asset may be interpreted either as flat money with a fixed own nominal return of zero, or as claims to productive capital which emits a fixed exogenous flow of the consumption good. We assume also that output may be produced by labor. However, only one of the two agents is productive at any instant in time. The duration of time over which a single agent is productive is assumed to be random, and, for analytical simplicity, is assumed to be generated by a Poisson counting process. The resulting allocation has the property that the agent who is not productive exchanges some of his stock of the asset in return for the consumption good supplied by the productive agent. If the nonproductive agent has none of the asset at a point in time, then he consumes nothing.

We do not attempt to derive this limited financial structure from more primitive economic considerations. At one extreme, we could imagine this setting to be relevant for a world in which debt contracts are simply unenforceable. More realistically, we take this

[1]Research supported by NSF Grants # SES 8026587 and # 7926726A03.

[2]We wish to thank Mordecai Kurz, Abraham Neyman, seminar participants at IMSSS at Stanford University and at the Money and Banking Workshop at the University of Chicago, and especially Mike Harrison who was instrumental for several of the sections. Coleman Kendall provided computational assistance.

Reprinted with permission:
Scheinkman, Jose A. and Laurence Weiss. "Borrowing Constraints and Aggregate Activity." *Econometrica* 54 (1986): 23–46

formulation to capture the qualitative properties of economic environments in which agents' labor productivities are not directly observable. In this case, the usual considerations of moral hazard and adverse selection would suggest that agents are unable to insure against unfavorable outcomes. We postpone until the conclusion a more complete discussion of the relevance of our simplified model to more complicated settings which take explicit account of the informational barriers underlying restrictions on intertemporal trades.

The absence of a complete insurance market in the face of idiosyncratic production disturbances gives rise to a precautionary demand for wealth. Agents accumulate assets while productive to provide for consumption during periods when they are unable to produce. This phenomenon has direct implications for aggregate economic activity. The model shows that, in contrast to a world with complete contingent claims, the resulting equilibrium will exhibit random fluctuations in aggregate output, labor input, and the relative price of the asset. Furthermore, even though the exogenous uncertainty (the realization of which agent is productive) is first order Markovian, the resulting time paths of the endogeneous variable will exhibit higher order serial correlation. Thus, the model is capable of replicating co-movements in aggregate time series which characterize actual business cycles. The model shows that an important determinant of aggregate economic activity is the cross-sectional distribution of nonhuman wealth. As this distribution evolves endogenously, the model is capable of producing rich dynamics from a rather simple specification of stochastic disturbances.

The main qualitative features of the equilibrium can be described simply. Consider an agent at the moment he switches from being nonproductive to being productive. Since he has just finished a spell of dissaving, he is most likely asset poor and he is willing to work hard, so output is high and prices low. Over time, the agent accumulates assets, so an income effect reduces labor supply and output and drives up prices. This continues until the two agents reverse roles which occurs at random exogenous points in time. Since, on average, the state change makes the poorer agent productive, it is associated with an upward jump in output and downward jump in prices.

This type of model can explain several empirical findings which appear to contradict earlier models of aggregate economic behavior. Unlike the labor supply behavior in [**13** or **14**] which portray aggregate employment fluctuations as arising from intertemporal substitution of leisure in response to perceived abnormal relative prices, the current analysis emphasizes the role of the cross-sectional distribution of asset holdings and hence income effects for affecting employment. In this way the model shows that fluctuations in employment are compatible with constant real wages, measured either as average real wages of those employed, or as the cross-sectional distribution of marginal products. Thus the model can explain the failure of tests of the intertemporal substitution hypothesis to explain aggregate employment fluctuations as in [**1** and **9**]. The inability to insure completely also implies that each individual's consumption will not be perfectly correlated with aggregate consumption. This can explain the failure of tests of models of asset returns and consumption which rely on conditions for treating *per capita* consumption as if it is chosen by a "representative" consumer. Among these tests are the variance tests of stock prices in [**5**] and tests of an aggregate Euler equation in [**6** or **16**].

The model is also capable of yielding nonlinear responses to various sorts of hypothetical interventions, which cannot arise in models whose solutions can be described as stochastic linear difference equations. For example, we consider the effects of an unanticipated increase in the money supply which distributes the new money equally between the two agents. As this affects the cross-section distribution of wealth it will have real effects. However the direction of this effect depends on the existing distribution of assets. In particular, when output is low monetary injections will raise output, but when output is high it will have the opposite effect. This finding suggests at the very least that the usual time series representation of economic aggregates might not reveal all economically interesting relationships.

The paper is organized as follows: In Section 2 we present the model and prove existence of competitive equilibria. In Section 3 we explore the effects of an unanticipated, once and for all increase in the money supply which is distributed equally between the two agents. In Section 4 we present results of various numerical simulations of the model to see how the equilibrium changes with various parameters. In Section 5 we compare the derived co-movements to actual business cycles. Section 6 is the conclusion.

2. The Model

We consider a model of two types of infinitely long-lived individuals, indexed by $i = 1, 2$. Each agent has preferences over streams of consumption and labor supply which is additive and time separable, viz.

$$U^i = \int_0^\infty e^{-\beta t}(u(c^i(t)) - l^i(t))\,dt \qquad (i = 1, 2). \tag{1}$$

The productivity of labor is state dependent. In state i, $i = 1, 2$, labor of type i can produce one unit of consumption per unit of labor input, both measured as flows per unit time. Labor of type $j \neq i$ in state i is not productive at all. The duration of time between state changes is random and has an exponential probability distribution with mean duration $1/\lambda$. In order to fix notation let $N_t(\omega)$ be a Poisson counting process with rate λ on a probability space $(\Omega, \mathcal{F}, P)$.[3] Define $s_t(\omega) = 1$ if $N_t(\omega)$ is odd and $s_t(\omega) = 2$ if $N_t(\omega)$ is even. In particular, $P\{s_{t+h}(\omega) = i | s_t(\omega) = j\} = \lambda h + o(h)$ if $i \neq j$.

Consumers are assumed to be able to observe the "histories" of the process $s_t(\omega)$. In order to make this precise let us write $\mathcal{F}_t$ for the smallest sub σ-algebra of $\mathcal{F}$ which makes all random variables $s_\tau(\omega)$, $\tau \leqslant t$ measurable. $\{\mathcal{F}_t\}_{t=0}^\infty$ is a nondecreasing family of σ-algebras and each $\mathcal{F}_t$ summarizes the information given by the histories. Consumer choices at time t should be $\mathcal{F}_t$ measurable, i.e., independent of future $s_\tau(\omega)$. *Every real valued function indexed by t that appears in the sequel is assumed to be $\mathcal{F}_t$ measurable* (i.e., the inverse image of a Borel subset of reals is assumed to belong to $\mathcal{F}_t$). Similarly all equations are to be interpreted as holding almost surely (e.g., $c(t, \omega) = 0$ means that for almost all (t, ω), $c(t, \omega) = 0$).

2.1 The Competitive Equilibrium With Complete Markets

Before proceeding with the competitive equilibrium under restrictions on trade, we will briefly discuss the market allocation which would prevail if there were complete sets of Arrow-Debreu contingent markets. Such markets would allow agents to purchase at time O at a price $Q(t, \omega)$ the rights to delivery of 1 unit of consumption in state ω at time t for all t and $\omega \in \Omega$.

The problem faced by agent i is to maximize the expected value of (1) subject to a budget constraint:

$$\int_0^\infty \int_\Omega Q(t, \omega)c^i(t, \omega)\,dP\,dt \leqslant \int_0^\infty \int_\Omega l^i(t, \omega)Q(t, \omega)\,dP\,dt$$

[3] That is, Ω is a set, $\mathcal{F}$ is a σ-algebra of subset of Ω, and P is a probability measure, and $N_0(\omega) = 0$, $N_t(\omega)$ has stationary and independent increments and $P\{N_h(\omega) = 1\} = \lambda h + o(h)$, $P\{N_h(\omega) \geqslant 2\}\tilde{o}(h)$, where $\lim_{h\to 0}\frac{|o(h)|}{|h|} = \lim_{h\to 0}\frac{|\tilde{o}(h)|}{|h|} = 0.$

subject to

$$l^i(t, \omega) = 0 \quad \text{if} \quad s_t(\omega) = j \neq i.$$

It is straightforward to verify that the competitive equilibrium[4] for this economy entails constant consumption; that is, $u^t(c^j(t, \omega)) = 1$, all t, j, and ω. The "price" of 1 unit of consumption with certainty at t, $\int_\Omega Q(t, \omega)\, dP$, falls at the rate of time preference, so that the implicit "interest rate" is equal to the (constant) rate of time discount. Labor supply of the productive agent, and hence aggregate labor input, is also time invariant, $L^j(t, j) = 2C$, where C satisfies $u'(C) = 1$.

The absence of aggregate fluctuations in this economy rates on the time separable specification of tastes and technologies. Relaxing this assumption could possibly generate some interesting dynamic relationships. However, we chose this specification to highlight the role played by borrowing constraints in causing aggregate movements.

2.2. The Competitive Equilibrium and Borrowing Constraints

We assume the existence of a good called "money" which can be neither augmented nor depleted. We choose units in such a way that when any one type holds a unit of it per capita, the other type must hold zero. Later we will comment on what happens when instead of money a capital good which emits a constant flow of $\delta \geqslant 0$ consumption goods per period is considered. Clearly when $\delta = 0$ we are back to the "money" case.

At each time, at each event $\omega \in \Omega$, let $q(t, \omega)$ denote the value of the aggregate capital stock. Agents of type i take as given $q(t, \omega)$ and choose $c^i(t, \omega)$, $l^i(t, \omega)$ to solve problem (P^i):

$$\text{Max } E\left\{ \int_o^\infty e^{-\beta t}[u(c^i(t, \omega)) - l^i(t, \omega)]\, dt \right\}$$

subject to

$$y^i(0, \omega) = y_0^i,$$

(2) $$\dot{y}^i(t, \omega) = (l^i(t, \omega) - c^i(t, \omega))/q(t, \omega) \quad \text{if} \quad s_t(\omega) = i,$$

(3) $$\dot{y}^i(t, \omega) = -c^i(t, \omega)/q(t, \omega) \quad \text{and}$$

$$l^i(t, \omega) = 0 \quad \text{if} \quad s_t(\omega) = j \neq i,$$

$$y^i(t, \omega) \geqslant 0, \quad l^i(t, \omega) \geqslant 0, \quad c^i(t, \omega) \geqslant 0.$$

In (P), notice that in state i individual i chooses both consumption and labor supply while in state $j \neq i$ it sets its labor supply at zero and chooses consumption. The constraint $y^i(t, \omega) \geqslant 0$ means that *no borrowing is allowed.*

An equilibrium is a stochastic process $q(t, \omega)$ defined on Ω that if $y^i(t, \omega)$ solves P^i given $q(t, \omega)$, then $y^1(t, \omega) + y^2(t, \omega) = 0$ or (since $y_0^i = 1 - y_0^j$)

(4) $$y^1(t, \omega) + y^2(t, \omega) \equiv 1.$$

Let $z(t, \omega)$ denote the average amount of the capital goods held by type 1 at time t in event ω. We will look for an equilibrium in which $q(t, \omega) = q(z(t, \omega), s_t(\omega))$. In order to treat the two types symmetrically we assume that $q(z, 1) = q(1 - z, 2)$ for each $0 \leqslant z \leqslant 1$.

[4]This competitive equilibrium is for the case where $P[s_0(\omega) = i] = \frac{1}{2}$. Further we assume that feasible consumptions are essentially bounded, i.e. ess $\sup_{t,\omega}|c(t, \omega)| < \infty$.

Thus we may think that consumers take $z(t, \omega)$ and the function q:$[0, 1] \times \{1, 2\} \rightarrow R$ as given and solve P^i.[5] We will further assume that consumers forecast that z will be an absolutely continuous function such that, where the derivative exists,

$$\dot{z}(t, w) = h(z, s_t(w)). \tag{5}$$

In particular, it only depends on z and the state.

With this structure we may redefine an equilibrium as a function q: $[0, 1] \times \{1, 2\} \rightarrow R$ with $q(z, 1) = q(1 - z, 2)$, and a stochastic process $z(t, \omega)$ with values in $[0, 1]$, such that if consumer i solves (P^i) with $q(t, \omega) = q(z(t, \omega), s_t(\omega))$ and $y_0^1 = z(0, \omega), y_0^2 = 1 - z(0, \omega)$, then $\dot{y}^i(t, \omega) = \dot{z}(t, \omega)$ and $\dot{y}^2(t, \omega) = -\dot{z}(t, \omega)$, i.e., type i holds the predicted amounts of capital.

Our strategy is first to motivate a candidate equilibrium in a purely heuristic fashion. We will then show rigorously that our candidate is, in fact, an equilibrium. We will do the latter using a variation for the stochastic case of the well known procedure of showing that a path that satisfies an "Euler equation" and a transversality condition is optimal if concavity is present. To achieve this we must derive a candidate path and support prices along such a path.

Let us write $p(z, i)$ as the marginal value of a unit of "money" for an agent of type 1, when the average holdings of type 1 is z and this agent also holds z, and state i prevails. We will assume that $l^1(t, w) - c^1(t, w) > 0$ when $s_t(w) = 1$ (which can be guaranteed if $u(0) = -\infty$). Since in equilibrium $y^1(t, w) = z(t, w)$, the linearity of the disutility of work implies when $s_t(w) = 1$ that

$$p(z, 1) = q\,(z, 1). \tag{6}$$

Similarly, in state 2, if we assume $c^1(z, 2) > 0$ if $z > 0$ (which again will follow from $u(0) = -\infty$), then

$$p(z, 2) = q(z, 2)u'(c^1(z, 2)). \tag{7}$$

Notice also that the linearity of the disutility of work implies that if $s_t(\omega) = 1$, then $c^1(t, \omega) = \overline{c}$ where $u'(\overline{c}) = 1$.

In equilibrium agent 1 is satisfied to hold z units when the average holdings of agents of type 1 is z. Since money yields no direct utility, in analogy with the exhaustible resource problem, one expects that the discounted marginal value forms a martingale, i.e., the expected discounted marginal value at $t + dt$ conditional on $\mathcal{F}_t$ is the discounted marginal value at t. Since $(z\,(t, \cdot), s_t(\cdot))$ forms a Markov process, and z is $\mathcal{F}_t$ measurable this is equivalent to conditioning on $z(t, \omega)$ and $s_t(\omega)$. Now, since $s_t(\omega)$ is defined by a Poisson process with parameter λ, for $0 < z < 1$,

$$E\{e^{-\beta(t+dt)}p(z(t + dt, \omega), s(t + dt, \omega))|\, z(t, \omega) = z, s_t(\omega) = 1\}$$
$$= e^{-\beta t}p(z, 1) + e^{-\beta t}\left\{\frac{d}{dz}p(z, 1)h(z, 1) - (\beta + \lambda)p(z, 1) - \lambda p(z, 2)\right\} dt + o(dt).$$

Making $dt \rightarrow 0$, we obtain

$$\left(\frac{d}{dz}p(z, 1)\right)h(z, 1) = (\beta + \lambda)p(z, 1) - \lambda p(z, 2) \tag{8}$$

[5] In our model, since we will show that $q(\cdot, 1)$ is invertible, knowing both q and the state i one knows z. But one may take as primitive that consumers observe z, i, and $q(z, i)$.

and similarly

$$\left(\frac{d}{dz}p(z,2)\right)h(z,2) = (\beta+\lambda)p(z,2) - \lambda p(z,1). \tag{9}$$

Now using (7) we obtain

$$h(z,2) = -\frac{c^1(z,2)}{q(z,2)} = -\frac{g(p(z,2)/q(z,2))}{q(z,2)}$$

where $g = u'^{-1}$. Since $q(z,2) = q(1-z,1) = p(1-z,1)$ (by (6)) we have,

$$h(z,2) = -\frac{g(p(z,2)/p(1-z,1))}{p(1-z,1)} \tag{10}$$

Also,

$$h(z,1) = -h(1-z,2) = \frac{g(p(1-z,2)/p(z,1))}{p(z,1)}. \tag{11}$$

Using (10) and (11) in (8) and (9), we have

$$\left(\frac{d}{dz}p(z,1)\right)\frac{g(p(1-z,2)/p(z,1))}{p(z,1)} = (\beta+\lambda)p(z,1) - \lambda p(z,2) \tag{12}$$

and

$$\left(\frac{d}{dz}p(z,2)\right)\frac{g(p(z,2)/p(1-z,1))}{p(1-z,1)} = \lambda p(z,1) - (\beta+\lambda)p(z,2). \tag{13}$$

Now if $u'(0) = \infty$, then

$$\lim_{z\to 0} p(z,2) = \infty. \tag{14}$$

Since when $z = 1$ we must have, in equilibrium, $h(1,1) = 0$, applying the same Martingale property as above, we get

$$(\beta+\lambda)p(1,1) = \lambda p(1,2). \tag{15}$$

The qualitative properties of the solutions can be read from the phase diagram in Figure 1. The only solutions of (2), (13), (14), and (15) that are positive must stay in region III. In particular, $dp(z,1)/dz \leqslant 0$, $dp(z,2)/dz \leqslant 0$. This is sufficient for Proposition 1.

PROPOSITION 1. *The value of the asset and both the consumption of the nonproductive agent and aggregate consumption increase (weakly) with the fraction of the asset held by the nonproductive agent.*

FIGURE 1

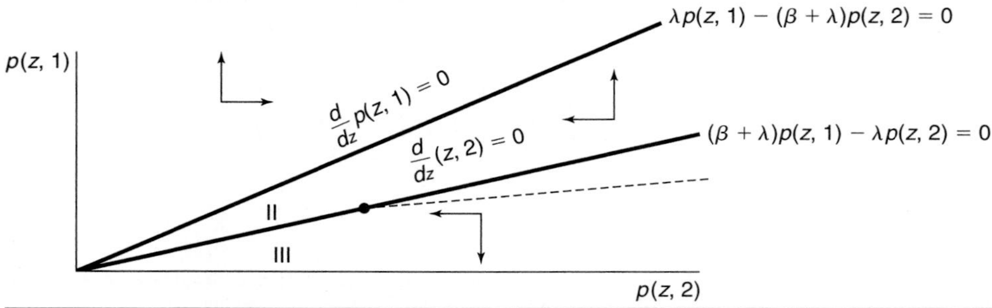

Proof:

$$0 \geqslant \frac{\frac{d}{dz}p(z,2)}{p(z,2)} = \frac{\frac{d}{dz}q(z,2)}{q(z,2)} + \frac{\frac{d}{dz}u'(c^1(z,2))}{u'(c^t(z,2))}$$
$$= \frac{\frac{d}{dz}q(z,2)}{q(z,2)} + \frac{u''(c^1(z,2))\cdot\frac{d}{dz}c^1(z,2)}{u'(c^1(z,2))}.$$

Now, $q(z, 2) = q(1 - z, 1) = p(1 - z, 1)$ and thus $dq(z, 2)/dz \geqslant 0$ (since $dp(z, 1)/dz \leqslant 0$). Thus, $dc^1(z, 2)/dz \geqslant 0$. Since $c^1(z, 1) = \bar{c}$ such that $u'(\bar{c}) = 1$, we have established the proposition. Q.E.D.

Equations (12)−(15) gives us a two-point boundary value problem with a delayed differential equation. For the case where $u(c) = \log c$ we may simplify it to get (writing $A(z) = p(z, 2)$ and $B(z) = p(z, 1)$):

(16) $$B'(z) = A(1 - z)\{(\beta + \lambda)B(z) - \lambda A(z)\},$$

(17) $$A'(z) = A(z)\{\lambda B(z) - (\beta + \lambda)A(z)\},$$

with

(18) $$\lim_{z\to 0} A(z) = \infty,$$

(19) $$\lambda A(1) = (\beta + \lambda)B(1).$$

In Appendix A it is shown that there exists a strictly positive solution to Equations (16) and (17) satisfying the boundary conditions (18) and (19). In Appendix B we demonstrate that the derived path of prices and quantities do, in fact, constitute a competitive equilibrium for this economy. We prove that if $A(z)$ and $B(z)$ solve (16) to (19) and we let $q(z, 1) = B(z)$, $h(z, 1) = (A(1 - z))^{-1}$, $h(z, 2) = -(A(z))^{-1}$ and if $z(t, \omega)$ solves (5) with $z(0, \omega)$ given, then $y^1(t, \omega) = z(t, \omega)$ and $y^2(t, \omega) = 1 - z(t, \omega)$ solve P^i when $y_0^1 = z(0, \omega)$ and $y_0^2 = 1 - z(0, \omega)$. Hence from the A's and B's we construct a price function and a stochastic process for the average holdings of type one that, if expected by agents, will result in an equilibrium.

2.3. The Stationary Distribution of Asset Holdings

Starting from an initial distribution of asset holdings and state of labor productivity at time t_0, the distribution of asset holdings and labor productivity at t_1 is random, as it depends upon the realization of the random path of labor productivity at time t_0, this distribution of asset holdings and labor productivity at t_1 is uniqueness of a pair of state dependent stationary cumulative probability distributions $F(Z, s)$, $s = 1, 2$, with the following property: Suppose $\Pr(z(t_0, \omega) \leqslant Z | s_{t_0}(\omega) = s) = F(Z, s)$ for $s_{t_0}(\omega) = 1, 2$. Then at any time $t_1 \geqslant t_0$ the $\Pr(z(t_1, \omega) \leqslant Z | s_{t_1}(\omega) = s) = F(Z, s)$. The derivation of these probability distributions will prove useful for numerical simulations in Section 4.

Consider time $t + dt$ when $s_{t+dt}(\omega) = 1$ and $z(t + dt, \omega) \leqslant Z$. There are two ways in which this state could have been reached: either $s_t(\omega) = 1$ and $z(t, \omega) \leqslant Z - h(Z, 1)\,dt$, or $s_t(\omega) = 2$ and $z(t, \omega) \leqslant Z - h(Z, 2)\,dt$. Conditional on $s_{t+dt}(\omega) = 1$, the probability of the latter is $\lambda\,dt$. Substituting from (10) and (11), $h(z, 1) = 1/A(1 - z)$ and $h(Z, 2) = -1/A(z)$ yields

$$F(z, 1, t + dt) = (1 - \lambda\, dt)\, F\left(z - \frac{dt}{A(1 - z)}, 1, t\right)$$
$$+\lambda\, dt\, F\left(z + \frac{dt}{A(z)}, 2, t\right).$$

Similarly,

$$F(z, 2, t + dt) = (1 - \lambda\, dt)\, F\left(z + \frac{dt}{A(z)}, 2, t\right)$$
$$+ \lambda\, dt\, F\left(z + \frac{dt}{A(1 - z)}, 1, t\right).$$

Expanding around $dt = 0$ and dropping terms of order $(dt)^2$ and dividing by dt, the condition that $F(z, s, t + dt) = F(z, s, t)$ implies:

$$f(z, 1) = A(1 - z)\, \lambda[F(z, 2) - F(z, 1)], \tag{20}$$

$$f(z, 2) = A(z)\, \lambda[F(z, 2) - F(z, 1)], \tag{21}$$

where $f(z, s) = \partial F(z, s)/\partial z$.

From (20) and (21) it can be seen immediately that $F(z, 2) - F(z, 1) \geqslant 0$; that $F(Z, 1)$ stochastically dominates $F(Z, 2)$. This has a straightforward economic intuition. It implies that the probability that $z < Z$ is always greater when agent 2 is productive than when agent 1 is productive—the productive agent has, on average, greater wealth.

To solve (20) and (21), note that $f(z, 1) = [A(1 - z)/A(z)]\, f(z, 2)$. Differentiating equation (21) with respect to z and substituting for $f(z, 2)$ yields

$$\frac{f'(z, 1)}{f(z, 2)} = \frac{A'(z)}{A(z)} + \lambda[A(z) - A(1 - z)]. \tag{22}$$

In Appendix C we show that there exists a unique solution $f(z, 2)$ to equation (22) satisfying $\int_0^1 f(z, 2)\, dz = 1$.

Since the system is obviously ergodic, it may also be shown that, starting from any initial state, the distribution of (z_t, s_t) will converge to this stationary distribution.

3. The Effects of a Monetary Injection

In this section we investigate the effects of a one time, unanticipated increase in the money supply which distributes the new money equally between the two agents. Such an infusion of new money is best thought of as a monetarily-financed government transfer payment. With only a single security there is no independent role in the model for monetary as opposed to fiscal policy.

Since the new money is introduced equally between the two agents, it will, generally, alter the distribution of asset holdings. Such a change in relative asset holdings will have real effects. However, the direction and size of these effects will depend on the initial state of the economy. In particular, we demonstrate that when output is low an increase in money will raise output and real balances, but when output is high it will have just the opposite effect.

Consider an unanticipated θ per cent increase in the money supply in state (z, s). This will change the distribution of assets held to (z', s) where $z' = (z + \frac{1}{2}\theta)/(1 + \theta)$. Note that $\partial z'/\partial\theta|_{\theta=0} = (\frac{1}{2} - z)$ so that an equal increase in money brings the distribution close to equality.

Since in the initial situation there was, by assumption, one unit of money, the price level is $\pi(z, s) = (q(z, s))^{-1}$. The reader may verify that the new equilibrium price level equals $\pi'(z', s) = (1 + \theta)\pi(z', s)$. Thus at $\theta = 0$, the change in the price level is given by

$$\pi(z, s) = \pi_z(\tfrac{1}{2} - z). \tag{23}$$

whereas the change in output is given by

$$x_z(\tfrac{1}{2} - z)\,. \tag{24}$$

Assume that $s = 2$. Proposition I implies that $x_z > 0$, $\pi_z = -q_z/q_z^2 < 0$. Hence if $z < \frac{1}{2}$, output will be relatively low and a 1 per cent increase in money will raise prices by less than 1 per cent and raise output. If $z > \frac{1}{2}$, output will be higher and a money increase will suppress output by making the productive agent richer. This will make prices rise by more than θ per cent. Since output is monotonic in the share of the asset held by the nonproductive agent, the current level of output is a sufficient statistic determining the share of assets held by both the productive and nonproductive agent and hence the effects of a monetary shock.

4. Simulations of the Model

In this section we present the results of numerical simulations of the model to investigate how changes in various parameters affect the time series properties of prices and output. All simulations are for the case $u(c) = \log c$.

The simulations were derived by approximating the differential equations (16) and (17) by finite difference equations with an exogenously fixed (taken to be 100). We first "guess" a pair $(A(\frac{1}{2}), B(\frac{1}{2}))$. From these the entire path of A and B can be determined. We then iterate on different values $A(\frac{1}{2})$, $B(\frac{1}{2})$ until the boundary conditions (equations (18), (19)) are satisfied.

We first investigate changes in β, the rate of time discount. In contrast to the Arrow-Debreu economy in which this parameter affects only prices, but not quantities, the simulations show that increases in β lead to lower output. Our interpretation of this result is that with higher rates of time preference agents are less willing to accumulate assets. This makes the real value of money less and hence makes the constraint that agents can consume only out of existing assets more effective. We conjecture that as β goes towards zero, the value of assets grows without bound and the borrowing constraints become ineffective such that the allocation approaches that of the Arrow-Debreu economy.

Changes in λ, the instantaneous rate of state change, would appear to have a non-monotonic effect on real balances. At one extreme, $\lambda = 0$, the productive agent would never accumulate real balances since he would never have the opportunity to spend them. The equilibrium value of real balances would also appear to approach 0 as $\lambda \to \infty$. In this case the duration of nonproductive spells grows sufficiently short so that agents have no incentive to accumulate more than infinitesimal wealth. We would expect that the effect of an increase in λ would be to increase mean equilibrium output, and in the limit, as $\lambda \to \infty$, for the allocation to approach that of a complete market economy. As the duration of nonproductive spells becomes shorter, there is less need to accumulate assets and the borrowing constraints become less effective. The numerical simulations bear out that a rise in λ increases output and, for the parameters chosen, equilibrium real balances also rise.

FIGURE 2

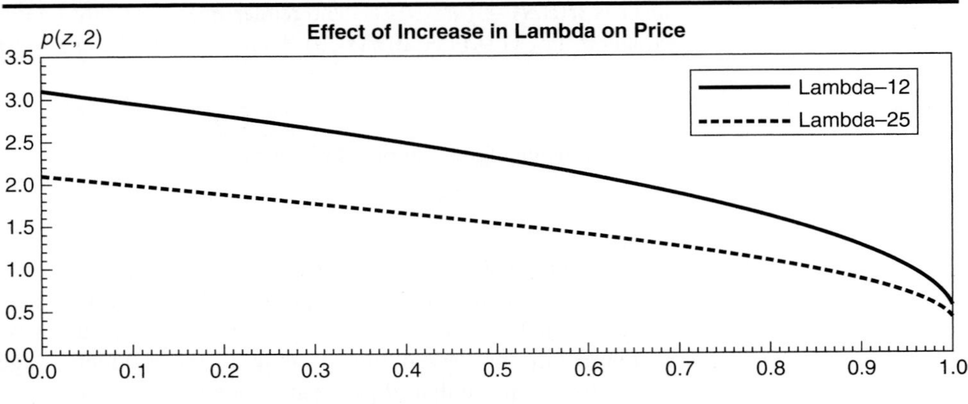

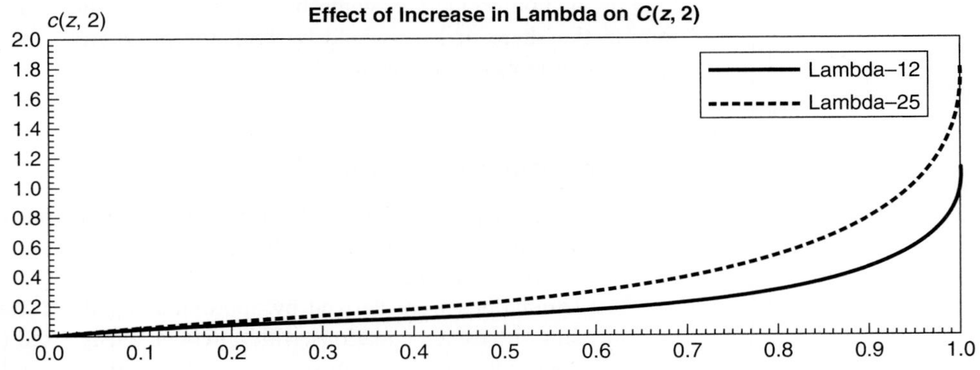

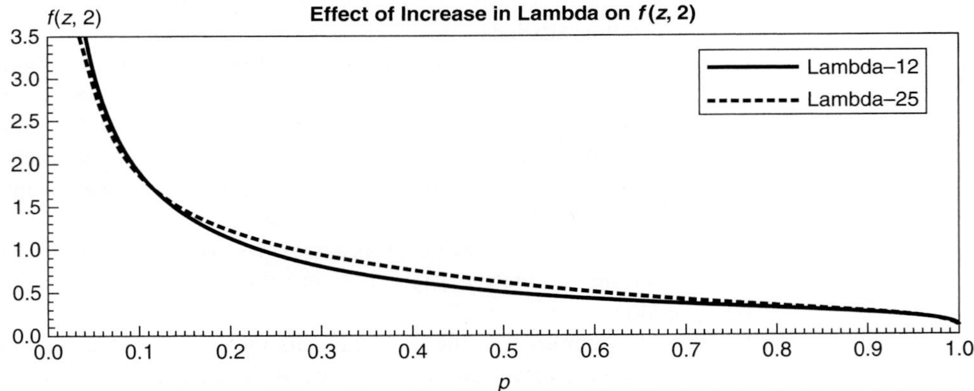

TABLE 1

β	α	δ	Mean *x*	Var *x*	Mean *P*	Var *P*
.5	.12	0	.058	.012	2.73	.248
.8	.12	0	.038	.005	6.05	1.15
.5	.25	0	.137	.035	1.78	.118
.5	.12	.25	.137	.036	.83	.03
.5	.12	.5	.27	.069	.79	.01

NOTES: *x* is amount of produced output sold to nonproductive agent; *P* is price level.

FIGURE 3 |

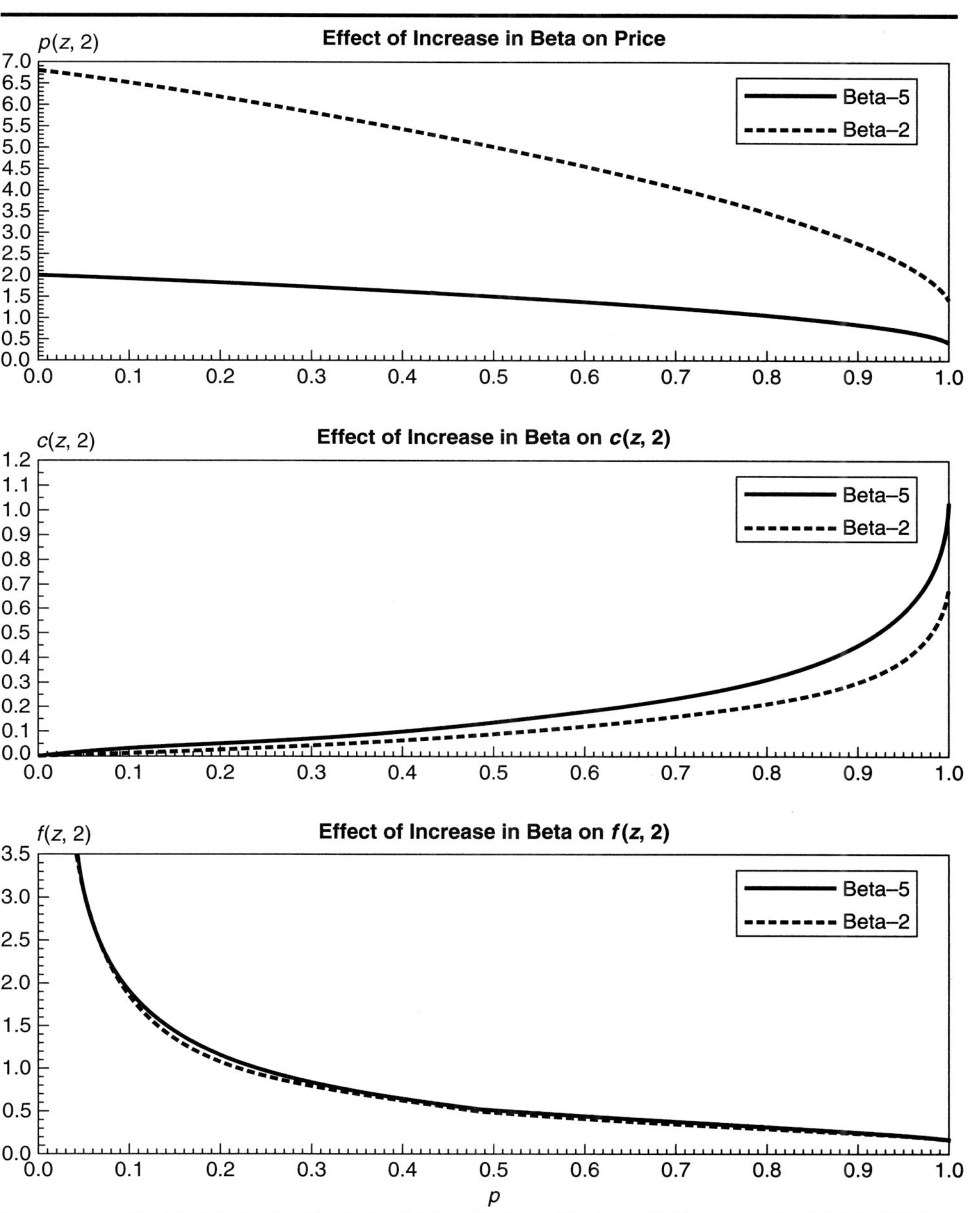

Perhaps the most interesting simulations show the effects of a change in δ, the flow of output emitted by nonhuman capital. Even though the theory developed above covers only the case $\delta = 0$, the modifications needed in equations (16) to (19) are rather obvious. The simulations show that as δ increases, so does equilibrium quantities of produced output exchanged between the two agents. Thus the model demonstrates that borrowing constraints give rise to a type of "complementarity" between human and nonhuman capital. The interpretation of this result is that as the value of nonhuman capital rises, the borrowing constraint becomes less effective as the risk that agents exhaust their wealth decreases. It is also interesting to note that the equilibrium value of assets varies less than the flow of dividends across alternative equilibria. This finding is similar to what one would find in models of overlapping, finitely lived agents. In both types of models there is an explicit need for wealth to intermediate intertemporal trade.

5. Comparison with Actual Business Cycles

The model presented in Section 2 gives rise to random fluctuations in output. Furthermore, the level of output is correlated with the level of prices. Thus, the model predicts systematic co-movements between different economic aggregates. In this section we compare these derived co-movements with actual behavior to assess the usefulness of models of this type for describing actual behavior.

The "Phillips Curve"—the statistical relationship between the rate of change of either prices or wages and measured unemployment—is perhaps the most famous, although far from the most empirically stable feature of macroeconomic fluctuations. The model predicts that, under a constant nominal money supply, there is a tight *negative* relationship between the *level* of prices and the *level* of output. This would appear to contradict the Phillips Curve. However, numerical simulations show that the model exhibits a positive relationship between the level of output and the expected rate of change of prices. These two aspects of the model are compatible because unexpected output changes (which arise from exogenous changes in the state of labor productivity) are generally associated with upward jumps in output and downward jumps in prices.

The model also displays that expected output changes and expected price changes are negatively related, an empirical point established in Litterman-Weiss [**12**]. Interpretation of this latter finding is somewhat problematic since that model contains only a single asset and thus identifies the expected inflation rate with the (negative) of the expected real rate. With this interpretation, the model predicts a positive correlation between expected output and consumption rates of change and ex ante real rates.

The model is also useful for explaining why asset prices may appear "too" volatile. For example, simulations show that the variance of expected price changes (equal to the variance in expected real returns) are far larger than the variance in expected consumption rates of change. With logarithmic utility we would expect these two quantities to be equal, as a 1 per cent increase in expected return is associated with a 1 per cent decline in the level of consumption. Similarly, the model shows why some variance bound tests which rely on conditions for treating per capita consumption as if it is chosen by a representative consumer might fail. This rejection stems from the fact that although the stochastic Euler equation holds for each agent separately, it will not hold for per capita consumption when agents' consumptions are not perfectly correlated. A similar sort of critique of tests of asset pricing is made in Bewley [**3**] and Mehra and Prescott [**17**].

6. Conclusion

This paper has presented a model in which the inability to insure against adverse productivity disturbances motivates a need for financial assets for intermediating intertemporal trade among agents with diverse labor productivity time profiles. This phenomenon has implications for both asset pricing and aggregate employment and output. The model emphasizes the importance of the cross sectional joint distribution of financial assets and marginal value products for affecting aggregate outcomes at a point in time. As this distribution evolves endogenously, the model is capable of generating more asset price variability relative to aggregate consumption and dividend variability than could be explained by earlier theories. In many ways the derived aggregate price and quantity co-movements resemble actual business cycles. Economic intuition suggests, and numerical simulations confirm, that the average level of output will be lower (i) the greater is the rate of pure time discount, (ii) the lower is the dividend flow from aggregate capital, (iii) the longer is the duration of time between productivity shocks. We emphasize that as a model of aggregate dynamics, the model rests crucially on there being movements over time in the cross-sectional joint distribution of marginal products and assets. For this to be true, it is necessary that the timing of changes in labor productivity, although not necessarily the magnitude of these shocks, be correlated across agents. Otherwise, as the analysis of Hellwig [**8**] shows, with many independent shocks the resulting aggregate equilibrium would, after an initial transitional stage, become time invariant. Thus the model implicates noninsurable real sectoral shifts which simultaneously effect nonnegligible masses of agents as the cause of cycles.

Since the occurrence of these epochs which alter productivity must be publicly observable, it seems natural to enquire further into why such risks are uninsurable. Clearly, it is necessary that each agent's own labor productivity itself be not publicly observable; otherwise he could purchase insurance directly. However, this condition is not sufficient to exclude possible gain from risk sharing. If changes in a particular agent's labor productivity were correlated with the value of some competitively traded financial asset, then the agent could arrange a portfolio, possibly involving derivative assets such as put and call options, which effectively insured him against unexpected outcomes. For the specification analyzed in this paper, each agent's own change in labor productivity is (locally) perfectly correlated with the value of the asset, so the derived equilibrium is sensitive to the introduction of derivative assets which could, in this case, provide complete opportunities for risk sharing.[6] However, in more complicated settings this will not necessarily be true. Consider a model with a continuum of agents in which at each epoch only one half of the productive agents become nonproductive and one half of the nonproductive agents become productive. In this environment, no agent's own history is perfectly correlated with asset prices, so everyone will necessarily bear some risk even with complete option markets. We conjecture that price and aggregate output movements in this economy will replicate those derived in our simple setting.

A natural question is whether borrowing constraints necessarily intensify aggregate cyclical variability relative to a complete market economy. Our analysis shows that by introducing the current distribution of wealth as a separate explanatory factor, borrowing constraints lead to a variety of possible outcomes for any given configuration of labor productivities. But whether this contributes to variation over time depends also on how borrowing constraints affect output across different states for a given distribution of wealth. Borrowing constraints tend to reduce each agent's ability to intertemporally substitute work effort in response to temporary, idiosyncratic productivity disturbances. Thus they tend to smooth out each individual's time profile of work effort relative to the complete markets case. In Appendix D we present a simple example of how this effect may reduce aggregate output variability. The crucial feature of this example is that, unlike our main model, there is variability over time in the distribution of labor productivities.

Do these fluctuations suggest that business cycles are a social problem? Since the allocation is not Pareto Optimal, there remains the possibility that some kinds of monetary and fiscal policies could be structured to improve welfare. The model suggests that these policies would be useful by transferring wealth to the nonproductive agent, which it was shown

[6] This intuition is not strictly correct since the introduction of derivative assets raises subtle issues concerning the existence of competitive equilibria. See Hart [**7**] for an example of when conditioning on endogenous asset prices, rather than exogenous events, prevents equilibrium from existing, despite the usual concavity assumptions.

could "improve" some appealing measures of social welfare at a point in time. However, such policies if implemented consistently would have some adverse incentive effects on individual labor supply. A full analysis would have to weigh the gains from wealth transfers from these adverse incentive effects.

University of Chicago
and
University of California-San Diego
Manuscript received September, 1983; final revision received March, 1985.

Appendix A

Equations (16) and (17) may be expressed as

$$\text{(A.1)} \qquad B(z) = B(y) + \int_F^z A(1-s)\{(\beta+\lambda)B(s) - \lambda A(s)\}\,ds,$$

$$A(z) = A(y) + \int_F^z A(s)\{\lambda B(s) - (\lambda+\beta)A(s)\}\,ds.$$

Given any $(A(\frac{1}{2}), B(\frac{1}{2}))$ one may use the contraction mapping theorem to solve (A.1) uniquely in an interval $(1-\varepsilon_1, \varepsilon_1)$ for some $\varepsilon_1 > \frac{1}{2}$. In turn give $(A(1-\varepsilon_1), B(1-\varepsilon_1))$ and $(A(\varepsilon_1), B(\varepsilon_1))$ one may again use the contraction mapping principle to solve (A.1) on $(1-\varepsilon_2, \varepsilon_2)$ where $\varepsilon_2 > \varepsilon_1$. This process will continue until either (a) solution is obtained in an open interval containing [0, 1] or (b) for some $\varepsilon \leqslant 1$

$$\lim_{z\to\varepsilon} \operatorname{Max}\{[(A(\varepsilon), B(\varepsilon))|, |(A(1-\varepsilon), B(1-\varepsilon))]\} = \infty$$

in which case we can construct a solution only on $(1-\varepsilon, \varepsilon)$.

Notice that, from the linearity of equation (16), this can only occur if

$$\lim_{z\to\varepsilon} \operatorname{Max}\{|A(z)|, |A(1-z)|\} = \infty.$$

From now on let $(A(z, x), B(z, x))$ denote the solution to (A.1) with $(A(\frac{1}{2}), B(\frac{1}{2})) = x$. Also let $\varepsilon = (x)$ denote the maximum interval of existence. It is a consequence of the contraction mapping principle that for any closed interval $I \subset \varepsilon(\bar{x})$, for x sufficiently near $\bar{x}$, $(A(z, x), B(z, x))$ is defined at least on the interval I, is C^1, and satisfies for $i = 1, 2$:

$$\text{(A.2)} \qquad \frac{d}{dz}\frac{\partial A(z,x)}{\partial x^i} = \frac{\partial A(z,x)}{\partial x^i}\{\lambda B(z,x) - (\beta+\lambda)\,A(z,x)\} + A(z,x)\left\{\lambda\frac{\partial B(z,x)}{\partial x^i} - (\beta+\lambda)\frac{\partial A(z,x)}{\partial x^i}\right\},$$

$$\frac{d}{dz}\frac{B(z,x)}{\partial x^i} = \frac{\partial A(1-z,x)}{\partial x^i}\{(\beta+\lambda)\,B(z,x) - \lambda A(z,x)\} + A(1-z,x)\left\{(\beta+\lambda)\frac{\partial B(z,x)}{\partial x^i} - \frac{\partial A(z,x)}{\partial x^i}\right\},$$

with

$$\frac{\partial A(\frac{1}{2},x)}{\partial x^1} = \frac{\partial B(\frac{1}{2},x)}{\partial x^2} = 1,$$

$$\frac{\partial A(\frac{1}{2},x)}{\partial x^2} = \frac{\partial B(\frac{1}{2},x)}{\partial x^1} = 0.$$

Solutions to (A.2) may be constructed as those for (A.1) in the same interval $\varepsilon(x)$.

LEMMA 1: *Let* $(A(z, x), B(z, x))$ *be a solution such that for* $z \leqslant \frac{1}{2}$, $A(z, x) \geqslant 0$, $B(z, x) \geqslant 0$, *and* $(\lambda + \beta) B(z, x) - \lambda A(z, x) \leqslant 0$ *(Region III in Figure* 1*). Then, if for some* $z \leqslant \frac{1}{2}$, $A(z, x) > 1/\beta z$ *then* $\varepsilon(x)$ *is contained in* $(0, 1)$. *Furthermore, if* $A(z, x) < 1/(\beta + \lambda)z$, *then* $\varepsilon(x)$ *contains* $[0, 1]$.

PROOF: From (17), for $s \leqslant \frac{1}{2}$

$$-\beta A^2(s, x) > A'(s, x) > -(\beta + \lambda)A^2(s, x). \tag{A.3}$$

Define the differential equation

$$\alpha'(s) = -\mu\alpha^2(s) \tag{A.4}$$

with $\alpha(z) = A(z, x)$. The solution to (A.4) is given by

$$\alpha(s) = ((A(z, x))^{-1} - \mu z + \mu s)^{-1}$$

If follows that, from the differential inequality (A.3) that for $s < \frac{1}{2}$

$$((A(z, x))^{-1} - \beta z + \beta s)^{-1} \leqslant A(s, x) \leqslant ((A(z, x))^{-1} + (\lambda + \beta)(s - z))^{-1}.$$

Thus, if $(A(z, x))^{-1} < \beta z$, $A(s, x) \rightarrow \infty$ as $s \rightarrow \bar{s} > 0$ and hence $\varepsilon(x) \subset (0, 1)$. Further if $(A(z, x))^{-1} > (\beta + \lambda)z$, for each $s \geqslant 0$, $A(s, x)$ is defined and finite so $\varepsilon(x) \supset [0, 1]$ provided $A(z, x)$ is bounded above for $z \in [\frac{1}{2}, 1]$. If the solution remains in region III of Figure 1, we are done since $A'(z, x) \leqslant 0$. If it leaves region III through $B = 0$, again we are done since, by equation (13), if A is small, $A^2 < A$ and thus $A' \geqslant A(\lambda B - \beta)$ which implies $A(z, x) \geqslant 0$. If it leaves III through II and does not reach region I, again we are done since $A' \leqslant 0$ and $A \geqslant 0$. Finally if it reaches region I, this implies $0 \leqslant A'(z, x) \leqslant \lambda A(z, x)B(z, x)$ and $B'(z, x) \leqslant A(1 - z, x)(\beta + \lambda)B(z, x)$ and since $A(1 - z, x)$ is bounded we have that $B(z, x)$ is bounded and consequently $A(z, x)$ is too.

LEMMA 2: *Suppose* $(\partial A(z, x)/\partial x^2, \partial B(z, x)/\partial x^2)$ *solves (A.3) and* $A(z, x)\, B(z, x)$ *is a positive solution defined on the interval* $\varepsilon(x) \supset (0, 1)$ *with* $(\lambda + \beta)B(z, x) - \lambda A(z, x) \leqslant 0$ *for* $z < 1$. *Then for* $z > \frac{1}{2}$

$$\frac{\partial B(z, x)}{\partial x^2} > \frac{\partial A(z, x)}{\partial x^2}, \tag{i}$$

$$\frac{\partial A(z, x)}{\partial x^2} > 0, \tag{ii}$$

and, (iii)

$$\frac{\partial A(1 - z, x)}{\partial x^2} < 0.$$

PROOF: Recall that

$$\frac{\partial B(\frac{1}{2}, x)}{\partial x^2} = 1, \qquad \frac{\partial A(\frac{1}{2}, x)}{\partial x^2} = 0$$

and that from (A.2)

$$\frac{d}{dz}\frac{\partial B(z, x)}{\partial x^2}\bigg|_{z-\frac{1}{2}} > \frac{d}{d_2}\frac{\partial A(z, x)}{\partial x^2}\bigg|_{z-\frac{1}{2}} > 0.$$

Hence there exists $\varepsilon > 0$ such that for all $y, \frac{1}{2} < y < \frac{1}{2} + \varepsilon$ (i), (ii), and (iii) hold. If the lemma is false, there exists $\hat{y} > \frac{1}{2}$ such that $\hat{y} = \text{Inf}\{y \geqslant \frac{1}{2} |$ either (i), (ii), or (iii) does not hold$\}$. By smooth dependence of solutions this implies that at least one of the above conditions holds as an equality at $\hat{y}$.

CASE (a): Assume

$$\frac{\partial B(\hat{y}, x)}{\partial x^2} = \frac{\partial A(\hat{y}, x)}{\partial x^2}$$

But, for all $z, \frac{1}{2} < z < \hat{y}$, (i) and (ii) hold, and since $A(1 - z, x) > A(z, x)$, we have

$$\frac{d}{dz}\frac{\partial B(z, x)}{\partial x^2} > \frac{d}{dz}\frac{\partial A(z, x)}{\partial x^2}$$

Since

$$\frac{\partial B(\frac{1}{2}, x)}{\partial x^2} > \frac{\partial A(\frac{1}{2}, x)}{\partial x^2},$$

this is impossible.

CASE (b): Assume

$$\frac{\partial A(\hat{y}, x)}{\partial x^2} = 0.$$

From (A.2)

$$\frac{\partial A(\hat{y}, x)}{\partial x^2} = 0$$

implies

$$\text{sgn}\left[\frac{d}{dz}\frac{A(z, x)}{x^2}\bigg|_{z=\hat{y}}\right] = \text{sgn}\left[\frac{B(z, x)}{x^2}\bigg|_{z=\hat{y}}\right].$$

Since

$$\frac{1}{2} < z < y \Rightarrow \frac{\partial A(z, x)}{\partial x^2} > 0$$

it must be that

$$\frac{d}{dz}\frac{\partial A(z, x)}{\partial x^2}\bigg|_{z=\hat{y}} \leqslant 0 \Rightarrow \frac{\partial B(\hat{y}, x)}{\partial x^2} \leqslant 0,$$

but from previous arguments, this is impossible.

CASE (c): Assume

$$\frac{\partial A(1 - \hat{y}, x)}{\partial x^2} = 0.$$

As in Case (b), this implies

$$\frac{\partial B(1 - \hat{y}, x)}{\partial x^2} \leqslant 0$$

since

$$\frac{\partial B(\frac{1}{2}, x)}{\partial x^2} > \frac{\partial A(\frac{1}{2}, x)}{\partial x^2};$$

this implies there exists $\frac{1}{2} < \hat{\hat{y}} < \hat{y}$ such that

$$\frac{\partial B(1 - \hat{\hat{y}}, x)}{\partial x^2} = \frac{\partial A(1 - \hat{\hat{y}}, x)}{\partial x^2} \leqslant 0$$

and

$$\frac{d}{dz}\frac{\partial B(1 - \hat{\hat{y}}, x)}{\partial x^2} \geqslant \frac{d}{dz}\frac{\partial A(1 - \hat{\hat{y}}, x)}{\partial x^2}$$

But, from (A.2)

$$\frac{d}{dz}\frac{\partial B(1 - \hat{\hat{y}}, x)}{\partial x^2} < 0$$

and

$$\frac{d}{dz}\frac{\partial A(1 - \hat{\hat{y}}, x)}{\partial x^2} > 0$$

which is impossible.

THEOREM: *There exists a solution to* (A.1) *defined on* (0, 1) *with* $\lim_{z\to 1}(\lambda + \beta)\cdot B(z) - \lambda A(z) = 0$ *and* $\lim_{z\to 0} A(z) = \infty$.

PROOF: Choose $x_1 = (A(\frac{1}{2}), B(\frac{1}{2}))$ with $A(\frac{1}{2}) < 1/2(\beta + \lambda)$, $B(\frac{1}{2}) < \lambda A(\frac{1}{2})/(\beta + \lambda)$. By Lemma 1, any solution to (A.1) is defined on [0, 1]. Also if $B(\frac{1}{2}) = 0$, $(\lambda + \beta)B(1, x_1) - \lambda A(1, x_1) < 0$, if $B(\frac{1}{2}) = \lambda A(\frac{1}{2})/(\beta + \lambda)$, then $(\lambda + \beta)B(1, x_1) - \lambda A(1, x_1) > 0$. By continuity of the solutions with respect to initial conditions, there exists $\bar{x}_1 = (A(\frac{1}{2}), B(\frac{1}{2}))$ such that $(\lambda + \beta)B(1, \bar{x}_1) - \lambda A(1, \bar{x}_1) = 0$. Let $\Omega = \{a \geqslant 0 \mid \exists b < \lambda a/(\beta + \lambda)$ such that for $x = (a, b)$, then $(A(z, x), B(z, x))$ is defined on [0, 1] and $(\lambda + \beta)B(1, x) - \lambda A(1, x) = 0\}$. Then Ω is nonempty and if $a \in \Omega$, $a \leqslant 1/2\beta$. Let $\bar{a} = \sup \Omega$. Thus there exists a sequence $a_n \to \bar{a}$, $a_n \in \Omega$. Let b_n be the unique choice of b, such that if $x_n = (a_n, b_n)$, $(\lambda + \beta) B(1, x_n) - \lambda A(1, x_n) = 0$. Since $b_n < \lambda a_n/(\beta + \lambda)$ choose a subsequence, if necessary, such that $\bar{b} = \lim_{n\to\infty} b_n$. We claim that for $\bar{x} = (\bar{a}, \bar{b})$, $\varepsilon(\bar{x})$ does not contain [0, 1]. For if $[0, 1] \subset \varepsilon(\bar{x})$ there exists a neighborhood of $\bar{x}$ such that for all x in this neighborhood $\varepsilon(x) \supset [0, 1]$. By Lemma 2, if $\hat{x} = \bar{x} + (0, \delta/2)$ then $(\lambda + \beta)B(1, \hat{x}) - \lambda A(1, \hat{x}) > 0$. Similarly if $\hat{\hat{x}} = \bar{x} - (0, \delta/2)$, then $(\lambda + \beta)B(1, \hat{\hat{x}}) - \lambda A(1, \hat{\hat{x}}) < 0$. Let L be a polygonal in the neighborhood of $\hat{x}$ connecting $\hat{x}$ to $\hat{\hat{x}}$ strictly to the right of $\bar{x}$. By continuity, there exists $x^* \in L$ such that $(\lambda + \beta)B(1, x^*) - \lambda A(1, x^*) = 0$. Since $x^* = (a^*, b^*)$ and $a^* > \bar{a}$, this is a contradiction so $\varepsilon(\bar{x}) \not\supset [0, 1]$. We now claim $\varepsilon(\bar{x}) = (0, 1)$. By Lemma 1, since for each x_n, $A(z, x_n)$ is defined on $[0, 1]$, $A(z, x_n) \leqslant (\beta z)^{-1}$ for $z \in (0, \frac{1}{2}]$. Thus $A(z, x)$ is well defined for each $0 < z < \frac{1}{2}$. Also, by (A.1)$(\lambda + \beta)\cdot B'(\frac{1}{2}, x_n) - \lambda A'(\frac{1}{2}, x_n) > 0$. If for some $\bar{z} < 1$, $(\lambda + \beta) B'(\bar{z}, x_n) - \lambda A'(\hat{z}, x_n) = 0$, then for all $z > \bar{z}$, $(\lambda + \beta)B'(z, x_n) - \lambda A'(z, x_n) < 0$. But this contradicts $(\lambda + \beta)B(1, x_n) - \lambda A(1, x_n) = 0$ and $(\lambda + \beta)B(z, x_n) - \lambda A(z, x_n) < 0$, all $z < 1$. Hence,

$$0 < (\lambda + \beta)B'(z, x_n) - \lambda A'(z, x_n) \leqslant \lambda(\beta + \lambda)A^2(z, x_n) \leqslant 2\lambda(\beta + \lambda)\beta^{-2} \quad \text{for} \quad z \geqslant \tfrac{1}{2}.$$

Since for $x = (a, b)$

$$(\lambda + \beta)B(1, x_n) - \lambda A(1, x_n) = (\lambda + \beta)b - \lambda a + \int_{1/2}^{1} [(\lambda + \beta)B'(s, x) - \lambda A'(s, x)]\, ds$$

it follows from the dominated convergence theorem

$$(\lambda + \beta)B(1, \underline{x}) - \lambda A(1, \underline{x}) = \lim_{n\to\infty} (\lambda + \beta)B(1, x_n) - \lambda A(1, x_n) = 0$$

so that $A(z, \bar{x})$, $B(z, \bar{x})$ is the desired solution.

Appendix B

We will show here that the solution obtained in Appendix A allows us to construct an equilibrium. Given the solutions $A(z)$ and $B(z)$ let $h(z, 1) = (A(1 - z))^{-1}$ and $h(z, 2) = -(A(z))^{-1}$. Suppose $z(t, \omega)$ solves (5) with given $z(0, \omega) = z_0 > 0$. We will show that if agents initial endowment is z_0 for type 1 and $1 - z_0$ for type 2 and if they predict that type 1 average holdings at (t, ω) will be $z(t, \omega)$ and that $q(z, 1) = B(z)$, $q(z, 2) = B(1 - z)$, then at each (t, ω) each agent of type 1 will hold $z(t, \omega)$ and each agent of type 2 will hold $1 - z(t, \omega)$. We recall that all functions indexed by t are assumed $\mathcal{F}_t$ measurable. Also, all equities are satisfied only a.e. We will just establish a preliminary result.

LEMMA 1: *Let $A(z)$ and $B(z)$ be a solution of* (16), (17) *satisfying* (18) *and* (19), *and for each ω, $z(t,)$ the associated path of average money building by agent* 1. *Then for each T, there exists $\delta > 0$ such that for $t \leqslant T$, $\inf_{\omega \in \Omega} z(t, \omega) > \hat{o}$,* $\sup_{\omega \in \Omega} z(t, \omega) < 1 - \delta$, and $\sup_{(t,\omega)} |\dot{z}(t, \omega)| < \infty$.

PROOF: *Clearly it suffices to prove the first result for ω such that $s_t(\omega) = 2$, for where $s_t(\omega) = 1$, $\dot{z}(t, \omega) \geqslant 0$. Since for such ω, $\dot{z}(t, \omega) = -A^{-1}(z) < 0$, the map $T \to z(T, \omega)$ is invertible and $dT/dz = -A(z)$. Thus*

$$T(\delta) = \int_{\delta}^{z_0} A(z)\, dz \geqslant \int_{\delta}^{z_0} \frac{1}{(\lambda + \beta)z}\, dz$$

(by Lemma 1, Appendix A). Thus, $\lim_{\delta \to 0} T(\delta) = \infty$, and this establishes the first part.

Also, $|\dot{z}(t, \omega)| \leqslant \sup |A^{-1}(\dot{z})| \leqslant (A(1))^{-1}$, since $A' \leqslant 0$. By an analogous bound as in Lemma 1 of Appendix A, $A(1) \geqslant 1/(\beta + \lambda)$ and thus $|\dot{z}(t, \omega)| \leqslant (\beta + \lambda)^{-1}$. *Q.E.D.*

We will now consider the problem (P)

$$\text{Max } E_0 \left\{ \int_0^\infty e^{-\beta t}[\log c(t, \omega) - l(t, \omega)]dt \right\}$$

subject to

$$y(0, \omega) = z(0, \omega) > 0,$$
$$\dot{y} = (l(t, \omega) - c(t, \omega))/q(z(t, \omega), 1) \quad \text{if} \quad s_t(\omega) = 1 \text{ and}$$
$$\dot{y} = -c(t, \omega)/q(z(t, \omega), 2) \quad \text{and} \quad l(t, \omega) = 0 \quad \text{if} \quad s_t(\omega) = 2$$
$$c(t, \omega) \geqslant 0, \quad y(t, \omega) \geqslant 0, \quad l(t, \omega) \geqslant 0.$$

Here $q(z(t, \omega), 1) = B(z(t, \omega))$ and $q(z(t, \omega), 2) = B(1 - z(t, \omega))$.

Our purpose is to show that $y(t, \omega) = z(t, \omega)$ is a solution to problem (P). We will only consider solutions to (P) such that ess sup $|\dot{y}(t, \omega)| < \infty$. By Lemma 1, $z(t, \omega)$ is one such solution. Now for each $y > 0$, $0 \leqslant z \leqslant 1$ let $L(y, \dot{y}, z, 1) = \sup \{\log C - L | s.t.\ L - c = q(z, 1)\dot{y}\} = -q(z, 1)\dot{y} - 1$. Also, for $y > 0$, $\dot{y} < 0$ let $L(y, \dot{y}, z, 2) = \log(-q(z, 2)\dot{y})$. Clearly if $y > 0$, $(0, -q(z, 1)) = \nabla L(y, \dot{y}, z, 1)$, and if $y > 0, \dot{y} < 0$, $(0, 1/\dot{y}) = \nabla L(\dot{y}, z, 2)$.

Notice that the logarithmic utility function assures us that if a path with finite expected utility exists we may restrict ourselves to paths where $y(t, \omega) < 0$ if $s_t(\omega) = 2$. Also, such a path clearly exists, since the price of goods is bounded above by $(B(1)^{-1} = (\beta + \lambda)/\lambda\,(A(1))^{-1} \leqslant 1/\lambda)$.

Now for fixed T, by concavity of L,

$$E_0 \int_0^T e^{-\beta t}(L(y, \dot{y}, z, s) - L(z, \dot{z}, z, s))\, dt$$

$$\leq E_0 \int_0^T e^{-\beta t} p(t, \omega)[\dot{z} - \dot{y}]\, dt, \quad \text{where}$$

$$p(t, \omega) = q(z(t, \omega), 1) = B(z(t, \omega)) \quad \text{if} \quad s_t(\omega) = 1,$$
$$p(t, \omega) = (\dot{z}(t, \omega))^{-1} = A(z(t, \omega)) \quad \text{if} \quad s_t(\omega) = 2.$$

Notice that by Lemma 1, for each $T > 0$, $\sup_{\omega, t=\tau}(p(t, \omega)) < \infty$ and since $p(t, \omega) = p(z(t, \omega), s_i(\omega))$ where p is a C^1 function of z for fixed $s_i(\omega)$ we have $dp(\cdot, i)/dz$ is bounded for $z = z(t, \omega)$, $t \leq T$.

LEMMA 2 *($p, \mathcal{F}_t$) forms a Martingale, i.e.,*

$$E\{e^{-\beta(t+\tau)} p(t + \tau, \omega) | \mathcal{F}_t\} = e^{-\beta t} p(t, \omega).$$

The proof of Lemma 2 is rather routine, so we only sketch it. As observed in Section 2,

$$\begin{aligned} E\{e^{-\beta(t+\tau)} p(t + \tau, \omega) | \mathcal{F}_t\} &= E\{e^{-\beta(t+\tau)} p(t + \tau, \omega) | z(t, \omega), s_i(\omega)\} \\ &= E\{e^{-\beta(t+\tau)} p(t + \tau, \omega) | p(t, \omega), s_i(\omega)\} \end{aligned}$$

since for fixed i, $p(z, i)$ is invertible.

Using the fact that $1 - \delta > z(t', \omega) > \delta$ for $t \leq t' \leq r + \tau$, (16) and (17), and the fact that $p(z, i)$ and $\dot{z}(z, i)$ C^1 on z for fixed i, we have that for each $t', \tau', t + \tau' \leq t + \tau, t \geq t'$,

$$E(e^{-\beta(t+\tau)} p(t' + \tau', \omega) | z(t', \omega), s_i(\omega)\} = 0_t(\tau', \omega) + e^{-\beta t} p(t', \omega)$$

where

$$\lim_{\tau^t \to 0} \frac{|o_t(\tau' \omega)|}{\tau^t} = 0$$

uniformly on ω and t'. In particular, for any $\varepsilon < 0$, $|o_{t'}(\tau', \omega)| < \tau' \varepsilon$, if τ' is chosen small enough. It follows from the law of iterated expectations that $|E(e^{-\beta(t+\tau)} p(t + \tau, \omega | \mathcal{F}_t\} - e^{-\beta t} p(t, \omega)| \leq \varepsilon$ for each $\varepsilon > 0$.

Now for each ω since $p(t, \omega)$ is of bounded variation (a.s.).

$$\int_0^T e^{-\beta t} p(t, \omega)\, [z\,(t, \omega) - \dot{y}(r, \omega]\, dt$$

$$= e^{-\beta T} p(t, \omega)[z(t, \omega) - y(T, \omega)] + \int_0^T [y(t, \omega) - z(t, \omega)] d(e^{-\beta t} p(t, \omega)).$$

Now, in each $[0, T]$, both y and z are essentially bounded. Thus the last integral is the limit of integrals of nonanticipative bounded step functions whose $E(\cdot|\mathcal{F}_0)$ is zero by Lemma 2, and the law of iterated expectations. Also,

$$\left| \int_0^T \phi(t, \omega)\, de^{-\beta t} p(t, \omega) \right| < 4T\, ess \sup_{(t, \omega)} |\phi(t, \omega)| \text{ess} \sup_{(t, \omega)} |p(t, \omega)| N_\tau(\omega)$$

where $N_\tau(\omega)$ is the value of the Poisson Process at T in event ω. The right-hand side of this last expression is clearly integrable, provided ess $\sup_{(t,\omega)}|\phi(t,\omega)| < \infty$ and thus by the dominated convergence theorem the last integral has zero expected value. (Alternatively we could have established this result using the theory of integration against square integrable Martingales as in Lipster and Shirayev [**11**].)

Also

$$\limsup_{(T\to\infty)} |e^{-\beta T} p(T,\omega)\, z\,(T,\omega)| \leq \limsup_{T\to\infty} e^{-\beta T} A(z(T,\omega))z(T,\omega) = 0$$

since $A(z) \leqslant 1/\beta z$. Thus, by Fatou's Lemma,

$$\limsup_{T\to\infty} E_0 \int_0^T e^{-\beta t}(L(y,\dot{y},z,s) - L(z,\dot{z},z,s))\,dt \leqslant 0.$$

Appendix C

In this Appendix we show that (22) has a unique solution $f(z,2) \geqslant 0$ satisfying $\int_o^t f(z,2)dz = 1$ and that if $f(z,1) = [A(1-z)/A(z)]f(z,2)$ then $\int_o^t f(z,1)dz = 1$.

For each $c > 0$,

$$\gamma(\mu,c) = c\exp\left(\int_{1/2}^{\mu} [A'(z)/A(z) + \lambda A(z) - \lambda A(1-z)]\,dz\right)$$

is the general new negative solution to (22). If the exponential term is integrable over [0, 1] and non-zero, we may choose c such that $\int_0^1 \gamma(\mu,c) = 1$. Such c will be unique. Now using equation (17) we know that $A'(z)/A(z) = \lambda B(z) - (\lambda+\beta)A(z)$ and thus

$$\lambda A(z) = \frac{\lambda^2}{\lambda+\beta}B(z) - \frac{\lambda}{\lambda+\beta}\frac{A'(z)}{A(z)}.$$

Thus since $B(z)$ is nonnegative on [0, 1] and bounded near 1, the exponential term will be integrable if and only if

$$\int_0^1 \left\{\exp\left(\int_{1/2}^{\mu} \frac{\beta}{\lambda+\beta}\frac{A'(z)}{A(z)}dz\right)\right\} d\mu$$

exists, or, if and only if,

(B.1) $$\int_0^1 (A(z))^{\beta/\lambda+\beta} dz < \infty.$$

Now write $g(z) = 1/A(z)$. Then $g'(z) = -A'(z)/A^2(z) = \lambda + \beta - \lambda B(z)g(z)$ and since $\lim_{z\to 0}(B(z)/A(z)) = 0$, $g'(0) = \lambda + \beta$. Hence for any $\varepsilon > 0$ there exists δ such that if $0 \leqslant z \leqslant \delta$, $g(z) \geqslant (\lambda+\beta)z - \varepsilon z$. Since $\beta/(\lambda+\beta) < 1$, (B.1) holds. Thus there exists unique $\bar{c}$ such that $\int_0^1 \gamma(\mu,\bar{c})\,d\mu = 1$. Let $f(z,2) = \gamma(\mu,\bar{c})$. Notice that $F(1,2) = 1$.

Using Lemma 1 of Appendix A, one can easily show that $\int_\Omega^\mu A(z)\,dz = \infty$ for each $\mu > 0$. This result also implies that $f(0,2) = \infty$ and $f(1,2) = 0$. Since $A(z) \neq 0$, from (21) we have that $F(1,1) = F(1,2) = 1$.

Appendix D

EXAMPLE 1: There are two types of agents, and 3 states of the world. The following table relates output per unit of labor of agent $i = 1, 2$ in date of the world $j = 1, 2, 3$:

FIGURE 4 |

$j \backslash i$	1	2
1	4	2
2	3	3
3	2	4

Output is perishable and the utility function of agent i is given by $E_0\Sigma_{t-1}^{\infty}\beta^t(\log c_j^i - l_j^i)$. States are i.i.d. and $\pi_1 = \pi_3 = .25$ and $\pi_2 = .5$, where π_i denotes the probability of state i. The symmetric Arrow-Debreu allocation requires $l_1^t = 2, l_2^t = 0$ if $j = 1$; $l_1^t = 0, l_2^t = 2$ if $j = 3$; $l_1^i = l_2^i = 1$ if $j = 2$. In any case, $l_1^t + l_2^t \equiv 2$ and aggregate consumption varies between 8 and 6 each with probability .5.

Now if borrowing constraints are present and if there is no money, then $l_1^t \equiv l_2^t \equiv 1$ for any j and aggregate consumption is 6 in any state. Notice that the constraints impede the "specialization" that causes the aggregate fluctuations in the complete market case. By using a nonlinear utility of leisure one could make a similar point about employment as opposed to output.

References

1. Altonji, J. G.: "The Intertemporal Substitution Model of Labour Market Fluctuations: An Empirical Analysis," *Review of Economic Studies*, 49(1982).
2. Bewley, T.: "The Permanent Income Hypothesis: A Theoretical Formulation," *Journal of Economic Theory*, 16(1977), 252–292.
3. ______: "Thoughts on Tests of the Intertemporal Asset Pricing Model," unpublished, Northwestern University, 1982.
4. Dynkin, E. B., *Markov Process, Vol.* 1. Berlin: Springer, 1975.
5. Grossman, S., and R. Shiller: "The Determinants of the Variability of Stock Market Prices," *American Economic Review*, 71(1981), 222–227.
6. Hansen, L., and K. Singleton: "Stochastic Consumption, Risk Aversion and the Temporal Behavior of Asset Returns," *Journal of Political Economy*, 91(1983), 249–266.
7. Hart, O.: "On the Optimality of Equilibrium when Markets are Incomplete," *Journal of Economic Theory*, 11(1975), 418–444.
8. Hellwig, M. F.: "Precautionary Money Holding and the Payment of Interest on Money," University of Bonn Discussion Paper # 92, 1982.
9. Hotz, V. J, F. Kydland, and G. Sedlacek: "Intertemporal Substitution and Labor Supply," Carnegie Mellon University Working Paper, 1982.
10. Kushner, H.: *Stochastic Stability and Control.* New York: Academic Press, 1967.
11. Lipster, R. S., and A. N. Shirayev: *Statistics of Random Processes I—General Theory.* New York: Springer-Verlag, 1977.

12. Litterman, R., and L. Weiss: "Money, Real Interest Rates and Output: A Reinterpretation on Postwar U.S. Data," NBER Discussion Paper # 1077, 1983.

13. Lucas, R., and L. Rapping: "Real Wages, Employment and the Price Level," *Journal of Political Economy*, 77(1969), 721–754.

14. Lucas, R.: "Expectations and the Neutrality of Money," *Journal of Economic Theory*, 4(1972), 103–124.

15. ——: "Asset Prices in an Exchange Economy," *Econometrica,* 46(1978), 1429–1445.

16. Mankiw, W., J. Rotenberg, and L. Summers: "Intertemporal Substitution in Macro-economics," NBER Discussion Paper # 898, 1982.

17. Mehra, R., and E. Prescott: "A Test of the Intertemporal Asset Pricing Model," FRB Minneapolis Working Paper # 194, 1982.

18. Schectman, J.: "An Income Fluctuation Problem," *Journal of Economic Theory*, 12(1976), 218–241.

Six

Nancy Stokey

Nancy Stokey first met Steve Ross as an undergraduate at the University of Pennsylvania. She received a Ph.D. from Harvard University in 1978. She started out at the Graduate School of Management, Northwestern University, and now works at the University of Chicago. •

Except for Steve, I probably would not have gone into economics. After a good beginning as an Econ major at Penn in the late 1960s, I signed up for Intermediate Macro (Honors Section). During the first lecture, the instructor turned to the blackboard and covered it with National Income Accounting definitions, identities, etc., finishing the hour more or less without turning around. I dropped the course and that was almost the end of my career in economics.

But the following year I was persuaded to try Intermediate Macro again, with a brand-new, rookie assistant professor who, my advisor claimed, would probably have a very different approach. Indeed, Professor Ross's section did not involve much National Income Accounting. Instead we learned how to solve some cool optimization problems in continuous time and came out with our enthusiasm for economics not only intact but enhanced.

Steve can also take some credit for getting "Information, Trade and Common Knowledge" into print. Steve was the editor who handled the paper, in fact soliciting it for the *Journal of Economic Theory* after hearing that the *Review of Economic Studies* viewed the results as "trivial," "obvious and well known," and "not very interesting." It is a special pleasure to include here.

Information, Trade and Common Knowledge

*Paul Milgrom and Nancy Stokey**
Northwestern University, Evanston, Illinois 60201

In any voluntary trading process, if agents have rational expectations, then it is common knowledge among them that the equilibrium trade is feasible and individually rational. This condition is used to show that when risk-averse traders begin at a Pareto optimal allocation (relative to their prior beliefs) and then receive private information (which disturbs the marginal conditions), they can still never agree to any non-null trade. On markets, information is revealed by price changes. An equilibrium with fully revealing price changes always exists, and even at other equilibria the information revealed by price changes "swamps" each trader's private information. Journal of Economic Literature *Classification Numbers: 021, 026, 313.*•

1. Introduction

Halfway through the growing season a grain trader receives a private report on the state of the crop. Should he use this information to speculate in grain futures? Or should he assume futures prices already impound so much information that his own information is valueless, and on that basis refrain from speculating?

Generally, how do traders who have rational expectations respond to new, private information? We investigate this question using a general model of voluntary trade, so that our results apply to, but are not limited to, competitive markets.

Our central result is that, regardless of the institutional structure, if the initial allocation is *ex ante* Pareto-optimal (as occurs, for example, when it is the outcome of a prior round of trading on complete, competitive markets), then the receipt of private information cannot create any incentives to trade.

From one perspective this no-trade result may seem surprising. The receipt of private information will generally lead the traders to hold different posterior beliefs, even if their prior beliefs are identical. This, in turn, will result in an inequality of the traders' marginal rates of substitution for wealth across states of the world. One might expect this to create incentives for trade. Why then, does no trade take place? Since the initial allocation is Pareto optimal, there can be no valid insurance motive or transactions motive for trading—a trader's only motive is his hope of finding an advantageous bet. Therefore, the mere willingness of the other traders to accept their parts of the bet is evidence to at least one trader that his own part is unfavorable. Hence no trade can be found that is acceptable to all traders.

This no-trade result depends crucially on the rational expectations assumption that it is *common knowledge* when a trade is carried out that the trade is feasible and that it is mutually acceptable to all of the participants. Informally, a fact or an event is common knowledge among members of a group if it is known by each of them, if each knows that it is

*We are grateful to John Geanakoplos, John Roberts, and Mark Satterthwaite for helpful discussions. Both authors received support from the Center for Advanced Study in Managerial Economics and Decision Sciences, Northwestern University. Milgrom's research was also supported by NSF Grant SES8001932.

Reprinted with permission:
Milgrom, Paul and Nancy Stokey. "Information, Trade and Common Knowledge."
Journal of Economic Theory 26 (1982): 17–27

known by each of them, if each knows that each knows that it is known, etc. An example is used below to illustrate why trading can be consistent with more limited kinds of inference, but not with rational expectations.

We then examine the information conveyed by equilibrium prices when there are markets both before and after traders receive private information. In Theorem 2 we show that a fully revealing equilibrium on *ex post* markets always exists. At this equilibrium the change in relative prices is a sufficient statistic for all agents' private information taken jointly (although, of course, no trade takes place). In Theorem 3 we show that at any *ex post* equilibrium, even if it is not fully revealing, the information conveyed by the change in relative prices "swamps" each agent's private information taken individually. That is, each agent's posterior beliefs given both price changes and his private signal depend only on the price changes. It is also shown that the change in relative prices is a purely informational phenomenon, i.e., the change is independent of traders' endowments, preferences, and prior beliefs.

This independence result is in contrast to the conclusions for static rational expectations models. In the static models most often studied in the literature, traders are assumed to make inferences based on the price vector observed at a single market date. To do this, a trader must know a great deal about underlying supply and demand conditions, since prices depend on these as well as on the various traders' information. In a dynamic model, on the other hand, relative prices change over time in a simple way in response to new information, so that traders can easily make inferences from price changes without knowing anything about other traders' endowments, preferences, or prior beliefs. The dynamic rational expectations model studied here is in this sense simpler, and perhaps more plausible, than many static models. (Note that price changes are in fact commonly studied by securities' traders to guide their investment decisions.)

In Section 2, common knowledge is formally defined and the no-trade theorem is proved. An example is used to illustrate the importance of the role of common knowledge. In Section 3, Theorems 2 and 3, which deal with the information revealed by equilibrium prices on *ex post* markets, are presented. The relationship between our results and previous work is discussed in Section 4.

2. Common Knowledge and Trade

In rational expectations models it is assumed that each agent infers whatever information he can from the market variables he observes, as well as from the non-market signals to which he has access. Furthermore, in these models each agent believes—and is justified in believing—that all other agents also make full use of the information available to them. Since prices (or other market signals) are potentially an important source of information in rational expectations settings, it is important to know what kind of information they convey.

Certainly, at an equilibrium of any voluntary trading process, in addition to his private information, each agent knows that the equilibrium trade is feasible and is acceptable to the other agents. Moreover, since each agent knows that all the other agents are rational, agent i knows that all agents $j \neq i$ know that the trade is feasible and is acceptable to the others, and that all know that all know that the trade is feasible and acceptable, etc. Under rational expectations this "etc" consists of an infinite sequence of statements.

These statements can be expressed very concisely using Aumann's [2] definition of common knowledge. Let the state of the world be described by $\omega \in \Omega$, and let each agent's information be represented by a partition on Ω. Let P_i denote agent i's partition, for $i = 1, \dots, n$, and for any $\omega \in \Omega$ define $P_i(\omega)$ to be the element of P_i that contains ω. This is to be interpreted as follows: when the state of the world is ω, trader i knows only that the state is in $P_i(\omega)$. Thus, trader i knows that an event A has occurred if $P_i(\omega) \subset A$. Let R be the meet of the partitions $P_1, \ldots, P_n$, and for any $\omega \in \Omega$ define $R(\omega)$ to be the element of R that contains ω. (The meet of a collection of partitions is their finest common coarsening.)

Definition[1] (Aumann). An event A is *common knowledge* at ω among agents $1, \ldots, n$ if $R(\omega) \subset A$.

In what follows, we distinguish between the information available to a trader at two nearby points in time. Trader i's information just prior to trading is represented by the partition $\hat{P}_i$. His information at the time of trading, including whatever he can infer from prices or from the behavior of other traders, is represented by P_i.

At a rational expectations equilibrium of any voluntary trading process, it is common knowledge among all agents at the time of trading that the agreed-upon trade is feasible and mutually acceptable. As will be shown below, the fact that this market information is common knowledge is sufficient to preclude trading based solely on differences in private information.

Consider a pure exchange economy with n traders in an uncertain environment. Let Ω be the (finite) set of possible states of the world, with generic element ω. For our purposes, it is convenient to think of ω as consisting of two components. Let $\Omega = \Theta \times X$ and $\omega = (\theta, x)$. The set Θ will be called the set of payoff-relevant events; endowments and utility functions may depend on θ. The set X consists of payoff-irrelevant events; these events do not affect endowments or tastes directly. However, x and θ may be statistically related.

There are l commodities in each state of the world, and for simplicity we assume that the consumption set of each trader in each state of the world is R^l_+. Each trader i is described by:

(a) his endowment, e_i: $\Theta \to R^l_+$;

(b) his utility function, U_i: $\Theta \times R^l_+ \to R$;

(c) his (subjective) prior beliefs about ω, $p_i(\cdot)$; and

(d) his (prior) informational partition, $\hat{P}_i$.

It is assumed that $U_i(\theta, \cdot)$: $R^l_+ \to R$ is increasing for all i, θ. If $U^i(\theta, \cdot)$ is concave (resp. strictly concave) for all θ, trader i is said to be *weakly* (resp. *strictly*) *risk-averse.*

A *trade* $t = (t_1, \ldots, t_n)$ is a function from Ω to R^{nl}, where $t_i(\omega)$ describes trader i's net trade of physical commodities in state ω. If the trade t can be described by a function from Θ to R^{nl}, it is called a *θ-contingent trade.* A trade is *feasible* if:

$$e_i(\theta) + t_i(\theta, x) \geqslant 0, \qquad \forall i, \theta, x. \tag{1}$$

$$\sum_{i=1}^{n} t_i(\theta, x) \leqslant 0, \qquad \forall \theta, x. \tag{2}$$

Assume that $p_i(\omega) > 0$ for every state ω and every trader i, and let $E_i[\cdot]$ denote the expectation under p_i. If

$$p_1(x \mid \theta) = \cdots = p_n(x \mid \theta), \qquad \forall x, \theta, \tag{3}$$

we will say that beliefs are *concordant.* When one thinks of x as information about θ, concordant beliefs mean (roughly) that the traders agree about how this information should be interpreted. Concordant beliefs arise naturally in statistical problems where θ is an unknown parameter about which traders may hold different views, and x is a statistic whose conditional distribution is objectively determined.

---

[1] An axiomatic characterization of common knowledge is given in Milgrom [10].

Note that if the agents are risk-averse and have concordant beliefs, then for any feasible trade t, the θ-contingent trade $t^* \equiv (E_1[t_1|\theta|, \ldots, E_n[t_n|\theta|])$ is feasible and weakly preferred by each trader.[2] Intuitively, t differs from t^* only in that it includes side bets about x. Risk-averse traders with concordant beliefs find such bets to be unattractive when the markets for θ-contingent claims are complete. It is only when these markets are incomplete that the side bets may become attractive as imperfect surrogates for θ-contingent trades.

Theorem 1. *Suppose that all traders are weakly risk-averse, that the initial allocation $e = (e_1, \ldots, e_n)$ is Pareto-optimal relative to θ-trades, that agents' prior beliefs are concordant, and that each trader i observes the private information conveyed by the partition $\hat{P}_i$. If it is common knowledge at ω that t is a feasible θ-trade and that each trader weakly prefers t to the zero trade, then every agent is indifferent between t and the zero trade. If all agents are strictly risk-averse then t is the zero trade.*[3]

Proof. Recall that P_i denotes the information partition of trader i which includes whatever information is conveyed at equilibrium by the trading process, and that R is the meet of $P_1, \ldots, P_n$. Suppose that it is common knowledge at $\omega' \equiv (\theta', x')$ that t is a feasible, mutually acceptable θ-trade. Then for every i and every $\omega \in R(\omega')$

$$E_i[U_i(\theta, e_i + t_i)|P_i(\omega)] \geqslant E_i[U_i(\theta, e_i)|P_i(\omega)]. \tag{4}$$

Suppose that the inequality in (4) is strict for trader j at ω', and consider the (θ, x)-trade t^* defined by:

$$t_i^* \equiv t_i \, 1_{R(\omega')}, \qquad \forall i,$$

(where $1_{R(\omega')} = 1$ if $\omega \in R(\omega')$, and $1_{R(\omega')} = 0$ otherwise). Since t is feasible, so is t^*. Also, viewing t^* *ex ante,* we find that for each trader i

$$\begin{aligned} E_i[U_i(\theta, e_i + t_i^*)] &= E_i[E_i[U_i(\theta, e_i + t_i \, 1_{R(\omega')}|P_i]] \\ &= E_i[E_i[U_i(\theta, e_i) \, 1_{R^c(\omega')}|P_i]] \\ &\quad + E_i[E_i[U_i(\theta, e_i + t_i) \, 1_{R(\omega')}|P_i]]. \end{aligned}$$

Since R is coarser than P_i, this expression is equal to:

$$\begin{aligned} &= E_i[1_{R^c(\omega')} E_i[U_i(\theta, e_i)|P_i]] + E_i[1_{R(\omega')} E_i[U_i(\theta, e_i + t_i)|P_i]] \\ &\geqslant E_i[1_{R^c(\omega')} E_i[U_i(\theta, e_i)|P_i]] + E_i[1_{R(\omega')} E_i[U_i(\theta, e_i)|P_i]] \\ &= E_i[U_i(\theta, e_i)], \end{aligned}$$

where R^c denotes the complement of R, and the inequality follows from (4). Moreover, the inequality is strict for trader j. Hence t^* is feasible and *ex ante* is strictly Pareto-superior to the null trade. Since agents' beliefs satisfy (3), the θ-trade $t^{**} = E[t^*|\theta]$ is feasible, and *ex ante* is strictly Pareto-superior to the null trade, contrary to our hypothesis about the initial allocation.

If traders are strictly risk averse, if t satisfies (4), and if t is not null, then $1/2t^{**}$ is a Pareto-improving θ-trade, contrary to the assumption that the initial allocation is Pareto-optimal. Q.E.D.

After the agents observe $\hat{P}_1(\omega), \ldots, \hat{P}_n(\omega)$, respectively, their posterior beliefs about θ do, in general, differ. Still they do not trade. Intuitively, if any agent is willing to accept a

[2]Marshall [9] shows that this is true if traders have identical prior beliefs, i.e., if $p_i(\omega) = p_j(\omega)$, $\forall i, j$, $\forall \omega$.

[3]Milton Harris has called this the Groucho Marx Theorem since it is reminiscent of Groucho's remark: "I'd never join any club that would have me for a member."

TABLE I

	$\theta = 1$	$\theta = 2$
$x = 1$	0.20	0.05
$x = 2$	0.05	0.15
$x = 3$	0.05	0.05
$x = 4$	0.15	0.05
$x = 5$	0.05	0.20

trade, he reveals something about the signal he has observed. If a trade takes place all agents must know that the claims balance and that each agent regards the trade as beneficial to himself. Theorem 1 shows that in some situations this common knowledge is enough to preclude trade completely. (Note that trader i need not observe either prices or the net trades of others. Of course, he does know that the net trades of the others sum to $-t_i$.)

If agents do not have rational expectations, each agent may know that a proposed trade is feasible and is acceptable to all agents, yet those facts may not be common knowledge. The distinction is illustrated by the following example.

Suppose that two agents hold the prior beliefs about the pair (θ, x) given in Table I. Let the information structures for agents 1 and 2, respectively, be described by the following partitions on X:

$$\hat{P}_1 : \{x = 1 \text{ or } 2\}, \{x = 3 \text{ or } 4\}, \{x = 5\},$$
$$\hat{P}_2 : \{x = 1\}, \{x = 2 \text{ or } 3\}, \{x = 4 \text{ or } 5\}.$$

Assume that both agents are risk-neutral and suppose that the following bet is proposed: if $\theta = 1$ agent 2 pays one dollar to agent 1, if $\theta = 2$ agent 1 pays one dollar to agent 2. Suppose that $x = 3$ occurs. Consider the following types of behavior which might occur.

Case A. *Naive behavior.* Since at $x = 3$, $p(\theta = 1 \mid P_1) = 2/3 > 1/2$, agent 1 accepts the bet. Similarly, since at $x = 3$, $p(\theta = 2 \mid P_2) = 2/3 > 1/2$, agent 2 accepts the bet.

Case B. *First-order sophistication.* Agent 1 reasons as follows:

> "I know that either $x = 3$ or $x = 4$. If $x = 3$, $p(\theta = 2 \mid P_2) = 2/3 > 1/2$, so I could expect agent 2 to accept the bet. If $x = 4$, $p(\theta = 2 \mid P_2) = 5/9 > 1/2$, so I could expect him to accept the bet. Therefore, the fact that agent 2 accepts the bet tells me nothing new. Since $p(\theta = 1 \mid P_1) = 2/3 > 1/2$, I will accept the bet."

Agent 2 reasons similarly, and also accepts the bet.

Case C. *Rational expectations.* Agent 1 reasons as follows:

> "If $x = 1$, agent 2 knows that $x = 1$ and will refuse the bet. Hence if agent 2 accepts the bet $x \neq 1$. Therefore, if I observe the partition element $\{1, 2\}$ *and* if agent 2 accepts the bet, then $x = 2$. If $x = 2$ the bet is disadvantageous to me. Hence if I observe $\{1, 2\}$ I should refuse to bet. Agent 2 will use a similar line of reasoning to conclude that he should refuse the bet if he observes $\{4, 5\}$.
>
> Hence I will refuse the bet if I observe $\{1, 2\}$ or $\{5\}$, and agent 2 will refuse the bet if he observes $\{1\}$ or $\{4, 5\}$. Since I am risk-neutral, I am indifferent between accepting and rejecting the bet if I observe $\{3, 4\}$, and it doesn't matter to me what agent 2 does when he observes $\{2, 3\}$."

Agent 2 will use a similar line of reasoning to conclude that he should refuse the bet if he observes $\{1\}$ or $\{4, 5\}$. Hence the bet is accepted by both only if $x = 3$.

If both agents are slightly risk-averse, the analysis is unchanged in Cases A and B, but in Case C agent 1 will decline the bet if he observes $\{3, 4\}$ (since it can take effect only if $x = 3$) and agent 2 will decline the bet if he observes $\{2, 3\}$.

If all information is public, beliefs need not be concordant to preclude trade from an initial position which was *ex ante* Pareto optimal relative to θ-trades. For concave, differentiable utility functions, if x is publicly announced, then further trade is precluded if and only if:

$$\frac{p_1(x\,|\,\theta)}{p_1(x\,|\,\theta')} = \cdots = \frac{p_n(x\,|\,\theta)}{p_n(x\,|\,\theta')}, \qquad \forall\, x, \theta, \theta'. \tag{5}$$

3. What Prices Reveal

Suppose that before any information about (θ, x) is revealed, a round of trading is conducted using a market mechanism. Let e denote the competitive equilibrium allocation and let $q(\theta) \in R^l_+$ denote the prices supporting e. Let Q be the join of $\hat{P}_1, \ldots, \hat{P}_n$. (The join of a collection of partitions is their coarsest common refinement.) Thus, Q conveys all of the information contained in $P_1, \ldots, P_n$, but no more.

If the signals $P_1(\omega), \ldots, P_n(\omega)$, are revealed to agents $1, \ldots, n$, respectively and markets reopen, we know from Theorem 1 that e is still a competitive equilibrium allocation. Theorem 2 concerns the price vector that supports e as a revealing rational expectations equilibrium.

Theorem 2. *Let* $e = (e_1, \ldots, e_n)$ *be an* ex ante *Pareto-optimal allocation relative to* θ*-trades, supported by the prices* $q(\theta)$*, and assume that agents' prior beliefs satisfy* (3). *If the signals* $\hat{P}_1(\omega), \ldots, \hat{P}_n(\omega)$ *are revealed to agents* $1, \ldots, n$, *respectively, and markets are reopened, the price vector* $\hat{q}(\theta\,|\,x)$ *given by:*

$$\hat{q}(\theta\,|\,x) = q(\theta)\, p(Q(\omega)\,|\,\theta),$$

together with the initial allocation, constitutes a fully revealing rational expectations equilibrium.

Proof. Since each agent observes $p(Q(\omega)\,|\,\theta)$ through the change in prices, using Bayes' Theorem i's posterior for θ is given by:

$$p_i(\theta\,|\,Q(\omega)) = p(Q(\omega)\,|\,\theta)p_i(\theta)/p_i(Q(\omega)),$$

so that the price vector is a sufficient statistic for all the private signals. It is straightforward to check that the initial allocation is a competitive equilibrium relative to the new prices and fully revealed information. Q.E.D.

Notice that it is the *change* in prices that reveals all of the information about θ available to all traders (i.e., $\hat{q}(\theta\,|\,x)/q(\theta)$ is a sufficient statistic for $P_1(\omega), \ldots, P_n(\omega)$). It does this in a very simple, easily interpretable way, and in a way that does not depend on any trader's preferences. In the usual rational expectations model, if traders' preferences are unknown, each trader must attempt to sort out θ-relevant information from information about preferences as he scrutinizes market prices.

There may be other rational expectations equilibria as well—equilibria that are less than fully revealing. However, the following theorem shows that in *any* equilibrium, information from an agent's private signal is "swamped" by price information, just as it is in the fully revealing equilibrium.

Theorem 3. *Assume that all agents are strictly risk-averse and have continuously differentiable utility functions $U_i(\theta,)$; that an* ex ante *round of trade on competitive θ-markets leaves agents at a Pareto-optimal allocation e supported by the price vector q; that $e_i \in R^l_{++}$, for all i; and that agents' prior beliefs satisfy* (3). *Suppose that agents* 1, . . . , *n observe the private signals $P_1(\omega), \ldots, P_n(\omega)$, respectively, and θ-markets reopen. By Theorem* 1, *e is still a competitive equilibrium allocation; let $\hat{q}(\theta|x)$ be any price vector supporting it. Then*

$$p_i(\theta|P_i(\omega), \hat{q}) = p_i(\theta|\hat{q}), \qquad \forall\theta, i. \tag{6}$$

Proof. For simplicity of notation take $l = 1$, and let U_i' denote the marginal utility of consumption. Since e is a competitive equilibrium allocation *ex ante,*

$$\frac{p_i(\theta)\, u_i'(\theta, e_i(\theta))}{p_i(\theta')\, u_i'(\theta, e_i(\theta'))} = \frac{q(\theta)}{q(\theta')}$$

and since it is still an equilibrium allocation *ex post,*

$$\frac{p_i(\theta|P_i(\omega), \hat{q})\, u_i'(\theta, e_i(\theta))}{p_i(\theta'|P_i(\omega), \hat{q})\, u_i'(\theta', e_i(\theta'))} = \frac{\hat{q}(\theta|Q(\omega))}{\hat{q}(\theta'|Q(\omega))} \qquad \forall\theta, \theta', i\,.$$

Together these conditions imply that:

$$\frac{p_i(\theta|P_i(\omega), \hat{q})}{p_i(\theta'|P_i(\omega), \hat{q})} = \frac{p_i(\theta)}{p_i(\theta')}\,\frac{\hat{q}(\theta|Q(\omega))/q(\theta)}{\hat{q}(\theta'|Q(\omega))/q(\theta')} \qquad \forall\theta, \theta', i; \tag{7}$$

The posterior probabilities $p_i(\theta|P_i(\omega), \hat{q})$ are completely determined by their ratios and the condition that the probabilities must sum to one. Then since the right-hand side of (7) depends on $Q(\omega)$ only through $\hat{q}$, Eq. (6) follows. Q.E.D.

Equation (7) shows that any *ex post* equilibrium prices supporting *e*, even if they are not fully revealing, have the following important property: the change in relative prices is independent of agents' endowments, utility functions, and prior beliefs, and is also independent of the initial allocation *e.*

4. Conclusions

The results above cast light on two issues that have been widely discussed in the literature on trade under uncertainty. The first is the value of private and public information when trading takes place *ex ante* and *ex post.* Marshall [9] shows that if all agents hold identical prior beliefs and if both *ex ante* and *ex post* markets are available, then the release of public information has neither private nor social value and leads to no further trading. Marshall also claims that although private information is socially valueless, it is valuable to the individual who receives it. As Hirshleifer [8] did, Marshall argues that an individual who receives private information can speculate profitably at (virtually) unchanged market prices. This argument rests on the assumption that an individual is "small" relative to the market.

Theorem 1 above shows that this argument is invalid if traders' expectations are rational; a trader with new information is never "small". On the contrary, any attempt to speculate on the basis of new information must result in that information becoming impounded in prices, so that profitable speculation is impossible. Hence, if beliefs are concordant, private information has neither private nor public value. The argument used in Theorem 1 can also be used to show that (5) is a necessary and sufficient condition for public information to be valueless.

The second issue addressed is the nature of the information revealed by prices in a rational expectations equilibrium. This is a question that has been addressed by Grossman [6], Radner [12], Allen [1], and others. It is a question that has proven hard to answer, at least in part because it is usually difficult to interpret the informational assumptions. In the work just cited, information about all agents' endowments, utility functions, and prior beliefs is commingled in market variables with information about their private signals about the state of the world.

Theorems 2 and 3 above show that when markets are available both before and after information is released, it is the *change* in relative prices that reveals information. This seems to us a more appealing conclusion than the claim that price levels reveal information. Moreover, Theorem 2 shows that when beliefs are concordant, the change in relative prices has a purely informational character: the changes do not depend on any characteristics of agents or on the initial allocation (except that it must be Pareto-optimal).

Finally, Theorem 3 shows that the information conveyed by any *ex post* equilibrium prices, whether or not they are fully revealing, "swamps" the private signal received by any agent. That is, after the equilibrium prices are formed each agent can afford to forget the signal he observed; to compute his posterior beliefs he only needs to remember how prices have changed.

Our results concerning rational expectations market equilibria raise anew the disturbing questions expressed by Beja [3], Grossman and Stiglitz [7], and Tirole [13]: Why do traders bother to gather information if they cannot profit from it? How does information come to be reflected in prices if informed traders do not trade or if they ignore their private information in making inferences? These questions can be answered satisfactorily only in the context of models of the price formation process[4]; and our central result, the no-trade theorem, applies to all such models when rational expectations are assumed.

References

1. B. Allen, Generic existence of completely revealing equilibria for economies with uncertainty when prices convey information, *Econometrica* **49** (1981), 1173–1199.
2. R. Aumann, Agreeing to disagree, *Ann. Statist.* **4** (1976), 1236–1239.
3. A. Beja, "The Limits of Price Information in Market Processes," N.Y.U. Working Paper #78-19 (1977).
4. P. Dubey and M. Shubik, "A Strategic Market Game with Price and Quantity Strategies," Cowles Foundation D.P. #521, April, 1979.
5. L. Glosten, "Strong Form Informational Efficiency in Stock Markets with Disequilibrium Trading," Northwestern University D.P. #400, September, 1979.
6. S. Grossman, The existence of futures markets, noisy rational expectations, and informational externalities, *Rev. Econ. Studies* **44** (1977), 431–449.
7. S. Grossman and J. Stiglitz, On the impossibility of informationally efficient markets, *Amer. Econ. Rev.* **70** (1980), 393–408.
8. J. Hirschleifer, The private and social value of information and the reward to inventive activity, *Amer. Econ. Rev.* **61** (1971), 561–574.

[4]Recent papers by Dubey and Shubik [4] and Wilson [14] address the question of how prices are formed. Glosten [5] and Milgrom [11] study models of price formation where the traders have unequal access to information.

9. J. Marshall, Private incentives and public information, *Amer. Econ. Rev.* **64** (1974), 373–390.

10. P. Milgrom, An axiomatic characterization of common knowledge, *Econometrica* **49** (1981), 219–222.

11. P. Milgrom, Rational expectations, information acquisition, and competitive bidding, *Econometrica* **49** (1981), 921–943.

12. R. Radner, Rational expectations equilibrium: Generic existence and information revealed by prices, *Econometrica* **47** (1979), 655–678.

13. J. Tirole, "On the Possibility of Speculation under Rational Expectation," mimeo, M.I.T., 1980.

14. R. Wilson, Competitive exchange, *Econometrica* **46** (1978), 577–586.

Seven

Raymond Chiang

Raymond Chiang received a Ph.D. from the University of Pennsylvania in 1979. He started out at the University of Florida. Raymond passed away in August 2002 at the age of fifty-two. •

Imperfect Price Discrimination and Welfare

Raymond Chiang
University of Florida

and

Chester S. Spatt
Carnegie-Mellon University

We develop a model in which a monopolist uses differences across consumers in their valuation of time to imperfectly price discriminate. Though it is customary to analyse price discrimination problems by the calculus of variations after postulating a continuum of types, we assume a finite number of types and exploit the geometry and duality of the contract set and the structure of the programming specification. We analyse in detail the qualitative properties of the model's solution and show by construction that our results exhaust the implications of the model for equilibrium contract pairs.

We show that imperfect discrimination is not bounded in welfare terms between perfect discrimination and single-price monopoly and that the deadweight loss, consumer surplus and output comparisons between single-price monopoly and imperfect discrimination are ambiguous.

1. Introduction

Monopolists use a variety of devices to extract extra surplus from consumers. Often a monopolist packages his commodity with a characteristic that is costly for the consumer. For example, airlines offer discount fares to consumers who satisfy various restrictions.[1] The extra profit the firm can earn by tying in this manner results from its ability to use the device to separate markets.[2] In order to acquire the ability to split markets a monopolist may be willing to operate inefficiently.

Economists have studied in recent years a variety of mechanisms in which an agent's selection of a contract reveals information in equilibrium about the agent's characteristics (e.g. see Spence (1974), Rothschild and Stiglitz (1976), and Riley (1979)). This approach has been applied to monopolistic imperfect price discrimination. Researchers have considered a variety of ways in which the monopolist can bundle his commodity with itself (i.e. non-linear pricing) or with other goods (or characteristics) in order to imperfectly price discriminate.[3]

In our model the monopolized commodity is bundled with time. The amount the consumer is required to pay for the commodity depends on the time cost he absorbs. In equilibrium consumers with a high cost of time use less time in purchasing the commodity (and pay a higher price). The time variable has several interpretations. We emphasize a spatial interpretation[4] in which all consumers live at one point on a line (i.e. the centre of the city) and the monopolist sets his branch locations and prices to discriminate by differences in the cost of travel (e.g. different opportunity costs). Outside the spatial context a monopolist may offer a lower price to a consumer who waits longer[5] (or goes to a store with longer waiting time) for

Reprinted with permission:
Chiang, Raymond and Chester S. Spatt. "Imperfect Price Discrimination and Welfare." *Review of Economic Studies* 49 (1982): 155–181
First version received May 1981, *final version accepted November* 1981 (*Eds.*).
We wish to thank Philip Dybvig and Stephen Ross for valuable suggestions, and workshop participants at Carnegie-Mellon University, Princeton University, Yale University, and the University of Pennsylvania, Oliver Hart, the referees and Tom Ross for helpful comments. Support from National Science Foundation Grant SES-8015086 is gratefully acknowledged.

service or to a consumer who haggles a long time before purchasing (based on demand side considerations alone). The consumer's time cost and the time-price contracts offered by the monopolist determine how high a price the consumer pays for the commodity. The idea of bundling the commodity with a "bad" is also developed in a similar model by Salop (1977) in which the bad is the level of search activity. The "bad" might denote other undesirable variable attributes of the commodity as illustrated by the restrictions on discount airline tickets.

An important analysis of price discrimination is the Mussa and Rosen (1978) model of product quality. The monopolist sets price to rise in quality more rapidly than does cost so that the monopolist can extract some of the incremental surplus of high valuation consumers. Unlike Mussa and Rosen (1978), we focus on an environment in which quality is not costly to the firm and in which there are a finite number of consumer types. We use a different solution technique and emphasize the exhaustiveness of certain of our results and the output and welfare comparisons between the discriminating solution and single-price monopoly.

Many of the other price discrimination models developed use a continuum of types of agents and exploit techniques in the calculus of variations.[6] Our methodological approach is a model with N types[7] and we describe the properties of our solution by exploiting linear programming results, the geometry of the contract set and analogues to the duality of consumer theory.[8] We feel that the use of geometric and dual techniques is expositionally attractive and emphasizes the strong analogy between the structure of our model and the traditional theory of the consumer. This geometric approach should prove helpful in analyzing other problems involving price discrimination (and the related optimal tax framework) and other models with informed and uninformed agents.

An interesting issue in many economic contexts is what are the complete set of implications of a model. The knowledge that one's implications are exhaustive strengthens the theoretical conclusions and suggests limits to the restrictions that can be analysed in empirical work. Using a constructive approach (as in integrability theory) we show our results are exhaustive using the equilibrium contract pairs as the observables. A similar technique could prove useful in other models with asymmetric information.

Though it might seem intuitive for imperfect discrimination to be bounded between single-price monopoly (no discrimination) and perfect discrimination, the comparison of output between single-price monopoly and third-degree discrimination (i.e. where the monopolist can charge a distinct price in each exogenously specified separate market) is ambiguous (see Pigou (1920), Robinson (1933), Samuelson (1947), Edwards (1950) and Schmalensee (1981*b*)). (A similar ambiguous comparison occurs between single-price monopoly and second-degree discrimination (see Kwoka (1979)).) Robinson (1933) observes that if discrimination leads to less output than single-price monopoly, then discrimination leads to more deadweight loss because of the greater exclusion and failure to distribute output to those who value it most.[9] Now suppose instead there are two markets and no one in the secondary market purchases in the single-price case so that the price in the primary market with discrimination matches the single-price. Then consumers in the primary market are indifferent between the single-price and discrimination solutions, but the monopolist and consumers in the secondary market are better off under discrimination so that third-degree discrimination can lead to less deadweight loss than single-price monopoly and discrimination can Pareto dominate the single-price solution.

In our model and much of the recent price discrimination literature, unlike the third-degree discrimination paradigm, the traders are endogenously separated into markets by their selection of contracts. Within our model we show ambiguous output and welfare comparisons between imperfect discrimination and single-price monopoly. Output in imperfect discrimination can be lower or higher than single-price monopoly and the deadweight loss in imperfect discrimination can be lower or higher than single-price monopoly, and, in fact, discrimination can make some consumers better off and none worse off and raise monopoly profits. This welfare result is in a similar spirit to Willig's (1978) theorem that a non-linear outlay schedule is Pareto-superior, though Willig does not examine the solution to the monopolist's profit maximizing discrimination problem. Similar kinds of ambiguous results are also obtained on expected output and the distribution of expected surplus for the resolution of uncertainty under imperfect discrimination. These results are similar in spirit to Hart's (1975) conclusions in an incomplete market context and the second-best paradoxes more generally.

The ambiguous results in the third-degree context are not driven by the exogenous separation of markets of third-degree discrimination *per se*, but most of the recent literature on imperfect discrimination through self-selection mechanisms does not emphasize these comparisons (however Adams and Yellin (1976) do focus on the ambiguous deadweight loss comparison in a model in which the tied commodity is monopolistically supplied and recently, Schmalensee (1981*a*) looks at the welfare implications of the two-part tariff and Katz (1982) analyzes various output and welfare issues in detail in the context of non-uniform pricing). Despite Scherer's (1970, p. 258) argument that "the correct question is, are resources allocated more or less efficiently under discriminating monopoly than under simple (uniform price) monopoly," much of the welfare evaluation of imperfect discrimination in the context of specific models is against competition. Discussion of antitrust policy on discriminatory practices (see Posner (1976) and Bork (1978)) would be enhanced by explicit output and welfare comparison of single-price monopoly and discrimination through self-selection mechanisms.

In Section 2 of the paper we describe our basic model. In Section 3 we analyse the model by exploiting its geometric, dual and programming structures. In Section 4 we present examples to demonstrate the ambiguous output and welfare effects of imperfect discrimination. We conclude the paper in Section 5 with a discussion of unresolved issues.

2. The Model

In our model a monopolist price discriminates by bundling his product with a second commodity that consumers dislike (which we call time). We assume a finite number of types of consumers indexed by $i = 1, \ldots, N$ where there are n_i agents of type i. The type i consumer regards each (divisible) unit of the unwanted commodity (which we take to be expenditure of time) as equivalent to an extra c_i (a wage rate) added to the purchase price of the good ($c_i > 0$). If the consumer purchases a unit (0–1 demand) of the monopolized commodity he selects the contract offered by the monopolist in which he has minimum expenditure. The type i consumer purchases a single unit of the monopolized commodity provided his total expenditure (including time costs) does not exceed his reservation price v_i.

The monopolist may offer the consumer the option of spending time to acquire the product. For example, a monopolist may offer a low price to consumers who travel to outlying stores, purchase at stores with slow service, or bargain at length in order to split the market by time costs (and potentially by reservation price). Our preference structure assumes the marginal disutility of time is constant (akin to the typical assumption of constant unit costs to search). This assumption seems reasonable if the amount of the time activity is relatively small. We exploit this in obtaining the convexity of the contract set and the resulting standard duality interpretation. By assumption we preclude the possibility of resale by one purchaser to another (i.e., the transaction cost of resale is too high as illustrated in the airline context) to prevent the lowest time cost agents from purchasing the product for everyone (the assumption of no resale is also discussed by Pigou (1920)).

If t represents the time required to purchase the commodity at price p and Ω denotes the set of contracts offered by the profit maximizing monopolist in (t, p) space, then a type i consumer purchases the commodity if

FIGURE 1 | Type i consumer purchases if some contract is in the shaded region.

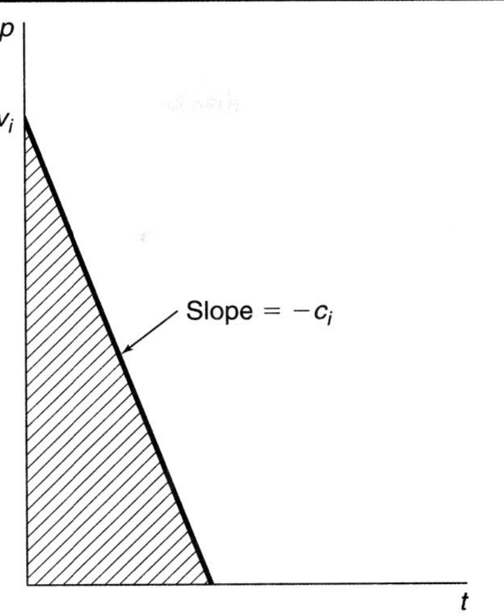

$$\min_{(t,\,p)\in\Omega}[p + tc_i] \leqq v_i.$$

We can plot in (t, p) space iso-expenditure curves for a type i consumer as lines with slope $-c_i$. The type i agent purchases the monopolized product only if the monopolist offers a contract in the triangle formed by the axes and the iso-expenditure line with slope $-c_i$ and intercept v_i (see Figure 1). There is no contract on an iso-expenditure line that is closer to the origin for a buyer than the one he selects (see Figure 2). We let $x_i = 0$ mean type i doesn't purchase the commodity and $x_i = 1$ mean type i does purchase the commodity and if $x_i = 1$ the consumer then picks (t, p) from Ω, the set of offered contracts, to maximize $(v_i - (p + tc_i))$. Without any loss of generality we assume $c_k \geqq c_j$ for $k < j$ and for expositional simplicity assume $c_k > c_j$ for $k < j$ (i.e., $c_1 > c_2 > \cdots > c_N$). The latter restriction precludes the possibility that agents with the same time cost differ in their reservation price (i.e., we rule out $c_k = c_j$ implies $v_k \neq v_j$ so that $v_i = v(c_i)$ where $v(\cdot)$ is a function).

FIGURE 2 | If the consumer of type i purchases with contract A, then no offered contract lies on a line closer to the origin with slope $-c_i$.

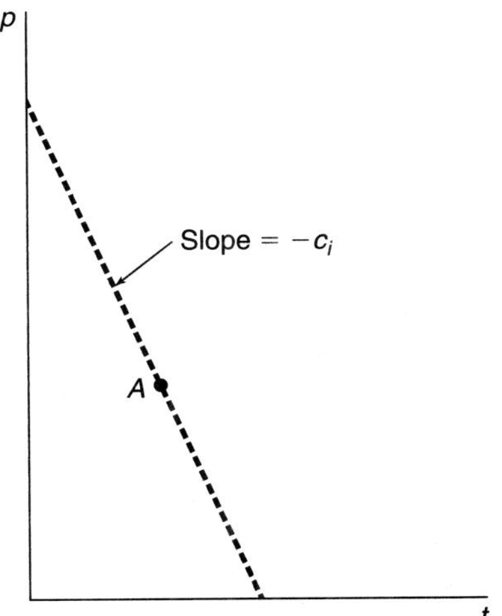

However, the reservation price increasing with the cost of time (i.e., $v(c_i)$ increasing everywhere) is not required, though the nature of $v(c_i)$ can affect the extent of sorting and correlation between cost of time and reservation price (suggested by the correlation between wage rates and income in cross-section) seems natural.

The monopolist's problem is to offer a set of contracts which maximizes profit subject to the constraints imposed by consumer maximization. We assume that the monopolist faces a constant unit cost of output which we take to be zero since we can rescale the reservation prices. Let n_i represent the number of type i agents, $d \geqq 0$ be any costs paid by the firm per unit of consumer time associated with the purchase (e.g. if the time is expended through bargaining then the consumer imposes costs on the firm) and $(t(c_i), p(c_i))$ denotes the contract selected by type i. (The assumption $d \geqq 0$ does preclude firm cost rising in quality.) The monopolist knows all the parameters of the model except for the type of individual agents. He knows the joint distribution of agents exactly. The firm's objective[10] becomes

$$\max \sum n_i x_i p(c_i) - d \sum n_i x_i t(c_i)$$

i.e., maximize revenue (net of costs of production) less any time costs borne by the firm. The constraints imposed by consumer maximization guarantee that every buyer i ($x_i = 1$) does not spend more than his reservation price for the commodity, i.e.,

$$p(c_i) + c_i t(c_i) \leqq v_i$$

(otherwise, he is better off not purchasing). Each buyer purchases the contract which is least costly to him, i.e., $x_i = 1$ implies

$$p(c_i) + c_i t(c_i) \leqq p + c_i t \quad \forall\, (t, p) \in \Omega.$$

In our model, unlike many of the other models of price discrimination, the private information of consumers is characterized by two parameters (c_i and v_i). A simple solution is obtained in our two-attribute model because the cost parameter determines the contract selection if the agent purchases and the reservation price determines whether the agent purchases. The monopolist's problem can be formalized as

$$\max \sum n_i x_i p(c_i) - d \sum n_i x_i t(c_i)$$

$$\text{s.t.} \quad x_i(p(c_i) + c_i t(c_i)) \leqq x_i v_i \quad \forall i, \tag{1.1}$$

$$x_i(p(c_i) + c_i t(c_i)) \leqq x_i(p + c_i t) \quad \forall (t, p) \varepsilon \Omega \text{ and } \forall i, \tag{1.2}$$

$$x_i \in \{0, 1\} \quad \forall i, \tag{1.3}$$

$$t(c_i) \geqq 0 \quad \forall i, \tag{1.4}$$

and

$$p(c_i) \geqq 0 \quad \forall i, \tag{1.5}$$

where $(t(c_i), p(c_i))$ is well-defined for $x_i = 1$. The last two sets of constraints represents the non-negative requirement on the contract space (t, p). Since the objective function is unchanged and the feasible set reduced by offering contracts not purchased in equilibrium (through the self-selection constraints) we restrict our attention to the case in which every offered contract is purchased by at least one type. Consequently, constraint (1.2) can be replaced in the monopolist's problem by

$$x_i x_j(p(c_i) + c_i t(c_i)) \leqq x_i x_j(p(c_j) + c_i t(c_j)) \quad \text{for all } i \neq j, \tag{1.2'}$$

i.e., each buyer i has no incentive to claim to be a different type (self-selection). The monopolist's maximization program is compact and non-empty (a feasible solution is $x_i = 1$,

$t(c_i) = 0$ and $p(c_i) = \min\{v_j\}$ for all j) and thus has an optimal solution. If we fix x at an optimal set of buyers then the program is linear in $t(c_i)$ and $p(c_i)$ and we can exploit the powerful techniques of linear programming to obtain additional restrictions.[11]

The solution to the firm's maximization problem is a monopoly equilibrium in the sense that no consumer can do strictly better than to follow these strategies given the set of contracts offered by the firm[12] and no other set of contracts leads to greater firm profits given the strategies of consumers. Inspection of any such equilibrium solution does point to the closure problem of this equilibrium concept,[13] but this problem is endemic to many price discrimination models. In our analysis we adopt the convention that an indifferent consumer acts in the firm's interest. For example, a purchaser selects the highest price contract on his minimum iso-expenditure line.

An alternative interpretation of our model to the one in which i indexes types of consumers is where i denotes states of the world.[14] In this perspective all consumers are identical, characteristics v_i and c_i are state dependent, n_i denotes the state probability (then $\sum n_i = 1$) and the firm maximizes expected profit and must fix the set of offered contracts before the state is revealed (and cannot change the set after some consumers purchase), though the consumers know the state when they select their contract. The assumption of no resale seems more attractive in this context than in our principal interpretation. Though all contracts offered are purchased in some state, the contracts need not be purchased in every state. A more general interpretation is that i is generated by a state and type pair. This leads to interesting examples on the impact of the resolution of state uncertainty (see Section 4).

3. General Structure of the Model

Many of the qualitative properties of equilibria in the model are developed by geometric analysis in the (t, p) contract space. Analogies to the theory of the consumer and its duality illuminate many of the results. Some of the equilibrium properties require only consumer maximization, though in others we exploit the profit maximization of the monopolist.[15] Proofs are in the indicated footnotes.

The assumption of consumer maximization (without requiring firm profit maximization) implies restrictions on the set of contracts in the equilibrium contract set.

Proposition 1. *In the equilibrium contract set, p and t are inversely related, i.e., if* $(t', p'), (t'', p'') \in \Omega$, *then* $t' < t''$ *if and only if* $p' > p''$.[16]

If the contract set is not monotone, then some contract does not minimize expenditure for any type. This illustrates Telser's (1979) result that the price of a tied commodity can be less than marginal cost. The consumer is actually bribed here (via reduction in price of the monopolized good) to accept some time, even though the consumer's time expenditure may be costly to the firm (and is at best costless).

Proposition 2. *The equilibrium contract set is strictly convex in the sense that if* $(t', p'), (t'', p''), (\lambda t' + (1 - \lambda)t'', \hat{p}) \in \Omega$ *for some* $\lambda \in (0, 1)$, *then* $\hat{p} < \lambda p' + (1 - \lambda)p''$.[17, 18]

The linearity of the iso-expenditure curves of consumers is sufficient to ensure that all consumers prefer at least one of the extreme contracts to the interior one (see Figure 3). Because each offered contract has the property that it minimizes a linear function there can be no contracts in the interior of the convex hull generated by the offered contracts.

Proposition 3. *The equilibrium contract set* Ω *need contain no more than N elements.*[19]

This restriction on the number of contracts offered exploits the hypothesized finite number of types of consumers.

FIGURE 3 | If *A* and *B* are contracts offered, then all consumers whose iso-surplus lines are at least as steep as the line segment connecting *A* and *B* prefer contract *A* to any contract with an intermediate price that lies above the line segment and all other consumers prefer *B* to any contract with an intermediate price that lies above the line segment.

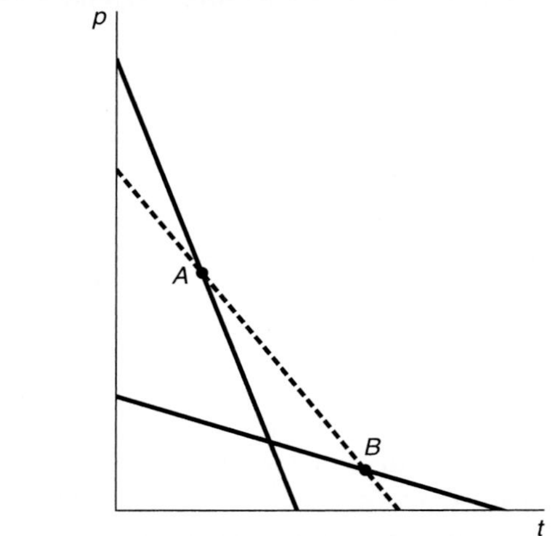

Some comparative statics results on the impact of time can be derived from consumer maximization without monopoly profit-maximization. If a consumer buys, he will select an element from the convex contract set (analogous to opportunity set) to minimize expenditure $E(c_i)$, where

$$E(c_i) = p(c_i) + c_i t(c_i).$$

The functions $t(\cdot)$ and $p(\cdot)$ are analogous to compensated demand functions and $E(\cdot)$ to the expenditure function in consumer or producer theory and several of our results are clearly equivalent to duality ideas in the theory of the consumer or firm.

Proposition 4. *The function $t(c_i)$ is non-increasing and $p(c_i)$ is non-decreasing.*[20]

The consumers with high cost of time substitute price for time. The variable c_i is the relative price of time for type i so that $t(c_i)$ and $p(1/c_i)$ are non-increasing is analogous to the standard result that compensated demand is non-increasing in its own price. This allows us to establish that many of the self-selection constraints are not binding.

Corollary 1. *If i, j, and k buy the commodity with $c_i > c_j > c_k$ and $(t(c_i), p(c_i))$, $(t(c_j), p(c_j))$ and $(t(c_k), p(c_k))$ are distinct, then $p(c_i) + c_i t(c_i) < p(c_k) + c_i t(c_k)$ and $p(c_k) + c_k t(c_k) < p(c_i) + c_k t(c_i)$.*[21]

This result is closely related to the strict convexity of the contract set. The hypothesis of consumer maximization also leads to comparative statics restrictions on the expenditure function.

Proposition 5. *The condition $c_i > c_j$ implies $E(c_i) \geqq E(c_j)$ (strict inequality for $t(c_i) > 0$) and $E(c_i)/c_i < E(c_j)/c_j$.*[22]

These results follow intuitively (see Figure 4) from the convexity of the contract set as $E(c_i)$ denotes the p-intercept and $E(c_i)/c_i$ the t-intercept of the line with slope $-c_i$ through the contract $(t(c_i), p(c_i))$. Notice that an increase in slope for a fixed contract is represented

FIGURE 4 | If $c_j < c_i$ then $(t(c_j), p(c_j))$ lies in triangle *ABC* and $E(c)$ and $E(c)/c$ are monotone.

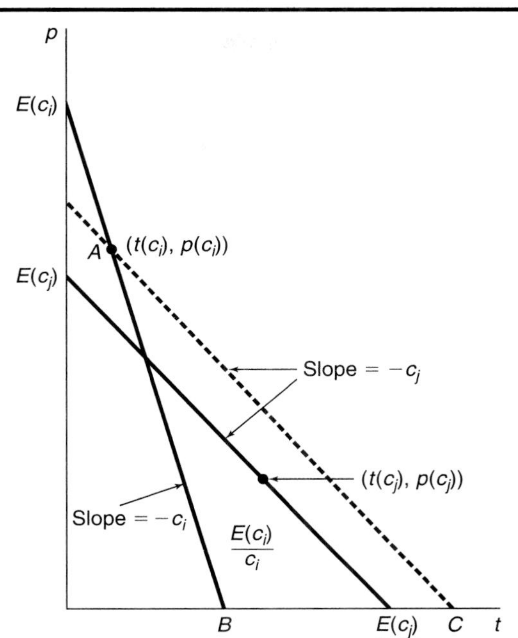

by pivoting the iso-expenditure line through the fixed contract. The monotonicity of $E(\cdot)$ is analogous to the monotonicity of the expenditure function in input prices in the theory of the consumer. As we later show by exploiting the firm maximization problem $E(\cdot)$ satisfies a version of Shepherd's Lemma, but the results presented so far do not require the monopoly market structure.

We now turn to the implications of our equilibrium that exploit the maximizing behaviour of the monopolist (taking into account the maximizing behaviour of consumers). We obtain these qualitative properties of the solution of the monopoly maximization problem by manipulating the algebraic formulation of the maximization problem or exploiting the geometry of the contract set.

Proposition 6. *In equilibrium the monopolist offers some contract with $t = 0$, i.e.* $\exists p \ni (0, p) \in \Omega$.

The geometry of the contract set shows this result. If there is no zero time contract the monopolist can increase profits by replacing the minimum time contract by one with zero time and a slightly higher price. Every purchaser of the earlier minimum time contract now purchases the zero time contract and other buyers and earlier non-buyers might substitute this very profitable contract for the firm. Under our spatial interpretation the result means that the discriminating monopolist always has a store at the centre of the city (where everyone lives). This suggests that the discriminating monopolist offers a contract that imposes no wastage costs (no undesirable tie-in) on the consumer, an important testable restriction. The result in Proposition 6 when combined with Proposition 4 implies that the buyer with the highest cost of travel must purchase the contract with $t = 0$.

Corollary 2. *The consumer with the highest reservation price always purchases the commodity.*

No price including that of the zero time contract can exceed the largest reservation price of all consumers. Clearly, the highest reservation price consumer prefers the zero time contract to not purchasing though he may elect to purchase another contract (we do not require him to have the highest time cost).

As we emphasized earlier in formulating the monopolist's maximization problem the equilibrium must satisfy self-selection constraints such that no consumer gains by selecting a contract not earmarked for him. If both consumers i and j purchase the product, then

$$p(c_i) + c_i t(c_i) \leqq p(c_j) + c_i t(c_j).$$

Proposition 7. *If agents i and k both purchase the commodity and no agent j with $c_i > c_j > c_k$ purchases, the equilibrium must satisfy $p(c_i) + c_i t(c_i) = p(c_k) + c_i t(c_k)$.*[23]

Under this condition the type i consumer is just indifferent between purchase of the contract intended for him and the contract with slightly lower price and higher time. The proof, illustrated in Figure 5, entails a similar perturbation of the contract set to that used in Proposition 6 to show that otherwise firm profits are not maximal. If $(t(c_i), p(c_i))$ and $(t(c_k), p(c_k))$ are distinct, then $p(c_k) + c_k t(c_k) < p(c_i) + c_k t(c_i)$. Other self-selection constraints also do not affect the solution (see, for example, Corollary 1). The binding constraint in Proposition 7 allows us to establish a discrete version of Shepherd's Lemma.[24]

Corollary 3. *If consumers i and k both purchase the commodity and no consumer j with $c_i > c_j > c_k$ purchases, then $(E(c_i) - E(c_k))/(c_i - c_k) = t(c_k)$.*[25]

The role of the binding self-selection constraint in the proof is akin to that of the first order condition in establishing the derivative property of the expenditure function (Shepherd's Lemma) in the theory of the consumer. (While the nature of the binding self-selection constraints is quite robust, our version of Shepherd's Lemma is much less likely to be robust.) A consumer with parameter c_i has the same expenditure under contract $(t(c_k), p(c_k))$ as in $(t(c_i), p(c_i))$. Consequently, in evaluating the change in expenditure corresponding to c_i compared with c_k we can fix the contract at $(t(c_k), p(c_k))$, hence, $E(c_i) - E(c_k) = c_i t(c_k) - c_k t(c_k)$. The slope property of our expenditure function together with $t(\cdot)$ non-increasing implies the expenditure function is concave (again analogous to standard microeconomic theory).

FIGURE 5 | The monopolist can raise profits by replacing $(t(c_k), p(c_k))$ by $(\hat{t}(c_k), \hat{p}(c_k))$.

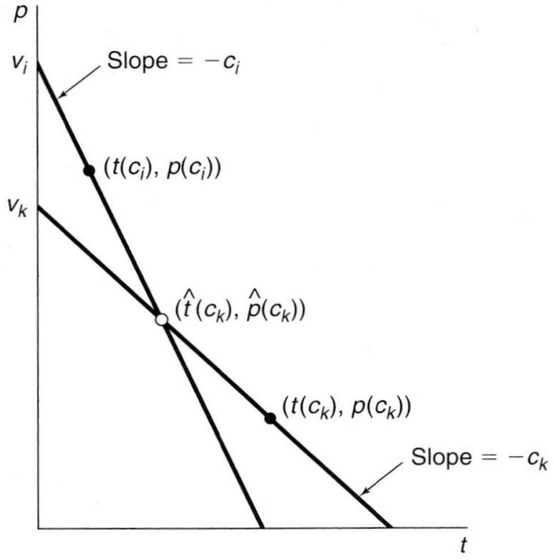

Corollary 4. If $c_i > c_j > c_k$, *agents i, j, k purchase the commodity, and no agents i′ and j′ with* $c_i > c_{i'} > c_j$ *and* $c_i > c_{j'} > c_k$ *purchase, then*

$$\frac{E(c_i) - E(c_j)}{c_i - c_j} \leqq \frac{E(c_j) - E(c_k)}{c_j - c_k}$$

i.e., $E(\cdot)$ *is concave.*

In addition to restriction on the self-selection conditions we can also describe some characteristics of the consumer surplus conditions.

Proposition 8. *Some consumer who purchases the lowest price and highest time contract must have zero consumer surplus.*[26]

Otherwise, the firm can raise the price of this low price contract and increase profits. The result that a trader at the bottom has no surplus under imperfect price discrimination is fairly common in price discrimination studies. Though it is easy to construct examples (see Section 4) in which the agent with the lowest reservation price among buyers does not have zero surplus (i.e., some other buyer of the low price contract has zero surplus), the low reservation buyer must purchase using the lowest price contract.

Corollary 5. *Any buyer with the lowest reservation price must purchase the lowest price contract.*[27]

Otherwise, the low reservation buyer expends more than any buyer of the low price contract (see Propositions 4 and 5) and thus none of the buyers of the low price contract can have zero surplus. We can exploit the programming structure of our model to demonstrate the following.

Proposition 9. *For each (optimal) grouping of buyers on m contracts there exists a profit maximal solution for the firm in which at least m types of consumers achieve only zero surplus.*[28]

The basic idea is to construct an artificial linear programme in $2m$ variables (i.e. two per contract) whose solutions generate maximal monopoly profit. The constructed linear programme has exactly $m - 1$ binding self-selection conditions and one binding non-negativity condition so in any corner solution at least m expenditure constraints must be satisfied with equality.

If the solution separates all consumers to purchase on distinct contracts (so $m = N$) then all N expenditure constraints must be satisfied with equality in any corner solution. But then there is only a single corner solution that completely separates (for $m < N$ we could have different combinations of m constraints satisfied with equality and obtain multiple corner solutions) and the separating solution is unique. In the unique separating solution no consumer has any surplus, i.e., $v_i = E(c_i)$. In order for complete separation to be feasible the relation $v(\cdot)$ must satisfy every restriction on $E(\cdot)$ that is a consequence of maximizing behaviour (e.g. expenditure must be non-decreasing and concave, and expenditure per unit time cost must decline with the cost of time—see Proposition 5 and Corollary 4).

Proposition 10. *The complete separating solution is* $t(c_1) = 0, p(c_1) = v_1$, *and for* $i = 2, \ldots, N$

$$t(c_i) = \frac{v_{i-1} - v_i}{c_{i-1} - c_i} \quad \textit{and} \quad p(c_i) = \frac{c_{i-1}v_i - c_iv_{i-1}}{c_{i-1} - c_i}.$$ [29]

This solution is obtained by solving recursively the $2N$ binding linear conditions that characterize the separating solution. Notice that the restrictions on $v(\cdot)$ implied by

$v(\cdot) = E(\cdot)$ emerge in the solution as requirements that $t(\cdot)$ be non-increasing, $t(c_i) \geqq 0$ and $p(c_i) > 0$.

The results in Propositions 9 and 10 are somewhat surprising. In most models of price discrimination similar results are not obtained as only the bottom purchaser has his surplus extracted. Typically, the bottom purchaser has no surplus in equilibrium, but any other consumer purchasing that contract has positive surplus so that the maximal choices of the other purchasers must also entail positive surplus. This argument does not apply to our particular specification. Our assumption of a constant marginal cost of time appears to play at least some role in our result, but linearity does not yield similar findings in at least some other price discrimination models (see the references in footnote 11).

Our results can be extended to environments in which the monopolist must pay a fixed cost per contract or the monopolist is exogenously restricted to offer only k contracts. Propositions 1 through 5 and their implications do not involve the firm side of the problem and therefore extend. Similarly, Propositions 6 through 8 and their corollaries use perturbations of the contract set that keep the number of stores fixed. (Some of our results do not obtain if the rent for a store depends on its location, for example, the discriminating monopolist may not choose to locate a store at the centre city if its rent is too high.) One illustration of our results occurs when the monopolist is restricted to only offer a single contract. The best single contract must set $t = 0$ (otherwise, replace the contract with $t > 0$ by one with $t = 0$ and a slightly higher price) and charge a price (i.e., the monopoly price) equal to the reservation value of some consumer.

In our analysis we found several restrictions in terms of observables in the contract space, i.e., the contract set is a finite set of points that is strictly monotone and strictly convex and has a contract with $t = 0$. These necessary conditions are also sufficient, i.e., any set of points satisfying these restrictions is a contract set for some economy that maximizes monopoly profit given the maximizing behaviour of consumers, so that our results in the contract space are exhaustive.[30] Our approach is constructive in that we calculate a particular supporting economy for each set of observations that satisfy the restrictions. This technique as well as the focus upon exhaustive implications is like the integrability issue in consumer theory.

Proposition 11. *An exhaustive description of the contract set is that it has a finite set of points that are strictly monotone and strictly convex and has a contract with* $t = 0$.

Proof. By Propositions 1, 2, 3 and 6 the contract set satisfies these properties. To show these are the only restrictions we construct a distribution of agent characteristics which imply that any contract set satisfying these conditions is maximal for the firm given the maximizing behaviour of consumers. We denote the given set as $\{(t_1, p_1), (t_2, p_2), \ldots, (t_m, p_m)\}$ where $p_1 > p_2 > \ldots > p_m$ and $0 = t_1 < t_2 < \ldots < t_m$ and proceed to construct a supporting economy. We let $c_i = (p_i - p_{i+1})/(t_{i+1} - t_i)$ for $i = 1, \ldots, m-1$ $(p_{i+1} + t_{i+1}c_i = p_i + t_i c_i)$, $c_m \in (0, c_{m-1})$ and $v_i = p_i + t_i c_i$. Under this construction the type i consumer maximizes by purchasing through contract (t_i, p_i), thereby satisfying feasibility in the firm's problem. We construct a set of weights $n_i > 0$ and $\sum_{i=1}^{m} n_i = 1$ such that the contract set hypothesized yields greater profit than any other (see footnote 31). *Q.E.D*

In our construction we generate an economy that supports the hypothesized contract set in which each type of trader purchases a distinct contract. Complete separation and no consumer receiving any surplus occurs for some economy for each possible equilibrium contract set. By an appropriate perturbation of our construction we can show that a supporting economy can always be obtained without complete separation and therefore, the supporting economy can never be uniquely identified. (We also note that one can show in a similar manner that Propositions 1, 2 and 3 are the only restrictions on the contract set that are implied by consumer maximization alone.) Richer spaces of observables or stronger assumptions are required in order to obtain more restrictions. In Spatt (1980) the constructive approach is used in a more general model with several spaces of observables. Examining exhaustively the implications of one's model is potentially useful in many settings with asymmetric information.

We also briefly describe some other results that exploit the programming structure of the monopolist's maximization problem. The solution satisfies various homogeneity restrictions. First note that multiplying all time costs (i.e., c vector and d) by λ preserves the solution except that the prior waiting times are divided by λ, i.e., the set of buyers, prices offered and corresponding expenditures on time are unchanged.[32] Second note that multiplying all reservation prices by λ causes the monopolist to rescale his set of offered contracts by multiplying both the price and time components of all contracts by λ.[33] The dual of the monopolist's programming problem in which an optimal set of buyers is specified also suggests some intuition about the solution. Fixing the vector x (i.e., the set of buyers) converts the monopolist's problem into a linear programme (whose dual, of course, is a linear programme). Deleting non-buyers the monopolist's problem is just

$$\max \sum n_i p(c_i) - \sum dn_i t(c_i)$$

$$\text{s.t.} \quad p(c_i) + c_i t(c_i) \leqq v_i, \tag{2.1}$$

$$p(c_i) + c_i t(c_i) \leqq p(c_j) + c_i t(c_j), \tag{2.2}$$

$$t(c_i) \geqq 0, \tag{2.3}$$

and

$$p(c_i) \geqq 0. \tag{2.4}$$

The dual[34] of this programme can be written as

$$\min \sum v_i w_i$$

$$\text{s.t.} \quad \sum\nolimits_{j \neq i} D_{ij} - \sum\nolimits_{j \neq i} D_{ji} + w_i \geqq n_i, \tag{3.1}$$

$$\sum\nolimits_{j \neq i} c_i D_{ij} - \sum\nolimits_{j \neq i} c_j D_{ji} + c_i w_i \geqq -dn_i, \tag{3.2}$$

$$D_{ij} \geqq 0, \tag{3.3}$$

and

$$w_i \geqq 0. \tag{3.4}$$

If n types of agents purchase the product this problem has n^2 variables and $2n$ constraints (beside the non-negativity constraints).

Constraints (3.1) are all binding since $p(c_i) > 0$ (if $p(c_i) = 0$ just call i a non-buyer). Combining these conditions yields $\sum w_i = \sum n_i$. The marginal impact on profit of a small reservation price shift in all consumers (assuming the set of optimal buyers is fixed) is the shift times the number of buyers. Notice that if $w_i < n_i$, then $\exists j \ni w_j > n_j$. Therefore, either $\exists j \ni w_j > n_j$ or $w_i = n_i \; \forall \, i$ (which corresponds to full information). If $w_i = n_i \, \forall i$ then the value of the dual objective is $\sum n_i v_i$. The linear programming duality insures $\sum n_i v_i$ is also the value of the primal, but this contradicts the infeasibility of perfect discrimination. Therefore $\exists j \ni w_j > n_j$. An increase in some trader's reservation price leads to an unexpectedly large increase in profit because of the interdependence of the contracts. This idea is discussed further in Section 4 with the help of the separating solution when there are only two types.

A similar argument exploiting constraint (3.2) shows that the highest cost buyer doesn't expend time. For any agent i with $t(c_i) > 0$ constraints (3.2) are binding so that

$$\sum\nolimits_{j \neq i} D_{ij} - \sum\nolimits_{j \neq i} \frac{c_j}{c_i} D_{ji} + w_i = \frac{-d}{c_i} n_i.$$

Combining this with the binding form of (3.1) yields

$$\sum\nolimits_{j \neq i} (c_j - c_i) D_{ji} = (c_i + d) n_i.$$

But the right-side is positive and $D_{ji} \geqq 0$ so that we obtain a contradiction of $t(c_i) > 0$ for the agent i with the largest cost of time. This duality proof is also an alternative proof of Proposition 6.

4. Examples and Welfare Results

In this section of the paper we present some examples that illustrate the general structure of our approach and the welfare comparison between imperfect discrimination and single-price monopoly. In single-price monopoly the monopolist offers the one contract that maximizes his profits. This contract must prescribe zero time (in the spatial interpretation of the model the monopolist locates his store where everyone lives). In the imperfect discrimination solution the monopolist offers the set of (one or more) contracts that maximizes his profits. We first compare these solutions in a two-type example.

With two types of agents the single-price monopoly and imperfect discrimination can potentially differ only if the monopolist finds it more profitable to offer 2 contracts rather than one. Therefore, we restrict our attention to $v_1 > v_2$ as $c_1 > c_2$.[35] One single contract solution is for the monopolist to charge the low reservation price (v_2) which yields profit as $\pi = (n_1 + n_2)\, v_2$. Under this solution the monopolist foregoes [sic] some surplus on the high reservation traders. The other single price solution is for the monopolist to charge the high reservation price and earn $\pi = n_1 v_1$ by foregoing [sic] sales to low reservation traders. Whether the monopolist earns more by charging the high or low reservation price depends on the steepness of the demand function (see Figure 6). The monopolist should charge the high reservation price if demand is inelastic enough (i.e., if $n_1/(n_1 + n_2) > v_2/v_1$).

Under imperfect discrimination the monopoly either offers a single contract or perfectly separates the traders by offering the pair of contracts

$$\left\{ \left(t(c_1), p(c_1) \right) = (0, v_1), (t(c_2), p(c_2)) = \left(\frac{v_1 - v_2}{c_1 - c_2}, \frac{c_1 v_2 - c_2 v_1}{c_1 - c_2} \right) \right\}$$

(see Proposition 10). The surplus of each consumer is fully extracted and the type 1 consumer is just indifferent to acting as a type 2 (see Figure 7). It is interesting to note that in this separating solution the positive time contract is increasing in c_2 because a greater wastage time is required to separate markets. The set of sorting contracts points to the asymmetry in the impact of the firm's and consumer's time cost; given that sorting occurs $p(c_2)$ is affected by small changes in c_1 and c_2 (through the sorting condition), but not by changes in d. The asymmetry occurs even though the monopoly extracts the entire consumer surplus and bears the consumer time costs. The profit of the firm that offers the separating pair of contracts is just

FIGURE 6 | The single-price monopoly solution (i.e., charge v_1 or v_2) depends on the steepness of the demand function, i.e., which of the shaded rectangles under portions of the demand curve is bigger.

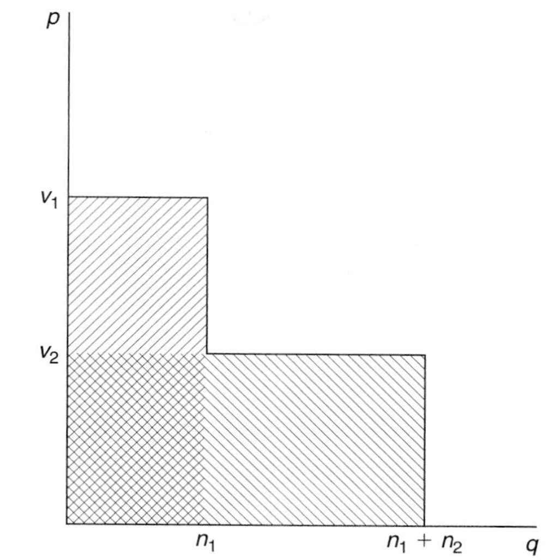

$$\pi = n_1 v_1 + n_2\left(\frac{(c_1 + d)v_2 - (c_2 + d)v_1}{c_1 - c_2}\right).$$

Notice that the profit from perfect discrimination ($n_1v_1 + n_2v_2$) exceeds that from sorting or either single contract solution. Sorting is more profitable than charging the high reservation price if

FIGURE 7 | In the two-type example the monopolist who sorts the traders offers contracts *A* and *B*. If he doesn't find it profitable to sort he offers either *A* or *C*.

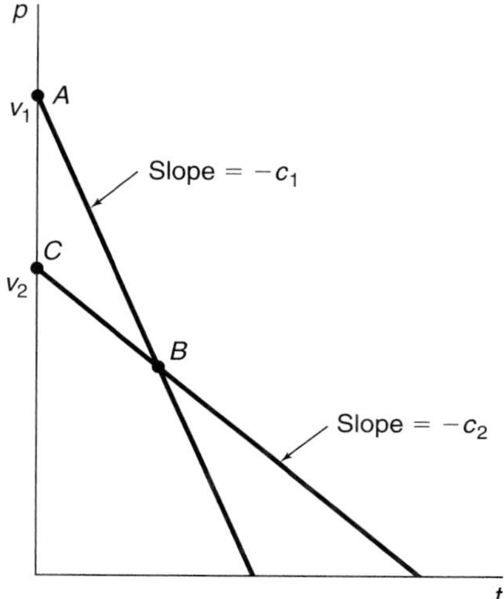

$$\frac{c_2 + d}{c_1 + d} < \frac{v_2}{v_1}$$

(otherwise, the second contract has too low a price and is not profitable). Similarly, the separating solution is more profitable than the low reservation price contract if

$$\frac{c_2 + d}{c_1 + d} < \frac{n_1}{n_1 + n_2}.$$

Otherwise, there are too few type 1 agents for it to be worthwhile to gain extra profit on the type 1's and less profit on the type 2's than just charging the low reservation price. Sorting is profitable if and only if

$$\frac{c_2 + d}{c_1 + d} < \min\left[\frac{v_2}{v_1}, \frac{n_1}{n_1 + n_2}\right].$$

If sorting is the most profitable strategy of the firm (and continues to be for small changes in v_2)

$$\Delta\pi = n_2 \Delta v_2 \frac{c_1 + d}{c_1 - c_2} > n_2 \Delta v_2.$$

Sorting causes the increase in reservation price of the low reservation trader to increase the profit of the monopolist by more than the number of these consumers because the increase in reservation prices reduces the time required for separation. This illustrates the earlier result that some trader has $w_i > n_i$ given a fixed set of buyers.

The deadweight loss comparison between standard monopoly and imperfect discrimination is ambiguous. We combine the firm profit and total consumer surplus to measure total surplus under our structure (deadweight loss is $n_1 v_1 + n_2 v_2$ minus surplus). We suppose

$$\frac{c_2 + d}{c_1 + d} < \min\left[\frac{v_2}{v_1}, \frac{n_1}{n_1 + n_2}\right]$$

so that sorting is used by a monopolist when it is allowed. Under sorting no consumer has any surplus as total surplus is firm profit. First suppose the single-price contract that the monopolist offers has the high price (i.e., $n_1/(n_1 + n_2) > v_2/v_1$). For this high price contract no consumer has any surplus so that total surplus is again firm profit. Since sorting has higher firm profit than offering the high reservation price contract, imperfect discrimination can lead to higher output, higher total surplus and less deadweight loss than single-price monopoly. If instead the single-price contract that is most profitable to the monopolist is the low reservation price contract (i.e., $n_1/(n_1 + n_2) < v_2/v_1$) then total surplus is $n_1 v_1 + n_2 v_2$ and deadweight loss is zero. Imperfect discrimination can lead to more deadweight loss (from time costs) and lower total surplus (and thus lower consumer surplus) than single-price monopoly.

We now develop two examples with three types of consumers to strengthen the welfare results. In these examples we assume $v_1 > v_2 > v_3$ (and $c_1 > c_2 > c_3$), $d = 0$, n_2 is "small" and $c_1 v_3 - c_3 v_1 > 0$. Since n_2 is "small" the monopolist in either an imperfect discrimination solution or single-price monopoly solution doesn't try to sell to type 2 or extract extra surplus from type 2 if it reduces profits from type 1 or type 3. In both examples if the firm separates types 1 and 3 it offers contracts

$$\left\{(0, v_1), \left(\frac{v_1 - v_3}{c_1 - c_3}, \frac{c_1 v_3 - c_3 v_1}{c_1 - c_3}\right)\right\}.$$

FIGURE 8 | The imperfect discriminating monopolist might offer contracts A and B (when n_2 is "small") excluding the type 2 consumers. These consumers would not be excluded under single-price monopoly when that solution is to offer contract C.

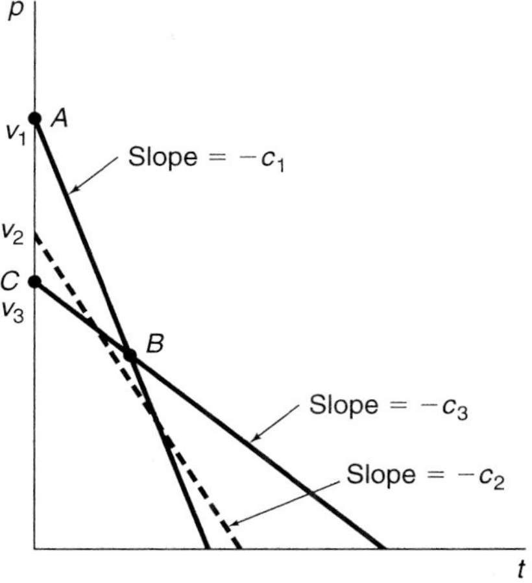

In the first example we assume

$$\frac{v_1 - v_3}{c_1 - c_3} < \frac{v_1 - v_2}{c_1 - c_2}.$$

This example can have the imperfect discriminating firm maximizing profits by contracts to sort types 1 and 3

$$\left\{(0, v_1), \left(\frac{v_1 - v_3}{c_1 - c_3}, \frac{c_1 v_3 - c_3 v_1}{c_1 - c_3}\right)\right\},$$

while the single-price firm offers the contract $\{(0, v_3)\}$. The structure of the imperfect discrimination solution is illustrated in Figure 8. Note that the type 2 agent doesn't purchase the commodity since he would have to spend more than v_2 to purchase it, which is a consequence of

$$\frac{v_1 - v_3}{c_1 - c_3} < \frac{v_1 - v_2}{c_1 - c_2}.^{36}$$

A consumer with an intermediate reservation price does not purchase the commodity in the example though those with high and low reservation prices do purchase.[37] Imperfect discrimination need not distribute the actual output to those who value it most. Since the single-price contract (lowest reservation price) entails no output restriction, our example also shows that imperfect discrimination can lead to more output restriction than single-price monopoly. In the earlier example with two types in which the single-price solution is the high reservation price we saw that imperfect discrimination can also lead to more output than monopoly so that imperfect discrimination and single-price monopoly lead to an ambiguous output comparison.

In a second example with the earlier hypothesized three type structure we assume

$$\frac{v_1 - v_3}{c_1 - c_3} > \frac{v_1 - v_2}{c_1 - c_2}.$$

This example can have the imperfect discriminating firm maximizing profits by offering contracts to sort types 1 and 3

FIGURE 9 | The imperfect discriminating monopolist might offer contracts *A* and *B* when n_2 is "small". Type 2 consumers earn positive surplus by purchasing contract *B,* although these consumers would be excluded and earn no surplus under single-price monopoly when that solution is *A.*

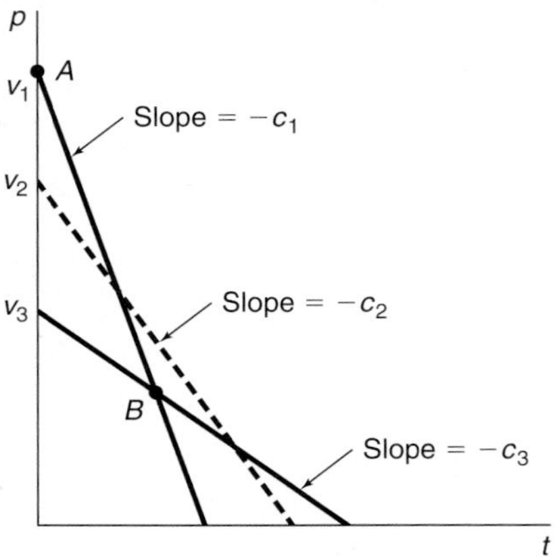

$$\left\{(0, v_1), \left(\frac{v_1 - v_3}{c_1 - c_3}, \frac{c_1 v_3 - c_3 v_1}{c_1 - c_3}\right)\right\},$$

while the single-price firm offers the contract $\{(0, v_1)\}$. The structure of the imperfect discrimination solution is illustrated in Figure 9. The type 2 agent purchases the commodity by contract

$$\left(\frac{v_1 - v_3}{c_1 - c_3}, \frac{c_1 v_3 - c_3 v_1}{c_1 - c_3}\right).$$

A consumer with an intermediate reservation price has positive surplus in the discrimination solution, while the entire surplus of the high and low reservation price consumers is extracted. Surplus is not monotone in reservation price. In the single-price solution $\{(0, v_1)\}$ no consumer earns any surplus and monopoly profits are lower than when types 1 and 3 are separated. The extra profits of imperfect discrimination need not come at the expense of any consumer and in fact, imperfect discrimination can make the firm and some consumer strictly better off and no consumers worse off. Total consumer surplus can rise under discrimination and consumers may prefer discrimination to single-price monopoly.

Proposition 12. *The output and deadweight loss comparisons between discrimination and single-price monopoly are ambiguous. In fact, discrimination can potentially Pareto dominate single-price monopoly.*

We next examine an example with three types of traders where $v_1 > v_2 > v_3$, $c_1 > c_2 > c_3$ and $d = 0$. We suppose that n_3 is "small" so that we can obtain the monopolist's contract set by focusing upon types 1 and 2. We suppose $c_1 v_2 - c_2 v_1 > 0$ so that it is profitable for the monopolist to service the type 2 traders, but also suppose most of the agents are type 1 so that discrimination is viable. The monopolist's contract set is

$$\left\{(0, v_1), \left(\frac{v_1 - v_2}{c_1 - c_2}, \frac{c_1 v_2 - c_2 v_1}{c_1 - c_2}\right)\right\}$$

FIGURE 10 | The imperfect discriminating monopolist might offer contracts *A* and *B* when n_3 is "small". Type 3 consumers earn positive surplus by purchasing contract *B*, though the type 2 agents earn zero surplus by purchasing *B*.

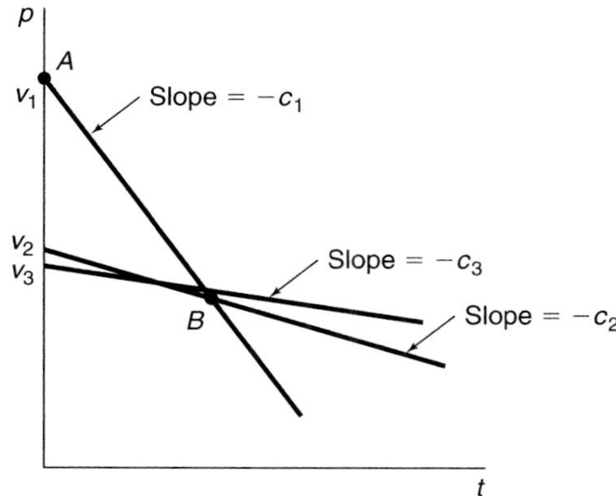

It is internally consistent for

$$\frac{c_1 v_2 - c_2 v_1}{c_1 - c_2} + c_3 \frac{v_1 - v_2}{c_1 - c_2} < v_3$$

(see Figure 10) so that it is possible for the agent with the lowest reservation value to have positive surplus, though he purchases a contract in which some buyer has zero surplus (see Corollary 5).

As we described in Section 2 the model can be interpreted in uncertainly contexts. Suppose the firm must specify its contract set before the state of nature is revealed, while the consumer selects after the state is revealed. Reinterpreting our previous example so that all consumers are identical and states are indexed shows the ambiguous effects on welfare and output of permitting the firm to offer several contracts. A related set of issues concerns the effect of the resolution of uncertainty where the firm can offer only a single contract (no matter what the information structure). If all consumers are identical then the comparison between the monopolist knowing the state before setting his single contract and determining the contract offered before the state is revealed is analogous to the distinction between *perfect* discrimination (first-degree price discrimination) and single-price monopoly. The resolution of uncertainty when all consumers are identical allows perfect discrimination so the resolution of uncertainty can neither cut expected output nor increase expected deadweight loss. Surprising results can occur if consumers differ so that the resolution of uncertainty does not eliminate asymmetric information.

We consider a pair of examples with two types and two states to illustrate the ambiguous impact of the resolution of uncertainty. We denote the reservation price of type i trader in state θ by v_i^θ and cost per unit time of type i in state θ by c_i^θ. In the first example we let $v_2 = v_2^1 = v_2^2$, $c_2 = c_2^1 = c_2^2$, $c_1 = c_1^1 = c_1^2$, $c_1 > c_2$ and $v_1^1 > v_1^2 > v_2$ (the type 1 traders have a higher reservation price in the "good" state (state 1) than state 2). We let n_1 and n_2 respectively denote the number of type 1 and 2 agents, α denote the probability of state 1 (and thus $1-\alpha$ is the probability of state 2). We assume

$$c_1 v_2 - c_2 v_1^1 < 0, \qquad c_1 v_2 - c_2 v_1^2 > 0$$

FIGURE 11 | Contracts *B* and *C* are offered by the monopolist before the state is revealed and in state 2, while contract *A* is offered in state 1.

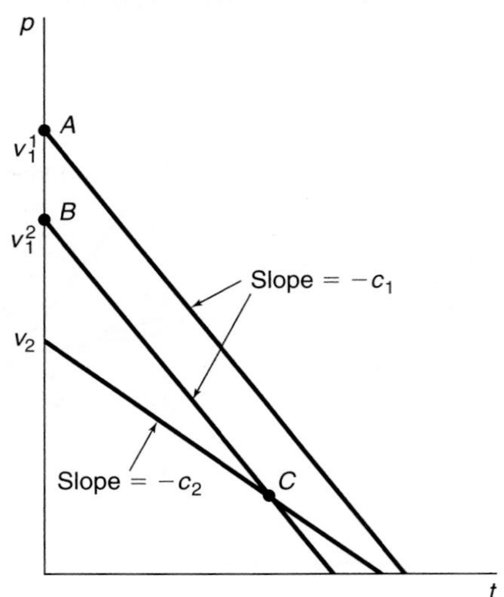

and n_2 is small. The monopolist offers

$$\left\{(0, v_1^2), \left(\frac{v_1^2 - v_2}{c_1 - c_2}, \frac{c_1 v_2 - c_2 v_1^2}{c_1 - c_2}\right)\right\}$$

in state 2 and $\{(0, v_1^1)\}$ in state 1 if the contract set is specified after the state is revealed. For small enough values of α it offers

$$\left\{(0, v_1^2), \left(\frac{v_1^2 - v_2}{c_1 - c_2}, \frac{c_1 v_2 - c_2 v_1^2}{c_1 - c_2}\right)\right\}$$

if the contract set must be specified before the state is revealed (see Figure 11). (If state 1 is unlikely enough, then it is optimal to avoid the discrete cost of designing the contract set to take into account this case.) The type 2 agent is excluded in the good state if the contract set is specified after the state is drawn, but both types of consumers purchase the output in both states if the contract set is specified before the state is revealed. The resolution of uncertainty can reduce expected output. In this example the ex ante contract set leads to some firm surplus on type 2 in state 1, while the ex post contract set excludes these traders so that no firm consumer surplus is earned on type 2 in state 1. The resolution of uncertainty can reduce expected total (consumer and firm) surplus. The reverse possibilities on expected total surplus and output are illustrated by the earlier discussion of n states and identical consumers.

In the second example we let $v_1^1 > v_1^2 > v_2$ and $c_1^1 > c_1^2 > c_2$ where $v_2 = v_2^1 = v_2^2$ and $c_2 = c_2^1 = c_2^2$. We let n_1 and n_2 respectively denote the number of type 1 and 2 agents and let α denote the probability of state 1. We suppose $c_1^1 v_2 - c_2 v_1^1 > 0$

and

$$v_1^2 < \lambda v_1^1 + (1 - \lambda) v_2$$

where

$$c_1^2 = \lambda c_1^1 + (1 - \lambda) c_2.$$

FIGURE 12 | Contracts A and C are offered by the monopolist before the state is revealed and in state 1, while contract B is offered in state 2.

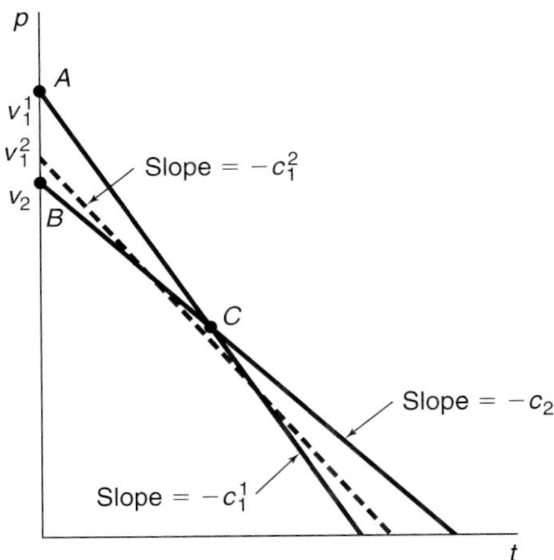

(This structure is similar to the first of the examples in which we compared single-price monopoly and imperfect discrimination.) We suppose the probability of state two is near zero (i.e., α almost 1). Then the monopolist offers the contract set

$$\left\{(0, v_1^1), \left(\frac{v_1^1 - v_2}{c_1^1 - c_2}, \frac{c_1^1 v_2 - c_2 v_1^1}{c_1^1 - c_2}\right)\right\}$$

if state 1 is revealed or if he is forced to determine his contracts before the state is revealed for appropriately large n_1/n_2. In neither case does any consumer purchasing the contract have positive surplus. For the smallest of the permissible n_1/n_2 the monopolist offers $\{(0, v_2)\}$ after state 2 is revealed (see Figure 12) and the type 1 has positive surplus. The expected monopoly profit and expected surplus of type 1 increases (and expected surplus of type 2 is constant) if the state of nature is revealed before the contract set is determined.

5. Conclusion

By exploiting its dual and geometrical structure we have analyzed a model of monopolistic price discrimination in which consumers with low time costs invest in time to pay a lower price for the monopolized commodity. We obtain implications on the structure of contracts offered by the monopolist (e.g., monotonicity, convexity, use of a zero time contract, possibility of less output in imperfect discrimination than single-price monopoly) and show that our implications exhaust the results that are observable when only the equilibrium contract pairs are observable. On the normative side, imperfect discrimination can (but need not) lead to more deadweight loss and output restriction relative to single-price monopoly. Alternatively, imperfect discrimination can raise monopoly profits and make some consumers better off and none worse off relative to single-price monopoly. The resolution of uncertainty has similar ambiguous effects.

Much research remains to be done on imperfect price discrimination. Some similarities appear in the analysis of diverse models (e.g., the monotonicity of the contract set, the substitution effect governing consumer choices, the importance and form of the set of binding self-selection constraints, the first-best efficiency of the uppermost contract and the extraction of surplus from a consumer in the bottom contract), though some qualitative properties are model specific. Our understanding of the general structure of the canonical price discrimination model (as posed, for example, in Stiglitz (1977)) needs development. For example, how should the monopolist choose among alternative (but not necessarily mutually exclusive) means of price discrimination and trade-off the inefficiency induced by various instruments against their separating power. Our knowledge of the welfare impacts of price discrimination seems to be at an especially primitive stage (see Katz (1982), Palfrey (1980), and Schmalensee (1981*a*) for recent characterizations of welfare issues in special settings). For example, the general conditions under which profit maximizing imperfect discrimination dominates in welfare terms or has less output than single-price monopoly require analysis (these issues are somewhat related to Willig's (1978) demonstration of the strict dominance of non-linear pricing). Insight in this area may also contribute to understanding of optimal pricing (see e.g. Spence (1977), Willig (1978), and Roberts (1979)). The literature on price discrimination has emphasized the behaviour of monopolists rather than discrimination in an oligopolistic market. The presence of some market power by firms without complete monopoly might be sufficient for discriminatory pricing to extract extra surplus under other equilibrium concepts besides joint maximization (e.g. Nash or the foresighted sequential entry equilibrium in Prescott and Visscher (1977)). Wright (1965) also makes this point in the monopolistic competition context (recent models of this type include Gal-or (1980, 1981), Jaynes (1978), Spence (1978), Spulber (1980*a*, 1980*b*, 1981) and Wilson, Oren and Smith (1980)). A spatial location model may be a useful approach in analysing oligopolistic discrimination (see Greenhut and Greenhut (1975)) and might also add more insight into monopolistic discrimination (in the spatial view of our model all consumers live at one point) as illustrated by the early work of Smithies (1941). (A recent detailed treatment of spatial pricing theory is Greenhut and Ohta (1975).) A general spatial model of monopolistic dicrimination (in which consumers live at diverse points in the space) is analysed by Spatt (1980). Imperfect discrimination can be used to explain various pricing policies of firms (e.g., Spatt (1981) explains periodic sales by a firm as a device to augment the firm's customer base).

Challenging problems remain in explaining the pricing policies of firms and in assessing the welfare effects of these actions in non-competitive markets.

Notes

[1]This airline example takes the view that the oligopoly is acting as a joint profit maximizer in the Chamberlain tradition. An interesting question for future research is what other oligopolistic solution concepts allow price discrimination.

[2]An alternative explanation is cost-based, e.g., it is less costly for the airline to transport a consumer under a restrictive ticket (these flyers might be forced to ticket far in advance or utilize excess capacity).

[3]A representative but incomplete bibliography of this literature includes Adams and Yellin (1976), Goldman, Leland and Sibley (1980), Harris and Raviv (1981), Leland and Meyer (1976), Maskin and Riley (1981), Mussa and Rosen (1978), Phillips (1979), Roberts (1979), Salop (1977), Spence (1977, 1980), Stiglitz (1977), Stokey (1979) and Telser (1979). A closely related literature focuses on optimal or profit-maximizing multi-part and multiblock pricing. A recent bibliography in this areas is in Auerbach and Pellechio (1978).

[4]An early price discrimination model in a spatial setting is the analysis of f.o.b. pricing by Smithies (1941). More recent studies include Greenhut and Ohta (1975), Greenhut and Greenhut (1975), and Phlips (1980).

[5]Nichols, Smolensky and Tideman (1971) introduce and Barzel (1974) extends the idea of waiting time in allocating merit goods by a public authority. Parks (1974) briefly considers price discrimination by wage rates and transactions costs in his general discussion of the consumer durable choice. Spence (1973) discusses time as a

signal in non-market contexts in a provocative essay. Prescott and Visscher (1977) have consumers differing by the disutility of time in some of the examples they develop to illustrate an oligopolistic equilibrium concept.

[6]Among authors using a continuum of types and the calculus of variations are Mussa and Rosen (1978), Salop (1977), Spence (1977), Stiglitz (1977) and Stokey (1979).

[7]Mussa and Rosen (1978) note they use a continuum of types as a mathematically convenient way to approximate N types. Both Harris and Raviv (1981) and Telser (1979) also exploit an N-type structure.

[8]We wish to thank Phil Dybvig and Steve Ross for suggesting that we examine the dual structure of our model. Littlechild (1975) examines a two-part tariff in a model with two types, but in his conclusion suggests the possibility of exploiting dual techniques in an N-type model. Roberts (1979) uses dual methods in analyzing optimal and monopolistic non-linear pricing. The dual approach to consumer theory is reviewed in Varian (1978).

[9]If output is greater in discrimination than single-price monopoly, then the deadweight loss need not be lower because output is not allocated in discrimination to those who value the commodity the highest (and in our model discrimination imposes direct costs). Scherer (1970) and Bork (1978) seem to overlook this in suggesting that greater output in discrimination than single-price monopoly implies that the deadweight loss in discrimination is lower (see Yamey (1977)) and Bork (1978) even argues that output provides a way to compare welfare that is free of interpersonal comparison problems. In many contexts (including our model) if output is lower in discrimination than single-price monopoly, then the deadweight loss is greater under discrimination. This results because of the combination of greater exclusion of buyers who are willing to cover cost, the direct cost (as in our case) of discrimination and discrimination not allocating the good to those who value it most.

[10]In the waiting time interpretation of our model it might be natural to think that maximizing behavior of consumers in selecting stores leads to the creation of queues in the equilibrium structure, i.e., the queuing structure is endogenous (see Katz and Yechiali (1979)). We do not pursue this possibility beyond observing that the action of a consumer then depends on the decisions of other consumers as well as the set of contracts offered. This is illustrated in the model of priority pricing for interruptible service by Harris and Raviv (1981).

[11]Linear programming techniques have also been used in the analysis of price discrimination by Spence (1980) and Harris and Raviv (1981). Spence (1980) uses a linear programming formulation to determine prices in a non-linear pricing setting after the quantities are set optimally.

[12]Our equilibrium does not permit the firm to change the contracts offered an individual once he makes his choice. If the consumer had ex ante anticipated the change in contracts then the sorting scheme would not be viable. Stokey (1979) also discusses this limitation of the price discrimination approach and Harris and Townsend (1981) show more generally that self-selection is a basic feasibility requirement. Dybvig and Spatt (1982) explicitly examine dynamic inference from equilibrium consumer choices in price discrimination environments.

[13]Consumers can do exactly as well for themselves given the contract set by following other strategies (implied by a binding self-selection constraint). Strict preference on the consumer side can in principle be obtained by a messy perturbation of the solution, though for any perturbation there exists another that is slightly more profitable for the firm.

[14]This formalism is noted by Leland and Meyer (1976), though they do not combine the type and state interpretations.

[15]Results in monopoly price discrimination models that rely only on consumer maximization and not firm behavior will be valid in other market structures.

[16]Suppose not. If $t' < t''$ and $p' \leqq p''$, or $t' \leqq t''$ and $p' < p''$, then $p' + t'c_i < p'' + t''c_i$ and contract (t'', p'') is not purchased by any trader. Similarly, if the inequalities are reversed (t', p') is not purchased.

[17]Suppose not. Then $\hat{p} \geqq \lambda p' + (1 - \lambda)p''$ which implies $\hat{p} + (\lambda t' + (1 - \lambda)t'')c_i \geqq \lambda(p' + t'c_i) + (1 - \lambda)(p'' + t''c_i) \geqq \min[p' + t'c_i, p'' + t''c_i]$. The last inequality is strict if $c_i \neq (p' - p'')/(t'' - t')$ so then $(\lambda t' + (1 - \lambda)t'', \hat{p})$ is not expenditure minimizing. Without loss of generality $p' > p''$ so that if $c_i = (p' - p'')/(t'' - t')$, then $p' + t'c_i = \hat{p} + (\lambda t' + (1 - \lambda)t'')c_i$ and consumers select (t', p') under our convention for indifferent consumers that each purchaser selects the highest price and lowest time contract on his minimum iso-expenditure line. Therefore, $(\lambda t' + (1 - \lambda)t'', \hat{p}) \not\in \Omega$, which is a contraction.

[18]The linearity in the iso-expenditure curve is utilised in the proof of Proposition 2. The convexity of the contract set can be lost with concave iso-expenditure curves in (t, p) space. The monotonicity and convexity of the contract set is strongly suggestive of analogy with the standard indifference curve (see Figure 13).

[19]Under our convention each consumer who purchases uses the highest price and lowest time contract on his minimum iso-expenditure locus. Thus each type purchases a unique contract and the monopolist need not offer more than N contracts. We consider only minimal equilibrium contract sets in which redundant contracts have been eliminated.

[20]The hypothesis that agents who purchase with time cost c_i and c_j $(c_i \neq c_j)$ purchase their most inexpensive contract implies $p(c_i) + c_i t(c_i) \leqq p(c_j) + c_i t(c_j)$ and $p(c_j) + c_j t(c_j) \leqq p(c_i) + c_j t(c_i)$. These together imply

FIGURE 13 | Contract set

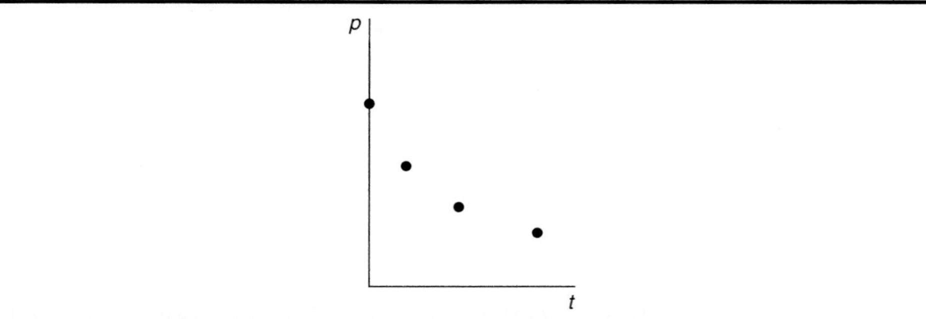

$$(c_i - c_j)\,[t(c_i) - t(c_j)] \leqq 0$$

and

$$\left(\frac{1}{c_i} - \frac{1}{c_j}\right)[p(c_i) - p(c_j)] \leqq 0$$

so that $t(\cdot)$ is non-increasing and $p(\cdot)$ is non-decreasing.

[21]From consumer maximization we obtain $p(c_i) + c_i t(c_i) \leqq p(c_j) + c_i t(c_j)$ and $p(c_j) + c_j t(c_j) \leqq p(c_k) + c_j t(c_k)$. But $t(c_j) < t(c_k)$ (from Proposition 4) and the second condition imply $p(c_j) + c_i t(c_j) < p(c_k) + c_i t(c_k)$ so that combining with the first condition we obtain $p(c_i) + c_i t(c_i) < p(c_k) + c_i t(c_k)$. To show $p(c_k) + c_k t(c_k) < p(c_i) + c_k t(c_i)$ we reverse all i's and k's in the above argument and replace $t(c_j) < t(c_k)$ by $t(c_j) > t(c_i)$.

[22]The condition $c_i > c_j$ implies $p(c_j) + c_j t(c_j) \leqq p(c_i) + c_j t(c_i) \leqq p(c_i) + c_i t\,(c_i)$ (with the latter inequality strict for $t(c_i) > 0$) or $E(c_i) \geqq E(c_j)$ (and $E(c_i) > E(c_j)$ for $t(c_i) > 0$). Similarly $c_i > c_j$ implies (for $p(c_j) > 0$)

$$\frac{p(c_j)}{c_j} + t(c_j) > \frac{p(c_j)}{c_i} + t(c_j) \geqq \frac{p\,(c_i)}{c_i} + t(c_i)$$

so

$$\frac{E(c_i)}{c_i} < \frac{E(c_j)}{c_j}.$$

[23]Suppose not. Then $p(c_i) + c_i t(c_i) < p(c_k) + c_i t(c_k)$. The type i agent is the one purchasing $(t(c_i), p(c_i))$ with smallest c_i since there is no buyer j with $c_i > c_j > c_k$. Without any loss of generality we can reinterpret the type k agent as the one with the smallest (rather than largest) time cost among the buyers of $(t(c_k), (p(c_k))$. We replace $(t(c_k), (p(c_k))$ by contract $(\hat{t}(c_k), \hat{p}(c_k))$ (see Figure 5) such that

$$\hat{p}(c_k) + c_i\hat{t}(c_k) = p(c_i) + c_i t(c_i)$$

and

$$\hat{p}(c_k) + c_k\hat{t}(c_k) = p(c_k) + c_k t(c_k).$$

Then

$$\hat{t}(c_k) = \frac{p(c_i) - p(c_k) + c_i t(c_i) - c_k t(c_k)}{c_i - c_k}$$

and substituting the non-binding self-selection constraint yields $\hat{t}(c_k) < t(c_k)$. But then agent k is indifferent to $(t(c_k), p(c_k))$ and $(\hat{t}(c_k), \hat{p}(c_k))$ so we have $\hat{p}(c_k) > p(c_k)$. For all agents with $c_{\bar{k}} \geqq c_k$ who purchase $(t(c_k), p(c_k))$, $\hat{p}(c_k) + c_{\bar{k}}\,\hat{t}(c_k) \leqq p(c_k) + c_{\bar{k}}\,t(c_k)$. Consequently, all earlier buyers of $(t(c_k), p(c_k))$ substitute the more profitable $(\hat{t}(c_k),, \hat{p}(c_k))$. Now we need only show that no earlier purchaser of a more profitable contract substitutes $(\hat{t}(c_k), \hat{p}(c_k))$. First recall that the self-selection constraints ensure $p(c_k) + c_k t(c_k) \leqq p(c_i) + c_k t(c_i)$ so that $\hat{p}(c_k) + c_k\hat{t}(c_k) \leqq p(c_i) + c_k t(c_i)$. But then $\hat{p}(c_k) + c_i\hat{t}(c_k) = p(c_i) + c_i t(c_i)$ implies $\hat{t}(c_k) \geqq t(c_i)$ and $\hat{p}(c_k) \leqq p(c_i)$. Since any agent $\bar{i}$ who previously purchased a more profitable contract for the firm than $(\hat{t}(c_k), \hat{p}(c_k))$ satisfies $c_{\bar{i}} \geqq c_i$ we obtain $\hat{p}(c_k) + c_{\bar{i}}\hat{t}\,(c_k) \geqq p(c_i) + c_{\bar{i}}\hat{t}(c_i)$. None of these consumers will prefer $(\hat{t}(c_k), \hat{p}(c_k))$ to their earlier more profitable contract. We have perturbed the contract set and increased profits so that the claimed solution in which the self-selection constraint is not binding is not joint profit maximal.

[24]In the theory of the consumer with the standard continuous choice set the derivative of the expenditure function is the compensated demand since any changes in demand must have a zero effect on the optimal expenditure for small price changes. In our discrete model the binding constraints in Proposition 7 mean that we can calculate the difference in expenditure between buyers adjacent in travel time as if they purchase by the same contract.

[25]By substitution

$$\frac{E(c_i) - E(c_k)}{c_i - c_k} = \frac{p(c_i) + c_i t(c_i) - p(c_k) - c_k t(c_k)}{c_i - c_k}.$$

If $(t(c_i), p(c_i)) = (t(c_k), p(c_k))$ the equation directly reduces to $t(c_k)$. If i and k purchase on distinct contracts, then Proposition 7 implies that the equation reduces to $t(c_k)$.

[26]If no consumer purchasing the lowest price contract has zero surplus its price can be increased without causing any buyers of it to withdraw from the market. The profits earned on buyers who earlier purchased the bottom contract must rise from a price hike since these buyers continue to buy this contract or substitute even more profitable ones for the firm. No consumer who purchased any other contract earlier will change his action (and the resulting firm profit he creates) as a result of a price hike on a contract he didn't purchase earlier. The monopolist is not maximizing his total profit unless some purchaser of the lowest price contract has zero surplus.

[27] Suppose not. Then some buyer with the lowest reservation price purchases by a contract which charges more than the minimum price in the contract set. Then by Proposition 4 all buyers of the lowest price contract have lower costs of travel and by Proposition 5 have lower expenditures. Then the expenditures of each agent in the lowest price contract are less than that of some agent with the lowest reservation price which in turn does not exceed the minimum reservation value among all buyers. Hence, all buyers of the minimum price contract have positive surplus, which is a contradiction.

[28]In any equilibrium we can observe which agents purchase and which agents use the same contract. We fix the set of buyers to correspond to the equilibrium and we impose constraints to dictate the grouping of consumers to contracts to an optimal arrangement (i.e., require all agents who use the same contract in the equilibrium to purchase the same contract). The programming problem is linear in 2 m variables (m contracts) and has an optimal solution which is a corner. Any such corner solution must have 2 m binding constraints in the restricted linear programme. From Proposition 7 and Corollary 1 there are exactly $m - 1$ binding self-selection constraints in addition to one binding non-negativity condition (i.e., $t = 0$ in the highest price contract) and thus at least m consumer surplus constraints are satisfied with equality in the corner solution.

[29]In the perfect sorting case there are N contracts. Any corner solution must then have all N surplus conditions binding along with a specified sequence of $N - 1$ self-selection constraints and one non-negativity constraint. Therefore, there is a only a single corner optimal and the optimal solution to the sorting problem is unique. The solution is obtained by solving

$$t(c_1) = 0$$

$$p(c_i) + c_i t(c_i) = v_i \quad \text{for } i = 1, \ldots, N,$$

and

$$p(c_i) + c_i t(c_i) = p(c_{i+1}) + c_i t(c_{i+1}) \quad \text{for all } i = 1, \ldots, N - 1.$$

But then

$$v_i = p(c_{i+1}) + c_i t(c_{i+1})$$

and

$$v_{i+1} = p(c_{i+1}) + c_{i+1} t(c_{i+1}) \quad \text{for } i = 1, \ldots, N - 1$$

and also

$$t(c_1) = 0 \quad \text{and} \quad p(c_1) = v_1.$$

The sorting solution is $t(c_1) = 0$ and $p(c_1) = v_1$ and for $i = 1, \ldots, N - 1$

$$p(c_i) = \frac{c_{i-1} v_i - c_i v_{i-1}}{c_{i-1} - c_i} \quad \text{and} \quad t(c_i) = \frac{v_{i-1} - v_i}{c_{i-1} - c_i}.$$

[30]We wish to thank Steve Ross for suggesting we examine the sufficiency of our results.

[31]We suppose almost all consumers are type 1. Then the monopolist wants these agents to purchase $(t^{(1)}, p^{(1)})$ that

$$\text{maximizes } p^{(1)}$$
$$\text{s.t. } p^{(1)} + c_1 t^{(1)} \leqq v_1 \quad \text{and} \quad t^{(1)} \geqq 0.$$

This implies $p^{(1)} = v_1$ and $t^{(1)} = 0$. We now recursively suppose that if we fix $n_1, \ldots, n_{k-1}$ then almost all of the agents of type at least k are in fact type k. Then the firm wants the type k agents (for $k = 2, \ldots, m$) to purchase contract $(t^{(k)}, p^{(k)})$ to

$$\text{Maximize } p^{(k)}$$
$$\text{s.t. } p^{(k)} + c_k t^{(k)} \leqq v_k,$$
$$p^{(k)} + c_j t^{(k)} \geqq p^{(j)} + c_j t^{(j)} \quad \text{for } j < k,$$

and

$$t^{(k)} \geqq 0.$$

This ensures that the type k consumer can purchase the contract intended for him and none of the earlier types prefer it to their own. By similar arguments to those in Proposition 7 and Corollary 1 we can show that the solution must satisfy

$$p^{(k)} + c_k t^{(k)} = v_k \quad \text{and} \quad p^{(k)} + c_{k-1} t^{(k)} = v_{k-1}.$$

It is then straightforward to verify that $(t_j, p_j) = (t^{(j)}, p^{(j)})$ so that each of the specified contracts are [sic] purchased by some consumer in our constructed economy.

[32]If all time costs (c_i and d) are multiplied by λ, then the monopolist will offer a contract $(t/\lambda, p) \in \Omega_\lambda$ for each $(t, p) \in \Omega$. The set Ω_λ must be feasible since the prices and total wastage expenditures of each consumer are identical to those in the feasible solution to the original problem Ω. If Ω_λ does not maximize firm profits then we contradict the assumption that Ω is profit-maximizing in the original problem.

[33]If all reservation prices are multiplied by λ, then the monopolist will offer a contract $(\lambda t, \lambda p) \in \Omega_\lambda$ for each $(t, p) \in \Omega$. The set Ω_λ must be feasible since Ω is feasible in the original problem. If Ω_λ is not profit-maximizing in the modified problem, then we contradict Ω profit-maximizing in the original problem.

[34]Gale (1960) is an excellent reference on duality in linear programming.

[35]If $c_1 > c_2$, then $p(c_1) \geqq p(c_2)$ is implied by consumer maximization. If $v_1 \leqq v_2$, then the monopolist cannot raise profit by offering a second contract.

[36]The type 2 agent does not purchase under discrimination by the contract $(0, v_1)$ since $v_1 > v_2$. The contract

$$\left(\frac{v_1 - v_3}{c_1 - c_3}, \frac{c_1 v_3 - c_3 v_1}{c_1 - c_3}\right)$$

would require the type 2 agent to spend

$$\left(\frac{v_1 - v_3}{c_1 - c_3}\right) c_2 + \frac{c_1 v_3 - c_3 v_1}{c_1 - c_3}, \text{ i.e. } \frac{(c_2 - c_3) v_1 + (c_1 - c_2) v_3}{c_1 - c_3}$$

or $\lambda v_t + (1 - \lambda) v_3$ where

$$\lambda = \frac{c_2 - c_3}{c_1 - c_3}.$$

The required expenditure exceeds v_2 if

$$\frac{v_1 - v_3}{c_1 - c_3} < \frac{v_1 - v_2}{c_1 - c_2}$$

(similarly, if

$$\frac{v_1 - v_3}{c_1 - c_3} > \frac{v_1 - v_2}{c_1 - c_2}$$

the type 2 agent has positive surplus in purchasing the contract earmarked for type 3).

[37]This contrasts with many other price discrimination models, see, for example, Mussa and Rosen (1978).

References

Adams, W. and Yellin, J. (1976), "Commodity Bundling and the Burden of Monopoly", *Quarterly Journal of Economics,* **90,** 475–488.

Auerbach, A. and Pellechio, A. (1978), "The Two-Part Tariff and Voluntary Market Participation", *Quarterly Journal of Economics,* **92,** 571–587.

Barzel, Y. (1974), "A Theory of Rationing by Waiting", *Journal of Law and Economics,* **17,** 73–95.

Bork, R. (1978) *The Antitrust Paradox: A Policy at War with Itself* (New York: Basic Books).

Dybvig, P. and Spatt, C. (1982), "Repeated Self-Selection Models" (in preparation).

Edwards, E. (1950), "The Analysis of Output Under Discrimination", *Econometrica,* **18,** 163–172.

Gale, D. (1960) *Theory of Linear Economic Models* (New York: McGraw-Hill).

Gal-or, E. (1980), "Nonlinear Pricing—Oligopoly Case" (unpublished manuscript, Graduate School of Business, University of Pittsburgh).

Gal-or, E. (1981), "Intertemporal Price Discrimination and Competition" (unpublished manuscript, Graduate School of Business, University of Pittsburgh).

Goldman, B., Leland, H. and Sibley, D. (1980), "Optimal Nonuniform Prices" (mimeo).

Greenhut, J. and Greenhut, M. (1975), "Spatial Price Discrimination, Competition and Locational Effects", *Economica,* **42,** 401–419.

Greenhut, M. and Ohta, H. (1975) *Theory of Spatial Pricing and Market Areas* (Durham, N.C.: Duke University Press).

Harris, M. and Raviv, A. (1981), "A Theory of Monopoly Pricing Schemes with Demand Uncertainty", *American Economic Review,* **71,** 347–365.

Harris, M. and Townsend, R. (1981), "Resource Allocation Under Asymmetric Information", *Econometrica,* **49,** 33–64.

Hart, O. (1975), "On the Optimality of Equilibrium When the Market Structure is Incomplete", *Journal of Economic Theory,* **11,** 418–443.

Jaynes, G. (1978), "Equilibria in Monopolistically Competitive Insurance Markets", *Journal of Economic Theory,* **19,** 394–422.

Katz, B. and Yechiali, U. (1979), "How Long will You Wait for What you Really Want or Optimal Strategies for Consumers and Producers When a Queue Forms for a Highly Desired Good" (working paper, New York University).

Katz, M. (1982), "Nonuniform Pricing, Output and Welfare Under Monopoly" (Woodrow Wilson School Discussion Paper, Princeton University).

Kwoka, J. (1979), "Output Under Second-Degree Price Discrimination" (FTC working paper No. 21).

Leland, H. and Meyer, R. (1976), "Monopoly Pricing Structures with Imperfect Discrimination", *Bell Journal of Economics,* **7,** 449–462.

Littlechild, S. C. (1975), "Two-Part Tariffs and Consumption Externalities", *Bell Journal of Economics,* **6,** 661–670.

Maskin, E. and Riley, J. (1981), "Multi-unit Auctions, Price Discrimination and Bundling" (UCLA Discussion Paper No. 201).

Mussa, M. and Rosen, S. (1978), "Monopoly and Product Quality", *Journal of Economic Theory,* **18,** 301–317.

Nichols, D., Smolensky, E. and Tideman, T. (1971), "Discrimination by Waiting Time in Merit Goods", *American Economic Review,* **61,** 312–323.

Palfrey, T. (1980), "Bundling Decisions by a Multiproduct Monopolist with Incomplete Information" (GSIA Working Paper No. 15–80–81, Carnegie-Mellon University).

Parks, R. (1974), "The Demand and Supply of Durable Goods and Durability", *American Economic Review,* **64,** 37–55.

Phillips, O. (1979), "Product Bundles, Price Discrimination and a Two-Product Firm" (Working Paper No. 79–07, Texas A & M University).

Phlips, L. (1980), "Intertemporal Price Discrimination and Sticky Prices", *Quarterly Journal of Economics,* **94,** 525–542.

Pigou, A. C. (1920) *The Economics of Welfare* (London: MacMillan).

Posner, R. (1976) *Antitrust Law: An Economic Perspective* (Chicago: University of Chicago Press).

Prescott, E. and Visscher, M. (1977), "Sequential Location Among Firms with Foresight", *Bell Journal of Economics* **8,** 378–393.

Riley, J. (1979), "Informational Equilibrium", *Econometrica,* **47,** 331–359.

Roberts, K. (1979), "Welfare Considerations of Nonlinear Pricing", *Economic Journal,* **89,** 65–83.

Robinson, J. (1933) *The Economics of Imperfect Competition* (London: MacMillan).

Rothschild, M. and Stiglitz, J. (1976), "Equilibrium in Competitive Insurance Markets: An Essay on the Economics of Imperfect Information", *Quarterly Journal of Economics,* **90,** 629–649.

Salop, S. (1977), "The Noisy Monopolist: Imperfect Information, Price Dispersion and Price Discrimination", *Review of Economic Studies,* **44,** 391–406.

Samuelson, P. (1947) *Foundations of Economic Analysis* (Cambridge, Mass: Harvard University Press).

Scherer, F. (1970) *Industrial Market Structure and Economic Performance* (Chicago: Rand McNally).

Schmalensee, R. (1981*a*), "Monopolistic Two-Part Pricing Arrangements", *Bell Journal of Economics,* **12,** 445–466.

Schmalensee, R. (1981*b*), "Output and Welfare Implications of Third-Degree Price Discrimination", *American Economic Review,* **71,** 242–247.

Smithies, A. (1941), "Monopolistic Price Policy in a Spatial Market", *Econometrica,* **9,** 63–73.

Spatt, C. (1980), "Imperfect Price Discrimination and Variety" (GSIA Working Paper No. 73–79–80, Carnegie-Mellon University).

Spatt, C. (1981), "An Intertemporal Theory of Sales" (GSIA Working Paper No. 48–80–81, Carnegie-Mellon University).

Spence, M. (1973), "Time and Communication in Economic and Social Interaction", *Quarterly Journal of Economics,* **87,** 651–660.

Spence, M. (1974) *Market Signalling: Informational Transfer in Hiring and Related Screening Processes* (Cambridge, Mass: Harvard University Press).

Spence, M. (1977), "Nonlinear Prices and Welfare", *Journal of Public Economics,* **8,** 1–18.

Spence, M. (1978), "Product Differentiation and Performance in Insurance Markets", *Journal of Public Economics,* **10,** 427–447.

Spence, M. (1980), "Multi-Product Quantity-Dependent Prices and Profitability Constraints", *Review of Economic Studies,* **47,** 821–841.

Spulber, D. (1980*a*), "Monopolistic Competition with Nonlinear Pricing" (Department of Economics Working Paper No. 80–6, Brown University).

Spulber, D. (1980*b*), "Nonlinear Price Competition in a Differentiated Industry" (Department of Economics Working Paper No. 80–23, Brown University).

Spulber, D. (1981), "Spatial Competition with Nonlinear Pricing" (presented at the American Economic Association meetings).

Stiglitz, J. (1977), "Monopoly, Non-linear Pricing and Imperfect Information: The Insurance Market", *Review of Economic Studies,* **44,** 407–430.

Stokey, N. (1979), "Intertemporal Price Discrimination", *Quarterly Journal of Economics,* **93,** 355–371.

Telser, L. (1979), "A Theory of Monopoly of Complementary Goods", *Journal of Business,* **52,** 211–230.

Varian, H. (1978) *Microeconomic Analysis* (New York: W. W. Norton).

Willig, R. (1978), "Pareto-superior Nonlinear Outlay Schedules", *Bell Journal of Economics,* **9,** 56–69.

Wilson, R., Oren, S. and Smith, S. (1980), "Competitive Tariffs" (unpublished manuscript).

Wright, J. F. (1965), "Some Reflections on the Place of Discrimination in the Theory of Monopolistic Competition", *Oxford Economic Papers,* **17,** 175–187.

Yamey, B. (1974), "Monopolistic Price Discrimination and Economic Welfare", *Journal of Law and Economics,* **17,** 377–380.

Eight

Chester S. Spatt

Chester S. Spatt received a Ph.D. from the University of Pennsylvania in 1979. He started out at Carnegie Mellon University and still works at Carnegie Mellon University. •

My earliest interactions with Steve Ross occurred during my first year in graduate school in economics at the University of Pennsylvania (spring 1976) when I helped Steve estimate the exponential parameter of constant elasticity of variance processes for equity price dynamics. These estimates were central to the use of such processes in options pricing models, which Steve had started to employ with John Cox and Mark Rubinstein for trading on the floor of the Chicago Board Options Exchange. I felt that I learned a lot from this exercise on many levels—the ease of estimation of one-dimensional problems (even then), the mathematical beauty of Fibonacci numbers and the golden ratio, the power of financial models for practical applications, and even Steve's extraordinary skills as a mentor. When I would report back to Steve on this small project, I always sensed he was several steps ahead of me. After a while I wondered to myself why it was useful for him to have my help. Only much later did I realize that wasn't the point—the project instead provided an effective way for him to mentor and teach me.

As this volume illustrates, Steve has been a master teacher of doctoral students and other aspiring researchers. I found Steve's mentoring (and, of course, his own work) to always emphasize the power of basic concepts and principles and the development of simple frameworks to tackle sophisticated issues in a broad array of market contexts—not just the more traditional studies of equity and fixed-income markets without frictions. He used simple tools and concepts to try to tease out fundamental and robust implications.

Among the specific concepts he emphasized to me when I was a student were the power of the absence of arbitrage, the importance of equilibrium considerations, optionality, dynamic optimization, rational expectations, and the importance of incentives and the structure of information. Over the last several decades, these have continued to be among the most central paradigms in modern financial economics. I benefited tremendously from Steve as a role model in both (a) appreciating the importance of and using the basic theoretical ideas discussed above and (b) developing the breadth of my substantive interests and research in addressing such topics as taxation, mortgages, commodity pricing, asset pricing under rational expectations, arbitrage, and limit order trading.

Among my research directions that I have been the most excited about is my work in recent years with Bob Dammon and Harold Zhang on asset allocation under realistic modeling of capital gains and other taxes. Taxation is an area that I started to learn about from Steve in graduate school. He reflected healthy skepticism about some of the published work at the time and, indeed, I still recall some brief comments that he made about original issue discount bonds—pointing to some interesting clientele and equilibrium effects that the marketplace (and the Treasury) didn't understand for another five years. His own academic contributions in this area were to come later, but I learned at the time that this was an area that was potentially quite rich and would benefit from approaching the problem from the perspectives of different types of agents. My work with Dammon and Zhang has built from some of the simple ideas that have been Steve's hallmark—dynamic optimization, arbitrage, and optionality. While we view taxes as among the most important frictions for investing, surprisingly, that has been a somewhat eclectic perspective among finance professors—but the virtue of being eclectic is another of the insights that's been a key lesson from Steve.

The paper I selected for this volume is Dammon, Spatt, and Zhang (2004), which explores asset location.[1] In particular, it addresses from various perspectives the question of how investors should locate their holdings of equity and debt between taxable personal accounts and tax-deferred retirement accounts, examining both contexts in which the investor can borrow without friction in his personal account and situations in which he faces borrowing constraints. It has been satisfying to hear from a number of distinguished finance professors that they have restructured their own asset location patterns after reading our paper. The paper utilizes for defined-contribution and taxable investing both (a) the arbitrage approach pioneered by Black and Tepper[2] in the context of locating assets between a corporate defined-benefit pension plan and the firm's general account and applies (b) the dynamic framework and numerical techniques developed in Dammon, Spatt, and Zhang (2001) for solving for optimal portfolio rebalancing given capital gains taxes triggered upon asset sales to situations in which the investor has both a taxable and tax-deferred account.[3] At a broader level, our paper on asset location offers a framework that can be used for integrating diverse tax treatments in different accounts into a dynamic portfolio setting.

[1]Dammon, R., C. Spatt, and H. Zhang, 2004, "Optimal Asset Location and Allocation with Taxable and Tax-deferred Investing," *Journal of Finance* 59, 999–1037.
[2]Black, F., 1980, "The Tax Consequences of Long-run Pension Policy," *Financial Analysts Journal* 36, 21–28, and Tepper, I., 1981, "Taxation and Corporate Pension Policy," *Journal of Finance* 36, 1–13.
[3]Dammon, R., C. Spatt, and H. Zhang, 2001, "Optimal Consumption and Investment with Capital Gains Taxes," *Review of Financial Studies* 14, 583–616.

Optimal Asset Location and Allocation with Taxable and Tax-Deferred Investing

*Robert M. Dammon, Chester S. Spatt, and Harold H. Zhang**

Abstract

We investigate optimal intertemporal asset allocation and location decisions for investors making taxable and tax-deferred investments. We show a strong preference for holding taxable bonds in the tax-deferred account and equity in the taxable account, reflecting the higher tax burden on taxable bonds relative to equity. For most investors, the optimal asset location policy is robust to the introduction of tax-exempt bonds and liquidity shocks. Numerical results illustrate optimal portfolio decisions as a function of age and tax-deferred wealth. Interestingly, the proportion of total wealth allocated to equity is inversely related to the fraction of total wealth in tax-deferred accounts. •

A central problem confronting investors in practice is how to efficiently invest the funds held in their taxable and tax-deferred savings accounts. The problem involves making both an optimal *asset allocation* decision (i.e., deciding how much of each asset to hold) and an optimal *asset location* decision (i.e., deciding which assets to hold in the taxable and tax-deferred accounts). Investors would like to make these decisions to reduce the tax burden of owning financial assets, while maintaining an optimally diversified portfolio over time. While only limited guidance is available to investors faced with this problem, the decision is crucial to the wealth accumulation and welfare of investors over their lifetimes.

In this paper, we examine the intertemporal portfolio problem for an investor with the opportunity to invest in both a taxable and tax-deferred savings account. In particular, we investigate how the opportunity for tax-deferred investing influences the investor's overall portfolio composition and how these asset holdings are allocated between the taxable and tax-deferred accounts. Our approach takes account of the investor's age, existing portfolio holdings, embedded capital gains, and available wealth levels in the taxable and tax-deferred accounts for the asset allocation and location decisions. This is in striking contrast to the traditional approach to financial planning, in which the interaction between the taxable and tax-deferred accounts is largely ignored.

The ability to invest on a tax-deferred basis is valuable to investors because it allows them to earn the pre-tax return on assets. However, because assets differ in terms of the tax

---

*Robert M. Dammon and Chester S. Spatt are from Carnegie Mellon University. Harold H. Zhang is from the University of North Carolina at Chapel Hill. We thank Gene Amromin, Peter Bossaerts, Jerome Detemple, Doug Fore, Richard Green, Mark Kritzman, Robert McDonald (the editor), Peter Schotman, two anonymous referees, and seminar participants at the California Institute of Technology, Fields Institute (Toronto), London Business School, New York University, the University of Pittsburgh, the University of Southern California, the University of Utah, Washington University in Saint Louis, the 2000 Western Finance Association Meetings at Sun Valley, the Stanford Institute for Economic Policy Research Asset Location Conference, and the Center for Economic Policy Research Summer Symposium at Gerzensee, Switzerland, for helpful comments. The financial support provided by the Teachers Insurance Annuity Association–College Retirement Equities Fund is gratefully acknowledged.
Reprinted with permission:
Dammon, Robert M., Chester S. Spatt, and Harold H. Zhang. "Optimal Asset Location and Allocation with Taxable and Tax-Deferred Investing." *The Journal of Finance* 59 (2004): 999–1037.

liabilities they create for investors, the value of tax-deferred investing depends upon which assets are held in the tax-deferred account. For example, it is well understood that holding municipal bonds in a tax-deferred account is tax inefficient because municipal bond interest is nontaxable. Our analysis of the optimal asset location policy focuses mainly on taxable bonds and equity. We show that there is a strong locational preference for holding taxable bonds in the tax-deferred account and equity in the taxable account. This preference reflects the higher tax burden on taxable bonds relative to equity. When held in the taxable account, equity generates less ordinary income than taxable bonds, provides the investor with a valuable tax-timing option to realize capital losses and defer capital gains, and allows the investor to avoid payment of the tax on capital gains altogether at the time of death. Our analysis also examines the circumstances under which equity ownership arises in the tax-deferred account despite its greater attractiveness in the taxable account.

When investors have unrestricted borrowing opportunities in the taxable account, the optimal asset location policy involves allocating the entire tax-deferred account to taxable bonds. Investors then combine either borrowing or lending with investment in equity in the taxable account to achieve their desired risk exposure. The optimal asset location policy with unrestricted borrowing opportunities follows directly from the arbitrage arguments made by Black (1980) and Tepper (1981), who analyze the optimal investment policy for corporations with defined-benefit pension plans.[1] Investors are indifferent to the location of their asset holdings only if capital gains and losses are taxed on an accrual basis (i.e., no deferral option) and at the same tax rate that applies to ordinary income. This implies that even the most tax-inefficient equity mutual funds (i.e., those that distribute a large fraction of their capital gains each year) are better suited for the taxable account than are taxable bonds.

In a series of recent papers, Shoven (1999), Shoven and Sialm (2003), and Poterba, Shoven, and Sialm (2001) question the tax-efficiency of holding equity in the taxable account and taxable bonds in the tax-deferred account when investors have the option to invest in tax-exempt bonds. They argue that because actively managed equity mutual funds distribute a large fraction of their capital gains each year, it can be optimal to locate them in the tax-deferred account and hold tax-exempt bonds in the taxable account. Using arbitrage arguments, we show that the strategy of holding an actively managed equity mutual fund in the tax-deferred account and tax-exempt bonds in the taxable account can be optimal only if the actively managed equity mutual fund (1) is highly tax inefficient and (2) substantially outperforms similar tax-efficient equity investments (e.g., individual stocks, passive index funds, or exchange-traded funds) on a risk-adjusted basis. Given the well-documented underperformance of actively managed equity mutual funds, we argue that investors are better off holding tax-efficient equity investments, locating them in the taxable account, and holding taxable bonds in the tax-deferred account. Of course, highly taxed investors who wish to hold a mix of stocks and bonds in the taxable account may still find tax-exempt bonds to be a better alternative than taxable bonds.

When investors are prohibited from borrowing, the optimal asset location policy is slightly more complicated. Although investors still have a preference for holding taxable bonds in the tax-deferred account, it may not be optimal to allocate the entire tax-deferred account to taxable bonds if doing so causes the overall portfolio to be overweighted in bonds. This is because offsetting portfolio adjustments in the taxable account are no longer possible when borrowing is prohibited. In this case, investors may hold a mix of stocks and

[1]Black (1980) and Tepper (1981) show that it is tax efficient for corporations to fully fund their pension plans, borrowing on corporate account if necessary, and to invest the pension plan assets entirely in taxable bonds. The implications of the Black–Tepper arbitrage results for optimal asset location for individual investors were first discussed in Dammon, Spatt, and Zhang (1999) and formally illustrated by Huang (2000).

bonds in their tax-deferred accounts, but only if they hold an all-equity portfolio in their taxable accounts. Investors may still hold a mix of stocks and (taxable or tax-exempt) bonds in the taxable account, but only if they hold a portfolio composed entirely of taxable bonds in their tax-deferred accounts. Investors do not simultaneously hold a mix of stocks and bonds in both the taxable and tax-deferred accounts.

With most or all of the taxable account allocated to equity, the investor may face liquidity problems if the value of equity declines substantially. With a dramatic decline in equity, the investor may be forced to liquidate a portion of the tax-deferred account to finance consumption. For some investors, withdrawing funds from the tax-deferred account may require the payment of a penalty. In principle, this can provide an incentive to hold some additional bonds in the taxable account to reduce the risk of needing to withdraw funds from the tax-deferred account. Contrary to this intuition, we find that the tax benefit of locating taxable bonds in the tax-deferred account generally outweighs the liquidity benefit of holding taxable bonds in the taxable account. Investors are willing to shift the location of taxable bonds from the tax-deferred account to the taxable account only if catastrophic shocks to consumption (or income) are highly negatively correlated with equity returns. Even in these cases, however, the demand for bonds in the taxable account for liquidity reasons is small relative to the total holding of bonds. The risk of a liquidity shock has a much larger impact on the investor's willingness to make additional contributions to the tax-deferred account.

We investigate numerically the investor's lifetime portfolio problem by incorporating a tax-deferred investment account into the intertemporal consumption–investment model developed by Dammon, Spatt, and Zhang (2001).[2] We illustrate how the relative wealth levels in the taxable and tax-deferred accounts influence the optimal asset location and allocation decisions. With the ability to borrow in the taxable account, the optimal overall holding of equity is relatively insensitive to the split of total wealth between the taxable and tax-deferred accounts. However, because the investor allocates 100% of the tax-deferred account to taxable bonds in this case, the proportion of the taxable account allocated to equity can exceed 100% (i.e., a levered equity position) at high levels of tax-deferred wealth. When investors are prohibited from borrowing, the holding of equity in the taxable account is capped at 100%. In this case, we find that equity can spill over into the tax-deferred account, but only at very high levels of tax-deferred wealth. However, because equity is less valuable when held in the tax-deferred account, the proportion of total wealth allocated to equity is lower at higher levels of tax-deferred wealth.

The results we derive on the optimal location of asset holdings are in sharp contrast to the financial advice that investors receive in practice. Financial advisors commonly recommend that investors hold a mix of stocks and bonds in both their taxable and tax-deferred accounts, with some financial advisors recommending that investors tilt their tax-deferred accounts toward equity. The asset location decisions made in practice mirror these recommendations, with many investors holding equity in a tax-deferred account and bonds in a taxable account. Poterba and Samwick (2003) report that 48.3% of investors who own taxable bonds in taxable accounts also own equity in tax-deferred accounts and that 41.6% of investors who own equity in tax-deferred accounts also own taxable bonds

[2]The intertemporal consumption-investment model of Dammon, Spatt, and Zhang (2001) incorporates many realistic features of the U.S. tax code, including the taxation of capital gains upon realization and the forgiveness of the tax on embedded capital gains at the time of death. The impact of optimal tax timing on the realization and trading behavior of investors is also studied by Constantinides (1983, 1984), Dammon, Dunn, and Spatt (1989), Dammon and Spatt (1996), and Williams (1985). In contrast to this earlier work, the Dammon, Spatt, and Zhang (2001) model incorporates an optimal intertemporal portfolio decision, which involves a tradeoff between the diversification benefits and tax costs of trading.

in taxable accounts. They also document that 53.1% of the owners of tax-exempt bonds also owned equity in tax-deferred accounts and that 11.3% of the owners of equity in tax-deferred accounts also owned tax-exempt bonds. Bergstresser and Poterba (2002) and Amromin (2001) report similar findings and document that a large proportion of investors have substantially more equity in their tax-deferred accounts than in their taxable accounts. We investigate the welfare costs of locating assets suboptimally between the taxable and tax-deferred accounts and find that these costs can be quite high, especially for young investors.

The paper is organized as follows. In Section I, we derive some general theoretical results regarding optimal asset location using basic arbitrage arguments. We examine the effects of borrowing and short-sale constraints, tax-exempt bonds, and liquidity shocks on the optimal asset location policy. In Section II, we present our numerical analysis of the investor's intertemporal portfolio problem, focusing on the case where there are restrictions on borrowing and short sales. Particular attention is given to the optimal asset allocation and location decisions as a function of age and the level of tax-deferred wealth. We also conduct a welfare analysis of the optimal asset location policy and investigate the effects of exogenous liquidity shocks on the asset location and retirement contribution decisions. Section III concludes the paper.

I. Optimal Asset Location

A. No Borrowing or Short-sale Constraints

In this section, we use arbitrage arguments to derive results on the optimal location of asset holdings. Our approach extends the arbitrage approaches used by Black (1980) and Tepper (1981) to analyze corporate pension policy and by Huang (2000) to analyze the asset location decision. The arbitrage approach involves making a risk-preserving change in the location of asset holdings to determine whether the after-tax return on the investor's portfolio can be improved. The objective is to identify the asset location policy that produces the highest expected utility of after-tax wealth for the investor.

We initially assume that investors are *forced* to realize all capital gains and losses each year (i.e., no deferral option) and have *unrestricted* borrowing and short-sale opportunities in their taxable accounts. (We later relax these assumptions to see what effect they have on the optimal location decision.) We also assume that the tax rate on ordinary income (dividends and interest), τ_d, is higher than the tax rate on capital gains and losses, τ_g. Under these conditions we show that investors prefer to allocate their entire tax-deferred wealth to the asset with the *highest yield.*[3] Investors then adjust the asset holdings in their taxable accounts, borrowing or selling short if necessary, to achieve their optimal overall risk exposure. For our purposes, we define *yield* as the fraction of total asset value (price) that is distributed as either dividends or interest.

We define the random pre-tax return on asset i as $\tilde{r}_i = (1 + d_i)(1 + \tilde{g}_i) - 1$, where d_i denotes the constant pre-tax yield on asset i and $\tilde{g}_i$ denotes the random pre-tax capital gain return on asset i. For the riskless taxable bond (asset 0), we assume that $\tilde{g}_0 = 0$ and $d_0 = r$. Consider an investor in this environment who has positive holdings of both the riskless taxable bond and risky asset i in the tax-deferred account. For this investor, a shift of one

[3]Under recent tax law changes, the tax rate on dividend income is less than the tax rate on interest income. In this case, it may not be optimal to hold the asset with the highest yield in the tax-deferred account. The implications of differential tax rates on dividend and interest income are discussed later.

after-tax dollar from asset i to the riskless taxable bond in the tax-deferred account, offset by a shift of x_i dollars from the riskless taxable bond (either through an outright sale or through borrowing) to asset i in the taxable account, leads to the following change in the investor's total wealth next period:[4]

$$\begin{aligned}\Delta \widetilde{W}_i &= \Delta \widetilde{W}_i^R + \Delta \widetilde{W}_i^T \\ &= \{r - [(1 + \widetilde{g}_i)(1 + d_i) - 1]\} \\ &\quad + x_i\{(1 + \widetilde{g}_i)(1 + d_i(1 - \tau_d)) - \widetilde{g}_i\tau_g - 1] - r(1 - \tau_d)\},\end{aligned} \tag{1}$$

where $\Delta \widetilde{W}_i^R = \{r - [(1 + \widetilde{g}_i)(1 + d_i) - 1]\}$ is the marginal change in tax-deferred (retirement) wealth and $\Delta \widetilde{W}_i^T = x_i\{[(1 + \widetilde{g}_i)(1 + d_i(1 - \tau_d)) - \widetilde{g}_i\tau_g - 1] - r(1 - \tau_d)\}$ is the marginal change in taxable wealth. Letting $x_i = (1 + d_i)/[1 + d_i(1 - \tau_d) - \tau_g]$, it is easily shown that for all values of $\widetilde{g}_i$,

$$\Delta \widetilde{W}_i = x_i\left[\frac{(r - d_i)(\tau_d - \tau_g)}{1 + d_i}\right] = C_i. \tag{2}$$

Since C_i is independent of $\widetilde{g}_i$, it represents a *risk-free* after-tax payoff that can be generated by shifting the location of asset holdings. However, because wealth in the tax-deferred account is more valuable than wealth in the taxable account, there is no guarantee that the change in the expected utility of total wealth has the same sign as C_i if the taxable and tax-deferred accounts are affected differently. To verify that the change in expected utility has the same sign as C_i, let $\widetilde{U}'$ denote the marginal utility of taxable wealth and $m\widetilde{U}'$ denote the marginal utility of tax-deferred wealth, where $m > 1$ is the *shadow price* of taxable wealth per dollar of tax-deferred wealth.[5] Then the change in expected utility is

$$\Delta E[\widetilde{U}] = E[\widetilde{U}'\Delta \widetilde{W}_i^T] + mE[\widetilde{U}'\Delta \widetilde{W}_i^R].$$

Because the investor has unrestricted borrowing and short-sale opportunities in the taxable account, there must be indifference between bonds and stocks at the margin in this account. This implies that the first-order optimality conditions must satisfy $E[\widetilde{U}'\Delta \widetilde{W}_i^T] = 0$. Using $\Delta \widetilde{W}_i^R = C_i - \Delta \widetilde{W}_i^T$, where C_i is given by equation (2), the change in expected utility becomes

$$\Delta E[\widetilde{U}] = mC_iE[\widetilde{U}'],$$

which clearly indicates that $\Delta E[\widetilde{U}]$ is of the same sign as C_i.

If $C_i > 0$, then the investor is strictly better off holding taxable bonds in the tax-deferred account and asset i in the taxable account. If $C_i < 0$, then the investor is strictly better off holding taxable bonds in the taxable account and asset i in the tax-deferred

[4]An *after-tax* dollar in the tax-deferred account refers to a dollar owned by the investor in that account. For example, if the investor contributes *pre-tax* income to the tax-deferred account, the government taxes withdrawals from the account as ordinary income. In this case, the investor owns the fraction $(1 - \tau_d)$ of his tax-deferred account and the government owns the fraction τ_d. A one-dollar shift of the investor's wealth in the tax-deferred account would then require an actual shift of $1/(1 - \tau_d)$ of the total account balance. This is equivalent to allowing investors to contribute *after-tax* income to the tax-deferred account and imposing no tax on withdrawals (e.g., Roth IRA). In this case, the investor owns 100% of his tax-deferred account.

[5]Wealth is more valuable in the tax-deferred account because of the ability to earn pre-tax returns in this account. The shadow price, m, is higher for investors who have longer horizons (i.e., younger investors) over which to benefit from tax-deferred savings. When investors are prohibited from borrowing, the shadow price of tax-deferred wealth may also be a function of the split of wealth between the taxable and tax-deferred accounts. Section II.D provides numerical estimates of the shadow prices in this case.

account. To determine the tax benefit of shifting one after-tax dollar from risky asset i to risky asset j in the tax-deferred account, with an offsetting adjustment in the taxable account, one simply needs to compute the difference $(C_i - C_j)$. Only if $C_i = 0$ for all i is the investor indifferent to the location of his asset holdings.

Since x_i is strictly positive, the sign of C_i depends upon the sign of $(r - d_i)(\tau_d - \tau_g)$. If $\tau_d = \tau_g$, then $C_i = 0$ for all i and the investor is indifferent to the location of his asset holdings. This indifference result is independent of the expected returns and yields on assets and only requires that the total returns on all assets be taxed identically each year. When $\tau_d > \tau_g$, the sign of C_i depends upon the sign of $(r - d_i)$, with the value of C_i monotonically *decreasing* in d_i. Thus, when $\tau_d > \tau_g$ the investor prefers to allocate his entire tax-deferred wealth to the asset with the *highest yield,* with all other assets held in the taxable account.[6] After allocating the entire tax-deferred wealth to the asset with the highest yield, the investor then adjusts the asset holdings in the taxable account, borrowing or selling short if necessary, to achieve the desired overall risk exposure. This asset location policy provides the investor with the highest level of tax efficiency while maintaining the risk profile of his overall portfolio. The optimal asset location policy is also independent of the joint distribution of asset returns and investors' preferences.

It is widely believed that because actively managed mutual funds distribute significant capital gains each year, it can be tax-efficient to hold these funds (to the extent that they are held at all) in a tax-deferred account. Similarly, it is believed that an investor who engages in active trading should do so in a tax-deferred account to avoid the payment of capital gains taxes. Our analysis of the optimal asset location policy sheds some light on this issue. Recall that our analysis is based upon the assumption that investors are *forced* to realize all capital gains and losses each year (i.e., no deferral option). Yet, despite the inability to defer capital gains, our analysis indicates that it is still optimal to locate the asset with the *highest yield* in the tax-deferred account provided $\tau_d > \tau_g$.[7] Thus, even though actively managed mutual funds distribute most, or even all, of their capital gains each year, they should not be held in the tax-deferred account if taxable bonds have higher yields. Only in the extreme case in which the actively managed mutual fund distributes 100% of its capital gains each year, with all gains realized *short term* so that $\tau_g = \tau_d$, would the investor be *indifferent* to holding the actively managed mutual fund or riskless taxable bond in the tax-deferred account.[8]

[6] When the tax rate on dividend income (τ_d) is lower than the tax rate on interest income (τ_0) the sign of C_i in Equation (2) depends upon the sign of $[r(\tau_0 - \tau_g) - d_i(\tau_i - \tau_g)]$, where τ_i is equal to τ_d if d_i is dividend income or τ_0 if d_i is interest income. In this case, it is optimal to hold the asset with the highest value of $d_i(\tau_i - \tau_g)$ in the tax-deferred account. Under recent changes to U.S. tax rates, dividends and capital gain income are taxed at the same rate, while interest income is taxed at a higher rate (i.e., $\tau_0 > \tau_d = \tau_g$). This implies that it is not optimal to hold equity in the tax-deferred account, regardless of the magnitude of the dividend yield on equity.

[7] For mutual funds that distribute both long-term and short-term capital gains, the capital gains tax rate is a weighted average of the long-term and short-term tax rates, with the weights determined by the proportion of the total capital gain that is of each type. If all capital gains are realized short-term each year, then $\tau_d = \tau_g$. Otherwise, $\tau_d > \tau_g$, even for the most active of mutual funds.

[8] When capital gain tax rates are allowed to differ across assets, the riskless taxable bond will still be held in the tax-deferred account provided it has the highest yield (i.e., $d_i < r$ for all i). However, if the dividend yields on some assets exceed the riskless taxable interest rate, then the asset with the highest yield may *not* be held in the tax-deferred account. In this case, the values of C_i in equation (2) for different assets depend upon both the yield and asset-specific capital gains tax rate.

B. Tax-exempt Bonds

According to the above analysis, it is tax efficient to hold equity (or equity mutual funds) in the taxable account and taxable bonds in the tax-deferred account if taxable bonds have higher yields. In a recent paper, Shoven and Sialm (2003) argue that this policy can be overturned if investors have the opportunity to invest in *tax-exempt* bonds. Rather than holding taxable bonds in the tax-deferred account and equity in the taxable account, they show that it can be optimal to hold tax-exempt bonds in the taxable account and equity in the tax-deferred account. Using our framework to analyze this alternative strategy, the risk-free change in total wealth from shifting one after-tax dollar from taxable bonds to equity in the tax-deferred account and $x = (1 + d)/[1 + d(1 - \tau_d) - \tau_g]$ dollars from equity to *tax-exempt* bonds in the taxable account is

$$\hat{C} = x\left[r(\tau_d - \tau_m) - \frac{(r - d)(\tau_d - \tau_g)}{1 + d}\right], \tag{3}$$

where τ_m is the implicit tax rate reflected in the yield differential between riskless taxable bond and riskless tax-exempt bonds.[9] Using arguments similar to those used earlier, one can show that the change in expected utility is of the same sign as $\hat{C}$. If $\tau_g > \tau_d - [r(\tau_d - \tau_m)(1 + d)]/(r - d)$, then $\hat{C} > 0$ and it is optimal for the investor to hold equity in the tax-deferred account and tax-exempt bonds in the taxable account. Assuming $r = 6\%$, $d = 2\%$, $\tau_d = 36\%$, and $\tau_m = 25\%$, $\hat{C} > 0$ for all $\tau_g > 19.17\%$.[10] For a tax-inefficient equity mutual fund that realizes 75% of its capital gains each year, two-thirds of which are short term and one-third of which are long term, the effective capital gains tax rate is $\tau_g = 23\%$. In contrast, for a tax-efficient index fund that realizes only 15% of its capital gains each year, 5% of which are short term and 95% of which are long term, the effective capital gains tax rate is only $\tau_g = 3.12\%$.[11] Clearly it can be optimal to hold equity in the tax-deferred account, and tax-exempt bonds in the taxable account, but only if the form of the equity holding is *highly* tax inefficient.

While the above analysis is instructive, it does not directly answer the question as to whether it is better to hold a tax-efficient index fund in the taxable account and taxable bonds in the tax-deferred account, or to hold an actively managed (tax-inefficient) equity mutual fund in the tax-deferred account and tax-exempt bonds in the taxable account. Assume that the two equity funds have identical dividend yields and are perfectly correlated on a pre-tax basis. Let τ_{gi} denote the effective capital gains tax rate on the tax-efficient index fund. It is straightforward to show that a shift of one after-tax dollar from taxable bonds to the actively managed equity mutual fund (asset j) in the tax-deferred account, offset by a

[9] Equation (3) applies only to those investors who do not borrow in their taxable accounts. If investors do borrow, then the U.S. tax code disallows the interest deduction on an amount of borrowing equal to the tax-exempt holdings. This has the effect of setting $\tau_d = \tau_m$ in equation (3) for each dollar of borrowing that is not allowed the tax deduction. The net effect is to lower the benefit of shifting equity into the tax-deferred account for investors that hold levered equity positions.

[10] The implicit tax rate $\tau_m = 25\%$ is the 30-year average for long-term municipal bonds reported by Shoven and Sialm (2003). The implicit tax rate on short-term municipal bonds is typically closer to the statutory marginal tax rate for high-income investors. Green (1993) provides an equilibrium model of the municipal term structure that relies on clientele arguments and is broadly consistent with the empirical evidence.

[11] The effective capital gains tax rate is based upon the assumption that long-term capital gains are taxed at 20%, short-term capital gains are taxed at 36%, and unrealized capital gains are untaxed by virtue of the fact that investors can defer the realization of capital gains until death, at which time the embedded tax liability is forgiven. The realization percentages used to calculate the effective capital gains tax rates for actively managed and index mutual funds are broadly consistent with those reported in Shoven and Sialm (2003).

shift of $x_{ij} = (1 + d_j)/[1 + d_j(1 - \tau_d) - \tau_{gi}]$ dollars from the index fund (asset i) to tax-exempt bonds in the taxable account, produces the following *riskless* after-tax cash flow:[12]

$$\hat{C}_{ij} = [d_j + \alpha_j(1 + d_j) - r] - x_{ij}[d_j(1 - \tau_d) - r(1 - \tau_m)], \tag{4}$$

where $\alpha_j = (\tilde{g}_j - \tilde{g}_i)$ is the *riskless* pre-tax capital gain return differential between the actively managed equity mutual fund and the tax-efficient index fund. Thus, we can interpret $\alpha_j(1 + d_j)$ as the *certainty-equivalent* pre-tax abnormal return (net of transaction costs and fees) on the actively managed equity mutual fund. Using the tax rates, dividend yields, and interest rates from above, the value of $\hat{C}_{ij}$ is strictly positive provided $\alpha_j(1 + d_j) > 0.00654$. This implies that it is optimal to hold the actively managed equity mutual fund in the tax-deferred account and municipal bonds in the taxable account (instead of taxable bonds in the tax-deferred account and the tax-efficient index fund in the taxable account) only if the actively managed equity mutual fund generates a certainty-equivalent pre-tax abnormal return (net of transaction costs and fees) of at least 65.4 basis points per year.[13] Moreover, since it is not uncommon for actively managed equity mutual funds to have expense ratios that are 100 basis points or more above that of a passive index fund, a certainty-equivalent pre-tax abnormal return (before transaction costs and fees) of 165 basis points or more may be necessary before it is beneficial to hold the actively managed equity mutual fund in the tax-deferred account. Given the well-documented underperformance of actively managed equity mutual funds (see, e.g., Gruber (1996) and Carhart (1997)), investors are more likely to benefit from holding taxable bonds in their tax-deferred accounts and tax-efficient equity investments (e.g., individual stocks, index funds, and exchange-traded funds) in their taxable accounts.

C. Borrowing Constraints and Liquidity

With unrestricted borrowing and short-sale opportunities, the investor optimally allocates his entire tax-deferred wealth to the asset with the highest yield (typically taxable bonds) and either borrows or sells short in the taxable account to achieve the desired risk exposure. If the investor faces restrictions on borrowing or selling short, then the optimal asset location policy is more complicated. In this case, the investor shifts his tax-deferred wealth into the asset with the highest yield until offsetting adjustments in the taxable account are no longer possible because of the borrowing or short-sale restrictions. The investor then begins to allocate the remaining tax-deferred wealth to the asset with the next highest yield until the restrictions again bind. The process continues with successively lower yielding assets until the investor's tax-deferred wealth has been completely allocated. Thus, with borrowing and short-sale constraints, the investor may hold a mix of taxable bonds and equity in the tax-deferred account, but only if the taxable account is invested entirely in assets with lower yields.[14]

---

[12]We are implicitly assuming that the financial markets are rich enough that a portfolio of securities can be constructed to match any risk and yield characteristics the investor desires. The assumption of perfect correlation implies that the return on asset j is of the following form: $\tilde{g}_j = \gamma_j \tilde{g}_i + \alpha_j$. Without loss of generality, we assume that $\gamma_j = 1$ in our analysis.

[13]If the dividend yields on both funds are zero, then the *certainty-equivalent* pre-tax abnormal return (net of transaction costs and fees) on the actively managed equity mutual fund must exceed 135.5 basis points per year.

[14]Our discussion here assumes that the tax rate on capital gains, τ_g, is identical across all risky assets. If not, then assets will be ranked on the basis of the values of $-C_i$ (with τ_{gi} replacing τ_g) in equation (2) instead of yields. Moreover, if dividends and capital gains are taxed at the same rate, while interest is taxed at a higher rate ($\tau_0 > \tau_d = \tau_g$), then dividend yields are irrelevant and the investor should never hold equity in the tax-deferred account at the same time taxable bonds are held in the taxable account.

While the optimal asset location policy maximizes the tax efficiency of the investor's overall portfolio, it also increases the risk of the taxable portfolio relative to the tax-deferred portfolio. With restrictions on borrowing and short sales, this shift in risk between the taxable and tax-deferred accounts may become important for some investors. For example, an investor with relatively little taxable wealth (relative to tax-deferred wealth) may wish to control the risk of his taxable portfolio to guarantee a minimum level of consumption. It is instructive, therefore, to investigate the extent to which liquidity considerations can affect the asset location decision.

Consider an investor who currently has all equity in the taxable account and a mix of taxable bonds and equity in the tax-deferred account. In the absence of liquidity considerations, this asset location choice is tax-efficient, as long as taxable bonds have a higher yield than equity. Now assume that the investor shifts one dollar from taxable bonds to equity in the tax-deferred account and $x = (1 + d)/[1 + d(1 - \tau_d) - \tau_g]$ dollars from equity to taxable bonds in the taxable account. As we have seen earlier, this shift in asset location is ex ante tax-inefficient. The benefit of the shift is that it will reduce the risk of the taxable account and potentially increase the funds available to finance any unforeseen consumption shocks, thereby reducing the need to withdraw funds from the tax-deferred account. The incremental wealth in the investor's taxable account as a result of the shift from equity to taxable bonds is

$$\Delta \widetilde{W}^T = x\{r(1 - \tau_d) - [(1 + \widetilde{g})(1 + d(1 - \tau_d)) - \widetilde{g}\,\tau_g - 1]\} = \widetilde{z}^T. \tag{5}$$

The change in wealth in the tax-deferred account as a result of the shift from taxable bonds to equity is

$$\Delta \widetilde{W}^R = \left[\frac{1 - \tau_d}{1 - \tau_d - p}\right]\widetilde{z}^T\widetilde{I} - \widetilde{z}^R, \tag{6}$$

where $\widetilde{z}^R = \{r - [(1 + \widetilde{g})(1 + d) - 1]\}$, p is the penalty per dollar withdrawn from the tax-deferred account, and $\widetilde{I} = 1$ if a consumption shock occurs next period that *exceeds* the investor's wealth in the taxable account and $\widetilde{I} = 0$ otherwise.[15] The shift in asset location has two effects on tax-deferred wealth. The first term in equation (6) is the incremental wealth in the tax-deferred account that must be liquidated to help finance a shortfall in the taxable account resulting from a large shock to consumption. The second term, $\widetilde{z}^R$, is the change in tax-deferred wealth resulting from the differential returns on bonds and stocks.

To determine whether it is beneficial for the investor to hold some bonds in the taxable account for liquidity reasons, we need to evaluate the effect of the shift in asset location on expected utility. Letting m denote the shadow price of taxable wealth per dollar of tax-deferred wealth, the change in expected utility is[16]

$$\begin{aligned}\Delta E[\widetilde{U}] &= E[\widetilde{U}'\Delta \widetilde{W}^T] + mE[\widetilde{U}'\Delta \widetilde{W}^R]\\ &= E[\widetilde{U}'\widetilde{z}^T] + \left[\frac{m(1 - \tau_d)}{1 - \tau_d - p}\right]E[\widetilde{U}'(\widetilde{z}^T\widetilde{I})],\end{aligned} \tag{7}$$

[15]Here we assume that the total amount of funds withdrawn from the tax-deferred account is subject to tax and penalty. In this case, the investor must withdraw $\widetilde{z}^T[(1 - \tau_d)/(1 - \tau_d - p)]$ of his after-tax retirement account wealth to generate $\widetilde{z}^T$ of incremental wealth in the taxable account after the payment of taxes and the penalty for early withdrawal. If withdrawals from the tax-deferred account are not subject to tax (e.g., Roth IRA), then the investor must withdraw $\widetilde{z}^T/(1 - p)$ to generate $\widetilde{z}^T$ of incremental wealth in the taxable account after the payment of the penalty.

[16]Although the shadow price of taxable wealth per dollar of tax-deferred wealth, m, will depend upon the split of wealth between the two accounts when investors cannot borrow, as a first approximation we shall treat m as a constant.

where $E[\tilde{U}'\tilde{z}^R] = 0$ by virtue of the fact that we have assumed that the investor holds both bonds and stocks in the tax-deferred account and, therefore, is indifferent between the two securities at the margin. Next, note that $(\tilde{z}^R - \tilde{z}^T)$ is equal to the positive risk-free after-tax payoff C (ignoring the i subscript) in equation (2). This implies that $E[\tilde{U}'\tilde{z}^T] = E[\tilde{U}'(\tilde{z}^R - C)] = -CE[\tilde{U}']$. Substituting this into the above equation, multiplying and dividing the right-hand side by $E(\tilde{U}')$, yields

$$\Delta E[\tilde{U}] = \left\{\left[\frac{m(1-\tau_d)}{1-\tau_d-p}\right]\hat{E}[\tilde{z}^T\tilde{I}] - C\right\}E[\tilde{U}'], \tag{8}$$

where $\hat{E}(\cdot)$ is the expectation operator under the risk-neutral measure.[17] The value of $\Delta E[\tilde{U}]$ is positive provided

$$\hat{E}[\tilde{z}^T\tilde{I}] > C\left[\frac{(1-\tau_d-p)}{m(1-\tau_d)}\right]. \tag{9}$$

There are some interesting properties of the expression for $\Delta E[\tilde{U}]$. First, note that if there is no uncertainty in $\tilde{I}$ (i.e., either $\tilde{I} = 0$ or $\tilde{I} = 1$ with certainty), the value of $\Delta E[\tilde{U}]$ is strictly negative (since $\hat{E}[\tilde{z}^T] = -C$). Hence, for investors who have sufficient wealth in their taxable accounts that a consumption shock can easily be financed without having to access the tax-deferred account ($\tilde{I} = 0$ with certainty), or for investors who are certain to have consumption needs that exceed the wealth in their taxable accounts ($\tilde{I} = 1$ with certainty), it is not optimal to hold taxable bonds in the taxable account for liquidity reasons. It is only those investors who face some uncertainty about being hit with a shock to consumption that exceeds their taxable wealth for whom liquidity risk may be important. Second, note that even if $\tilde{I}$ is uncertain, but is either uncorrelated or negatively correlated with $\tilde{z}^T$ under the risk-neutral measure, the value of $\Delta E[\tilde{U}]$ will again be negative. This implies that the benefits of shifting taxable bonds into the taxable account to hedge against liquidity shocks can be optimal only when the liquidity shocks are positively correlated with $\tilde{z}^T$ (i.e., negatively correlated with equity returns) under the risk-neutral measure. The last thing to note is that the value of $\Delta E[\tilde{U}]$ can be positive even if there is no penalty for early withdrawal (i.e., if $p = 0$). This is because withdrawing funds from the tax-deferred account and forgoing the opportunity to earn pre-tax returns is costly to the investor.

The above analysis provides some useful insights regarding the conditions under which liquidity considerations can influence the asset location decision. It requires a positive probability (less than one) of a shock to consumption that exceeds the investor's resources in the taxable account (including any borrowing opportunities), combined with a sufficiently negative correlation between these shocks and equity returns. While this may be a concern for some investors, it is not likely to be a major concern for most investors. For investors who can access their tax-deferred accounts without penalty (i.e., investors older than $59\frac{1}{2}$ or who become disabled), there is little benefit from maintaining significant liquidity in the taxable account. Many investors also receive nonfinancial (labor) income and have some ability to borrow to smooth consumption. On the whole, we do not believe that liquidity shocks alone can generate significant hedging demand for bonds in the taxable account. We investigate numerically the effect of liquidity shocks on asset location and retirement contribution decisions in Section II.E.

[17]The derivation of the expression for $E(\tilde{U})$ is based upon the assumption that the investor holds all equity in the taxable account and a mix of bonds and equity in the tax-deferred account. If, instead, the investor holds all bonds in the tax-deferred account and a mix of bonds and equity in the taxable account, then the only change is that the shadow price, m, does not appear on the right-hand side of the expression.

D. Tax-timing Considerations

While the analysis in the preceding sections highlights the importance of tax efficiency, it largely ignores the benefits of optimal tax timing. In practice, investors are not forced to realize capital gains and losses each year, but have the ability to time these realizations optimally. With the ability to realize losses and defer gains, holding equity in the taxable account can further increase tax efficiency. Not only can investors exploit the tax-timing option by realizing losses and deferring gains, but because of the reset (or step-up) provision at death, the embedded capital gain tax liability can be completely avoided through deferral. Thus, even in situations where equity generates higher ordinary income than a riskless taxable bond, the value of the tax-timing option may still be high enough to overcome the disadvantage of the higher yield.

Although the optimal asset location policy is difficult to derive analytically in the presence of tax-timing options, it is intuitive that assets with relatively lower yields and higher volatilities (typically individual stocks, index funds, and exchange-traded funds) should be held in the taxable account. However, since yields tend to increase with risk for some assets (e.g., taxable corporate bonds), it is unclear which assets are most appropriate for the tax-deferred account. Depending upon the tradeoff between yield and volatility, low-risk government bonds or high-yield corporate bonds may be found in the tax-deferred account.[18] In our numerical analysis in the next section, we incorporate the tax-deferral option on equity when investigating the interaction between the optimal asset allocation and location decisions.

II. Numerical Analysis of the Intertemporal Portfolio Problem

Section I focused on the investor's optimal asset location policy. In this section we investigate numerically how the optimal asset *allocation* decision interacts with the optimal asset *location* decision. Because the interaction between asset allocation and asset location is most pronounced when the investor faces borrowing and short-sale constraints, we focus our numerical analysis on this case. The model is briefly discussed in Section II.A. In Section II.B, we solve numerically for the optimal decision rules as a function of the state variables. We conduct a simulation analysis of the optimal portfolio decisions over an investor's lifetime in Section II.C. A welfare analysis is presented in Section II.D. Finally, in Section II.E, we investigate the effects of liquidity shocks on the optimal asset location and retirement contribution decisions.

A. The Model

Our model builds upon the specification in Dammon, Spatt, and Zhang (2001) by incorporating a tax-deferred (retirement) savings account together with a taxable savings account into an intertemporal model of optimal consumption and portfolio choice. Since the model itself is not the main contribution or focus of the paper, we restrict our discussion in this section to the important features of the model and refer the interested reader to the appendix for the details. The model assumes that the investor makes decisions annually starting at age 20 and lives for at most another 80 years (until age 100). The investor's annual mortality rates are calibrated to match those for the U.S. population. This allows us to directly

[18] Constantinides and Ingersoll (1984) derive optimal tax-timing policies for taxable bonds. The benefits of optimal tax-timing for taxable bonds have been reduced by subsequent changes in the U.S. tax code that require market discounts and premiums to be amortized as ordinary income over the life of the bond. This effectively eliminates the option of treating market discounts on bonds as capital gains.

consider the impact of the investor's age (and increasing mortality) upon the optimal location and allocation decisions.

Investors in the economy derive utility from consuming a single consumption good. We assume that investors receive annual endowment income prior to retirement at age 65. Although investors do not make an endogenous labor-leisure choice in our model, we interpret the endowment income as nonfinancial (or labor) income. Throughout the analysis we assume that pre-tax nonfinancial income is a constant fraction, l, of the investor's contemporaneous total wealth (taxable plus tax-deferred wealth) prior to retirement. This assumption is needed in our numerical analysis to keep the problem homogeneous in wealth and to limit the number of state variables. Because investors are assumed to receive nonfinanical income throughout their working years, young investors with significant future nonfinancial income will adjust the risk of their portfolios by holding slightly more equity (as a proportion of total financial wealth) than they would without nonfinancial income. Finally, the existence of nonfinancial income makes it less likely that the investor will encounter liquidity problems in financing consumption.

Investors can trade two assets in the financial markets: a riskless taxable one-period bond (equivalent to a one-year Treasury bill) and a risky stock index.[19] No transaction costs are incurred for trading these assets. The pre-tax nominal return on the taxable bond is denoted r and is assumed to be constant over time. The pre-tax nominal return on the risky stock index is $\tilde{r}_s = (1 + d)(1 + \tilde{g}) - 1$, where d is the constant dividend yield and $\tilde{g}$ is the random pre-tax capital gain return. To derive numerical solutions, we assume that $\tilde{g}$ follows a binomial process with a constant mean and variance.

Investors can hold financial assets in two different types of accounts: a taxable account and a tax-deferred retirement account. We assume that investors are not allowed to borrow or sell short in either account. Nominal dividend and interest payments generated from the financial assets held in the taxable account are taxed at the ordinary tax rate of τ_d. *Realized* capital gains (and losses) on stock held in the taxable account are taxed (rebated) at a constant rate of τ_g. All *unrealized* capital gains and losses remain untaxed. To calculate the nominal capital gain, we assume that the tax basis is equal to the weighted average purchase price of all shares held by the investor at the time of sale. This modeling approach, first introduced by Dammon, Spatt, and Zhang (2001), facilitates our numerical analysis by limiting the number of state variables. The assumption that there is a single risky asset and the use of the average basis rule cause the value of the tax-timing option on equity to be understated and induce the investor to hold less equity than would be the case with multiple risky assets and separate tax bases for each asset purchase.

The treatment of the investor's retirement account is broadly consistent with practice. Prior to retirement, the investor is assumed to contribute a constant fraction k of pre-tax nonfinacial income to a retirement account each year. The investor allocates his tax-deferred wealth to the taxable bond and the risky stock index and is allowed to rebalance his portfolio holdings in the retirement account without paying capital gains taxes or transaction costs. Nominal dividends, interest, and capital gains generated from the financial assets held in the retirement account are not subject to immediate taxation, but are tax deferred. After retirement, the investor is required to withdraw the fraction h_t of the remaining tax-deferred wealth at age t, where h_t is the inverse of the investor's remaining life

[19]We do not include tax-exempt bonds in our analysis because, as discussed in Section I, the existence of tax-exempt bonds does not alter the asset location decision when investors have the opportunity to invest in equity that is relatively tax efficient (e.g., exchange-traded funds, passive index mutual funds, or individual stocks). With tax-exempt bonds, the only change that would occur in our analysis is that high-tax bracket investors (those with $\tau_d > \tau_m$) would prefer to hold tax-exempt bonds instead of taxable bonds in the taxable account.

expectancy at age t.[20] We assume that the investor contributes the maximum to the retirement account during his working years and withdraws the minimum from the retirement account during his retirement years. Withdrawals from the retirement account are fully taxed as ordinary income at the rate τ_d. Although investors in practice are allowed to withdraw funds from their retirement accounts prior to age $59\frac{1}{2}$ with a 10% penalty, we assume that the investor is not allowed to withdraw funds from the tax-deferred account prior to retirement. We relax these assumptions in Section II.E and allow the investor to optimize the retirement contributions and withdrawals, including withdrawals prior to retirement, when analyzing liquidity shocks.

The investor's problem is to maximize the discounted expected utility of lifetime consumption, given the initial endowment of assets and wealth, subject to an intertemporal budget constraint. Since the investor has a positive probability of death at each date, the treatment of terminal wealth is important. We assume that at the time of death, the asset holdings in the taxable account are liquidated without incurring a capital gains tax. This is consistent with the *reset (or step-up) provision* of the current U.S. tax code, which requires the tax bases of all inherited assets to be costlessly reset to current market prices at the time of the investor's death. We also assume that the assets held in the investor's retirement account are liquidated at the time of death and that the proceeds are taxed as ordinary income. At the time of death, the investor's total wealth is liquidated and distributed as a bequest to his beneficiary. For simplicity, we assume that the investor derives utility from his bequest equal to the utility his beneficiary would derive if the bequest were used to purchase an annuity contract that provided a constant amount of *real* consumption for H periods. Higher values for H indicate a stronger bequest motive for the investor.

The value of the investor's asset holdings (i.e., the after-tax value of the retirement account plus the pre-tax value of the taxable account) serves as our measure of total wealth at each date. To eliminate total wealth as a state variable, we assume that the investor has constant relative risk-averse preferences. After normalizing by total wealth, the investor's intertemporal consumption and portfolio problem involves the following control (choice) variables: The consumption-wealth ratio, c_t; the fraction of taxable wealth allocated to equity, f_t; the fraction of taxable wealth allocated to riskless taxable bonds, b_t; and the fraction of tax-deferred wealth allocated to equity, θ_t. Given f_t and b_t, the fraction of the investor's taxable portfolio allocated to equity is $f_t/(f_t + b_t)$. The relevant state variables for the normalized optimization problem are the incoming proportion of equity in the taxable account, s_t; the basis-price ratio on the incoming equity holdings, p^*_{t-1}; the fraction of the investor's incoming total wealth that is held in the retirement account, y_t; and the investor's age, t. Because investors are allowed to rebalance their retirement account portfolios without incurring any transaction costs or taxes, the incoming asset holdings in this account are not relevant state variables for the investor's decision problem.

B. Numerical Solutions for the Optimal Policies

The *base-case* parameter values for our numerical analysis are summarized in Table I and discussed below. We assume that the nominal pre-tax interest rate on the riskless taxable bond is $r = 6\%$ per year; the nominal dividend yield on the stock index is $d = 2\%$ per year; and the annual inflation rate is $i = 3.5\%$. Inflation is relevant in our model because taxes are levied on nominal quantities. The nominal annual capital gains return on the stock index

[20]Recently, the IRS has adopted a minimum withdrawal schedule that is based upon the joint life expectancy of the individual and a hypothetical beneficiary. Consequently, our withdrawal rates are somewhat higher than those required by the new regulations issued by the IRS. Although we assume that the balance in the retirement account is subject to immediate taxation at the time of the investor's death, the recently adopted IRS regulations allow the beneficiary to withdraw the remaining funds according to his own life expectancy. Consequently, our analysis somewhat understates the potential benefits of tax-deferred investing.

TABLE I | Base-case Parameter Values

The table provides the base-case parameter values that are used to conduct the numerical analysis in Section II. The bequest parameter (H) is the number of years of consumption the investor wishes to provide his beneficiary following his death. Higher values of H imply a stronger bequest motive. Labor income is assumed to be a constant proportion (l) of the investor's total wealth. The retirement contribution rate (k) is stated as a proportion of the investor's pre-tax labor income. Retirement contributions are mandatory prior to retirement. The retirement withdrawal rate (h_t) is stated as a proportion of the investor's tax-deferred wealth. Investors are not allowed to withdraw funds from their tax-deferred accounts prior to retirement.

Parameters of the Model	Notation	Base-case Value
Asset Returns:		
Riskless one-period taxable interest rate	r	6.0%
Dividend yield on equity	d	2.0%
Expected capital gain return on equity	$\overline{g}$	9.0%
Standard deviation of capital gain return	σ	20.0%
Inflation rate	i	3.5%
Tax Rates:		
Ordinary income tax rate	τ_d	36%
Capital gain tax rate	τ_g	20%
Utility and Bequest Functions:		
Utility discount factor	β	0.96
Relative risk aversion	α	3.0
Bequest parameter	H	20
Labor Income and Retirement Savings		
Labor income	l	15%
Retirement contribution rate	k	20%
Retirement withdrawal rate	h_t	1/life expectancy
Mandatory retirement age	J	65

is assumed to follow a binomial process with a constant mean and standard deviation of $\overline{g} = 9\%$ and $\sigma = 20\%$, respectively. We assume that the tax rate on dividends and interest is $\tau_d = 36\%$ and that the tax rate on *realized* capital gains and losses is $\tau_g = 20\%$. Because the pre-tax expected return on the stock index is given by $\overline{r}_s = (1 + \overline{g})(1 + d) - 1$, the annual pre-tax equity risk premium (above the riskless interest rate) is 5.18%. While this equity risk premium is relatively low compared to the historical average equity risk premium of about 8%, Fama and French (2002) and others have argued that the expected future equity risk premium should be substantially lower than the historical average. For reasonable levels of risk aversion, the lower equity risk premium also ensures that the investor's optimal portfolio will consist of less than 100% equity.

The investor is assumed to have power utility with an annual subjective discount factor of $\beta = 0.96$ and a risk aversion parameter of $\gamma = 3.0$. We set $H = 20$ in the bequest function, indicating that the investor values the bequest as though it provided a 20-year annuity of constant real consumption for his beneficiary.[21] We assume that pre-tax nonfinancial income is a constant $l = 15\%$ of the investor's total beginning-of-period wealth prior to age 65 and $l = 0\%$ thereafter. Before retirement at age 65, the investor is assumed to invest $k = 20\%$ of pre-tax nonfinancial income in the tax-deferred retirement account

[21] We also calculated the optimal decision rules for higher and lower values of H. A weaker (stronger) bequest motive increases (reduces) the optimal consumption-wealth ratio, especially at late ages, but has relatively little effect on the investor's optimal portfolio holdings across the state space.

FIGURE 1 | Optimal equity proportions as a function of retirement wealth and age. The figure shows the optimal equity proportions in the taxable account (top panel), retirement account (middle panel), and overall portfolio (bottom panel) as a function of age and the fraction of total wealth held in the retirement account. The basis-price ratio is set at $p^* = 1.0$.

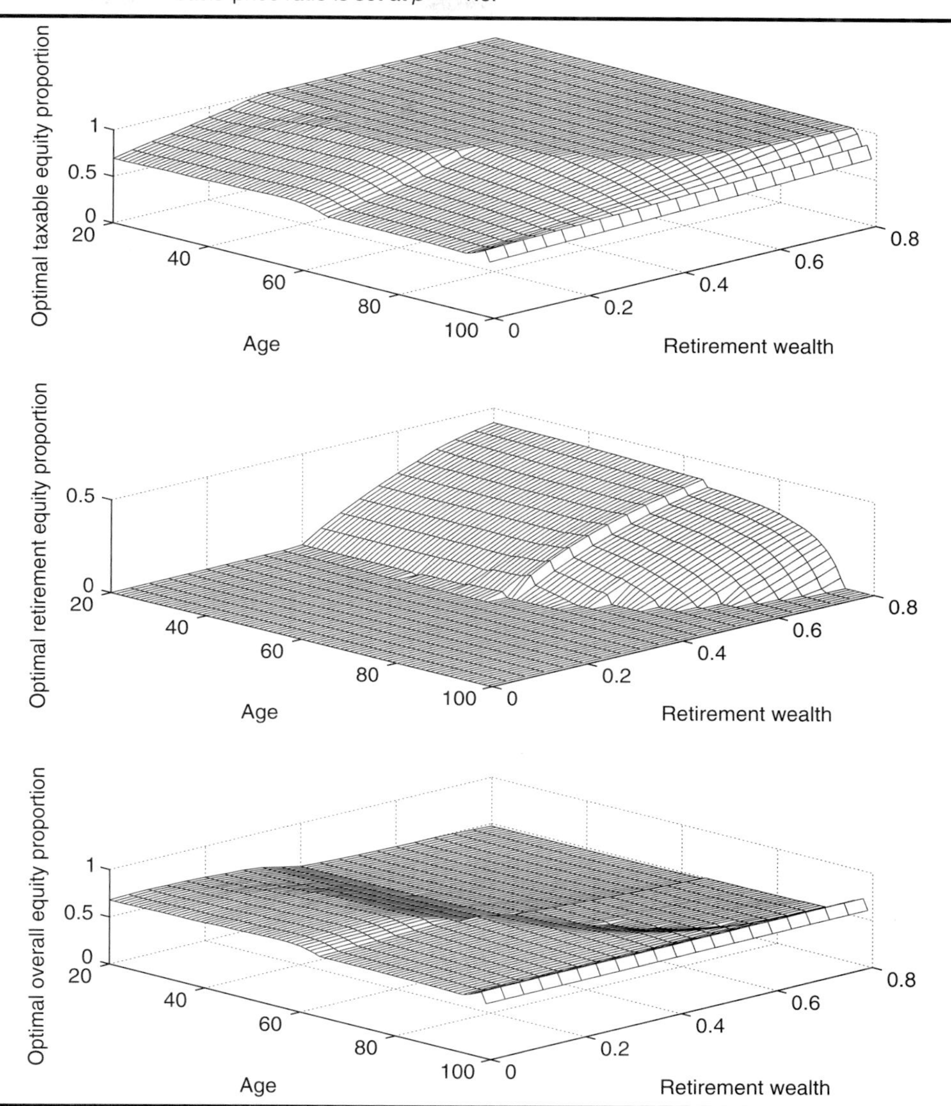

each year. This contribution rate is the maximum allowed in the U.S. for self-employed individuals with defined contribution plans. Although withdrawals from tax-deferred retirement accounts can be deferred until age $70\frac{1}{2}$ under current IRS rules, we assume that the investor is forced to begin withdrawing funds from the retirement account at age 65 in accordance with the withdrawal schedule h_t.

Figure 1 shows the optimal equity proportions for the taxable account (top panel), the tax-deferred retirement account (middle panel), and the overall portfolio (bottom panel).

FIGURE 2 | Optimal equity proportions at ages 35 and 75.

The figure shows the optimal equity proportions in the taxable account (dash-dotted line), tax-deferred account (dashed line), and overall portfolio (solid line) at age 35 (top panel) and age 75 (bottom panel). The optimal equity proportions are shown as a function of the fraction of total wealth held in the retirement account. The basis-price ratio is set at $p^* = 1.0$.

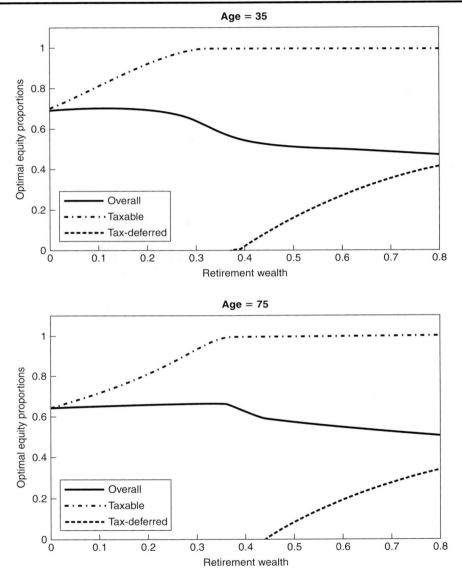

These optimal equity proportions are shown as a function of the investor's age and the fraction of beginning-of-period total wealth held in the retirement account. A two-dimensional representation of these optimal equity proportions is shown in Figure 2 for age 35 (top panel) and age 75 (bottom panel). Figures 1 and 2 are constructed using the base-case parameter values and assuming that the basis-price ratio is $p^* = 1.0$. With a basis-price ratio of $p^* = 1.0$, the investor has neither a gain nor a loss on existing equity holdings and can rebalance the portfolio in the taxable account without incurring a tax cost. We refer to these optimal equity proportions as the *zero-gain optimum* equity holdings.

As the fraction of wealth in the retirement account increases, the optimal equity proportion in the taxable account increases. This reflects the preference for holding taxable bonds in the retirement account, thus making it necessary for the investor to increase the proportion of equity in the taxable account in order to maintain an optimal overall portfolio mix. Note, however, that because of the prohibition on borrowing, the proportion of equity in the taxable account is bounded above by 100%. The top panels of Figures 1 and 2 show that prior to retirement, the investor allocates 100% of the taxable account to equity whenever the tax-deferred wealth exceeds about 30% of total wealth. In contrast, with *unrestricted borrowing* (not shown), the optimal holding of equity in the taxable account would continue to increase beyond 100% as the investor borrows to invest in equity in the taxable account. For example, with 50% of total wealth held in the retirement account, investors in their working years hold approximately 175% of their taxable wealth in equity when they are allowed to borrow.

Figure 1 (middle panel) and 2 show that the optimal equity proportion in the tax-deferred account can be nonzero when investors are prohibited from borrowing. Note, however, that the investor does not hold equity in the tax-deferred account until the tax-deferred wealth exceeds approximately 40% of total wealth. The reason the investor does not add equity to the retirement account as soon as he is constrained in the taxable account is because equity is much less valuable when held in the retirement account. For this reason, the investor holds equity in the retirement account only when the level of tax-deferred wealth is sufficiently high and refrains from holding a mix of stocks and bonds in both the taxable and tax-deferred accounts simultaneously. In fact, over a range of tax-deferred wealth, the investor holds an all-equity portfolio in the taxable account and an all-bond portfolio in the retirement account. These findings are in contrast to the unrestricted borrowing case (not shown) in which the investor always allocates his entire tax-deferred wealth to taxable bonds (see Section I.A).

Figures 1 (bottom panel) and 2 show the optimal proportion of *total wealth* allocated to equity for the no-borrowing case. The figures illustrate that optimal asset allocation for an investor's overall portfolio depends upon the split of wealth between the taxable and tax-deferred accounts. In fact, the optimal overall equity proportion (weakly) declines as the fraction of total wealth held in the retirement account increases. The optimal overall equity proportion is relatively flat in the level of tax-deferred wealth as long as the investor holds less than 100% equity in the taxable account. Once the investor is constrained in the taxable account, however, the optimal overall equity proportion begins to decline. This reflects the investor's reluctance to substitute equity for taxable bonds in the retirement account. At sufficiently high levels of tax-deferred wealth, the investor begins to add equity to the retirement account to avoid becoming too underweighted in equity. This causes the optimal overall equity proportion to level off once again. In contrast, when the investor has unrestricted borrowing opportunities (not shown), the optimal overall equity proportion is relatively constant across all levels of tax-deferred wealth.[22] For young investors with unrestricted borrowing opportunities, the optimal overall equity proportion is approximately 70%.

[22]With unrestricted borrowing, the optimal overall equity proportion increases slightly with the level of tax-deferred wealth. Higher levels of tax-deferred wealth allow the investor to generate higher levels of riskless tax-arbitrage profits. By investing the incremental tax-deferred wealth in bonds, and borrowing in the taxable account to invest in equity, the investor is able to increase his total wealth without incurring additional risk. The investor responds to this risk-free increase in wealth by increasing slightly his overall exposure to equity.

The effect of age on the overall equity proportion is also shown in the bottom panel of Figure 1. While the overall equity proportion remains relatively constant during the working years, there is a slight decline between the ages of 60 and 65. The drop in the optimal overall equity proportion at these ages reflects the anticipated loss of the relatively low-risk nonfinancial income after retirement. This effect is less pronounced at high levels of retirement wealth, where the exposure to equity has already been reduced at young ages because of the restrictions on borrowing. After retirement, the optimal overall equity proportion *increases* slightly with age. This reflects the higher value of equity for elderly investors, who because of their higher mortality rates, benefit the most from the forgiveness of capital gains taxes at death.

Figures 1 and 2 were constructed assuming that the basis-price ratio for equity held in the taxable account was $p^* = 1.0$. With an embedded capital loss (i.e., $p^* > 1.0$), the investor optimally sells his entire equity holding in the taxable account to benefit from the tax rebate and immediately rebalances to the zero-gain optimum equity holdings shown in Figure 1. With an embedded capital gain (i.e., $p^* < 1.0$), the investor's optimal equity holdings will differ from those shown in Figure 1. If the investor's taxable account is initially *underweighted* in equity, his equity holdings following optimal rebalancing will be slightly lower than the zero-gain optimum equity holdings. This is because the averaging rule used to compute the tax basis reduces the value of holding additional equity when existing shares have an embedded capital gain. The smaller the embedded capital gain, the closer the optimal equity holdings are to the zero-gain optimum. If the investor's taxable account is initially *overweighted* in equity, there exists a tradeoff between the diversification benefits and tax costs of rebalancing. The willingness of the investor to realize embedded capital gains to rebalance his portfolio depends upon a number of factors. Smaller embedded capital gains, larger deviations from the zero-gain optimum equity holdings, lower mortality risk, and lower levels of future nonfinancial income increase the amount of rebalancing that is optimal. However, because rebalancing is costly in this case, the optimal equity holdings are higher than the zero-gain optimum equity holdings. The age and basis effects discussed above are similar to those derived by Dammon, Spatt, and Zhang (2001) in a model without a tax-deferred account.

Our results illustrate a preference for holding equity in the taxable account and taxable bonds in the tax-deferred account to the extent possible. We also have discussed how the investor's overall asset allocation depends upon age, the basis-price ratio, and the split of wealth between the taxable and tax-deferred accounts.[23] In the next section, we investigate the time-series profile of the investor's optimal consumption and portfolio allocation decisions using simulation analysis.

C. Simulation Analysis

Given the investor's optimal consumption and investment policies defined on the state space, we can obtain time-series profiles of optimal consumption and portfolio allocations by simulating the capital gain return on the risky stock index. Using our base-case parameter values, the simulation begins for an investor at age 20 with an initial basis-price ratio of $p^* = 1$. The investor is prohibited from borrowing and is assumed to have no tax-deferred wealth at age 20. Table II shows the age profiles for the optimal consumption,

[23]Reichenstein (2001) uses a one-period mean-variance model to generate a series of numerical examples that illustrate the interaction between the asset location and asset allocation decisions. His model, however, does not consider the impacts of age, basis-price ratio, or the split of wealth between the taxable and tax-deferred accounts on the optimal decisions.

portfolio holdings, and level of retirement wealth. The values reported in the table are *averages* at each age taken across 5,000 simulation trials.

Table II shows that the investor's optimal consumption-wealth ratio slowly falls as the investor ages during his working years and then slowly rises as he ages during his retirement years. The decline in the investor's optimal consumption-wealth ratio during his working years reflects the anticipated loss of nonfinancial income after retirement. The increase in the investor's consumption-wealth ratio during his retirement years reflects the bequest motive. With $H = 20$, the bequest provides the investor the same utility as his beneficiary would receive from consuming a 20-year annuity stream. Hence, as the investor ages (and mortality risk increases), the optimal consumption-wealth ratio increases in an attempt to equate the expected marginal utility of the investor's own consumption with that of his beneficiary. With a stronger bequest motive ($H = \infty$), the investor's optimal consumption-wealth ratio declines with age during retirement.

The investor contributes $k = 20\%$ of pre-tax nonfinancial income to the retirement account each year. Given the high levels of consumption, these retirement contributions represent the bulk of the investor's overall savings during his working years. As a result, the fraction of total wealth held in the retirement account increases rapidly at young ages. The fraction of total wealth held in the retirement account reaches its maximum of 45% at age 55, well before the investor reaches retirement age.[24] The decline in the fraction of total wealth held in the retirement account in the years prior to retirement reflects two things: (1) the lower fraction of total after-tax savings allocated to the retirement account at these ages and (2) the relatively low average return earned on the assets (primarily taxable bonds) held in the retirement account. Because of the mandatory distributions from the tax-deferred account during his retirement years, the investor's after-tax retirement account declines rapidly after age 65. By the time the investor reaches age 80, the after-tax wealth in the retirement account is only slightly more than 12% of total wealth on average.

The last six columns of Table II provide information about the investor's optimal lifetime portfolio choices. Because of the relatively high equity risk premium, the investor's overall demand for equity is extremely high and frequently exceeds the available resources in the taxable account. As Table II indicates, a large proportion of simulation trials result in an all-equity portfolio in the taxable account at some point during the investor's lifetime. Most (but not all) of these cases result in some positive holdings of equity in the retirement account. Since equity is less valuable when held in the retirement account, the overall holding of equity declines in these cases. While the investor has limited opportunities at early ages to realize losses on equity held in the taxable account, the profile of the average basis-price ratio in Table II indicates that he quickly becomes locked in to a capital gain. During the retirement years, the average proportion of tax-deferred wealth allocated to equity declines rapidly as the investor begins to liquidate the equity holdings in the retirement account to fund his mandatory distributions. However, as a proportion of total wealth, the investor's equity holdings continue to increase during his retirement years. This reflects the increased holdings of equity in the taxable account and the investor's reluctance to sell equity with an embedded capital gain.[25]

---

[24]Across the 5,000 simulations, there is considerable variation in the magnitude of tax-deferred wealth. For example, at age 55 the minimum and maximum values of tax-deferred wealth are 13% and 81%, respectively, of total wealth. The timing of when tax-deferred wealth reaches its maximum is also somewhat variable, although it typically occurs between the ages of 50 and 60.

[25]If the investor is allowed to borrow, the optimal holding of equity in the taxable account is likely to exceed 100% at late ages. This is because the investor prefers to sell bonds and borrow to finance consumption rather than selling equity with embedded capital gains. At death, the investor's equity holdings are liquidated without payment of the capital gains tax, all borrowing is repaid, and the remaining wealth is used to finance his bequest.

TABLE II Monte Carlo Simulation Analysis

The table summarizes the results of the Monte Carlo simulation analysis conducted in Section II.C. The numbers reported in the table are averages at each age taken over 5,000 simulation trials, starting at age 20 and ending at age 100. The simulations utilize the base-case parameter values outlined in Table I. The table reports the average consumption-wealth ratio; the fraction of total wealth in the retirement account; the overall equity proportion; the equity proportion in the taxable account; the basis-price ratio of the equity in the taxable account; the frequency of reaching 100% equity in the taxable account; the frequency of positive equity holdings in the retirement account; and the proportion of retirement wealth allocated to equity conditional on positive equity holdings in the retirement account.

Age	Consumption-Wealth Ratio	Fraction of Total Wealth Held in the Retirement Account	Overall Equity Proportion	Equity Proportion in the Taxable Account	Basis-Price Ratio	Frequency of 100% Equity in the Taxable Account	Frequency of Positive Equity in the Retirement Account	Conditional Equity Proportion in the Retirement Account
20	9.30%	1.91%	67.88%	69.35%	1.000	0.00%	0.00%	—
25	9.19%	11.11%	71.72%	81.66%	0.666	0.00%	0.00%	—
30	9.12%	19.70%	70.58%	90.08%	0.488	0.24%	0.24%	0.00%
35	8.92%	27.32%	67.13%	95.79%	0.367	3.62%	3.62%	5.19%
40	8.58%	33.93%	62.57%	98.36%	0.281	3.90%	3.90%	18.36%
45	8.10%	39.38%	58.56%	98.53%	0.218	1.78%	1.74%	29.53%
50	7.37%	43.14%	56.05%	98.12%	0.195	59.36%	55.04%	10.37%
55	6.35%	44.68%	55.37%	97.71%	0.233	64.70%	59.80%	11.90%
60	5.14%	43.50%	56.04%	96.70%	0.321	61.60%	60.64%	11.05%
65	3.86%	36.21%	53.76%	81.61%	0.379	10.90%	10.90%	20.02%
70	3.85%	28.96%	61.39%	87.27%	0.314	6.24%	6.24%	15.08%
75	3.90%	20.55%	66.27%	84.71%	0.244	1.98%	1.98%	9.19%
80	4.03%	12.19%	68.64%	78.91%	0.186	0.46%	0.18%	1.11%
85	4.24%	5.41%	70.83%	75.08%	0.141	0.00%	0.00%	—
90	4.51%	1.47%	75.70%	76.87%	0.109	0.00%	0.00%	—
95	4.88%	0.12%	86.32%	86.42%	0.084	0.00%	0.00%	—
99	5.37%	0.00%	98.99%	98.99%	0.071	0.00%	0.00%	—

The results of the simulation analysis illustrate the time-series properties of the investor's optimal consumption, portfolio allocation, and asset location decisions. In the next section, we investigate the welfare benefits from following the optimal asset location policies and illustrate the value of tax-deferred investing.

D. Alternative Investment Policies and Welfare Analysis

Because many individuals in practice hold a mix of bonds and stocks in both their taxable and tax-deferred accounts, and in some cases actually tilt their retirement accounts toward equity, we want to examine the utility costs of following these suboptimal policies. We examine two alternative investment strategies. In the first, investors hold the same mix of bonds and stocks in both their taxable and tax-deferred accounts. In the second, investors first allocate their holdings of equity to the retirement account before holding equity in their taxable accounts. Given our earlier analysis, this latter policy is the worst possible choice in terms of asset location. For both of the alternative investment policies, we allow the investor to choose the optimal mix of stocks and bonds as a function of the state variables. We then conduct a welfare analysis by computing the amount of additional wealth (allocated entirely to the taxable account) that is needed to equate the investor's total expected utility under the suboptimal location policy to that under the optimal location policy. This allows us to quantify the cost of ignoring the optimal location of securities across the taxable and tax-deferred accounts.

The welfare analysis is conducted using our base-case parameter values. The one exception is that we assume that future nonfinancial income and retirement contributions are zero. This allows us to focus on the welfare costs associated with the suboptimal location policies when applied to the pre-existing wealth levels. The optimal asset location decision is unaffected by the elimination of nonfinancial income and retirement account contributions.

The top panel of Figure 3 shows the utility costs for an investor who is forced to hold the same portfolio mix in both the taxable and tax-deferred accounts. The middle panel of Figure 3 shows the utility costs for an investor who is not allowed to hold equity in the taxable account unless 100% of his tax-deferred wealth is allocated to equity. The utility costs are shown as a function of the investor's age and level of tax-deferred wealth. The figures are drawn for a basis-price ratio of $p^* = 1.0$. Since there is no embedded capital gain or loss on the investor's portfolio, the initial equity proportion in the taxable account has no effect on the optimal decision rules or utility costs.

The utility costs depicted in these two figures exhibit a strong age effect. Other things being equal, younger investors incur a higher utility cost because they have longer horizons over which the suboptimal asset location policy is in effect. The utility costs are also hump-shaped in the level of tax-deferred wealth at young and middle ages. Intuitively, the utility costs of being constrained to follow the suboptimal policy are highest when the investor's wealth is split relatively evenly across the taxable and tax-deferred accounts and smallest when concentrated in one or the other of these two accounts.[26]

In the top panel of Figure 3, the utility costs are generally less than 5% across all ages, with the exception that young investors with moderate levels of retirement account wealth

[26]Because the split of wealth between the taxable and tax-deferred accounts is changing over time, the utility costs depend upon more than just the investor's current distribution of wealth across these two accounts. In general, it will also depend upon the investor's age, anticipated future retirement account contributions and withdrawals, level of nonfinancial income, consumption plans, and asset returns. This explains why the level of retirement account wealth that produces the highest utility cost is not equal to 0.5 and why it is not the same across all ages.

FIGURE 3 | Utility costs and shadow prices.

The top panel shows the utility costs of following the suboptimal policy of holding the same portfolio mix in both the taxable and tax-deferred accounts. The middle panel shows the utility costs of following the suboptimal policy of allocating equity to the tax-deferred account before allocating equity to the taxable account. The utility costs are measured as the percentage increase in total wealth (allocated entirely to the taxable account) needed to compensate the investor for following the suboptimal policy. The bottom panel shows the shadow prices for an additional dollar of tax-deferred wealth. The shadow price is the amount of taxable wealth the investor is willing to pay to receive an additional after-tax dollar in his retirement account. The basis-price ratio is set at $p^* = 1.0$ and future nonfinancial income and retirement contributions are assumed to be zero.

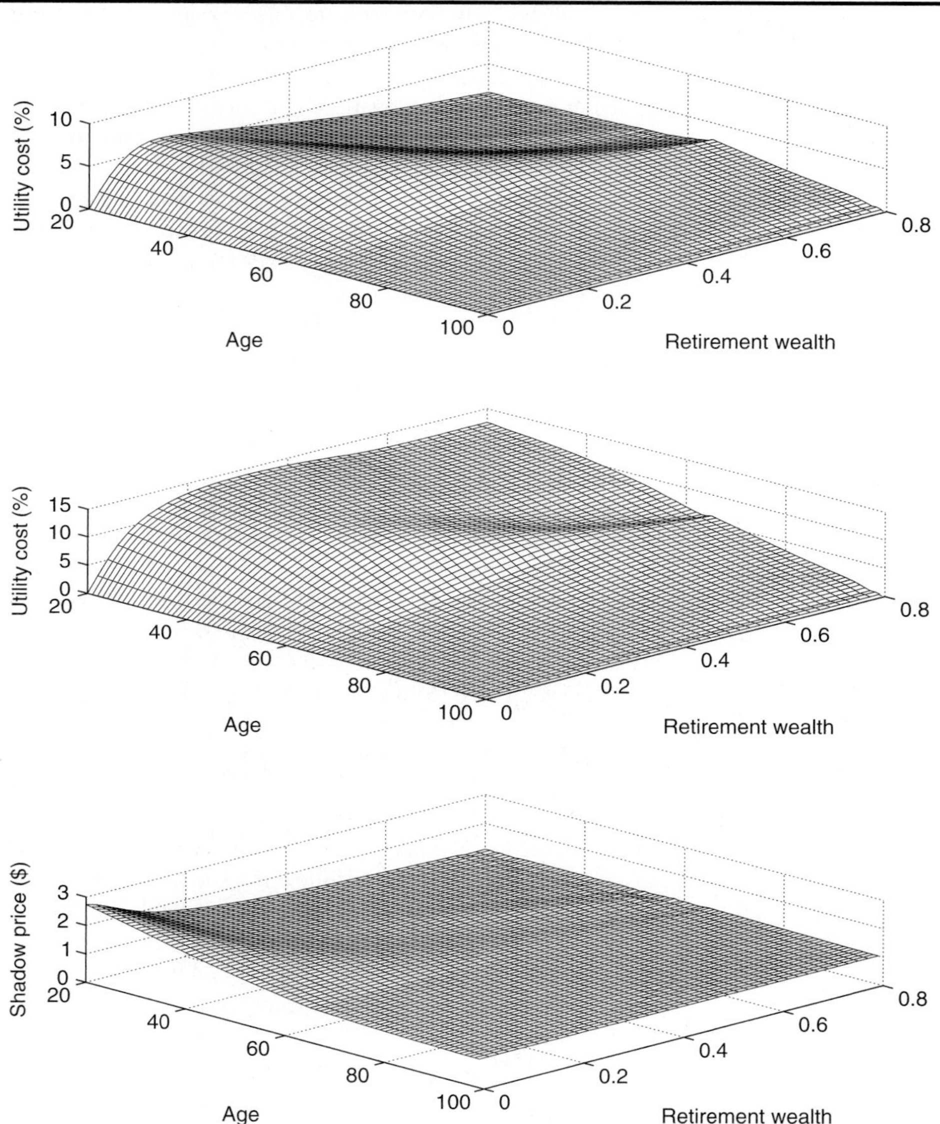

have slightly higher utility costs. The utility costs depicted in the middle panel of Figure 3 are higher than those depicted in the top panel. This is to be expected, since locating equity in the tax-deferred account before locating it in the taxable account is the worst possible policy for asset location. For young investors with moderate levels of tax-deferred wealth, the utility costs are nearly 15%. These utility costs would be even higher if the investor contributed additional funds to the retirement account over time. The overall impression given by these two figures is that the benefits from optimally locating equity in the taxable account and bonds in the tax-deferred account can be large, especially for young and middle-aged investors.

Our model also can be used to measure the welfare benefits of tax-deferred investing. Using the base-case parameters (without nonfinancial income and retirement contributions), and an assumed basis-price ratio of $p^* = 1.0$, the bottom panel of Figure 3 shows the shadow prices for tax-deferred wealth. The shadow price measures the amount of taxable wealth the investor is willing to give up in order to receive one additional dollar of wealth in the tax-deferred account. The shadow prices depicted in Figure 3 are all greater than 1.0, indicating that it is beneficial for the investor to have a higher fraction of total wealth in the retirement account.[27] The shadow prices are highest for young investors, who have longer horizons over which to benefit from tax-deferred investing, and for investors with lower levels of tax-deferred wealth, who can efficiently allocate their tax-deferred wealth to taxable bonds.[28] Since investors are forced to liquidate their tax-deferred accounts during their retirement years, the shadow prices for additional tax-deferred wealth decline rapidly after age 65.

E. Effects of Liquidity on Optimal Asset Location

The tax-efficient location policy involves holding equity in the taxable account and taxable bonds in the tax-deferred account, to the extent possible. While this location policy does not alter the risk of the investor's overall portfolio, it does shift most of the risk exposure to the taxable account. The higher risk exposure in the taxable account should have little or no effect on investors with substantial wealth in their taxable accounts, low labor income risk, easy access to borrowing, or penalty-free access to their tax-deferred accounts. For other investors, however, the higher risk exposure in the taxable account can create a potential liquidity problem. If equity values decline significantly, it may be necessary for these investors to incur a penalty to liquidate a portion of their tax-deferred accounts to finance consumption. In principle, this can create demand for holding taxable bonds in the taxable account to reduce liquidity risk. In Section I.C, we show that deviations from the tax-efficient asset location policy require a positive probability of a liquidity shock that exceeds the wealth in the taxable account, combined with a sufficiently negative correlation (under the risk-neutral measure) between these liquidity shocks and equity returns. In this section, we use numerical analysis to explore the effects of liquidity on the intertemporal asset location and retirement contribution decisions.

While liquidity shocks can be modeled in a number of different ways, we choose to model them as an exogenous shock to consumption. The numerical analysis of these consumption

[27]Since consumption must be financed exclusively from the resources held in the taxable account, the shadow prices can be less than 1.0 for extremely high levels of tax-deferred wealth.

[28]For an investor at age 20 with no wealth in the tax-deferred account, the shadow price in Figure 3 is \$2.71. To understand the magnitude of this shadow price, consider the following simple example. Investing one dollar of tax-deferred wealth in bonds earning a pre-tax return of 6% per year will grow to \$24.65 after 55 years (the life expectancy of a 20-year-old). To produce the same terminal value after 55 years, an investor would need to invest \$3.10 of taxable wealth in bonds earning an after-tax return of 3.84% per year.

shocks is conducted using our base-case parameter values. However, unlike in our earlier analysis, we allow investors to endogenously determine their optimal contributions to the retirement account during their working years (subject to a contribution limit of $k = 20\%$) and their optimal withdrawals from the tax-deferred account during their retirement years (subject to the minimum withdrawal schedule). Investors are also allowed to withdraw funds from their tax-deferred accounts prior to retirement, but must pay ordinary income taxes and a 10% penalty on early withdrawals. Because the taxable account is the preferred location for equity, even without the benefits of optimal tax timing, we simplify our analysis by assuming that all capital gains and losses are realized each year and taxed at the rate of $\tau_g = 20\%$. This assumption is consistent with the analysis in Section I.C and allows us to drop the incoming equity proportion in the taxable account and the basis-price ratio as state variables.

We first analyze a situation in which the investor faces a *known* "consumption gulp" of 50% of total wealth at age 30.[29] The purchase of a home or college tuition are examples of the type of consumption expenditures we have in mind. At age 30, the investor withdraws funds from the retirement account and pays the 10% penalty only if the wealth in the taxable account is insufficient to finance the required "consumption gulp." Figure 4 illustrates the optimal holding of taxable bonds in the taxable account (top panel) and equity in the tax-deferred account (middle panel) as a function of the investor's age and the level of tax-deferred wealth. Under the tax-efficient asset location policy, positive holdings of taxable bonds in the taxable account (top panel) should not coincide with positive holdings of equity in the tax-deferred account (middle panel). Except for a few years prior to age 30, and for levels of tax-deferred wealth between about 45 to 55% of total wealth, the investor follows the tax-efficient asset location policy. Investors who deviate from the tax-efficient location policy are those for whom negative equity returns might otherwise force a liquidation of a portion of the tax-deferred account at age 30. To reduce this risk, these investors shift some taxable bonds to the taxable account and some equity to the tax-deferred account. Note, however, that the holding of taxable bonds in the taxable account is small relative to the overall holding of taxable bonds. For all other investors, the correlation between equity returns and a liquidity crisis at age 30 is not sufficiently negative to warrant a deviation from the tax-efficient asset location policy.

The bottom panel of Figure 4 shows the optimal contributions to the tax-deferred account prior to age 30. Investors with substantial tax-deferred wealth reduce (or eliminate) the contributions to the retirement account prior to age 30 to increase the wealth in the taxable account and reduce (or eliminate) the penalty for early withdrawal. The higher the level of tax-deferred wealth, the earlier the age at which the investor eliminates the retirement contributions. Note that some investors reduce (or eliminate) contributions to the retirement account, but continue to follow the optimal asset location policy. Investors older than age 30 (not shown) maximize the contributions to the retirement account during their working years and withdraw the minimum from their retirement accounts during their retirement years.

[29]Huang (2000) analyzes the asset location decision for an investor who faces a one-time tax on total wealth at a known future date. The wealth tax is a dead-weight loss for the investor in her model. In contrast, the "consumption gulp" in our model serves as a constraint on the minimum level of consumption. We model the "consumption gulp" as a fixed percentage of total wealth for simplicity. If the "consumption gulp" is a fixed dollar amount, instead of a fixed percentage of total wealth, then two complications arise. First, it is necessary to introduce wealth as an additional continuous state variable. Second, it is necessary to define a penalty function, in the event that the investor's wealth is not sufficient to meet the required "consumption gulp." In this case, the severity of the penalty function will determine the extent to which the investor hedges in the taxable account.

FIGURE 4 | Optimal asset allocations and retirement contributions with a known "consumption gulp."

The figure shows the optimal bond proportion in the taxable account, equity proportion in the retirement account, and retirement contributions for the case in which the investor has a known "consumption gulp" of 50% of total wealth at age 30. A 10% penalty is enforced on withdrawals from the retirement account prior to age 65. The optimal asset allocations and retirement contributions are shown as a function of age and the fraction of total wealth held in the retirement account. The top panel depicts the optimal bond proportion in the taxable account, the middle panel depicts the optimal equity proportion in the tax-deferred account, and the bottom panel depicts the optimal retirement contributions (as a percentage of pre-tax non-financial income).

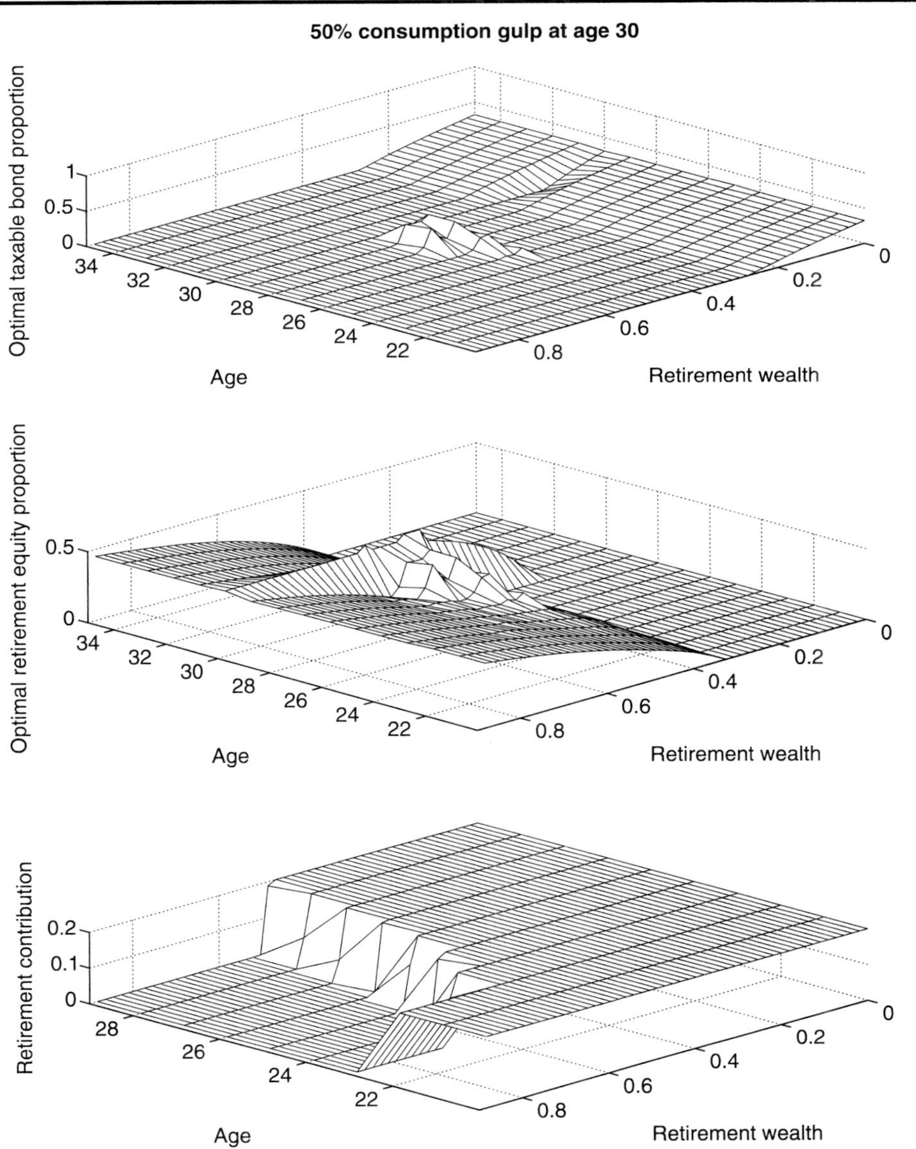

The above analysis assumes that the timing of the "consumption gulp" is known with certainty. Another approach is to assume that the investor faces a constant *per-period* probability of a liquidity shock that requires consumption to be 50% of total wealth.[30] The consumption shocks are assumed to occur with a 10% probability each period and are independent over time. The first case we consider assumes that the consumption shocks are *independent* of equity returns. In this case, the numerical results (not shown) indicate that the tax-efficient asset location policy is optimal for all investors and for all levels of tax-deferred wealth. With zero correlation between the consumption shocks and equity returns, shifting taxable bonds to the taxable account is not an effective hedge against liquidity risk and is highly tax inefficient. Rather than deviating from the tax-efficient asset location policy, investors younger than retirement age hedge the risk of a liquidity shock by reducing (or eliminating) the contributions to the retirement account in order to increase the wealth in the taxable account. Since younger investors face a higher cumulative probability of a liquidity crisis prior to retirement, they contribute to the retirement account only at low levels of tax-deferred wealth.

The second case we consider assumes that consumption shocks are *negatively* correlated with equity returns. We maintain the assumption that the consumption shock requires consumption to be 50% of total wealth. Conditional on a negative equity return, the probability of a consumption shock is assumed to be 18%. Conditional on a positive equity return, the probability of a consumption shock is assumed to be 2%. Therefore, with an equal probability of a negative or positive equity return, the unconditional probability of a consumption shock is 10% per period. Figure 5 illustrates the numerical results for this case.

Figure 5 shows the optimal holding of taxable bonds in the taxable account (top panel), the optimal holding of equity in the tax-deferred account (middle panel), and the optimal contributions to the retirement account prior to age 65 (bottom panel). Because equity is riskier when its returns are negatively correlated with consumption shocks, investors hold substantially less equity (and more bonds) as a proportion of total wealth. Except for a few years prior to retirement, investors again follow the tax-efficient asset location policy. The deviations from the tax-efficient asset location policy are driven by a horizon effect; at age 65 the investor is allowed to withdraw funds from the tax-deferred account without penalty. This alters the trade-off between the liquidity benefits and tax costs of hedging for investors as they approach retirement age.

For young investors, the cumulative probability of a liquidity crisis prior to retirement is so high that deviating from the tax-efficient asset location policy is not optimal. For these investors, a shift from equity to bonds in the taxable account, offset by a shift from bonds to stocks in the tax-deferred account, involves a significant tax cost and has virtually no effect on the probability or severity of a future consumption shock. In contrast, investors approaching retirement age face a more favorable trade-off between the liquidity benefits and tax costs of hedging. For these investors, a deviation from the tax-efficient asset location policy may reduce the probability and severity of a consumption shock prior to retirement, especially if the current level of taxable wealth is only slightly below the level of the shock. The largest deviation from the tax-efficient asset location policy occurs at age 63, when the investor shifts his entire taxable account to taxable bonds if the level of taxable

[30]This approach is similar in spirit to the random shocks to nonfinancial income analyzed by Amromin (2001). Despite the potential for a catastrophic loss of nonfinancial income for an extended period of time, he finds that the hedging demand for taxable bonds in the taxable account is still small relative to the overall holding of taxable bonds.

FIGURE 5 | Optimal asset allocations and retirement contributions with a random "consumption gulp."

The figure shows the optimal bond proportion in the taxable account, equity proportion in the retirement account, and retirement contributions for the case in which the investor faces a 10% probability each period of a shock to consumption requiring him to consume 50% of total wealth. The consumption shocks are assumed to be independent over time and are negatively correlated with equity returns. A 10% penalty is enforced on withdrawals from the retirement account prior to age 65. The optimal asset allocations and retirement contributions are shown as a function of age and the fraction of total wealth held in the retirement account. The top panel depicts the optimal bond proportion in the taxable account, the middle panel depicts the optimal equity proportion in the tax-deferred account, and the bottom panel depicts the optimal retirement contributions (as a percentage of pre-tax non-financial income).

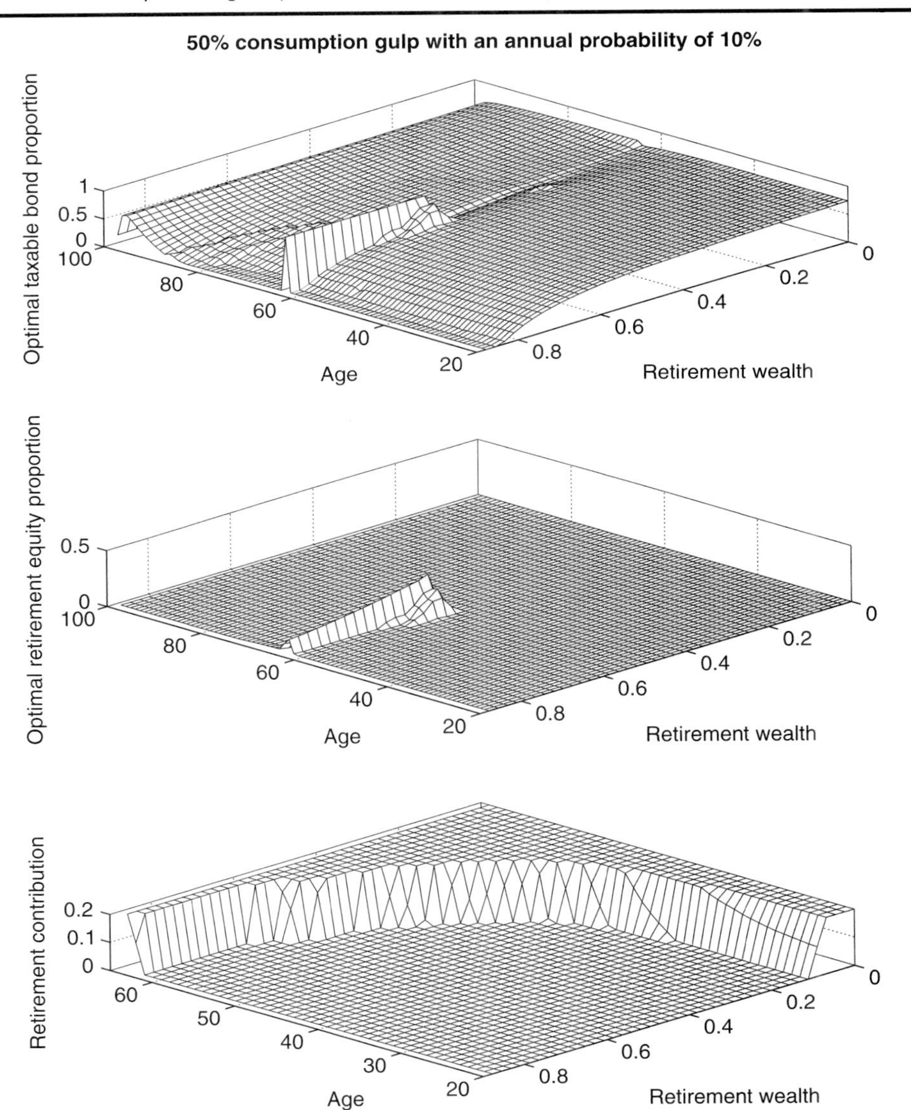

wealth is less than that required to meet an unforeseen consumption shock next period (at age 64). Since this investor has insufficient funds in the taxable account to finance a consumption shock next period, he attempts to minimize the potential penalty for withdrawing funds from the tax-deferred account by hedging against the simultaneous occurrence of a consumption shock and negative equity returns. The pattern of retirement contributions shown in the bottom panel of Figure 5 also reflects the desire of young investors to build liquidity in their taxable accounts.

III. Summary and Conclusion

In this paper, we analyze the optimal dynamic asset allocation and location decisions for an investor with both taxable and tax-deferred investment opportunities. Our results indicate that investors have a strong preference for locating taxable bonds in the tax-deferred retirement account and locating equity in the taxable account. This preference reflects the higher tax burden on taxable bonds relative to equity. When investors can borrow without restrictions in their taxable accounts, it is optimal for them to invest their entire retirement account wealth in taxable bonds and either borrow or lend in the taxable account to achieve an optimal overall portfolio mix. Moreover, the opportunity to invest in tax-exempt bonds does not alter the optimal asset location policy provided equity can be held in a relatively tax-efficient form (e.g., as individual stocks, index mutual funds, or exchange-traded funds).

When investors are prohibited from borrowing, the optimal asset location policy depends upon whether investors face liquidity shocks to consumption. In the absence of liquidity shocks, investors may optimally hold a mix of stocks and bonds in the tax-deferred account, but only if they hold an all-equity portfolio in the taxable account. In the presence of liquidity shocks, investors with insufficient resources in the taxable account to meet the potential need for liquidity tend to reduce their future contributions to the tax-deferred account. Whether investors also adjust the location of their bond holdings to reduce the risk of the taxable portfolio depends upon the magnitude and likelihood of the liquidity shocks and the correlation between these shocks and equity returns. We find that the probability and magnitude of the liquidity shocks need to be rather large and highly negatively correlated with equity returns in order to induce investors to deviate from the tax-efficient asset location policy.

Our analysis points to an important "asset location puzzle" in which the asset location decisions observed in practice deviate substantially from the predictions of our model. Amromin (2001), Poterba and Samwick (2003), Bergstresser and Poterba (2002), and Ameriks and Zeldes (2000) document that investors in practice commonly hold a mix of bonds and stocks in both their taxable and tax-deferred accounts, and in many instances tilt their tax-deferred investments toward equity. While liquidity considerations may help explain some of the observed behavior, we do not believe that liquidity concerns alone can fully account for the magnitude of the deviations that are observed in practice, especially for investors who can borrow and for elderly investors who have unrestricted access to their retirement savings. Our welfare analysis suggests that many investors would benefit considerably from shifting the location of their asset holdings to more closely conform to the tax-efficient policies derived in this paper.

Appendix: Derivation of the Model

Our model builds upon the model developed in Dammon, Spatt, and Zhang (2001) by incorporating tax-deferred investing with taxable investing. The investor's intertemporal consumption-investment problem can be stated as follows:

$$\max_{C_t,n_t,B_t,\theta_t} E\left\{\sum_{t=0}^{T}\beta^t\left[F(t)u\left(\frac{C_t}{(1+i)^t}\right)\right.\right.$$
$$\left.\left. + [F(t-1)-F(t)]\sum_{k=t+1}^{t+H}\beta^{k-t}u\left(\frac{A_H W_t}{(1+i)^t}\right)\right]\right\}, \quad \text{(A1)}$$

s.t.

$$W_t = W_t^T + Y_t(1-\tau_d), \quad t = 0,\ldots,T, \quad \text{(A2)}$$

$$W_t^T = L_t(1-\tau_d) + n_{t-1}[1+(1-\tau_d)d]P_t$$
$$+ B_{t-1}[1+(1-\tau_d)r], \quad t=0,\ldots,T, \quad \text{(A3)}$$

$$Y_t = W_{t-1}^R[\theta_{t-1}(1+g_t)(1+d)+(1-\theta_{t-1})(1+r)], \quad t=1,\ldots,T, \quad \text{(A4)}$$

$$C_t = W_t - \tau_g G_t - n_t P_t - B_t - W_t^R(1-\tau_d), \quad t=0,\ldots,T-1, \quad \text{(A5)}$$

$$W_t^R = Y_t + kL_t, \quad t=0,\ldots,J-1, \quad \text{(A6)}$$

$$W_t^R = Y_t(1-h_t), \quad t=J,\ldots,T-1, \quad \text{(A7)}$$

$$C_t \ge 0, \quad n_t \ge 0, \quad B_t \ge 0, \quad 0 \le \theta_t \le 1, \quad t=0,\ldots,T-1, \quad \text{(A8)}$$

$$n_T = 0, \quad B_T = 0, \quad W_T^R = 0, \quad \text{(A9)}$$

where t denotes time (or age); $F(t)$ is the probability of living through period t; $u(\cdot)$ denotes the investor's utility function; β is the subjective discount factor for utility; C_t is nominal consumption; n_t is the number of shares of stock held in the taxable account; B_t is the amount invested in bonds in the taxable account; θ_t is the fraction of tax-deferred wealth allocated to equity; W_t is total wealth; W_t^T is the wealth in the taxable account after payment of ordinary income taxes but prior to the payment of capital gains taxes; Y_t is the pre-tax wealth in the tax-deferred account before contributions (withdrawals) in period t; W_t^R is the wealth in the tax-deferred account after contributions (withdrawals) in period t; L_t is the pre-tax nonfinancial income; kL_t is the contribution to the retirement account in period t; h_tY_t is the withdrawal from the retirement account in period t; P_t is the per share stock price; d is the nominal dividend yield; r is the nominal riskless interest rate; g_t is the nominal pre-tax capital gain return; i is the constant rate of inflation; G_t is the total realized capital gain in period t; τ_d is the ordinary tax rate; and τ_g is the capital gains tax rate. The initial portfolio holdings, n_{-1} and B_{-1}, initial nonfinancial income, L_0, and initial tax-deferred wealth, Y_0, are assumed to be non-negative. The value of $F(t)$ in equation (A1) is given by:

$$F(t) = \exp\left(-\sum_{j=0}^{t}\lambda_j\right), \quad \text{(A10)}$$

where $\lambda_j > 0$ is the single-period hazard rate for period j with $\lambda_T = \infty$.

The expression inside the square brackets in equation (A1) is the investor's probability-weighted utility at date t. The first term measures the utility of consumption in period t weighted by the probability of living through period t, while the second term is the utility of the investor's bequest weighted by the probability of dying in period t. As written, the bequest provides the investor with a constant level of real consumption for a period of H years, where $A_H = (r^*(1+r^*)^H)/((1+r^*)^H - 1)$ is the H-period annuity factor and $r^* = [(1-\tau_d)r - i]/(1+i)$ is the real after-tax interest rate.

Equation (A2) defines the investor's total wealth as the sum of his taxable wealth and the fraction $(1 - \tau_d)$ of his retirement account balance. Equations (A3) and (A4) define the wealth in the taxable and tax-deferred accounts, respectively. Equation (A5) is the investor's intertemporal budget constraint. The realized capital gain (loss) in equation (A5) is given by

$$G_t = \{I(P^*_{t-1} > P_t)n_{t-1} + [1 - I(P^*_{t-1} > P_t)] \max(n_{t-1} - n_t, 0)\} (P_t - P^*_{t-1}), \quad \text{(A11)}$$

where P^*_{t-1} is the investor's tax basis on shares held at the beginning of period t and $I(P^*_{t-1} > P_t)$ is an indicator function that takes the value of one if there is an embedded capital loss (i.e., $P^*_{t-1} > P_t$) and zero otherwise. Following Dammon, Spatt, and Zhang (2001), we assume that the tax basis is the weighted average purchase price for shares held in the taxable account. The nominal tax basis follows the law of motion:

$$P^*_t = \begin{cases} \dfrac{n_{t-1}P^*_{t-1} + \max(n_t - n_{t-1}, 0)P_t}{n_{t-1} + \max(n_t - n_{t-1}, 0)}, & \text{if } P^*_{t-1} < P_t, \\ P_t, & \text{if } P^*_{t-1} \geq P_t. \end{cases} \quad \text{(A12)}$$

This formulation takes into account that, in the absence of transaction costs, the investor optimally sells his entire holding of equity to realize a tax loss when $P^*_{t-1} \geq P_t$ and immediately repurchases equity to rebalance his portfolio. In this case, the tax basis of the newly acquired shares is the current market price, P_t. Also, when the investor has an embedded capital gain on existing shares (i.e., $P^*_{t-1} < P_t$), the tax basis is unchanged, unless the investor purchases additional shares in period t (i.e., $n_t > n_{t-1}$).

Equations (A6) and (A7) impose constraints on contributions to and withdrawals from the retirement account. Equation (A8) requires consumption to be non-negative and prohibits short sales and borrowing in the taxable and tax-deferred accounts. If investors are allowed to borrow or sell short in the taxable account, the non-negativity constraints on B_t and n_t are relaxed. Finally, equation (A9) requires the investor to liquidate his holdings at date T.

We assume that the investor's preferences can be expressed as follows

$$u\left[\frac{C_t}{(1+i)^t}\right] = \frac{\left[\dfrac{C_t}{(1+i)^t}\right]^{1-\gamma}}{1-\gamma}, \quad \text{(A13)}$$

where γ is the investor's relative risk aversion coefficient. Note that the summation appearing in the second term of the objective function can be rewritten as follows:

$$\sum_{k=t+1}^{t+H} \beta^{k-t} u\left[\frac{A_H W_t}{(1+i)^t}\right] = \frac{\beta(1-\beta^H)\left[\dfrac{A_H W_t}{(1+i)^t}\right]^{1-\gamma}}{(1-\beta)(1-\gamma)}.$$

Letting X_t denote the vector of state variables at date t, we can write the Bellman equation for the above maximization problem as follows:

$$V(X_t) = \max_{C_t, n_t, B_t, \theta_t} \left\{ \frac{e^{-\lambda_t}\left[\dfrac{C_t}{(1+i)^t}\right]^{1-\gamma}}{1-\gamma} + \frac{(1-e^{-\lambda_t})\beta(1-\beta^H)\left[\dfrac{A_H W_t}{(1+i)^t}\right]^{1-\gamma}}{(1-\beta)(1-\gamma)} + e^{-\lambda_t}\beta E_t[V(X_{t+1})] \right. \quad \text{(A14)}$$

for $t = 0, \ldots, T-1$, subject to equations (A2)–(A9). The sufficient state variables for the investor's problem at date t are denoted by the following vector:

$$X_t = [P_t, P^*_{t-1}, n_{t-1}, W^T_t, Y_t, L_t]'. \tag{A15}$$

We simplify the investor's optimization problem by normalizing by the investor's total wealth, W_t, and assuming that the investor's nonfinancial income is a constant fraction of total wealth, $l = L_t/W_t$. Let $s_t = n_{t-1}P_t/W^T_t$ be the beginning-of-period equity proportion in the taxable account; $f_t = n_t P_t/W^T_t$ be the fraction of taxable wealth allocated to equity after trading at date t; $b_t = B_t/W^T_t$ be the fraction of taxable wealth allocated to taxable bonds after trading at date t; $y_t = Y_t(1-\tau_d)/W_t$ be the fraction of the investor's beginning-of-period total wealth that is held in the retirement account before trading at date t; $w^R_t = W^R_t/W_t$ be the fraction of the investor's beginning-of-period wealth that is held in the retirement account after trading at date t; and $p^*_{t-1} = P^*_{t-1}/P_t$ be the investor's tax basis–price ratio on the initial equity holdings in the taxable account. Then, the gross nominal rate of return on the investor's taxable portfolio from period t to $t+1$, after the tax on dividends and interest, but prior to the payment of capital gain taxes, is

$$\mu^T_{t+1} = \frac{f_t[1+(1-\tau_d)d](1+g_{t+1}) + [1+(1-\tau_d)r]b_t}{f_t + b_t}, \tag{A16}$$

and the gross rate of return on the investor's tax-deferred portfolio from period t to $t+1$ is

$$\mu^R_{t+1} = \theta_t(1+d)(1+g_{t+1}) + (1-\theta_t)(1+r). \tag{A17}$$

Using this notation, equation (A2) can be written as the following linear dynamic wealth equation:

$$W_{t+1} = \left[\mu^T_{t+1}(f_t + b_t)\frac{1-y_t}{1-l(1-\tau_d)} + \mu^R_{t+1}\frac{w^R_t(1-\tau_d)}{1-l(1-\tau_d)}\right]W_t. \tag{A18}$$

Similarly, the intertemporal budget constraint in equation (A5) can be written as follows:

$$c_t = 1 - \tau_g\delta_t(1-y_t) - (f_t + b_t)(1-y_t) - w^R_t(1-\tau_d), \tag{A19}$$

where $c_t = C_t/W_t$ is the consumption–wealth ratio for period t,

$$\delta_t = G_t/W_t = \{I(p^*_{t-1} > 1)s_t + [1 - I(p^*_{t-1} > 1)]\max(s_t - f_t, 0)\}(1 - p^*_{t-1}) \tag{A20}$$

is the fraction of beginning-of-period wealth that is taxable as *realized* capital gains in period t, and p^*_{t-1} is given by

$$p^*_{t-1} = \begin{cases} \dfrac{[s_{t-1}p^*_{t-2} + \max(f_{t-1} - s_{t-1}, 0)]/(1+g_t)}{s_{t-1} + \max(f_{t-1} - s_{t-1}, 0)}, & \text{if } p^*_{t-2} < 1, \\[2ex] \dfrac{1}{1+g_t}, & \text{if } p^*_{t-2} \geq 1. \end{cases} \tag{A21}$$

The linearity of the dynamic wealth equation and the assumption of constant relative risk-averse preferences ensure that our model has the property that the consumption and portfolio decision rules, $\{c_t, f_t, b_t, \theta_t\}$, are independent of total wealth, W_t. Furthermore, with the above normalization, the relevant state variables for the investor's problem become $x_t = \{s_t, p^*_{t-1}, y_t\}$. Defining $v(x_t) = V(X_t)/[W_t/(1+i)^t]^{1-\gamma}$ to be the normalized value function and $\rho_{t+1} = W_{t+1}/[W_t(1+i)]$ to be one plus the *real* growth rate in wealth from period t to period $t+1$ the investor's problem can be restated as follows:

$$v(x_t) = \max_{c_t, f_t, b_t, \theta_t} \left\{ \frac{e^{-\lambda_t} c_t^{1-\gamma}}{1-\gamma} + \frac{(1 - e^{-\lambda_t})\beta(1 - \beta^H)A_H^{1-\gamma}}{(1-\beta)(1-\gamma)} + e^{-\lambda_t}\beta E_t\left[v(x_{t+1})\rho_{t+1}^{1-\gamma}\right] \right\},$$
$$t = 0, \ldots, T-1, \tag{A22}$$

s.t.

$$\rho_{t+1} = \left(\frac{\mu_{t+1}^T}{1+i}\right)(f_t + b_t)\frac{1 - y_t}{1 - l(1-\tau_d)} + \left(\frac{\mu_{t+1}^R}{1+i}\right)\frac{\omega_t^R(1-\tau_d)}{1 - l(1-\tau_d)}, \quad t = 0, \ldots, T-1, \tag{A23}$$

$$w_t^R = \frac{y_t}{1-\tau_d} + kl, \quad t = 0, \ldots, J-1, \tag{A24}$$

$$w_t^R = \frac{y_t}{1-\tau_d}(1 - h_t), \quad t = J, \ldots, T-1, \tag{A25}$$

$$c_t \geq 0, \quad f_t \geq 0, \quad 0 \leq \theta_t \leq 1, \tag{A26}$$

where c_t is given by equation (A19), δ_t is given by equation (A20), and p_{t-1}^* is given by equation (A21).

The above problem can be solved numerically using backward recursion. To do this, we discretize the lagged endogenous state variables, $x_t = \{s_t, p_{t-1}^*, y_t\}$, into a grid of $(101 \times 101 \times 21)$ over the following ranges: $s_t \in [0, 0.999]$, $p_{t-1}^* \in [0, 1.1]$, and $y_t \in [0, 0.8]$. At the terminal date T, the investor's value function takes the known value

$$v_T = \frac{\beta(1-\beta^H)A_H^{1-\gamma}}{(1-\beta)(1-\gamma)} \tag{A27}$$

at all points in the state space. The value function at date T is then used to solve for the optimal decision rules for all points on the grid at date $T - 1$. The procedure is repeated recursively for each time period until the solution for date $t = 0$ is found. Tri-linear interpolation is used to calculate the value function for points in the state space that lie between the grid points.

References

Ameriks, John, and Stephen Zeldes, 2000, How do household portfolio shares vary with age? Unpublished manuscript, Columbia University.

Amromin, Gene, 2001, Portfolio allocation choices in taxable and tax-deferred accounts: An empirical analysis of tax efficiency, Unpublished manuscript, University of Chicago.

Bergstresser, Daniel, and James Poterba, 2002, Asset allocation and asset location: Household evidence from the Survey of Consumer Finances, Unpublished manuscript, Massachusetts Institute of Technology.

Black, Fischer, 1980, The tax consequences of long-run pension policy, *Financial Analysts Journal* 36, 21–28.

Carhart, Mark, 1997, On persistence in mutual fund performance, *Journal of Finance* 52, 57–82.

Constantinides, George, 1983, Capital market equilibrium with personal taxes, *Econometrica* 51, 611–636.

Constantinides, George, 1984, Optimal stock trading with personal taxes: Implications for prices and the abnormal January returns, *Journal of Financial Economics* 13, 65–89.

Constantinides, George, and Jonathan Ingersoll, 1984, Optimal bond trading with personal taxes: Implications for bond prices and estimated tax brackets and yield curves, *Journal of Financial Economics* 13, 299–335.

Dammon, Robert, Kenneth Dunn, and Chester Spatt, 1989, A reexamination of the value of tax options, *Review of Financial Studies* 2, 341–372.

Dammon, Robert, and Chester Spatt, 1996, The optimal trading and pricing of securities with asymmetric capital gains taxes and transaction costs, *Review of Financial Studies* 9, 921–952.

Dammon, Robert, Chester Spatt, and Harold Zhang, 1999, Optimal asset allocation with taxable and tax-deferred investing, Unpublished manuscript, Carnegie Mellon University.

Dammon, Robert, Chester Spatt, and Harold Zhang, 2001, Optimal consumption and investment with capital gains taxes, *Review of Financial Studies* 14, 583–616.

Fama, Eugene, and Kenneth French, 2002, The equity premium, *Journal of Finance* 57, 637–659.

Green, Richard, 1993, A simple model of the taxable and tax-exempt yield curves, *Review of Financial Studies* 6, 233–264.

Gruber, Martin, 1996, Another puzzle: The growth in actively managed mutual funds, *Journal of Finance* 51, 783–810.

Huang, Jennifer, 2000, Taxable or tax-deferred account? Portfolio decision with multiple investment goals, Unpublished manuscript, Massachusetts Institute of Technology.

Poterba, James, and Andrew Samwick, 2003, Taxation and household portfolio composition: U.S. evidence from the 1980s and 1990s, *Journal of Public Economics* 87, 5–38.

Poterba, James, John Shoven, and Clemens Sialm, 2001, Asset location for retirement savers, in W. Gale, J. Shoven, and M. Warshawsky, eds: *Private Pensions and Public Policies* (Brookings Institution, Washington, D.C.).

Reichenstein, William, 2001, Asset allocation and asset location decisions revisited, *Journal of Wealth Management* 4 (Summer), 16–26.

Shoven, John, 1999, The location and allocation of assets in pension and conventional savings accounts, Working paper no. 7007, National Bureau of Economic Research.

Shoven, John, and Clemens Sialm, 2003, Asset location in tax-deferred and conventional savings accounts, *Journal of Public Economics* 88, 23–38.

Tepper, Irwin, 1981, Taxation and corporate pension policy, *Journal of Finance* 36, 1–13.

Williams, Joseph, 1985, Trading and valuing depreciable assets, *Journal of Financial Economics* 14, 283–308.

The Yale University Generation

Nine

Philip H. Dybvig

Phillip H. Dybvig received a Ph.D. from Yale University in 1979. He started out at Princeton University, and now works at Washington University in Saint Louis. •

How did I get the greatest living finance scholar as a thesis advisor?

Mostly luck. I first met Steve Ross on April 14, 1976. Steve was well-established then but probably still viewed by most people as a rising star rather than a top scholar. I was an undergraduate at Indiana University, and I had to decide by April 15 where to go to graduate school. I had fellowship offers from the University of Pennsylvania and the University of Rochester, and Steve Ross came to give a seminar at Indiana on the 14th. This was one piece of luck. It was another piece of luck that Michael Magill, my professor at Indiana, had encouraged me to come to finance seminars and read the papers beforehand. I usually prepared a question for the speaker; I was lucky that this was a smart thing to do because I did not have a smart reason for doing it: I asked a question just to stay awake in the seminar. I read Steve's seminar paper, the classic incentive-signalling model of capital structure.[1] I was having trouble finding a good question, and reading a couple of Steve's other papers did not help. So, I decided to take the easy way out. It is usually a safe question to ask why a model's story is different from the traditional story. In Steve's leading example, the firm chooses a high debt-equity ratio to signal it is tough; choosing to take on a lot of debt signals a good firm. I asked a friend who is a business major what it means to have a high debt-equity ratio. She responded that such a firm could have cash flow problems and might be headed for trouble. In the seminar, I asked how Steve knew that the firms in his model took on lots of debt to show they were tough and how did we know they were not in trouble and borrowing money in a last-ditch effort to stay in business. This was a very lucky question, much better than I realized, because this is why the example is a parable and should not be taken too literally.

After the seminar, there were beers with the speaker at Nick's Pub. I was underage so I borrowed the picture ID of a friend who looked nothing like me. I was lucky I was not arrested for using a fake ID, and I was lucky that after looking down at the ID and up at me for about five minutes, the girl at Nick's shrugged and let me in. I monopolized Steve. We sat at a table next to the wall: Steve was at the end and I sat next to him. I asked him why I should choose Penn over Rochester and he gave me a long and charming sales pitch. Then I asked the crucial question. I had been offered a Wharton Econometric Forecasting Associates Fellowship, and all the examples in the offer letter talked about doing empirical work. Was there any way I could ensure working with a theorist, such as Steve, Cass, Shell, or Pollak? Steve replied that he would be happy to work with me. Lucky again!

I walked home from Nick's slightly tipsy and very happy. The truth is that I had no idea just how lucky I was. Steve didn't care that I looked a mess at the time, too skinny with long

[1]Stephen A. Ross, (1977) "The Determination of Financial Structure: the Incentive-Signalling Approach," *Bell Journal of Economics* **8,** 23–40.

straggly hair and acne; all he cared about was my potential. Everyone in the profession knows that Steve is blazingly smart and fast, and that he has made fundamental contributions to every area of finance. A lot of people also know that Steve has a talent for making everything he talks about magical and that he is great at explaining to people how things work and what is important and why.

Steve's students know much more. Once Steve latches on to a student, he gives the student unwavering support. He helps the student in whatever ways he can, works around or through any flaws the student may have. He is patient when patience is called for and prodding when prodding is needed. He enlists other people to help, too. He also says nice flattering (sometimes exaggerated) things about his students, even at his own expense. In short, Steve has the sort of selfless commitment to his students that is a hallmark of a great teacher.

The paper I picked for this volume bears Steve's mark. The paper looks at the feasible set in a portfolio problem in terms of distributions instead of state-payouts. Steve taught me to look at problems from different angles, and turning a problem on its head this way is the sort of thing he would do.

Inefficient Dynamic Portfolio Strategies or How to Throw Away a Million Dollars in the Stock Market

Philip H. Dybvig
Yale University

A number of portfolio strategies followed by practitioners are dominated because they are incompletely diversified over time. The payoff distribution pricing model is used to compute the cost of following undiversified strategies. Simple numerical examples illustrate the technique, and computer-generated examples provide realistic estimates of the cost of some typical policies, using reasonable parameter values. The cost can be substantial and should not be ignored by practitioners. A section on generalizations shows how to extend the analysis to term structure models and other general models of returns. •

Portfolio managers regularly use a number of dynamic portfolio strategies that have not received careful theoretical analysis; some examples are lock-in strategies, stop-loss strategies, rolling over portfolio insurance, and contingent immunization. The lack of analysis has been due largely to the inadequacy of the traditional theoretical tools. Specifically, mean-variance analysis is not valid when the portfolio return is nonlinearly related to market returns, as it will be under these strategies.[1] Cox and Leland (1982) have shown that when the riskless rate is constant and the risky asset follows geometric Brownian motion or a geometric binomial process, strategies such as these are inefficient; unfortunately, the Cox-Leland approach, while elegant and insightful, does not tell us the *magnitude* of the inefficiency. The purpose of this article is to use the payoff distribution pricing model [Dybvig (1980, 1988)] to compute directly the cost of the inefficiency. As a result, we can now compare the cost of a failure to diversify over time with nonmodeled costs, such as trading commissions. The results indicate that the inefficiency costs of the strategies are substantial and should not be ignored by practitioners.

A common misconception among students first learning about the efficient markets hypothesis is that portfolio managers can do no damage. Of course, this is not true, because managers choosing random or poorly diversified portfolios throw away investors' money by obtaining them less return than is justified for the amount of risk taken on. For example,

I am grateful for helpful discussions with Michael Brennan, Stephen Brown, Kent Dybvig, David Feldman, Mike Granito, Roger Ibbotson, Jon Ingersoll, Alan Kraus, Steve Ross, Eduardo Schwartz, and participants in various seminars. I am also grateful for financial support from the Sloan Research Fellowship Program.

[1]See Dybvig and Ingersoll (1982) for a discussion of the difficulty of using mean-variance analysis for evaluating options and other nonlinear claims, and Dybvig and Ross (1985a, 1985b) for a general discussion of why mean-variance performance measures may not be valid even in the absence of measurement error.

The Review of Financial Studies 1988, Volume 1, number 1, pp. 67–88, © 1988. The Review of Financial Studies 0021-9398/88/5904-013 $1.50

Reprinted with permission:
Dybvig, Phillip H. "Inefficient Dynamic Portfolio Strategies, or How to Throw Away a Million Dollars in the Stock Market." *Review of Financial Studies* 1 (1988): 67–88.

in the mean-variance world an efficient portfolio choice could have given the investors the same mean and variance of terminal wealth at a lower cost. In an intertemporal context, things get a bit more complicated. Besides the importance of diversification across assets, an efficient portfolio choice must also be diversified across time. Furthermore, a nonconstant portfolio choice over time may be optimal, but such a portfolio choice must react appropriately to information arrival.

Fortunately, there is a simple way of viewing the multiperiod problem. As Ross (1978) has emphasized, the space of feasible consumption bundles is quite generally a linear space. Therefore, if all consumption takes place at the end, we can replace the original dynamic problem with an equivalent one-period problem that has the appropriate terminal state prices.[2] The use of state prices to reduce a multiperiod problem to a one-period problem is the basis of Cox and Leland (1982) and has been emphasized by many others, starting perhaps with Ross (1976) and Rubinstein (1976).[3]

Once we assume that all consumption takes place at the end, we apply the payoff distribution pricing model (PDPM), which allows us to calculate a lower bound on the cost of the efficiency loss. Here are the assumptions of the PDPM [see Dybvig (1988) for a formal development of the PDPM]:

1. Agents' preferences depend only on the probability distribution of terminal wealth.
2. Agents prefer more to less. That is, given a choice between two ordered random terminal wealths, an agent will always choose the larger.
3. The market faced by an individual comes from our standard model of a perfect market (no taxes, transaction costs, or information asymmetries) that is complete over finitely many equally probable terminal states or over some atomless continuum of states. Such a market allows short sales without penalty.

Informally, the assumptions are (1) state independence of preferences, (2) preference of more to less, and (3) completeness of frictionless complete markets with equally probable states.[4]

The first assumption says that preferences depend only on the probability distribution of terminal consumption. This assumption allows von Neumann-Morgenstern preferences over wealth, or more generally Machina (1982) preferences over wealth, but it precludes state-dependent preferences (including those induced by nontraded wealth). The second assumption, preference of more to less, would not be reasonable for ice cream but is certainly reasonable for wealth. The third assumption, completeness of markets over equally probable or continuous terminal states, is a natural assumption in the presence of continuous trading or a complete set of options. The assumption of equally probable terminal states is for convenience; it allows us to use first-order stochastic dominance. If we allow terminal state probabilities to be unequal and assume concavity of preferences, the analysis is messier, but exactly the same numerical results are valid [see Appendix I of Dybvig (1988)].

These assumptions imply that any optimal strategy purchases more consumption in terminal states in which consumption is cheaper. What is new to the PDPM is the idea of

[2]Consumption will always be assumed to occur at the end. More generally, if preferences are time-separable, the analysis is unchanged if we treat consumption at each date separately.

[3]Other papers emphasizing state prices and the reduction of a multiperiod problem to one period include: Banz and Miller (1978); Brennan and Solanki (1981); Cox and Leland (1982); Cox, Ross, and Rubinstein (1979); Cox and Huang (1985); and Pliska (1986).

[4]By definition, any atomless distribution has equally probable states each having probability 0. (An *atom* is an indivisible state with positive probability.) *Continuum* will be taken to mean a nonatomic continuum.

computing how much the cheapest portfolio generating a given *distribution function* of consumption should cost, and the development of simple machinery for doing so. This cost is given by the change in price in response to swapping consumption across terminal states to make the consumption a decreasing function of the state-price density while maintaining the same marginal distribution.

Section 1 contains simple numerical examples. Section 2 presents some computer generated numerical results for reasonable parameter values. Section 3 discusses generalizations, particularly to term structure models. The article is intended to be self-contained in the sense that it does not require any prior knowledge of the PDPM.

1. Some Numerical Examples

Here are some simple examples designed to illustrate the principle behind applying the PDPM to measuring inefficiency. These examples use the binomial model of stock returns introduced by Cox, Ross, and Rubinstein (1979). For convenience, numerically simple parameters are chosen: the initial wealth level and initial stock price are both 16, the riskless rate is always zero, and in each period the stock doubles in price or halves in price, each with probability ½. A four-period model is required, since, given the other assumptions, this is the shortest time span over which the analysis does not degenerate.[5] Obviously, these examples are for illustration only; more realistic examples will be analyzed in Section 3, using the general form of the PDPM.

Before moving to the examples, let us review some important properties of the binomial model (all these properties have appeared in the literature in one form or another) and a few PDPM concepts and results.

The Binomial Model and the PDPM

In the binomial model, stock and bond returns are shown graphically in Table 1. For binomial models, it is most common to represent the stock-price movements by an *ingrown tree.* An expanded tree in which all possible stock-price paths are distinguished will also be useful, since we will be studying portfolio strategies for which the terminal portfolio value will depend on the whole path of stock prices and not just on the final stock price. The bond price is constant over time and in all states and is represented by a line segment.

We can see from Table 1 that the usual convention of representing the stock price in terms of an ingrown tree is simply a shorthand that combines all the states in which the stock price is the same. In the expanded tree, each state has the same probability, $1/16 = (1/2)^4$, because at each node the up and down probabilities are both ½. We could write the bond in an expanded tree in the same way, but the result would be a boring tree with 16 at each node.

From option pricing theory [and explicitly Cox, Ross, and Rubinstein (1979)], we know that every contingent claim paying off various amounts in the last period can be

[5] Readers who are familiar with the path independence results of Cox and Leland (1982) may find this confusing, since the strategies we will consider have path-dependent strategies in three or even in two periods. However, these strategies will not be inefficient for agents who have concave preferences that are not necessarily strictly concave. To get inefficiency for these general agents, we need something slightly stronger than path independence, which is that a path with strictly higher state price should have strictly higher consumption. For a general discussion of the relation between the amount of regularity assumed of utility functions and the first-order conditions in terms of the state-price density, see Dybvig and Ross (1982), especially in Table 1 and the related discussion.

TABLE 1 | Security returns, state probabilities, and state prices

Bond:

16—16—16—16—16

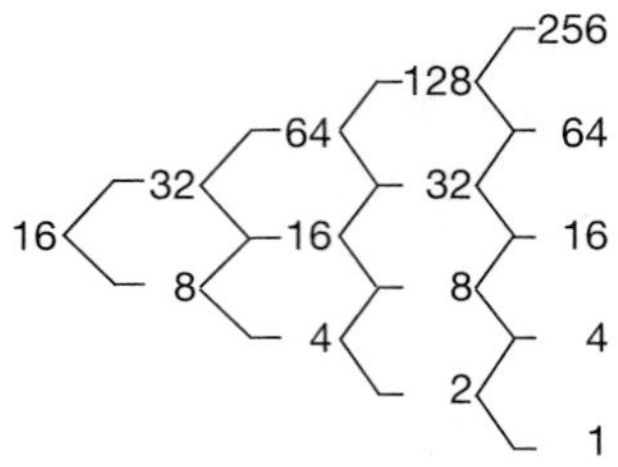

Stock:	State probability	State price	State-price density
256	1/16	1/81	16/81
64	4/16	8/81	32/81
16	6/16	24/81	64/81
4	4/16	32/81	128/81
1	1/16	16/81	256/81
Stock (expanded):			
256	1/16	1/81	16/81
64	1/16	2/81	32/81
64	1/16	2/81	32/81
16	1/16	4/81	64/81
64	1/16	2/81	32/81
16	1/16	4/81	64/81
16	1/16	4/81	64/81
4	1/16	8/81	128/81
64	1/16	2/81	32/81
16	1/16	4/81	64/81
16	1/16	4/81	64/81
4	1/16	8/81	128/81
16	1/16	4/81	64/81
4	1/16	8/81	128/81
4	1/16	8/81	128/81
1	1/16	16/81	256/81

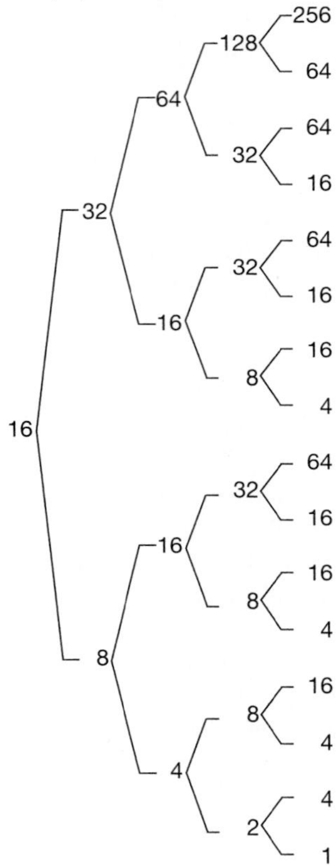

priced, because each contingent claim can be duplicated by some hedging strategy. In particular, we can price a claim that pays 1 in a given state and 0 in all other states. By definition, the price of this claim is called the *state price* of the given state. State prices are useful because the value of any security can be written as the sum across states of the state price times the value of the security in the state.

To compute the state price for the binomial model, look first to a single period. Suppose that the value of an asset next period is v_1 if the stock goes up and is v_2 if the stock goes down. We want to duplicate holding the asset. If we invest an amount v_s in stock and an amount v_B in bond, tomorrow we will have $2v_s + v_B$ if the stock goes up and $v_s/2 + v_B$ if the stock goes down. If this investment duplicates the asset's value, then we have

$$v_1 = 2v_s + v_B \quad \text{and} \quad v_2 = v_s/2 + v_B$$

Solving for v_s and v_B, we get $v_s = 2\,(v_1 - v_2)/3$ and $v_B = (4v_2 - v_1)/3$, which is the hedging strategy. Note that $v_s + v_B = v_1/3 + 2v_2/3$, which is the one-period pricing relation. In other words, the up state has price ⅓ and the down state has price ⅔.

Of course, we can use this procedure to obtain the state price of any node and, by extension, the value of any claim. In particular, the state price of any node equals the price of a claim that pays 1 in that state at that time and 0 otherwise. By folding back, we conclude that the state price of any node is $(1/3)^u\,(2/3)^d$, where u is the number of times the stock price goes up and d is the number of times the stock price goes down. This formula applies to all time intervals. For example, the value of a security at any point is equal to ⅓ times the value one period later if the stock goes up plus ⅔ times the value one period later if the stock goes down. Working backward a period at a time using state prices is analogous to solving the Black and Scholes (1973) differential equation, while valuing a claim directly by summing over the four-period prices is analogous to using the Rubinstein (1976) integral approach to option pricing. From now on we will focus on the approach using state prices. Keep in mind, however, that the derivation of the state prices tells us explicitly how to compute the amounts of stock and bond held at each point in time in the dominating strategy.

The one aspect of Table 1 that remains to be discussed is the *state-price density* (or *state price per unit probability*), which is simply the state price divided by the probability.[6] It is useful to think in terms of this ratio, which plays a central role in the PDPM. For one thing, maximizing a von Neumann-Morgenstern utility function gives the first-order condition that the marginal utility is proportional to the terminal state-price density. Suppose that an agent solves the following problem:

Choose c_i's to
maximize $\sum \pi_i u(c_i)$
subject to $\sum p_i c_i = w_0$

where c_i is consumption in terminal state i, π_i is the probability of terminal state i, $u(\cdot)$ is the agent's utility function, and p_i is the state price of terminal state i. If $u(\cdot)$ is differentiable, then the first-order condition is that for some λ,

$$\pi_i\, u'(c_i) = \lambda p_i$$

or

$$u'(c_i) = \lambda p_i/\pi_i \equiv \lambda \rho_i \tag{1}$$

which is to say that the agent's marginal utility of wealth in terminal state i is proportional to the terminal state-price density $\rho_i \equiv p_i/\pi_i$.[7] A second important feature of the state-price density is that if we combine states with the same state-price density, the combined aggregate state will also have the same state-price density. Perhaps more importantly, we can define

[6]One special feature of Table 1 is that the terminal state-price density is a function only of the terminal stock price. This is a very special feature of this particular example and of certain other examples, including economies with geometric i.i.d. stock-price movements [see Cox and Leland (1982)]. Especially in models of the term structure (with random interest rate movements), it is not reasonable to assume that the state-price density is a function only of the natural state variables. Fortunately, as we will see in Section 3, the approach in this article does not require the state price to be a function only of the state variables driving asset returns.

[7]It $u(\cdot)$ is concave but not everywhere differentiable, $u'(\cdot)$ should be interpreted as some element of the marginal utility correspondence, which is the closed interval bounded by the right and left derivatives. See Dybvig and Ross (1982).

the state-price density even if there is a nonatomic continuum of states (in which case both the state price and the probability are zero), as in the diffusion models. The state-price density is defined at each node as the ratio of the state price to the probability of the node. The state-price density follows a multiplicative process whose movements locally price all assets correctly. In our specialized binomial model, the state-price density at a node following u ups and d downs is given by $\rho_n = p_n/\pi_n = [(1/3)^u(2/3)^d]/[(1/2)^u(1/2)^d] = (2/3)^u(4/3)^d$.

We will need a few concepts and results of the payoff distribution pricing model (PDPM). An *asset pricing model* (such as the CAPM, the APT, or the Black-Scholes model) gives us the price of a random cash flow, as in the budget constraint to the agent's maximization problem above. For discrete models with complete markets, the asset pricing model is $P_A(c) = \Sigma_i p_i c_i$. The PDPM assigns a price to a distribution function of consumption by assigning to it the price of the least expensive consumption pattern having that payoff. In other words, we can write the distributional pricing function as $P_D(F) = \min\{P_A(c) \mid c \sim F\}$, where ~ means "is distributed as." For the extensions in Section 3, I will refer to a general formula for this minimum cost in terms of the distribution functions of c and ρ, but for now all we need is the following theorem, which combines several results from Dybvig (1988).

Theorem 1. *The following are equivalent:*

1. *The consumption pattern c is chosen by some agent who has strictly increasing von Neumann-Morgenstern preferences over terminal wealth.*
2. *The consumption pattern has an asset price equal to the distributional price of its distribution function; that is,* $P_A(c) = P_D(F_c)$.
3. *Consumption is nondecreasing in the terminal state-price density.*

Proof. See theorems 1 and 2 in Dybvig (1988).

This theorem is useful to us for two different reasons. First, it says that $P_A(c) - P_D(F_c)$ is a tight lower bound on the amount of initial wealth an agent would pay to switch from c to an optimal strategy, given that we do not know the agent's actual preferences. [This is a bound because all agents are indifferent between c and the strategy underlying $P_D(c)$, and the bound is tight because the theorem tells us that there is some agent who would follow that underlying strategy, implying that the bound is achieved for this agent.] Second, it tells us how to compute the bound: namely, by swapping consumption across terminal states, leaving the distribution function unchanged, until consumption is nondecreasing in the terminal state-price density.

Now that the binomial model and the PDPM have been reviewed, we are ready to proceed to the examples. All the examples use the concepts and tools of the PDPM to quantify the amount of damage done by following an inefficient policy, that is, a policy for which consumption is not non-increasing in the terminal state-price density. The first example examines a policy of holding stock initially but limiting potential losses by switching from the stock to the bond if ever the portfolio value falls too much. Let us call this policy a stop-loss strategy.

Example 1: Stop-loss strategy

The rule under this strategy is to invest in the stock until the portfolio value falls to 8 and to stay in the bond from then on. The value of the portfolio under this strategy is given in the ingrown tree in Table 2. The probabilities are computed by adding up the number of paths to the terminal node and multiplying by 1/16. For example, there are three paths (up-up-up-down, up-up-down-up, and up-down-up-up) having a terminal wealth of 64 and two paths (up-up-down-down and up-down-up-down) having a terminal wealth of 16.

TABLE 2 | The stop-loss strategy (limit = 8) and a dominating strategy

Here is the stop-loss strategy:

					Probability
				256	1/16
			128		
		64		64	3/16
	32		32		
16		16		16	2/16
	8	8	8	8	10/16

Here is a dominating strategy (which is itself undominated). This strategy costs only $15\frac{65}{81}$ (=1280/81) but gives the same terminal probability distribution of wealth (in different states).

				Dominating payoff	Stop-loss payoff	State-price density
1280/81	832/27	64	128	256	256	16/81
				64	64	32/81
			32	64	64	32/81
				16	16	64/81
		128/9	80/3	64	64	32/81
				8	16	64/81 ←
			8	8	8	64/81
				8	8	128/81
	224/27	80/9	32/3	16	8	32/81 ←
				8	8	64/81
			8	8	8	64/81
				8	8	128/81
		8	8	8	8	64/81
				8	8	128/81
			8	8	8	128/81
				8	8	256/81

Horizontal paths corresponding to holding the bond have to be counted twice *per period the bond is held,* since the horizontal line captures both states. Therefore, there are 10 paths with a terminal wealth of 8 (up-down-down-up, up-down-down-down, down-up-up-up, down-up-up-down, down-up-down-up, down-up-down-down, down-down-up-up, down-down-up-down, down-down-down-up, and down-down-down-down).

The second strategy in Table 2 was chosen to obtain the same distribution of terminal wealth (allocated differently across states) but with consumption ordered the opposite of the terminal state-price density, which, from Table 1, is ordered the opposite of the stock price. To do this, we walk down the two probability distributions together. First, we assign the $1/16$ probability of 256 to the terminal state in which the stock reaches 256. Next, we assign the $3/16$ probability of 64 to three of the four terminal states in which the stock price reaches 64. Now, we assign $1/16$ of the $2/16$ probability of getting 16 to the remaining terminal state in which the stock is 64, and the remaining $1/16$ to one of the terminal states in which the stock is 16. In all the remaining terminal states (10 of them) the amount we get is 8. Because this selection makes consumption nonincreasing in the terminal state-price density, by Theorem 1 the resulting portfolio strategy is efficient. The values earlier on in the tree are computed by walking back period by period using the $1/3$, $2/3$ weighting rule. We find that this portfolio strategy, while giving exactly the same probability distribution of terminal wealth as the stop-loss strategy, costs only $15\,65/81$ (as compared to 16).

What is really going on here? If we compare the two strategies' terminal wealth state by state, we find that they differ only in the two marked states, up-down-up-down and down-up-up-up. Since the later state has more ups and fewer downs, the terminal state-price density is lower. The efficient dominating strategy has its higher consumption in that state (16 versus 8), while the stop-loss strategy has it reversed (8 versus 16). The savings is the difference in cost of the two strategies ($16 - 1280/81 = 16/81$), which is the probability ($1/16$) times the difference in terminal state-price density ($64/81 - 32/81 = 32/81$) times the amount of consumption moved ($16 - 8 = 8$). In richer examples with more periods or more elaborate strategies, there would be more terminal states in which the inefficient and dominating strategies disagree; nonetheless, the concept would be the same: The dominating strategy would move consumption from expensive terminal states to cheaper states.

The second example is in the same spirit as the first, but in reverse. The policy is to hold stock initially, but to switch into bonds (to lock in the gain) if there is sufficient improvement in the portfolio value. Let us refer to this policy as a lock-in strategy.

Example 2: Lock-in strategy

The rule under this strategy is to invest in the stock until the portfolio value rises to 32 and to stay in the bond from then on. The value of the portfolio is given by the ingrown tree in Table 3. In terms of which paths can occur (and therefore the probabilities of the outcomes), the ingrown tree is just the same as the stop-loss tree of Example 1 in Table 2, only upside down. The efficiency loss is different, however, since the quantities and terminal state prices are different when we turn the tree upside down.

The second strategy in Table 3 was chosen to obtain the same terminal distribution of terminal wealth as the lock-in strategy but with consumption ordered the opposite of the terminal state-price density. This process is just as in Example 1, except that it starts from the opposite side. Computing the initial investment required for this strategy, we find that it costs only $15\,17/81$ (as compared to 16).

As in Example 1, if we compare the terminal wealth of the lock-in strategy with its dominating strategy state by state, we find that the two differ only in the two marked states (up-down-down-down and down-up-down-up). The improvement made by the dominating strategy is to move the larger consumption from the more expensive of the two states to the cheaper one.

In the third example, we compute the potential cost of hiring someone who claims to have timing ability but actually may not.

Example 3: Random market timing strategy (market timer who cannot)

The rule under this strategy is to invest in the stock in some two of the four periods (half the time) and to invest in the bond in the other two. The timing is based on any random rule

TABLE 3 | The lock-in strategy (limit = 32) and a dominating strategy

Here is the lock-in strategy:

					Probability
	32	32	32	32	10/16
16		16		16	2/16
	8		8		
		4		4	3/16
			2		
				1	1/16

Here is a dominating strategy (which is itself undominated). This strategy costs only 15 17/81 (=1232/81) but gives the same terminal probability distribution of wealth (in different states).

				Dominating payoff	Lock-in payoff	State-price density
1232/81	736/27	32	32	32	32	16/81
				32	32	32/81
			32	32	32	32/81
				32	32	64/81
		224/9	32	32	32	32/81
				32	32	64/81
			64/3	32	32	64/81
				16	32	128/81 ←
	248/27	176/9	32	32	32	32/81
				32	32	64/81
			40/3	32	16	64/81 ←
				4	4	128/81
		4	8	16	16	64/81
				4	4	128/81
			2	4	4	128/81
				1	1	256/81

that is independent of market returns. The distribution of terminal wealth is the same whatever the timing; two examples (*A* and *B*) are illustrated in Table 4. Strategy *A* has the stock investment in the first two periods. Strategy *B* has the stock investment in the first and last periods. Since the terminal distribution is the same independent of the random choice, the unconditional distribution is the same under each choice.

As before, the way to dominate the strategy is to move the large amounts of consumption to terminal states in which consumption is cheaper. From Table 4, we can see that the move to the dominating strategy requires two switches (both marked), one between

TABLE 4 | Random market timing strategy (50 percent stock) and a dominating strategy

Here is random market timing strategy A:

					Probability
16	32	64	64	64	4/16
	8	16	16	16	8/16
		4	4	4	4/16

Here is random market timing strategy B:

					Probability
16	32	32	32	64	4/16
	8	8	8	16	8/16
				4	4/16

Here is a dominating strategy (which is itself undominated). This strategy costs only 14⅔ (=129/9) but gives the same terminal probability distribution of wealth (in different states).

				Dominating payoff	Timing *A*	State-price density
128/9	256/9	128/3	64	64	64	16/81
				64	64	32/81
			32	64	64	32/81
				16	64	64/81 ←
		64/3	32	64	16	32/81 ←
				16	16	64/81
			16	16	16	64/81
				16	16	128/81
	64/9	32/3	16	16	16	32/81
				16	16	64/81
			8	16	16	64/81
				4	16	128/81 ←
		16/3	8	16	4	64/81 ←
				4	4	128/81
			4	4	4	128/81
				4	4	256/81

up-up-down-down and up-down-up-up, and the other between down-up-down-down and down-down-up-up. The first switch reduces the cost by the product of the probability $1/16$, the amount 48 (=64 − 16) of consumption moved, and the difference $32/81$ (= $64/81 - 32/81$) in terminal state-price density, for a cost reduction $1\,5/27$ (= $32/27$). The second switch reduces the cost by the product of the probability $1/16$, the amount 12 (=16 − 4) of consumption moved, and the difference $64/81$ (= $128/81 - 64/81$) in terminal state-price density, for a cost reduction of $16/27$. Combining these two changes, we have a total cost reduction of $1\,7/9$ (=$1\,21/27$), which reduces the initial cost from 16 to $14\,2/9$.

This concludes the simple numerical examples. Section 2 reports computer-based calculations of the loss under more reasonable parameter values.

2. Realistically, How Large Is the Cost?

Section 1 examined three numerical examples that showed the theoretical principle behind measuring the cost of following a dominated strategy. Now we compute the cost in more realistic situations. The calculations approximate continuous lognormal stock movements using a binomial process with a daily grid. To approximate current conditions with a round number, the short riskless rate is assumed to be 8 percent. To approximate historical returns on well-diversified portfolios, the stock is assumed to have an expected return of 16 percent (i.e., an excess return of 8 percent annually) and an annual standard deviation of about 20 percent (in logs).

Table 5 summarizes how these parameter assumptions map into per-period returns. As the time increment Δt gets smaller and smaller, the stochastic process described in Table 5 and the corresponding pricing converge to a standard lognormal diffusion model for the stock price [as is consistent with Black and Scholes (1973) with a constant mean return].

TABLE 5 | One-period returns in terms of the underlying parameters

Parameters used in numerical work:

$r = .08$ annual interest rate = 8%, continuous compounding

$\mu = .16$ annual expected return = 16%, for an 8% risk premium

$\sigma = .2$ annual proportional standard deviation = 20%

$\Delta t = 1/360 \approx .0027778$ daily

$\sqrt{\Delta t} \approx .0527046$

Here is the one-period bond return:

$$1 \longrightarrow 1 + r\Delta t \approx 1.0002222$$

Here is the one-period stock return:

	Probability
$1 + \mu\Delta t + \sigma\sqrt{\Delta t} \approx 1.0109854$	.5
$1 + \mu\Delta t - \sigma\sqrt{\Delta t} \approx 0.9899035$	.5

State price density:

$$1 \begin{cases} \dfrac{1}{1 + r\Delta t}\left(1 - \dfrac{(\mu - r)\Delta t}{\sigma\sqrt{\Delta t}}\right) \approx 0.9787007 \\[2ex] \dfrac{1}{1 + r\Delta t}\left(1 + \dfrac{(\mu - r)\Delta t}{\sigma\sqrt{\Delta t}}\right) \approx 1.0208550 \end{cases}$$

FIGURE 1 | Efficiency loss of a stop-loss strategy
The efficiency loss is shown in basis points (hundredths of 1 percent of the initial investment). Under the stop-loss strategy, the manager invests the entire portfolio in stocks until the portfolio value reaches or falls below the limit value. When the limit value is at or above 100 percent of the initial wealth, the switch takes place immediately and the strategy is the same as just holding the bond (and is therefore efficient). The size of the efficiency loss can be dramatic: at its worst it is nearly 1 percent of the portfolio value in only a year!

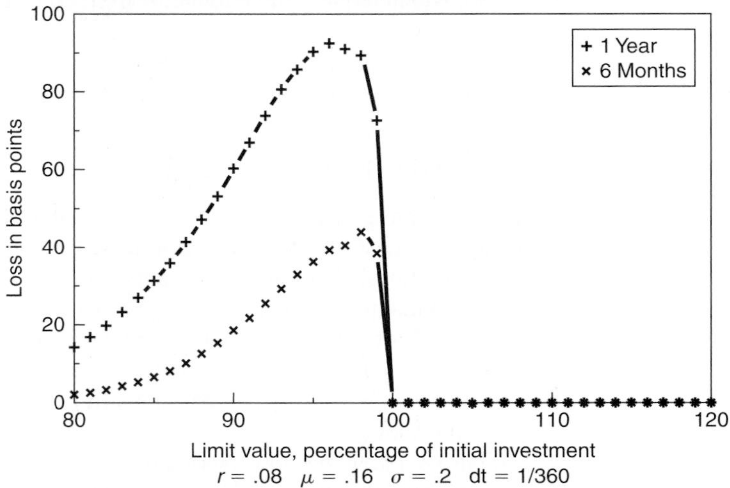

[For related analyses, see Banz and Miller (1978); Brennan and Solanki (1981); Cox and Leland (1982); Cox, Ross, and Rubinstein (1979); Garman (1976); Ross (1976); and Rubinstein (1976).] Therefore, the numerical results can be considered an approximation to what would be obtained in continuous time.

Now we are ready to look at some numerical results. Figures 1, 2, and 3 are plots of numerical estimates of the cost of following the three inefficient strategies described in Section 1. The estimates were made by using a set of routines for analyzing probability distributions. These routines were written in the SCHEME programming language, which is a dialect of LISP [see R. K. Dybvig (1987)]. The program computes the minimum cost by matching consumption levels in reverse order of the terminal state-price density as described in Section 1. In computing the terminal distribution, the routines manage the size of the problem by combining indistinguishable states along the way.

Figure 1 shows the cost of following a stop-loss strategy, as a function of the limit value. (The "jaggedness" of the plot comes from the coarseness of the daily binomial approximation to the diffusion; the plot became smoother when the computations were repeated for a half-day interval.) For example, assume that the current portfolio value is \$2 billion and that we plan to switch into stock if the value falls to \$1.8 billion or below; then the limit value is 90 percent (=1.8/2.0). Figure 1 says that we will be throwing away about 60 basis points, or \$12 million, by following the stop-loss strategy for a year, as compared to following the efficient strategy giving the same distribution of terminal wealth. While this ignores transaction costs for the two strategies, 60 basis points over a year is a large number, and we can surely do better than a stop-loss strategy. When the limit value is small, the efficiency loss is small, since the limit is rarely achieved and the portfolio strategy is nearly the same as holding the stock (which is efficient). Similarly, as the limit value approaches 100 percent from below, the probability of hitting the limit close to the starting

FIGURE 2 | Efficiency loss of a lock-in strategy

The efficiency loss is shown in basis points (hundredths of 1 percent of the initial investment). Under the lock-in strategy, the manager invests the entire portfolio in stocks until the portfolio value reaches or exceeds the limit value. When the limit value is at or below 100 percent of the initial wealth, the switch takes place immediately and the strategy is the same as just holding the bond (and is therefore efficient). Again, the size of the efficiency loss can be dramatic: at its worst it is roughly 0.8 percent of the portfolio value in only a year. (It is not exactly the same as for the very similar stop-loss strategy, since the state prices are not symmetric for increases and decreases.)

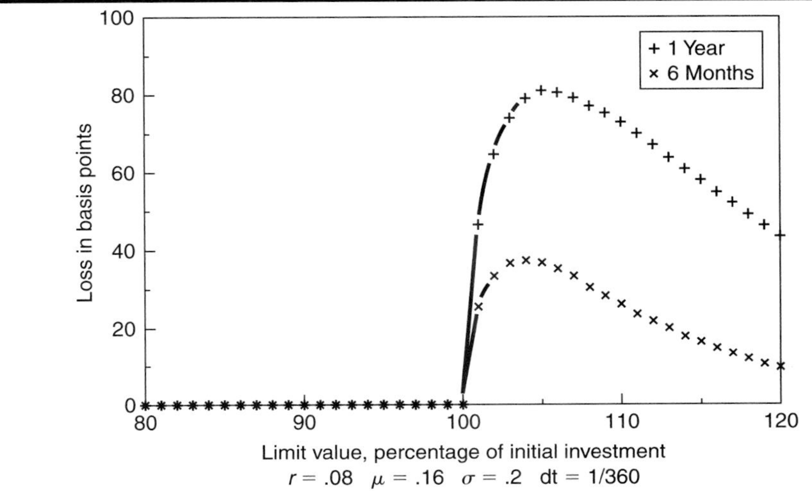

time increases to 1 and the strategy looks more and more like holding the bond (which is also efficient). When the limit value is 100 percent or more, the strategy switches immediately to the bond and the strategy is precisely holding the bond (which is efficient). Intuitively, the loss is largest when there is a large chance both of hitting and of missing the limit soon after the start. This is consistent with Figure 1, which shows the largest loss at a limit of about 96 percent (with a one-year horizon), which is one-fourth of the one-year standard deviation of the stock.

Figure 2 shows the efficiency loss of a lock-in strategy, which is in some sense a mirror image of a stop-loss strategy. The loss is not exactly symmetric, since the terminal state-price density is higher for lower stock prices. This means that the damage done by the stop-loss strategy (which usually occurs when the stock has gone down) is more costly than the damage done by the lock-in strategy; nonetheless, the cost of following a lock-in strategy is substantial and should not be ignored by practitioners.

Figure 3 shows the efficiency loss of a random timing strategy (a "timer who cannot") as a function of the fraction of time the timer holds the stock. The efficiency loss of this strategy can be as high as 200 basis points over a year, or \$40 million for a \$2 billion portfolio! While Figure 3 contains numerical results, this is one of the few cases we can actually solve analytically for the diffusion model. The random timer follows a strategy which holds the stock a fixed fraction f of the time and which holds the bond a fraction $(1 - f)$ of the time. (Because there are assumed to be no transaction costs, the exact allocation does not matter—it only matters that the stock is held exactly a fraction f of the time.) If w_0 is the initial wealth, then the wealth $\tilde{w}_T$ at the end (time T) is lognormally distributed, as

$$\log(\tilde{w}_T) \sim N(\log(w_0) + \mu f T + r(1 - f)T + \sigma^2 f T/2, \sigma^2 f T) \tag{2}$$

FIGURE 3 | Efficiency loss of a random timing strategy

A random timing strategy is a strategy followed by an agent who claims to have market timing ability but really does not. By assumption, such a manager spends a fixed fraction of the time fully invested in the stock and a fixed fraction of the time fully invested in the bond, using a rule that is independent of security returns. For the limits with 0 percent or 100 percent of the time spent invested in the stock, the strategy is efficient, because these limits correspond to buying and holding the bond or the stock, respectively. For other cases, the efficiency loss is even larger than for the stop-loss and lock-in strategies: at its worst it is nearly 2 percent of the portfolio value in only a year!

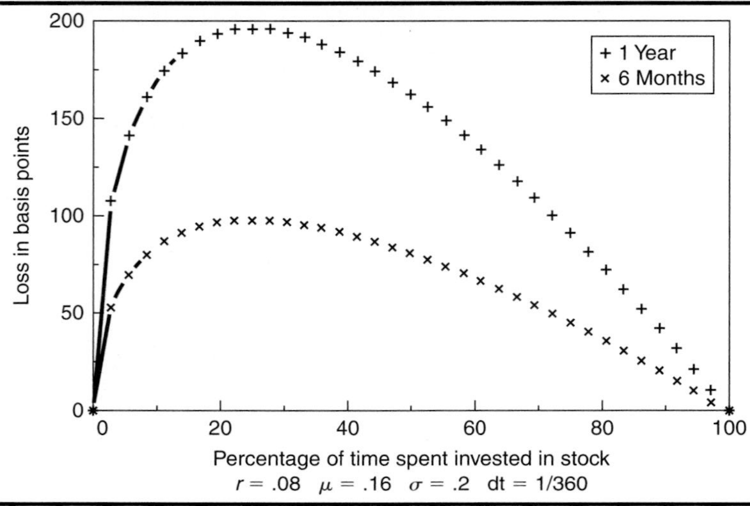

An alternative strategy with initial wealth x_0 and a fixed portfolio weight α is also lognormally distributed and is efficient for $\alpha > 0$. Its terminal distribution is

$$\log(\tilde{x}_T) \sim N(log(x_0) + \mu\alpha T + r(1 - \alpha)T + \sigma^2\alpha^2 T/2, \sigma^2\alpha^2 T) \tag{3}$$

To give these two the same distribution (for $\alpha > 0$), we must choose $\alpha = \sqrt{f}$ to match variances and then choose

$$log(x_0) = log(w_0) - (\sqrt{f} - f)(\mu - r)T \tag{4}$$

to match means. In log terms, $(\sqrt{f} - f)(\mu - r)T$ is the loss, and up to scaling this is essentially what is plotted in Figure 3.[8]

Figure 4 shows the efficiency loss of a strategy, not analyzed in Section 1, that uses portfolio insurance repeatedly. (Because of the technical limitations of my computer program, I have chosen slightly different parameters and weekly rebalancing for this example;

[8]The formula for the loss in the random timer case is linear in T. Another way of saying this is that if you split the time interval into two parts, the value as a percentage of the potential on the whole period is the product of the value as a percentage of the potential on each half. This is a special case of a general result. Suppose that security returns are independent over time and that the return to the inefficient portfolio strategy in the two subperiods is independent; then the value as a percentage of the potential on the whole period is less than or equal to the product of the values as a percentage of the potential on the subperiods. To prove this, consider making the dominated strategies on the subperiods your strategy over the whole period. This may not be optimal over the whole period, but it achieves a value that proves the bound. This result says that when stock returns are independent, you cannot recover from past inefficient policies. As an example of applying this result, rolling over portfolio insurance each year is efficient in each period but inefficient over two years (an example of inequality). The result implies that rolling over portfolio insurance each year over four years is at least twice as bad (measured in logs) as rolling over portfolio insurance each year for two years (and in fact it is even worse).

FIGURE 4 | Efficiency loss of repeated portfolio Insurance
Under portfolio insurance, a dynamic strategy based on option pricing theory varies th portfolio mix between stocks and bonds to create a payoff at the end of the insurance horizon that is the larger of the initial investment and a proportion of the terminal stock price. This plot shows that while following this strategy for one year is efficient, following it repeartely with a one year horizon is poorly diversified over time and is very costly in 10 years, the strategy throws away over 5 percent of the initial investment!

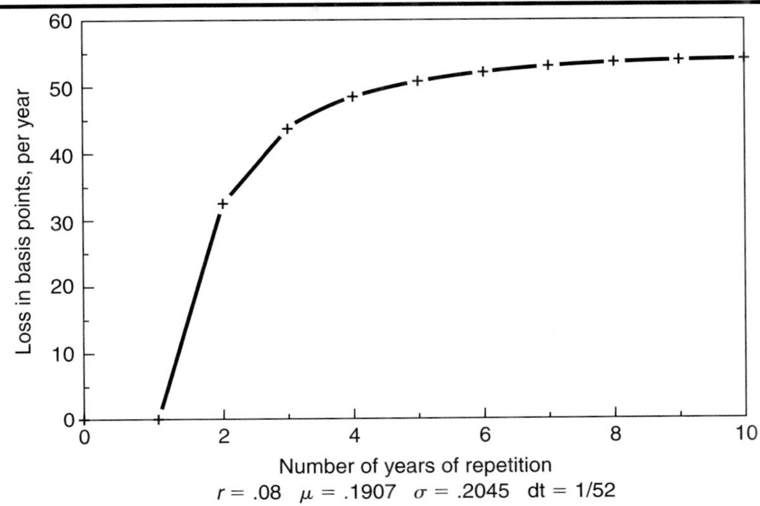

both choices reduce the number of terminal nodes and help keep the size manageable in spite of exponential growth.) Since many managers create synthetic portfolio insurance with a one-year horizon repeated annually, the large size of the efficiency loss shown in Figure 4 (over 5 percent in 10 years) is especially troubling.

3. Generalizations

This section derives a formula for the state-price density in the general case when asset prices follow general *Itô* processes. The main economic assumptions we need are completeness of markets and the absence of arbitrage.[9] We then turn to applications involving the term structure of interest rates. While numerical analysis like that in Section 2 has not been performed for the term structure applications, doing such computations is a promising avenue for future research.

State-price density in continuous-time models

The state-price density ρ gives a representation of the linear pricing rule of Ross (1978). Letting P be the vector of reinvested price series, then in terms of ρ and the price at a later time t, the price at time s is

$$\rho_s P_s \equiv E_s(\tilde{\rho}_t \tilde{P}_t) \tag{5}$$

[9]There are some additional technical assumptions that would be required in a more formal analysis. See, for example, Harrison and Pliska (1981), Cox and Huang (1985), or Dybvig and Huang (1986) for related results. In these papers the emphasis is on the risk-neutral probabilities (called martingale probabilities). The state-price density is equal to a discount factor times the Radon-Nikodyn derivative of the risk-neutral probabilities applied to indicator sets, with respect to the probability measure.

or in particular, if we take $\rho = 1$ at $s = 0$, we have

$$P_0 \equiv E_0(\tilde{\rho}_t \tilde{P}_t) \tag{6}$$

Equation (5) says that ρP is a martingale, which implies that ρP has no drift.

Assume that prices follow an *Itô* process. Specifically, the n-vector of risky asset price changes is given by

$$\frac{d\tilde{P}}{P} = \mu\, dt + \sigma\, d\tilde{Z} \tag{7}$$

where the division is componentwise, μ is the n-vector of expected returns, $\tilde{Z}$ is a k-dimensional Wiener process, and σ is an $(n \times k)$ matrix of risk exposures. Under reasonable assumptions, ρ itself follows an *Itô* process involving only $\tilde{Z}$; taking this as given, we have

$$\frac{d\tilde{\rho}}{\rho} = a\, dt + b'\, d\tilde{Z} \tag{8}$$

where $\rho_0 = 1$, or equivalently

$$\tilde{\rho}_t = \exp\left(\int_{s=0}^{t} a\, ds + \int_{s=0}^{t} b'\, d\tilde{Z}_s - \frac{1}{2}\int_{s=0}^{t} b'b\, ds\right) \tag{9}$$

for some random one-dimensional process a and some k-dimensional process b. Since Equation (5) holds for all assets,

$$\frac{d(\tilde{\rho}\tilde{P})}{\rho P} = \frac{d\tilde{\rho}}{\rho} + \frac{d\tilde{P}}{P} + \frac{d\tilde{\rho}}{\rho}\frac{d\tilde{P}}{P} \tag{10}$$

has no drift, or by *Itô's* lemma this implies that

$$0 = \text{drift}\left(\frac{d(\tilde{\rho}\tilde{P})}{\rho P}\right) = ae + \mu + \sigma b \tag{11}$$

where e is an n-vector of 1s. If we eliminate locally redundant assets, completeness implies that σ is square and nonsingular, and therefore

$$a = -r \tag{12}$$

and

$$b = -\sigma^{-1}(\mu - re) \tag{13}$$

where r is the local riskless rate. Generally, a and b are solutions to Equation (11), even if we have not eliminated locally redundant assets. Of course, completeness of markets implies that there is a locally riskless portfolio.

To use Equations (8), (11), and (12) with the payoff distribution pricing model, we have to use the continuous state-space analogue of valuation using consumption ordered in reverse of the terminal state-price density. This analogue implies that the cost of the dominating portfolio (the distributional price) is

$$P_D = \int_{\gamma=0}^{1} F_{\rho}^{-1}(\gamma) F_{c}^{-1}(1-\gamma)\, d\gamma \tag{14}$$

which is Equation (3) of Dybvig (1988). This is a general expression for the expectation of the product of two variables ρ and c that are perfectly inversely related. F_{ρ}^{-1} has the same units as ρ (state price over probability), F_{c}^{-1} has units of consumption, and γ has units of probability. The arguments γ and $1 - \gamma$ signify inverse ordering, and the integral corresponds to summing across states in the finite model.[10]

Term structure models

To illustrate the evolution of the state-price density in continuous-time models, this section computes the state-price density in closed form for a class of models with interest rate uncertainty. Because interest rates can move randomly, there is a nontrivial term structure of interest rates in these models. Throughout the rest of this section, it will be assumed either that preferences are over nominal payoffs or that we are expressing all returns in real terms (which is formally equivalent).

To illustrate the computation of ρ, let us assume that the vector b of asset risk premiums is constant. Then we can write the state-price density (9) as

$$\widetilde{\rho}_t = \exp\left(- \int_{s=0}^{t} r_s \, ds + \int_{s=0}^{t} b' \, d\widetilde{Z}_s - \frac{t}{2} b' b \right) \tag{15}$$

In particular, if $b = 0$, we have the local expectations hypothesis [see Cox, Ingersoll, and Ross (1981)], which is a reasonable assumption if all the assets in our list are bonds or derivative of bonds. In this case, every efficient portfolio has a terminal value that is a nondecreasing function of the compounded return on rolling over shorts. One interesting implication of this result is that contingent immunization is not an efficient strategy.[11] This is formally true from Equation (15) whenever the local expectations hypothesis holds; more generally, Equations (9) and (12) tell us that we would have to make a bizarre assumption about the movement of the vector b of risk premiums to make contingent immunization efficient.

To apply our analysis to a term structure model, we would want to use Equation (14), for which we need to know the distribution of the state-price density. The state-price density's process is given by Equation (15). In general, we can compute the density numerically, and in this article we will consider a special case in which the distribution can be computed analytically. We will use a special case of Vasicek (1977). Loosely speaking, Vasicek showed that if interest rates follow a Gaussian process, then we can compute bond prices. (One has to make an assumption about risk premiums as well; the assumption that the vector b of risk premiums is a constant is sufficient.) Vasicek's model is attractive analytically because the normality makes it tractable. (Unfortunately, however, it is not a good approximation to the actual movement of interest rates, except perhaps over very short periods of time.[12]) From Equations (6) and (15), we can see how

---

[10]For details, see Dybvig (1988). To define the inverse distribution function for discrete variables (or more generally at mass points), we put "risers" on the step function. For example, suppose that a random variable is either 1 or 2, each with probability ½; then the inverse distribution function is defined to be 1 on (0, ½) and 2 on (½, 1). The values assigned to the endpoints 0 and 1 do not matter, because they do not affect the integral in Equation (14).

[11]Intuitively, a contingent immunization strategy switches from one risky portfolio into an immunized portfolio using a cutoff rule that is qualitatively similar to the stop-loss strategy, if we consider the initial portfolio as the stock and the immunized portfolio as the bond. (Using the immunized portfolio as *numeraire* makes the analogy almost exact.) Therefore, while the qualitative properties of the efficiency loss should be as in Figure 1, without further analysis we cannot be sure of the magnitude of the loss. It does seem, however, that if the size of the loss we are insuring is significant, the efficiency loss will be significant too.

[12]For example, interest rates can go arbitrarily negative in Vasicek's model, and they will go negative frequently under reasonable variance assumptions. Also, it has been shown empirically that the variance of interest rates changes over time in a way that can be predicted by looking at yield curves, contradicting the assumption of constant variance; see Brown and Dybvig (1986).

to compute bond prices in the Vasicek model. By Equation (6), the price at time 0 of a bond paying 1 at t is $E_0(\widetilde{\rho}_t/\rho_0) = E_0(\widetilde{\rho}_t)$. If r and Z are jointly normal (as they are in Vasicek's model), we can compute this expectation using the normal moment generating function.

For our extended example, assume that r follows the following simple mean-reverting process:

$$dr = \kappa(\bar{r} - r)\,dt + \Sigma^t\,d\widetilde{Z} \tag{16}$$

where κ, $\bar{r}$, and Σ are known and constant and where $\widetilde{Z}$ is the k-dimensional Wiener process that drives security prices. Then we have

$$r_t = \bar{r} + (r_0 - \bar{r})e^{-\kappa t} + \int_{\tau=0}^{t} e^{-\kappa(t-\tau)}\Sigma^t\,d\widetilde{Z}_\tau \tag{17}$$

and
$$\int_{s=0}^{t} r_\tau\,d\tau = \bar{r}t + (r_0 - \bar{r})\frac{1 - e^{-\kappa t}}{\kappa} + \int_{\tau=0}^{t}\left(\frac{1 - e^{-\kappa(t-\tau)}}{\kappa}\right)\Sigma^t\,d\widetilde{Z}_\tau \tag{18}$$

From Equations (15) and (18), we have

$$\log(\rho_t) = -\left(\frac{b'b}{2} + \bar{r}\right)t - (r_0 - \bar{r})\frac{1 - e^{-\kappa t}}{\kappa} + \int_{\tau=0}^{t}\left(b' - \frac{1 - e^{-\kappa(t-\tau)}}{\kappa}\Sigma^t\right)d\widetilde{Z}_\tau \tag{19}$$

Therefore, ρ_t is normally distributed with mean

$$M = -\left(\frac{b'b}{2} + \bar{r}\right)t - (r_0 - \bar{r})\frac{1 - e^{-\kappa t}}{\kappa} \tag{20}$$

and variance

$$\begin{aligned} V &= \int_{\tau=0}^{t}\left(b - \frac{1 - e^{-\kappa(t-\tau)}}{\kappa}\Sigma\right)^t\left(b - \frac{1 - e^{-\kappa(t-\tau)}}{\kappa}\Sigma\right)d\tau \\ &= \left(b'b - \frac{2b'\Sigma}{\kappa} + \frac{\Sigma'\Sigma}{\kappa^2}\right)t + \frac{2}{\kappa}\left(b'\Sigma - \frac{\Sigma'\Sigma}{\kappa}\right)\frac{1 - e^{-\kappa t}}{\kappa} \\ &\quad + \frac{\Sigma'\Sigma}{\kappa^2}\,\frac{1 - e^{-2\kappa t}}{2\kappa} \end{aligned} \tag{21}$$

Therefore, ρ_t is distributed lognormally, and $\log(\rho_t)$ has mean M and variance V. By the normal moment generating function, then, the bond price is given by $\exp(M + \frac{1}{2}V)$.

The lognormality of ρ_t implies that it is possible (although not done here) to compute analytically the cost of some types of random timing strategies. Of course, more numerical work is required in order to compute the cost of following other dominated strategies. In numerical work, having a closed-form expression for the distribution of the state-price density is very useful, because computing it numerically requires us to keep track of two state variables, r and ρ. In some sense, this is why term structure models are difficult to solve analytically: the state-price density is not a function of the natural state variable (the interest rate).

4. Conclusion

The numerical results reported in this article show that the efficiency loss to inefficient strategies may in fact be very large, even given very realistic assumptions. The strategies we have considered—stop-loss, lock-in, random timer, and repeated portfolio insurance—are very similar to strategies used in practice. It is interesting to note that the efficiency loss is the same whether or not the strategy was "planned" in advance; in other words, a manager deciding to lock in the gains at the time a boundary is reached has the same terminal distribution of wealth as a manager who planned from the start to follow this strategy.

Much work remains. In one direction, it would be nice to extend the analysis to include transaction costs explicitly. Short of that, we can add the transaction cost to the cost described here to get an overall measure of the cost of a given policy, and it would be useful to have a collection of examples of this sort to aid our understanding. Along other lines, it is possible to measure the efficiency loss of other strategies. For example, it would be nice to know the magnitude of loss from contingent immunization and other fixed-income strategies.

References

Banz, R., and M. Miller, 1978, "Prices for State-Contingent Claims: Some Estimates and Applications," *Journal of Business,* 51, 653–672.

Black, F., and M. Scholes, 1973, "The Pricing of Options and Corporate Liabilities," *Journal of Political Economy,* 81, 637–654.

Brennan, M., and R. Solanki, 1981, "Optimal Portfolio Insurance," *Journal of Financial and Quantitative Analysis,* 16, 279–300.

Brown, S. J., and P. H. Dybvig, 1986, "The Empirical Implications of the Cox, Ingersoll, Ross Theory of the Term Structure of Interest Rates," *Journal of Finance,* 41, 617–632.

Cox, J. C., and C. Huang, 1985, "A Variational Problem Arising in Financial Economics with an Application to a Portfolio Turnpike Theorem," working paper, MIT.

Cox, J. C., J. E. Ingersoll, Jr., and S. A. Ross, 1981, "A Re-examination of Traditional Hypotheses about the Term Structure of Interest Rates," *Journal of Finance,* 36, 769–799.

Cox, J. C., and H. Leland, 1982, "On Dynamic Investment Strategies," *Proceedings of the Seminar on the Analysis of Security Prices,* 26(2), Center for Research in Security Prices, University of Chicago.

Cox, J. C., S. A. Ross, and M. Rubinstein, 1979, "Option Pricing: A Simplified Approach," *Journal of Financial Economics,* 7, 229–263.

Dybvig, P. H., 1980, "Some New Tools for Testing Market Efficiency and Measuring Mutual Fund Performance," working paper, Yale University.

Dybvig, P. H., 1988, "Distributional Analysis of Portfolio Choice," *Journal of Business,* forthcoming in July.

Dybvig, P. H., and C. Huang, 1986, "Nonnegative Wealth, Absence of Arbitrage, and Feasible Consumption Plans," working paper, Yale University.

Dybvig, P. H., and J. E. Ingersoll, Jr., 1982, "Mean-Variance Theory in Complete Markets," *Journal of Business,* 55, 233–251.

Dybvig, P. H., and S. A. Ross, 1982, "Portfolio Efficient Sets," *Econometrica,* 50, 1525–1546.

Dybvig, P. H., and S. A. Ross, 1985a, "The Analytics of Performance Measurement Using a Security Market Line," *Journal of Finance,* 40, 401–416.

Dybvig, P. H., and S. A. Ross, 1985b, "Differential Information and Performance Measurement Using a Security Market Line," *Journal of Finance,* 40, 384–399.

Dybvig, R. K., 1987, *The Scheme Programming Language,* Prentice-Hall, Englewood Cliffs, N.J.

Garman, M., 1976, "A General Theory of Asset Valuation Under Diffusion State Processes," working paper, University of California, Berkeley.

Harrison, J. M., and S. Pliska, 1981, "Martingales and Stochastic Integrals in the Theory of Continuous Trading," *Stochastic Processes and Their Applications,* 11, 215–260.

Machina, M., 1982, "'Expected Utility' Analysis Without the Independence Axiom," *Econometrica,* 50, 277–323.

Pliska, S., 1986, "A Stochastic Calculus Model of Continuous Time Trading: Optimal Portfolios," *Mathematics of Operations Research,* 11.

Ross, S. A., 1976, "Options and Efficiency," *Quarterly Journal of Economics,* 90, 75–89.

Ross, S. A., 1978, "A Simple Approach to the Valuation of Risky Streams," *Journal of Business,* 51, 453–475.

Rubinstein, M., 1976, "The Valuation of Uncertain Income Streams and the Pricing of Options," *Bell Journal of Economics,* 7, 407–425.

Vasicek, O., 1977, "An Equilibrium Characterization of the Term Structure," *Journal of Financial Economics,* 5, 177–188.

Ten

Douglas W. Diamond

Douglas W. Diamond received a Ph.D. from Yale University in 1980. He started out at the University of Chicago, Graduate School of Business, and still works at the University of Chicago, Graduate School of Business. •

"Financial Intermediation and Delegated Monitoring" is the first paper that I wrote about banks and financial intermediaries. It asks why investors would choose to invest via an intermediary instead of investing directly, by lending to entrepreneurs and how such an intermediary is optimally structured. This paper is part of my dissertation at Yale, and Steve Ross was the chair. Steve changed my approach to economics. I would not have been able to complete a good theoretical dissertation on this topic without Steve's customized guidance.

I met Steve at the end of my second year in graduate school when he served as an examiner for my oral field examination in finance. Steve was to join the Yale faculty the following fall. It would have been easier to have Steve as an examiner after taking a course from him. Thankfully, he decided that I passed. I took Steve's course the next year and learned a lot more finance, and especially how to approach unsolved problems. I was very impressed with Steve's insights and mentoring, and I wanted to share this knowledge. I encouraged Greg Connor, Mark Grinblatt, and Paul Pfleiderer, who were students in the macroeconomics course where I was the teaching assistant, to take Steve's course. All became students of Steve's. They probably would have found him on their own, but my tip improved their timing. I later learned a lot from them (especially from Greg Connor), and from the two great students brought from Penn: Phil Dybvig and Chester Spatt.

Steve's influence on my research output and style can be illustrated by a trick that he played on me. Before meeting Steve, I had built several models with implications that I could not understand fully. I brought a draft of a chapter from my dissertation to Steve, and as was his style, he had me present the model to him on the blackboard of his office. Steve told me to go home and take every complication out until I no longer had a model, then put an important one back in to deliver at least some of the results. I came back in with a much simpler model that was easy to both solve and interpret. Steve said that he thought that this simpler model captured my idea, to forget about the more complicated model, and to make this chapter 1 of my thesis. I was shocked, but it was the right advice. This illustrates two of the reasons that Steve is a wonderful advisor. First, he could see what problem I was having with the economics before I knew my results. This would not be the right advice for everyone or every problem. Steve often understands others' work better than they do. Second, he does not try to impose his current research interests on his students. He pushes each of us to go in our own direction. He is still a mentor, friend, and valued colleague.

When I applied Steve's advice to "Financial Intermediation and Delegated Monitoring," which was chapter 3, I had a very nice two-state example that showed the value of diversification in delegated monitoring. Unfortunately, my referee did not study with Steve Ross, and it was taken out of the paper published in the *Review of Economic Studies.* I found that the example was the best way to teach the paper to students and later published it as Diamond [1996]. I wish that I had kept it in the 1984 paper. I try not to forget Steve's advice and have passed it along to some of my students.

Financial Intermediation and Delegated Monitoring

Douglas W. Diamond

University of Chicago

This paper develops a theory of financial intermediation based on minimizing the cost of monitoring information which is useful for resolving incentive problems between borrowers and lenders. It presents a characterization of the costs of providing incentives for delegated monitoring by a financial intermediary. Diversification within an intermediary serves to reduce these costs, even in a risk neutral economy. The paper presents some more general analysis of the effect of diversification on resolving incentive problems. In the environment assumed in the model, debt contracts with costly bankruptcy are shown to be optimal. The analysis has implications for the portfolio structure and capital structure of intermediaries. •

Introduction

This paper develops a theory of financial intermediation based on minimum cost production of information useful for resolving incentive problems. An intermediary (such as a bank) is delegated the task of costly monitoring of loan contracts written with firms who borrow from it. It has a gross cost advantage in collecting this information because the alternative is either duplication of effort if each lender monitors directly, or a free-rider problem, in which case no lender monitors. Financial intermediation theories are generally based on some cost advantage for the intermediary. Schumpeter assigned such a "delegated monitoring" role to banks,

> . . . the banker must not only know what the transaction is which he is asked to finance and how it is likely to turn out but he must also know the customer, his business and even his private habits, and get, by frequently "talking things over with him", a clear picture of the situation (Schumpeter (1939), p. 116).

The information production task delegated to the intermediary gives rise to incentive problems for the intermediary; we can term these delegation costs. These are not generally analysed in existing intermediation theories, and in some cases one finds that the costs are so high that there is no net advantage in using an intermediary. Schumpeter made a similar point, although he did not consider incentives explicitly:

> . . . traditions and standards may be absent to such a degree that practically anyone can drift into the banking business, find customers, and deal with them according to his own ideas. . . . This in itself . . . is sufficient to turn the history of capitalist evolution into a history of catastrophes (Schumpeter (1939), p. 116).

I am grateful to S. Bhattacharya, G. Connor, P. Dybvig, B. Grundy, O. Hart, B. Holmström, M. Machiuna, D. Ryle, D. Romer, S. Ross, J. Tobin and R. Verrecchia for helpful comments. An earlier version of this paper was part of my dissertation submitted to the Yale University Department of Economics.

Reprinted with permission:
Diamond, Douglas W. "Financial Intermediation and Delegated Monitoring." *Review of Economic Studies* 51 (1984): 393–414.

This paper analyses the determinants of delegation costs, and develops a model in which a financial intermediary has a *net* cost advantage relative to direct lending and borrowing.

Diversification within the intermediary is key to the possible net advantage of intermediation. This is because there is a strong similarity between the incentive problem between an individual borrower and lender and that between an intermediary and its depositors. The possibility of diversification within the intermediary can make the incentive problems sufficiently different to make it feasible to hire an agent (the intermediary) to monitor an agent (the borrower). Diversification proves to be important even when everyone in the economy is risk neutral.

This model is related to two literatures. It relates to the single agent-single principal literature (e.g., Harris–Raviv (1979), Holmström (1979) and Shavell (1979)) which develops conditions when monitoring additional information about an agent will help resolve moral hazard problems. The analysis here extends this to costly monitoring in a many principals setting, where principals are security holders of a firm or depositors in an intermediary. The other related literature is that of financial intermediation based on imperfect information. Several interesting papers analyse the gross benefits of delegating some informational task to an intermediary without presenting explicit analysis of the costs and feasibility of this delegation (e.g., Leland–Pyle (1977) and Chan (1982)). In addition to developing a model in which overall feasibility of financial intermediation is analysed, we briefly apply our results to determine conditions when intermediation is feasible in the Leland–Pyle model.

The basic model developed is of an ex-post information asymmetry between potential lenders and a risk neutral entrepreneur who needs to raise capital for a risky project. In this environment, debt is shown to be the optimal contract between an entrepreneur and lenders. Because of the wealth constraint that an entrepreneur cannot have negative consumption (pay lenders more than he has), the debt contracts with which the entrepreneur can raise funds involve some costs. As an alternative to incurring these costs, it is possible for lenders (who contract directly with the entrepreneur) to spend resources monitoring the data which the entrepreneur observes. In the class of contracts written directly between entrepreneurs and lenders, the less costly of these two is optimal. However, the cost of monitoring may be very high if there are many lenders. If there are m outside security holders in a firm and it costs $K > 0$ to monitor, the total cost of direct monitoring is $m \cdot K$. This will imply either a very large expenditure on monitoring, or a free rider problem where no securityholder monitors because his share of the benefit is small. The obvious thing to do is for some securityholders to monitor on behalf of others, and we are then faced with analysing the provision of incentives for delegated monitoring.

There are many methods by which delegated monitoring might be implemented. We assume that the information monitored by a given person cannot be directly observed without cost by others. The analysis here focuses on a financial intermediary who raises funds from many lenders (depositors), promises them a given pattern of returns, lends to entrepreneurs, and spends resources monitoring and enforcing loan contracts with entrepreneurs which are less costly than those available without monitoring. The financial intermediary monitors entrepreneurs' information, and receives payments from the entrepreneurs which are not observed by depositors.

An example of useful costly information in a loan contract is a covenant which is costly to monitor. A common covenant is a promise that the firm's working captial will not fall below some minimum, unless "necessary for expansion of inventory". (See Smith–Warner (1979).) If it is costly to determine whether a shortfall is "necessary", and each of the bondholders has to incur this cost to enforce the contract, the contract using costly information is unlikely to be used if the number of bondholders is large. A contract specifying an uncontingent working capital requirement might be substituted, when the contingency would have been specified if there had been a single principal. In practice, loan covenants in bank loan contracts specify coarse contingencies which define a "default". Conditional on such a default, the intermediary monitors the situation and uses the information to renegotiate the contract with new interest rates and contingent promises. A financial intermediary must choose an incentive contract such that it has incentives to monitor the information, make proper use of it, and make sufficient payments to depositors to attract deposits. Providing these incentives is costly, but we show that diversification serves to reduce these costs. As the number of loans to entrepreneurs with projects whose returns are independent (or independent conditional on observables) grows without bound, we show that costs of delegation approach zero, and that for some finite number of loans financial intermediation becomes viable, considering all costs.

Financial intermediaries in the world monitor much information about their borrowers in enforcing loan covenants, but typically do not directly announce the information or serve such an auditor's function. The intermediary in this model similarly does not announce the information monitored from each borrower, it simply makes payments to depositors. We show that debt is the optimal contract between the intermediary and depositors. The result that the delegation costs go to zero implies that asymptotically no other delegated monitoring structure will have lower costs. If there is an independent demand by entrepreneurs for monitoring without disclosure of the information monitored, for example to keep competitors from learning the information as suggested by Campbell (1979), then well diversified financial intermediaries can provide it (in addition to simple monitoring services) at almost no cost disadvantage.

Diversification is key to this theory, and it is interesting that because of the wealth constraint, diversification is important despite universal risk neutrality. To develop a more general intuition into the role of diversification, some analysis is presented of a related model with risk averse agents but no wealth constraint. Two types of diversification are considered in the context of two alternative financial intermediary models; one is the traditional diversification by subdividing independent risks, while the other is diversification by adding more independent risks of given scale. The latter is what Samuelson (1963) has termed a "fallacy of large numbers", because it does not always increase expected utility. This section may be of independent interest because it provides some conditions when the fallacy of large numbers is not a fallacy.

The basic model is outlined in Section 2. Delegated monitoring by a financial intermediary in the context of the basic model is analysed in Section 3. Section 4 explores the extension of the basic model to risk averse agents. Section 5 applies the analysis of section 4 to the model of Leland–Pyle. Section 6 concludes the paper.

2. A Simple Model of Firm Borrowing

A model of risk neutral entrepreneurs who need to raise capital to operate a large investiment project is used to capture many of the aspects of the agency relationship between commerical borrowers and lenders. We specify a simple environment, and characterize optimal direct contracts between borrower and lender.

There are N entrepreneurs indexed by $i = 1, \ldots, N$ in the economy. For the balance of Section 2, we examine one of them, and do not use the index. The entrepreneur is endowed with the technology for an indivisible investment project with stochastic returns. The scale of inputs for the project greatly exceeds both his personal wealth and the personal wealth of any single lender. For simplicity, the entrepreneur's wealth is zero. Assume a one good economy with all consumption at the end of the period. The project requires inputs of the good today, and will produce output in one period. Normalize the required initial amount of inputs to one. The expectation of the output that will be produced at the end of the period exceeds R, the competitive interest rate in the economy. Therefore, the project would be undertaken if the risk neutral entrepreneur had available to him enough capital inputs.

The other investors in the economy are also risk neutral: call them lenders. To undertake the project, the entrepreneur must borrow sufficient resources from them to operate it at its scale of one. Because the interest rate is R, i.e. the lenders have access to a technology which will return R per unit of input, the entrepreneur must convince potential lenders that the rate of return which he will pay to them has an expected value of at least R. Each lender has available wealth of $1/m$, thus the entrepreneur must borrow from $m > 1$ lenders. The capital market is competitive—if convinced that their expected return equals or exceeds R (R/m per lender), lenders will make the loan.

Let the total output of the project be the random variable $\tilde{y}$. Assume that $\tilde{y}$ is bounded between zero and $\tilde{y} < \infty$. The entrepreneur and all lenders agree on the probability distribution of $\tilde{y}$, in particular all agree that $E_{\tilde{y}}(\tilde{y}) > R + K$ (where $K > 0$ and is defined below) and that $y = 0$ is possible. The realization of $\tilde{y}$ does not depend on any actions of the entrepreneur.

A simple information asymmetry is introduced which will make the loan contracting problem non-trivial. The realization of $\tilde{y}$ is freely observed only by the entrepreneur. With output observed by the entrepreneur alone, he must be given incentives to make payments to lenders. At the end of the period, he will pay a liquidating dividend. It is always feasible for him to claim a very low value of y, and keep for himself the difference between the actual value and what he pays the others.

Let $z \geqq 0$ be the aggregate payment which the entrepreneur pays to the m lenders. If the realization of output is $\tilde{y} = y$, he then keeps $y - z$ for himself. Because consumption cannot be negative the payment which he pays cannot feasibly exceed y (plus any personal wealth he might have, assumed here to be zero). To induce the entrepreneur to select a value of $z > 0$, he must be provided with incentives. To raise captial to undertake the project, lenders must believe that the expectation of the value of z which he will select is at least R. The entrepreneur must choose an incentive contract which depends only on observable variables and makes lenders anticipate a competitive expected dividend. The only costlessly observable variable is the payment z itself.

Lenders know the distribution of $\tilde{y}$, and know that the entrepreneur chooses the payment z which is best for him given a realization $\tilde{y} = y$, and that $z \in [0, y]$. If y exceeded R with probability one, then a full information optimal contract would be feasible—the risk neutral entrepreneur would offer an uncontingent payment of R. (See Harris–Raviv (1979).)

It might appear that the assumption that $y = 0$ is a possible outcome of the project rules out any borrowing, because $z = 0$ must be feasible, and it does not appear incentive compatible for an entrepreneur to choose a payment $z > 0$ when he can choose $z = 0$ and retain the rest. However, we will allow contracts with non-pecuniary penalties: penalties where the entrepreneur's loss is not enjoyed by the lenders. This allows the agent's utility function to be defined over negative values of its domain without allowing negative consumption to "produce" goods. We will see that these penalties are best interpreted as bankruptcy penalties. Some examples include a manager's time spent in bankruptcy proceedings, costly "explaining" of poor results, search costs of a fired manager, and (loosely) the manager's loss of "reputation" in bankruptcy. Physical punishment is a less realistic example. Projects which could not be undertaken at all without the penalties can be operated using the penalties.

The optimal contract maximizes the risk neutral entrepreneur's expected return, given a minimum expected return to lenders of R. Let the function ϕ, from the non-negative reals to the non-negative reals, be the non-pecuniary penalty function, which depends on z, the payment to lenders selected by the entrepreneur. Assume that if the entrepreneur is indifferent between several values of z, he chooses the one preferred by the lender. The optimal contract with penalties $\phi^*(\cdot) \geqq 0$ solves[1]

$$\max_{\phi(\cdot)} E_{\tilde{y}}[\max_{z\epsilon[0,\tilde{y}]} \tilde{y} - z - \phi(z)] \tag{1a}$$

$$\text{Subject to} \quad z \in \arg\max_{z\in[0,y]} y - z - \phi(z) \tag{1b}$$

and

$$E_{\tilde{y}}[\arg\max_{z\in[0,\tilde{y}]} \tilde{y} - z - \phi(z)] \geqq R, \tag{1c}$$

where the notation "arg max "denotes the set of arguments that maximize the objective function that follows.

Proposition 1. *The optimal contract which solves* (1) *is given by* $\phi^*(z) = \max(h - z, 0)$, *where* h *is the smallest solution to*

$$(P(\tilde{y} < h) \cdot E_{\tilde{y}}[\tilde{y} \mid y < h]) + (P(\tilde{y} \geqq h) \cdot h) = R. \tag{2}$$

That is, it is a debt contract with face value h *and a non-pecuniary bankruptcy penalty equal to the shortfall from face,* h, *where* h *is the smallest face value which provides lenders with an expected return of* R.

Proof. Given $\phi^*(z)$,

$$\arg\max_{z\in[0,y]} y - z - \phi^*(z) = \begin{cases} y & \text{if } y < h \\ h & \text{if } y \geqq h. \end{cases}$$

Using (2), this satisfies with equality the constraint (1c) of providing a competitive return to lenders. By construction, h is the smallest number such that if the constraints $z \leqq y$ and $z \leqq h$ are satisfied, the expectation of $\tilde{z}$ is at least R. Hence, to satisfy (1c), there must exist some payment $h^+ \geqq h$ which is incentive compatible. If $z = h^+$ is incentive compatible (fulfills (1b) given contract $\phi(z)$), it must be true that

$$y - h^+ - \phi(h^+) \geqq \max_{z'\in[0,h^+]} y - z' - \phi(z')$$

or for all $z' \in [0, h^+]$,

$$\begin{aligned} \phi(z') &\geqq h^+ + \phi(h^+) - z' \\ &\geqq h + \phi(h^+) - z' \\ &\geqq h - z' \\ &= \phi^*(z'). \end{aligned}$$

The final inequality follows from the requirement $\phi(z) \geqq 0$ for all z. Combined with the result that $\phi^*(z) = 0$ for all $z \geqq h$, this implies that $\phi^*(z)$ gives the smallest penalties such that it is incentive compatible to fulfill (1c), implying that $\phi^*(z)$ maximizes (1).||

The necessity of a positive probability of incurring the non-pecuniary penalty means that even the optimal contract is costly. Entrepreneurs could be made better off without making lenders worse off if $\tilde{y}$ were observable. In a one entrepreneur-one lender setting, where $\tilde{y}$ could be observed at some cost, it would be observed so long as the cost were less than the expected non-pecuniary bankruptcy penalty, $E_{\tilde{z}}[\phi^*(\tilde{z})] = E_{\tilde{y}}[\phi^*(\tilde{y})]$.

In a setting where it is not possible to make $\tilde{y}$ observable to lenders at some cost, the contracting problem is not influenced by the number of lenders—a contract with one lender

[1]Note that this formulation is without loss of generality, and contract $\phi(z)$, which specifies a payment of goods to the entrepreneur by the lender and is not a non-pecuniary penalty, can be expressed as a net payment $\hat{z} = \phi(z) - z$.

who loans one unit is equivalent to a contract with m lenders who each loan[s] $1/m$ units and the entrepreneur incurs a penalty of $\phi^*(z_j)/m$ on the basis of payments z_j to lender j. However, this is not true when costly monitoring is possible. By spending $K > 0$ in resources, a lender can observe $\tilde{y}$, but other lenders do not automatically observe $\tilde{y}$ as a result and other lenders cannot observe the payments by an entrepreneur to the lender who monitors. As a result, an entrepreneur and a given lender consider only the effect on a given lender's loan of $1/m$ units when deciding between a contract with costly penalties and one that avoids the bankruptcy penalties by costly monitoring.

We analyse the impact of an information technology which allows costly monitoring of the exact realization of output, y, for each entrepreneur. This information costs $K > 0$ for each principal to monitor, and the cost must be incurred before the output realization is known to anyone, including the entrepreneur. See Townsend (1979) for some interesting analysis of the optimal contingent monitoring policy when the decision to monitor can be made *after* the entrepreneur has made a payment to a lender. This additional complication is not introduced because given some specified probability of monitoring it would not influence our results.

If it is possible for lenders to observe the outcome at some cost, there are three types of contracting situations possible. The contract can be as described above, with no monitoring. A second possibility is for each of the m lenders to spend resources to monitor the outcome. Thirdly, the lenders can delegate the monitoring to one or more monitoring agents. The least costly of these will be selected.

If there were a single lender so $m = 1$ (rather than $m > 1$ as we assume), monitoring would be valuable if its cost were less than the expected deadweight penalty without monitoring or $K \leqq E_{\tilde{y}}[\phi^*(\tilde{y})]$. With many lenders and direct contracting between the entrepreneur and lenders, if each lender monitors, monitoring is valuable if and only if $m \cdot K \leqq E_{\tilde{y}}[\phi^*(\tilde{y})]$. When m is large this is unlikely because each lender's loan is small. Even if this condition for valuable monitoring is satisfied, it implies a large expenditure on monitoring and some sort of delegated monitoring might be desirable in this case.

To obtain the benefits of monitoring, when m is large the task must be delegated rather than left to each individual lender. The entity doing the monitoring ("the monitor") must be provided with incentives to monitor and enforce the contract. We assume that the actions taken and the information observed by the monitor are not directly observed by the lenders. It will generally be costly to provide incentives to the monitor, and below we analyse these costs. The total cost of delegated monitoring is the physical cost of monitoring by the monitor, K, plus the expected cost of providing incentives to the monitor, which we call the cost of delegation and denote the cost per project by D. Delegated monitoring pays when

$$K + D \leq \min\,[E_{\tilde{y}}[\phi^*(\tilde{y})], (m \cdot K)].$$

The costs of delegation are analysed when the monitor is a financial intermediary who receives payments from entrepreneurs and makes payments to principals.

3. Delegated Monitoring by a Financial Intermediary

A financial intermediary obtains funds from lenders and lends them to entrepreneurs. Economists have tried to explain this intermediary role by arguing that the financial intermediary has a cost advantage in certain tasks. When such tasks involve unobserved actions by the intermediary or the observation of private information, then an agency/incentive problem for the intermediary may exist. Any theory which tries to explain the role of intermediaries by an information cost advantage must net out the costs of providing incentives to the intermediary from any cost savings in producing information. Existing intermediary theories do not make this final step. We now introduce a financial intermediary between entrepreneurs and lenders (whom we call depositors from now on), and examine conditions when this intermediary function is viable considering all costs.

A financial intermediary is a risk neutral agent, with personal wealth equal to zero. The intermediary receives funds from depositors to lend to entrepreneurs and is delegated the task of monitoring the outcomes of entrepreneurs' projects on behalf of depositors. Monitoring the i-th entrepreneur costs the intermediary K units of goods.[2] Depositors can observe the payment they receive from the intermediary, but cannot observe the project outcomes, payments by entrepreneurs to the intermediary, or the resources expended by the intermediary in monitoring the outcomes.

Each entrepreneur's project requires one unit of initial capital. Each depositor has available capital of $1/m$, as in Section 2. An intermediary which contracts with N entrepreneurs has $m \cdot N$ depositors.

To analyse the conditions when intermediation is beneficial (when the monitoring cost savings exceed the delegation costs of providing incentives) we must first characterize the delegation costs. If the intermediary could monitor at no cost, it could enforce contracts with entrepreneurs which imposed no deadweight bankruptcy costs on them. However, there would remain an incentive problem for the intermediary, because the payments it receives from entrepreneurs are not observed by depositors. The intermediary could claim that payments from entrepreneurs were low, and pay a small amount to depositors. We now extend the results in Section 2 to analyse the optimal contract to provide incentives for an intermediary to make payments to depositors. We later show that it provides incentives to monitor as well.

Let us re-introduce the subscript i on the outcome y_i of the i-th entrepreneur. For $i = 1, \ldots,$ N, the $\tilde{y}_i$ are distributed independently and all are bounded below by zero and above by the real number $\bar{y}$. The probability distribution functions of the $\tilde{y}_i$ are common knowledge to all. Let $g_i(\cdot)$ be the non-negative real valued function which is the payment to the intermediary by the i-th entrepreneur as a function of the outcome y_i, assuming the intermediary monitors y_i. Because y_i is then observed by the intermediary, this implies no deadweight penalties will be imposed on the i-th entrepreneur. If the intermediary does not monitor, it must use a contract with deadweight bankruptcy penalties, as in Section 2, but in that case there would be no reason to have an intermediary. Due to the constraint that an entrepreneur can pay only what he has, we require $g_i(y_i) \leqq y_i$. The intermediary monitoring N entrepreneurs receives total payments G_N when $\tilde{y}_1 = y_1$, $\tilde{y}_2 = y_2, \ldots,$ $\tilde{y}_N = y_N$ equal to

$$G_N = \sum_{i=1}^{N} g_i(y_i).$$

Let $\tilde{G}_N$ be the random variable with realization G_N. It is bounded above by $\overline{G}_N$, and below by zero.

The intermediary must make total payments to depositors with expectation R per project, or $N \cdot R$ in total. Let Z_N be the total payment to depositors by entrepreneurs. The intermediary can pay only what it has, thus $Z_N \leqq G_N$. By an argument identical to that of

[2]There are two equivalent ways to model the monitoring cost. One, mentioned in the text, is for the financial intermediary to experience no disutility from monitoring and enforcement, but to spend K in resources. In this case, to avoid messy notation, re-normalize so that "one unit" is defined as the sum of the amount each project requires plus K, the amount spent on monitoring by the intermediary. Alternatively, one can assume that monitoring does not require resources, but that the intermediary experiences disutility from monitoring and has the linear utility function of wealth $U(W, N) = W - NK$, where N is the number of entrepreneurs monitored. In this case, no renormalization is required.

Section 2, we see that deadweight bankruptcy penalties must be imposed on the intermediary unless the intermediary will always receive aggregate payments of at least $N \cdot R$, or $P(\tilde{G}_N \geqq N \cdot R) = 1$. Because of the constraint that entrepreneurs can pay the intermediary at most y_i, we know $P(\tilde{G}_N \geqq N \cdot R) \leqq P(\sum_{i=1}^{N} \tilde{y}_i \geqq N \cdot R)$. Any entrepreneur, i, with $P(\tilde{y}_i \geqq R) = 1$ could finance directly, with no bankruptcy penalties, thus entrepreneurs who choose to use intermediaries will lead the intermediary to incur expected deadweight bankruptcy penalties.

Let $\Phi(Z_N)$ be the deadweight non-pecuniary penalty imposed on the intermediary when payment Z_N is made to depositors. From Proposition 1, the optimal $\Phi(Z_N)$ which gives incentives to make payments with expectation $N \cdot R$, is given by

$$\Phi(Z_N) = \max[H_N - Z_N, 0],$$

where the constant H_N is the smallest solution to

$$\{(P(\tilde{G}_N < H_N) \cdot E_{\tilde{G}_N}[\tilde{G}_N | G_N < H_N]) + ([1 - P(\tilde{G}_N < H_N)] \cdot H_N)\} \geqq N \cdot R.$$

With this contract in place, the expected return of the intermediary is $E_{\tilde{G}_N}[\tilde{G}_N] - H_N$; therefore the intermediary chooses monitoring expenditure to maximize $E_{\tilde{G}_N}[\tilde{G}_N]$. The intermediary uses the same decision rule in the decision to monitor as it would if its expenditure on monitoring were freely observable. This implies that it contracts only with entrepreneurs for whom the value of monitoring exceeds its physical and delegation costs, and chooses to monitor them. The minimum cost contract which provides incentives for payment to depositors also provides incentives for monitoring. This implies that the optimal contract between the intermediary and depositors is also a debt contract.

Diversification and the Viability of Intermediation

For a financial intermediary to be viable, three conditions must be fulfilled. The depositors must receive an expected return of R per unit deposited. The intermediary must receive an expected return net of monitoring costs and any deadweight penalties incurred which is at least zero. Finally, each entrepreneur must retain an expected return at least as high as he would by contracting directly with depositors.

Everyone in the economy is risk netural, implying that a complete description of the optimality of any feasible set of contracts is the sum of monitoring costs and expectation of total deadweight bankruptcy penalties.

A financial intermediary which contracts with one entrepreneur (and m depositors) is not viable. This follows, immediately from the constraint $g_1(y_1) \leqq y_1$, that the entrepreneur can pay no more than the outcome y_1, and the constraint $Z \leqq G_1 = g_1(y_1)$, that the intermediary can pay no more than it receives from the entrepreneur. An entrepreneur incurs a deadweight penalty whenever $y_1 < h$; an intermediary with one entrepreneur who pays g_i must also incur a penalty of at least the same magnitude when $g_i \leqq y_i \leqq H_1$ (and it is necessary that $H_1 \geqq h$ to provide depositors with a competitive return). The intermediary is not viable because it incurs at least as high a deadweight cost and in addition spends resources on monitoring.

The case of one entrepreneur demonstrates the potential hazard of neglecting the costs of delegation when considering financial intermediation. The per-entrepreneur cost of providing incentives to the intermediary is reduced as it contracts with more entrepreneurs with independently distributed projects. With independent and identically distributed projects, the per-entrepreneur cost, D_N, is a monitonically decreasing function of the number of entrepreneurs, N, because deadweight penalties are incurred when returns are in the extreme lower tail, and the probability of the average return across projects being in that tail is monitonically decreasing.[3]

The argument in footnote 3 shows that for all projects with less than perfect correlation, the delegation cost for N projects monitored by a single intermediary is less than the sum of the delegation costs for monitoring proper subsets of them by several intermediaries. Increasing returns to scale from delegation cost savings is a very general result. The assumption of independence allows a stronger result, The expected delegation cost per entrepreneur monitored by the intermediary gets arbitrarily small as N, the number of entrepreneurs with independently distributed projects, grows without bound. This implies that the total cost (per entrepreneur) of providing monitoring converges to K, the physical cost of monitoring. This is Proposition 2.

Proposition 2. *The cost of delegation, per entrepreneur monitored, D_N, approaches zero as $N \to \infty$ if entrepreneurs' projects have bounded returns, distributed independently.*

Proof. Choose payment schedules $g_i = g_i(y_i)$ to the intermediary for entrepreneurs $i = 1, \ldots, N$, such that

$$E_{\tilde{g}_i}[\tilde{g}_i] = R + K + D_N, \quad \text{where } D_N > 0 \text{ is a real number.}$$

This provides the i-th entrepreneur with an expected return given by

$$E_{\tilde{g}_i}[\tilde{g}_i] - R - D_N.$$

Choose the non-pecuniary bankruptcy penalties of the intermediary as

$$\Phi_N(Z_N) = \max[(H_N - Z_N), 0]$$

where $H_N = N \cdot (R + D_N/2)$.

Given this contract, the intermediary will choose payments Z_N to depositors equal to

$$Z_N = \begin{cases} G_N & \text{if } G_N \leqq H_N \\ H_N & \text{if } G_N > H_N. \end{cases}$$

The expected return of the intermediary net of expenditure NK on monitoring is

$$E_{\tilde{G}_N}(\tilde{G}_N) - H_N - NK = [N \cdot (R + K + D_N)] - \left[N \cdot \left(R + \frac{D_N}{2}\right)\right] - (N \cdot K)$$

$$= \frac{N}{2} D_N > 0,$$

(satisfying the constraint that this be non-negative.)

---

[3]For example, in the identically distributed case with 1 project, the delegation cost is

$$D_1 = E_{\tilde{g}_1}[H_1 - \tilde{g}_1 | g_1 \leqq H_1],$$

while with 2 projects the per project delegation cost is

$$D_2 = \tfrac{1}{2} E_{\tilde{g}_1} E_{\tilde{g}_2}[H_2 - \tilde{g}_1 - \tilde{g}_2 | g_1 + g_2 \leqq H_2].$$

We know that the minimum feasible value of $H_2 \leqq 2H_1$ because if $H_2 = 2H_1$, the expected return to depositors is at least $2R$. This implies $D \leqq D_1 - C$, where

$$C = P(\Omega) E[H_2 - \tilde{g}_1 - \tilde{g}_2 | \Omega]$$

and Ω is the event "$g_1 + g_2 \geqq H_1 \cdot 2$, and either [$g_1 \leqq H_1$ or $g_2 \leqq H_1$]". If $\tilde{g}_1$ and $\tilde{g}_2$ have continuous distributions, $P(\Omega) > 0$ unless they are perfectly correlated, implying $C > 0$.

The aggregate expected return to depositors is given by

$$P_N \cdot E_{\tilde{G}_N}[\tilde{G}_N | G_N \leqq H_N] + (1 - P_N) \cdot H_N \quad \text{where } P_N \equiv P(\tilde{G}_N \leqq H_N).$$

Notice that $G_N \geqq 0$ implying $E_{\tilde{G}_N}[\tilde{G}_N | G_N \leqq H_N] \geqq 0$ and that the aggregate expected rerurn of depositors is greater than or equal to:

$$(1 - P_N) \cdot H_N = (1 - P_N) \cdot N \cdot \left(R + \frac{D_N}{2}\right)$$
$$> N \cdot R \quad \text{for small } P_N > 0$$

i.e., for $P_N \in (0, (D_N/2)/(R + D_N/2))$.

There exists $N^* < \infty$ such that $P_N < \delta$ for all $\delta > 0$, by the (weak) law of large numbers, because $E_{\tilde{G}_N}[\tilde{G}_N] > H_N$. This implies that the delegation cost D_N can be made arbitrarily small for large N. ||

Proposition 2 demonstrates the key role of diversification in the provision of delegated monitoring. The intermediary need not be monitored because it takes "full responsibility" and bears all penalties for any short-fall of payments to principals. The diversification of its portfolio makes the probability of incurring these penalties very small and allows the information collected by the intermediary to be observed only by the intermediary.

Proposition 1 characterized the optimal incentive compatible mechanism for financial intermediation, and this is the optimal incentive compatible mechanism with "privacy". It was the optimal mechanism when the agent monitoring entrepreneurs was constrained not to announce the values of the project outcomes he observed and could only use the information privately to enforce his contract with each entrepreneur. Proposition 2 shows that financial intermediation is, asymptotically, the optimal incentive compatible mechanism for financing entrepreneurs' projects, without imposing the constraint of "privacy".

If the number of entrepreneurs monitored is $N = 1$, then delegation costs are so large that intermediation is never viable. If $N \to \infty$, then expected delegation costs approach zero, and intermediation is viable whenever direct monitoring pays. There exists some $N > 1$ at which intermediation becomes just viable (when $D_N \leqq \min[E_{\tilde{y}}[\phi^*(\tilde{y})], m \cdot K]$). If the assumption is made that each entrepreneur's project has the same variance, then the expected delegation costs are a monotonically decreasing function of N. This leads to increasing returns to scale due to diversification, but asymptotic constant returns to scale because expected delegation costs per project are bounded below by zero, and they may be small for moderate values of N.

The incentive contract is debt with bankruptcy penalties and high leverage. Asymptotically, the debt is riskless (as $D_N \to 0$). The leverage is high, as the face value of the debt is $H(N) = N \cdot (R + D_N/2)$, while the expected future value of the intermediary (including value of the debt) is $N \cdot (R + D_N + K)$.

The importance of the diversification is not simply a way for principals to hold well-diversified portfolios. Principals are risk neutral, and are not made directly better off by the diversification. Diversification within the financial intermediary organization is important, and cannot be replaced by diversification across intermediaries by principals.

Correlated Returns of Entrepreneurs

The assumption of independently distributed project returns across entrepreneurs is quite strong. It can be weakened somewhat. Instead of independence, assume that entrepreneur's project returns depend on several common factors which are observable. Factors might include GNP, interest rates, input prices, etc. Since these are observable, they can be used as the basis for contingent contracts. There might exist futures markets for these variables, and the financial intermediary could hedge changes in these factors in those markets. An example is a bank's hedging of interest rate risk using interest rate futures. If there are not active futures markets, then the intermediary can write contracts with depositors which depend on the values of these factors, rather than taking responsibility for all risks. An example of this is matching the maturity of assets and liabilities by banks, which places all interest rate risk on depositors. In either case, the intermediary retains responsibility for (and potentially fails as a result of) all risks which are not observable.

The result of Proposition 2, that $D_N \to 0$ as $N \to \infty$ follows given this alternative assumption in place of independence. This is stated in the following corollary.

Corollary to Proposition 2. *If it is common knowledge that the returns of the projects of entrepreneurs $i = 1, \ldots N$, are given by*

$$\tilde{y}_i = \Sigma_{j=1}^{M}[\beta_{ij} \cdot \tilde{F}_j] + \tilde{\varepsilon}_i$$

where the $\tilde{F}_j$ are observable ex post, the $\tilde{\varepsilon}_i$ are independent and bounded and $E[\tilde{y}_i] > R + K$, then the result of Proposition 2 follows.

Proof. Choose $g_i(y_i) = \alpha_i \cdot y_i$ where

$$\alpha_i = \frac{R + K + D_N}{E_{\tilde{y}}[\tilde{y}_i]}.$$

Let the penalty contract be either

$$\phi(Z) = Z + [\Sigma_{i=1}^{N} \Sigma_{j=1}^{M} \alpha \cdot \beta_{ij} \cdot F_j] - H(N)$$

where

$$H(N) = \left[N \cdot \left(R + \frac{D_N}{2}\right)\right] - E[\Sigma_{i=1}^{N} \Sigma_{j=1}^{M} \alpha_i \cdot \beta_{ij} \cdot \tilde{F}_j],$$

or let $\phi(Z)$ be as in Proposition 2, and let the position in the futures market be $\Sigma_{i=1}^{N} \alpha_i \cdot \beta_{ij}$ in futures markets $j = 1, \ldots, M$. The transformed random variables are now independent, and the result Proposition 2 follows. ||

The intermediary monitors firm-specific information, which is independent across entrepreneurs, and hedges out all systematic risks. The description of the process generating project returns is consistent with the Arbitrage Pricing Theory of Ross (1976).

The intuition behind this result is that the intermediary must bear certain risks for incentive purposes, but that risks which have no incentive component because they are common information should be shared optimally.[4] There has been a debate among various bankers and bank regulators over the desirability of allowing hedging in futures markets by banks. Our analysis suggests a reason why it is desirable.

4. Risk Aversion and Diversification

Diversification proved to be important to reduce delegation costs despite universal risk neutrality because of the wealth constraint of non-negative consumption and the asymmetry of information about project outcomes. The wealth constraint gives rise to a special type of

[4]See Diamond–Verrecchia (1982) and Holmström (1982) for implications of this observation for the theory of managerial capital budgeting.

"risk aversion". In this section, we investigate the role of diversification within the intermediary when the agents within the intermediary are risk averse in the usual sense. To focus on risk sharing issues, we drop the wealth constraint to allow any promise to be made good. A complete re-analysis of the model of Section 2 is not presented. This section does not present a realistic intermediary model, but simply a further investigation of the role of diversification in reducing the costs of delegation.

The basic setup is as in Section 2, each entrepreneur is endowed with a project with outcome $\tilde{y}_i$ which is freely observed only by the entrepreneur, which has zero as a possible realization. Absent monitoring by lenders, no incentive compatible payment schedule can depend on the realization y_i, because the entrepreneur could always claim a low value occurred. For simplicity, assume that all agents in the economy, including the entrepreneurs, are identical and risk averse. Risk aversion implies that the payment to lenders will be a constant, rather than a random amount independent of $\tilde{y}_i$, (see Holmström (1979)). This implies that, absent monitoring, the risk averse entrepreneur bears all of the risk from fluctuations in $\tilde{y}_i$. This is inconsistent with the optimal risk sharing which would occur if $\tilde{y}_i$ were observed, and this provides a potential benefit from monitoring $\tilde{y}_i$. In this risk averse setting, we could introduce other actions, e.g., effort, which the entrepreneur could privately select to give rise to a more general motivation for monitoring. This would not change the essence of our results.

We focus again on delegated monitoring by a financial intermediary. A financial intermediary raises funds from depositors who do not monitor, lends these funds to entrepreneurs, and can offer improved risk sharing with an entrepreneur because the intermediary's monitoring reduces or eliminates the incentive problem. In Section 2, we showed that an intermediary monitoring a single entrepreneur would have an incentive problem just as severe as would an entrepreneur. Almost the same result is true here. Because depositors do not monitor the intermediary and cannot observe its information, incentive compatible payments from the intermediary to depositors cannot depend on outcomes, and will be constant. It is true, however, that a single intermediary and a single entrepreneur can now share $\tilde{y}_i$ risk, but this has little to do with intermediation. Any lender who spends resources to monitor $\tilde{y}_i$ can share risk with the entrepreneur without being called an "intermediary".

For a financial intermediary in an economy where everyone is risk averse to viably provide delegated monitoring services, it must have lower delegation costs than an entrepreneur. Equivalently, since risk sharing is the issue here, a viable financial intermediary which monitors many entrepreneurs with independently distributed projects must charge a lower Arrow-Pratt risk premium for bearing the risk of an entrepreneur's project than does the entrepreneur. This will carry over to more general settings, because if the intermediary can bear risks at a lower risk premium it will generally face a less severe trade-off between risk sharing and incentives, and can thus efficiently be delegated a monitoring task.

Two Types of Diversification

There are two ways in which an intermediary in an economy of risk averse agents might use diversification. They correspond to two different models of an intermediary. One model increases the number of agents working together within the intermediary organization as the intermediary monitors a larger number of entrepreneurs. The second model assumes that the intermediary consists of a *single* agent who monitors a large number of entrepreneurs with independent projects.

Beginning with the first model, assume that each identical agent ("banker") in the intermediary is risk averse, and that by spending resources to monitor, each banker within the intermediary can observe the information monitored by all other bankers within the intermediary. This implies that there are no incentive problems within the intermediary. The extreme assumption that incentive problems are absent is intended to capture the idea that there may be a different mechanism for controlling incentive problems within an organization. This approach is followed in Ramakrishnan–Thakor (1983), to generalize the risk neutral analysis we present in Section 2. This model leads to the traditional "risk subdividing" type of diversification. This type of diversification works because each independent risk is shared by an increasing number of bankers. For example, each risk averse agent will obtain a higher expected utility if each of N agents invests in a fraction $1/N$ of N identical independent gambles than in any single one of the gambles.

The second type of diversification, "adding risks", occurs in the second model where a single banker bears 100% of N independent risks, with diversification occurring as N grows. This is quite different from risk subdivision, because it is not a form of risk sharing at all. The total risk imposed on the agent rises with N, while with subdivision of risks it falls with N. Samuelson (1963) termed diversification by adding risks a "fallacy of large numbers", because it is not true for all risk averse utility functions that the risk aversion toward the N-th independent gamble is a decreasing function of N. Samuelson provides no analysis of conditions when this type of diversification is beneficial, and I know of none in the literature.[5] We provide a partial characterization of conditions when the certainty equivalent of a given gamble is higher (and the risk premium lower) when another independent risky gamble is also held. That is, when is the per-asset certainty equivalent higher with $N = 2$ than with $N = 1$?

We turn first to the relatively straightforward model of diversification by subdivision of risks. Assume that it takes one banker in the intermediary to monitor one entrepreneur, and this requires an expenditure in goods of K (or that the disutility of this monitoring task is additively separable). All bankers are identical, have increasing, concave utility of wealth functions $U(W)$. By spending K to monitor their entrepreneur, each banker can also observe information monitored by the other bankers within the intermediary, implying that there is no incentive problem within the intermediary. Depositors are not assumed to be able to observe any of the information generated within the intermediary, and are paid a fixed unconditional payment of NR. As $N \to \infty$, Ramakrishnan–Thakor (1983) shows that each banker bears an arbitrarily small risk, with perfect risk sharing within the intermediary.

The interpretation of this result is that the diversification which occurs when bankers within the intermediary can share independent risks does serve to reduce the severity of its incentive problem. This occurs because the incentive problem here imposes a constraint on optimal risk sharing, and if there is improved risk sharing within the intermediary (where incentive problems may be controlled directly, or absent as assumed here), then this is analogous to reducing the risk aversion of a single agent, which reduces the tradeoff between risk sharing and the provision of incentives.

In the second model, where the intermediary consists of a single agent, diversification by adding risks is at work. The intermediary agent monitoring N loans, receives payments from each entrepreneur and bears all of the risk because he pays an unconditional return, $N \cdot R$, to depositors. The financial intermediary can provide monitoring and risk sharing services superior to an individual lender if and only if his risk aversion toward the Nth independent risk is a decreasing function of N. Put another way, when there is no wealth constraint an intermediary monitoring a single entrepreneur ($N = 1$) is equivalent to direct monitoring

[5]Some analysis is presented of risk aversion measured from a stochastic initial "wealth" position in Kihlstrom, Romer and Williams (1981), Machina (1982), and Ross (1981). These papers do not address the problem of adding risks.

by a lender. Intermediation becomes potentially viable when the delegation cost (equal to the risk premium here) is reduced by the centralization of monitoring to a single intermediary. This is therefore equivalent to the conditions when adding independent risks reduces per-entrepreneur risk aversion, which are the conditions when the fallacy of large numbers is not a fallacy.

To provide a partial characterization of conditions when the per-risk risk premium declines, we initially focus on the case of two risks. That is, given two bounded and independent random variables $\tilde{g}_1$ and $\tilde{g}_2$, when is the risk premium for bearing the risk of the bounded random variable $\tilde{g}_1 + \tilde{g}_2$ less than the sum of the two risk premia for bearing either risk separately. If both random variables represent payment schedules from entrepreneurs which a risk averse intermediary would voluntarily accept, both must have expectation greater than $R + K$, because the intermediary promises $N \cdot R$ to depositors and spends $N \cdot K$ on monitoring. It will ease exposition to provisionally assume $E_{\tilde{g}_1}[\tilde{g}_1] = R + K$. In addition, define $x_i \equiv g_i - R - K$, for $i = 1, 2$. With this notation, the net effect of contracting to monitor an entrepreneur with payment schedule $\tilde{g}_1$ is equivalent to receiving the random variable $\tilde{x}_1$. (In this notation, our temporary assumption is $E_{\tilde{x}_1}[\tilde{x}_1] = 0$.)

An agent has a four times differentiable, increasing and strictly concave von Neuman-Morgenstern utility function $U(W)$, and initial wealth W_0. The random variables $\tilde{x}_1$ and $\tilde{x}_2$ are bounded and independent. The risk premium, ρ_i, for bearing the risk, of the single random variable $x_i (i = 1, 2)$, satisfies

$$E_{\tilde{x}_i}[U(W_0 + \tilde{x}_i + \rho_i)] = U(W_0 + E_{\tilde{x}_i}[\tilde{x}_i]).$$

The risk premium, ρ_{1+2}, for bearing the risk of the random variable $\tilde{x}_1 + \tilde{x}_2$, satisfies

$$E_{\tilde{x}_1} E_{\tilde{x}_2}[U(W_0 + \tilde{x}_1 + \tilde{x}_2 + \rho_{1+2})] = U(W_0 + E_{\tilde{x}_1}[\tilde{x}_1] + E_{\tilde{x}_2}[\tilde{x}_2]).$$

Adding risks reduces the risk premium if

$$\rho_{1+2} < \rho_1 + \rho_2.$$

If $\tilde{x}_2$ is a small gamble, its risk premium is proportional to the Arrow-Pratt measure of absolute risk aversion or $-U''(W_0)/U'(W_0)$. Treating $\tilde{x}_1$ as part of the agent's endowment define the indirect utility function $V(x_2)$ of increments to wealth x_2, which is also von Neuman-Morgenstern and defined as

$$V(x_2) = E_{\tilde{x}_1}[U(W_0 + \tilde{x}_1 + x_2)].$$

The expected utility of the agent bearing the risk of $\tilde{x}_1 + \tilde{x}_2$ is now expressed as $E_{\tilde{x}_2} V(\tilde{x}_2)$.

The incremental risk premium for bearing the risk of $\tilde{x}_2$, given that $\tilde{x}_1$ is in one's endowment, is given by the Arrow-Pratt measure for the utility function $V(\cdot)$. The condition for $\rho_{1+2} < \rho_1 + \rho_2$ is for $V(\cdot)$ to be less risk averse than $U(\cdot)$, or

$$-\frac{E_{\tilde{x}_1}[U''(W_0 + \tilde{x}_1)]}{E_{\tilde{x}_1}[U'(W_0 + x_1)]} < -\frac{U''(W_0)}{U'(W_0)}.$$

Given our assumption that $E_{x_1}[\tilde{x}_1] = 0$, a sufficient condition can be directly obtained from Jensen's inequality. A sufficient condition is for the function $-U''(w)$ to be concave and $U'(w)$ to be convex, or $U''''(\cdot) \geqq 0$ and $U'''(\cdot) \geqq 0$ (with one inequality strict) over the range of $W_0 + \tilde{x}_1 + \tilde{x}_2$. (Clearly, $U'''' \leqq 0$ and $U''' \leqq 0$ (with one inequality strict) is sufficient for the reverse condition).

The assumption that $E_{\tilde{x}_1}[\tilde{x}_1] = 0$ is invalid if $\tilde{x}_1$ is a gamble which the agent accepts voluntarily. It is necessary to have $E_{\tilde{x}_1}[\tilde{x}_1] > 0$. Adding a voluntarily chosen gamble $\tilde{x}_1$ will not only place a mean preserving spread onto intitial wealth, it will increase mean wealth. To take account of the effect of this higher mean wealth on risk aversion, we augment the sufficient conditions described above with the condition for decreasing absolute risk aversion. This provides sufficient conditions for the "fallacy of large numbers" to be correct, rather than a fallacy, (for proof that this is equivalent to decreasing risk aversion, see Pratt (1964, Theorem 5) or Kihlstrom, Romer and Williams (1981, Corollary 2)).

The condition for decreasing absolute risk aversion at a point W is

$$U'''(W) > \frac{U''(W)^2}{U'(W)} > 0,$$

thus a sufficient condition is that over the entire domain of W

$$U'''(W) > \frac{U''(W)^2}{U'(W)}.$$

Combined with $U'''' \geqq 0$, we have a sufficient condition for diversification by adding risks to reduce the risk premium. Stronger characterizations can be obtained from stronger assumptions about the random variables $\tilde{x}_1$ and $\tilde{x}_2$.

These conditions extend beyond the case of $N = 2$, because if over the relevant domain $U'''(\cdot) \geqq 0$ then $V'''(\cdot) \geqq 0$ and if $U''''(\cdot) \geqq 0$ then $V''''(\cdot) \geqq 0$. Finally, straight forward extension of Pratt (1964, theorem 5) shows that if $-U''/U'$ is decreasing in the relevant domain, then $-V''/V'$ is decreasing as well. A third independent gamble will further reduce the risk premium: $\rho_{1+2+3} < \rho_{1+2} + \rho_3 < \rho_1 + \rho_2 + \rho_3$.

A few examples may help to illustrate what is at work. With constant absolute risk aversion ($-U''(W)/U'(W) = k$ for all W), increasing the mean initial wealth is of no consequence and in addition,

$$\frac{-V''}{V'} = k\frac{E_{\tilde{W}}[U'(\tilde{W})]}{E_{\tilde{W}}[U'(W)]} = k,$$

implying that diversification by adding independent risks is of no consequence, because there are no wealth levels of lower risk aversion over which to average. The quadratic utility function $U(W) = W - (b/2)W^2$ has $U'''(\cdot) = U''''(\cdot) = 0$, therefore adding a zero mean gamble $\tilde{x}_1$ does not influence the risk aversion toward the independent gamble $\tilde{x}_2$. However, a voluntarily chosen gamble $\tilde{x}_1$ will have a positive expectation, and quadradic utility implies increasing absolute risk aversion. The per-gamble risk premium will *increase* and diversification will "hurt".

A simple example of a utility function which satisfies the conditions for diversification by adding risks to be beneficial is $U(W) = 0.05W^3 - 60W^2 + 50{,}000\,W - 4{,}450{,}000$ which is increasing and concave and has $U'''(\cdot) > 0$, $U''''(\cdot) = 0$, and decreasing absolute risk aversion over the domain $W \in [0, 400)$. Suppose initial wealth is 100, notice that $U(100) = 0$. The gamble

$$\tilde{x}_1: \quad \begin{cases} +32{\cdot}1983 & \text{with probability } \tfrac{1}{2} \\ -30 & \text{with probability } \tfrac{1}{2} \end{cases}$$

will be just acceptable; that is $E_{\tilde{x}_1}[U(100 + \tilde{x}_1)] = 0$. If $\tilde{x}_2$ is an independent identically distributed gamble, we find $E_{\tilde{x}_1}E_{\tilde{x}_2}[U(100 + \tilde{x}_1 + \tilde{x}_2)] = 209.6$. The risk aversion toward the second gamble is reduced by accepting the first.

In contrast to diversification by subdividing risk, the value of diversification by adding risks depends critically on the form of agent's utility function. Given the lack of observability of preferences in practice, this limits the testability of this result on diversification when there is no binding wealth constraint. The results in Section 3, where the value of diversification arises only from binding wealth constraints, provide strong and testable results.

5. Comparison with Leland–Pyle (1977) Results

Leland–Pyle (1977) (L–P hereafter) develops an interesting model of costly signalling by entrepreneurs selling shares to the public. In contrast to the ex-post information asymmetry analysed in this paper, they focus on an *ex-ante* information asymmetry, where entrepreneurs know more than investors. This gives rise to an adverse selection problem, because if entrepreneurs of different types cannot be distinguished, all must sell securities at the same price, and there would be a large supply of securities by entrepreneurs with worthless projects. The model allows the entrepreneur an endogenous choice of investing in other assets or retaining equity in his project. L–P show that retained equity serves as a costly signal of the entrepreneur's information about value. It is costly, because in equilibrium a risk averse entrepreneur retains some "project specific risk" of his project which would be avoided under full information.

Some preliminary thoughts on a theory of financial intermediation are presented in L–P although no analysis is developed. They suggest that financial intermediaries might expend resources to observe entrepreneur's *ex-ante* information and use the information to offer to buy securities from entrepreneurs, offering improved risk sharing. Intermediaries might do this to capture cost savings compared with information collection by investors, or to solve underproduction of information problems analysed by Grossman–Stiglitz (1980) and Chan (1983). Although L–P do not mention diversification, they seem to suggest that the intermediary collects information about many entrepreneurs and then signals the *ex-ante* prospects of its portfolio using the same "retained equity" costly signal which entrepreneurs can use individually. Such intermediation will be viable only if the per-entrepreneur risk sharing cost of signalling by the intermediary is lower than the per-entrepreneur cost of direct signalling without an intermediary. This is analogous to the conditions for viable intermediation in the delegated monitoring model analysed above. It is interesting to investigate whether the types of diversification analysed in Section 4 facilitate intermediation here. In the process of doing this, we correct an error in L–P which was not criticial to their analysis of individual entrepreneur signalling, but which is central to our extending the analysis to diversification and intermediation.[6] We present results in the text, and sketch the analysis in the Appendix.

The formal L–P signalling model analyses an entrepreneur endowed with a project which has a mean return observed only by him. It is common knowledge that it has a normal distribution with known variance σ^2. The entrepreneur and all investors have exponential utility (constant absolute risk aversion). The entrepreneur's preferences are common knowledge. Traded securities are valued in the market using the Capital Asset Pricing Model and public information. This implies that known market wide risks are "priced", while "specific risks" (those uncorrelated with the market portfolio) are not priced. The market will bear specific risks at no risk premium. The entrepreneur signals by issuing

[6]The analysis of L–P presented here was stimulated by a referee's noting that this paper's results seemed opposed to those of Proposition III of L–P, and his conjecture that L–P Proposition III might be incorrect.

unlimited liability (riskless) debt, and equity at market prices, and by trading in the "market portfolio", with signalling conditions enforced by retaining a non-trivial amount of equity and its associated specific risk. This signalling is costly because of imperfect risk sharing—the risk averse entrepreneur retains a large amount of specific risk which could be sold off to the market with no risk premium under full information.

We introduce financial intermediation and diversification into the L–P model by assuming that there are N entrepreneurs with projects whose returns are distributed independently and identically and are independent of the market portfolio. (The results extend to the case where projects are correlated with the market portfolio, but independent conditional on the observed market portfolio). In the Appendix, we demonstrate that the results of Section 4 carry over to the L–P model.

Diversification by adding independent risks occurs if the intermediary is modeled as a single agent who like everyone else in the L–P model has exponential utility. As is suggested by the analysis in Section 4, such diversification has no effect, because with constant absolute risk aversion the risk aversion toward any gamble is not affected by the presence of any other independent gambles. This implies that an agent signalling a given project will choose to retain a given fraction of its equity in a signalling equilibrium, irrespective of other independent projects he must signal, and that the marginal impact on his expected utility is not influenced by other independent projects he must signal. This implies that financial intermediation based on diversification by adding risks is not viable given the L–P model because the intermediary signalling costs will be just as high as an entrepreneur's.

Diversification by subdividing risks occurs if there are N bankers working in the intermediary who all observe the *ex-ante* information of N entrepreneurs, and signal by each retaining equity in the intermediary's portfolio. Focusing for simplicity on the case of bankers with identical utility functions and identical independent projects with mean μ, and variance σ^2, this implies that each banker in the intermediary retains a fraction $1/N$ of total equity retained by insiders, and an equal fraction of each project. Because all bankers can observe each other's information and actions, they face no group moral hazard problem. Because of their risk sharing, we show that each banker's signalling decision is equivalent to that of a single entrepreneur signalling a project with mean $N\mu/N = \mu$ and variance $(1/N)^2 N\sigma^2 = \sigma^2/N$. As a result, diversification by subdividing risks has the same effect on each banker's expected utility as reducing the known variance of specific risk of a single project signalled directly by a single entrepreneur. We show in the Appendix that this diversification improves the expected utility of the agents in the intermediary (expected utility is a decreasing function of variance), implying that diversified intermediation is potentially viable. Put another way, the intermediary's signalling costs are lower than an entrepreneur's, because the intermediary's costs are equivalent to the signalling costs of an entrepreneur with a smaller variance of specific risk. This analysis corrects the erronous Proposition III in L–P, which states that an entrepreneur's expected utility is an *increasing* function of variance, and would have implied that even diversification by subdividing risk was counterproductive.

The results of our delegated monitoring intermediation model are consistent with the extension of the L–P analysis to intermediation. In particular, if the *ex-ante* information about the N entrepreneurs who contract with the intermediary is observed by the N bankers who as a team are the intermediary (diversification by subdividing risks), then the "delegated signalling" costs approach zero. The implication of this is an intermediary with primarily debt (deposits) in its capital structure and very little outside equity.

6. Conclusion

Diversification within the financial intermediary is the key to understanding why there is a benefit from delegating monitoring to an intermediary which is not monitored by its depositors. The intuitive reason for the value of diversification is slightly different in the model with risk neutral agents from the one with risk averse agents. In the risk neutral model, diversification is important because it increases the probability that the intermediary has sufficient loan proceeds to repay a fixed debt claim to depositors; in the limit, this probability is one, and the probability of incurring necessary bankruptcy costs goes to zero. In the model with risk aversion, but no binding constraints on non-negative consumption, diversification increases the intermediary's risk tolerance toward each loan, allowing the risk bearing necessary for incentive purposes to be less costly. The general importance of diversification in financial intermediary theories is demonstrated by the similar results obtained from our analysis of a Leland–Pyle signalling model of intermediation.

Financial intermediaries allow better contracts to be used and allow Pareto superior allocations. This provides a positive role for financial intermediaries. The delegated monitoring model predicts well-diversified financial intermediaries with a capital structure which is mainly debt (deposits), with despite this high leverage, a low probability of default. These predictions are in line with reality for most intermediaries. In addition, the insight that intermediaries must bear certain risks for incentive purposes has an important implication for the regulatory controversy involving the desirability of allowing banks to hedge in interest rate futures markets. Because interest rate risk is freely observable, it ought to be shared optimally, and permitting banks to sell such risk in the futures market effectively allows them to do so. Because risk sharing within the intermediary is constrained by binding incentive compatibility constraints, there is a reason to allow the bank to hedge against these risks (although a possible alternative is for the bank to force borrowers to do this hedging).

Commerical banks and insurance companies are the most obvious applications of this model. Another interesting application of the diversification by subdividing model is conglomerate firms. To the extent that members of subsidiary divisions can monitor each others' actions at low cost, the conglomerate can allow the managers of the divisions to share the risks which they as a group must bear for incentive purposes. In Diamond–Verrecchia (1982), it is argued that the risks which managers must bear for incentive purposes are the firm-specific risks because these are not observable elsewhere. If the cost of within conglomerate monitoring is fixed, a possible implication of our results is that firms with high firm-specific risk will be most likely to join together into conglomerates.

An interesting implication of the delegated monitoring model is that intermediary assets will be illiquid. This is because the intermediary is delegated the task of observing information about each loan which no one else but the entrepreneur/borrower observes. In one sense, such assets are totally illiquid, as the intermediary contracts to hold them and enforce the contract, rather than sell them. If the intermediary were to sell a loan and transfer the monitoring and enforcement to someone else, the acquirer would have to incur the monitoring costs again, duplicating the effort of the first intermediary. These costs would be in addition to any physical costs of transfering ownership. Adverse selection of which loan an intermediary chooses to sell could be another complication caused by the private information possessed by the intermediary. The centralization of monitoring each loan by a single intermediary will mean that there are no active markets for these assets. All of these phenomena are related to the concept of illiquidity. The resulting illiquidity of assets leads to another reason why financial intermediaries might improve on the allocations provided by competitive exchange markets; see Diamond–Dybvig (1983), where asset illiquidity is simply a result of the specified production technology. An interesting extension of these two models would be a model of the liqudity implications of private information within an intermediary.

Many "markets" for information services induce the delegated private information production analysed in this paper. Further study of the implications of this arrangement should produce new insights into financial markets and institutions, and possibly other types of markets and organizations.

Appendix

To focus on the role of diversification in reducing the signalling costs of an intermediary below those of individual entrepreneurs, we compare signalling costs for $N = 1$ and $N = 2$. We view the intermediary as equivalent to an entrepreneur with 2 projects. We assume that the projects of entrepreneurs monitored by the intermediary are mutually independent and uncorrelated with the "market portfolio", the one other traded risky asset in the L–P model. We follow L–P and assume that projects are so small that we can neglect the effect of adding them to the market. This implies we can alternatively assume that the projects are independent conditional on the market portfolio, because trade in the market allows optimal linear sharing of market risk, and L–P analyze only linear risk sharing.

Agents in the intermediary have identical known exponential utility of wealth functions, $U(W) = -e^{-bW}$ where $b > 0$. Project i has returns $\tilde{x}_i + \mu_i$, where $\tilde{x}_i$ has a normal distribution with zero mean and known variance $\sigma^2_{x_i}$, and μ_i is known by the entrepreneur and intermediary, but not investors in the market. Given information which will be available to the market, the project is valued at its expectation, discounted by the rate of interest, r (because the project is uncorrelated with the market, or alternatively, because investors are risk neutral). The intermediary chooses to retain a fraction α_i of the equity in the ith project, selling the remainder to outside investors and also issuing unlimited liability (riskless) debt. Absent some sort of self-selection or signalling mechanism, there will be a severe adverse selection problem. L–P solve for a fully separating signalling equilibrium, with sorting based on the value of α_i.

Using notation similar to L–P, define:

α_i = the fraction of the i-th project retained by the intermediary.

$\mu_i(\alpha_i)$ = the market's valuation schedule, expressing the μ_i inferred on the basis of α_i selected.

$V_i(\alpha_i)$ = the total market value of project i implied by the schedule $\mu_i(\alpha_i)$. $V_i(\alpha_i) = \mu_i(\alpha_i)/(1 + r)$.

W_0 = the initial wealth of the intermediary.

$\tilde{M}$ = the random return on the market portfolio.

β = the fraction of the market portfolio held by the intermediary.

V_M = price of the market portfolio.

K_i = initial outlay required for the i-th project.

D_i = current value of riskless debt issued against the i-th project (promise to pay $D_i(1 + r)$).

Y = current value of riskless debt issued on "personal account". (The distinction between D_i and Y is not used here; we present it this way to be consistent with L–P.

r = riskless rate of interest.

W_1 = final wealth of intermediary.

$\sigma^2_{W_i}$ = variance of final wealth.

Given the assumption of exponential utility, and normal distributions of the projects and market portfolio, the intermediary maximizes $E[\widetilde{W}_i] - (b/2)\sigma^2_{w_i}$. The budget constraint is:

$$W_0 + \alpha_1 D_1 + \alpha_2 D_2 + (1 - \alpha_1)V_1(\alpha_1) + (1 - \alpha_2)V_2(\alpha_2) - K_1 - K_2 - \beta V_M - Y = 0. \quad \text{(A1)}$$

Final wealth is

$$\widetilde{W}_1 = \alpha_1[\widetilde{x}_1 + \mu_1 - (1 + r)D_1] + \alpha_2[\widetilde{x}_2 + \mu_2 - (1 + r)D_2] + \beta\widetilde{M} + (1 + r)Y. \quad \text{(A2)}$$

Substituting (A2) into (A1),

$$\widetilde{W}_1 = \alpha_1[\widetilde{x}_1 + \mu_1 - \mu_1(\alpha_1)] + \alpha_2[\widetilde{x}_2 + \mu_2 - \mu_2(\alpha_2)] + \beta\widetilde{M} - (1 + r)\, V_M$$
$$+ (W_0 - K_1 - K_2)(1 + r) + \mu_1(\alpha_1) + \mu_2(\alpha_2). \quad \text{(A3)}$$

The intermediary chooses α_1, α_2 and β to maximize $E[\widetilde{W}_1] - (b/2)\sigma^2_{\widetilde{W}_1}$. Noting that $\widetilde{x}_1$, $\widetilde{x}_2$, and $\widetilde{M}$ are independent, the optimal α_1^*, α_2^*, and β^* satisfy:

$$[\mu_1 - \mu_1(\alpha_1^*)] + (1 - \alpha_1^*)\mu_{\alpha_1}(\alpha_1) - \alpha_1 b\sigma^2_{x_1} = 0, \quad \text{(A4)}$$

$$[\mu_2 - \mu_2(\alpha_2^*)] + (1 - \alpha_2^*)\mu_{\alpha_2}(\alpha_2) - \alpha_2 b\sigma^2_{x_2} = 0, \quad \text{(A5)}$$

and

$$[E[\widetilde{M}] - (1 + r)V_M] - \beta b\sigma^2_M = 0. \quad \text{(A6)}$$

In a separating signalling equilibrium $\mu_i(\alpha_i) = \mu_i$. Solving (A4) and (A5) given this constraint yields

$$(1 - \alpha_i)\mu_{\alpha_i}(\alpha_i) = b\alpha_i\sigma^2_{x_i} \quad \text{for } i = 1, 2. \quad \text{(A7)}$$

Solving the differential equation (A7) yields

$$\mu_i(\alpha_i) = -b\sigma^2_{x_i}[\log(1 - \alpha_i) + \alpha_i] + (1 + r)K_i, \quad \text{(A8)}$$

plus an arbitrary constant. The least cost solution not subject to unraveling, is shown in L–P to have the constant = 0, implying that the market value of the ith project is

$$V_i(\alpha_i) = \frac{1}{1 + r}[-b\sigma^2_{x_i}[\log(1 - \alpha_i) + \alpha_i]] + K_i. \quad \text{(A9)}$$

For simplicity we analyse the case of independent and identically distributed (i.i.d.) projects, where $\mu_1 = \mu_2 = \mu$ and $\sigma^2_{x_1} = \sigma^2_{x_2} = \sigma^2_x$.

Diversification by *subdividing* risks occurs with an intermediary which consists of two agents each with risk aversion b who each retain[s] a fraction $\alpha/2$ of each of two projects. Because their decisions are separable, they each make a decision for each project which is equivalent to that of a single agent endowed with a single project with mean $\mu/2$ and variance $\sigma^2_x/4$. This, in turn, is equivalent to a project with mean $= \mu$ and variance $= \sigma^2_x/2$, because from (A8), if α_i solves $\mu_i = [\log(1 - \alpha_i) + \alpha_i]\,\sigma^2_{x_i}$, it also solves $a\mu_i = [\log(1 - \alpha_1) + \alpha_1] \cdot a\sigma^2_{x_i}$. We can therefore analyse the comparative static effect of diversification by sub-dividing risks on an intermediary's expected utility by analysing the effect of reducing the variance of specific risk of a single project $i = 1$, holding its mean constant (we suppress the subscript "i"). This is given by

$$\frac{dE[U(\widetilde{W}_1)]}{d\sigma^2_x} = \frac{dE[\widetilde{W}_1]}{d\sigma^2_x} - \frac{b}{2}\frac{d\sigma^2 w_1}{d\sigma^2_x}. \quad \text{(A10)}$$

Because $E[\tilde{x}_i] = 0$ and $\mu = \mu(\alpha)$, (A3) shows that $dE[\tilde{W}_1]/d\sigma_x^2 = 0$. Turning to the variance of final wealth, note that it is given by $\sigma_{W_i}^2 = \alpha^2\sigma_x^2 + \beta^2\sigma_M^2$, implying

$$\frac{d\sigma_{W_1}^2}{d\sigma_x^2} = 2\sigma_x^2\alpha\frac{d\alpha}{d\sigma_x^2} + \alpha^2\frac{d\sigma_x^2}{d\sigma_x^2} + \frac{d(\beta^2\sigma_M^2)}{d\sigma_x^2}. \tag{A11}$$

Inspecting (A4) and (A6), $d(\beta^2\sigma_M^2)/d\sigma_x^2 = 0$, and by definition $d\sigma_x^2/d\sigma_x^2 = 1$. In equilibrium $\mu(\alpha) = \mu$, so one can apply the implicit function theorem to (A8), and obtain

$$\frac{d\alpha}{d\sigma_x^2} = -\frac{d\mu(\alpha)/d\sigma_x^2}{d\mu(\alpha)/d\alpha} = \frac{(1-\alpha)[\log(1-\alpha)+\alpha]}{\alpha\sigma_x^2}.$$

Inserting this into (A10) and (A11), one obtains

$$\frac{dE[U(\tilde{W}_i)]}{d\sigma_x^2} = -b\left[(1-\alpha)[\log(1-\alpha)+\alpha] + \frac{\alpha^2}{2}\right] < 0.$$

This is negative because it is defined over $\alpha \in (0,1)$, is zero at zero, and decreasing in α. This corrects Proposition III in L–P, where the final α^2 term was omitted, leading them to conclude that the sign of the entire expression was positive. The intuition behind the correct result is clear: signalling is costly because of inferior risk sharing, if there is very little risk, the cost is low (if $\sigma^2 = 0$, there is no risk for the entrepreneur to bear, and no need to go public). Thus diversification by subdividing risks can serve as a basis for viable financial intermediation in a L–P setting. As N, the number of independent projects, and number of bankers within the intermediary, grows without bound, the per-project risk premium goes to zero, because the total variance of wealth, per banker in the intermediary (σ_x^2/N) goes to zero.

Diversification by *adding independent* risks is modelled by adding a second i.i.d. project to the intermediary's portfolio, while the intermediary consists of a single agent with constant risk aversion of b. Inspecting (A4) and (A5), one finds that no terms involving another independent project enter, thus $\alpha_1 = \alpha_2$ and both are equal to the level that would prevail if there were only one project. Therefore, adding additional i.i.d. projects is equivalent to adding i.i.d. lotteries, and given exponential utility the analysis in Section 4 shows that the risk premium per project is not influenced by the number of independent projects. Therefore, diversification by adding i.i.d. projects does not reduce signalling costs in the L–P model and cannot serve as a basis for viable financial intermediation. It would be interesing to extend the L–P model to a utility function which implies that this type of diversification has value.

References

Campbell, T. (1979), "Optimal Investment Decisions and the Value of Confidentiality", *Journal of Financial and Quantitative Analysis*, **14,** 913–924.

Chan, Y. (1983), "On the Positive Role of Financial Intermediation in Allocation of Venture Capital in a Market with Imperfect Information", *Journal of Finance*, **38,** 1543–1568.

Diamond, D. W. and Dybvig, P. H. (1983), "Bank Runs, Deposit Insurance and Liquidity", *Journal of Political Economy*, **91,** 401–419.

Diamond, D. W. and Verrecchia, R. E. (1982), "Optimal Managerial Contracts and Equilibrium Security Prices", *Journal of Finance*, **37,** 275–287.

Harris, M. and Raviv, A. (1979), "Optimal Incentive Contracts with Imperfect Information", *Journal of Economic Theory*, **20,** 231–259.

Holmström, B. (1979), "Moral Hazard and Observability", *Bell Journal of Economics*, **10,** 74–91.

Holmström, B. (1982), "Moral Hazard in Teams", *Bell Journal of Economics*, **13,** 324–340.

Kihlstrom, R., Romer, D. and Williams, S. (1981), "Risk Aversion with Random Initial Wealth", *Econometrica*, **49,** 911–920.

Leland, H. and Pyle, D. (1977), "Informational Asymmetries, Financial Structure, and Financial Intermediation", *Journal of Finance*, **32,** 371–387.

Machina, M. (1983), "Temporal Risk and the Nature of Induced Preferences" (Working paper, University of California-San Diego, Department of Economics).

Pratt, J. (1964), "Risk Aversion in the Small and the Large", *Econometrica*, **69,** 122–136.

Ramakrishnan, R. and Thakor, A. (1983), "Information Reliability and a Theory of Financial Intermediation" (Working paper, Indiana University).

Ross, S. A. (1976), "The Arbitrage Theory of Capital Asset Pricing", *Journal of Economic Theory*, **13,** 341–360.

Ross, S. A. (1981), "Some Stronger Measures of Risk Aversion in the Small and the Large with Applications", *Econometrica*, **49,** 621–638.

Samuelson, P. (1963), "Risk and Uncertainty: A Fallacy of Large Numbers", *Scientia.*

Schumpeter, J. (1939) *Business Cycles* (New York: McGraw-Hill).

Shavell, S. (1979), "Risk Sharing and Incentives in the Principal and Agent Relationship", *Bell Journal of Economics*, **10,** 55–73.

Smith, C. W. and Warner, J. B. (1979), "On Financial Contracting: An Analysis of Bond Covenants", *Journal of Financial Economics*, **7,** 117–161.

Townsend, R. M. (1979), "Optimal Contracts and Competitive Markets with Costly State Verification", *Journal of Economic Theory*, **21,** 1–29.

Eleven

Gur Huberman

Gur Huberman received a Ph.D. from Yale University in 1980. He started out at the University of Chicago Graduate School of Business, and now works at the Columbia School of Business. •

I came to Yale to study operations research in September 1977, having been an undergraduate student in mathematics at Tel Aviv and having received a Masters in applied mathematics from UBC in Vancouver. At that point I knew that I would not excel in mathematics and was seeking some second-best subject. Operations research seemed to offer that opportunity.

I took all the required courses in the area, including a course in stochastic processes in the department of statistics in which I met two other first-year graduate students: Greg Connor and Mark Grinblatt. Both were in the economics department, both impressed me with their smarts and technical ability, thereby inspiring in me a general respect for economists. I also attended the weekly faculty seminar in operations research. An occasional attendee was a young professor who, when present, would make some of the quickest and most insightful comments: Steve Ross.

By the following September I took his doctoral class in financial economics (yes, Mark and Greg were in it) and asked him to supervise my thesis. Naturally, he covered the APT in the class, presenting it with a beautifully compelling argument. (The rest of the course was as compelling and as pretty.)

At least in those days, the culture in operations research, perhaps inspired by laboratory set-ups in schools of engineering, was that the advisor assigns a problem to a student. Steve obliged. It was a dynamic portfolio choice problem, which kept me busy for many months. My failures and successes with the problem were excuses for regular meetings with Steve. Other students who were knocking on Steve's door at the time were Chester Spatt, Phil Dybvig, Doug Diamond, and Paul Pfleiderer. Their presence turned the waiting times for Steve into informal seminars in their own right.

The meetings with Steve were a lot of fun. He was quick, he was incisive, he had a broad view of what could be accomplished and what could not, and why. He was warm, he was supportive, always a great teacher. I got a sense from him that economics was fun, and was about the real world.

In the fall of 1979, having written a few papers in operations research, I was ready to look for an academic job. Steve suggested that I read the work of Grossman and Stiglitz, saying that it was an indispensable part of the education of anybody seeking to join a finance faculty. As I was reading those now-famous papers, I pointed out to Steve that the Israeli market for indexed bonds was very similar to the setup in those papers on rational expectations with asymmetric information. Steve immediately encouraged me to get those data and turn my observation into an empirical piece. His Rolodex even had the number of Bank Leumi in New York. (An aside: when I asked Steve why he had the number, he said that they would do things other banks wouldn't. I still wonder what those things were.)

The Leumi folks did give me the initial data, and the work eventually appeared as a collaboration with Bill Schwert. Steve was an enthusiastic guide at the project's most crucial point: its inception.

My contribution to this volume, "A Simple Approach to Arbitrage Pricing Theory," was also born in the late fall of 1979. Steve asked me to write a referee's report on a paper on the subject. Being a very serious graduate student, I thought that the occasion called for my thorough understanding of the topic, which meant going back to reading Steve's original papers. Challenged by the complexity of Steve's work, I tried to produce a simpler proof of the theory. When I showed it to Steve, he was enthusiastic and welcoming of this approach. In fact, he was kind enough to advertise it, which of course was very helpful on my job search.

Many of the contributors to this volume had made up their minds to be economists before they met Steve. Some had even expected to be financial economists. I came to Yale as a graduate student in operations research, and left a budding financial economist. I have enjoyed my career very much. Clearly, I could not imagine this happy turn in my life without Steve.

A Simple Approach to Arbitrage Pricing Theory

*Gur Huberman**
Graduate School of Business, University of Chicago, Chicago, Illinois 60637

1. Introduction

The arbitrage theory of capital asset pricing was developed by Ross [9, 10, 11] as an alternative to the mean-variance capital asset pricing model (CAPM), whose main conclusion is that the market portfolio is mean-variance efficient. Its formal statement entails the following notation. A given asset i has mean return E_i and the market portfolio has mean return E_m and variance σ_m^2. The covariance between the return on asset i and the return on the market portfolio is σ_{im}, and the riskless interest rate is r. The CAPM asserts that

$$E_i = r + \lambda b_i, \tag{1.1}$$

where

$$\lambda = E_m - r,$$

and

$$b_i = \sigma_{im}/\sigma_m^2 \tag{1.2}$$

is the "beta coefficient" of asset i.

Normality of the returns of the capital assets or quadratic preferences of their holders are the assumptions which lead to (1.1)–(1.2). Theoretically and empirically it is difficult to justify the assumptions of the CAPM. Moreover, the CAPM has been under strong criticism because of its dubious empirical content (cf. [7]). The market portfolio is practically not observable, and a statement on the market portfolio (such as the CAPM) is difficult to test empirically. Yet the linear relation (1.1) is appealing in its simplicity and in its ready interpretations. The arbitrage pricing theory [10, 11] is an alternative theory to mean-variance theories, an alternative which implies an approximately linear relation like (1.1). In [10] Ross elaborated on the economic interpretation of the arbitrage pricing theory and its relation to other models, whereas in [11] he provided a rigorous treatment of the theory. Recent interest in the APT is evident from papers elaborating on the theory (e.g., Chamberlin and Rothschild [1], Connor [4] and Kwon [5, 6]) as well as on its empirical aspects (e.g., Chen [2, 3] and Roll and Ross [8]).

The main advantage of Ross' arbitrage pricing theory is that its empirical testability does not hinge upon knowledge of the market's portfolio. Unfortunately, Ross' analysis is difficult to follow. He does not provide an explicit definition of arbitrage and his proof—unlike the intuitively appealing introductory remarks in [11]—involves assumptions on agents' preferences as well as "no arbitrage" assumptions.

---

*This is a modified version of the third chapter in my Ph.D. dissertation which was written at Yale University. I am grateful to Gregory Connor, who inspired some of the ideas in the paper. Comments from my advisor, Steve Ross, as well as from Jon Ingersoll, Uriel Rothblum and Michael Rothschild were helpful in my attempts to bring this work to a lucid form. This research was supported by NSF Grants ENG-78-25182 and SOC-77-22301.

Reprinted with permission:
Huberman, Gur. "A Simple Approach to Arbitrage Pricing Theory." *Journal of Economic Theory* 28 (1982): 183–191

Here arbitrage is defined and the intuition is formalized to obtain a simple proof that no arbitrage implies Ross' linear-like relation among mean returns and covariances. The main lines of the proof are illustrated in the following paragraphs.

Consider an economy with n risky assets whose returns are denoted by $\tilde{x}_i$ $(i = 1, \ldots, n)$ and they are generated by a factor model

$$\tilde{x}_i = E_i + \beta_i \tilde{\delta} + \tilde{\varepsilon}_i \qquad (i = 1, \ldots, n), \tag{1.3}$$

where the expectations $E\tilde{\delta} = E\tilde{\varepsilon}_i = 0$ $(i = 1, \ldots, n)$, the $\tilde{\varepsilon}_i$ are uncorrelated and their variances are bounded. Relying on results from linear algebra, express the vector E (whose ith component is E_i) as a linear combination of the vector e (whose ith component is 1), the vector β (whose ith component is β_i) and a third vector c which is *orthogonal* both to e and to β.[1] In other words, one can always find a vector c such that

$$E = \rho e + \gamma\beta + c, \tag{1.4}$$

where ρ and γ are scalars,

$$ec \equiv \sum_{i=1}^{n} c_i = 0, \tag{1.5}$$

and

$$\beta c \equiv \cdot\sum_{i=1}^{n} \beta_i c_i = 0. \tag{1.6}$$

Next, consider a portfolio which is proportional to c, namely αc (α is a scalar). Note that it costs nothing to acquire such a portfolio because its components (the dollar amount put into each asset) sum to zero by (1.5). We shall call such a portfolio an arbitrage portfolio. Also, by (1.6) this is a zero-beta portfolio. The return on this portfolio is

$$\alpha\tilde{x}c = \alpha \sum_{i=1}^{n} \tilde{x}_i c_i = \alpha \sum_{i=1}^{n} c_i^2 + \alpha \sum_{i=1}^{n} c_i \tilde{\varepsilon}_i, \tag{1.7}$$

by virtue of the decomposition (1.4) and the orthogonality relations (1.5) and (1.6). It is important to notice that the expected return on the portfolio αc is proportional to α (and $\sum_{i=1}^{n} c_i^2$), whereas an upper bound on the variance of its return is proportional to α^2 (and $\sum_{i=1}^{n} c_i^2$).

Suppose now that the number of assets n increases to infinity. Think of arbitrage in this environment as the opportunity to create a sequence of arbitrage portfolios whose expected returns increase to infinity while the variances of their returns decrease to zero. If the sum $\sum_{i=1}^{n} c_i^2$ increased to infinity as n did, then one could find such arbitrage opportunities as follows. Set $\alpha = 1/(\sum_{i=1}^{n} c_i^2)^{3/4}$ and use the portfolio αc. The reason why such a choice of α will create the arbitrage is that the expected return on the portfolio is proportional to α (and with $\alpha = 1/(\sum_{i=1}^{n} c_i^2)^{3/4}$ it equals $\alpha\sum_{i=1}^{n} c_i^2 = (\sum_{i=1}^{n} c_i^2)^{1/4}$), while its variance is proportional to α^2 (and with $\alpha = 1/(\sum_{i=1}^{n} c_i^2)^{3/4}$ it equals $\alpha^2 \sum_{i=1}^{n} c_i^2 = 1/(\sum_{i=1}^{n} c_i^2)^{1/2} j$).

Therefore, if there are no arbitrage opportunities (as described above) the sum $\sum_{i=1}^{n} c_i^2$ cannot increase to infinity as n does. In particular, when the number of assets n is large, most of the c_i's are small and approximately zero. Going back to the original decomposition (1.4) we conclude that $E_i \approx \rho + \gamma\beta_i$ for most of the assets.

When motivating his proof, Ross [11, p. 342] emphasized the role of "well-diversified" arbitrage portfolios. He indicated that the law of large numbers was the driving force behind the diminishing contribution of the idiosyncratic risks $\tilde{\varepsilon}_i$ to the overall risks of the arbitrage

[1] Gregory Connor used this idea in an earlier work of his [4].

portfolios. The portfolios presented above, αc, need not be well diversified, but they satisfy the orthogonality conditions (1.5) and (1.6). It is the judicious choice of the scalar α that enables us to apply an idea, which is in the spirit of the proof of the law of large numbers.

Section 2 of this paper presents the formal model, a precise statement of the result and a rigorous proof. In the closing section an attempt is made to interpret the linear-like pricing relation and to justify the no-arbitrage assumption in an equilibrated economy of von Neumann–Morgenstern expected utility maximizers.

2. Arbitrage Pricing

The arbitrage pricing theory considers a sequence of economies with increasing sets of risky assets. In the nth economy there are n risky assets whose returns are generated by a k-factor model (k is a fixed number). Loosely speaking, arbitrage is the possibility to have arbitrarily large returns as the number of available assets grows. We will show that in the absence of arbitrage a relation like (1.1) holds, namely (2.9).

Formally, in the nth economy, we consider an array of returns on risky assets $\{\tilde{x}_i^n: i = 1, \ldots, n\}$. These returns are generated by a k-factor linear model of the form

$$\tilde{x}_i^n = E_i^n + \beta_{i1}^n \tilde{\delta}_1^n + \beta_{i2}^n \tilde{\delta}_2^n + \cdots + \beta_{ik}^n \tilde{\delta}_k^n + \tilde{\varepsilon}_i^n \qquad (i = 1, 2, \ldots, n), \tag{2.1}$$

where

$$E\tilde{\delta}_j^n = 0 \qquad (j = 1, \ldots, k), \qquad E\tilde{\varepsilon}_i^n = 0 \qquad (i = 1, \ldots, n), \tag{2.2}$$

$$E\tilde{\varepsilon}_i^n \tilde{\varepsilon}_j^n = 0 \qquad \text{if} \quad i \neq j, \tag{2.3}$$

$$\text{and Var } \tilde{\varepsilon}_i^n \leqslant \bar{\sigma}^2 \qquad (i = 1, \ldots, n), \tag{2.4}$$

where $\bar{\sigma}^2$ is a fixed (positive) number. Using standard matrix notation we can rewrite (2.1) as

$$\tilde{x}^n = E^n + \beta^n \tilde{\delta}^n + \tilde{\varepsilon}^n, \tag{2.5}$$

where β^n is the $n \times k$ matrix whose elements are β_{ij}^n ($i = 1, \ldots, n$; $j = 1, \ldots, k$).

A portfolio $c^n \in R^n$ in the nth economy is an *arbitrage portfolio* if $c^n e^n = 0$, where $e^n = (1, 1, \ldots, 1) \in R^n$. The return on a portfolio c is

$$\tilde{z}(c) = c\tilde{x}^n = cE^n + c\beta^n\tilde{\delta}^n + c\tilde{\varepsilon}^n. \tag{2.6}$$

Arbitrage is the existence of a subsequence n' of arbitrage portfolios whose returns $\tilde{z}(c^{n'})$ satisfy

$$\lim_{n' \to \infty} E\tilde{z}(c^{n'}) = +\infty, \tag{2.7}$$

and

$$\lim_{n' \to \infty} \text{Var } \tilde{z}(c^{n'}) = 0. \tag{2.8}$$

In Section 3 we relate (2.7)–(2.8) to standard probabilistic convergence concepts, and discuss how von Neumann–Morgenstern expected utility maximizers view (2.7)–(2.8).

In Theorem 1 we show that the absence of arbitrage implies an approximation to a linear relation like (1.1).

Theorem 1. *Suppose the returns on the risky investments satisfy* (2.1)–(2.4) *and there is no arbitrage. Then for* $n = 1, 2, \ldots,$ *there exists* ρ^n, $\gamma_1^n, \ldots, \gamma_k^n$, *and an* A *such that*

$$\sum_{i=1}^{n} \left(E_i^n - \rho^n - \sum_{j=1}^{k} \beta_{ij}^n \gamma_j^n \right)^2 \leqslant A, \qquad \textit{for} \quad n = 1, 2, \ldots, \tag{2.9}$$

Proof. Using the orthogonal projection of E^n into the linear subspace spanned by e^n and the columns of β^n, one obtains the representation

$$E^n = \rho^n e + \beta^n \gamma^n + c^n, \tag{2.10}$$

where

$$\gamma^n \in R^k,$$
$$e^n c^n = 0, \tag{2.11}$$

and

$$\beta^n c^n = 0. \tag{2.12}$$

Note that $\|c^n\|^2 \equiv \sum_{i=1}^n (c_i^n)^2 = \sum_{i=1}^n (E_i^n - \rho^n - \sum_{j=1}^k \gamma_j^n \beta_{ij}^n)^2$, and assume that the result is false. Consequently, there is an increasing subsequence (n') with

$$\lim_{n'\to\infty} \|c^{n'}\| = +\infty \tag{2.13}$$

Let p be fixed between -1 and $-1/2$, and consider the portfolio $d^{n'} = \alpha_{n'} c^{n'}$, where

$$\alpha_{n'} = \|c^{n'}\|^{2p}. \tag{2.14}$$

By (2.11), $d^{n'}$ is an arbitrage portfolio for each n'. Use (2.10)–(2.12) to see that its return

$$\tilde{z}(d^{n'}) = \alpha_{n'} \|c^{n'}\|^2 + \alpha_{n'} c^{n'} \tilde{\varepsilon}^{n'}. \tag{2.15}$$

Note that

$$E\tilde{z}(d^{n'}) = \alpha_{n'} \| c^{n'}\|^2 = \| c^{n'}\|^{2+2p}, \tag{2.16}$$

so (by (2.13)–(2.14)),

$$\lim_{n'\to\infty} E\tilde{z}(d^{n'}) = +\infty. \tag{2.17}$$

On the other hand (using (2.3), (2.4))

$$\text{Var } \tilde{z}(d^{n'}) \leqslant \bar{\sigma}^2 \alpha_{n'}^2 \|c^{n'}\|^2 = \bar{\sigma}^2 \|c^{n'}\|^{2+4p}, \tag{2.18}$$

so (by (2.13)),

$$\lim_{n'\to\infty} \text{Var } \tilde{z}(d^{n'}) = 0,$$

thus completing the proof.

Next, consider a stationary model, in which $E_i^n = Ei$ and $\beta_{ij}^n = \beta_{ij}$ for all i,j and n. In other words, (2.5) is replaced by

$$\tilde{x}^n = E + \beta\tilde{\delta}^n + \tilde{\varepsilon}^n. \tag{2.5$'$}$$

The stationary model is the one considered originally by Ross [11]. The nonstationary model is more general than the stationary model but its result (2.9) is not as elegantly presentable as the result in the stationary case (2.9′).

Theorem 2. *Suppose the returns on the risky investments satisfy* (2.5′), (2.2)–(2.4), *and there is no arbitrage. Then there exist* $\rho, \gamma_1, \ldots, \gamma_k$ *such that*

$$\sum_{i=1}^{\infty}\left(E_i - \rho - \sum_{j=1}^{k} \beta_{ij}\gamma_j\right)^2 < \infty. \tag{2.9$'$}$$

Proof. Consider the $n \times (k+1)$ matrix B^n whose (i,j) entry is 1 if $j = 1$ and β_{ij-1} if $1 < j \leqslant k+1$. Let $r(n)$ be the rank of B^n. Since $1 \leqslant r(n) \leqslant r(n+1) \leqslant k+1$ for all n, and $r(n)$ is an integer, there is an $\overline{n}$ such that $r(n) = r(\overline{n})$ for all $n \geqslant \overline{n}$. Let $n \geqslant \overline{n}$ be fixed. By permuting the columns of B^n we may assume that its first $r(\overline{n})$ columns can be expressed as linear combinations of the first $r(\overline{n})$ columns. Define the set H^n by

$$H^n = \left\{(\rho, \gamma_1, \ldots, \gamma_k): \sum_{i=1}^{n}\left(E_i - \rho - \sum_{j=1}^{k}\beta_{ij}\gamma_j\right)^2 \leqslant A, \gamma_j = 0, \quad \text{for} \quad r(\overline{n}) < j \leqslant k\right\},$$

where A is the A whose existence was asserted in Theorem 1. Note that H^n is nonempty (by Theorem 1), compact for $n \geqslant \overline{n}$ and $H^n \subset H^{n+1}$. Therefore, $\bigcap_{n=1}^{\infty} H^n$ is nonempty. Since every $k+1$ tuple $(\rho, \gamma_1, \ldots, \gamma_k) \in \bigcap_{n=1}^{\infty} H^n$ satisfies (2.9′), the proof is complete.

Finally, we turn attention to the case where a risk free asset exists, i.e., where there is an additional asset in the nth economy, whose return, say, x_0^n, satisfies

$$x_0^n = r_0^n. \tag{2.19}$$

Now look at excess returns of the risky assets (excess relative to the riskless rate), i.e., at

$$\tilde{y}_i^n \equiv \tilde{x}_i^n - r_0^n, \qquad i = 1, 2, \ldots, n.$$

Note that any arbitrage portfolio $(c_0, c_1, \ldots, c_n) \in R^{n+1}$ of $x_0^n, \tilde{x}_1^n, \ldots, \tilde{x}_n^n$ (which of course satisfies $\sum_{i=0}^{n} c_i = 0$) is equivalent to a vector $(c_1, \ldots, c_n) \in R^n$ indicating a wealth allocation among the risky assets. Using this idea one can go through the same analysis as in Theorem 1 with the excess returns vector $\tilde{y}^n$, the decomposition (2.10) replaced by

$$E^n - r_0^n e = \beta^n \gamma^n + c^n, \tag{2.10′}$$

and (2.11) deleted.

Consequently, one has

Corollary. *Suppose the returns on the risky investments satisfy* (2.1)–(2.4), *there is a risk free asset satisfying* (2.19) *and there is no arbitrage. Then there exist* $\gamma_1^n, \gamma_2^n, \ldots, \gamma_k^n$ *such that*

$$\sum_{i=1}^{n}\left(E_i^n - r_0^n - \sum_{j=1}^{k}\beta_{ij}^n\gamma_j^n\right)^2 \leqslant A \qquad \textit{for} \quad n = 1, 2, \ldots. \tag{2.20}$$

Remark Analogously, a similar result holds for the stationary model.

3. Discussion

The interpretation of (2.9) or (2.9′) is straightforward: for most of the assets in a large economy, the mean return on an asset is approximately linearly related to the covariances of the asset's returns with economy-wide common factors. As the number of assets becomes large, the linear approximation improves and most of the assets' mean returns are almost exact linear functions of the appropriate covariances.

Next, consider the probabilistic implications of arbitrage returns satisfying (2.7)–(2.8). Given a sequence of random returns $\tilde{z}(c^{n'})$ which satisfy (2.7)–(2.8), we can apply Chebychev's inequality to see that along this sequence $\lim_{n' \to \infty} \tilde{z}(c^{n'}) = +\infty$ in probability (i.e., for all $M > 0$, $\lim_{n' \to \infty} \Pr\{\tilde{z}(c^{n'}) \geqslant M\} = 1$). Furthermore, along a subsequence $\hat{n}$, a stronger convergence holds: $\lim_{\hat{n} \to \infty} \tilde{z}(c^{\hat{n}}) = +\infty$ almost surely (i.e., for all $M > 0$, $\Pr\{\liminf_{\hat{n} \to \infty} \tilde{z}(c^{\hat{n}}) \geqslant M\} = 1$).

Are arbitrage portfolio which satisfy (2.7)–(2.8) desirable for an expected utility maximizer? In other words, do (2.7)–(2.8) suffice to assert that $\lim_{n\to\infty} EU(\tilde{z}(c^n)) = U(+\infty)$ for any monotone concave utility function U? The negative answer is illustrated by the following examples.

The first example considers a utility function which is $-\infty$ for nonpositive wealth levels, whereas the second example is for an exponential utility which takes finite values for finite wealth levels.

1. The returns $\tilde{z}(c^n)$ are 0, n and $2n$ with probabilities $1/n^3$, $1 - 2/n^3$, and $1/n^3$, respectively. The utility function $U(x) = -1/x$ for $x > 0$ and $U(x) = -\infty$ for $x \leqslant 0$. Then $EU(\tilde{z}(c^n)) = -\infty$ although $\tilde{z}(c^n)$ satisfies (2.7)–(2.8).
2. The returns $\tilde{z}(c^n)$ are $-n$, n, and $3n$ with probabilities $1/n^3$, $1 - 2/n^3$, and $1/n^3$, respectively. The utility function is $U(x) = -\exp(-x)$. Then $EU(\tilde{z}(c^n)) \leqslant -n^3 \exp(n)$, so $\lim_{n\to\infty} EU(\tilde{z}(c^n)) = -\infty$, although (2.7)–(2.8) are met.

General conditions which assert that (2.7)–(2.8) imply $\lim_{n'\to\infty} EU(t(\tilde{z}(c^{n'})) = U(+\infty)$ are not known. As shown in [11, Appendix 2], utility functions which are bounded below or uniformly integrable utility functions will possess this property.

We conclude that one needs to make assumptions on agents' preferences in order to relate existence of equilibria to absence of arbitrage. This task is beyond the scope of this paper. However, it is straightforward to see that if the economies satisfy the assumptions made by Ross (see [11], especially the first paragraph on p. 349 and Appendix 2), then no arbitrage can exist. In fact, a result of the type "no arbitrage implies a certain behavior of returns," should involve no consideration of the preference structure of the agents involved. Our analysis is in this spirit, because it involves no assumptions on utilities. Other than the simple proof, this may be another contribution of this work.

References

1. G. Chamberlain and M. Rothchild, Arbitrage and mean-variance analysis of large asset markets, mimeo, University of Wisconsin–Madison, 1980.
2. Nai-Fu Chen, Empirical evidence of the arbitrage pricing theory, mimeo, UCLA, 1980.
3. Nai-Fu Chen, The arbitrage pricing theory: Estimation and applications, mimeo, UCLA, 1980.
4. G. Connor, "Asset Prices in a Well-Diversified Economy," Technical Report No. 47, Yale School of Organization and Management, July 1980.
5. Y. Kwon, Counterexamples to Ross' arbitrage asset pricing model, mimeo, University of Kansas, 1980.
6. Y. Kwon, "On the negligibility of diversifiable risk components at the capital market equilibrium," mimeo, University of Kansas, 1980.
7. R. Roll, A critique of the asset pricing theory's tests: Part I: On past and potential testability of the theory, *Financial Econ.* **4** (1977), 129–179.
8. R. Roll and S. Ross, An empirical investigation of the arbitrage pricing theory, *Journal of Finance* **35** (1980), 1073–1103.
9. S. Ross, "The General Validity of the Mean-Variance Approach in Large Markets," Discussion Paper No. 12–72, Rodney L. White Center for Financial Research, University of Pennsylvania.
10. S. Ross, Return, risk and arbitrage, in "Risk and Return in Finance" (I. Friend and J. Bicksler, Eds.), Ballinger, Cambridge, Mass., 1977.
11. S. Ross, The arbitrage theory of capital asset pricing, *J. Econ. Theory* **13**, No. 3 (1976), 341–360.

Twelve

Gregory Connor

Gregory Connor received a Ph.D. from Yale University in 1982. He started out at the Kellogg School, Northwestern University, and now works at the London School of Economics. •

Stephen Ross had a profound influence on my academic career, through his inspiration and guidance. I entered the Yale Ph.D. program in economics resolved to pursue a research agenda in industrial organization. The Nelson-Winter research program using an evolutionary approach to industrial structure and technical change was in its infancy; there was much excitement about it at Yale. My planned secondary field (we were required to have two fields, for our field exams) was to be either economic theory or mathematical economics. It was natural for me to take Stephen Ross's Financial Economics course in year two since it related to both mathematical economics and economic theory (and even a bit to industrial organization). The course was inspiring, and beautiful in the way that good mathematics or scientific theory can be beautiful. Mark Grinblatt and I had long hours of enjoyment together codifying and re-proving the results from Ross's lectures, as part of our "swatting" for the course.

In year three, I was faced with a stark choice. The third-year Nelson-Winter Industrial Organization seminar was scheduled at exactly the same time as Ross's third-year Financial Economics seminar. It was time to fish or cut bait, and for the first lecture of the term, I stuck with my plan to continue in Industrial Organization. I missed the first Financial Economics seminar for this reason: I was at the Nelson-Winter seminar.

During the first Financial Economics seminar, Stephen Ross looked around the room at the assembled group of students and said aloud to them, "Where's Greg?" Three different people reported it back to me: Mark Grinblatt, Gur Huberman, and Paul Pfleiderer. At that point in my short career, this little remark was probably the highest compliment I had ever received as an economist. Ross's two-word remark changed my career plan permanently—if Stephen Ross thought I belonged in the financial economics research stream, and cared enough to ask after me, the decision seemed obvious. I switched my fields to Financial Economics and Industrial Organization, with the major focus on Financial Economics. I enthusiastically joined Ross's very talented team of doctoral students. The rest is, well, personal history, and I have never regretted the decision. It was an exciting place to be and we were the envy of our Yale classmates.

A Unified Beta Pricing Theory*

Gregory Connor
J. L. Kellogg Graduate School of Management,
Northwestern University, Evanston, Illinois 60201

This paper derives Ross's mutual fund separation theory and a new, equilibrium version of Ross's arbitrage pricing theory as special cases of a general theory. The paper also reveals that the two theories are identical in their predictions of asset prices and portfolio returns. The capital asset pricing model (a restricted case of the mutual fund separation theory) receives special treatment. Journal of Economic Literature *Classification Numbers: 021, 313.*

1. Introduction

This paper proves fundamental similarities between two asset pricing theories. It compares the mutual fund separation theory (the general case of the popular capital asset pricing model) with a new, competitive equilibrium version of the well-known arbitrage pricing theory. The paper presents both a theoretical and empirical unification of the two theories. First, it derives both of the theories simultaneously as two cases of a general theory. Second, the paper shows that the testable implications of the two are empirically indistinguishable if the analyst only observes asset prices and investors' portfolio returns.

The capital asset pricing model (CAPM) receives special treatment as an important restricted case of the mutual fund separation theory (MFST). Previous authors have remarked that the CAPM provides a convenient "black box" which mimics the intuitive understanding of portfolio choice and asset pricing in a large, diverse economy. This paper goes a step further: it formally constructs a model which follows this intuitive understanding, and shows an exact empirical equivalence between this model and the CAPM.

Some of the results of this paper have appeared elsewhere in different form. The mutual fund separation theory is due to Ross [10]. The version described herein simplifies some of the arguments in his proof but sacrifices the generality of his result. The arbitrage pricing theory (APT) is also due to Ross [8]. This paper derives a competitive equilibrium version of the APT. Ross's arbitrage theory describes the prices of a large, but unspecified, subset of the assets. This competitive equilibrium theory describes the prices of all the assets in the economy. The competitive equilibrium approach also makes it possible to see close relationships between the pricing of assets in a large economy and classic principles of market efficiency and portfolio diversification.

Section 2 defines a *factor economy* as an economy in which asset payoffs obey a factor model. The theory applies both to a factor economy with a finite number of assets and to one with an infinite number of assets. Although these two types of economies seem quite different, the general theory rarely needs to distinguish between them. The paper uses general-dimensional linear algebra to treat both cases simultaneously.

---

* This is a revised version of the second chapter of my Ph.D. dissertation, completed under the direction of Stephen Ross at the Department of Economics, Yale University. I would like to thank Carol Mershon Connor, Philip Dybvig, Jonathan Ingersoll, Alvin Klevorick, Stephen Ross, Daniel Siegel, and Ludo van der Heyden for their many helpful comments.

Reprinted with permission:
Connor, Gregory. "A Unified Beta Pricing Theory." *Journal of Economic Theory* 34 (1982): 13–31

Section 3 defines *market insurance* as the ability of market trading to completely eliminate idiosyncratic risk from investor portfolios. Section 4 proves the general pricing theory for any factor economy obeying the market insurance conditions.

Section 5 proves that it is impossible to empirically distinguish the finite assets from the infinite assets version of the theory. Section 6 focuses on the CAPM as a special case of the finite assets model, and argues that the CAPM serves well as an "as if" model, mimicking the predictions of the more intuitive limit theory. Section 7 provides a summary of the paper.

2. The Definition of a Factor Economy

This section gives some basic definitions for an economy in which asset payoffs follow a factor model.

The vector of per-share, gross payoffs for the ν risky assets can be written as[1]

$$x = c + Bf + i. \tag{1}$$

The κ-vector of random variables, $f = (f_1, f_2, \ldots, f_\kappa)$, consists of the *market factors.* The market factors describe the economy-wide random influences which (linearly) affect the payoffs of assets. They are normalized so that $E[f_\lambda] = 0$.

The *beta matrix* B is a $(\nu \times \kappa)$-matrix of constants; the γth row of B is the vector of *factor betas* for the γth asset. Without loss of generality, it can be assumed that B has full column rank. Otherwise, there would exist an equivalent factor model with fewer factors. (See Appendix 1 of [3] for a discussion of equivalent factor models.)

The nonrandom ν-vector c measures the per-share expected payoffs of the assets. The paper assumes throughout that there exists a riskless asset with per-share payoff x_0.

The vector of *idiosyncratic variates*, $i = (i_1, i_2, \ldots, i_\nu)$, represents the extra random variation specific to individual assets. These random variates are normalized so that $E[i_\gamma] = 0$. The covariance matrix of idiosyncratic terms is assumed to exist and is denoted by V:

$$V = E[ii'].$$

If V is singular, let V^{-1} denote the Moore–Penrose inverse[2] of V.

The paper assumes that none of the ν risky assets is redundant, and therefore $E[(x - c)(x - c)']$ is nonsingular. A *portfolio* (a_0, a) is a linear functional on $R^{\nu+1}$. The product of a portfolio with the asset payoffs $a_0 x_0 + a'x$ is the *portfolio payoff.* A norm is defined on the space of portfolios by using the second moment of the portfolio payoffs:

$$\|(a_0, a)\| = E[(a_0 x_0 + a'x)^2]^{1/2}.$$

Ross's arbitrage pricing theory uses a sequential-economy approach. Ross considers a sequence of economies with an increasing number of assets and proves an approximate pricing result. The approximation increases in accuracy as the number of assets grows large.

Chamberlain and Rothschild [2] have recently shown that many of Ross's results can be succinctly restated by examining a *fixed* economy with an *infinite* number of assets. This allows the approximating properties of the sequential model to become exact properties. This paper adapts the Chamberlain–Rothschild technique to a competitive equilibrium version of the APT.[3]

---

[1]Throughout the paper, upper case Roman letters represent matrices, lower case letters represent either vectors or functions, and Greek letters represent scalars. Subscripted terms are an exception to this rule: x_3 would be a scalar, the third component of the vector x. An apostrophe denotes the transpose of a vector or matrix.

[2]For any finite matrix X there exists a unique matrix X^{-1} (the Moore–Penrose inverse of X) having the properties: $XX^{-1}X = X$, $X^{-1}XX^{-1} = X^{-1}$, $(XX^{-1})' = XX^{-1}$, and $(X^{-1}X)' = X^{-1}X$.

[3]See [4] for a sequential-economy model of the equilibrium arbitrage pricing theory.

The paper models an economy with a countably infinite collection of risky assets whose payoffs obey a factor model:

$$x = c + Bf + i, \tag{2}$$

where the terms have the same definitions as in the finite case, replacing vectors in R^ν with vectors in R^∞. Again, I assume that there exists a riskless asset with payoff x_0.

For simplicity, the limit model is specified with a finite number of investors. Without loss of rigor, one can view each of these investors as representing an infinite number of investors of μ different types. Within each type, all investors are identical.

As in the finite number case, a *portfolio,* (a_0, a), is a linear functional on the space of asset payoffs, R^∞. The product of a portfolio with the asset payoffs $a_0x_0 + a'x$ is the *portfolio payoff.* Portfolios are restricted to those linear functionals whose payoffs have a finite second moment:

$$E[(a_0x_0 + a'x)^2] < \infty.$$

This second moment defines the norm on the space:

$$\|(a_0, a)\| = E[(a_0x_0 + a'x)^2]^{1/2}. \tag{3}$$

This definition of a portfolio means that two collections of asset holdings which produce identically the same portfolio payoff constitute the same portfolio.[4] The definition eliminates spuriously different portfolios. The space of portfolios is a Hilbert space.

An example will illustrate the definition. An investor might choose to hold one share of the riskless asset and one-half share of each of the first two risky assets. This portfolio could be represented by the array of real numbers: $(1, \frac{1}{2}, \frac{1}{2}, 0, 0, 0, \ldots)$; or the investor might hold $\frac{1}{3}$ share of the first three risky assets: $(1, \frac{1}{3}, \frac{1}{3}, \frac{1}{3}, 0, 0, 0, \ldots)$. This can be extended to any number ν of assets: $(1, 1/\nu, 1/\nu, \ldots, 1/\nu, 0, 0, \ldots)$. This model also lets an investor hold the limit of such a sequence:

$$\underset{\nu\to\infty}{\text{limit}}(1/\nu, 1/\nu, 1/\nu, \ldots).$$

Although such a portfolio cannot be represented by a fixed array of real numbers, it is well defined as an element in the vector space of linear functionals on R^∞ under the norm (3).

Define B^ν as the matrix consisting of the first ν rows of B and i^ν as the vector consisting of the first ν elements of i. Let $V^\nu = E[i^\nu i^{\nu'}]$. In the infinite assets case it will be assumed that B^ν has full column rank and V^ν is nonsingular for every ν. Note that the sequence must begin at some value of ν greater than or equal to κ.

The following definitions apply to both the finite and limit factor economies. Let (q_0, q) be the market portfolio, that is, the per-capita supply of assets.

A vector of *asset prices* (p_0, p) is a vector of real numbers with dimension equal to the number of assets. The *cost* of a portfolio (a_0, a) is the product $a_0p_0 + a'p$.

An *allocation* $\{(a_0^1, a^1), (a_0^2, a^2), \ldots, (a_0^\mu, a^\mu)\}$ is a collection of portfolios, one for each investor, which satisfies the resource constraint:

$$\sum_{\gamma=1}^{\mu} a^\gamma = \mu q, \qquad \sum_{\gamma=1}^{\mu} a_0^\gamma = \mu q_0,$$

[4]Using this norm creates equivalence classes containing all linear functionals whose difference in payoff has a zero second moment. That is, if (a_0, a) and (b_0, b) are such that $E[(a_0x_0 + a'x - b_0x_0 - b'x)^2] = 0$ then $(a_0, a) = (b_0, b)$.

where μ is the number of investors. This is just the economy-wide constraint and does not include any budget constraint.

An *initial allocation* $\{(e_0^1, e^1), \ldots, (e_0^\mu, e^\mu)\}$ is an allocation representing the endowments of investors. A *competitive equilibrium* consists of an *equilibrium allocation* $\{(a_0^1, a^1), \ldots, (a_0^\mu, a^\mu)\}$ and *equilibrium prices* (p_0, p) such that

$$\text{(budget feasibility)} \qquad a_0^\gamma p_0 + a^{\gamma\prime} p \leqslant e_0^\gamma p_0 + e^{\gamma\prime} p$$

and

$$\text{(optimality)} \qquad E[u^\gamma(a_0^\gamma x_0 + a^{\gamma\prime} x)] \geqslant E[u^\gamma(g_0 x_0 + g' x)]$$

for any portfolio (g_0, g) which is budget feasible.

The main assumptions of the theory will be summarized in two definitions. A *finite factor economy* is a set of investors, assets, and endowments such that:

(Fl) There are μ investors, all of whom have risk-averse, von Neumann–Morgenstern utility functions.

(F2) There are ν risky assets with per-share payoffs obeying (l), and $V = E[ii']$ and $E[ff']$ exist.

(F3) There exists a riskless asset with per-share payoff x_0.

(F4) $(B'B)$ and $E[(x - c)(x - c)']$ are nonsingular.

(F5) $E[i \mid f] = 0$.

(F6) The economy has a competitive equilibrium.

A *limit economy* is a set of investors, assets, and endowments such that:

(Ll) There are μ investors all of whom have risk-averse von Neumann–Morgenstern utility functions.

(L2) There is a countably infinite collection of risky assets obeying (2), and $V^\nu = E[i^\nu i^\nu]$ and $E[ff']$ exist for every ν.

(L3) There exists a riskless asset with per-share payoff x_0.

(L4) $(B^{\nu\prime} B^\nu)$ and V^ν are nonsingular for every ν.

(L5) $E[i \mid f] = 0$.

Note that in the finite economy the covariance matrix of idiosyncratic terms may be singular. If the matrix is nonsingular, it is not possible to completely eliminate idiosyncratic risk from portfolios with a finite number of assets. In the limit economy, one does not need singularity—investors can eliminate idiosyncratic risk by diversifying (i.e., holding many assets, each in very small quantity).

Assumption (F6) can be made exogenous by using Hart's [5] results.[5] The existence of equilibrium in the limit case will follow from its existence in the finite case (Theorem 4).

3. Insurable Factor Economies

This section gives conditions under which all investors in a factor economy (finite or limit case) are able to diversify away idiosyncratic risk. It also shows, by a Pareto-efficiency argument, that if investors can diversify away idiosyncratic risk, they will do so in competitive equilibrium.

[5] If one adds the distributional assumptions that i, f are bounded and that $x \geqslant 0$, then Hart's Theorem 3.3 applies and competitive equilibrium exists.

First, the section defines a well-diversified portfolio as one with zero idiosyncratic risk. It defines an insured allocation as one in which all portfolios are well diversified. An economy is insurable if there exists an insured allocation for every distribution across investors of expected payoff and market risk. It is shown that if an economy is insurable then the competitive equilibrium allocation is insured.

It is unnecessary to distinguish between the finite and limit cases of the theory in this section. The linear algebra is general dimensional, covering both cases simultaneously.

Definition. A *well-diversified portfolio* (w_0, w) is one with no idiosyncratic risk: $E[(w'i)^2] = 0$.

Although the definition is the same in the finite and limit cases, the "diversification mechanism" behind it differs in the two cases. In the finite assets model, investors eliminate risk by exploiting the singularity in the covariance matrix of idiosyncratic terms. Investors hold particular combinations of assets whose idiosyncratic risks exactly offset one another. In the infinite assets model, investors diversify by holding many assets, each in small quantity. The infinite number formalism of the model expresses the limit of this process: investors hold an infinite number of assets, each in infinitesimally small quantity.

An investor who holds a well-diversified portfolio is effectively insured against idiosyncratic risk. If assets are allocated so that all investors hold well-diversified portfolios, then all investors are insured.

Definition. An allocation is *insured* if it consists entirely of well-diversified portfolios.

The next definition of this section draws an equivalence between portfolios which have identical expected payoffs and factor risk but different idiosyncratic risk.

Definition. Two portfolios (a_0, a) and (w_0, w) are *factor equivalent* if $a'B = w'B$ and $a_0x_0 + a'c = w_0x_0 + w'c$. Two allocations,

$$\{(a_0^1, a^1), (a_0^2, a^2), \ldots, (a_0^\mu, a^\mu)\} \qquad \text{and} \qquad \{(w_0^1, w^1), (w_0^2, w^2), \ldots, (w_0^\mu, w^\mu)\},$$

are *factor equivalent* if all of their corresponding portfolios are factor equivalent: (a_0^γ, a^γ) is factor equivalent to (w_0^γ, w^γ) for $\gamma = 1, 2, \ldots, \mu$.

Economies in which all investors can be assigned well-diversified portfolios, for any distribution of expected payoff and factor risk, are called *insurable.*

Definition. A factor economy is *insurable* if for any allocation there exists a factor-equivalent, insured allocation.

The next theorem gives the insurability conditions for any factor economy.

Theorem 1 *A factor economy is insurable if and only if*

$$E[(q'i)^2] = 0 \tag{4}$$

and for any κ-vector b there exists a well-diversified portfolio (a_0, a) such that

$$a'B = b'. \tag{5}$$

The Appendix states condition (5) in terms of the primitive elements of the factor model.

Proof (Necessity). Given that an economy is insurable, let $\{(w_0^1, w_1), (w_0^2, w^2), \ldots, (w_0^\mu, w^\mu)\}$ be any insured allocation. Note that

$$0 = \frac{1}{\mu}\sum_{\gamma=1}^{\mu} E[(w^{\gamma\prime}i)^2]^{1/2} \geqslant E[(q'i)^2]^{1/2},$$

where the inequality follows from the Cauchy–Schwartz inequality. Therefore $E[(q'i)^2] = 0$.

Let b be any κ-vector. Since B has full column rank, for any b there exists a portfolio (z_0, z) such that $z'B = b'$. Under the hypothesis of insurability there exists a well-diversified portfolio (w_0, w) which is factor equivalent to (z_0, z); hence,

$$w'B = z'B = b',$$

which proves that condition (5) is necessary for insurability.

(Sufficiency) Let $\{(a_0^1, a^1), (a_0^2, a^2), \ldots, (a_0^\mu, a^\mu)\}$ be any allocation. Replace $a^1, a^2, \ldots, a^{\mu-1}$ with well-diversified, factor-equivalent portfolios $w^1, w^2, \ldots, w^{\mu-1}$. Let

$$w^\mu = \mu q - \sum_{\gamma=1}^{\mu-1} w^\gamma$$

$$w_0^\gamma = \frac{1}{x_0}(a_0^\gamma x_0 + a^{\gamma\prime}c - w^{\gamma\prime}c).$$

The allocation $\{(w_0^1, w^1), (w_0^2, w^2), \ldots, (w_0^\mu, w^\mu)\}$ is an insured factor-equivalent alternative to $\{(a_0^1, a^1), (a_0^2, a^2), \ldots, (a_0^\mu, a^\mu)\}$. It is insured because $w^1, w^2, \ldots, w^{\mu-1}$ are well diversified by construction, and w^μ is well diversified by the Cauchy–Schwartz inequality:

$$E[(w^{\mu\prime}i)^2]^{1/2} \leqslant \mu E[(q'i)^2]^{1/2} + \sum_{\gamma=1}^{\mu-1} E[(w^{\gamma\prime}i)^2]^{1/2}.$$

It is factor equivalent because $w^1, w^2, \ldots, w^{\mu-1}$ are factor equivalent by construction and for w^μ:

$$w^{\mu\prime}B = \mu q'B - \sum_{\gamma=1}^{\mu-1} w\gamma'B = \mu q'B - \sum_{\gamma=1}^{\mu-1} a^{\gamma\prime}B = a^{\mu\prime}B.$$

The collection of portfolios is an allocation because

$$\sum_{\gamma=1}^{\mu} w^\gamma = \mu q - \sum_{\gamma=1}^{\mu-1} w^\gamma + \sum_{\gamma=1}^{\mu-1} w^\gamma = \mu q$$

and

$$\sum_{\gamma=1}^{\mu} w_0^\gamma = \sum_{\gamma=1}^{\mu} a_0^\gamma + \frac{1}{x_0}(\mu q'c - \mu q'c) = \mu q_0.$$

Q.E.D

Given the assumptions of a factor economy, an investor prefers a well-diversified portfolio to a factor-equivalent, undiversified one.

Remark 1 In a factor economy, any investor strictly prefers a well-diversified portfolio to a factor-equivalent portfolio with nonzero idiosyncratic variance.

Proof Let (w_0, w) be well diversified and factor equivalent to (a_0, a) which has nonzero idiosyncratic variance. Using $w_0 x_0 + w'c = a_0 x_0 + a'c$ and $w'B = a'B$:

$$\begin{aligned} &E[u(a_0 x_0 + a'x)] \\ &\quad = E[u(w_0 x_0 + w'c + w'Bf + a'i)] < E[u(w_0 x_0 + w'c + w'Bf)] \\ &\quad = E[u(w_0 x_0 + w'x)], \end{aligned}$$

where the inequality follows from $E[i \mid f] = 0$ and Jensen's inequality.

Q.E.D.

The next result is fundamental. It is based on the classic principle that competitive markets efficiently allocate risk. Since insured allocations are preferable (by Remark 1) and possible (in an insurable economy), the Pareto-efficiency of competitive equilibrium guarantees that the competitive allocation is insured.

Theorem 2 *In an insurable factor economy, the competitive allocation is insured.*

Proof Let $\{(a_0^1, a^1), \ldots, (a_0^\mu, a^\mu)\}$ be a competitive allocation. Construct the factor-equivalent, insured allocation $\{(w_0^1, w^1), (w_0^2, w^2), \ldots, (w_0^\mu, w^\mu)\}$ described in Theorem 1. By Remark 1, $E[u(w_0^\gamma x_0 + w^{\gamma\prime} x)] \geqslant E[(a_0^\gamma x_0 + a^{\gamma\prime} x)]$, where the inequality is an equality if (a_0^γ, a^γ) is well diversified. Comparing the two allocations gives

$$\begin{aligned} E[u(w_0^1 x_0 + w^{1\prime} x)] &\geqslant E[u(a_0^1 x_0 + a^{1\prime} x)] \\ E[u(w_0^2 x_0 + w^{2\prime} x)] &\geqslant E[u(a_0^2 x_0 + a^{2\prime} x)] \\ \vdots \qquad & \qquad \vdots \\ E[u(w_0^\mu x_0 + w^{\mu\prime} x)] &\geqslant E[u(a_0^\mu x_0 + a^{\mu\prime} x)]. \end{aligned}$$

Unless all of the inequalities are equalities, the allocation $\{(w_0^1, w^1), (w_0^2, w^2), \ldots, (w_0^\mu, w^\mu)\}$ Pareto-dominates $\{(a_0^1, a^1), (a_0^2, a^2), \ldots, (a_0^\mu, a^\mu)\}$. Therefore, by efficiency, the competitive allocation $\{(a_0^1, a_1), (a_2^2, a^2), \ldots, (a_0^\mu, a^\mu)\}$ is insured.

Q.E.D.

Theorem 2 has as a corollary a mutual fund separation theorem.

Corollary 2.1 *In an insurable factor economy, each investor's equilibrium portfolio consists of a linear combination of $\kappa + 1$ mutual funds.*

Proof By condition (5) there exists a well-diversified portfolio for every factor beta position. Construct the κ well-diversified portfolios $\{(a_0^1, a^1), (a_0^2, a^2), \ldots, (a_0^\kappa, a^\kappa)\}$ with factor beta positions:

$$a^{1\prime}B = \begin{bmatrix} 1 \\ 0 \\ 0 \\ \vdots \\ 0 \end{bmatrix}, \qquad a^{2\prime}B = \begin{bmatrix} 0 \\ 1 \\ 0 \\ \vdots \\ 0 \end{bmatrix}, \qquad \ldots, \qquad a^{\kappa\prime}B = \begin{bmatrix} 0 \\ 0 \\ 0 \\ \vdots \\ 1 \end{bmatrix}.$$

Theorem 2 implies that each investor holds a portfolio which can be described as a linear combination of these "mutual fund" portfolios and the riskless asset.

Q.E.D.

The standard statement of mutual fund separation is that investors are *indifferent* between a mutual fund portfolio and any other portfolio. Corollary 2.1 may seem surprisingly strong—they always *hold* a mutual fund portfolio. This is due to the different definition of a portfolio. The usual definition distinguishes between portfolios which have the same return (i.e., redundant portfolios) whereas the definition used in this paper does not.

The separation result of the CAPM (Sharpe [14]) is a special case of Corollary 2.1. Corollary 2.1 is less general than Ross's [10] portfolio separation theorem for the MFST since Ross describes sufficient *and* necessary conditions. However, this paper's version has the strength that it extends Ross's small-economy theory to the large-economy case.

Ross also treats the pricing consequences of his portfolio separation theorem. The pricing results in the next section parallel his, but apply to both the finite and limit versions of the theory.

4. Price Linearity in an Insurable Factor Economy

This section proves the paper's pricing thorem. Equilibrium prices in an insurable factor economy are linear in the expected payoffs and factor betas of the assets. All of the theorems in this section apply to both the finite and limit cases. Most of the linear algebra is general dimensional: separate proofs for the finite and limit cases are rarely necessary.

The proof of the pricing theorem relies on the result that investors hold well-diversified portfolios. An investor with such a portfolio is risk neutral at the margin with respect to idiosyncratic risk. This "marginal risk neutrality" means that the investor cannot be in competitive equilibrium unless prices are linear in the factor coefficients. Otherwise, he can improve his expected utility by undiversifying his portfolio.

Definitions Let (p_0, p) be the vector of per-share prices of the assets. Normalize the prices so that the per-dollar return on the riskless asset equals one $(x_0/p_0 = 1)$. This normalization on prices is retained throughout the paper. Prices are *linear* if a vector m exists such that

$$p_0 = x_0, \quad p = c + Bm.$$

The vector m is called the vector of *factor prices*.

A portfolio with zero cost, zero risk, and a positive expected payoff is an arbitrage portfolio. The next lemma treats a portfolio which is "almost" an arbitrage portfolio, except that it contains idiosyncratic risk.

Lemma 1 *In any factor economy there exists a portfolio* (h_0, h) *with zero cost, zero factor risk, and positive expected payoff:*

$$h_0 p_0 + h'p = 0, \qquad h'B = 0, \qquad h_0 x_0 + h'c > 0,$$

if and only if prices are not linear.

Proof (Sufficiency) Consider first a finite economy. Suppose that prices are not linear. Let m be the vector which minimizes the sum of squares $d'd$ in the equation

$$p = c + Bm + d.$$

By a well-known property of least-squares residuals, the vector d so chosen is orthogonal to B. Construct the portfolio

$$h_0 = \frac{1}{x_0}(c'd + d'd), \qquad h = -d.$$

This portfolio has zero cost, zero factor risk, and an expected payoff of

$$h_0 x_0 + h'x = c'd + d'd - c'd = d'd$$

which is greater than zero whenever $d \neq 0$.

For the limit economy case, construct the ν-vector p^ν which consists of the first ν elements of p. Similarly, construct the vector c^ν and the $(\nu \times \kappa)$-matrix B^ν. Let m^ν be the vector which minimizes the sum of squares $d^{\nu\prime} d^\nu$ in the equation

$$p^\nu = c^\nu + B^\nu m^\nu + d^\nu.$$

If $d^\nu = 0$ for all ν, then $m^\nu = m^* = (B^{\nu\prime} B^\nu)^{-1}(p^\nu - c^\nu)$ for all ν. This implies that $p = c + Bm^*$.

Given that $d^\nu \neq 0$ for some ν, in the limit economy let $d^* = (d^\nu, 0, 0, 0, \ldots)$ and construct the zero cost, zero factor risk portfolio:

$$h_0 = \frac{1}{x_0}(d^{*\prime}c + d^{*\prime}d^*), \qquad h = -d^*$$

which has an expected payoff of $d^{\nu\prime}d^\nu > 0$.

(Necessity, both finite and limit case) Suppose that prices are linear. Let (h_0, h) be any hedge portfolio. It has cost:

$$h_0 p_0 + h'p = h_0 x_0 + h'c + h'd.$$

Since $d = 0$, $h'd = 0$. Hence

$$h_0 p_0 + h'p = h_0 x_0 + h'c > 0$$

and the portfolio has positive cost. Q.E.D.

Lemma 1 above shows that if prices are not linear, then there exists some "risk premium" for idiosyncratic risk: an investor can costlessly earn positive expected profit by incurring idiosyncratic risk. The next theorem shows that there cannot exist any such risk premium in an insurable factor economy. Therefore, prices must be linear.

Theorem 3 *In an insurable factor economy, competitive equilibrium prices are linear.*

Proof Let (a_0, a) be the competitive equilibrium portfolio of some investor. By Theorem 2 it is well diversified. Let (h_0, h) be any zero cost, zero factor risk portfolio. By the optimality of (a_0, a) and the zero cost of (h_0, h):

$$\frac{d}{d\varepsilon} E[u(a_0 x_0 + a'x + \varepsilon(h_0 x_0 + h'x))]_{\varepsilon=0} = 0, \tag{6}$$

otherwise the investor could costlessly increase expected utility by adding an increment of (h_0, h) to his portfolio. Solving for the derivative (6):

$$(h_0 x_0 + h'c)E[u'(a_0 x_0 + a'x)] + E[(h'i)u'(a_0 x_0 + a'x)].$$

Using $E[i \mid f] = 0$ and $a'i \equiv 0$ gives

$$(h_0 x_0 + h'c)E[u'(a_0 x_0 + a'x)]. \tag{7}$$

Since (7) $= 0$ from (6), and $E[u'(a_0 x_0 + a'x)] > 0$ by the risk-aversion assumption, this implies

$$(h_0 x_0 + h'c) = 0,$$

and this is equivalent to price linearity. Q.E.D.

The finite economy case in Theorem 3 is the same as Ross's MFST pricing theorem. The limit economy case is a strengthened version of Ross's APT.[6] The next section unifies these two theories in another way by showing an empirical equivalence.

5. The Factor Pricing Theory Isomorphism

This section shows that an insurable finite economy and an insurable limit economy are not empirically distinguishable. Given identity of investor preferences and endowments in the two economies, the economies produce "isomorphic" competitive equilibria. The equilibrium portfolio return of each investor is the same in the two economies, and the linear formula for competitive equilibrium prices is the same as well.

Definition A finite economy and a limit economy *correspond* if they have the same investor preferences and the same market factors, and their endowments are factor equivalent.

A price vector in a finite economy p and one in a corresponding limit economy p^* are superficially different, since one belongs to R^{ν} and the other to R^{∞}. However, if each of the price vectors is linear in the expected payoffs and factor betas of its assets:

$$p = c + Bm, \qquad p^* = c^* + B^*m,$$

and the factor price vector m is the same in each, then the price vectors represent identical prices. The "underlying prices" (factor prices) are identical. A portfolio in a finite economy and a portfolio in a corresponding limit economy are superficially different, since one belongs to the dual space of $R^{\nu+1}$ and the other to the dual space of R^{∞}. However, if the portfolio payoffs are identical, then in an important sense the two portfolios are the same.

Definition Competitive equilibria of a finite economy and of a corresponding limit economy are *isomorphic* if prices are linear in each economy, the factor prices are the same in each, and every investor has the same portfolio payoff in the two equilibrium allocations.

The use of the term "isomorphic" deserves explanation. Note that in either economy there is a linear function from an asset's expected payoff and factor betas to its equilibrium price. If the two competitive equilibria are isomorphic, then this function is the same in each economy. Similarly, for any investor (specified by preferences and an endowment of factor risk and expected payoff) there is a function[7] to an equilibrium portfolio payoff. If two economies are isomorphic then this function is the same. The term "isomorphic" denotes the equivalence across these two functions.

---

[6]Ross's APT guarantees that the sum of squared deviations from price linearity are bounded. That is, there exists m, d, ω such that $p_0 = x_0$, $p = c + Bm + d$, and $d'd < \omega < \infty$. This finite bound on the total sum of squares implies that the mean-squared pricing error goes to zero:

$$\lim_{\nu\to\infty} (1/\nu)\sum_{\gamma=1}^{\nu} (d^{\gamma})^2 = 0. \tag{8}$$

The competitive equilibrium version guarantees that

$$d = 0. \tag{9}$$

See Shanken [13] for a discussion of the difference in testable implications between (8) and (9).

[7]If there are multiple competitive equilibria then this will be a relation rather than a function, but that causes no difficulty.

Theorem 4 *Consider an insurable finite economy and a corresponding insurable limit economy. For any competitive equilibrium in either economy there is an isomorphic one in the other economy.*

Proof Consider a competitive allocation $\{(a_0^1, a^1), \ldots, (a_0^\mu, a^\mu)\}$ and price vector (p_0, p) in an insurable finite economy. By Theorem 2, the allocation is insured. Construct (see Theorem 1) a factor-equivalent, insured allocation in the corresponding limit economy, $\{(a_0^{*1}, a^{*1}), \ldots, (a_0^{*\mu}, a^{*\mu})\}$ Construct the price vector:

$$p_0 = x_0, \qquad p^* = c^* + B^* m,$$

where m is the factor price vector from the linear prices in the finite economy. This allocation and price vector form a competitive equilibrium in the limit economy. Competitive equilibrium requires two properties, budget feasibility and budget optimality.

(Budget Feasibility) Budget feasibility of the competitive equilibrium in the finite economy requires

$$e_0^\gamma p_0 + e^{\gamma\prime} p \geqslant a_0^\gamma p_0 + a^{\gamma\prime} p.$$

If two economies have linear prices with the same factor prices, then factor-equivalent portfolios in them have the same cost (as the reader can quickly prove). By the correspondence of the two economies, each investor's endowments are factor equivalent and $e_0^\gamma p_0 + e^{\gamma\prime} p = e_0^{*\gamma} p_0 + e^{*\gamma\prime} p^*$. Hence $(a_0^{*\gamma}, a^{*\gamma})$ is budget feasible:

$$e_0^{*\gamma} p_0 + e^{*\gamma\prime} p^* \geqslant a_0^{*\gamma} p_0 + a^{*\gamma\prime} p^*.$$

(Budget Optimality) In an insurable economy with linear prices, an investor only needs to consider well-diversified portfolios to find his optimal portfolio. For any poorly diversified portfolio, there exists a factor-equivalent (and therefore equal cost) portfolio which he will strictly prefer.

Let (g_0, g) be any budget-feasible portfolio in the finite economy. By the optimality of competitive portfolios, (a_0, a) is weakly preferred to (g_0, g). Let (g_0^*, g^*) be any budget-feasible portfolio in the limit economy. If $E[u(g_0^* x_0 + g^{*\prime} x)] > E[u(a_0^* x_0 + a^{*\prime} x)]$ then there is a budget-feasible (g_0, g) in the finite economy such that $E[u(g_0 x_0 + g' x)] > E[u(a_0 x_0 + a' x)]$, contradicting the competitive equilibrium in the finite economy.

The proof reverses exactly for the mapping from an equilibrium in the limit economy to an isomorphic one in the finite economy. Let $\{(a_0^{1*}, a^{1*}), \ldots (a_0^{\mu *}, a^{\mu *})\}$, (p_0^*, p^*) be an equilibrium in the limit economy. By Theorem 3 the prices are linear: $p^* = c^* + B^* m$. Construct the factor equivalent, insured allocation, $\{(a_0^1, a^1), \ldots, (a_0^\mu, a^\mu)$ in the finite economy and define p by $p = c + Bm$, using the factor price vector from the limit economy equilibrium. Repeat the proof of feasibility and optimality given above. Q.E.D.

Theorem 4 is my second step in building upon Ross's evidence that the APT and MFST are closely related theories (Ross [10, p. 278]). My first step is the unified derivation of the MFST and (equilibrium) APT presented in Section 4. Theorem 4 provides a more formal connection. It is an "impossibility theorem": one can never distinguish between the finite and limit models of this paper, i.e., between the MFST and equilibrium APT, based on prices or portfolio returns. This is true even if one fully knows the prices which will occur in competitive equilibrium under the two models (see Scarf [12] for how one might compute the prices). It would be treacherous to claim that there is absolutely *no* testable distinction between the two. The theorem only guarantees that portfolio return and asset price observations alone will not suffice to distinguish them.

6. Choosing between the Cases

Most of this paper has been dedicated to minimizing the distinctions between the finite and limit cases of the theory. This section attempts to choose which provides a better model of asset pricing based on the differences that remain. It argues that the limit case is superior, since it requires a weaker assumption on asset supplies. However, the CAPM, a restricted version of the finite-assets case, avoids this untenable assumption.

The most telling comparison of the finite and limit cases centers on the assumption that the market portfolio is well diversified:

$$E[(q'i)^2] = 0. \tag{4}$$

As discussed earlier, the "diversification mechanism" behind (4) differs between the two cases. In the finite case, asset supplies must be in a particular proportion such that the idiosyncratic risks exactly cancel out of the market portfolio. This "singularity" assumption is very restrictive on asset supplies. It is also nongeneric: a perturbation of asset supplies would almost surely destroy this property.

In the limit case, (4) arises naturally. Asset supplies need not be in any special ratio. Rather, the supply of each asset must be "very small" (infinitesimal) on a per-capita basis. Together with reasonable bounds on the correlations of the idiosyncratic variates this guarantees (4).

The CAPM does not use the framework of the more general MFST and does not require the strong assumption on asset supplies. The CAPM does not assume that a factor model *generates* asset payoffs. Instead, it uses asset payoffs to *construct* a factor model. Given a market portfolio q and asset payoffs x consider the *market model* defined by:

$$\begin{aligned} f &= q'x - E[q'x] \\ c &= E[x] \\ B &= \operatorname{cov}(x, q'x)/\operatorname{var}(q'x) \\ x &= c + Bf + i. \end{aligned}$$

This is an "ex-post" factor model: asset payoffs determine the factor value, rather than the factor value affecting asset payoffs. The CAPM uses this "ex-post" factor model to generate the finite-case theory while avoiding its untenable restriction on asset supplies. The well-diversified condition on the market portfolio follows immediately from the definition of the factor model, since $q'i = q'x - 1\operatorname{var}(q'x)/\operatorname{var}(q'x))q'x \equiv 0$. If x is joint normal (the usual CAPM assumption), then the market model satisfies the other distributional requirement ($E[i\,|\,f] = 0$) and price linearity follows by the theorems of Section 4.

The CAPM obviously has been a useful model of asset pricing. Some theorists have objected to the model because its derivation is unintuitive. This paper provides a formal justification for the simple model. The CAPM produces the same empirical predictions as a more sophisticated theory which follows the analyst's intuition. The CAPM provides a convenient "black box" which mimics the structure of asset prices and portfolio returns in a large, diverse economy.

7. Summary

This paper unifies the mutual fund separation theory with a new, equilibrium version of the arbitrage pricing theory. It considers two economies, one with a fixed, finite number of assets and another with an infinite number of assets. The mutual fund separation theory is proven on the finite assets economy and the equilibrium-version arbitrage pricing theory on the infinite assets economy. The paper describes a common framework of assumptions for the two economies and proves the two theories simultaneously under this framework.

The paper next proves an empirical equivalence. Given that investor preferences and endowments are the same in the two economies, it demonstrates that equilibrium prices and portfolio returns are identical in them. Hence it is impossible to distinguish between the two theories by observing competitive equilibrium prices or portfolio returns.

Although the capital asset pricing model is mathematically a special case of the finite assets model, it requires separate treatment. The CAPM takes a different viewpoint from the more general MFST. By doing so, it avoids the finite model's most objectionable assumption.

Various authors (e.g., Roll and Ross [7]) have argued that the CAPM is flawed because it does not capture the intuition which motivates its use. Others have countered that the model seems to serve as a convenient "black box"—generating predictions similar to those one would expect from a more intuitively plausible model. This paper supports the "black box" justification of the CAPM with a more rigorous argument. The infinite assets theory herein directly follows the large-economy intuition that motivates the CAPM. The finite assets theory is empirically identical to this infinite assets theory. The CAPM, a restricted version of the finite assets theory, is empirically identical to a (restricted version of) the infinite assets theory. Hence the CAPM provides a remarkably accurate black box representation of the large-economy intuition.

Appendix

Lemma 2 *In a finite factor economy, condition* (5) *holds if and only if* $(I - V^{-1}V)B$ *has full column rank.*

Proof (Sufficiency) Suppose $(I - V^{-1}V)B$ has full column rank. Then for any b there exists a solution z to the equation:

$$z'(I - V^{-1}V)B = b'.$$

For any b the portfolio of risky assets $w = (I - V^{-1}V)z$ is well diversified and solves the equation:

$$w'B = b';$$

hence condition (5) holds.

(Necessity) Suppose condition (5) holds. Then for any b there exists a w such that

$$w'B = b' \qquad \text{and} \qquad w'V = 0.$$

The second condition implies that $w'(I - V^{-1}V) = w'$; therefore, for any b there exists a w such that

$$w'(I - V^{-1}V)B = b'$$

which implies that $(I - V^{-1}V)B$ has full column rank. Q.E.D.

Let $\|\cdot\|_\kappa$ denote a matrix norm on $R^{\kappa\times\kappa}$. In general, any norm will do since all norms on $R^{\kappa\times\kappa}$ generate the same neighborhood of zero. For convenience, the proof below uses the Euclidean norm

$$\|X\|_\kappa = \max_{\substack{g'g=1 \\ g\in R^\kappa}} |g'Xg|.$$

Lemma 3 *In a limit factor economy, condition* (5) *holds if*

$$\lim_{\nu\to\infty} \|(B^{\nu\prime}(V^\nu)^{-1}B^\nu)^{-1}\|_\kappa = 0.$$

Proof Suppose that $\lim_{v\to\infty} \|(B^{v\prime}(V^v)^{-1}B^v)^{-1}\|_\kappa = 0$. Consider the sequence of risky asset portfolios defined by

$$w^v = (V^v)^{-1}B^v(B^{v\prime}(V^v)^{-1}B^v)^{-1}b'$$
$$w^{*v} = (w^v, 0, 0, 0, \ldots).$$

Each portfolio in this sequence has a factor beta vector of b because

$$w^{*v\prime}B = w^{v\prime}B^v = b'.$$

The variances of the portfolios are:

$$w^{*v\prime}Vw^{*v} = w^{v\prime}V^vw^v = b'(B^{v\prime}(V^v)^{-1}B^v)^{-1}b \leqslant (b'b)\|(B^{v\prime}(V^v)^{-1}B^v)^{-1}\|_\kappa.$$

Given $\lim_{v\to\infty} \|(B^{v\prime}(V^v)^{-1}B^v)^{-1}\|_\kappa = 0$, this implies $\lim_{v\to\infty} w^{v\prime}V^vw^v = 0$. The sequence of portfolios (w^{*v}) has constant factor risk and idiosyncratic variance approaching zero. Therefore, the sequence converges. Let $w = \lim_{v\to\infty} w^{*v}$. Note that

$$w'B = b' \qquad \text{and} \qquad E[(w'i)^2] = 0. \qquad \text{Q.E.D.}$$

References

1. G. Chamberlain, A characterization of the distributions that imply mean-variance utility functions, *J. Econom. Theory* **29** (1983), 185–201.
2. G. Chamberlain and M. Rothschild, Arbitrage, factor structure, and mean-variance analysis on large asset markets, *Econometrica* **51** (1983), 1281–1304.
3. G. Connor, Asset pricing theory in factor economies, Ph.D. dissertation, Yale University, Department of Economics, December 1982.
4. G. Connor, "A Factor Pricing Theory for Capital Assets," mimeograph, Northwestern University, 1982.
5. O. D. Hart, On the existence of equilibrium in a securities model, *J. Econom. Theory* **9** (1974), 293–311.
6. E. Malinvaud, The allocation of individual risks in large markets, *J. Econom. Theory* **4** (1972), 312–328.
7. R. Roll and S. A. Ross, An empirical investigation of the arbitrage pricing theory, *J. Finance* **35** (1979), 1073–1103.
8. S. A. Ross, The arbitrage theory of capital asset pricing, *J. Econom. Theory* **13** (1976), 341–360.
9. S. A. Ross, Return, risk, and arbitrage, *in* "Risk and Return in Finance" (I. Friend and J. L. Bicksler, Eds.), Vol. I, pp. 189–218, Ballinger, Cambridge, Mass., 1977.
10. S. A. Ross, Mutual fund separation in financial theory—the separating distributions, *J. Econom. Theory* **17** (1978), 254–286.
11. M. Rothschild and J. E. Stiglitz, Increasing risk. I. A definition, *J. Econom. Theory* **2** (1970), 225–243.
12. H. E. Scarf, with the collaboration of T. Hansen, "The Computation of Economic Equilibria," Cowles Foundation for Research Economics at Yale University Monograph No. 24, Yale Univ. Press, New Haven, Conn., 1973.
13. J. Shanken, The arbitrage pricing theory: Is it testable?, *J. Finance* **37** (1982), 1129–1140.
14. W. Sharpe, Capital asset prices: A theory of market equilibrium under conditions of risk, *J. Finance* **19** (1964), 425–442.

Thirteen

Mark Grinblatt

Mark Grinblatt received a Ph.D. from Yale University in 1982. He started out at the UCLA Anderson School of Management. He still works there. •

In the mid-1980s, I began a line of research in the area of portfolio performance evaluation, initially with Sheridan Titman and later with Sheridan, Russ Wermers, and Kent Daniel. The paper in this volume is a theoretical piece that synthesizes many of the issues that perplexed researchers at the time. It combines two areas of financial economics. One of these is asymmetric information. At some level, superior information is what performance evaluation is trying to detect. The other area is asset pricing because performance evaluation inherently involves some sort of adjustment for risk.

I owe a debt of gratitude to Steve Ross for any skill I possess in these two areas. In the late 1970s, Steve sensed that research on asymmetric information was an area that was about to reach a level of preeminence in economics and finance that it had never reached before. Of course, by that time, he was already a seminal contributor to this area with papers on financial signaling and agency. However, it was as a teacher and mentor that he kept directing many of his grad students of that era to the work of Grossman and Stiglitz. He also asked many of us to interact with Larry Weiss, who was doing fascinating asymmetric information modeling with an innovation known today as "noise trading." Quite a number of Steve's students at Yale, myself among them, wrote papers on rational expectations equilibria for their dissertations. This was great training for any future research that required modeling of private versus public information.

Steve's emphasis on the importance of asset pricing, both in his research and his teaching, was also key. His influence on the way I viewed the subject is clearly observable from this piece. I learned from Steve that factor models are the most natural way to think about risk. Indeed, much of the intuition for the CAPM found in today's finance textbooks is rooted in factor structures, even though the CAPM is not a model generated by the assumption that securities returns have common factors. I carried this strong intuition about risk to my research on performance evaluation. "Portfolio Performance Evaluation: Old Issues and New Insights" tries to understand the issues of risk adjustment in the presence of asymmetric information, while skirting the benchmark issues pointed out by Richard Roll.

In my graduate school days, Steve was constantly emphasizing how important Roll's contribution in this area was. One of the ways this was imparted to us was through an informal seminar he insisted that his students put on. The group of seminar participants included many of the contributors to this volume, as well as Steve. The seminars would consist of student presentations of someone else's research rather than our own. Steve insisted that we present and try to defend both good and bad papers, so that we could learn to distinguish strong from weak research. A number of these seminars revolved around the topic of Roll's benchmarking issues and performance evaluation. Many of these seminars ended with heated debates on the feasibility of performance evaluation and the merits of various pieces of research in the area.

I recall one debate in which Phil Dybvig started running with a group of ideas. Ultimately, those ideas culminated in a couple of influential performance evaluation papers by Dybvig and Ross in the *Journal of Finance* in the mid 1980s. The issues stuck with me for many years, until my long-time co-author and friend, Sheridan Titman, began a conversation on performance evaluation as a natural outgrowth of our conversations on asset pricing and factor models.

It is quite obvious to me that without the mentorship of Stephen Ross, and those internal seminars at Yale, I would not have produced either the paper I am contributing to this volume or the line of research that is most associated with my name. Thank you, Steve, for your intellectual guidance and personal concern for me throughout my career.

Portfolio Performance Evaluation: Old Issues and New Insights

Mark Grinblatt
Sheridan Titman
University of California, Los Angeles

This article presents a model that provides insights about various measures of portfolio performance. The model explores several criticisms of these measures. These include the problem of identifying an appropriate benchmark portfolio, the possibility of overestimating risk because of market-timing ability, and the failure of informed investors to earn positive risk-adjusted returns because of increasing risk aversion. The article argues that these need not be serious impediments to performance evaluation. •

One of the widely held "folk theorems" in finance is that informed investors can achieve a better risk–return trade-off than uninformed investors. Risk, however, is difficult to define and measure in markets with asymmetric information, especially when one considers that it must be evaluated by an uninformed observer. For this reason, there has been a great deal of controversy over whether the performance measures proposed by Treynor (1965), Sharpe (1966), and Jensen (1968, 1969) can identify investors with superior information.

Jensen's alpha, which measures the deviation of a portfolio from the securities market line, has been the focus of most of the controversy because it is the most widely used in academic empirical studies. One criticism of the Jensen measure is that it is based on an upwardly biased estimate of systematic risk for a market-timing investment strategy. Examples provided by Jensen (1972), Admati and Ross (1985), and Dybvig and Ross (1965) demonstrate that, because of this, the Jensen measure can assign negative performance to a market timer.

Figure 1, which graphs the excess return of the evaluated portfolio (above a risk-free rate) against the excess return of the benchmark portfolio, illustrates this deficiency of the Jensen measure. The portfolio manager is constrained here to select a high or low beta portfolio, represented by the steeper and gentler sloped solid lines, respectively. (If the benchmark is mean-variance efficient, both of these lines pass through the origin.) Suppose that the manager receives one of two signals: that the benchmark excess return will be r_H, which is above its unconditional mean, or it will be r_L, which is below its mean. If he acts as a market timer, he will select a high beta portfolio and be at point A upon receipt of the high return signal and at point B if he receives the low return signal. An uninformed observer

S.T. gratefully acknowledges financial support from the Batterymarch Fellowship program. The authors are grateful to Michael Brennan for helpful discussions and comments on earlier drafts of this article. They also thank Anat Admati, Thomas Copeland, Brad Cornell, Philip Dybvig, David Hirshleifer, Jonathan Ingersoll, Ronald Masulis, Krishna Ramaswamy, Richard Roll, Stephen Ross, Walter Torous, Brett Trueman, Robert Verrecchia, Arthur Warga, an anonymous referee, and seminar participants at Chicago, Michigan, Northwestern, Wharton, UCLA/USC, and the European Finance Association for their comments.

Reprinted with permission:
Grinblatt, Mark and Sheridan Titman. "Portfolio Performance Evaluation: Old Issues and New Insights." *Review of Financial Studies* 2 (1989): 393–421.

FIGURE 1 | An example of a negative Jensen measure for a market timer
The two solid lines plot the excess return of a managed portfolio consisting of a risk-free investment and an investment in the risky efficient portfolio against the latter's excess return for two different choices of beta. A market-timing strategy, constrained to choose between the two betas, would plot at point *A* (point *B*) if information indicated that the excess return of the efficient portfolio was expected to be r_H (r_L). The slope of the dotted line is the estimated beta in the Jensen measure regression, and the intercept is the Jensen measure.

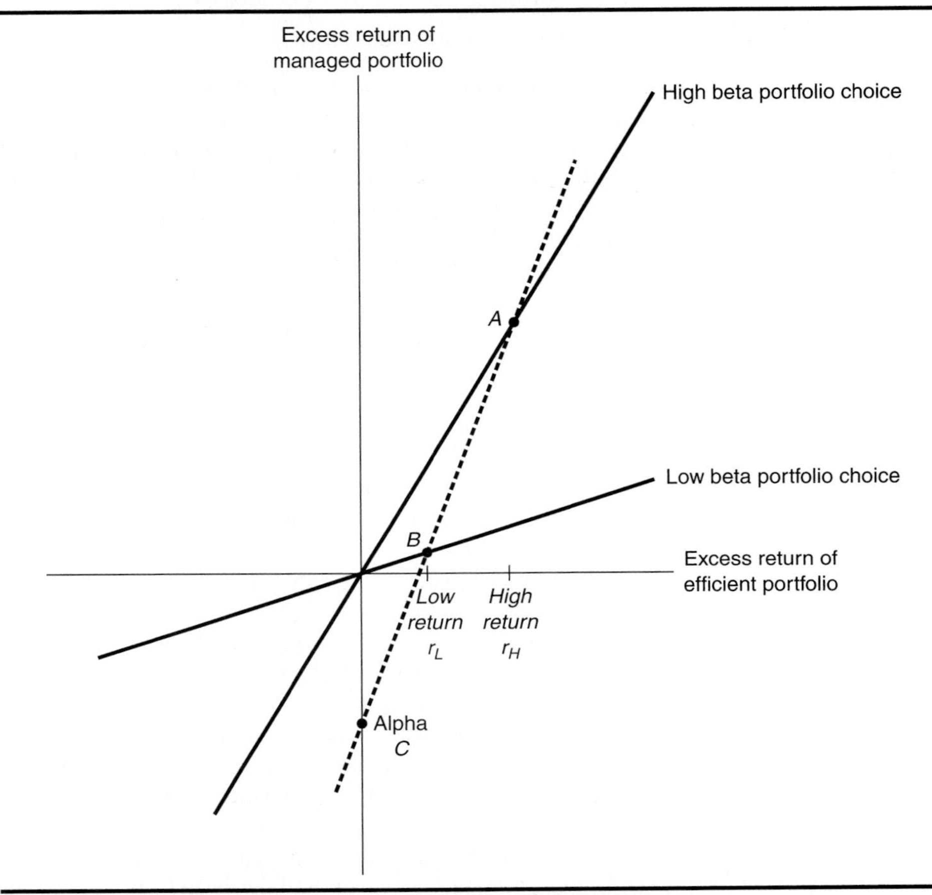

would estimate the risk of this investment strategy as the slope of the dotted line connecting points *A* and *B*, which exceeds the risk of the portfolio in either information state. Moreover, it is even possible, as in this example, that the Jensen measure, which is the intercept of the dotted line at *C*, may be negative, erroneously indicating that the informed investor is an inferior performer.

The most important contribution of this article is the development of the *positive period weighting measure*, which is an alternative performance measure that has the same data requirements as the Jensen measure but which correctly identifies informed investors as positive performers. In addition to demonstrating that this measure is not distorted by the timing-related problem discussed above, the article addresses two additional criticisms of the Jensen measure that are also relevant for our new measure.

One of these criticisms, advanced by Roll (1978, 1979), is that the Jensen measure of a portfolio bears no reliable relation to its true performance because there is no appropriate benchmark portfolio with which to compute beta. The CAPM (capital asset pricing model)-related empirical anomalies documented in the past decade lend weight to this criticism as it applies to traditional benchmark portfolios. Since it is undesirable to classify uninformed investors who engage in passive strategies (e.g., buy and hold small firms) as superior performers, index portfolios that yield such "anomalies" are inappropriate as performance benchmarks.

It is well known that a Jensen measure employing a mean-variance efficient benchmark portfolio correctly classifies uninformed investors as zero performers. However, we demonstrate that the mean-variance efficient portfolio is the appropriate benchmark for both Jensen's alpha and our new measure in that it also correctly classifies informed investors as positive performers. Moreover, in contrast to the market portfolio in tests of the CAPM, which requires the observability of all assets, this benchmark may consist of a relatively small set of assets, since it can be limited to those assets that are managed by the evaluated investor or that he considers tradable. Such a benchmark also provides correct inferences in cases in which the evaluated investor does not optimally select a portfolio on the mean-variance efficient frontier, as we show by allowing for nontraded assets.

The third criticism was raised by Verrecchia (1980), who presented an example in which an informed investor realizes average returns below that expected by uninformed observers who know the risk of the portfolio. This means that informed investors can realize negative risk-adjusted returns, even when returns are properly adjusted for risk. Thus, the example challenges the validity of all measures of portfolio performance.[1] We demonstrate, however, that counterexamples in the class described by Verrecchia can only occur when the informed investor has unrealistic preferences.

These three criticisms are analyzed within a framework that decomposes the Jensen measure into a bias-in-beta term, a selectivity term reflecting the ability to select investments that will do well relative to the benchmark portfolio, and a timing term representing the contribution to performance of the ability to forecast the return of the benchmark portfolio. In addition to providing insights about the Jensen measure, this decomposition suggests two other new performance measures, the selectivity measure and the timing measure, which have desirable properties for evaluating performance. We also show that the measure proposed by Cornell (1979) captures the sum of the timing and selectivity terms.

1. The Measures of Performance and Their Decomposition

Our analysis assumes the existence of N risky assets, which trade in frictionless markets (i.e., no transaction costs, taxes, short sales restrictions, etc.), at dates t, $t = 1, \ldots, T$. We plan to evaluate the performance of an investor over the T periods by examining risk-adjusted portfolio returns that are given by the returns of these assets. We will also assume that a risk-free asset exists and define excess returns relative to the risk-free return. Let

$\widetilde{R}_{jt}$ = excess return of asset j from holding asset j between dates t and $t+1$

$\widetilde{x}_{jt}$ = the investor's period t portfolio weight on asset j

$\widetilde{r}_{pt} = \sum_{j=1}^{N} \widetilde{x}_{jt} \widetilde{R}_{jt}$ = period t excess return of the investor's portfolio of the N risky assets

[1]Dybvig and Ross (1985) first pointed out that Verrecchia's example applies to the measure of performance proposed by Cornell (1979)

where $\tilde{x}_{jt}$ is random, since the investor may alter his portfolio in response to (real or imagined) information. Similarly, let $\tilde{r}_{Et}$ denote the period t excess return of the portfolio of risky assets that is mean-variance efficient from the perspective of an uninformed observer. It has population mean $\bar{r}_E$ and variance σ_E^2.

The excess returns of each asset can then be expressed as

$$\tilde{R}_{jt} = \beta_j \tilde{r}_{Et} + \tilde{\epsilon}_{jt}$$

where

$$\beta_j = \frac{\text{cov}(\tilde{R}_{jt}, \tilde{r}_{Et})}{\sigma_E^2}$$

and, given the efficiency of the benchmark, the mean of $\tilde{\epsilon}_{jt}$ is zero. The excess return of the investor's portfolio can then be expressed as

$$\tilde{r}_{pt} = \tilde{\beta}_{pt} \tilde{r}_{Et} + \tilde{\epsilon}_{pt} \tag{1}$$

where

$$\tilde{\beta}_{pt} = \sum_{j=1}^{N} \tilde{x}_{jt} \beta_j \qquad \text{and} \qquad \tilde{\epsilon}_{pt} = \sum_{j=1}^{N} \tilde{x}_{jt} \tilde{\epsilon}_{jt}$$

Note that $\bar{r}_E$, σ_{E1}^2 and β_j are not subscripted by t. Throughout the article, the means, variances, and covariances of the excess returns of assets are calculated from the perspective of an uninformed observer who, by assumption, views the excess-return vector as being drawn from an i.i.d. (independently and identically distributed) distribution (henceforth, "the unconditional distribution"). Although the distribution of asset returns, conditioned on the information signals of informed investors, is nonstationary, the model is consistent with a general equilibrium as long as the effect of informed traders on market-clearing prices is negligible.[2]

I.i.d. unconditional returns imply that the unconditional mean-variance efficient portfolio has constant portfolio weights and that the beliefs of an uninformed investor, and hence his portfolio weights and portfolio beta, must be independent of the realizations of $\tilde{r}_{Et}$ and each $\tilde{R}_{jt}$. In contrast, an informed investor may change his portfolio weights in response to new information, inducing a nonzero covariance between his portfolio weights and asset returns.

In later sections, we demonstrate that the ability of various measures to capture superior performance depends on whether the informed investor's information relates to $\tilde{r}_{Et}$ or to the $\tilde{\epsilon}_{jt}$'s. For this reason, it is convenient to distinguish between these types of information.

Definition. *An investor is said to have timing information if the expected value of $\tilde{r}_{Et}$, conditioned on his information, is not equal to $\bar{r}_E$ for at least one time period.*

Definition. *An investor is said to have selectivity information if the expected value of $\tilde{\epsilon}_{jt}$, conditioned on his information, is nonzero for at least one asset in one time period.*

[2]The i.i.d. assumption is required because it is otherwise impossible for an uninformed observer to distinguish between performance and changes in the parameters of the return-generating process. Indeed, any taxonomy that distinguishes between these possibilities is necessarily based on the number of investors who are assumed to observe the nonstationarities. In a market with traders who have special information, only a few investors observe the nonstationarities, whereas in a market with nonstationary parameters, virtually all investors observe the nonstationarities (and only the evaluator is naive). For the analysis of some of the performance measures, this strong stationarity assumption can be relaxed. For example, if the observer can identify the unconditional mean-variance efficient portfolio each period, our results still apply.

These definitions of timing and selectivity are closely related to their common usage by investment professionals. The two types of information will be explicitly modeled in Section 2.

1.1 The decomposition of the Jensen measure and its relation to other measures of abnormal performance

This subsection examines the large sample value (or probability limit) of the Jensen measure in order to derive a decomposition that simplifies and synthesizes our analysis.

The Jensen measure is

$$J = \hat{r}_p - b_p \hat{r}_E \tag{2}$$

where b_p = the probability limit of the least squares slope coefficient from the time-series regression of excess returns of the evaluated portfolio against the excess returns of the efficient benchmark portfolio

$\hat{r}_p$ = the probability limit of the sample mean of $\tilde{r}_{p1}, \tilde{r}_{p2}, \ldots, \tilde{r}_{pT}$

$\hat{r}_E$ = the probability limit of the sample mean of $\tilde{r}_{E1}, \ldots, \tilde{r}_{ET} = \tilde{r}_E$

In general, we denote

$$\hat{q} = \text{plim}\left[\frac{1}{T}\sum_{t=1}^{T} \tilde{q}_t\right]$$

as the limiting sample mean of a sequence of random variables $\tilde{q}_1, \ldots, \tilde{q}_T$. Wherever necessary, this probability limit is assumed to exist. (Note that b_p is not necessarily the same as $\hat{\beta}_p$. For example, in Figure 1, $\hat{\beta}_p$ is a weighted average of the slopes of the two solid lines, while b_p is the slope of the dotted line.)

Using Equation (1), the limiting large-sample mean of the excess return of the portfolio can be expressed as

$$\hat{r}_p = \text{plim}\left[\frac{1}{T}\sum_{t=1}^{T} (\tilde{\beta}_{pt}\tilde{r}_{Et} + \tilde{\epsilon}_{pt})\right]$$

$$= \hat{\beta}_p \hat{r}_E + \text{plim}\left[\frac{1}{T}\sum_{t=1}^{T} \tilde{\beta}_{pt}(\tilde{r}_{Et} - \hat{r}_E)\right] + \hat{\epsilon}_p \tag{3}$$

Substituting Equation (3) into Equation (2) yields the decomposition:

$$J = (\hat{\beta}_p - b_p)\hat{r}_E + \text{plim}\left[\frac{1}{T}\sum_{t=1}^{T} \tilde{\beta}_{pt}(\tilde{r}_{Et} - \hat{r}_E)\right] + \hat{\epsilon}_p \tag{4}$$

The three terms in Equation (4) will be referred to respectively as the component of performance that results from large sample biases in estimated beta, the component that results from timing, and the component that results from selectivity.

If the weights of the evaluated investor's portfolio are observable, the elements of the decomposition can be separately identified. The selectivity measure is constructed by estimating the period t beta of a portfolio as period t's portfolio-weighted average of the individual asset betas. Multiplying this beta by r_{ET}, subtracting from r_{pt}, and averaging yields a measure with an asymptotic value of

$$S = \hat{r}_p - \text{plim}\left[\frac{1}{T}\sum_{t=1}^{T} \tilde{\beta}_{pt}\tilde{r}_{Et}\right]$$

After substitution of Equation (3), this can be expressed as

$$S = \hat{\epsilon}_p \tag{5}$$

The counterpart of the selectivity measure, the timing measure, is defined as the sample covariance between the portfolio beta and the excess return of the benchmark portfolio. Its asymptotic value is

$$\mathrm{TM} = \operatorname{plim}\left[\frac{1}{T}\sum_{t=1}^{T}\tilde{\beta}_{pt}(\tilde{r}_{Et} - \hat{r}_E)\right] \tag{6}$$

Cornell (1979) proposed a measure that averages the difference between the holding-period return of an investor's portfolio and the return realized with the same portfolio weights in a benchmark time period outside of the holding period.[3] If asset returns in the benchmark period are distributed independently of their respective portfolio weights in the holding period (which is assumed throughout this article), the asymptotic value of this measure can be expressed as

$$C = \hat{r}_p - \hat{\beta}_p \hat{r}_E$$

which, upon substitution of Equation (3), yields

$$C = \operatorname{plim}\left[\frac{1}{T}\sum_{t=1}^{T}\tilde{\beta}_{pt}(\tilde{r}_{Et} - \hat{r}_E)\right] + \hat{\epsilon}_p \tag{7}$$

Thus, the Cornell measure captures the sum of the timing and selectivity components.

The components of abnormal performance are analyzed separately in Sections 3, 4, and 5. Section 3 analyzes the bias-in-beta component, Section 4 analyzes the selectivity components, and Section 5 examines conditions under which the timing component of performance is positive for informed investors.

1.2 The measured abnormal performance of an uninformed investor

A minimum requirement of an "appropriate" performance measure is that, in large samples, it assigns zero performance to the portfolios of uninformed investors. As a preliminary to showing that all the above measures satisfy this criterion, we demonstrate that the bias-in-beta component can be nonzero only if there is timing information.

Lemma 1. *$\hat{\beta}_p = b_p$ for an investor who lacks market timing information.*

Proof. Using Equation (1), the portfolio's excess return in period t can be written as

$$\tilde{r}_{pt} = \hat{\epsilon}_p + \hat{\beta}_p \tilde{r}_{Et} + [(\tilde{\beta}_{pt} - \hat{\beta}_p)\tilde{r}_{Et} + (\tilde{\epsilon}_{pt} - \hat{\epsilon}_p)]$$

where $\hat{\epsilon}_p$ and $\hat{\beta}_p$, respectively, represent the theoretical intercept and slope coefficient of a regression. Without timing information, the bracketed expression, which can be regarded as the regression residual, is asymptotically uncorrelated with $\tilde{r}_{En}$ so that the least-squares procedure yields a consistent estimator of the slope coefficient, $\hat{\beta}_p$.

With this lemma, the next result is straightforward.

Proposition 1. *The portfolio of an investor who lacks both timing and selectivity information exhibits zero performance with either the Jensen measure, the Cornell measure,*

[3]Copeland and Mayers (1982) pointed out that the Cornell approach should be modified by measuring securities' benchmark returns in periods after they were held by investors, rather than before, because trading strategies may be based on past returns. This, however, introduces survivorship bias.

the selectivity measure, or the timing measure in large samples. Moreover, if the investor lacks timing (selectivity) information, his portfolio has a zero timing (selectivity) measure in large samples.

Proof. Examine the three elements in Equation (4). Lemma 1 implies that the bias-in-beta component is zero if the investor lacks timing information. The absence of timing information also implies that $\tilde{\beta}_{pt}$ is uncorrelated with $\tilde{r}_{Et}$, so that the timing component is zero. Finally, if the investor lacks selectivity information, $\tilde{x}_{jt}$ and $\tilde{\epsilon}_{jt}$ are uncorrelated, which (along with the zero mean of $\tilde{\epsilon}_{jt}$) implies that the selectivity component is zero. The result follows immediately from Equations (4) to (7).

2. The Informed Investor

Observe that the first part of Proposition 1 is a very general result requiring only a minimal set of assumptions: frictionless markets, i.i.d. returns, an efficient benchmark portfolio (for measures that employ one), and the existence of a risk-free asset. If one were willing to accept negative as well as positive deviations from zero abnormal performance as an indication of superior information, the analysis could end here. The ability to measure performance would then be an empirical issue that hinges on benchmark observability, the stationarity of returns, data availability, and the small sample properties of the various techniques.

However, since negative measured performance can arise from high transaction costs or embezzlement as well as from superior information, the properties of the performance measures in frictionless markets are not necessarily indicative of their ability to identify superior investment performance in a more realistic setting. Thus, it is useful to demonstrate that the measures are generally positive for investment strategies that utilize superior information.[4] Although others have pointed out that this more stringent criterion is not always met, we will argue that it can be met under plausible conditions.

To demonstrate this, a model of information and portfolio choice is developed. The model analyzes the signs of unconditional means of the random variables $\tilde{\epsilon}_{pt}$ and $\tilde{\beta}_{pt}(\tilde{r}_{Et} - \bar{r}_E)$ and determines the conditions under which they (and hence their asymptotic counterparts, the selectivity and timing components) are positive. Because the analysis of the unconditional means does not depend on the time period, time subscripts can be omitted to simplify notation. With this simplification, it is convenient to refer to $E(\tilde{\epsilon}_p)$ and $\text{cov}(\tilde{\beta}_p, \tilde{r}_E)$, respectively, as the selectivity and timing components.

The model assumes that an investor's wealth consists of an evaluated portion (i.e., investments in the N tradable assets) and an unevaluated portion (i.e., nontradable assets). In addition, the model abstracts from issues that can arise in the multiperiod consumption–investment optimization problem and assumes a form of myopia. Each period's investment decision is assumed to be determined by maximizing the (possibly time-dependent) expected utility of end-of-period wealth,

$$E[U(\tilde{W} + \tilde{W}_H)]$$

[4]It would be better if performance measures could also select the more informed of two investors. Unfortunately, risk aversion and preferences for higher-order moments also affect these measures, making it impossible, except for special cases, to extract the information-related component of performance. See, for example, Henriksson and Merton (1981), Admati and Ross (1985), Admati et al (1986), and Connor and Korajczyk (1986).

conditioned on information available just prior to trading in that period, where

W_H = end-of-period wealth from nontradable assets
W = end-of-period wealth from managed (i.e., tradable) assets $W_0\,(R_F + r_p)$, where
W_0 = wealth available at the beginning of the period for investment in managed assets
R_F = one plus the risk-free rate

Let the return of the mean-variance efficient portfolio be expressed as

$$\tilde{r}_E = \bar{r}_E + \tilde{m} + \tilde{y}$$

where m is a timing signal observed by the informed investor and y is the realization of uncorrelated random noise. Similarly, the unconditional return of the mean zero residual $\tilde{\epsilon}_j$ in the regression,

$$\tilde{R}_j = \beta_j \tilde{r}_E + \tilde{\epsilon}_j$$

can be expressed as

$$\tilde{\epsilon}_j = \tilde{s}_j + \tilde{z}_j \qquad j = 1, \ldots, N$$

where s_j is a selection signal observed by the informed investor and z_j is the realization of uncorrelated noise. The private information signals, m and s_j, are observed before trading in the period and are mean zero by definition.

The information structure is summarized by the equations

$$\tilde{R}_j = \beta_j(\underline{r}_E + \tilde{m} + \tilde{y}) + \tilde{s}_j + \tilde{z}_j$$

for individual assets and for the evaluated portfolio by

$$\tilde{r}_p = \tilde{\beta}_p(\bar{r}_E + \tilde{m} + \tilde{y}) + \tilde{s}_p + \tilde{z}_p$$

where

$$\tilde{s}_p = \sum_{j=1}^{N} \tilde{x}_j \tilde{s}_j \qquad \text{and} \qquad \tilde{z}_p = \sum_{j=1}^{N} \tilde{x}_j \tilde{z}_j$$

which implies $\tilde{\epsilon}_p = \tilde{s}_p + \tilde{z}_p$. Note that the portfolio-weighted averages of the $\tilde{z}_j$'s and $\tilde{s}_j$'s of constant-weight portfolios have unconditional expectations of zero because of the efficiency of the benchmark and the independence of $\tilde{s}_j$ and $\tilde{z}_j$. The portfolios of informed investors, by contrast, change dynamically in response to information. We represent this in a single period as a random vector of portfolio weights. Such portfolios necessarily have $\tilde{z}_p$'s with means of zero but may have $\tilde{s}_p$'s with nonzero expected values if the portfolio weights are correlated with their respective $\tilde{s}_j$'s.

To summarize the information structure for nontradable wealth, we first separate the ratio W_H/W_0 into a market and nonmarket component,

$$\tilde{W}_H/W_0 = \alpha_H + \beta_H \tilde{r}_E + \tilde{\epsilon}_H$$

where β_H is the population regression coefficient of $\tilde{W}_H/W_0$ on $\tilde{r}_E$. As with the tradable assets, we assume that $\tilde{\epsilon}_H = \tilde{s}_H + \tilde{z}_H$, where $\tilde{s}_H$ is observable.

All the $\tilde{s}_j$'s, $\tilde{z}_j$'s, and $\tilde{y}$ are assumed to be jointly normal. Hence, the random vector $(\tilde{\epsilon}_1, \ldots, \tilde{\epsilon}_N, \tilde{\epsilon}_H, \tilde{r}_E)$ is multivariate normally distributed, both unconditionally and conditionally, with unconditional mean $(0, 0, \ldots, 0, \bar{r}_E)$ and mean $I = (s_1, \ldots s_N, s_H, \bar{r}_E + m)$ conditional on private information.

Given this information structure, it is possible to characterize the optimal portfolio of the evaluated investor. This follows directly from the standard first order conditions for portfolio optimality,

$$E[U'(\tilde{W} + \tilde{W}_H)\tilde{\mathbf{R}}|I] = \mathbf{0}$$

Using Stein's Lemma,[5] this can be rewritten as[6]

$$\begin{aligned} E(\tilde{\mathbf{R}}|I) &= a(I)\operatorname{cov}(\tilde{W} + \tilde{W}_H, \tilde{\mathbf{R}}|I) \\ &= aW_0 \operatorname{cov}(\tilde{R}_p + R_H, \tilde{\mathbf{R}}|I) \end{aligned} \tag{8}$$

where the positive parameter $a = a(I)$, termed "the Rubinstein (1973) measure of absolute risk aversion," is defined by

$$a(I) = -\frac{E[U''(\tilde{W} + \tilde{W}_H)|I]}{E[U'(\tilde{W} + \tilde{W}_H)|I]}$$

The informed investor is said to have decreasing (increasing) Rubinstein risk aversion if this measure is a monotonically decreasing (increasing) function of expected utility. This means that with decreasing Rubinstein risk aversion, information that increases (decreases) $E[U(\tilde{W} + \tilde{W}_H)|I]$ will decrease (increase) $a(I)$.

Section 3 discusses estimation problems that exist for investors with timing information. It is assumed in this analysis that the investor always increases his beta as his information about the market becomes more favorable (i.e., $\partial\beta_p/\partial m > 0$). As we discuss in Section 5, this behavioral assumption does not hold for all utility functions. However, as Lemma 2 demonstrates, investors with independent timing and selectivity information and nonincreasing Rubinstein absolute-risk aversion will behave in this manner.

Lemma 2. *If an investor has independent timing and selectivity information and nonincreasing Rubinstein absolute risk aversion, then $\partial\beta_p/\partial m > 0$.*

Proof. See the Appendix.

3. Timing-Related Estimation Problems and Their Solutions

3.1 The bias-in-beta component

Consider an investor with timing information but no selectivity information, as defined by the model in Section 2. We now formally demonstrate the result, illustrated in Figure 1, that a superior investor may display a negative Jensen measure. Here, we assume that the beta response function is monotonically increasing in the timing signal and symmetric about the long-run target beta, denoted $\tilde{\beta}_p$, that is,

$$\tilde{\beta}_p = \hat{\beta}_p + f(\tilde{m})$$

where $f(m) = -f(-m)$, $f(0) = 0$, and $f'(m) = \partial\beta_p/\partial m > 0$.

This model of beta adjustment implies [after substitution into Equation (1)] that

$$\tilde{r}_p = \hat{\beta}_p\tilde{r}_E + f(\tilde{m})(\bar{r}_E + \tilde{m} + \tilde{y}) + \tilde{\epsilon}_p$$

[5]$\operatorname{cov}[\tilde{u}, g(\tilde{v})] = E[g'(\tilde{v})]\operatorname{cov}(\tilde{u}, \tilde{v})$ if $g(\cdot)$ is continuously differentiable, all expectations are finite, and $(\tilde{u}, \tilde{v})$ is bivariate normally distributed. See Stein (1973) or Rubinstein (1973) for a proof.

[6]The intermediate algebraic steps can be found in Grinblatt and Titman (1983, p. 501).

The large-sample least-squares estimate of the Jensen measure beta is then

$$
\begin{aligned}
b_p &= \frac{\operatorname{cov}(\tilde{r}_p, \tilde{r}_E)}{\sigma_E^2} \\
&= \frac{\hat{\beta}_p \sigma_E^2}{\sigma_E^2} + \frac{\operatorname{cov}[(\tilde{\beta}_p - \hat{\beta}_p)(\bar{r}_E + \tilde{m} + \tilde{y}), \tilde{r}_E]}{\sigma_E^2} + \frac{\operatorname{cov}(\tilde{\epsilon}_p, \tilde{r}_E)}{\sigma_E^2} \\
&= \hat{\beta}_p + \left\{ \frac{E[(\tilde{\beta}_p - \hat{\beta}_p)\bar{r}_E \tilde{r}_E]}{\sigma_E^2} + \frac{E[f(\tilde{m})(\tilde{m} + \tilde{y})^2]}{\sigma_E^2} \right\} \\
&= \hat{\beta}_p + \frac{\bar{r}_E}{\sigma_E^2} \operatorname{cov}(\tilde{\beta}_p, \tilde{r}_E)
\end{aligned}
$$

which tends to overestimate the average risk of the portfolio by a factor proportional to the timing component.

Substituting the above expression for b_p into Equation (4) yields the large-sample estimate of the Jensen measure,

$$
\left(1 - \frac{\bar{r}_E^2}{\sigma_E^2}\right) \operatorname{cov}(\tilde{\beta}_p, \tilde{r}_E)
$$

The positive derivative for $f(\cdot)$ implies a positive timing component. Hence, this expression is negative for positive timing $[\operatorname{cov}(\tilde{\beta}_p, \tilde{r}_E) > 0]$ if the absolute value of the Sharpe ratio of the benchmark, $\bar{r}_E/\sigma_E$, exceeds one. In terms of our decomposition, we have shown that the bias-in-beta component can be negative and of larger magnitude than the timing component.[7]

3.2 Period weighting measures

This defect of the Jensen measure, that it may assign negative performance to market timers, is overcome by the Cornell, selectivity, and timing measures at the cost of acquiring information about the security holdings of the evaluated portfolio. This subsection introduces a new measure that does not require the observation of portfolio holdings and is not subject to this timing-related problem.

We begin by studying a general class of "period weighting" performance measures, which are weighted sums of the period-by-period portfolio excess returns:

$$
\alpha^* = \sum_{t=1}^{T} w_t r_{pt} \tag{9}
$$

where $w_t = w(r_{Et}, T)$ satisfies

$$
\operatorname{plim}\left[\sum_{t=1}^{T} w_t r_{Et}\right] = 0 \tag{10}
$$

[7]If $f'(m) = \partial\beta_p/\partial m < 0$, so that the investor times perversely, $\hat{\beta}_p$ will be underestimated in large samples. If this is the case, the analysis above indicates that the positive bias-in-beta component would dominate the negative timing component if $\bar{r}_E > \sigma_E$, resulting in a positive Jensen measure. The Jensen measure would thus correctly identify the investor as having superior information, but it would fail to indicate that he was using the information in a contrary manner—to lower returns rather than to increase them.

of which the Jensen measure is a special case.[8] To ensure that the measure's variance converges to zero as T approaches infinity, the weights, w_t, are scaled to sum to one and each weight is assumed to approach zero at a sufficiently rapid rate as the time series gets large.

To show that the Jensen measure is a period weighting measure,[9] let

$$w_t = \frac{v_E - (r_{Et} - r_E^*)r_E^*}{Tv_E} \tag{11}$$

where v_E denotes the (maximum-likelihood) sample variance of $r_{E1}, \ldots, r_{ET}$ and r_E^* the sample mean. Using the weights from Equation (11), it is easy to verify that the weights (11) satisfy condition (10). Substituting Equation (11) into Equation (9) yields

$$\sum_{t=1}^{T} w_t r_{pt} = r_p^* - b_p^* r_E^* \quad \text{the (small-sample) Jensen measure}$$

where r_p^* and b_p^* are, respectively, the sample mean and the sample beta of the portfolio returns $r_{p1}, \ldots, r_{pT}$.

For large r_{Et}, the weights (11) implicit in the Jensen measure are negative. For a positive market timer, the large positive portfolio returns that tend to occur when the benchmark's return is extremely high are multiplied by negative weights, reducing the Jensen measure and possibly making it negative. This suggests that an improved measure, which would not yield this perverse result, could be constructed by replacing the negative weights with positive weights and adjusting the other weights accordingly. This intuition is confirmed in the following proposition:

Proposition 2. *Let*

$$\tilde{\alpha}^* = \sum_{t=1}^{T} \tilde{w}_t \tilde{r}_{pt}$$

where

$$\tilde{w}_t = w(\tilde{r}_{Et}, T)$$

$$\text{plim}\left[\sum_{t=1}^{T} \tilde{w}_t \tilde{r}_{Et}\right] = 0$$

$$|\text{plim}[Tw_t]| < \infty$$

$$\sum_{t=1}^{T} \tilde{w}_t = 1$$

[8]Many of the results in the next three sections assume that the timing signal is uncorrelated with each of the selectivity signals (which may be correlated with each other). This has been a fairly standard assumption in the performance literature [e.g., see Jensen (1972) and Admati et al. (1986)]. An example of a selectivity signal that provides no information about the market would be inside information about which of two defense contractors will win a large government contract. Good news to one firm is offset by bad news to the other, so that the overall effect on the economy is unchanged. While information of this type certainly exists, it is unreasonable to assume that all selectivity signals are independent of information about the broader economy. For instance, inside information that the United Auto Workers will strike General Motors affects ϵ_{GM}, but it also has repercussions throughout the economy and can thus affect the "market return." Correlated timing and selectivity information, however, presents technical difficulties in generalizing some of the subsequent results. The technical problems, which only arise when there are wealth effects in addition to correlated timing and selectivity information, are discussed in more detail in later sections.

[9]The intercept in the Treynor and Mazuy (1966) regression also falls in this class and is subject to the same bias-in-beta problem as the Jensen measure.

define a class of performance measures called period weighting measures.

a. *The large-sample period weighting measure of an uninformed investor's portfolio,* $\text{plim}[\tilde{\alpha}^*] = 0$.

b. $\text{plim}[\tilde{\alpha}^*] > 0$ *for the portfolio of an informed investor with selectivity ability but no timing ability.*

c. *If the period weights additionally satisfy* $\tilde{w}_t > 0$, $t = 1, \ldots, T$, *and if* $\partial\beta_{pt}/\partial m_t > 0$ *for all realizations of the signals of an informed investor with selectivity and/or independent timing information, then* $\text{plim}[\tilde{\alpha}^*] > 0$.

Proof. See the Appendix.

Thus, the positive period weighting measures assign zero performance to uninformed investors and positive performance to selectivity ability or timing ability or both, provided that the selectivity and timing information is independent and the investor is a positive market timer. Technical problems associated with wealth effects prevent us from relaxing these assumptions. However, as Proposition A1 in the Appendix demonstrates, the positive period weighting measure is always positive for informed investors with constant absolute-risk aversion, even when timing and selectivity information is correlated.

An interesting interpretation of the period weighting measures can be made if we substitute expectations for the summations and interpret the weights w_t as marginal utilities.[10] Equation (10) then becomes the first-order condition for maximizing the expected utility of an uninformed investor who holds the benchmark portfolio, and Equation (9) then measures this investor's marginal change in utility from adding a small amount of the evaluated portfolio's excess return to his existing portfolio,

$$E\{U'[W_0(R_F + \tilde{r}_E)]\tilde{r}_p\}.$$

If this quantity is positive, it indicates that an uninformed investor, with marginal utilities equal to the weights used to evaluate performance, wishes to add some of the evaluated portfolio to his unconditionally optimal portfolio.

The Jensen measure weights of Equation (11) are linear in r_{Et} and are thus the marginal utilities of a quadratic utility investor. The perverse behavior of the Jensen measure in assigning negative performance to positive performers can thus be explained in terms of negative marginal utilities at wealth levels that exceed the satiation point of the quadratic utility investor.[11,12]

---

[10] We thank Michael Brennan for this insight.

[11] An interpretation of the Dybvig and Ross example is that an uninformed quadratic utility investor may not wish to marginally add the returns of an informed exponential utility investor's portfolio to his existing portfolio. On the other hand, the large-sample Jensen measure of a portfolio that is managed by an informed quadratic utility investor is positive even with timing ability and arbitrary asset return distributions. This is because an uninformed investor with quadratic utility will prefer to add a portion of the portfolio of his more informed counterpart, even it his risk-aversion parameter or initial endowment differs. To see this, note that $E[U'(\tilde{W}^u)\tilde{r}_p] > 0$ for concave utility functions, where r_p represents the excess return of the portfolio of an informed investor with utility function U and W^u represents the wealth from the optimal investment of an uninformed investor with the same utility function. (A proof is available on request.)

One can infer from this that Verrecchia's "counterexample," in which an informed quadratic utility investor displays a negative risk-adjusted return, does not apply to the Jensen measure. We confirmed this numerically for Verrecchia's parameterization of the example, which has a positive bias-in-beta component of performance. The latter more than outweighs a negative component of performance from timing plus selectivity, and results in a Jensen measure of 0.0005. In this example, which has correlated timing and selectivity information, the selectivity component is negative and larger in absolute magnitude than the timing component, which is positive, resulting in a negative Cornell measure.

[12] The positive period weighting measure has been implemented on hypothetical data in Grinblatt (1986/1987) and on the 1975–1984 monthly returns of 279 mutual funds in Grinblatt and Titman (1988). In the latter case, a power utility function with a risk-aversion parameter of eight was selected to generate the weights.

4. The Component of Abnormal Performance That Is Due to Selectivity

Since the Jensen measure is a period weighting measure, Proposition 2 can be used to generalize the Mayers and Rice (1979) and Dybvig and Ross (1985) result, that the Jensen measure assigns positive performance to investors with selectivity information, to settings in which the informed investor is not a mean-variance optimizer (since we allow for nontraded assets). Hence, the Jensen measure can provide appropriate inferences in cases where the mean-variance diagram (or the Sharpe ratio) cannot be used to evaluate performance. A second implication of Proposition 2 is that the selectivity component is positive if the timing and selectivity signals are independent.[13] These results are developed in two corollaries.

Corollary 1. *In the absence of timing information, the asymptotic Jensen, Cornell, and selectivity measures (and, hence, the selectivity component) of an informed investor's portfolio are positive.*

Proof. The result immediately follows from part *b* of Proposition 2 for the Jensen measure, since, by Equation (10), the Jensen measure is a period weighting measure. In addition, when there is no timing information, the timing component is zero by Proposition 1, and by Lemma 1 the bias-in-beta component is zero. In conjunction with Equations (4), (5), and (7), this implies that the asymptotic values of all three measures are identical, since each equals the selectivity component.

Corollary 2. *The selectivity component of performance of an informed investor's portfolio (and, hence, the asymptotic selectivity measure), is positive if the investor's selectivity signal for each asset is distributed independently of the timing signal.*

Proof. This is identical to the proof of part (*b*) of Proposition 2, which follows from the proof of part (*c*).

5. The Timing Component of Abnormal Performance

5.1 Verrecchia's example: the Giffen good effect

Verrecchia (1980), responding to some of the restrictive assumptions in the Mayers and Rice model, presented a counterexample to what he called the "broader hypothesis" that "the superior investor will on average achieve a greater return than the uninformed investors expect." Corollaries 1 and 2 imply that the negative performance of an informed investor in Verrecchia's counterexample must result from timing information, since his assumption of quadratic utility has the same implications for portfolio choice as our assumption that returns are normally distributed. We contend that Verrecchia's critique is linked to perverse income or wealth effects [in the sense of the income/substitution effects and the superior/inferior goods classification in Hicks (1939)]. In Verrecchia's example, the preferences of the informed investor make the efficient portfolio of risky assets a Giffen good (i.e., less is purchased as its expected return increases). Quadratic utility functions have the property that increases in wealth always increase risk aversion, so that information that increases expected wealth, such as a signal of a large "market" return (i.e., large *m*), can make an investor with quadratic utility so much more averse to risk that he holds less of that portfolio, rather than more. This wealth effect can induce a negative correlation between $\tilde{\beta}_p$ and $\tilde{r}_E$ and hence a negative timing component.

[13] Proposition A2 in the Appendix demonstrates that with constant absolute-risk aversion, the selectivity component of performance is positive, even with correlated timing and selectivity information.

This type of behavior is probably pathological. One expects the portfolio beta of most investors to be an increasing, not a decreasing, function of m. If this is the case, an investor with timing information exhibits a positive timing component, as shown in the next proposition.

Proposition 3. *The timing component is positive if $\partial\beta_p/\partial m > 0$ for all realizations of the signals of an investor with timing information and possibly uncorrelated selectivity information.*

Proof. It suffices to show that $E(\tilde{\beta}_p\tilde{m}) > 0$. Using the multivariate version of Stein's lemma,[14]

$$E(\tilde{\beta}_p\hat{m}) = E\left(\frac{\partial\beta_p}{\partial m}\right)\text{var}(\tilde{m}) + \sum_{j=1}^{N} E\left(\frac{\partial\beta_p}{\partial s_j}\right)E(\tilde{m}\tilde{s}_j)$$

$$= E\left(\frac{\partial\beta_p}{\partial m}\right)\text{var}(\tilde{m}) > 0$$

Corollary 3. *Under the conditions specified in Proposition 3, the large-sample timing and Cornell measures of an informed investor will be positive.*

Proof. This follows trivially from Equations (6) and (7), Corollary 2, and Proposition 3.

One can examine the class of utility functions that make $\partial\beta_p/\partial m > 0$ and ask whether this class is broad enough to represent the behavior of most investors. Lemma 2 demonstrated that if the timing and selectivity signals are independent, a sufficient (but not necessary) condition for this inequality to hold is that the investor have nonincreasing Rubinstein absolute-risk aversion (defined in Section 2).

Corollary 4. *The timing component of the portfolio of an investor with independent timing and selectivity information and nonincreasing Rubinstein absolute-risk aversion (and hence the large-sample timing and Cornell measures) is positive.*

Proof. This follows trivially from Lemma 2, Corollary 2, and Proposition 3.

We have not been able to prove that Corollary 4 generalizes to cases where timing and selectivity information are correlated. However, the following proposition proves that the sum of timing and selectivity (and by extension, the large-sample Cornell measure) is positive in this case for an informed investor with nonincreasing Rubinstein absolute-risk aversion.[15,16]

Proposition 4. *If all assets are tradable, and if an informed investor exhibits nonincreasing Rubinstein absolute-risk aversion, then the sum of his portfolio's timing and selectivity components (and, hence, its large-sample Cornell measure) is positive.*

---

[14] Let $\tilde{\mathbf{v}} = (\tilde{v}_1, \ldots, \tilde{v}_n)$.

$$\text{cov}[\tilde{u}, g(\tilde{\mathbf{v}})] = \sum_{j=1}^{N} E\left(\frac{\partial g}{\partial v_j}\right)\text{cov}(\tilde{u}, \tilde{v}_j)$$

if $g(\cdot)$ is a continuously differentiable function, all expectations are finite, and $(\tilde{u}, \tilde{v})$ is multivariate normally distributed. See Losq and Chateau (1982) for a proof.

[15] In a complete markets framework, Verrecchia (1980) implicitly demonstrated that the sum of the timing and selectivity components of the portfolio of an informed investor with constant absolute- or relative-risk aversion is positive, even if the timing and selectivity signals are correlated.

[16] Furthermore, Proposition A2 in the Appendix demonstrates that with constant absolute-risk aversion, the timing component of abnormal performance is positive, even with correlated timing and selectivity information.

Proof. See the Appendix.

The requirement in Proposition 4 that all assets be tradable is dictated by the same technical difficulties that prevent a generalization of Propositions 2 and 3 to a model in which timing and selectivity signals are correlated.[17] However, counterexamples to Propositions 2 to 4 in a more general setting are probably unrealistic, since they are necessarily founded on the unlikely possibility that changes in risk aversion will dominate substitution effects.

5.2 Why the timing and selectivity components are fundamentally different

Note that both timing and selectivity signals can affect expected wealth and hence the risk aversion of an informed investor. However, with independent timing and selectivity signals, only the timing information can potentially lead to pathological behavior. Consider, for example, the case of an investor who, with neutral selectivity information [i.e., $E(\tilde{\epsilon}_j) = 0$], holds the mean-variance efficient portfolio along with IBM stock to hedge against variability in the value of his human capital. If this investor receives favorable private information about IBM that is independent of the "market," his expected wealth increases. However, regardless of how his risk aversion increases or decreases in response to this change in expected wealth, he will always increase his holdings of IBM when he receives favorable private information. To illustrate this, consider the self-financing portfolio consisting of $1 long in IBM stock, β_{IBM} dollars short in the efficient portfolio, and $1 - \beta_{IBM}$ dollars short in the risk-free asset, which has end-of-period value $\tilde{\epsilon}_{IBM}$. With neutral information, this self-financing portfolio has an expected end-of-period value of zero (i.e., no risk premium) and the investor will hold the amount of this portfolio that minimizes the unsystematic variance of his total wealth (tradable plus nontradable "nonmarket" risk). Since the portfolio weights of this minimum unsystematic variance portfolio are fixed, changes in the portfolio in response to information always increase risk and will only be taken to increase expected return. Hence, favorable information about IBM always increases the investor's holdings of IBM's unsystematic disturbance, while unfavorable information always decreases the investor's holdings. The same cannot be said for information about the unconditional efficient portfolio, since it carries a risk premium $\bar{r}_E$. Thus, the different effects of timing and selectivity ability on measured performance stem from timing information being related to priced risk and selectivity information being related to non-priced risk.

6. The Appropriate Benchmark Portfolio

The preceding sections present conditions under which the unconditional mean-variance efficient portfolio of tradable assets can be used to evaluate portfolio performance. This benchmark portfolio is used with all the measures analyzed here except for the Cornell measure. The intuition for the appropriateness of this portfolio is quite simple. The efficiency of any particular index portfolio will be rejected if a portfolio with constant weights

[17] In both cases, there are realizations of information for which the investor is shorting an asset (but shorting less than for the average information realization) when he knows its expected return will be slightly larger than average. This is because the short position hedges unforecastable changes in the value of other assets in his portfolio—in the case of Proposition 4's generalization, the nontraded assets. For these realizations, an increase in the expected return of the asset decreases expected utility and makes him more risk-averse. With hedging now relatively more valuable, he may increase his short position in response to the information rather than decrease it.

realizes a nonzero performance measure with respect to it.[18] Hence, if a managed portfolio realizes significant positive performance and if the efficiency of the index used to compute the performance cannot be rejected, the positive performance must be due to portfolio weights that change in response to superior information.

In his reply to Mayers and Rice (1979), Roll (1979) suggested that choosing an appropriate benchmark portfolio may be particularly difficult if uninformed investors need to include real estate and other nonequity assets in their optimal portfolio, as the CAPM suggests. However, our results indicate that the appropriate benchmark portfolio consists only of those assets that can be included in the portfolio being evaluated. For example, portfolio managers who select the oil stocks in a larger portfolio can be evaluated with a mean-variance efficient benchmark portfolio consisting only of oil stocks.[19] This is because, from the perspective of these managers, non-oil investments in the complete portfolio may be regarded as nontraded assets. A related example is the case of partially delegated portfolio management, where an investment manager, aware that his clients invest a portion of their assets on their own or with other professionals, regards those investments as nontraded assets. A rational manager should select a portfolio that partly hedges the unmanaged wealth of a representative client. Our results suggest that portfolio performance can be evaluated in these circumstances.[20]

7. Summary and Conclusions

The ability to evaluate portfolio performance has been questioned in a number of papers. We analyzed the various criticisms of existing performance measures and introduced new measures that we believe have desirable properties.

We extended the well-known result that an investor with selectivity but without timing information achieves a positive Jensen measure to settings in which the investor holds nontraded assets, so that the evaluated portfolio is not mean variance efficient. We also showed that the counterexample to what Verrecchia (1980) called the "Mayers/Rice conjecture" occurs only for investors with timing information who have (what we consider) pathological preferences. Finally, we showed that the problems with the Jensen measure resulting from timing-related estimation problems, advanced by Jensen (1972), Dybvig and Ross (1985), and Admati and Ross (1985) can be overcome with a new measure that we call the positive period weighting measure.

This article also addressed the issue of the appropriate benchmark portfolio. Because of its mathematical (and not its equilibrium) properties, the unconditional mean-variance efficient portfolio of assets that are considered tradable by the evaluated investor provides correct inferences about the investor's performance. This indicates that the missing-asset problem, which is important in tests of the CAPM, does not apply to the evaluation of managed portfolios that consist of traded stocks or bonds.

[18]For a strategy with constant portfolio weights, all the measures that employ benchmark portfolios, with the exception of the timing measure, are asymptotically identical, regardless of the efficiency of the benchmark.

[19]This assumes that the covariance between the personally managed portion of the client's wealth and that portion under the jurisdiction of the manager is independent of the manager's information.

[20]Performance may also be detectable with an efficient benchmark portfolio that includes additional assets not contained in the investor's choice set (e.g., the efficient portfolio of NYSE stocks is an appropriate benchmark for evaluating a portfolio of NYSE oil stocks). If the investor's information provides no information about either the unconditional mean-variance efficient portfolio of assets within his choice set or the larger portfolio used as the benchmark, our propositions apply to measures that use the larger benchmark. We have not, however, been able to determine the extent to which this can be generalized.

Roll's (1977) critique of CAPM tests led some authors to question the appropriateness of the Jensen methodology.[21] However, our analysis illustrated that links between performance measures and particular equilibrium models are not necessary. Equilibrium models, such as the arbitrage pricing theory, do nothing more than suggest candidates for mean-variance efficient benchmarks.[22]

An i.i.d. return-generating process was assumed for this analysis. If unconditional returns are nonstationary, a portfolio with constant weights that is ex ante efficient for each time period may not exist. However, the Jensen measure and the positive period weighting measure may still be of interest in this case. After all, many investors would like to know if there are strategies with changing portfolio weights that dominate simple buy-and-hold strategies or rebalancing strategies with constant portfolio weights. If some evaluated portfolios exhibit positive Jensen or positive period weighting measures, it indicates that either the managers of these funds have special information or that the composition of the mean-variance efficient portfolio is changing over time. In either case, the evidence indicates that simple passive strategies can be beaten.

Appendix

This Appendix is organized in the following order:

1. Preliminaries for all but Proposition 5
2. Proof of Lemma 2
3. Proof of Proposition 2
4. Proposition A1
5. Proposition A2
6. Proof of Proposition 4

All of the results here assume that returns and information are multivariate normal and that the informed investor maximizes the expected utility of end-of-period wealth.

Preliminaries

The proofs presented here, except for the proof of Proposition 4, are simplified without limiting their generality by considering an equivalent economy formed from N portfolios of the tradable risky assets. In the repackaged securities market, the excess returns of the redefined assets can be written as

$$\tilde{\mathbf{R}} = \begin{bmatrix} \tilde{R}_1 \\ \tilde{R}_2 \\ \tilde{R}_3 \\ \vdots \\ \tilde{R}_N \end{bmatrix} = \begin{bmatrix} \tilde{r}_E \\ \tilde{\epsilon}_2 \\ \tilde{\epsilon}_3 \\ \vdots \\ \tilde{\epsilon}_N \end{bmatrix} = \begin{bmatrix} \bar{r}_E + \tilde{m} \\ \tilde{s}_2 \\ \tilde{s}_3 \\ \vdots \\ \tilde{s}_N \end{bmatrix} + \begin{bmatrix} \tilde{y} \\ \tilde{z}_2 \\ \tilde{z}_3 \\ \vdots \\ \tilde{z}_N \end{bmatrix}$$

Prior to repackaging, the efficient portfolio's weighting of the N ("market model") residuals was zero, implying linear dependence. This dependence has been eliminated in the repackaged market.

[21] See, for example, Cornell (1979, p. 390) and Wallace (1980).

[22] This does not necessarily imply that a one-factor model is superior to the multifactor approach employed by Lehmann and Modest (1997) and Connor and Korajczyk (1986). Indeed, one may prefer multiple index benchmarks because they generally yield more powerful test statistics and intuition suggests that they are less likely to be inefficient than a single index. The propositions in this article apply directly to multiple indexes if the index portfolios are locally mean-variance efficient, as defined in Grinblatt and Titman (1987).

We also assume, without loss of generality, that the $N \times N$ covariance matrix of asset returns conditioned on the information signals, $\mathbf{V} = \text{var}(\tilde{y}, \tilde{\mathbf{z}}^T)$, ($T$ denotes "transpose"), is positive definite. If $\tilde{m}$ and $\tilde{s}_j$ are uncorrelated, $\tilde{y}$ and $\tilde{z}_j$ are uncorrelated, implying that elements V_{1j} and V_{j1} of this matrix are zero for $j \neq 1$. $\mathbf{V}^{-1}$ also has off-diagonal elements of zero in the first row and column in this case.

Letting

$$\mathbf{e} = \text{the first column of the identity matrix}$$

$$\boldsymbol{\sigma} = \text{cov}(\tilde{\epsilon}_H, \tilde{\mathbf{R}})$$

$$\mathbf{s} = \begin{bmatrix} 0 \\ s_2 \\ \vdots \\ s_N \end{bmatrix} \quad \mathbf{z} = \begin{bmatrix} 0 \\ z_2 \\ \vdots \\ z_N \end{bmatrix} \quad \text{and} \quad \mathbf{x} = \begin{bmatrix} \beta_p \\ x_2 \\ \vdots \\ x_N \end{bmatrix}$$

the first-order condition [Equation (8)] for selecting the vector of optimal portfolio weights, $\mathbf{x}$, can be rewritten as

$$\mathbf{e}(\bar{r}_E + m) + \mathbf{s} = aW_0[\mathbf{V}\mathbf{x} + (\beta_H V_{11}\mathbf{e} + \boldsymbol{\sigma})],$$

which yields portfolio weights

$$\mathbf{x} = \mathbf{V}^{-1}[(\mathbf{e}(\bar{r}_E + m)) + \mathbf{s}/(aW_0) - (\beta_H V_{11}\,\mathbf{e} + \boldsymbol{\sigma})] \tag{A1}$$

Note that a, the Rubinstein risk-aversion measure, is unconditionally a random variable because it depends on information. An exception to this, in Propositions A1 and A2, occurs when the investor has constant absolute-risk aversion, in which case the Arrow-Pratt and Rubinstein measures are identical.

In addition to Equation (A1), Propositions (A1) and (A2) make use of the following

Lemma A1. *If a symmetric matrix* $\mathbf{M}$ *is positive definite, then for all i, the product of the ith diagonal element of* $\mathbf{M}$ *and that in* $\mathbf{M}^{-1}$ *equals or exceeds one.*

Proof: Available from authors on request.

Proof of Lemma 2

By Equation (A1),

$$\beta_p = \frac{(\mathbf{e}^T\mathbf{V}^{-1}\mathbf{e})\,(\bar{r}_E + m) + \mathbf{e}^T\mathbf{V}^{-1}\mathbf{s}}{aW_0} - \mathbf{e}^T\mathbf{V}^{-1}(\beta_H V_{11}\mathbf{e} + \boldsymbol{\sigma})$$

$$\frac{\partial\beta_p}{\partial m} = -\frac{1}{a^2\,W_0}\frac{\partial a}{\partial m}aW_0[\beta_P + \mathbf{e}^T\mathbf{V}^{-1}(\beta_H V_{11}\mathbf{e} + \boldsymbol{\sigma})] + \frac{1}{aW_0}\mathbf{e}^T\mathbf{V}^{-1}\mathbf{e}$$

$$= -\frac{1}{a}\frac{\partial a}{\partial m}(\beta_p + \beta_H) + \frac{1}{aW_0}\mathbf{e}^T\mathbf{V}^{-1}\mathbf{e}$$

with the last equality following from the independence of the timing and selectivity signals, which makes the (1,1) element of $\mathbf{V}^{-1}$ equal to $1/V_{11}$ and the first entry of $\boldsymbol{\sigma}$ zero. This expression is positive because the quadratic form on the right side is $1/\text{var}(\tilde{y})$ and $\partial a(I)/\partial m$ is zero or of the opposite sign of $\beta_p + \beta_H$. To see the latter, note that if $\beta_p + \beta_H$ is positive (negative), an increase (decrease) in m, ceteris paribus, results in an expected utility increase even if the investor's portfolio weights do not change. Consequently, expected utility increases (and risk aversion decreases) even more after portfolio weights shift in response to these information changes.

Proof of Proposition 2

The large-sample expectations encountered here easily translate into a more notationally convenient "one-period framework." Because $\tilde{r}_{Et}$ has a stationary distribution, we can view the infinite sequence of time-series drawings of r_{Et} and Tw_t as random drawings from a population distribution. In this framework, we use the realizations of $\tilde{w}$ and $\tilde{r}_E$ to represent some time period t's outcome of Tw_t and r_{Et}. Thus, $E(\tilde{w}) = 1$, $E(\tilde{\alpha}^*) = E(\tilde{w}\tilde{r}_p)$, and $E(\tilde{w}\tilde{r}_E) = 0$.

For parts *(a)* and *(b)*, consider an investor who lacks timing ability. In this case, we first show that the period weighting measure equals the selectivity component.

$$E(\tilde{w}\tilde{r}_p) = E[\tilde{w}(\tilde{\beta}_p\tilde{r}_E + \tilde{\epsilon}_p)] = E(\tilde{w}\tilde{r}_E)\,E(\tilde{\beta}_p) + E(\tilde{w})\,E(\tilde{\epsilon}_p)$$
$$= E(\tilde{w})\,E(\tilde{\epsilon}_p) = E(\tilde{\epsilon}_p) \qquad \text{(A2)}$$

where the first equality follows from Equation (1) and, in the absence of timing ability, the second follows from the independence of $\tilde{\epsilon}_p$ and $\tilde{w}$ and of $\tilde{w}\tilde{r}_E$ and $\tilde{\beta}_p$.

a. Equation (A2) is zero since $E(\tilde{\epsilon}_p) = 0$ by the proof of Proposition 1.
b. Equation (A2) is positive, since, with selectivity ability, $E(\tilde{\epsilon}_p)$ is shown to be positive by substituting "1" for "$\tilde{w}$" in part (c) and following the steps in the proof of part (c), below, that demonstrate $E(\tilde{w}\tilde{\epsilon}_p) > 0$.
c. $E(\tilde{w}\tilde{r}_p) = E(\tilde{w}\tilde{r}_E\tilde{\beta}_p) + E(\tilde{w}\tilde{\epsilon}_p)$ by Equation (1).

We first demonstrate that $E(\tilde{w}\tilde{\epsilon}_p) = E(\tilde{w}\tilde{s}_p) = E(\tilde{w}\tilde{\mathbf{s}}^T\tilde{\mathbf{x}}) > 0$. Using Equation (A1),

$$E(\tilde{w}\tilde{s}_p) = E\left[\frac{\tilde{w}\tilde{\mathbf{s}}^T\mathbf{V}^{-1}\mathbf{e}(\tilde{r}_E + \tilde{m})}{\hat{a}W_0}\right] + E\left(\frac{\tilde{w}\tilde{\mathbf{s}}^T\mathbf{V}^{-1}\tilde{\mathbf{s}}}{\tilde{a}W_0}\right) - E[\tilde{w}\tilde{\mathbf{s}}^T\mathbf{V}^{-1}(\beta_H V_{11}\mathbf{e} + \boldsymbol{\sigma})]$$

With selectivity signals that are independent of the timing signal, the off-diagonal elements in the first row and column of $\mathbf{V}^{-1}$ are zero. Hence, the term inside the first expectation on the right side of the equation is zero. The last expectation is zero because $\tilde{\mathbf{s}}$ has a mean of zero and is independent of $\tilde{w}$. Hence,

$$E(\tilde{w}\tilde{s}_p) = E\left(\frac{\tilde{w}\tilde{\mathbf{s}}^T\mathbf{V}^{-1}\tilde{\mathbf{s}}}{\tilde{a}W_0}\right) > 0$$

because $\tilde{a} > 0$, $\tilde{w} > 0$, and $\mathbf{V}^{-1}$ is positive definite.

The proof is completed by demonstrating that $E(\tilde{w}\tilde{r}_E\tilde{\beta}_p) \geq 0$. By the law of iterated expectations,

$$E(\tilde{w}\tilde{r}_E\tilde{\beta}_p) = E_E(\tilde{w}\tilde{r}_E\tilde{\beta}_p|r_E)$$

and since $\tilde{w}\tilde{r}_E$ is nonstochastic conditional on r_E,

$$\begin{aligned}
E(\tilde{w}\tilde{r}_E\tilde{\beta}_p) &= E_{r_E}[E(\tilde{w}\tilde{r}_E|r_E)E(\tilde{\beta}_p|r_E)] \\
&= E_{(r_E:r_E\geq 0)}[E(\tilde{w}\tilde{r}_E|r_E)E(\tilde{\beta}_p|r_E)]\Pr[\tilde{r}_E \geq 0] \\
&\quad + E_{(r_E:r_E<0)}[E(\tilde{w}\tilde{r}_E|r_E)]E(\tilde{\beta}_p|r_E)\Pr[\tilde{r}_E < 0] \\
&> E_{(r_E:r_E\geq 0)}[E(\tilde{w}\tilde{r}_E|r_E)\beta_p^*]\Pr[\tilde{r}_E \geq 0] \\
&\quad + E_{(r_E:r_E<0)}[E(\tilde{w}\tilde{r}_E|r_E)\beta_p^*]\Pr[\tilde{r}_E < 0]
\end{aligned}$$

where $\beta_p^* = E(\tilde{\beta}_p | \tilde{r}_E = 0)$. The inequality follows from $\tilde{w} > 0$ and $\partial\beta_p/\partial m > 0$. The latter assumption makes $E(\tilde{\beta}_p | r_E)$ an increasing function of r_E.[23]

Note that β_p^* is independent of $\tilde{r}_E$. Thus,

$$E(\tilde{w}\tilde{r}_E\tilde{\beta}_p) > \beta_p^* E_{(r_E:r_E \geq 0)}[E(\tilde{w}\tilde{r}_E | r_E)]\Pr[\tilde{r}_E \geq 0] + \beta_p^* E_{(r_E:r_E<0)}[E(\tilde{w}\tilde{r}_E | r_E)]\Pr[\tilde{r}_E < 0) = \beta_p^* E(\tilde{w}\tilde{r}_E) = 0$$

since $E(\tilde{w}\tilde{r}_E) = 0$.

Proposition A1. *If the Rubinstein measure of absolute risk aversion, a, is constant over all the information realizations of an informed investor, then the expectation of the investor's positive period weighting measure, $E(\tilde{w}\tilde{r}_p)$, is positive.*

Proof. Using Equation (1)

$$E(\tilde{w}\tilde{r}_p) = E(\tilde{w}\tilde{r}_E\tilde{\beta}_p) + E(\tilde{w}\tilde{\boldsymbol{\epsilon}}^T\tilde{\mathbf{x}})$$

where the first element of $\tilde{\boldsymbol{\epsilon}}$ is 0 and the ith element is $\tilde{\epsilon}_i$. Using Equation (A1) and noting that $\tilde{w}\tilde{r}_E$ is nonstochastic conditional on r_E, the timing term

$$\begin{aligned} E(\tilde{w}\tilde{r}_E\tilde{\beta}_p) &= E\left\{\tilde{w}\tilde{r}_E\left[\frac{\mathbf{e}^T\mathbf{V}^{-1}\mathbf{e}\bar{r}_E}{aW_0} - \mathbf{e}^T\mathbf{V}^{-1}(\beta_H V_{11}\mathbf{e} + \boldsymbol{\sigma})\,\mathrm{d}\right.\right\} \\ &\quad + \frac{1}{aW_0}E_{r_E}\{wr_E[\mathbf{e}^T\mathbf{V}^{-1}\mathbf{e}E(\tilde{m}|\tilde{r}_E = r_E) + \mathbf{e}^T\mathbf{V}^{-1}E(\tilde{\mathbf{s}}|\tilde{r}_E = r_E)]\} \\ &= \frac{1}{aW_0}E_{r_E}\left\{wr_E^2\left[(\mathbf{e}^T\mathbf{V}^{-1}\mathbf{e})\frac{\mathrm{var}\,(\tilde{m})}{\sigma_E^2} + \mathbf{e}^T\mathbf{V}^{-1}\frac{E(\tilde{\mathbf{s}}\tilde{m})}{\sigma_E^2}\right]\right\} \\ &> E\left(\frac{\tilde{w}\tilde{r}_E^2}{\sigma_E^2 aW_0}\right)[\mathbf{e}^T\mathbf{V}^{-1}E(\tilde{\mathbf{s}}\tilde{m})] \\ &= E\left(\frac{\tilde{w}\tilde{r}_E^2}{\sigma_E^2 aW_0}\right)[\mathbf{e}^T\mathbf{V}^{-1}(-\mathbf{V}\mathbf{e} + V_{11}\mathbf{e})] \end{aligned}$$

This is positive because $(wr_E^2)/(\sigma_E^2 aW_0)$ is positive, and Lemma A1 implies that the latter factor is positive. The last equality stems from $\tilde{\epsilon}_j$ and $\tilde{r}_E$ being uncorrelated, $j = 2, \ldots, N$, which implies

$$E(\tilde{\mathbf{s}}\tilde{m}) = -E(\tilde{\mathbf{z}}\tilde{y}) = -(\mathbf{V}\mathbf{e} - V_{11}\mathbf{e})$$

Using Equation (A1), the selectivity term,

$$\begin{aligned} E(\tilde{w}\tilde{\boldsymbol{\epsilon}}^T\tilde{\mathbf{x}}) &= E\left\{\tilde{w}\left[\frac{\tilde{\boldsymbol{\epsilon}}^T\mathbf{V}^{-1}\mathbf{e}\bar{r}_E}{aW_0} - \tilde{\boldsymbol{\epsilon}}^T\mathbf{V}^{-1}(\beta_H V_{11}\mathbf{e} + \boldsymbol{\sigma})\right]\right\} \\ &\quad + \frac{1}{aW_0}E[\tilde{w}(\tilde{\boldsymbol{\epsilon}}^T\mathbf{V}^{-1}\tilde{\mathbf{s}} + \tilde{m}\tilde{\boldsymbol{\epsilon}}^T\mathbf{V}^{-1}\mathbf{e})] \end{aligned}$$

[23]Let $g(m|r_E)$ represent the conditional density function of $\tilde{m}$ given $\tilde{r}_E = r_E$. $\tilde{m}$ and $\tilde{r}_E$ are normally distributed. Thus, for any constant $c > 0$, there exists a unique critical value $m^* = m^*(r_E, c)$ where the conditional density functions $g(m|r_e)$ and $g(m|r_E + c)$ are equal (i.e., where they cross). For all $m > m^*$, $g(m|r_E + c) > g(m|r_E)$. For $m < m^*$, $g(m|r_E + c) < g(m|r_E)$. This implies chat the conditional expectation of m given $\tilde{r}_E = r_E + c$ exceeds the conditional expectation of m given $\tilde{r}_E = r_E$. It also implies that any monotonic increasing function of m has the same property. Since β_p is a monotonic increasing function of m holding the selectivity signals constant, and since the selectivity signal vector is independent of $\tilde{r}_E$, $E(\tilde{\beta}_p|r_E + c) > E(\tilde{\beta}_p|r_E)$.

$$= \frac{1}{aW_0} E_{r_E}[wE(\tilde{\epsilon}^T \mathbf{V}^{-1}\tilde{\mathbf{s}} + \tilde{m}\tilde{\epsilon}^T \mathbf{V}^{-1}\mathbf{e} \mid r_E)]$$

$$= \frac{1}{aW_0} E\{\tilde{w}[E(\tilde{\epsilon}^T \mathbf{V}^{-1}\tilde{\mathbf{s}}) + E(\tilde{m}\tilde{\epsilon}^T \mathbf{V}^{-1}\mathbf{e})]\}$$

$$= \frac{1}{aW_0} E\{\tilde{w}[E(\tilde{\mathbf{s}}^T \mathbf{V}^{-1}\tilde{\mathbf{s}}) + E(\tilde{m}\tilde{\mathbf{s}}^T \mathbf{V}^{-1}\mathbf{e})]\} > 0 \qquad \text{(A3)}$$

The second equality stems from the zero mean of $\tilde{\epsilon}$ and $\tilde{w}$ being nonstochastic conditional on r_E. In the third equality, the independence of $\tilde{\epsilon}$ and $\tilde{r}_E$ implies the equality of the unconditional and conditional expectations. To see this, regress $\tilde{m}$ and $\tilde{\mathbf{s}}$ onto $\tilde{r}_E$ and note that the covariances of the regression residuals with $\tilde{\epsilon}$ are identical to the covariances of $\tilde{m}$ and $\tilde{\mathbf{s}}$ with $\tilde{\epsilon}$. Finally, the first interior expectation in Equation (A3) is positive because its argument is a quadratic form in a positive definite matrix. The second interior expectation is positive by Lemma A1, as demonstrated in the first part of the proof. Since $w > 0$, the exterior expectation is positive as well.

Proposition A2. *If the Rubinstein measure of absolute risk aversion, a, is constant over all the information realizations of an informed investor, then both the investor's selectivity component and timing component are positive.*

Proof.

1. By Equation (A1), the selectivity component of performance is

$$\begin{aligned} E(\tilde{s}_p) &= E(\tilde{\mathbf{s}}^T\tilde{\mathbf{x}}) \\ &= \frac{E(\tilde{\mathbf{s}}^T \mathbf{V}^{-1}\mathbf{e}\tilde{r}_E)}{aW_0} - E[\tilde{\mathbf{s}}^T \mathbf{V}^{-1}(\beta_H V_{11}\mathbf{e} + \boldsymbol{\sigma})] + \frac{E(\tilde{\mathbf{s}}^T \mathbf{V}^{-1}\tilde{\mathbf{s}} + \tilde{\mathbf{s}}^T \mathbf{V}^{-1}\mathbf{e}\tilde{m})}{aW_0} \\ &= \frac{1}{aW_0}[E(\tilde{\mathbf{s}}^T \mathbf{V}^{-1}\tilde{\mathbf{s}}) + E(\tilde{m}\tilde{\mathbf{s}}^T \mathbf{V}^{-1}\mathbf{e})] \\ &> \frac{1}{aW_0} E(\tilde{m}\tilde{\mathbf{s}}^T \mathbf{V}^{-1}\epsilon) \\ &= (-\mathbf{e}^T\mathbf{V} + V_{11}\mathbf{e}^T)\mathbf{V}^{-1}\mathbf{e} \end{aligned}$$

which is positive by Lemma A1. The last equality stems from $\tilde{\epsilon}_j$ and $\tilde{r}_E$ being uncorrelated, $j = 2, \ldots, N$, which implies

$$E(\tilde{m}\tilde{\mathbf{s}}^T) = -E(\tilde{y}\tilde{\mathbf{z}}^T) = -(\mathbf{e}^T\mathbf{V} - V_{11}\mathbf{e}^T)$$

2. From Equation (A1), the timing component,

$$\begin{aligned} E(\tilde{\beta}_p\tilde{m}) &= E\left[\frac{1}{aW_0}\mathbf{e}^T\mathbf{V}^{-1}(\mathbf{e}\tilde{m} + \tilde{\mathbf{s}})\tilde{m}\right] \\ &\quad + E\left[\frac{\mathbf{e}^T\mathbf{V}^{-1}\mathbf{e}\tilde{r}_E\tilde{m}}{aW_0} + \mathbf{e}^T\mathbf{V}^{-1}(\beta_H V_{11}\mathbf{e} + \boldsymbol{\sigma})\tilde{m}\right] \\ &= \frac{1}{aW_0}[(\mathbf{e}^T\mathbf{V}^{-1}\mathbf{e})\operatorname{var}(\tilde{m}) + \mathbf{e}^T\mathbf{V}^{-1}E(\tilde{\mathbf{s}}\tilde{m})] \\ &> \frac{1}{aW_0}\mathbf{e}^T\mathbf{V}^{-1}E(\tilde{\mathbf{s}}\tilde{m}) \end{aligned}$$

which is positive, as shown in part (1).

Proof of Proposition 4

To simplify the proof without loss of generality, redefine the tradable primitive assets in the economy so that

$$\text{cov}(\beta_j\tilde{y} + \tilde{z}_j, \beta_i\tilde{y} + \tilde{z}_i) = 0 \qquad \text{for } i \neq j$$

By forming portfolios, one can always repackage the primitive assets to have this covariance structure, although this will not permit the repackaging used for the other proofs, Investors are indifferent to such repackagings since they can be undone in their personal portfolios. Moreover, if the sum of the timing and selectivity components of performance is positive in the repackaged economy, it is positive in the original economy because the two sums are identical.

This repackaging allows us to rewrite the standard first-order condition, Equation (8), as

$$\overline{R}_j + \beta_j m + s_j = aW_0 x_j \text{var}(\beta_j\tilde{y} + \tilde{z}_j) \tag{A4}$$

Without loss of generality, one can express the deviations of conditional mean returns from unconditional mean returns with the factor model

$$\beta_j\tilde{m} + \tilde{s}_j = \sum_{i=1}^{N} \gamma_{ji}\tilde{f}_i \qquad \text{for } j = 1, \ldots, N$$

where the normally distributed factors $\tilde{f}_1, \ldots, \tilde{f}_N$ are normalized to have zero mean and zero covariance with each other.

Taking the partial derivative of Equation (A4) with respect to f_k, holding f_i constant for $i \neq k$, implies

$$\gamma_{jk} = aW_0\text{var}(\beta_j\tilde{y} + \tilde{z}_j)\left(\frac{x_j}{a}\frac{\partial a}{\partial f_k} + \frac{\partial x_j}{\partial f_k}\right)$$

or

$$\gamma_{jk}\frac{\partial x_j}{\partial f_k} = \frac{\gamma_{jk}^2}{aW_0\text{var}(\beta_j\tilde{y} + \tilde{z}_j)} - \frac{x_j\gamma_{jk}}{a}\frac{\partial a}{\partial f_k}$$

Summing over j and noting that γ_{jk} is a constant yields

$$\sum_{j=1}^{N}\frac{\partial(x_j\gamma_{jk})}{\partial f_k} = \frac{1}{a}\left[\sum_{j=1}^{N}\frac{\gamma_{jk}^2}{W_0\text{var}(\beta_j\tilde{y} + \tilde{z}_j)} - \frac{\partial a}{\partial f_k}\sum_{j=1}^{N}x_j\gamma_{jk}\right]$$

This is positive because with nonincreasing Rubinstein absolute-risk aversion, $\partial a/\partial f_k$ is zero or of opposite sign of $\sum_{j=1}^{N} x_j\gamma_{jk}$. Thus, the sum of the timing and selectivity components of performance,

$$E\left[\sum_{j=1}^{N}\tilde{x}_j(\tilde{R}_j - \overline{R}_j)\right] = E\left(\sum_{k=1}^{N}\sum_{j=1}^{N}\tilde{x}_j\gamma_{jk}\tilde{f}_k\right)$$

is positive because

$$E\left(\sum_{j=1}^{N}\tilde{x}_j\gamma_{jk}\tilde{f}_k\right) = E_{fi,\, i\neq k}\text{cov}\left(\sum_{j=1}^{N}x_j\gamma_{jk}, \tilde{f}_k | f_i, i \neq k\right)$$

and the conditional covariance is positive because

$$\frac{\partial\left(\sum_{j=1}^{N} x_j \gamma_{jk}\right)}{\partial f_k} = \sum_{j=1}^{N} \frac{\partial(x_j \gamma_{jk})}{\partial f_k} > 0$$

as shown above.

References

Admati, A., and S, Ross, 1985, "Measuring Investment Performance in a Rational Expectations Equilibrium Model," *Journal of Business*, 58, 1–26.

Admati, A., S. Bhattacharya, P. Pfleiderer, and S. Ross, 1986, "On Timing and Selectivity," *Journal of Finance*, 41, 715–730.

Connor, G., and R. Korajczyk, 1986, "Performance Measurement with the Arbitrage Pricing Theory: A New Framework for Analysis," *Journal of Financial Economics*, 15, 373–394.

Copeland, T., and D. Mayers, 1982, "The Value Line Enigma (1965–1978): A Case Study of Performance Evaluation Issues," *Journal of Financial Economics*, 10, 239–322.

Cornell, B., 1979, "Asymmetric Information and Portfolio Performance Measurement," *Journal of Financial Economics*, 7, 381–391.

Dybvig, P., and S. Ross, 1985, "Differential Information and Performance Measurement using a Security Market Line," *Journal of Finance*, 40, 383–399.

Grinblatt, M., 1986/1987, "How to Evaluate a Portfolio Manager," *Financial Markets and Portfolio Management*, 1(2), 97–112.

Grinblatt, M., and S. Titman, 1983, "Factor Pricing in a Finite Economy," *Journal of Financial Economics*, 12, 497–507.

Grinblatt, M., and S. Titman, 1987, "The Relation Between Mean-Variance Efficiency and Arbitrage Pricing," *Journal of Business*, 60, 97–112.

Grinblatt, M., and S. Titman, 1988, "The Evaluation of Mutual Fund Performance: An Analysis of Monthly Returns," working paper, University of California, Los Angeles.

Grinblatt, M., and S. Titman, 1989, "Mutual Fund Performance: An Analysis of Quarterly Portfolio Holdings," *Journal of Business*, 62, 393–416.

Henriksson, R., and R. Merton, 1981, "On Market Timing and Investment Performance II: Statistical Procedures for Evaluating Forecasting Skills," *Journal of Business*, 54, 513–533.

Hicks, J., 1939, *Value and Capital*, Oxford University Press, London.

Jensen, M., 1968, "The Performance of Mutual Funds in the Period 1945–1964," *Journal of Finance*, 23, 389–416.

Jensen, M., 1969, "Risk, the Pricing of Capital Assets, and the Evaluation of Investment Portfolios," *Journal of Business*, 42, 167–247.

Jensen, M., 1972, "Optimal Utilization of Market Forecasts and the Evaluation of Investment Portfolio Performance," in G. Szego and K. Shell (eds.), *Mathematical Methods in Investment and Finance*, North Holland, Amsterdam.

Lehmann, B., and D. Modest, 1987, "Mutual Fund Performance Evaluation: A Comparison of Benchmarks and Benchmark Comparisons," *Journal of Finance*, 42, 233–265.

Losq, E., and J. Chateau, 1982, "A Generalization of the CAPM Based on a Property of the Covariance Operator," *Journal of Financial and Quantitative Analysis*, 17, 783–797.

Mayers, D., and E. Rice, 1979, "Measuring Portfolio Performance and the Empirical Content of Asset Pricing Models," *Journal of Financial Economics*, 7, 3–29.

Roll, R., 1977, "A Critique of the Asset Pricing Theory's Tests; Part I: On Past and Potential Testability of the Theory," *Journal of Financial Economics*, 4, 129–176.

Roll, R., 1978, "Ambiguity When Performance Is Measured by the Securities Market Line," *Journal of Finance*, 33, 1051–1069.

Roll, R., 1979, "A Reply to Mayers and Rice," *Journal of Financial Economics*, 7, 391–400.

Rubinstein, M., 1973, "A Comparative Statics Analysis of Risk Premiums," *Journal of Business*, 46, 605–615.

Sharpe, W., 1966, "Mutual Fund Performance," *Journal of Business*, 39, 119–138.

Stein, C., 1973, "Estimation of the Mean of a Multivariate Normal Distribution," *Proceedings of the Prague Symposium on Asymptotic Statistics.*

Treynor, J., 1965, "How to Rate Management of Investment Funds," *Harvard Business Review*, 43, 63–75.

Treynor, J., and F. Mazuy, 1966, "Can Mutual Funds Outguess the Market?" *Harvard Business Review*, 44, 131–136.

Verrecchia, R., 1980, "The Mayers-Rice Conjecture: A Counterexample," *Journal of Financial Economics*, 8, 87–100.

Wallace, A., 1980, "Is Beta Dead?" *Institutional Investor*, 20, 23–30.

Fourteen

Paul Pfleiderer

Paul Pfleiderer received a Ph.D. from Yale University in 1982. He started out at the Graduate School of Business, Stanford University, and has been there ever since. •

Most people can look back and identify a serendipitous encounter that had a profound effect on their life. Mine occurred in 1978 when I (almost literally) ran into Doug Diamond in the crowded administrative offices of the Yale Economics department. I was there to sign up for my second year of Ph.D. courses, and Doug, who was two years ahead of me in the program, suggested that I consider taking a course on finance taught by this new guy the department had hired from Penn, someone named Steve Ross. Doug knew Steve and absolutely and unconditionally guaranteed that I would find Steve's course both interesting and valuable. I protested that I was not at all excited by finance and I naively claimed that there could not be much of economic interest to be found in the workings of the stock market, beyond what had already been revealed by mean/variance models. Doug insisted that I give Steve and the course a chance. Doug was so relentless in his praise for Steve that I had to give in. I showed up for the first class session with a closed mind and the comforting assurance that I could always drop the course and sign up for something else. After little more than twenty minutes of Steve's introduction had passed, I was completely hooked—hooked on both Steve and finance. As anyone who has taken a course from Steve knows, Steve has this uncanny ability to almost instantly communicate just how fascinating finance is and how exciting it is to solve its many puzzles. It seemed to me that in that first session he was inviting everyone who was interested to join him in the fun. I was interested, I did join him, and it was and continues to be fun.

In the late 70s and the early 80s there was much interest in applying models of asymmetric information to problems in finance. Steve had already made significant contributions in this area (e.g., modeling the agency relationship and showing how managers' private information can be revealed through capital structure choice). At this time Steve was (among other things) quite interested in performance evaluation and particularly how one would determine when a portfolio manager was acting on valuable private information. I can remember some interesting discussions with Steve about how information comes to be distributed throughout markets and how active fund management might be thought of as a way of selling information.

These discussions with Steve must have made an impression on me, since when I arrived at Stanford I started thinking off and on about how information might be sold in financial markets. Fortunately for me, another serendipitous event occurred the year after I joined the Stanford faculty and that was Anat Admati's decision to come to Stanford as well. She too was very much interested in the distribution and flows of information in financial markets, no doubt inspired by similar discussions with Steve, and we found that with our common background as Steve's students, we approached problems in the same way and seemed to speak a common language. We wrote several papers on markets for information and the different ways information can be sold for use in trading.

I owe Steve a debt of gratitude for sparking my interest in finance (as mentioned above, something that only took him 20 minutes), but much more importantly for inspiring me (and all of his other students) through his example to think about fundamental questions and not take any shortcuts in seeking answers. None of us students had any reasonable hope of making the large number of significant contributions Steve has made to finance and economics, contributions that cut across so many areas. But we all benefited from trying to chase after him to the extent we could.

Direct and Indirect Sale of Information

By Anat R. Admati and Paul Pfleiderer[1]

In this article we compare two methods for a monopolist to sell information. In a direct sale buyers observe the seller's signal (or noisy versions of it) and subsequently use what they observe to make investment decisions. In an indirect sale the seller creates a portfolio based on his private information and then sells shares to the traders. Indirect sale allows the seller to control more effectively the buyers' reactions to the information, but may not allow as much surplus to be extracted as is possible with direct sale. We show how the optimal selling method depends on the extent to which information is revealed by assets' equilibrium prices.

KEYWORDS: *Markets for information, mutual funds, newsletters, monopoly.* •

1. Introduction

This paper explores different strategies for selling information to traders in a financial market. One method involves the sale of the information (or versions of it) *directly.* Newsletters are an example of this. In a direct sale buyers of information can use it as they see fit in making their portfolio decisions, i.e., they purchase the unrestricted use of the information. The direct sale of information is analyzed in Admati and Pfleiderer (1986). In this paper we explore another selling method for information, which we call *indirect.* When he sells information indirectly, the seller creates a fund whose portfolio choices exploit the information he has, and the sale of information amounts to selling shares in this fund to traders. Mutual funds that are involved in "active management" are an example of this. In an indirect sale traders do not observe the seller's information but pay for the response to the information taken on their behalf. We will find the optimal strategy for selling information indirectly, and compare direct and indirect sale of information.

An important characteristic of information as a commodity which our model captures is the externality in its valuation—if more agents observe a piece of information, its value (and the value of related pieces of information) is generally diminished. This phenomenon is typically due to competition among informed traders. In our model there is also leakage of information through the asset prices, which means that traders can free-ride on the information of others. Because of this externality in the valuation of the information, the information seller typically wishes to control the response of his clients to the information they purchase. One way to restrict the usage of information is to add noise to the information before selling it. As is shown in Admati and Pfleiderer (1986), this may be desirable for the seller if information is sold directly. We show here that when information is sold indirectly, it is never desirable to add noise. Adjusting the unit price for the fund is a more effective way to control the usage of the information.

To focus on how the information seller controls the usage of the information we abstract from some other important features of information exchange. In particular, we assume away any incentive problems between the seller and buyers—the seller provides truthfully the promised information if information is sold directly and makes the promised investments on

[1] We would like to thank Xavier de Groot, Martin Hellwig, Myron Scholes, Mark Wolfson, three referees, and especially David Kreps for helpful comments and suggestions. The financial support of the Stanford Program in Finance, Batterymarch Financial Management, and the Sloan Foundation is gratefully acknowledged.

Reprinted with permission:
Admati, Anat R. and Paul Pfleiderer. "Direct and Indirect Sale of Information." *Econometrica* 58 (1990): 901–928.

behalf of the traders if information is sold indirectly. Also, buyers do not resell information. We further assume that the information seller does not trade on his own account in the financial market or that, if he trades on his own account, he behaves competitively.[2]

We first analyze the case in which the shares of the fund are priced linearly. (Linear pricing seems realistic, especially if there exists a secondary market for shares of the fund.) We show that in this case there is a tradeoff between selling directly and indirectly. Because it is assumed that information buyers are homogeneous, the seller of direct information is able to extract all the surplus the information generates. This is not the case with indirect sale and linear pricing. However, in an indirect sale the seller controls the usage of the information more effectively than the direct seller is able to with the tools at his disposal (namely added noise or limiting the number of buyers). We find that indirect sale is more profitable when the externality in the valuation of information is relatively intense, which in our model occurs when traders are relatively risk tolerant or when there is little noise in supply. Conversely, when the externality is relatively mild, direct sale is more profitable.

If the fund manager is not restricted to linear pricing, then with homogenous buyers the optimal pricing scheme involves a per share price and a fixed participation fee. The optimal two part pricing scheme is strictly more profitable than the direct sale. The extent to which two part pricing improves profits relative to direct sale or to indirect sale with linear pricing depends on the degree to which the asset's price reveals the seller's information. If the price is very informative, then restricting the usage of the information is very important. In this case most profits in the two part scheme are derived from the per share pricing of the fund and the fixed fee is small. On the other hand, if the price is not very informative, then most profits are derived from the fixed fee, and in the limit the optimal selling strategy becomes equivalent to direct sale.

The situation is more complex if traders are heterogeneous in the type and amount of private information they have. One problem with the creation of a fund is that different traders may wish to use information differently, depending on the information they observe from other sources. We illustrate how with more than one risky asset (and assuming that the information seller cannot sell as many products as there are types of traders), there may be an advantage to selling information directly. This is because in a direct sale traders can "unbundle" a vector of information signals and combine them optimally with their particular private information signals. By contrast, the particular usage of the information that is priced in the indirect sale is likely to be suboptimal for some of the traders given their private information endowments. Indeed, direct sale may lead to strictly higher profits than indirect sale even if the fund manager can use a two part pricing scheme.

The paper is organized as follows. Section 2 describes the basic model. In Section 3 we briefly review the main results in Admati and Pfleiderer (1986). Section 4 introduces the indirect method of selling information. In Section 5 we discuss the optimal strategy and the resulting profits for the fund manager if he is restricted to linear pricing. Section 6 compares the direct method and indirect method with linear pricing. In Section 7 we discuss general pricing schemes. Section 8 is concerned with the case of heterogeneous traders and discusses the bundling problem. Concluding remarks, which include a discussion

[2] The information seller may commit to not trading on his own account so that buyers will not be concerned with his incentives. Also, if the information seller is risk averse (and his information is imperfect), then in our model he will never choose to take a trading position large enough to affect the asset's price—in other words, he will behave competitively in the asset market. He will, however, have an incentive to misrepresent his information to information buyers. For analyses of the incentive problem in the provision of information, see Allen (1986) and Bhattacharya and Pfleiderer (1985).

of some related literature, are offered in Section 9. Unless otherwise noted, proofs which are not in the text are in the Appendix.

2. The Model

The basic setting of our model is similar to that in Admati and Pfleiderer (1986). There are three time periods and a continuum of traders $v \in [0, 1]$. In period zero, information may be acquired by traders as discussed below. Trading in the securities market takes place in period one, and involves, in the basic model, one risky asset and a riskless asset, which is the numeraire. (A simple extension to more than one risky asset is straightforward.) In period one, the price of the risky asset is determined in equilibrium. In period two, each share of the riskless asset pays off one unit of a single consumption good, each share of the risky asset pays off a random amount $\tilde{F}$, and consumption takes place.

We assume:

(A1) COMPETITIVE RATIONAL EXPECTATIONS EQUILIBRIUM: *The market for the risky asset clears, and each trader maximizes the expected utility of final consumption conditional on all the information available to him, including the asset equilibrium price. Traders take the price distribution and price realizations as given.*

(A2) NOISY SUPPLY: *The per capita supply of the risky asset is a random variable $\tilde{Z}$, which is independent of any information that traders have.*

Assumption (A2) guarantees that information is valuable in equilibrium.[3]

The following parametric assumptions are made for analytical tractability.

(A3) CONSTANT ABSOLUTE RISK AVERSION: *Traders have negative exponential utility functions.*

(A4) NORMAL DISTRIBUTIONS: *The random variables $\tilde{F}$, $\tilde{Z}$, and all information signals are jointly normally distributed.*

We normalize the variance of the payoff $\tilde{F}$ to be 1 (without loss of generality), and also assume for simplicity that all the random variables in the model have zero mean. (Since in our context the valuation of information never depends on expected values, this assumption does not affect our results in any important way.) For a random variable $\tilde{X}$ we denote its variance by σ_x^2 and its standard deviation by σ_x.

We make a strong assumption of homogeneity, namely:

(A5) IDENTICAL TRADERS: *Traders have the same coefficient of risk tolerance ρ, and they all possess a priori the same information. (Their beliefs are summarized by the distribution of the payoff.)*

This assumption clearly affects our results in important ways, since it allows the information seller to extract all the surplus his information generates when he charges a fixed fee. However, the assumption allows us to focus on aggregation of information in prices

[3]The source of the randomness in supply is not modeled here, but it can be interpreted in a variety of ways, e.g., via randomness in endowments or trading by liquidity traders. Diamond and Verrecchia (1981) model randomness in endowments explicitly. Independence of supply and traders' information is assumed for simplicity, as is standard in the literature; see, for example, Grossman and Stiglitz (1980) and Hellwig (1980). It can be dropped (at a substantial cost in terms of tractability), as long as aggregate supplies are not perfectly correlated with traders' information.

and its effects on the optimal selling strategies of an information seller without having to deal with complex issues of price discrimination. Section 8 touches on some of the issues that arise if traders are heterogeneous.

Finally, we introduce the information seller.

(A6) INFORMATION SELLER: *There is a single information seller. The seller is endowed with a signal* $\widetilde{F} + \widetilde{\theta}$ *, where* $\widetilde{\theta}$ *is normally distributed and independent of* $\widetilde{F}$*. He does not trade on his own account in the financial market.*[4]

3. Direct Sale of Information

In the direct sale of information the product being sold is the *unrestricted* right to use the information signal for trading. Each buyer of information observes some version of the seller's signal which can be used in trading in the financial market. We assume that traders cannot resell the information. (This is a reasonable assumption if the information is only useful for a short period of time, for example.) Of course, the sale of information takes place before buyers (or even the seller) can observe the signal realization, and the amount buyers are willing to pay depends on the statistical characteristics of both the signal they purchase and the information they can get from other sources. In particular, traders realize that if others purchase information, this information will be aggregated and partially revealed by the equilibrium prices.

Admati and Pfleiderer (1986) show that in a direct sale of information the seller may prefer to sell noisier versions of the information he has or to restrict the fraction of informed traders. To see most clearly why adding noise may be desirable, consider the case in which the seller has perfect information. If any positive fraction of the traders knows $\widetilde{F}$ perfectly, then the asset price is fully revealing (and equal to the payoff), since otherwise informed traders' demand is unbounded. Thus, information has no value and the seller's profits are zero. This occurs because traders use perfect information extremely aggressively, and this causes it to be reflected perfectly in equilibrium prices. In general, as traders in the aggregate acquire more information the price becomes more informative, and the value of information to any individual trader declines. This effect is stronger when the signal sold is more precise, causing the seller to add noise to his information in some cases.

Suppose that the seller provides to trader ν a signal of the form $\widetilde{Y}_\nu = \widetilde{F} + \widetilde{\theta} + \widetilde{\varepsilon}_\nu$, where $\widetilde{F}$, $\widetilde{\theta}$, and $\widetilde{\varepsilon}_\nu$, $\nu \in [0, 1]$, are jointly normally distributed. (This includes the possibility that the variance of $\widetilde{\varepsilon}_\nu$ is infinite, so that trader ν is uninformed.) Admati and Pfleiderer (1986) discuss the choice of joint distributions of $\widetilde{\varepsilon}_\nu$, focusing on "photocopied" noise, which is the same across traders who purchase information ($\widetilde{\varepsilon}_\nu \equiv \widetilde{\varepsilon}_{\nu'}$ for all traders ν and ν' who buy information), and "personalized" noise, in which the $\widetilde{\varepsilon}_\nu$'s are independent across traders. That paper shows that adding personalized noise is optimal within a broad set of selling strategies. In general, to enhance the value of each signal sold, any added noise should not affect the equilibrium price realization. In the optimal strategy the seller sells indentically distributed signals to all traders. For later use in this paper, we state the following result.

[4]As we remarked above, if the information seller also traded, then his incentives to provide the information truthfully would be distorted. In the absence of such incentive problems, the trading profits in our model would be negligible relative to selling profits if the information owner is a price taking trader. In general, an information owner may prefer to sell information rather than trade because he is more risk averse than other traders. See Admati and Pfleiderer (1988) for a discussion of trading vs. selling information in a model with imperfect competition.

Proposition 3.1 (Admati and Pfleiderer (1986)): *The optimal profits for a direct seller of information are given by*

$$\frac{\rho}{2}\log\left(1 + \frac{g\sigma_Z^2}{\rho(1 + \sigma_\theta^2 + g^2\sigma_Z^2)}\right), \tag{3.1}$$

where

$$g = \max\left(\frac{\sigma_\theta^2}{\rho}, \frac{\sqrt{1 + \sigma_\theta^2}}{\sigma_Z}\right). \tag{3.2}$$

If $g = \sqrt{1 + \sigma_\theta^2}/\sigma_Z$, then the seller adds (personalized) noise to his information before selling it to all traders. Otherwise the seller sells his information $\tilde{F} + \tilde{\theta}$ to all traders.

4. Indirect Sale of Information

The possible addition of noise in the direct sale of information is due to the seller's desire to restrict the usage of his information. If the seller could observe the response of each trader to the information, he might wish to charge each buyer as a function of his response. Since it is not realistic to assume that each buyer's trading position can be monitored, we now assume the seller sells his information indirectly through a managed fund whose investment positions are a function of the seller's information.

In period zero the information owner, who will be called the fund manager in this case, determines the fund's investment strategy and a price schedule for shares in the fund. Given this price schedule, each trader chooses a nonnegative number of shares of the fund. In addition, traders can trade in the risky asset and the riskless asset on their own account, and these investment decisions can be made contingent on the asset equilibrium price. Each trader chooses the number of shares of the fund and determines a price-contingent demand function for the risky asset to maximize his expected utility. This is done using the correct joint distribution of all random variables, including the asset price. At the beginning of the next period the fund manager observes his signal and establishes the portfolio position for the fund, and trading takes place in the financial market. Payoffs are realized in the final period.

In general, the position of the fund in the risky asset may be any function of the manager's signal $\tilde{F} + \tilde{\theta}$, the price $\tilde{P}$, and possibly some noise. (As we will argue later, however, it can be taken without loss of generality to be a function of the signal only.) We will restrict attention to trading rules which are linear functions of $\tilde{F} + \tilde{\theta}$, since with nonlinear rules the asset price is no longer normally distributed and the model becomes intractable. The fund manager's objective is to maximize his profits from the sale of shares in the fund given the demand function for shares, as elaborated later.

Clearly, the fund is a "large" trader in the sense that its total holding of the risky asset affects the asset's price. However, since traders can invest on their own account using the asset price and they have rational expectations, the fund manager cannot benefit by attempting to affect the price realization—traders will simply undo on their own account any investment of the fund that is measurable with respect to the asset price.[5] To see this, note that for each share of the fund a trader purchases, the fund will take a position in the

[5]This observation is similar to the notion that a cartel has no market power if cartel members are free to trade whatever quantities they want to trade on their own account.

risky asset that can be represented by $c(\tilde{F} + \tilde{\theta}) + H(\tilde{P})$ where c is a positive constant and $H(\cdot)$ is some function. On his own account a trader can take a position represented by $G(\tilde{P})$ where $G(\cdot)$ is again some function. Since the trader knows the investment policy of the fund given by c and $H(\cdot)$, he will choose $G(\cdot)$ so that his total position in the risky asset, given by $x(c(\tilde{F} + \tilde{\theta}) + H(\tilde{P})) + G(p)$, is optimal, where x is the number of shares of the fund purchased. Clearly $G(\cdot)$ will be chosen so that $xH(\tilde{P}) + G(\tilde{P})$ is the optimal response to $\tilde{P}$ given that $xc(\tilde{F} + \tilde{\theta})$ shares of the risky asset are purchased in response to the information signal $\tilde{F} + \tilde{\theta}$. The fund manager cannot affect the demand for the risky asset by varying $H(\cdot)$ since $xH(\tilde{P}) + G(\tilde{P})$ is independent of $H(\cdot)$.

The above argument uses the assumption that the fund manager does not trade on his own account and does not retain any shares of the fund. This assumption distinguishes the information seller in our model from a large strategic trader as in Grinblatt and Ross (1985) or Kyle (1989), for example. The seller's profits arise from the value of his information to traders with rational expectations who can trade on their own account based on the price. By contrast, the profits of a large informed trader arise from trading on his own account against liquidity or uninformed traders. The objective functions are quite different.[6]

Although we allow the fund manager to add noise to his information before creating the fund's position, we will show later that this is never desirable. Thus, without further loss of generality we assume that on behalf of a trader who has bought x shares in the fund, the manager purchases $x(\tilde{F} + \tilde{\theta})$ shares of the risky asset. This position is financed by borrowing $x(\tilde{F} + \tilde{\theta})\tilde{P}$ of the riskless asset. In period two, when the risky asset pays off, each trader's account in the fund is credited by the payoff of the risky asset position minus what is needed to pay back the loan used to finance the initial investment. Thus, if a trader buys x shares, his payoff from the fund in the final period is $x(\tilde{F} + \tilde{\theta})(\tilde{F} - \tilde{P})$.[7] In addition, each trader receives the payoff from investments undertaken on his own account.

As noted in the introduction, our analysis ignores possible incentive problems between the fund manager and the traders. In the context of our model, however, the incentive problems are not as severe as one might expect. First, the information seller has no financial stakes in the fund. Thus, assuming that he actually has information with the assumed statistical properties, the fund manager has no incentive not to follow the assumed trading strategy. Also, our analysis may be consistent with the existence of certain contracts designed to induce the fund manager to take the appropriate position. For example, if the manager has perfect information, the following approach can be taken. The fees the manager collects in period zero are put into escrow. In period one the investor in the fund observes $\tilde{P}$ and in period two he observes $\tilde{F}$ and the value of his holdings in the fund. The fees placed in escrow are paid to the fund manager if and only if the payoff from the fund divided by $x(\tilde{F} - \tilde{P})$ is equal to $\tilde{F}$. Otherwise the fees are refunded to the investor. A similar scheme can be used in the case of an imperfectly informed manager if the realization of the manager's signal can be observed in period two.[8]

[6]The sale of information in a market with strategic traders, who can only submit market orders is discussed in Admati and Pfleiderer (1988). In that model traders never wish to trade on their own account and, as a result, the fund does behave as if it is one large strategic trader.

[7]It may be more realistic to assume that the fund uses money invested up front by its customers rather than borrow in order to make its investment. This will not change our analysis.

[8]Without ex post observability of the manager's signal, first best solutions are not generally available. However, contracts that lead the manager to reveal truthfully the quality of his information and to take the appropriate position may still exist. (See, for example, Allen (1986) and Bhattacharya and Pfleiderer (1985).) It is not clear how the incorporation of these contracts would affect our analysis.

Turning to the traders' choice problem, suppose there exist constants a and b such that the asset equilibrium price is given by

(4.1) $$\widetilde{P} = a(\widetilde{F} + \widetilde{\theta}) - b\widetilde{Z}\,.$$

(This assumption will be verified in equilibrium.) Then the price reveals a noisy version of $\widetilde{F} + \widetilde{\theta}$, which traders can use to determine their demand for the risky asset on their own account. The informativeness of the price is an increasing function of a/b. The following result establishes that when the price is given by (4.1), each trader's investment on his own account is linear in the price. Note that this linearity does not follow from known results on optimal demand functions with normal payoffs and exponential utility functions, since with nonzero investment in the fund the second period wealth of the trader is not normally distributed conditional on prices.

Proposition 4.1 *Suppose the asset's price is given by $\widetilde{P} = a(\widetilde{F} + \widetilde{\theta}) - b\widetilde{Z}$ for some constants a and b. Consider a trader who holds x shares of the fund. There exists a constant $k(x) > 0$ such that the optimal number of shares for the trader to buy on his own account is $-k(x)\widetilde{P}$.*

It follows that if the total demand of each trader for the risky asset is $x(\widetilde{F} + \widetilde{\theta}) - k\widetilde{P}$, where x is the number of shares in the fund and $-k\widetilde{P}$ is the trading of the agent on his own account, then the market clearing price $\widetilde{P}$ satisfies

(4.2) $$x(\widetilde{F} + \widetilde{\theta}) - k\widetilde{P} = \widetilde{Z}\,.$$

Thus, under the conditions mentioned above the coefficients a and b in equation (4.1) are given by $a = x/k$ and $b = 1/k$. Since $a/b = x$ in equilibrium, the informativeness of the price is increasing in x. This is intuitive—the asset price is more informative when traders hold more shares of the fund. This result is important when we analyze the demand for shares in the fund and the manager's problem in the rest of the paper.

5. Linear Pricing of Shares

In this section we analyze the information acquisition stage under the assumption that the pricing of shares in the fund is linear. That is, if a trader buys x shares in the fund, he pays δx for some $\delta > 0$ chosen by the seller in the initial stage of the model. Linear pricing seems to be the most commonly observed way in which mutual funds are priced. Some reasons for it may be that if pricing is linear then there are no incentives for traders to form syndicates in order to exploit any nonlinearities in the pricing function.[9] Also, in a richer model there may be a secondary market in shares of the fund, and this may restrict the pricing schemes available to the fund manager. The analysis of linear pricing is also useful for the discussion of general pricing schemes later.

The following proposition derives the individual inverse demand function for shares in the fund and shows how it depends on the price coefficients.

Proposition 5.1 *Consider an individual trader who believes that the asset equilibrium price is $\widetilde{P} = a(\widetilde{F} + \widetilde{\theta}) - b\widetilde{Z}$ for some constants a and b. The trader's inverse demand function for the fund, i.e., the value of an additional share when the trader already has x shares of the fund, is given by*

[9] The incentives to share fixed costs may exist in the direct sale as well, but if information is short lived, it may be difficult to share it.

$$d(x; a/b) = \frac{\rho(\rho - \sigma_\theta^2 x)}{\rho(\rho + 2x) - \sigma_\theta^2 x^2 + \rho^2 \left(\frac{a}{b}\right)^2 \left(\frac{1 + \sigma_\theta^2}{\sigma_Z^2}\right)}. \tag{5.1}$$

Proof Suppose the trader has initial wealth W_0.[10] If he purchases x shares in the managed fund at a price d per share and $-k\widetilde{P}$ shares of the risky asset on his own account, his wealth in period two is

$$\widetilde{W}_2 = W_0 + (x(\widetilde{F} + \widetilde{\theta}) - k\widetilde{P})(\widetilde{F} - \widetilde{P}) - xd. \tag{5.2}$$

Define $\widetilde{u}$ to be the random vector $(\widetilde{F}, \widetilde{F} + \widetilde{\theta}, \widetilde{P})$, and let S be its variance-covariance matrix. Also define

$$A \equiv \begin{pmatrix} 0 & x & -k \\ x & 0 & -x \\ -k & -x & 2k \end{pmatrix}. \tag{5.3}$$

Then the trader's wealth in period two can be written as $\widetilde{W}_2 = W_0 + \frac{1}{2}\widetilde{u}'A\widetilde{u} - xd$.[11] If x and k are such that the matrix $\rho^{-1}A + S^{-1}$ is positive definite, then ex ante expected utility is[12]

$$\begin{aligned} \mathscr{E}(-\exp(-\rho^{-1}\widetilde{W}_2)) &= \frac{-\exp(\rho^{-1}(-W_0 + xd))}{(2\pi)^{3/2}|S|^{1/2}} \\ &\quad \times \int_{\mathfrak{R}^3} \exp\left[-\frac{1}{2\rho}\widetilde{u}'A\widetilde{u} - \frac{1}{2}\widetilde{u}'S^{-1}\widetilde{u}\right] d\widetilde{u} \\ &= \frac{-\exp(\rho^{-1}(-W_0 + xd))}{|S|^{1/2}|\rho^{-1}A + S^{-1}|^{1/2}} \\ &= \frac{-\exp(\rho^{-1}(-W_0 + xd))}{|\rho^{-1}SA + I|^{1/2}}. \end{aligned} \tag{5.4}$$

Substituting the optimal value of $k(x)$ from the proof of Proposition 4.1 into the first order condition for optimization of (5.4) over x gives the result. *Q.E.D.*

Note that for a finite σ_Z^2 the demand for the fund depends on the ratio a/b (see the last term in the denominator of (5.1)). This is because the price reveals some of the information on which the fund's position is based. As the supply variance σ_Z^2 grows, the price provides less payoff-relevant information. In the limit as $\sigma_Z^2 \to \infty$ the demand for the fund becomes independent of the price coefficients. Also, as is intuitive, the more informative is the asset price, i.e., the higher is a/b, the lower is the price a trader is willing to pay for an additional share in the fund.

[10] We assume for analytical simplicity that traders have endowments in the riskless asset only. Relaxing this assumption will not change our results, due to the assumed constant absolute risk aversion.

[11] If $\sigma_\theta^2 = 0$, then the same expressions hold with $\widetilde{u} = (\widetilde{F}, \widetilde{P})$ and with the second row and second column of A and S deleted.

[12] Values of x and k for which the expected utility integral diverges to negative infinity need not be considered, since the trader will always prefer to set x and k at values for which the integral converges rather than set them at values for which it does not.

The inverse demand function (5.1) is defined for an individual trader who takes the equilibrium price function as given. As already noted, market clearing (equation (4.2)) implies that if all traders take a position x in the fund, then in equilibrium $a/b \equiv x$. The aggregate demand relation $\delta(x)$ that the manager faces is therefore given by $\delta(x) = d(x; x)$. The manager's profits as a function of x are

$$x\delta(x) = \frac{\rho x \sigma_Z^2(\rho - \sigma_\theta^2 x)}{x^2(\rho^2(1 + \sigma_\theta^2) - \sigma_\theta^2\sigma_Z^2) + \rho\sigma_Z^2(\rho + 2x)}. \tag{5.6}$$

The following result is straightforward, and its proof is omitted.

Proposition 5.2 *Under linear pricing the fund manager's profits are maximized when each trader holds x^* shares in the fund, where*

$$x^* = \frac{\rho\left(\sigma_Z\sqrt{(1 + \sigma_\theta^2)(\rho^2 + \sigma_\theta^2\sigma_Z^2)} - \sigma_\theta^2\sigma_Z^2\right)}{\rho^2(1 + \sigma_\theta^2) + \sigma_\theta^2\sigma_Z^2}. \tag{5.7}$$

This is obtained by announcing the per share price $\delta^* = \delta(x^*) = d(x^*; x^*)$. In particular, if $\sigma_\theta^2 = 0$, then each trader holds $x^* = \sigma_Z$ shares of the fund.

From the above we can show the following corollary.

Corollary 5.1 *The fund manager's profits are* (i) *increasing in the supply noise, σ_z^2,* (ii) *increasing in the risk tolerance of traders, ρ, and* (iii) *decreasing in the variance of the error in the seller's signal, σ_θ^2.*

The proof is based on showing that these comparative statics results hold for the aggregate inverse demand at the optimum $\delta(x^*)$. Parts (i) and (ii) are also based on the fact that for any finite and positive σ_Z^2 and ρ, $x^* < \rho/\sigma_\theta^2$. Details are omitted.

An increase in σ_Z^2 means that prices are less informative and leads to an increase in the manager's profits since traders are willing to pay more for information when less of it is revealed through the price. Similarly, an increase in risk tolerance ρ increases the number of shares in the fund a trader is willing to purchase at any price δ. The aggregate inverse demand function $\delta(x)$ is therefore an increasing function of ρ, so profits are increasing in ρ.

So far we have not allowed the fund manager to add noise to his information, i.e., to base the fund's position on a noisier signal than that which he observes. (Recall that in many situations a direct seller of information chooses to add noise to his signal before selling it.) From Corollary 5.1, the manager's profits are decreasing in σ_θ^2, his error variance. It follows that the manager does not want to add photocopied noise to his signal, as adding such noise would amount to a voluntary increase in σ_θ^2. The next result shows that the manager never wishes to add personalized noise either.

Proposition 5.3 *If the manager buys $\tilde{F} + \tilde{\theta} + \tilde{\omega}_\nu$ shares of the risky asset for each share in the fund that trader ν purchases, where the $\tilde{\omega}_\nu$ are mutually independent and independent of $\tilde{F} + \tilde{\theta}$, then profits are maximized when $\sigma_{\omega_\nu}^2 = 0$ for all $\nu \in [0,1]$.*

Proof Assume that each trader purchases x shares in the fund and that the position taken in the fund for trader ν is $x(\tilde{F} + \tilde{\theta} + \tilde{\omega}_\nu)$. It can be shown that the optimal position in the risky asset on a trader's own account is independent of $\sigma_{\omega_\nu}^2$. This, together with the fact that $\tilde{\omega}_\nu$, $\nu \in [0, 1]$ are mutually independent implies that the joint distribution of $\tilde{F}$, $\tilde{\theta}$, and $\tilde{P}$ does not depend upon $\sigma^2_{\omega_\nu}$, $\nu \in [0, 1]$. It follows that the second period wealth of trader ν when $\sigma^2_{\omega_\nu} > 0$ is distributed as the second period wealth when $\sigma^2_{\omega_\nu} = 0$ plus the added noise $x\tilde{\omega}_\nu(\tilde{F} - \tilde{P})$. Thus for each x, second period wealth when $\sigma^2_{\omega_\nu} = 0$ stochastically dominates the wealth if $\sigma^2_{\omega_\nu} > 0$. Since all traders are risk averse, for any x each is willing to pay a higher per share price when $\sigma^2_{\omega_\nu} = 0$ than when $\sigma^2_{\omega_\nu} > 0$. Profits are therefore highest when $\sigma^2_{\omega_\nu} = 0$. *Q.E.D.*

The intuition behind this result is that the manager can control the leakage of his information through the asset price by adjusting the per share price. Since the fund charges for each unit of "use" of the information, there is no need to dilute its value by adding noise. By contrast, the direct seller of information cannot control traders' use of the information through pricing. The only way for him to control the leakage of information when the effect of externality is intense is to sell noisier versions of his information.

6. Comparison with Direct Sale

In this section we compare the profits obtained by direct sale and indirect sale with linear pricing. To develop some intuition, we plot three inverse demand curves, two of which we have already introduced. For simplicity we assume that the information seller has perfect information ($\sigma^2_\theta = 0$). Recall that the individual inverse demand function $d(x; \hat{x})$ gives the price a trader would pay for an additional share in the managed fund when the trader has x shares and all others have $\hat{x}$ shares. The aggregate inverse demand is $\delta(x) = d(x; x)$. At the optimal solution for the manager, the relevant individual inverse demand function is $d(x; x^*)$, which, applying Proposition 5.2 with $\sigma^2_\theta = 0$, equals $d(x; \sigma_z) = \rho/(2(\rho + x))$.

The third inverse demand function, which is relevant for the direct sale of information, is essentially the individual inverse demand function for shares in a hypothetical fund whose positions are based on the signals sold in a direct sale. Suppose that if trader ν holds x shares of this fund, then the fund buys $x(\tilde{F} + \tilde{\varepsilon}_\nu)$ shares of the risky asset, where $\{\tilde{\varepsilon}_\nu\}$ are independent and identically distributed. We define $D(x; \sigma^2_\varepsilon, \hat{x})$ to be the amount trader ν would be willing to pay for a unit increase in x, assuming that all other traders hold $\hat{x}$ shares in this fund and the variance of $\tilde{\omega}_\nu$ is σ^2_ε. From Admati and Pfleiderer (1986), the optimal strategy for a direct seller when $\sigma^2_\theta = 0$ is to set $\sigma^2_\varepsilon = \rho/\sigma_Z$. In this case the optimal coefficient of the signal in trader υ's demand is $\hat{x} = \sigma_Z$.[13] Thus, the appropriate inverse demand function is given by

$$D(x; \rho/\sigma_Z, \sigma_Z) = \frac{\rho\sigma_Z(\sigma_Z - x)}{2\rho\sigma^2_Z + 2\sigma^2_Z x - \sigma_Z x^2}. \tag{6.1}$$

Figure 1 shows the three functions discussed above assuming $\rho = \sigma_Z = 1$. With linear pricing, the fund manager charges a per share price of $\delta = .25$ and receives profit equal to the area of $\mathscr{B}$ and $\mathscr{C}$. The lost consumer surplus is the combined area of $\mathscr{A}$ and $\mathscr{D}$. Since the direct seller adds noise to his signal, $D(x; \rho/\sigma_Z, \sigma_Z)$ is more steeply sloped than $d(x; \sigma_Z)$, and it crosses the x axis at σ_Z.[14] The direct seller extracts part of the surplus that the fund

[13] Note that the same number of shares are sold by the fund manager under linear pricing—as already noted, when $\sigma^2_\theta = 0$, $x^* = \sigma_Z$. This is special to the case $\sigma^2_\theta = 0$. See Propositions 6.4 and 6.5.

[14] Note that $d(x; \sigma_Z)$ does not intersect the x axis; if the per share price of the fund were zero, demand would be unbounded. This is only true because the seller has perfect information. For $\sigma^2_\theta > 0$ there is an x at which $d(x; \hat{x})$ is zero. Note also that $D(0; \rho/\sigma_Z, \sigma_Z) = d(0; \sigma_Z)$. At $x = 0$ the incremental value of a "share" is the same whether noise is present or not. This is because the effect of the noise added by the direct seller is second order relative to the mean effect.

FIGURE 1 | The three inverse demand functions, $\delta(x)$, $d(x;\,\sigma_Z)$, and $D(x;\,\rho/\sigma_Z,\,\sigma_Z)$, are graphed against x for $\rho = 1$ and $\sigma_Z = 1$. The total area of regions $\mathscr{B}$ and $\mathscr{C}$ is equal to the profit under indirect sale with linear pricing, while the total area of regions $\mathscr{A}$ and $\mathscr{B}$ is equal to the profit under direct sale.

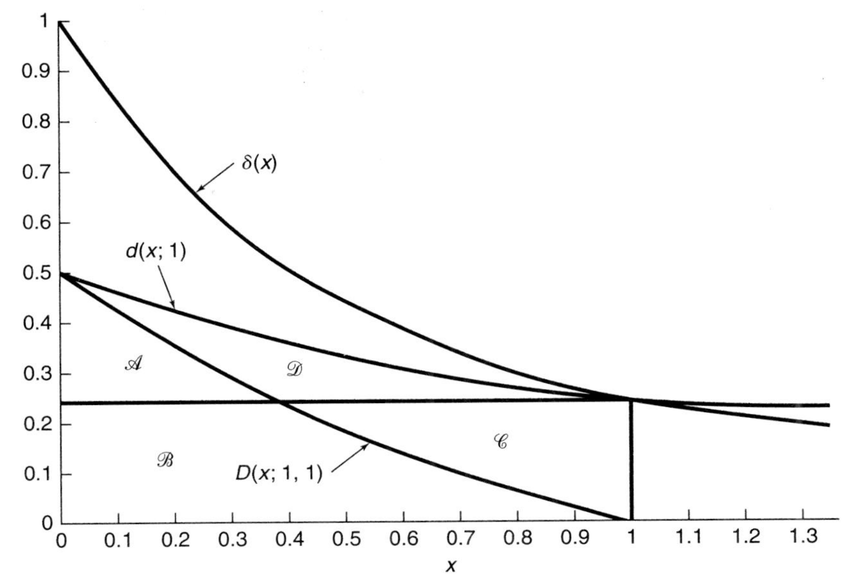

manager forgoes, namely the region $\mathscr{A}$, but because of the noise he adds, he gives up areas $\mathscr{C}$ and $\mathscr{D}$. Direct sale of information dominates indirect sale with linear pricing if and only if the area of $\mathscr{A}$ exceeds that of $\mathscr{C}$, which is not the case in Figure 1. Thus, for these parameters the fund manager with linear pricing earns higher profits than the direct seller.

Suppose that traders are more risk tolerant. For example, in Figure 2 we show the three demand curves for $\rho = 5$ and $\sigma_Z = 1$. Now $d(x;\,\sigma_Z)$ is less steeply sloped. As x increases, the overall risk of a trader's portfolio is increased, but for a very risk tolerant trader this has a small effect on the ex ante utility. Since the expected payoff of a share in the fund is independent of the level of x, the demand curve is virtually flat.[15] Thus, the fund manager gives up very little surplus when linear pricing is used. In the limit as $\rho \to \infty$, the fund manager essentially extracts all the surplus using only linear pricing (areas $\mathscr{A}$ and $\mathscr{D}$ vanish). The direct seller, at the same time, must add more and more noise to control traders' responses as they become more risk tolerant. In the limit the direct seller earns only half the profits of the fund manager (area $\mathscr{B}$ becomes equal to area $\mathscr{C}$), and $D(x;\,\rho/\sigma_Z,\,\sigma_Z)$ is linearly decreasing in x.

We now formalize the above discussion. Denote the optimal profits of the fund manager who uses linear pricing (namely $x^*\,\delta(x^*)$) by π^* and the optimal profits of the direct seller by π^d. Let $m = \rho/\sigma_Z$ measure the degree of externality in the valuation of information, where a larger m corresponds to a more intense externality. The following result concerns the case where m goes to infinity. It verifies the intuition obtained from Figure 2.

[15]Note, however, that even for large values of ρ the aggregate demand curve $\delta(x)$ is downward sloping. This is because traders' aggregate response affects the terms of trade and therefore the mean return on any particular portfolio.

FIGURE 2 | The three inverse demand functions, $\delta(x)$, $d(x; \sigma_Z)$, and $D(x; \rho/\sigma_Z, \sigma_Z)$, are now graphed against x for $\rho = 5$ and $\sigma_Z = 1$. With the higher value of ρ, $d(x, 1)$ is more elastic and less surplus is given up under indirect selling with linear pricing.

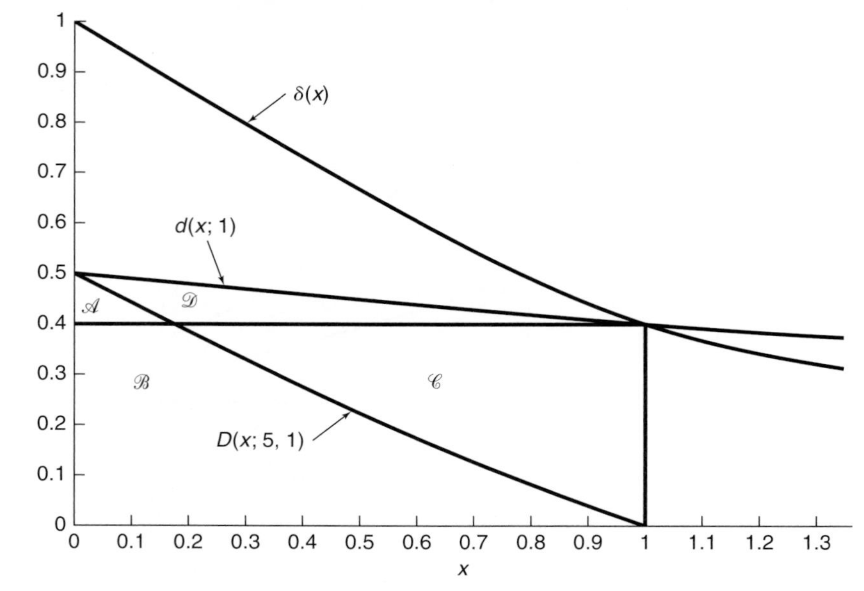

Proposition 6.1 $\lim_{m\to\infty} \pi^*/\pi^d = 2$.

When the externality is intense, restricting traders' use of the information is very important. Since the price of the fund's shares is a more effective tool for doing so than is the addition of noise, profits are higher for indirect sale. The intuition for the factor of 2 was explained graphically above. Note that as $\sigma_Z \to 0$ both π^d and π^* converge to zero, while when $\rho \to \infty$ both converge to a positive limit.

In the other extreme case, in which the $m = \rho/\sigma_Z$ vanishes, there is less need to control traders' use of the information. (Indeed, an imperfectly informed direct seller of information does not add noise to his information when ρ/σ_Z is small enough.) Since the fund manager is unable to extract surplus with linear pricing, it is not surprising that profits are higher with direct sale.

Proposition 6.2 $\lim_{m\to 0} \pi^*/\pi^d < 1$.

To summarize, Figure 3 illustrates the comparison between direct sale and indirect sale with linear prices in terms of the parameters σ_θ^2 and σ_Z^2. (We normalize ρ to be equal to 1.) For parameters in region $\mathscr{A}$, where σ_Z^2 and σ_θ^2 are relatively small, the fund manager obtains higher profits, while for parameters in regions $\mathscr{B}$ and $\mathscr{C}$ the direct seller obtains higher profits. In regions $\mathscr{A}$ and $\mathscr{B}$ the direct seller adds noise. Note that the addition of noise in a direct sale does not imply that indirect sale with linear pricing is more profitable—for parameters in region $\mathscr{B}$ the direct seller adds noise and still obtains higher profits than the fund manager.[16]

[16] The reader familiar with Admati and Pfleiderer (1986) may wonder what happens if the direct seller is restricted to selling one photocopied signal to all buyers. It turns out that in this case all possible relations between the strategies and profits of the two selling methods are possible. That is, it is possible that the direct seller adds photocopied noise and/or restricts the fraction of informed traders while obtaining higher/lower profits than the fund manager. Again, the fund manager obtains higher profits for parameters in a region similar to $\mathscr{A}$ in Figure 3.

FIGURE 3 | The parameter space is divided into three regions. For parameters in region $\mathscr{A}$, indirect sale with linear pricing dominates direct sale ($\pi^* > \pi^d$) and the direct seller adds noise ($\sigma_\varepsilon^2 > 0$). In region $\mathscr{B}$ direct sale is superior ($\pi^* < \pi^d$), but noise is still added to the direct seller's signal before it is sold. Finally, in region $\mathscr{C}$ direct sale is still superior but no noise is added.

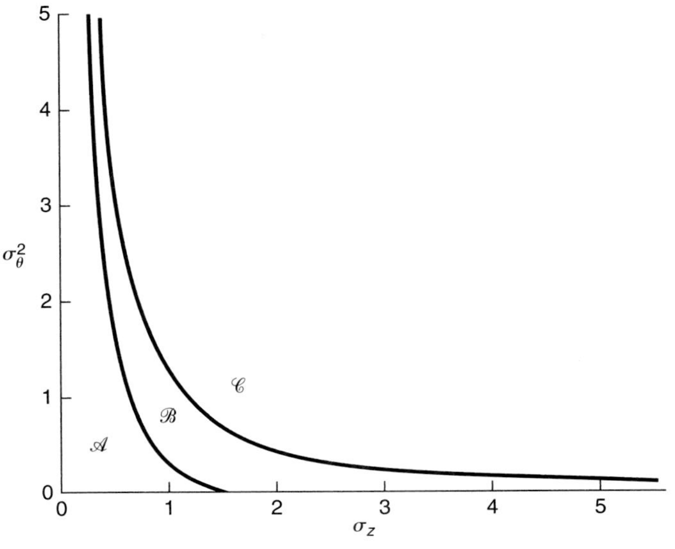

It is not clear that direct and indirect sale should be viewed as separate alternatives. The information owner might be able to set up a mutual fund and also sell information directly.[17] It turns out, however, that, at least for the case of perfect information, this is not desirable for the seller, so that allowing the information owner to sell information both directly and indirectly will not change our analysis. We assume that the seller does not bundle the direct and indirect sale, i.e., that traders can determine how many shares of the fund to buy as well as whether to purchase information directly. Of course, the directly sold information must be noisier than the indirect information for a trader to purchase both.[18]

Proposition 6.3 *Assume that $\sigma_\theta^2 = 0$ and that the pricing of shares in the fund is linear. Then it is always preferable for the seller only to sell information indirectly rather than to offer both direct and indirect information. The overall optimal strategy is to sell information either exclusively directly or exclusively indirectly, depending on ρ/σ_Z as in Figure* 3.

To gain some intuition note that, taking the distribution of the price (i.e., other traders' actions) as given, the ex ante expected utility of a potential direct information buyer who does not buy the information is higher if information is available indirectly, than if it is not. If a fund exists, then a trader who does not buy information directly can buy more shares in the fund (as well as adjust the investment on his own account). If a fund is not available,

[17]We are grateful to an anonymous referee for suggesting this to us.

[18]We have been unable to extend this result to the case where the seller's information is imperfect due to the analytical complexity of the problem. It is possible that the result is special to the case of perfect information. However, since only information that is noisier than the seller's signal can be sold directly if shares in the fund are offered, it seems that it would be even less desirable in this case to sell information directly in addition to selling indirectly.

then he can only adjust the investment on his own account. Clearly, the availability of the fund increases his ex ante expected utility relative to the situation in which no fund is available, keeping other traders' actions constant. The remaining surplus to be extracted is therefore smaller, particularly since noise must be added in the direct sale. In other words, the surplus extraction advantage of direct sale relative to indirect sale with linear pricing is weaker when both direct and indirect information is available. Note, however, that in a model with heterogeneous traders it is possible that a seller may wish to offer both direct and indirect information as a means of screening different types of traders.

7. General Pricing Schemes

We now drop the restriction that the pricing of the fund's shares be linear. The discussion of general pricing schemes for the fund unifies the analysis so far, since it also covers direct sale as a special case—direct sale corresponds to the sale of shares in a fund (with noise possibly added) with a fixed fee equal to the value of the information in the fund's position and a zero per share price. In fact, it is easy to show, using the same arguments that prove Corollary 5.1 and Proposition 5.2, that the fund manager never wishes to add noise if he can charge a per share price. This immediately implies that with general pricing the fund manager's profits are strictly higher than those of the direct seller when the direct seller adds noise.

Turning to the optimal pricing strategy note that with general pricing the fund manager may be able to sell different numbers of shares to different traders. (For example, he can restrict the number of traders who buy shares in the fund by adjusting the fixed fee.) The next result shows that this is never desirable, so that we can restrict attention to symmetric allocations of shares.

Proposition 7.1 *Suppose the manager can sell x^ν shares in the fund to each trader ν and can extract the full value of these shares. Then the optimal profits are obtained if $x^\nu = x^{\nu'}$ for all ν and ν'.*

Proof Suppose the equilibrium price is given by $\tilde{P} = a(\tilde{F} + \tilde{\theta}) - b\tilde{Z}$, and that the seller charges $f(x)$ for x shares in the fund. As shown in the proof of Proposition 5.1, the ex ante expected utility of the trader who purchases x shares in the fund is

$$\text{(7.1)} \qquad \frac{-\exp(\rho^{-1}(-W_0 + f(x)))}{|\rho^{-1}SA + I|^{1/2}},$$

where S and A are defined in the proof of Proposition 5.1.

A trader who does not purchase shares in the fund has expected utility

$$\text{(7.2)} \qquad \frac{-\exp(-\rho^{-1}W_0)}{|\rho^{-1}S_0A_0 + I|^{1/2}},$$

where S_0 and A_0 are obtained from S and A by deleting the second row and column.

The consumer surplus, which is equal to $f(x)$ if profits are maximized, is therefore given by

$$\text{(7.3)} \qquad \frac{\rho}{2}\log\left(\frac{|\rho^{-1}SA + I|}{|\rho^{-1}S_0A_0 + I|}\right) = \frac{\rho}{2}\log\left(1 + \frac{x\sigma_Z^2(2\rho - x\sigma_\theta^2)}{\rho^2((a/b)^2(1 + \sigma_\theta^2) + \sigma_Z^2)}\right).$$

It is straightforward but tedious to show that the consumer surplus is a concave function of x. This implies that if the allocation of shares of the fund is asymmetric in that one group of traders hold a different number of shares than another group, then the fund manager can obtain strictly higher profits in a symmetric allocation of shares. *Q.E.D.*

The following result shows that in fact it is sufficient to consider two part pricing schemes. This is hardly surprising in the context of a model with identical traders.

Proposition 7.2 *For any pricing scheme f(x) there exists a two part pricing scheme* $\delta x + \gamma$ *which yields the same profits to the fund manager.*

Proof Suppose that given the pricing scheme $f(x)$ each trader chooses to hold $\bar{x}$ shares of the fund. Since the aggregate demand function $\delta(\cdot)$ is strictly decreasing over the range for which the expected utility integral converges, the seller can implement any feasible x by an appropriate choice of per share price $\delta(x)$. Let $\delta = \delta(\bar{x})$ and let $\gamma = f(\bar{x}) - \delta\bar{x}$. The pricing scheme $\delta x + \gamma$ is feasible and yields the same profits for the fund manager as $f(x)$. *Q.E.D.*

We are now ready to find the optimal two part pricing strategy.

Proposition 7.3 *If pricing is not restricted, the fund manager's profits are maximized by setting the per share price* $\delta^{**} = \delta(x^{**})$, *where*

$$x^{**} = \frac{\sigma_Z\sqrt{\sigma_\theta^4\sigma_Z^2 + 4\rho^2(1+\sigma_\theta^2)} - \sigma_\theta^2\sigma_Z^2}{2\rho(1+\sigma_\theta^2)}, \tag{7.4}$$

and setting the fixed fee as

$$\gamma^{**} = \frac{\rho}{2}\log\left(\frac{(x^{**})^2(\rho^2(1+\sigma_\theta^2) - \sigma_\theta^2\sigma_Z^2) + \rho\sigma_Z^2(\rho + 2x^{**})}{\rho^2((x^{**})^2(1+\sigma_\theta^2) + \sigma_Z^2)}\right) - \delta^{**}x^{**}. \tag{7.5}$$

Proof From (7.3) it follows that the manager's problem is equivalent to choosing x to maximize

$$1 + \frac{x\sigma_Z^2(2\rho - x\sigma_\theta^2)}{\rho^2(x^2(1+\sigma_\theta^2) + \sigma_Z^2)}. \tag{7.6}$$

It is straightforward to show that the optimal value of x is given by (7.4). To induce the choice of x^{**} shares the manager should set δ^{**} as the per share price. The relevant fixed fee is constructed to extract all consumer surplus. *Q.E.D.*

As can be expected, the extent to which profits under two part pricing are higher than those with linear pricing or with direct sale depends on the intensity of the externality. Note that, going back to Figures 1 and 2, with two part pricing the seller obtains profits equal to the area under $d(x;\sigma_Z)$, or the combined area of $\mathcal{A}$, $\mathcal{B}$, $\mathcal{C}$ and $\mathcal{D}$. As ρ grows, i.e., the externality becomes intense, the advantage of the two part scheme over the linear scheme vanishes, as the demand function becomes flat—it is possible to extract essentially all the consumer surplus with the per share fee alone. Thus, both the linear and the two part selling schemes earn in the limit twice as much as the direct seller. On the other hand, when the externality is not strong, the two part scheme coincides with the direct sale in the sense that most profits are obtained from the fixed fee, and the per share price vanishes.

Formally, let π^{**} be the optimal profits under two part pricing, and recall that π^* are the optimal profits under proportional pricing and π^d are the optimal profits from direct sale. Again, let $m = \rho/\sigma_Z$ measure the externality.

Proposition 7.4 (i) $\lim_{m\to\infty}\pi^{**}/\pi^* = 1$, *and* (ii) $\lim_{m\to 0}\pi^{**}/\pi^d = 1$.

To conclude this section, we compare the number of shares sold under the linear and two part selling schemes, and then compare the informativeness of the equilibrium price under the three selling methods. It is easy to see that absent the externality in the valuation of information, the manager would sell more shares under the two part scheme than under linear pricing. (This is a general property of the solutions to the monopoly problem with linear and two part pricing schemes.) We now show that a similar result also holds for finite values of σ_Z^2. Thus, when profits are only derived from linear pricing, the manager sets the per share price higher than he does in a two part scheme.

Proposition 7.5 *If $\sigma_\theta^2 > 0$, then $x^{**} > x^*$; otherwise $x^{**} = x^*$.*

An immediate implication of the above proposition is that the asset price is more informative with two part pricing than with linear pricing. Comparing this with the case of direct sale, the following result shows that the price is generally more informative with direct sale than with indirect sale of information. This is consistent with the intuition that controlling the usage of information is more costly when information is sold directly than when it is sold indirectly, so that less control is exercised by the seller in equilibrium with direct sales, and more is revealed through the price.[19]

Proposition 7.6 *If $\sigma_\theta^2 > 0$, then the asset price provides more precise information about $\tilde{F}$ when information is sold directly than when it is sold indirectly. If $\sigma_\theta^2 = 0$, these precisions are equal.*

8. Heterogeneous Traders and the Bundling Problem

We have shown that if the two part pricing scheme is feasible, then a monopolist will never sell information directly. This and other results of the previous sections depend on the assumption that traders are identical. Models with heterogeneous traders present a host of complex issues. For example, if perfect price discrimination is not possible, then the direct seller of information may choose to offer signals having different precisions, with different signals aimed for different traders. If these signals are personalized, however, some traders may wish to buy more than one signal and obtain a higher precision. It thus becomes important to specify whether the seller can control the number of signals each trader buys. Moreover, it may be desirable to offer information both directly and indirectly as a screening device. The seller's problem is clearly quite complex, as these issues are combined with the tradeoffs already discussed in the previous sections. A complete analysis of the case of heterogeneous traders is therefore beyond the scope of this paper. In this section we provide a brief discussion of how the results of the previous sections may change when traders have heterogeneous private information.

Suppose that traders are endowed with or otherwise acquire different pieces of information. Also suppose that for various reasons it is not possible for the information seller to offer as many products as there are types of traders. For simplicity, let us assume that the information seller can only offer one product, i.e., either one newsletter or one managed fund. An important difference between direct and indirect sale of information is that if the seller's information has many components (e.g., if it concerns more than one asset) then in a direct sale, where the buyers actually observe the information, the components of the information can be unbundled and used optimally with other information signals the trader may have. With indirect sale, however, the managed fund provides a particular usage of

[19] However, this result depends on the direct seller's ability to obtain the optimal profits of the personalized allocations. If the seller is restricted to selling photocopied information, for example, then for small σ_θ^2 the precision of prices is smaller than that obtained if information is sold using the two part scheme.

information which will typically not be optimal for all individual traders. This limits the value of the information that is sold indirectly.

Indeed, it is possible to create examples where the direct information seller obtains strictly higher profits than the fund manager even if the fund manager can use two part pricing. For example, suppose there are two risky assets with independent payoffs, and suppose half of the traders have information only about the first asset while the other half have information only about the second asset. The information seller has imperfect information about both assets. Clearly, if information is sold directly, then each trader will put different weights on the different components of the information. In an indirect sale traders with different private information are forced to give the same relative weights to the two components of the seller's signal, and this lowers the surplus for the fund manager.[20] The bundling problem is particularly severe if the seller's information and traders' private information are complements rather than substitutes (see Admati and Pfleiderer (1987)), since in this case traders benefit greatly from the ability to combine their private information with the seller's information.

9. Concluding Remarks

This paper analyzes a particular case of the general problem of how information is sold by a monopolist to agents who can use the information in a subsequent market. The focus of our analysis has been on the externality that occurs when the usage of information by one trader reduces its value to other traders. We have studied this problem in the context of a financial market, but information sales are clearly relevant in many other contexts. In order to provide additional insights into our results and relate our analysis to other models involving information sales, it is useful to cast the problem in more general terms.

In our setup the information seller is given three types of potential choice variables. They include (i) a fixed fee paid by all buyers of any information, (ii) a linear price for some unit measuring the use of the information, which we can term the "usage price," and (iii) a variable, which we will call "noise," that transforms the information that is sold (thereby affecting its usage). In what we have called *direct sale* the seller can add noise and determine a fixed fee for the information, but he cannot otherwise control the usage of the information. In what we called *indirect sale* the seller can add noise and can also determine a usage price in the form of the per share price of the fund. In addition, if two part pricing is allowed, the seller can also determine a fixed fee. (Of course, in other models it may be more natural to think of the "indirect" seller as actually giving the information to the buyers and charging for its use by royalties; see below.)

In general, if a fixed fee can be charged and agents are identical, the information seller attempts to maximize the surplus generated by his information, which he then extracts by the fee. Because of the externality in the use of information, this surplus, which is related

[20] Consider the following numerical example. There are two risky assets with payoffs $\tilde{F}_1$ and $\tilde{F}_2$, where $\text{Var}(\tilde{F}_1) = \text{Var}(\tilde{F}_2) = 1$. The assets have random supplies $\tilde{Z}_1$ and $\tilde{Z}_2$, with $\text{Var}(\tilde{Z}_1) = \text{Var}(\tilde{Z}_2) = 10$. Half of the traders observe the signal $\tilde{F}_1 + \tilde{\theta}_1 + \tilde{\varepsilon}_1$, before trading begins, and the other half of the traders observe $\tilde{F}_2 + \tilde{\theta}_2 + \tilde{\varepsilon}_2$. The information seller observes the vector of signals $\tilde{Y}_1^S = \tilde{F}_1 + \tilde{\theta}_1 + \tilde{\eta}_1$ and $\tilde{Y}_2^S = \tilde{F}_2 + \tilde{\theta}_2 + \tilde{\eta}_2$. Assume all of the errors in the information signals are independent of each other and of $\tilde{F}$. If information is sold indirectly, then, because of the symmetry, the fund manager will invest $\tilde{Y}_i^S$ in asset i, $i = 1, 2$. It can be shown that the fund manager always sets the fixed fee so that all traders buy shares in the fund. Moreover, all traders will choose to purchase the same number of shares in the fund. If $\text{Var}(\tilde{\theta}_i) = 10$, and $\text{Var}(\tilde{\varepsilon}_v) = \text{Var}(\tilde{\eta}_i) = 1$, then the fund manager, using a two part scheme, sells 0.08443 shares to each trader and his profits are 1.0921. The direct seller, selling the bundle $(\tilde{Y}_1^S, \tilde{Y}_2^S)$ to all traders, earns $1.0951 > 1.0921$. Of course, the direct seller may still do better by adding noise or restricting the number of buyers.

to the difference in expected utility (net of fees) between informed and uninformed agents, depends on the total usage of the information by agents. The seller would generally like to control this usage to maximize surplus. This might be done by adjusting the usage price and/or by adding noise, if these controls are available.

The property of our model which drives our results is that *it is valuable for the seller to restrict the usage of the information.* This suggests why the seller might want to add noise in a direct sale of information. However, adding noise is costly in the sense that the signal sold is less precise and therefore, other things equal, less valuable to an individual agent. As a result, restricting the use of the information by pricing usage directly (selling shares in the fund) is a more efficient means for controlling the usage of the information. This advantage of indirect sale is particularly important in situations where traders wish to use their information relatively aggressively (since they are risk tolerant) or when information gets readily reflected in the asset price (since there is little supply noise). In these situations surplus extraction, which can be accomplished by the fixed fee, is less important than controlling the usage of the information efficiently, since the total surplus is diminishing quickly by the excessive usage of the information. As a result, the seller's profits in the two part scheme are mostly derived from the linear pricing of shares, and these profits are strictly larger than those obtained in a direct sale even when no fixed fee for the fund can be charged. On the other hand, the fixed fee is an important source of the seller's profits in cases where the usage of the information has less effect on the aggregate surplus. In these cases direct sale performs better than indirect sale with linear pricing. In fact, if both fixed fee and usage price can be controlled, the usage price vanishes in the limit, and indirect sale with two part pricing coincides with direct sale.

It is interesting to compare our results to those of Kamien and Tauman (1986), who consider the sale of a cost-reducing innovation by a single patent holder to firms in an oligopolistic market. They show that in a linear Cournot model, fees yield higher profits for the seller than royalties. The distinction between indirect sale with linear pricing and direct sale of information in our model is clearly analogous to that between royalties and fees in the sale of technology. In our model, however, royalties may be preferred to fees. The key difference between the two models is that, in contrast to our model, in the linear Cournot model the seller of the technology wishes to *encourage* firms who bought the innovation to be aggressive in its use, as that would hurt uninformed firms and therefore increase the total surplus. In fact, it can be shown that if the seller in Kamien and Tauman's model is allowed to use a two part pricing scheme including both fees and royalties, then he would either set the royalty to zero or, if possible, would set it to be *negative*![21] It is therefore not surprising that using royalty is inferior to using fees in this environment—if the seller can only obtain profits through royalties he is forced in effect to move in the wrong direction in terms of inducing the optimal usage of the information, since he must restrict the usage of the innovation by making usage costly. Moreover, he cannot extract the full surplus generated by the innovation.

Another distinction between our model and that of Kamien and Tauman (1986) is that in their model there is no leakage of information—firms that do not purchase the innovation do not obtain a cost reduction when others purchase it. This partly explains why no analog of noise addition seems to be desirable in that model or in simple variations of it. We should

[21] While the possibility of two part pricing was not considered by Kamien and Tauman, it can be shown that the optimal two part scheme for the seller is such that it induces only one firm to buy the innovation and, by subsidizing its production through negative royalties (if the innovation is not already so called drastic), causing all other firms to stop producing. This gives the seller the monopoly profits, which are clearly highest, and obviates the need for controlling the usage of the information.

note, however, that the fact that a direct seller may wish to add noise to his information is neither necessary nor sufficient for our results. The desire to add noise is only an extreme manifestation of the desire of the information seller to restrict its use. Although adding noise as a means of restricting the use of information may be desirable in other contexts, in our model it seems to be particularly related to the fact that agents can free ride on the information of others by observing the asset price. For example, Admati and Pfleiderer (1988) analyze information sales in a model where traders can only submit market orders and therefore cannot use the price for investing on their own account. In that context it is shown that a direct seller of information never wishes to add noise to his information. In this and other senses, this model is similar to the linear Cournot model. However, in that model, as in the model of the current paper, the seller would like to restrict the usage of the information—if information is sold indirectly using a two part pricing, the per share price is strictly positive and the seller generally obtains strictly higher profits than he obtains with direct sale.[22]

An implicit assumption in our analysis has been that the fund manager can trade anonymously, i.e., that the fund's position is not observable to other traders. In the models we have considered, the fund's position is a one to one function of the information on which this position is taken. If traders could costlessly observe the fund's position, then selling information in this way would be impossible. This problem may not be so severe either if observing the fund's position is costly, or if only extremely large positions are observablel.[23]

A number of important issues are still to be explored. First, as noted in Section 8, the case of heterogeneous traders is yet to be fully analyzed. Second, we have only analyzed the case of a single seller. With imperfect competition among sellers of information (whose information is different, for example) indirect sale may emerge as optimal, since surplus extraction is imperfect due to competition. Finally, there are obvious incentive problems involved in selling information. It is important to understand how information markets are affected by such problems, and how these problems may be dealt with through contracts and long term relationships.

Appendix

Proof of Proposition 4.1 Begin by assuming that the price is a linear function of the fund manager's signal, $\tilde{F} + \tilde{\theta}$, and the noise $\tilde{Z}$, with $\tilde{P} = a(\tilde{F} + \tilde{\theta}) + b\tilde{Z}$. Consider an investor who holds x shares in the fund. That investors wealth in period 2 is given by

$$\tilde{W}_2 = W_0 + (x(\tilde{F} + \tilde{\theta}) - q)(\tilde{F} - \tilde{P}) - f(x), \tag{A1}$$

where $f(x)$ is the fee paid to the manager for managing x units of the fund and $-q$ is equal to the number of shares of the risky asset the investor purchases on his own account. The

[22]We note that if traders are risk neutral in Admati and Pfleiderer (1988), then there is no benefit to indirect sale because in that case the highest profits are obtained when only one trader buys the information. Controlling the usage is irrelevant. (This is analogous to the Kamien and Tauman result for the case of a drastic innovation.) For the case of risk averse traders it is not possible in this model to derive in closed form the demand function for shares in the fund. We cannot therefore perform the comparison between direct sale and indirect sale with linear pricing in that context. Although tradeoffs between controlling the usage of the information and surplus extraction, similar to those found in the current paper, will arise there as well, it is not clear how the net benefits stack up. For example, it is possible that in that model surplus extraction will be always more important than controlling usage for all parameters, so that direct sale will always dominate indirect sale with linear pricing. We conjecture, however, that results will depend on the parameters of the model as in the current paper.

[23]Information about the portfolio positions of potentially informed traders in financial markets seems to be actively collected and even sold. It also seems that the larger the position taken, the more "visible" or costly (in terms of transaction costs) the trade is.

value of q is chosen at the time the price $\widetilde{P}$ is observed. The investor therefore chooses q to maximize $\mathscr{E}(-\exp(-\widetilde{W}_2/\rho)|P)$. The distribution of $\widetilde{F}$ and $\widetilde{\theta}$ conditional on P is normal:

$$\begin{pmatrix} \widetilde{F} \\ \widetilde{\theta} \end{pmatrix} \Bigg| P \sim N\left(\begin{pmatrix} h^{-1}ap \\ h^{-1}a\sigma_\theta^2 P \end{pmatrix}, \begin{pmatrix} h^{-1}(a^2\sigma_\theta^2 + b^2\sigma_Z^2) & -h^{-1}a^2\sigma_\theta^2 \\ -h^{-1}a^2\sigma_\theta^2 & h^{-1}\sigma_\theta^2(a^2 + b^2\sigma_Z^2) \end{pmatrix}\right),$$

where $h = a^2(1 + \sigma_\theta^2) + b^2\sigma_Z^2$.

We now use the following lemma whose proof is omitted:

Lemma *Let $\widetilde{\eta}_1$ and $\widetilde{\eta}_2$ be jointly normally distributed with means μ_1 and μ_2 and variance covariance matrix Σ. Then $\mathscr{E}(-\exp(-\widetilde{\eta}_1\widetilde{\eta}_2))$ equals*

$$\text{(A2)} \quad -|\Sigma|^{-1/2}\left|\Sigma^{-1} + \begin{pmatrix} 0 & 1 \\ 1 & 0 \end{pmatrix}\right|^{-1/2} \exp\left(-\mu_1\mu_2 + \tfrac{1}{2}(\mu_2 \;\; \mu_1)\left(\Sigma^{-1} + \begin{pmatrix} 0 & 1 \\ 1 & 0 \end{pmatrix}\right)^{-1}\begin{pmatrix} \mu_2 \\ \mu_1 \end{pmatrix}\right).$$

Now let $\widetilde{\eta}_1 = x(\widetilde{F} + \widetilde{\theta}) - q$ and $\widetilde{\eta}_2 = (\widetilde{F} - P)/\rho$. Then the investor's expected utility is proportional to the expression given in (A2) with

$$\text{(A3)} \quad \mu_1 = xh^{-1}a(1 + \sigma_\theta^2)P - q,$$

$$\text{(A4)} \quad \mu_2 = (h^{-1}aP - P)/\rho,$$

$$\text{(A5)} \quad \Sigma_{11} = h^{-1}(x^2(1 + \sigma_\theta^2)b^2\sigma_Z^2),$$

$$\text{(A6)} \quad \Sigma_{12} = h^{-1}(xb^2\sigma_Z^2)/\rho,$$

and

$$\text{(A7)} \quad \Sigma_{22} = h^{-1}(a^2\sigma_\theta^2 + b^2\sigma_Z^2)/\rho^2.$$

Since Σ does not depend upon q, maximizing expected utility with respect to q is equivalent to maximizing

$$\text{(A8)} \quad -\mu_1\mu_2 + \frac{1}{2}(\mu_2 \;\; \mu_1)\left(\Sigma^{-1} + \begin{pmatrix} 0 & 1 \\ 1 & 0 \end{pmatrix}\right)^{-1}\begin{pmatrix} \mu_2 \\ \mu_1 \end{pmatrix}.$$

The first order condition is given by

$$\text{(A9)} \quad -\mu_2 + (\mu_2 \;\; \mu_1 + q)\left(\Sigma^{-1} + \begin{pmatrix} 0 & 1 \\ 1 & 0 \end{pmatrix}\right)^{-1}\begin{pmatrix} 0 \\ -1 \end{pmatrix}$$

$$= (0 \;\; q)\left(\Sigma^{-1} + \begin{pmatrix} 0 & 1 \\ 1 & 0 \end{pmatrix}\right)^{-1}\begin{pmatrix} 0 \\ -1 \end{pmatrix}.$$

Since $\mu_1 + q$ and μ_2 are both proportional to P, it is easy to see that q will also be proportional to P. In fact the solution is given by

$$\text{(A10)} \quad q = \left(\frac{b^2\sigma_Z^2(\rho + x) + \rho a^2(1 + \sigma_\theta^2) + a(\sigma_\theta^2 x - \rho)}{a^2\sigma_\theta^2 + b^2\sigma_Z^2}\right)P.$$

This completes the proof. *Q.E.D.*

Proof of Proposition 5.1 Let $m = \rho/\sigma_Z$, and consider the direct seller. For any (finite) σ_θ^2, there is an $\hat{m}$ such that for all $m > \hat{m}$, the seller adds noise to the signal being sold. For $m > \hat{m}$, profits are

$$\text{(A11)} \quad \pi^d = \frac{\rho}{2}\log\left(1 + \frac{g\sigma_Z^2}{\rho(1 + \sigma_\theta^2 + g^2\sigma_Z^2)}\right) = \frac{\rho}{2}\log\left(1 + \frac{\sigma_Z}{2\rho\sqrt{1 + \sigma_\theta^2}}\right),$$

since when noise is added $g = \sqrt{1 + \sigma_\theta^2}/\sigma_Z$. This means that

$$\text{(A12)} \qquad \lim_{m\to\infty} \frac{\pi^d}{\sigma_Z} = \lim_{m\to\infty} \frac{m}{2} \log\left(1 + \frac{1}{2m\sqrt{1 + \sigma_\theta^2}}\right) = \frac{1}{4\sqrt{1 + \sigma_\theta^2}}.$$

For the fund manager we get, by direct calculation,

$$\text{(A13)} \qquad \lim_{m\to\infty} \frac{\pi^*}{\sigma_Z} = \lim_{m\to\infty} \frac{m^2\sqrt{1 + \sigma_\theta^2} - m\sigma_\theta^2}{2m^2(1 + \sigma_\theta^2) + 2m\sqrt{1 + \sigma_\theta^2} - \sigma_\theta^2} = \frac{1}{2\sqrt{1 + \sigma_\theta^2}}.$$

The result now follows immediately. *Q.E.D.*

Proof of Proposition 5.2 Again, let $m = \rho/\sigma_Z$. From the results in Admati and Pfleiderer (1986) we have

$$\text{(A14)} \qquad \lim_{m\to 0} \frac{\pi^d}{\rho} = \frac{1}{2} \log\left(1 + \frac{1}{\sigma_\theta^2}\right).$$

Turning to the fund manager from Proposition 5.2 we have

$$\text{(A15)} \qquad \lim_{m\to 0} \frac{x^*}{\rho} = \lim_{m\to\infty} \frac{\sqrt{(1 + \sigma_\theta^2)(m^2 + \sigma_\theta^2)} - \sigma_\theta^2}{\sigma_\theta^2 + m^2(1 + \sigma_\theta^2)} = \frac{\sqrt{1 + \sigma_\theta^2}}{\sigma_\theta} - 1.$$

It follows that

$$\text{(A16)} \qquad \lim_{m\to 0} \frac{\pi^*}{\rho} = \lim_{m\to 0} \frac{(x^*/\rho)\,(1 - \sigma_\theta^2(x^*/\rho))}{(x^*/\rho)^2\,(m^2(1+\sigma_\theta^2) - \sigma_\theta^2) + 2(x^*/\rho) + 1} = \frac{1}{2}\left(1 - \frac{\sigma_\theta}{\sqrt{1 + \sigma_\theta^2}}\right).$$

To show that $\lim_{m\to 0}\pi^*/\rho < \lim_{m\to 0}\pi^d/\rho$, we must show that $\log(1 + 1/\sigma_\theta^2) > 1 - \sigma_\theta/\sqrt{1 + \sigma_\theta^2}$. Let $y = \sigma_\theta/\sqrt{1 + \sigma_\theta^2}$. Since $\log(z) > (z - 1)/z$ for $z > 1$, $\log(1 + 1/\sigma_\theta^2) = \log(1/y^2) > 1 - y^2 > 1 - y$ where the last inequality holds because $y < 1$. *Q.E.D.*

Proof of Proposition 6.3 Assume that $\rho = 1$. This can be done without loss of generality for the purpose of this proof. To see this, consider an economy in which $\rho \neq 1$. Now consider the same economy with the units of the consumption good redefined so that one unit in the old system of measurement is equal to $1/\rho$ units in the new. Let $\tilde{W}$ be the wealth of a trader as measured in the old system and $\tilde{W}'$ be his wealth as measured in the new. It is easy to see that $\tilde{W}' = \tilde{W}/\rho$ and that risk tolerance, as measured in the new system, is equal to 1. If we continue to define shares of the risky asset in the same way, the variance of the payoff of a share of the risky asset in the new system of measurement is $1/\rho$. To restore the variance of the risky asset to 1 we must redefine shares so that ρ old shares are equal to one new share. This makes the variance of $\tilde{Z}'$, the random supply in the new system, equal to σ_Z^2/ρ. Thus an economy in which risk tolerance is equal to ρ and supply variance is equal to σ_Z^2 is equivalent to an economy in which risk tolerance is 1 and the supply variance is σ_Z^2/ρ.

Now suppose the information seller offers shares in a mutual fund, which are priced linearly, as well as personalized signals $\tilde{F} + \tilde{\varepsilon}^v$ with $\text{Var}(\tilde{\varepsilon}^v) = s$. Consider a situation in which $x > 0$ shares of the fund are purchased by each trader. Then a trader's total demand for the risky asset if he buys the information directly as well can be written as

$x\tilde{F} + \nu(\tilde{F} + \tilde{\varepsilon}) - k\tilde{P}$, where x is the number of shares of the fund and ν and $-k$ are the coefficients on the signal and on the price respectively. Assuming that $\tilde{P} = a\tilde{F} - b\tilde{Z}$, we can derive the inverse demand function for the fund using methods similar to those in the proof of Proposition 1. This involves finding the optimal solution for ν and k and deriving the first order condition for the choice of x. Let $p = 1/s$ measure the precision of the information sold directly. The optimal value of ν can be shown to be equal to p, independent of x, and

$$d(x; p, a/b) = \frac{1}{2x + 1 + p + \left(\frac{a}{b}\right)^2\left(\frac{1}{\sigma_Z^2}\right)}.$$

The market clearing condition implies that in equilibrium $a/b = x + \nu = x + p$, so the aggregate inverse demand function for shares in the fund, given the value of p, is $\delta(x; p) = d(x; p, x + p)$, and the profits from indirect sale of information are equal to $x\delta(x; p)$.

Turning to the direct sale, we first derive a relation between the optimal number of shares in the fund that an informed trader would buy and the number of shares that an uninformed trader buys (keeping the price function constant). The inverse demand function of an uninformed [trader] can be found from the above inverse demand function with $p = 0$. (In fact, this is the same function as (5.3).) It follows that, for any given price for a share in the fund and asset price function, if an informed trader optimally holds x shares, then an uninformed trader optimally holds $x + p/2$ shares.

The profits derived from the direct sale of information are equal to the value of the signal to each trader. This involves the calculation of ex ante expected utility both when information is bought directly and when it is not. (Of course, each case involves a different number of shares in the fund, and different levels of investment on own account, i.e., different k's.) It turns out that the difference between the certainty equivalent of profits of informed and uninformed traders in this model is exactly equal to the cost of the extra shares in the fund that an uninformed trader purchases. This implies that the profits of the seller from direct sale are equal to $(p/2)\delta(x; p)$. In sum, the total profits to the seller are equal to $(x + p/2)\delta(x; p)$. Maximizing this function subject to the constraint that the expected utility integral converges leads to the conclusion that $p = 0$ is always optimal, so that direct sale is never desirable. *Q.E.D.*

Proof of Proposition 7.4 We first prove (i). Let $m = \rho/\sigma_Z$. Using equation (7.4) we can show that

(A17) $$\lim_{m\to\infty} \frac{x^{**}}{\sigma_Z} = \frac{1}{\sqrt{1 + \sigma_\theta^2}}.$$

From (7.4) and (7.5) it follows that profits in the two part pricing scheme are

(A18) $$\pi^{**} = \frac{\rho}{2}\log\left(\frac{(x^{**})^2\,(\rho^2(1 + \sigma_\theta^2) - \sigma_\theta^2\sigma_Z^2) + \rho\sigma_Z^2(\rho + 2x^{**})}{\rho^2((x^{**})^2(1 + \sigma_\theta^2) + \sigma_Z^2)}\right).$$

Substituting $x^{**} = \sigma_Z(1 + \sigma_\theta^2)^{-1/2}$ into (A18) and simplifying we have

(A19) $$\lim_{m\to\infty} \frac{\pi^{**}}{\sigma_Z} = \lim_{m\to\infty} \frac{m}{2}\log\left(1 + \frac{1}{m\sqrt{1 + \sigma_\theta^2}} - \frac{\sigma_\theta^2}{2m^2(1 + \sigma_\theta^2)}\right).$$

Now let $h = 1/m$. Then

$$\text{(A20)} \quad \lim_{m\to\infty} \frac{\pi^{**}}{\sigma_Z} = \lim_{h\to 0} \frac{1}{2h} \log\left(1 + \frac{h}{\sqrt{1+\sigma_\theta^2}} - \frac{h^2\sigma_\theta^2}{2(1+\sigma_\theta^2)}\right)$$

$$= \lim_{h\to 0} \frac{1}{2}\left(1 + \frac{h}{\sqrt{1+\sigma_\theta^2}} - \frac{h^2\sigma_\theta^2}{2(1+\sigma_\theta^2)}\right)^{-1}\left(\frac{1}{\sqrt{1+\sigma_\theta^2}} - \frac{h\sigma_\theta^2}{1+\sigma_\theta^2}\right)$$

$$= \frac{1}{2\sqrt{1+\sigma_\theta^2}}.$$

(The second equality follows from L' Hospital's rule.) Comparing (A20) with (A12) yields the result.

We now prove (ii). Again using (7.4), it can be shown that

$$\text{(A21)} \quad \lim_{m\to 0} \frac{x^{**}}{\rho} = \frac{1}{\sigma_\theta^2}.$$

Substituting this into (A18) and simplifying gives

$$\text{(A22)} \quad \lim_{m\to 0} \frac{\pi^{**}}{\rho} = \lim_{m\to 0} \frac{1}{2}\log\left(1 + \frac{1}{\sigma_\theta^2}\left(1 + \frac{m^2(1+\sigma_\theta^2)}{\sigma_\theta^4}\right)^{-1}\right) = \frac{1}{2}\log\left(1 + \frac{1}{\sigma_\theta^2}\right).$$

Comparing this with (A14) gives the second part of the proposition. *Q.E.D.*

Proof of Proposition 7.5 Assume that $\rho = 1$, without loss of generality. The first order conditions for linear pricing imply that x^* solves

$$\text{(A23)} \quad \sigma_Z^2 - x^2(1 + \sigma_\theta^2 + \sigma_\theta^2\sigma_Z^2) - 2\sigma_\theta^2\sigma_Z^2 x = 0.$$

For two part pricing the first order condition implies that x^{**} solves

$$\text{(A24)} \quad \sigma_Z^2 - x^2(1 + \sigma_\theta^2) - \sigma_\theta^2\sigma_Z^2 x = 0.$$

Note first that if $x = 0$, the left hand sides of both (A23) and (A24) are both equal to $\sigma_Z^2 > 0$ and both decrease as x is increased. Subtracting the left hand side of (A24) from the left hand side of (A23), we obtain $x\sigma_\theta^2\sigma_Z^2(1 + x)$ which is positive for $\sigma_\theta^2 > 0$. Thus, for positive σ_θ^2, $x^{**} > x^*$ and for $\sigma_\theta^2 = 0$, $x^{**} = x^*$. *Q.E.D.*

Proof of Proposition 7.5 Assume again that $\rho = 1$. When information is sold directly the normalized price is $\tilde{F} + \tilde{\theta} - g\tilde{Z}$ where $g = \max(\sigma_\theta^2, \sqrt{(1+\sigma_\theta^2)}/\sigma_Z)$. Thus, we need to show that $1/g \geqslant x^{**}$, with strict inequality when $\sigma_\theta^2 > 0$, equality when $\sigma_\theta^2 = 0$. This will follow if we show that $x^{**} \leqslant 1/\sigma_\theta^2$ and $x^{**} \leqslant \sigma_Z/\sqrt{1+\sigma_\theta^2}$. First note that

$$\text{(A25)} \quad x^{**} - \frac{1}{\sigma_\theta^2} = \frac{\sigma_\theta^2\sigma_Z\sqrt{\sigma_\theta^4\sigma_Z^2 + 4\sigma_\theta^2 + 4} - (\sigma_\theta^4\sigma_Z^2 - 2\sigma_\theta^2 - 2)}{2\sigma_\theta^2(1+\sigma_\theta^2)}.$$

Since

$$\text{(A26)} \quad \left(\sigma_\theta^2\sigma_Z\sqrt{\sigma_\theta^4\sigma_Z^2 + 4\sigma_\theta^2 + 4}\right)^2 - (\sigma_Z^4\sigma_Z^2 - 2\sigma_\theta^2 - 2)^2 = -4(1+\sigma_\theta^2)^2,$$

the difference in (A25) is always negative. This proves the first inequality. Now consider the difference

$$\text{(A27)} \quad x^{**} - \frac{\sigma_Z}{\sqrt{1+\sigma_\theta^2}} = \frac{\sigma_Z\sqrt{\sigma_\theta^4\sigma_Z^2 + 4\sigma_\theta^2 + 4} - 2\sigma_Z\sqrt{1+\sigma_\theta^2} - \sigma_\theta^2\sigma_Z^2}{\sigma_\theta^2(1+\theta_\theta^2)}$$

This is also always negative for $\sigma_\theta^2 > 0$ since

$$\text{(A28)} \qquad \sigma_Z^2(\sigma_\theta^4\sigma_Z^2 + 4\sigma_\theta^2 + 4) - \left(2\sigma_Z\sqrt{1+\sigma_\theta^2} + \sigma_\theta^2\sigma_Z^2\right)^2 = -4\sigma_\theta^2\sigma_Z^3\sqrt{1+\sigma_\theta^2}.$$

If $\sigma_\theta^2 = 0$, then $g = 1/\sigma_Z$ and (A28) is the relevant difference. Since it is zero in this case, $1/g = x^{**}$. *Q.E.D.*

References

Admati, Anat R., and Paul Pfleiderer (1986): "A Monopolistic Market for Information," *Journal of Economic Theory*, 39, 400–438.

—— (1987): "Viable Allocations of Information in Financial Markets," *Journal of Economic Theory*, 43, 76–115.

—— (1988): "Selling and Trading on Information in Financial Markets," *American Economic Review, Papers and Proceedings*, 78, 96–103.

Allen, Franklin (1986): "Contracts to Sell Information," Working Paper, Wharton School, University of Pennsylvania.

Bhattacharya, Sudipto, and Paul Pfleiderer (1985): "Delegated Portfolio Management," *Journal of Economic Theory*, 36, 1–25.

Diamond, Douglas W., and Robert E. Verrecchia (1981): "Information Aggregation in a Noisy Rational Expectations Economy," *Journal of Financial Economics*, 9, 221–235.

Grinblatt, Mark S., and Stephen A. Ross (1985): "Market Power in a Securities Market with Endogenous Information," *Quarterly Journal of Economics*, 100, 1143–1167.

Grossman, Sanford J, and Joseph E. Stiglitz (1980): "On the Impossibility of Informationally Efficient Markets," *American Economic Review*, 70, 393–408.

Hellwig, Martin F. (1980): "On the Aggregation of Information in Competitive Markets," *Journal of Economic Theory*, 22, 477–498.

Kamien, Morton I., and Yair Tauman (1986): "Fees versus Royalties and the Private Value of a Patent," *Quarterly Journal of Economics*, 101, 471–491.

Kyle, Albert S. (1989): "Informed Speculation with Imperfect Competition," *Review of Economic Studies*, 56, 317–355.

Fifteen

Anat R. Admati

Anat R. Admati received a Ph.D. from Yale University in 1983. She started out at the Stanford Graduate School of Business, and still works at the Stanford Graduate School of Business. •

When I arrived to Yale in 1979 as an operations research student, there was already a "buzz" about Steve Ross. The word was that one absolutely *had to* take the Ross finance course, offered every Monday morning in the fall, 9 a.m. to noon. So, alongside my classmate Shmuel Kandel, I took the famed Ross course in the fall of 1980. As will likely be echoed by others in this volume, this was an incredible course, and the exposure to Steve was transforming. His enthusiasm was contagious; he got a number of us, including me, to think finance was fascinating. And it was clear as well that he would be a wonderful mentor. I think it would have been quite unlikely for me to have become interested in finance at that point if not for Steve's influence.

My interest in information economics was first sparked by a seminar early in September 1980 in which Bob Weber presented his paper with Milgrom on auctions. This led me to take a reading course on the subject with John Geanakoplos that same fall. While Steve's research in the '70s focused mainly on portfolio theory, risk aversion measures, APT, options, and term structure models, he recognized the significance of information in financial markets and had already contributed to this literature (e.g., with his papers on agency). At that time, Steve was particularly interested in performance measurement. He wrote about it with Phil Dybvig, and he got me interested in it as well. (Mark Grinblatt and Paul Pfleiderer also worked on the topic later.) The breadth of Steve's interests and research has always amazed me.

Being one of Steve's students during that period required tolerating his busy schedule, and occasionally missed or overbooked appointments. But the benefits were overwhelming. Even a brief meeting with Steve was extremely valuable. Not only was it productive and fun to discuss research with him; his support and good cheer kept many of us going during the ups and downs of the dissertation stage. A bonus was having such a great set of fellow students around, some working on similar issues. And then there was also Mary Polverari, Steve's assistant, who "mothered" his students and kept us company outside his office.

Steve's impact on my research is pervasive and profound, and is still felt many years after I graduated. Through his course, through the elegant models and beautiful insights of his papers, and in many conversations, Steve taught me about the role of theory in helping us understand financial markets. He taught me to keep the big picture as I immerse in the analytical details, to construct the simplest possible model that would allow the analysis of an issue, to make sure to understand the intuition behind results, to work through examples, and also to have fun! And in all the years since I graduated, Steve has continued to be an amazing colleague, friend, and mentor.

In my case, Steve's impact becomes magnified. One of his older students, Phil Dybvig, was also on my dissertation committee. And I've been lucky enough to have Paul Pfleiderer as a colleague and frequent co-author. I first met Paul when he was my TA in microeconomics in the fall of 1979; then we both worked with Steve on related topics; and then, of course, we both found ourselves at Stanford, and it did not take long for us to start collaborating. The shared heritage of research values and style that Steve has instilled in us has certainly made it easier for us to connect and has continued to guide us over the years. I believe Steve's impact can be seen in all of our research. This includes in particular the papers on intraday trading patterns and on direct and indirect sale of information, both of which are included in this volume. I can't say enough how much I admire Steve and how grateful I am to him for all he has done and been for me since the fall of 1980.

A Theory of Intraday Patterns: Volume and Price Variability

Anat R. Admati
Paul Pfleiderer
Stanford University

This article develops a theory in which concentrated-trading patterns arise endogenously as a result of the strategic behavior of liquidity traders and informed traders. Our results provide a partial explanation for some of the recent empirical findings concerning the patterns of volume and price variability in intraday transaction data. •

In the last few years, intraday trading data for a number of securities have become available. Several empirical studies have used these data to identify various patterns in trading volume and in the daily behavior of security prices. This article focuses on two of these patterns; trading volume and the variability of returns.

Consider, for example, the data in Table 1 concerning shares of Exxon traded during 1981.[1] The U-shaped pattern of the average volume of shares traded—namely, the heavy trading in the beginning and the end of the trading day and the relatively light trading in the middle of the day—is very typical and has been documented in a number of studies. [For example, Jain and Joh (1986) examine hourly data for the aggregate volume on the NYSE, which is reported in the *Wall Street Journal*, and find the same pattern.] Both the variance of price changes and the variance of returns follow a similar U-shaped pattern. [See, for example, Wood, McInish, and Ord (1985).] These empirical findings raise three questions that we attempt to answer in this article:

- Why does trading tend to be concentrated in particular time periods within the trading day?
- Why are returns (or price changes) more variable in some periods and less variable in others?
- Why do the periods of higher trading volume also tend to be the periods of higher return variability?

To answer these questions, we develop models in which traders determine when to trade and whether to become privately informed about assets' future returns. We show that the

We would like to thank Michihiro Kandori, Allan Kleidon, David Kreps, Pete Kyle, Myron Scholes, Ken Singleton, Mark Wolfson, a referee, and especially Mike Gibbons and Chester Spatt for helpful suggestions and comments. We are also grateful to Douglas Foster and S. Viswanathan for pointing out an error in a previous draft. Kobi Boudoukh and Matt Richardson provided valuable research assistance. The financial support of the Stanford Program in Finance and Batterymarch Financial Management is gratefully acknowledged.

[1] We have looked at data for companies in the Dow Jones 30, and the patterns are similar. The transaction data were obtained from Francis Emory Fitch, Inc. We chose Exxon here since it is the most heavily traded stock in the sample.

Reprinted with permission:
Admati, Anat R. and Paul Pfleiderer. "A Theory of Intraday Patterns: Volume and Price Variability." *Review of Financial Studies* 1 (1988): 3–40.

TABLE 1 | The Intraday Trading Pattern of Exxon Shares in 1981

	10 A.M. TO 12 NOON	12 NOON TO 2 P.M.	2 P.M. TO 4 P.M.
Average volume	179,349	103,024	122,670
SD (price changes)	0.34959	0.28371	0.37984

The first row gives the average volume of Exxon shares traded in 1981 in each of the three time periods. The second row gives the standard deviation (SD) of price changes, based on the transaction prices closest to the beginning and the end of the period.

patterns that have been observed empirically can be explained in terms of the optimizing decisions of these traders.[2]

Two motives for trade in financial markets are widely recognized as important: information and liquidity. Informed traders trade on the basis of private information that is not known to all other traders when trade takes place. Liquidity traders, on the other hand, trade for reasons that are not related directly to the future payoffs of financial assets—their needs arise outside the financial market. Included in this category are large traders, such as some financial institutions, whose trades reflect the liquidity needs of their clients or who trade for portfolio-balancing reasons.

Most models that involve liquidity (or "noise") trading assume that liquidity traders have no discretion with regard to the timing of their trades. [Of course, the timing issue does not arise in models with only one trading period and is therefore only relevant in multiperiod models, such as in Glosten and Milgrom (1985) and Kyle (1985).] This is a strong assumption, particularly if liquidity trades are executed by large institutional traders. A more reasonable assumption is that at least some liquidity traders can choose the timing of their transactions strategically, subject to the constraint of trading a particular number of shares within a given period of time. The models developed in this article include such discretionary liquidity traders, and the actions of these traders play an important role in determining the types of patterns that will be identified. We believe that the inclusion of these traders captures an important element of actual trading in financial markets. We will demonstrate that the behavior of liquidity traders, together with that of potentially informed speculators who may trade on the basis of private information they acquire, can explain some of the empirical observations mentioned above as well as suggest some new testable predictions.

It is intuitive that, to the extent that liquidity traders have discretion over when they trade, they prefer to trade when the market is "thick"—that is, when their trading has little effect on prices. This creates strong incentives for liquidity traders to trade together and for trading to be concentrated. When informed traders can also decide when to collect information and when to trade, the story becomes more complicated. Clearly, informed traders also want to trade when the market is thick. If many informed traders trade at the same time that liquidity traders concentrate their trading, then the terms of trade will reflect the increased level of informed trading as well, and this may conceivably drive out the liquidity traders. It is not clear, therefore, what patterns may actually emerge.

In fact, we show in our model that as long as there is at least one informed trader, the introduction of more informed traders generally *intensifies* the forces leading to the concentration of trading by discretionary liquidity traders. This is because informed traders

[2]Another paper which focuses on the strategic timing of trades and their effect on volume and price behavior is Foster and Viswanathan (1987). In contrast to our paper, however, this paper is mainly concerned with the timing of informed trading when information is long lived.

compete with each other, and this typically improves the welfare of liquidity traders. We show that liquidity traders always benefit from more entry by informed traders when informed traders have the same information. However, when the information of each informed trader is different (i.e., when information is diverse among informed traders), then this may not be true. As more diversely informed traders enter the market, the amount of information that is available to the market as a whole increases, and this may worsen the terms of trade for everyone. Despite this possibility, we show that with diversely informed traders the patterns that generally emerge involve a concentration of trading.

The trading model used in our analysis is in the spirit of Glosten and Milgrom (1985) and especially Kyle (1984, 1985). Informed traders and liquidity traders submit market orders to a market maker who sets prices so that his expected profits are zero given the total order flow. The information structure in our model is simpler than Kyle (1985) and Glosten and Milgrom (1985) in that private information is only useful for one period. Like Kyle (1984, 1985) and unlike Glosten and Milgrom (1985), orders are not constrained to be of a fixed size such as one share. Indeed, the size of the order is a choice variable for traders.

What distinguishes our analysis from these other papers is that we examine, in a simple dynamic context, the interaction between strategic informed traders and strategic liquidity traders. Specifically, our models include two types of liquidity traders. *Nondiscretionary liquidity traders* must trade a particular number of shares at a particular time (for reasons that are not modeled). In addition, we assume that there are some *discretionary liquidity traders*, who also have liquidity demands, but who can be strategic in choosing when to execute these trades within a given period of time, e.g., within 24 hours or by the end of the trading day. It is assumed that discretionary liquidity traders time their trades so as to minimize the (expected) cost of their transactions.

Kyle (1984) discusses a single period version of the model we use and derives some comparative statics results that are relevant to our discussion. In his model, there are multiple informed traders who have diverse information. There are also multiple market makers, so that the model we use is a limit of his model as the number of market makers grows. Kyle (1984) discusses what happens to the informativeness of the price as the variance of liquidity demands changes. He shows that with a fixed number of informed traders the informativeness of the price does not depend on the variance of liquidity demand. However, if information acquisition is endogenous, then price informativeness is increasing in the variance of the liquidity demands. These properties of the single period model play an important role in our analysis, where the variance of liquidity demands in different periods is determined in equilibrium by the decisions of the discretionary liquidity traders.

We begin by analyzing a simple model that involves a fixed number of informed traders, all of whom observe the same information. Discretionary liquidity traders can determine the timing of their trade, but they can trade only once during the time period within which they must satisfy their liquidity demand. (Such a restriction may be motivated by per-trade transaction costs.) We show that in this model there will be patterns in the volume of trade; namely, trade will tend to be concentrated. If the number and precision of the information of informed traders is [sic] constant over time, however, then the information content and variability of equilibrium prices will be constant over time as well.

We then discuss the effects of endogenous information acquisition and of diverse private information. It is assumed that traders can become informed at a cost, and we examine the equilibrium in which no more traders wish to become informed. We show that the patterns of trading volume that exist in the model with a fixed number of informed traders become more pronounced if the number of informed traders is endogenous. The increased level of liquidity trading induces more informed trading. Moreover, with endogenous information acquisition we obtain patterns in the informativeness of prices and in price variability.

Another layer is added to the model by allowing discretionary liquidity traders to satisfy their liquidity needs by trading more than once if they choose. The trading patterns that emerge in this case are more subtle. This is because the market maker can partially predict the liquidity-trading component of the order flow in later periods by observing previous order flows.

This article is organized as follows. In Section 1 we discuss the model with a fixed number of (identically) informed traders. Section 2 considers endogenous information acquisition, and Section 3 extends the results to the case of diversely informed traders. In Section 4 we relax the assumption that discretionary liquidity traders trade only once. Section 5 explores some additional extensions to the model and shows that our results hold in a number of different settings. In Section 6 we discuss some empirically testable predictions of our model, and Section 7 provides concluding remarks.

1. A Simple Model of Trading Patterns

1.1 Model Description

We consider a single asset traded over a span of time that we divide into T periods. It is assumed that the value of the asset in period T is exogenously given by

$$\tilde{F} = \bar{F} + \sum_{t=1}^{T} \tilde{\delta}_t \tag{1}$$

where $\tilde{\delta}_t$, $t = 1, 2, \ldots, T$, are independently distributed random variables, each having a mean of zero. The payoff $\tilde{F}$ can be thought of as the liquidation value of the asset: any trader holding a share of the asset in period T receives a liquidating dividend of $\tilde{F}$ dollars. Alternatively, period T can be viewed as a period in which all traders have the same information about the value of the asset and $\tilde{F}$ is the common value that each assigns to it. For example, an earnings report may be released in period T. If this report reveals all those quantities about which traders might be privately informed, then all traders will be symmetrically informed in this period.

In periods prior to T, information about $\tilde{F}$ is revealed through both public and private sources. In each period t the innovation $\tilde{\delta}_t$ becomes public knowledge. In addition, some traders also have access to private information, as described below. In subsequent sections of this article we will make the decision to become informed endogenous; in this section we assume that in period t, n_t traders are endowed with private information. A privately informed trader observes a signal that is informative about $\tilde{\delta}_{t+1}$. Specifically, we assume that an informed trader observes $\tilde{\delta}_{t+1} + \tilde{\varepsilon}_t$, where $\text{var}(\tilde{\varepsilon}_t) = \phi_t$. Thus, privately informed traders observe something about the piece of public information that will be revealed one period later to all traders. Another interpretation of this structure of private information is that privately informed traders are able to process public information faster or more efficiently than others are. (Note that it is assumed here that all informed traders observe the same signal. An alternative formulation is considered in Section 3.) Since the private information becomes useless one period after it is observed, informed traders only need to determine their trade in the period in which they are informed. Issues related to the timing of informed trading, which are important in Kyle (1985), do not arise here. We assume throughout this article that in each period there is at least one privately informed trader.

All traders in the model are risk-neutral. (However, as discussed in Section 5.2, our basic results do not change if some traders are risk-averse.) We also assume for simplicity and ease of exposition that there is no discounting by traders.[3] Thus, if $\tilde{\Phi}_t$ summarizes all the information observed by a particular trader in period t, then the value of a share of the asset to that trader in period t is $E(\tilde{F}|\tilde{\Phi}_t)$, where $E(\cdot|\cdot)$ is the conditional expectation operator.

In this section we are mainly concerned with the behavior of the liquidity traders and its effect on prices and trading volume. We postulate that there are two types of liquidity traders. In each period there exists a group of *nondiscretionary liquidity traders* who must trade a given number of shares in that period. The other class of liquidity traders is composed of traders who have liquidity demands that need not be satisfied immediately. We call these *discretionary liquidity traders* and assume that their demand for shares is determined in some period T' and needs to be satisfied before period T'', where $T' < T'' < T$.[4] Assume there are m discretionary liquidity traders and let $\tilde{Y}^j$ be total demand of the jth discretionary liquidity trader (revealed to that trader in period T'). Since each discretionary liquidity trader is risk-neutral, he determines his trading policy so as to minimize his expected cost of trading, subject to the condition that he trades a total of $\tilde{Y}^j$ shares by period T''. Until Section 4 we assume that each discretionary liquidity trader only trades once between time T' and time T''; that is, a liquidity trader cannot divide his trades among different periods.

Prices for the asset are established in each period by a market maker who stands prepared to take a position in the asset to balance the total demand of the remainder of the market. The market maker is also assumed to be risk-neutral, and competition forces him to set prices so that he earns zero expected profits in each period. This follows the approach in Kyle (1985) and in Glosten and Milgrom (1985).[5]

Let $\tilde{x}_t^i$ be the ith informed trader's order in period t, $\tilde{y}_t^j$ be the order of the jth discretionary liquidity trader in that period, and let us denote by $\tilde{z}_t$ the *total* demand for shares by the nondiscretionary liquidity traders in period t. Then the market maker must purchase $\tilde{\omega}_t = \sum_{i=1}^n \tilde{x}_t^i + \sum_{j=1}^m \tilde{y}_t^j + \tilde{z}_t$ shares in period t. The market maker determines a price in period t based on the history of public information, $\tilde{\delta}_1, \tilde{\delta}_2, \ldots, \tilde{\delta}_t$, and on the history of order flows, $\tilde{\omega}_1, \tilde{\omega}_2, \ldots, \tilde{\omega}_t$.[6] Let $\tilde{\Delta}_t = (\tilde{\delta}_1, \tilde{\delta}_2, \ldots, \tilde{\delta}_t)$ and let $\tilde{\Omega}_t = (\tilde{\omega}_1, \tilde{\omega}_2, \ldots, \tilde{\omega}_t)$. The zero expected profit condition implies that $\tilde{P}_t$, the price set in period t by the market maker, satisfies

$$\tilde{P}_t = E(\tilde{F}|\tilde{\Delta}_t, \tilde{\Omega}_t) \tag{2}$$

[3]This assumption is reasonable since the span of time covered by the T periods in this model is to be taken as relatively short and since our main interests concern the volume of trading and the variability of prices. The nature of our results does not change if a positive discount rate is assumed.

[4]In reality, of course, different traders may realize their liquidity demands at different times, and the time that can elapse before these demands must be satisfied may also be different for different traders. The nature of our results will not change if the model is complicated to capture this. See the discussion in Section 5.1.

[5]The model here can be viewed as the limit of a model with a finite number of market makers as the number of market makers grows to infinity. However, our results do not depend in any important way on the assumption of perfect competition among market makers. The same basic results would obtain in an analogous model with a finite number of market makers, where each market maker announces a (linear) pricing schedule as a function of his own order flow and traders can allocate their trade among different market makers. In such a model, market makers earn positive expected profits. See Kyle (1984).

[6]If the price were a function of individual orders, then anonymous traders could manipulate the price by submitting canceling orders. For example, a trader who wishes to purchase 10 shares could submit a purchase order for 200 shares and a sell order for 190 shares. When the price is solely a function of the total order flow, such manipulations are not possible.

Finally, we assume that the random variables

$$(\tilde{Y}^1, \tilde{Y}^2, \ldots, \tilde{Y}^m, \tilde{z}_1, \tilde{z}_2, \ldots, \tilde{z}_{T-1}, \tilde{\delta}_1, \tilde{\delta}_2, \ldots, \tilde{\delta}_T, \tilde{\varepsilon}_1, \tilde{\varepsilon}_2, \ldots, \tilde{\varepsilon}_{T-1})$$

are mutually independent and distributed multivariate normal, with each variable having a mean of zero.

1.2 Equilibrium

We will be concerned with the (Nash) equilibria of the trading game that our model defines among traders. Under our assumptions, the market maker has a passive role in the models.[7] Two types of traders do make strategic decisions in our model. Informed traders must determine the size of their market order in each period. At time t, this decision is made knowing $\tilde{\Omega}_{t-1}$, the history of order flows up to period $t-1$; $\tilde{\Delta}_t$, the innovations up to t; and the signal, $\tilde{\delta}_{t+1} + \tilde{\varepsilon}_t$. The discretionary liquidity traders must choose a period in $[T', T'']$ in which to trade. Each trader takes the strategies of all other traders, as well as the terms of trade (summarized by the market maker's price-setting strategy), as given.

The market maker, who only observes the total order flow, sets prices to satisfy the zero expected profit condition. We assume that the market maker's pricing response is a linear function of $\tilde{\Omega}_t$ and $\tilde{\Delta}_t$. In the equilibrium that emerges, this will be consistent with the zero-profit condition. Given our assumptions, the market maker learns nothing in period t from past order flows ($\tilde{\Omega}_{t-1}$) that cannot be inferred from the public information $\tilde{\Delta}_t$. This is because past trades of the informed traders are independent of $\tilde{\delta}_{t+1}, \tilde{\delta}_{t+2}, \ldots, \tilde{\delta}_T$ and because the liquidity trading in any period is independent of that in any other period. This means that the price set in period t is equal to the expectation of $\tilde{F}$ conditional on all public information observed in that period plus an adjustment that reflects the information contained in the current order flow $\tilde{\omega}_t$:

$$\begin{aligned} \tilde{P}_t(\tilde{\Delta}_t, \tilde{\Omega}_t) &= E(\tilde{F}|\tilde{\Delta}_t) + \lambda_t \tilde{\omega}_t \\ &= \bar{F} + \sum_{\tau=1}^{t} \tilde{\delta}_\tau + \lambda_t \tilde{\omega}_t \end{aligned} \tag{3}$$

Our notation conforms with that in Kyle (1984, 1985). The reciprocal of λ_t is Kyle's market-depth parameter, and it plays an important role in our analysis.

The main result of this section shows that in equilibrium there is a tendency for trading to be concentrated in the same period. Specifically, we will show that equilibria where all discretionary liquidity traders trade in the same period always exist and that only such equilibria are robust to slight changes in the parameters.

Our analysis begins with a few simple results that characterize the equilibria of the model. Suppose that the total amount of discretionary liquidity demands in period t is $\sum_{j=1}^{m} \tilde{y}_t^j$, where $\tilde{y}_t^j = \tilde{Y}^j$ if the jth discretionary liquidity trader trades in period t and where $\tilde{y}_t^j = 0$ otherwise. Define $\Psi_t \equiv \text{var}(\sum_{j=1}^{m} \tilde{y}_t^j + \tilde{z}_t)$; that is, Ψ_t is the total variance of the liquidity trading in period t. (Note that Ψ_t must be determined in equilibrium since it depends on the trading positions of the discretionary liquidity traders.) The following lemma is proved in the Appendix.

Lemma 1. *If the market maker follows a linear pricing strategy, then in equilibrium each informed trader i submits at time t a market order of* $\tilde{x}_t^i = \beta_t^i(\tilde{\delta}_{t+1} + \tilde{\epsilon}_t)$, *where*

$$\beta_t^i = \sqrt{\frac{\Psi_t}{n_t(\text{var}(\tilde{\delta}_{t+1}) + \phi_t)}} \tag{4}$$

---

[7]It is actually possible to think of the market maker also as a player in the game, whose payoff is minus the sum of the squared deviations of the prices from the true payoff.

The equilibrium value of λ_t is given by

$$\lambda_t = \frac{\text{var}(\tilde{\delta}_{t+1})}{n_t + 1}\sqrt{\frac{n_t}{\Psi_t(\text{var}(\tilde{\delta}_{t+1}) + \phi_t)}} \tag{5}$$

This lemma gives the equilibrium values of λ_t and β_t for a given number of informed traders and a given level of liquidity trading. Most of the comparative statics associated with the solution are straightforward and intuitive. Two facts are important for our results. First, λ_t is decreasing in Ψ_t, the total variance of liquidity trades. That is, the more variable are the liquidity trades, the deeper is the market. Less intuitive is the fact that λ_t is decreasing in n_t, the number of informed traders. This seems surprising since it would seem that with more informed traders the adverse selection problem faced by the market maker is more severe. However, informed traders, all of whom observe the same signal, compete with each other, and this leads to a smaller λ_t. This is a key observation in the next section, where we introduce endogenous entry by informed traders.[8]

When some of the liquidity trading is discretionary, Ψ_t is an endogenous parameter. In equilibrium each discretionary liquidity trader follows the trading policy that minimizes his expected transaction costs, subject to meeting his liquidity demand $\tilde{Y}^j$. We now turn to the determination of this equilibrium behavior. Recall that each trader takes the value of λ_t (as well as the actions of other traders) as given and assumes that he cannot influence it. The cost of trading is measured as the difference between what the liquidity trader pays for the security and the security's expected value. Specifically, the expected cost to the jth liquidity trader of trading at time $t \in [T', T'']$ is

$$\text{E}((P_t(\tilde{\Delta}_t, \tilde{\Omega}_t) - \tilde{F})\ \tilde{Y}^j|\tilde{\Delta}_t, \tilde{\Omega}_{t-1}, \tilde{Y}^j) \tag{6}$$

Substituting for $P_t(\tilde{\Delta}_t, \tilde{\Omega}_t)$—and using the fact that $\tilde{z}_t$, $\tilde{y}^i_t$, $i \neq j$ and $\tilde{\delta}_\tau$ where $\tau = t+1$, $t+2, \ldots T$ are independent of $\tilde{\Delta}_t$, $\tilde{\Omega}_{t-1}$, and $\tilde{Y}^j$ (which is the information of discretionary liquidity trader j)—the cost simplifies to $\lambda_t(\tilde{Y}^j)^2$. Thus, for a given set of λ_t, $t \in [T', T'']$, the expected cost of liquidity trading is minimized by trading in that period $t^* \in [T', T'']$ in which λ_t is the smallest. This is very intuitive, since λ_t measures the effect of each unit of order flow on the price and, by assumption, liquidity traders trade only once.

Recall that from Lemma 1, λ_t is decreasing in Ψ_t. This means that if in equilibrium the discretionary liquidity trading is particularly heavy in a particular period t, then λ_t will be set lower, which in turn makes discretionary liquidity traders concentrate their trading in that period. In sum, we obtain the following result.

Proposition 1. *There always exist equilibria in which all discretionary liquidity trading occurs in the same period. Moreover, only these equilibria are robust in the sense that if for some set of parameters there exists an equilibrium in which discretionary liquidity traders do not trade in the same period, then for an arbitrarily close set of parameters (e.g., by perturbing the vector of variances of the liquidity demands $\tilde{Y}^j$), the only possible equilibria involve concentrated trading by the discretionary liquidity traders.*

---

[8]More intuition for why λ_t is decreasing in n_t can be otained from statistical inference. Recall that λ_t is the regression coefficient in the forecast of $\tilde{\delta}_{t+1}$, given the total order flow $\tilde{\omega}_t$. The order flow can be written as $a(\tilde{\delta}_{t+1} + \tilde{\varepsilon}_t) + \tilde{u}$, where $a(\tilde{\delta}_{t+1} + \tilde{\varepsilon}_t)$ represents the total trading position of the informed traders and $\tilde{u}$ is the position of the liquidity traders with $\text{var}(\tilde{u}) = \Psi$. As the number of informed traders increases, a increases. For a given level of a, the market maker sets λ_t equal to $\lambda(a) = a/(a^2(1 + \phi) + \Psi)$. This is an increasing function of a if and only if $a \leq \sqrt{\Psi/(1 + \phi)}$, which in this model occurs if and only if $n_t \leq 1$. We can think of the market maker's inference problem in two parts: first he uses $\tilde{\omega}_t$ to predict $a\tilde{\delta}_{t+1}$; then he scales this down by a factor of $1/a$ to obtain his prediction of $\tilde{\delta}_{t+1}$. The weight placed upon $\tilde{\omega}_t$ in predicting $a\tilde{\delta}_{t+1}$ is always increasing in a, but for a large enough value of a the scaling down by a factor of $1/a$ eventually dominates, lowering λ_t.

Proof. Define $h \equiv \text{var}(\sum_{j=1}^{m} \tilde{Y}^j)$, that is, the total variance of discretionary liquidity demands. Suppose that all discretionary liquidity traders trade in period t and that the market maker adjusts λ_t and informed traders set β_t accordingly. Then the total trading cost incurred by the discretionary traders is $\lambda_t(h)h$, where $\lambda_t(h)$ is given in Lemma 1 with $\Psi_t = h + \text{var}(\tilde{z}_t)$.

Consider the period $t^* \in [T', T'']$ for which $\lambda_t(h)$ is the smallest. (If there are several periods in which the smallest value is achieved, choose the first.) It is then an equilibrium for all discretionary traders to trade in t^*. This follows since $\lambda_t(h)$ is decreasing in h, so that we must have by the definition of t^*, $\lambda_t(0) \geq \lambda_{t^*}(h)$ for all $t \in [T', T'']$. Thus, discretionary liquidity traders prefer to trade in period t^*.

The above argument shows that there exist equilibria in which all discretionary liquidity trading is concentrated in one period. If there is an equilibrium in which trading is not concentrated, then the smallest value of λ_t must be attained in at least two periods. It is easy to see that any small change in $\text{var}(\tilde{Y}^j)$ for some j would make the λ_t different in different periods, upsetting the equilibrium.

Proposition 1 states that concentrated-trading patterns are always viable and that they are generically the only possible equilibria (given that the market maker uses a linear strategy). Note that in our model all traders take the values of λ_t as given. That is, when a trader considers deviating from the equilibrium strategy, he assumes that the trading strategies of other traders and the pricing strategy of the market maker (i.e., λ_t) do not change.[9] One may assume instead that liquidity traders first announce the timing of their trading and then trading takes place (anonymously), so that informed traders and the market maker can adjust their strategies according to the announced timing of liquidity trades. In this case the only possible equilibria are those where trading is concentrated. This follows because if trading is not concentrated, then some liquidity traders can benefit by deviating and trading in another period, which would lower the value of λ_t in that period.

We now illustrate Proposition 1 by an example. This example will be used and developed further in the remainder of this article.

Example Assume that $T = 5$ and that discretionary liquidity traders learn of their demands in period 2 and must trade in or before period 4 (i.e., $T' = 2$ and $T'' = 4$). In each of the first four periods, three informed traders trade, and we assume that each has perfect information. Thus, each observes in period t the realization of $\tilde{\delta}_{t+1}$. We assume that public information arrives at a constant rate, with $\text{var}(\tilde{\delta}_t) = 1$ for all t. Finally, the variance of the nondiscretionary liquidity trading occurring each period is set equal to 1. We are interested in the behavior of the discretionary liquidity traders. Assume that there are two of these traders, A and B, and let $\text{var}(\tilde{Y}^A) = 4$ and $\text{var}(\tilde{Y}^B) = 1$. First assume that A trades in period 2 and B trades in period 3. Then $\lambda_1 = \lambda_4 = 0.4330$, $\lambda_2 = 0.1936$ and $\lambda_3 = 0.3061$. This cannot be an equilibrium, since $\lambda_2 < \lambda_3$, so B will want to trade in period 2 rather than in period 3. The discretionary liquidity traders take the λ's as fixed and B perceives that his trading costs can be reduced if he trades earlier. Now assume that both discretionary liquidity traders trade in period 3. In this case $\lambda_1 = \lambda_2 = \lambda_4 = 0.4330$ and $\lambda_3 = 0.1767$.

[9]Interestingly, when $n_t = 1$ the equilibrium is the same whether the informed trader takes λ_t as given or whether he takes into account the effect his trading policy has on the market maker's determination of λ_t. In other words, in this model the Nash equilibrium in the game between the informed trader and the market maker is identical to the Stackelberg equilibrium in which the trader takes the market maker's response into account.

This is clearly a stable trading pattern. Both traders want to trade in period 3 since λ_3 is the minimal λ_t.

1.3 Implications for Volume and Price Behavior

In this section we show that the concentration of trading that results when some liquidity traders choose the timing of their trades has a pronounced effect on the volume of trading. Specifically, the volume is higher in the period in which trading is concentrated both because of the increased liquidity-trading volume and because of the induced informed-trading volume. The concentration of discretionary liquidity traders does not affect the amount of information revealed by prices or the variance of price changes, however, as long as the number of informed traders is held fixed and is specified exogenously. As we show in the next section, the results on price informativeness and on the variance of price changes are altered if the number of informed traders in the market is determined endogenously.

It is clear that the behavior of prices and of trading volume is determined in part by the rate of public-information release and the magnitude of the nondiscretionary liquidity trading in each period. Various patterns can easily be obtained by making the appropriate assumptions about these exogenous variables. Since our main interest in this article is to examine the effects of traders' *strategic* behavior on prices and volume, we wish to abstract from these other determinants. If the rate at which information becomes public is constant and the magnitude of nondiscretionary liquidity trading is the same in all periods, then any patterns that emerge are due solely to the strategic behavior of traders. We therefore assume in this section that $\mathrm{var}(\tilde{z}_t) = g$, $\mathrm{var}(\tilde{\delta}_t) = 1$, and $\mathrm{var}(\tilde{\varepsilon}_t) = \phi$ for all t. Setting $\mathrm{var}(\tilde{\delta}_t)$ to be constant over time guarantees that public information arrives at a constant rate. [The normalization of $\mathrm{var}(\tilde{\delta}_t)$ to 1 is without loss of generality.]

Before presenting our results on the behavior of prices and trading volume, it is important to discuss how volume should be measured. Suppose that there are k traders with market orders given by $\tilde{s}_1, \tilde{s}_2, \ldots, \tilde{s}_k$. Assume that the $\tilde{s}_i$ are independently and normally distributed, each with mean 0. Let $\tilde{s}_i^+ = \max(\tilde{s}_i, 0)$ and $\tilde{s}_i^- = \max(-\tilde{s}_i, 0)$. The total volume of trade (including trades that are "crossed" between traders) is $\max(\tilde{S}^+, \tilde{S}^-)$, where $\tilde{S}^+ = \sum_{i=1}^k \tilde{s}_i^+$ and $\tilde{S}^- = \sum_{i=1}^k \tilde{s}_i^-$. The expected volume is

$$E(\max(\tilde{S}^+, \tilde{S}^-)) = \frac{1}{2}\sum_{i=1}^{k} E|\tilde{s}_i| + \frac{1}{2}E\left|\sum_{i=1}^{k} \tilde{s}_i\right|$$

$$= \frac{1}{\sqrt{2\pi}}\left(\sum_{i=1}^{k} \sigma_i + \sqrt{\sum_{i=1}^{k} \sigma_i^2}\right) \tag{7}$$

where σ_i is the standard deviation of $\tilde{s}_i$.

One may think that $\mathrm{var}(\tilde{\omega}_t)$, the variance of the total order flow, is appropriate for measuring the expected volume of trading. This is not correct. Since $\tilde{\omega}_t$ is the net demand presented to the market maker, it does not include trades that are crossed between traders and are therefore not met by the market maker. For example, suppose that there are two traders in period t and that their market orders are 10 and -16, respectively (i.e., the first trader wants to purchase 10 shares, and the second trader wants to sell 16 shares). Then the total amount of trading in this period is 16 shares, 10 crossed between the two traders and 6 supplied by the market maker ($\tilde{\omega}_t = 6$ in this case). The parameter $\mathrm{var}(\tilde{\omega}_t)$, which is represented by the last term in Equation (7), only considers the trading done with the market maker. The other terms measure the expected volume of trade across traders. In light of the above discussion, we will focus on the following measures of trading volume, which identify the contribution of each group of traders to the total trading volume:

$$V_t^I \equiv \sqrt{\operatorname{var}\left(\sum_{i=1}^{n} \tilde{x}_t^i\right)} = \sqrt{\operatorname{var}(n_t\beta_t(\tilde{\delta}_{t+1} + \tilde{\varepsilon}_t))} \tag{8}$$

$$V_t^L \equiv \sum_{j=1}^{m} \sqrt{\operatorname{var}(\tilde{y}_t^j)} + \sqrt{\operatorname{var}(\tilde{z}_t)} \tag{9}$$

$$V_t^M \equiv \sqrt{\operatorname{var}(\tilde{\omega}_t)} \tag{10}$$

$$V_t \equiv V_t^I + V_t^L + V_t^M \tag{11}$$

In words, V_t^I and V_t^L measure the expected volume of trading of the informed traders and the liquidity traders, respectively, and V_t^M measures the expected trading done by the market maker. The total expected volume, V_t, is the sum of the individual components. These measures are closely related to the true expectation of the actual measured volume.[10]

Proposition 1 asserts that a typical equilibrium for our model involves the concentration of all discretionary liquidity trading in one period. Let this period be denoted by t^*. Note that if we assume that n_t, $\operatorname{var}(\tilde{\delta}_t)$, $\operatorname{var}(\tilde{\varepsilon}_t)$, and $\operatorname{var}(\tilde{z}_t)$ are independent of t, then t^* can be any period in $[T', T'']$.

The following result summarizes the equilibrium patterns of trading volume in our model.

Proposition 2. *In an equilibrium in which all discretionary liquidity trading occurs in period t^*,*

1. $V_{t^*}^L > V_t^L$ *for* $t \neq t^*$
2. $V_{t^*}^I > V_t^I$ *for* $t \neq t^*$
3. $V_{t^*}^M > V_t^M$ *for* $t \neq t^*$

Proof. Part 1 is trivial, since there is more liquidity trading in t^* than in other periods. To prove part 2, note that

$$V_t^I = \sqrt{\operatorname{var}(n_t\beta_t(\tilde{\delta}_{t+1} + \tilde{\varepsilon}))} = \sqrt{n_t\Psi_t} \tag{12}$$

Thus, an increase in Ψ_t, the total variance of liquidity trading, decreases λ_t and increases the informed component of trading. Part 3 follows immediately from parts 1 and 2.

This result shows that the concentration of liquidity trading increases the volume in the period in which it occurs not only directly through the actual liquidity trading (an increase in V_t^L) but also indirectly through the additional informed trading it induces (an increase in V_t^I). This is an example of trading generating trading. An example that illustrates this phenomenon is presented following the next result.[11]

We now turn to examine two endogenous parameters related to the price process. The first parameter measures the extent to which prices reveal private information, and it is defined by

$$Q_t \equiv \operatorname{var}(\tilde{\delta}_{t+1} \mid \tilde{P}_t) \tag{13}$$

[10]Our measure of volume is proportional to the actual expected volume if there is exactly one nondiscretionary liquidity trader; otherwise, the trading crossed between these traders will not be counted, and V_t^L will be lower than the true contribution of the liquidity traders. This presents no problem for our analysis, however, since the amount of this trading in any period is independent of the strategic behavior of the other traders.

[11]Note that the amount of informed trading is independent of the precision of the signal that informed traders observe. This is due to the assumed risk neutrality of informed traders.

The second is simply the variance of the price change:

$$R_t \equiv \mathrm{var}(\tilde{P}_t - \tilde{P}_{t-1}) \tag{14}$$

Proposition 3. *Assume that $n_t = n$ for every t. Then*

1. $Q_{t*} = Q_t$ *for every t*
2. $R_{t*} = R_t = 1$ *for every t*

Proof. It is straight forward to show that in general

$$Q_t = \left(1 + \frac{n_t}{1 + \phi + n_t\phi}\right)^{-1} \tag{15}$$

and

$$R_t = \frac{1}{1+\phi}\left(\frac{n_t}{1+n_t} + \frac{1}{1+n_{t-1}} + \phi\right) \tag{16}$$

The result follows since both R_t and Q_t are independent of Ψ_t, and $n_t = n$.

As observed in Kyle (1984, 1985), the amount of private information revealed by the price is *independent* of the total variance of liquidity trading. Thus, despite the concentration of trading in t^*, $Q_{t*} = Q_t$ for all t. The intuition behind this is that although there is more liquidity trading in period t^*, there is also more informed trading, as we saw in Proposition 2. The additional informed trading is just sufficient to keep the information content of the total order flow constant.

Proposition 3 also says that the variance of price changes is the same when n informed traders trade in each period as it is when there is no informed trading. [When there is no informed trading, $\tilde{P}_t - \tilde{P}_{t-1} = \tilde{\delta}_t$, so $R_t = \mathrm{var}(\tilde{\delta}_t) = 1$ for all t.] With some informed traders, the market gets information earlier than it would otherwise, but the overall rate at which information comes to the market is unchanged. Moreover, the variance of price changes is independent of the variance of liquidity trading in period t. As will be shown in the next section, these results change if the number of informed traders is determined endogenously. Before turning to this analysis, we illustrate the results of this section with an example.

Example (continued) Consider again the example introduced in Section 1.2. Recall that in the equilibrium we discussed, both of the discretionary liquidity traders trade in period 3. Table 2 shows the effects of this trading on volume and price behavior. The volume-of-trading measure in period 3 is $V_3 = 13.14$, while that in the other periods is only 4.73. The difference is only partly due to the actual trading of the liquidity traders. Increased trading by the three informed traders in period 3 also contributes to higher volume. As the table shows, both Q_t and R_t are unaffected by the increased liquidity trading. With three informed traders, three quarters of the private information is revealed through prices no matter what the magnitude of liquidity demand.

2. Endogenous Information Acquisition

In Section 1 the number of informed traders in each period was taken as fixed. We now assume, instead, that private information is acquired at some cost in each period and that traders acquire this information if and only if their expected profit exceeds this cost. The number of informed traders is therefore determined as part of the equilibrium. It will be shown that endogenous information acquisition intensifies the result that trading is

TABLE 2 | Effects of Discretionary Liquidity Trading on Volume and Price Behavior When the Number of Informed Traders Is Constant over Time

t	n_t	λ_t	V_t	V_t^I	V_t^L	V_t^M	Q_t	R_t
1	3	0.43	4.73	1.73	1.00	2.00	0.25	
2	3	0.43	4.73	1.73	1.00	2.00	0.25	1.00
3	3	0.18	13.14	4.24	4.00	4.90	0.25	1.00
4	3	0.43	4.73	1.73	1.00	2.00	0.25	1.00

A four-period example, with $n_t = 3$ informed traders in each period. For $t = 1, 2, 3, 4$, the table gives λ_t, the market-depth parameter; V_t, a measure of total trading volume; V_t^I, a measure of the informed-trading volume; V_t^L, a measure of liquidity-trading volume; V_t^M a measure of the trading volume of the market maker; Q_t, a measure of the amount of private information revealed in the price; and R_t, the variance of the price change from period $t - 1$ to period t.

concentrated in equilibrium and that it alters the results on the distribution and informativeness of prices.

Let us continue to assume that public information arrives at a constant rate and that $\text{var}(\tilde{\delta}_t) = 1$ and $\text{var}(\tilde{z}_t) = g$ for all t. Let c be the cost of observing $\tilde{\delta}_{t+1} + \tilde{\varepsilon}_t$ in period t, where $\text{var}(\tilde{\varepsilon}_t) = \phi$. We assume that $c < 0.5\sqrt{g/(1+\phi)}$. This will guarantee that in equilibrium at least one trader is informed in each period. We need to determine n_t the equilibrium number of informed traders in period t.[12]

Define $\pi(n_t, \Psi_t)$ to be the expected trading profits of an informed trader (over one period) when there are n_t informed traders in the market and the total variance of all liquidity trading is Ψ_t. Let $\lambda(n_t, \Psi_t)$ be the equilibrium value of λ_t under these conditions. (Note that these functions are the same in all periods.)

The total expected cost of the liquidity traders is $\lambda(n_t, \Psi_t)\Psi_t$. Since each of the n_t informed traders submits the same market order, they divide this amount equally. Thus, from Lemma 1 we have

$$\pi(n_t, \Psi_t) = \frac{1}{n_t}\lambda(n_t, \Psi_t)\Psi_t = \frac{1}{n_t + 1}\sqrt{\frac{\Psi_t}{n_t(1+\phi)}} \tag{17}$$

It is clear that a necessary condition for an equilibrium with n informed traders is $\pi(n_t, \Psi_t) \geq c$; otherwise, the trading profits of informed traders do not cover the cost of acquiring the information. Another condition for an equilibrium with n_t informed traders is that no additional trader has incentives to become informed.

We will discuss two models of entry. One approach is to assume that a potential entrant cannot make his presence known (that is, he cannot credibly announce his presence to the rest of the market). Under this assumption, a potential entrant takes the strategies of all other traders and the market maker as given and assumes that they will continue to behave as if n_t traders are informed. Thus we still have $\lambda = \lambda(n_t, \Psi_t)$. The following lemma gives the optimal market order for an entrant and his expected trading profits under this assumption. (The proof is in the Appendix.)

[12]Note that we are assuming that the precision of the information, measured by the parameter $\phi = \text{var}(\tilde{\varepsilon}_t)$, together with the cost of becoming informed, are constant over time. If the precision of the signal varied across periods, then there might also be a different cost to acquiring different signals. We would then need to specify a cost function for signals as a function of their precision.

TABLE 3 | Expected Trading Profits of Informed Traders When the Variance of Liquidity Demand Is 6

n	$\pi(n, 6)$	$\frac{1}{4}\pi(n, 6)$
1	1.225	0.306
2	0.577	0.144
3	0.354	0.088
4	0.245	0.061
5	0.183	0.046
6	0.143	0.038
7	0.116	0.029

For some possible number of informed traders, n, the table gives $\pi(n, 6)$, the expected profits of each of the informed traders, assuming that the variance of total liquidity trading is 6; and $\pi(n, 6)/4$, the profits of an entrant who assumes that all other traders will use the same equilibrium strategies after he enters as an informed trader. If the cost of information is 0.13, then the equilibrium number of informed traders is $n \in \{3, 4, 5, 6\}$ in the first approach and $n = 6$ in the second.

Lemma 2. *An entrant into a market with n_t informed traders will trade exactly half the number of shares as the other n_t traders for any realization of the signal, and his expected profits will be $\pi(n_t, \Psi_t)/4$.*

It follows that with this approach n_t is an equilibrium number of informed traders in period t if and only if n_t satisfies $\pi(n_t, \Psi_t)/4 \leq c \leq \pi(n_t, \Psi_t)$. If c is large enough, there may be no positive integer n_t satisfying this condition, so that the only equilibrium number of informed traders is zero. However, the assumption that $c < 0.5\sqrt{g/(1 + \phi)}$ guarantees that this is never the case. In general, there may be several values of n_t that are consistent with equilibrium according to this model.

An alternative model of entry by informed traders is to assume that if an additional trader becomes informed, other traders and the market maker change their strategies so that a new equilibrium, with $n_t + 1$ informed traders, is reached. If liquidity traders do not change their behavior, the profits of each informed trader would now become $\pi(n_t + 1, \Psi_t)$.[13] The largest n_t satisfying $\pi(n_t, \Psi_t)/4 \leq c \leq \pi(n_t, \Psi_t)$ is the (unique) n satisfying $\pi(n_t + 1, \Psi_t) < c \leq \pi(n_t, \Psi_t)$, which is the condition for equilibrium under the alternative approach. This is illustrated in the example below.

Example (continued) Consider again the example introduced in Section 1.2 (and developed further in Section 1.3). In period 3, when both of the discretionary liquidity traders trade, the total variance of liquidity trading is $\Psi_3 = 6$. Assume that the cost of perfect information is $c = 0.13$. Table 3 gives $\pi(n, 6)$ and $\pi(n, 6)/4$ as a function of some possible values for n.

With $c = 0.13$, it is not an equilibrium to have only one or two informed traders, for in each of these cases a potential entrant will find it profitable to acquire information. It is also not possible to have seven traders acquiring information since each will find that his equilibrium expected profits are less than $c = 0.13$. Equilibria involving three to six informed traders are clearly supportable under the first model of entry. Note that $n_3 = 6$ also has the property that $\pi(7, 6) < 0.13 < \pi(6, 6)$, so that if informed traders and the market maker

[13] In fact, the same equilibrium obtains if liquidity traders were assumed to respond to the entry of an informed trader, as will be clear below.

TABLE 4 | Expected Trading Profits of Informed Traders When the Variance of Liquidity Demand Is 3

n	$\pi(n, 1)$	$\frac{1}{4}\pi(n, 1)$
1	0.500	0.125
2	0.236	0.059
3	0.144	0.036
4	0.100	0.025

For some possible number of informed traders, n, the table gives $\pi(n, 1)$, the expected profits of each of the informed traders, assuming that the variance of total liquidity trading is 1; and $\pi(n, 1)/4$, the profits of an entrant who assumes that all other traders will use the same equilibrium strategies after he enters as an informed trader. If the cost of information is 0.13, then the equilibrium number of informed traders is $n \in \{1, 2, 3\}$ in the first approach and $n = 3$ in the second.

(as well as the entrant) change their strategies to account for the actual number of informed traders, each informed trader makes positive profits, and no additional trader wishes to become informed.

As is intuitive, a lower level of liquidity trading generally supports fewer informed traders. In period 2 in our example, no discretionary liquidity traders trade, and therefore $\Psi_2 = g = 1$. Table 4 shows that if the cost of becoming informed is equal to 0.13, there will be no more than three informed traders. Moreover, assuming the first model of entry, the lower level of liquidity trading makes equilibria with one or two informed traders viable.

To focus our discussion below, we will assume that the number of informed traders in any period is equal to the maximum number that can be supported. With $c = 0.13$ and $\Psi_t = 6$, this means that $n_t = 6$, and with the same level of cost and $\Psi_t = 1$, we have $n_t = 3$. As noted above, this determination of the equilibrium number of informed traders is consistent with the assumption that an entrant can credibly make his presence known to informed traders and to the market maker.

Does endogenous information acquisition change the conclusion of Proposition 1 that trading is concentrated in a typical equilibrium? We know that with an increased level of liquidity trading, more informed traders will generally be trading. If the presence of more informed traders in the market raises the liquidity traders' cost of trading, then discretionary liquidity traders may not want to trade in the same period.

It turns out that in this model the presence of more informed traders actually *lowers* the liquidity traders' cost of trading, intensifying the forces toward concentration of trading. As long as there is some informed trading in every period, liquidity traders prefer that there are more rather than fewer informed traders trading along with them. Of course, the best situation for liquidity traders is for there to be no informed traders, but for $n_t > 0$, the cost of trading is a decreasing function of n_t. The total cost of trading for the liquidity traders was shown to be $\lambda(n_t, \Psi_t)\Psi_t$. That this cost is decreasing in n follows from the fact that $\lambda(n_t, \Psi_t)$ is decreasing in n_t.

Thus, endogenous information acquisition intensifies the effects that bring about the concentration of trading. With more liquidity trading in a given period, more informed traders trade, and this makes it even more attractive for liquidity traders to trade in that period. As already noted, the intuition behind this result is that competition among the privately informed traders reduces their total profit, which benefits the liquidity traders.

TABLE 5 | Effects of Discretionary Liquidity Trading on Volume and Price Behavior When the Number of Informed Traders Is Endogenous

t	n_t	λ_t	V_t	V_t^I	V_t^L	V_t^M	Q_t	R_t
1	3	0.43	4.73	1.73	1.00	2.00	0.25	
2	3	0.43	4.73	1.73	1.00	2.00	0.25	1.00
3	6	0.14	16.48	6.00	4.00	6.48	0.14	1.11
4	3	0.43	4.73	1.73	1.00	2.00	0.25	0.90

A four-period example in which the number of informed traders, n_t, is determined endogenously, assuming that the cost of information is 0.13. For $t = 1, 2, 3, 4$, the table gives λ_t, the market-depth parameter; V_t, a measure of total trading volume; V_t^I, a measure of the informed-trading volume; V_t^L, a measure of liquidity-trading volume; V_t^M, a measure of the trading volume of the market maker; Q_t, a measure of the amount of private information revealed in the price; and R_t, the variance of the price change from period $t - 1$ to period t.

The following proposition describes the effect of endogenous information acquisition on the trading volume and price process.[14]

Proposition 4. *Suppose that the number of informed traders in period t is the unique n_t satisfying $\pi(n_t + 1, \Psi_t) < c \leq \pi(n_t, \Psi_t)$ (i.e., determined by the second model of entry). Consider an equilibrium in which all discretionary liquidity traders trade in period t^*. Then*

1. $V_{t^*} > V_t$ *for* $t \neq t^*$
2. $V_{t^*}^I > V_t^I$ *for* $t \neq t^*$
3. $Q_{t^*} < Q_t$ *for* $t \neq t^*$
4. $R_{t^*} > R_{t^*-1} > R_{t^*+1}$

Proof. The first three statements follow simply from the fact that V_t and V_t^I are increasing in n_t, and that Q_t is decreasing in n_t. The last follows from Equation (16).

Example (continued) We consider again our example, but now with endogenous information acquisition. Suppose that the cost of acquiring perfect information is 0.13. In periods 1, 2, and 4, when no discretionary liquidity traders trade, there will continue to be three informed traders trading, as seen in Table 4. In period 3, when both of the discretionary liquidity traders trade, the number of informed traders will now be 6, as seen in Table 3. Table 5 shows what occurs with the increased number of informed traders in period 3.

With the higher number of informed traders, the value of λ_3 is reduced even further, to the benefit of the liquidity traders. It is therefore still an equilibrium for the two discretionary liquidity traders to trade in period 3. Because three more informed traders are present in the market in this period, the total trading cost of the liquidity traders (discretionary and nondiscretionary) is reduced by 0.204, or 19 percent.

The addition of the three informed traders affects the equilibrium in significant ways. First note that the volume in period 3 is even higher now relative to the other periods. With the increase in the number of informed traders, the amount of informed trading has increased. Increased liquidity trading generates trade because (1) it leads to more informed trading by a given group of informed traders and (2) it tends to increase the number of informed traders.

[14]A comparative statics result analogous to part 3 is discussed in Kyle (1984).

More importantly, the change in the number of informed traders in response to the increased liquidity trading in period 3 has altered the behavior of prices. The price in period 3 is more informative about the future public-information release than are the prices in the other periods. Because of the increased competition among the informed traders in period 3, more private information is revealed and $Q_3 < Q_t$ for $t \neq 3$. With endogenous information acquisition, prices will generally be more informative in periods with high levels of liquidity trading than they are in other periods.

The variance of price changes is also altered around the period of higher liquidity trading. From Equation (16) we see that if $n_t = n_{t-1}$, then $R_t = 1$. When the number of informed traders is greater in the later period, $R_t > 1$. This is because more information is revealed in the later period than in the earlier one. When the number of informed traders decreases from one period to the next, $R_t < 1$, since more information is revealed in the earlier period.

It is interesting to contrast our results in this section with those of Clark (1973), who also considers the relation between volume and the rate of information arrival. Clark takes the flow of information to the market as exogenous and shows that patterns in this process can lead to patterns in volume. In our model, however, the increased volume of trading due to discretionary trading leads to changes in the process of private-information arrival.

3. A Model with Diverse Information

So far we have assumed that all the informed traders observe the same piece of information. In this section we discuss an alternative formulation of the model, in which informed traders observe different signals as in Kyle (1984). The basic results about trading and volume patterns or price behavior do not change. However, the analysis of endogenous information acquisition is somewhat different.

Assume that the ith informed trader observes in period t the signal $\tilde{\delta}_{t+1} + \tilde{\varepsilon}_t^i$ and assume that the $\tilde{\varepsilon}_t^i$ are independently and identically distributed with variance ϕ. Note that as n increases, the total amount of private information increases as long as $\phi > 0$. The next result, which is analogous to Lemma 1 for the case of identical private signals, gives the equilibrium parameters for a given level of liquidity trading and a given number of informed traders. (The proof is a simple modification of the proof of Lemma 1 and is therefore omitted).

Lemma 3. *Assume that n_t informed traders trade in period t and that each observes an independent signal $\tilde{\delta}_{t+1} + \tilde{\varepsilon}_t^i$, where var v$\tilde{\delta}_{t+1}$] = 1 and var$(\tilde{\varepsilon}_t^i) = \phi_t$ for all i. Let Ψ_t be the total variance of the liquidity trading in period t. Then*

$$\lambda_t = \frac{1}{1 + n_t + 2\phi_t}\sqrt{\frac{n_t(1 + \phi_t)}{\Psi_t}} \tag{18}$$

The ith informed trader submits market order $\beta_t^i(\tilde{\delta}_{t+1} + \tilde{\varepsilon}_t^i)$ in each period t with

$$\beta_t^i = \frac{1}{\lambda_t(1 + n_t + 2\phi_t)} = \sqrt{\frac{\Psi_t}{n_t(1 + \phi_t)}} \tag{19}$$

Note that, as in the case of identical signals, λ_t is decreasing in Ψ_t. This immediately implies that Proposition 1 still holds in the model with diverse signals. Thus, if the number of informed traders is exogenously specified, the only robust equilibria are those in which trading by all discretionary liquidity traders is concentrated in one period.

Recall that the results when information acquisition is endogenous were based on the observation that when there are more informed traders, they compete more aggressively with each other. This is favorable to the liquidity traders in that λ_t is reduced, intensifying the effects that lead to concentrated trading. However, when informed traders observe different pieces of information, an increase in their number also means that more private information is actually generated in the market as a whole. Indeed, unlike the case of identical signals an increase in n_t can now lead to an increase in λ_t. It is straightforward to show that (with $\phi_t = \phi$ for all t as before)

$$\text{sign}\left(\frac{\partial\lambda(n_t, \Psi_t)}{\partial n_t}\right) = \text{sign}\,(1 - n_t + 2\phi) \tag{20}$$

If the information gathered by informed traders is sufficiently imprecise, an increase in n_t will increase λ_t. An increase in n_t has two effects. First, it increases the degree of competition among the informed traders and this tends to reduce λ_t. Second, it increases the amount of private information represented in the order flow. This generally tends to increase λ_t. For large values of ϕ and small values of n_t, an increase in n_t has a substantial effect on the amount of information embodied in the order flow and this dominates the effect of an increase of competition. As a result, λ_t increases.

The discussion above has implications for equilibrium with endogenous information acquisition. In general, since the profits of each informed trader are increasing in Ψ, there would be more informed traders in periods in which discretionary liquidity traders trade more heavily. When signals are identical, this strengthens the incentives of discretionary liquidity traders to trade in these periods, since it lowers the relevant λ_t further. Since in the diverse information case λ_t can actually increase with an increase in n_t, the argument for concentrated trading must be modified.

Assume for a moment that n_t is a continuous rather than a discrete parameter. Consider two periods, denoted by H and L. In period H, the variance of liquidity trading is high and equal to Ψ_H; in period L, the variance of liquidity trading is low and equal to Ψ_L. Let n_H (respectively n_L) be the number of traders acquiring information in period H (respectively L). To establish the viability of the concentrated-trading equilibrium, we need to show that with endogenous information acquisition, $\lambda(n_H, \Psi_H) \leq \lambda(n_L, \Psi_L)$. If n is continuous, then endogenous information acquisition implies that profits must be equal across periods:

$$\begin{aligned}\pi(n_H, \Psi_H) &= \frac{1}{1 + n_H + 2\phi}\sqrt{\frac{\Psi_H(1 + \phi)}{n_H}} \\ &= \pi(n_L, \Psi_L) \\ &= \frac{1}{1 + n_L + 2\phi}\sqrt{\frac{\Psi_L(1 + \phi)}{n_L}}\end{aligned} \tag{21}$$

Since $\Psi_H > \Psi_L$, it follows that $n_H > n_L$. To maintain equality between the profits with $n_H > n_L$, it is necessary that $\Psi_H/n_H > \Psi_L/n_L$. Since $\lambda(n, \Psi) = n\pi(n, \Psi)/\Psi$, it follows that $\lambda(n_H, \Psi_H) < \lambda(n_L, \Psi_L)$. Thus, if n were continuous, the value of λ would always be lower in periods with more liquidity trading, and the concentrated-trading equilibria would always be viable. These equilibria would also be generic as in Proposition 1.

The above is only a heuristic argument, establishing the existence of concentrated-trading equilibria with endogenous information acquisition in the model with diverse information. Since n_t is discrete, we cannot assert that in equilibrium the profits of informed traders are equal across periods. This may lead to the nonexistence of an equilibrium for some parameter values, as we show in the Appendix. It can be shown, however, that

- An equilibrium always exists if the variance of the discretionary liquidity demand is sufficiently high.
- If an equilibrium exists, then an equilibrium in which trading is concentrated exists. Moreover, for almost all parameters for which an equilibrium exists, only such concentrated-trading equilibria exist.

We now show that, when an equilibrium exists, the basic nature of the results we derived in the previous sections do not change when informed traders have diverse information. We continue to assume that $\phi_t = \phi$ for all t. Consider first the trading volume. It is easy to show that the variance of the total order flow of the informed traders is given by

$$\operatorname{var}\left(\sum_{i=1}^{n} \beta_i(\tilde{\delta}_{t+1} + \tilde{\varepsilon}_t^i)\right) = \frac{\Psi_t(n_t + \phi)}{1 + \phi} \tag{22}$$

This is clearly increasing in Ψ_t and in n_t. Since informed traders are diversely informed, there will generally be some trading within the group of informed traders. (For example, if a particular informed trader draws an extreme signal, his position may have an opposite sign to that of the aggregate position of informed traders.) Thus, V_t^I, the measure of trading volume by informed traders, will be greater than the expression in Equation (22). The amount of trading within the group of informed traders is clearly an increasing function of n_t. Thus, this strengthens the effect of concentrated trading on the volume measures: more liquidity trading leads to more informed traders, which in turn implies an even greater trading volume.

The basic characteristics of the price process are also essentially unchanged in this model. First consider the informativeness of the price, as measured by $Q_t = \operatorname{var}(\tilde{\delta}_{t+1}|\tilde{P}_t)$. With diverse information it can be shown that

$$Q_t = \left(1 + \frac{n_t}{1 + 2\phi}\right)^{-1} \tag{23}$$

As in Kyle (1984), an increase in the number of informed traders increases the informativeness of prices. This is due in part to the increased competition among the informed traders. It is also due to the fact that more information is gathered when more traders become informed. This second effect was not present in the model with common private information. The implications of the model remain the same as before: with endogenous information acquisition, prices will be more informative in periods with higher liquidity trading (i.e., periods in which the discretionary liquidity traders trade).

In the model with diverse private information, the behavior of R_t (the variance of price changes) is very similar to what we saw in the model with common information. It can be shown that

$$R_t = \frac{n_t}{1 + n_t + 2\phi} + \frac{1 + 2\phi}{1 + n_{t-1} + 2\phi} \tag{24}$$

As before, if $n_t = n$ for all t, then $R_t = 1$, and $R_t > 1$ if and only if $n_t > n_{t-1}$.

4. The Allocation of Liquidity Trading

In the analysis so far we have assumed that the discretionary liquidity traders can only trade once, so that their only decision was the timing of their single trade. We now allow discretionary liquidity traders to allocate their trading among the periods in the interval $[T', T'']$, that is, between the time their liquidity demand is determined and the time by which it must be satisfied. Since the model becomes more complicated, we will illustrate what happens in this case with a simple structure and by numerical examples.

Suppose that $T' = 1$ and $T'' = 2$, so that discretionary liquidity traders can allocate their trades over two trading periods. Suppose that there are n_1 informed traders in period 1 and n_2 informed traders in period 2 and that the informed traders obtain perfect information (i.e., they observe $\tilde{\delta}_{t+1}$ at time t). Each discretionary liquidity trader must choose α, the proportion of the liquidity demand $\tilde{Y}^j$ that is satisfied in period 1. The remainder will be satisfied in period 2. Discretionary liquidity trader j therefore trades $\alpha\tilde{Y}^j$ shares in period 1 and $(1 - \alpha)\ \tilde{Y}^j$ shares in period 2.

To obtain some intuition, suppose that the price function is as given in the previous sections; that is,

$$\tilde{P}_t = \bar{F} + \sum_{\tau=1}^{t} \tilde{\delta}_\tau + \lambda_t \tilde{\omega}_t \tag{25}$$

where λ_t is given by Lemma 1. Note that the price in period t depends only on the order flow in period t. In this case the discretionary liquidity trader's problem is to minimize the cost of liquidity trading, which is given by

$$(\alpha^2\lambda_1 + (1 - \alpha)^2\lambda_2)(\tilde{Y}^j)^2 \tag{26}$$

It is easy to see that this is minimized by setting $\alpha = \lambda_2/(\lambda_1 + \lambda_2)$. For example, if $\lambda_1 = \lambda_2$, then the optimal value of α is $\frac{1}{2}$. Thus, if each price is independent of previous order flows, the cost function for a liquidity trader is convex, and so discretionary liquidity traders divide their trades among different periods. It is important to note that the optimal α is independent of $\tilde{Y}^j$. This means that all liquidity traders will choose the same α.

If the above argument were correct, it would seem to upset our results on the concentration of trade. However, the argument is flawed, since the assumption that each price is independent of past order flows is no longer appropriate. Recall that the market maker sets the price in each period equal to the conditional expectation of $\tilde{F}$, given all the information available to him at the time. This includes the history of past order flows. In the models of the previous sections, there is no payoff-relevant information in past order flows $\tilde{\Omega}_{t-1}$ that is not revealed by the public information $\tilde{\Delta}_t$ in period t. This is no longer true here, since past order flows enable the market maker to forecast the liquidity component of current order flows. This improves the precision of his prediction of the informed-trading component, which is relevant to future payoffs. Specifically, since the information that informed traders have in period 1 is revealed to the market maker in period 2, the market maker can subtract $n_1\beta_1\delta_2$ from the total order flow in period 1. This reveals $\alpha\Sigma_j Y^j + \tilde{z}_1$, which is informative about $(1 - \alpha)\ \Sigma_j Y^j$, the discretionary liquidity demand in period 2.

Since the terms of trade in period 2 depend on the order flow in period 1, a trader who is informed in both periods will take into account the effect that his trading in the first period will have on the profits he can earn in the second period. This complicates the analysis considerably. To avoid these complications and to focus on the behavior of discretionary liquidity traders, we assume that no trader is informed in more than one period.

Suppose that the price in period 1 is given by

$$\tilde{P}_1 = P_0 + \tilde{\delta}_1 + \lambda_1\tilde{\omega}_1 \tag{27}$$

where

$$\tilde{\omega}_1 = n_1\beta_1\tilde{\delta}_2 + \alpha\sum_j \tilde{Y}^j + \tilde{z}_1 \tag{28}$$

and that the price in period 2 is given by

$$\tilde{P}_2 = P_0 + \tilde{\delta}_1 + \tilde{\delta}_2 + \lambda_2 \tilde{\omega}_2^p \tag{29}$$

where

$$\tilde{\omega}_2^p = n_2 \beta_2 \tilde{\delta}_3 + (1 - \alpha) \sum_j \tilde{Y}^j + \tilde{z}_2 - (1 - \alpha) E\left(\sum_j \tilde{Y}^j \middle| \tilde{\omega}_1, \tilde{\delta}_2 \right) \tag{30}$$

Note that the form of the price is the same in the two periods, but the order flow in the second period has been modified to reflect the prediction of the discretionary liquidity-trading component based on the order flow in the first period and the realization of $\tilde{\delta}_2$. Let γ be the coefficient in the regression of $\Sigma_j \tilde{Y}^j$ on $\alpha\, \Sigma_j \tilde{Y}^j + \tilde{z}_1$. Then it can be shown that the problem each discretionary liquidity trader faces, taking the strategies of all other traders and the market maker as given, is to choose α to minimize

$$\alpha^2 \lambda_1 + (1 - \alpha)^2 \lambda_2 - \alpha(1 - \alpha)\lambda_2 \gamma$$

The solution to this problem is to set

$$\alpha = \frac{\lambda_2(\gamma + 2)}{2(\lambda_1 + \lambda_2(\gamma + 1))} \tag{31}$$

Given that discretionary liquidity traders allocate their trades in this fashion, the market maker sets λ_1 and λ_2 so that his expected profit in each period (given all the information available to him) is zero. It is easy to show that in equilibrium λ_t and β_t are given by Lemma 1, with

$$\Psi_1 = g + \alpha^2 h \tag{32}$$

and

$$\Psi_2 = g + (1 - \alpha)^2 \left(\frac{1}{h} + \frac{\alpha^2}{g} \right)^{-1} \tag{33}$$

While it can be shown that this model has an equilibrium, it is generally impossible to find the equilibrium in closed form. We now discuss two limiting cases, one in which the nondiscretionary liquidity component vanishes and one in which it is infinitely noisy; we then provide examples in which the equilibrium is calculated numerically.

Consider first the case in which most of the liquidity trading is nondiscretionary. This can be thought of as a situation in which $g \to \infty$. In this situation the market maker cannot infer anything from the information available in the second period about the liquidity demand in that period. It can then be shown that $\gamma \to 0$, so that past order flows are uninformative to the market maker. Moreover,

$$\alpha \to \left(1 + \sqrt{\frac{n_1}{n_2}} \left(\frac{1 + n_2}{1 + n_1} \right) \right)^{-1} \tag{34}$$

For example, if $n_1 = n_2$, then $\alpha \to 1/2$. Not surprisingly, this is the solution we would obtain if we assumed that the price in each period is independent of the previous order flow. When discretionary liquidity trading is a small part of the total liquidity trading, we do not obtain a concentrated-trading equilibrium.

Now consider the other extreme case, in which $g = \text{var}(\tilde{z}_t) \to 0$. In this case almost all the liquidity trading is discretionary, and therefore the market maker can predict with great precision the liquidity component of the order flow in the second period, given his information. It can be shown that in the limit we get $\alpha = 1$, so that all liquidity trading is

TABLE 6 | Volume and Price Behavior When Discretionary Liquidity Traders Allocate Trading across Several Periods

t	n_t	λ_t	V_t	V_t^I	V_t^L	V_t^M	Q_t	R_t
1	3	0.43	4.73	1.73	1.00	2.00	0.25	
2	4	0.30	7.84	2.67	2.19	2.99	0.20	1.05
3	3	0.38	6.51	2.12	1.95	2.45	0.25	0.95
4	3	0.40	6.31	2.06	1.87	2.38	0.25	1.00

A four-period example in which the number of informed traders, n_t, is determined endogenously, assuming that the cost of information is 0.13 and that liquidity traders can allocate their trade in different periods between 2:00 P.M. and 4:00 P.M. For $t = 1, 2, 3, 4$, the table gives λ_t, the market-depth parameter; V_t, a measure of total trading volume; V_t^I, a measure of the informed-trading volume; V_t^L, a measure of liquidity-trading volume; V_t^M a measure of the trading volume of the market maker; Q_t, a measure of the amount of private information revealed in the price; and R_t, the variance of the price change from period $t - 1$ to period t.

concentrated in the first period. Note that since there is no liquidity trading in the second period, $\lambda_2 \to \infty$; thus, in a model with endogenous information acquisition we will get $n_2 = 0$ and there will be no trade in the second period.[15]

In general, discretionary liquidity traders have to take into account the fact that the market maker can infer their demands as time goes on. This causes their trades to be more concentrated in the earlier periods, as is illustrated by the two examples below. Note that, unlike the concentration result in Proposition 1, it now matters whether trading occurs at time T' or later; the different trading periods are not equivalent from the point of view of the discretionary liquidity traders. This will have implications when information acquisition is endogenous. Consider the following two examples.

In the first example we make all the parametric assumptions made in our previous examples, except that now we allow the discretionary liquidity traders A and B to allocate their trades across periods 2, 3, and 4. If information acquisition is endogenous and if the cost of perfect information is $c = 0.13$, then we obtain the equilibrium parameters given in Table 6. In this example, each discretionary liquidity trader j trades about $0.4\tilde{Y}^j$ in period 2, $0.31\tilde{Y}^j$ in period 3, and $0.29\tilde{Y}^j$ in period 4. Note that the measure of liquidity-trading volume is highest in period 2 and then falls off in periods 3 and 4. Three informed traders are present in each of the periods except period 2, when it is profitable for a fourth to enter. The behavior of prices is therefore similar to that when traders could only time their trades.

In the second example, illustrated in Table 7, we assume that there is less nondiscretionary liquidity trading. Specifically, we set the variance of nondiscretionary liquidity trading to be 0.1. With the cost of information at $c = 0.04$ and with endogenous information acquisition, we obtain pronounced patterns. For example, there are 11 informed traders in period 2 and three informed traders in each of the other periods. Liquidity trading is much heavier in period 2 as well, and the patterns of the volume and price behavior are very pronounced. In this example, each discretionary liquidity trader j trades $0.74\tilde{Y}^j$ in period 2, $0.14\tilde{Y}^j$ in period 3, and $0.12\tilde{Y}^j$ in period 4.

[15]Note that if indeed there is no trading by either the informed or the liquidity traders, then λ is undetermined, if we interpret it as a regression coefficient in the regression of $\tilde{\delta}_{t+1}$ on $\tilde{\omega}_t^p$. However, with no liquidity trading the market maker must refuse to trade. This is equivalent to setting λ_t to infinity.

TABLE 7 | An Example of Pronounced Patterns of Volume and Price Behavior When Discretionary Liquidity Traders Allocate Trading across Several Periods

t	n_t	λ_t	V_t	V_t^I	V_t^L	V_t^M	Q_t	R_t
1	3	1.37	1.50	0.55	0.32	0.63	0.25	
2	11	0.16	13.95	5.59	2.54	5.83	0.08	1.17
3	3	1.35	2.40	0.77	0.74	0.89	0.25	0.83
4	3	1.35	2.23	0.72	0.68	0.83	0.25	1.00

The same example as in Table 6, except that the variance of nondiscretionary liquidity trading is lower (0.1). The cost of information is assumed to be $c = 0.04$.

5. Extensions

In this section we discuss a number of additional extensions of our basic model. We show that the main conclusions of the model do not change in more general settings. This indicates that our results are robust to a variety of models.

5.1 Different Timing Constraints for Liquidity Traders

For simplicity, we have assumed so far that the demands of all the discretionary liquidity traders are determined at the same time and must be satisfied within the same time span. In reality, of course, different traders may realize their liquidity demands at different times, and the time that can elapse before these demands must be satisfied may also be different for different traders. Our results can be extended to this more general case, and their basic nature remains unchanged.

For example, suppose that there are three discretionary liquidity traders, *A*, *B*, and *C*, whose demands have the variances 5, 1, and 7, respectively. Suppose that trader *A* realizes his liquidity demand at 9:00 A.M. and must satisfy it by 2:00 P.M. that day. Trader *B* realizes his demand at 11:00 A.M. and must satisfy if by 4:00 P.M., and trader *C* realizes his demand at 2:30 P.M. and must satisfy it by 10:00 A.M. on the following day. If each of these traders trades only once to satisfy his liquidity demands, then it is an equilibrium that traders *A* and *C* trade at the same time between 9:00 A.M. and 10:00 A.M. (e.g., 9:30 A.M.) and that trader *B* trades sometime between 11:00 A.M. and 4:00 P.M.

Now suppose that the variance of *B*'s demand is 9 instead of 1. Then the equilibrium described above is possible only if trader *B* trades before 2:30 P.M.; otherwise, trader *C* would prefer to trade at the same time that *B* trades rather than at the same time that *A* trades, and the equilibrium would break down. Two other equilibrium patterns exist in this situation. In one, traders *B* and *C* trade at the same time between 2:30 P.M. and 4:00 P.M. (e.g., 3:00 P.M.), and trader *A* trades sometime between 9:00 A.M. and 2:00 P.M. In another equilibrium, traders *A* and *B* trade at the same time between 11:00 A.M. and 2:00 P.M. (e.g., 11:30 A.M.), and trader *C* trades sometime between 4:00 P.M. and 10:00 A.M. of the next morning. All these equilibria involve trading patterns in which two of the traders trade at the same time. If informed traders can enter the market, then their trading would also be concentrated in the periods with heavier liquidity trading. Thus, we obtain trading patterns similar to those discussed in the simple model.

5.2 Risk-Averse Liquidity Traders

We now ask whether our results change if, instead of assuming that all traders are risk-neutral, it is assumed that some traders are risk-averse. We focus on the discretionary liquidity traders, since their actions are the prime determinants of the equilibrium trading patterns we have identified. In the discussion below we continue to assume that informed traders and the market maker are risk-neutral. (A model in which these traders are also risk-averse is much more complicated and is therefore beyond the scope of this article.)

A risk-averse liquidity trader, say trader j, is concerned with more than the conditional expectation of $\tilde{Y}^j(\tilde{P}_t - \tilde{F})$ given his own demand $\tilde{Y}^j$. Since he submits market orders, the price at which he trades is uncertain. In those periods in which a large amount of liquidity trading takes place, the variance of the order flow is higher. One may think that since this will make the price more variable, it will discourage risk-averse liquidity traders from trading together. In fact, the reverse occurs; that is, risk-averse liquidity traders have an even greater incentive to trade together than do risk-neutral traders.

The following heuristic discussion uses the basic model of Sections 1 to 3. Given our assumptions, the conditional distribution of $\tilde{P}_t - \tilde{F}$ is normal, given $\tilde{Y}^j$ and the public information available at time t. Thus, liquidity trader j is concerned only with the first two moments of this conditional distribution. Consider first the unconditional variance of $\tilde{P}_t - \tilde{F}$. Since $\tilde{P}_t$ is the expectation of $\tilde{F}$, given the order flow at time t (and public information), the variance of $\tilde{P}_t - \tilde{F}$ is the variance of the prediction error. Suppose that all liquidity traders trade in period t^*. Recall from Section 1 that because of the more intense trading by informed traders at t^*, the prediction variance (which is related to Q_t) is *independent of* Ψ_t, the variance of liquidity trading. Thus, as long as the number of informed traders is constant over time, the concentration of liquidity trading in period t^* does not increase the variance of $\tilde{P}_{t^*} - \tilde{F}$ relative to other periods. We have also seen that the prediction variance is *decreasing* in n_t, the number of informed traders. This implies that with endogenous information acquisition, since more informed traders trade in period t^*, the prediction variance is even lower.

Now, liquidity trader j also knows his own demand $\tilde{Y}^j$, so we must consider the conditional variance of $\tilde{P}_t - \tilde{F}$, given $\tilde{Y}^j$. If $f_t(n_t)$ is the unconditional variance discussed above, then the conditional variance is equal to $f_t(n_t) - \lambda_t^2 \operatorname{var}(\tilde{Y}^j)$ if trader j trades in period t and is equal to $f_t(n_t)$ if he trades in a different period. It is clear now that the fact that trader j knows $\tilde{Y}^j$ does not change the direction of the results outlined in the preceding paragraph; if all discretionary liquidity traders trade in period $t^* \in [T', T'']$, then $f_{t^*}(n_t^*) - \lambda_{t^*}^2 \operatorname{var}(\tilde{Y}^j) < f_t(n_t)$ for all $t \in [T', T'']$ and $t \neq t^*$ and for all j. Thus, the equilibrium in which discretionary liquidity traders concentrate their trading in one period is still viable even if these traders are risk-averse.

5.3 Correlated Demands of Liquidity Traders

We have assumed that the demands of discretionary liquidity traders are independent of each other. This assumption seems to be reasonable if liquidity demands are driven by completely idiosyncratic life-cycle motives that are specific to individual traders. If liquidity demands are correlated across traders because of some common factors affecting these demands, and if these factors are observed by the market maker before he forms prices, then our analysis is still valid, with the interpretation that liquidity trading corresponds to the unpredictable part of these demands.

It is possible to extend our analysis to the case where common factors in liquidity demands are not observable (or, in general, to the case of correlated liquidity demands). Two considerations arise in this case. First, if liquidity traders trade in different periods, then past order flows may provide information to the market maker concerning the liquidity component in the current order flow. Second, if more than one liquidity trader trades in a given period, then the cost of trading in this period, which is proportional to the correlation of his demands with the total order flow, involves an additional term that reflects the correlation of the trader's demand with the other liquidity demands.

If liquidity demands are negatively correlated, then it can be shown that concentrated-trading equilibria always exist, so our results are still valid. The same is true if the variance of nondiscretionary liquidity demands is small enough, that is, if there is very little nondiscretionary liquidity trading. The results may be different if liquidity demands are positively correlated. In this case it is possible that an equilibrium in which trading is completely concentrated does not exist, or that equilibria in which different traders trade in different periods also exist, in addition to the concentrated-trading equilibria (and they are robust to slight perturbations in the parameters). Examples are not difficult to construct.

6. Empirical Implications

The result that trading is concentrated in particular periods during the day and that the variability of price changes is higher in periods of concentrated trading is clearly consistent with empirical observations of financial markets, as discussed in the Introduction and in the following section. Our models also provide a number of more specific predictions, examples of which we will spell out below. For simplicity, we will mostly use the model of Sections 1 to 3, where discretionary liquidity traders trade only once within the period in which they have to satisfy their liquidity demands.

In the context of our model, it seems reasonable to treat prices $\tilde{P}_t$ and order flows $\tilde{\omega}_t$ as observables. Specifically, if we define the periods to be, say, 30 minutes long, then the relevant price would be the last transaction price of the interval, and the order flow would be the net change in the position of the market maker during the interval. (It should be noted, however, that in practice the order-flow data may not be easily available from market makers.)

Suppose for simplicity that trading periods are divided into two types, those with high trading volume and those with low trading volume. We will use H and L to denote the set of periods with high and low trading volumes, respectively. (We also use superscript parameters accordingly.) The basic pricing equation in our model is

$$\tilde{P}_t = \sum_{\tau=1}^{t} \tilde{\delta}_\tau + \lambda^H \tilde{\omega}_t \tag{35}$$

for periods with high volume ($t \in H$) and

$$\tilde{P}_t = \sum_{\tau=1}^{t} \tilde{\delta}_\tau + \lambda^L \tilde{\omega}_t \tag{36}$$

for periods with low volume ($t \in L$).

Three hypotheses follow directly from our results in Sections 1 to 3.

Hypothesis 1. $\lambda^H < \lambda^L$.

That is, our model predicts that the market-depth coefficient (defined by $1/\lambda_t$) is higher when the volume is lower. This hypothesis can easily be tested by using standard statistical procedures, as long as we can estimate λ^H and λ^L from price and order-flow observations. To see how this can be done, define

$$\tilde{m}_t \equiv \tilde{P}_{t+1} - \tilde{P}_{t-1} = \tilde{\delta}_{t+1} + \tilde{\delta}_t + \lambda_{t+1}\tilde{\omega}_{t+1} - \lambda_{t-1}\tilde{\omega}_{t-1} \tag{37}$$

An estimate of λ^H can be obtained by regressing the observations of $\tilde{m}_t$ for $t \in H$ on the order-flow observations $\tilde{\omega}_t$. This follows because all the terms in the above expression, except $\tilde{\delta}_{t+1}$, are independent of $\tilde{\omega}_t$ and because, by construction, λ_t is set by the market maker as the regression coefficient in the prediction of $\tilde{\delta}_{t+1}$, given $\tilde{\omega}_t$. Similarly, a regression of the observations of $\tilde{m}_t$ for $t \in L$ on $\tilde{\omega}_t$ would give an estimate of λ^L.[16]

Hypothesis 2. *If $t \in H$ and $t' \in L$, then $Q_t < Q_{t'}$; that is, $var(\tilde{\delta}_{t+1}|\tilde{P}_t) < var(\tilde{\delta}_{t'+1}|\tilde{P}_{t'})$.*

This simply says that prices are more informative in periods in which the trading volume is heavier. Although it is less transparent to see, Hypothesis 2 can also be tested empirically using price and order-flow observations. This is shown in the Appendix.

Hypothesis 3. *The variance of the price change from $t \in L$ to $t + 1 \in H$ is larger than the variance of the price change from $t \in L$ to $t + 1 \in L$, and this exceeds the variance of the price change from $t \in H$ to $t + 1 \in L$.*

It is straightforward to test this hypothesis, given price and volume observations.

Cross-sectional implications can also be derived from our analysis. For example, it is reasonable to assume that a typical discretionary liquidity trader is a large institutional trader. Our models predict that trading patterns will be more pronounced for stocks that are widely held by these institutional traders.

7. Concluding Remarks

This article has presented a theory of trading patterns in financial markets. Some of the conclusions of our theory are these:

- In equilibrium, discretionary liquidity trading is typically concentrated.
- If discretionary liquidity traders can allocate their trades across different periods, then in equilibrium their trading is relatively more concentrated in periods closer to the realization of their demands.
- Informed traders trade more actively in periods when liquidity trading is concentrated.
- If information acquisition is endogenous, then in equilibrium more traders become privately informed in periods of concentrated liquidity trading, and prices are more informative in those periods.

We have obtained our results in models in which the information process and the amount of nondiscretionary liquidity trading are completely stationary over time. All the patterns we have identified in volume and price variability emerge as consequences of the interacting strategic decisions of informed and liquidity traders. The main innovation in our theory is the explicit inclusion of *discretionary liquidity* traders, who can time their trading. As discussed in the Introduction, observations similar to the last two points above have been made as comparative statics results in Kyle (1984), where the variance of liquidity trading is parametrically varied in a single period model. We have shown that these results continue to hold in equilibrium when the timing of liquidity trading is endogenized. As we have seen, it is a delicate matter whether the strategic interaction between liquidity traders and informed traders actually leads to pronounced patterns of trading over time. Among other things, what is important in this regard is the degree of competition among informed traders. When informed traders observe highly correlated signals, competition between

[16]Note that in the model of Section 4, where liquidity traders can allocate their trades, previous order flows must be included in the regression as well, since they (indirectly) provide relevant information in predicting $\tilde{\delta}_{t+1}$.

them is intense, and this improves the terms of trade for liquidity traders, promoting concentration of trading. If private signals are weakly correlated, however, then competition among informed traders is less intense, and an increase in the number of informed traders can actually worsen the terms of trade. This may lead to the nonexistence of an equilibrium. However, despite the complexity of the strategic interaction among traders, our analysis shows that whenever an equilibrium exists, it is characterized by the concentration of liquidity and informed trading and by the resulting patterns in volume and price behavior.

The actual timing and shape of trading patterns in financial markets are determined by a number of factors and parameters that are exogenous to the model, such as the rate of arrival of public information, the amount of nondiscretionary liquidity trading, and the length of the interval within which each discretionary liquidity trader trades. As we noted, empirical observations suggest that the *daily* patterns in trading volume and returns are quite profound. In particular, there is heavier trading at the beginning and end of the trading day than there is in the middle of the day, and the returns and price changes are more variable.

There are a few hypotheses that, combined with our results, may explain the concentration of trading at the open and the close. The open and close are distinguished by the fact that they fall just after and just before the exchange is closed: that is, after and before a period of time in which it is difficult or impossible to trade. This may cause an increase in (nondiscretionary) liquidity trading at the open and close. As a result, discretionary liquidity trading (as well as informed trading) will also be concentrated in these periods, as implied by our results. In this case the forces we have identified for concentration would be intensified.

The concentration of trading at the end of the trading day may also be due to the settlement rules that are followed by many exchanges. Under these rules all trades undertaken on a particular day are actually settled by the close several days later. While delivery depends on the day in which the transaction takes place, the exact time within a day in which the trade occurs has no effect on delivery. This suggests that the interval within which many discretionary liquidity traders must trade terminates at the close of a trading day, (i.e., that for many liquidity traders T'' is the close of a trading day). Since T', the time at which liquidity demands are realized, may vary across traders, there will be a tendency for trading to be concentrated at the close, when there is the most overlap among the intervals available to different liquidity traders. (See Section 5.1 for an intuitive discussion of this in the context of a related example.)

Note that the model of Section 4, in which discretionary liquidity traders can allocate their trades over different periods, predicts that trading will be concentrated in "earlier" trading periods (i.e., in periods closer to the time in which the liquidity demand is realized). For example, if many discretionary liquidity traders realize their liquidity demands after the market closes, then our model predicts that they will satisfy them as soon as the market opens the next day. If, on the other hand, liquidity demands are realized late in the trading day, then we will observe heavy trading by discretionary liquidity traders and informed traders near the close of the market.

Our analysis may also shed some light on the finding discussed in French and Roll (1986) that the variance of returns over nontrading periods is much lower than the variance of returns over trading periods. If the liquidity-trading volume is higher at the end of the trading day, then more informed traders will trade at this time. As a result, the prices quoted at the end of the trading day will reflect more of the information that will be released publicly during the following nontrading hours (see Hypothesis 2 in Section 6). While this effect may explain some of these findings, it is probably not sufficiently strong to account for the striking differences in variances reported in French and Roll (1986).

It is interesting to ask whether our results can account for the actual magnitudes of the observed patterns. A satisfactory answer to this question requires a serious empirical investigation, something we will not attempt here. However, casual calculations suggest that the predictions from the model may accord well with the observed magnitudes. For example, consider again the Exxon data presented in Table 1. Suppose that there are four informed traders in period 1 (10 A.M. to 12 noon), one informed trader in period 2 (12 noon to 2 P.M.), and three informed traders in period 3 (2 P.M. to 4 P.M.). These values are roughly consistent with the pattern of trading volume. Suppose also that $\phi = 0$; that is, informed traders in period t have perfect information about $\tilde{\delta}_{t+1}$. Finally, let $\sigma_\delta^2 = 0.115661$, the average of the variance of the price changes in the three periods. Then we can calculate the variance of price change in each period as predicted by our model using Equation (16), modified to include σ_δ. (In doing this calculation we ignore the overnight period and assume that the third period of one day immediately precedes the first period of the next.)

$$R_1^{1/2} = \left(\frac{n_1}{1 + n_1} + \frac{1}{1 + n_3}\right)^{1/2} \sigma_\delta = 0.34849$$

$$R_2^{1/2} = \left(\frac{n_2}{1 + n_2} + \frac{1}{1 + n_1}\right)^{1/2} \sigma_\delta = 0.28454$$

$$R_3^{1/2} = \left(\frac{n_3}{1 + n_3} + \frac{1}{1 + n_2}\right)^{1/2} \sigma_\delta = 0.38023$$

These values are quite close to the observed values (0.34959, 0.28371, 0.37984).[17] The foregoing should in no way be construed as a test of the model. We simply conclude that the effects the model predicts can be of the same magnitude as those seen in the data.

In closing, we note that many intraday phenomena remain unexplained. For example, a number of studies have shown that mean returns also vary through the day. [See, for example, Jain and Joh (1986); Harris (1986); Marsh and Rock (1986); and Wood, McInish, and Ord (1985).] In our model, prices are a martingale, so patterns in means do not arise. This is due in part to the assumption of risk neutrality. [Williams (1987) analyzes a model that is related to ours in which risk aversion plays an important role and mean effects do arise.] Developing additional models that produce testable predictions for transaction data is an important task for future research.

Appendix

Proof of Lemma 1

Consider the informed traders' decisions. The ith informed trader chooses x_t^i, the amount to trade in period t, to maximize the expected profits, which are given by

$$E(x_t^i(\tilde{F} - P_t(\tilde{\Delta}_t, \tilde{\Omega}_t)) \mid \tilde{\Delta}_t, \tilde{\Omega}_{t-1}, \tilde{\delta}_{t+1} + \tilde{\varepsilon}_t) \tag{A1}$$

Given the form of the price function in Equation (3), this can be written as

$$E(x_t^i(\tilde{\delta}_{t+1} - \lambda_t \tilde{\omega}_t) \mid \tilde{\delta}_{t+1} + \tilde{\varepsilon}_t) \tag{A2}$$

Suppose that informed trader i conjectures that the market order of the other $n - 1$ informed traders is equal to $\beta_t(\tilde{\delta}_{t+1} + \tilde{\varepsilon}_t)$. Then the total order flow is

[17]We have in fact searched over a number of possible candidates for (n_1, n_2, n_3) and have obtained the best fit with (4, 1, 3).

$\tilde{\omega}_t = x_t^i + (n_t - 1)\beta(\tilde{\delta}_{t+1} + \tilde{\varepsilon}_t) + \Sigma_{j=1}^{m}\tilde{y}_t^j + \tilde{z}_t$, and the ith informed trader chooses x_t^i to maximize

$$E\left[x_t^i\tilde{\delta}_{t+1} - x_t^i\lambda_t\left(x_t^i + (n_t - 1)\beta_t(\tilde{\delta}_{t+1} + \tilde{\varepsilon}_t) + \sum_{j=1}^{m}\tilde{y}_t^j + \tilde{z}_t\right)\middle|\, \tilde{\delta}_{t+1} + \tilde{\varepsilon}_t\right] \tag{A3}$$

which is equal to

$$\frac{x_t^i \operatorname{var}(\tilde{\delta}_{t+1})}{\operatorname{var}(\tilde{\delta}_{t+1}) + \phi_t}(\tilde{\delta}_{t+1} + \tilde{\varepsilon}_t) - x_t^i\lambda_t(x_t^i + (n_t - 1)\beta_t(\tilde{\delta}_{t+1} + \tilde{\varepsilon}_t)) \tag{A4}$$

It is easily seen that the expected profits of the ith informed trader in period t are maximized if x_t^i is set equal to

$$\left(\frac{\operatorname{var}(\tilde{\delta}_{t+1})}{2\lambda_t(\operatorname{var}(\tilde{\delta}_{t+1}) + \phi_t)} - \frac{(n_t - 1)\beta_t}{2}\right)(\tilde{\delta}_{t+1} + \tilde{\varepsilon}_t) \tag{A5}$$

The Nash equilibrium is found by setting the above equal to $\beta_t(\tilde{\delta}_{t+1} + \tilde{\varepsilon}_t)$ and solving for β_t.[18] We obtain

$$\beta_t = \frac{\operatorname{var}(\tilde{\delta}_{t+1})}{(n_t + 1)\lambda_t(\operatorname{var}(\tilde{\delta}_{t+1}) + \phi_t)} \tag{A6}$$

We now determine the value of λ_t for a given set of strategies by all traders. Recall that the total amount of discretionary liquidity demands in period t is $\Sigma_{j=1}^{m}\tilde{y}_t^j$, where $\tilde{y}_t^j = \tilde{Y}^j$ if the jth discretionary liquidity trader trades in period t and where $\tilde{y}_t^j = 0$ otherwise. The zero-profit condition for the market maker implies that

$$\lambda_t = \frac{\operatorname{cov}(\tilde{\delta}_{t+1}, \tilde{\omega}_t)}{\operatorname{var}(\tilde{\omega}_t)} = \frac{n_t\beta_t \operatorname{var}(\tilde{\delta}_{t+1})}{n_t^2\beta_t^2(\operatorname{var}\tilde{\delta}_{t+1}) + \phi_t) + \Psi_t} \tag{A7}$$

Substituting Equation (A6) for β_t, we obtain a cubic equation for λ_t. The unique positive root gives the equilibrium value for the assumed level of liquidity trading. This is the value given in Equation (5).

Proof of Lemma 2

As shown in the proof of Lemma 1, when n_t traders are informed, each places in period t a market order of $\beta_t(\tilde{\delta}_{t+1} + \tilde{\varepsilon}_t)$ shares, where

$$\beta_t = \frac{1}{(n_t + 1)\lambda(n_t, \Psi_t)(1 + \phi)} \tag{A8}$$

[We assume here that $\operatorname{var}(\tilde{\delta}_{t+1}) = 1$ and $\phi_t = \phi$.] Now consider a deviant trader who acquires information in addition to the other n traders. He will demand x_t, shares, where x_t maximizes

$$E[x_t(\tilde{\delta}_{t+1} - \lambda(n_t, \Psi_t)\,(x_t + n_t\beta_t(\tilde{\delta}_{t+1} + \tilde{\varepsilon}_t) + \tilde{u}_t)) \mid \tilde{\delta}_{t+1} + \tilde{\varepsilon}_t] \tag{A9}$$

[18] It is straightforward to prove that the equilibrium among informed traders is always unique.

where $\tilde{u}_t$ is the total liquidity demand in period t. This is maximized at

$$x_t = \left(\frac{1}{2\lambda(n_t, \Psi_t)(1+\phi)} - \frac{n_t\beta_t}{2}\right)(\tilde{\delta}_{t+1} + \tilde{\varepsilon}_t) \tag{A10}$$

or substituting for β_t,

$$x_t = \left(\frac{1}{2\lambda(n_t, \Psi_t)(1+\phi)} - \frac{n_t}{2(n_t+1)\lambda(n_t, \Psi_t)(1+\phi)}\right)(\tilde{\delta}_{t+1} + \tilde{\varepsilon}_t)$$

$$= \frac{1}{2(n_t+1)\lambda(n_t, \Psi_t)(1+\phi)}(\tilde{\delta}_{t+1} + \tilde{\varepsilon}_t)$$

$$= \frac{\beta_t}{2}(\tilde{\delta}_{t+1} + \tilde{\varepsilon}_t) \tag{A11}$$

The expected profits earned by the deviant trader, $\pi^d(n_t, \Psi_t)$, will be

$$E\left[\frac{\beta_t}{2}(\tilde{\delta}_{t+1} + \tilde{\varepsilon}_t)\left(\tilde{\delta}_{t+1} - \lambda(n_t, \Psi_t)\left(\frac{(2n_t+1)\beta_t(\tilde{\delta}_{t+1} + \tilde{\varepsilon}_t)}{2} + \tilde{u}_t\right)\right)\right] \tag{A12}$$

which is

$$\frac{\beta_t}{2}\left(1 - \frac{\lambda(n_t, \Psi_t)}{2}(2n_t+1)\beta_t(1+\phi)\right) \tag{A13}$$

Substituting for β_t and $\lambda(n_t, \Psi_t)$, we can simplity this to

$$\pi^d(n_t, \Psi_t) = \frac{1}{4(n_t+1)}\left(\frac{\Psi_t}{n_t(1+\phi)}\right)^{1/2} = \frac{\pi(n_t, \Psi_t)}{4} \tag{A14}$$

This completes the proof.

An Example of the Nonexistence of an Equilibrium

Assume that there are two discretionary liquidity traders, A and B, with $\mathrm{var}(\tilde{Y}^A) = 0.6$ and $\mathrm{var}(Y^B) = 0.4$. Assume that the cost of trader i observing in period t the signal $\tilde{\delta}_{t+1} + \tilde{\varepsilon}_t^i$ is 0.11 for all i and that var $(\tilde{\varepsilon}_t^i) = \phi = 10$, again for all i. Finally, assume that the variance of the nondiscretionary liquidity trading is 1. Is it an equilibrium for both discretionary liquidity traders to trade in the same period? If they do, the total variance of liquidity trading in that period will be 2, and in all other periods it will be 1. Table 8 shows the profits earned by informed traders as a function of the number informed and of the variance of the liquidity trading. It also shows the value of λ in each case.

From the first two columns of the table it follows that in equilibrium there will be one informed trader in the market if $\Psi = 1$ and $c = 0.11$, and three informed traders when $\Psi = 2$. This creates a problem, since $\lambda(3, 2) = 0.169 > \lambda(1, 1) = 0.151$. Taking λ_t as given, neither of the two discretionary liquidity traders will be content to trade in the period they are assumed to trade in. If each assumes that he can move to another period without affecting other traders' strategies, then each will want to move to one of the periods with $\lambda = 0.151$.

Having shown that it is not an equilibrium for both A and B to trade in the same period, we now show that it is also not an equilibrium for each discretionary liquidity trader to trade in a different period. From the third and fourth columns of the table it follows that if each discretionary liquidity trader trades in a different period, then there will be two informed traders in each period. However, in the period in which A trades, $\lambda = \lambda(2, 1.6) = 0.161$, while in the

TABLE 8 | An Example of the Nonexistence of an Equilibrium

n	$\pi(n, 1)$	$\pi(n, 2)$	$\pi(n, 1.4)$	$\pi(n, 1.6)$	$\lambda(n, 1)$	$\lambda(n, 2)$	$\lambda(n, 1.4)$	$\lambda(n, 1.6)$
1	0.151	0.213	0.178	0.191	0.151	0.107	0.127	0.119
2	0.102	0.144	0.121	0.129	0.204	0.144	0.172	0.161
3	0.080	0.113	0.094	0.101	0.239	0.169	0.202	0.189
4	0.066	0.094	0.078	0.084	0.265	0.188	0.224	0.210
5	0.057	0.081	0.067	0.072	0.285	0.202	0.241	0.226
6	0.050	0.071	0.059	0.063	0.301	0.213	0.254	0.238
7	0.045	0.063	0.053	0.057	0.313	0.222	0.265	0.248

For each number of informed traders, n, this table gives $\pi(n, 1)$, the profits of each informed trader if no discretionary liquidity trader trades in that period; $\pi(n, 2)$, the profits of each informed trader if both discretionary liquidity traders trade in that period; $\pi(n, 1.4)$, the profits of each informed trader if only discretionary liquidity trader B trades in that period; and $\pi(n, 1.6)$, the profits of each informed trader if only discretionary liquidity trader A trades in that period. Similarly, for each n and each of these four values of Ψ, the table gives the equilibrium value of λ_t, which measures the cost of liquidity trading under the assumed traders' composition.

period in which B trades, $\lambda = \lambda(2, 1.4) = 0.172$. If B takes the strategies of all other traders and λ_t as given, he will want to trade in the period in which A is trading.

A Statistical Test of Hypothesis 2

Note first that $Q_t = \text{var}(\hat{\delta}_{t+1} - E(\tilde{\delta}_{t+1}|\tilde{\omega}_t)) = \text{var}(\tilde{\delta}_{t+1} - \lambda_t\tilde{\omega}_t)$. Thus, Hypothesis 2 is equivalent to the hypothesis that if $t \in H$ and $t' \in L$, then

$$\text{Var}(\tilde{\delta}_{t+1} - \lambda_t\tilde{\omega}_t) < \text{var}(\tilde{\delta}_{t'+1} - \lambda_{t'}\tilde{\omega}_{t'}) \tag{A15}$$

Since $\tilde{\delta}_t = \tilde{P}_{t+1} - \tilde{P}_t - \lambda_{t+1}\tilde{\omega}_{t+1} + \lambda_t\tilde{\omega}_t$, Equation (A15) is equivalent to

$$\text{var}(\tilde{P}_{t+1} - \tilde{P}_t - \lambda_{t+1}\tilde{\omega}_{t+1}) < \text{var}(\tilde{P}_{t'+1} - \tilde{P}_{t'} - \lambda_{t'+1}\tilde{\omega}_{t'+1}) \tag{A16}$$

Denote the estimates of λ^H and λ^L, obtained by the regression described after Hypothesis 1, by $\hat{\lambda}^H$ and $\hat{\lambda}^L$. Suppose that these are estimated out of sample. Also assume for simplicity that both $t + 1$ and $t' + 1$ are periods with low trading volume.[19] Then Hypothesis 2 can be tested by comparing $\text{var}(\tilde{P}_{t+1} - \tilde{P}_t - \hat{\lambda}^L\tilde{\omega}_{t+1})$ with $\text{var}(\tilde{P}_{t'+1} - \tilde{P}_{t'} - \hat{\lambda}^L\tilde{\omega}_{t'+1})$. To see this, note that

$$\begin{aligned}\text{var}(\tilde{P}_{t+1} - \tilde{P}_t - \hat{\lambda}^L\tilde{\omega}_{t+1}) &= \text{var}(\tilde{P}_{t+1} - \tilde{P}_t - \lambda^L\tilde{\omega}_{t+1}) + \text{var}(\lambda^L - \hat{\lambda}^L)\,\text{var}(\tilde{\omega}_{t+1}) \\ &\quad + 2\,\text{cov}((\lambda^L - \hat{\lambda}^L)\tilde{\omega}_{t+1}, \tilde{P}_{t+1} - \tilde{P}_t - \lambda^L\tilde{\omega}_{t+1})\end{aligned} \tag{A17}$$

The covariance term is zero (since $\hat{\lambda}^L$ is estimated out of sample), and the second term on the right-hand side is the same whether the trading volume is high or low at time t, as long as the trading volume is low in period $t + 1$. Thus, Equation (A16) can be tested by comparing $\text{var}(\tilde{P}_{t+1} - \tilde{P}_t - \hat{\lambda}^L\tilde{\omega}_{t+1})$ with $\text{var}(\tilde{P}_{t'+1} - \tilde{P}_{t'} - \hat{\lambda}^L\tilde{\omega}_{t'+1})$.

[19]The case in which both are periods with high trading volume is completely analogous. Otherwise, the discussion can be modified in a straightforward manner.

References

Clark, P. K., 1973, A Subordinated Stochastic Process Model with Finite Variance for Speculative Prices, *Econometrica*, 41, 135–155.

Foster, F. D., and S. Viswanathan, 1987, Interday Variations in Volumes, Spreads and Variances: I. Theory, Working Paper 87-101, Duke University, The Fuqua School of Business, October.

French, K. R., and R. Roll, 1986, Stock Return Variances; the Arrival of Information and the Reaction of Traders, *Journal of Financial Economics*, 17, 5–26.

Glosten, L. R., and P. R. Milgrom, 1985, Bid, Ask and Transaction Prices in a Specialist Market with Heterogeneously Informed Traders, *Journal of Financial Economics*, 14, 71–100.

Harris, L., 1986, A Transaction Data Survey of Weekly and Intraday Patterns in Stock Returns, *Journal of Financial Economics*, 16, 99–117.

Jain, P. J., and G. Joh, 1986, The Dependence Between Hourly Prices and Trading Volume, working paper, University of Pennsylvania, Wharton School.

Kyle, A. S., 1984, "Market Structure, Information, Futures Markets, and Price Formation," in *International Agricultural Trade: Advanced Readings in Price Formation, Market Structure, and Price Instability*, ed. by Gary G. Storey, Andrew Schmitz, and Alexander H. Sarris. Boulder and London: Westview Press, 45–64.

Kyle, A. S., 1985, Continuous Auctions and Insider Trading, *Econometrica*, 53, 1315–1335.

Marsh, T. A., and K. Rock, 1986, The Transaction Process and Rational Stock Price Dynamics, working paper, Berkeley, University of California.

Williams, J., 1987, Financial Anomalies Under Rational Expectations: A Theory of the Annual Size and Related Effects, working paper, New York University, Graduate School of Business Administration.

Wood, R. A., T. H. McInish, and J. K. Ord, 1985, An Investigation of Transaction Data for NYSE Stocks, *Journal of Finance*, 40, 723–741.

Sixteen

Shmuel Kandel

Shmuel Kandel received a Ph.D. from Yale University in 1983. He started out at the University of Chicago, Graduate School of Business. Shmuel passed away in January 2007 at the age of 55. This essay is one of the last things he wrote. •

All the contributors to this volume were at one point or another protégées of Steve Ross. All of us tried to spend as much time with him as he would give, for time with Steve was a learning experience, a constant stimulation by his wisdom and wit, and, of course, sheer good conversation.

Trouble was, claimants on Steve's time were many, within and without the circle of his students. The way I got face time with Steve was by waiting outside his office door at the appointed time, and, once he showed up, I would state that I wanted a mere three minutes of his time. Such a modest request Steve would not turn down. Once engaging Steve in a conversation, I frequently looked at my watch, and when the three minutes were over, I offered to leave. The originality of my tactic, no matter how often I had repeated it, would lead Steve to ask me to continue the conversation.

In one of our conversations, I explained to Steve how two points can be interpreted with eight parabolas in different spaces. Surrealistic as this may sound, that conversation was a milestone in the road to my doctoral thesis, which was about the geometry of mean-variance space and its econometric implications.

My contribution to this volume, "Mean-Variance Spanning," is co-authored with Gur Huberman, a fellow Ross student, a high school friend whom I lured to the empirical side of finance in general and asset pricing in particular. It complements Gibbons, Ross, and Shanken ("A Test of the Efficiency of a Given Portfolio," *Econometrica* 1989), which in turn grew out of a working paper written by Steve in the early 1980s. I was fortunate to be exposed to that paper as a student.

The bulk of my work has been empirical. I would like to think that it is based on careful thinking regarding the suitability of the methodology to the question at hand. Much of that careful thinking and tight link between methodology and data work owe to those supposedly three-minute conversations in Steve's office. It is impossible to imagine the counterfactual—how my career would have evolved without those extensive and very satisfying conversations.

Mean-Variance Spanning

*Gur Huberman and Shmuel Kandel**

Abstract

The authors propose a likelihood-ratio test of the hypothesis that the minimum-variance frontier of a set of K *assets coincides with the frontier of this set and another set of* N *assets. They study the relation between this hypothesis, exact arbitrage pricing, and mutual fund separation. The exact distribution of the test statistic is available. The authors test the hypothesis that the frontier spanned by three size-sorted stock portfolios is the same as the frontier spanned by thirty-three size-sorted stock portfolios.* •

Investors' choices of portfolios of assets and the implications of these choices for assets' prices are major topics in financial economics. Students of the first topic—portfolio theory—often strive to derive separation results, i.e., seek conditions under which each investor allocates all of his or her savings among a small number of separating funds. These separating funds are the same across investors.

The second topic entails a study of the aggregate behavior of security market participants. Students of the pricing issues derive equilibrium restrictions on security prices.

We focus on the relations among mean-variance efficiency, mutual fund separation, and two prominent security-pricing models in finance: the CAPM and the APT.

The investment universe under consideration includes $K + N$ risky assets with returns that have a nonsingular covariance matrix. In addition, it may include a risk-free asset. We are particularly interested in forming K portfolios of the $N + K$ original assets and then studying the relation between the minimum-variance frontier spanned by the K derived assets and the frontier of the original $N + K$ assets. The returns on the derived K assets are denoted by the $K \times 1$ vector $\underline{R}$, and the returns on the other N assets are denoted by the $N \times 1$ vector $\underline{r}$. (The investment opportunity set of the derived K assets and the other N assets is equal to the investment opportunity set of the original $N + K$ assets.) The following linear model is assumed:

$$\underline{r} = \underline{a} + B\underline{R} + \underline{e}, \tag{1}$$

where $\underline{r}$, $\underline{a}$, and $\underline{e}$ are $N \times 1$ vectors, $\underline{R}$ is a $K \times 1$ vector, and B is an $N \times K$ matrix. The vectors $\underline{r}$, $\underline{R}$, and $\underline{e}$ are random. The random vector $\underline{e}$ is uncorrelated with the random vector $\underline{R}$, and the expected value of each element of $\underline{e}$ is 0.

Consider the following statements:

1. The minimum-variance frontier of $\underline{R}$ intersects the minimum-variance frontier of $\underline{R}$ and $\underline{r}$.
2. The minimum-variance frontier of $\underline{R}$ intersects the minimum-variance frontier of $\underline{R}$, $\underline{r}$, and the risk-free asset.
3. The minimum-variance frontier of $\underline{R}$ is the same as the minimum-variance frontier of $\underline{R}$ and $\underline{r}$.

---

*Huberman is from the University of Chicago and Tel Aviv University; Kandel is from the University of Chicago. An earlier version of this paper was titled "Likelihood Ratio Tests of Asset Pricing and Mutual Fund Separation". We are grateful to Eugene Fama, Wayne Ferson, Jon Ingersoll, Steve Ross, Robert Stambaugh, an anonymous referee, and especially Nai-fu Chen for useful conversations and comments and to the University of Chicago's Center for Research in Security Prices for financial support.

Reprinted with permission:
Huberman, Gur and Shmuel Kandel. "Mean-Variance Spanning." *The Journal of Finance* 48 (1987): 873–888.

The first and second statements are closely related to exact arbitrage pricing, and the third implies (under (1)) K-fund separation. These relations are discussed in Sections I and II, respectively.

In Section I (in Proposition 1), we show that, under (1), the first statement above is equivalent to the existence of a constant w_0 such that

$$\underline{a} = w_0[\underline{i}_N - B\underline{i}_K], \tag{2}$$

where $\underline{i}$ is the vector with elements all equal to 1. The dimensionality of these vectors varies with the context. For instance, $\underline{i}_K$ is the $K \times 1$ vector with elements all equal to 1.

The second statement above implies that the scalar w_0 is the return on the risk-free asset. In this case, (2) is a set of linear constraints.

In Section II (in Proposition 3), we show that, under (1), the third statement above (spanning) is equivalent to

$$\underline{a} = \underline{0} \tag{3a}$$

and

$$B\underline{i}_K = \underline{i}_N, \tag{3b}$$

where $\underline{0}$ is the vector with elements all equal to 0.

In Section III, we review multivariate tests of the first two statements and propose a multivariate test of the third statement. The exact small-sample distributions of the test statistics are available for the test of (3) and for tests that assume the presence of a risk-free asset.

In Section IV, the likelihood-ratio test of spanning is illustrated by applying it to the hypothesis that the monthly returns on three size-based indices of NYSE stocks span the minimum-variance frontier of the monthly returns on thirty-three size-sorted portfolios. We test this hypothesis because the size-based indices can potentially proxy for factors in the context of the APT. This factor-proxying property is suggested by the work of Huberman, Kandel, and Karolyi [17], who observe that returns on stocks of firms of a similar size are more correlated with each other than with returns on stocks of firms of different sizes and that the returns on three size-based stock indices capture most of that cross-correlation.

Concluding remarks are offered in Section V.

I. Asset Pricing and Mean-Variance Intersection

The main result of the Capital Asset Pricing Model (CAPM), as developed by Sharpe [32], Lintner [22], and Black [3], is that a capital asset's expected return is linearly related to the covariance of the asset's return with the return on the market portfolio. This linear relation holds for all assets if and only if the market portfolio is on the minimum-variance frontier, (Fama [10], Roll [24], and Ross [27] make this observation.) Therefore, a test of the CAPM may be interpreted as an examination of the distance (in mean-variance space) between a given market index and the minimum-variance frontier of a given set of assets.

The Arbitrage Pricing Theory (APT) of Ross [26, 28] is a one-period model in which the $N \times 1$ vector $\underline{r}$ of returns on capital assets satisfies the generating model

$$\underline{r} = \underline{E} + B\underline{f} + \underline{e}, \tag{4}$$

where $\underline{f}$ is a $K \times 1$ vector of random factors, B is an $N \times K$ matrix of factor loadings, and $\underline{e}$ is an $N \times 1$ vector of residuals. With no loss of generality, normalize (4) to obtain $\mathrm{E}\{\underline{f}\} = \mathrm{E}\{\underline{e}\} = 0$ and $\mathrm{E}\{\underline{f}\underline{f}'\} = I$, where $\mathrm{E}\{\cdot\}$ denotes expectation and I is the identity matrix, so that $\underline{E}$ is the vector of mean returns. Assume further that the matrix B is of rank K. Restrictions on the diagonality of the covariance matrix $E\{\underline{e}\underline{e}'\}$ and on the relation between the eigenvalues of that covariance matrix and those of BB' (as N becomes large) are required for proofs of the APT. (Huberman [16] reviews the APT literature.)

Exact arbitrage pricing obtains if an exact linear pricing of $\underline{r}$ (and the risk-free asset if such an asset exists) holds with respect to the factors $\underline{f}$, i.e.,

$$\underline{E} = \underline{i}r_0 + B\underline{u}, \tag{5}$$

where r_0 is the return on a riskless asset if that asset exists and $\underline{u}$ is a $K \times 1$ vector of risk premiums. Chamberlain [6], Chen and Ingersoll [8], and Connor [9] provide conditions under which (5) holds. Exact arbitrage pricing is the tested form of the APT, e.g., by Roll and Ross [25], Chen [7], and Lehmann and Modest [21].

Empirical investigations of the APT often involve the formation of investment positions with payoffs that are intended to mimic the realizations of the K factors, i.e., to be used in place of the factors for pricing the subset's assets (e.g., Lehmann and Modest [21]). Huberman, Kandel, and Stambaugh [18] define and characterize the sets of mimicking positions and discuss their properties.

Grinblatt and Titman [15] and Jobson and Korkie [19] derive results that imply that exact arbitrage pricing is equivalent to the mean-variance efficiency of a portfolio of the mimicking portfolios. Thereby, they show that Chamberlain's [6] result for an infinite economy holds also for a finite set of assets.

The equivalence between the pricing equation (5) and the parameter restriction (2) on the returns-generating model is known for the case $K = 1$ (CAPM, consumption CAPM), as well as for $K > 1$ (intertemporal CAPM, APT). See, for example, Black, Jensen, and Scholes [4], Breeden, Gibbons, and Litzenberger [5], and Shanken [30].

Proposition 1 combines the above results and summarizes the relations among mean-variance intersection, exact linear pricing, and the restrictions on the regression model. To keep the paper self-contained, we provide a simple proof of the proposition.

Proposition 1 *Suppose the linear structure* (1) *holds. The following statements are equivalent.*

1. *There exists a portfolio of the vector of asset returns $\underline{R}$ that is on the minimum-variance frontier of $(\underline{R}, \underline{r})$ but is not the global minimum-variance portfolio.*
2. *Exact linear pricing of $\underline{r}$ holds with respect to $\underline{R}$.*
3. *There exists a scalar w_0 such that*

$$\underline{a} = w_0[\underline{i}_N - B\underline{i}_K]. \tag{6}$$

The scalar w_0 is the expected return on any portfolio of $(\underline{R}, \underline{r})$ with a return that is uncorrelated with the portfolio of $\underline{R}$ that is on the minimum-variance frontier of $(\underline{R}, \underline{r})$.

Proof The following notation is used in the proof. Let $\underline{x}$ and $\underline{y}$ be $n \times 1$ and $m \times 1$ vectors of random variables. The (i, j) element of the $n \times m$ matrix $\text{cov}(\underline{x}, \underline{y})$ is the covariance between x_i and y_j.

It is well known that the following two statements are equivalent.

i) There exists a portfolio $\underline{p}$ of $\underline{R}(\underline{p}'\underline{i} = 1)$, with return $y = \underline{p}'\,\underline{R}$, on the mean-variance frontier of $(\underline{R}, \underline{r})$, but y is not the global minimum-variance portfolio.

ii) There exist scalars w_0 and $w \neq 0$ that satisfy

$$\text{E}\{\underline{R}\} = \underline{i}w_0 + \text{cov}(\underline{R}, y)w \tag{7}$$

and

$$\text{E}\{\underline{r}\} = \underline{i}w_0 + \text{cov}(\underline{r}, y)w. \tag{8}$$

This characterization of the mean-variance frontier can be proved by considering the first-order conditions of the optimization problem that seeks a variance-minimizing portfolio with a specified mean.

Since, for every random vector $\underline{x}$, $\text{cov}(\underline{x}, y) = \text{cov}(\underline{x}, \underline{p}'\underline{R}) = \text{cov}(\underline{x}, \underline{R})\underline{p}$, equations (7) and (8) can be rewritten as

$$\text{E}\{\underline{R}\} = \underline{i}w_0 + \text{cov}(\underline{R}, \underline{R})\underline{p}w \tag{9}$$

and

$$\text{E}\{\underline{r}\} = \underline{i}w_0 + \text{cov}(\underline{r}, \underline{R})\underline{p}w. \tag{10}$$

Equation (9) implies that

$$\underline{p}w = \text{cov}(\underline{R}, \underline{R})^{-1}[\text{E}\{\underline{R}\} - \underline{i}w_0]. \tag{11}$$

Substituting (11) into (10) gives

$$\text{E}\{\underline{r}\} = \underline{i}w_0 + \text{cov}(\underline{r}, \underline{R})\text{cov}(\underline{R}, \underline{R})^{-1}[\text{E}\{\underline{R}\} - \underline{i}w_0]. \tag{12}$$

The linear structure (1) implies that

$$B = \text{cov}(\underline{r}, \underline{R})\text{cov}(\underline{R}, \underline{R})^{-1} \tag{13}$$

and

$$\text{E}\{\underline{r}\} = \underline{a} + B\text{E}\{\underline{R}\}. \tag{14}$$

Combine (12) and (13) to infer that the existence of a portfolio of $\underline{R}$ on the frontier of $(\underline{R}, \underline{r})$ is equivalent to exact linear pricing of $\underline{r}$ with respect to $\underline{R}$. Combine (12) to (14) to conclude that the existence of a portfolio of $\underline{R}$ on the frontier is equivalent to the existence of a scalar w_0 that satisfies (6). Equation (8) implies that w_0 is the expected return on any portfolio with a return that is uncorrelated with the intersecting portfolio. Q.E.D.

II. Mutual Fund Separation and Mean-Variance Spanning

The vector of assets $\underline{R}$ is separating relative to the investment universe that consists of the vector $(\underline{R}, \underline{r})$, if, for every portfolio of $(\underline{R}, \underline{r})$ with a return y, there exists a portfolio of $\underline{R}$ with a return z, such that $\text{E}U(z) \geq \text{E}U(y)$ for every concave monotone utility function U. In other words, under K-fund separation, the optimal investment portfolio of each risk-averse individual can be described as a portfolio of the K separating funds. Ross [29] characterizes the class of random variables for which a weaker form of this separation holds.

Mutual fund separation is a stronger property than exact arbitrage pricing relative to the separating funds. Relations between the Arbitrage Pricing Theory and mutual fund separation are pointed out by Chamberlain [6] and Ross [29]. They show that augmentation of the assumptions underlying the APT gives rise to a mutual fund separation.

In this section, we study the relation between mean-variance spanning and K-fund separation, assuming that the multivariate-regression model (1) holds.

Proposition 2 *Suppose that* (1) *and* (3) *hold and the vector of conditional expectations* $\text{E}\{\underline{e}|\underline{R}\} = 0$. *Then* $\underline{R}$ *is a separating vector relative to the investment universe that consists of the vector* $(\underline{R}, \underline{r})$.

Proof Let $y = \underline{p}_R'\underline{R} + \underline{p}_r'\underline{r}$, where $\underline{p}_R'\underline{i}_K + \underline{p}_r'\underline{i}_N = 1$. The return y is a return on a portfolio of $(\underline{R}, \underline{r})$. Let $\underline{p}' = \underline{p}_R' + \underline{p}_r'B$. Equation (3b) implies that $\underline{p}'\, \underline{i}_K = 1$, so $z = \underline{p}'\,\underline{R}$ is a return on a portfolio of $\underline{R}$. Moreover, $z = \mathrm{E}\{y|z\}, y - z = \underline{p}_r'\underline{e}$, and $\mathrm{E}\{\underline{p}_r'\underline{e}|z\} = 0$. Apply Jensen's inequality to conclude that $\mathrm{E}U(z) \geq \mathrm{E}U(y)$ for every monotone concave utility function U, which completes the proof. Q.E.D.

An interpretation of (3) in the context of minimum-variance set geometry is provided in Proposition 3.

Proposition 3 *Suppose that* (1) *holds and the minimum-variance frontier of* $\underline{R}$ *contains at least two points with different expected returns. Every minimum-variance portfolio of* $(\underline{R}, \underline{r})$ *is a portfolio of* $\underline{R}$ *if and only if* (3) *holds, i.e.,* $\underline{a} = \underline{0}$ and $B\underline{i}_K = \underline{i}_N$.

Proof Since every minimum-variance frontier of risky assets is spanned by two portfolios, it is sufficient to show that (3) holds if and only if at least two distinct portfolios of $\underline{R}$ are on the minimum-variance frontier of $(\underline{R}, \underline{r})$.

Equations (3) hold if and only if (6) holds with any value of w_0. Apply Proposition 1 to conclude that (3) holds if and only if, for each w_0, there is a minimum-variance portfolio of $\underline{R}$ with a return that is uncorrelated with the assets that have expected returns equal to w_0. Therefore, (3) is equivalent to the existence of more than one minimum-variance portfolio of $\underline{R}$. Q.E.D.

III. Multivariate Tests of Mean-Variance Intersection and Spanning

We apply Propositions 1 and 3 to review multivariate tests of mean-variance intersection and propose a multivariate test of mean-variance spanning.

The following hypotheses are considered for the two vectors of asset returns, $\underline{R} = (R_1, \ldots, R_K)$ and $\underline{r} = (r_1, \ldots, r_N)$.

H_1: $\underline{R}$ spans $(\underline{R}, \underline{r})$.

H_2: $\underline{R}$ intersects $(\underline{R}, \underline{r})$.

H_3: $\underline{R}$ does not intersect $(\underline{R}, \underline{r})$.

If there exists a risk-free asset with a rate of return that is known and equal to r_f and if r_f is not equal to the expected return on the global minimum-variance portfolio of risky assets, then the minimum-variance frontier of all assets is spanned by the risk-free asset and a portfolio of the risky assets. Propositions 1 and 3 can be used to show that the following are equivalent:

1. The mean-variance frontier of $\underline{R}$ and the risk-free asset is equal to the frontier of $\underline{R}$, $\underline{r}$, and the risk-free asset.
2. The mean-variance frontier of $\underline{R}$ intersects the mean-variance frontier of $\underline{R}$, $\underline{r}$, and the risk-free asset.
3. Equation (2) holds with $w_0 = r_f$ in the regression of $\underline{r}$ on the vector $\underline{R}$.
4. Equation (3a) holds in the regression of the vector of excess returns $\underline{r} - r_f\underline{i}$ on the vector $\underline{R} - r_f\underline{i}$.

For the case where a risk-free asset with a known return exists, we consider also H_4 and H_5:

H_4: $\underline{R}$ intersects $(\underline{R}, \underline{r}, r_f)$.

H_5: $\underline{R}$ does not intersect $(\underline{R}, \underline{r}, r_f)$.

It is noteworthy that no assumption about normality or about the correlations of the disturbance terms (the e's) is necessary in (1) in order to derive Propositions 1 and 3. However, in order to conduct tests suggested by H_1 to H_5, one has to specify the distribution of the vector of disturbance terms $\underline{e}$, conditioned on the vector $\underline{R}$. We assume that it is multivariate normal with mean zero and an unknown $N \times N$ covariance matrix V.

Let L_i be the maximized value of the likelihood function under the hypothesis H_i, and let V_i be the associated maximum-likelihood estimator of the covariance matrix V. Let

$$V^{ij} = |V_j|/|V_i|. \tag{15}$$

The maximized log-likelihood values, the L_i's, satisfy $2[L_i - L_j] = T\log(V^{ij})$. These log-likelihood ratios are asymptotically distributed as chi-square under H_i, the null hypothesis against H_j. This chi-square statistic has $2N$ degrees of freedom when H_1 is tested against H_3; it has $N + 1$ degrees of freedom when H_1 is tested against H_2; and it has $N - 1$ degrees of freedom when H_2 is tested against H_3. If the return on a risk-free asset is known, then set $r_0 = w_0$ in (2), and the chi-square statistic has $N - 2$ degrees of freedom when H_4 is tested against H_5.

Proposition 4 provides the small-sample distribution of a monotone transformation of the likelihood-ratio statistic for the case where a risk-free asset with a known return is assumed to exist. It is also in Gibbons, Ross, and Shanken [14] and Jobson and Korkie [19]. The proposition can be proven by applying results from Anderson [1] (Section 8.4).

Proposition 4 *Suppose that there exists a risk-free asset with a known return. Consider testing H_0: H_4 against H_A: H_5. The statistic $[1/V^{45} - 1](T - K - N)/N$ is a monotone transformation of the likelihood-ratio test statistic, which, under H_4, has an F distribution with $N - 1$ and $T - K - (N - 1)$ degrees of freedom.*

When a risk-free asset does not exist, the restriction (2) is nonlinear. For the test of H_0: H_2 against H_A: H_3, the zero-beta rate has to be estimated and the exact small-sample distribution of the test statistic is unknown. Gibbons [12] performs such a test in the case $K = 1$. He resorts to a one-step Gauss-Newton procedure in order to compute the restricted-regression coefficient estimates and thereby calculate the likelihood-ratio test statistic. Kandel [20] also considers this case and obtains an exact maximum-likelihood estimator of the zero-beta rate and closed-form solution for the test statistic. Shanken [30, 31] introduces a multivariate cross-sectional regression test for this case and derives an approximate small-sample distribution for the test statistic. He also obtains bounds on the exact distribution function of the test statistics for this test and for the likelihood-ratio test and an exact maximum-likelihood estimator of the zero-beta rate for the case $K > 1$.

We propose a test of mean-variance spanning. It is an alternative to tests of mean-variance intersection in the case without a risk-free asset. The test involves only linear restrictions on the regression coefficients, and the exact distribution of the test statistic under the null hypothesis is known. The spanning test is a test of a more stringent hypothesis than mean-variance intersection.

Proposition 5 *Suppose that there is no risk-free asset. Consider testing H_0: H_1 against H_A: H_3. The statistic $[1/\sqrt{V^{13}} - 1](T - K - N)/N$ is a monotone transformation of the likelihood-ratio test statistic, which, under H_1, has an F distribution with $2N$ and $2(T - K - N)$ degrees of freedom.**

Proof Apply Theorem 8.4.6 in Anderson [1]. Q.E.D.

*This statement of the proposition corrects a typographical error that appeared in the original *Journal of Finance* article.

IV. A Size-Based Example

In this section, the likelihood-ratio test of spanning is illustrated by applying it to the hypothesis that the monthly returns on three size-based indices of NYSE stocks span the minimum-variance frontier of the monthly returns on thirty-three size-sorted portfolios. Huberman, Kandel, and Karolyi [17] observe that the contemporaneous correlations of the disturbance terms in the market model depend on the difference in the size of the firms with stock returns that are used as independent variables. The more similar the firms are in size, the higher the correlation. A linear structure of stock returns (1) in which similarity of firm size implies similarity of slope coefficients could give rise to this pattern.

We estimate the linear structure (1) with the returns on $K = 3$ size-sorted indices as the explanatory variables and the returns on $N = 30$ size-sorted portfolios as the dependent variables. We then inquire whether the three size-based indices span the minimum-variance frontier of the larger set of size-sorted portfolios. We describe the data in Subsection *A*, discuss temporal variations of the regression coefficients in Subsection *B*, present the results in Subsection *C*, and relate them to the size effect in Subsection *D*.

A. The Data

The raw data consist of monthly returns on all stocks that traded on the New York Stock Exchange (NYSE) from January 1964 until December 1983. At the beginning of each year, we rank the stocks on the NYSE according to the market value of their equity in December of the previous year and construct thirty-three size-sorted sets of stocks. The returns on the equally weighted portfolios of these size-sorted sets are denoted $r_1, \ldots, r_{33}$. ($r_1(t)$ indicates the time-t returns on the portfolio of the smallest stocks.)

The return on the small-stock index is the equally weighted average of $r_1, \ldots, r_{21}$. Similarly, the returns on the medium- and large-stock indices are the equally weighted averages of $r_{12}, \ldots, r_{22}$ and $r_{23}, \ldots, r_{33}$. The returns on the three indices are denoted by the 3×1 vector $\underline{R}(t) = (R_1(t), R_2(t), R_3(t))'$.

We consider the multivariate regression (1) with the vector $\underline{R}$ as the vector of explanatory variables. As Proposition 5 requires that the contemporaneous covariance matrix of the residuals V be nonsingular, we use only thirty of the thirty-three returns. The vector of independent variables in the example is

$$r(t) = (r_1(t), \ldots, r_5(t), r_7(t), \ldots, r_{16}(t), r_{18}(t), \ldots, r_{27}(t), r_{29}(t), \ldots, r_{33}(t)).$$

B. A Test of Temporal Constancy of Regression Coefficients

The estimation of the regression model (1) entails the assumption that $\underline{a}$ and B are constant over the estimation period. We study the temporal constancy of $\underline{a}$ and B with a multivariate Chow test. We break the overall period into two subperiods and estimate the following regression:

$$\underline{r}_t = \underline{a} + \underline{a}^1 D_t + (B + B^1 D_t)\underline{R}_t + \underline{e}_t, \tag{16}$$

where D_t is a dummy variable set equal to one in the first subperiod and to zero in the second subperiod. The vector $\underline{a}^1$ and the matrix B^1 are of the same dimensions as the vector $\underline{a}$ and the matrix B.

Constancy of the coefficients implies that

$$\underline{a}^1 = \underline{0} \text{ (the } N \times 1 \text{ zero vector)} \tag{17a}$$

and

$$B^1 = 0 \text{ (the } N \times K \text{ zero matrix).} \tag{17b}$$

TABLE I | Multivariate Chow Tests of the Coefficients in Equation (1)[a]

Years	U_1	*p*-Value	U_2	D.F.	*p*-Value
64–83	168	.003	1.44	825	.003
64–73	157	.013	1.36	348	.016
74–83	146	.056	1.25	348	.063
64–68	133	.200	1.09	110	.315
69–73	168	.003	1.55	110	.010
74–78	150	.035	1.35	110	.079
79–83	180	.000	1.75	110	.002

[a]Restrictions (17) are imposed on (16) for different test periods. The tests use monthly returns over different test periods. The statistic U_1 is distributed asymptotically as chi-square, with 120 degrees of freedom. The statistic U_2 is distributed approximately as F_1 with 120 and D.F. degrees of freedom.

The likelihood-ratio test of (17) is similar to the test discussed in Proposition 5. The test statistic is

$$U = |V_0|/|V_A|, \tag{18}$$

where $|V_0|$ and $|V_A|$ denote the determinants of the covariance matrices of the residuals under the restricted system (i.e., (16) and (17)) and under the unrestricted system (i.e., (16) alone).

Unfortunately, the small-sample distribution of the test statistic (under (16) and (17)) is unavailable. Asymptotically, the test statistic

$$U^1 = -(T - 21.5)\ln U$$

has a chi-square distribution with 120 degrees of freedom, where T is the number of observations.

Rao's small-sample approximation (Anderson [1], Section 8.5.4) uses the statistics

$$U^2 = [1/U^{1/s} - 1]((T - 21.5)s - q)/120,$$

where $s = 3.975$ and $q = 59$. Under (16) and (17), the distribution of U^2 is approximately F, with 120 and $(T - 21.5)s - q$ degrees of freedom. Test results for different periods, ranging from the whole twenty-year period to four nonoverlapping five-year periods, are reported in Table I. It seems that the coefficients in (1) do change over time.

C. A Test of Mean-Variance Spanning

Temporal instability of regression coefficients is well known in finance. It led researchers to choose fairly short time periods for tests of asset pricing (e.g., Fama and MacBeth [11], Gibbons [12], and Roll and Ross [25]). The justification for this approach is that, although the coefficients vary, their short-run variation is negligible to the extent that the tested pricing relation is unlikely to be rejected due to the temporal variation of the coefficients. We follow this approach in this example.

In Parts A and B of Table II, we report the regression estimates for the ten-year periods 1964 to 1973 and 1974 to 1983. The F-test statistics mentioned in Proposition 5 have 60 and 174 degrees of freedom. They are 1.08 and 0.97 for the first and second ten-year periods. Their p-values are 0.34 and 0.55, so restrictions (3) are not rejected for either period at the conventional significance levels. The point estimates of the slope coefficients display an interesting pattern, discussed by Huberman, Kandel, and Karolyi [17]: the coefficients of R_1

TABLE II | Estimates of $r_i = a_i + b_{i1}R_1 + b_{i2}R_2 + b_{i3}R_3 + e_i$, Where r_i Is the Monthly Return on Size-Sorted Portfolio *i* and R_j Is the Monthly Return on Size-Based Index j[a]

Dependent Variable	a	b_1	b_2	b_3	$b_1 + b_2 + b_3$	F	p	R^2
				Part A: Estimation Period 1964 to 1973				
r_1	0.46	1.89	−0.81	−0.16	0.91	4.23	0.02	0.92
	0.19	0.15	0.28	0.20				
r_2	0.28	1.49	−0.45	−0.08	0.96	1.79	0.17	0.93
	0.16	0.12	0.24	0.17				
r_3	0.00	1.26	−0.10	−0.13	1.02	0.15	0.86	0.94
	0.15	0.12	0.23	0.16				
r_4	−0.15	1.24	−0.61	0.40	1.03	1.23	0.30	0.96
	0.12	0.09	0.18	0.12				
r_5	0.00	0.88	0.04	0.10	1.02	0.10	0.91	0.93
	0.16	0.12	0.24	0.17				
r_7	0.12	0.78	0.31	−0.07	1.01	0.49	0.62	0.95
	0.14	0.10	0.20	0.14				
r_8	−0.21	0.77	0.18	0.09	1.05	1.76	0.18	0.95
	0.14	0.10	0.20	0.14				
r_9	−0.14	0.65	0.51	−0.20	0.96	1.57	0.21	0.95
	0.12	0.09	0.18	0.13				
r_{10}	−0.09	0.68	0.36	0.00	1.04	0.68	0.51	0.95
	0.13	0.10	0.20	0.14				
r_{11}	−0.03	0.32	0.67	0.03	1.02	0.17	0.85	0.95
	0.12	0.09	0.18	0.13				
r_{12}	0.21	0.03	1.31	−0.37	0.97	1.55	0.22	0.95
	0.13	0.10	0.19	0.14				
r_{13}	0.06	0.03	1.26	−0.35	0.95	1.00	0.37	0.94
	0.13	0.10	0.19	0.14				
r_{14}	−0.05	0.09	0.99	−0.07	1.01	0.12	0.89	0.95
	0.12	0.09	0.17	0.12				
r_{15}	0.01	−0.01	1.05	−0.07	0.97	0.37	0.69	0.94
	0.12	0.10	0.19	0.13				

r_{16}	−0.26	0.08	0.93	0.00	1.00	3.43	0.04	0.96
	0.10	0.08	0.15	0.11				
r_{18}	−0.12	0.14	0.71	0.15	1.00	0.56	0.57	0.95
	0.12	0.09	0.18	0.13				
r_{19}	0.03	0.07	0.61	0.36	1.04	0.91	0.41	0.95
	0.11	0.09	0.17	0.12				
r_{20}	−0.25	−0.19	1.28	−0.08	1.01	2.26	0.11	0.95
	0.12	0.09	0.18	0.12				
r_{21}	0.17	−0.18	1.15	0.01	0.98	1.47	0.23	0.96
	0.10	0.08	0.16	0.11				
r_{22}	0.05	−0.34	1.07	0.34	1.08	4.26	0.02	0.96
	0.10	0.08	0.15	0.11				
r_{23}	−0.06	0.03	0.35	0.72	1.10	4.35	0.02	0.94
	0.12	0.09	0.18	0.13				
r_{24}	0.08	−0.05	0.44	0.68	1.07	3.89	0.02	0.96
	0.10	0.08	0.15	0.11				
r_{25}	−0.07	0.11	−0.06	1.03	1.07	2.71	0.07	0.93
	0.12	0.09	0.18	0.13				
r_{26}	0.05	−0.01	0.43	0.59	1.00	0.13	0.88	0.95
	0.10	0.08	0.16	0.11				
r_{27}	0.07	−0.15	0.27	0.85	0.97	0.74	0.48	0.94
	0.10	0.08	0.16	0.11				
r_{29}	0.03	0.03	−0.13	1.07	0.97	0.47	0.63	0.94
	0.10	0.08	0.15	0.11				
r_{30}	−0.08	0.00	−0.19	1.17	0.98	0.85	0.43	0.95
	0.09	0.07	0.14	0.10				
r_{31}	0.01	−0.06	−0.07	1.04	0.90	8.80	0.00	0.94
	0.09	0.07	0.14	0.10				
r_{32}	−0.08	0.04	−0.50	1.45	0.99	0.45	0.64	0.94
	0.09	0.07	0.14	0.10				
r_{33}	0.24	0.04	−0.54	1.34	0.83	14.09	0.00	0.87
	0.12	0.09	0.18	0.13				

(*continued*)

TABLE II | *(continued)*

Dependent Variable	a	b_1	b_2	b_3	$b_1 + b_2 + b_3$	F	p	R^2
Part B: Estimation Period 1974 to 1983								
r_1	−0.22	2.45	−1.54	0.12	1.03	0.45	0.64	0.94
	0.26	0.15	0.33	0.21				
r_2	−0.16	1.68	−0.83	0.16	1.01	0.46	0.63	0.96
	0.17	0.10	0.22	0.14				
r_3	−0.05	1.34	−0.41	0.04	0.96	0.67	0.51	0.95
	0.18	0.10	0.23	0.15				
r_4	0.14	1.03	0.01	−0.07	0.97	0.57	0.56	0.95
	0.17	0.09	0.21	0.14				
r_5	0.26	0.93	−0.01	0.06	0.98	1.25	0.29	0.95
	0.17	0.09	0.21	0.14				
r_7	0.02	0.61	0.45	−0.02	1.05	1.32	0.27	0.95
	0.15	0.09	0.20	0.12				
r_8	0.07	0.62	0.39	0.00	1.01	0.25	0.78	0.96
	0.14	0.08	0.18	0.11				
r_9	0.04	0.70	0.31	−0.02	0.99	0.09	0.91	0.95
	0.15	0.08	0.19	0.12				
r_{10}	−0.02	0.25	1.00	−0.27	0.98	0.33	0.72	0.94
	0.16	0.09	0.20	0.13				
r_{11}	0.04	0.37	0.80	−0.19	0.98	0.30	0.74	0.96
	0.13	0.07	0.17	0.11				
r_{12}	0.01	0.11	0.99	−0.10	1.01	0.03	0.97	0.94
	0.14	0.08	0.18	0.12				
r_{13}	−0.19	0.11	1.16	−0.21	1.06	3.28	0.04	0.96
	0.13	0.07	0.16	0.10				
r_{14}	−0.05	−0.12	1.47	−0.32	1.03	0.73	0.49	0.95
	0.13	0.07	0.17	0.11				
r_{15}	0.14	0.17	0.79	0.07	1.04	1.99	0.14	0.96
	0.13	0.07	0.16	0.10				
r_{16}	−0.09	−0.08	1.36	−0.34	0.94	3.56	0.03	0.95
	0.12	0.07	0.16	0.10				
r_{18}	0.12	0.04	1.00	−0.10	0.94	3.21	0.04	0.95
	0.12	0.07	0.16	0.10				

r_{19}	−0.11	0.04	0.81	0.08	0.93	5.49	0.01	0.95
	0.12	0.07	0.15	0.10				
r_{20}	0.25	−0.14	1.01	0.14	1.01	2.70	0.07	0.96
	0.12	0.06	0.15	0.09				
r_{21}	−0.07	−0.09	0.88	0.20	0.99	0.39	0.67	0.96
	0.11	0.06	0.14	0.09				
r_{22}	−0.01	−0.07	0.59	0.57	1.08	6.15	0.00	0.95
	0.13	0.07	0.16	0.10				
r_{23}	−0.13	0.03	0.60	0.38	1.01	0.64	0.53	0.96
	0.11	0.06	0.14	0.09				
r_{24}	0.05	0.04	0.30	0.71	1.05	2.69	0.07	0.95
	0.12	0.07	0.15	0.10				
r_{25}	0.21	0.05	0.20	0.77	1.02	2.30	0.11	0.95
	0.11	0.06	0.14	0.09				
r_{26}	0.05	0.12	0.04	0.83	0.99	0.12	0.89	0.96
	0.11	0.06	0.14	0.09				
r_{27}	0.10	0.05	−0.06	1.02	1.01	0.90	0.41	0.96
	0.10	0.05	0.12	0.08				
r_{29}	−0.11	0.05	−0.05	0.98	0.98	1.48	0.23	0.97
	0.09	0.05	0.12	0.07				
r_{30}	0.08	−0.17	0.03	1.12	0.99	0.32	0.73	0.95
	0.11	0.06	0.14	0.09				
r_{31}	−0.06	0.01	−0.21	1.16	0.96	2.43	0.09	0.95
	0.10	0.06	0.13	0.08				
r_{32}	−0.15	−0.25	−0.09	1.37	1.04	2.38	0.10	0.96
	0.10	0.06	0.13	0.08				
r_{33}	0.06	0.01	−0.77	1.71	0.94	1.68	0.19	0.89
	0.16	0.09	0.21	0.13				

[a]F is the test statistic that $a = 0$ and $b_1 + b_2 + b_3 = 1$; p is the p-value corresponding to that F-statistic. Standard errors are below the point estimates of the coefficients.

decrease as we go down the table; the coefficients of R_3 increase as we go down the table; and the coefficients of R_2 reach their higher values in the middle of the table.

We also calculate the F-statistics testing restrictions (3) of (1) for the twenty-year period 1964 to 1983 and for the four nonoverlapping five-year subperiods of these twenty years. These F-statistics are 1.6, 0.68, 0.86, 0.59, and 0.91. Their corresponding p-values are 0.0046, 0.93, 0.72, 0.98, and 0.65. The subperiod results can be aggregated. Following Gibbons and Shanken [13], our aggregate test statistic is minus two times the sum of the natural logarithms of the p-values of the nonoverlapping subperiods. This statistic has a chi-square distribution, with twice as many degrees of freedom as the number of time-series observations. Our results for the two ten-year subperiods give rise to the chi-square statistic of 2.88. Under the null hypothesis, the probability of having this value or higher is greater than fifty percent. This chi-square statistic for the four five-year subperiods is 0.95. Under the null hypothesis, the probability of having this value or higher is greater than 99.5 percent.

When ten or five years are used to construct the test statistic (or when the subperiod results are aggregated), the data seem to support the null hypothesis. When twenty years of data are considered, the data do not support the spanning hypothesis. It is possible, however, that the spanning hypothesis is correct but that temporal instability of the coefficients of the underlying returns-generating model, as discussed in Subsection B, accounts for the high values of the test statistic when twenty years of data are used.

D. Mean-Variance Spanning of Size Portfolios and the Size Effect

Banz [2] and Reinganum [23] show that mean returns on small-firm stocks are higher than those on large-firm stocks even after controlling for covariation with the market (beta) as usually measured. Using a multivariate test, Shanken [30] concludes that the CAPM is rejected when size is used to form portfolios. Put differently, the market portfolio is not on the minimum-variance frontier of size-sorted portfolios, contrary to the prediction of the CAPM.

The pattern of covariation of returns on size-sorted portfolios, documented by Huberman, Kandel, and Karolyi [17], leads us to inquire whether the frontier of the size-sorted portfolios is spanned by the three indices. If one accepts that restrictions (3) hold in our size-based example and if one accepts the size-based indices as mimicking portfolios in the context of the APT, then exact arbitrage pricing holds and the size effect is not a mispricing phenomenon. The evidence presented here, however, does not explain the size-related covariation pattern reported by Huberman, Kandel, and Karolyi [17], and it remains for future research to study it closely.

V. Conclusion

This paper puts together results about mean-variance efficiency, exact arbitrage pricing, and K-fund separation. These results imply restrictions on an underlying return-generating process. When the restrictions are linear, the small-sample distributions of some multivariate tests are available.

Most of the empirical research on asset pricing has consisted of tests of mean-variance efficiency. In the absence of a risk-free asset, the restrictions are not linear and the small-sample distribution of the test statistic can only be approximated. The mean-variance spanning test proposed here is a test of a stronger hypothesis than exact pricing, but its statistic is easily computed and the statistics small-sample distribution is available.

The multivariate test of spanning is applied to the hypothesis that the monthly returns on three size-based indices of NYSE stocks span the minimum-variance frontier of the monthly returns on thirty-three size-sorted portfolios. When twenty years of data are considered, the data do not support the spanning hypothesis. It is possible, however, that the spanning hypothesis is correct but that temporal instability of the coefficients of the underlying return-generating model accounts for the high values of the test statistic when twenty years of data are used. When ten or five years are used to construct the test statistic or when subperiod results are aggregated, the data seem to support the hypothesis.

References

T. W. Anderson. *An Introduction to Multivariate Analysis.* New York: John Wiley and Sons, Inc., 1984.

Rolf Banz. "The Relationship between Return and Market Value of Common Stocks." *Journal of Financial Economics* 9 (March 1981), 3–18.

Fischer Black. "Capital Market Equilibrium with Restricted Borrowing." *Journal of Business* 45 (July 1972), 444–54.

———, Michael C. Jensen, and Myron Scholes. "The Capital Asset Pricing Model: Some Empirical Tests." In Michael C. Jensen (ed.), *Studies in the Theory of Capital Markets.* New York: Praeger, 1972.

Douglas Breeden, Michael Gibbons, and Robert Litzenberger. "Empirical Tests of the Consumption-Oriented CAPM." Working paper, Stanford University, 1986.

Gary Chamberlain. "Funds, Factors and Diversification in Arbitrage Pricing Models." *Econometrica* 51 (September 1983), 1305–23.

Nai-fu Chen. "Some Empirical Tests of the Theory of Arbitrage Pricing." *Journal of Finance* 38 (December 1983), 1393–1414.

——— and Jonathan Ingersoll. "Exact Pricing in Linear Factor Models with Infinitely Many Assets: A Note." *Journal of Finance* 38 (June 1983), 985–88.

Gregory Connor. "A Unified Beta Pricing Theory." *Journal of Economic Theory* 34 (October 1984), 13–31.

Eugene Fama. "Risk, Return and Equilibrium." *Journal of Political Economy* 79 (January 1971), 30–55.

——— and James D. MacBeth. "Risk, Return, and Equilibrium: Empirical Tests." *Journal of Political Economy* 81 (May 1973), 607–36.

Michael R. Gibbons. "Multivariate Tests of Financial Models: A New Approach." *Journal of Financial Economics* 10 (March 1982), 1–27.

——— and Jay Shanken. "Subperiod Aggregation and the Power of Multivariate Tests of Portfolio Efficiency." Working paper, Stanford University, 1986.

Michael R. Gibbons, Stephen A. Ross, and Jay Shanken. "A Test of the Efficiency of a Given Portfolio." Working paper, Stanford University, 1986.

Mark Grinblatt and Sheridan Titman. "The Relation between Mean-Variance Efficiency and Arbitrage Pricing." *Journal of Business* 60 (January 1987), 97–112.

Gur Huberman. "A Review of the Arbitrage Pricing Theory." Working Paper, University of Chicago, 1986. Forthcoming in *The New Palgrave: A Dictionary of Economic Theory and Doctrine.*

———, Shmuel Kandel, and G. Andrew Karolyi. "Size and Industry Related Covariation of Stock Returns." Working paper, University of Chicago, 1987.

Gur Huberman, Shmuel Kandel, and Robert F. Stambaugh. "Mimicking Portfolios and Exact Arbitrage Pricing." *Journal of Finance* 42 (March 1987), 1–9.

J. D. Jobson and Bob Korkie. "Some Tests of Linear Asset Pricing with Multivariate Normality." *Canadian Journal of Administrative Sciences* 2 (June 1985), 114–38.

Shmuel Kandel. "Likelihood Ratio Test Statistics of Mean Variance Efficiency without a Riskless Asset." *Journal of Financial Economics* 13 (December 1984), 575–92.

Bruce Lehmann and David Modest. "The Empirical Foundations of the Arbitrage Pricing Theory I: The Empirical Tests." Working paper, Columbia University, 1985.

John Lintner. "The Valuation of Assets and the Selection of Risky Investments in Stock Portfolios and Capital Budgets." *Review of Economics and Statistics* 48 (February 1965), 13–37.

Mark R. Reinganum. "Misspecification of Capital Asset Pricing: Empirical Anomalies Based on Earning's Yields and Market Values." *Journal of Financial Economics* 9 (March 1981), 19–46.

Richard Roll. "A Critique of the Asset Pricing Theory's Tests; Part 1: On Past and Potential Testability of the Theory." *Journal of Financial Economics* 4 (March 1977), 129–76.

——— and Stephen A. Ross. "An Empirical Investigation of the Arbitrage Pricing Theory." *Journal of Finance* 35 (December 1980), 1073–1103.

Stephen A. Ross. "The Arbitrage Theory of Capital Asset Pricing." *Journal of Economic Theory* 13 (December 1976), 341–60.

———. "The Capital Asset Pricing Model (CAPM), Short Sale Restrictions and Related Issues." *Journal of Finance* 32 (March 1977), 341–60.

———. "Risk, Return and Arbitrage." In Irwin Friend and James L. Bicksler (eds.), *Risk and Return in Finance.* Cambridge, MA: Ballinger Books, 1977.

———. "Mutual Fund Separation in Financial Theory—The Separating Distributions." *Journal of Economic Theory* 17 (April 1978), 254–83.

Jay Shanken. "Multivariate Tests of the Zero-Beta CAPM." *Journal of Financial Economics* 14 (September 1985), 327–48.

———. "Further Results on Testing Portfolio Efficiency When the Zero-Beta Is Unknown." Working paper, University of Rochester, 1986.

William Sharpe. "Capital Asset Prices: A Theory of Market Equilibrium under Conditions of Risk." *Journal of Finance* 19 (September 1984), 425–42.

Seventeen

John Y. Campbell

John Y. Campbell received a Ph.D. from Yale University in 1984. He started teaching at Princeton University, and now works at Harvard University. •

My first memory of Steve Ross is of the opening of his legendary finance course in the Yale Ph.D. program. With energy, style, and a dash of ferocity, Steve let us know we were studying a discipline, finance, with its own intellectual tradition that should inspire pride and dedication in its students. It was Marine boot camp for economists.

My second memory of Steve Ross is of the oral exam that he administered along with Jim Tobin. At that time, Yale students talked in whispers of the "Tobin spiral," caused when Tobin asked an easy question, the student assumed there must be a catch and froze up, prompting Tobin to ask an even easier question, and so on towards failure. I was actually more intimidated by Steve than by Jim, but escaped a Ross spiral when Steve asked what seemed to me abundantly difficult questions.

Throughout my time at Yale, I was inspired by the finance theory that Steve laid out so elegantly. At the same time, I knew I was cut out to be an applied economist, and I looked for a way to use econometrics to understand asset price behavior. When Bob Shiller arrived at Yale, I was able to do this by following Bob's lead. But even then, my intellectual development proceeded in large part by arguing (silently for the most part, in my own thoughts) with Steve. I was even cheeky enough to write a chapter of my Ph.D. dissertation pushing back against the work of Cox, Ingersoll, and Ross—not their famous 1985 *Econometrica* papers, but their 1981 *Journal of Finance* paper. This later became my first solo publication, in the *Journal of Finance* in 1986.

In the early 1990s I became fascinated by the question of what determines the risk prices in factor asset pricing models. I realized that Bob Merton's intertemporal CAPM in principle determined those prices that were left as free parameters in Steve's Arbitrage Pricing Theory. The challenge was to find explicit solutions for the risk prices, given the dynamics of interest rates and risk premia. My 1993 *American Economic Review* paper, reprinted in this volume, was my response to this challenge. Working on it, and coming to understand more deeply the connections between Steve's work and other traditions in asset pricing, was the most intense experience of my research career.

In 1998–99 I was lucky enough to visit the Sloan School at MIT and to renew my acquaintance with Steve Ross. Interactions with Steve were some of the most exciting moments of the year, not only intellectually, but also physically, as when Steve gave me a short ride across the Charles River in his Porsche, breaking my land speed record (if not his) in the middle of the Longfellow Bridge.

It is a great honor and pleasure to join Steve's many students in this celebration of his life and work.

Intertemporal Asset Pricing without Consumption Data

By *John Y. Campbell**

This paper proposes a new way to generalize the insights of static asset pricing theory to a multiperiod setting. The paper uses a loglinear approximation to the budget constraint to substitute out consumption from a standard intertemporal asset pricing model. In a homoscedastic lognormal setting, the consumption–wealth ratio is shown to depend on the elasticity of intertemporal substitution in consumption, while asset risk premia are determined by the coefficient of relative risk aversion. Risk premia are related to the covariances of asset returns with the market return and with news about the discounted value of all future market returns. (JEL G12). •

For the last 25 years an important goal of financial research has been to generalize the insights of the simple one-period capital asset pricing model (CAPM) to a multiperiod setting. Such a generalization is difficult to achieve because the multiperiod consumption and portfolio-choice problem is inherently nonlinear. A complete solution is obtained by combining the consumer's Euler equation with the intertemporal budget constraint, but the budget constraint is a nonlinear equation except in very special cases.

In response to this difficulty Robert C. Merton (1969, 1971, 1973) suggested reformulating the consumption and portfolio-choice problem in continuous time. Doing this in effect linearizes by taking the decision interval as infinitely small, so that the model becomes linear over this interval. However, this kind of linearity is only local, so it does not allow one easily to study longer-run aspects of intertemporal asset pricing theory.

In this paper I take a different approach. Instead of assuming that the time interval is small, I assume that variation in the consumption–wealth ratio is small. This makes the intertemporal budget constraint approximately loglinear, allowing me to solve the consumption and portfolio-choice problem in closed form. My approach clarifies the relation between the time-series properties of market returns and the time-series properties of consumption. It also leads to a simple expression relating assets' risk premia to their covariances with the market return and news about future market returns. This formula unifies the large body of research on time-series properties of aggregate stock returns with the equally large literature on cross-sectional patterns of mean returns.

The formula for risk premia derived in this paper can be tested without using data on consumption. This is potentially an important advantage, for empirical work using

---

*Woodrow Wilson School, Robertson Hall, Princeton University, Princeton, NJ 08544. I am grateful to the London School of Economics Financial Markets Group for its hospitality during the academic year 1989–1990, to the National Science Foundation and the Sloan Foundation for financial support, to Kevin Carey for research assistance, and to Hyeng Keun Koo for invaluable help with numerical calculations. Andrew Abel, Fischer Black, Doug Breeden, Steve Cecchetti, John Cochrane, George Constantinides, Silverio Foresi, Ravi Jagannathan, Bob Merton, Lars Svensson, Philippe Weil, Steve Zeldes, and two referees made helpful comments on earlier drafts, which carried the title "Intertemporal Asset Pricing Without Consumption."

Reprinted with permission:
Campbell, John Y. "Intertemporal Asset Pricing Without Consumption Data." *American Economic Review* 83 (1993): 487–512.

aggregate consumption data in the manner suggested by Robert E. Lucas, Jr. (1978), Douglas T. Breeden (1979, 1986), and Sanford J. Grossman and Robert J. Shiller (1981) has generally rejected the model restrictions or has estimated implausible parameter values. These problems occur both with a simple power specification for utility (Lars P. Hansen and Kenneth J. Singleton, 1982, 1983; Rajnish Mehra and Edward Prescott, 1985; N. Gregory Mankiw and Matthew D. Shapiro, 1986) and with more elaborate specifications that allow for durable goods and habit formation (Kenneth B. Dunn and Singleton, 1986; George M. Constantinides, 1990; Wayne E. Ferson and Constantinides, 1991) or a divergence between the coefficient of relative risk aversion and the elasticity of intertemporal substitution (Lawrence Epstein and Stanley Zin, 1989, 1991; Philippe Weil, 1989, 1990; Alberto Giovannini and Philippe Jorion, 1989). The difficulty may well be inherent in the use of aggregate consumption data. These data are measured with error and are time-aggregated, which can have serious consequences for asset pricing relationships (Grossman et al., 1987; Simon Wheatley, 1988; Breeden et al., 1989; John Heaton, 1991; David A. Wilcox, 1992). More fundamentally, the consumption of asset-market participants may be poorly proxied by aggregate consumption. Predictable movements in aggregate consumption growth are correlated with predictable growth in current disposable income, which suggests that a large fraction of the population is liquidity-constrained or fails to optimize intertemporally (Campbell and Mankiw, 1989), and micro evidence shows that the consumption of stockholders behaves differently from the consumption of nonstockholders (Mankiw and Stephen P. Zeldes, 1991).

Of course, the approach of this paper does not resolve all measurement issues. The formula for risk premia derived here requires that one be able to measure the return on the market portfolio, which should in general include human capital. The difficulties with this have been forcefully pointed out by Richard Roll (1977) in his critique of tests of the static CAPM. At the very least, however, the results of the paper enable one to use the imperfect data on both market returns and consumption in new and potentially fruitful ways.

Section I of this paper shows how to obtain a loglinear approximation to the intertemporal budget constraint. Section II develops implications for asset pricing when asset returns are jointly lognormal and homoscedastic and when consumers have the objective function proposed by Epstein and Zin (1989, 1991) and Weil (1989,1990). This objective function implies that the consumption–wealth ratio is constant whenever the intertemporal elasticity of substitution is equal to 1, so it provides a natural benchmark case in which the loglinear approximation of this paper holds exactly. Importantly, the intertemporal asset pricing model differs from a one-period asset pricing model even in this benchmark case. This section of the paper derives several alternative expressions for risk premia and discusses how they might be tested empirically. Section III allows for changing second moments of asset returns. Section IV assesses the accuracy of the approximation to the intertemporal budget constraint, and conclusions are presented in Section V.

I. A Loglinear Approximation to the Intertemporal Budget Constraint

I consider a representative-agent economy in which all wealth, including human capital, is tradable. I define W_t to be total wealth, including human capital, at the beginning of period t, C_t to be consumption at time t, and $R_{\mathrm{m},\,t+1}$ to be the gross simple return on wealth invested from period t to period $t+1$. The subscript m denotes the fact that total invested wealth is the "market portfolio" of assets. The representative agent's dynamic budget constraint can then be written as

$$W_{t+1} = R_{\mathrm{m},\,t+1}(W_t - C_t)\,. \tag{1}$$

Labor income does not appear explicitly in this budget constraint because of the assumption that the market value of tradable human capital is included in wealth. The budget constraint can be solved forward, imposing a condition that the limit of discounted future wealth is zero, to obtain the highly nonlinear present-value budget constraint

$$W_t = C_t + \sum_{i=1}^{\infty} \frac{C_{t+i}}{\left(\prod_{j=1}^{i} R_{m,\,t+j}\right)}. \tag{2}$$

The loglinear approximation begins by dividing (1) through by W_t, to obtain

$$\frac{W_{t+1}}{W_t} = R_{m,\,t+1}\left(1 - \frac{C_t}{W_t}\right) \tag{3}$$

or in logs (indicated by lowercase letters)

$$\Delta W_{t+1} = r_{m,t+1} + \log(1 - \exp(c_t - w_t)) \tag{4}$$

The second term on the right-hand side is a nonlinear function of the log consumption–wealth ratio. Consider this as a function of some variable $x_t = \log(X_t)$, and take a first-order Taylor expansion around the mean $\bar{x}$. The resulting approximation is

$$\log(1 - \exp(x_t)) \approx \log(1 - \exp(\bar{x})) - \frac{\exp(\bar{x})}{1 - \exp(\bar{x})}(x_t - \bar{x}). \tag{5}$$

If x_t is a constant $x = \log(X)$, then the coefficient $-\exp(\bar{x})/[1 - \exp(\bar{x})]$ equals $-X/(1 - X)$. In the present application, when the log consumption–wealth ratio is a constant the coefficient equals $-C/(W-C)$, the constant ratio of consumption to invested wealth. Of course, when x_t is random then by Jensen's inequality the coefficient no longer equals the average ratio of consumption to invested wealth.

Figures 1 and 2 give a visual impression of the approximation (5). In each figure, the horizontal axis measures the consumption–wealth ratio, using a log scale. The vertical axis measures the "net growth rate of wealth," that is, the growth rate of wealth less the market return $\Delta w_{t+1} - r_{m,\,t+1}$. The solid line shows the exact relationship $\Delta w_{t+1} - r_{m,\,t+1} = \log(1 - \exp(c_t - w_t))$, while the dashed straight line shows the approximation (5). These lines are plotted over a horizontal range three standard deviations on either side of the mean log consumption–wealth ratio, where the standard deviation of the log consumption–wealth ratio is calculated for an example calibrated in Section IV using equation (46). Figure 1 assumes that the consumer has an elasticity of intertemporal substitution in consumption (σ) equal to 2 (or zero, since the standard deviation of the log consumption–wealth ratio depends on the distance of this elasticity from 1), while Figure 2 assumes an elasticity of intertemporal substitution equal to 4. In this example the approximation is clearly very accurate when the variability of the log consumption–wealth ratio is as low as implied by an elasticity of 2, but much less accurate when the variability is as high as implied by an elasticity of 4. Section IV of the paper discusses approximation accuracy in greater detail.

It will be helpful to rewrite the coefficient $-\exp(\bar{x})/[1-\exp(\bar{x})]$ in (5) as $1 - 1/\rho$ where $\rho \equiv 1 - \exp(\bar{x})$. When the log consumption–wealth ratio is constant, then ρ can be interpreted as $(W - C)/W$, the constant ratio of invested wealth to total wealth. Putting together (4) and (5), the approximation to the intertemporal budget constraint is

$$\Delta w_{t+1} \approx r_{m,\,t+1} + k + \left(1 - \frac{1}{\rho}\right)(c_t - w_t) \tag{6}$$

where the constant k can be calculated directly from (5).

FIGURE 1 | Loglinear Approximation for $\sigma = 2$

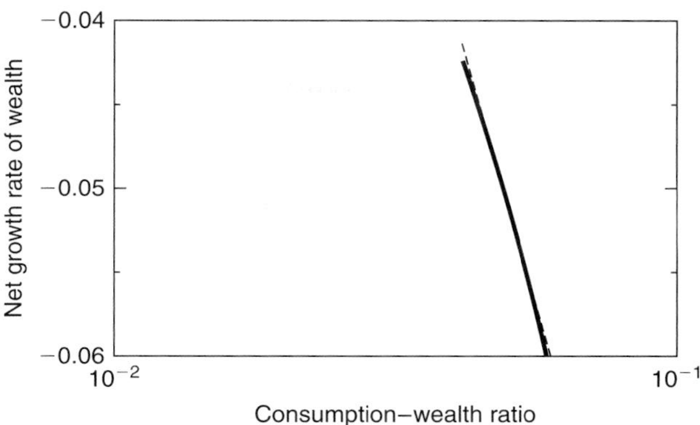

Notes: The horizontal axis shows the annualized consumption–wealth ratio, using a log scale from 1 percent to 10 percent. The vertical axis shows the annualized net growth rate of wealth $\Delta w_{t+1} - r_{m,\,t+1}$. The solid curve is the exact relationship $\Delta w_{t+1} - r_{m,\,t+1} = \log(1 - \exp(c_t - w_t))$, while the dashed straight line is the approximation given by equation (5) in the text. These curves are plotted over a range from three standard deviations below to three standard deviations above the mean log consumption–wealth ratio. The standard deviation of the log consumption–wealth ratio is calculated from equation (46) in the text using the parameter values discussed in Section IV and assuming $\sigma = 2$.

The next step is to use the trivial equality

$$\Delta w_{t+1} = \Delta c_{t+1} + (c_t - w_t) - (c_{t+1} - w_{t+1}). \tag{7}$$

Equating the left-hand sides of (6) and (7), one obtains a difference equation in the log consumption–wealth ratio, $c_t - w_t$. This can be solved forward, assuming that $\lim_{j\to\infty} \rho^j(c_{t+j} - w_{t+j}) = 0$, to yield

$$c_t - w_t = \sum_{j=1}^{\infty} \rho^j(r_{m,\,t+j} - \Delta c_{t+j}) + \frac{\rho k}{1 - \rho}. \tag{8}$$

FIGURE 2 | Loglinear Approximation for $\sigma = 4$

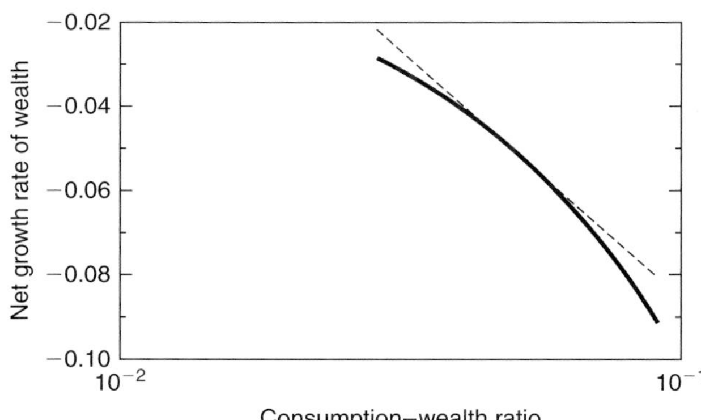

Notes: The horizontal axis shows the annualized consumption–wealth ratio, using a log scale from 1 percent to 10 percent. The vertical axis shows the annualized net growth rate of wealth $\Delta w_{t+1} - r_{m,\,t+1}$. The solid curve is the exact relationship $\Delta w_{t+1} - r_{m,\,t+1} = \log(1 - \exp(c_t - w_t))$, while the dashed straight line is the approximation given by equation (5) in the text. These curves are plotted over a range from three standard deviations below to three standard deviations above the mean log consumption-wealth ratio. The standard deviation of the log consumption–wealth ratio is calculated from equation (46) in the text using the parameter values discussed in Section IV and assuming $\sigma = 4$.

This equation is the loglinear equivalent of the nonlinear expression (2). It says that a high consumption–wealth ratio today must be followed either by high returns on invested wealth or by low consumption growth. This holds simply by virtue of the intertemporal budget constraint; there is no model of optimal behavior in equation (8).

Equation (8) holds *ex post*, but it also holds *ex ante*; if one takes expectations of (8) at time t, the left-hand side is unchanged, and the right-hand side becomes an expected discounted value:

$$c_t - w_t = E_t \sum_{j=1}^{\infty} \rho^j (r_{\mathrm{m},\, t+j} - \Delta c_{t+j}) + \frac{\rho k}{1-\rho}. \tag{9}$$

Equation (9) can be substituted into (6) and (7) to obtain

$$\begin{aligned} c_{t+1} - E_t c_{t+1} = {} & (E_{t+1} - E_t) \sum_{j=0}^{\infty} \rho^j r_{\mathrm{m},\, t+1+j} \\ & - (E_{t+1} - E_t) \sum_{j=1}^{\infty} \rho^j \Delta c_{t+1+j}. \end{aligned} \tag{10}$$

Equation (10) says that an upward surprise in consumption today must correspond to an unexpected return on wealth today (the first term in the first sum on the right-hand side of the equation), or to news that future returns will be higher (the remaining terms in the first sum), or to a downward revision in expected future consumption growth (the second sum on the right-hand side). This is similar to the equation discussed in Campbell (1991) for an arbitrary stock portfolio. Here consumption plays the role of dividends in the earlier analysis; aggregate wealth can be thought of as an asset whose dividends are equal to consumption. In the next section, a loglinear Euler equation will be used to eliminate expected future consumption growth from the right-hand side of (10), leaving only current and expected future asset returns.

II. Intertemporal Asset Pricing with Constant Variances

In this section I explore asset pricing relationships assuming that the conditional joint distribution of asset returns and consumption is homoscedastic. This assumption is unrealistic, since there is strong evidence that asset-return variances change through time, but it simplifies the analysis considerably. In the next section I allow for heteroscedasticity.

The loglinear approximate budget constraint of the previous section can be combined with a loglinear Euler equation. To obtain such an Euler equation, I further assume that the joint conditional distribution of asset returns and consumption is lognormal. Below I show that this is an approximate implication of the more fundamental assumption that returns and news about future returns are jointly lognormal. The lognormality assumption can also be relaxed if one is willing to work with a second-order Taylor approximation to the Euler equation.[1]

Along with these distributional assumptions, I use the non-expected-utility model proposed by Epstein and Zin (1989, 1991) and Weil (1989, 1990) to generate a loglinear Euler equation that distinguishes the coefficient of relative risk aversion and the elasticity of intertemporal substitution. In the standard model of time-separable power utility, relative risk aversion

[1] Conditional joint lognormality and homoscedasticity are also assumed by Hansen and Singleton (1983). Note that conditional lognormality does not imply unconditional lognormality unless conditional expected returns are constant through time. Constant expected returns and unconditional lognormality are assumed in Merton's (1969, 1971) continuous-time model, where all asset returns follow geometric Brownian motions; the assumption used here is weaker.

is the reciprocal of the elasticity of intertemporal substitution, but as will be seen, these concepts play quite different roles in the asset pricing theory. The non-expected-utility model also allows intertemporal considerations to affect asset prices even when the ratio of consumption to wealth is constant, something which is not possible with time-separable power utility.

A. The Euler Equation for a Simple Non-Expected-Utility Model

The objective function for a simple non-expected-utility model is defined recursively by

$$U_t = \{(1-\beta)C_t^{(1-\gamma)/\theta} + \beta(E_t U_{t+1}^{1-\gamma})^{1/\theta}\}^{\theta/(1-\gamma)}. \tag{11}$$

Here, γ is the coefficient of relative risk aversion, σ is the elasticity of intertemporal substitution, and θ is defined, following Giovannini and Weil (1989), as

$$\theta = (1-\gamma)/[1-(1/\sigma)].$$

Note that in general the coefficient θ can have either sign. Important special cases of the model include the case in which the coefficient of relative risk aversion γ approaches 1, so that θ approaches 0; the case in which the elasticity of intertemporal substitution σ approaches 1, so that θ approaches infinity; and the case in which $\gamma = 1/\sigma$, so that $\theta = 1$. Inspection of (11) shows that this last case gives the standard time-separable power utility function with relative risk aversion γ. When both γ and σ equal 1, the objective function is the time-separable log utility function.

Building on the work of David Kreps and E. Porteus (1978), Epstein and Zin (1989, 1991) have established several important properties of this objective function. First, when consumption is chosen optimally the value function (the maximized objective function) is given by

$$\begin{aligned} V_t &= \max U_t \\ &= \left[(1-\beta)^{-\sigma}\frac{C_t}{W_t}\right]^{1/(1-\sigma)} W_t. \end{aligned} \tag{12}$$

The objective function (11) has been normalized so that the value function is linearly homogeneous in wealth (for a given consumption–wealth ratio). It is conventional to normalize the time-separable power utility function so that wealth appears in the value function raised to the power $1-\gamma$, but the normalization in (11) turns out to be convenient here. Naturally the normalization makes no difference to the solution of the model.[2]

Second, the Euler equation for asset i's return, $R_{i,\,t+1}$, can be written as

$$1 = E_t\left[\left\{\beta\left(\frac{C_{t+1}}{C_t}\right)^{-1/\sigma}\right\}^{\theta}\left\{\frac{1}{R_{\mathrm{m},\,t+1}}\right\}^{t-\theta} R_{i,\,t+1}\right]. \tag{13}$$

For the market portfolio itself, this takes the simpler form

$$1 = E_t\left[\left\{\beta\left(\frac{C_{t+1}}{C_t}\right)^{-1/\sigma} R_{\mathrm{m},\,t+1}\right\}^{\theta}\right]. \tag{14}$$

These equations collapse to the familiar expressions for power utility when $\theta = 1$.

When asset returns and consumption are jointly conditionally homoscedastic and lognormally distributed, the Euler equations (13) and (14) can be rewritten in log form. This

[2] The notation used here is similar to that in Epstein and Zin (1991). However their parameter ρ corresponds to $1-(1/\sigma)$ here. Their parameter α corresponds to $1-\gamma$ here. Thus the parameter θ here is ρ/α in their notation. Note also that there are errors in equations (10)–(12) of their paper. Equation (12) here is a corrected version of their equation (12). Giovannini and Weil (1989) also give the correct formula for the value function, although they normalize the objective function in the conventional manner for power utility.

rewriting can also be justified as a second-order Taylor approximation if asset returns and consumption are jointly conditionally homoscedastic. The log version of (14) takes the form

$$0 = \theta \log \beta - \frac{\theta}{\sigma} E_t \Delta c_{t+1} + \theta E_t r_{\mathrm{m},\,t+1} + \frac{1}{2}\left[\left(\frac{\theta}{\sigma}\right)^2 V_{cc} + \theta^2 V_{mm} - \frac{2\theta^2}{\sigma} V_{cm}\right]. \tag{15}$$

Here lowercase letters are again used for logs. V_{cc} denotes

$$\mathrm{Var}_t(\Delta c_{t+1}) = \mathrm{Var}(\Delta c_{t+1} - E_t \Delta c_{t+1})$$

where the equality holds because of the assumption of conditional homoscedasticity, and other expressions of the form V_{xy} are defined in analogous fashion (with subscript m representing r_{m}).

Equation (15) implies that there is a linear relationship between expected consumption growth and the expected return on the market portfolio, with a slope coefficient equal to the intertemporal elasticity of substitution σ. The relationship is

$$\begin{aligned} E_t \Delta c_{t+1} &= \mu_{\mathrm{m}} + \sigma E_t r_{\mathrm{m},\,t+1} \\ \mu_{\mathrm{m}} &= \sigma \log \beta + \frac{1}{2}\left[\left(\frac{\theta}{\sigma}\right) V_{cc} + \theta\sigma V_{mm} - 2\theta V_{cm}\right] \\ &= \sigma \log \beta + \frac{1}{2}\left(\frac{\theta}{\sigma}\right) \mathrm{Var}_t[\Delta c_{t+1} - \sigma r_{\mathrm{m},\,t+1}]. \end{aligned} \tag{16}$$

The intercept term μ_{m} is related to the variance of the error term in the *ex post* version of the linear relationship (16), that is, the degree of uncertainty about consumption growth relative to the return on the market. If θ is positive, a high value of this variance will cause consumers to increase the slope of their consumption growth path by postponing consumption to the future. If θ is negative, on the other hand, consumers will accelerate their consumption in response to increased uncertainty.

The log version of the general Euler equation (13) can be used for cross-sectional asset pricing. It takes the more complicated form

$$\begin{aligned} 0 = \theta \log \beta &- \frac{\theta}{\sigma} E_t \Delta c_{t+1} + (\theta - 1) E_t r_{\mathrm{m},\,t+1} + E_t r_{i,\,t+1} \\ &+ \frac{1}{2}\left[\left(\frac{\theta}{\sigma}\right)^2 V_{cc} + (\theta - 1)^2 V_{mm} + V_{ii} - \frac{2\theta}{\sigma}(\theta - 1) V_{cm} \right. \\ &\left. - \frac{2\theta}{\sigma} V_{ci} + 2(\theta - 1) V_{im}\right]. \end{aligned} \tag{17}$$

When the asset under consideration is a risk-free real return $r_{\mathrm{f},\,t+1}$, this expression simplifies because some variances and covariances drop out. Subtracting the risk-free version of (17) from the general version and rearranging, one obtains

$$E_t r_{i,\,t+1} - r_{\mathrm{f},\,t+1} = -\frac{V_{ii}}{2} + \theta \frac{V_{ic}}{\sigma} + (1 - \theta) V_{im}. \tag{18}$$

Equation (18) is the implication of the model emphasized by Giovannini and Weil (1989). In this expression all risk premia are constant over time because of the assumption that asset returns and consumption are homoscedastic. Equation (18) says that the expected excess log return on an asset is determined by its own variance (a Jensen's inequality effect) and by a weighted average of two covariances. The first covariance is with consumption growth divided by the intertemporal elasticity of substitution; this gets a weight of θ. The second covariance is with the return on the market portfolio; this gets a weight of $1 - \theta$.[3]

Three special cases are worth noting. When the objective function is a time-separable power utility function the coefficient $\theta = 1$, and the model collapses to the loglinear consumption CAPM of Hansen and Singleton (1983). When the coefficient of relative risk aversion $\gamma = 1$, then $\theta = 0$, and a logarithmic version of the static CAPM pricing formula holds. Most important for the present paper, as the elasticity of intertemporal substitution σ approaches 1 the coefficient θ goes to infinity. At the same time, the variability of the consumption–wealth ratio decreases so that the covariance V_{ic} approaches V_{im}. It does not follow, however, that the risk premium is determined only by V_{im} in this case. Giovannini and Weil (1989) show that the convergence rates are such that asset pricing is not myopic when $\sigma = 1$ unless also $\gamma = 1$ (the log-utility case). In the next subsection I give an exact expression for the risk premium in the $\sigma = 1$ case.

B. Substituting Out Consumption

The loglinear Euler equations derived above can now be combined with the approximate loglinear budget constraint of Section I. Substituting (16) into (9), one obtains

$$c_t - w_t = (1 - \sigma)E_t \sum_{j=1}^{\infty} \rho^j r_{\mathrm{m},\, t+j} + \frac{\rho(k - \mu_{\mathrm{m}})}{1 - \rho}. \tag{19}$$

The log consumption–wealth ratio is a constant, plus $(1 - \sigma)$ times the discounted value of expected future returns on invested wealth. If σ is less than 1, the consumer is reluctant to substitute intertemporally, and the income effect of higher returns dominates the substitution effect, raising today's consumption relative to wealth. If σ is greater than 1, the substitution effect dominates, and the consumption–wealth ratio falls when expected returns rise. Thus equation (19) extends to a dynamic context the classic comparative statics results of Paul A. Samuelson (1969) and Merton (1969).

Note that the coefficient of relative risk aversion, γ, does not appear in (19) except indirectly through the [sic] the parameter of linearization, ρ. Shmuel Kandel and Robert F. Stambaugh (1991) have used a numerical solution method to show that σ rather than γ is the main determinant of the variability of expected market returns in a model with exogenous consumption and endogenous returns. Equation (19) provides a simple way to understand their finding.

As discussed above, the case $\sigma = 1$ is the borderline case where consumption is a constant fraction of wealth. As σ approaches 1, θ approaches infinity, and it is easy to see from (16) that the variance terms in μ_{m} must cancel if expected consumption growth is to be finite. This cancellation occurs when consumption is a constant fraction of wealth. Furthermore, by substituting the definitions of k and ρ into (19), one can show that when $\sigma = 1$ the consumption–wealth ratio equals $1 - \beta$, while the parameter of linearization ρ equals β. Since the consumption–wealth ratio is constant when $\sigma = 1$, the approximate budget constraint and asset pricing formulas of this paper hold exactly in this case if one sets $\rho = \beta$.

The approximation (19) can be used to restate the value function (12) in terms of exogenous variables. Taking logs of (12), one obtains

[3] Zhiwu Chen (1991) discusses a similar result in a model with a von Neumann-Morgenstern utility function that is directly affected by the level of wealth.

$$(20) \qquad v_t = w_t + \left(\frac{1}{1-\sigma}\right)(c_t - w_t)$$
$$= w_t + E_t \sum_{j=1}^{\infty} \rho^j r_{m,t+j}.$$

The value function is determined by the level of wealth and by the discounted value of all future expected market returns, a measure of long-run investment opportunities.

Equation (19) can also be used to express the innovation in consumption as a function of the return on the market and news about future returns on the market. Substituting (16) into (10), one obtains

$$(21) \qquad c_{t+1} - E_t c_{t+1} = r_{m,t+1} - E_t r_{m,t+1}$$
$$+ (1-\sigma)(E_{t+1} - E_t) \sum_{j=1}^{\infty} \rho^j r_{m,t+1+j}.$$

The intuition here is much the same as for equation (19). An unexpected return on invested wealth has a one-for-one effect on consumption, no matter what the parameters of the utility function. [This follows from the scale independence of the objective function (11).] An increase in expected future returns raises or lowers consumption depending on whether σ is greater or less than 1.

Equation (21) can be used in several different ways. First, it shows the conditions on the return process that are necessary to justify the original assumption of this section that consumption growth and asset returns are jointly lognormal. To a first approximation, consumption growth will be lognormal if the return on the market and revisions of expectations about future returns are jointly lognormal; thus the assumption of joint lognormality of consumption growth and asset returns can be approximately consistent with equilibrium.

Second, the equation shows when consumption will be smoother than the return on the market. There is some evidence that innovations in current stock returns are negatively correlated with revisions in expectations of future returns. According to (21), this reduces the variability of consumption growth if the elasticity of intertemporal substitution σ is less than 1. It amplifies the volatility of consumption growth, however, if σ is greater than 1.

To understand this more clearly, it may be helpful to consider a simple example in which the market return follows a univariate stochastic process: $r_{m,t+1} = A(L)\varepsilon_{t+1}$. Here the polynomial in the lag operator $A(L) \equiv 1 + a_1 L + a_2 L^2 + \cdots$, where the coefficients a_i are the moving-average coefficients of the market-return process. Similarly, one can define $A(\rho) \equiv 1 + a_1\rho + a_2\rho^2 + \cdots$, the infinite sum of moving-average coefficients discounted at rate ρ. Since ρ is close to 1, $A(\rho)$ is approximately the sum of the moving-average coefficients, a measure of the impact of today's return innovation on long-run future wealth. In this special case, (21) can be rewritten as

$$c_{t+1} - E_t c_{t+1} = \varepsilon_{t+1} + (1-\sigma)[A(\rho) - 1]\varepsilon_{t+1}$$
$$= \sigma\varepsilon_{t+1} + (1-\sigma)A(\rho)\varepsilon_{t+1}.$$

The innovation in consumption is a weighted combination (with weights σ and $1 - \sigma$) of the current market-return innovation ε_{t+1} and the discounted long-run impact of the return innovation $A(\rho)\varepsilon_{t+1}$. In this example a negative correlation between current return innovations and revisions in expected future returns is equivalent to "mean-reversion," or negative serial correlation in realized returns. Evidence for mean-reversion has been reported by Eugene F. Fama and Kenneth R. French (1988a) and James M. Poterba and Lawrence H.

Summers (1988). Mean-reversion in the market return makes $A(\rho) < 1$, which reduces the variability in consumption if $\sigma < 1$.[4]

Third, equation (21) can be used to clarify the interpretation of the intercept coefficient μ_{m} in the equation relating consumption growth and the expected return on the market. Substituting (21) into (16), μ_{m} can be written as

$$\begin{aligned}(22)\qquad \mu_{\mathrm{m}} &= \sigma \log \beta + \left(\frac{1}{2}\right)(1-\sigma)^2\left(\frac{\theta}{\sigma}\right)\mathrm{Var}_t\left[(E_{t+1}-E_t)\sum_{j=0}^{\infty}\rho^j r_{\mathrm{m},\,t+1+j}\right] \\ &= \sigma \log \beta + \left(\frac{1}{2}\right)(1-\sigma)^2\left(\frac{\theta}{\sigma}\right)\mathrm{Var}_t v_{t+1}.\end{aligned}$$

The summation in (22) runs from zero to infinity, since the uncertainty that affects μ_{m} includes both the variance of this period's market return and the variance of news about future market returns. The second equality in (22) follows from the solution for the value function (20). Equation (22) shows that the conditional variance of expected long-run investment opportunities (equivalently, the conditional variance of the value function) is the correct measure of risk in this model. As discussed above, the sign of θ determines whether consumers will postpone or accelerate consumption in response to this risk.

Finally, equation (21) implies that the conditional covariance of any asset return with consumption growth can be rewritten in terms of conditional covariances with the return on the market and revisions in expectations of future returns on the market.[5] The conditional covariance satisfies

$$(23)\qquad \mathrm{Cov}_t(r_{i,\,t+1}, \Delta c_{t+1}) \equiv V_{ic} = V_{im} + (1-\sigma)V_{ih}$$

where

$$(24)\qquad V_{ih} = \mathrm{Cov}_t\left(r_{i,\,t+1}, (E_{t+1}-E_t)\sum_{j=1}^{\infty}\rho^j r_{\mathrm{m},\,t+1+j}\right).$$

V_{ih} is defined to be the covariance of asset i's return with good news about future returns on the market (i.e., upward revisions in expected future returns).[6]

Substituting (23) into (18) and using the definition of θ in terms of the underlying parameters σ and γ, I obtain a cross-sectional asset pricing formula that makes no reference to consumption:

$$(25)\qquad E_t r_{i,\,t+1} - r_{\mathrm{f},\,t+1} = -\frac{V_{ii}}{2} + \gamma V_{im} + (\gamma - 1)V_{ih}.$$

Equation (25) has several striking features. First, assets can be priced without direct reference to their covariances with consumption growth, using instead their covariances with the

[4] One should recognize that this example is special. In more general examples, such as the one developed in Section IV, innovations in returns can be negatively correlated with revisions in expectations of future returns even when realized returns are serially uncorrelated (Campbell, 1991). Thus, in general, the univariate properties of market returns do not pin down the behavior of consumption.

[5] Equally, (21) could be used to rewrite the covariance with the market in terms of covariances with consumption and revisions in expectations of future investment opportunities. The contribution of (21) is to show that only two of these three covariances need be measured accurately in order to have a testable asset pricing theory.

[6] The notation V_{ih} is chosen to accord with Campbell (1991). It recalls the standard terminology of "hedge portfolios" (e.g., Jonathan E. Ingersoll, Jr., 1987).

return on invested wealth and with news about future returns on invested wealth. This is a discrete-time analogue of Merton's (1973) continuous-time model in which assets are priced using their covariances with certain "hedge portfolios" that index changes in the investment opportunity set.

Second, the only parameter of the utility function that enters (25) is the coefficient of relative risk aversion γ. The elasticity of intertemporal substitution σ does not appear once consumption has been substituted out of the model. This is in striking contrast with the important role played by σ in the consumption-based Euler equation (18). Intuitively, this result comes from the fact that σ plays two roles in the theory. A low value of σ reduces anticipated fluctuations in consumption [equation (16)], but it also increases the risk premium required to compensate for any contribution to these fluctuations [equation (18)]. These offsetting effects lead σ to cancel out of the asset-based pricing equation (25). Narayana Kocherlakota (1990) and Lars E. O. Svensson (1989) have already shown that σ is irrelevant for asset pricing when asset returns are independently and identically distributed over time. This is not surprising, since with independently and identically distributed returns there is no interesting role for intertemporal substitution in consumption. The present result is approximate but is much stronger, since it holds in a world with changing conditional mean asset returns.

Third, equation (25) expresses the risk premium (net of the Jensen's inequality effect) as a weighted sum of two terms. The first term is the asset's covariance with the market portfolio; the weight on this term is the coefficient of relative risk aversion γ. The second term is the asset's covariance with news about future returns on the market; this receives a weight of $\gamma - 1$. When γ is less than 1, assets that do well when there is good news about future returns on the market have lower mean returns, but when γ is greater than 1, such assets have higher mean returns. The intuitive explanation is that such assets are desirable because they enable the consumer to profit from improved investment opportunities, but undesirable because they reduce the consumer's ability to hedge against a deterioration in investment opportunities. When $\gamma < 1$ the former effect dominates, and consumers are willing to accept a lower return in order to hold assets that pay off when wealth is most productive. When $\gamma > 1$ the latter effect dominates, and consumers require a higher return to hold such assets.

There are several possible circumstances under which assets can be priced using only their covariances with the return on the market portfolio, as in the logarithmic version of the static CAPM. These cases have been discussed in the literature on intertemporal asset pricing, but equation (25) makes it particularly easy to understand them. First, if the coefficient of relative risk aversion $\gamma = 1$, then the opposing effects of covariance with investment opportunities cancel out so that only covariance with the market return is relevant for asset pricing. Giovannini and Weil (1989) emphasize this result, and it has been long understood for the special case of log utility, where not only $\gamma = 1$, but also $\sigma = 1$. Second, if the investment opportunity set is constant, then V_{ih} is zero for all assets, so again assets can be priced using only their covariances with the market return. Fama (1970) and Merton (1969, 1971) stress this result. Third, if the return on the market follows a univariate stochastic process, then news about future returns is perfectly correlated with the current return. Using the notation introduced above, in this case $V_{ih} = [A(\rho) - 1]V_{im}$ for all assets i, and the risk premium (ignoring the Jensen's inequality term) is $\{\gamma + (\gamma - 1)[A(\rho) - 1]\}V_{im}$. Giovannini and Weil (1989) and Merton (1990 Ch. 16) present results of this type in discrete time and continuous time, respectively.

One obvious application of formula (25) is to the equity premium, the risk premium on the market itself. When innovations in the market return are uncorrelated with revisions in expectations of future market returns, then $V_{mh} = 0$, and the equity premium net of the Jensen's inequality effect is just γV_{mm}. In this case, the coefficient of relative risk aversion can be estimated in the manner of Irwin Friend and Marshall E. Blume (1975) by taking the ratio of the equity premium to the variance of the market-return innovation. This procedure can be seriously misleading, however, if market-return innovations are correlated with innovations in expected future market returns. To see this, consider the special case in which the market-return process is univariate so that correlation between return innovations and revisions in expectations of future returns is equivalent to serial correlation in market returns. In this case the equity premium net of the Jensen's inequality term is $\{\gamma + (\gamma - 1)[A(\rho) - 1]\}V_{mm}$. Mean-reversion in stock returns [the case $A(\rho) < 1$] reduces the equity premium when $\gamma > 1$ but increases it when $\gamma < 1$. The Friend and Blume estimate of risk aversion will be off by $(\gamma - 1)[A(\rho) - 1]$. This error can be substantial, particularly if γ is very large as suggested by Kandel and Stambaugh (1991) among others. Fischer Black (1990) also emphasizes that mean-reversion can affect the relation between short-run market volatility and the equity premium.

C. The Term Structure of Real Interest Rates

Real bonds, which make fixed payments of consumption goods, play a special role in asset pricing theory because they have no payoff uncertainty. The only uncertainty in their return comes from changes in the real interest rates used to discount their payoffs. In this section I show that in a lognormal homoscedastic model, the unexpected return on a real consol bond is approximately equal to minus the news about future returns on invested wealth. This means that the covariance with good news about future returns can also be written as minus the covariance with the return on a real consol.

Let p_{bt} denote the log price at time t of a real consol bond paying one unit of the consumption good each period, with no maturity date. The log return on this bond is

$$r_{b,t+1} \equiv \log(1 + \exp(p_{b,t+1})) - p_{bt}. \tag{26}$$

Linearizing this expression with a first-order Taylor expansion in the manner of Section I, one obtains the approximation

$$r_{b,t+1} \approx k_b + \rho_b p_{b,t+1} - p_{bt} \tag{27}$$

where ρ_b is the reciprocal of the average gross, simple return on the consol: $\rho_b = 1/\overline{R}_b$.

This implies that p_{bt} is determined by the discounted value of expected future returns on the bond or, equivalently, by the discounted value of expected future returns on invested wealth (in the homoscedastic model these are the same, up to a constant risk premium):

$$p_{bt} = E_t \sum_{j=1}^{\infty} \rho_b^j r_{m,t+j} + k^* \tag{28}$$

for some constant k^*. Substituting (28) back into (27), one obtains

$$r_{b,t+1} - E_t r_{b,t+1} = -(E_{t+1} - E_t) \sum_{j=1}^{\infty} \rho_b^j r_{m,t+1+j}. \tag{29}$$

In general ρ_b does not equal the parameter of linearization for the intertemporal budget constraint, ρ. However the difference is likely to be small, and it will have little effect on a discounted value like the right-hand side of (29) if news about future returns on the market dies out fairly rapidly. Thus,

$$\text{Cov}_t(r_{i,t+1}, r_{b,t+1}) \equiv V_{ib} \approx -V_{ih} \tag{30}$$

and the asset pricing equation (25) can be rewritten as

$$E_t r_{i,\,t+1} - r_{f,\,t+1} = -\frac{V_{ii}}{2} + \gamma V_{im} + (1 - \gamma)V_{ib}. \tag{31}$$

Equation (31) says that the expected log return on any asset is determined by its own conditional variance and by a weighted average of its conditional covariances with the market portfolio and with a real consol bond. The weights on the market and the consol are γ and $1 - \gamma$, respectively, where as before γ is the coefficient of relative risk aversion.

Equation (31) is reminiscent of the formula in Merton (1973) that expresses the expected excess return on any asset as a linear function of its covariances with the market and with the return on an asset perfectly correlated with changes in short-term interest rates (loosely, a long-term bond).[7] However, the present model differs from Merton's in two important respects. First, Merton's result depends on the assumption that all changes in investment opportunities are summarized by the change in a single state variable, the instantaneous interest rate. Here, the short-term interest rate summarizes the current investment opportunity set (because all asset returns move in parallel in the homoscedastic model), but it does not summarize all changes in investment opportunities (because there can be many sources of news about future returns). Another way to see the difference is to note that in Merton's model long-term bond returns and changes in short-term rates are perfectly correlated instantaneously, whereas this need not be the case in the present model.[8] Second, Merton's (1973) model gives the prices of the two sources of risk only in terms of the derivatives of the consumer's value function, which are endogenous to the model. Here, the risk prices are explicitly determined by the primitive parameters of the consumer's utility function.

D. A Vector Autoregressive Factor-Pricing Model

The results of the previous section would be useful for empirical work if real consol returns were observable. Unfortunately, such assets do not exist; the closest equivalent may be finite-maturity index bonds in the United Kingdom, and even these have been actively traded only in recent years. Another approach is needed to derive testable implications of the basic asset pricing equation (25).

Here I adapt the vector autoregressive approach of Campbell (1991).[9] I assume that the return on the market can be written as the first element of K-element state vector $\mathbf{z}_{t+1}$. The other elements are variables that are known to the market by the end of period $t + 1$ and are relevant for forecasting future returns on the market. I assume that the vector $\mathbf{z}_{t+1}$ follows a first-order vector autoregression (VAR):

$$\mathbf{z}_{t+1} = \mathbf{A}\mathbf{z}_t + \boldsymbol{\varepsilon}_{t+1}. \tag{32}$$

The assumption that the VAR is first-order is not restrictive, since a higher-order VAR can always be stacked into first-order (companion) form in the manner discussed by Campbell and Shiller (1988a). The matrix $\mathbf{A}$ is known as the companion matrix of the VAR.[10]

---

[7] This is equation (32) of Merton (1973), reprinted as equation (15.32) in Merton (1990). Mark Rubinstein (1981), Breeden (1986), and Peter Bossaerts and Richard C. Green (1989) also emphasize the importance of real bonds in asset pricing.

[8] In another respect, however, Merton's (1973) model is more general, because it allows variances to depend on the interest rate. In the next section, I allow for changing variances in the present framework.

[9] Campbell (1991) uses this approach to decompose the overall market return into news about dividends and news about future market returns. In the present homoscedastic context the latter component is just the return on a real consol, as discussed above. Equation (25) says that the dividend news component of the market return has risk price γ, while the return news component has risk price $1 - \gamma$.

[10] As is well known, VAR systems can be normalized in different ways. For example, the variables in the state vector can be orthogonalized so that the variance-covariance matrix of the error vector $\boldsymbol{\varepsilon}$ is diagonal. The results given here hold for any observationally equivalent normalization of the VAR system.

Next I define a K-element vector $\mathbf{e1}$, whose first element is one and whose other elements are all zero. This vector picks out the real stock return $r_{m,\,t+1}$ from the vector $\mathbf{z}_{t+1}$: $r_{m,\,t+1} = \mathbf{e1}'\mathbf{z}_{t+1}$, and $r_{m,\,t+1} - E_t r_{m,\,t+1} = \mathbf{e1}'\boldsymbol{\varepsilon}_{t+1}$. The first-order VAR generates simple multiperiod forecasts of future returns:

$$E_t r_{m,\,t+1+j} = \mathbf{e1}'\mathbf{A}^{j+1}\mathbf{z}_t. \tag{33}$$

It follows that the discounted sum of revisions in forecast returns can be written as

$$\begin{aligned}\left(E_{t+1} - E_t\right)\sum_{j=1}^{\infty}\rho^j r_{m,\,t+1+j} &= \mathbf{e1}'\sum_{j=1}^{\infty}\rho^j\mathbf{A}^j\boldsymbol{\varepsilon}_{t+1}\\ &= \mathbf{e1}'\rho\mathbf{A}(\mathbf{I} - \rho\mathbf{A})^{-1}\boldsymbol{\varepsilon}_{t+1}\\ &= \boldsymbol{\lambda}'\boldsymbol{\varepsilon}_{t+1}\end{aligned} \tag{34}$$

where $\boldsymbol{\lambda}'$ is defined to equal $\mathbf{e1}'\rho\mathbf{A}(\mathbf{I} - \rho\mathbf{A})^{-1}$, a nonlinear function of the VAR coefficients. The elements of the vector $\boldsymbol{\lambda}$ measure the importance of each state variable in forecasting future returns on the market. If a particular element $\boldsymbol{\lambda}_k$ is large and positive, then a shock to variable k is an important piece of good news about future investment opportunities.

I now define

$$V_{ik} \equiv \mathrm{Cov}_i(r_{i,\,t+1}, \varepsilon_{k,\,t+1}) \tag{35}$$

where $\varepsilon_{k,\,t+1}$ is the kth element of $\boldsymbol{\varepsilon}_{t+1}$. Since the first element of the state vector is the return on the market, $V_{i1} = V_{im}$. Then equations (34), (35), and (25) imply that

$$E_t r_{i,\,t+1} - r_{f,\,t+1} = -\frac{V_{ii}}{2} + \gamma V_{i1} + (\gamma - 1)\sum_{k=1}^{K}\lambda_k V_{ik} \tag{36}$$

where λ_k is the kth element of $\boldsymbol{\lambda}$. This is a standard K-factor asset pricing model, and its general form could be derived in any number of ways: perhaps most straightforwardly by using the arbitrage pricing theory of Stephen A. Ross (1976).

The contribution of the intertemporal optimization problem is a set of restrictions on the risk prices of the factors. The first factor (the innovation in the market return) has a risk price of $\gamma + (\gamma - 1)\lambda_1$. The sign of λ_1 is the sign of the correlation between market-return innovations and revisions in expected future market returns. This sign affects the risk price of the market factor; with a negative λ_1, for example, the market factor risk price is reduced if γ is greater than 1.

The other factors in this model have risk prices of $(\gamma - 1)\lambda_k$. Factors here are variables that help to forecast the return on the market, and their risk prices are proportional to their forecasting importance as measured by the elements of the vector $\boldsymbol{\lambda}$. If a particular variable has a positive value of λ_k, this means that innovations in that variable are associated with good news about future investment opportunities. Following the analysis in subsection II-B, such a variable will have a negative risk price if the coefficient of relative risk aversion γ is less than 1, and a positive risk price if the coefficient of relative risk aversion is greater than 1.

Thus, the intertemporal model suggests that priced factors should be found not by running a factor analysis on the covariance matrix of returns (Roll and Ross, 1980), nor by selecting important macroeconomic variables (Nai-fu Chen et al., 1986). Instead, variables that have been shown to forecast stock-market returns should be used in cross-sectional asset pricing studies. Recent empirical work suggests that dividend yields, interest rates, and other financial variables are likely to be important (Fama and G. William Schwert, 1977; Donald B. Keim and Stambaugh, 1986; Campbell, 1987, 1991; Campbell and Shiller, 1988a, b; Fama and French, 1988b, 1989).

III. Intertemporal Asset Pricing with Changing Variances

In this section, I relax the unrealistic assumption of the previous section that all variances and covariances of log asset returns and consumption are constant through time. Relaxing this assumption has no effect on the log-linearization of the budget constraint in Section I or the formulation of the intertemporal optimization problem in Section II. What it does is change the log form of the Euler equations for this problem. If asset returns and consumption are jointly lognormal, but heteroscedastic rather than homoscedastic, equations (15)–(18) hold with time-t subscripts on the variances and covariances; constants of the form V_{xy} become variables of the form $V_{xy,t}$. These modified log Euler equations also hold as second-order Taylor approximations if asset returns and consumption are not lognormal.

The more general form of equation (16) is

$$(37)\qquad \begin{aligned} E_t\,\Delta c_{t+1} &= \mu_{\mathrm{m},t} + \sigma E_t r_{\mathrm{m},t+1} \\ \mu_{\mathrm{m},t} &= \sigma \log \beta + \frac{1}{2}\left[\left(\frac{\theta}{\sigma}\right)V_{cc,t} + \theta\sigma V_{mm,t} - 2\theta V_{cm,t}\right] \\ &= \sigma \log \beta + \frac{1}{2}\left(\frac{\theta}{\sigma}\right)\mathrm{Var}_t[\Delta c_{t+1} - \sigma r_{\mathrm{m},t+1}]. \end{aligned}$$

The intercept $\mu_{\mathrm{m},t}$, which was previously constant, now changes over time with the variance of consumption growth relative to the market return. This means that, when (37) is substituted into the approximate loglinear budget constraint (9), extra terms appear in the formulas for the log consumption–wealth ratio and the innovation in log consumption. Equation (21) becomes

$$(38)\qquad \begin{aligned} c_{t+1} - E_t c_{t+1} = {} & r_{\mathrm{m},t+1} - E_t r_{\mathrm{m},t+1} \\ & + (1-\sigma)(E_{t+1} - E_t)\sum_{j=1}^{\infty}\rho^j r_{\mathrm{m},t+1+j} \\ & -(E_{t+1} - E_t)\sum_{j=1}^{\infty}\rho^j \mu_{\mathrm{m},t+j}. \end{aligned}$$

The new term in equation (38) reflects the influence of changing risk on saving. The variable $\mu_{\mathrm{m},t}$ is proportional to the conditional variance of consumption growth less σ times the return on invested wealth. As this changes, consumers may be induced to accelerate or postpone consumption. The difficulty is that equation (38), unlike the homoscedastic equivalent (21), still makes reference to consumption growth on the right-hand side through the variable $\mu_{\mathrm{m},t}$, which is a function of the second moments of consumption. Thus, equation (38) cannot be used to substitute consumption growth out of the intertemporal asset pricing model without further assumptions.

There are, however, several special cases in which consumption can be substituted out of the model with changing variances. First, if the coefficient of relative risk aversion $\gamma = 1$, then $\theta = 0$, and μ_{m} remains constant even in the heteroscedastic case. Thus, when $\gamma = 1$ a logarithmic version of the static CAPM holds with changing conditional variances. Second, if the elasticity of intertemporal substitution $\sigma = 1$, then θ is infinite, and the conditional variance in (37) must be zero. In this case the intertemporal asset pricing formula (25) continues to hold with time subscripts on the conditional variances. Presumably this formula is a good approximation if σ is not too far from 1 or if conditional variances are not highly variable or persistent. Third, the asset pricing formula (25) describes any asset returns that are uncorrelated with revisions in expectations of future intercepts $\mu_{\mathrm{m},t+j}$. Fernando Restoy (1991), building on the analysis of this paper, has shown that (25) describes the equity premium if the variance of market returns follows a generalized autoregressive conditionally heteroscedastic (GARCH) process that is uncorrelated with the return on the market.

A final special case assumes, in the spirit of John C. Cox et al. (1985), that the intercept $\mu_{m,t}$ is a linear function of the expected return on the market. Suppose that

$$\mu_{m,t} = \mu_0 + \psi E_t r_{m,t+1} \tag{39}$$

for some coefficient ψ.[11] Then the innovation in consumption can be rewritten as

$$c_{t+1} - E_t c_{t+1} = r_{m,t+1} - E_t r_{m,t+1} + (1 - \sigma - \psi)(E_{t+1} - E_t) \sum_{j=1}^{\infty} \rho^j r_{m,t+1+j}. \tag{40}$$

It follows that the covariance of any asset return with consumption growth can be written as

$$\text{Cov}_t(r_{i,t+1}, \Delta c_{t+1}) \equiv V_{ic,t} = V_{im,t} - (1 - \sigma - \psi) V_{ih,t} \tag{41}$$

and the expected excess return on any asset is given by

$$E_t r_{i,t+1} - r_{f,t+1} = -\frac{V_{ii,t}}{2} + \gamma V_{im,t} + \left[(\gamma - 1) - \frac{\theta\psi}{\sigma}\right] V_{ih,t}. \tag{42}$$

This formula for the risk premium is the same as before, with the addition of a term involving the sensitivity of the consumption intercept to the expected return on the market, ψ. This term may be positive or negative in general, and it is interpreted as follows. A 1-percent increase in the expected return on the market lowers consumption by ψ percent through the precautionary saving channel. The market price of consumption risk is θ/σ, so the market price of investment-opportunity-set risk includes a term $-\theta\psi/\sigma$.

It is important to find conditions on the exogenous process for asset returns that justify the assumption on $\mu_{m,t}$ given in (39). One can show that $\mu_{m,t}$ will satisfy (39) if the variances and covariance of the return on the market and news about future returns on the market are linear functions of the expected return on the market. In other words, if for $\{x, y\} = \{m, h\}$ one has that

$$V_{xy,t} = V^0_{xy} + V^1_{xy} E_t r_{m,t+1} \tag{43}$$

then (39) is satisfied.[12] This assumption on returns is a discrete-time analogue of the assumption used in Cox et al. (1985).

In this model the variance-covariance matrix of the return on the market and news about future returns on the market changes with one underlying variable, the expected return on the market. This means that the expected excess return on the market, as given by equation (42) for asset i = m, can be written as a linear function of the conditional variance of the return on the market. Substituting (43) into (42) for asset i = m, one obtains

$$E_t r_{m,t+1} - r_{f,t+1} = \beta_0 + \beta_1 V_{mm,t} \tag{44}$$

$$\beta_0 = \left(\gamma - 1 - \frac{\theta\psi}{\sigma}\right)\left(V^0_{mh} - \frac{V^1_{mh} V^0_{mm}}{V^1_{mm}}\right)$$

$$\beta_1 = \gamma - \frac{1}{2} + \left(\gamma - 1 - \frac{\theta\psi}{\sigma}\right)\frac{V^1_{mh}}{V^1_{mm}}.$$

[11] This condition is slightly problematic in a discrete-time model, because strictly speaking it is inconsistent with the normality of conditional expected returns on the market and the positivity of the variances defining μ_m. Whether this is a serious problem will depend on the parameter values of the model.

[12] However, some values of the slope coefficients in (43) may give a complex (rather than real) solution for ψ.

This result sheds new light on the large empirical literature that estimates a linear relation between the conditional mean and variance of the return on the aggregate stock market (e.g., Merton, 1980; French et al., 1987; Timothy Bollerslev et al., 1988). It is sometimes argued that linearity will hold in a fully specified intertemporal asset pricing model only if agents have log utility. The model of this section provides a counterexample to this claim. It is important to note, however, that the market price of conditional volatility, given by the coefficient β_1 in equation (44), does not generally equal the coefficient of relative risk aversion γ.

IV. How Accurate Is the Log-Linear Approximation?

Earlier sections of the paper have stated some strikingly simple results about the determination of expected asset returns. These results are based on a log-linear approximation to the intertemporal budget constraint that will be accurate when the log consumption–wealth ratio is "not too" variable. In this section I try to characterize more precisely the circumstances under which the approximation works well. To do this, I assume a specific market-return process and consider alternative parameter values for the representative consumer's objective function. For each set of parameter values, I calculate optimal consumption functions numerically and compare them with the approximate analytical solutions derived above.

To reduce the complexity of the problem, I first specialize the model of Section II to a simple example discussed in Campbell (1991). In this example, the expected return on the market portfolio follows a univariate AR(1) process with coefficient ϕ, while the realized return is the expected return plus a white-noise error. This should not be confused with the special case discussed in previous sections in which the market return itself is a univariate process. The model considered here is

$$r_{m,t+1} = E_t r_{m,t+1} + \varepsilon_{1,t+1} \qquad (45)$$
$$E_{t+1} r_{m,t+2} = \phi E_t r_{m,t+1} + \varepsilon_{2,t+1}.$$

The free parameters of this model are the coefficient ϕ and the second moments V_{11}, V_{12}, and V_{22}.

The next step is to pick reasonable values for these parameters. Campbell (1991) estimates persistence measures for expected returns using monthly data on value-weighted U.S. stock returns over the period 1927–1988. The persistence measures are estimated using a VAR system of the type discussed in Subsection II-D, rather than the simple AR(1) model (45). However, it is straightforward to calculate the AR(1) parameter that would correspond to any VAR persistence measure. The estimates of Campbell (1991) imply $\phi = 0.79$ over the full 1927–1988 sample period, and a similar value of $\phi = 0.83$ in the postwar 1952–1988 sample period. Thus $\phi = 0.8$ is a realistic benchmark value to use in the AR(1) model. This value of ϕ implies a half-life for expected-return shocks of just over three months.

Once one has a value of ϕ, the innovation variance of expected returns can be found by using the fact that the variance of expected returns $\mathrm{Var}(E_t r_{m,t+1})$ equals $V_{22}/(1-\phi^2)$. The variance of expected returns is given by the variance of the fitted value in a regression of returns on the relevant information, or equivalently by the overall variance of returns and the R^2 statistic from the regression. The estimates in Campbell (1991) imply that $V_{11} = (0.0563)^2$ and $V_{22} = (0.0063)^2$ in the 1927–1988 sample period. The implied standard deviation for monthly expected returns, when $\phi = 0.8$, is just over 1 percent at a monthly rate. Since the overall standard deviation of the monthly *ex post* return is 5.7 percent, this implies a monthly R^2 statistic of just over 3 percent. The standard deviation for monthly expected returns can also be compared with the mean return of 6.5 percent at an annual rate, or just over 0.5 percent at a monthly rate. Finally, the correlation between innovations in realized returns and revisions in expectations of future returns is estimated to be about −0.8, and I pick this value for the example here. These estimates imply substantial variability in expected returns and also considerable mean-reversion in the market-return process.

Approximate loglinear consumption rules are straightforward to derive in this example. The log consumption–wealth ratio is

$$c_t - w_t = \frac{(1-\sigma)\rho}{1-\rho\phi} E_t r_{\mathrm{m},t+1} + \frac{\rho(k-\mu_{\mathrm{m}})}{1-\rho} \tag{46}$$

while the consumption growth rate is

$$\Delta c_{t+1} = \mu_{\mathrm{m}} + \sigma E_t r_{\mathrm{m},t+1} + \varepsilon_{1,t+1} + \frac{(1-\sigma)\rho}{1-\rho\phi}\varepsilon_{2,t+1}. \tag{47}$$

Note that negative correlation between $\varepsilon_{1,t+1}$ and $\varepsilon_{2,t+1}$ makes consumption smoother if $\sigma < 1$ but more volatile if $\sigma > 1$.

The exact optimal consumption function can only be calculated numerically. Building on the work of George Tauchen and Robert Hussey (1991), I use Gaussian quadrature to approximate the normal distribution of the expected return in (45) by a nine-state Markov process. I then use an iterative procedure to calculate the optimal consumption–wealth ratio in each state and the corresponding value function. Full details are given in Campbell and Hyeng K. Koo (1992); here I simply summarize the results.

Table 1 shows the mean value function for a wealth level of 100 (i.e., the mean value function as a percentage of wealth), calculated numerically for a grid of six values of σ and six values of γ: σ is set equal to 0.05, 0.5, 1, 2, 3, and 4, while γ is 0, 0.5, 1, 2, 3, and 4. The smallest value of σ is 0.05 rather than 0 because the program encounters some numerical difficulties when σ is extremely small. All the results reported assume that the mean market return is 6.5 percent at an annual rate and that the discount factor β is the 12th root of 0.94, giving the monthly equivalent of a 6-percent annual discount rate.

Table 1 also shows, in parentheses, the percentage losses in the mean objective function that result from using various approximate consumption rules. Since the objective function has been normalized to be linear in wealth, these losses have the same units as reductions in wealth. The second number in each block is the percentage utility loss when the loglinear consumption rule (46) is used with ρ obtained from (5) and the true optimal value of the mean log consumption–wealth ratio. The third number in each block is the percentage utility loss when (46) is used with ρ set equal to β, its value for the $\sigma = 1$ case. The former procedure gives a more accurate approximation, but it requires knowledge of the true mean log consumption–wealth ratio. The latter procedure is less accurate but easier to implement in practice.

Finally, the fourth number in each block gives the percentage utility loss from setting the consumption–wealth ratio equal to the constant value that would be optimal if returns were independently and identically distributed with the same unconditional distribution as the mean-reverting process (45). This is a much cruder, traditional approximation that ignores variation in the consumption–wealth ratio altogether as suggested by David P. Brown and Michael R. Gibbons (1985) and others.

As one would expect, the utility losses from using approximate consumption rules increase as σ moves further from unity. The losses are zero when $\sigma = 1$, for then all the approximations are exact. When $\sigma = 0.5$ or 2, the approximate consumption functions based on (46) cost less than 0.01 percent of wealth unless γ is at its highest value of 4.

TABLE 1 | Mean Value Function with Percentage Losses from Approximate Consumption Rules

γ	σ 0.05	0.50	1.00	2.00	3.00	4.00
0.00	0.608	0.612	0.617	0.629	0.646	0.670
	(0.002)	(0.000)	(0.000)	(0.000)	(0.001)	(0.003)
	(0.238)	(0.002)	(0.000)	(0.010)	(0.137)	(0.724)
	(—)[b]	(0.806)	(0.000)	(1.74)	(13.4)	(—)[a]
0.50	0.574	0.576	0.578	0.583	0.589	0.596
	(0.002)	(0.000)	(0.000)	(0.000)	(0.001)	(0.003)
	(0.048)	(0.000)	(0.000)	(0.002)	(0.023)	(0.102)
	(—)[b]	(0.260)	(0.000)	(0.377)	(1.50)	(4.54)
1.00	0.540	0.541	0.542	0.543	0.544	0.546
	(0.002)	(0.000)	(0.000)	(0.000)	(0.001)	(0.002)
	(0.006)	(0.000)	(0.000)	(0.000)	(0.002)	(0.008)
	(2.28)	(0.065)	(0.000)	(0.065)	(0.174)	(0.295)
2.00	0.473	0.474	0.475	0.477	0.479	0.481
	(0.004)	(0.000)	(0.000)	(0.000)	(0.001)	(0.002)
	(0.021)	(0.000)	(0.000)	(0.000)	(0.004)	(0.016)
	(14.3)	(1.04)	(0.000)	(0.724)	(1.47)	(1.96)
3.00	0.407	0.412	0.417	0.426	0.433	0.438
	(0.007)	(0.000)	(0.000)	(0.000)	(0.000)	(0.002)
	(0.867)	(0.004)	(0.000)	(0.010)	(0.085)	(0.268)
	(38.9)	(4.54)	(0.000)	(1.91)	(3.05)	(3.45)
4.00	0.341	0.354	0.366	0.384	0.397	0.407
	(0.010)	(0.000)	(0.000)	(0.000)	(0.000)	(0.001)
	(—)[b]	(0.029)	(0.000)	(0.055)	(0.426)	(1.21)
	(76.3)	(11.7)	(0.000)	(3.15)	(4.29)	(4.43)

Notes: The first number in each block is the mean value function, expressed as a percentage of wealth, for an agent facing the return process (45). The remaining numbers, in parentheses, are losses from using approximate consumption rules, expressed as percentages of the exact mean value function. The second number in each block is the loss from using the loglinear approximate consumption rule (46) with the true ρ, the third number is the loss from using (46) with $\rho = \beta$, and the fourth number is the loss from picking the constant consumption–wealth ratio that would be optimal if returns were independently and identically distributed with the unconditional distribution of the return process (45).

[a] The approximate consumption rule is undefined for these parameters.

[b] Calculation of loss from the approximate consumption rule failed to converge.

When $\sigma = 0.05$, 3, or 4, the approximate consumption function (46) with the correct ρ still costs no more than 0.01 percent of wealth, but the approximate consumption function (46) setting $\rho = \beta$ is noticeably less accurate. As an extreme case, when both σ and γ are at their maximum values of 4, this approximation costs 1.2 percent of wealth. All these losses are generally an order of magnitude smaller than the losses incurred by the traditional approximation that fixes the consumption–wealth ratio.[13]

Table 2 shows mean optimal consumption as a percentage of wealth. Since β and the expected return process are fixed, the mean consumption–wealth ratio varies considerably

[13]The traditional approximation is not defined when $\sigma = 4$ and $\gamma = 0$, because the optimization problem with independently and identically distributed returns has no solution in this case. In addition, the numerical calculation of utility losses failed to converge for the traditional approximation when $\sigma = 0.05$ and $\gamma = 0$ or 0.5, and for the approximation (46) with $\rho = \beta$ when $\sigma = 0.05$ and $\gamma = 4$. These convergence problems are associated with excessively large mean consumption–wealth ratios, shown in Table 2, and with utility losses that continue to increase with each iteration of the numerical solution method.

TABLE 2 | Mean Optimal Consumption–Wealth Ratio with Percentage Errors of Approximate Consumption Rules

	σ					
γ	**0.05**	**0.50**	**1.00**	**2.00**	**3.00**	**4.00**
0.00	0.603	0.561	0.514	0.421	0.329	0.237
	(0.090)	(0.017)	(0.000)	(0.170)	(0.635)	(1.43)
	(1.40)	(0.396)	(0.000)	(2.01)	(9.55)	(27.9)
	(15.1)	(8.54)	(0.000)	(−22.9)	(−58.8)	(—)[a]
0.50	0.571	0.544	0.514	0.455	0.396	0.336
	(0.103)	(0.024)	(0.000)	(0.153)	(0.583)	(1.30)
	(0.659)	(0.183)	(0.000)	(0.868)	(3.76)	(9.45)
	(7.97)	(4.40)	(0.000)	(−10.6)	(−24.4)	(−43.1)
1.00	0.539	0.527	0.514	0.488	0.463	0.437
	(0.117)	(0.032)	(0.000)	(0.134)	(0.535)	(1.21)
	(0.228)	(0.063)	(0.000)	(0.265)	(1.08)	(2.49)
	(−0.034)	(−0.018)	(0.000)	(0.040)	(0.086)	(0.137)
2.00	0.475	0.494	0.514	0.556	0.597	0.639
	(0.151)	(0.049)	(0.000)	(0.103)	(0.470)	(1.10)
	(0.439)	(0.127)	(0.000)	(0.393)	(1.59)	(3.54)
	(−19.2)	(−9.74)	(0.000)	(17.3)	(32.1)	(44.9)
3.00	0.412	0.460	0.514	0.623	0.733	0.843
	(0.195)	(0.068)	(0.000)	(0.078)	(0.427)	(1.04)
	(2.44)	(0.642)	(0.000)	(1.97)	(7.42)	(15.9)
	(−44.5)	(−20.9)	(0.000)	(30.7)	(52.0)	(67.5)
4.00	0.348	0.427	0.514	0.691	0.869	1.05
	(0.254)	(0.091)	(0.000)	(0.059)	(0.397)	(0.991)
	(6.95)	(1.68)	(0.000)	(4.77)	(17.5)	(37.6)
	(−79.1)	(−33.9)	(0.000)	(41.4)	(65.4)	(80.6)

Notes: The first number in each block is the mean optimal consumption–wealth ratio, expressed as a percentage of wealth, for an agent facing the return process (45). The remaining numbers, in parentheses, are the differences between mean consumption–wealth ratios when approximate consumption rules are used and the mean optimal consumption–wealth ratio, expressed as percentages of the mean optimal consumption–wealth ratio. The second number corresponds to the loglinear consumption rule (46) with the true ρ, the third number corresponds to (46) with $\rho = \beta$, and the fourth number corresponds to the constant consumption–wealth ratio that would be optimal if returns were independently and identically distributed with the unconditional distribution of the return process (45).

[a]The approximate consumption rule is undefined for these parameters.

as the parameters γ and σ vary. The smallest value in the table is 0.237 percent (2.84 percent at an annual rate) when $\sigma = 4$ and $\gamma = 0$. The largest value is 1.05 percent (12.6 percent at an annual rate) when $\sigma = 4$ and $\gamma = 4$. The table also reports the differences between the exact and approximate mean consumption–wealth ratios, expressed as percentages of the exact mean consumption–wealth ratio. These differences are again zero when $\sigma = 1$, but they increase quite rapidly as σ moves away from 1. When the approximation uses (46) and the true ρ, the error is between 0.05 percent and 0.25 percent of the exact mean consumption–wealth ratio when $\sigma = 0.05$ or 2, increasing to almost 1.5 percent of the exact mean consumption–wealth ratio when $\sigma = 4$. When the approximation uses (46) and $\rho = \beta$, the errors can be many times larger. The traditional approximation with a fixed consumption–wealth ratio does well when $\sigma = 1$ or $\gamma = 1$, but very poorly otherwise.

If one is interested in the dynamic behavior of consumption and its implications for asset pricing, errors in the mean consumption–wealth ratio are relatively unimportant. What is important is to approximate accurately the variation of the consumption–wealth ratio and the consumption growth rate around their means. Table 3 gives the standard deviation of the optimal log consumption–wealth ratio, along with the percentage errors of the

TABLE 3 | Standard Deviation of Optimal Log Consumption–Wealth Ratio with Percentage Errors of Approximate Consumption Rules

	σ					
γ	**0.05**	**0.50**	**1.00**	**2.00**	**3.00**	**4.00**
0.00	0.048 (0.760) (1.20)	0.025 (0.756) (0.986)	0.000 (—) (—)	0.051 (0.750) (0.287)	0.103 (0.749) (−0.178)	0.155 (0.748) (−0.640)
0.50	0.048 (0.759) (1.04)	0.025 (0.755) (0.902)	0.000 (—) (—)	0.051 (0.752) (0.454)	0.102 (0.755) (0.156)	0.154 (0.760) (−0.141)
1.00	0.048 (0.758) (0.876)	0.025 (0.754) (0.818)	0.000 (—) (—)	0.051 (0.754) (0.622)	0.102 (0.760) (0.492)	0.153 (0.771) (0.361)
2.00	0.048 (0.754) (0.558)	0.025 (0.753) (0.650)	0.000 (—) (—)	0.051 (0.757) (0.958)	0.101 (0.768) (1.16)	0.151 (0.788) (1.37)
3.00	0.049 (0.750) (0.239)	0.026 (0.751) (0.482)	0.000 (—) (—)	0.051 (0.759) (1.30)	0.101 (0.773) (1.84)	0.150 (0.798) (2.39)
4.00	0.049 (0.746) (−0.078)	0.026 (0.749) (0.314)	0.000 (—) (—)	0.050 (0.760) (1.63)	0.100 (0.775) (2.52)	0.148 (0.802) (3.42)

Notes: The first number in each block is the standard deviation of the optimal log consumption–wealth ratio for an agent facing the return process (45). The remaining numbers, in parentheses, are the differences between the standard deviations of log consumption–wealth ratios when approximate consumption rules are used and the standard deviation of the optimal log consumption–wealth ratio, expressed as percentages of the standard deviation of the optimal log consumption–wealth ratio. The second number corresponds to the loglinear consumption rule (46) with the true ρ, and the third number corresponds to (46) with $\rho = \beta$. The approximation with a constant consumption–wealth ratio is not included in this table because it implies a difference of 100 percent in every column.

two approximations that use equation (46), The log ratio is used because it is approximately normally distributed, and the traditional approximation is omitted from the table because it implies errors of 100 percent whenever $\sigma \neq 1$. The table shows that as σ approaches 1, the approximation error for the log standard deviation goes to zero at almost the same rate as the log standard deviation itself. Thus, in percentage terms the approximation error is almost constant and small at about 0.75 percent of the true standard deviation.

Table 4 reports the standard deviation of the optimal log consumption growth rate, once again with the percentage errors of the various approximations. The consumption-smoothing effect of mean-reversion when σ is low is clearly visible in this table. The approximations using (46) tend to understate the variability of log consumption growth when σ is low and tend to overstate the variability when σ is high. However, the errors are quite small, never much above 0.5 percent of the true standard deviation when the correct value of ρ is used. The approximation setting $\rho = \beta$ should be used more cautiously, as its maximum error is four times greater than the approximation error using the true ρ. The traditional approximation does much worse, since it forces the standard deviation of log consumption growth to equal the standard deviation of the log market return.

These results are encouraging for several reasons. First, they are obtained using a model in which the expected return on the market is highly variable. Less-extreme variability in the expected-return process would increase approximation accuracy by reducing the variability of the optimal consumption–wealth ratio. Second, the approximation developed in this paper does well in cases where a more traditional approach, ignoring variation

TABLE 4 | Standard Deviation of Optimal Log Consumption Growth Rate with Percentage Errors of Approximate Consumption Rules

γ	σ					
	0.05	**0.50**	**1.00**	**2.00**	**3.00**	**4.00**
0.00	0.037	0.045	0.057	0.085	0.115	0.147
	(−0.251)	(−0.175)	(0.000)	(0.260)	(0.401)	(0.482)
	(−0.394)	(−0.228)	(0.000)	(0.100)	(−0.088)	(−0.392)
	(52.2)	(26.0)	(0.000)	(−32.9)	(−50.6)	(—)[a]
0.50	0.037	0.045	0.057	0.085	0.115	0.146
	(−0.251)	(−0.175)	(0.000)	(0.260)	(0.403)	(0.490)
	(−0.341)	(−0.209)	(0.000)	(0.158)	(0.087)	(−0.081)
	(52.3)	(26.0)	(0.000)	(−32.8)	(−50.5)	(−61.1)
1.00	0.037	0.045	0.057	0.085	0.115	0.146
	(−0.250)	(−0.175)	(0.000)	(0.260)	(0.405)	(0.496)
	(−0.289)	(−0.189)	(0.000)	(0.215)	(0.263)	(0.235)
	(52.4)	(26.0)	(0.000)	(−32.8)	(−50.4)	(−60.90)
2.00	0.037	0.045	0.057	0.085	0.114	0.145
	(−0.249)	(−0.175)	(0.000)	(0.261)	(0.408)	(0.506)
	(−0.184)	(−0.151)	(0.000)	(0.331)	(0.620)	(0.882)
	(52.5)	(26.1)	(0.000)	(−32.7)	(−50.2)	(−60.7)
3.00	0.037	0.045	0.057	0.085	0.114	0.144
	(−0.247)	(−0.174)	(0.000)	(0.261)	(0.410)	(0.511)
	(−0.080)	(−0.112)	(0.000)	(0.447)	(0.988)	(1.56)
	(52.7)	(26.1)	(0.000)	(−32.7)	(−50.1)	(−60.5)
4.00	0.037	0.045	0.057	0.085	0.114	0.143
	(−0.246)	(−0.174)	(0.000)	(0.261)	(0.410)	(0.512)
	(0.025)	(−0.074)	(0.000)	(0.565)	(1.37)	(2.29)
	(52.8)	(26.2)	(0.000)	(−32.6)	(−49.9)	(−60.3)

Notes: The first number in each block is the standard deviation of the optimal log consumption growth rate for an agent facing the return process (45). The remaining numbers, in parentheses, are the differences between the standard deviations of log consumption growth rates when approximate consumption rules are used and the standard deviation of the optimal log consumption growth rate, expressed as a percentage of the standard deviation of the optimal log consumption growth rate. The second number corresponds to the loglinear consumption rule (46) with the true ρ, the third number corresponds to (46) with $\rho = \beta$, and the fourth number corresponds to the constant consumption–wealth ratio that would be optimal if returns were independently and identically distributed with the unconditional distribution of the return process (45).

[a]The approximate consumption rule is undefined for these parameters.

in the consumption–wealth ratio, does extremely poorly. Third, a number of authors (Robert E. Hall, 1988; Campbell and Mankiw, 1989; Giovannini and Weil, 1989; Kandel and Stambaugh, 1991) have argued from direct evidence on consumption and asset price behavior that σ is more likely to be very small than very large. Tables 3 and 4 show that a loglinear approximation to the intertemporal budget constraint is workably accurate when σ is close to zero, even if the true value of ρ is unknown.

V. Conclusions

In this paper I have argued that intertemporal asset pricing theory has become unnecessarily tangled in complications caused by the nonlinearity of the intertemporal budget constraint. I have proposed a loglinear approximation to the constraint as a way to cut this Gordian knot. In a simple example calibrated to U.S. stock-return data, the approximation seems to be workably accurate when the elasticity of intertemporal substitution is less than about 3.

I assume that all assets, including human capital, are freely tradable, that asset returns and news about future returns are jointly lognormal and homoscedastic, and that there is a representative agent who maximizes the objective function proposed by Epstein and Zin (1989, 1991) and Weil (1987). This objective function has many of the appealing features of the time-separable power utility function, but it separates the elasticity of intertemporal substitution σ from the coefficient of relative risk aversion γ rather than forcing these parameters to be reciprocals of one another as in the power utility case. The loglinear approximation to the budget constraint then yields some simple propositions about consumption behavior and intertemporal asset pricing.

(i) The log consumption–wealth ratio equals a constant, plus $(1 - \sigma)$ times the discounted value of all future expected returns on invested wealth including human capital (the "market portfolio"). The innovation to log consumption equals the innovation to the log return on the market portfolio, plus $(1 - \sigma)$ times the revision in the discounted value of future market returns. As one would expect, the coefficient σ, rather than γ, governs the response of consumption to changing expected asset returns.

(ii) The expected excess log return on any asset over the risk-free return is the sum of three terms. The first term is minus one-half the own variance of the log asset return, a Jensen's inequality effect. The second term is γ times the covariance of the asset return with the return on the market, as in a logarithmic version of the static CAPM. The third term is $(\gamma - 1)$ times the covariance of the asset return with news about future returns on the market. As one would expect, the coefficient γ rather than σ determines the size and sign of asset risk premia.

(iii) In the homoscedastic model, the log return on a real consol bond is approximately equal to minus the news about future returns on the market. Thus, the expected excess return on any asset, net of the Jensen's inequality effect, can also be written as a weighted average of the asset's covariance with the market and with the consol. The weights are γ and $1 - \gamma$, respectively.

(iv) If the return on the market can be written as one element of a state vector that follows a homoscedastic vector autoregression (VAR), then the intertemporal theory delivers a set of restrictions on the risk prices of a factor asset pricing model. The factors are variables that are relevant for forecasting the market and hence enter the VAR state vector. Their risk prices are proportional to their importance in forecasting the discounted value of future returns on the market.

(v) The results above can be generalized to allow a restricted form of heteroscedasticity in asset returns. If the conditional variance-covariance matrix of the return on the market and news about future returns on the market is linear in the expected return on the market, then the asset pricing model goes through as before, except that the price of covariance with news about future returns is no longer equal to $\gamma - 1$. With this form of heteroscedasticity, the expected excess return on the market is linear in the conditional variance of the return on the market, as commonly assumed in empirical work. The homoscedastic results also generalize straightforwardly if σ or γ is sufficiently close to 1.

These results have pedagogic value as a simple way to understand the vast and complicated literature on intertemporal asset pricing. They also raise the hope that this subject can be brought into a closer relationship with the equally large body of work on cross-sectional factor asset pricing models. An important topic for future research will be to test the restrictions placed by the approximate intertemporal model on cross-sectional factor risk prices.

The main difficulty in conducting such a test is that, as emphasized by Roll (1977), the return on the market portfolio is imperfectly measured. If neither consumption data nor market-return data are adequate, then it may be necessary to develop a more explicit general equilibrium model in which macroeconomic variables help to identify the returns on physical and human capital. Such a model might also be used to relax the assumption made here that human capital is tradable. The loglinear approximation of this paper has already been used to solve real-business-cycle models by Robert G. King et al. (1987), Lawrence J. Christiano (1988), Campbell (1992), and others, and the application of macroeconomic models to asset pricing promises to be another active area of research.

References

Black, Fischer, "Mean Reversion and Consumption Smoothing," *Review of Financial Studies*, 1990, *3* (1), 107–14.

Bollerslev, Timothy, Engle, Robert F. and Wooldridge, Jeffrey, "A Capital Asset Pricing Model with Time Varying Covariances," *Journal of Political Economy*, February 1988, *96*, 116–31.

Bossaerts, Peter and Green, Richard C., "A General Equilibrium Model of Changing Risk Premia: Theory and Tests," *Review of Financial Studies*, 1989, *2* (4), 467–93.

Breeden, Douglas T., "An Intertemporal Asset Pricing Model with Stochastic Consumption and Investment," *Journal of Financial Economics*, September 1979, *7*, 265–96.

———, "Consumption, Production, Inflation, and Interest Rates: A Synthesis," *Journal of Financial Economics*, May 1986, *16*, 3–39.

Breeden, Douglas T., Gibbons, Michael R. and Litzenberger, Robert H., "Empirical Tests of the Consumption-Oriented CAPM," *Journal of Finance*, June 1989, *44*, 231–62.

Brown, David P. and Gibbons, Michael R., "A Simple Econometric Approach for Utility-Based Asset Pricing Models," *Journal of Finance*, June 1985, *40*, 359–81.

Campbell, John Y., "Stock Returns and the Term Structure," *Journal of Financial Economics*, June 1987, *18*, 373–99.

———, "A Variance Decomposition for Stock Returns," *Economic Journal*, March 1991, *101*, 157–79.

———, "Inspecting the Mechanism: An Analytical Approach to the Stochastic Growth Model," National Bureau of Economic Research (Cambridge, MA) Working Paper No. 4188, October 1992.

——— and Koo, Hyeng K., "A Numerical Solution for the Consumption Wealth Ratio in a Model with Nonexpected Utility Using Nystrom's Method," unpublished manuscript, Princeton University, 1992.

——— and Mankiw, N. Gregory, "Consumption, Income, and Interest Rates: Reinterpreting the Time Series Evidence," in Olivier J. Blanchard and Stanley Fischer, eds., *NBER Macroeconomics Annual 1989*, Cambridge, MA: MIT Press, 1989, pp. 185–216.

——— and Shiller, Robert J., (1988a) "The Dividend–Price Ratio and Expectations of Future Dividends and Discount Factors," *Review of Financial Studies*, 1988, *1* (3), 195–228.

——— and ——— (1988b) "Stock Prices, Earnings, and Expected Dividends," *Journal of Finance*, July 1988, *43*, 661–76.

Chen, Nai-fu, Roll, Richard and Ross, Stephen A., " Economic Forces and the Stock Market," *Journal of Business*, July 1986, *59*, 383–403.

Chen, Zhiwu, "Consumer Behavior and Asset Pricing When Taste Formation Depends on Wealth," Graduate School of Business, University of Wisconsin Working Paper No. 7-91-7, 1991.

Christiano, Lawrence J., "Why Does Inventory Investment Fluctuate So Much?" *Journal of Monetary Economics*, March/May 1988, *21*, 247–80.

Constantinides, George M., "Habit Formation: A Resolution of the Equity Premium Puzzle," *Journal of Political Economy*, June 1990, *98*, 519–43.

Cox, John C., Ingersoll, Jonathan E., Jr. and Ross, Stephen A., "A Theory of the Term Structure of Interest Rates," *Econometrica*, March 1985, *53*, 385–408.

Dunn, Kenneth B. and Singleton, Kenneth J., "Modelling the Term Structure of Interest Rates under Habit Formation and Durability of Goods," *Journal of Financial Economics*, September 1986, *17*, 27–55.

Epstein, Lawrence and Zin, Stanley, "Substitution, Risk Aversion, and the Temporal Behavior of Consumption and Asset Returns: A Theoretical Framework," *Econometrica*, July 1989, *57*, 937–69.

——— and ———, "Substitution, Risk Aversion, and the Temporal Behavior of Consumption and Asset Returns: An Empirical Analysis," *Journal of Political Economy*, April 1991, *99*, 263–86.

Fama, Eugene F., "Multiperiod Consumption–Investment Decisions," *American Economic Review*, March 1970, *60*, 163–74.

——— and French, Kenneth R., (1988a) "Permanent and Temporary Components of Stock Prices," *Journal of Political Economy*, April 1988, *96*, 246–73.

——— and ———, (1988b) "Dividend Yields and Expected Stock Returns, *Journal of Financial Economics*, October 1988, *22*, 3–25.

——— and ———, "Business Conditions and Expected Returns on Stocks and Bonds," *Journal of Financial Economics*, November 1989, *25*, 23–49.

——— and Schwert, G. William, "Asset Returns and Inflation," *Journal of Financial Economics*, November 1977, *5*, 115–46.

Ferson, Wayne E. and Constantinides, George M., "Habit Persistence and Durability in Aggregate Consumption: Empirical Tests," National Bureau of Economic Research (Cambridge, MA) Working Paper No. 3631, February 1991.

French, Kenneth R., Schwert, G. William and Stambaugh, Robert F., "Expected Stock Returns and Volatility," *Journal of Financial Economics*, September 1987, *19*, 3–29.

Friend, Irwin and Blume, Marshall E., "The Demand for Risky Assets," *American Economic Review*, December 1975, *65*, 900–22.

Giovannini, Alberto and Jorion, Philippe, "Time-Series Tests of a Non-expected Utility Model of Asset Pricing, National Bureau of Economic Research (Cambridge, MA) Working Paper No. 3195, December 1989.

——— and Weil, Philippe, "Risk Aversion and Intertemporal Substitution in the Capital Asset Pricing Model," National Bureau of Economic Research (Cambridge, MA) Working Paper No. 2824, January 1989.

Grossman, Sanford J., Melino, Angelo and Shiller, Robert J., "Estimating the Continuous-Time Consumption Based Asset Pricing Model," *Journal of Business and Economic Statistics*, July 1987, *5*, 315–28.

Grossman, Sanford J. and Shiller, Robert J., "The Determinants of the Variability of Stock Market Prices," *American Economic Review*, May 1981 (*Papers and Proceedings), 71*, 222–7.

Hall, Robert E., "Intertemporal Substitution in Consumption," *Journal of Political Economy*, April 1988, *96*, 221–73.

Hansen, Lars P. and Singleton, Kenneth J., "Generalized Instrumental Variables Estimation of Nonlinear Rational Expectations Models," *Econometrica*, September 1982, *50*, 1269–85.

——— and ———, "Stochastic Consumption, Risk Aversion, and the Temporal Behavior of Asset Returns," *Journal of Political Economy*, April 1983, *91*, 249–65.

Heaton, John, "An Empirical Investigation of Asset Pricing with Temporally Dependent Preference Specifications," Working Paper No. 3245-91-EFA, Massachusetts Institute of Technology, February 1991.

Ingersoll, Jonathan E., Jr., *Theory of Financial Decision Making*, Totowa, NJ: Rowman and Littlefield, 1987.

Kandel, Shmuel and Stambaugh, Robert F., "Asset Returns and Intertemporal Preferences," *Journal of Monetary Economics*, February 1991, *27*, 39–71.

Keim, Donald B. and Stambaugh, Robert F., "Predicting Returns in the Stock and Bond Markets," *Journal of Financial Economics*, December 1986, *17*, 357–90.

King, Robert G., Plosser, Charles I. and Rebelo, Sergio T., "Production, Growth and Business Cycles: Technical Appendix," unpublished manuscript, University of Rochester, 1987.

Kocherlakota, Narayana, "Disentangling the Coefficient of Relative Risk Aversion from the Elasticity of Intertemporal Substitution: An Irrelevance Result," *Journal of Finance*, March 1990, *45*, 175–90.

Kreps, David and Porteus, E., "Temporal Resolution of Uncertainty and Dynamic Choice Theory," *Econometrica*, January 1978, *46*, 185–200.

Lucas, Robert E., Jr., "Asset Prices in an Exchange Economy," *Econometrica*, November 1978, *46*, 1429–46.

Mankiw, N. Gregory and Shapiro, Matthew D., "Risk and Return; Consumption versus Market Beta," *Review of Economics and Statistics*, August 1986, *68*, 452–9.

——— and Zeldes, Stephen P., "The Consumption of Stockholders and Nonstockholders," *Journal of Financial Economics*, March 1991, *29*, 97–112.

Mehra, Rajnish and Prescott, Edward, "The Equity Premium: A Puzzle," *Journal of Monetary Economics*, March 1985, *15*, 145–61.

Merton, Robert C., "Lifetime Portfolio Selection Under Uncertainty: The Continuous Time Case," *Review of Economics and Statistics*, August 1969, *51*, 247–57.

———, "Optimum Consumption and Portfolio Rules in a Continuous-Time Model," *Journal of Economic Theory*, December 1971, *3*, 373–413.

———, "An Intertemporal Capital Asset Pricing Model," *Econometrica*, September 1973, *41*, 867–87.

———, "On Estimating the Expected Return on the Market: An Exploratory Analysis," *Journal of Financial Economics*, December 1980, *8*, 323–61.

———, *Continuous Time Finance*, Cambridge, MA: Blackwell, 1990.

Poterba, James M. and Summers, Lawrence H., "Mean Reversion in Stock Prices: Evidence and Implications," *Journal of Financial Economics*, October 1988, *22*, 27–59.

Restoy, Fernando, "Optimal Portfolio Policies Under Time-Dependent Returns," unpublished manuscript, Harvard University, 1991.

Roll, Richard R., "A Critique of the Asset Pricing Theory's Tests, Part 1: On Past and Potential Testability of the Theory," *Journal of Financial Economics*, March 1977, *4*, 129–76.

Roll, Richard R. and Ross, Stephen A., "An Empirical Investigation of the Arbitrage Pricing Theory," *Journal of Finance*, December 1980, *35*, 1073–1103.

Ross, Stephen A., "Arbitrage Theory of Capital Asset Pricing," *Journal of Economic Theory*, December 1976, *13*, 341–60.

Rubinstein, Mark, "A Discrete-Time Synthesis of Financial Theory," in Haim Levy, ed., *Research in Finance 3*, Greenwich, CT: JAI Press, 1981.

Samuelson, Paul A., "Lifetime Portfolio Selection by Dynamic Stochastic Programming," *Review of Economics and Statistics*, August 1969, *51*, 239–46.

Svensson, Lars E. O., "Portfolio Choice with Non-expected Utility in Continuous Time," *Economics Letters*, 1989, *30* (4), 313–17.

Tauchen, George and Hussey, Robert, "Quadrature-Based Methods for Obtaining Approximate Solutions to Nonlinear Asset Pricing Models," *Econometrica*, March 1991, *59*, 371–96.

Weil, Philippe, "The Equity Premium Puzzle and the Risk-Free Rate Puzzle," *Journal of Monetary Economics*, November 1989, *24*, 401–21.

———, "Nonexpected Utility in Macroeconomics," *Quarterly Journal of Economics*, February 1990, *105*, 29–42.

Wheatley, Simon, "Some Tests of the Consumption-Based Asset Pricing Model," *Journal of Monetary Economics*, September 1988, *22*, 193–215.

Wilcox, David A., "The Construction of U.S. Consumption Data: Some Facts and Their Implications for Empirical Work," *American Economic Review*, September 1992, *82*, 922–41.

Eighteen

Jonathan Tiemann

Jonathan Tiemann received a Ph.D. from Yale University in 1986. He started out at the Harvard Business School, and is now the president of Tiemann Investment Advisors, LLC. •

No influence in my professional life, in academia or as an investment practitioner, approaches in importance my time as a student of Steve Ross's at Yale. As a prospective graduate student, going into my first meeting with Steve, I didn't even know whether I would find finance an interesting subject. In a single session, he introduced me to this wonderful discipline, with its mathematical rigor, its economic substance, and its exceptional practical application. I was hooked, and I remain happily so, 25 years later.

Steve's teaching, and especially his advising, was much like our initial meeting. In a few words, Steve can elucidate a problem that has vexed a student for weeks. As I wrestled with my dissertation, any 10 minutes with Steve seemed to advance the cause further than any week of other effort. My paper in this book, drawn from that dissertation, illustrates Steve's care well.

Prof. Ross marks his scholarship and teaching with a stubborn insistence on a few principles: That finance is a science, and any academic work that does not respect the demands of a scientific approach isn't worth the effort. That no theory is interesting unless it produces predictions that are subject to empirical testing. That neoclassical finance provides the right null hypotheses, and establishes the right framework for explaining market phenomena. That from a remarkably weak condition—the absence of arbitrage, equivalent to the nonexistence of perpetual motion—proceed a galaxy of interesting conclusions.

Steve's principles continue to inform my approach to investment management. My professional colleagues, reared in the rough-and-tumble of real-world markets, often criticize as unrealistic the stylized models of the academic world. But as my understanding of how markets really work has deepened, so has my appreciation for the importance of the theoretic kernel of neoclassical finance, and of the training I received from Steve. Markets do often appear to behave in ways that, in some sense, they ought not behave. Solid theory, correctly understood and applied, doesn't ignore these divergences, or sweep them under the rug. By describing the underlying economic logic of an idealized market, solid theory shows us where to look for the explanations.

Whether I'm trying to understand a market that breaks because a large player reaches the limits of leverage; an army of highly paid salespeople that foist closed-end funds with large sales charges on an unsuspecting public; or a hedge fund that "paints the tape" at year-end to goose performance, increase its incentive fee, and gather more assets (in effect running a Ponzi scheme), the theoretical foundation and scientific skepticism I received as Steve's student have reliably pointed me in the direction of the answers. Solid theory allows us to spot apparent anomalies, and either debunk them, correct their underlying causes, or profit from them. No theoretical alternative to neoclassical finance even remotely approaches this power.

My debt to Steve runs deep. He has given me a systematic way of thinking about securities and markets. And on reflection, he also gave me many of the mathematical tools that are so much the stuff of my daily work that I've forgotten learning them. Steve Ross gave me the basis of my profession.

Exact Arbitrage Pricing and the Minimum-Variance Frontier

*Jonathan Tiemann**

Abstract

The author examines the relationship between the Arbitrage Pricing Theory of Ross and mean-variance analysis. In particular, conditions are derived on the vector of the factor risk premia that are equivalent to the existence of a strictly positively weighted portfolio on the minimum-variance frontier. Also, a sufficient condition is given under which the existence of a positive minimum-variance portfolio of all the assets in the economy will imply the existence of a positive minimum-variance portfolio on a subset. This means that rejection of the hypothesis of the existence of a positive minimum-variance portfolio on a subset satisfying this condition implies rejection for the whole set. •

A growing body of literature explores the relationship between the Arbitrage Pricing Theory (APT) of Ross [13, 14] and the mean-variance model. Among the early work in this direction were the papers of Chamberlain and Rothschild [2] and Chamberlain [1]. These papers examine a sequence of economies and characterize the relationship in the limit between the mean and portfolio cost functionals and the minimum-variance frontier. Chamberlain [1] also gives a condition under which exact arbitrage pricing will hold. Dybvig [4] and Grinblatt and Titman [7] examine equilibrium models in an APT context for a finite economy. They derive sharp bounds on the deviation from exact arbitrage pricing.

Recent papers by Huberman, Kandel, and Stambaugh [9] and Grinblatt and Titman [8] explore the relationship between the APT and the mean-variance model by studying portfolios that can be used as proxies for the factors and examining the relationship these portfolios bear to the minimum-variance frontier. These two papers also deal with equilibrium models.

In spite of the number and variety of equilibrium-APT models, the question of the pricing of factor risk in equilibrium remains largely unexplored. This paper makes some progress in addressing that issue by looking at a given equilibrium restriction and studying the constraints it imposes on the vector of factor premia itself.

The most familiar equilibrium restriction we might study is the central implication of the Capital Asset Pricing Model (CAPM), that the market portfolio is efficient. In particular, no portfolio with the same expected return as the market portfolio has a smaller variance. The restriction we actually study is weaker than this. Since the market portfolio has strictly

---

*Graduate School of Business Administration, Harvard University. I would like to thank Richard Green and Stephen Ross for several helpful conversations. Eric Denardo and Kurt Anstreicher helped me clarify ideas regarding the role of duality. I am also grateful to an anonymous referee for many thoughtful comments.

Reprinted with permission:
Tiemann, Jonathan. "Exact Arbitrage Pricing and the Minimum-Variance Frontier." *The Journal of Finance* 43 (1988): 327–338.

positive elements, the existence of a strictly positive portfolio on the minimum-variance frontier is a necessary condition for the CAPM. We study the behavior of the factor-premia vector under the restriction that there exists a minimum-variance portfolio with all-positive components.

The existence of such a portfolio is an interesting issue in its own right for several reasons. First, an empirical test that rejected the hypothesis that a positive minimum-variance portfolio exists would reject the hypothesis that the CAPM holds. In addition, there are other, practical reasons for being interested in positive portfolios. Professional portfolio managers tend to invest their clients' wealth almost exclusively in long positions. Indeed, many managers, such as those managing pensions, are legally precluded from taking short positions. Also, as Green [6] points out, mutual funds and index funds tend to have the same feature. This suggests that a large number of investors believe that portfolio efficiency does not require short positions, and a finding to the contrary would be interesting. In addition, short-sale restrictions and high transaction costs for short sales may represent constraints that are not present in the usual asset-pricing models, and an examination of the existence of positive efficient portfolios can shed light on the issue of whether these constraints are binding.

This paper studies the joint implications of two conditions: that exact arbitrage pricing holds and that some positive portfolio lies on the minimum-variance frontier. The first major result provides conditions on the factor-premia vector λ that are equivalent under exact arbitrage pricing to the existence of such a portfolio. Roughly speaking, the result is that a positive minimum-variance portfolio will exist if the factor premia lie in a range that compensates investors for bearing the factor risk of some long position in each asset. The second major result in the paper concerns the empirical matter of testing the mean-variance model under exact arbitrage pricing when we observe only a subset of the assets in the economy. It gives conditions on the relationship between the missing assets and the included assets that imply that rejection of the model on the subset implies rejection on the whole set. The condition is that the included assets be representative of the missing ones in the sense that the covariance vector of the missing asset can be replicated with a positive portfolio of the included ones.

Section I of the paper specifies the form of the APT under study and reviews a result due to Green [6]. Section II gives the basic characterization result and Section III an interpretation. Section IV then discusses testing on subsets and gives the second major result. Section V provides concluding remarks.

I. Preliminaries

We model asset returns as arising from a factor model, in which some number, say k, of zero-mean (or de-meaned) factors f influence asset returns according to (1):

$$\tilde{R}_i = E_i + \sum \beta_{ij}\tilde{f}_j + \tilde{e}_i, \tag{1}$$

where $\tilde{R}_i$ is the random return on the ith asset, E_i is its expected return, the $\tilde{f}_j$ are the k factors, $\tilde{e}_i$ is an independent noise term for asset i, and β_{ij} is the factor loading pertaining to asset i and factor j. This linear structure implies that the matrix $\mathbf{V}$ of the covariances of the assets in the market will be

$$\mathbf{V} = \mathbf{BB}' + \mathbf{D}, \tag{2}$$

where the i, jth element of $\mathbf{B}$ is β_{ij} and $\mathbf{D}$ is a diagonal matrix with an ith diagonal element that is $\text{var}(\tilde{e}_i)$. Ross [13, 14] shows that, in the absence of arbitrage, the expected return vector E will be approximately

$$E = \rho\underline{1} + \mathbf{B}\lambda, \tag{3}$$

where λ is the vector of factor premia and $\underline{1}$ is a vector of ones. We will assume throughout that **B** is of full rank, that **V** is positive definite and therefore nonsingular, and that the pricing relation (3) is exact. When (3) holds, we shall say that the APT holds. A portfolio will be a vector y satisfying $y'\,\underline{1} = 1$ (where $\underline{1}$ is a vector of ones), and an arbitrage portfolio or hedge portfolio will be a vector y satisfying $y'\underline{1} = 0$.

In this framework, we examine the problem of the existence of minimum-variance portfolios with only strictly positive components. We start with a result of Green [6] that gives conditions on **V** and E in a general framework under which there does not exist a minimum-variance portfolio with all-positive portfolio weights. We repeat Green's main theorem below.

Theorem 1 *There exists some strictly positive minimum-variance portfolio if and only if there exists no y satisfying*

$$\mathbf{V}y > 0,$$
$$y'E = 0,$$

and

$$y'\underline{1} = 0. \tag{4}$$

In vector expressions, we write "$\geq$" to mean that in every component the relation is $\geq$, "$>$" to mean that the inequality is strict in some component, and "$\gg$" to mean that the inequality is strict in every component.

Theorem 1 implies that, if there exists a zero-mean hedge portfolio that has a non-negative covariance with every asset (and positive covariance with some asset), then there can be no positively weighted portfolio on the minimum-variance frontier. The idea is that, if y satisfies (4), then, for any positive portfolio a, $a - \gamma y$ has the same mean return as a and a smaller variance for sufficiently small, positive γ. The proof of the result is essentially an exercise in duality and may be obtained by applying Farkas' Lemma.

Although a one-factor model always has a positive minimum-variance portfolio, a multiple-factor APT model need not. Green shows that the following model with two factors and three assets has no positive portfolio on the minimum-variance frontier. Suppose that (2) and (3) hold with

$$\mathbf{B} = \begin{bmatrix} 6 & 4 \\ 7 & 2 \\ 11 & 0 \end{bmatrix}, \quad \lambda = [1 \quad 1]', \quad \rho = 0.1, \quad \text{and} \quad \mathbf{D} = \mathbf{I}.$$

In this market, all hedge portfolios with mean zero are proportional to the vector $y = [-1, \frac{1}{2}, \frac{1}{2}]'$, but this vector has a non-negative covariance with every asset. By Theorem 1, then, no positive minimum-variance portfolio exists. The reason for this lies in the choice of the factor risk premia, λ. In this model, the two factors command the same premium, even though the first factor has heavier loadings. However, a mean-variance investor will hedge or diversify risk that does not offer adequate compensation. If such an investor is to hold a positive amount of every asset, the return to bearing factor risk must reflect a premium for bearing that risk.

To see why in a mean-variance framework we might expect factors with heavier loadings to command greater premia, consider the model of Dybvig [4]. As an illustrative example, normalize the factors so that $\mathrm{E}\tilde{f}_j = 0$, $\mathrm{E}\tilde{f}_j^2 = 1$, and $\mathrm{E}\tilde{f}_j\tilde{f}_k = 0$ when $j \neq k$. From Dybvig's development we have that

$$\lambda \propto \mathrm{E}[\tilde{f}_j u'(w)],$$

where

$$w = a'x$$

for some efficient portfolio a, and

$$x_i = E_i + \sum_j \beta_{ij} \tilde{f}_j + \tilde{e}_i$$

represents the payoff on an investment of one dollar in asset i. The simplest CAPM-motivated example relevant here is the case of quadratic utility. With quadratic utility, $u'(w)$ is proportional to w. Thus, λ_j is proportional to $\mathrm{E}[\tilde{f}_j w]$, which equals

$$\begin{aligned}\mathrm{E}[\tilde{f}_j w] &= \mathrm{E}\Big[\tilde{f}_j \sum a_i \sum \beta_{ik}\tilde{f}_k] + \mathrm{E}[\tilde{f}_j] \sum a_i(E_i) + \mathrm{E}[\tilde{f}_j \sum \tilde{e}_i\Big] \\ &= \mathrm{E}\Big[\sum a_i \beta_{ij} \tilde{f}_j^2\Big] \\ &= \sum a_i \beta_{ij}.\end{aligned}$$

If a is a positive efficient portfolio, then this means that λ_j must be a positive combination of the β_{ij}. This paper studies a model somewhat different from Dybvig's in that, in this paper, we assume that the arbitrage-pricing equation holds exactly. The results in the next section thus differ correspondingly from the conclusion that any positive combination of the assets' factor-loading vectors will be a factor-premia vector that admits the existence of a positive efficient portfolio. The difference lies in the importance of the own-variance matrix **D.** This should not be surprising since exact arbitrage pricing depends in some models (see, for instance, Chamberlain [1]) on the ability to diversify idiosyncratic risk away, that is, on **D**'s being somehow inconsequential.

II. Characterization of Risk-Compensating Factor Premia

Naturally, Green's example gives rise to the question of whether there will always be a set of factor premia that permits the existence of a positive portfolio on the minimum-variance frontier. The first result in this section shows that such a vector of premia will always exist.

Because the existence of a positive minimum-variance portfolio depends on the condition that each factor premium rewards investors sufficiently for taking on factor risk so that some mean-variance investor will hold a positive portfolio rather than try to hedge the factor risk away with a short position, we say that, when the APT holds, a vector λ of factor premia is factor-risk compensating or risk compensating if and only if there exists a positive minimum-variance portfolio when the factor premia are λ. This allows us to state succinctly the first result:

Proposition 1 *If the APT holds, then the factor-premia vector* $\lambda = \mathbf{B}'\mathbf{D}^{-1}\underline{1}$ *is risk compensating. Furthermore, if* $\lambda = \mathbf{B}'\mathbf{D}^{-1}\underline{1}$, *then an equal idiosyncratic-variance index* $\mathbf{D}^{-1}\underline{1}/(\underline{1}'\mathbf{D}^{-1}\underline{1})$ *will be mean-variance efficient.*

Proof We require that, if $\lambda = \mathbf{B}'\mathbf{D}^{-1}\underline{1}$, then there must be no y satisfying $\mathbf{V}y > 0$, $y'E = 0$, and $y'\underline{1} = 0$. Suppose that y is a zero-mean hedge portfolio. The requirements that $y'\underline{1} = 0$ and $y'E = 0$, together with (3), imply that

$$y'\mathbf{B}\lambda = y'\mathbf{B}\mathbf{B}'\mathbf{D}^{-1}\underline{1} = 0. \tag{5}$$

The requirement that

$$y'\mathbf{V} > 0$$

implies that

$$y'\mathbf{V}\mathbf{D}^{-1}\underline{1} > 0.$$

However,

$$
\begin{aligned}
y'\mathbf{V}\mathbf{D}^{-1}\,\underline{1} &= y'\mathbf{B}\mathbf{B}'\mathbf{D}^{-1}\,\underline{1} + y'\mathbf{D}\mathbf{D}^{-1}\,\underline{1} \\
&= y'\mathbf{D}\mathbf{D}^{-1}\,\underline{1} \\
&= y'\,\underline{1} \\
&= 0,
\end{aligned}
$$

which is a contradiction. To show that the second statement is true, let $a = \underline{1}'\mathbf{D}^{-1}\,\underline{1}$. If the vector $a\mathbf{V}^{-1}E + a(1-\rho)\mathbf{V}^{-1}\,\underline{1}$ is a portfolio, then it is mean-variance efficient since $a > 0$. Substituting in $E = \mathbf{B}\lambda + \rho\underline{1}$, we have

$$
\begin{aligned}
a\mathbf{V}^{-1}E + a(1-\rho)\mathbf{V}^{-1}\,\underline{1} &= \mathbf{V}^{-1}[(a\rho + a(1-\rho))\underline{1} + a\mathbf{B}\mathbf{B}'\mathbf{D}^{-1}\,\underline{1}] \\
&= a\mathbf{V}^{-1}[(\mathbf{I} + \mathbf{B}\mathbf{B}'\mathbf{D}^{-1})\underline{1}] \\
&= \mathbf{D}^{-1}\,\underline{1}/(\underline{1}'\mathbf{D}^{-1}\,\underline{1}).
\end{aligned}
$$

However, this is the required portfolio, which completes the proof. Q.E.D.

This result serves to demonstrate the existence of a risk-compensating factor-premia vector. Intuitively, the proof proceeds by showing that, if $\lambda = \mathbf{B}'\mathbf{D}^{-1}\,\underline{1}$, then the index portfolio proportional to $\mathbf{D}^{-1}\,\underline{1}$ is both minimum variance and uncorrelated with every zero-mean arbitrage portfolio. We will see later that the expression for λ in Proposition 1 figures in our complete characterization of the set of risk-compensating factor-premia vectors.

Under the mean-variance model, we know that the minimum-variance frontier corresponds to the range space of $[\mathbf{V}^{-1}E \mid \mathbf{V}^{-1}\,\underline{1}]$, a fact used in proving Proposition 1. Thus, the existence of a positive minimum-variance portfolio is equivalent to the condition that this range space intersects the positive orthant. Thus, if $\mathbf{V}^{-1}\,\underline{1} \gg 0$, then the global minimum-variance portfolio is positive, and so any factor premia will be risk compensating. Failing that, λ will be risk compensating if and only if there exist numbers $\alpha \neq 0$ and γ and a vector $z^* \gg 0$ such that

$$
\begin{aligned}
\alpha\mathbf{B}\lambda + \gamma\underline{1} &= \mathbf{V}z^* \\
&= (\mathbf{D} + \mathbf{B}\mathbf{B}')z^*.
\end{aligned} \tag{8}
$$

We will assume that $\alpha > 0$ since this is the case in which the positive portfolio is on the upward-sloping portion of the frontier. We can rewrite, saying that λ is risk compensating if and only if for some number γ there is a $z \gg 0$ such that

$$\mathbf{B}\lambda + \gamma\underline{1} = (\mathbf{I} + \mathbf{B}\mathbf{B}'\mathbf{D}^{-1}\,\underline{1})z,$$

or

$$\mathbf{B}\lambda = \mathbf{B}\mathbf{B}'\mathbf{D}^{-1}z + (z - \gamma\underline{1}). \tag{9}$$

This $z = \mathbf{D}z^*/\alpha$. This suggests that risk-compensating λ's look like $\mathbf{B}'\mathbf{D}^{-1}z + q$, where $\mathbf{B}q = z - \gamma\underline{1}$. In fact, this is exactly the case. If equation (9) holds, then $z - \gamma\underline{1}$ is in the range space of $\mathbf{B}$. This implies that there is some q such that $\mathbf{B}q = z - \gamma\underline{1}$, or $\mathbf{B}q + \gamma\underline{1} = z$. However, if z is strictly positive, then $\gamma > -\min(\mathbf{B}q)_i$. Hence, equation (9) implies that, for some q and some $\gamma > -\min(\mathbf{B}q)_i$,

$$\mathbf{B}\lambda = \mathbf{B}\mathbf{B}'\mathbf{D}^{-1}(\mathbf{B}q + \gamma\underline{1}) + \mathbf{B}q. \tag{10}$$

Since $\mathbf{B}$ has full column rank, it also has a left inverse, so we can rewrite (10) as

$$\lambda = (\mathbf{B}'\mathbf{D}^{-1}\mathbf{B} + \mathbf{I})q + \gamma\mathbf{B}'\mathbf{D}^{-1}\,\underline{1}. \tag{11}$$

We can also reverse the calculation so that, if we choose any vector q and any $\gamma > -\min(\mathbf{B}q)_i$ and if we calculate λ using (11) and let $z = \mathbf{B}q + \gamma\underline{1}$, then λ, z, and γ will satisfy (9).

If $\alpha < 0$, then equation (9) is the same, except that we require z^* to be strictly negative, and $-z^*$ will be the positive portfolio on the minimum-variance frontier. The same argument goes through as above, but now we need $\gamma < -\max(\mathbf{B}q)_i$. In fact, λ is risk compensating by this argument, using q and γ in equation (11) if and only if $-\lambda$ is risk compensating by the first argument using $-q$ and $-\gamma$. We state all of this as Theorem 2.

Theorem 2 (Characterization Theorem) *A vector λ is risk compensating if and only if $-\lambda$ is risk compensating as well. They will be risk compensating if and only if, for one or the other (say λ), there exist a vector q and a number γ, such that $\gamma > -\min(\mathbf{B}q)_i$, that satisfy*

$$\lambda = (\mathbf{B}'\mathbf{D}^{-1}\mathbf{B} + \mathbf{I})q + \gamma\mathbf{B}'\mathbf{D}^{-1}\,\underline{1}. \tag{11}$$

This is a complete characterization of the set of risk-compensating prices. Note that Proposition 1 is the special case with $q = 0$ and $\gamma = 1$. We can add to this the observation that the set of risk-compensating λ's is a cone omitting the origin since, if λ, q, and γ satisfy equation (11) and $\gamma > -\min(\mathbf{B}q)_i$, then, for any positive number θ, $\theta\lambda$, θq, and $\theta\gamma$ will solve (11) also, and $\theta\gamma > -\min(\mathbf{B}(\theta q))_i$.

We also note that, if the original α in equation (8) is positive, then the positive efficient portfolio z^* is a combination of the global minimum-variance portfolio and the tangency portfolio proportional to $\mathrm{V}^{-1}E$ and includes a positive weighting of that portfolio. Therefore, these λ correspond to the existence of a positive portfolio on the upward-sloping portion of the minimum-variance frontier—a positive, mean-variance efficient portfolio. If $\alpha < 0$, then the positive minimum-variance portfolio $-z^*$ lies on the downward-sloping portion of the frontier. In other words, one half of the cone of risk-compensating λ's corresponds to minimum-variance portfolios on the mean-variance efficient portion of the minimum-variance frontier, and the other half corresponds to the downward-sloping branch.

It is also the case that each half of the cone is convex. Suppose that λ_1, q_1, γ_1 and λ_2, q_2, γ_2 are two triplets satisfying (11) and that we have $\gamma_1 > -\min(\mathbf{B}q_1)_i$ and $\gamma_2 > -\min(\mathbf{B}q_2)_i$, so that λ_1 and λ_2 are both risk compensating. Then for $0 \le \theta \le 1$, $\lambda = \theta\lambda_1 + (1-\theta)\lambda_2$, $q = \theta q_1 + (1-\theta)q_2$, and $\gamma = \theta\gamma_1 + (1-\theta)\gamma_2$ satisfy (11), and $\gamma > -\min(\mathbf{B}q)_i$, so λ is risk compensating as well.

III. Interpretation of the Characterization Theorem

This section provides two ways of interpreting (11). Proposition 1 states that one risk-compensating factor-premia vector is $\lambda = \gamma\mathbf{B}'\mathbf{D}^{-1}\,\underline{1}$, which is proportional to an idiosyncratic risk-weighted average of the assets' vectors of factor loadings. In particular, if one factor tends, "on average" in this sense, to have a much heavier loading on the assets than another, then risk-compensating factor pricing requires that the more heavily weighted factor command a larger premium. Going back to Green's example, the first factor has a larger loading than the second on every asset. As Green shows, a factor-premia vector giving each factor the same premium is not risk compensating. However, $\lambda = \gamma\mathbf{B}'\mathbf{D}^{-1}\,\underline{1} = [4\ 1]'$ is risk compensating.

Theorem 2 specifies exactly the extent to which factor premia can deviate from this average and still be risk compensating. Recall that the risk-compensating λ's lie in a convex cone, so that, if λ is risk compensating, then so is any vector proportional to λ. Consider the vector $\lambda = \gamma\mathbf{B}'\mathbf{D}^{-1}\,\underline{1}$, which is risk compensating as long as $\gamma \neq 0$.

Noting that, for any q, we can write $q = \mathbf{B}'p$ for some (not necessarily unique) p, rewrite (11) as

$$\lambda = (\mathbf{B}'\mathbf{D}^{-1}\mathbf{B} + \mathbf{I})\mathbf{B}'p + \gamma\mathbf{B}'\mathbf{D}^{-1}\underline{1}, \tag{12}$$

with the restriction on p being that $\mathbf{B}\mathbf{B}'p + \gamma\underline{1} \gg \underline{0}$. Then if we think of p as an investment position after the fashion of Huberman, Kandel, and Stambaugh [9] (not necessarily a portfolio since $p'\underline{1}$ need not equal one), the restriction requires us to consider only investment positions with a factor-borne covariance with each asset (that is, $(\mathbf{B}\mathbf{B}'p)_i$ for asset i) that is greater than $-\gamma$. We can further rewrite (12) as

$$\begin{aligned}\lambda &= (\mathbf{B}'\mathbf{D}^{-1}\mathbf{B}\mathbf{B}' + \mathbf{B}')p + \gamma\mathbf{B}'\mathbf{D}^{-1}\underline{1}\\ &= \mathbf{B}'\mathbf{D}^{-1}(\mathbf{B}\mathbf{B}' + \mathbf{D})p + \gamma\mathbf{B}'\mathbf{D}^{-1}\underline{1}\\ &= \mathbf{B}'\mathbf{D}^{-1}(\mathbf{V}p + \gamma\underline{1}).\end{aligned} \tag{13}$$

In other words, risk-compensating λ's must be linear combinations of $\mathbf{B}'\mathbf{D}^{-1}$, the ith weight of which can be written as γ plus the covariance of some position p with asset i, where p meets the "factor-borne" covariance restriction. Notice that this does not rule out negative weights. A negative weight may arise if $(\mathbf{B}\mathbf{B}'p + \gamma\underline{1})_i$ is close to zero, $p_i < 0$, and d_i is relatively large. Since $\mathbf{D}^{-1}$ has all-positive diagonal elements, the set of risk-compensating λ's is nearly, but not quite, the cone of positive linear combinations of the assets' factor-loading vectors. Note further that, since a negative weight typically requires d_i to be relatively large, the presence of $\mathbf{D}^{-1}$ in expression (13) reduces the impact of a negative weight when it can arise. Conversely, it is also a simple matter to construct examples of positive weightings that do not yield risk-compensating factor premia.

A second way of looking at (11) may also be helpful. This interpretation relates to statistical estimation of the factors from realized returns, using the GLS projection that minimizes the variance of the residual ascribed to idiosyncratic (that is, **D**) risk.

To see this, rewrite (11) as

$$\begin{aligned}\lambda &= \mathbf{B}'\mathbf{D}^{-1}(\mathbf{B}q + \gamma\underline{1}) + q\\ &= \mathbf{B}'[\mathbf{D}^{-1}(\mathbf{B}q + \gamma\underline{1}) + \mathbf{D}^{-1}\mathbf{B}(\mathbf{B}'\mathbf{D}^{-1}\mathbf{B})^{-1}q].\end{aligned} \tag{14}$$

Again writing $q = \mathbf{B}'p$, the second term in brackets gives the GLS predictor of the portion of the return to p due to the factors,

Huberman, Kandel, and Stambaugh [9] show that, under exact arbitrage pricing, $\mathbf{D}^{-1}\mathbf{B}(\mathbf{B}'\mathbf{D}^{-1}\mathbf{B})^{-1}$ can be used in place of the factors to price all assets. They also note (as do Grinblatt and Titman [8]) that this matrix gives the maximum-likelihood factor-analysis portfolios. Thus, (14) provides that λ must be a linear combination of the assets' factor loadings such that the weights are a positive vector plus a specific combination, q, of the maximum-likelihood estimates of the factors.

IV. An Application to Testing on Subsets

One important practical question that arises with respect to empirical testing concerns Roll's [12] critique that we only observe a subset of the assets available in the market. At issue is the validity of empirical tests on such subsets. In this section, we show that, in the APT setting under consideration here, some tests on subsets still may produce valid results. We show that, if the factor-loading vectors of the assets included in a sample are in some sense representative of the factor loadings of those omitted, then rejection of the existence of a positive efficient portfolio on the subset implies rejection of the existence of a positive efficient portfolio on the entire set. As in Kandel [10], we may identify a collection of omitted assets with a single asset—the portfolio formed from those assets. Proposition 3 defines the sense in which the included assets must be representative; the omitted asset's factor loadings must be nearly a positive combination of the included assets', permitting a deviation from positive weights similar to that in Theorem 2. Proposition 4 ties this result to one in Kandel [10].

Proposition 3 *Consider an economy with n assets, in which* (2) *and* (3) *hold, and for which* λ *is risk compensating. Suppose that asset n's factor-loading vector,* β_n*, can be written*

$$\beta_n = (\mathbf{B}'\mathbf{D}^{-1}\mathbf{B} + \mathbf{I})a, \quad \textit{where} \quad \mathbf{B}a > 0. \tag{15}$$

Here, **B, D,** *and* **I** *refer to the first* $n - 1$ *assets. Then* λ *is risk compensating in the economy restricted to the first* $n - 1$ *assets as well.*

Proof Suppose that λ is risk compensating for all n assets and that β_n satisfies (15). Then for some q and γ we can write

$$\lambda = [\mathbf{B}' \ \ \beta_n]\begin{bmatrix} \mathbf{D}^{-1} & 0 \\ 0 & d_n^{-1} \end{bmatrix}\begin{bmatrix} \mathbf{B} \\ \beta_n \end{bmatrix} q + \gamma[\mathbf{B}' \ \ \beta_n]\begin{bmatrix} \mathbf{D}^{-1} & 0 \\ 0 & d_n^{-1} \end{bmatrix}\underline{1},$$

where $\mathbf{B}q + \gamma\underline{1} \gg 0$ and $\beta'_n q + \gamma > 0$. Rewriting,

$$\begin{aligned} \lambda &= (\mathbf{B}'\mathbf{D}^{-1}\mathbf{B} + \mathbf{I})q + \gamma\mathbf{B}'\mathbf{D}^{-1}\underline{1} + (\gamma/d_n)(\mathbf{B}'\mathbf{D}^{-1}\mathbf{B} + \mathbf{I})a \\ &\quad + (\beta'_n q/d_n)(\mathbf{B}'\mathbf{D}^{-1}\mathbf{B} + \mathbf{I})a \\ &= (\mathbf{B}'\mathbf{D}^{-1}\mathbf{B} + \mathbf{I})(q + a(\beta'_n q + \gamma)/d_n) + \gamma\mathbf{B}'\mathbf{D}^{-1}\underline{1}. \end{aligned}$$

Now $\mathbf{B}a \gg 0$, so $\mathbf{B}a(\beta'_n q + \gamma)/d_n \gg 0$, so $\mathbf{B}(q + a(\beta'_n q + \gamma)/d_n) \gg 0$. Thus, λ is risk compensating for the subset as well. Q.E.D.

This proof is a simple calculation showing that, if (11) holds on the whole set, then (15) guarantees that (11) holds on the subset as well, with γ unchanged and q modified but still meeting the restriction $\mathbf{B}q + \gamma\underline{1} \gg 0$.

Proposition 3 is a special case (under exact arbitrage pricing) of a more general result that derives directly from Theorem 1. That result, Proposition 4, should clarify further the meaning of Proposition 3.

Proposition 4 *Consider a market with n assets with mean-returns vector E and variance matrix* **V**. *Write* $\mathbf{V}_{-i}$ *and* E_{-i} *for the variance submatrix and mean vector for the subset omitting the ith asset. Suppose that there exists a positive mean-variance efficient portfolio, and suppose that* σ_i*, the vector of the covariances between the ith asset and the others, can be written*

$$\sigma_i = \mathbf{V}_{-i}a, \quad a > 0.$$

Then there exists a positive minimum-variance portfolio on the subset omitting the ith asset.

Proof We prove the contrapositive. Suppose without loss of generality that $i = n$, and suppose that there is no positive minimum-variance portfolio on the subset. Then there is an $(n - 1)$-vector y such that

$$\begin{aligned} \mathbf{V}_{-n}y &> 0, \\ y'E_{-n} &= 0, \\ y'\underline{1} &= 0. \end{aligned}$$

Note that

$$\mathbf{V} = \begin{bmatrix} \mathbf{V}_{-n} & \sigma_n \\ \sigma_n & \mathbf{V}_{nn} \end{bmatrix} = \begin{bmatrix} \mathbf{V}_{-n} & \mathbf{V}_{-n}a \\ a'\mathbf{V}_{-n} & \mathbf{V}_{nn} \end{bmatrix}.$$

Then

$$\mathbf{V}\begin{bmatrix} y \\ 0 \end{bmatrix} = \begin{bmatrix} \mathbf{V}_{-n}y \\ a'\mathbf{V}_{-n}y \end{bmatrix} > 0 \quad \text{since} \quad a > 0.$$

$$[y' \quad 0]E = y'E_{-n} + 0 = 0,$$

$$[y' \quad 0]\underline{1} = y'\underline{1} + 0 = 0$$

Hence, $[y' \ 0]$ meets the conditions for Theorem 1, so there is no positive minimum-variance portfolio on the whole set. Q.E.D.

This proposition is similar in flavor to Theorem 4 in Kandel [10]. That theorem examines the existence of σ_n and $\mathbf{V}_{nn}$, which give mean-variance efficiency for a portfolio consisting of a specific portfolio of the included assets (Kandel's α) and the true portfolio of the missing assets. This proposition exploits Theorem 1 to obtain a sufficient condition on σ_n for the existence of a positive minimum-variance portfolio when the true portfolio of the missing assets is added to the set. This sufficient condition is that it be possible to duplicate the covariances of the added asset by forming a non-negative portfolio of the other assets. The result says in particular that the expected return on the added asset is not important.

As in Kandel, if we have no information regarding σ_n or the variance of the missing asset, we can say nothing about the existence of a positive minimum-variance portfolio when we add the missing asset. However, it also shows that we can make some statement about the existence of the positive minimum-variance portfolio on the strength of only partial information about the missing asset.

To see that Proposition 3 is a special case of Proposition 4, note that the variance matrix for the whole set is

$$\mathbf{V} = \begin{bmatrix} \mathbf{BB}' + \mathbf{D} & \mathbf{B}\beta_n \\ \beta_n'\mathbf{B}' & \beta_n'\beta_n + d_n \end{bmatrix}.$$

If $\beta_n = (\mathbf{B}'\mathbf{D}^{-1}\mathbf{B} + \mathbf{I})a$, then

$$\sigma_n = \mathbf{B}\beta_n = (\mathbf{BB}'\mathbf{D}^{-1} + \mathbf{I})\mathbf{B}a = (\mathbf{BB}' + \mathbf{D})\mathbf{D}^{-1}\mathbf{B}a, \quad \text{with} \quad \mathbf{D}^{-1}\mathbf{B}a > 0.$$

Proposition 3 says that adding an asset with such factor loadings cannot widen the cone of risk-compensating λ. To see that adding such an asset can narrow it, consider Green's example. Suppose that $\lambda = [3 \ 2]'$. Then λ satisfies (11) with

$$q = \begin{bmatrix} \frac{15}{111} & \frac{30}{111} \end{bmatrix}' \quad \text{and} \quad \gamma = -\frac{163}{111}. \qquad \text{Note that } \min\,(\mathbf{B}q)_i = \frac{165}{111}.$$

However, suppose we add a fourth asset and suppose that $\beta_4 = [5\ 1]'$ are its factor loadings. Then β_4 satisfies (15) with $\alpha = \begin{bmatrix} \frac{67}{2903} & \frac{17}{2903} \end{bmatrix}'$ since $\mathbf{B}a > 0$. Assuming that $d_4 = 1$, the augmented variance matrix is

$$\mathbf{V} = \begin{bmatrix} 53 & 50 & 66 & 34 \\ 50 & 54 & 77 & 37 \\ 66 & 77 & 122 & 55 \\ 34 & 37 & 55 & 27 \end{bmatrix}$$

and

$$\mathbf{B}\lambda = \begin{bmatrix} 26 \\ 25 \\ 33 \\ 17 \end{bmatrix}.$$

Then $y = [0\ \ -1\ \ ½\ \ ½]'$ has $y'\mathbf{B}\lambda = 0$, $y'\underline{1} = 0$, and $\mathbf{V}y = [0\ \ 3\ \ 11.5\ \ 4]' > 0$. Hence, $\lambda = [3\ \ 2]'$ is no longer risk compensating on the subset.

Theorem 2 and Proposition 3 say that, if the assets that we examine are in this sense representative of the assets in the market, then rejection of the existence of a positive efficient portfolio on the subset under exact arbitrage pricing implies rejection on the whole set. The example serves to demonstrate that the reverse is not true. That is, it may be the case that a factor-premia vector would be risk compensating on the subset but not on the larger set.

V. Conclusion

In this paper, we have added to the discussion of the relationship between the Arbitrage Pricing Theory and mean-variance analysis. In particular, we have studied the conditions under which exact arbitrage pricing is compatible with the existence of a positive portfolio on the minimum-variance frontier and, therefore, (weakly) compatible with the Capital Asset Pricing Model. By approaching the issue from the standpoint of studying the behavior of the vector of factor premia, we have also contributed insight to the issue of how factor prices should look in equilibrium, an issue that has received rather little attention. We have also shown that the conditions derived here can in principle be used to reject the null hypothesis of the existence of a positive efficient portfolio when we only have in hand a subset of the total universe of assets, if we know enough about the relationship between the included assets and the excluded ones.

References

Gary Chamberlain. "Funds, Factors, and Diversification in Arbitrage Pricing Models." *Econometrica* 51 (September 1983), 1305–23.

—— and Michael Rothschild. "Arbitrage, Factor Structure, and Mean-Variance Analysis on Large Asset Markets." *Econometrica* 51 (September 1983), 1281–1304.

Gregory Connor. "A Factor Pricing Theory for Capital Assets." Working paper, Kellogg School, 1982.

Philip H. Dybvig. "An Explicit Bound on Individual Assets' Deviations from APT Pricing in a Finite Economy." *Journal of Financial Economics* 12 (December 1983), 483–96.

——and Stephen A. Ross. "Yes, the APT is Testable." *Journal of Finance* 40 (September 1985), 1173–88.

Richard C. Green. "Positively Weighted Portfolios on the Minimum-Variance Frontier." *Journal of Finance* 41 (December 1986), 1051–68.

Mark Grinblatt and Sheridan Titman. "Factor Pricing in a Finite Economy." *Journal of Financial Economics* 12 (December 1983), 497–507.

——. "The Relation between Mean-Variance Efficiency and Arbitrage Pricing." *Journal of Business* 60 (January 1987), 97–112.

Gur Huberman, Shmuel Kandel, and Robert F. Stambaugh. "Mimicking Portfolios and Exact Arbitrage Pricing." *Journal of Finance* 42 (March 1987), 1–9.

Shmuel Kandel, "On the Exclusion of Assets from Tests of the Mean-Variance Efficiency of the Market Portfolio." *Journal of Finance* 39 (March 1984), 63–75.

Marjorie B. McElroy and Edwin Burmeister. "Joint Estimation of Factor Sensitivities and Risk Premia for the Arbitrage Pricing Theory." Working paper, Duke University and University of Virginia, 1986.

Richard Roll. "A Critique of the Asset Pricing Theory's Tests." *Journal of Financial Economics* 4 (March 1977), 129–76.

Stephen A. Ross. "Risk, Return, and Arbitrage." In I. Friend and J. Bicksler (eds.), *Risk and Return in Finance.* Cambridge, MA: Ballinger, 1976, 189–218.

——. "The Arbitrage Theory of Capital Asset Pricing." *Journal of Economic Theory* 13 (December 1976), 341–60.

Nineteen

Yasushi Hamao

Yasushi Hamao received a Ph.D. from Yale University in 1987. He started out at the Graduate School of International Relations and Pacific Studies, University of California, San Diego, and now works at the Marshall School of Business, University of Southern California. •

I went to Yale as an MBA student, without knowing what financial economics was. Steve's introductory finance course, even though it was for MBAs, had so many intellectual subtleties that I became curious about what exists beyond it. So I stayed for a Ph.D. I have been working on mostly Japanese financial markets, a rather peculiar focus in the United States, especially these days. Once when I was bogged down with frustrations, Steve, who has never failed to encourage me along the way, said, "You have written these articles. You have taught us something new." These words, coming from Steve Ross, were deeply humbling.

Correlations in Price Changes and Volatility across International Stock Markets

Yasushi Hamao
University of California, San Diego

Ronald W. Masulis
Vanderbilt University

Victor Ng
University of Michigan

The short-run interdependence of prices and price volatility across three major international stock markets is studied. Daily opening and closing prices of major stock indexes for the Tokyo, London, and New York stock markets are examined. The analysis utilizes the autoregressive conditionally heteroskedastic (ARCH) family of statistical models to explore these pricing relationships. Evidence of price volatility spillovers from New York to Tokyo, London to Tokyo, and New York to London is observed, but no price volatility spillover effects in other directions are found for the pre-October 1987 period. •

The extent of international financial integration has received much attention in recent years. However, its empirical implications for the functioning of individual capital markets has received far less attention. In this study, we consider the short-term relations among security prices across three major stock markets: Tokyo, London, and New York. We are interested in (1) the extent to which security price changes in one market influence the opening prices in the next market to trade and (2) whether changes in price volatility in one market are positively related to changes in price volatility observed in the next market to trade. The financial press strongly suggests that such a relation exists.[1]

Earlier research has examined the correlation of asset prices across international markets. Hilliard (1979) studied the contemporaneous and lagged correlation in daily closing price changes across 10 major stock markets. Jaffe and Westerfield (1985a, 1985b) examined daily closing prices in the Australian, British, Canadian, Japanese, and U.S. stock markets. Eun and Shim (1989) studied daily stock returns across nine national stock markets,

[1] This point is exemplified by the following quote: "A sharp downward movement in the New York stock market last week triggered fear here in Japan and the Tokyo market experienced the largest drop this year." [*Nihon Keizai Shimbun (Japan Economic Journal)*, May 22, 1988].

The authors thank participants at the American Finance Association Meetings in Atlanta; the European Finance Association Meetings in Stockholm; the Western Finance Association Meetings in Seattle; TIMS Meetings in Osaka; the finance workshops at Berkeley, Carnegie Mellon, Houston, Northwestern, USC, Vanderbilt, and Wisconsin; and the statistics workshop at SMU where earlier versions of this article were presented for helpful suggestions. The authors also thank Tim Bollerslev, Robert Engle, Michael Gibbons (the editor), Ravi Jaganathan, Robert Korajczyk, Josef Lakonishok, Rex Thompson, and an anonymous referee for their valuable comments. Any remaining errors are our own.

Reprinted with permission:
Hamao, Yasushi, Ronald W. Masulis, and Victor Ng. "Correlations in Price Changes and Volatility across International Stock Markets." *Review of Financial Studies* 3 (1990): 281–307.

while Barclay, Litzenberger, and Warner (1990) examined daily price volatility and volume for common stocks dually listed on the New York and Tokyo stock exchanges. They all report evidence of positive correlations in daily close-to-close returns across individual stock exchanges.

We examine the transmission mechanisms of the conditional first and second moments in common stock prices across international stock markets and allow for changing conditional variances as well as conditional mean returns.[2] As Engle (1982) notes, it is reasonable for stock return variances to be conditional on current information given that their means are conditional on this data set.

Unlike earlier studies, we divide daily close-to-close returns into their close-to-open and open-to-close components. This enables us to analyze separately the spillover effects of price volatility in foreign markets on the opening price in the domestic market and on prices after the opening of trading. This separation is relevant since spillover effects from foreign markets on the conditional means of the close-to-open return (which reflect effects on opening prices in the domestic market) are predicted by international asset pricing models, while spillover effects on conditional means of the open-to-close return (which reflect effects on prices in the domestic market after the opening of trading) are predicted not to occur.[3] In addition, volatility spillovers onto the conditional variances of the close-to-open and open-to-close returns of the domestic market can occur, a question on which little theoretical work exists. Such volatility spillovers could represent a causal phenomenon across markets that trade sequentially; alternatively, they could reflect global economic changes that concurrently alter stock-return volatility across international stock markets.

Prior statistical analysis of common stock daily returns has documented mild serial correlation over very short periods of time.[4] Previous analyses of daily and monthly U.S. common stock returns have found that "large price changes tend to be followed by large changes—of either sign—and small changes tend to be followed by small changes . . ." [see Mandelbrot (1963, p. 418); also see Fama (1965, pp. 85–87)]. There is also evidence that percentage changes in stock prices and indices exhibit fatter tails than that predicted by a stationary normal distribution [e.g., see Westerfield (1977) and Kon (1984)].

The autoregressive conditional heteroskedastic (ARCH) model recognizes the temporal dependence in the second moment of stock returns and exhibits a leptokurtic distribution for the unconditional errors from the stock returns generating process. This model was introduced by Engle (1982) and generalized by Bollerslev (1986, 1987) and Engle, Lilien, and Robins (1987). Examining the descriptive validity of these models, French, Schwert, and Stambaugh (1987) find that the generalized autoregressive conditional heteroskedastic-in-mean (GARCH-M) model is an attractive representation of daily stock-return behavior in the United States, successfully capturing the effects of time-varying volatility on a stock's expected return.

---

[2] In related research, Engle, Ito, and Lin (1990) apply the generalized autoregressive conditional heteroskedastic (GARCH) model to test for spillovers in daily exchange rate volatility across Japanese and American foreign exchange markets. They find that changes in volatility in the foreign exchange market previously open are positively correlated with changes in volatility in the next market to open trading based on close-to-close price data.

[3] See Stulz (1981), Solnik (1983), Errunza and Losq (1985), and Cho, Eun, and Senbet (1986) for examples of international asset pricing models.

[4] See, in particular, the evidence of serial correlation in daily stock returns of U.S. stocks found by Fama (1965) and studied by Scholes and Williams (1977). For evidence on the statistical properties of the Nikkei daily return series, see Tse (1989).

1. Data

In this article, we examine daily and intraday stock-price activity over the three-year period, April 1, 1985, to March 31, 1988. We study daily open and close data from three stock markets: Tokyo, London, and New York.[5] In each market, we chose the most comprehensive and diversified stock index that met the previously mentioned data requirements. For the Tokyo Stock Exchange, we used the Nikkei 225 Stock Index. This index of "first section" stocks includes the largest 225 firms in Japan and represents 52.2 percent of the total equity capitalization of the Tokyo Stock Exchange at the end of 1987.[6] The Nikkei 225 is a share price weighted index (similar to the Dow Jones stock index, which has no dividend reinvestment). However, cash dividends paid on most Japanese stocks are relatively small, so this dividend omission is of little consequence.[7] The price data were obtained from Nihon Keizai Shimbun Sha. Opening price data were recorded at 9:15 A.M. until December 18, 1987, and at 9:01 A.M. thereafter, while closing prices are recorded at 3:00 P.M. Tokyo time.

In the London stock market, we used the Financial Times–Stock Exchange 100 Share (FTSE) Index, which represents 70 percent of the equity capitalization of all United Kingdom equities at the end of 1987. This is an equity value weighted arithmetic index. The opening price data were recorded at 9:00 A.M., while the closing price data (legal closing) were recorded at 3:30 P.M. London time. The data sources were the London International Stock Exchange and the *Financial Times.*

In the New York stock market, we used the Standard & Poors 500 Composite Index. This represented 76 percent of the equity capitalization of the NYSE as of midyear 1989, though it currently includes a small number of AMEX and OTC stocks. The S&P 500 is an equity value weighted arithmetic index. The primary data source was S&P's monthly "500 Information Bulletin." The opening stock price was measured at 10:01 A.M. until September 30, 1985, and at 9:31 A.M. thereafter and the close is at 4:00 P.M. EST. From these daily opening and closing prices, we compute daily close-to-close, close-to-open, and open-to-close returns for our three stock indices.[8]

Figure 1 shows trading hours of the three exchanges in Eastern Standard Time. With the exception of the morning trading in New York, which represents late afternoon trading in London, the trading activity in these markets is not concurrent. To minimize the trading overlap between the London and New York stock markets to one hour, we measured the London closing price at the 3:30 legal close rather than the 5:00 official close of the exchange.[9] A technical problem in studying pricing relations across markets was the existence

[5] A description of the basic institutional features of these stock exchanges can be found in Cohen et al. (1986, chap. 2).

[6] While an equity value weighted index for the Tokyo Stock Exchange (TOPIX) exists, data on opening prices of this index were not available.

[7] Campbell and Hamao (1989) document the dividend–price ratio foe the Tokyo market.

[8] These three indices are each composed of only common stocks of companies headquartered in the nation where the stock market is based.

[9] However, differences in daylight savings time in the United Kingdom and the United States can cause some minor variability in concurrent trading periods. In 1985–1986, daylight savings time began on the last Sunday in April in the United States and the last Sunday in March in the United Kingdom. Since 1987, daylight savings time has begun on the first Sunday in April in the United States. Daylight savings time ends the last Sunday in October in both countries. This difference in conventions caused the trading overlap between the two markets to decrease by an hour for the month of March in 1985–1986 and for the last week of March in 1987–1989.

FIGURE 1 | Exchange Trading Hours

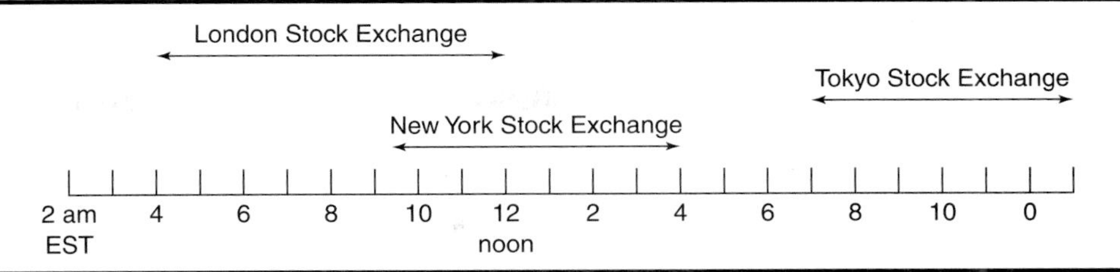

of nonsynchronous holidays and twice monthly Saturday trading on the Tokyo Exchange. When measuring spillover effects from foreign markets in periods where one or both foreign markets were closed, we substitute the most recent "volatility surprise" (defined below) available for the foreign exchange that was closed.[10]

In the case of the S&P and the Nikkei, the use of index prices near the open of trading can present some difficulties. When individual stocks of the index have not yet opened trading, the previous day's closing price quotes are substituted into the index. For the S&P 500 index, Stoll and Whaley (1988) report that stocks on average begin trading 5 to 7 minutes after the exchange open. For Nikkei, we have been unable to determine the exact extent of the problem, though for most of the time series we are using prices 15 minutes after the official open, which should minimize the effects of stale prices. In the case of the FTSE index, firm quotes rather than transaction prices are used, and these quotes must be available while the exchange is open. The result of this substitution procedure for the S&P and the Nikkei is to induce higher serial correlation between close-to-open and open-to-close returns in adjacent days. It can also artificially induce positive serial correlation in the open-to-close return data. For New York, we also studied the use of noon-to-close returns in place of open-to-close returns. This has the added benefit of eliminating overlapping trading between London and New York.

Our sample period includes October 1987 when all major stock exchanges experienced large declines in prices. Since the "crash" took place in the three markets we are analyzing sequentially across a 24-hour period, it may seriously influence the estimation of the first and second moment spillover effects.[11] To separate out any "crash" effect, we have also estimated our models over the subperiod prior to the stock market crash (i.e., from April 1, 1985, to September 30, 1987).

2. Methodology

We begin with a brief review of the ARCH family of statistical models. To capture the effect of changing volatility in a time series, Engle (1982) developed the ARCH model where the conditional variance h is a linear function of past squared errors, ϵ's, as well as possible

[10] We also estimated our model dropping out domestic returns for any days where at least one of the two foreign markets was closed. Qualitatively similar spillover effects were observed.

[11] Roll(1988) discusses the international transmission of the crash in detail.

exogenous variables X. The simplest representation of this model is an ARCH(1) which has the form

$$R_t = \alpha + \epsilon_t \qquad \text{where } \epsilon_t \mid \mathcal{F}_{t-1} \sim \mathcal{N}(0, h_t)$$

and

$$h_t = a + c\epsilon_{t-1}^2 + fX_t \qquad \text{where } a > 0 \text{ and } c, f \geq 0$$

The conditional variance at time t is a positive function of the square of last period's error. While the ARCH models do not allow the conditional variance at time t to have a stochastic component, the models can incorporate additional squared error terms from prior periods. For example, in an ARCH(2) model the conditional variance is a linear function of the squared errors from the most recent prior two periods.

Bollerslev (1986) generalized this model by allowing the conditional variance h to be a function not only of last period's error squared but also of its conditional variance. The GARCH(1,1) model defines the conditional variance of R at time t to be of the form

$$h_t = a + bh_{t-1} + c\epsilon_{t-1}^2 + fX_t$$

The GARCH formulation can also be extended to include squared errors from prior periods, for example, a GARCH(1, 2) model includes squared errors from the prior two periods in the conditional variance equation. For stability of the volatility process, the coefficients of the lagged errors and lagged conditional variances must sum to less than 1. Engle, Lilien, and Robins (1987) extend the GARCH model to allow the conditional mean to be a function of the conditional variance at time t. This GARCH(1, 1)-M model takes the form

$$R_t = \alpha + \beta h_t + \epsilon_t$$

where the conditional variance is defined in the same way as the GARCH(1, 1) model.

Several characteristics of stock price indices need to be addressed. Scholes and Williams (1977) and Cohen et al. (1980) examine how nonsynchronous trading in individual stocks, bid–ask spreads, and minimum-size price changes can cause serial correlation in stock and index returns. Because the above institutional factors can induce a small, short-lived serial correlation in these returns, while the ARCH models assume that the conditional error is serially uncorrelated, it is necesssary to extract this serial correlation from the stock return's first moment. Bollerslev (1987) and French, Schwert, and Stambaugh (1987) adjust the conditional mean return for a first-order moving average, MA(1), so that the equation for R is altered in the following way:

$$R_t = \alpha + \beta h_t - \gamma\epsilon_{t-1} + \epsilon_t$$

French (1980) and Gibbons and Hess (1981) document negative mean returns for U.S. stocks on Mondays, while Fama (1965) and Godfrey, Granger, and Morgenstern (1964) document higher return variances for U.S. stocks on Mondays. Because of holidays and the high variability of daily stock returns, these Monday effects will not be clearly captured by an MA(5). To take these potential Monday effects directly into account in the three markets being studied, we include a dummy variable for the day following a weekend or holiday in both the conditional mean and variance equations.

Nonlinear optimization techniques are used to calculate the maximum-likelihood estimates based on the Berndt–Hall–Hall–Hausman algorithm.[12] The primary specification

[12] Initial values must be chosen in using this estimation method. For this purpose, for example, the first-order autocorrelation coefficient of the returns squared is used as the initial value for the ARCH(1) coefficient in the variance equation. When an exogenous variable is added to the equation, we start with some small number for the coefficients of the new variable, while scaling down the existing coefficients. The R-squared convergence criterion used in our estimation was 0.001 in almost all cases.

tests for the model involve the Ljung-Box statistic, which is used to test for a lack of serial correlation in the model residuals and in the residuals squared. This statistic has been shown by McLeod and Li (1983) to be asymptotically chi-square distributed. Skewness and kurtosis coefficients for the normalized residuals are also reviewed. The descriptive validity of the estimated model can be evaluated with a likelihood ratio (LR) statistic that is chi-square distributed.

We use daily open and closing price data (last market's open-to-close return to predict the next market's close to-open and open-to-close conditional mean returns and conditional variances). Finally, we test for spillovers in conditional mean and volatility across countries using correlation analysis and the inclusion of lagged returns and estimated squared residuals from the other stock markets in the ARCH models.[13]

To address formally the issue of spillover effects from one stock exchange to another, we divide the daily close-to-close return into its close-to-open and open-to-close components. This allows us to analyze separately the effects of foreign stock trading on both the market's opening price (from its close-to-open return) and the market's subsequent pricing behavior until its daily close (from its open-to-close return). We focus primarily on the open-to-close returns and the question of price volatility spillover effects, though we do document that the close-to-open return is positively correlated with prior open-to-close returns in foreign markets measured over periods when the domestic market is closed.

We estimate the Nikkei, FTSE, and S&P indexes' close-to-open and open-to-close daily return processes with a GARCH-M model. The primary purpose of this initial estimation is to evaluate the descriptive validity of the GARCH-M model and to determine the appropriate specifications for the three-stock-return time series. The GARCH-M specification that best fits the data is employed when we examine the empirical significance of cross-country return and volatility spillovers. Nested specification tests using likelihood ratio (LR) statistics are undertaken to determine the most parsimonious and descriptively accurate GARCH-M model.

3. Data Analysis of Daily and Intraday Stock Return Series

We begin with an examination of the serial correlation of the close-to-close, close-to-open, and open-to-close returns on the three stock exchange indices for the full sample period and the pre-October 1987 subperiod. Table 1, Panel A shows the estimated serial correlations for the full sample period. Table 1, Panel B shows estimates for the precrash subperiod.

For the full sample period, we find evidence in the close-to-close return series of the Tokyo and New York markets of negative correlation at lag 2 and positive correlation at lags 5, 9, and 10 (which potentially reflects the documented "day of the week" effect). For the open-to-close returns, we also find evidence of negative correlation at lag 2 and positive correlation at lag 5. When the stock crash and subsequent period are excluded, the serial correlations of the returns for the various stock indices tend to exhibit large positive correlations at lag 1 and much diminished correlations at lag 2. Large positive correlations at lags 5, 9, and 10 continue to be observed.

[13] Since these residuals are proxies for the true unobservable innovations, an estimated regressor problem exists. Thus, the t-statistics for the associated parameter estimates will not be strictly t-distributed though these estimates remain consistent and likelihood ratios can also be used to measure the importance of these effects.

TABLE 1 | Data Summary, Close-to-Close, Open-to-Close, and Close-to-Open Returns

Panel A: Sample period: April 1, 1985–March 31, 1988

	Number of obs.	Mean	Standard deviation	Autocorrelations Lag 1	2	3	4	5	6	7	8	9	10
NK C-C[1]	836	.0936	1.1237	.0188	−.1136	−.0023	−.0676	.1185	−.0643	−.0544	.0101	.0112	.0057
				(.0346)	(.0346)	(.0350)	(.0350)	(.0352)	(.0357)	(.0358)	(.0359)	(.0359)	(.0359)
NK O-C	837	.0201	1.0790	−.0265	−.1028	.0200	−.0717	.1277	−.0447	−.0390	.0264	.0160	.0031
				(.0346)	(.0346)	(.0350)	(.0350)	(.0351)	(.0357)	(.0358)	(.0358)	(.0358)	(.0358)
NK C-O	836	.0739	0.2243	.1634	.0060	.0713	.0829	.0860	.0587	−.0544	.0379	.1152	.0765
				(.0346)	(.0355)	(.0355)	(.0357)	(.0359)	(.0362)	(.0363)	(.0364)	(.0364)	(.0368)
FTSE C-C	760	.0488	1.2607	−.0120	.0930	.0229	.0380	.0595	−.1037	.0962	.0529	.1214	.0005
				(.0363)	(.0363)	(.0366)	(.0366)	(.0367)	(.0368)	(.0372)	(.0375)	(.0376)	(.0381)
FTSE O-C	760	−.0102	0.8619	−.0192	−.0540	.1015	.0631	−.0201	−.0589	.0890	.1585	.0854	−.0314
				(.0363)	(.0363)	(.0364)	(.0368)	(.0369)	(.0369)	(.0370)	(.0373)	(.0382)	(.0385)
FTSE C-O	760	.0581	0.8282	−.1114	.0940	−.0091	−.0435	.0769	−.0664	.0313	−.0570	.0755	−.0141
				(.0363)	(.0367)	(.0370)	(.0370)	(.0371)	(.0373)	(.0375)	(.0375)	(.0376)	(.0378)
S&P C-C	760	.0574	1.3823	.0427	−.1169	−.0547	−.0666	.0924	.0353	.0307	.0012	−.0124	−.0414
				(.0363)	(.0363)	(.0368)	(.0369)	(.0371)	(.0374)	(.0374)	(.0375)	(.0375)	(.0375)
S&P O-C	760	.0586	1.3609	.0387	−.1088	−.0494	−.0591	.0918	.0422	.0274	−.0059	−.0094	−.0435
				(.0363)	(.0363)	(.0368)	(.0368)	(.0370)	(.0373)	(.0373)	(.0374)	(.0374)	(.0374)
S&P C-O	760	−.0012	0.1528	−.0059	−.0045	−.1199	.0162	.0816	−.0320	.0271	−.1515	.0130	.0726
				(.0363)	(.0363)	(.0363)	(.0368)	(.0368)	(.0370)	(.0371)	(.0371)	(.0379)	(.0379)

Correlation coefficients[2]

	NK O-C		FTSE O-C		S&P O-C
S&P O-C (−1)	.48583	NK O-C	−.00561	FTSE O-C	.41200
FTSE O-C (−1)	.36397	SP O-C (−1)	−.24117	NK O-C	.11673

Panel B: Sample period: April 1, 1985–September 30, 1987

	Number of obs.	Mean	Standard deviation	Autocorrelations Lag 1	2	3	4	5	6	7	8	9	10
NK C-C[1]	701	.1062	0.8470	.1965	−.0526	−.0828	.0025	.0520	−.0347	−.0591	−.0668	.0167	.0626
				(.0378)	(.0392)	(.0393)	(.0396)	(.0396)	(.0397)	(.0397)	(.0398)	(.0400)	(.0400)
NK O-C	702	.0191	0.7883	.1328	−.0255	−.0487	−.0002	.0654	.0182	−.0278	−.0405	.0277	.0598
				(.0377)	(.0384)	(.0384)	(.0385)	(.0385)	(.0387)	(.0387)	(.0387)	(.0388)	(.0388)
NK C-O	702	.0875	0.2392	.1475	−.0152	.0568	.0702	.0654	.0433	−.0756	.0238	.1069	.0600
				(.0377)	(.0386)	(.0386)	(.0387)	(.0389)	(.0390)	(.0391)	(.0393)	(.0393)	(.0397)
FTSE C-C	632	.1014	0.8782	.0451	.0500	−.0501	−.0328	.0055	−.0562	.0403	.0421	.1614	.0564
				(.0398)	(.0399)	(.0400)	(.0401)	(.0401)	(.0401)	(.0402)	(.0403)	(.0404)	(.0414)
FTSE O-C	632	.0089	0.6547	−.0113	.0304	−.0283	−.0281	−.0258	−.0446	.0633	.0117	.0950	.1035
				(.0398)	(.0398)	(.0398)	(.0399)	(.0399)	(.0399)	(.0400)	(.0402)	(.0402)	(.0405)
FTSE C-O	632	.0923	0.5614	−.0917	−.0158	−.0119	−.0322	.0270	−.0040	.0689	.0106	.0995	.0454
				(.0398)	(.0401)	(.0401)	(.0401)	(.0402)	(.0402)	(.0402)	(.0404)	(.0404)	(.0408)
S&P C-C	633	.0950	0.8657	.0915	−.0345	.0177	−.0492	−.0697	−.0183	−.0069	.0307	.0182	.0634
				(.0398)	(.0401)	(.0401)	(.0401)	(.0402)	(.0404)	(.0404)	(.0404)	(.0405)	(.0405)
S&P O-C	633	.0920	0.8460	.0800	−.0077	.0265	−.0276	−.0802	−.0111	−.0210	.0346	.0232	.0616
				(.0398)	(.0400)	(.0400)	(.0400)	(.0401)	(.0403)	(.0403)	(.0403)	(.0404)	(.0404)
S&P C-O	633	.0033	0.1566	−.0090	−.0004	−.1422	.0268	.0977	−.0275	0335	−.1875	.0110	.0740
				(.0398)	(.0398)	(.0398)	(.0406)	(.0406)	(.0409)	(.0410)	(.0410)	(.0424)	(.0424)

Correlation coefficient[2]

	NK O-C		FTSE O-C		S&P O-C
S&P O-C (−1)	.11604	NK O-C	.05259	FTSE O-C	.11989
FTSE O-C (−1)	.00597	SP O-C (−1)	−.10882	NK O-C	.09540

[1] C-C, O-C, and C-O stand for close-to-close, open-to-close, and close-to-open, respectively. To minimize the trading overlap between London and New York, FTSE close is measured at 3:30 P.M. legal close. Returns are measured in percent. Numbers in parentheses are standard errors.

[2] (−1) denotes one-period lag. For example, corr(NK, S&P(−1)) gives a correlation coefficient between Nikkei and S&P on the prior trading day (when the New York market closes several hours prior to the Tokyo market).

For the close-to-open returns, we find positive correlation at lags 1 and 9 for Tokyo, and negative correlation at lags 3 and 8 for New York. However, over the precrash period these higher-order lagged correlations are much less important. This serial correlation is likely to reflect the effects of late opening and early closing of trading in individual stocks comprising the indices especially in the case of the New York and Tokyo exchanges, as well as the effects of bid–ask spreads on all three exchanges. Estimating the GARCH-M model with higher-order MA processes specified produced no evidence supporting the significance of moving-average parameters of a higher order than an MA(1). This suggests that at least part of the observed serial correlation is induced by the GARCH in mean effect. Given the lack of consistent evidence of significant higher-order serial correlation beyond a possible "day of the week" effect, we follow the approach of Bollerslev (1987) and French, Schwert, and Stambaugh (1987) by specifying an MA(1) process in conjunction with a GARCH-M model, which we apply to all three stock return series. We also include a dummy variable for the trading day following a weekend or holiday in both the conditional mean and variance equations to capture potential "day of the week" effects.

Table 1 also presents estimated contemporaneous and first-order lagged correlations of open-to-close returns across our three major stock markets. Since an international dateline separates the New York and Tokyo stock markets, lagged correlations of the returns of the S&P and the FTSE indices are also reported. We find large positive correlations between "contemporaneous" Tokyo and London returns, London and New York returns, and lagged New York and Tokyo returns, while a large negative correlation is observed between lagged New York and London returns and a smaller positive correlation between "contemporaneous" New York and Tokyo returns. In the precrash subperiod, the cross correlations of contemporaneous and lagged index returns tend to be predictably weaker in size and statistical significance. Comparing the mean returns and standard deviations in the two tables also yields the not surprising conclusion that mean returns are higher and standard deviations smaller if the stock crash and subsequent period are excluded. The evidence in Table 1 suggests the need to estimate our GARCH models for both time intervals to ensure the robustness of our conclusions.

4. Spillover Effects in Open-to-Close Stock Returns

To assess the appropriateness of the GARCH-M specification for open-to-close daily stock returns, we employ an MA(1)-GARCH(1, 1)-M model, as discussed in Section 2, which has the following form:

$$\begin{aligned} R_t &= \alpha + \beta h_t + \delta D_t + \gamma \epsilon_{t-1} + \epsilon_t \\ h_t &= a + b h_{t-1} + c \epsilon_{t-1}^2 + d D_t \end{aligned} \qquad (1)$$

where h represents the conditional variance of the stock index return, R, at time t, and D represents a dummy variable that takes a value of 1 on days following weekends and holidays and is 0 otherwise. This formulation more clearly tests the spillover effect often asserted to exist when ovelapping close-to-close returns of several stock exchanges are studied. By using open-to-close returns for stock markets without concurrent trading, stock returns across markets are measured in such a way that their trading periods do not overlap in time, thus eliminating the spillover effect in opening prices predicted by international capital asset pricing models.

Table 2 shows the results of our initial estimation of the GARCH-M model for the open-to-close returns series in the U.S., U.K., and Japanese markets.[14] The likelihood ratio [LR(4)] statistics, which allow us to test the null hypothesis that the returns are normally distributed against the alternative that they are generated by an MA(1)–GARCH(1, 1)-M model, are significant at the 1 percent level in all three markets. No indications of serious model misspecification are observed; for example, none of the Ljung-Box values for the first 12 normalized residuals or residuals squared are significant at conventional levels. Of somewhat greater concern are the coefficients of kurtosis for the normalized residuals that take on values of 7.66 for the Nikkei, 22.78 for the FTSE, and 7.74 for the S&P, relative to a predicted value of 3.0[15] These coefficients, however, are much smaller for the subperiod prior to the October 1987 stock market crash as seen in Panel B of Table 2.[16] Finally, it is noteworthy that the conditional variance has a significant effect only on the conditional mean in the precrash subperiod and then only in the Tokyo and London markets.

We next introduce an exogenous variable into the conditional variance that captures the potential volatility spillover effect from the previously open foreign stock market into the domestic stock market. Interpreting the squared residual from the above model as a "volatility surprise", we take the most recent squared residual derived from model (1), denoted by X, using open-to-close returns in the foreign market that trades most recently (i.e., Tokyo for London, London for New York, and New York for Tokyo), and append it to the domestic market's conditional variance specification:[17]

$$R_t = \alpha + \beta h_t + \delta D_t + \gamma \epsilon_{t-1} + \epsilon_t$$
$$h_t = a + b h_{t-1} + c \epsilon_{t-1}^2 + d D_t + f X_t \tag{2}$$

In this GARCH specification, X_t can be interpreted as the most recent volatility surprise observed in the foreign markets.

The results of estimating this model for both the full sample period and the precrash subperiod are shown in Table 3. For the full sample period, the effect of a volatility surprise in the most recent foreign market to trade on the return volatility in the domestic market is statistically significant for all three stock exchanges. More precisely, the parameter estimate on the foreign volatility surprise is positive and statistically significant for all three markets, and the LR statistics for inclusion of this spillover effect variable are 83.68 for the Nikkei, 51.89 for the FTSE, and 18.68 for the S&P, which are all significant at the 1 percent level. On the other hand, when the post-October 1987 period is removed from the sample, the effect becomes less pervasive, as seen in Panel B. Only in one of the three markets is a statistically significant volatility spillover effect observed, namely, from the United States to Japan.[18]

Next, we expand the exogenous variables in the conditional variance equation by including the squared residuals from the GARCH-M model of the open-to-close returns for

[14] We also estimated more complicated GARCH-M specifications that consistently indicated that the simpler specification was more strongly supported by the data.

[15] The higher kurtosis in London may be in part a manifestation of the smaller number of stocks in this index which a more diversified index would lessen.

[16] We explored a volatility spillover model that included lagged high–low spread squared in the conditional variance. This alternative formulation fit the data rather poorly.

[17] We also used the most recent h_t from the previously open foreign market as X_t. The results were essentially unchanged.

[18] We also converted the Japanese stock returns into U.S. dollars using the open (9:00 A.M.) and close (3:00 P.M.) spot interbank exchange rate quotations (yen/dollar), S_o and S_c from the Tokyo foreign exchange market:

$$\text{Return in dollars} = (S_o/S_c)_1\,(1 + \text{return in yen}) - 1$$

TABLE 2 | Estimation of a GARCH Model Using Open-to-Close Stock Returns

$$R_t = \alpha + \beta h_t + \delta D_t + \gamma \epsilon_{t-1} + \epsilon_t$$
$$h_t = a + bh_{t-1} + \alpha^2_{t-1} + dD_t$$

where R_t = open-to-close return, h_t = conditional variance of R_t, and D_t = weekend dummy variable that equals 1 on a day following a weekend or holiday or 0 otherwise.

Panel A: Sample period: April 1, 1985–March 31, 1988

	Japan stock market Nikkei 225 Stock Index		U.K. stock market FTSE 100 Stock Index		U.S. stock market S&P 500 Stock Index	
Number of obs.	837		760		760	
Log-likelihood	−969.32		−874.84		−1072.07	
	Coeff.	***t*-stat.**	**Coeff.**	***t*-stat.**	**Coeff.**	***t*-stat.**
α	.0623	2.01	.1175	2.60	.1214	2.46
β	.0377	0.95	−.1465	−1.89	.0124	0.28
γ	.1227	2.57	−.0368	−0.87	.0544	1.08
δ	−.0580	−1.50	−.1299	−2.10	−.0327	−0.47
a	.1237	5.98	.0316	2.10	.0091	0.47
b	.2720	6.77	.8551	42.88	.7937	45.72
c	.8403	16.41	.0847	4.95	.2056	16.77
d	.0284	0.86	−.0059	−0.13	.1519	2.18
LR(6) for H_0: $\beta = \gamma = \delta = b = c = d = 0$[1]	562.97		180.26		480.01	
Coefficient of skewness for normalized residuals	−0.87		−2.05		−0.91	
Coefficient of kurtosis for normalized residuals	7.66		22.78		7.74	
Ljung-Box(12) for normalized residuals[2]	8.99		14.68		5.41	
Ljung-Box(12) for normalized squared residuals[2]	4.13		5.09		3.78	

both foreign markets that complete their trading cycles while the domestic market is closed. This yields the following modification of the model:

$$R_t = \alpha + \beta h_t + \delta D_t + \gamma \epsilon_{t-1} + \epsilon_t$$
$$h_t = a + bh_{t-1} + c\epsilon^2_{t-1} + dD_t + f_1 X_{1t} + f_2 X_{2t} \tag{3}$$

This enables us to examine separate volatility spillover effects from both foreign markets. If the spillover effect reflects the influence of a common economic effect on the volatility of all three stock market indices, introducing the second foreign market is unlikely

---

Although the Japanese foreign currency market is closed on Saturdays, the Tokyo Stock Exchange is open on the first and fourth Saturday of the month for two hours. In order to align Japanese returns consistently with the U.S. returns, Saturday trading is ignored. This conversion allows us to assess whether our findings are mitigated or exacerbated by the conversion into a single currency. We reestimated models (1) and (2) for the dollar-denominated Nikkei index. The outcomes were very similar to the local-currency case, demonstrating the robustness of our results. (The exchange rate data were provided by Nihon Keizai Shimbun Sha.)

TABLE 2 | *(Continued)*

Panel B: Sample period: April 1, 1985–September 30, 1987						
	Japan stock market Nikei 225 Stock Index		U.K. stock market FTSE 100 Stock Index		U.S. stock market S&P 500 Stock Index	
Number of obs.	702		632		633	
Log-likelihood	−733.18		−618.05		−772.44	
	Coeff.	***t*-stat.**	**Coeff.**	***t*-stat.**	**Coeff.**	***t*-stat.**
α	−.0447	−1.01	.2805	2.35	.1464	1.53
β	.2208	2.42	−.5596	−1.89	−.0483	−0.32
γ	.1228	2.80	−.0335	−0.76	.0685	1.62
δ	−.1247	−2.31	−.1513	−2.36	−.0376	−0.50
a	.0268	3.10	.0295	1.33	−.0180	−1.14
b	.7782	34.55	.8789	16.64	.9192	38.95
c	.1825	7.35	.0610	2.37	.0552	3.92
d	.0031	0.08	−.0223	−0.39	.1671	2.63
LR(6) for H_0: $\beta = \gamma = \delta = b = c = d = 0$[1]	190.80		20.97		38.79	
Coefficient of skewness for normalized residuals	−0.66		−0.36		−0.41	
Coefficient of kurtosis for normalized residuals	5.42		3.70		5.03	
Ljung-Box(12) for normalized residuals[2]	8.39		19.11		8.39	
Ljung-Box(12) for normalized squared residuals[2]	13.68		20.10		5.55	

[1] $\chi^2(6)$ critical values: 10.64 (10%), 12.59 (5%), 16.81 (1%).

[2] $\chi^2(12)$ critical values: 18.55 (10%), 21.03 (5%), 26.22 (1%).

to add much incremental explanatory power. Table 4 shows estimates for the two sample periods. For the full sample period, all three markets are affected by the volatility surprises of the two previously open foreign markets, with the exception that Tokyo has no significant influence on New York. We also find that the New York market's spillover effect is larger than that of the other foreign market in its effect on either London or Tokyo stock market volatility. Overall, the inclusion of a second foreign market does not appear to diminish the volatility spillover effect of the first foreign market and for the most part both foreign markets appear to have equally important spillover effects. These observed relations appear unlikely to be the result of a common economic effect manifesting itself in all three markets.

The results for the precrash subperiod are consistent with the single foreign market spillover case and show a distinctive asymmetry, that is, there is no significant volatility spillover to the London and New York markets, but there is an equally significant spillover effect from both London and New York to the Tokyo stock market. While the inclusion of the post-October 1987 period does increase the measured spillover effect, the main finding is clear: the Japanese market is most sensitive to volatility spillover effects from foreign markets, while the other two major stock exchanges are at most moderately sensitive, if at all, to volatility spillovers from foreign stock markets.

TABLE 3 | Volatility Spillovers Estimated from a GARCH Model Using Open-to-Close Stock Returns of the Domestic Market and One Foreign Market

$$R_t = \alpha + \beta h_t + \delta D_t + \gamma \epsilon_{t-1} + \epsilon_t$$

$$h_t = a + b h_{t-1} + c \epsilon_{t-1}^2 + d D_t + f X_t$$

where R_t = the domestic open-to-close return, h_t = conditional variance of R_t, D_t = weekend/holiday dummy variable which equals 1 on a day following a weekend or holiday and 0 otherwise, and X_t = most recent squared residual derived from an MA(1)–GARCH(1,1)-M model applied to the open-to-close return of the previously open foreign market.

Panel A: Sample period: April 1, 1985–March 31, 1988

	From U.S. to Japan		From Japan to U.K.		From U.K. to U.S.	
Number of obs.	837		760		760	
Log-likelihood	−927.48		−848.89		−1062.73	
	Coeff.	***t*-stat.**	**Coeff.**	***t*-stat.**	**Coeff.**	***t*-stat.**
α	.0355	0.97	.0774	1.76	.1223	2.35
β	.0634	1.27	−.0831	−1.11	−.0093	−0.19
γ	.1357	3.17	−.0330	−0.82	.0603	1.32
δ	−.1216	−2.40	−.1203	−1.97	−.0330	−0.43
a	.0389	3.57	.0376	2.13	.0058	0.30
b	.6104	15.24	.8390	30.00	.7790	34.40
c	.2685	6.69	.0447	2.03	.1349	5.81
d	.0442	1.27	−.0120	−0.20	.1135	1.89
f	.0464	5.24	.0312	5.36	.1459	6.54
LR(1) for H_0: $f = 0$[1]	83.68		51.89		18.68	
LR(7) for H_0: $\beta = \gamma = \delta = b = c = d = f = 0$[2]	646.66		232.15		498.69	
Coefficient of skewness for normalized residuals	−0.55		−1.41		−0.82	
Coefficient of kurtosis for normalized residuals	5.65		13.90		6.62	
Ljung-Box(12) for normalized residuals[3]	9.01		15.75		6.17	
Ljung-Box(12) for normalized squared residuals[3]	6.51		4.98		4.69	

This asymmetry in influences across national stock markets is consistent with evidence uncovered in a recent study by Eun and Shim (1989). They employ a vector autoregression model to investigate the international transmission mechanism of stock market movements across nine major stock markets. Eun and Shim report that "innovations in the United States are rapidly transmitted to other markets in a clearly recognizable fashion, whereas no single foreign market can significantly explain the U.S. market movements." The underlying economic explanation for this result is far from resolved.[19]

[19] We also explored the effect of estimating this model using close-to-close returns. The qualitative results especially with regard to spillover effects turned out to be very similar.

TABLE 3 | *(Continued)*

Panel B: Sample period: April 1, 1985–September 30, 1987						
	From U.S. to Japan		**From Japan to U.K.**		**From U.K. to U.S.**	
Number of obs.	702		632		633	
Log-likelihood	−728.40		−616.99		−772.43	
	Coeff.	***t*-stat.**	**Coeff.**	***t*-stat.**	**Coeff.**	***t*-stat.**
α	−.0383	−0.85	.2757	2.23	.1474	1.56
β	.2145	2.31	−.5573	−1.80	−.0457	−0.31
γ	.1208	2.63	−.0296	−0.68	.0657	1.58
δ	−.1177	−2.21	−.1397	−2.14	−.0413	−0.55
a	.0174	2.28	.0248	1.12	−.0202	−1.26
b	.7271	25.84	.8754	17.06	.9197	39.53
c	.1988	6.87	.0558	2.21	.0527	3.85
d	.0193	0.57	.0015	0.02	.1576	2.63
f	.0347	3.90	.0043	0.99	.0123	0.82
LR(1) for H_0: $f = 0$[1]	9.54		2.12		0.03	
LR(7) for H_0: $\beta = \gamma = \delta = b = c = d = f = 0$[2]	200.34		23.09		38.82	
Coefficient of skewness for normalized residuals	−0.69		−0.35		−0.43	
Coefficient of kurtosis for normalized residuals	5.94		3.58		5.10	
Ljung-Box(12) for normalized residuals[3]	7.77		19.38		8.31	
Ljung-Box(12) for normalized squared residuals[3]	10.28		17.79		5.18	

[1] $\chi^2(1)$ critical values: 2.71 (10%), 3.84 (5%), 6.64 (1%).

[2] $\chi^1(7)$ critical values: 12.02 (10%), 14.07 (5%), 18.48 (1%).

[3] $\chi^1(12)$ critical values: 18.55 (10%), 21.03 (5%), 26.22 (1%).

5. Spillover Effects on the Conditional Means of Stock Returns

We next consider the possibility of a spillover effect in the stock returns of one market on the conditional *mean* as well as conditional variance in the next market to trade, again using open-to-close returns data. We modify the specification in model (2) by expanding the definition of the conditional mean to include the current open-to-close return of the most recent foreign market to trade, Y, and define the exogenous variable X in the conditional variance equation to be the most recent squared residual from model (1) for the open-to-close return of the same foreign market. The form of the model is

$$R_t = \alpha + \beta h_t + \delta D_t + \phi Y_t + \gamma \epsilon_{t-1} + \epsilon_t$$
$$h_t = a + bh_{t-1} + c\epsilon_{t-1}^2 + dD_t + fX_t \quad (4)$$

The results of this estimation for the full sample period are shown in Table 5, Panel A. In all three markets, the parameter estimates did not change significantly from those

TABLE 4 | Volatility Spillovers Estimated from a GARCH Model Using Open-to-Close Stock Returns of the Domestic Market and Two Foreign Markets

$$R_t = \alpha + \beta h_t + \delta D_t + \gamma \epsilon_{t-1} + \epsilon_t$$
$$h_t = a + bh_{t-1} + c\epsilon_{t-1}^2 + dD_t + f_t X_{1t} + f_2 X_{2t}$$

where R_t = the domestic open-to-close return, h_t = conditional variance of R_t, D_t, = weekend/holiday dummy variable that equals 1 on a day following a weekend or holiday and 0 otherwise, and X_{it} = squared residuals derived from an MA(1)–GARCH(1,1)-M model applied to the open-to-close, return of the two foreign markets.

Panel A: Sample period: April 1, 1985–March 31, 1988

	From U.S. (f_1) & U.K. (f_2) to Japan		From Japan (f_1) & U.S. (f_2) to U.K.		From U.K. (f_1) & Japan (f_2) to U.S.	
Number of obs.	837		760		760	
Log-likelihood	−923.28		−820.37		−1062.47	
	Coeff.	***t*-stat.**	**Coeff.**	***t*-stat.**	**Coeff.**	***t*-stat.**
α	.0429	1.29	.0731	1.69	.1310	2.54
β	.0620	1.35	−.0728	−0.99	−.0226	−0.47
γ	.1191	2.70	−.0276	−0.69	.0617	1.34
δ	−.1080	−2.14	−.1186	−1.99	−.0291	−0.37
a	.0262	1.90	.0422	2.23	.0020	0.10
b	.5211	11.71	.8273	22.16	.7776	29.82
c	.3055	6.27	.0389	1.52	.1328	5.70
d	.0258	0.84	−.0317	−0.47	.1370	2.05
f_1	.0519	4.76	.0185	2.51	.1418	6.53
f_2	.0995	3.59	.0159	8.88	.0078	0.76
LR(1) for H_0: $f_2 = 0$[1]	8.40		57.03		0.53	
LR(2) for H_0: $f_1 = f_2 = 0$[2]	92.08		103.93		19.21	
LR(8) for H_0: $\beta = \gamma = \delta = b = c = d = f_1 = f_2 = 0$[3]	655.05		289.19		499.22	
Coefficient of skewness for normalized residuals	−0.54		−0.70		−0.82	
Coefficient of kurtosis for normalized residuals	5.85		6.00		6.59	
Ljung-Box(12) for normalized residuals[4]	8.50		16.78		6.23	
Ljung-Box(12) for normalized squared residuals[4]	6.40		8.48		5.17	

obtained for model (4). However, statistically significant mean spillover effects, associated with Y_t, are observed in both the New York and Tokyo markets. In other words, the conditional mean return exhibits a positive spillover effect from the prior market; a high return in the New York (London) market is followed by a high return in the Tokyo (New York) market, but such a relation is not found between Tokyo and London. This contrasts with the conditional variance that exhibits a spillover effect in all three markets for the entire sample period. For the New York market, where the mean spillover effect is largest and most

TABLE 4 | *(Continued)*

Panel B: Sample period: April 1, 1985–September 30, 1987						
	From U.S. (f_1) & U.K (f_2) to Japan		From Japan (f_1) & U.S. (f_2) to U.K.		From U.K. (f_1) & Japan (f_2) to U.S.	
Number of obs.	702		632		633	
Log-likelihood	−726.73		−616.53		−771.86	
	Coeff.	***t*-stat.**	**Coeff.**	***t*-stat.**	**Coeff.**	***t*-stat.**
α	−.0260	−0.62	.2489	2.29	.1363	1.39
β	.1918	2.12	−.4926	−1.79	−.0368	−0.24
γ	.1052	2.20	−.0299	−0.68	.0693	1.64
δ	−.1015	−1.80	−.1408	−2.21	−.0409	−0.53
a	.0017	0.17	.0221	0.98	−.0220	−1.37
b	.6701	20.18	.8615	15.17	.9297	40.15
c	.2228	6.15	.0607	2.08	.0484	3.57
d	.0355	1.04	−.0002	−0.003	.1575	2.45
f_1	.0353	3.82	.0027	0.58	.0127	0.88
f_2	.0743	3.36	.0111	1.72	−.0027	−0.64
LR(1) for H_0: $f_1 = 0$[1]	3.35		0.94		1.13	
LR(2) for H_0: $f_1 = f_2 = 0$[2]	12.89		3.06		1.15	
LR(8) for H_0: $\beta = \gamma = \delta = b = c = d = f_1 = f_2 = 0$[3]	203.69		24.03		39.95	
Coefficient of skewness for normalized residuals	−0.72		−0.36		−0.43	
Coefficient of kurtosis for normalized residuals	6.35		3.76		5.09	
Ljung-Box(12) for normalized residuals[4]	7.24		19.63		8.45	
Ljung-Box(12) for normalized squared residuals[4]	6.72		19.21		5.11	

[1] $\chi^2(1)$ critical values: 2.71 (10%), 3.84 (5%), 6.64 (1%).

[2] $\chi^2(2)$ critical values: 4.61 (10%), 5.99 (5%), 9.21 (1%).

[3] $\chi^2(8)$ critical values: 13.36 (10%), 15.51 (5%), 20.09 (1%).

[4] $\chi^2(12)$ critical values: 18.55 (10%), 21.03 (5%), 26.22 (1%).

significant, the likely explanation is the one-hour overlap in trading with London. For the Tokyo market, the positive mean spillover effect is more difficult to explain, though it may reflect the use of stale quotes for stocks in the Nikkei index experiencing a delayed opening of trading.

Turning to the pre-stock crash estimates shown in Panel B of Table 5, we find some interesting differences in spillover effects for the open-to-close returns. The spillover in conditional mean in this subperiod is diminished in all three markets and becomes marginally insignificant for the Tokyo market. Since over this subperiod the Nikkei open was recorded 15 minutes after the start of trading, the effects of stale quotes on the opening price and the open-to-close return are minimized. The use of these more accurate opening

TABLE 5 | Mean and Volatility Spillovers Estimated from a GARCH Model Using Open-to-Close Returns

$$R_t = \alpha + \beta h_t + \delta D_t + \phi Y_t + \gamma \epsilon_{t-1} + \epsilon_t$$
$$h_t = a + b h_{t-1} + c\epsilon_{t-1}^2 + dD_t + fX_t$$

where R_t = the domestic open-to-close return, h_t = conditional variance of R_t, D_t = weekend/holiday dummy variable that equals 1 on a day following a weekend or holiday and 0 otherwise, X_t = most recent squared residual derived from an MA(1)–GARCH(1,1)-M model applied to the open-to-close return of the previously open foreign market, and Y_t = open-to-close return of the previously open foreign market.

Panel A: Sample period: April 1, 1985–March 31, 1988

	From U.S. to Japan		From Japan to U.K.		From U.K. to U.S.	
Number of obs.	837		760		760	
Log-likelihood	−921.52		−847.68		−1051.83	
	Coeff.	***t*-stat.**	**Coeff.**	***t*-stat.**	**Coeff.**	***t*-stat.**
α	.0272	0.67	.0753	1.71	.1008	1.71
β	.0595	1.09	−.0812	−1.10	−.0128	−0.24
γ	.1430	3.22	−.0341	−0.84	.0784	1.57
δ	−.1530	−2.58	−.1162	−1.86	−.0149	−0.17
ϕ	.1007	3.42	.0156	0.47	.2559	4.53
a	.0475	3.11	.0378	2.11	−.0007	−0.03
b	.5719	11.29	.8380	28.76	.7886	32.07
c	.2778	5.90	.0441	1.99	.1307	5.21
d	.1250	2.89	−.0110	−0.18	.1725	2.26
f	.0498	4.71	.0323	5.33	.1481	5.44
LR(1)for H_0: $\phi = 0$[1]	11.92		2.42		21.80	
Coefficient of skewness for normalized residuals	−0.46		−1.39		−0.81	
Coefficient of kurtosis for normalized residuals	5.45		13.49		6.58	
Ljung-Box(12) for normalized residuals[2]	6.99		16.02		8.76	
Ljung-Box(12) for normalized squared residuals[2]	7.68		5.15		4.22	

prices for the Nikkei should also lower the S&P spillover into the Nikkei conditional mean, which is consistent with the observed marginally insignificant mean spillover effect. More interesting, the spillover in conditional variances is lowered in all three markets, though it remains relatively large and significant for Tokyo.

The spillover effects observed in New York for open-to-close returns are likely to be influenced by the fact that the London market does not close until after the open of trading in New York. One approach to eliminating the effects of this overlapping trading across markets and the effects of stale quotes being used at the S&P's open is to replace open-to-close returns with noon-to-close returns for the S&P index. By reestimating model (4) for the New York market using noon-to-close returns, we can then compare these results to those in Table 5. This comparison allows us to assess the influence on conditional means and variances in the New York market. The basic model (1) is also reestimated to determine

TABLE 5 | *(Continued)*

Panel B: Sample period: April 1, 1985–September 30, 1987						
	From U.S. to Japan		**From Japan to U.K.**		**From U.K. to U.S.**	
Number of obs.	702		632		633	
Log-likelihood	−725.17		−616.59		−768.95	
	Coeff.	***t*-stat.**	**Coeff.**	***t*-stat.**	**Coeff.**	***t*-stat.**
α	−.0746	−1.42	.1686	1.60	.1220	1.11
β	.2570	2.49	−.3058	−1.24	−.0335	−0.20
γ	.1256	2.69	−.0184	−0.40	.0886	1.99
δ	−.1505	−2.38	−.1148	−1.71	−.0119	−0.15
ϕ	.0632	1.98	.0114	0.33	.1038	2.05
a	.0166	.172	.0265	1.13	−.0148	−0.78
b	.7589	23.90	.8730	17.58	.9240	35.00
c	.1667	6.04	.0473	1.91	.0499	3.30
d	.0598	1.31	−.0091	−0.13	.1386	2.07
f	.0275	3.17	.0194	2.09	.0127	0.77
LR(1) for H_0: $\phi = 0$[1]	6.46		0.81		6.95	
Coefficient of skewness for normalized residuals	−0.63		−0.31		−0.42	
Coefficient of kurtosis for normalized residuals	5.46		3.21		5.20	
Ljung-Box(12) for normalized residuals[2]	7.30		19.39		9.33	
Ljung-Box(12) for normalized squared residuals[2]	12.80		13.71		5.65	

[1] $\chi^2(1)$ critical values: 2.71 (10%), 3.84 (5%), 6.64 (1%).

[2] $\chi^2(12)$ critical values: 18.55 (10%), 21.03 (5%), 26.22 (1%).

whether or not the GARCH-M model is an appropriate specification for the S&P noon-to-close return series.

Table 6 shows the results of these two estimations for the full period and the precrash subperiod. For the basic MA(1)–GARCH(1, 1)-M model defined by (1), we find that noon-to-close returns of the S&P index are well characterized by the GARCH model for both periods. This result supports our reestimation of the spillover effects using model (4) and these same noon-to-close returns. We find that the spillover effect in conditional mean is no longer significant, while the spillover effect in conditional variance is strengthened in both the full period and subperiod cases. The above evidence supports our earlier conclusions that significant spillovers in conditional variances occur across all three markets.

6. Spillover Effects in Close-to-Open Stock Returns

Prior studies of spillover effects have used close-to-close returns to estimate these effects. This tends to confuse several alternative causes of correlation in return processes across these markets since the time interval represented by these returns overlap[s]. With a significant level of international financial integration, an overlap in the stock return time intervals across markets should induce positive correlation in the measured returns

TABLE 6 | Mean and Volatility Spillovers Estimated from a GARCH Model Using Noon-to-Close S&P Returns

Base model:
$R_t = \alpha + \beta h_t + \delta D_t + \gamma \epsilon_{t-1} + \epsilon_t$
$h_t = a + bh_{t-1} + c\epsilon_{t-1}^2 + dD_t$

Spillover model from U.K. to U.S.:
$R_t = \alpha + \beta h_t + \delta D_t + \phi Y_t + \gamma \epsilon_{t-1} + \epsilon_t$
$h_t = a + bh_{t-1} + c\epsilon_{t-1}^2 + dD_t + fX_t$

where R_t = S&P noon-to-close return, h_t = conditional variance of R_t, D_t = weekend/holiday dummy variable that equals 1 on a day following a weekend or holiday and 0 otherwise, X_t = most recent squared residual derived from an MA(1)–GARCH(1,1)-M model applied to the FTSE open-to-close returns and Y_t = most recent FTSE open-to-close return.

Panel A: Sample period: April 1, 1985–March 31, 1988

	Base model			**Spillover model from U.K. to U.S.**	
Number of obs.	760			760	
Log-likelihood	−813.48			−796.36	
	Coeff.	***t*-stat.**		**Coeff.**	***t*-stat.**
α	.0594	1.44	α	.0706	2.21
β	.0109	0.13	β	−.0126	−0.21
γ	−.0955	−2.06	γ	−.1057	−2.19
δ	.0820	1.46	δ	.0780	1.27
a	.0635	3.26	ϕ	.0475	1.28
b	.6218	15.47	a	.0456	2.11
c	.2635	18.63	b	.4962	10.64
d	.0814	1.83	c	.3188	7.55
			d	.1289	2.62
			f	.1471	5.88
LR(6) for H_0 $\beta = \gamma = \delta = b = c = d = 0$[1]	435.42		LR(2) for H_0 $\phi = f = 0$[2]	34.25	
Coefficient of skewness for normalized residuals	−1.11			−0.81	
Coefficient of kurtosis for normalized residuals	8.08			5.85	
Ljung-Box(12) for normalized residuals[3]	6.19			5.56	
Ljung-Box(12) for normalized squared residuals[3]	7.67			10.66	

and possibly in return volatility. The extent to which previously documented positive correlations in returns across stock markets are due to overlapping time intervals can be evaluated by studying the spillover effects of concurrent open-to-close returns in the foreign market on close-to-open returns in the domestic market. This essentially accounts for the impact of "overnight" foreign trading on the opening price in the domestic market. The subsequent spillover effects in the domestic market after the opening of trading are captured in the open-to-close returns documented in the prior sections of this article. In estimating the spillover effects in both the conditional mean and conditional variance of the close-to-open returns in the domestic market, we use model (4) where the exogenous variables Y and X are defined as the most recent

TABLE 6 | *(Continued)*

Panel B: Sample period: April 1, 1985–September 30, 1987

	Base model			**Spillover model from U.K. to U.S.**	
Number of obs.	633			633	
Log-likelihood	−572.45			−570.70	
	Coeff.	***t*-stat.**		**Coeff.**	***t*-stat.**
α	.1168	1.87	α	.0957	1.52
β	−.1552	−0.87	β	−.0982	−0.57
γ	−.0727	−1.68	γ	−.0775	−1.66
δ	.1134	1.93	δ	.1029	1.61
a	.0103	1.00	ϕ	.0022	0.06
b	.8353	21.94	a	.0041	0.32
c	.0823	4.36	b	.8063	15.58
d	.0921	3.22	c	.0914	3.92
			d	.1287	3.42
			f	.0229	1.38
LR(6) for H_0 $\beta = \gamma = \delta = b = c = d = 0$[1]	48.67		LR(2) for H_0 $\phi = f = 0$[2]	3.50	
Coefficient of skewness for normalized residuals	−0.69			−0.68	
Coefficient of kurtosis for normalized residuals	5.61			5.51	
Ljung-Box(12) for normalized residuals[3]	9.86			9.51	
Ljung-Box(12) for normalized squared residuals[3]	4.84			4.62	

[1] $\chi^2(6)$ critical values: 10.64 (10%), 12.59 (5%), 16.81 (1%).

[2] $\chi^2(2)$ critical values: 4.61 (10%), 5.99 (5%), 9.21 (1%).

[3] $\chi^2(12)$ critical values: 18.55 (10%), 21.03 (5%), 26.22 (1%).

open-to-close return and its squared residual using model (1) in the two foreign markets that trade in this time interval.

The results of estimating the spillover effects on the close-to-open returns of the domestic market are shown in Table 7, Panel A for the April 1985–March 1988 period. For all three stock markets, we find clear evidence that the most recent open-to-close returns of the two foreign markets consistently have positive influences on the opening price in the next market to trade with at least one of these two foreign markets exhibiting statistical significance. We also find that, for at least one of the two foreign markets, the residual from the GARCH model in that market has a significant positive spillover effect on the conditional volatility of the close-to-open return in the next market to open trading. Comparing these results with those for spillover effects measured by the open-to-close returns in Table 5, Panel A, we find very similar spillover patterns with Tokyo's market return having little influence on the London opening price. Also, the influence of London on the opening price in New York is likely to be attenuated by the fact that the close in London occurs after the open in New York as a result of the overlap in trading periods. Further, the magnitude

TABLE 7 | Mean and Volatility Spillovers Estimated from a GARCH Model Using Close-to-Open Stock Returns of the Domestic Market and Open-to-Close Stock Returns of Two Foreign Markets

$$R_t = \text{ga} + \beta h_1 + \delta D_t + \phi_1 Y_{1t} + \phi_2 Y_{2t} + \gamma \epsilon_{t-1} + \epsilon_t$$
$$h_t = bh_{t-1} + c\epsilon_{t-1}^2 + dD_t + f_t X_{1t} + f_2 X_{2t}$$

where R_t = the domestic close-to-open return, h_t = conditional variance of R_t, D_t = weekend/holiday dummy variable that equals 1 on a day following a weekend or holiday and 0 otherwise, Y_{it} = open-to-close returns in the two foreign markets, and X_{it} = squared residuals derived from an MA(1)–GARCH(1,1)-M model applied to the open-to-close returns of the two foreign markets.

Panel A: Sample period: April 1, 1985–March 31, 1988

	From U.S. (ϕ_1, f_1) & U.K. (ϕ_2, f_2) to Japan		**From Japan (ϕ_1, f_1) & U.S. (ϕ_2, f_2) to U.K.**		**From U.K. (ϕ_1, f_1) & Japan (ϕ_2, f_2) to U.S.**	
Number of obs.	837		760		760	
Log-likelihood	454.56		−597.06		648.71	
	Coeff.	***t*-stat.**	**Coeff.**	***t*-stat.**	**Coeff.**	***t*-stat.**
α	.0132	3.41	.0297	1.29	.0043	2.03
β	.8021	4.71	−.0233	−0.41	−.1706	−1.94
γ	.1423	3.69	−.1666	−4.14	−.1064	−2.83
δ	.0084	1.19	.0639	1.42	−.0468	−8.63
ϕ_1	.0181	7.69	.0304	1.10	.0084	2.57
ϕ_2	.0017	0.47	.3200	13.92	.0027	1.10
a	.0001	0.51	.0126	1.96	.0002	1.45
b	.8827	110.44	.8529	47.52	.3182	9.58
c	.1284	9.65	.0253	1.72	1.1154	9.67
d	−.0002	−0.45	−.0358	−1.25	.0115	21.99
f_1	.00004	2.46	.0123	3.02	.0012	13.42
f_2	−.0001	−1.20	.0268	5.51	−.0002	−7.20
LR(10) for H_0: $\beta = \gamma = \delta = \phi_1 = \phi_1 = b = c = d = f_1 = f_2 = 0$[1]	780.38		675.06		597.59	
Coefficient of skewness for normalized residuals	0.21		−0.41		−0.93	
Coefficient of kurtosis for normalized residuals	5.23		4.57		28.38	
Ljung-Box(12) for normalized residuals[2]	15.00		11.24		9.95	
Ljung-Box(12) for normalized squared residuals[2]	26.95		4.66		1.33	

of the volatility spillover effect is much stronger in the conditional variance of the open-to-close returns.

The results of restricting the observations to the pre-October 1987 period are shown in Panel B of Table 7. In comparing these estimated spillover effects in the conditional mean and conditional variance of the close-to-open return with those of Panel A, we generally find similar results. However, one notable difference is observed for the spillovers in the conditional mean for the New York market; specifically, Japan has much greater influence

TABLE 7 | *(Continued)*

Panel B: Sample period: April 1, 1985–September 30, 1987						
	From U.S. (ϕ_1, f_1) & U.K. (ϕ_2, f_2) to Japan		From Japan (ϕ_1, f_1) & U.S. (ϕ_2, f_2) to U.K.		From U.K. (ϕ_1, f_1) & Japan (ϕ_2, f_2) to U.S.	
Number of obs.	702		632		633	
Log-likelihood	305.16		−412.85		589.73	
	Coeff.	***t*-stat.**	**Coeff.**	***t*-stat.**	**Coeff.**	***t*-stat.**
α	.0175	4.05	−.0400	−0.86	.0017	1.24
β	.7084	4.15	.2827	1.46	−.1597	−1.92
γ	.1477	3.33	−.1176	−2.58	−.1340	−3.26
δ	.0142	1.89	.1198	2.48	−.0285	−4.89
ϕ_1	.0236	8.00	.0206	0.72	.0012	0.35
ϕ_2	.0022	0.61	.3051	12.51	.0024	1.71
a	.0002	1.23	.0143	2.20	−.0000	−0.07
b	.8659	93.78	.8636	23.22	.3478	9.97
c	.1538	9.22	.0424	2.13	1.1279	8.94
d	.0000	0.00	−.0386	−1.54	.0061	19.64
f_1	−.0000	−0.86	.0106	2.24	.0015	18.45
f_2	−.0002	−2.88	.0155	2.95	−.0003	−5.37
LR(10) for H_0: $\beta = \gamma = \delta = \phi_1 = \phi_2 = b = c = d = f_1 = f_2 = 0$[1]	593.08		237.21		627.23	
Coefficient of skewness for normalized residuals	0.21		−0.24		0.45	
Coefficient of kurtosis for normalized residuals	5.59		4.17		27.53	
Ljung-Box(12) for normalized residuals[2]	11.44		15.76		10.37	
Ljung-Box(12) for normalized squared residuals[2]	22.30		10.04		1.50	

[1] $\chi^2(10)$ critical values: 15.99 (10%), 18.31 (5%), 23.21 (5%).

[2] $\chi^2(12)$ critical values: 18.55 (10%), 21.03 (5%), 26.22 (1%).

than does London in the precrash period. Over this subperiod the Nikkei open was recorded 15 minutes after the start of trading; thus, the effects of using stale quotes on the open price and the close-to-open return of the Nikkei stock index are minimized. This should strengthen the spillover in conditional mean from Tokyo to London. It should also strengthen the spillover in conditional mean from New York to Tokyo, which may explain why this spillover effect is not noticeably weakened when estimated over the shorter pre-crash subperiod. With respect to spillovers in the conditional variance, we find that the spillovers from London and Tokyo to New York are significantly strengthened while the spillover from New York to Tokyo becomes small and statistically insignificant.

In comparing the parameter estimates for the weekend/holiday dummy variables in the conditional mean and variance equations for the open-to-close returns and the close-to-open returns, we uncover some interesting patterns. For the open-to-close returns, there are consistently significant negative parameter estimates for the weekend/holiday dummy variable in the conditional mean of the Japanese and U.K. markets but not for the U.S. market. On the other hand, there is a significant positive parameter estimate in the conditional variance of the U.S. market but not for the Japanese and U.K. markets. In contrast, when we estimate the model with close-to-open returns, we observe a highly significant negative parameter estimate for the conditional mean and a significant positive parameter estimate for the conditional variance in the U.S. market and insignificant parameter estimates for the other two markets.[20] This concentration of the negative weekend effect on the opening price in the United States is consistent with the Smirlock and Starks (1986) finding that in the post-1974 period the negative weekend effect is concentrated near the opening for the U.S. market.

7. Conclusions

This study documents the existence of price change and price volatility effects from one international stock market to the next. We find daily stock returns measured from close-to-open and open-to-close to be approximated by a GARCH(1,1)-M model. For the conditional variance, we find spillover effects from the U.S. and the U.K. stock markets to the Japanese market. This effect shows an intriguing asymmetry: while the volatility spillover effect on the Japanese market is significant, the spillover effects on the other two markets are much weaker. This result is not affected by whether returns are converted into a single currency.

Unexpected changes in foreign market indices are associated with significant spillover effects on the conditional mean of the domestic market for both open-to-close and close-to-open returns. While the effect on the open-to-close returns suggests some informational inefficiencies in these markets, further examination of this evidence indicates that overlapping trading between London and New York and the inclusion of stale quotes in the calculation of the Nikkei and S&P opening prices are more likely explanations. For the close-to-open returns, this effect on the conditional mean is consistent with international financial integration, while the magnitude of volatility spillover is generally much less in this case.

References

Barclay, M. J., R. H. Litzenberger, and J. B. Warner, 1990, "Private Information, Trading Volume, and Stock-Return Variances," *Review of Financial Studies,* 3, 233–253.

Bollerslev, T., 1986, "Generalized Autoregressive Conditional Heteroskedasticity," *Journal of Econometrics,* 31, 307–327.

Bollerslev, T., 1987, "A Conditionally Heteroskedastic Time Series Model for Speculative Prices and Rates of Return," *Review of Economics and Statistics,* 69, 542–547.

Campbell, J., and Y. Hamao, 1989, "Predictable Stock Returns in the United States and Japan: A Study of Long-Term Capital Market Integration," working paper, National Bureau of Economic Research.

Cho, C., C. Eun, and L. Senbet, 1986, "International Arbitrage Pricing Theory: An Empirical Investigation," *Journal of Finance,* 41, 313–329.

[20] It is noteworthy that our spillover estimates are very insensitive to the inclusion or exclusion of weekend/holiday dummy variables in the model specification.

Cohen, K., G. Hawawini, S. Maier, R. Schwartz, and D. Whitcomb, 1980, "Implications of Microstructure Theory for Empirical Research on Stock Price Behavior," *Journal of Finance,* 35, 249–257.

Cohen, K., S. Maier, R. Schwartz, and D. Whitcomb, 1986, *The Microstructure of Security Markets,* Prentice-Hall, Englewood Cliffs, N.J.

Engle, R. F., 1982, "Autoregressive Conditional Heteroskedasticity with Estimates of the Variance of United Kingdom Inflation," *Econometrica,* 50, 987–1007.

Engle, R. F., T. Ito, and W-L. Lin, 1990, "Meteor Showers or Heat Waves?: Heteroskedastic Intra-Daily Volatility in the Foreign Exchange Market," forthcoming in *Econometrica.*

Engle, R., D. Lilien, and R. Robins, 1987, "Estimating Time Varying Risk Premia in the Term Structure: the ARCH-M Model," *Econometrica,* 55, 391–407.

Errunza, V., and E. Losq, 1985, "International Asset Pricing under Mild Segmentation: Theory and Test," *Journal of Finance,* 40, 105–124.

Eun, C., and S. Shim, 1989, "International Transmission of Stock Market Movements," *Journal of Financial and Quantitative Analysis,* 24, 241–256.

Fama, E., 1965, "The Behavior of Stock Market Prices," *Journal of Business,* 38, 34–105.

French, K., 1980, "Stock Returns and the Weekend Effect," *Journal of Financial Economics,* 8, 55–69.

French, K. R., G. W. Schwert, and R. F. Stambaugh, 1987, "Expected Stock Returns and Volatility,"' *Journal of Financial Economics,* 19, 3–29.

Gibbons, M. R., and P. Hess, 1981, "Day of the Week Effects and Asset Returns," *Journal of Business,* 54, 579–596.

Godfrey, M., C. Granger, and O. Morgenstern, 1964, "The Random Walk Hypothesis of Stock Market Behavior," *Kylos,* 17, 1–30.

Hilliard, J., 1979, "The Relationship between Equity Indices on World Exchanges," *Journal of Finance,* 34, 103–114.

Jaffe, J., and R. Westerfield, 1985a, "Patterns in Japanese Common Stock Returns: Day of the Week and Turn of the Year Effects," *Journal of Financial and Quantitative Analysis,* 20, 261–272.

Jaffe, J., and R. Westerfield, 1985b, "The Week-End Effect in Common Stock Returns: The International Evidence," *Journal of Finance,* 40, 433–454.

Kon, S., 1984, "Models of Stock Returns—A Comparison," *Journal of Finance*, 39, 147–165.

Mandelbrot, B., 1963, "The Variation of Certain Speculative Prices," *Journal of Business,* 36, 394–419.

McLeod, A., and W. Li, 1983, "Diagnostic Checking ARMA Time Series Models Using Squared-Residual Autocorrelations," *Journal of Time Series Analysis,* 4, 269–273.

Roll, R., 1988, "The International Crash of October 1987," in R. Kamphuis, R. Kormendi, and H. Watson (eds.), *Black Monday and the Future of Financial Markets,* Irwin, Homewood, Ill.

Scholes, M., and J. Williams, 1977, "Estimating Betas from Nonsynchronous Data," *Journal of Financial Economics*, 5, 309–327.

Smirlock, M., and L. Starks, 1986, "Day-of-the-Week and Intraday Effects in Stock Returns," *Journal of Financial Economics,* 17, 197–210.

Solnik, B., 1983, "International Arbitrage Pricing Theory," *Journal of Finance,* 38, 449–457.

Stoll, H., and R. Whaley, 1988, "Stock Market Structure and Volatility: Preliminary Results," working paper, Vanderbilt University.

Stulz, R., 1981, "A Model of International Asset Pricing," *Journal of Financial Economics,* 9, 383–406.

Tse, Y. K., 1989, "Price and Volume in the Tokyo Stock Exchange: An Exploratory Study," working paper, University of Illinois at Urbana–Champaign.

Westerfield, R., 1977, "The Distribution of Common Stock Price Changes: An Application of Transaction Time and Subordinated Stochastic Models," *Journal of Financial and Quantitative Analysis,* 12, 743–765.

Twenty

Anant K. Sundaram

Anant K. Sundaram received a Ph.D. from Yale University in 1987. He started out at the Tuck School of Business, Dartmouth University, and, after stints at the University of Michigan and the Thunderbird School of Management, is now back at the Tuck School of Business. •

Much will be said in this volume about Steve's stupendous influence as a scholar. Please allow me to add a couple of thoughts on Steve Ross as a teacher.

Someone once said—I am paraphrasing—that mediocre teachers explain ideas, good teachers inspire some ideas, but truly *great* teachers inspire us to teach ourselves and, in turn, others. In the process, a great teacher affects eternity.

Let me give you an example. I still remember the awe I felt—indeed, the sense that scales seemed to fall from my brain, and the feeling that suddenly, all was revealed—when I heard Steve explain in class the link between the no-arbitrage principle and linear pricing (Ross [1973]). One can use attributes such as centrality, simplicity, profundity, and clarity to gauge the significance of an idea. Using just about any such measure, rarely have I heard in the classroom something that meant more to me before, or since. The notion that "supply" and "demand" are awkward (and not even necessary) constructs to understand the concept of equilibrium (I am paraphrasing Steve) was nothing short of a revelation.

It never ceases to amaze me how this link underlies just about every significant conceptual development in our profession. Equally, I continue to be confidently suspicious of (and unimpressed by) ideas in our profession that cannot pass the smell-test of "no-arbitrage in equilibrium." In every class I teach, whether for MBAs or for executives, I devote time not only to the link between no-arbitrage and linear pricing, but the minimally necessary behavioral condition that Steve repeatedly stressed, that "all else equal, people prefer more wealth to less." Of course, I substitute slightly looser language, such as "something for nothing" in place of "arbitrage" and "value additive" for "linear prices." (It comes as a surprise to even seasoned Wall Street types when I point out—leave aside fancy stuff such as options, forwards, and swaps—that one couldn't, for instance, value an annuity as a combination of two perpetuities if it weren't for this idea!)

I could provide many such examples, but this one will suffice. (OK, one additional mini-example: His favorite saying about empirical analysis used to be "mere data can't change a good theory," which seemed to follow, for some strange reason, from his travels in Turkey where he seemed to have picked up some insights about getting "data" to "squeal.")

Once every so often, as a teacher, it brings me the utmost joy when I see that sense of awe from this idea—as revealed by that gleam in the student's eye—and know that it has been passed on. And that, somehow, somewhere, it will be passed on yet again. *Ad infinitum.*

What follows is perhaps "tortured" data, but also a model that passes the smell-test of equilibrium!

An Empirical Analysis of Strategic Competition and Firm Values: The Case of R&D Competition

Anant K. Sundaram*
University of Michigan School of Business, Ann Arbor, MI 48109, USA
Teresa A. John
Stern Graduate School of Business, New York University, New York, NY 10012, USA
Kose John
Stern Graduate School of Business, New York University, New York, NY 10012, USA

Abstract

We operationalize a firm's competitive strategy through a new empirical measure, and develop a framework for empirical analysis of the market value of strategic behavior. Using this framework, we study announcement effects of R&D spending. The announcing firm's stock prices are positively influenced by a change in spending, and negatively by our competitive strategy measure (CSM). Competitors' stock prices are positively influenced by the interaction between the market's reaction to the announcing firm and the CSM. Our results are consistent with positive effects of 'accommodating' competition with strategic substitutes, and nonpositive effects of 'tough' competition with strategic complements. •

Key Words: Strategic substitutes; Strategic complements; Competitive strategy; R&D; Event study
JEL Classification: G31; L22

*Corresponding author.
We are grateful to Carliss Baldwin (the referee) and to Michael Jensen and Richard Ruback (the editors) for extensive comments on earlier drafts. We thank Christopher Pears, Nicholas Hall, and Dorothy Bower for research assistance, and Clas Bergstrom, James Brickley, Su Chan, Mark Hirschey, William Kracaw, Baruch Lev, James McKeown, Joshua Ronen, Dennis Sheehan, Clifford Smith, René Stulz, Jerold Warner, and Josef Zechner for comments on previous drafts. Earlier versions of the paper were presented at the 1993 American Economic Association meetings, the 1993 European Finance Association meetings, the 1994 Mitsui Conference in Finance and Accounting at the University of Michigan, University of Rochester, Pennsylvania State University, and the Stockholm School of Economics. Anant Sundaram acknowledges support from the Tuck Associates Research Program, Teresa John from a Stern School summer research grant, and Kose John from a Bank and Financial Analysts Faculty Fellowship.

Reprinted with permission:
John, Kose, Teresa John, and Anant K. Sundaram. "An Empirical Analysis of Strategic Competition and Firm Values: The Case of R&D Competition." *Journal of Financial Economics* 40 (1996): 459–486.

1. Introduction

In settings characterized by imperfect product markets, incomplete contracting, or imperfect information, strategic interaction can affect outcomes of financial policy and investment choices.[1] Theory predicts that the nature of competitive interaction—whether competition is tough or accommodating—affects the wealth of companies and the value of their shares. Therefore, the nature of competitive interaction in an industry should affect individual firms' share-price response to the announcement of new strategic initiatives.

In this paper, we test the hypothesis that 'competition matters' when firms announce new strategic initiatives, using a sample of firms announcing changes in R&D expenditures. We operationalize the nature of competitive interactions by constructing an empirical measure of the responsiveness of a firm's profits to changes in its competitors' revenues. Our measure is negative or positive, depending on whether competition is in 'strategic substitutes' (accommodating or complaisant competition) or in 'strategic complements' (tough or aggressive competition). The empirical framework we develop here is applicable to the study of the effects of competitive interaction across many investment and financial decisions, e.g., capital structure changes, share repurchases, dividend changes, capital expenditures, and so forth.

The choice of R&D investment as the instrument of competition is prompted by two considerations. First, among financial economists, there has been considerable interest in R&D expenditures and the links to corporate governance mechanisms and managerial incentives (see, for instance, Jensen, 1993). A second reason for looking at R&D is the presence of an extensive theoretical literature on the spillover effects of R&D investment and technical change. [See Reinganum (1989) for a survey of the theoretical literature on strategic competition in R&D.] Although the role of strategic interaction has been a major preoccupation, the issue has been largely neglected in the empirical literature. [The absence of empirical testing in this area, and some of the difficulties in operationalizing the theoretical models of R&D, have been stressed in a survey of empirical work by Cohen and Levin (1989).]

In this paper, we develop and implement a framework that uses standard data sources in finance [e.g., Center for Research in Security Prices (CRSP) and Compustat] and its methodologies (e.g., the event-study methodology) to address long-outstanding theoretical questions on strategic interaction. We propose a measure that categorizes the nature of competitive strategy in product markets, and we relate that measure to the wealth effects of the shareholders of the firm announcing R&D expenditure changes, as well as to the wealth effects of their rivals' shareholders.

Our first step is to study the stock-price response of firms that announce changes in R&D expenditures. The evidence thus far is somewhat mixed. Some of the earlier studies (e.g., Chan, Martin, and Kensinger, 1990; hereafter, CMK) found a positive announcement effect, while others (e.g., Doukas and Switzer, 1992) found an insignificant average announcement effect. While we also find an insignificant average announcement effect, our focus is on examining how individual effects depend on the nature of strategic interaction in the industry.

[1]The linkage between strategic interaction and financial variables has been explored in a growing theoretical literature. In a setting of oligopolistic competition, Brander and Lewis (1986) argued that firms may choose leveraged capital structures as a way of precommitting to larger output levels. Gertner, Gibbons, and Scharfstein (1988) explored how the choice of firms' financial policies balance the gains from revelation of private information to investors with the losses from revealing it to competitors. Other theoretical papers that have examined similar issues include the analysis of share repurchases in Rotemberg and Scharfstein (1990), dividend announcements and capital structure in Sundaram and John (1992), and capital structure in Allen (1985), Glazer (1989), Maksimovic (1988), and Glazer and Israel (1990). Although empirical literature is sparse, Chevalier (1993a, b) is a notable exception.

To characterize the nature of competition in an empirically implementable way, we categorize competitive behavior as 'strategic substitutes' or 'strategic complements'. Intuitively, the idea of strategic substitutes is that competitors accommodate a firm's strategic move, and thus act complaisantly. With strategic complements, competitors match a firm's strategic move, thereby escalating competition. As argued by Fudenberg and Tirole (1984), Bulow, Geanakoplos, and Klemperer (1985), Tirole (1988), and Milgrom and Roberts (1990a, 1990b), many results found in oligopoly theory can be understood in terms of strategic substitutes or complements. Sundaram and John (1992) argued that empirical studies that examine only the *average* announcement effect may be missing important dichotomous effects that arise from market structure distinctions among firms: Announcement effects can depend totally on whether the market is characterized by strategic substitutes or complements. Results can often be reversed, depending on whether one or the other type of strategic interaction prevails.

Using data from June 1985 to December 1991, we examine the effect of R&D expenditure announcements on stock prices of announcing firms, as well as those of their competitors in the industry. We find that while the average announcement effect of an R&D announcement is not significantly different from zero, it is significantly related to the nature of competitive strategy. When the announcing firm competes in strategic substitutes, the announcement effect of R&D spending is positive; when the firm competes in strategic complements, the announcement effect is negative. In other words, when the sample is taken as a whole, an insignificant *average* effect masks the significant effects with opposite signs that are found in the two strategic interaction subsamples comprising the whole sample.

We also examine the announcement effect on competitor firms in the industry. We find that the average effect on competing firms is negative and significant, although there is evidence of positive interfirm R&D spillover effects. We also find that the effect of the interaction between the announcing firm's abnormal return and our measure of competitive strategy is positive and significant.

The rest of the paper is organized as follows. Section 2 develops a model of strategic interaction among firms that are making changes in their R&D expenditures. This model is the source of several hypotheses tested in the rest of the paper. Section 3 describes our data, their sources, and sample characteristics, and provides the basic results on announcement effects in the sample. Section 4 develops the measure of strategic interaction, and examines the cross-sectional impact of this measure on both the own-firm and the competitor firms' returns. Section 5 concludes.

2. A Model of Strategic Interaction in R&D

Consider two duopolistic firms (say, firm A and firm B) who are engaged in Cournot (i.e., quantity-setting) competition in their cost-reducing R&D spending. When firm A increases its R&D spending, it signals to its competitors that it is likely to lower its costs, and hence increase its profits (see, e.g., Spence, 1984). Such profit increases should have a positive impact on A's stock prices.

The actual profit of A depends on how firm B reacts to the increase in R&D spending. If B accommodates A by 'staying put' (the usual assumption that is made in most models of oligopolistic competition), then the net effect of increased R&D spending is to increase A's profits and market share, and in the process reduce B's profit and market share. In the oligopoly literature, this situation is referred to generically as competition in 'strategic substitutes' (Bulow, Geanakoplos, and Klemperer, 1985). Under this competitive scenario, the stock-price effect resulting from the R&D announcement would be positive for firm A and negative for firm B.

But B's reaction to A's strategy may not be accommodating: B can respond by increasing its own R&D spending. If this happens, then the profit and market share effects on A become ambiguous. For instance, if A and B are *ex ante* identical and B reacts to A's move by adopting an identical strategy, then both their costs would fall, outputs increase, and market shares remain the same as before—but industry profits may fall. The reason is that the joint higher industry output lowers industry prices. In the oligopoly literature, such a competitive scenario is referred to generically as competition in 'strategic complements'. The stock-price effect resulting from the R&D spending announcement would be at best ambiguous and could even be negative, depending on the specifics of market structure.

The intuition that announcement effects of important strategic moves in oligopolistic settings can be positive or not, depending on whether competition is in strategic substitutes or strategic complements, is the essence of our empirical effort here. However, to measure these ideas, we must define strategic substitutes and complements more precisely.

Whether or not the competitor adopts an accommodating or nonaccommodating strategy depends on the effects of A's moves on its competitor's marginal profits. Intuitively, the reasoning is as follows. Assume that the firms are already in an initial equilibrium prior to the announcement, i.e., both firms have already set their marginal revenues equal to marginal costs, or their marginal profits to zero. Now, if firm A changes its strategy in this equilibrium, it would affect both its own and firm B's marginal profits. Given this change, both firms would re-optimize, based on what happens to their marginal profits, to reach a new equilibrium. If firm B re-optimizes by accommodating a move by firm A—i.e., it competes in strategic substitutes—then its marginal profits must be decreasing. On the other hand, if firm B re-optimizes by responding with its own similar move—i.e., it competes in strategic complements—then its marginal profits must be increasing.[2]

Thus, what determines strategic substitutes and complements is the sign of the change in marginal profits of each firm with respect to changes in both its own and its competitor's output. When the change in marginal profits is negative, competition is said to be in strategic substitutes; when the change is positive, competition is said to be in strategic complements.

To implement the idea of strategic substitutes and complements empirically, we first measure a firm's marginal profits (i.e., the change in a firm's profit relative to its own output). Following that, we measure how this marginal profit changes relative to its competitor's output. We describe our empirical implementation of these ideas in Section 4.1.

Our model leads to the following testable predictions for the announcing firm: (i) The announcement effect of R&D spending on the stock prices for firms competing in strategic substitutes will be positive; for firms competing in strategic complements, the announcement effect could be negative or zero. (ii) The announcement effect will increase as the percentage change in R&D spending announced increases. (iii) If the sample consists of equal proportions of firms competing in strategic substitutes and complements, the average announcement effect will not be significantly different from zero.

With respect to competitors, our model should predict that the impact of an R&D announcement on competitors' stock prices will depend on the interaction of the announcing firm's abnormal return and the competitive strategy variable, as follows: (i) If the announcing firm has a positive abnormal return and competition is in strategic substitutes,

[2]A detailed explanation of the reasons why marginal profits can be increasing or decreasing around the equilibrium is beyond the scope of this paper. Suffice it to say, for our purposes, that it depends on particular combinations of three sets of variables: (i) the nature of the demand curves in the industry, (ii) the nature of cost curves in the industry, and (iii) the nature of competition—whether firms compete on the basis of Cournot (quantity) competition, Bertrand (price) competition, etc.—in the industry.

then the competitors' abnormal return will be negative. (ii) If the announcing firm has a negative abnormal return and competition is in strategic complements, then the competitors' abnormal return will be positive.

3. Sample Design, Descriptive Statistics, and Abnormal Stock Returns

This section describes how we derive the sample firms, their characteristics, and the stock-price effects of their R&D spending announcements. Following this, in Section 4, we examine the stock-price effects of the competitive strategy measure on both the announcing firm and its competitors.

3.1. Sample Design and Descriptive Statistics

Our sample consists of firms that voluntarily announced plans to increase, decrease, or leave unchanged from their previous fiscal year their company sponsored R&D expenditures for the forthcoming fiscal year. The sample covers the period June 1985 to December 1991. Announcement dates are obtained from the *Dow Jones News Retrieval Service* database, which provides news-service articles and selected stories from the *Dow Jones News Wire* (DJNW, also called the 'Broad Tape'), the *Wall Street Journal* (WSJ), and *Barron's*.

We employ a model of investor expectations about the firm's R&D expenditure that assumes that only changes from the previous year represent new information in the R&D expenditure announcement. Such changes could exceed previous years' levels, in which case they reflect the total announced change in R&D expenditures, or they could represent changes over and above a past trend, in which case they reflect a surprise in the change.

We eliminate several announcements from the initial list of 201 R&D announcements. Following the criteria in CMK (1990, pp. 258–259) and Doukas and Switzer (1992, pp. 100–103), we omit: (1) announcements by foreign firms, (2) announcements lacking specificity in the form of either a dollar value or a percentage change over the previous year's spending (e.g., we exclude vague statements such as 'we expect R&D to grow', 'the company plans to continue its emphasis on R&D spending', etc.), (3) those that duplicate earlier statements about R&D spending plans, (4) those that involve noncompany-sponsored R&D spending (e.g., with funding from customers or from government contracts), and (5) those that contain multi-year R&D commitments. This gives us 160 announcements. By imposing the additional criterion that the announcing firms be listed on either the NYSE or the AMEX, our effective sample size is 125 announcements by 65 firms, which is comparable to the sample size of 95 announcements in the CMK study.

Table 1, column 2, provides data on the distribution of announcing firms. Of the 125 announcements, 99 announce increases in R&D spending for the forthcoming fiscal year compared to the previous year's spending levels, while the rest announce either no change or a decline in R&D spending. Of the 125 announcements, only 21 are 'pure' R&D announcements; the rest are made simultaneously with announcements related to earnings and/or capital expenditures. Indeed, 81 announcements in the sample are made concurrently with earnings announcements. (The concurrent earnings announcements in our sample raise the issue of the R&D announcement effects being confounded with earnings announcement effects. We address this issue in detail in Section 4.)

The firms in our sample are large, with average annual sales of \$7.8 billion in the year of announcement (median = \$4.7 billion) and average assets of \$7.3 billion (median = \$4.5 billion). Compared to an average announced R&D expenditure of \$426 million (median = \$270 million), the average actual expenditure on R&D is \$471 million (median = \$303 million) in the announcement year. The average percentage increase in announced R&D expenditure during the announcement year is 14.5%. (The average annual percentage

TABLE 1 | Abnormal Stock Performance over Two-Day Announcement Period of 125 Announced R&D Expenditure Changes by NYSE and AMEX Firms, by Type of Announcement: 1985–1991

Type of announcement	# observations	*CAR* (day 0 + day 1; %)[a]	*t*-statistic[b]
1. Pure R&D announcement	21	0.69	1.39
2. R&D and earnings announcements			
a. Earnings up	38	0.83	1.66
b. Earnings down or flat	11	−3.65	2.30
3. R&D and capital expenditure announcements			
a. Capital expenditure up	13	0.99	1.52
b. Capital expenditure down or flat	10	0.00	0.00
4. R&D, earnings, and capital expenditure announcements			
a. Capital expenditure up, earnings up	16	0.91	1.61
b. Capital expenditure up, earnings down/flat	8	1.36	1.16
c. Capital expenditure down/flat, earnings up	0		
d. Capital expenditure down/flat, earnings down/flat	8	−0.07	0.07
Total sample	125	0.43	1.54
a. Firms announcing R&D increases	99	0.46	1.54
b. Firms announcing R&D decreases/staying flat	26	0.33	0.43

[a] *CAR* is the cumulative abnormal return aggregated over the two-day announcement period, day 0 and day 1.

[b] The *t*-statistic for the total sample is $CAR_k \div (\sigma_{AAR}\sqrt{k})$, where σ_{AAR} is the standard deviation estimated from the time series of *AAR* in the event window (excluding the day of announcement and the day after), *AAR* is the portfolio average abnormal return on each event day, and k is the number of days in the announcement period.

increase in actual spending in the three years prior to the announcement year is 13.8%.) Firms in the sample have higher-than-average market-to-book ratios (2.59) and a 29% higher R&D intensity compared to their industry counterparts. (We define R&D intensity as the ratio of the firms' R&D spending divided by its net sales to the industry R&D spending divided by industry net sales. All data on industry-level R&D spending are drawn from the various annual issues of the *BusinessWeek R&D Scoreboard.*)

Examining the expected and actual R&D spending in the sample, the announced spending increase (14.5%) compares well with the actual increase during the announcement year (12.1%), the increase prior to the announcement year (12.6%), and the average annual increase over three years prior to the announcement year (13.8%). For those firms who make R&D announcements in one particular year but did not in the previous year, the average increase in actual R&D spending during the previous year is 12.3%.

When we compare the industry distribution of our sample's R&D spending with the population, the sample firms' actual R&D expenditures during the announcement year are 8.3% of net sales, which is much higher than the average of 3.5% for all nonfinancial firms. However, the sample firms are representative of their industry's population, since the sample industries themselves average 7.1% of net sales. Indeed, our sample is dominated by industries such as aerospace, chemicals, pharmaceuticals, semiconductors, medical products, etc., which tend to be R&D-intensive industries. Therefore, our results can be cautiously interpreted as applying to large firms in R&D-intensive industries that choose to make announcements about their R&D expenditures. In other words, our study pertains to firms that compete on R&D. (More detailed data on our sample firms is available on request.)

3.2. Computing Abnormal Stock Returns

To measure the stock market's response to R&D announcements, we use the standard event-study methodology to evaluate market- and risk-adjusted prediction errors. We define the event window to include days −30 through +12 in relation to the announcement. We use the equally weighted CRSP index as a proxy for market returns, and estimate the parameters of the market model by using data for the 248 days surrounding the event window. The estimation period includes days −141 through −31 and days +13 through +151.

To remove any bias that might result if a beta shift accompanied the announcement, we use the procedure in Ruback (1982). The parameters before the announcement date are estimated on data from the pre-event estimation period; those on or after the event are estimated from the post-event estimation period. Market-model parameters estimated from the pre-event estimation period are used to calculate abnormal returns for days −30 to −1. Similarly, we use parameters estimated from the post-event estimation period to calculate abnormal returns for days 0 to 12.

We test for shifts in the firm's beta between the pre-event and post-event estimation periods using the following regression model in which D_t is a dummy variable that takes a value of zero for the pre-event estimation period and one for the post-event estimation period, R_{jt} is the return on stock j at time t, and R_{mt} is the return on the market portfolio at time t:

$$R_{jt} = a_j + b_{j1}D_t + b_{j2}R_{mt} + b_{j3}D_tR_{mt} + e_j. \tag{1}$$

We find no cases experiencing a statistically significant change in the slope.

We average the abnormal returns across the sample's announcements on each event day to form a portfolio average abnormal return (*AAR*). These *AAR*s are then cumulated over selected intervals in the event period to form cumulative average abnormal returns (*CAR*s). The test statistic for the significance of *CAR* for k days from t through $t + k$ is as follows: The t-statistic for $CAR = CAR_k/(\sqrt{k}\sigma_{AAR})$, in which σAAR is the standard deviation estimated from the time series of AAR_t in the event window, excluding the day of announcement and the day after. If $k = 1$, the t-statistic is equivalent to the t-statistic for AAR on day t (see Dodd, 1980; Holthausen and Leftwich, 1986). We replicate the variance estimation by using the time series of *AAR*s in the pre-event and post-event estimation periods, and find no significant difference between these estimates and those obtained using the event period. We also adjust for first-order autocorrelation in the *AAR*s using Ruback's (1982) methodology. Again, the results are robust. (In these procedures, we follow the CMK 1990 study.)

3.3. Abnormal Returns of Announcing Firms

The average abnormal stock performance of the firms announcing R&D expenditure changes is given in column 3 of Table 1. The average announcement effect for the entire sample is 0.43% for days 0 and +1. This abnormal return, while positive, is not significantly different from zero. Compare this with the announcement effect documented in CMK, in which they find an announcement period abnormal return of +1.38%, which is statistically significant. (Their sample covers the period 1979–85.) Doukas and Switzer (1992), using a longer period of data (1965–84) and only pure R&D announcements, find results similar to ours: In the two-day event window surrounding the announcement, they find an insignificant average abnormal return of 0.31%.

We also examine the announcement effect of R&D changes for subsamples separated according to whether they are pure R&D announcements, or concurrent with information about earnings changes and/or capital expenditure changes. While those making pure R&D announcements do not have significant positive average announcement effects, there does seem to be a *prima facie* effect associated with firms announcing R&D expenditures with contemporaneous earnings declines. Even when we examine only firms announcing R&D spending increases, the average announcement effect is 0.46%. While positive, this is not significantly different from zero.[3]

Table 2 presents the effect of several variables on the announcement effect of R&D changes, and makes a comparison with a similar set of regressions run by CMK. We examine variables such as R&D intensity of the firm (*RDINT*, measured as the ratio of firm R&D spending/net sales divided by the industry average R&D spending/industry net sales); whether or not the firm is in a high- or low-technology industry (*HILO*, based on the definitions in CMK); the percentage change in announced R&D spending over the previous year's spending (*RDCHNG*); the announced percentage increase or decrease over the past three years' percentage change in R&D spending (*RDSURP*, as a measure of the 'surprise' change in R&D spending[4]); whether or not the firm is dominant firm within the industry

[3]We conduct all of following analyses both for all the firms in our sample as well as for only those firms announcing R&D spending increases. The results are similar for both groups of firms. In the interest of brevity and since our model allows for firms to decrease their R&D expenditures as well, we present here the data for all firms in the sample. The results for only the subsample of the 99 firms announcing R&D spending increases are available on request.

[4]We also construct three other measure[s] of R&D spending 'surprise': the announced percentage increase or decrease over the previous year's percentage change in R&D spending, the percentage change over the past three years' R&D spending relative to the firm's sales, and the percentage change over the previous year's R&D spending relative to sales. In all instances, the results are nearly identical, and similar to those for the percentage change in R&D spending (*RDCHNG*). Henceforth, from Table 3 and on, we present only the results for *RDCHNG*. The other results are available on request.

TABLE 2 | Cross-Sectional Regression Estimates and Independent Variables from Regressing Two-Day Announcement Period Abnormal Return on R&D Intensity (*RDINT*), Technology Type (*HILO*), % R&D Change Announced (*RDCHNG*), % 'Surprise' in R&D Change Announced (*RDSURP*), Firm Dominance (*DOM*), and Industry Concentration (*CONC*) for 125 Announcements of R&D Spending Changes by NYSE and AMEX Firms (and Comparison with CMK Results in Panel 2): 1985–1991 (OLS Estimates; *t*-Statistics in Parentheses)

Regression model	Intercept	*RDINT*[a]	*HILO*[b]	*RDCHNG*[c]	*RDSURP*[d]	*DOM*[e]	*CONC*[f]	*RDINT** *HILO*	*RDCHNG** *RDCHNG*	Adj. R^2	*F*	*N*
Panel 1. Results of this study												
(1)	0.0001			0.0287						0.073	10.83***	125
	(0.03)			(3.29)***								
(2)	0.0021	−0.0015		0.0286						0.068	5.52***	125
	(0.42)	(0.52)		(3.28)***								
(3)	0.0026	−0.0016	−0.0003	0.0454		0.0023	0.0053	−0.0183	−0.0021	0.045	1.83	125
	(0.23)	(0.52)	(0.05)	(2.88)***		(0.39)	(0.28)	(0.59)	(0.18)			
(4)	−0.0052	−0.0012	0.0019		0.0377	0.0047	0.0089	−0.0097	−0.0007	0.039	1.70	125
	(0.42)	(0.39)	(0.26)		(2.57)***	(0.78)	(0.46)	(0.32)	(0.06)			
Panel 2. Results of CMK study												
(1)	−2.07	−0.29	0.34	0.98		0.51	0.02	1.68	−0.26	0.200	3.79***	79
	(1.08)	(0.30)	(0.18)	(0.66)		(0.62)	(0.81)	(1.62)*	(1.12)			
(2)	−0.36	−0.28						1.83		0.214	11.61***	79
	(0.47)	(0.50)						(3.94)***				

[a]Ratio of firm R&D/firm net sales to 4-digit SIC industry R&D/industry net sales.

[b]Dummy variable equal to 1 if firm is high-tech and 0 otherwise, where the definitions of 'high' and 'low' are based on CMK Table 2, p. 261.

[c]Percentage change in R&D spending announced.

[d]Excess of announced percentage change in R&D spending over the average of the previous three years' actual R&D spending.

[e]Dummy variable equal to 1 if in terms of sales the firm is one of the four top-ranked firms in the industry.

[f]Concentration ratio measured as the market share percentage (of sales) contributed by the four largest firms in the industry; this ratio is computed using the data from the *BusinessWeek R&D Scoreboard* at the end of the year preceding the announcement.

Asterisks indicate significance at the 1% (***), 10% (*) level in a one-tail test.

(*DOM*, a dummy variable equal to one if the announcing firm is one of the four top-ranked firms in the industry in terms of net sales, and zero otherwise); industry concentration (*CONC*, measured as the net sales market share of the four largest firms in the industry); and interaction variables (*RDINT*∗*HILO* and *RDCHNG*∗*RDCHNG*). We find that with the exception of *RDCHNG* and *RDSURP*, both of which have a positive and significant impact on *CAR*s, none of the other variables has an impact on the announcement effect of R&D changes. We also examine the effect of several other variables, such as market-to-book ratio, P/E ratio, free cash flow, firm size, net income, and capital expenditures, and find that none of these is significant.

CMK find that the interaction between firms R&D intensity (relative to industry intensity) and whether or not the firm was in a high- or low-technology industry affects *CAR*s (see panel 2, Table 2). However, we do not find this result in our sample. CMK find that *RDCHNG* had no cross-sectional impact on *CAR*s in their sample. In our sample, we find that *RDCHNG* (as well as *RDSURP*, our proxy for 'surprise' in such change) has a significant cross-sectional impact on *CAR*s.

In Table 2, we document that the announcement effect is systematically related to the percentage change announced in R&D spending. This suggests that while the market shows an insignificant average response to the direction of change announced, it responds favorably to the extent of change announced, i.e., the higher the percentage change announced, the greater the market reaction.

4. Competitive Strategy and Announcement Effects

In this section, we operationalize the notion of strategic substitutes and complements and examine its effect on share price reactions. In what follows, we call our measure the 'Competitive Strategy Measure' (*CSM*). Section 4.1 describes how we construct the Competitive Strategy Measure, and Section 4.2 describes its empirical properties. Sections 4.3 and 4.4 examine the cross-sectional effect of the *CSM* on both own-firm and competitor firms' *CAR*s.

4.1. Construction of the Competitive Strategy Measure

As we noted in Section 2, the concept of strategic substitutes and complements requires us to measure the impact of changes in quantity on the marginal (as opposed to total) profit of firms in an industry. Thus our concept is defined by the responsiveness of the change in a firm's marginal profits relative to its own output, with respect to a change in competitors' output.

To construct this measure, we need data on the profits and outputs of the announcing firms and their 'competitors'. Since our definition of strategic substitutes and complements is based on how competitors respond to a move made by the announcing firm, we require data on: (i) the change in the firm's competitors' total profit relative to changes in their outputs and (ii) changes in the own-firm's output. However, because of data difficulties in identifying competitor profits, we measure empirically how the announcing firm will respond to a move made by the competition, and treat this measure as a proxy for how the competition would behave. We justify this empirical construction by making the common assumption that a firm and its competitors adopt symmetric strategies to compete with each other. In other words, if a firm competes in strategic substitutes, so do its competitors; if it competes in strategic complements, so do its competitors.

In constructing this measure, we must first define the set of competitors. We define the set of competitors as all the firms in the industry at the level of the Compustat four-digit primary SIC code except the announcing firm. Next, we need a proxy for the firm's profit. We define this as the net income of the announcing firm. Finally, we need a proxy for firm and competitor outputs. We define this as the net sales, assuming that the change in product prices at the SIC four-digit level is constant and the same across a firm and its competitors. From Compustat, we obtained 40 quarters (i.e., ten years) of data on net income and net sales, up to and including the quarter prior to the announcement quarter.[5]

To compute the measure, our first step is to derive a firm's marginal profit. To do so, we consider the ratio of change in a firm's net income (call it $\Delta\pi^f$) to change in its net sales (call it ΔS^f), i.e., the change in a firm's profit margin. The $\Delta\pi^f/\Delta S^f$ ratio measures the change in a firm's total profit as a function of its own output. Next, we derive the change in the competitors' output (call it ΔS^c). We now have two measures, $\Delta\pi^f/\Delta S^f$ and ΔS^c, for 39 quarters prior to the announcement quarter. We then compute the coefficient of correlation between $\Delta\pi^f/\Delta S^f$ against ΔS^c, and call this variable the Competitive Strategy Measure. Going back to our discussion in Section 2, note that $\Delta\pi^f/\Delta S^f$ is a direct proxy for the first derivative of profit, $\partial\pi^A/\partial q^A$. The coefficient of correlation between $\Delta\pi^f/\Delta S^f$ and ΔS^c is a direct proxy of the second derivative of profit with respect to own quantity and the competitors' quantity, $\partial^2\pi^A/\partial q^A\partial q^B$. [This second derivative is the basis for the precise definition of strategic substitutes and complements; when it is less than zero, it defines strategic substitutes, and when it is greater than zero, it defines strategic complements; see Bulow, Geanakoplos, and Klemperer (1985).]

Given this construction, when the *CSM* is less than zero, it corresponds to strategic substitutes; when it is greater than zero, it corresponds to strategic complements; when equal to zero, it corresponds to neither strategic substitutes nor complements.

This measure is available for 106 out of our total sample of 125 announcements. An appendix to this paper lists the firms in our sample, ranked by their *CSM*.

4.2. Empirical Properties of the CSM

The average *CSM* in our sample is -0.02 (median $= -0.02$), and since it is less than zero, it implies that the average sample firm competes on the basis of strategic substitutes. (Sixty-seven firms in the sample have $CSM < 0$ and 39 firms have $CSM > 0$.) There is considerable range in the measure ($+0.40$ to -0.55). The skewness of the *CSM* is 0.255 (not significantly different from zero). When the same firm makes multiple announcements (see the Appendix for the list of firms and their *CSM*s), we examine the temporal stability of the *CSM* and find that the values are quite close. This should not be surprising, since a number of overlapping quarters are used in constructing the measure for the same sample firm with multiple announcements across different years.

Table 3 lists the industries in our sample (for whom data are available) and the associated industry average *CSM*s. Given the small sample sizes in many of the industries, it is difficult to draw any generalizations. However, for those industries where we have more than ten announcements, the *CSM*s are as follows: aerospace $+0.03$ (strategic complements), chemicals -0.08 (strategic substitutes), and pharmaceuticals -0.01 (strategic substitutes).

---

[5] Given our sample time period of 1985–91, this means that we go back to the first quarter of 1975 for the earliest Compustat data point. We are able to find reasonably accurate data on firm net income and sales, and rest-of-industry (i.e., competitor) sales. These data are available for 106 of the 125 announcements in our sample. However, rest-of-industry net income data, which has to be constructed as the aggregate of the net incomes of each of the competitor firms, are available for far fewer firms.

TABLE 3 | Average Industry Competitive Strategy Measure (*CSM*) for 106 R&D Expenditure Change Announcements by NYSE and AMEX Firms During 1985–1991

Industry	Average *CSM*[a]	# announcements
Aerospace	0.03	11
Aluminum	0.14	2
Chemicals	−0.08	20
Computers	−0.03	6
Conglomerates	0.03	2
Electronics	0.04	1
Food	−0.16	3
Instruments	−0.00	4
Leisure products	0.07	5
Machine/hand tools	−0.09	1
Medical products	−0.03	7
Office equipment	−0.05	1
Paper	−0.21	1
Peripherals	0.19	1
Personal care	0.08	4
Pharmaceuticals	−0.01	26
Semiconductors	−0.03	6
Telecommunications	0.01	5

[a]The *CSM* of strategic substitutes or strategic complements is defined as the coefficient of correlation between: (i) ratio of change in firm's quarterly net income to change in firm's quarterly net sales and (ii) change in the rest-of-industry's quarterly net sales, over the period of 40 quarters prior to announcement quarter. A positive correlation indicates strategic complements, and a negative correlation indicates strategic substitutes.

In Table 4, we examine the determinants of the Competitive Strategy Measure, i.e., what makes firms interact on the basis of strategic substitutes or strategic complements. We examine as independent variables the firm's R&D intensity (*RDINT*),whether the firm is in a high- or low-technology industry (*HILO*), the percentage change in R&D spending announced (*RDCHNG*), free cash flow as a percentage of sales (*CFPCTS*), whether the firm is dominant in the industry (*DOM*), and the degree of industry concentration (*CONC*). The four significant variables are *CONC, RDCHNG, RDINT*, and *CFPCTS.* The coefficient of *CONC* is positive, the coefficient of *RDCHNG* is negative, the coefficient of *RDINT* is negative, and the coefficient of *CFPCTS* is positive (all significant). In other words, the more concentrated the industry, the more the firm competes in strategic complements; the greater the R&D spending announced, the less the firm competes in strategic complements; the more R&D-intensive the firm, the less it competes in strategic complements; and the greater the free cash flow in the firm, the more the firm competes in strategic complements.

The picture that emerges is that firms in more concentrated industries with greater free cash flow are likely to escalate competition. On the other hand, as a firm's R&D intensity increases, it is likely to adopt a more accommodating competitive stance. To the extent that more concentrated industries are likely to be more oligopolistic, our results suggest that normal behavior for such industries involves strategic complements, rather than strategic substitutes. Thus, our *CSM* results are contrary to most theoretical models of imperfect competition, which usually assume strategic substitutes. The positive relation between the *CSM* and free cash flow suggests that firms with greater free cash flow are more likely to make R&D investments in response to competitors' announcements of such expenditures.

TABLE 4 | Cross-Sectional Regression Estimates and Independent Variables from Regressing the Competitive Strategy Measure (Measure of Strategic Substitutes and Complements, *CSM*) against Technology Type (*HILO*), R&D Intensity (*RDINT*), % R&D Change Announced (*RDCHNG*), Firm Dominance (*DOM*), Industry Concentration (*CONC*), and Free Cash Flow (*CFPCTS*) for 125 Announcements of R&D Spending by NYSE and AMEX Firms: 1985–1991 (OLS Estimates; *t*-Statistics in Parentheses; $N = 106$ in All Three Regressions)

***Dependent variable*: Competitive strategy measure**[a]

Regression model	Intercept	*RDINT*[b]	*HILO*[c]	*RDCHNG*[d]	*DOM*[e]	*CONC*[f]	*CFPCTS*[g]	Adj. R^2	*F*
(1)	−0.112			−0.069		0.154	0.098	0.071	3.67**
	(2.08)**			(1.79)**		(1.88)**	(1.78)**		
(2)	−0.118	−0.041	0.021	−0.064	0.015	0.191	0.182	0.101	2.94**
	(1.90)**	(2.28)***	(0.84)	(1.70)**	(0.59)	(1.99)**	(2.76)***		
(3)	−0.125					0.180		0.037	5.01***
	(2.49)***					(2.24)***			

[a]The measure of strategic substitutes or strategic complements, *CSM*, is defined as the coefficient of correlation between: (1) ratio of change in firm's quarterly net income to change in firm's quarterly net sales and (ii) change in the rest-of-industry's quarterly net sales, over the period of 40 quarters prior to the announcement quarter. A positive correlation indicates strategic complements, and a negative correlation indicates strategic substitutes.

[b]Ratio of firm R&D/firm net sales to four-digit SIC industry R&D/industry net sales.

[c]Dummy variable equal to 1 if firm is high-tech and 0 otherwise, where the definitions of 'high' and 'low' are based on CMK (Table 2, p. 261).

[d]Percentage change in R&D spending announced.

[e]Dummy variable equal to 1 if in terms of sales the firm is one of the four top-ranked firms in the industry.

[f]Concentration ratio measured as the market share percentage (of sales) contributed by the four largest firms in the industry; this ratio is computed using the data from the *BusinessWeek R&D Scoreboard* at the end of the year preceding the announcement.

[g]Free cash flow as a percentage of net sales.

Asterisks indicate significance at the 1% (***), 5% (**) levels in a two-tail test.

TABLE 5 | Categorical Analysis of the *CSM*: Announcement Effects for 106 Announcements of R&D Expenditure Changes Made by NYSE and AMEX Firms, Categorized by Strategic Substitutes (SS), Strategic Complements (SC), and Neither Strategic Substitutes nor Complements (Neither SS nor SC): 1985–1991

Category[a]	*N*	*CAR* (day 0 + day 1)[b]	*t*-statistic[c]
SS	41	0.008	1.45
Neither SS nor SC	39	0.005	1.17
SC	26	−0.006	−0.96
Difference in mean *CAR*s of SS and SC		0.014	1.78**

[a]SS are defined as firms with *CSM* less than −0.05, SC to be firms with *CSM* greater than +0.05, and neither SS nor SC firms as those with $-0.05 \leqslant CSM \leqslant 0.05$. The measure of strategic substitutes or complements, *CSM*, is defined as the coefficient of correlation between: (i) ratio of change in firm's quarterly net income to change in firm's quarterly net sales and (ii) change in the rest-of-industry's quarterly net sales, over the period of 40 quarters prior to the announcement quarter. A positive correlation indicates strategic complements, and a negative correlation indicates strategic substitutes.

[b]Cumulative abnormal returns aggregated over days 0 and 1.

[c]Cross-sectional *t*-statistic.

Asterisks (**) indicate significance at the 5% level in a one-tail test.

4.3. Announcement Effects and the Competitive Strategy Variable

We now examine the cross-sectional explanatory power of the Competitive Strategy Measure. Recall the hypotheses that (i) firms competing in strategic substitutes ($CSM < 0$) will have a positive announcement effect, and firms competing in strategic complements ($CSM > 0$) will have a nonpositive announcement effect; and (ii) when measured as a continuous variable, *CAR* decreases in the *CSM*.

We examine hypothesis (i) in Table 5. We divide the sample into three subgroups in which strategic substitutes firms are defined as those whose *CSM* is less than −0.05; strategic complements as those whose *CSM* is greater than +0.05; and the rest as those firms competing on the basis of neither strategic substitutes nor complements. As predicted, the announcement effect is positive for strategic substitutes firms (0.8%) and negative for strategic complements firms (−0.6%); for the in-between group, it is 0.5%. The difference in the mean *CAR* between firms competing on the basis of strategic substitutes and complements is 1.4%, a statistically significant difference at the 5% level in a one-tail test.

Table 6 examines hypothesis (ii), and goes on to examine the possible confounding effects of contemporaneous earnings announcements. Regression 1 in Table 6 (the effect of *RDCHNG*) confirms what we would expect from Table 2, that the larger the percentage change in R&D, the greater the announcement effect. (These results remain the same regardless of whether total change in R&D spending or R&D spending surprises are considered.) Regression 2 shows that the *CSM*'s coefficient is negative and significant, as hypothesis (ii) predicts. This suggests that the announcement effect is highest when the competitive interaction is one of strategic substitutes, and that the abnormal returns are negative when the competition is one of strategic complements. The regression with both *RDCHNG* and the *CSM* (regression 3) reveals that both variables jointly affect *CAR*s.

The evidence, therefore, indicates that even though the average announcement effect is not significant, the nature of competitive interaction seems to be a major factor in determining the announcement effect. The insignificant *average* effect seems to be the result of

TABLE 6 | Cross-Sectional Regression Estimates and Independent Variables from Regressing Two-Day Announcement Period Abnormal Return on the Measure of Strategic Substitutes/Complements, *CSM*, % R&D Change Announced (*RDCHNG*), Earnings Announcement Dummies (*EDUMPLUS* and *EDUMNOAN*) and Percentage Change in Earnings Announced (*EARNCHNG*), for 125 Announcements of R&D Spending Changes by NYSE and AMEX Firms: 1985–1991 (OLS Estimates; *t*-Statistics in Parentheses)

Model	Intercept	*RDCHNG*[a]	*CSM*[b]	*EDUMPLUS*[c]	*EDUMNOAN*[d]	*EARNCHNG*[e]	Adj. R^2	*F*	*N*
(1)	0.0001	0.0287					0.073	10.83***	125
	(0.03)	(3.29)***							
(2)	0.0030		−0.0600				0.053	6.83***	106
	(0.88)		(2.61)***						
(3)	−0.0020	0.0270	−0.0460				0.120	8.13***	106
	(0.50)	(2.98)***	(2.04)**						
(4)	−0.0161	0.0262	−0.0536	0.0131	0.0145		0.015	1.91	106
	(1.04)	(2.97)***	(2.73)***	(1.74)*	(1.82)*				
(5)	−0.0058	0.0279	−0.0749			0.0018	0.102	3.62**	75[f]
	(1.21)	(1.65)*	(2.23)**			(1.35)			

[a]Percentage change in R&D spending announced.

[b]The measure of strategic substitutes or strategic complements. Measured as the coefficient of correlation between: (i) ratio of change in firm's quarterly net income to change in firm's quarterly net sales and (ii) change in the rest-of-industry's quarterly net sales, during the period of 40 quarters prior to the announcement quarter. A positive correlation indicates strategic complements, and a negative correlation indicates strategic substitutes.

[c]The dummy variable *EDUMPLUS* = 1 for all firms making positive earnings announcements, and 0 otherwise.

[d]The dummy variable *EDUMNOAN* = 1 for all firms making no earnings announcements, and 0 otherwise.

[e]The variable *EARNCHNG* is the percentage change in earnings announced (for those firms making simultaneous earnings announcements).

[f]Out of the 81 firms announcing earnings changes, we do not have data on the *CSM* for 6 firms.

Asterisks indicate significance at the 1% (***), 5% (**), 10% (*) level in a two-tail test.

TABLE 7 | Regression Analysis of Percentage Change in Earnings Announced, *EARNCHNG* with *RDCHNG* as Dependent Variable (Panel A), and the Residual from Panel A, *RESIDL, EARNCHNG.* and the *CSM* with the Two-Day Announcement Period Abnormal Return as the Dependent Variable (Panel B), for 81 R&D Expenditure Change Announcements Made by NYSE and AMEX Firms: 1985–1991

Panel A. Dependent variable: RDCHNG[a]

Intercept	*EARNCHNG*[b]	Adj. R^2	*F*	*N*
0.1376 (5.12)***	0.0098 (0.30)	0.001	0.88	81

Panel B. Dependent variable: Two-day announcement period abnormal return

	Intercept	*CSM*[c]	*RESIDL*[d]	*EARNCHNG*[b]	Adj. R^2	*F*	*N*
(1)	0.0033 (0.88)		0.0290 (1.87)**		0.029	3.50**	81
(2)	−0.0011 (0.66)	−0.0715 (2.16)**	0.0277 (1.65)*		0.089	4.38**	75
(3)	−0.0020 (0.48)	−0.0749 (2.26)**	0.0279 (1.64)*	0.0019 (1.41)	0.102	3.62**	75

[a]Percentage change in R&D spending announced.

[b]Percentage change in earnings announced.

[c]The measure of strategic substitutes or complements, *CSM*, is defined as the coefficient of correlation between: (i) ratio of change in firm's quarterly net income to change in firm's quarterly net sales and (ii) change in the rest-of-industry's quarterly net sales, during the period of 40 quarters prior to the announcement quarter. A positive correlation indicates strategic complements and a negative correlation indicates strategic substitutes.

[d]Residual from the regression in panel A.

Asterisks indicate significance at the 1% (***), 5% (**), 10% (*) levels in a two-tail test.

positive effects canceling out the negative effects. Positive effects in our data come from strategic substitutes interaction, and negative or zero effects come from strategic complements interaction.

This result is similar to that predicted by Sundaram and John (1992, p. 20) who argue that: (i) Modeling choices that rationalize only *average* announcement effects may be missing crucial driving factors, such as the underlying market structure; (ii) unless data sets are preanalyzed and firms classified as competing in either strategic substitutes or strategic complements, we could obtain average results that might not apply to a particular firm or industry; (iii) in many empirical studies, we should not be surprised to find insignificant average announcement effects, since the opposite effects of the two competitive phenomena—strategic substitutes and complements—could be canceling each other out.

Regressions 4 and 5 in Table 6 and the regressions in Table 7 attempt to filter out the possible contaminating effects of concurrent earnings announcements. Given that 81 out of the 125 announcements in our sample also make joint earnings announcements, there are likely to be confounding effects of earnings surprises on R&D spending surprises. The announcement effects of earnings surprises are well documented in both the finance and the accounting literatures.

We undertake the analysis to filter out the possible contaminating effects of concurrent earnings announcements in three stages. First, we examine the marginal impact of earnings announcements (see regression 4, Table 6) using a categorical analysis. In addition to *RDCHNG* and the *CSM*, we add two dummy variables. The first dummy is set to one for firms that announce positive surprises in earnings (and zero otherwise), and the other dummy is set to one for all firms that make no earnings announcements (and zero otherwise). The effect of firms announcing negative earnings surprises (or flat earnings) is picked up by the intercept term in this regression. We observe from regression 4, Table 6, that there is a positive and significant announcement effect associated with positive earnings surprises, but a negative and nonsignificant announcement effect associated with negative earnings surprises. We find that *RDCHNG* and the *CSM* continue to have strong explanatory power ($t = 2.97$ and $t = 2.73$, respectively; both are significant at the 1% level), with magnitudes and directions of effects similar to those reported in regressions 1–3, Table 6.

Second, we examine the marginal impact of earnings announcements (regression 5, Table 6) by using a continuous earnings variable, the percentage change in announced earnings for those firms making earnings announcements. While percentage earnings change data are available for 81 firms, we can use only 75, since we do not have the *CSM* data for six firms. We note that the coefficient of the earnings variable is positive, although not significant at conventional levels. However, the coefficient of the *CSM* continues to he negative and significant ($t = 2.23$), and *RDCHNG* continues to be positive and significant ($t = 1.65$), although the effects of both are slightly lower than before.

Finally, to account for the possibility that *RDCHNG* might itself be affected by earnings surprises, we examine whether there is a residual effect of *RDCHNG* in a simultaneous specification. We first regress *RDCHNG* against the percentage change in announced earnings (panel A, Table 7), and then regress the own-firm *CAR* against the R&D residuals from this regression and the *CSM*, as reported in regressions 1–3, panel B, Table 7. Earnings have a positive, although nonsignificant, effect on *RDCHNG*, but the R&D residual has a positive and significant effect ($t = 1.87$) and the *CSM* continues to have a negative and significant effect ($t = 2.16$) on *CAR*s.

In summary, although own-firm *CAR*s are affected by earnings announcements, both the percentage change in R&D spending announced and the strategic interaction variable have strong announcement effects, independent of the earnings announcement effect.

4.4. Announcement Effect on Competitors' Stock Prices

Table 8 examines the average announcement effect on competitor firms (*CCAR*). We note from line (1) of Table 8 that the average excess return is −0.16%, which is negative and statistically significant. The announcement effect is economically small, and the statistical significance could also be due to the unusually low standard errors resulting from averaging the returns across a number of firms within each four-digit SIC code. Given that our sample has 67 cases of strategic substitutes, but only 39 cases of strategic complements, this negative announcement effect is not surprising. We would expect, from the arguments in Section 2, that the average competitor effect of a value-enhancing strategic move would be negative for competitor firms that compete in strategic substitutes.

The relationship of competitor return to the Competitive Strategy Measure and the own-firm announcement effect (*FCAR*) is examined in more detail in lines (2)–(5) of Table 8. When the own-firm announcement effect is positive, then the competitors' announcement effect for strategic complements interaction is higher (less negative) than that for strategic substitutes interaction. In other words, the output-increasing response of strategic complements interaction elicits a better announcement effect for the competing firm when the own-firm's R&D spending is viewed by the market as value-enhancing. On the other hand,

TABLE 8 | Competitors' Abnormal Stock Performance over Two-Day Announcement Period Categorized by Positive or Negative Firm *CAR*, and Strategic Substitutes (SS)[a] or Strategic Complements (SC)[a] for 125 R&D Expenditure Change Announcements by NYSE and AMEX Firms: 1985–1991

	Category	*N*	*CAR* (day 0 + day 1)[b]	*t*-statistic[c]
(1)	Total competitor sample *of which*	121[d]	−0.0016	3.26***
(2)	*FCAR* > 0 and SC	21	−0.0008	0.54
(3)	*FCAR* ⩽ 0 and SS	29	−0.0010	0.99
(4)	*FCAR* > 0 and SS	35	−0.0023	3.49***
(5)	*FCAR* ⩽ 0 and SC	16	−0.0025	1.14

[a]SS is defined as *CSM* < 0, and SC is defined as *CSM* ⩾ 0. The measure of strategic substitutes or complements, the *CSM*, is defined as the coefficient of correlation between: (i) ratio of change in firm's quarterly net income to change in firm's quarterly net sales and (ii) change in the rest-of-industry's quarterly net sales, during the period of 40 quarters prior to the announcement quarter. A positive correlation indicates strategic complements, and a negative correlation indicates strategic substitutes.

[b]*CAR* is the cumulative abnormal return aggregated over the two-day announcement period, day 0 and day 1.

[c]The *t*-statistic for the total sample is $CAR_k \div (\sigma_{AAR}\sqrt{k})$, in which σ_{AAR} is the standard deviation estimated from the time series of *AAR* in the event window (excluding the day of announcement and the day after). *AAR* is the portfolio average abnormal return on each event day, and *k* is the number of days in the announcement period.

[d]We could not find sufficient competitor data in the case of four announcements.

Asterisks (***) indicate significance at the 1% level in a two-tail test.

when the own-firm effect is negative, then strategic substitutes interaction by the competitor elicits a better announcement effect for the competitor. In other words, the output-decreasing response of strategic substitutes interaction elicits a better announcement effect for the competing firm when the own-firm's R&D spending is viewed by the market as value-reducing.

Regressions 1–3 in Table 9 examine the determinants of the competitor announcement effect using continuous values for the *CSM* and *FCAR*. From regression 1, we see that the abnormal return of competing firms is positively related to the return of the announcing firm, and that the relation is statistically significant. However, from regression 2, we see that the direct effect of the *CSM* is not significant.

But the most interesting results involve the interaction variable in regression 3, i.e., the *CSM* multiplied by the two-day abnormal return of the announcing firm, *FCAR*. The competitor return is positively related to this interaction variable and the coefficient is statistically significant ($t = 4.78$).

Next, to examine potential confounding effects of contemporaneous earnings announcements, we conduct an analysis similar to that for the own-firm effect. The results of this analysis are shown in regressions 4 and 5 of Table 9. Regression 4 presents our analysis of categorical variables for contemporaneous earnings announcements. The first dummy variable is set to one for all firms that announce positive surprises in earnings (and zero otherwise), and the second dummy variable is set to one for all firms that make no earnings announcements (and zero otherwise). We observe that the interaction variable, $FCAR*CSM$, continues to be positive and highly significant ($t = 4.56$), and all the other variables (including the earnings dummies) are nonsignificant. Regression 5 does a similar analysis for the continuous variable, the percentage change in earnings announced (*EARNCHNG*). Again, note that the only variable that emerges as significant is the interaction variable, $FCAR*CSM$.

TABLE 9 | Cross-Sectional Regression Estimates and Independent Variables from Regressing Competitors' Two-Day Announcement Period Abnormal Return on Firms' Two-Day *CAR* (*FCAR*), the *CSM*, Earnings Announcement Dummies (*EDUMPLUS* and *EDUMNOAN*), % Change in Earnings Announced (*EARNCHNG*), and Interaction Variable *FCAR*∗*CSM* for 121 Announcements of R&D Spending Changes by NYSE and AMEX Firms: 1985–1991 (OLS Estimates; *t*-Statistics in Parentheses)

***Dependent variable*: Competitors' two-day announcement period abnormal return**

Regression model	Intercept	*FCAR*[a]	*CSM*[b]	*FCAR*∗ *CSM*[c]	*EDUMPLUS*[d]	*EDUMNOAN*[e]	*EARNCHNG*[f]	Adj. R^2	*F*	*N*
(1)	−0.0020	0.0280						0.02	3.46**	121
	(3.48)***	(1.86)**								
(2)	−0.0020	0.0390	−0.0010					0.03	2.46**	102
	(3.21)***	(2.11)**	(0.13)							
(3)	−0.0010	0.0220	0.0040	0.4250				0.20	9.61***	102
	(2.37)***	(1.27)	(0.89)	(4.78)***						
(4)	−0.0024	0.0170	0.0033	0.4139	0.0022	0.0015		0.20	6.07***	102
	(2.06)**	(0.97)	(0.75)	(4.56)***	(1.31)	(0.75)				
(5)	−0.0012	0.0134	0.0041	0.4409			0.0001	0.21	5.43***	71[g]
	(1.60)***	(0.61)	(0.63)	(4.12)***			(0.97)			

[a]The two-day announcement period cumulative abnormal return of sample firms.

[b]The *CSM* is measured as the coefficient of correlation between: (i) ratio of change in firm's quarterly net income to change in firm's quarterly net sales and (ii) change in the rest-of-industry's quarterly net sales, during the period of 40 quarters prior to the announcement quarter. A positive correlation indicates strategic complements, and a negative correlation indicates strategic substitutes.

[c]The interaction between *FCAR* and *CSM*.

[d]*EDUMPLUS* = 1 for firms making positive announcements, and 0 otherwise.

[e]*EDUMNOAN* = 1 for firms making no earnings announcements, and 0 otherwise.

[f]Percentage change in announced earnings for firms making contemporaneous earnings announcements.

[g]Out of the total sample of 81 firms making contemporaneous earnings announcements, we have no competitor returns data for 4 firms, and we have no data on the competitive strategy measure for 6 firms; thus, the sample size in this regression is 71.

Asterisks indicate significance at the 1% (***), 5% (**), 10% (*) levels in a two-tail test.

We further examine whether a subset of sample, those 35 firms with $FCAR > 0$ and strategic substitutes, are driving these results, since it would appear from line (4), Table 8, that this subgroup is the only one for which competitor *CAR*s are significantly different from zero. We find, however, that all the previous regression results continue to hold even when we take out this group of 35 firms, suggesting that this subgroup is not driving our competitor results. In the interest of brevity, we do not report these regressions here, but can provide them on request.

In summary, our interaction between the own-firm announcement effect and the Competitive Strategy Measure continues to have a strong effect on competitor *CAR*s, even in the presence of contemporaneous earnings announcements.

5. Conclusion

Although the role of strategic interaction in R&D investment and technical change has been analyzed extensively in theoretical models, there has been very little empirical work. One objective of this paper is to examine strategic interactions by using the stock-price reactions for both firms announcing changes in R&D spending, and their competitors. We operationalize strategic interaction by constructing a new measure (the Competitive Strategy Measure) to determine if competition is characterized by strategic substitutes or strategic complements.

As theory predicts, we find that the announcement effect of the firm announcing the R&D expenditure change is negatively and significantly related to the Competitive Strategy Measure. The percentage change in R&D expenditure announced also has a significant positive impact on the stock price of the announcing firm. These effects remain even after controlling for the possible confounding effects of earnings announcements that are concurrently made with R&D announcements.

For the entire sample, the announcement effect of R&D expenditure changes is not significantly different from zero, a result that is at variance with that reported in CMK (who examine the sample period 1979–85, compared to our sample period of 1985–91). However, this result should not be surprising. Our evidence is consistent with that reported in Hall (1993), who finds that the stock market's valuation of the intangible capital created by R&D investment in the U.S. manufacturing sector fell dramatically (by a factor of three to four times) in the middle and later part of the 1980s, compared to the 1970s and the early 1980s. Hall reports that '. . . although intangible R&D assets from 1973 through 1983–84 were about equally valued with tangible capital, this relationship broke down completely during the mid 1980s' (p. 259). She surmises that the reasons for this include the possibility that the private rate of return to R&D has fallen; R&D capital depreciates much more rapidly than it used to; and the wave of mergers and leveraged buyouts in consumer products firms during the 1980s had a role in shifting valuation effects away from an intangible factor, such as R&D, towards other intangible factors, such as advertising.

We also have some novel results on the determinants of the *CSM.* We find that industry concentration and free cash flow show a consistent relationship with the measure of strategic interaction: More concentrated industries and firms with large amounts of free cash flow are characterized by competition in strategic complements, that is, aggressive competition. If concentration is interpreted as being associated with industry structures that are more oligopolistic in nature, then our evidence suggests that theoretical work should pay closer attention to exploring the implications of strategic-complements competitor behavior, rather than strategic-substitutes behavior (as is usually assumed in many models). Our results also suggest that firms with high free cash flow are more likely to match their competitors' strategic moves.

The nature of the strategic interaction has a significant effect on the abnormal returns of competitors, which is consistent with our predictions. For competitor firms in the announcing firm's industry, the average announcement effect, although small in absolute terms, is negative and significant. Further, the competitor announcement effect is positively and significantly affected by the announcing firm's abnormal return, as well as the interaction between the *CSM* and the announcing firm's abnormal return. We interpret these results as follows: The market responds more favorably to cases in which competitors react with output-increasing strategies to value-enhancing R&D expenditures, or competitors react with output-reducing strategies to value-reducing R&D expenditures; the market reacts less favorably to the other two cases. The intuitive implication is straightforward: Financial markets appear to be saying that if a firm adopts value-reducing R&D, the competitor is better off 'staying put'. On the other hand, if a firm adopts value-enhancing R&D, the competitor is better off matching the move.

It should be pointed out that most announcements of R&D changes are made by large firms in R&D-intensive industries such as aerospace, pharmaceuticals, and semiconductors. This caveat should be kept in mind while interpreting our results.

There has been growing interest in both theoretical and empirical literature in examining the interaction between financial policies and product market competition. The concepts of strategic substitutes and complements are generally understood as crucial to categorizing and understanding the effects of strategic interaction (see, for example, Tirole, 1988). In this paper, we have made what is to our knowledge the first attempt to operationalize these concepts. We find that this measure is a major factor in explaining the market's reaction to announcements of R&D spending. We hope that our measure will be useful for a closer examination of the nature of competition in other contexts as well.

Appendix

TABLE 10 | List of Firms and Their Average Competitive Strategy Measure (*CSM*) in Ascending Order, for 106 R&D Expenditure Announcements Made by Firms on NYSE and AMEX: 1985–1991

Firm	# announcement	Industry[a]	Primary SIC (4-digit)	Average *CSM*[b]	Range of *CSM*[c] (for multiple announcements only)
Cray Research Inc.	1	Computers	3571	−0.55	−0.55
Kellogg Co.	1	Food	2040	−0.24	−0.24
Kimberly Clark Corp.	1	Paper	2621	−0.21	−0.21
Sundstrand Corp.	1	Aerospace	3728	−0.19	−0.19
W.R. Grace & Co.	5	Chemicals	2800	−0.18	−0.15 to −0.20
National Semiconductor	3	Semiconductors	3674	−0.16	−0.12 to −0.19
Procter & Gamble Co.	2	Personal care	2840	−0.15	−0.15 to −0.15
Engelhard Corp.	4	Chemicals	3330	−0.12	−0.09 to −0.14
Gerber Products Corp.	1	Food	2030	−0.12	−0.12
Nabisco Co.	1	Food	2000	−0.12	−0.12
Teradyne Inc.	1	Instruments	3825	−0.12	−0.12
Hercules Inc.	2	Chemicals	2821	−0.10	− 0.09 to −0.10
Black and Decker Corp.	1	Machinery, tools	3540	−0.09	−0.09
Syntex Corp.	4	Pharmaceuticals	2834	−0.09	− 0.03 to −0.13
Boeing Co.	5	Aerospace	3721	−0.07	− 0.04 to −0.13
Bolar Pharmaceutical	1	Pharmaceuticals	2834	−0.05	−0.05
Monsanto Co.	1	Chemicals	2800	−0.05	−0.05
Diebold Inc.	1	Office equipment	3578	−0.05	−0.05
Merck & Co. Inc.	5	Pharmaceuticals	2834	−0.05	− 0.01 to −0.08
Abbott Laboratories	3	Pharmaceuticals	2834	−0.05	−0.05 to −0.05
Lockheed Corp.	2	Aerospace	3760	−0.05	−0.04 to −0.06
Johnson & Johnson	2	Pharmaceuticals	2834	−0.04	−0.01 to −0.06
E.I Du Pont de Nemours	2	Chemicals	2820	−0.04	−0.03 to −0.05
Bristol Myers Co.	1	Pharmaceuticals	2834	−0.03	−0.03

(*Continued*)

TABLE 10 | *(Continued)*

Firm	# announcement	Industry[a]	Primary SIC (4-digit)	Average *CSM*[b]	Range of *CSM*[c] (for multiple announcements only)
Northern Telecom Ltd.	4	Telecommunication	3661	−0.02	0.00 to −0.05
Dow Chemical Co.	3	Chemicals	2800	−0.02	0.00 to −0.03
Schering Plough Corp.	7	Pharmaceuticals	2834	−0.01	0.01 to −0.03
Genentech Inc.	2	Pharmaceuticals	2834	0.00	0.00 to 0.00
IBM	2	Computers	3570	0.00	0.00 to 0.00
Pfizer Inc.	1	Pharmaceuticals	2834	0.01	0.01
Amdahl Corp.	1	Computers	3571	0.02	0.02
Baxter International Inc.	2	Pharmaceuticals	2834	0.02	0.02 to 0.02
Allied Signal Inc.	2	Conglomerate	3724	0.03	0.02 to 0.04
Dexter Corportation	1	Chemicals	2821	0.03	0.03
Knogo Corp.	1	Electronics	3669	0.04	0.04
Honeywell Inc.	2	Instruments	3822	0.04	0.04 to 0.04
Beckman Instruments Inc.	1	Instruments	3826	0.04	0.04
Warner Lambert Co.	4	Pharmaceuticals	2834	0.06	0.02 to 0.08
Eastman Kodak Co.	5	Leisure products	3861	0.07	0.05 to 0.09
Texas Instruments Inc.	3	Semiconductors	3674	0.09	0.08 to 0.10
Eli Lilly & Co	1	Pharmaceuticals	2834	0.10	0.10
American Cyanamid Co.	2	Chemicals	2800	0.11	0.06 to 0.14
AT&T Corp.	1	Telecommunication	4813	0.12	0.12
General Dyanmics Corp.	1	Aerospace	3721	0.13	0.13
Alcoa Internationals	2	Aluminum	3334	0.14	0.14 to 0.14
NCR	1	Computers	3570	0.19	0.19
Xerox Corp.	1	Peripherals	3861	0.19	0.19
Data General Co.	1	Computers	3570	0.19	0.19
Gillette Co.	1	Personal care	3420	0.22	0.22
Grumman Corp.	2	Aerospace	3721	0.39	0.33 to 0.45
International Flavors & Fragrances Inc.	1	Personal care	2844	0.40	0.40

[a]Industry definition is based on the *BusinessWeek R&D Scoreboard.*

[b]Average *CSM* for the various years, in the case of multiple announcements by the same firm.

[c]Only one value in the case of firms with one announcement.

References

Allen, F., 1985, Capital structure and imperfect competition in product markets, Discussion paper (University of Pennsylvania, Philadelphia, PA).

Brander, James and Tracey Lewis, 1986, Oligopoly and financial structure: The limited liability effect, American Economic Review 76, 956–970.

Bulow, Jeremy, John Geanakoplos, and Paul Klemperer, 1985, Multimarket oligopoly: Strategic substitutes and complements, Journal of Political Economy 93, 488–511.

Chan, Su Han, John Martin, and John Kensinger, 1990, Corporate research and development expenditures and share value, Journal of Financial Economics 26, 255–276.

Chevalier, J., 1993a, Debt and product market competition: An event study of supermarket LBOs, Working paper (Harvard University, Cambridge, MA).

Chevalier, J., 1993b, Capital structure and product market competition: A study of supermarket pricing, Working paper (Harvard University, Cambridge, MA).

Cohen, Wesley and Richard Levin, 1989, Empirical studies of innovation and market structure, in: R. Schmalensee and R.D. Willig, eds., Handbook of industrial organization, Vol. II (Elsevier Science Inc., New York, NY).

Dodd, Peter, 1980, Merger proposals, management discretion and stockholder wealth, Journal of Financial Economics 8, 105–137.

Doukas, John and Lorne Switzer, 1992, The stock market's valuation of R&D spending and market concentration, Journal of Economics and Business 44, 95–114.

Fudenberg, Drew and Jean Tirole, 1984, The fat-cat effect, the puppy dog ploy, and the lean and hungry look, American Economic Review Papers and Proceedings 74, 361–366.

Gertner, R., R. Gibbons, and D. Scharfstein, 1988, Simultaneous signalling to the capital and product markets, Rand Journal of Economics 19, 173–190.

Glazer, J., 1989, Live and let live: Collusion among oligopolists with long-term debt, Working paper (Boston University, Boston, MA).

Glazer, J. and R. Israel, 1990, Managerial incentives and financial signalling in product-market competition, International Journal of Industrial Economics 8, 271–280.

Hall, Bronwyn H., 1993, The stock market's valuation of R&D investment during the 1980s, American Economic Review Papers and Proceedings 83, 259–264.

Houlthausen, Robert W. and Richard W. Leftwich, 1986, The effect of bond rating changes on common stock prices, Journal of Financial Economics 17, 57–89.

Jensen, M., 1993, The modern industrial revolution, exit, and the failure of internal control systems, Journal of Finance 48, 831–880.

Maksimovic, V., 1988, Capital structure in repeated oligopolies, Rand Journal of Economics 19, 308–407.

Milgrom, Paul and John Roberts, 1990a, The economics of modern manufacturing, American Economic Review 80, 511–528.

Milgrom, Paul and John Roberts, 1990b, Rationalizability, learning and equilibrium in games with strategic complementarities, Econometrica 58, 1255–1278.

Rotemberg, Julio and David Scharfstein, 1990, Shareholder value maximization and product market competition, Review of Financial Studies 3, 367–393.

Reinganum, Jennifer, 1989, The timing of innovation: Research, development and diffusion, in: R. Schmalensee and R.D. Willig, eds., Handbook of industrial organization, Vol. II (Elsevier Science Inc., New York, NY).

Ruback, Richard S., 1982, The effects of discriminatory price control decisions on equity values, Journal of Financial Economics 10, 83–105.

Spence, A.M., 1984, Cost reduction, competition, and industry performance, Econometrica 52, 101–121.

Sundaram, Anant and Kose John, 1992, Signalling models and product market games in finance: Do we know what we know?, Working paper (NYU Stern School of Business, New York, NY).

Tirole, J., 1988, Theory of industrial organization (MIT Press, Cambridge, MA).

Twenty-One

Jaime F. Zender

Jaime F. Zender received a Ph.D. from Yale University in 1988. He started out at the Business School at the University of Utah, and now works at the Leeds School of Business at the University of Colorado. •

It is not an exaggeration to say that I wouldn't be working in finance today if it weren't for Steve Ross. I entered Yale's Doctoral program in economics intending to study macroeconomics. I changed my career plans in the first two weeks of Steve's seminar in finance due to the clarity of his presentation style and his enthusiasm for the subject. To this day, every time I develop a new lecture for any class, I try to envision how Steve would communicate the material. Even as a student, it was stunning to me how much understanding he could convey with a single question.

My strongest memory of Steve during the time I was writing my dissertation is that, no matter how hard I worked on a problem, whenever I walked into his office something was wrong. What was worse was that he always managed to point it out in the first minute of our conversation. It was so consistent that it became a standing joke between my roommate and me. There was one month during the third year in my doctoral program that I was feeling unusually good about my work and I consciously avoided seeing him altogether. Looking back, I often wonder what I missed.

The paper I have chosen for this volume is a chapter of my dissertation. "Capital Structure and Dividend Irrelevance with Asymmetric Information" was published in the *Review of Financial Studies* in 1991. This paper made sense not only because it bases its main argument on a "Ross style agency model" but also because my co-author is Phil Dybvig. Phil was also one of Steve's students, making me a "grandson" in Steve's academic family. This work followed the appearance of a number of papers that developed signaling or agency cost models of capital structure or dividend policy relevance. A common feature of many of these models was the reliance on an *ad hoc* incentive contract for the decision maker. Our approach was to consider in a general framework the implications of using an optimal incentive contract. Perhaps not surprisingly, for a broad set of models, financial policies are irrelevant once an optimal managerial contract is selected.

Steve also heavily influenced another of my papers in the agency/contract design area. "Do Incentives Matter? Managerial Contracts for Dual-Purpose Funds" (joint work with my colleagues Mike Lemmon and Jim Schallheim) was published in the *Journal of Political Economy* in 2000. This paper, using an almost ideal setting, shows the strong correlation between actual behavior and expected compensation maximizing behavior. Despite the publication date, this project was started shortly after I left Yale as an attempt on my part to learn more about option pricing. Shortly after we began looking at the data, we realized that something very interesting was going on. The realization came that it was driven by incentives; this was heavily influenced by my association with Steve. During our discussions on the topic, he had always emphasized the important influence on the behavior of fund managers. This is one of my papers of which I am most proud, despite the fact that I still know very little about option pricing.

Steve, for your time, your enthusiasm, and the excitement of my career, I thank you.

Capital Structure and Dividend Irrelevance with Asymmetric Information

Philip H. Dybvig
Washington University in St. Louis

Jaime F. Zender
University of Utah

The Modigliani and Miller propositions on the irrelevancy of capital structure and dividends are shown to be valid in a large class of models with asymmetric information. The main assumption is that managerial compensation is chosen optimally. This differs from most of the recent articles on this topic, which impose by fiat a suboptimal contract. Even when imperfections internal to the firm preclude optimal investment, there is a separation between incentives and financing. We conclude that corporations should move toward contracts with better incentives, and that new models should be built that recognize the limitations to optimal contracting. •

The Modigliani and Miller (1958, 1963; Miller and Modigliani, 1961) irrelevancy propositions imply that capital structure and dividend policy are matters of irrelevance in the absence of transaction costs, taxes, and informational asymmetries. If the irrelevancy propositions accurately explain the world, then we cannot hope to develop any model that can predict or prescribe capital structure or dividend policy. More interestingly, irrelevancy propositions indicate where not to look for predictive and prescriptive models. Furthermore, irrelevancy propositions provide a framework for classifying different potential models in which capital structure or dividend policy is relevant, based on how the assumptions of the irrelevancy propositions have been violated. For these reasons, the irrelevancy propositions have been the benchmark against which models of capital structure and dividend policy have been evaluated. The purpose of this article is to extend the irrelevancy propositions to a large class of models with asymmetric information.

The irrelevancy propositions in this article may seem to be logically inconsistent with a number of articles presenting models in which asymmetric information does make capital structure or dividend policy matter.[1] The main difference between this article and most of the existing literature is in the manager's assumed incentives: while we determine the manager's incentives as an optimal choice, most articles in the literature assume suboptimal

[1]Some examples of important articles in this literature are Bhattacharya (1980), Miller and Rock (1985), Myers and Majluf (1984), Harris and Raviv (1985), and Ross (1977). This article is closest in spirit to the Ross article, since the optimal incentive contract is discussed (but not derived) in that article. The article by Myers and Majluf also recognizes this issue, and explores several incentive contracts that seem "natural," but does not examine an optimal contract.

An earlier version of this article appeared as a chapter of Zender's Ph.D. thesis [Zender (1988)]. Dybvig is grateful for support under the Sloan Research Fellowship program. We are grateful for helpful comments from Jeff Borland, Joel Demskt, Doug Diamond, Thomas George, Jon Ingersoll, Saman Majid, Merton Miller, Steve Ross, Chester Spatt, and many seminar participants at different schools.

Reprinted with permission:
Dybvig, Phillip H. and Jaime F. Zender. "Capital Structure and Dividend Irrelevance with Asymmetric Information." *Review of Financial Studies* 4 (1991): 201–219.

incentives. Some of these articles also assume implicitly that it is useful for managers to signal information about the firm to the market. In fact, if the information possessed by managers is firm-specific, this implicit assumption is probably incorrect.[2]

The starting point for our analysis is Myers and Majluf (1984), a distinguished representative of the literature we are criticizing. Myers and Majluf consider several suboptimal objectives for managers, but we will focus on their leading case of a manager who is assumed to act on behalf of existing shareholders who hold their investment until the end, when the firm is liquidated. While this may sound like a reasonable managerial objective, Myers and Majluf demonstrate that it implies suboptimal investment. Specifically, suppose that the manager has private information about existing assets and about a potential new project. A manager who observes very good news about the existing projects would refrain from taking on a new project that is only modestly profitable, because a stock offering at a price based on public information would imply too much of a dilution of the existing shares. Of course, this suboptimal behavior is anticipated by investors and results in an initial offering price that is lower than it would be under an optimal investment policy.

We develop a series of models based on the framework of Myers and Majluf but solving for optimal contracts using the approach to agency theory pioneered by Ross (1973). In these models, we show that investment is optimal, while capital structure and dividend policy are irrelevant. The optimality of investment is due to the special feature of Myers and Majluf's model: there are no imperfections within the firm related to agency problems of costly managerial effort. We also derive the more general result of separation of financing and incentives: financing does not affect the value of the firm in the presence of imperfect information, provided that the market does not generate information (in its valuation of the firm's obligations) that is valuable to the manager or to those agents evaluating the manager, and provided that costly information gathering does not depress the market price.[3] All these results are in Section 1.

An important implicit assumption of our analysis is that financial claims and control rights can be assigned equally well to different outside claimants. This assumption seems to be reasonable for a firm with publicly traded claims, provided that the law does not include arbitrary restrictions to contracting. For example, it would be inconsistent with our assumptions to have a legal system in which the equityholders can always fire the manager at will and introduce a new manager with a new incentive contract. It seems reasonable that it is possible for equityholders to commit not to do this because of restrictions or incentives built into the corporate charter, bond indentures, offering statements, and other contracts entered into by the firm. (One interesting potential reason for having a particular type of claim is to make sure that some agent has a vested interest in making sure that contracts are enforced, although this concept is outside of our model, which assumes that contracting on observables is not a problem.) Note that if managerial incentives or actions by equity's representatives are simply unobservable, it is unclear how the holders of publicly traded equity can verify that the manager has an incentive to act on their behalf in the first place.

---

[2]Earlier drafts of the article contained a section on the value of early release of information by a firm. That analysis showed that earlier release of information does not, in itself, make shareholders better off or the firm more valuable ex ante. The section also contained a very simple and general proof of the resolution uncertainty result of Ross (1989) on which our analysis is based. It also included an example that shows that learning about a firm's beta is idiosyncratic risk. That entire analysis can be found in Dybvig and Zender (1990).

[3]Several information economists have suggested to us that the real surprise is not that there is a separation of financing and incentives, but rather that anyone would ever think otherwise. [See, e.g., Hart and Hölmstrom (1987, p. 90).] Our analysis shows how and under what circumstances the information economists' perspective applies to existing models in finance.

If we were to consider a sole proprietorship, however, the assignability of control rights seems much less obvious: for example, the manager may also be the main equityholder. This is why we think of our model as being most clearly applicable to publicly traded firms.

To tie our analysis to the empirical literature, we present an example showing that the Modigliani–Miller irrelevancy propositions are consistent with the stylized empirical facts. The idea behind the example is that in very good states, the existing project generates the funds needed to undertake any new project, and therefore a new issue is bad news. If the manager has good news about the new project but bad news about the old project, the manager raises debt, which is only slightly bad news. If the manager has bad news about both new and old projects, the manager raises equity, which is very bad news. All of this is consistent with optimal investment. Therefore, even if the empirical evidence agrees more or less with Myers and Majluf, this agreement is not convincing proof that their story is correct; the same empirical evidence is consistent with optimal investment in a world in which the Modigliani and Miller irrelevancy propositions hold. The example is in Section 2.

1. The Model

In the simplest model of Myers and Majluf (1994), the manager is assumed to act on behalf of original shareholders who plan to hold their stock until liquidation of the firm. The manager has private information both about the value of existing assets in place and about the value of a new potential investment. When the new project is marginally profitable and the existing asset is sufficiently more profitable than is typical, the manager knows that the issue price of the new shares will be significantly less than their intrinsic value. Because of the manager's assumed objective, the manager will perceive a loss due to the underpricing of new shares. If this perceived loss is larger than the profitability of the investment, the manager will refrain from making the new investment. The perceived loss is not an economic loss (it is a transfer), which is why a profitable project may be passed by. This rejection of profitable projects is the inefficiency in the Myers and Majluf model.

1.1. Optimal Investment

Our first model follows Myers and Majluf's first model very closely, except that the manager's incentive contract is chosen endogenously.[4] We study a single firm existing over three periods (0, 1, and 2). In period 0, the firm is established by an entrepreneur who invests an amount I^a in the firm's initial project, hires a manager, and chooses the manager's contract $s(\cdot)$, anticipating the manager's reactions to the incentives created by the contract. In this initial period, all agents have the same information, which includes knowledge of the distributions of the exogenous random variables (a and b, to be introduced shortly) and the structure of the problems faced by all agents, At the end of this initial period, the entrepreneur sells the new firm by making an equity issue (an initial public offering or IPO).[5] In period 1, the manager learns two pieces of private information: the realization a of the profit a (payoff in excess of I^a) to capital in place, and the realization b of the prospective profit b (payoff in excess of I^b) of a prospective investment opportunity requiring

[4]As mentioned in note 1, Myers and Majluf did consider several alternative managerial contracts, but not any optimal contract.

[5]It is only a matter of convenience that we are looking at an initial public offering. An ongoing firm with bad incentives in place may not find it desirable to move instantly to the optimal contract (because of potential information asymmetries), but should be able to plan such a change at some time in the future when the usefulness of most information now available will have evaporated. Because of the prospective efficiency gain, there are some terms on which this arrangement will be attractive to all interested parties.

an investment I^b. After observing a and b, the manager chooses whether to undertake the new investment project. We code the manager's choice as d: $d = 1$ if the manager undertakes the new investment, and $d = 0$ if not. The manager's choice is made known to the public, and if the new investment is undertaken, the firm issues new equity worth I^b to finance the project. (We consider later the possibility that the manager may choose to issue debt instead.) In period 2, all payoffs are realized, and the public learns the total profit $a + bd$. It is reasonable that the public learns $a + bd$ but not a and b separately, because we think of the new project as being inextricably tied to the original project. For example, the new project may be an upgrading of the capital used in the original project. (If the payoffs were ultimately separable, there is no reason in the model why the new project could not be spun off with separate accounting.) At the end of period 2, the manager is compensated and the residual goes to the shareholders.[6]

We retain Myers and Majluf's assumptions that all agents are risk-neutral and that there is no discounting. End-of-period prices of the original equity issue, denoted by P_0, P_1, and P_2, are formed rationally. The price at each time can depend only on the public's information at that time; therefore, we can write the equilibrium pricing functions as P_0 (there is "no" public information at 0), $P_1(d)$, and $P_2(d, a + bd)$.[7] The manager's choice of d is based on the manager's information at time 1, namely, a and b, and therefore we write the decision rule as $d(a, b)$. The agent's compensation scheme (sharing rule) $s(a + bd, d, P_1, P_2)$ is permitted to depend on all information that is publicly available at the end of time 2.[8] As in Myers and Majluf, the manager cannot trade on his own account to undo the incentive contract with the firm, and the incentive contract is common knowledge. Rents extracted from the manager are limited by the agent's reservation utility level $U^* > 0$. We assume that $U^* < E[a]$, which is sufficient to ensure that it is optimal to form the firm in the first place. We also assume that a and b both have compact support; to avoid discussions of ties, we assume that the probability that $b = 0$ is zero.

The entrepreneur faces Problem 1, given in Table 1. An informal representation of the decision problem is as follows: Choose a compensation scheme, an equilibrium investment decision rule, and prices to maximize the initial value of the IPO subject to (i) the manager's equilibrium payoff (just a definition), (ii) the rationality of stock prices, (iii) the incentive compatibility of the investment decision rule, and (iv) the manager's reservation utility constraint. The main difference between our model and that of Myers and Majluf is that the manager's objective [here embodied in the contract $s(a + bd, d, P_1, P_2)$] is determined endogenously. The objective most emphasized by Myers and Majluf is to act on behalf of shareholders who plan to hold to the end, which amounts to taking $s(a + bd, d, P_1, P_2)$ to be equal to a constant plus a tiny proportion of P_2. Another difference between our model and that of Myers and Majluf is that we assume that the profit levels a and b are

[6]Taken literally, the formal statements of the choice problems imply that shareholders are also assessed for any shortfall. This is an inessential feature of the model. We could assume instead that $I^a + a$ and $I^b + b$ are never negative and that $s(\cdot)$ is constrained to leave nonnegative residual, and none of this would change the optimal value of our problem (and a nonempty subset of the set of optimal solutions would remain feasible), provided the manager's reservation utility level is not too large.

[7]We could make P_2 depend on P_1 as well, but this is redundant, because there are no game-theoretic issues of perfection.

[8]As with P_1, it is formally redundant to include P_1 and P_2. In fact, this simple observation is one theme of the article: optimal contracting is independent of financing because using market prices cannot improve on contracts that already exploit the public information on which the market prices are based. (Of course, it is possible that the market price aggregates information not available within the firm, but it seems like a good approximation that the value of this information in evaluating the manager is small.) Including P_1 and P_2 is required, if we want to admit explicitly the contracts implicit in Myers and Majluf's model.

TABLE 1 | Entrepreneur's Choice Problem 1

Choose $s(a + bd, d, P_1, P_2)$, $d^*(a, b)$, $P_1(d)$, and $P_2(d, a + bd)$, to maximize $P_0 = E[I^a + a + bd^*(a, b) - s^*(a, b)]$, subject to

(i) $s^*(a, b) = s(a + bd^*(a, b), d^*(a, b), P_1(d^*(a, b)), P_2(d^*(a, b)), a + bd^*(a, b)))$

(iia) $P_1(d) = E[I^a + a + bd - s^*(a, b) | d^*(a, b) = d]$

(iib) $P_2(d, a + bd) = \dfrac{P_1(d)}{P_1(d) + I^b d}[I^a + I^b d + (a + bd) - s(a + bd, d, P_1(d), P_2(d, a + bd))]$

(iii) $d^*(a, b)$ uniquely solves:
Choose $d(a, b)$ to
$\max E[s(a + bd(a, b), d(a, b), P_1(d(a, b)), P_2(d(a, b), a + bd(a, b)))]$
s.t. $(\forall a, b) d(a, b) = 0$ or 1
$(\forall a, b) s(a + bd(a, b), d(a, b), P_1(d(a, b)), P_2(d(a, b), a + bd(a, b))) \geq 0$

(iv) $E[s^*(a, b)] \geq U^*$

not separately observable by the public at the end, or else we could trivially obtain the first best directly using a forcing contract to induce the manager to follow the first-best decision rule. On a related point, Myers and Majluf assume that $b \geq 0$ with probability 1. We want to relax this assumption (to allow $b < 0$ with positive probability), or else the first best would obtain trivially under a forcing contract enforcing $d = 1$.

For simplicity, it is assumed that the entrepreneur retains no equity. The issue price P_0 for the initial public offering is the sunk investment I^a in place plus the expectation of profit $a + bd(a, b)$, less the expectation of manager's compensation $s^*(a, b)$. This is because the issue price of stock in a competitive market includes a rational assessment of all net rents (including an allowance for any inefficiency of investment). Also, we assume that the firm has no financial slack, because the existence of slack does not affect our results.

The first constraint in Problem 1 simply defines the manager's equilibrium payoff, which is based on equilibrium prices and the equilibrium decision rule. The first rationality-of-prices constraint (iia) follows directly from competitive risk-neutral pricing in the securities market. This expression is the same as the expression for P_0, except conditioned on public information at time 1. The second rationality-of-prices constraint (iib) takes into account the liquidation value of the firm and the dilution from the share issue (if any) at time 1. The factor $P_1(d)/(P_1(d) + I^b d)$ is the fraction of terminal firm ownership represented by the original shares. This factor multiplies the realized total value of investments less the manager's compensation.

The third constraint is the standard incentive-compatibility constraint for the manager. In this constraint, the requirement of a unique optimum rules out paying a constant and assuming the manager (who is therefore indifferent) follows a first-best investment rule. This requirement of a strict incentive is an imperfect substitute for the costly effort (see Problem 4) that would rule out paying a constant in a more complete model than that of Myers and Majluf. Finally, the reservation utility constraint ensures that the manager is paid enough to accept the position.

The first-best optimum is the solution to the entrepreneur's problem in the absence of incentive problems. In other words, we would maximize the offering price, subject to constraints (i), (ii), and (iv), and the *constraints* to the incentive compatibility problem [$d(a, b) = 0$ or 1 and $s \geq 0$]. Because of risk neutrality, the solution to this problem is trivial, since the form of the sharing rule does not matter so long as the reservation-utility constraint holds with equality. Therefore, the first-best choice problem reduces to

$$\text{Choose } d(a, b) \text{ to maximize } P_0 = E[I^a + a + bd(a, b)] - U^* .$$

Only the third term in the expectation is not a constant; therefore, the optimal strategy is to maximize the third term—that is, to take $d(a, b) = 1$ whenever $b > 0$, and to take $d(a, b) = 0$ whenever $b < 0$. To fill out a solution, we must choose a compensation scheme and equilibrium pricing rules. However, we can simply choose $s(\cdot) \equiv U^*$, defining the price function by the rationality constraints. In other words, the first-best optimum is characterized by efficient production: profitable new projects are always undertaken and money-losing projects are never undertaken.

Our first result is that we can obtain the first-best solution as the solution to the second-best problem, Problem 1 (including the incentive compatibility constraint), if we choose the sharing rule

$$s(a + bd, d, P_1, P_2) = \alpha + \beta(a + bd), \tag{1}$$

where α and $\beta > 0$ are constants chosen to make the reservation-utility constraint an equality and $s^*(a, b) > 0$. (This is feasible for β sufficiently small because a and b both have compact support.) This sharing rule clearly gives the manager a strict incentive to undertake the optimal investment rule

$$d^*(a, b) = \begin{cases} 1, & \text{for } b > 0, \\ 0, & \text{otherwise.} \end{cases} \tag{2}$$

Together with rationally determined prices $P_1(d)$ and $P_2(d, a + bd)$ [given by (iia) and (iib) in Problem 1], we have a solution to Problem 1 that implements the first best.

Because we can use P_1 and P_2 to measure $a + bd$ indirectly, the form of the optimal contract is indeterminant [beyond the choice of β in (1)]. One economically interesting alternative is to take

$$s(a + bd, d, P_1, P_2) = \alpha' + \beta'\left(P_2 + I^b d \frac{P_2 - P_1}{P_1}\right), \tag{3}$$

which also implements the optimal investment rule (2) as a solution of Problem 1, given rational pricing and provided α' and $\beta' > 0$ are chosen to maintain positivity and the reservation-utility constraint. Contract (3) is equivalent to (1) with $\beta = \beta'/(1 + \beta')$ and $\alpha = (\alpha' + \beta' I^a)/(1 + \beta')$, as can be seen by substituting constraint (iib) of Problem 1 into (3) and solving for s. Therefore, the incentives are the same. The interpretation of contract (3) is that the manager is paid a constant plus a term proportional to the portfolio of the initial stock plus a pro rata purchase and participation in new issues. In this way, if P_1 is out of line (based on the manager's information), the effect on compensation of any mispricing of existing shares is exactly offset by the effect on the pro rata purchase of new shares. For example, if the manager knows that a is very large, the prospective capital loss on the existing shares (the dilution effect) is exactly offset by the windfall gain on the implicit purchase of underpriced new shares. The net effect is to make the manager indifferent about the price at which the new issue is made, and to care only about the fundamental value of the firm. The share price is correct on average, but does not fully reflect the manager's information in each state of nature.[9]

How does this solution relate to that of Myers and Majluf? The main difference is that Myers and Majluf assume by fiat the objective function of the manager. The objective function assumed by Myers and Majluf is consistent with the compensation scheme

$$s(a + bd, d, P_1, P_2) = \alpha'' + \beta'' P_2, \tag{4}$$

[9]It may surprise the reader that this informational inefficiency of prices does not represent an economic (Pareto) inefficiency that is reflected in the price of the firm. Intuitively, this is because the timing of resolution of idiosyncratic risk does not matter when investors are equally informed.

for α'' and sufficiently small $\beta'' > 0$, chosen to satisfy positivity and the reservation-utility constraint. This rule is compared most simply to the optimal rule of the form given in (3), with $\alpha' = \alpha''$ and $\beta' = \beta''$. The term that differs is the term $\beta' I^b d(P_2 - P_1)/P_1$, which neutralizes the manager's preferences over mispricing in the middle period. Without this term, the manager has an incentive to forgo investment (set $d = 0$) when b is small and an offer would imply a price $P_1(d = 1)$ significantly less than the manager's assessment $P_2(1, a + b)$.

1.2. Capital Structure

In Problem 1, we assumed that the manager financed all new investments using equity exclusively. In this section, we look at an analogous problem (Problem 2), which allows the manager to finance new investments using a mix of debt and equity selected by the manager. Problem 2 is contained in Table 2. The introduction of debt is the main change from Problem 1. This corresponds to the introduction of a new choice variable, F, which is the face value of debt issued at the end of period 1. Rational bond prices are formed as conditional expectations given all public information, just as stock prices are, only all public information now includes the size of the debt issue. Furthermore, we include the effect of leverage on the stock price, and a constraint (v) that the size of the bond issue does not exceed the value of the firm.[10]

TABLE 2 | Entrepreneur's Choice Problem 2

Choose $s(a + bd, d, P, P_1, P_2, B_1, B_2)$, $d^*(a, b)$, $F^*(a, b)$, $P_1(d, F)$, $P_2(d, F, a + bd)$, $B_1(d, F)$, and $B_2(d, F, a + bd)$, to maximize $P_0 = E[I^a + a + bd^*(a, b) - s^*(a, b)]$, subject to

(i) $s^*(a, b) = s(a + bd^*(a, b), d^*(a, b), F^*(a, b), P_1(d^*(a, b), F^*(a, b)), P_2(d^*(a, b), F^*(a, b), a + bd^*(a, b)), B_1(d^*(a, b), F^*(a, b)), B_2(d^*(a, b), F^*(a, b), a + bd^*(a, b)))$

(iia) $P_1(d, F) = E[I^a + a + bd - s^*(a, b) \mid d^*(a, b) = d, F^*(a, b) = F]$

(iib) $P_2(d, F, a + bd) = \dfrac{P_1(d, F)}{P_1(d, F) + I^b d - B_1(d, F)}[\max(0, I^a + I^b d + (a + bd) - F - s(a + bd, d, F, P_1(D, F), P_2(d, F, a + bd), B_1(d, F), B_2(d, F, a + bd)))]$

(iic) $B_1(d, F) = E[\min(F, I^a + I^b d + a + bd - s^*(a, b)) \mid d^*(a, b) = d, F^*(a, b) = F]$

(iid) $B_2(d, F, a + bd) = \min(F, I^a + I^b d + (a + bd) - s(a + bd, d, F, P_1(d, F), P_2(d, F, a + bd), B_1(d, F), B_2(d, F, a + bd)))$

(iii) Together, $d^*(a, b)$ and $F^*(a, b)$ uniquely solve:
Choose $d(a, b)$ and $F(a, b)$ to
$\max E[s(a + bd(a, b), d(a, b), F(a, b), P_1(d(a, b), F(a, b)), P_2(d(a, b), F(a, b), a + bd(a, b)), B_1(d(a, b), F(a, b)), B_2(d(a, b), F(a, b), a + bd(a, b)))]$
s.t. $(\forall a, b) d(a, b) = 0$ or 1
$(\forall a, b)\ s(a + bd(a, b), d(a, b), F(a, b), P_1(d(a, b), F(a, b)), P_2(d(a, b), F(a, b), a + bd(a, b)), B_1(d(a, b), F(a, b)), B_2(d(a, b), F(a, b), a + bd(a, b))) \geq 0$

(iv) $E[s^*(a, b)] \geq U^*$

(v) $(\forall a, b)\ B_1(d^*(a, b), F^*(a, b)) < P_1(d^*(a, b), F^*(a, b)) + I^b d^*(a, b)$

[10] As a technical aside, there is in principle an issue of how the conditional expectation in (iia) should be formed if the choice of debt issue is not in the support of the set of values anticipated by shareholders. In game-theoretic terms, this is an issue of perfection, which deals with the equation of how to form expectations on events thought to be impossible [see Rasmusen (1989, chap. 5) for an introductory discussion of perfection]. However, this whole problem is not an issue given the optimal contract, since the manager does not care about the market price in the middle period.

Other features of the new choice problem represent an attempt to avoid unneeded complexity. For example, we have not precluded a "short" bond issue—that is, issuing equity to buy bonds—nor have we precluded a swap of equity for debt. (We *have* precluded a swap of debt for equity, but only "accidentally," since we start with an all-equity firm.) These assumptions keep the choice problem from becoming even messier without affecting the economic message.

As before, the first-best solution (i.e., the solution in the absence of the incentive-compatibility constraint) includes an investment policy of undertaking only the new projects that are economically profitable, while paying the manager the reservation utility in expectation. Subject to the constraint of leaving some equity in the firm (which we have imposed a priori), capital structure is irrelevant to the value of this problem. Given any capital structure, we can solve out the remaining constraints of the problem (with reservation utility as an equality) to obtain an expression that is the expected value of the firm, net of the reservation utility and expected investment expenditure. This is essentially the irrelevancy of capital structure in the absence of informational asymmetries, because the first-best solution is what arises if all information is shared.

As in Problem 1, if we did not require uniqueness for the solution to Problem 2, we would obtain a trivial solution with a constant salary and directions to follow the optimal strategy. Given our requirement of uniqueness, it is necessary for the debt issue $F^*(a, b)$ to depend on a and b only through d and $a + bd$, which is the information that can be verified ex post by the market.[11] In any first-best solution, knowing d tells us precisely whether $b \gtreqless 0$. Therefore, we can obtain positive incentives for no issue, equity, or debt when $b < 0$. We also can simultaneously provide positive incentives to issue equity only when $a + bd < 0$, and debt only when $a + bd \geq 0$. This policy (with optimal investment and the asset prices then implied by rationality of pricing) is supported by the compensation scheme

$$\begin{aligned} s(a + bd, d, F, P_1, P_2, B_1, B_2) \\ = \alpha + \beta(a + bd) - d\delta(d, a + bd, F), \end{aligned} \tag{5}$$

where

$$\delta(d, a + bd, F) = \begin{cases} 0, & \begin{cases} \text{if } a + bd < 0 \text{ and } B_1(d_1 F) = 0, \text{ or} \\ \text{if } a + bd \geq 0 \text{ and } B_1(d_1 F) = I^b, \end{cases} \\ \\ k, & \text{otherwise,} \end{cases} \tag{6}$$

$B_1(\cdot)$ is the rational bond price under the stated policy, and the constants are chosen for feasibility (β and k chosen small enough for positivity, and α chosen to make the reservation-utility constraint an equality). Of course, this is not the only optimal scheme: "any" rule for issue of debt and equity as a function of the optimal d and $a + bd$ can be implemented in an equilibrium with first-best investment (where "any" means subject only to nonnegative equity and rational pricing).

While the formal analysis in this section applies only to a split between debt and equity, it should be clear by now that the same arguments will work for many sorts of financial issues, including not only straight debt and equity but also subordinated debt, preferred stock, warrants, convertible bonds, and the like.

[11]The restrictions to functions of d and $a + bd$ are not needed if we are willing to forgo uniqueness of the capital-structure choice in the incentive-compatibility constraint.

1.3. Dividend Policy

Problem 3 deviates from Problem 1 in giving the informed manager a choice of dividend policy. To avoid unneeded complexity, we restrict the manager to issuing only equity, although irrelevancy of dividend policy is obviously not dependent on this assumption. The formal statement of the problem appears in Table 3. The problem is solved by the sharing rule given in (1) but modified to punish inappropriate dividend policy, optimal investment, and any dividend strategy restricted to depend on a and b only through d and $a + bd$, which is the information that can be verified ex post by the market.[12] An optimal sharing rule based on market prices, similar to (3), can easily be derived. This sharing rule differs from (3) in that the manager receives a pro rata share of any dividends paid.

1.4. Separation of Incentives and Financing

In previous subsections, we have studied models in which equilibrium investment is optimal. This feature is special to the Myers and Majluf framework we have considered. One degenerate feature of the Myers and Majluf model is that there is no costly effort. If the model included costly effort on the part of a risk-averse manager, we would have the traditional trade-off between incentives and risk-sharing that occurs in all significant agency problems. This trade-off would imply a second-best solution in which there is suboptimal investment. Nonetheless, financing would not matter in the sense that the degree of suboptimality of investment does not depend on financing. The reason is that the "real" set of feasible contracts to the manager does not depend on financing.

To obtain the general result, we assume there are no taxes or transaction costs (to avoid the traditional violations of Modigliani and Miller), and the additional assumption that the information available to the public (and potentially revealed through the stock price) is a function of information known by the manager and those evaluating the manager. (Or, more generally, we could assume that the public information is not marginally useful to the

TABLE 3 | Entrepreneur's Choice Problem 3

Choose $s(a + bd, d, D, P_1, P_2)$, $d^*(a, b)$, $D^*(a, b)$, $P_1(d, D)$ (ex-dividend), and $P_2(d, D, a + bd)$, to maximize $P_0 = E[I^a + a + bd^*(a, b) - s^*(a, b)]$, subject to

(i) $s^*(a, b) = s(a + bd^*(a, b), d^*(a, b), D^*(a, b), P_1(d^*(a, b), D^*(a, b)), P_2(d^*(a, b), D^*(a, b), a + bd^*(a, b)))$

(iia) $P_1(d, D) = E[I^a + a + bd - s^*(a, b) \mid d^*(a, b) = d, D^*(a, b) = D]$

(iib) $$P_2(d, D, a + bd) = \frac{P_1(d, D)}{P_1(d, D) + I^b d + D}[I^a + I^b d + (a + bd) - s(a + bd, d, D, P_1(d, D), P_2(d, D, a + bd))]$$

(iii) Together, $d^*(a, b)$ and $D^*(a, b)$ uniquely solve:
Choose $d(a, b)$ and $D(a, b)$ to
$\max E[s(a + bd(a, b), d(a, b), D(a, b), P_1(d(a, b), D(a, b)), P_2(d(a, b), D(a, b), a + bd(a, b)))]$
s.t. $(\forall a, b) d(a, b) = 0$ or 1
$(\forall a, b) D(a, b) \geq 0$
$(\forall a, b) s(a + bd(a, b), d(a, b), D(a, b), P_1(d(a, b), D(a, b)), P_2(d(a, b), D(a, b), a + bd(a, b))) \geq 0$

(iv) $E[s^*(a, b)] \geq U^*$

(v) $(\forall a, b)\ P_1(d^*(a, b), D^*(a, b)) > 0$

[12] The restrictions to functions of d and $a + bd$ are not needed if we are willing to forgo uniqueness of the dividend-policy choice in the incentive-compatibility constraint.

manager for making investment decisions or to the people evaluating the manager, given their information sets.) In the absence of this assumption, capital structure may influence the usefulness of the information revealed through prices. Once this assumption is satisfied, separation of incentives and financing is quite generally valid.

Because of risk-neutrality, it is implicitly assumed there are no imperfections in the capital market and no risk premium or liquidity premium. The results would be robust to competitive risk-pricing and discounting, provided the manager's information is idiosyncratic and not significantly predictive of market returns (as only seems reasonable). The results are not generally robust to the existence of a liquidity premium. In principle, anticipated information revelation by the manager could make the stock more liquid in the middle period and increase its initial offering price [see Diamond (1985)]. These issues were explored in more detail in an earlier draft (see note 2).

Here is the idea behind the proof, which uses composition of functions just like the proof of the revelation principle. Suppose a manager's compensation depends on market prices, the manager's actions, information that is publicly available (at some date), and fundamentals within the firm. We know that market prices depend only on the publicly available information in a known way. Therefore, we can "see through" the dependence of the compensation on market price, understanding that this is just an alternative way of introducing dependence on publicly available information. Furthermore, the manager's real actions can be retained, and the actions about financing can be changed to announcements. Once we realize this, we can rewrite the compensation directly as a function of publicly available information, the manager's actions and announcements, and fundamentals within the firm. This form of the compensation schedule is completely independent of the financial structure of the firm. Therefore, real choices (and consequently any market values) that are feasible under one financial policy are also feasible under all other financial policies.

Problem 4 (in Table 4) presents the entrepreneur's choice problem for a case that involves costly effort by a risk-averse manager. Problem 4 is a variation on Problem 1, with the following differences. Now, in addition to the investment decision that the manager

TABLE 4 | Entrepreneur's Choice Problem 4

Choose $s(a + bd, d, \theta, P_1, P_2)$, $d^*(\eta, \theta)$, $x^*(\eta, \theta)$, $P_1(d, \theta)$, and $P_2(d, \theta, a + bd)$, to maximize $P_0 = E[I^a + a^* + b^*d^*(\eta, \theta) - s^*(\eta, \theta)]$, subject to

(i) $s^*(\eta, \theta) = s(a^* + b^*d^*(\eta, \theta), d^*(\eta, \theta), \theta, P_1(d^*(\eta, \theta), \theta), P_2(d^*(\eta, \theta), \theta, a^* + b^*d^*(\eta, \theta)))$

(ii) $a^* = a(x^*(\eta, \theta), \eta, \theta)$ and $b^* = b(x^*(\eta, \theta), \eta, \theta)$

(iiia) $P_1(d, \theta) = E[I^a + a^* + b^*d - s^*(\eta, \theta) | \theta, d^*(\eta, \theta) = d]$

(iiib) $$P_2(d, \theta, a + bd) = \frac{P_1(d, \theta)}{P_1(d, \theta) + I^b d}[I^a + I^b d + (a(x, \eta, \theta) + b(x, \eta, \theta)d) - s(a(x, \eta, \theta) + b(x, \eta, \theta)d, d, \theta, P_1(d, \theta), P_2(d, \theta, a(x, \eta, \theta) + b(x, \eta, \theta)d))]$$

(iv) $d^*(\eta, \theta)$ and $x^*(\eta, \theta)$ solve:

Choose $d(\eta, \theta)$ and $x(\eta, \theta)$ to

$\max E[U(s(a(x(\eta, \theta), \eta, \theta) + b(x(\eta, \theta), \eta, \theta)\, d(\eta, \theta), d(\eta, \theta), \theta, P_1(d(\eta, \theta), \theta), P_2(d(\eta, \theta), \theta, a(x(\eta, \theta), \eta, \theta) + b(x,(\eta, \theta), \eta, \theta)\, d(\eta, \theta))), x(\eta, \theta))]$

s.t. $(\forall \eta, \theta)\ d(\eta, \theta) = 0$ or 1

$(\forall \eta, \theta)\ s(a(x(\eta, \theta), \eta, \theta) + b(x(\eta, \theta), \eta, \theta)\, d(\eta, \theta), d(\eta, \theta), \theta, P_1(d(\eta, \theta), \theta), P_2(d(\eta, \theta), \theta, a(x(\eta, \theta), \eta, \theta) + b(x(\eta, \theta), \eta, \theta)\, d(\eta, \theta))) \geq 0$

$(\forall \eta, \theta)\ x(\eta, \theta) \geq 0$

(v) $E[U(s^*(\eta, \theta), x^*(\eta, \theta))] \geq U^*$

must make on behalf of the shareholders, the manager must also choose a level of effort. The manager's effort is assumed to increase the profitability of the projects a and b, and the effectiveness of effort is allowed to depend upon the state of nature. The problem includes a public signal θ observed by all agents in the economy at time 1, and a private signal η observed only by the manager. These signals are interpreted as indicators of the realized state of nature (i.e., they contain information on the productivity of effort.)[13] In this problem, the manager chooses an investment policy $d(\eta, \theta)$ and effort policy $x(\eta, \theta)$ in order to maximize expected utility. We write the manager's utility generally as $U(s(\cdot), x(\cdot))$, and interpret $U(\cdot)$ as increasing in $s(\cdot)$ and decreasing in $x(\cdot)$.[14]

Demonstration of the irrelevance of the firm's capital structure in this problem follows the argument given above. The optimal sharing rule in this case can be written contingent on any of the publicly observable variables. This naturally includes P_1 and P_2. However, P_1 and P_2 are themselves known functions of other publicly available information. Therefore, any action that can be implemented using a sharing rule of the form $s(a + bd, d, \theta, P_1, P_2)$ can also be implemented by a contract of the form $s(a + bd, d, \theta)$, and the potential value of the firm is not affected by capital structure.

Note that in this problem efficient, or "first-best," investment is not generally achieved. The usual agency-model trade-offs between incentives and risk-sharing imply that the manager will not, at the entrepreneur's optimum, expend a first-best level of effort. New projects that would be profitable under the first-best rule will not be undertaken in this world. Therefore, we have shown irrelevance of capital structure and dividend policy, even when there are agency problems that prevent attainment of the first-best investment policy. This irrelevance is due to the separation between incentives and financing: the real choices (and, in particular, investment) implemented using an optimal contract are the same, independent of financing.

2. Reaction of Stock Prices to New Issues: Theory and Empirics

In this section we demonstrate, through the use of a simple numerical example, that the existing empirical evidence is consistent with the model presented here. The existing evidence on stock-price reaction to issues of new securities can be summarized as follows.[15] New security issues, in general, seem to be interpreted by the market to indicate bad news. The stock price of firms seeking new financing appears to drop at the announcement date of the new issues. The size (and statistical significance) of this drop is related to the type of security offered. Seasoned offerings of equity appear to be particularly bad news, whereas new issues of debt have a less negative (and statistically less significant or insignificant) impact on the stock price of the issuing firm.

Our example shows that the observed price reactions are consistent with optimal investment. We are not claiming that the story in this article is necessarily *the* correct story, Rather, we are pointing out that the existing empirical evidence does not discriminate

[13]The choice problem in Table 4 actually assumes that η and θ represent all the exogenous noise in the model, but this is convenience only. More generally, we could add another random argument ϵ to the functions $a(\cdot)$ and $b(\cdot)$ and our economic arguments would be unchanged (although the choice problem would be even messier).

[14]Much more structure is required to ensure the existence of a solution to Problem 4. As in most agency problems, even the usual concavity and Inada conditions are not enough to ensure the existence or even to make the agent's first-order conditions necessary and sufficient, since the endogenous choice of sharing function may undo the concavity of the agent's objective function. Formally, our results say that *if* there is a solution, it is independent of capital structure.

[15]See, for example, Asquith and Mullins (1984), Dann (1981). Dann and Mikkelson (1984), Eckbo (1986), Masulis and Korwar (1986), and Mikkelson and Partch (1986).

between a Myers-Majluf world and a world with efficient investment. In other words, interpretation of the empirical evidence should be in the context of a well-specified alternative against which the empirical test has power.

One idea behind the example is that, in very good states, the existing project generates the funds needed to undertake any new project; therefore, the fact that a firm requires new financing is bad news. In order to stay within the existing outline of our model, our example assumes that no new project is available in the very good state. (Another way of thinking of this is that in the very good state there is no new project *that requires outside financing.*)

The example follows. We assume there are three realizations to the value of the asset in place (project a) and the new project (b), if any. The three equally probable realizations of a and b are given by

State	*a*	*b*
1	1000	−100
2	100	100
3	100	300

Recall that in our model, at time 1, the manager is assumed to observe the realizations of a and b. This is equivalent to observing the realized state of nature. The ex ante expectations of these random variables are given by $\overline{a} = 400$ and $\overline{b} = 100$. We assume that the manager is given a compensation scheme that is similar to that given in Equations (5) and (6). Specifically, $s(\cdot)$ is given by

$$\begin{aligned} s(a + bd, d, F, P_1, P_2, B_1, B_2) \\ = \alpha + \beta(a + bd) - d\delta(d, a + bd, F), \end{aligned} \tag{7}$$

where

$$\delta(d, a + bd, F) = \begin{cases} 0, & \begin{cases} \text{if } a + bd = 200 \text{ and } B_1(d, F) = 0, \text{ or} \\ \text{if } a + bd = 400 \text{ and } B_1(d, F) = I^b, \end{cases} \\ k, & \text{otherwise.} \end{cases} \tag{8}$$

This contract gives the manager incentives to invest only in profitable new projects and to issue debt in state 3 and equity in state 2. We can interpret this as a financing strategy that aims to stabilize the debt/equity ratio of the firm or move it toward an industry average. Stabilizing the debt/equity ratio or moving toward the industry average is an arbitrary policy, but that is what many of today's managers have been taught to do; moreover, under the assumptions of this article, the policy is harmless.

Under the optimal investment policy, $d = 1$ if $b > 0$ and $d = 0$ otherwise (since there are no ties), and $E[a + bd] = 533.33$. Therefore, we can write the time 0 price of the original equity offering as $P_0 = I^a + 533.33$, where we have ignored the manager's compensation, which we think of as being negligible compared to the size of the firm. Now, consider the market-price reaction to issues of new securities. Under this contract, if the market, at time 1, observes a new issue being made by the firm, the market expects that state 2 or 3 has been realized. The new issue is bad news. If debt is offered by the firm at time 1, the market expects that state 3 has been realized and the time 1 price of the original equity becomes $P_1^D = I^a + 400$. If equity is offered by the firm at time 1, the market price of the original equity becomes $P_1^E = I^a + 200$. On the other hand, if no new financing is sought by the firm at time 1, the market price of the shares is given by $P_1^n = I^a + 1000$.[16]

We have shown that the existing empirical evidence on the price impact of security issues is consistent with a model in which investment is optimal. In this model, having to issue securities is bad news because it indicates an inability to generate funds internally. Equity issues are particularly bad news, while debt issues are only slightly bad news (or, under a slightly different choice of parameters, would be neutral or slightly good news), Therefore, although the evidence is roughly consistent with the story told by Myers and Majluf, the empirical evidence is not convincing proof that Myers and Majluf are correct. This same empirical evidence is consistent with an optimal (endogenous) investment policy in a world with asymmetric information in which the Modigliani and Miller irrelevancy propositions hold. In fact, it seems that this type of example can be used to explain any rational price process.

3. Conclusion

This article has shown that the Modigliani and Miller irrelevancy propositions hold for a large class of models with asymmetric information and endogenous investment. This type of irrelevancy result is important primarily because it tells where *not* to look for reasons for optimal capital structure. In light of this article, many (or most) of the existing articles in theoretical corporate finance tell us why it is not efficient to have managers act on behalf of shareholders.

The research in this article suggests two directions. One direction is to accept provisionally that the type of model in this article is useful, and to conclude that we should advocate corporate charters, corporate law, and contractual structures that will give better incentives to managers. Another direction is to view the models in this article as unrealistic, and to conclude that we should build models that make explicit whatever practical limitations exist that prevent us from achieving the optimal contracts described here.[17] Ideally, any attempt to describe these limitations should also derive, from fundamentals, what securities (debt and equity or whatever) should be offered. This derivation should determine not only the state-contingent cash flows accruing to each claimant but also the allocation of control rights. This second approach does not generally bring us back to the models in which managers act on behalf of a specific claimant (e.g., shareholders), since it hardly seems possible that the practical limitations that rule out our efficient contracts do not also rule out contracts that induce managers to act on behalf of shareholders.

---

[16]It might seem that there would be an upward jump in the stock price in the absence of a new issue, and that this has not been documented in the data. However, there is no single date on which the public learns that there will not be a new issue and, consequently, there is a small increase (in addition to the usual noise) on each of a large number of days.

[17]Some examples of such limitations may be an inability to precommit to a particular managerial incentive contract; restrictions on indentured servitude, which make it hard to ensure a manager will stay with the firm in bad states; and corporate governance rules that make firms that do not maximize the value of equity subject to takeovers. Another model that implies a violation of our model in a different direction is given by Diamond (1985), who points out that the amount of information released can be relevant beyond the cash flows if there is a liquidity premium based on the degree of investors' information asymmetry.

A Critique of Size-Related Anomalies

Jonathan B. Berk
University of British Columbia

This article argues that the size-related regularities in asset prices should not be regarded as anomalies. Indeed, the opposite result is demonstrated. Namely, a truly anomalous regularity would be if an inverse relation between size and return was not observed. We show theoretically (1) that the size-related regularities should be observed in the economy and (2) why size will in general explain the part of the cross-section of expected returns left unexplained by an incorrectly specified asset pricing model. In light of these results we argue that size-related measures should be used in cross-sectional tests to detect model misspecifications. •

Over the past 30 years researchers have identified a number of related regularities in asset prices that have come to be regarded as anomalies.[1] It has been found that the ratio of per-share earnings to price (E/P), the dividend yield and other yield surrogates, the amount of leverage, the size of the firm (as measured by the market value of equity), and the ratio of the book value of equity to the market value of equity (book-to-market equity) are all correlated (in the cross-section) with future asset returns. Moreover, these variables have been shown to explain the cross-sectional variation in asset returns better than the capital asset pricing model (CAPM) or any other (multi) factor model.[2] In this article we argue that, rather than being examples of asset pricing anomalies, these regularities are all consistent with an economy in which all asset returns satisfy any one of the well-known asset pricing models.

The size-related empirical regularities are widely regarded as anomalous because most researchers believe that they cannot be explained within the current asset pricing paradigm. The size anomaly, in particular, is generally recognized as the most prominent contradiction of the paradigm [see Fama and French (1992, p. 427)]. Schwert (1983, p. 9), reflecting on the profession's understanding of the size anomaly, sums it up in this way:

---

[1]Keim (1988, p. 35) traces the term *anomaly* to "Kuhn (1970) in his classic book *The Structure of Scientific Revolutions.* Kuhn maintains that research activity in any normal science will revolve around a central paradigm and that experiments are conducted to test the predictions of the underlying paradigm and to extend the range of the phenomena it explains. Although the research most often supports the underlying paradigm, eventually results are found that don't conform. Kuhn (1970, pp. 52–3) terms this stage 'discovery': 'Discovery commences with the awareness of *anomaly*, i.e., with the recognition that nature has somehow violated the paradigm-induced expectations that govern normal science," (Keim's emphasis).

[2]A comprehensive review of the anomaly literature is beyond the scope of this article. The interested reader is referred to the many excellent reviews of the subject [e.g., Dimson (1988), Fama (1991), Ziemba (1994), or the special issue of the *Journal of Financial Economics* (vol. 12, no. 1)].

The author thanks Sandra Betton, Fischer Black, Michael Brennan, Kent Daniel, Glen Donaldson, Espen Eckbo, Gene Fama, Campbell Harvey, Rob Heinkel, Burton Hollifield, Ravi Jagannathan, Alan Kraus, Usha Mittoo, Richard Roll, Steve Ross, Eduardo Schwartz, Andy Snell, Raman Uppal, and Bill Ziemba for their insights, comments, and suggestions. A special note of thanks is due to the editor, Rob Stambaugh, and an anonymous referee. Financial support from the Institute for Quantitative Research in Finance (the Q Group) is gratefully acknowledged. Earlier versions of this article were entitled: "Does Size Really Matter?"

Reprinted with permission:
Berk, Jonathan B. "A Critique of Size-Related Anomalies." *Review of Financial Studies* 8 (1995): 275–286.

> The search for an explanation of this anomaly has been unsuccessful. Almost all authors of papers on the "size effect" agree that it is evidence of misspecification of the capital asset pricing model, rather than evidence of inefficient capital markets. On the other hand, none of the attempts to modify the CAPM to account for taxation, transaction costs, skewness preference, and so forth have been successful at discovering the "missing factor" for which size is a proxy. Thus, our understanding of the economic or statistical causes of the apparently high average returns to small firms' stocks is incomplete. It seems unlikely that the "size effect" will be used to measure the opportunity cost of risky capital in the same way the CAPM is used because it is hard to understand why the opportunity cost of capital should be substantially higher for small firms than for large firms.

As Schwert notes, it is generally recognized that the observed relation between the anomaly variables and return implies that these variables proxy for risk.[3] Nevertheless, economists have had little success explaining these regularities. Hence, Lo and MacKinlay (1990) and Black (1992) have recently objected to empirical procedures that implicitly use size as a proxy for risk. They point out that no satisfactory theoretical reason has been identified that predicts such a relation.

This article provides a theoretical explanation of *why* relative firm size measures risk. The distinction between the theoretical explanation in this article and all previous work is that our explanation does not rely on a presumed relation between a particular characteristic of the firm and its risk.[4] Instead we argue that, regardless of what process generates the return of the firm, the empirically demonstrated relation between these variables and expected return should always be observed.

The intuition underlying the above observation can best be illustrated by the following thought experiment. Consider a one-period economy in which all investors trade off risk and return. Assume that all firms in this economy are exactly the same size; that is, assume that the expected value of every firm's end-of-period cashflow is the same. Since the riskiness of each firm's cashflow is different [i.e., the correlation of the cashflows with the underlying risk factor(s) will vary across firms], the market value of each firm must also differ. Given that all firms have the same expected cashflow, riskier firms will have lower market values and so, by definition, will have higher expected returns. Thus, even though all firms are the same size, if market value is used as the measure of size, then it will predict return.

The thought experiment illustrates the main contribution of this article. The reason for the relation between the anomaly variables and the expected return of the firm is not related to the *operating* characteristics these variables measure (e.g., earnings, firm size). Rather, they predict expected return because of the theoretical risk premium contained in the *market* characteristics of these variables. For example, the market value of equity is negatively correlated to average return because it is theoretically inversely related to the risk of the firm. That is, the market value of equity of a firm is affected by (at least) two things. First,

[3]See Fama (1976), Ball (1978), Chen (1988), and Keim (1988). Recently, however, Black (1992) has taken issue with this conclusion.

[4]For instance, in their theoretical explanations, Ball (1978), Chen (1988), and Jagannathan and Wang (1992) explicitly assume that the operating aspects of their respective explanatory variables are affected by the same risk factors that determine the expected return. Ball assumes that the P/E ratio and risk are related because *earnings* proxies for unmeasured risk. Chen's argument is based on a relation between size (smaller firms are assumed to fluctuate more with business cycles) and risk. Jagannathan and Wang argue that firms that have lost value will have larger systematic risk. Alternatively, Jagannathan and Viswanathan (1988) assume that the systematic risk of firms' cashflows does not vary through time but that the overall expected cashflows (or operating size) of firms do vary through time. They then show that this will induce a negative relation between the systematic risk of a dollar invested in the firm and its relative size.

relatively bigger firms have relatively higher market values. Second, riskier firms have relatively lower market values. Therefore, so long as there is no *positive* correlation between the operating size of a firm and its risk, a firm with a low market value is more likely to be riskier than a firm with a high market value.

This article is organized as follows. In the next section we formally derive the theoretical relation between market value and expected return. Next, we provide conditions that imply a similar relation between market value and the part of expected return not explained by an asset pricing model. Finally, we discuss the magnitude of the effect and provide an explanation for the empirical observation that book-to-market equity is a better predictor of return than market value. Section 2 concludes the article.

1. The Predictive Power of Market Value

In this section we formalize the arguments discussed in the introduction. In the context of a one-period model, we show why, even in an economy in which firm size and risk are *unrelated*, the logarithm of a firm's market value always measures the firm's discount rate. The logarithm of market value variable is used because it has received the lion's share of attention in the literature. However, the logic can be applied to explain the predictive power of other anomaly variables such as E/P, dividend yield, book-to-market equity, or simply market value itself. It is also easily extended to a multiperiod framework.

1.1. The Relation Between Market Value and Return

Consider a one-period economy that consists of a set of firms, I, each of which is a claim to an uncertain end-of-period cashflow, $\tilde{c}_i$, where $i \in I$. The firms are traded on a spot market at the beginning of the period. The value of the ith firm on this spot market is denoted p_i. The continuously compounded return is given by $\tilde{r}_i = \log(\frac{\tilde{c}_i}{p_i})$.[5] Each firm in this economy is parameterized by the expected value of the logarithm of its cashflow,[6] $E[\log \tilde{c}_i]$, and its (continuously compounded) expected return, $E[\tilde{r}_i] = E[\log(\frac{\tilde{c}_i}{p_i})]$. The economic interpretation of these two variables is that they separately measure firm size and risk, respectively. We will henceforth define $C_i \equiv E[\log \tilde{c}_i]$ and $R_i \equiv E[\tilde{r}_i]$.

The (cross-sectional) distribution of firms in this economy is given by $L : \Re^2 \to [0, 1]$, a function of the firms' parameters (i.e., expected log cashflow, C, and expected return, R).[7] Therefore, $L(c, r)$ is the probability that any randomly selected stock will have an expected log cashflow of c or less and an expected return of r or less. We will assume that the cross-sectional distribution of expected log cashflow in the economy is independent of the cross-sectional distribution of expected return. The economic interpretation of this assumption is that the size of the firm is unrelated to its riskiness. Formally then,

$$L(C, R) = G(C)H(R), \tag{1}$$

[5]The empirical studies that have documented the size anomaly have generally used the one-month return. However, as a consequence of the fact that we take the logarithm of market value, continuously compounded returns are expositionally simpler to handle and are theoretically more appealing. The difference between the monthly and continuously compounded return is very small: if $\tilde{r}_m$ and $\tilde{r}_c$ is [sic] the return expressed on a monthly and continuously compounded basis, respectively, then a second-order Taylor expansion gives $E[\tilde{r}_m - \tilde{r}_c] \approx \frac{1}{2}E[r_m^2] = 0.2$ percent for the market portfolio. Using continuously compounded returns greatly simplifies the article without affecting the inferences.

[6]We again take logs to maintain consistency.

[7]In the cross-section, C and R are random variables (since they differ from firm to firm). We adopt the convention that without a subscript (e.g., R) denotes the random variable, while with the subscript (e.g., R_i) denotes a realization of the random variable (i.e., the expected return of the ith firm).

where $G : \Re_+ \rightarrow [0, 1]$, and $H : \Re \rightarrow [0, 1]$ are the cross-sectional distribution functions of C and R, respectively.[8]

With no further assumptions, it is possible to show that the logarithm of market value is, by itself, a predictor of expected return. To see this, consider a cross-sectional regression of the expected return of each stock onto the logarithm of its beginning of period market value:

$$R_i = \alpha + \theta \log p_i + \epsilon_i. \tag{2}$$

From the definition of R_i we have that,

$$\log p_i = C_i - R_i. \tag{3}$$

The coefficient θ (i.e., the value if the regression is "run" in the population) is

$$\begin{aligned} \theta &= \frac{\operatorname{cov}(\log p, R)}{\operatorname{var}(\log p)} \\ &\equiv \frac{\int_{\Re^2}(c - r) r dL(c, r) - \int_{\Re^2}(c - r) dL(c, r) \int_{\Re} r dH(r)}{\int_{\Re^2}(c - r)^2 dL(c, r) - \left(\int_{\Re^2}(c - r) dL(c, r)\right)^2}. \end{aligned} \tag{4}$$

The denominator of θ is strictly positive; hence, we investigate the sign of the numerator:

$$\begin{aligned} \operatorname{cov}(\log p, R) &= \operatorname{cov}(C - R, R) \\ &= \operatorname{cov}(C, R) - \operatorname{cov}(R, R) \\ &= -\operatorname{var}(R) < 0. \end{aligned} \tag{5}$$

Since $\theta < 0$, any cross-sectional regression of average return onto the logarithm of market value should produce a negative coefficient. The empirical result that average return and the logarithm of market value are negatively correlated is therefore no more anomalous than the observation that risk and return are related. Even when firm size (as measured by expected cashflow) is assumed to be unrelated to riskiness (as measured by expected return), market value will be theoretically inversely correlated with realized return.

1.2. The Relation between Market Value and the Unexplained Part of Return

In this section we will show why market value can add additional explanatory power in any test of an asset pricing model that does not completely explain expected return. The intuition behind this result is straightforward. In an economy in which the operating size of the firm is unrelated to its riskiness, market value is negatively correlated with all risk factors. Therefore, so long as an omitted risk factor is unrelated to the firm's operating size, market value will also be negatively correlated with the omitted risk factor. Consequently, market value will always provide additional explanatory power in any test of an asset pricing model that omits relevant risk factors that are uncorrected with operating size. We will use the same economy as in the previous section to show this formally.

Let $\hat{R}$ be the continuously compounded expected return predicted by the asset pricing model that is being tested. In addition to the assumptions made in the previous section, we assume that $\hat{R}$ and C are distributed independently.[9] That is, like the actual expected return, we assume that the expected return predicted by the asset pricing model is not related to the

[8]We assume independence for expositional simplicity. All that is actually required is that the expected log cashflow of a firm not be too *positively related* to its expected return, that is, $\operatorname{cov}(C,R) \leq \operatorname{var}(R)$.

[9]Again, independence is assumed for expositional simplicity. Assuming $\operatorname{cov}(C, R) \leq 0$ and $\operatorname{cov}(\hat{R}, C) = 0$ will provide the same result.

operating size of the firm. Of course, if $\hat{R}$ and C were related to each other, then, because we have assumed that R and C are unrelated, this relation alone would be evidence that the asset pricing model being tested was misspecified.[10] Formally, then, the asset pricing model assigns a (continuously compounded) expected return $\hat{R}_i$ to the ith firm and this determines $M : \Re \to [0, 1]$, the cross-sectional distribution of $\hat{R}$ in the economy. The joint distribution function of C and $\hat{R}$ is then given by $M(\hat{R})G(C)$.

Consider a cross-sectional regression test of the asset pricing model in the economy:

$$R_i = \omega + \beta\hat{R}_i + \epsilon_i. \tag{6}$$

The part of expected return not explained by the model (the abnormal return) is the part of R orthogonal to $\hat{R}$. Therefore, ϵ_i is the part of firm i's expected return not explained by the model. Since this regression is "run" in the population, if the asset pricing model explains expected returns exactly, then $\epsilon_i = 0, \forall i \in I$. If, on the other hand, the asset pricing model only partially explains expected returns, then ϵ will be different from zero. It turns out that whenever ϵ is different from zero, market value will be inversely related to it and must provide additional explanatory power over and above the asset pricing model. To see this, consider cross-sectionally regressing ϵ (i.e., the residuals of the above regression) onto the logarithm of market value:

$$\epsilon_i = \eta + \gamma \log p_i + \zeta_i. \tag{7}$$

The theoretical value of the regression coefficient γ is

$$\gamma = \frac{\text{cov}(\log p, \epsilon)}{\text{var}(\log p)}.$$

As before, the denominator of γ is strictly positive; hence, we investigate the sign of the numerator:

$$\begin{aligned}
\text{cov}(\log p, \epsilon) &= \text{cov}(C - R, \epsilon) \\
&= \text{cov}(C, R - \omega - \beta\hat{R}) - \text{cov}(R, \epsilon) \\
&= -\text{cov}(R, \epsilon) \\
&= -\text{cov}(\omega + \beta\hat{R} + \epsilon, \epsilon) \\
&= -\text{var}(\epsilon) < 0.
\end{aligned}$$

Thus, whenever $\epsilon \neq 0$, the logarithm of market value is always negatively correlated to it. In an economy in which operating size is unrelated to both expected return and the prediction of the model being tested, the logarithm of market value will always provide additional explanatory power in any test in which the expected return predicted by the model differs from the actual expected return.

There are, of course, many reasons why the expected return predicted by an asset pricing model might differ from the actual expected return. The obvious reason is that the asset pricing model is misspecified and therefore does not correctly price all relevant factors. It is important to appreciate that this is not the only possible explanation. The asset pricing model might well price risk correctly, but the empirical specification may be incorrect or inappropriate. For example, the CAPM (or single beta model) might in reality hold perfectly, but the test may be conducted using a proxy portfolio that is not mean-variance efficient. The expected return calculated using this proxy would then differ from the actual

[10] One way to "fix" this misspecification would be to project $\hat{R}$ onto C to get the part of $\hat{R}$ orthogonal to C. If this is then used as the prediction of the asset pricing model, the model would no longer be misspecified, a priori, and the results in this section could be applied.

expected return and so, by the above logic, market value will have additional explanatory power. Similarly, even if the proxy portfolio is mean-variance efficient, the beta of each stock may be estimated with error. *Any* error in the beta estimate must induce an error in the expected return predicted by the model, and so market value will provide additional explanatory power. Thus, the observation that market value explains the part of return not explained by the CAPM, by itself, is not necessarily evidence that the CAPM is misspecified.

1.3. Magnitude of the Effect

The previous subsections demonstrate that market value is theoretically negatively correlated to both expected return and the part of expected return that is not explained by the asset pricing model being tested. Yet neither section addresses how much of the cross-sectional variation in expected return will be explained by market value. It turns out that the fraction of the cross-sectional variation in expected return that is explained by market value depends on how the cross-sectional variation of C compares to the cross-sectional variation of R. The most effective way to demonstrate this is to calculate explicitly the theoretical value of the R-squared statistic ($\mathcal{R}^2$) for the regression in Section 1.1:

$$\begin{aligned}\mathcal{R}^2 &= \frac{\text{var}(\theta \log p)}{\text{var}(R)} = \theta^2 \frac{\text{var}(\log p)}{\text{var}(R)} \\ &= |\theta| = \frac{\text{var}(R)}{\text{var}(C - R)} = \frac{\text{var}(R)}{\text{var}(C) + \text{var}(R)},\end{aligned}$$

where we have used Equations (4) and (5). If the cross-sectional variation in C is small, then $\mathcal{R}^2$ is close to 1 and market value will explain most of the cross-sectional variation in R. On the other hand, if the cross-sectional variation in C is large, then $\mathcal{R}^2$ is close to 0 and market value will explain only a small fraction of the cross-sectional variation in R.[11]

Unfortunately, C is difficult to observe empirically, so that actual differences in the cross-sectional variation in C and R are not easily observable. There is, however, some evidence that the relative cross-sectional variation in R is large enough so that the effect identified in this article could completely account for the observed relation between market value and return. Specifically, the only way the existing empirical evidence on the size effect could be consistent with a relatively small cross-sectional variance in R is if C is cross-sectionally negatively correlated with R. That is, the observed inverse relation between market value and return is due primarily to a relation between operating size and risk. However, a follow-up paper [Berk (1994)] finds no evidence of such a relation. Therefore, the empirically observed relation between market value and return must be explained solely by the effect identified in this article.

Perhaps a more sensible approach is to avoid this problem by simply adjusting the market value measure so that it is insensitive to the variation in C. Since we have assumed that C and R are unrelated, one way to do this without affecting the theoretical results derived in the previous section is to normalize market value by expected cashflow. For example, define a new measure: $Q \equiv E[\log \frac{\tilde{c}}{p}] = C - \log p$. It should be clear that results similar to those in Sections 1.1 and 1.2 can be derived for this variable. Yet, unlike the variable $\log p$, the fraction of the cross-sectional variation in R that is explained by Q is

[11] Similar results can be obtained for the regression in Section 1.2; that is, $\mathcal{R}^2 = \frac{\gamma^2 \text{var}(\log p)}{\text{var}(\epsilon)} = |\gamma| = \frac{\text{var}(\epsilon)}{\text{var}(C - R)} = \frac{\text{var}(\epsilon)}{\text{var}(C) + \text{var}(R)}$.

independent of the cross-sectional variation in C. That is, if $\Delta \equiv \frac{\text{cov}(Q,R)}{\text{var}(Q)}$ is the coefficient of a cross-sectional regression of R on Q, then

$$\mathcal{R}^2 = \frac{\text{var}(\Delta Q)}{\text{var}(R)} = \Delta^2 \frac{\text{var}(C - \log p)}{\text{var}(R)} = 1.$$

Thus, Q explains all of the cross-sectional variation in expected returns. Unfortunately, the expected cashflow is not readily observable and so no researcher has undertaken such an empirical study. However, something quite similar has been done.

Like the expected cashflow, the book value of equity is a measure of the size of the firm that does not theoretically contain a risk premium. As such, one would expect these two measures to be correlated. So long as there is some correlation between the expected cashflow and book value of equity, book equity can be used as a control for the cross-sectional variation in expected cashflows. Therefore, the logarithm of the ratio of book equity to market equity is, in principle, a better measure of the continuously compounded expected return than is the logarithm of market equity alone. In light of the above argument, it is not surprising that Fama and French (1992, Table III) find that the logarithm of book-to-market equity is a much better predictor of return than the logarithm of market equity alone.

2. Conclusion

Banz's original paper (1981) and the subsequent literature on the size anomaly documented two important empirical regularities. First, it showed that the logarithm of a stock's market value is an inverse predictor of its return. Second, when risk is controlled for by using an asset pricing model like the CAPM, it demonstrated that market value has explanatory power over the part of return not explained by the model (the abnormal return). We have shown that, even in an economy in which firm size and risk are unrelated, the logarithm of market value will be inversely related to expected return. Consequently, market value and expected returns will be negatively correlated in the cross-section. Furthermore, if either the asset pricing model is misspecified or the empirical specification is incorrect, we demonstrate that, so long as this misspecification does not imply a positive relation between operating size and the return predicted by the model, the logarithm of market value will be inversely correlated with the part of return not explained by the model. Our results therefore provide a theoretical explanation of the size effect within the current asset pricing paradigm.

An "empirical anomaly" is, by definition, an empirical fact that cannot be supported by the prevailing theory. As such, an important implication of this article is that it is misleading to refer to the size effect as an "anomaly." The fact that return and market value have been found to be inversely related certainly cannot be regarded as evidence against any asset pricing theory. Similarly, since empiricists usually do not expect the asset pricing models they test to hold exactly,[12] the fact that they do not and that market value is left with additional explanatory power should not surprise anyone. The empirical findings therefore provide no theoretical justification for researchers to look for, in Schwert's words, "the 'missing factor' for which size is a proxy." There is no one factor that market value "proxies" for. Market value is inversely correlated with unmeasured risk, so the type of risk it will "proxy" for is entirely determined by the asset pricing model that is being tested. If two different asset pricing models miss different factors in the risk premium, then size will "proxy" for different factors in the two tests.

[12]For instance, the fact that it is empirically obvious that all agents do not hold the market portfolio has not stopped researchers from attempting to test the CAPM. Generally, researchers themselves explicitly recognize the existence of measurement error in their tests [e.g., Fama and French (1992, pp. 431 and 439–440)].

The empirically observed size effect is not, by itself, evidence of a relation between firm size and risk. Nevertheless, based on the empirical evidence, we certainly cannot rule out the possibility of such a relation. This question can only be resolved empirically, and it is therefore the focus of a follow-up paper, Berk (1994). In this paper we find no evidence of such a relation. That is, using four measures of size that do not contain adjustments for risk,[13] we find no evidence that the size of the firm is in any way correlated to either return or the part of return not explained by the CAPM.

Though our results show that there is no reason to regard the size effect as an asset pricing anomaly, they do provide a sound theoretical justification for using market value related measures to increase the power of an empirical test. For instance, the portfolios used in asset pricing tests can be assured to exhibit substantial cross-sectional variation in their expected returns if market value is used to construct these portfolios. Although previous empirical studies have used market value in this way, Lo and MacKinlay (1990) have pointed out that the authors of these studies provide no theoretical basis for their methodology. Consequently, Lo and MacKinlay (1990) have questioned the conclusions of these empirical studies. Our arguments imply that the results in these empirical studies are indeed valid.

The theoretical arguments in this article demonstrate that variables such as market value have an important role to play in future empirical tests. Since these variables always explain any unmeasured risk, they can be used as a measure of how much of the risk premium remains unexplained by the model being tested. In particular, if a specific asset pricing model claims to explain all relevant risk factors, then, at a minimum, it must leave any market value related measure with no residual explanatory power. As such, the market value related variables loom as natural yardsticks by which all asset pricing models could potentially be measured. Although the econometric work remains to be done, developing the statistical foundations of such a testing procedure is an important task for future researchers.

References

Ball, R., 1978, “Anomalies in Relations between Securities’ Yields and Yield-Surrogates,” *Journal of Financial Economics*, 6, 103–126.

Banz, R. F., 1981, “The Relation between Return and Market Value of Common Stocks,” *Journal of Financial Economics*, 9, 3–18.

Berk, J. B., 1994, “An Empirical Re-examination of the Size Relation between Firm Size and Returns,” working paper, University of British Columbia, August.

Black, F., 1992, “Beta and Return,” presentation at the Berkeley Program in Finance: “Are Betas Irrelevant? Evidence and Implications for Asset Management.”

Chen, N., 1988, “Equilibrium Asset Pricing Models and the Firm Size Effect,” in E. Dimson (ed.), *Stock Market Anomalies*, Cambridge University Press, Cambridge, U.K.

Dimson, E. (ed.), 1988, *Stock Market Anomalies*, Cambridge University Press, Cambridge, U.K.

Fama, E. F., 1976, *Foundations of Finance*, Basic Books, New York.

[13]Book value of assets; book value of property, plant, and equipment; number of employees; and total value of annual sales.

Fama, E. F., 1991, "Efficient Capital Markets: II" *Journal of Finance*, 46, 1575–1618.

Fama, E. F., and K. R. French, 1992, "The Cross-Section of Expected Stock Returns," *Journal of Finance*, 47, 427–466.

Jagannathan, R., and S. Viswanathan, 1988, "Linear Factor Pricing, Term Structure of Interest Rates and the Small Firm Anomaly," working paper, Kellogg Graduate School of Management, Northwestern University.

Jagannathan, R., and Z. Wang, 1992, "The Cross-Section of Expected Stock Returns: Do Size and Book to Market Equity Measure Systematic Risk Better than Beta?" presentation at the Berkeley Program in Finance: "Are Betas Irrelevant? Evidence and Implications for Asset Management."

Kleim, D. B., 1988, "Stock Market Regularities: A Synthesis of the Evidence and Explanations," in E. Dimson (ed.), *Stock Market Anomalies*, Cambridge University Press, Cambridge, U.K.

Kuhn, T., 1970, *The Structure of Scientific Revolutions*, University of Chicago Press.

Lo, A. W., and A. C MacKinlay, 1990, "Data-Snooping Biases in Tests of Financial Asset Pricing Models," *Review of Financial Studies*, 3, 431–468.

Schwert, G. W., 1983, "Size and Stock Returns, and Other Empirical Regularities," *Journal of Financial Economics*, 12, 3–12.

Ziemba, W. T., 1994, "World Wide Security Market Regularities," *European Journal of Operational Research*, 74, 198–229.

Twenty-Three

Zhiwu Chen

Zhiwu Chen received a Ph.D. from Yale University in 1990. He started out at the University of Wisconsin-Madison Graduate School of Business, and now works at the School of Management, Yale University. •

My venture into financial economics was totally unplanned, if I may borrow a term from the terminology familiar to people in my native country, China. Before applying to the Yale Ph.D. Program in Management Sciences in 1985, all of my education had been in engineering and science. The only economics to which I was exposed was Marxist political economy, and my real-life economic experience was mostly limited to a planned economy. When I applied to the Yale Program and wrote to Professor Martin Shubik in 1985, my goal was to apply mathematics to study political science and economics. Upon receiving the admissions materials, I saw that one of the areas of focus in the Yale Program was finance, a subject that was totally foreign to me. Even after a friend tried to explain to me what finance was, I still had no clue about this subject matter. With no knowledge of finance, I came to study at Yale in 1986. I am deeply indebted to Martin Shubik for making this opportunity possible.

During my first year at Yale, I hit an intellectual jackpot and had the honor to be exposed to such scholars as Steve Ross, Martin Shubik, Jon Ingersoll, Phil Dybvig, and Joel Demski. I wrote my first-year paper on multi-period stochastic dominance with Steve and Phil. Steve not only mentored me throughout the process, but also corrected my English writing on various drafts. In this process, Steve together with Phil and Jon opened the world of financial economics to me. Steve's way to conceptualize even complicated issues in a simple, crystallized framework is just magical and has to this day guided me in my research on not only finance, but also economics and institutions. I still remember how Steve in an MBA class proved mathematically why diversification pays. He did it so beautifully that even the MBA students found the rigorous math to be intuitive and easy. You sometimes run into individuals who are Nobel-quality researchers, superb teachers or genuinely nice persons, but not necessarily all of the above. Steve is one of God's rare gifts, and he has them all. Steve's influence has changed my intellectual and professional life. I have been so fortunate to have had him as my mentor.

My co-author, Gurdip Bakshi, and I are so honored to have a joint paper included in this special volume. This paper originated in one of my dissertation chapters advised by Steve. In neoclassic economic models, the value of wealth accumulation is no more than the material consumption potential that wealth generates. But, in real life, the subjective value of wealth to an individual is much more than its material consumption potential. For example, one may pursue more wealth simply for the sake of wealth or for spiritual enrichment. "Feeling good" because of wealth-induced relative social status can be a strong motive for wealth maximization. Given that stock markets are mostly participated in by the wealthy segment of the population whose wealth is already beyond satisfying material consumption needs, we find the model to perform much better in explaining stock market volatility once wealth-dependent social status is included in the utility function.

For the insights that I have gained in this and other studies in which I have been involved, I am deeply indebted to Steve.

The Spirit of Capitalism and Stock-Market Prices

*By Gurdip S. Bakshi and Zhiwu Chen**

In existing theory, wealth is no more valuable than its implied consumption rewards. In reality investors acquire wealth not just for its implied consumption, but for the resulting social status. Max M. Weber refers to this desire for wealth as the spirit of capitalism. We examine, both analytically and empirically, implications of Weber's hypothesis for consumption, savings, and stock prices. When investors care about relative social status, propensity to consume and risk-taking behavior will depend on social standards, and stock prices will be volatile. The spirit of capitalism seems to be a driving force behind stock-market volatility and economic growth. (JEL G1, G10, G11, G12) •

In neoclassic economic models, the accumulation of wealth is often taken to be solely driven by one's desire to increase consumption rewards. This assumption is best demonstrated by the objective function in most consumption-portfolio and growth models:

$$\max_{C_\tau,\, \alpha_\tau \,:\, \tau \in [\tau, \infty]} E_t \int_t^\infty u(C_\tau, \tau) d\tau,$$

subject to certain lifetime budget constraints, where $u(\cdot, \cdot)$ is the utility of consumption; W_t and C_t are respectively time t wealth and consumption; and α_t stands for some other controls, such as portfolio weights. In those models, wealth is clearly no more valuable than the maximum amount of consumption utility that it can bring. Because consumption rewards are the only things that matter, everything has to be valued according to its relation with consumption. Thus, for instance, the equilibrium price of an asset is completely determined by its consumption beta (Douglass T. Breeden, 1979; Robert E. Lucas Jr., 1978).

While the aforementioned motive is an important—perhaps the most important—motive for wealth accumulation, it is, however, not the only important motive behind the sometimes relentless acquisition of wealth, in part because biological needs as well as social norms and customs put a limit on how much an individual can consume. To quote from Lee Iacocca (1988):

> Once you reach a certain level in a material way, what more can you do? You can't eat more than three meals a day; you'll kill yourself. You can't wear two suits one over the other. You might now have three cars in your garage—but six! Oh, you can indulge yourself, but only to a point. [Iacocca, 1988 p. 67]

---

*Department of Economics and Finance, University of New Orleans, New Orleans, LA 70148, and University of Maryland; Fisher College of Business, Ohio State University, 1775 College Road, Columbus, OH 43210, respectively. We have benefitted from comments by William Brock, Tzu-Kuan Chiu, George Constantinides, William Goetzmann, Stephen Heston, Jon Ingersoll, David Mauer, R. Preston McAfee (the editor), Yuki Naka, Steve Ross, Robert Shiller, Ken West, Heng-Fu Zou, and particularly, three anonymous referees. We would also like to thank the seminar participants at Columbia University, Emory University, Northwestern University, Tulane University, University of California-Irvine, University of Houston, University of New Orleans, and University of Wisconsin-Madison. Any remaining errors are ours alone.

Reprinted with permission:
Bakshi, Gurdip S. and Zhiwu Chen. "The Spirit of Capitalism and Stock-Market Prices." *American Economic Review* 86 (1996): 133–157.

Harold L. Cole et al. (1992) argue that the consumption motive fails to explain why such already rich individuals as Donald Trump "continue to work long days, endure substantial amounts of stress, and take enormous risks," for "he seems to have more money than he could spend in several life times" (pp. 1115–16). A possible counter argument to Iacocca and Cole et al. is that they save and acquire more wealth not just for themselves but also for their offspring. This argument, however, is not consistent with the empirical evidence that no significant difference exists in the rate of asset decumulation between the elderly with and without children (Michael D. Hurd, 1986). Given that increasing consumption rewards cannot be the sole motive behind wealth acquisition, it may not be surprising that consumption-based asset pricing, savings, and growth models have failed to consistently explain the relevant real-life data. Among the most damaging pieces of evidence, aggregate consumption is too smooth to justify the volatile stock returns.[1]

Building on work by Chen (1990), Cole et al. (1992), Arthur J. Robson (1992), and Heng-Fu Zou (1992, 1994), we examine in the present paper, both analytically and empirically, the implications for consumption, portfolio holdings and stock-market prices of the hypothesis that investors accumulate wealth not only for the sake of consumption but also for wealth-induced social status. According to Max M. Weber (1958), this hypothesis essentially captures the spirit of capitalism:

> Man is dominated by the making of money, by acquisition as the ultimate purpose of his life. Economic acquisition is no longer subordinated to man as the means for the satisfaction of his material needs. This reversal of what we should call the natural relationship, so irrational from a naive point of view, is evidently a leading principle of capitalism. (Weber, 1958 p. 53)

This view of the capitalistic spirit has been shared by many other contemporary and past economists including Adam Smith, John S. Mill, J. Schumpeter, and John M. Keynes.[2] In the case of Keynes (1971), he wrote:

> . . . society was so framed as to throw a great part of the increased income into the control of the class least likely to consume it. The new rich . . . preferred the power which investment gave them to the pleasures of immediate consumption . . . Herein lay, in fact, the main justification of the capitalist system. . . And so the cake increased; but to what end was not clearly contemplated . . . Saving was for old age or their children; but this was only in theory—the virtue of the cake was that it was never to be consumed, neither by you nor by your children after you. (pp. 11–12)

As in Robson (1992), we formalize the spirit-of-capitalism hypothesis by assuming each investor's lifetime preferences are representable in the following form

$$\int_0^\infty e^{-\rho t} E_t\{u(C_t, S_t)\}\, dt,$$

where S_t is the investor's relative social standing. We postulate S_t is strictly increasing in wealth (so as to reflect the spirit of capitalism) but decreasing in social-wealth standards (so that status is only relative). In explaining why in a capitalist society the pursuit of wealth is in part for the sake of wealth-enhanced status, Robert H. Frank (1985) observes that human beings face constant contests for position in society and relative status often dictates who

[1]For empirical studies on the consumption-based pricing theory, see, among others, Lars P. Hansen and Ravi Jagannathan (1991, 1994), Hansen and Kenneth J. Singleton (1982), and Rajnish Mehra and Edward C. Prescott (1985). The general conclusion is that the smooth consumption process cannot explain the observed stock prices, unless the representative agent's risk aversion is unrealistically high.

[2]See Zou (1992, 1994) for a review of the history of economic thought and more references on this topic.

gets to receive the prizes. Cole et al. (1992), for instance, argue that wealth determines status, which in turn regulates such things as marriage patterns.[3] In particular, they show that if that is the case, the reduced form preferences of investors will take the general structure as given above. In this sense, we can treat their analysis as providing a micro foundation for the preferences studied here.

Economices populated with status-conscious investors exhibit characteristics distinct from those with the standard agents. To mention a few examples, optimal consumption-portfolio plans will be functions of not only one's own wealth and preference parameters but also social-wealth standards. Under one of three parametrized-preference models in this paper, the optimal propensity to consume is increasing in both one's relative social standing and own wealth but decreasing in (i) social-wealth standards (so as to "catch up with the Joneses"), (ii) the investor's aversion to poverty, and (iii) the degree to which the investor cares about status. Further, the investor is more averse to wealth risk (i) the more he cares about status, (ii) the higher the social-wealth standards, or (iii) the lower the investor's social standing. These and other characterizations have many important implications for consumption, savings, and portfolio choice behavior. In such economies, even if the consumption process is smooth, stock prices can be quite volatile. The spirit of capitalism is a driving force behind stock-market volatility.

To test the spirit-of-capitalism hypothesis that wealth acquisition is more than just for its consumption rewards, we subject the asset-pricing equation under one parametrized-preference model to monthly U.S. data. The test methods used include the Hansen and Jagannathan (1991) volatility-bound diagnostics, Hansen and Jagannathan (1994) specification-error tests, and the Hansen (1982) generalized method of moments (GMM) tests. Overall, the estimated values and signs of the preference parameters are supportive of the hypothesis. In particular, when compared to the standard expected-utility theory, our preference model that takes into account concerns about wealth-induced status does a better job in explaining empirically observed stock prices.

The paper is organized as follows. In Section I, we first introduce the preference structure as well as three parametrized models, and then define the investor's consumption-portfolio problem. A general asset-pricing result is also given there. Section II studies closed-form solutions to the consumption-portfolio problem under the parametrized-preference models. Section III presents results from the empirical tests. Section IV offers concluding remarks. Proof of each result is given in Appendix A, and description of the data used in the tests is provided in Appendix B.

I. A General Framework with the Spirit of Capitalism

In this section, we first outline a class of preferences that depend on relative wealth status and then offer a general characterization of the consumption-portfolio problem. Asset-pricing equations are also presented without assuming parametric functional forms for the preferences.

A. Preferences

Assume there is a sole perishable consumption good that is also used as the value numeraire. For a generic investor, let his consumption (flow) and relative wealth status be,

[3]They quote from Madonna's song *Material Girl* that "The boy with the cold hard cash is always Mister Right . . ." and from Harold J. Perkin (1969) that "the pursuit of wealth *was* the pursuit of social status, not merely for oneself but for one's family."

respectively, C_t and S_t, from time t to $(t + \Delta t)$. The preferences of this infinitely-lived investor are assumed to be representable by

$$(1) \qquad \sum_{t \in [0, \Delta t, 2\Delta t, \ldots]} e^{-\rho t} E_0[u(C_t, S_t)] \, \Delta t,$$

where ρ is the time-preference parameter and Δt the time length in-between decision points. In addition to requiring that $u(C_t, S_t)$ be twice continuously differentiable, we impose the following restrictions: $u_C > 0$ (more consumption is strictly better), $u_S > 0$ (higher status is strictly preferred), and $u_{CC} < 0$ (utility increases in consumption but at a decreasing speed), where a subscript on u denotes the partial derivative of u with respect to the corresponding argument. In Robson (1992), u is assumed to be convex in status, that is, $u_{SS} < 0$. As for the cross partial derivative, u_{CS}, it can take either sign. If the Harry M. Markowitz (1952) hypothesis holds,[4] we will have $u_{CS} < 0$; otherwise, $u_{CS} \geq 0$. For our general discussion, we leave both second-order derivatives unrestricted in sign.

The relative wealth-status variable, S_t, deserves a few clarifications. First, assume S_t is strictly increasing in the investor's absolute wealth at time t, denoted by W_t, so that higher wealth means higher status regardless of the wealth distribution for the group of people with whom the investor has social or professional contacts. Second, assume S_t is a function of the social group to which the investor belongs, so that for a given level of wealth W_t, the investor's relative status will be high (low) if he compares himself to a group of low-income (high-income) consumers.[5] While the investor's relative status should in general depend on the entire wealth distribution of his reference group, we assume that S_t is only a function of W_t and V_t:

$$(2) \qquad S_t = f(W_t, V_t),$$

for some $f(\cdot, \cdot)$ such that $f_W > 0$ and $f_V < 0$, where V_t is what determines '"middle class" within the investor's reference group. We refer to V_t as the *social-wealth index.* It should be emphasized that for different consumers, their wealth references, V_t, can be quite different, depending on the social or professional groups to which they compare themselves. The higher the incomes of the members in the reference group, the higher V_t. Substituting (2) into the period utility $u(C_t, S_t)$ gives the induced utility: $U(C_t, W_t, V_t) \equiv u[C_t, f(W_t, V_t)]$, where $U(C_t, W_t, V_t)$ is also twice continuously differentiable, with $U_C > 0$, $U_{CC} < 0$, $U_W > 0$, $U_V < 0$.

The following three parametrized models of preferences are useful for later sections.

Model 1.—Absolute wealth is status: $S_t = W_t$, with the period utility given by

$$(3) \qquad U(C_t, W_t, V_t) = \frac{C_t^{1-\gamma}}{1-\gamma} W_t^{-\lambda},$$

[4]According to Markowitz (1952), an increase (or decrease) in wealth will shift an investor's utility-of-consumption curve to the right (or the left). An interpretation of his hypothesis is that each time an investor's wealth status changes, it essentially causes him to go back and rerank the entire consumption set, such that the wealthier the investor, the less utility from a given unit of consumption. In some sense, this means an increase in wealth can "spoil" the investor's tastes.

[5]This assumption seems natural in light of James S. Duesenberry's (1949 p. 48) observation: "Consider two groups with the same incomes. One group associates with people who have the same income as they have. The other group associates with people who have higher incomes than the members of the group. . . . The two groups have the same income but the first will be better satisfied with its position than the second. Its members will make fewer unfavorable comparisons. . ." (Duesenberry also provides early survey data demonstrating a positive connection between relative status and happiness.) Frank (1985) refers to status relative to one's group of close association as *local status.* He emphasizes that local status is of more concern to consumers than *global status*, because "Negative feelings are much more strongly evoked by adverse comparisons with our immediate associates than by those with people who are distant in place or time" (p. 9). In this sense, per-capita wealth for the whole country, for instance, may not be a good wealth reference for *every individual.*

where $\gamma > 0$, and $\lambda \geq 0$ when $\gamma \geq 1$ and $\lambda < 0$ otherwise. The magnitude, $|\lambda|$, measures the extent to which the investor cares about status.

This specification is consistent with those in Mordecai Kurz (1968), Chen (1990), and Zou (1992, 1994) as well as with the previous quotes from Weber (1958) and Keynes (1971). Note that since any reasonable notion of the spirit of capitalism must have status strictly increasing in wealth W_t, we can think of Model 1 as capturing the first-order effect of wealth on status determination and hence on the period utility. This is particularly true when the wealth distribution for the reference group and V_t are constant over time, because in that case the utility in (3) can be treated as the reduced-form of $u[C_t, f(W_t, V_t)]$.

Model 2.—The ratio of one's own wealth to the social-wealth index determines status: $S_t = W_t/V_t$, with the utility given by

$$U(C_t, W_t, V_t) = \frac{C_t^{1-\gamma}}{1-\gamma}\left(\frac{W_t}{V_t}\right)^{-\lambda}, \tag{4}$$

where the parameters are as restricted Model 1. This model also coincides with one in which the wealth contribution to utility is purely external.

Here, an investor is said to be in the middle class if $S_t = 1$, in the lower-wealth class if $S_t < 1$, and in the upper class otherwise. Model 2 collapses to Model 1 when the index V_t is constant over time.

Model 3.—Self-perception determines happiness: $S_t = W_t/V_t$ but the utility given by

$$U(C_t, W_t, V_t) = \frac{C_t^{1-\gamma}}{1-\gamma}(W_t - \kappa V_t)^{-\lambda}, \tag{5}$$

for some constant $\kappa \geq 0$, where γ and λ are as restricted in Model 1 and κV_t is the investor's self-assessed reservation or subsistence wealth level.

Two points are worth noting. First, the utility in (5) is increasing both in W_t/V_t, which measures relative standing in the *objective wealth* distribution, and in $(W_t - \kappa V_t)$, which is the perceived position relative to the investor's reservation-wealth level. Second, W_t in Model 3 should never be less than or equal to the subsistence level κV_t (because otherwise the utility function would not be well defined). For a given κ value, this puts a strong restriction on the investor's consumption-portfolio behavior. An intuitive interpretation of this restriction follows. Suppose $\kappa = 1$. Then, the investor will never tolerate a wealth level below the social-wealth index (average) V_t, that is, the investor cannot tolerate the possibility of descending to the middle- or lower-wealth class. Since the coefficient κ reflects part of the investor's preferences, different investors will have different values for κ. Presumably, a consumer who was born to a low-wealth family can absorb economic hardships much better than someone born to a well-to-do family, in which case the former will have a lower κ value, or is said to be less averse to poverty, than the latter. Based on this observation, we refer to κ as *the poverty-aversion coefficient.* Of course, if one's wealth is low, it may not be feasible to have a high κ value. In this sense, the poor cannot feasibly imitate the rich by showing off with a high aversion to poverty. When $\kappa = 0$, Model 3 also becomes Model 1.

In some sense, Models 2 and 3 share the same spirit with, respectively, (i) Andrew B. Abel's (1990) "catching up with the Joneses" model in which he defines the period utility as a function of the ratio of one's own to aggregate consumption and (ii) John Y. Campbell and John H. Cochrane's (1995) habit formation model in which consumption felicity is a function of the difference between one's own and aggregate consumption. In drawing this comparison, however, one should keep in mind that in our case the wealth reference V_t is group specific and not necessarily the aggregate wealth.

B. The Consumption-Portfolio Problem

To introduce the investor's consumption portfolio problem, assume that traded in this frictionless economy is one risk-free asset, with its constant rate of return given by r_0, and N risky assets with their prices at time t denoted by $P_{i,t}$, for $i = 1, \ldots, N$ and $t \in [0, \infty)$. These asset prices follow a vector-diffusion process:

$$\text{(6)} \qquad \frac{dP_{i,t}}{P_{i,t}} = \mu_{i,t}dt + \sigma_{i,t}d\omega_{i,t}$$

where $\mu_{i,t}$ and $\sigma_{i,t}$ are, respectively, the conditional expected value and standard deviation of the rate of return on asset i per unit time, and $\omega_{i,t}$ is a standard Wiener process. The variables, $\mu_{i,t}$ and $\sigma_{i,t}$, generally depend on the time t state of the economy.

To maintain a level of simplicity, assume that *one individual investor's* consumption-portfolio decision will have at most a negligible impact on the social-wealth index V_t (thinking of this index as reflecting a *large group's* average wealth level). Consumption-portfolio rebalancing by the investor takes place at discrete intervals of length Δt. Let the portfolio vector, $\alpha_t \equiv (\alpha_{0,t}, \alpha_{1,t}, \ldots, \alpha_{N,t})$, be such that $\alpha_{i,t}$ is the fraction of time t savings invested in asset i and $\Sigma_{i=0}^{N} \alpha_{i,t} = 1$. The infinitely-lived capitalistic investor then chooses a plan, $\{(C_t, \alpha_t): t = 0, \Delta t, \ldots\}$, so as to

$$\text{(7)} \qquad \max_{(C_t,\alpha_t)} \sum_{t=0}^{\infty} e^{-\rho t} E_0 U(C_t, W_t, V_t)\, \Delta t$$

subject to the budget constraints

$$\text{(8)} \qquad W_{t+\Delta t} - W_t = \left\{ r_0 W_t - C_t + W_t \sum_{i=1}^{N} \alpha_{i,t}(\mu_{i,t} - r_0) \right\} \Delta t + W_t \sum_{i=1}^{N} \alpha_{i,t}\sigma_{i,t}\, \Delta\omega_{i,t} \qquad \forall t = 0, \Delta t, \ldots.$$

Assume that $\{(C_t^*, \alpha_t^*): t = 0, \Delta t, \ldots\}$ is an optimal plan for (7). Following a variational argument in Sanford J. Grossman and Robert J. Shiller (1982), we arrive at the necessary Euler equation:

$$\text{(9)} \qquad P_{i,t} = e^{-\rho\Delta t} E_t \left\{ \frac{U_C(C_{t+\Delta t}^*, W_{t+\Delta t}^*, V_{t+\Delta t})}{U_C(C_t^*, W_t^*, V_t)} + \frac{U_W(C_{t+\Delta t}^*, W_{t+\Delta t}^*, V_{t+\Delta t})\Delta t}{U_C(C_t^*, W_t^*, V_t)} P_{i,t+\Delta t} \right\}.$$

The price of an asset should thus equal the expected future benefit that the asset can generate in terms of today's utility. This Euler equation differs from its state-independent expected-utility-based counterpart in that the intertemporal marginal rate of substitution in consumption (IMRS), denoted by m_t, is now a function of the investor's consumption, his wealth and the social-wealth index. Therefore, in an economy populated with capitalistic investors, we expect its IMRS to be volatile when the individual wealth processes and the social-wealth index are so. This is true even if the individual-consumption processes are quite smooth.

The discrete-time Euler equation in (9) is the basis for the empirical tests reported in Section IV. Other than for the empirical tests, we are, from now on, mainly interested in characterizing solutions to (7) in the continuous-time limit (i.e., as $\Delta t \to 0$). We first present a pricing characterization in Subsection C below.

C. Asset-Price Restrictions

Assume that in the continuous-time limit both the investor's optimal consumption and the social-wealth index follow a diffusion process:

$$\frac{dC_t^*}{C_t^*} = \mu_{c,t}\,dt + \sigma_{c,t}\,d\omega_{c,t}\,, \tag{10}$$

$$\frac{dV_t}{V_t} = \mu_{v,t}dt + \sigma_{v,t}\omega_{v,t}, \tag{11}$$

where $\mu_{c,t}$, $\sigma_{c,t}$, $\mu_{v,t}$, and $\sigma_{v,t}$ generally depend on the state of the economy, and $\omega_{c,t}$, and $\omega_{v,t}$, are standard Wiener processes. A justification for this assumption is that when asset prices and optimal consumption follow diffusion processes, the resulting social-wealth index should be expected to follow a diffusion as well. In particular, based on (8), each individual investor's optimal wealth must then follow a diffusion.

Proposition 1. *Suppose that in the continuous-time limit, the vector-diffusion process* $\{(C_t^*, W_t^*): t \in [0, \infty)\}$ *is the investor's optimal consumption-wealth path. Then, the risk premium on asset i must satisfy*

$$\mu_{i,t} - r_0 = -\frac{C_t^* U_{CC}}{U_C}\sigma_{i,c} - \frac{W_t^* U_{CW}}{U_C}\sigma_{i,w} - \frac{V_t U_{CV}}{U_C}\sigma_{i,v}, \tag{12}$$

$$\forall i = 0, 1, \ldots, N,$$

where $\sigma_{i,c}$, $\sigma_{i,w}$, and $\sigma_{i,v}$ are the covariance, of asset i's return with, respectively, the individual investor's consumption growth, his wealth growth, and the growth on the social-wealth index, that is, $\sigma_{i,c}\,dt \equiv \mathrm{cov}_t(dP_{i,t}/P_{i,t}, dC_t^*/C_t^*)$, $\sigma_{i,w}\,dt \equiv \mathrm{cov}_t(dP_{i,t}/P_{i,t}, dW_t^*/W_t^*)$, and $\sigma_{i,v}\,dt \equiv \mathrm{cov}_t(dP_{i,t}/P_{i,t}, dV_t/V_t)$, with $\mathrm{cov}_t(\cdot, \cdot)$ being the conditional covariance operator.

Equation (12) implies that in an economy populated with capitalistic investors, consumption risk is not the only risk that should be compensated for in equilibrium, as Breeden's (1979) consumption-based capital-asset-pricing model (CAPM) predicts. Instead, the expected-risk premium for a risky asset is determined by its covariation with each investor's consumption, his wealth, and the social-wealth index. Intuitively, when investors care about relative social standing, they will hedge not only against future consumption uncertainty but also against those factors that affect their future status. Since one's social status is determined by both his own wealth and the social-wealth index, risks that are correlated with these two variables should be compensated for.

To further appreciate Proposition 1, apply the utility of Model 1 to (12) to yield

$$\mu_{i,t} - r_0 = \gamma\sigma_{i,c} + \lambda\sigma_{i,w}\,, \tag{13}$$

which appears to resemble the pricing equation of Larry G. Epstein and Stanley E. Zin (1991 eq. 24) or Darrell J. Duffie and Epstein (1992 eq. 21) in the sense that equilibrium risk premium is determined by the covariance of the asset with both consumption and wealth growth. But, their model is fundamentally different from ours. In the case of Epstein and Zin where they examine a particular class of recursive preferences, wealth enters the pricing equation and the IMRS as a stand-in for tomorrow's utility index, whereas here wealth risk also matters because the investor cares about wealth-induced status. As will be noted later, however, the *discrete-time pricing equation under Model* 1 is distinct from the counterpart in Epstein and Zin (eq. 16). Besides, the two models impose different restrictions on γ and λ. To see this, recall that under Model 1, $\lambda \geq 0$ if $\gamma \geq 1$ and $\lambda < 0$ otherwise. Under Epstein and Zin's model, the restriction is that $\gamma > 0$ if $\lambda < 1$; $\gamma < 0$ if $\lambda > 1$;

and $\gamma = 0$ if $\lambda = 1$. This is the case because the parameters λ and γ here have the following correspondence with their notation:

$$\lambda = 1 - \overline{\gamma} \quad \text{and} \quad \gamma = \frac{1 - \lambda}{\overline{\sigma}},$$

where $\overline{\gamma}$ is their "γ" and $\overline{\sigma} > 0$ is their elasticity coefficient (σ). Thus, one can still empirically distinguish our Model 1 from their model.

Substituting the utility in (4) of Model 2 into (12) yields

$$\text{(14)} \qquad \mu_{i,t} - r_0 = \gamma\sigma_{i,c} + \lambda\sigma_{i,w} - \lambda\sigma_{i,v}.$$

Given $\gamma \geq 1$ and $\lambda > 0$, this implies that if an asset is positively correlated with the investor's consumption or wealth, it deserves a positive consumption or wealth-risk premium. In the mean time, the more positively correlated an asset is with the social-wealth index, the less risk premium it deserves, which may not come as a surprise. To see this, note that fixing the investor's wealth level, a rise in V_t leads to a decline in the investor's social status ($S_t = W_t/V_t$). Thus, an asset that is positively correlated with V_t should be desirable to the investor because adding it to the portfolio will increase the correlation between W_t and V_t, which helps better insure against future status uncertainty and allows the investor to "catch up with the Joneses."

Under the class of preferences in Model 3, equation (12) becomes

$$\text{(15)} \qquad \mu_{i,t} - r_0 = \gamma\sigma_{i,c} + \lambda\frac{W_t^*}{W_t^* - \kappa V_t}\sigma_{i,w} - \lambda\frac{\kappa V_t}{W_t^* - \kappa V_t}\sigma_{i,v}.$$

Again, the more positively correlated an asset is with V_t, the less risk premium it deserves. Unlike in Model 2, however, this type of economy will typically experience stochastic investment opportunities in the sense that the risk premium, $(\mu_{i,t} - r_0)$, will depend on W_t^* and V_t.

Before closing this section, note that if we adopt the common assumption of identical preferences but possibly different endowments across investors in the economy, the pricing restriction in (14) under Model 2 (and hence Model 1) also applies to aggregate consumption and wealthy—*so long as all investors compare themselves to the same exogenous wealth standard* V_t. To briefly see this, suppose that there are K exogenous state variables, $x_t \equiv (x_{i,t}, \ldots, x_{K,t})$, following a joint vector-diffusion process. By using the solution method in Subsections A and B (see also Robert C. Merton, 1971), we have the optimal consumption for Model 2 given by: $C_t^* = g(x_t, t)W_t^*$, for some '"well-behaved" function $g(x_t, t)$. Substituting this solution into (14) and applying Ito's lemma, we arrive, upon rearranging, at (16) below. Since investors are identical (except in endowments), the propensity to consume, g, is also identical for them. Summing this equation across all investors and reversing the above derivation yield (17) below, where $\overline{W}$, is aggregate wealth at t, and $\sigma_{i,\overline{c}}$ ($\sigma_{i,\overline{w}}$) is the covariance between return on asset i and aggregate-consumption (wealth) growth. This substantiates our

$$\text{(16)} \quad W_t^*(\mu_{i,t} - r_0) =$$

$$W_t^*\left[\gamma\sum_{k=1}^{K}\frac{1}{g}\frac{\partial g}{\partial x_k}\frac{1}{dt}\operatorname{cov}_t\left(\frac{dP_{i,t}}{P_{i,t}}, dx_{k,t}\right) - \lambda\sigma_{i,v}\right] + (\gamma + \lambda)\frac{1}{dt}\operatorname{cov}_t\left(\frac{dP_{i,t}}{P_{i,t}}, dW_t^*\right)$$

$$\text{(17)} \quad \mu_{i,t} - r_0 = \gamma\frac{1}{dt}\operatorname{cov}_t\left(\frac{dP_{i,t}}{P_{i,t}}, \sum_{k=1}^{K}\frac{1}{g}\frac{\partial g}{\partial x_k}dx_{k,t} + \frac{d\overline{W}_t}{\overline{W}_t}\right) + \gamma\sigma_{i,\overline{w}} - \lambda\sigma_{i,v}$$

$$= \gamma\sigma_{i,\overline{c}} + \gamma\sigma_{i,\overline{w}} - \lambda\sigma_{i,v}$$

claim.[6] If investors differ in preferences or in wealth reference groups, however, aggregation may be difficult to obtain. In addition, as the solution structure in Subsection C implies, aggregation may not obtain under Model 3 even, when investors have identical preferences.

II. Consumption, Saving, and Portfolio Choice

This section uses the parametrized preferences in Models 1, 2, and 3 to study optimal consumption, saving, and portfolio rules in detail. To economize the discussion, assume that there are only two traded assets, a risky stock and a risk-free bond, and that trading and consumption decision making takes place continuously over time. The price of the stock and the social-wealth index follow two separate geometric Brownian motions, that is, the coefficients in (6) and (11) are all constants: $\mu_{1,t} = \mu$, $\sigma_{1,t} = \sigma$, $\mu_{v,t} = \mu_v$, and $\sigma_{v,t} = \sigma_v$, for some positive μ, σ, μ_v, and σ_v. Under this and the continuous decision-making assumption, the investor's problem in (7) can be reexpressed as solving at each time $t \in [0, \infty)$

$$J(W_t,V_t) \equiv \max_{Ct,\, \alpha_t:\, t\in[t,\infty]} E_t\left\{ \int_t^{\infty} e^{-p(s-t)} \times U(C_s,W_s,V_s)\, ds \right\}, \tag{18}$$

subject to

$$dW_t = \{W_t[r_0 + \alpha_t(\mu - r_0)] - C_t\}\, dt + \alpha_t \sigma W_t d\omega_r, \tag{19}$$

where α_t is now the fraction of savings invested in the risky stock, ω_t the standard Wiener process governing the return on the stock, and the other notation is the same as before. Let $\sigma_{1,v}$ be the covariance between the return on the risky stock and the growth rate of V_t. The first-order condition for (18) yields

$$J_W(W_t, V_t) = U_C(C_t, W_t, V_t) \tag{20}$$

$$\alpha_t = \frac{1}{\text{RRA}} \frac{\mu - r_0}{\sigma^2} - \frac{V_t J_{VW}}{W_t J_{WW}} \frac{\sigma_{1,v}}{\sigma^2}, \tag{21}$$

where $\text{RRA} = -(W_t J_{WW}/J_W)$ is the Arrow-Pratt relative risk aversion in wealth. The optimal proportion of savings invested in the risky asset is thus linear in both the market price of risk and the investor's relative risk tolerance. However, unlike in the case of the standard state-independent expected utility, the optimal portfolio also depends on both how the investor cares about social standing and how the risky stock is correlated with the social-wealth level.

A. Model 1: Absolute Wealth Is Status

Let's first examine the case of Model 1 because it represents a relatively simple benchmark that renders the comparative statics easier to see. Since Model 1 is a special case of Model 2, we report the-general result under Model 2 below.

---

[6]Since Model 1 is free of V_t, the above aggregation argument holds even if investors face different wealth standards. In the case of Model 2, however, not only should the investors refer to the same wealth standard, but also the wealth standard should be exogenous to the model, in order for this aggregation argument to go through. The assumption of an exogenous wealth standard may not be restrictive when examining an individual's consumption-portfolio decision, but when aggregation is the concern this seems quite restrictive. It is hard to imagine that the wealth index in the aggregate is still exogenous, and in a true general equilibrium the social-wealth index should be endogenized, which is a topic beyond the scope of die present paper.

Proposition 2. *Let the utility be as given in (4). Then, the optimal solution to the consumption-portfolio problem in (18) is*

$$C_t^* = \eta W_t^* \tag{22}$$

$$\alpha_t^* = \frac{\mu - r_0}{\sigma^2}\frac{1}{\gamma + \lambda} + \frac{\sigma_{1,v}}{\sigma^2}\frac{\lambda}{\gamma + \lambda} \tag{23}$$

$$J(W_t, V_t) = \frac{\eta^{-\gamma}}{1 - \gamma - \lambda} W_t^{1-\gamma-\lambda} V_t^{-\lambda}, \tag{24}$$

where

$$\eta \equiv \frac{\gamma - 1}{\gamma(\gamma + \lambda - 1)}\left\{\rho + (\gamma + \lambda - 1)r_0 - \lambda\mu_v - \frac{1}{2}\lambda(\lambda - 1)\sigma_v^2 + \frac{1}{2}\frac{\gamma + \lambda - 1}{\gamma + \lambda}\left(\frac{\mu - r_0 + \lambda\sigma_{1,v}}{\sigma}\right)^2\right\}, \eta \geq 0, \gamma + \lambda \geq 1.$$

The restriction that $\eta \geq 0$ and $\gamma + \lambda \geq 1$ is demanded by the transversality condition for the infinite-horizon problem. Given the utility of wealth in (24), the relative risk aversion in wealth is simply RRA $= \gamma + \lambda$, which is in contrast with the fact that under the standard expected utility, the relative-risk-aversion coefficient is γ. As noted earlier, when the investor prefers higher social status, we have $\lambda \geq 0$ if $\gamma \geq 1$ and $\lambda < 0$ if $\gamma < 1$. Since the above solution requires $\gamma + \lambda \geq 1$, *the internally permissible parameter values can only be:* $\gamma \geq 1$ and $\lambda > 0$, which is what the remainder of this section is based on. The more the investor cares about status, the more risk averse he becomes.

Model 1 is obtained from Model 2 by letting V_t be a constant, which means by choosing $\mu_v = 0$ and $\sigma_v = 0$. Substituting these values into (22) and (23) yields *the optimal policy under Model 1:*

$$C_t^* = \overline{\eta} W_t^* \tag{25}$$

$$\alpha_t^* = \frac{\mu - r_0}{\sigma^2}\frac{1}{\gamma + \lambda}, \tag{26}$$

where

$$\overline{\eta} \equiv \frac{\gamma - 1}{\gamma}\left\{r_0 + \frac{\rho}{\gamma + \lambda - 1} + \frac{1}{2}\frac{1}{\gamma + \lambda}\left(\frac{\mu - r_0}{\sigma}\right)^2\right\}.$$

By (26), the optimal proportion invested the risky stock is decreasing in both γ and λ: $\partial\alpha_t^*/\partial\gamma < 0$ and $\partial\alpha_t^*/\partial\lambda < 0$. Then, the more the investor cares about wealth status, the higher the coefficient λ and hence the less the investor will hold of the risky stock. This is because in this case caring about wealth status makes the investor more risk averse.

By (25), the propensity to consume, $\overline{\eta}$, is decreasing in λ: $\partial\overline{\eta}/\partial\lambda < 0$. The more the investor cares about status, the higher the savings rate. To see the implications of this for economic growth, note that (19) and (25) together result in

$$\frac{dC_t^*}{C_t^*} = \frac{dW_t^*}{W_t^*} = \mu_w\, dt + \frac{\mu - r_0}{\sigma(\gamma + \lambda)} d\omega_t, \tag{27}$$

where $\mu_w \equiv r_0/\gamma + ((\gamma + 1)/2\gamma(\gamma + \lambda))((\mu - r_0)/\sigma)^2 + \rho(\gamma - 1)/\gamma(1 - \gamma - \lambda)$. The impact of an increase in λ on μ_w and μ_c is clouded by two opposite effects: the portfolio effect and the savings effect. On the one hand, when the investor cares more about status (i.e., λ is higher), his risk aversion in wealth, RRA $= \gamma + \lambda$, will increase, which means holding less of the risky stock and a Lower α_t^*. This implies the first part of expected wealth growth in (19) will be lower. Consequently, the increased risk aversion asserts a negative effect on wealth growth. On the other hand, an increase in λ induces the investor to consume less and raise the savings rate, which means the second part of expected growth in (19) will be higher.

In economic growth models the existence of a sole investment asset is often assumed, presumably to isolate the savings effect from the portfolio effect. To adopt that assumption here, let the sole asset be the risky stock. Then, there is no portfolio choice involved and every dollar saved is fully invested in the sole asset: $\alpha_t^* = 1$. Substituting this into (19), (25), and (26) and rearranging the terms yield a new set of wealth dynamics:

$$\frac{dC_t^*}{C_t^*} = \overline{\mu}_c \, dt + \sigma \, d\omega_t = \frac{dW_t^*}{W_t^*} = \overline{\mu}_w \, dt + \sigma \, d\omega_t, \tag{28}$$

where $\mu_w = \mu_c \equiv \mu/\gamma + ((\gamma - 1)/\gamma)(\sigma^2(\gamma + \lambda)/2 + \rho/(1 - \gamma - \lambda))$.

Clearly, the expected wealth growth $\overline{\mu}_w$ is increasing in λ, as $\partial\mu_w/\partial\lambda > 0$. Using such a conventional-growth-model framework, we are thus able to show that the stronger the spirit of capitalism or the more the investor cares about status, the faster the capital stock (or wealth) will grow. This formally justifies the reasoning by, among others, Weber (1958) and Keynes (1971) that the spirit of capitalism is the underlying driving force for fast economic growth.

As an aside, note that by definition the elasticity of intertemporal substitution in consumption is given by the response of $\overline{\mu}_c$ to a change in the marginal product of capital,[7] which means the elasticity coefficient here is just the reciprocal of γ, as $\partial\mu_c/\partial\mu = 1/\gamma$. Since RRA $= \gamma + \lambda$, we conclude that in an economy with capitalistic investors the intertemporal-elasticity and the risk-aversion coefficients are no longer reciprocal.

B. Model 2: Ratio of One's Own Wealth to Social Index Determines Status

When making consumption-portfolio decisions, investors under Model 2 will have to take into account what happens to the social-wealth index so that their relative status will not suddenly sink below a certain level. In Proposition 2, the optimal proportion invested in the risky stock, α_t^*, precisely reflects this concern. The first term in (23), $((\mu - r_0)/\sigma^2)$ $(I/(\gamma + \lambda))$, is dictated by the investor's aversion to wealth risk. In particular, since caring about status makes the investor more risk averse, he will hold less of the risky stock than someone who does not care about status ($\lambda = 0$).

The second term in (23), $(\sigma_{1,v}/\sigma^2)$ $(\lambda/(\gamma + \lambda))$, deserves more comments. This part of the optimal holding depends critically on how the risky stock is correlated with the social-wealth index V_t. (i) Suppose $\sigma_{1,v} > 0$, that is, the stock is positively correlated with the index V_t. Then, as discussed earlier, adding this stock to the portfolio will increase the correlation between W_t^* and V_t, which serves to insure against future

[7]See, among others, George M. Constantinides (1990) and Epstein and Zin (1991). It is discussed there that under the standard expected utility the elasticity coefficient and the relative risk aversion are reciprocal of one another and captured by the same parameter.

uncertain declines in status that can result from rises in social-wealth standards. Consequently, the second term in (23) is positive and increasing in $\sigma_{1,v}$, and the investor puts a higher proportion into the stock than dictated by risk aversion alone. The intensity of the investor's desire to insure against status falls is indicated by $\lambda/(\gamma + \lambda)$, which is increasing in λ. The more the investor cares about status, the more of the risky stock he will hold for insurance purposes, (ii) Suppose $\sigma_{1,v} = 0$, that is, the stock is uncorrected with V_t. Then, the risky asset is of no status-insurance value. As a result, the second term is zero and the investor's holding is completely dictated by the investor's aversion to wealth risk. (iii) Finally, suppose $\sigma_{1,v} < 0$. In this case, holding too much of the stock will only work toward reducing the investor's status some further when V_t rises. To avoid such a "double penalty," the investor will hold less of the risky stock than determined by risk aversion.

For the same reason as given above, the propensity to consume under Model 2, η, has a mixed response to an increase in the extent to which the investor cares about status, that is, $\partial\eta/\partial\lambda$ can take either sign. The propensity to consume decreases as the expected growth rate in the social-wealth index increases: $\partial\eta/\partial\mu_v < 0$. Intuitively, when V_t is expected to grow faster, the investor will have to consume less in order to maintain a desired social status. An increase in the volatility of V_t, σ_v^2, can lead to either a decrease or an increase in the propensity to consume, depending on whether $\lambda > 1$ or not. If the investor cares a lot about status in the sense that $\lambda > 1$, an increase in σ_v^2 will lead to a lower η: $\partial\eta/\partial\sigma_v^2 < 0$. This is to say that savings rates will be high in an economy where investors care much about status and where the social-wealth standards grow fast and volatilely.

The optimal-wealth and consumption-growth dynamics under Model 2 are given below:

$$\frac{dC_t^*}{C_t^*} = \frac{dW_t^*}{W_t^*} = \mu_w' \, dt + \frac{\mu - r_0 + \lambda\sigma_{1,v}}{\sigma(\gamma + \lambda)} \, d\omega_t, \tag{29}$$

where

$$\mu_w' \equiv \frac{r_0}{\gamma} + \frac{(\gamma - 1)(\lambda\mu_v - \rho + \frac{1}{2}\lambda(\lambda - 1)\sigma_v^2)}{\gamma(\gamma + \lambda - 1)} + \frac{(\gamma + 1)(\mu - r_0 + \lambda\sigma_{1,v})^2}{2\sigma^2\gamma(\gamma + \lambda)} - \frac{2\gamma\lambda\sigma_{1,v}(\mu - r_0 + \lambda\sigma_{1,v})}{2\sigma^2\gamma(\gamma + \lambda)}.$$

It is clear that expected wealth growth is in creasing in μ_v and, if $\lambda > 1$, in the volatility σ_v^2 as well. Therefore, when social-wealth standards grow fast, the desire to "catch up with the Joneses" will make the capital stock also grow fast. Next, the impact of an increase in λ on expected wealth growth will be determined by the joint working of three effects; the portfolio effect, the savings effect, and the status-hedging effect. As in Model 1, the more the investor cares about status, the more averse to wealth risk (*causing wealth to grow slower*) and the higher the savings rate (*causing wealth to grow faster*). But, unlike in Model 1, this also increases the investor's desire to insure against status declines, which means investing more in the risky stock (assuming the stock has a positive correlation with V_t) and *causing wealth to grow faster.* Depending on which effect dominates, a higher λ can mean higher or lower expected wealth growth. However, as in the previous subsection, if we adopt the common assumption from the growth literature of a sole investment asset, the portfolio and the hedging effects due to caring about status will not matter and only the savings effect will play a role. This is to say that in that case economic growth will be faster as investors care more about status.

C. Model 3: Self-Perception Determines Happiness

With the preferences of Model 3, the complexity of the consumption-portfolio problem rises significantly.[8] For our purpose, assume V_t grows at a deterministic rate:

$$\frac{dV_t}{V_t} = r_0\,dt\,, \tag{30}$$

that is, set $\mu_{v,t} = r_0$ and $\sigma_{v,t} = 0$ in (11). The wealth standard grows at the risk-free rate.

Proposition 3. *Let the utility and the V_t process be respectively as given in (5) and (30). Then,*

$$C_t^* = \xi(W_t^* - \kappa V_t) \tag{31}$$

$$\alpha_t^* = \frac{\mu - r_0}{\sigma^2}\frac{1}{\gamma + \lambda}\left(1 - \kappa\frac{V_t}{W_t^*}\right) \tag{32}$$

$$J(W_t, V_t) = \frac{\xi^{-\gamma}}{1 - \gamma - \lambda}(W_t - \kappa V_t)^{1-\gamma-\lambda}, \tag{33}$$

where $$\xi = \frac{\gamma - 1}{\gamma}\left\{r_0 + \frac{\rho}{\gamma + \lambda - 1} + \frac{1}{2}\frac{1}{\gamma + \lambda}\left(\frac{\mu - r_0}{\sigma}\right)^2\right\}, \xi \geq 0, \gamma + \lambda \geq 1.$$

The above result has many intuitively appealing implications. First, optimal consumption is proportional to the difference between the investor's wealth and his subsistence reference. The optimal proportion, ξ, is strictly decreasing and convex in λ: caring about status induces the investor to consume less, but the speed at which the investor lowers the optimal proportion increases as the extent to which the investor cares about status increases. Unlike in Models 1 and 2, the propensity to consume here depends on the investor's relative status:

$$\pi_t \equiv \xi\left[1 - \kappa\left(\frac{W_t^*}{V_t}\right)^{-1}\right] \geq 0\,, \tag{34}$$

which means that (i) the higher the poverty-aversion coefficient (κ), the lower the propensity to consume; (ii) the higher the investor's relative social status as measured by W_t^*/V_t, the higher the propensity to consume; and (iii) π_t is increasing in wealth W_t^* but decreasing in social-wealth index V_t. Therefore, in a society where status is crucial and where members compete to get into the upper-wealth class (by setting high κ values), the propensity to consume will be relatively low and the savings rate will be relatively high. Since W_t^* follows a diffusion process, so will π_t.

Second, based on (33), the implied relative risk aversion is

$$\text{RRA} = (\gamma + \lambda)\frac{W_t^*}{W_t^* - \kappa V_t} > 0, \tag{35}$$

which is increasing in γ, λ, κ and V_t but decreasing in W_t^*. In words, an investor will become more averse to wealth risk as (i) the investor cares more about status; (ii) he becomes more averse to poverty; (iii) the social-wealth standard goes higher; (iv) the investor's wealth goes lower; and (v) the investor's social status declines. Thus, including

[8] The Hamilton-Jacobi-Bellman equation in (46) is difficult to solve in closed form even when, for example, V_t follows a geometric Brownian motion as in the last two subsections. The case which tenders a closed-form solution obtainable by us is the one examined in this subsection.

status in the preferences allows us to relate an investor's risk aversion to both his relative standing in the wealth distribution and the degree to which the investor can handle poverty.

Third, since the wealth index V_t follows a deterministic process, there is no social-wealth uncertainty to hedge against. Consequently, the optimal proportion of savings invested in the risky stock is entirely determined by the investor's relative risk aversion, RRA, and the market price of risk. As before, higher relative risk aversion means lower investment in the risky stock. The comparative statics of α_t^* with respect to λ, κ, V_t, W_t^*, and W_t^*/V_t are exactly the opposite of those of RRA with respect to the respective parameters and variables (see the paragraph above).

Next, the growth process of wealth is as follows:

$$\frac{dW_t^*}{W_t^*} = \mu_{w,t}\,dt + \frac{1}{\gamma+\lambda}\,\frac{\mu - r_0}{\sigma}\,\frac{W_t^* - \kappa V_t}{W_t^*}\,d\omega_t, \tag{36}$$

where

$$\mu_{w,t} \equiv r_0 + \left(\frac{(\gamma+1)(\mu - r_0)^2}{2\gamma(\gamma+\lambda)\sigma^2} - \frac{\gamma - 1}{\gamma} r_0 - \frac{\rho(\gamma-1)}{\gamma(\gamma+\lambda-1)}\right) \times \frac{W_t^* - \kappa V_t}{W_t^*}. \tag{37}$$

As in Model 1, caring about status may mean lower or higher expected wealth growth (i.e., $\partial\mu_{w,t}/\partial\lambda$ can take either sign), depending on whether its portfolio effect dominates its savings effect.

Unlike in Models 1 and 2, however, expected wealth growth $\mu_{w,t}$ is decreasing in the poverty-aversion coefficient κ and the social-wealth level V_t.[9] Note that even though an increase in κ or V_t will lead to a decrease in consumption and hence an increase in savings, it will also imply an increase in risk aversion and thus a decrease in risky investment. The latter results in a decline in expected wealth growth. Here, the risk-aversion effect of a higher κ or V_t dominates the savings effect, making its overall impact on wealth growth negative. Higher wealth, on the other hand, means higher expected wealth growth. To see this, an increase in W_t^* causes the investor both to consume more (and thus save less) and to be less risk averse. But, in this case, the positive effect (on risk taking) dominates the negative effect (on savings), rendering the overall impact on wealth growth positive.

Finally, the growth process for consumption is no longer the same as that for wealth:

$$\frac{dC_t^*}{C_t^*} = \mu_{c,t}\,dt + \frac{1}{\gamma+\lambda}\,\frac{\mu - r_0}{\sigma}\,d\omega_t, \tag{38}$$

where $\mu_{c,t} \equiv (r_0/\gamma - \rho(\gamma-1)/\gamma(\gamma+\lambda-1) + (\gamma+1)(\mu - r_0)^2/2\gamma(\gamma+\lambda)\sigma^2)$. While the optimal consumption *level* is decreasing in κ and increasing in W_t^*/V_t, consumption *growth* is independent of these two factors, Note that in this economy both the return process on the risky stock and the consumption-growth process are independently-and-identically-distributed random walks, whereas the growth process for wealth has both its drift and diffusion terms state and time dependent. In this sense, Model 3 not only offers many empirically plausible features but also leads to richer economic dynamics.

---

[9] This statement relies on the fact that

$$\left(\frac{(\gamma+1)(\mu - r_0)^2}{2\gamma(\gamma+\lambda)\sigma^2} - \frac{\gamma - 1}{\gamma} r_0 - \frac{\rho(\gamma-1)}{\gamma(\gamma+\lambda-1)}\right) \geq 0.$$

To see why this expression in (37) must be nonnegative, suppose, to the contrary, that it were negative. Then, W_t^* would be expected to grow at a rate, $\mu_{w,t}$, lower than the risk-free rate r_0 at which κV_t grows. This means $(W_t^* - \kappa V_t)$ would become negative in the long run, which contradicts the restriction that $(W_t^* - \kappa V_t) > 0$ at each t.

III. Empirical Tests

Like the standard expected-utility theory, models of preferences that take into account concerns about relative status are ultimately judged on how well they fare empirically. Following standard practice, one can test such preference models by examining the empirical validity of their implied Euler equations. That is, we can achieve this goal by testing the discrete-time Euler equation in (9) or the continuous-time pricing equation in (12). Since all economic data is collected at discrete time intervals, we chose to focus efforts on the Euler equation in (9).

Applying the preferences of Models 2 and 3 to (9), one obtains two parametrized versions of the Euler equation and both are testable—so long as all required data can be collected. In addition to stock prices, one needs data on consumption, wealth and the social-wealth index in order to test the two models. Whereas proxies for consumption and wealth, at either the individual or aggregate level, are available at some sacrifice of quality, the choice of proxies for the social-wealth index is not apparent. At the aggregate level, it's not clear what the social-wealth reference for the "representative investor" corresponds to in reality, not to mention collecting such data. By definition, the "representative investor" will always be exactly in the middle class: $\overline{S}_t = \overline{W}_t/\overline{W}_t = 1$, if we use per-capita wealth as the wealth standard, where a bar indicates it's the per-capita counterpart of the variable. Under Model 2, for instance, this effectively means that even if individual investors care about status, the representative investor will not, because no matter what this so-defined investor does he cannot get out of the middle-class status. As such, even though we showed that aggregation does obtain for Model 2 under certain conditions, it may not make sense to test Model 2 using aggregate data because the very feature of caring about status will not be present in the Euler equation for the representative investor. In the case of Model 3, it is probably even less justified to subject the corresponding Euler equation to aggregate data because in that case aggregation may not obtain even under the assumption of identical preferences across investors. For this reason, it may make more sense to subject the Euler equations for Models 2 and 3 to individual consumer data. But, as discussed before, two consumers who are in two distinct reference groups will have two different social-wealth indices to which they compare themselves. This means that possibly *for each individual* a social-wealth index may have to be constructed and collected, in order to have the two models tested on cross-sectional consumer data. To maintain the scope of this paper, we leave such an investigation for a follow-up project.

We are thus led to focus on Model 1 as this preference model is independent of any social-wealth index, and yet captures an important part of investors' desire to improve relative social standing. Alternatively, if we assume that wealth standards stayed unchanged in the United States during the sample period 1959–1991, we can interpret our tests of Model 1 as tests of Model 2 because the latter in that case collapses to the former. In any case, as shown earlier, aggregation obtains under Model I if we adopt the assumption of identical preferences across investors. This means that under this assumption it is justified to subject the Euler equation for Model 1 to aggregate data. The Euler equation below is used for the empirical tests to follow:

$$E[m_{t+1}R_{i,t+1} \mid Z_t] = 1, \tag{39}$$

which is obtained by substituting the utility function of Model 1 into (9) and setting $\Delta t = 1$, where $\beta \equiv e^{-\rho}$, $R_{i,t+1}$ is the gross return on asset i, Z_t the time t information set with respect to which the conditional expectation is taken, and

$$m_{t+1} \equiv \beta R_{c,t+1}^{-\gamma} R_{w,t+1}^{-\gamma} \times \left(1 + \frac{\lambda}{\gamma - 1}\frac{C_{t+1}}{W_{t+1}}\right), \tag{40}$$

letting $R_{c,t+1} \equiv C_{t+1}/C_t$ and $R_{w,t+1} \equiv W_{t+1}/W_t$. Note that when $\lambda = 0$, this IMRS collapses to that implied by the standard constant-relative-risk-aversion (CRRA) power utility. The IMRS in Epstein and Zin (1991 eq. 20) can, following our notation, be expressed as

$$m_{t+1}^{\epsilon 2} \equiv \beta R_{c,t+1}^{-\gamma} R_{w,t+1}^{-\lambda}, \tag{41}$$

which is clearly different from the m_{t+1} in (40). Indeed, using discrete-time data, one can distinguish our Model 1 from their parametrized model.

To identify the IMRS in empirical tests, we need three time series: $\{R_{c,t}\}$, $\{R_{w,t}\}$, and $\{C_t/W_t\}$. Following standard practice, we choose the real-growth series for per-capita nondurables and services consumption as a proxy for $R_{c,t}$. The proxy choice of $R_{w,t}$ is nontrivial. As Richard W. Roll (1977) argues, aggregate wealth or the market portfolio is almost impossible to estimate because a major portion of it is not traded and hence its value is not observable. For this reason, researchers often have to look for some observable proxy. Following Cochrane and Hansen (1992), Epstein and Zin (1991), and Robert E. Hall (1978), we use the return on the New York Stock Exchange (NYSE) value-weighted index as a stand-in for $R_{w,t}$. The time series for consumption-to-wealth ratio, $\{C_t/W_t\}$, is constructed as follows. Note that $C_t = C_0\Pi_{\tau=1}^{t} R_{c,\tau}$ and $W_t = W_0 \Pi_{\tau=1}^{t} R_{w,\tau}$, which gives

$$\frac{C_t}{W_t} = \frac{C_0}{W_0}\prod_{\tau=1}^{t}\frac{R_{c,\tau}}{R_{w,\tau}}.$$

Given that we have chosen the real-life counterparts for $R_{c,t}$ and $R_{w,t}$, we only need the starting value, C_0/W_0, in order to construct the time series for C_t/W_t. The starting value, C_0/W_0 is chosen via a calibration exercise such that the mean of the resulting time series for C_t/W_t is consistent with what has been reported in the literature. This criterion has lead to a monthly initial value of $C_0/W_0 = 0.0076$ (i.e., for the first month of 1959), which corresponds to an annualized initial consumption-to-wealth ratio of 9.12 percent. The mean of the resulting time series for C_t/W_t is an annualized 6.83 percent.[10] Since the estimate for β was close to one in all pre-tried estimations, we set $\beta = 1$ in all reported tests so that there is one less parameter to estimate.

The data set used, a detailed description of which is in Appendix B, contains monthly observations on stock and bond returns, per-capita consumption, and returns on the NYSE value-weighted index. Monthly data has been used in numerous empirical studies of asset pricing including, among others, Epstein and Zin (1991), Wayne Ferson and George M. Constantinides (1991), Hansen and Jagannathan (1991, 1994), and Hansen and Singleton (1982).

To aid the discussion to follow, recall that according to the spirit-of-capitalism hypothesis, the preference parameters should be such that $\lambda > 0$ when $\gamma \geq 1$ and $\lambda < 0$ when $\lambda < 1$. If this hypothesis is empirically true, we should expect the resulting asset-pricing model to perform better when the values of γ and λ are consistent with this restriction.

A. Hansen-Jagannathan Bound Diagnostics

We first apply the Hansen and Jagannathan (1991) diagnostic method to check whether the IMRS in (40) satisfies the volatility bounds for any admissible IMRS or *stochastic discount factor*. Let $\mathbf{R}$ be the N vector of payoffs to the N assets included in the investigation, $\mathbf{q}$ the

[10] Lawrence Christiano (1991), for example, reports that the average consumption-to-GNP ratio (per capita) is about 0.73, while the average capital stock-to-GNP ratio is about 10.59. The implied average consumption-to-capital stock ratio is then about 6.89 percent, which is roughly the same as the annualized mean of our monthly time series for C_t/W_t, as constructed above. Also see Campbell (1993).

N vector of prices for the payoffs, and Σ_R the covariance matrix of **R.** Then, if our asset-pricing model in (39) can empirically explain the pricing structure for the N assets, it is, according to Hansen and Jagannathan (eq. 12), *necessary* that its IMRS in (40) satisfy

$$\sigma_m \geq \sigma_{\mathbf{R}} \equiv ([E(\mathbf{q}) - \mu_m E(\mathbf{R})]' \Sigma_{\mathbf{R}}^{-1} \times [E(\mathbf{q}) - \mu_m E(\mathbf{R})])^{1/2}, \tag{42}$$

where μ_m and σ_m are, respectively, the unconditional mean and standard deviation of the proposed IMRS. For any given value of μ_m, the volatility bound is constructed by estimating the mean vector $E(\mathbf{R})$ and the matrix $\Sigma_{\mathbf{R}}$. We refer the reader to Hansen and Jagannathan (1991) for detailed derivation and interpretation of this diagnostic.

As for the choice of assets in **R,** Hansen and Jagannathan (1991) suggest that including returns generated by using conditioning information should sharpen the volatility bounds considerably. Guided by their suggestion, we include in **R**: (i) real returns respectively on the NYSE value-weighted index and on long-term government bonds and (ii) scaled returns constructed via multiplying each of these two assets, separately, by their lagged returns and the lagged real return on the smallest decile of NYSE stocks. Thus, **R** contains a total of 8 assets (2 primitive and 6 scaled). The resulting Hansen-Jagannathan bounds are shown as the □-curve in Figure 1. The ◊-curve in Figure 1 indicates the (μ_m, σ_m) pairs obtained via fixing the value of γ and varying the value of λ, and the △-curve by fixing λ and varying γ.

FIGURE 1 | Hansen-Jagannathan Volatility Bounds

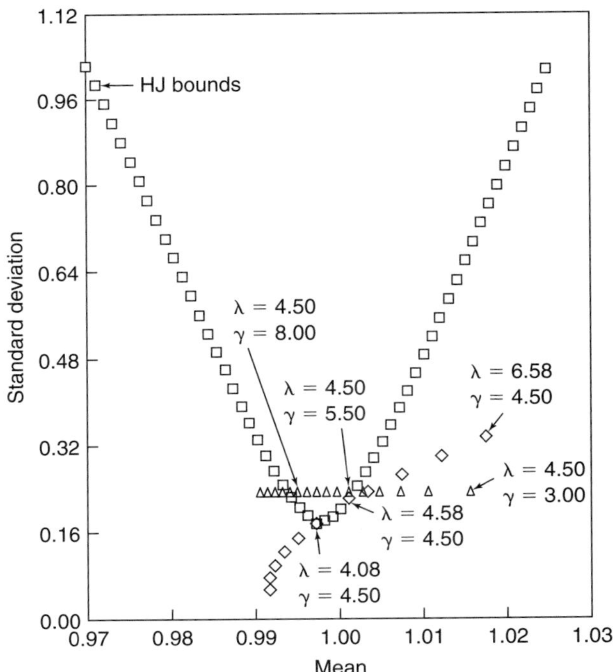

Note: The Hansen-Jagannathan bounds are illustrated by the □-curve. The candidate IMRS is given by

$$m_{t+1} \equiv \beta\left(\frac{C_{t+1}}{C_t}\right)^{-\gamma}\left(\frac{W_{t+1}}{W_t}\right)^{-\lambda}\left(1 + \frac{\lambda}{\gamma - 1}\frac{C_{t+1}}{W_{t+1}}\right)$$

The ◊-curve stands for the mean-standard deviation pairs of the IMRS obtained by fixing $\beta = 1$, $\gamma = 4.50$, and varying λ. The △-curve stands for the mean and standard deviation pairs of the IMRS obtained by fixing $\beta = 1$, $\lambda = 4.50$, and varying γ.

For certain $[\gamma, \lambda]$ values, the resulting (μ_m, σ_m) pairs for the IMRS are inside the Hansen-Jagannathan acceptance region. For instance, the Hansen-Jagannathan bounds are not violated when γ is fixed at 4.50 and λ is in the range 4.08–4.58, or when λ is fixed at 4.50 and γ is in the range 5.50–8.50. In these cases, the implied relative risk aversion in wealth, RRA $= \gamma + \lambda$, is around 9. This is in sharp contrast with the finding of Hansen and Jagannathan (1991) that the relative risk aversion needs to be in excess of 100 in order for the standard expected-utility model to satisfy the volatility bounds.

Observe that the $\triangle$-curve (corresponding to a fixed value for λ) is virtually flat, whereas the $\lozenge$-curve (corresponding to a fixed value for γ) is not. This is the case because, with the consumption growth series being smooth, varying the value of γ by a small value will mostly change the mean, but not the standard deviation, of the IMRS. On the other hand, given the volatility of wealth growth, changing the value of λ even by a small amount can lead to a large change in the volatility of the IMRS. Therefore, the ability of our model to generate a volatile IMRS comes mostly from the impact of the spirit of capitalism.

Stephen G. Cecchetti et al. (1994) argue that the original Hansen-Jagannathan bound diagnostic is not a statistical test as it involves comparing the point estimates of the volatility bound with those of the standard deviation of the IMRS. To take into account sampling errors, we follow their procedure to test whether $\sigma_m \geq \sigma_R$ for a given value of μ_m and whether σ_m lies within two standard errors from the Hansen-Jagannathan bounds.[11] Table 1 presents the results of such an investigation for several values of λ and γ. The reported t statistic tests the one-sided null hypothesis that $\sigma_m - \sigma_R \leq 0$. As in Cecchetti et al., the standard errors for this t test are calculated using the method in Whitney K. Newey and Kenneth D. West (1987a) with 11 lags (the results were quantitatively similar when alternate numbers of lags, such as 6, 9, or 15, were employed). The appropriate critical values for this test statistic are -1.65 and -2.33 for the 5- and 1-percent significance levels, respectively. That is, an absolute t value below 1.65 means a rejection of the null at the 5-percent significance level, and an absolute t value below 2.33 a rejection at the 1-percent level.

Start with the IMRS implied by the standard CRRA expected utility, which corresponds to our IMRS with $\lambda = 0$. Table 1 indicates that the standard IMRS is not volatile enough even for large values of γ, and the t values for the null that $\sigma_m - \sigma_R \leq 0$ are much higher in absolute value than the critical value, 1.65. Therefore, the standard model fails to satisfy the volatility bounds even when sampling errors are taken into consideration.

In contrast, when $\lambda > 0$, the results are substantially different. For instance, let $\lambda = 2$. Then, the resulting IMRS is volatile and the null hypothesis that $\sigma_m \leq \sigma_R$ is rejected at the 5-percent significance level when γ is between 4.0 and 6.0. This implies that with sampling errors taken into consideration, the Hansen-Jagannathan bounds are not violated when the relative risk aversion varies between 6 and 8. Similar conclusions emerge when $\lambda = 4.0$ and γ varies between 3 and 15, with the implied relative risk aversion between 7 and 19.

Also note that when $\gamma < 1$ and $\lambda > 0$ (i.e., the first three rows in Table 1), the parameter restriction implied by the spirit-of-capitalism hypothesis is violated. In these cases, the volatility bounds are overwhelmingly violated as well. Together with the other results in Table 1, this suggests that parameter values consistent with the spirit-of-capitalism hypothesis lead to better-performing IMRS models.

[11]See Cecchetti et al. (1994) for details regarding the test method and technical results on the asymptotic-distribution theory. Also see Hansen et al. (1995). We thank Nelson Mark for providing us with his code for their test procedure.

TABLE 1 | Cecchetti-Lam-Mark Volatility Bound Tests

	$\lambda = 0$			$\lambda = 2$			$\lambda = 4$		
γ	σ_m	σ_R	t value	σ_m	σ_R	t value	σ_m	σ_R	t value
0	0.000	0.224	−4.10	0.091	0.488	−2.71	0.192	0.744	−3.71
0.50	0.002	0.206	−3.78	0.091	0.912	−4.99	0.187	1.591	−3.85
0.75	0.003	0.200	−3.65	0.088	1.743	−7.98	0.178	3.265	−7.20
2	0.007	0.183	−3.25	0.095	0.319	−1.91	0.203	0.855	−1.90
3	0.011	0.189	−3.30	0.095	0.183	−1.69	0.201	0.409	−0.68
4	0.016	0.210	−3.52	0.096	0.220	−1.14	0.200	0.253	−0.22
5	0.019	0.024	−3.74	0.097	0.278	−1.32	0.200	0.190	−0.11
6	0.023	0.028	−3.91	0.098	0.338	−1.56	0.201	0.187	−0.13
7	0.027	0.032	−4.05	0.099	0.395	−1.79	0.201	0.218	−0.07
8	0.031	0.037	−4.14	0.100	0.450	−2.01	0.202	0.263	−0.21
9	0.034	0.417	−4.22	0.102	0.504	−2.20	0.203	0.312	−0.34
10	0.038	0.465	−4.29	0.104	0.556	−2.38	0.214	0.363	−0.47
15	0.057	0.704	−4.48	0.114	0.806	−3.02	0.209	0.609	−1.01

Notes: The volatility bound tests reported here are based upon Cecchetti et al. (1994). The IMRS being tested is

$$m_t = \beta\left(\frac{C_t}{C_{t-1}}\right)^{-\gamma}\left(\frac{W_t}{W_{t-1}}\right)^{-\lambda}\left(1 + \frac{\lambda}{\gamma - 1}\frac{C}{W_t}\right)$$

The asset vector used includes eight assets: $RVWI_t$, $RLTGB_t$, $RVWI_t \cdot RVWI_{t-1}$, $RVWI_t \cdot RLTGB_{t-1}$, $RLTGB_t \cdot RVWI_{t-1}$, $RLTGB_t \cdot RLTGB_{t-1}$, $RVWI_t \cdot RDEC_{1,t-1}$, $RLTGB_t \cdot RDEC_{1,t-1}$, where RVWI, RLTGB, and $RDEC_1$ denote, respectively, the real returns on the NYSE value-weighted index, long-term government bonds and the lowest decile of NYSE stocks. The asymptotic standard errors are based on Cecchetti et al. (eq. 19) and a lag length of 11 is used in the computation of the Newey-West (1987a) covariance matrix. For each estimation, set $\beta = 1$. The reported *t* value tests the null hypothesis that $\sigma_m - \sigma_R \leq 0$, where σ_m and σ_R are, respectively, the standard deviation of the IMRS and the volatility bound. The critical *t* value, above which the null is rejected, is −1.65 at the 5-percent and −2.33 at the 1-percent significance level.

The above Hansen-Jagannathan bound-based results are robust to the inclusion of other assets in **R.** In most cases, values for the preference parameters that support the volatility bounds are similar to those reported in Table 1.

B. Hansen-Jagannathan Specification Error Tests

Hansen and Jagannathan (1994) propose the following distance measure to reflect the performance of an asset-pricing model in pricing the assets in **R**:

$$\delta = [(E(\mathbf{q}) - E(m\mathbf{R}))'[E(\mathbf{RR}')]^{-t} \times (E(\mathbf{q}) - E(m\mathbf{R}))]^{1/2}, \tag{43}$$

where all variables are as defined before and m is the IMRS implied by the pricing model. They show that this δ measures the minimum distance between the candidate m and the set of admissible stochastic discount factors. It can also be interpreted as measuring the maximum pricing error induced by the IMRS over the unit ball in the payoff span of **R.** A nice property of this measure is that if two-asset pricing models lead to two different δ values, we can say the one with the smaller δ performs better than the other in pricing the assets in **R.** An admissible pricing model is one whose δ value is zero. For further discussion, see Hansen and Jagannathan.

Using the same set of assets from Subsection A, we report in Table 2 specification error estimates for the IMRS in (40). The standard errors are calculated with the help of Proposition 3.2 in Hansen et al. (1995) and by using 11 lags in the Newey-West (1987a) correction procedure. Again, the case with $\lambda = 0$ corresponds to the standard time-separable

TABLE 2 | Hansen-Jagannathan Specification Error Tests

	δ					
γ	$\lambda = 0$	$\lambda = 0.50$	$\lambda = 1.00$	$\lambda = 1.50$	$\lambda = 2.00$	$\lambda = 2.50$
0.50	0.184 (0.049)	0.180 (0.049)	0.178 (0.049)	0.178 (0.049)	0.181 (0.050)	0.186 (0.050)
2	0.183 (0.049)	0.179 (0.049)	0.177 (0.049)	0.177 (0.050)	0.180 (0.050)	0.184 (0.052)
5	0.183 (0.050)	0.179 (0.050)	0.177 (0.050)	0.177 (0.050)	0.179 (0.050)	0.184 (0.051)
10	0.181 (0.050)	0.178 (0.050)	0.176 (0.050)	0.177 (0.050)	0.179 (0.050)	0.184 (0.051)
15	0.181 (0.050)	0.177 (0.050)	0.176 (0.050)	0.177 (0.050)	0.180 (0.050)	0.184 (0.051)
20	0.180 (0.050)	0.177 (0.050)	0.176 (0.050)	0.177 (0.050)	0.180 (0.050)	0.185 (0.051)
25	0.180 (0.050)	0.177 (0.050)	0.177 (0.050)	0.178 (0.050)	0.181 (0.050)	0.186 (0.051)
30	0.180 (0.050)	0.177 (0.050)	0.177 (0.050)	0.178 (0.050)	0.182 (0.050)	0.187 (0.051)
Minimum $\delta = 0.176$ obtained at $\gamma = 6.40$ and $\lambda = 1.07$						
Constrained minimum $\delta = 0.180$ obtained at $\gamma = 29.44$ and λ fixed at 0						

Notes: Estimation of the specification error, δ, is based on Hansen and Jagannathan (1994 eq. 2.10). The standard errors, reported in parentheses, are estimated following Hansen et al. (1995 Proposition 3.2). A lag length of 11 is employed for the Newey-West (1987a) correction. The payoff vector used includes eight assets: $RVWI_t$, $RLTGB_t$, $RVWI_t \cdot RVWI_{t-1}$, $RVWI_t \cdot RLTGB_{t-1}$, $RLTGB_t \cdot RVWI_{t-1}$, $RLTGB_t \cdot RLTGB_{t-1}$, $RVWI_t \cdot RDEC_{1,t-1}$, $RLTGB_t \cdot RDEC_{1,t-1}$, where RVWI, RLTGB, and $RDEC_1$ denote, respectively, the real returns on the NYSE value-weighted index, long-term government bonds and the lowest decile of NYSE stocks. For each estimation, set $\beta = 1$. The reported minimum is obtained by choosing γ and λ, in the unconstrained case, and γ, in the constrained case, to minimize die Hansen-Jagannathan specification error.

model. In Table 2, δ values for the standard model are between 0.180 to 0.184. When $\lambda > 0$, the implied IMRS typically leads to lower δ values. For example, when λ varies between 0.5 and 2.0, the value of δ corresponding to any given γ is consistently smaller than when $\lambda = 0$. The Last two rows in Table 2 report the minimum δ values obtained, respectively, by the choice of both γ and λ and by the choice of γ subject to the constraint $\lambda = 0$. The constrained minimum δ is 0.180, with the estimated γ at 29.44, whereas its unconstrained counterpart is 0.176, with the estimated γ at 6.40 and λ at 1.07. Thus, when concerns about status are reflected in preferences, the resulting asset-pricing model generates smaller pricing errors.

We can also use the Hansen-Jagannathan specification error measure to compare the performance of our IMRS, m_{t+1}, versus that of Epstein and Zin's (1991) IMRS, $m_{t+1}^{\epsilon z}$, as given in (41). Recall that in the case of Epstein and Zin, the parameter restriction is that $\gamma > 0$ if $\lambda < 1$; $\gamma < 0$ if $\lambda > 1$; and $\gamma = 0$ if $\lambda = 1$. Under the spirit-of-capitalism hypothesis, however, it should be that $\lambda > 0$ when $\gamma \geq 1$ and $\lambda < 0$ when $\gamma < 1$. As the first example, fix $\lambda = 1.07$. Then, in the case of Epstein and Zin, the minimum δ among all $m_{t+1}^{\epsilon z}$ corresponding to the permissible range for γ (i.e., $\gamma < 0$) is 0.178, whereas in our case the minimum δ obtainable at $\lambda = 1.07$ is 0.176, with $\gamma = 6.40$ (see Table 2). As another example, fix $\lambda = 2.0$. The minimum δ within the permissible γ value range for the Epstein-Zin model is 0.180, while that for our Model 1 within γ values consistent with the spirit-of-capitalism hypothesis is 0.179. Therefore, taking the parameter restrictions into account, our Model 1 does slightly better than Epstein and Zin's. The parameter range, ($\gamma \geq 1$, $1 \geq \lambda \geq 0$), is consistent with both our hypothesis and their model. Within this range, both models generate virtually identical pricing errors and perform equally well (for this reason, the corresponding specification error values for m_{t+1}^{ez} are not reported in Table 2).

C. Criterion-Based Inferences and GMM Tests of the Euler Equation

The purpose of this subsection is to apply Hansen's (1982) generalized method of moments (GMM) to test the Euler equation in (39). To briefly explain the implementation, suppose the ith portfolio is included in the test and define the disturbance:

$$\varepsilon_{i,t+1} \equiv \beta R_{c,t+1}^{-\gamma} R_{w,t+1}^{-\lambda}\left(1 + \frac{\lambda}{\gamma - 1}\frac{C_{t+1}}{W_{t+1}}\right) \times R_{i,t+1} - 1.$$

Stack all $\varepsilon_{i,t+1}$ into the vector $\boldsymbol{\varepsilon}_{t+1}$. Under the null that the model holds, we have $E(\boldsymbol{\varepsilon}_{t+1} \otimes \mathbf{Z}_t) = 0$, that is, the disturbance must be orthogonal to the information variables in $\mathbf{Z}_t$. Each GMM estimation is based on minimizing the quadratic form, $G_T' \boldsymbol{\Omega}_T \mathbf{G}_T$, where T is the number of monthly observations, $\mathbf{G}_T$ the sample analog of the process $(\boldsymbol{\varepsilon}_{t+1} \otimes \mathbf{Z}_t) = 0$, and $\boldsymbol{\Omega}_T$ a positive-definite, symmetric-weighting matrix. The minimized value of the quadratic form multiplied by T, called the J_T statistic, is χ^2 distributed under the null that the model is true, with degrees of freedom, df, equal to the number of orthogonality conditions net of the number of parameters to be estimated. The J_T statistic provides a goodness-of-fit measure for the model: a higher value means a more misspecified model.

The choice of information instruments in $\mathbf{Z}_t$ is an important one and in this regard theory has little guidance (Hansen and Singleton, 1982). Based on previous research, $\mathbf{Z}_t$ is chosen to contain a constant and two lags each of the default premium, the term premium, and the nominal returns on the NYSE value-weighted index (except that when more than one portfolio is included in the test, only one lag of each instrument is used so as to keep the number of moment conditions at a proper level, i.e., 8). To check robustness, we experimented with alternate sets of instruments and found that the results do not differ significantly. To save space, we concentrate on the said set of instruments.

Table 3 reports results from estimations using a broad set of portfolios. For instance, estimates of (γ, λ) in the first three rows are obtained each by including a size-based portfolio, RDEC_1, RDEC_5, or RDEC_{10}. The standard errors reported in parenthesis are calculated using the simple covariance matrix outlined in Hansen (1982). The p value in brackets tests the null that the estimated parameter equals zero. The p value reported below the J_T statistic indicates the probability that a χ^2 variate exceeds the minimized sample value of the GMM criterion function.

Start with results from estimations in which λ and γ are unrestricted. When only one portfolio is included, the estimated range for γ is 2.27–3.08. Note that the magnitude of γ tends to decrease with firm size. For instance, the point estimate of γ is 3.08 in the case of decile 1, while in the cases of deciles 5 and 10 the estimates are 2.67 and 2.27, respectively. This is consistent with the fact that small stocks are generally more volatile than large ones. When more than one asset is included the test, the value of γ varies between 2.29–2.38. In all cases, the estimated value for γ is more than two standard errors away from zero and the p value is less than 5 percent.

The point estimates for λ are in the range 0.75–1.27, and in all cases they are many standard errors away from zero, with the lowest p value being 0 percent. For example, when decile 10 and a portfolio of long-term government bonds are included in the test, the

TABLE 3 | GMM Tests of The Euler Equation

Assets	Unrestricted λ & γ			Restricted $\lambda = 0$		Restricted $\gamma = 0$	
	γ	λ	$J_{r,u}$	γ	J_r	λ	J_r
$RDEC_1$	3.08 (0.91) [0.00]	1.16 (0.34) [0.00]	22.71 [0.00] (5)	5.44 (1.60) [0.00]	8.51 [0.00]	0.90 (0.22) [0.00]	3.76 [0.05]
$RDEC_5$	2.67 (0.37) [0.00]	1.27 (0.18) [0.00]	7.05 [0.22] [5]	4.50 (0.87) [0.00]	44.18 [0.00]	0.89 (0.11) [0.00]	12.80 [0.00]
$RDEC_{10}$	2.27 (0.13) [0.00]	0.84 (0.07) [0.00]	10.90 [0.06] (5)	3.38 (0.32) [0.00]	150.20 [0.00]	0.60 (0.06) [0.00]	18.41 [0.00]
$RDEC_5$ & $RDEC_{10}$	2.38 (0.15) [0.00]	0.82 (0.07) [0.00]	17.51 [0.00] [6]	4.22 (0.34) [0.00]	100.81 [0.00]	0.58 (0.04) [0.00]	18.87 [0.00]
$RDEC_{10}$ & RLTGB	2.29 (0.15) [0.00]	0.75 (0.08) [0.00]	13.21 [0.04] (6)	3.44 (0.37) [0.00]	85.08 [0.00]	0.55 (0.04)	18.47 [0.00]

Notes: Estimation of the following Euler equation is based on Hansen's (1982) generalized method of moments,

$$\beta E\left\{\left(\frac{C_{t+1}}{C_t}\right)^{-\gamma}\left(\frac{W_{t+1}}{W_t}\right)^{-\lambda}\left(1+\frac{\lambda}{\gamma-1}\frac{C_{t+1}}{W_{t+1}}\right)R_{1,t+1} \mid Z_t\right\} = 1,$$

where Z_t contains a constant and two lags (one lag when two assets are included in the test) each of term premium, default premium and the nominal returns of the NYSE value-weighted index. The standard errors reported in parentheses are based on the simple covariance-matrix estimator as outlined in Hansen. The p value in brackets indicates the probability that the estimated parameter equals zero. The degree of freedom df (reported in curly brackets) is the number of moment conditions minus the number of parameters to be estimated. The J_T statistic, $J_{T,U}$, tests whether the overidentifying restrictions of the model are true with the degrees of freedom, df. The statistic, $\bar{J}_T = J_{T,R} - J_{T,U}$, is $\chi^2(1)$-distributed, with $J_{T,R}$ being the GMM criterion function value from the restricted estimation. For each estimation, set $\beta = 1$. $RDEC_i$ is the real return on the ith decile of NYSE stocks and RLTGB the real return on a portfolio of long-term government bonds.

estimate for λ is 0.75, with a standard error of 0.08 and a p value of 0.00. Note that the point estimates for γ are uniformly greater than 1 and those for λ uniformly positive, which is consistent with the restriction implied by the spirit-of-capitalism hypothesis. Together the implied relative risk aversion in wealth, $\gamma + \lambda$, is in the range 3.04–4.24, which is in line with the estimates of Irvin Friend and Marshall E. Blume (1975), who report relative risk aversion coefficients higher than 2.0.

In two out of the three single-portfolio cases, the overidentifying restrictions imposed by the model are not rejected, as indicated by the p values below the J_T statistic (if we use the 5-percent acceptance criterion).[12] In the two cases that involve more than one portfolio, the p values below the J_T statistic are smaller than 5 percent, which means the overidentifying restrictions are rejected by the data. In Euler equation-based tests of the standard consumption-based asset pricing theory, rejections of the over-identifying restrictions are not

[12] The above estimation results are robust to a change in the measure of aggregate consumption. For example, we reestimated the parameters in the Euler equation, separately using seasonally-adjusted nondurables consumption and services consumption. But, that did not lead to any qualitatively different results. The estimates for γ and λ are also similar in both magnitude and statistical significance, for the two subperiods: 1959:1–1974:12 and 1975:1–1991:12. Thus, our conclusion regarding the goodness-of-fit of the model as well as the spirit-of-capitalism hypothesis is robust.

uncommon (e.g., Hansen et al., 1994 and the references therein). Thus, some rejections of the model in (39) based on the GMM criterion function should not come as a surprise.

Since the standard CRRA model is nested within our model, GMM criterion function-based inferences can be conducted (e.g., Martin Eichenbaum et al., 1988; Hansen et al., 1994; and Newey and West, 1987b). First, keep the weighting matrix from the unrestricted GMM estimation; second, use this weighting matrix in the restricted GMM estimation by assuming $\lambda = 0$ or $\gamma = 0$; then, compare the minimized GMM-criterion value (multiplied by T) from the restricted estimation, denoted by $J_{T,R}$, to that from the unrestricted, denoted by $J_{T,U}$.

$$\widetilde{J}_T = J_{T,R} - J_{T,U}.$$

This test statistic, $\widetilde{J}_T$, is asymptotically χ^2-distributed with degrees of freedom equal to the number of exclusion restrictions. Results from this exercise of imposing either $\lambda = 0$ or $\gamma = 0$ are reported in columns marked "Restricted" in Table 3. With either restriction, $\lambda = 0$ or $\gamma = 0$, the GMM-criterion function value increases substantially. In the case of $\lambda = 0$, for example, when the long-term government bond portfolio and decile 10 are included in this likelihood-ratio test, the estimate of γ is 3.44 and the $\widetilde{J}_T$ statistic equals 85.08 with a p value of 0 percent. The hypothesis that restricting the value of λ to zero does not change the GMM-criterion value is therefore overwhelmingly rejected. The same conclusion holds when γ is restricted to zero.

In summary, results from the GMM tests are consistent with those from the Hansen-Jagannathan bound and the Hansen-Jagannathan specification error-tests reported earlier, all supporting the claim that incorporating the spirit of capitalism, or concerns about status, into the investor's preferences improves the ability of the asset-pricing model to explain both stock and bond price movements. The magnitudes and signs of the estimated γ and λ are supportive of spirit-of-capitalism hypothesis.

IV. Concluding Remarks

In this paper, we examined the implications for consumption, portfolio choice, and stock prices, of the hypothesis that investors acquire wealth not just for its implied consumption but also for its induced status. We formalized the spirit-of-capitalism hypothesis in a way that is compatible with the more formal models of asset pricing that have been the prevailing mode of analysis in the past two decades. Among other things, we found that when investors care about status and about "catching up with the Joneses," they will be more conservative in risk taking and more frugal in consumption spending. Their consumption and risk taking will depend both on their relative social standing and on the prevailing wealth standards at the time. Further, stock prices tend to be more volatile than when the spirit of capitalism is absent.

Our work adds to the recent literature on the economic implications of social norms, customs, and culture.[13] Cole et al. (1992) study how the desire to increase social status may affect wealth accumulation and economic growth. In some sense, our preference structure can be viewed as a parametrization of their wealth-is-status equilibrium. Zou (1992, 1994) also assumes a direct utility function that has wealth as a variable to discuss economic growth and savings issues. By focusing attention on implications of the capitalistic spirit for risk taking and investment behavior, our exercise has lead to explicitly-testable restrictions relating concerns for status to stock prices and other economic

[13] See Chaim Fershtman and Yoram Weiss (1993) for more references on this topic.

variables.[14] The reported empirical results are supportive of the spirit-of-capitalism hypothesis and the resulting asset-pricing model performs better than the standard expected-utility model.

As noted earlier, wealth enters the IMRS under both our Model 1 and Epstein and Zin's (1991) parametrized recursive utility. In our discussion, this occurs due to investors' concern about wealth-induced status, whereas in theirs it is due to investors' concern about the timing of uncertainty resolution. In reality, both types of concern may exist simultaneously. In order for a preference model to capture these distinct concerns, one can substitute our Model 1, for instance, for the period utility in their recursive structure so that the two concerns are separately parametrized. Such a parametrization is potentially useful for empirical work since it allows one to estimate how much the effect of wealth on the IMRS is due to the timing concern and how much to the status concern. Along the same line, one can incorporate the concern for status into the habit-forming preferences of Constantinides (1990) and John Heaton (1995). Such extensions will generally be more complex, but should nonetheless make modelled preferences closer to their real-life counterparts.

Appendix A: Proof of Results

Proof of Proposition 1:

Rewrite equation (9) as follows:

$$\text{(A1)}\qquad e^{-\rho\Delta t}E_t\left\{\frac{U_C(C^*_{t+\Delta t}, W^*_{t+\Delta t}, V_{t+\Delta t})}{U_C(C^*_t, W^*_t, V_t)} + \frac{U_W(C^*_{t+\Delta t}, W^*_{t+\Delta t}, V_{t+\Delta t})\cdot\Delta t}{U_C(C^*_t, W^*_t, V_t)} \times\left(1+\frac{\Delta P_{i,t}}{P_{i,t}}\right)\right\} = 1$$

for any risky asset i and the risk-free asset, where $\Delta P_{i,t} \equiv P_{i,t+\Delta t} - P_{i,t}$. Subtracting the risk-free asset counterpart of (A1) from equation (A1) yields (A2):

$$\text{(A2)}\qquad E_t\left\{\frac{U_C(C^*_{t+\Delta t}, W^*_{t+\Delta t}, V_{t+\Delta t})}{U_C(C^*_t, W^*_t, V_t)} + \frac{U_W(C^*_{t+\Delta t}, W^*_{t+\Delta t}, V_{t+\Delta t})\cdot\Delta t}{U_C(C^*_t, W^*_t, V_t)} \times\left(\frac{\Delta P_{i,t}}{P_{i,t}} - r_0\Delta t\right)\right\} = 0.$$

Note that the term $U_W(C^*_{t+\Delta t}, W^*_{t+\Delta t}, V_{t+\Delta t})\cdot\Delta t$ in (A2) becomes negligible as $\Delta t \to 0$. Then, we can take the Taylor series of $U_C(C^*_{t+\Delta t}, W^*_{t+\Delta t}, V_{t+\Delta t})$ around the point (C^*_t, W^*_t, V_t) in equation (A2) and apply Ito's lemma to the resulting equation. Simplifying and rearranging the final terms will yield equation (12).

Proof of Proposition 2:

The Hamilton-Jacobi-Bellman equation for (18) is

$$\text{(A3)}\qquad 0 = \max(U(C_t, W_t, V_t) + \tfrac{1}{2}\alpha_t^2\sigma^2 W_t^2 J_{ww} + \{W_t[r_0 + \alpha_t(\mu - r_0)] - C_t\}J_w + \tfrac{1}{2}\sigma_v^2 V_r^2 J_{vv} + \mu_v V_e J_v + \alpha_t\sigma_{1,v}W_t V_t J_{vw} - \rho J\},$$

[14] For a different study on wealth-dependent preferences and asset prices, see Tzu-Kuan Chiu (1993).

the first-order conditions of which are stated in (20) and (21). Conjecturing that the value function has the form: $J(W, V) = \eta^{-\gamma}(W^{1-\gamma-\lambda})/(1-\gamma-\lambda))V^{-\lambda}$, we substitute it into (20), (21), and (A3) and solve the system jointly for C_t^*, α_t^* and η, which will give the desired result. See Merton (1971) for further details of the solution technique.

Proof of Proposition 3:

The solution steps are the same as in the proof of Proposition 2 except that the conjectured value function is $J(W, V) = \xi^{-\gamma}((W - {}_{\kappa}V)^{1-\gamma-\lambda}/(1-\gamma-\lambda))$.

Appendix B: Data Description

The variables employed in our tests and their sources are explained below:

C_t: per-capita real consumption in nondurables and services during month t. Source: CITIBASE. It equals real consumption expenditures divided by the residential population. The variable DCON, is the percentage change in C_t from month $(t-1)$ to month t.

INF_t: percentage change in the nondurables plus services consumption deflator from month $(t-1)$ to t. Source: CITIBASE.

$RDEC_{i,t}$: real return on the ith decile stock portfolio in month t, for $i = 1, \ldots, 10$. The decile portfolios are the 10 standard CRSP size-based portfolios, with each monthly return for any decile portfolio given by the value-weighted average of the component stock returns in that decile. Decile 1 includes the smallest 10 percent stocks; decile 2 the next smallest 10 percent; and so on. The nominal returns on the deciles are then adjusted by the nondurables and services consumption deflator to get the real returns. The data source for the nominal returns is the Center of Research for Security Prices (CRSP), University of Chicago.

$TBILL_t$: real return on one-month Treasury bills, which is the nominal return, obtained from Ibbotson Associates, adjusted by the non-durables and services consumption deflator.

$RLTGB_t$: real return on a portfolio of long-term government bonds (source: Roger G. Ibbotson and Rex A. Sinquefield, 1992). It is the nominal return minus the nondurables and services inflation rate.

$RLTCB_t$: real return on a portfolio of long-term corporate bonds. It is again the nominal return (source: Ibbotson and Sinquefield) minus the nondurables and services inflation rate.

$TERM_t$: term premium, which is the difference between the nominal return on a portfolio of long-term government bonds and the nominal return on the Treasury bills (source: Ibbotson and Sinquefield).

DEF_t: default premium, which is the excess return on long-term corporate bonds over the short-term interest rate from the one-month Treasury bills (source: Ibbotson and Sinquefield).

$RVWI_t$: real rate of return on the New York Stock Exchange value-weighted index.

Table 4 reports the summary statistics for the variables. Many of the stylized facts about consumption and asset returns are known. For instance, decile 1 (the smallest firms) has the highest average return and the highest standard deviation while decile 10 has the lowest standard deviation and the lowest average return. The average real-consumption growth is 0.0016 with a standard deviation of 0.004, which is quite smooth relative to the volatility of stock returns.

TABLE 4 | Summary Statistics

Variable	Mean	STD	θ_1	θ_2	θ_3	θ_6	θ_{12}	θ_{24}
RVWI	0.0053	0.044	0.07	−0.05	0.00	−0.06	0.03	0.00
$RDEC_1$	0.0106	0.082	0.20	0.00	−0.02	−0.03	0.31	0.13
$RDEC_5$	0.0071	0.061	0.15	−0.02	−0.02	−0.01	0.13	0.01
$RDEC_{10}$	0.0047	0.043	0.03	−0.04	0.01	−0.06	0.04	−0.00
RLTGB	0.0014	0.031	0.05	−0.01	−0.13	0.04	0.04	−0.07
RLTCB	0.0026	0.026	0.18	−0.03	−0.04	0.07	0.11	−0.04
TBILL	0.0011	0.002	0.51	0.45	0.36	0.42	0.31	0.24
TERM	0.0003	0.031	0.04	−0.03	−0.13	0.03	0.03	−0.08
DEF	0.0015	0.026	0.16	−0.04	−0.05	0.05	0.10	−0.05
DCON	0.0016	0.004	−0.24	0.06	0.15	0.05	−0.04	−0.15
INF	0.0039	0.003	0.64	0.60	0.52	0.57	0.45	0.31
C/W	0.0057	0.002	0.97	0.95	0.93	0.85	0.73	0.55

Notes: All variables are in monthly values. $RDEC_1$ through $RDEC_{10}$ are the value-weighted real returns on the 10 size-based portfolios. RVWT is the real return on the value-weighted index of the NYSE stocks. RLTGB and RLTCB are the real returns of a portfolio of long-term government bonds and a portfolio of long-term corporate bonds, respectively. TBILL is the nominal Treasury bill return, minus the nondurables and services inflation rate. TERM is the total return on a portfolio of long-term government bonds minus the nominal Treasury bill return. DEF is the total return on a portfolio of corporate bonds minus the nominal Treasury bill rate. DCON is the real growth rate of per-capita nondurables plus services consumption. INF is the nondurables and services inflation rate, C/W is the consumption-to-wealth ratio. θ_τ denotes autocorrelation at lag τ. The sample period is 1959: 1–1991:12 (396 observations).

References

Abel, Andrew B. "Asset Prices under Habit Formation and Catching Up with the Joneses." *American Economic Review*, March 1990, *80*(1), pp. 38–42.

Breeden, Douglass T. "An Intertemporal Asset Pricing Model with Stochastic Consumption and Investment Opportunities." *Journal of Financial Economics*, September 1979, *7*(3), pp. 265–96.

Campbell, John Y. "Intertemporal Asset Pricing Without Consumption Data." *American Economic Review*, June 1993, *83*(3), pp. 487–512.

Campbell, John Y. and Cochrane, John H. "By Force of Habit: A Consumption-Based Explanation of Aggregate Stock Market Behavior." Working Paper, Harvard University and University of Chicago, 1995.

Cecchetti, Stephen G.; Lam, Pok-Sang and Mark, Nelson C. "Testing Volatility Restrictions on Intertemporal Marginal Rates of Substitution Implied by Euler Equations and Asset Returns." *Journal of Finance*, March 1994, *49*(1), pp. 123–52.

Chen, Zhiwu. "Changing Tastes and Asset Pricing in Multiperiod Economies." Ph.D. Dissertation, Yale University, 1990.

Chiu, Tzu-Kuan. "Wealth-Dependent Preferences and Asset Prices in General Equilibrium: Theoretical Implications." Working Paper, University of Pennsylvania, 1993.

Christiano, Lawrence. "Modelling the Liquidity Effect of a Money Shock." *Quarterly Review*, Federal Reserve Bank of Minneapolis, Winter 1991, pp. 3–34.

Cochrane, John H. and Hansen, Lars P. "Asset Pricing Explorations for Macroeconomics," in *NBER Macroeconomics Annual.* Cambridge, MA: MIT Press, 1992, pp. 115–65.

Cole, Harold L.; Mailath, George J. and Postlewaite, Andrew. "Social Norms, Saving Behavior and Growth." *Journal of Political Economy*, December 1992, *100*(6), pp. 1092–125.

Constantinides, George M. "Habit Formation: A Resolution of the Equity Premium Puzzle." *Journal of Political Economy*, June 1990, *98*(3), pp. 519–43.

Duesenberry, James S. *Income, Saving and the Theory of Consumer Behavior*. Cambridge, MA: Harvard University Press, 1949.

Duffie, Darrell J. and Epstein, Larry G. "Asset Pricing with Stochastic Differential Utility." *Review of Financial Studies*, 1992, *5*(3), pp. 411–36.

Eichenbaum, Martin; Hansen, Lars P. and Singleton, Kenneth J. "A Time Series Analysis of Representative Agent Models of Consumption and Leisure Under Uncertainty." *Quarterly Journal of Economics*, February 1988, *103*(1), pp. 51–78.

Epstein, Larry G. and Zin, Stanley E. "Substitution, Risk Aversion, and the Temporal Behavior of Consumption and Asset Returns: An Empirical Analysis." *Journal of Political Economy*, April 1991, *99*(2), pp. 263–86.

Fershtman, Chaim and Weiss, Yoram. "Social Status, Culture and Economic Performance." *Economic Journal*, July 1993, *103*(141), pp. 946–59.

Ferson, Wayne and Constantinides, George M. "Habit Persistence and Durability in Aggregate Consumption: Empirical Tests." *Journal of Financial Economics*, October 1991, *29*(2), pp. 199–240.

Frank, Robert H. *Choosing the Right Pond: Human Behavior and the Quest for Status.* New York: Oxford University Press, 1985.

Friend, Irvin and Blume, Marshall E. "The Demand for Risky Assets." *American Economic Review*, December 1975, *65*(5), pp. 900–22.

Grossman, Sanford J. and Shiller, Robert J. "Consumption Correlatedness and Risk Measurement in Economics with Non-Traded Assets and Heterogeneous Information." *Journal of Financial Economics*, July 1982, *10*(2), pp. 195–210.

Hall, Robert E. "Stochastic Implications of the Life Cycle-Permanent Income Hypothesis: Theory and Evidence." *Journal of Political Economy*, December 1978, *86*(6), pp. 971–87.

Hansen, Lars P. "Large Sample Properties of Generalized Method of Moments Estimators." *Econometrica*, September 1982, *50*(6), pp. 1029–179.

Hansen, Lars P.; Heaton, John and Luttmer, Erzo G. "Econometric Evaluation of Asset Pricing Models." *Review of Financial Studies* 1995, *8*(2), pp. 237–74.

Hansen, Lars P.; Heaton, John and Yaron, Amir "Finite Sample Properties of Some Alternative GMM Estimators." Working Pape No. 2728-94-EFA, Massachusetts Institute of Technology, 1994.

Hansen, Lars P. and Jagannathan, Ravi. "Implications of Security Market Data for Model; of Dynamic Economies." *Journal of Political Economy*, April 1991, *99*(2), pp. 225–62.

______. "Assessing Specification Errors in Stochastic Discount Factors." Working Paper, University of Chicago and University of Minnesota, 1994.

Hansen, Lars P. and Singleton, Kenneth J. "Generalized Instrumental Variable Estimation of Nonlinear Rational Expectations Models." *Econometrica*, September 1982, *50*(6), pp. 1269–86.

Heaton, John. "An Empirical Investigation of Asset Pricing with Temporally Dependent Preference Specifications." *Econometrica,* May 1995, *63*(3), pp. 681–717.

Hurd, Michael D. "Savings and Bequests." National Bureau of Economic Research (Cambridge, MA) Working Paper No. 1708–1986.

Iacocca, Lee. *Talking straight.* New York: Bantam Books, 1988.

Ibbotson, Roger G. and Sinquefield, Rex A. *Stocks, bonds, bills and inflation: 1992 yearbook.* Chicago: Ibbotson Associates, 1992.

Keynes, John M. *The economic consequence of the peace*. London: St. Martin's Press, 1971.

Kurz, Mordecai. "Optimal Economic Growth and Welfare Effects." *International Economic Review*, October 1968, *9*(3), pp. 348–57.

Lucas, Robert E., Jr. " Asset Prices in an Exchange Economy." *Econometrica*, November 1978, *46*(6), pp. 1429–45.

Markowitz, Harry M. "The Utility of Wealth," *Journal of Political Economy*, April 1952, *60*(2), pp. 151–58.

Mehra, Rajnish and Prescott, Edward C. "The Equity Premium: A Puzzle." *Journal of Monetary Economics*, March 1985, *15*(2), pp. 145–61.

Merton, Robert C. "Optimal Consumption and Portfolio Rules in a Continuous Time Model." *Journal of Economic Theory*, December 1971, *3*(4), pp. 373–413.

Newey, Whitney K. and West, Kenneth D. "A Simple Positive Semi-Definite Heteroskedasticity and Autocorrelation Consistent Covariance Matrix." *Econometrica*, July 1987a, *55*(4), pp. 703–8.

______. "Hypothesis Testing with Efficient Method of Moments Estimation," *International Economic Review*, October 1987b, *28*(3), pp. 777–87.

Perkin, Harold J. *The origins of modern english society, 1780–1880.* London: Routledge and Kegan Paul, 1969.

Robson, Arthur J. "Status, the Distribution of Wealth, Private and Social Attitudes to Risk." *Econometrica*, July 1992, *60*(4), pp. 837–57.

Roll, Richard W. "A Critique of Asset Pricing Theory Tests-Part 1: On Past and Potential Testability of the Theory." *Journal of Financial Economics*, March 1977, *4*(2), pp. 129–76.

Weber, Max M. *The protestant ethic and the spirit of capitalism.* New York: Charles Scribner's Sons, 1958.

Zou, Heng-Fu. "The Capitalist Spirit and a Resolution of the Savings Puzzle." Working Paper, World Bank, 1992.

______. "The Spirit of Capitalism and Long-Run Growth." *European Journal of Political Economy*, July 1994, *10*(2), pp. 279–93.

Twenty-Four

William N. Goetzmann

William N. Goetzmann received a Ph.D. from Yale University and joined Columbia Business School in 1990 as an Assistant Professor. He is now the Edwin J. Beinecke Professor of Finance and Management Studies at the Yale School of Management, and Director of its International Center for Finance. •

I owe an unusual debt of gratitude to Steve Ross as mentor. We first met when I took Steve's Topics in Finance class as an MBA student at the Yale School of Management. I had no background or previous training in finance or economics—the class simply looked interesting. His mentorship began with an empirical project that my fellow student Mark Garry and I conducted on S&P listings and delistings in 1985—a topic Steve introduced in his class. With Steve Ross's and Stephen Brown's guidance, Mark and I did an event study of the index changes consequent on the AT&T break-up. As a result, we were both suddenly hooked on empirical finance. Mark went to industry, and eventually become a principal in Roll and Ross asset management. After my MBA, Steve encouraged me to pursue a Ph.D. in Operations Research at Yale. When I said I could not afford it, he got me consulting work that helped finance my education.

In some ways, I suspect it was a mischievous experiment on the part of the Yale faculty to see whether a former museum-director and Art History major could survive linear algebra, real analysis, linear and non-linear optimization, stochastic processes and the theory of choice. Of course, I owe my entire professional career to their willingness to take that risk. When I pore over the dozens of doctoral applications Yale receives each year, I ask myself whether I have the judgment and insight to take a similar risk on an unconventional student.

"Global Stock Markets in the Twentieth Century," co-authored with Philippe Jorion, has an interesting intellectual ancestry that speaks to the crucial role a mentoring relationship and intellectual collaboration plays in research. The paper grew out of my research with Stephen Brown and Steve Ross on survivorship biases and financial markets. In our earlier paper "Survival" we explored the possibility that the *ex post* observed equity premium in the U.S. capital markets could be due to luck. Steve Ross's own interest in this topic grew out of his paper "Regression to the Max," a provocative work arguing that any econometric analysis motivated by an extreme economic event will impose subtle biases. For example, when you perform a regression that is motivated by an outlier, the results will be tipped towards rejection of the null. From the perspective of the intellectual history of the discipline, "Regression to the Max" was an important "Post-Modernist" theory. It demanded a self-conscious awareness of the analyst's relationship with the phenomenon of interest.

The analytical results in our "Survival" paper about the equity premium led to an empirical question—was the U.S. historical equity premium different? Does survival correlate to an ex post observed premium? "Global Stock Markets in the Twentieth Century" tackles these issues by collecting and analyzing historical returns for a broad set of equity markets.

Global Stock Markets in the Twentieth Century

*Philippe Jorion and William N. Goetzmann**

Abstract

Long-term estimates of expected return on equities are typically derived from U.S. data only. There are reasons to suspect that these estimates are subject to survivorship, as the United States is arguably the most successful capitalist system in the world. We collect a database of capital appreciation indexes for 39 markets going back to the 1920s. For 1921 to 1996, U.S. equities had the highest real return of all countries, at 4.3 percent, versus a median of 0.8 percent for other countries. The high equity premium obtained for U.S. equities appears to be the exception rather than the rule. •

In a now-famous article, Mehra and Prescott (1985) argue that standard general equilibrium models cannot explain the size of the risk premium on U.S. equities, which averages about 6 percent over the 1889–1978 period. They show that one would need a very large coefficient of risk aversion, largely in excess of the usual value of two, to generate such a premium. This unsettling result has sparked a flurry of theoretical research that explores alternative preference structures, including dropping the expected utility assumption and introducing habit formation.[1] Such efforts, however, come at the cost of losing the intuition of standard models.[2]

Rather than searching for preference structures that fit historical data, other explanations focus on the limitations of the data. Rietz (1988) proposes a solution to the puzzle that involves infrequently occurring "crashes." Assuming a crash where output falls by 50 (or 25) percent of its value with a probability of 0.4 percent (or 1.4 percent), Rietz generates ex ante equity premiums consistent with those observed in the United States and risk aversion of five (or ten).

A related argument is advanced in Brown, Goetzmann, and Ross (1995), who claim that survival of the series imparts a bias to ex post returns. They show that an ex ante equity premium of zero can generate a high ex post positive premium by simply conditioning on the

*Jorion is with the University of California at Irvine; Goetzmann is with the Yale School of Management. We thank seminar participants at the University of California at Los Angeles, Carnegie-Mellon, Indiana University, the London Business School, the Stockholm School of Economics, the University of Houston, the University of Michigan, the University of Notre Dame, the University of Southern California, the 1997 European Finance Association meetings, and the 1997 Western Finance Association meetings for useful comments. The referee and the editor, René Stulz, also provided valuable comments. Able research support was provided by Robin Brooks. George Bittlingmayer kindly provided a copy of the German data. This research received financial support from the Institute for Quantitative Research in Finance, for which we are grateful.

[1]See Epstein and Zin (1991) for nonadditive utility functions and Constantinides (1987) for habit formation. Bansal and Coleman (1996) suggest that liquidity services provided by cash partly explain why returns on cash are so low.

[2]Burnside and McCurdy (1992) provide a good review of the equity premium puzzle.

Reprinted with permission:
Jorion, Philippe and William N. Goetzmann. "Global Stock Markets in the Twentieth Century." *The Journal of Finance* 54 (1999):953–980.

market surviving an absorbing lower bound over the course of a century.[3] The implication is that risk aversion cannot be inferred from the empirical analysis of historical data whose observation is conditional on survival. Although the Rietz (1988) argument leads to higher ex ante equity premiums, the survival argument points to biases in ex post premiums.

Unfortunately, these arguments are nearly impossible to sort out based on a century of U.S. equity data. Consider, for instance, a 0.4 percent annual probability of a large crash. We would then expect one crash to occur every 250 years. Even if we observed such a long sample series, our estimate of the crash probability would still be subject to enormous estimation error.

The only solution to this dilemma is to expand the sample by collecting additional cross-sectional data. In this paper, we reconstruct real capital appreciation series for equity markets in 39 countries over much of the twentieth century. We include not only those markets that survived, but also those markets that experienced both temporary and permanent interruptions. We use this new database to estimate the long-term returns to investing in global markets over the twentieth century.

The first part of our analysis treats each market separately. In effect, it takes all stock market histories as draws from one urn. Under these conditions, we show that the process of discarding markets with interruptions creates serious biases in the measurement of expected returns. Such an experiment assumes that all markets have the same statistical characteristics. This framework is valid when markets are segmented due, for instance, to capital controls. The assumption of constraints on such diversification is not unreasonable for the time period under study.

This paper provides the first comprehensive long-run estimates of return on equity capital across a broad range of markets. To date, virtually the only long-run evidence regarding equity rates of return is derived from the United States, for which we have continuous stock price history going back to 1802. We are able to augment the U.S. experience with a wide range of different global equity market histories.

We find striking evidence in support of the survival explanation for the equity risk premium. Over our sample period, the United States has the highest uninterrupted real rate of appreciation, at 4.3 percent annually. For other countries, the median real appreciation rate is approximately 0.8 percent. This strongly suggests that estimates of equity premiums obtained solely from the U.S. market are biased upward by survivorship. An alternative line of explanation is that of fundamentally different risk premiums. With segmented markets, risk premiums are determined by local market conditions. Thus differing expected returns could be due to different investor expectations about risk or to different risk aversion.

Beyond its potential value for shedding light on the equity premium puzzle, this global database allows a broad investigation into the behavior of equity markets over the very long run. We have been able to construct monthly real and dollar-valued capital appreciation indices for virtually all the equity markets that existed during the twentieth century. This enables us to examine markets in crisis and to compare the behavior of losing markets to the behavior of winning markets.

In the second part of the study, we construct a world market appreciation index in order to examine the potential experience of a diversified global investor. This allows us to analyze the benefits of international diversification, comparing return and risk measures across the U.S. and the global portfolios. We estimate the return that such an investor would have earned had it been possible to hold the world market from the early 1920s. Even though one

[3]A similar argument is advanced by Goetzmann and Jorion (1996). They argue that many so-called "emerging markets" are in fact "reemerging markets" as they have longer histories than commonly believed. Few analysts, however, bother to track the histories of markets that have disappeared.

could argue that few investors could have held globally diversified portfolios during these turbulent times, this is still an informative experiment as a guide for future investing.

This paper is organized as follows. Section I motivates the search for differences in return on capital. Section II describes the construction of the global market database. Section III compares the performance of global stock markets and discusses biases affecting the construction of a global stock market index. Section IV contains some concluding comments.

I. The Importance of Compound Growth

In September 1626, Pierre Minuit, the Governor of the West India Company, purchased Manhattan Island from the local Indians for the total sum of 60 guilders, or about 24 dollars. At first sight, this seems like the deal of the century.

Yet, slight differences in the time value of money over long horizons can result in vastly different conclusions. If one compounds this payment at a 5 percent rate of interest, it would have grown in 1995 to about 1.6 billion in current dollars, which seems expensive for 31 square miles of undeveloped land. Compounding at 3 percent, however, results in a much lower current price of $1.3 million—a thousandfold difference! This story shows that differences in rates of return on capital can lead to drastically different numbers when compounded over long horizons.

Our estimates of the rate of return on equity capital are typically based on a century of U.S. data, which reveals an equity premium of about 6 percent. As shown in this example, however, small differences in rates of return can have momentous implications over the long run. How much faith can we have in this number?

Not much, given the volatility of stock returns. Consider, for instance, a market that grows at a 6 percent annual rate with a standard deviation of 20 percent. The question is, how many years do we require to establish that growth is positive with statistical confidence? Using the standard t-test at the 5 percent level, we require that the statistic

$$t = \frac{\hat{\mu}}{\hat{\sigma}\ /\sqrt{N}} = \frac{0.06}{0.20/\sqrt{N}} \tag{1}$$

be greater than two. This requires N to be at least 44 years. In other words, we need approximately half a century of returns to be confident that this 6 percent equity premium is positive. If the expected return is 3 percent instead, we will need more than 178 years of data to establish statistical significance.

Another problem is that we have reasons to suspect that estimates of return on capital from the United States are affected by survival. At the beginning of the century, active stock markets existed in a number of countries, including Russia, France, Germany, Japan, and Argentina. All of these markets have been interrupted for a number of reasons, including political turmoil, war, and hyperinflation. Assuming there was some probability of disruption for the U.S. market, this probability is not reflected in the observed U.S. data. In turn, this will bias our estimates of the equity premium.

As small differences in estimates on equity capital have dramatic implications for long-term growth, we feel it is important to extend our knowledge of equity premiums to a large cross-sectional sample of long-term data.

II. A Global Stock Market Database

The standard data sources on international stock prices are *Morgan Stanley Capital International Perspectives* (MSCIP) for developed markets and the International Finance Corporation (IFC) for emerging markets. Both are relatively recent.

MSCIP started to construct equity indices in January 1970 for a sample of 19 markets from industrial (developed) countries. These indices are built using a uniform methodology and include income and currency effects. A similar approach was undertaken by the IFC, which in 1980 started to build indices for nine emerging markets, which were expanded to 26 by 1995.

Beyond these databases, unfortunately, there is little systematic information on the long-term performance of global stock markets. The United States is a rare exception, as monthly stock market indices have been constructed by Standard and Poor's and, prior to 1926, by Alfred Cowles (1939), going back into the 1870s.[4]

For the non-U.S. data, we must turn to a variety of sources. The first is the International Monetary Fund (IMF), which publishes monthly stock price indices as reported by the local authorities in its *International Financial Statistics* (IFS) publication. The published indices generally represent monthly averages, as opposed to the end-of-month MSCIP and IFC data, and do not include dividends.[5] The IMF also publishes price indices and exchange rates, which can be used to compute real returns and dollar returns. We use the Wholesale Price Index (WPI) to deflate nominal returns, whenever available. The WPI measure offers a number of advantages, in that the WPI indices generally have longer histories than consumer indices, are less affected by differences in domestic consumption patterns, and are more responsive to monetary disturbances than other inflation measures.[6]

One drawback of this dataset is that it does not allow us to measure directly the equity premium, usually defined as the difference between the total return on stocks minus the Treasury bill rate. Decomposing the total return on stocks (R_S) into capital return (CR_S) and income return (IR_S), and the Treasury bill rate (R_{TB}) into the inflation component and the real rate, we can write

$$\begin{aligned}\text{Equity Premium} &= R_S - R_{TB} \\ &= [CR_S + IR_S] - [\text{Inflation} + \text{Real Rate}] \\ &= [CR_S - \text{Inflation}] + [IR_S - \text{Real Rate}]. \qquad (2)\end{aligned}$$

Our methodology measures the capital return in excess of inflation, which is the first bracketed term. To the extent that cross-sectional variations in the second bracketed term are small, this allows comparisons of equity premiums across countries. Some evidence on the quality of this approximation is presented later.

The first IFS publication was issued in 1948. Prior to the IMF, our source is the *Statistical Yearbooks* of the League of Nations (various issues), which include data on the capital appreciation of market indices in the period from 1929 through 1944. This collection effort was bridged by the United Nations' *Monthly Bulletin of Statistics* from 1945 to 1948.

[4]For evidence on long-term U.S. data, see Wilson and Jones (1987), Schwert (1990), Siegel (1992), and Goetzmann and Ibbotson (1994). There is some long-term evidence from the U.K. markets; for instance, see Goetzmann (1993), DeLong and Grossman (1993), and Goetzmann and Jorion (1995). Parsons (1974), Mirowski (1981), and Neal (1987, 1990) provide data on the Amsterdam and London exchanges in the eighteenth century.

[5]Relative to more modern data, the IFS data suffer from two drawbacks: possible noncomparability in the construction of the series and use of monthly average instead of end-month price. The Cowles indices, the standard data source before 1926 for U.S. data, however, have similar drawbacks because prices are measured as the average of high and low values during the month.

[6]There are a few instances where we have to use Consumer Price Index data (e.g., post-1947 data for Belgium, France, New Zealand, Peru, and Israel). Because nominal prices in Germany were distorted during the hyperinflation period, we measure nominal prices for 1921–1923 in gold marks.

Finally, the *International Abstract of Economic Statistics* publications (ICES 1934, 1938) have stock market data going back to 1919.[7]

By connecting data from these sources, we are able to reconstruct histories for a number of stock markets going back to the early 1920s. This is a challenging effort, because of erratic data reporting.[8] The IMF, for example, provides a CD-ROM with data starting in 1957. Unfortunately, this database suffers from sample selection biases, as a number of markets that were followed in the 1960s are not contained in the CD-ROM. Data for these markets have to be collected from the IFS monthly publications. More recent emerging market data, when not available from the IFS publication, are available from the IFC database.

In order to minimize survivorship biases, we follow all markets that were reported by the League of Nation or the IMF at any point during the 1929 to 1970 period. After 1970, a flurry of new markets opened (or reopened). These emerging markets, however, have relatively short histories and are not included in the database as they have been already extensively analyzed. We obtain a total of 39 markets.[9] All in all, this involves a total of approximately 76,000 data points.

Whenever data sources do not overlap, we attempt to link series by comparing annual averages. This is the case for Austria, for instance, whose price history was interrupted by the Anschluss (German annexation) in April 1938. Fortunately, the United Nations' publications provide annual averages from 1946 on and going back to 1935; allowing us to reconstruct a long-term history for Austria, albeit with an 8-year gap during the war.

Initially, we begin by collecting annual data. We find, however, that the monthly data create more precise estimates. In particular, we notice discrepancies between returns using monthly and annual data.[10] We also find that monthly data lead to cleaner linkages between various sources, which is particularly important as we sometimes have to patch series together. Finally, the monthly data allow us to perform event studies centered around specific dates.

Note that, despite all our efforts, this database is still not free from selection biases. The first type of bias occurs when backfilling of an index uses only stocks that are in existence at the end of the sample. In the case of Austria, for instance, even though the stock market has recovered, some companies may have fared badly or disappeared during the war. Therefore, a selection bias is induced if these companies are not included in the index.

The second type of remaining bias is much more serious. The UN–IMF data sources do not allow us to link gaps for six countries. In particular, there appears to be no link between stock market prices of Germany and Japan before and after the war in standard data sources. As these two countries did not fare well during these gaps, we can surmise

[7]Alfred Cowles, founder of the Cowles Commission for Research in Economics, was apparently the first scholar to document time-series data on global stock markets. We learned of the League of Nations data from the appendix to his 1939 publication which lists periodical sources for stock market data in 20 countries. A recent source of global stock market information which uses the League of Nations data, as well as information from other historical sources, is the Global Financial Markets database collected by Bryan Taylor, which we learned of after submission of this paper for publication. Taylor's database covers similar markets to ours; there are, however, some differences in the data sources and in particular during the breaks. For instance, we find the German stock price data collected by Gielen (1994) to be an excellent source for reconstruction of the German markets during the early part of the 20th century.

[8]The measurement of exchange rates also proves quite difficult. The League of Nations, for instance, reports rates in percentage of their 1929 gold parity value, from which current spot rates relative to the dollar have to be reconstructed. Many currencies also changed units or denomination during this century. Around World War II, trading in some currency pairs was either nonexistent or subject to heavy governmental control.

[9]The only market we deliberately omit is Lebanon, for which we cannot find inflation data.

[10]The difference can be particularly pronounced over short periods when the data are monthly or annual averages. As an illustration, comparing returns on the S&P index total returns series over 1926–1945, we find the annual growth to be 7.2 percent and 6.6 percent, respectively, for monthly and annual data.

FIGURE 1 | Real Returns on Global Stock Markets

The figure displays average real returns for 39 markets over the period 1921 to 1996. Markets are sorted by years of existence. The graph shows that markets with long histories typically have higher returns. An asterisk indicates that the market suffered a long-term break.

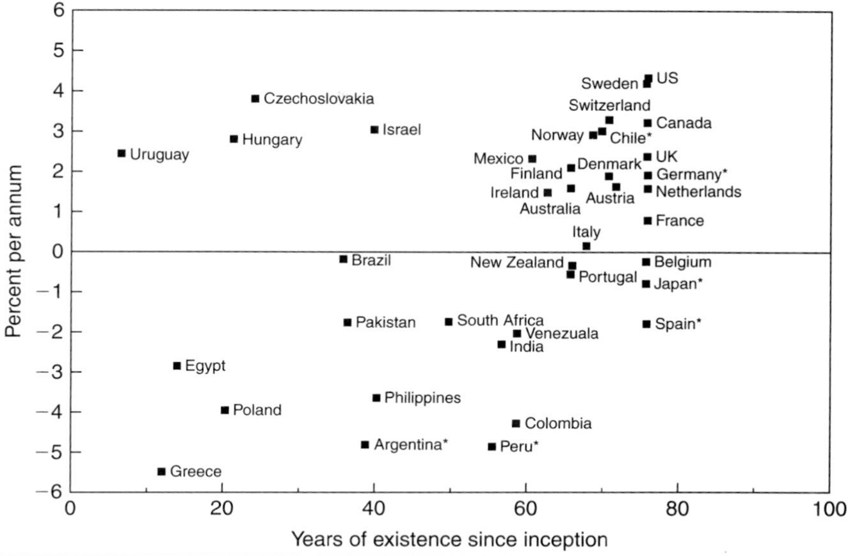

that omitting the gaps misses important negative information. We attempt to correct for this by turning to other data sources for bridging these gaps.[11]

III. Empirical Analysis

A. Performance of Global Stock Markets

We calculate returns using three different numéraires; the local currency, a real price index, and the dollar. Because of wide differences in inflation across time and countries, we primarily focus on WPI-deflated returns. Returns in dollars as a common currency should give similar results over the long run if exchange rates move in line with inflation differentials—that is, if Purchasing Power Parity holds. Differences between real and dollar returns, however, may be induced when exchange rates are pegged by central banks at artificial levels, or when official exchange rates do not reflect the actual rates facing international investors.

Table I presents geometric returns for 39 markets grouped by regions, compounded annually. These results are striking. Of the sample of 39 countries, real returns are the highest for the United States, at 4.32 percent per annum. There is no country with a higher return over the total period. Therefore, the high U.S. equity premium seems to be the exception rather than the rule.

These results are perhaps better visualized in Figure 1, which plots the compound return for each market against its observed "life" since 1921. Longer lives lead to more

[11]We have permanent gaps in the series for Chile, Germany, Japan, Peru, Portugal, and Argentina. The gap for Chile is filled using data from publications from the Chilean Central Bank. The gap for Germany is covered using data spliced by Gielen (1994). The gap for Japan is bridged using Bank of Japan (1966) data. The gap for Peru is filled using data received by the Lima stock exchange. To cover the gap for Portugal, we use information from the Portuguese Central Bank. Overall, Argentina is the only remaining country with a permanent break over July 1965 to December 1975, which is the first date for which we have data from the IFC. We have been unable to find data to bridge the gap.

TABLE I | Long-Term Performance of Global Equity Markets (Compound Return in Percentage per Annum)

The table compares the long-term performance of global equity markets with annually compounded data. The sample period varies across country and is reported in the second column. Data for subperiods are reported within brackets. Percentage returns are measured in nominal terms in the local currency, in real terms—deflating by the Wholesale Price Index, and translated into U.S. dollars. The last column reports the inflation rate. * indicates a break in the series that has been bridged; + indicates a permanent discontinuity in the series.

Country	Period	Nominal Return	Real Return	Dollar Return	Inflation
United States	1/21–12/96	6.95	4.32	6.95	2.52
Canada	1/21–12/96	5.78	3.19	5.35	2.51
Austria*	1/25–12/96	5.64	1.62	5.00	3.95
Belgium	1/21–12/96	4.45	−0.26	3.51	4.73
Denmark	1/26–12/96	5.87	1.87	5.19	3.93
Finland	1/31–12/96	10.23	2.07	6.19	7.99
France	1/21–12/96	9.09	0.75	4.29	8.28
Germany*	21–96	4.43	1.91	5.81	2.47
Germany	1/21–7/44	[3.29]	[2.23]	[5.59]	[1.04]
Germany	1/50–12/96	[8.46]	[6.00]	[10.78]	[2.32]
Ireland	1/34–12/96	7.00	1.46	5.14	5.45
Italy	12/28–12/96	10.10	0.15	3.22	9.94
Netherlands	1/21–12/96	3.71	1.55	4.47	2.12
Norway	1/28–12/96	7.13	2.91	6.29	4.10
Portugal*	31–96	6.89	−0.58	3.78	7.51
Portugal	12/30–4/74	[5.21]	[1.16]	[4.96]	[4.00]
Portugal	3/77–12/96	[20.11]	[5.63]	[11.92]	[13.71]
Spain*	1/21–12/96	4.66	−1.82	1.53	6.61
Sweden	1/21–12/96	7.42	4.29	7.00	3.00
Switzerland	1/26–12/96	4.83	3.24	6.84	1.54
United Kingdom	1/21–12/96	6.30	2.35	5.20	3.86
Czechoslovakia	1/21–4/45	4.33	3.79	9.50	0.52
Greece	7/29–9/40	−2.12	−5.50	−8.08	3.58
Hungary	1/25–6/44	6.29	2.80	9.07	3.40
Poland	1/21–6/39	−7.00	−3.97	−4.30	−3.15
Romania	12/37–6/41	−5.36	−28.06	−14.64	31.55
Australia	1/31–12/96	7.06	1.58	6.29	5.39
New Zealand	1/31–12/96	5.69	−0.34	3.63	6.01
Japan*	21–96	7.33	−0.81	1.80	8.21
Japan	1/21–5/44	[1.23]	[−0.34]	[−1.83]	[1.58]
Japan	4/49–12/96	[8.30]	[5.52]	[10.90]	[2.63]
India	12/39–12/96	5.10	−2.33	0.80	7.60
Pakistan	7/60–12/96	7.79	−1.77	0.59	8.57
Philippines	7/54–12/96	5.95	−3.65	−0.30	9.96
Argentina+	47–65, 75–96	87.48	−4.80	−1.43	96.92
Argentina	9/47–7/65	[-5.78]	[−25.09]	[−23.64]	[25.78]
Argentina	12/75–12/96	[236.29]	[16.71]	[22.43]	[188.15]
Brazil	2/61–12/96	142.34	−0.17	4.68	147.52
Mexico	12/34–12/96	20.13	2.30	6.12	17.43

TABLE I | *(Continued)*

Country	Period	Nominal Return	Real Return	Dollar Return	Inflation
Chile*	27–96	37.12	2.99	6.38	33.16
Chile	1/27–3/71	[12.98]	[−5.37]	[−4.23]	[19.39]
Chile	1/74–12/96	[64.19]	[15.52]	[20.94]	[42.13]
Colombia	12/36–12/96	10.15	−4.29	−0.88	15.09
Peru*	41–96	45.29	−4.85	3.45	52.68
Peru	3/41–1/53	[2.03]	[−12.36]	[2.03]	[16.41]
Peru	1/57–12/77	[1.53]	[−9.88]	[−7.40]	[12.66]
Peru	12/88–12/96	[340.95]	[30.45]	[50.92]	[232.18]
Uruguay	3/38–11/44	6.70	2.42	10.01	4.19
Venezuela	12/37–12/96	9.67	−2.04	0.78	11.95
Egypt	7/50–9/62	−1.46	−2.84	−1.63	1.42
Israel	1/57–12/96	37.05	3.03	7.21	33.02
South Africa	1/47–12/96	6.13	−1.76	1.48	8.03
All 39 countries					
Mean			−0.47	3.11	
Median			0.75	4.68	
11 countries with continuous histories into the 1920s					
Mean			1.88	5.09	
Median			2.35	5.20	

precise, less volatile, estimates of expected returns. Moving to the right of the figure, we observe that the U.S. market has the highest realized return of all markets.

At the bottom of Table I we show average and median returns for all countries, as well as for a group of countries for which we have data going to the 1920s. The median real returns for all 39 countries is 0.75 percent. By way of contrast, we also analyze countries with continuous histories going back to the 1920s; the median return for this group is also much higher, at 2.35 percent. These results strongly suggest that the 4.3 percent real capital appreciation return for the United States is highly unusual. As it is also one of the few series without any break, this high return could be ascribed to survival.

An alternative explanation is that the United States had a higher level of risk than any other market over the period. In perfectly integrated capital markets, a high equity premium can simply compensate for a high β. Of course, this is a difficult proposition to test directly because survivorship affects not only returns but also capital weights. Ex post, the most successful index will represent the largest share of the market.

Other high returns, however, are obtained in some cases. Over 1921 to 1996, Swedish equities displayed returns quite close to the 4.32 percent obtained in the United States, perhaps not surprisingly as Sweden also avoided major upheavals in this century. Higher returns are observed over more recent periods. For instance, Germany experienced a steep run-up in prices, 6 percent in real terms, over the period 1950 to 1996. But this high return must be offset against mediocre growth up to July 1944; additionally, during the five-year break in our series, German equities fell by 72 percent in real terms. As a result, the long-term growth of the German market is only 1.91 percent when evaluated over most of this century. The story is similar for Japan, where we observe a sharp difference between the postwar return of 5.52 percent and the prewar return of −0.34 percent. During the 1944 to 1949 break, the market fell by 95 percent in real terms.

Other markets that gapped, such as Portugal, Chile, and Peru, also did well recently, but not so well when going back further in time. These are typical "reemerging markets," whose recent performance appears to be, on the surface, nothing short of stellar. Our analysis shows that the performance of the same markets has also been mediocre at other times.

Table I also reports dollar returns. As expected, rankings for this column are very similar to those obtained with real returns.[12] In general, dollar returns for other currencies are slightly closer to U.S. returns than real returns. For example, the difference between U.S. equities and the median is $4.32 - 0.75 = 3.57$ percent when measured in real terms; the difference is $6.95 - 4.68 = 2.27$ percent in dollar terms. This discrepancy reflects the slight depreciation of the dollar, relative to its Purchasing Power Parity value, over the sample period.

In addition to geometric returns, which represent returns to a buy-and-hold strategy, it is also useful to consider arithmetic averages, which give equal weight to each observation interval. Table II presents conventional measures of annualized average (arithmetic) capital appreciation returns and standard deviations.[13] Data are presented in the local currency, in real terms, and in dollars. The table shows that the 16.2 percent volatility of the U.S. market is not particularly high when compared with other stock markets. Therefore the high return obtained in the United States does not seem to compensate for higher risk as measured by volatility (which would be the appropriate measure of risk under segmented capital markets).

The table also reports the results from standard statistical tests of significance of the real capital appreciation return premium. At the 99 percent level, we can only reject the hypothesis of a zero long-run appreciation return for the United States and Sweden. Over shorter periods, we observe significantly positive returns for Germany and Japan in the postwar period. When averaged with prewar data, however, these returns look less impressive.

B. The Effect of Dividend Omission

The previous section has revealed a striking result: long-term returns on the U.S. stock market appear to be greater than those of any other market during this century. One question that arises is whether this result could be due to the omission of dividends. To shed light on this issue, Table III presents performance numbers for markets for which we have dividend data.

Panel A reports data for the more recent MSCIP indices, which mainly cover industrial countries since 1971. The table displays compound real returns, with and without reinvestment of dividends. The difference due to the omission of dividends is shown in the third column. The fourth column reports the average level of inflation. Presumably, the results in the previous section could simply reflect a bias due to the omission of dividends. For this bias to be effective, other markets must systematically display a higher income component of return than the United States.

Table III clearly shows that this is not the case. Over the 1970–1995 period, the dividend effect for the United States was 4.14 percent, which is quite close to the group average of 4.25 percent. Therefore, there is no indication that the high return obtained for U.S. equities in Table I is due to dividend bias. If anything, the bias is in the opposite direction.

---

[12]Uruguay and Czechoslovakia had higher returns than U.S. equities, but this was over shorter periods during which currencies were subject to controls; hence, these returns are not representative.

[13]Since price data are monthly averages, it should be noted that the reported standard deviations are lower than those from using month-end data. Additionally, averaging induces spurious positive autocorrelation in the return series.

TABLE II | Return and Risk of Global Equity Markets (Arithmetic Return in Percentage per Annum)

The table compares average stock returns and their standard deviations. Percentage returns are measured in nominal terms in the local currency, in real terms, deflating by the Wholesale Price Index, and translated into U.S. dollars. The arithmetic average return is obtained from the monthly average multiplied by 12; the standard deviation is annualized by multiplying the monthly volatility by the square root of 12. For series with breaks, (1), (2), (3) refer to different subperiods.

		Nominal Return		Real Return		Dollar Return	
Country	Period	Average	(Std.Dev.)	Average	(Std.Dev.)	Average	(Std.Dev.)
United States	1/21–12/96	8.09**	(16.20)	5.48**	(15.84)	−8.09**	(16.20)
Canada	1/21–12/96	7.06**	(16.81)	4.54*	(16.65)	6.88**	(18.17)
Austria	1/25–12/96	6.77**	(18.92)	2.32	(19.49)	7.22**	(21.49)
Belgium	1/21–12/96	6.25**	(17.92)	1.49	(18.97)	5.77**	(21.80)
Denmark	1/26–12/96	6.43**	(12.04)	2.65	(12.69)	6.10**	(14.36)
Finland	1/31–12/96	10.74**	(16.56)	3.50	(17.07)	8.18**	(20.49)
France	1/21–12/96	11.19**	(21.57)	3.16	(21.25)	7.76**	(25.50)
Germany (1)	1/21–7/44	10.22	(40.24)	7 62	(34.26)	12.54	(40.49)
Germany (2)	1/50–12/96	9.35**	(15 50)	7.06**	(15.60)	11.75**	(17.19)
Ireland	1/34–12/96	7.88**	(14.85)	2.59	(15.02)	6.43**	(16.73)
Italy	12/28–12/96	12.62**	(26.01)	3.15	(25.66)	3.15	(25.66)
Netherlands	1/21–12/96	4.78**	(15.12)	2.78*	(14.80)	5.85**	(16.50)
Norway	1/28–12/96	8.49**	(17.90)	4.47*	(17.90)	7.97**	(19.33)
Portugal (1)	12/30–4/74	6.50**	(15.15)	2.34	(14.69)	7.40**	(15.03)
Portugal (2)	3/77–12/96	27.08**	(46.38)	14.69	(47.68)	20.42	(47.11)
Spain	1/21–12/96	6.77**	(18.92)	−0.51	(16.00)	2.44	(28.89)
Sweden	1/21–12/96	8.56**	(16.61)	5.60**	(16.65)	8.38**	(17.69)
Switzerland	1/26–12/96	5.83**	(14.79)	4.28*	(14.73)	7.91**	(15.97)
United Kingdom	1/21–12/96	7.25**	(15.43)	3.60*	(15.68)	6.66**	(17.57)
Czechoslovakia	1/21–4/45	5.04*	(12.53)	4.56	(12.84)	10.50**	(17.12)
Greece	7/29–9/40	−0.09	(21.77)	−3.44	(21.61)	−5.31	(25.50)
Hungary	1/25–6/44	9.34	(25.84)	6.20	(26.58)	11.99**	(26.02)
Poland	1/21–6/39	13.60	(71.20)	14.40	(65.69)	16.69	(71.54)
Romania	12/37–6/41	0.14	(33.31)	−27.30	(31.38)	−9.45	(35.06)
Australia	1/31–12/96	7.78**	(13.49)	2.57	(13.94)	7.68**	(18.06)
New Zealand	1/31–12/96	6.20**	(12.12)	0.55	(12.50)	4.98**	(15.97)
Japan (1)	1/21–5/44	2.72	(17.51)	0.89	(15.79)	−0.35	(17.40)
Japan (2)	4/49–12/96	9.79**	(18.78)	7.21**	(18.90)	12.61**	(20.97)
India	12/39–12/96	6.18**	(15.53)	−1.07	(16.13)	2.37	(17.46)
Pakistan	7/60–12/96	7.46**	(14.37)	−0.64	(15.23)	2.39	(17.50)
Philippines	7/54–12/96	10.62	(37.35)	1.21	(37.21)	5.30	(38.91)
Argentina (1)	9/47–7/65	−1.13	(31.91)	−23.32**	(32.73)	−18.17	(40.11)
Argentina (2)	12/75–12/96	179.34	(133.55)	49.68	(87.83)	57.85**	(93.68)
Brazil	2/61–12/96	110.69**	(68.22)	12.92	(51.93)	18.45*	(53.44)
Mexico	12/34–12/96	21.97**	(26.79)	5.37	(24.45)	10.46**	(29.09)
Chile (1)	1/27–3/71	14.51**	(22.45)	−3.91	(21.85)	−0.12	(28.64)
Chile (2)	12/73–12/96	57.19**	(40.34)	20.48**	(36.25)	25.94**	(38.59)
Colombia	12/36–12/96	11.66**	(21.56)	−2.32	(21.78)	1.67	(23.39)
Peru (1)	3/41–1/53	3.02	(12 90)	−12.08**	(14.15)	3.39	(16.58)

TABLE II | *(Continued)*

Country	Period	Nominal Return Average	Nominal Return (Std.Dev.)	Real Return Average	Real Return (Std.Dev.)	Dollar Return Average	Dollar Return (Std.Dev.)
Peru (2)	1/57–12/77	1.89	(8.62)	−9.94**	(9.08)	−6.61*	(13.66)
Peru (3)	12/88–12/96	200.64**	(118.38)	55.55	(87.98)	71.95*	(87.18)
Uruguay	12/36–11/44	10.55	(28.98)	6.67	(29.66)	13.80	(29.63)
Venezuela	12/37–12/96	12.03**	(24.65)	0.88	(24.84)	4.85	(28.08)
Egypt	7/50–9/62	−0.83	(11.50)	−2.11	(12.54)	−0.19	(17.33)
Israel	1/57–12/96	35.18**	(26.07)	5.68	(22.96)	10.07*	(24.33)
South Africa	1/47–12/96	7.24**	(15.75)	−0.46	(15.89)	3.34	(18.87)

*, **Significantly different from zero at the 5 and 1 percent levels, respectively.

For example, Japanese equities, which by now constitute the largest market outside the United States, paid an income return of 1.84 percent over the past 25 years, which is much lower than that of U.S. equities.

Panel B of Table III reports the only long-term data with dividends that we are aware of.[14] To maintain comparability with the original data sources, we use the Consumer Price Index (CPI) to deflate returns, except for Denmark where the WPI is employed. Including dividends, the United States displays the highest real equity returns since 1921, at 8.22 percent. Britain, another long-term survivor, is a close second; other markets provide returns that are lower by 109 to 334 basis points. Another way to look at the data is to notice that the ranking of returns is essentially the same with and without dividends. Therefore, there is no evidence that the performance of U.S. equities is artificially high because of relatively low U.S. dividend payments.

C. Evidence on the Equity Premium Puzzle

The data we present thus far do not explicitly solve the equity premium puzzle, as theoretically formulated. Strictly speaking, the equity premium puzzle concerns the spread of expected total return on the market portfolio of equities over the return of a riskless security. Siegel (1994) points out that defaults on "riskless" government securities have often occurred in periods of global stress—which of course raises the question of what the riskless asset might actually be and whether the stylized, single economy, two-asset formulation of the equity premium puzzle is robust.

In the absence of a riskless asset that is immune to the crisis events imagined by Rietz (1988), it seems reasonable to substitute physical storage of goods (i.e., inflation rates for T-bill rates). In this case, using real returns as a proxy for the equity premium clearly supports the hypothesis that the ex post observed U.S. premium is higher because the United States was a winner. This evidence, in turn, is consistent with the "survival" hypothesis suggesting that the magnitude of ex post observed equity returns may be higher than their ex ante expectation.

[14] Data sources are as follows: For the U.S. market, Ibbotson (1995) and prior to that, Cowles (1939); for the U.K., Barclays deZoete Wedd (1993); for Switzerland, Wydler (1989); for Sweden, Frenneberg and Hansson (1992); and for Denmark, Timmerman (1992). All of the data have been updated to 1995 using the MSCIP indices.

TABLE III | Comparison of Real Returns with and without Dividends

The table compares stock returns with and without dividends. Returns are measured in real terms and are annually compounded. The top part reports Morgan Stanley Capital International Perspective (MSCIP) data; the bottom part presents long-term data, obtained from various sources.

Country		Compound Return with Dividend (% pa)	Compound Return without Dividend (% pa)	Difference Due to Dividend	Inflation (% pa)
Panel A: Markets Covered by MSCIP, 1970–1995					
Australia		3.65	−0.71	4.36	6.79
Austria		4.89	2.07	2.82	2.75
Belgium		12.97	4.05	8.92	2.46
Canada		4.34	0.65	3.69	5.78
Denmark		6.54	2.71	3.83	5.62
France		4.45	−0.29	4.74	7.40
Germany		5.52	1.44	4.08	3.09
Italy		−0.26	−2.95	2.69	9.87
Japan		8.59	6.75	1.84	2.18
Netherlands		8.84	3.09	5.74	3.41
Norway		6.03	2.78	3.26	5.90
Spain		2.30	−4.00	6.31	8.40
Sweden		8.79	5.03	3.76	7.42
Switzerland		5.72	3.06	2.66	2.54
United Kingdom		6.39	1.23	5.16	8.35
United States		6.15	2.01	4.14	4.89
Average		5.93	1.68	4.25	5.43
Panel B: Long-Term Markets					
Denmark	1923–95	4.88	0.64	4.24	3.72
Germany	1924–95	4.83	1.21	3.63	2.47
Sweden	1926–95	7.13	3.30	3.83	3.64
Switzerland	1921–95	5.57	2.12	3.45	2.49
United Kingdom	1921–95	8.16	2.99	5.17	3.75
United States	1921–95	8.22	3.38	4.84	2.69
United States	1871–1920	5.43	0.27	5.16	0.59

Is there any evidence in the data supporting the Rietz (1988) hypothesis that the ex ante equity premium is as high as supposed? The issue is whether there was some probability of the U.S. market experiencing a large crash. In fact, this problem is akin to the "peso problem" in the foreign exchange market, where peso forward rates appeared to be biased forecasts of future spot rates over short sample periods, essentially because they account for a nonzero probability of devaluation that is not observed. More generally, peso problems can be interpreted as a failure of the paradigm of rational expectations econometrics, which requires that the ex post distribution of endogenous variables be a good approximation to the ex ante distribution that agents think may happen. The failure may not be that of the economic agent, but that of the econometrician, who only analyzes series with continuous histories. Unusual events with a low probability of occurrence but severe effects on prices, such as wars or nationalizations, are not likely to be well represented in samples and may be totally omitted from survived series.

Our cross-sectional data provide evidence about major market crashes not present in U.S. data. We have, for example, 24 markets for which we have data in 1931. Of these, seven experienced no interruption (the United States, Canada, the United Kingdom, Australia, New Zealand, Sweden, and Switzerland), seven experienced a temporary suspension of trading (less than one year), and the remaining 10 markets suffered long-term closure. Even though these events are not independent, they indicate that market failure is not a remote possibility. Under the assumption that market risks are "priced" individually, rather than under the assumption of integration, the frequency of failure would provide clear justification for a peso problem explanation.

Although it is entirely possible that the magnitude of the observed equity premium is due both to survival bias and to the "pricing" of an infrequently occurring crash, it is difficult to believe that the ex ante premium for the United States should be higher than for other markets. The increased probability of a large crash may explain a higher average equity premium, but if past crash frequency is any indication of future crash probability, then the Rietz (1988) hypothesis would suggest that markets with more interruptions should have a higher equity premium. If we believe that the magnitude of the equity premiums for each country is related to the ex post historical real appreciation, then the opposite appears to be the case. Absent survival effects, the Rietz hypothesis is inconsistent with cross-sectional differences in historical global equity market returns. In the next section, we investigate the possibility that markets anticipate major crashes.

Table III provides additional evidence on the equity premium puzzle by comparing the performance of U.S. equities during the recent period with longer term, 1871–1920, Cowles data. The last line in the table shows that the high real capital return obtained since 1921 is much higher than that obtained in the preceding 50 years—3.38 percent during 1921–1995 against 0.27 percent during 1871–1920. Siegel (1992) also points out that the U.S. equity premium is particularly high during this century. Put differently, this large premium seems not only large in a cross-country comparison but also by historical standards. Siegel concludes that "investors in . . . 1872 did not universally expect the United States to become the greatest economic power in the next century." If so, returns on U.S. equities this century cannot be viewed as representative of global stock markets.

D. Disappearance as an Event

To understand how risk premiums respond to the probability of major market crashes, we can examine the behavior of markets around interruptions. Sample selection of markets will create a bias if the performance of interrupted markets is systematically poor before the break. By the same token, falling stock prices prior to a market break may be indicative of investor assessment of increasing probability that the market will fail.

To test this hypothesis, we adopt the event-study methodology by constructing an equally weighted index in which real returns are aligned on the interruption date. We identify a sample of 25 breaks for which the data series are clearly interrupted. Table IV identifies each of these events. Many are of a global nature, such as the Second World War, or the depression of the early 1930s. A number of events, however, are country-specific, involving a banking crisis or political turmoil.

Figure 2 plots the time-series of the portfolio value, starting one year before the break. It shows prices falling on average by 21 percent relative to their peak. The *t*-test based on the

TABLE IV | Analysis of Stock Prices around Breaks

The table describes the behavior of stock prices measured in real terms around major breaks. It reports the break date, the return in the year previous to the break, the series restart date, and subsequent change, when available. Real returns are in excess of the Wholesale Price Index for the corresponding countries. * indicates that equities were effectively subject to price controls; + indicates that the subsequent change was obtained from alternative data sources.

Country	Break Date	Previous Year Return	Series Restart Date	Subsequent Change	Comment
Hungary	7/31	−0.222	9/32	0.125	Financial crisis, country in default
Germany	7/31	−0.316	4/32	−0.232	Credit crisis
Greece	10/31	−0.099	12/32	−0.581	Financial crisis, drought
Spain	7/36	−0.113	3/40	−0.147	Civil War
Austria	4/38	−0.179	12/46	0.941	Annexation by Germany
Czechoslovakia	10/38	−0.205	1/40	0.015	Session of land to Germany
Poland	7/39	0.169			Invaded by Germany (Sep 30)
Finland	12/39	−0.192	3/40	−0.101	Invaded by Soviets (Nov 30)
Denmark	4/40	−0.328	6/40	−0.084	Invaded by Germany (Apr 9)
Norway	4/40	−0.274	6/40	−0.154	Invaded by Germany (Apr 11)
Netherlands	5/40	−0.231	9/40	0.105	Invaded by Germany (May 10)
Belgium	5/40	−0.267	12/40	0.850	Invaded by Germany (May 10)
Switzerland	5/40	−0.193	7/40	−0.207	Mobilization
France	6/40	−0.122	4/41	0.824	Invaded by Germany (Jun 14)
Greece	10/40	−0 249	none		Invaded by Germany (Oct 28)
Romania	7/41	−0.396	none		Enters war
Czechoslovakia*	7/43	−0.141	none		War
Japan*	6/44	−0.211	4/49	−0.949+	War
Hungary*	7/44	−0.491	none		War
Belgium*	8/44	0.161	6/45	−0.145	War
Germany*	8/44	−0.013	1/50	−0.838+	Invaded by Allies (Sep 15)
Egypt	10/62	−0.126	none		Arab socialism
Argentina	8/65	−0.692	N/A		Widespread unrest, hyperinflation
Chile	4/71	−0.543	1/74	1.618+	State takes control of economy (Apr 4) Junta reverses policies (Sep 11, 73)
Portugal	4/74	−0.112	3/77	−0.860+	Takeover by leftist junta (Apr 27)

standard deviation of monthly changes in the previous year is −4.95 for this number, which is highly significant. However large, this fall of 21 percent in real terms understates the true loss of value to equities. During World War II, in particular, prices were kept artificially high through price controls and do not represent transaction prices as liquidity dried up.[15]

[15] In Germany, Italy, and German-occupied territories, dealing in shares was subject to strict controls, ranging from taxes on profits and capital gains to the rationing of purchases and to the compulsory declaration of securities holdings. In June 1942, for instance, the sale of German shares became prohibited unless they were first offered to the Reichsbank. The Reichsbank had the option to buy them at December 1941 prices in exchange for bonds that remained in the bank's possession. It is no wonder that this confiscatory system led to a sharp fall in trading activity. There were also rigid price controls in Japan during the war; see for instance Adams and Hoshii (1971). Therefore many of these price indices do not represent market-determined prices.

FIGURE 2 | Real Stock Prices Before Interruption

The figure displays the performance of an equally weighted index where real returns are aligned on the interruption date. The total sample of 25 is further divided into a sample for which the interruption turns out to be temporary, and a sample for which the interruption is permanent.

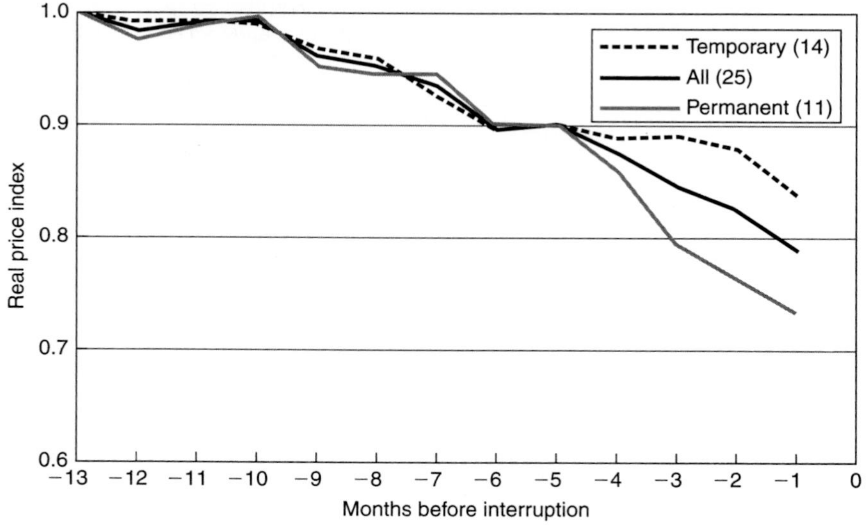

Eventually, reality prevailed. Figure 3 compares the performance of markets sorted by country involvement during the war.[16] As the figure shows, the advent of the war led to a sharp fall of about 20 percent in the value of equities of Allied countries (including the United States, Canada, the United Kingdom, and Commonwealth countries) for the next two months. A similar fall was suffered by neutral countries (Sweden and Switzerland). The index for occupied countries, in contrast, registered steady gains, which were only wiped out later as stock prices started to reflect transaction prices and as inflation became apparent. Five years later, the index moved below that of Allied countries, as we would have expected. In reality, the index should have been even lower if we had accounted for those markets that disappeared in the process (such as Germany, Hungary, and Czechoslovakia.)

Table IV also details the performance around each individual break. All markets suffered a substantial drop before the break, reaching 69 percent for Argentina. One exception is Poland, which experienced a slight price increase, possibly because the series was stopped in July, three months before Poland was invaded, or because the advent of the war was unanticipated. As explained before, the price drops in Germany and occupied Europe are also unusual, for artificial reasons. In all other cases, the event creating the market closure was anticipated.

In eleven of these cases, the UN–IMF equity series are interrupted without restarting later (or there are no continuous series spanning the interruption). These cases include

[16]The index for occupied countries includes Belgium, Czechoslovakia, France, Denmark, Finland, Germany, Hungary, Italy, Netherlands, and Norway.

FIGURE 3 | Real Stock Prices During World War II

The figure displays the performance of portfolios of equities measured in real terms during the war. The sample is divided into occupied, allied, and neutral countries.

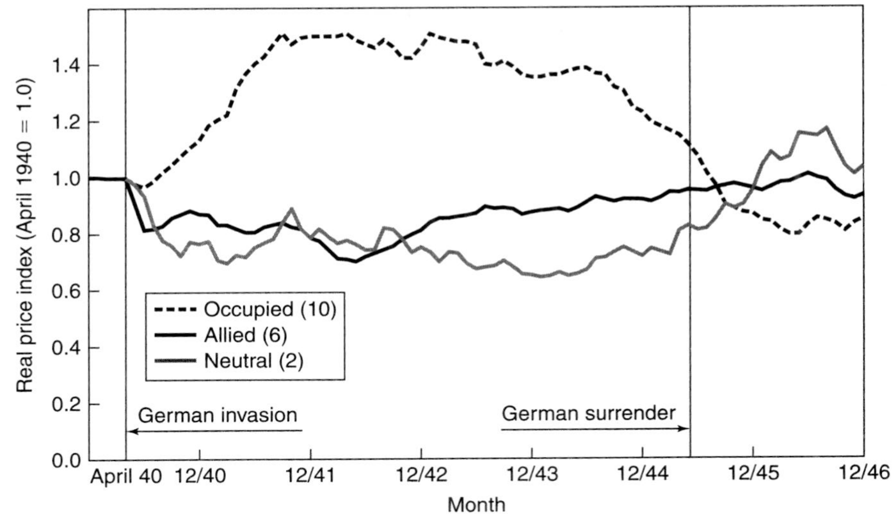

Germany, Japan, Eastern European countries taken over by the Soviet Union, Greece, Egypt, Chile, Argentina, and Portugal. Some of these were the result of a foreign occupation and widespread destruction due to war. In Egypt and Chile, the state took control of the economy. The Buenos Aires Stock Exchange, the oldest in Latin America, virtually disappeared as a result of inflation and interest rate policies in the late 1960s; reportedly, investors lost all interest in the market. These are precisely the situations where we would expect equities to fare most badly.

We have to turn to other data sources to bridge these "permanent" breaks. We find that, over the 1944–1949 break in Japan, equities fell by 95 percent in real terms.[17] For Germany, we find that equities fell by 84 percent in real terms over 1944–1950. Another example is the Portuguese stock market, which closed in April 1974 as a military junta took over the country, reopened in March 1977, then traded intermittently. The stock price series suffered a fall of 86 percent in real terms during the interruption in trading. In contrast, most of the loss for the Chilean stock market occurred before the interruption; the market recovered somewhat over the 1971–1974 break, as the military junta reversed the socialist policies of the Allende government.[18] Furthermore, these numbers probably underestimate the true loss in value by ignoring companies that failed during

[17]The Bank of Japan (1966) estimates that the material damage due to World War II was to reduce national wealth from 253 to 189 billion yen, which is a fall of 64 billion yen (not accounting for human losses), or about $15 billion. For comparison purposes, the market value of equities in 1945 was about 40 billion yen.

[18]The market lost 54 percent in the year to April 1971 during the Allende ascent to power, but then increased by 62 percent later, which is only a partial recovery. Assuming a starting value of 100, the market fell to 46, then recovered to 1.62 times 46, or 74, ending with a net loss in value relative to the starting point.

the interruption, as indices are backfilled from companies quoted before and after the break.

Going back to Figure 2, we have separated markets that were temporarily interrupted from those that disappeared, or "died," later. Markets that became extinct dropped by 27 percent the year before the break; markets that subsequently recovered dropped by only 16 percent before the break. To the extent that the event causing the break was anticipated, the market seems to have been able to gauge the gravity of unfolding events. Price declines before breaks are consistent with increasing demand for risk compensation for a catastrophic event.

E. A Global Stock Index

The global equity data provide a unique opportunity to construct a global equity index—an index that for the first time includes defunct as well as surviving countries and extends back 75 years. Because we have no data on market capitalization going back that far, we assign weights based on Gross Domestic Product (GDP). Annual GDP information is obtained from Mitchell (1992, 1993, 1995) and converted to U.S. dollars using annual averages. At the beginning of each decade, we construct a cross section of national GDPs, which are used to construct initial weights.

To minimize rebalancing, we adopt a portfolio value-weighted approach. Our global indices are therefore similar to market capitalization indices, except that the weights are reset to GDP weights at the beginning of each decade. A value-weighted scheme is more appropriate for measurement of investor returns when survival is an issue. As our analysis in the previous section demonstrates, markets that die tend to have less weight when they do so.

The indices represent the return an investor would have earned had it been possible to hold the market since the 1920s. This is a hypothetical experiment, however, because it would have been difficult to maintain such a portfolio. Constraints on cross-border capital flows and on liquidation of equity positions were acute during crises—precisely the times when the ability to diversify is most beneficial. In this period, investors were sometimes involuntarily separated from their assets, due to expropriations or nationalizations. As a result, it is not clear whether, for example, a U.S. investor could have continued to hold German or Japanese equities during World War II.

Table V presents the GDP weights at three points in time; 1920, 1950, and 1990. The table reveals a number of interesting observations. The United States accounts for about one-half of the world's output until the 1950s; the proportion then declines to approximately 30 percent. This decline is due to faster growth in other countries such as Japan and Germany. Japan, in particular, zooms from 4 percent of world GDP to 16 percent over this period, even after dipping below 2 percent after the war.

The GDP-based weights can be compared to stock market capitalization-based weights, which are reported in the last column. We observe that the stock market capitalization percentages of the United States, the United Kingdom, Japan, and South Africa are generally greater than those of other countries. Continental Europe, for example, has a history of relying on bank lending rather than raising funds through capital issues. Overall, however, the GDP weights are roughly of the same order of magnitude as market weights.

Biases can be introduced in the measured performance in a number of ways. The first is backfilling, and the second is due to interruptions. There is not much the researcher can do about backfilling if the series are the only ones available. As for interruptions, the problem is that data before the interruption are commonly ignored. Interruptions can be of two

TABLE V | Relative Importance of Economies (Percentage Weights Based on U.S. Dollar Prices)

The table describes the percentage of each country in the total Gross Domestic Product (GDP) in 1920, 1950, and 1990. The last column shows the percentage weight based on stock market capitalization.

	GDP Weights			Stock Market Capitalization
Country	**1920**	**1950**	**1990**	**1995**
United States	46.17%	51.52%	30.59%	41.03%
Canada	2.40%	3.16%	3.17%	2.16%
Austria	0.48%	0.47%	0.87%	0.24%
Belgium	0.73%	1.27%	1.09%	0.66%
Denmark	0.55%	0.56%	0.72%	0.37%
Finland	0.17%	0.42%	0.76%	0.26%
France	6.14%	5.19%	6.61%	3.27%
Germany	6.04%	4.19%	8.29%	3.75%
Ireland	0.42%	0.19%	0.24%	0.16%
Italy	1.67%	2.43%	6.07%	1.16%
Netherlands	0.98%	0.89%	1.57%	1.97%
Norway	0.56%	0.38%	0.59%	0.28%
Portugal	0.62%	0.25%	0.33%	0.12%
Spain	2.16%	0.82%	2.72%	0.99%
Sweden	1.22%	1.11%	1.26%	1.14%
Switzerland	0.84%	0.80%	1.25%	2.60%
United Kingdom	10.36%	6.57%	5.41%	8.77%
Czechoslovakia	0.52%	0.31%	0.25%	0.10%
Greece	0.33%	0.39%	0.37%	0.11%
Hungary	0.38%	0.71%	0.18%	0.02%
Poland	1.82%	0.35%	0.03%	
Romania		0.00%	0.21%	—
Australia	2.31%	1.07%	1.63%	1.59%
New Zealand	0.15%	0.35%	0.24%	0.21%
Japan	4.06%	1.96%	16.24%	23.19%
India	6.92%	3.54%	1.68%	0.82%
Pakistan		0.67%	0.22%	0.06%
Philippines		0.63%	0.24%	0.38%
Argentina	1.20%	0.90%	0.78%	0.24%
Brazil	0.75%	2.84%	2.66%	0.96%
Mexico	0.66%	0.85%	1.34%	0.59%
Chile	0.19%	0.75%	0.15%	0.48%
Colombia		0.72%	0.22%	0.12%
Peru		0.19%	0.20%	0.08%
Uruguay		0.18%	0.05%	0.00%
Venezuela		0.57%	0.27%	0.02%
Egypt		0.45%	0.31%	0.05%
Israel		0.24%	0.29%	0.24%
South Africa	1.03%	0.65%	0.56%	1.82%
Memorandum:				
GDP (millions)	$198,200	$556,500	$18,049,700	
Market cap (m)				$15,448,900

types: temporary closure of an exchange, with the series starting again later, or permanent interruption of these series, with no information about the continuity of prices across the interruption.

We take two approaches to the construction of the global index:

(i) Our "survived markets" index includes all markets since the last interruption, which can be a temporary break or a permanent closure; only markets in existence at the end of the sample are considered. As of December 1996, we have a total of 32 markets; of which only 18 had continuous histories to December 1940, for instance.

(ii) Our "all markets" index extends the sample to all markets in existence in our sample, including returns before temporary and permanent closures. As of December 1940, this "comprehensive" series yields 29 markets, adding Austria, Belgium, and France (which suffered a temporary interruption of trading during World War II), Chile, Germany, Japan, Portugal, Uruguay, and three markets that suffered a permanent break during the war: Czechoslovakia, Hungary, and Romania.

We expect the bias to decrease as we move from (i) to (ii). The difficult part, of course, is to estimate market losses during a permanent interruption such as war or nationalization. We have 11 occurrences of permanent breaks (or "deaths") out of our sample of 39 markets. For some of these, such as Germany, Japan, Portugal, we are able to trace the fall in value, which we evenly spread over the time period of the interruption. This smoothing preserves the geometric return, but induces an artificially low volatility and therefore increases the arithmetic return. We should note, however, that the same problem occurs when reported prices are controlled or do not represent transaction data. For the few remaining markets that suffered a permanent interruption, we assume that the market fell by 75 percent the following month.[19]

Table VI presents the performance of the various global stock indices. We focus on performance data first and discuss volatility later. Over the past 76 years, the U.S. stock market provided an arithmetic capital return of 5.48 percent, measured in real terms. Its geometric growth was 4.32 percent over this period. Figure 4 plots the performance of the U.S., global, and non-U.S. real capital growth indices (using the comprehensive series).

The differences in the performance of the global indices point to the importance of accounting for losing markets. The "survived markets" index has a compound return of 4.33 percent; it accounts only for markets in existence in 1996 and examined since their last break. The "all markets" index has a compound return of 4.04 percent; it accounts for all markets and attempts to interpolate returns over major breaks in the series. Going from the first to the second estimate should move us closer to a true, unbiased measure of long-term return.

At first sight, the difference between the long-term performance of the U.S. index and of the global comprehensive index appears to be small, at only 29 basis points. This result may appear puzzling in light of the evidence in Table I that all non-U.S. markets have lower long-term growth than the United States, often significantly so. One reason for the narrow difference lies in the temporal variation in weights. Consider the Japanese market, for instance. In the first half of the century, the performance of Japanese

[19] The markets affected were Czechoslovakia, Egypt, Greece, Hungary, Poland, and Romania. The 75 percent imputed drop is in line with the fall in value of markets that suffered a severe breakdown. The arbitrariness of the charge is mitigated by the fact that all of these markets are relatively small.

TABLE VI | Performance of Global Stock Index: 1921–1996 (Real Returns in Percentage per Annum)

The table displays the risk and return of real returns on stock market indices, measured in excess of the Wholesale Price Index inflation. Arithmetic return is obtained from the monthly average multiplied by twelve; risk is monthly volatility multiplied by the square root of twelve; Sharpe ratio is the ratio of monthly average to monthly volatility; geometric return uses annual compounding. Ending wealth reports the final value of $1 invested on December 1920 at the end of the sample. "Survived markets" series includes only markets in our sample in existence in 1996, taken since the last interruption (temporary or permanent). "All markets" series accounts for all markets in the sample, imputing a 75 percent loss in the month the series permanently disappears, or the actual loss spread over the period of the break.

Index	Arithmetic Return	Risk	Monthly Sharpe	Geometric Return	Ending Wealth
U.S. index	5.48	15.83	0.0999	4.32	27.3
Global index					
Survived markets	4.98	12.08	0.1190	4.33	27.3
All markets	4.59	11.05	0.1199	4.04	21.9
Non-U.S. index					
Survived markets	4.52	10.02	0.1301	4.09	22.2
All markets	3.84	9.96	0.1114	3.39	13.1

equities was mediocre. At that time the market carried a weight of less than 4 percent in the global index. In the second half of the century, however, Japanese equities outperformed U.S. equities, precisely at a time when their weight in the index was rising, reaching 16 percent in 1990. Another reason is the large weight in the U.S. market at the

FIGURE 4 | A Global Stock Market Index

The figure displays the performance of the U.S., global, and non-U.S. real capital growth indices. The latter indices are obtained using GDP weights and all existing markets, even if they fail later.

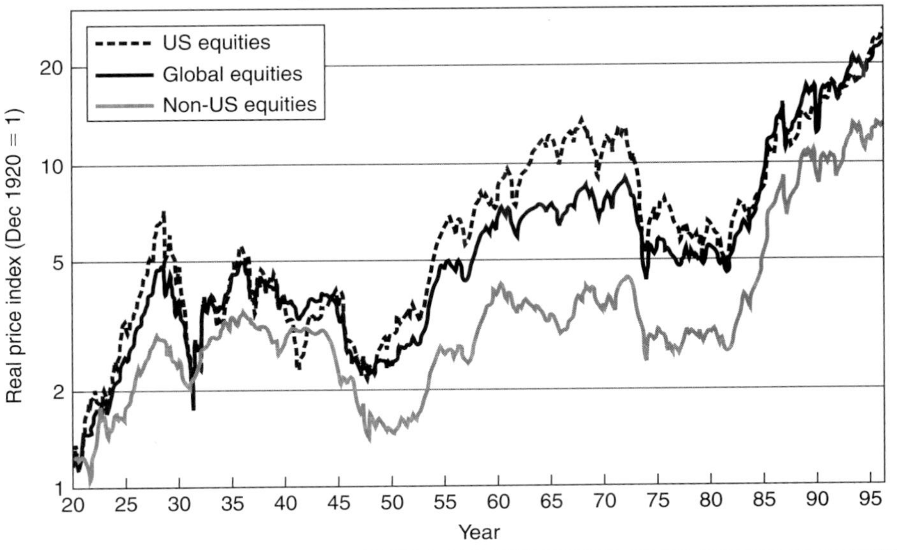

TABLE VII | Performance of Global Stock Index: 1921–1996 (Nominal Returns in U.S. Dollars, Percentage per Annum)

The table displays the risk and return of dollar returns on stock market indices, translated into U.S. dollars at the official rate. Arithmetic return, is obtained from the monthly average multiplied by twelve; risk is monthly volatility multiplied by the square root of twelve; Sharpe ratio is the ratio of monthly average to monthly volatility; geometric return uses annual compounding. Ending wealth reports the final value of $1 invested on December 1920 at the end of the sample. "Survived markets" series includes only markets in our sample in existence in 1996, taken since the last interruption (temporary or permanent). "All markets" series accounts for all markets in the sample, imputing a 75 percent loss in the month the series permanently disappears, or the actual loss spread over the period of the break.

Index	Arithmetic Return	Risk	Monthly Sharpe	Geometric Return	Ending Wealth
U.S. index	8.04	16.19	0.1433	6.95	171.2
Global index					
Survived markets	7.98	13.34	0.1728	7.32	222.9
All markets	7.76	12.14	0.1845	7.25	211.2
Non-U.S. index					
Survived markets	7.53	12.17	0.1785	7.00	176.5
All markets	7.28	12.08	0.1740	6.75	146.2

beginning of the century. Consider, for example, a \$100 investment in global stocks starting in 1921. From the GDP weights in Table V, the amount to allocate to U.S. stocks was \$46.17. Over the next 76 years, this amount grew to \$1149, using the 4.32 percent U.S. growth rate. Let us make now an extreme assumption, which is that all of the money invested outside the United States is lost. Using the \$1149-to-\$100 ratio, the rate of growth is still 3.26 percent. The large initial size of the U.S. market therefore ensures that the growth on the global index must be within 100 basis points of the U.S. growth number.

The last column in Table VI shows that a difference of 29 basis points can be quite significant over 76 years. Assuming a dollar invested in the U.S. index and in the comprehensive global index, the investments would have grown to 27.3 and 21.9 in real terms, which is a substantial difference.

Table VI also shows that a non-U.S. stock market index, based on our "comprehensive" measure, has grown at the rate of 3.39 percent, which is a full 93 basis points below U.S. equities. If one ignores survivorship issues, however, the return of the non-U.S. index appears to be 4.09 percent. Survival bias therefore induces a difference of 70 basis points in this index, which is quite substantial when accumulated over 76 years.

Table VII presents similar data, measured in nominal U.S. dollars. Over 1921 to 1996, the compound capital return on U.S. equities was 6.95 percent. The return on the global survived index was 7.32 percent; the return on the global comprehensive index was 7.25 percent. Similarly, the average return on the non-U.S. index was 7.00 percent and 6.75 percent. Here the survival bias is on the order of 25 basis points.

As in Table I, we observe that the difference between U.S. and non-U.S. returns is smaller when returns are measured in dollars instead of in real terms. In fact, the return on the unbiased global index is now variation in weights and the real appreciation of most other currencies discussed previously. Also, the return on the value-weighted global index appears not too sensitive to the survivorship issue.

Tables VI and VII also provide estimates of the volatility of the various indices. Using real returns, the volatility of the U.S. index is 15.8 percent. All other indices display lower volatility. For instance, the volatility of the non-U.S. indices is about 10 percent, which is much lower than that of the U.S. market alone, reflecting the fact that the portfolio is spread over a greater number of markets, thus benefiting from imperfect correlations across markets. Next, the risk of our global indices is also driven by correlations. Over the 76 years, the correlation coefficient between returns on the U.S. index and on the comprehensive non-U.S. index is 0.460 in real terms and about the same, 0.452, in dollar terms.[20] As a result of lower volatility for foreign markets and a low correlation coefficient, the risk of the global portfolio is substantially lower than that of U.S. equities. The "comprehensive" global index, for example, displays a volatility of 11.05 percent. Based on these long-term series, the main benefit of going international appears to be risk reduction rather than increased returns.

Taking into account survivorship decreases returns slightly, but also decreases volatility. This is partly due to the (artificial) interpolation of returns when markets are closed, but also because of additional diversification resulting from the inclusion of more markets. We measure the trade-off between risk and return with the Sharpe ratio, defined as average monthly returns divided by their volatility. These are reported in the third columns of Tables VI and VII. With real returns, the Sharpe ratio of the global index is 0.1199, which is higher than that of U.S. equities at 0.0999. With dollar returns, the Sharpe ratio of the global indices is about 0.1845, also higher than that of U.S. equities, at 0.1433. These differences, however, are not statistically significant.[21]

Systematic differences in return can be attributed to two classes of explanations. The first is survivorship, an ex post explanation. The second is rational, ex ante, differences in risk profiles. For example, if markets can be viewed as integrated, a higher return for U.S. equities could be explained by the fact that the U.S. market has a higher world β. Indeed, over the 1921–1996 period, U.S. equities had the highest beta, with a value of 1.24. A regression of real returns on real betas reveals a correlation of 0.53, which is significantly positive.

Testing this proposition is not straightforward because estimation of β with respect to the world index depends on survival issues as well. Had the outcome of the Second World War been different, for example, the β of the United States on the world index would likely have been different, The regression is also afflicted by data and econometric problems. The variables are estimated over different periods and thus have quite different sampling variability. Additionally, the betas that include periods of price controls or infrequent trading are not reliable. Thus it seems difficult to disentangle the higher systematic risk explanation from survivorship to explain the high returns on U.S. equities.

To understand the momentous implications of differences in long-term rates of return reported here, consider the following experiment. First, let us record the current capitalization of non-U.S. equity markets, which was approximately \$9,000 billion at the end of 1996. From Table VI, these markets have grown at an average rate of 3.39 percent, which is less than the 4.32 percent growth rate for the United States. Going back to 1921, this implies that the market capitalization of non-U.S. equities was \$9,000 billion divided by $(1 + 3.39\%)^{76}$, which amounts to \$714 billion in current dollars.

Next, assume that all markets have grown at the U.S. rate of growth. The market value of these equities would then be \$714 billion times $(1 + 4.32\%)^{76}$, which amounts to \$17,775

[20] As for the measurement of volatilities, correlations may be too low because of the smoothing of the series during the breaks. However, the correlation with the survived series is very close, at 0.510 in real terms and 0.520 in dollars. This suggests that the bias is not large.

[21] Using the performance tests developed by Jobson and Korkie (1981).

billion. In other words, the opportunity cost of growing at about 3.4 percent instead of the 4.3 percent U.S. rate is $8,775 billion in today's dollars. Foreign markets would be double their current size if they had grown only 1 percent faster than they did. Viewed in this context, survival biases of 70 basis points recorded in Table VI are quite significant.

IV. Conclusion

"Financial archaeology" involves digging through reams of financial data in search for answers. Sometimes this involves relying on poor quality data from which to draw inferences about markets in states of crisis. Even so, these data provide invaluable information to help understand long-term histories of capital markets. If one relies on historical data as the basis for estimates of long-term market growth, there is no reason to look at U.S. data only. This is why our paper paints a broad picture of the performance of global stock markets over more than 75 years of a turbulent century for financial markets.

The main lesson from our long-term data is that global capital markets have been systematically subject to dramatic changes over this century. Major disruptions have afflicted nearly all the markets in our sample, with the exception of a few such as the United States. Markets have been closed or suspended due to financial crises, wars, expropriations, or political upheaval.

No doubt this explains our finding that the 4.3 percent real capital appreciation return on U.S. stocks is rather exceptional, as other markets have typically had a median return of only 0.8 percent. These results suggest that the large equity premium obtained in the United States is at least partly to the result of conditioning estimates on the best performing market. This conditioning may also create time-variation in expected returns; for instance, we expect markets that have done well to exhibit more mean-reversion than others because periods of large losses must be followed by periods of upswings.[22]

This line of analysis treats each market separately. Another approach is to track the hypothetical performance of a diversified global investment. Interestingly, we find that the performance of a globally diversified portfolio is much closer to the performance of U.S. equities, averaging 4.0 percent. This is partly because markets with large capitalization at the beginning of the century performed well. This result also reflects the benefits of diversification, which spreads the risk of dramatic events over a large portfolio.

Whether similar disruptions will happen again is an open question. By now, however, it should be clear that if we fail to account for the "losers" as well as the "winners" in global equity markets, we are providing a biased view of history which ignores important information about actual investment risk.

References

Adams, Thomas, and Iwao Hoshii, 1971, *A Financial History of the New Japan* (Kodansha, Tokyo, Japan).

Bank of Japan, 1966, *A Hundred Years of Statistics of Japanese Economy* (Bank of Japan, Tokyo, Japan).

Bansal, Ravi, and Wilbur Coleman, 1996, A monetary explanation of the equity premium, term premium, and risk-free rate puzzles, *Journal of Political Economy* 104, 1135–1171.

[22] Goetzmann and Jorion (1995) also show that survival should induce other effects of interest, such as predictability based on dividend yields.

Barclays de Zoete Wedd, 1993, The BZW Equity Gilt Study: Investment in the London Stock Market since 1918 (Barclays deZoete Wedd, London, United Kingdom).

Brown, Stephen J., William Goetzmann, and Stephen Ross, 1995, Survival, *Journal of Finance* 50, 853–873.

Burnside, Craig, and Thomas McCurdy, 1992, The equity premium puzzle; in Peter Newman, Murray Milgate, and John Eatwell, eds.: *The New Palgrave Dictionary of Money and Finance* (Stockton Press, New York).

Constantinides, George, 1987, Habit formation: A resolution of the equity premium puzzle, *Journal of Political Economy* 98, 519–543.

Cowles, Alfred, 1939, *Common Stock Indices, 1871–1937* (Cowles Commission for Research in Economics, Monograph no. 3, Principia Press, Bloomington, Ind.).

Epstein, Larry, and Stanley Zin, 1991, Substitution, risk aversion and the temporal behaviour of consumption and asset returns: An empirical investigation, *Journal of Political Economy* 99, 263–286.

Frenneberg, Per, and Bjorn Hansson, 1992, Swedish stocks, bonds, bills, and inflation (1919–1990), *Applied Financial Economics* 2, 79–86.

Gielen, Gregor, 1994, *Konnen Aktienkurse Noch Steigen?* (Gabler, Wiesbaden, Germany).

Goetzmann, William N., 1993, Patterns in three centuries of stock market prices, *Journal of Business* 66, 249–270.

Goetzmann, William N., and Roger Ibbotson, 1994, An emerging market, the New York Stock Exchange 1816–1872, *Journal of Business* 68, 483–508.

Goetzmann, William N., and. Philippe Jorion, 1995, A longer look at dividend yields, *Journal of Business* 68, 483–508.

Goetzmann, William N., and Philippe Jorion, 1997, Re-emerging markets, (mimeo) University of California at Irvine.

Ibbotson, Roger, 1995, *Stocks, Bonds, Bills, and Inflation: 1995 Yearbook* (Ibbotson Associates, Chicago, Ill).

International Conference of Economic Services, 1934, *International Abstract of Economic Statistics* (ICES, London, United Kingdom).

International Conference of Economic Services, 1938, *International Abstract of Economic Statistics* (International Statistical Institute, Permanent Office, The Hague, The Netherlands).

International Finance Corporation, 1995, *The IFC Indexes: Methodology, Definitions, and Practices* (International Finance Corporation, Washington, DC).

International Monetary Fund, various issues, *International Financial Statistics* (International Monetary Fund, Washington, D.C.).

Jobson, J. D., and B. Korkie, 1981, Performance hypothesis testing with the Sharps and Treynor measures, *Journal of Finance* 36, 888–908.

League of Nations, various issues, *Statistical Yearbook* (League of Nations, Geneva, Switzerland).

Mehra, Rajnish, and Edward Prescott, 1985, The equity premium: A puzzle, *Journal of Monetary Economics* 15, 145–161.

Mehra, Rajnish, and Edward Prescott, 1988, The equity premium: A puzzle?, *Journal of Monetary Economics* 22, 133–136.

Mirowski, Philip, 1981, The risk (and retreat) of a market: English joint stock shares in the eighteenth century, *Journal of Economic History* 41, 559–577.

Mitchell, Brian, 1992, *International Historical Statistics: Europe, 1750–1988* (Stockton Press, New York).

Mitchell, Brian, 1993, *International Historical Statistics: The Americas, 1750–1988* (Stockton Press, New York)

Mitchell, Brian, 1995, *International Historical Statistics: Africa, Asia & Oceania, 1750–1988* (Stockton Press, New York).

Neal, Larry, 1987, The integration and efficiency of the London and Amsterdam stock markets in the eighteenth century, *Journal of Economic History* 47, 97–115.

Neal, Larry, 1990, *The Rise of Financial Capitalism: International Capital Markets in the Age of Reason* (Cambridge University Press, Cambridge, Mass.).

Parsons, Brian, 1974, The behavior of prices on the London stock market in the early eighteenth century, Ph.D. dissertation, University of Chicago.

Rietz, Thomas, 1988, The equity premium: A solution, *Journal of Monetary Economics* 22, 117–131.

Schwert, William, 1990, Indexes of U.S. stock prices from 1802 to 1987, *Journal of Business* 63, 399–426.

Siegel, Jeremy, 1992, The equity premium: Stock and bond returns since 1802, *Financial Analysts Journal* 48, 28–38.

Siegel, Jeremy, 1994, *Stocks for the Long Run* (Richard D. Irwin, New York).

Timmerman, Allan, 1992, Changes in Danish stock prices 1914–1990, *Nationalokonomisk Tidsskrift* 130, 473–482.

United Nations, various issues, *Monthly Bulletin of Statistics* (United Nations, New York).

Wilson, Jack, and Charles Jones, 1987, A comparison of annual common stock returns, *The Journal of Business* 60, 239–258.

Wydler, Daniel, 1989, Swiss stocks, bonds, and inflation: 1926–1987, *Journal of Portfolio Management* 15, 27–32.

Twenty-Five

Torben G. Andersen

Torben G. Andersen received a Ph.D. from Yale University in 1992. He started out at the Kellogg School of Management, Northwestern University, and still works at the Kellogg School of Management, Northwestern University. •

I am a slight anomaly among the Steve Ross students ending up in academia, as I have worked primarily within financial econometrics rather than more mainstream finance theory and empirics. Even so, I am hugely indebted to Steve Ross for the inspiration to enter the field as well as for my core perspectives and specific insights that permeate my contributions to the field.

I entered the Yale Economics PhD program with an intention to work in International Economics along with an interest in international financial markets and exchange rate determination. Given my statistics background, I took the advanced econometrics sequence. In addition, I added to my first year schedule by taking the finance classes at the Yale SOM. These choices had a dramatic effect on my career and life. Over the next few years I interacted with two very different but truly awe-inspiring scholars and advisors, namely Peter C.B. Phillips and Steve Ross. The former combined intuition, flair, discipline and technical prowess in a package that is stunning. Steve Ross offers a different style of broad economic intuition, of immediate grasp of ideas and cutting to the core issues, an incredible sense for applicability of technical tools on important questions, and a breathtakingly quick mind. I recall working on my dissertation and meeting regularly with Steve to describe my progress. He would take a moment to catch up and then, to my perpetual dismay and admiration, take off and further develop my hypotheses in natural directions. It was both intimidating and inspiring to experience him in relaxed playful intellectual fashion, on the spot, jump ahead of my own reasoning and point to issues that I should consider and develop further. On the other hand, there was never a sense of showing off or judging others' intellect. It was simply an effective way of demonstrating how exciting the process of intellectual exploration can be and to try to share it. Steve's inquiry and questions were always driven by a desire for deeper understanding and curiosity about the nature of the logic, arguments and facts. My reaction was to prepare more diligently for these meetings but, of course, I never managed to predict the ways of Steve's mind. Mind you, this is not news to those who have experienced Steve at academic presentations. He often asks a string of early questions revealing ignorance of the basic setup, then catches on and over the next hour periodically asks questions that push the speaker into unknown and unexpected territory, thus transforming the seminar into exchanges involving new hypotheses and research questions. Hence, my own experience was in line with his "standard operating procedures."

In the following years, I have also seen how he is the focus of dinner conversations and cocktail parties. By way of sheer raw intellect, charm, and quickness of thought, Steve naturally draws attention—not because he seeks it but because people instinctively direct their observations and questions towards him. This obviously puts him in high demand. To have been the recipient of persistent intellectual attention from Steve over a long period is one thing that I will always cherish as one of the great experiences of my academic life. Obviously, this is not to say that I agree with everything Steve says, writes or does. Any mature scholar knows that nobody has all the answers. It's just that I remain more interested in what Steve thinks than anybody else, because I learn more from his reactions than any other person I know.

In writing these comments, I pondered how Steve ever developed and honed his package of skills. I cannot imagine him without them, but he cannot have been as universally knowledgeable as a newly minted assistant professor. It must have been a rapid process of growth, building on a set of latent talents. Recently, I heard Steve speak about his career, and he may just have nailed it for me. It is quite simple—he loves solving puzzles and that is what he does. By extension, that is what he does when discussing dissertation work or attending a seminar. He perpetually challenges himself by seeking out questions (puzzles) and immediately starts solving them. This constant training of the creative side of the brain is part of the answer, I think. And it serves as a source of inspiration for all of us in the privileged position of making a good living from exploring ideas: in the midst of teaching, administration, publishing, refereeing, consulting and family demands, never forget the fun, inquisitive, and challenging parts of the job, as this is what drives good work and keeps us sharp. Not that we will catch up to Steve, but at least we will be in the running, have more fun, and just maybe we will also develop ideas and results of lasting value.

I now briefly turn to Steve's inspiration for my own research. For over a decade, I have been involved in work on using high-frequency data for measurement, modeling, estimation and forecasting of return volatilities and correlations. This has been carried out through close collaboration with Tim Bollerslev and other scholars including Frank Diebold, Nour Meddahi, Luca Benzoni, and Peter Christoffersen. The piece included in this volume bears a number of hallmarks that I associate with Steve Ross's imprint on me. First, Steve emphasizes the extent to which the simple no-arbitrage idea can lead to strong and insightful conclusions. Well, the absence of arbitrage is a basic feature of our volatility models. Moreover, this perspective is fundamental for the extension into the continuous-time setting in which our approach naturally leads to the concept of realized volatility defined as the cumulative sum of high-frequency intraday returns. The latter quantity is a model-free estimator of the quadratic variation of a semi-martingale, and asset return processes must satisfy this property if the no-arbitrage condition applies. Second, the interpretation of volatility as driven by information flow is related to work published by Steve during my years at Yale on information revelation and timing irrelevancy. Third, a critical component is that asset prices are impacted by a set of distinct factors. The implications are here mapped out for a single volatility process, but the intuition is reminiscent of the Arbitrage Pricing Theory developed by Steve much earlier. This set of basic principles contributed to the discovery of many novel features of volatility, including the robust finding of long-memory style dynamics and transient short-run components, whose further study has helped sustain my academic career and curiosity ever since.

Steve, I am enormously grateful for the inspiration to pursue the field of finance and the example you have set for all of us!

Heterogeneous Information Arrivals and Return Volatility Dynamics: Uncovering the Long-Run in High Frequency Returns

*Torben G. Andersen and Tim Bollerslev**

Abstract

Recent empirical evidence suggests that the interdaily volatility clustering for most speculative returns are best characterized by a slowly mean-reverting fractionally integrated process. Meanwhile, much shorter lived volatility dynamics are typically observed with high frequency intradaily returns. The present article demonstrates, that by interpreting the volatility as a mixture of numerous heterogeneous short-run information arrivals, the observed volatility process may exhibit long-run dependence. As such, the long-memory characteristics constitute an intrinsic feature of the return generating process, rather than the manifestation of occasional structural shifts. These ideas are confirmed by our analysis of a one-year time series of five-minute Deutschemark-U.S. Dollar exchange rates. •

Among the most puzzling issues is the behavior of volatility. While the general properties of volatility remain elusive, perhaps the most intriguing feature revealed by empirical work on volatility is its long persistence. Such behavior has sparked a search, almost akin to that for the Holy Grail, for the perfect GARCH *model, but the underlying question of why such volatility persistence endures remains unanswered. We conjecture that the ability to analyze higher frequency data may be particularly useful in pursuing this issue.*
(Goodhart and O'Hara (1997))

The pronounced volatility clustering is arguably one of the most striking features of financial price series recorded at daily or weekly intervals, and a large body of literature seeking to characterize this aspect of speculative returns has emerged over the past decade.[1] At the same time, convincing theoretical explanations for the underlying sources of long-run persistence in volatility remain elusive. The recent advent of comprehensive high-frequency

*Andersen is from the J.L. Kellogg Graduate School of Management of Northwestern University. Bollerslev is from the University of Virginia and is a research associate at the National Bureau of Economic Research. We gratefully acknowledge the financial support provided by a research grant from the Institute for Quantitative Research in Finance (the Q-Group). Special thanks are due to Olsen and Associates for making the intradaily exchange rate quotes and Reuter's News Tape available. We have received valuable comments from Wake Epps, Clive W.J. Granger, Stephen F. Gray, J. Huston McCulloch, as well as seminar participants at the December 1996 Triangle Econometrics Workshop, the 1997 AFA Meetings in New Orleans, Academia Sinica, the Wharton School, USC, and Georgetown and York universities. We remain fully responsible for the content.

[1]See Bollerslev, Chou, and Kroner (1992) for a survey of this literature using ARCH type models.

Reprinted with permission:
Bollerslev, Tim and Torben G. Andersen. "Heterogeneous Information Arrivals and Return Volatility Dynamics: Uncovering the Long-Run in High Frequency Returns." *The Journal of Finance* 52(1997): 975–1005.

data sets has added substantially to our knowledge of the higher frequency features of the returns process, but the findings have tended to deepen rather than resolve the puzzle surrounding the persistence in the volatility dynamics. In particular, while studies using daily or lower frequency returns generally point to a very high degree of intertemporal volatility dependence, the dynamic impact of identifiable intraday volatility shocks seem rather low, with any noticeable effects on the overall volatility typically gone in a matter of hours or less.[2]

These findings have led to a certain fragmentation of the literature, with most market microstructure studies focusing predominantly on the highly significant patterns in the intradaily price movements (time-of-day effects), ignoring the longer-run inter-daily volatility dependencies. This separation may appear entirely natural, if not inevitable. High-frequency returns generally cover only shorter time-spans, and given the evidence of near covariance non-stationarity of the return volatility process, as indicated by the findings of (near) integrated general autoregressive conditional heteroskedasticity (IGARCH) type models (Bollerslev and Engle (1993)), it may seem futile to search for insights regarding volatility persistence over a short horizon. This intuition is further bolstered by the lessons from the extant time series literature, which has documented that only very long time-spans, as opposed to more frequent observations, can provide genuine information about the presence of a unit root in a borderline stationary series.[3] At the same time, the assumption of structural stability, or invariance of the return generating process, may be unreasonable for very long time-spans. Specifically, if a structural break is present, and ignored, then the appearance of strong persistence may emerge artificially. This issue has been hotly debated in the context of modeling the level of economic time series and has led to the development of an extensive literature on testing for structural breaks; see e.g., Perron (1989). The same idea carries over to the volatility setting; see, e.g., Lamoureux and Lastrapes (1990).

This article advocates an approach that speaks directly to this important issue, while avoiding the analysis of excessively long time-spans of return data. The basic premise holds that shorter time-spans of high frequency returns—in contrast to widely, if implicitly, held notions—are in fact very informative about longer-run volatility dependencies. The rationale is closely related to the observation of Merton (1980), that whereas it is not possible to learn much about the drift (mean) of the price process by sampling more frequently, high frequency observations may greatly enhance estimates of the volatility (variance). In fact, in a strict diffusion setting volatility can be measured perfectly by sampling the price process continuously; see, e.g., Nelson (1990, 1992). In reality, market microstructure features such as the bid-ask spread and discrete price quotes, combined with the presence of strong intraday volatility patterns render this infeasible. Moreover, these short-run effects are generally large relative to the return component that provides information regarding the innovation in the long-run volatility. However, these effects may be controlled for in ways that allows an investigation of the long-run volatility features based on high-frequency return series covering only a relatively short time-span.

Our empirical findings along these lines clearly points towards the existence of long-run volatility persistence in high frequency returns.[4] Meanwhile, the empirical analysis also provides distinct evidence for the existence of multiple volatility components at the

---

[2]For a recent survey of this literature see Goodhart and O'Hara (1997).

[3]Shiller and Perron (1985) provide some of the first simulation based evidence along these lines.

[4]This is consistent with the recent findings of long-memory in the volatility of different daily return series, as formally modeled by Baillie, Bollerslev, and Mikkelsen (1996) and Ding and Granger (1996), among others.

intradaily frequencies. This evidence of multiple volatility components, along with the apparent long-memory characteristics, motivates our theoretical developments, in which we formulate a version of the mixture-of-distributions hypothesis (MDH) for returns that explicitly accommodates numerous heterogeneous information arrival processes. Even though each of the constituent information flow processes exhibit only short-run memory, we demonstrate how the aggregate volatility process may display the dependency associated with a long-memory process. In addition, we show that this degree of volatility persistence should be invariant to temporal aggregation.

The MDH interpretation of market volatility as resulting from the aggregation of numerous components type processes apply equally well across most financial markets and instruments. However, for concreteness the empirical analysis in the article is focused on the foreign exchange market, and a one-year time-span of five-minute Deutschemark–U.S. Dollar (DM–$) returns. While our empirical analysis is performed predominantly in the frequency domain, we also develop a low-pass filtering technique that purges all intraday volatility components with periodicities of less than one day. As such, the low-pass filter is designed to annihilate the strong intraday patterns, while retaining all the low-frequency information that pertains to the interdaily frequencies. The resulting high-frequency series thus speaks directly to the long-run features of the return series, and affords a direct time-domain analysis of the volatility persistence from the high frequency data. We verify that this approach yields results that are consistent with more standard frequency-based procedures, and also illustrate the usefulness of the filtered series for direct analysis of the longer run volatility implications of different macroeconomic announcements. The fact that our estimates for the degree of long-run volatility persistence are very similar across all intradaily sampling frequencies, and strikingly close to the estimates for a daily time series covering a much longer time-span, lend further support to the notion of long-memory dependence as an inherent feature of the return generating process, rather than an artifact of infrequent structural shifts, or changes in regimes.

The plan for the remainder of the article is as follows. Section I briefly reviews some of the existing literature on the intradaily dependencies in the foreign exchange market. This section also presents preliminary estimation results for specific announcement effects that point to the existence of multiple volatility components and long-run dependencies. The mixture-of-distributions hypothesis and the temporal aggregation argument are presented in Section II, where we show that, under suitable assumptions concerning the underlying component structure, the spectrum for the overall volatility process implies an eventual slow hyperbolic rate of decay in the autocorrelations for the absolute returns, irrespective of the sampling frequency. The theoretical developments are validated by the empirical analysis in Section III, which reports the results obtained from two alternative spectral-domain estimators for the degree of fractional integration in the volatility process across a range of different intradaily sampling frequencies. These findings are entirely consistent with the time-domain estimate for the fractional order of integration determined by the hyperbolic rate of decay in the autocorrelations for the low-pass filtered absolute returns presented in Section IV. This section also illustrates how the low-pass filtered absolute returns allow for important new insights into the structure behind the determination of the observed volatility. Section V concludes.

I. Preliminary Data Analysis

In order to motivate the subsequent theoretical developments, the following section describes the salient empirical features of the volatility in the DM–$ foreign exchange market. However, the general ideas and empirical results apply equally well to other financial markets and high frequency return series; see, e.g., Andersen and Bollerslev (1997a) for a discussion of the parallels between the empirical properties of high frequency foreign exchange and equity index returns. The DM–$ exchange rate data under study consist of all the quotes that appeared on the interbank Reuters network during the October 1, 1992 through September 29, 1993 sample period. The data were collected and provided by Olsen and Associates. Each quote contains a bid and an ask price along with the time to the nearest even second. The exchange rate corresponding to the endpoint of a given five-minute interval was determined as the interpolated average between the preceding and immediately following quotes weighted linearly by their inverse relative distance to this endpoint. The nth five-minute return for day τ, $R_{\tau,n}$, is then simply defined as the difference between the midpoint of the logarithmic bid and ask at the appropriately spaced time intervals. All 288 five-minute returns during the 24-hour daily trading cycle are used, but in order to avoid confounding the evidence by the decidedly slower trading patterns over the weekends, all returns from Friday 21:00 Greenwich Mean Time (GMT) through Sunday 21:00 GMT were excluded; see Bollerslev and Domowitz (1993) for a detailed analysis of the quote activity in the DM–$ interbank market and a justification for this "weekend" definition. Similarly, to preserve the number of returns associated with one week we make no corrections for any worldwide or country specific holidays that occurred during the sample period. All in all, this leaves us with a sample of 260 days, for a total of 74,880 five-minute intraday return observations; i.e., R_t, $t = 1, 2, \ldots, 74{,}880$, where $R_{(\tau-1)\cdot 288+n} \equiv R_{\tau,n}$, for $n = 1, 2, \ldots, 288$, and $\tau = 1, 2, \ldots, 260$. For further discussion of the data construction we refer to Andersen and Bollerslev (1997a), where the same dataset has previously been analyzed from a different perspective.

Aside from the numerically small, but statistically significant, negative first order autocorrelation coefficient of -0.040, the five-minute returns appear to be well approximated by a martingale process.[5] However, the returns are clearly not independent, as the first order autocorrelation coefficient for $|R_t|$ equals 0.309. Also, the Ljung–Box statistic for up to tenth order serial correlation in the absolute returns takes a value of 36,680, which is highly significant in the corresponding asymptotic chi-square distribution.

While the latter statistics are strongly suggestive of intraday volatility clustering, their overwhelming significance is in part attributable to the strong intradaily volatility pattern that is present in most financial markets. The importance of this phenomenon for the DM–$ rates is obvious from Figure 1, which graphs an estimate of the spectrum for the intradaily absolute five-minute returns.[6] The spectrum has a distinct peak at the daily frequency of approximately $2 \cdot \pi/288 \approx 0.0218$, along with well defined peaks at the corresponding seasonal harmonics of $4 \cdot \pi/288 \approx 0.0436$, $6 \cdot \pi/288 \approx 0.0654$, $8 \cdot \pi/288 \approx 0.0873$. This pronounced daily periodicity is also evident in the autocorrelogram for the absolute 5-minute returns depicted out to a lag of 2880, or ten days, in Figure 2. The intradaily

[5]The small negative autocorrelation may be explained by the asymmetric positioning of quotes by the foreign exchange dealers as a way to manage their inventory positions, thus causing the midpoint of the quoted prices to move around in a fashion analogous to the well documented bid–ask bounce effect on organized exchanges. This is also consistent with the results in Bollerslev and Domowitz (1993), who find similarly constructed five-minute DM–$ returns over a 3-month period in 1989 to be negatively correlated, while the first order autocorrelation for artificial constructed five-minute pseudo transactions price returns is actually positive. Similarly, the foreign exchange transactions prices analyzed by Goodhart, Ito, and Payne (1996) show no negative correlation between subsequent returns.

[6]The spectrum is estimated as the smoothed sample periodogram based on a triangular kernel with a bandwidth of ten; see, e.g., Hamilton (1994) or Priestley (1981). To allow for easier interpretation of the subsequent results, the plot is given on a double logarithmic scale.

FIGURE 1 | The Figure Graphs the Spectrum for the Five-Minute Absolute Returns on an Open Position in the Deutschemark–U.S. Dollar Spot Exchange Rate Market from October 1, 1992 Through September 29, 1993; i.e., $|R_t| \equiv |\ln(P_t) - \ln(P_{t-1})|$ where $t = 1, 2, \ldots, 74{,}880$.

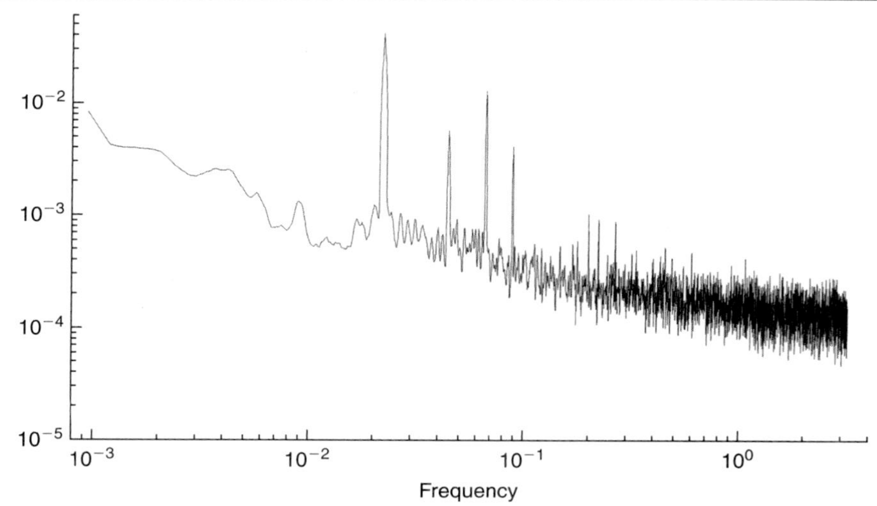

The spectrum is estimated as the smoothed sample periodogram using a triangular kernel with bandwidth of ten.

pattern induces a distorted U-shape in the sample autocorrelations across each day, with the autocorrelations spaced half-a-day apart actually turning negative. The shape of the underlying intradaily volatility pattern over the 24-hour trading cycle in the foreign exchange market, and the close connection to the market activity in the various financial centers around the world, have previously been documented by Andersen and Bollerslev (1997a),

FIGURE 2 | The Figure Graphs the Sample Autocorrelogram for the Five-Minute Absolute Returns on an Open Position in the Deutschemark–U.S. Dollar Spot Exchange Rate Market from October 1, 1992 Through September 29, 1993; i.e., $|R_t| \equiv |\ln(P_t) - \ln(P_{t-1})|$ where $t = 1, 2, \ldots, 74{,}880$.

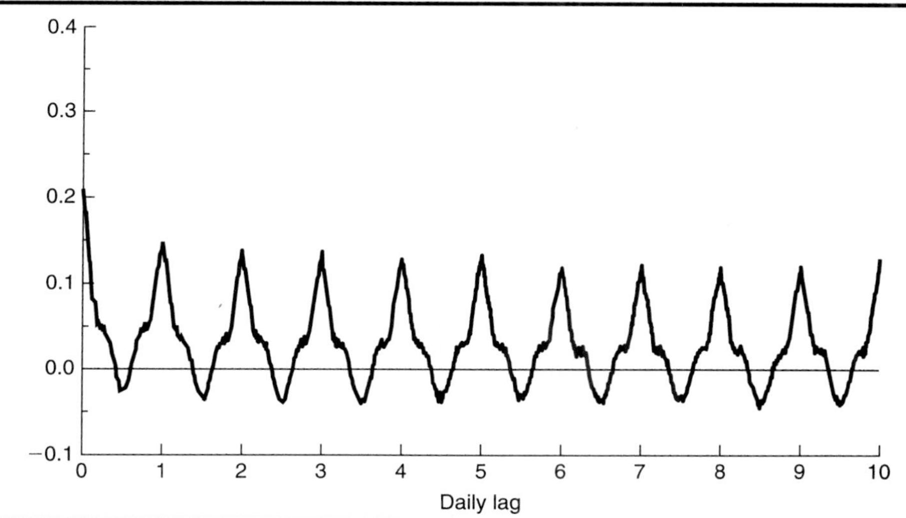

Baillie and Bollerslev (1991), Dacorogna et al. (1993), Ito, Lyons, and Melvin (1996), among others.[7]

Taken together, these results clearly point to the importance of appropriately accounting for the strong intradaily volatility patterns when analyzing high frequency dynamic dependencies, both within and across different markets. However, even after explicitly modeling the typical intradaily patterns, several recent studies have found that the estimation of standard GARCH type models for the nonperiodic intradaily volatility clustering tends to falter, in the sense that the estimated parameters obtained for different intradaily sampling frequencies are at odds with the temporal aggregation results developed by Drost and Nijman (1993) and the continuous record asymptotic in Nelson (1990); for existing evidence along these lines pertaining to the DM–$ rates analyzed here, see Andersen and Bollerslev (1997a). Thus, it appears that multiple volatility components are necessarily required in order to fully explain the complex intradaily dependencies that are present in all the major financial markets.[8]

The attempt to associate each of the underlying volatility components with explicit economic factors seems destined to fail. Meanwhile, the regularly scheduled releases of macroeconomic figures have been shown to induce heightened overall volatility immediately following the "news" release for a number of different financial instruments; for studies on the impact of macroeconomic announcements on high-frequency foreign exchange rates see, e.g., Andersen and Bollerslev (1997b), Ederington and Lee (1993), Goodhart et al. (1993), Hogan and Melvin (1994), and Ito and Roley (1987). Not surprisingly, the actual effect tends to vary according to the type of announcement. From the analysis in Andersen and Bollerslev (1997b) the three regularly scheduled macroeconomic announcements with the largest instantaneous impact on DM–$ volatility during the present sample period are the U.S. Employment Report, the biweekly Bundesbank meetings, and the U.S. Durable Goods figures.[9] To gauge the dynamic impact of each of these events, we consider the following simple AR(1) model for the standardized five-minute DM–$ absolute returns, augmented by a separate short-lived AR(1) component,

$$|\tilde{R}_t| = \gamma + \gamma_N \cdot I_N(t) + \phi \cdot |\tilde{R}_{t-1}| + \phi_N \cdot D_N(t) \cdot |\tilde{R}_{t-1}| + \varepsilon_t, \tag{1}$$

where the $I_N(t)$ indicator variable equals unity if an announcement of the given type, N, occurred during the tth time interval and zero otherwise, while the "news" dummy, $D_N(t)$, equals unity for the two hours immediately following the event; i.e., $D_N(t) \equiv I_N(t) + I_N(t - 1r) + \ldots + I_N(t - 23)$. In order to avoid confounding the dynamic dependencies by the strong intradaily volatility patterns, the returns in equation (1) are standardized by the average absolute return for the particular five-minute interval; i.e., $|\tilde{R}_t| \equiv 260 \cdot |R_{(\tau-1)\cdot 288+n}| \cdot (\sum_{\tau=1}^{260} |R_{(\tau-1)\cdot 288+n}|)^{-1}$ for $n = 1, 2, \ldots, 288$, and $\tau = 1, 2, \ldots, 260$.[10] The first order sample autocorrelation for these standardized returns, i.e., $I_N(t)$ and $D_N(t) \equiv 0$ for all t, equals $\hat{\phi} = 0.273$. However, the estimates obtained from the simple descriptive model in equation (1) suggest that the three major announcements result in

[7]Equally pronounced patterns have been documented for other financial markets, including the well known intradaily U-shape for equity market volatility; see, e.g., Wood, McInish, and Ord (1985) and Harris (1986).

[8]Multiple components ARCH models have been proposed by Müller *et al.* (1997) and Ghose and Kroner (1996) to capture this phenomenon in the modeling of high-frequency foreign exchange returns.

[9]The U.S. Employment Report, Durable Goods figures, and Business Inventories analyzed below, are all announced on a monthly schedule.

[10]Much more elaborate standardization procedures for characterizing the average intradaily volatility patterns have recently been developed by Andersen and Bollerslev (1997a, 1997b) and Dacorogna et al. (1993).

their own distinct volatility response pattern. Specifically, for the Employment Report $\hat{\gamma}_N = 5.346$ (1.424) and $\phi_N = -0.081$ (0.050), respectively, where the numbers in parentheses represent robust standard errors. These estimates therefore indicate an immediate increase in the volatility, but largely unaltered short-run dynamic dependencies in the two hours following the release of the report. Meanwhile, the estimates for the Bundesbank biweekly meetings are 1.394 (0.651) and 0.102 (0.054), suggestive of a slower rate of decay in the volatility component associated with this "news" release. The Durable Goods report also elevates volatility, $\hat{\gamma}_N = 1.801$ (0.687), but the estimated short-run decay is actually faster than average with $\hat{\phi}_N = -0.130$ (0.037), *or* $\hat{\phi} + \hat{\phi}_N = 0.144$. Many other announcements share this dynamic pattern. For instance, for the Business Inventory figures the same two parameters are 0.021 (0.110) and −0.094 (0.045), respectively.

This relatively rapid decay of the readily identifiable "news" effects at the intradaily frequencies is in sharp contrast to the well documented highly persistent volatility clustering that is present at the lower interdaily sampling frequencies. In fact, the daily dependencies have often been modeled by an integrated autoregressive conditional heteroskedasticity (ARCH) variance process; see Bollerslev, Chou, and Kroner (1992) for a survey of this voluminous literature. More recently however, Baillie, Bollerslev, and Mikkelsen (1996), Dacorogna et al. (1993), and Harvey (1994), have questioned these earlier findings, on the grounds that the long-run dependence in the volatility of interdaily foreign exchange returns is better characterized by a slowly mean-reverting fractionally integrated process.[11] While shocks to the daily volatility process are highly persistent, it appears that they eventually dissipate, albeit at a very slow hyperbolic rate. As discussed in Section III, the approximate linear behavior of the estimated spectrum for $|R_t|$, when plotted on the double logarithmic scale in Figure 1, is consistent with this long-memory type dependence. Similarly, the rapid initial decay followed by the decidedly slower rate of dissipation for the longer-run autocorrelations in Figure 2 also indicate the existence of long-memory type dependencies, although the marked intradaily periodicity severely complicates the interpretation of the overall pattern in the autocorrelogram for the raw absolute returns.

II. The Theoretical Volatility Model

This section demonstrates that the mixture-of-distribution hypothesis, originally advocated by Clark (1973), Epps and Epps (1976), and Tauchen and Pitts (1983) provides a framework for rationalizing the complicated, and seemingly conflicting, behavior of the return volatility dynamics that exist at the inter- and intradaily frequencies; see also the analyses in Andersen (1996), Harris (1987), Ross (1989), and Taylor (1994). Intuitively, the mixture-of-distributions hypothesis stipulates that the return generating process reflects the impact of a large number of innovations to the information processes associated with the economic factors of relevance for the valuation of the asset in question. While the innovations, by definition, are serially uncorrelated, they are not likely to be independent since information of a particular kind tends to be positively autocorrelated, thus inducing the kind of dependence in the absolute, or second order, moments of the returns discussed above.

To formalize these ideas, consider the following representation for the intradaily returns,

$$R_t = r_t - m_t = V_t^{1/2} \cdot Z_t, \tag{2}$$

[11]Similar long-run dependencies in daily stock market volatility have been observed by Bollerslev and Mikkelsen (1996), Breidt, Crato, and de Lima (1997), Ding, Granger, and Engle (1993), Granger and Ding (1996, 1997), among others.

where m_t denotes the conditional mean of the raw returns, r_t, Z_t is an independent identical distribution (i.i.d.) stochastic process with mean zero and variance one, and the nonnegative, positively serially-correlated mixing variable, V_t, serves as a proxy for the aggregate amount of information flow to the market. Equation (2) takes the typical form associated with the discrete time ARCH class of models in which both m_t and V_t are assumed measurable with respect to the time $t-1$ observable information set, so that the conditional variance of the return equals $\mathrm{Var}_{t-1}(R_t) = \mathrm{Var}_{t-1}(r_t) = V_t$. More generally, however, the information flow is not directly observable, and V_t is naturally modeled as a latent, or stochastic, volatility process. Of course, lacking additional assumptions regarding the temporal dependencies in the V_t process, the model in equation (2) is void of testable empirical implications in regards to the observed volatility dynamics.

The rest of this section develops a specific representation of equation (2) that affords an interpretation of volatility as governed by heterogeneous information arrivals, while retaining the capacity of reconciling the seemingly conflicting evidence regarding volatility at the various return frequencies, and producing interesting empirical implications that are directly testable.

A. Volatility as a Manifestation of Heterogeneous Information Arrivals

Motivated by the empirical observations in Section I, we assume that the volatility process reflects the aggregate impact of N distinct information arrival processes; say $V_{j,t} \geq 0$, where $j = 1, 2, \ldots, N$. Also, following Andersen (1994), the temporal dependence of each constituent component is expressed in terms of a standard log-normal stochastic volatility, or Exponential SARV, model,

$$\nu_{j,t} = \alpha_j \cdot \nu_{j,t-1} + \varepsilon_{j,t}, \tag{3}$$

where $\nu_{j,t} \equiv \ln(V_{j,t}) - \mu_j$, $\mu_j \equiv E[\ln(V_{j,t})]$, and the $\varepsilon_{j,t}$s are assumed to be i.i.d. $N(0, \sigma_j^2)$ for all $j = 1, 2, \ldots, N$. The logarithmic formulation in equation (3) ensures that the number of information arrivals dictated by the jth component process, $V_{j,t} \equiv \exp(\nu_{j,t} + \mu_j)$, is positive. The autoregressive coefficient, α_j, reflects the degree of persistence in the jth information arrival process. Consistent with the notion of positively serially-correlated but stationary "news" arrivals, we restrict these parameters to fall within the unit interval; i.e., $0 \leq \alpha_j < 1$.

According to the mixture-of-distributions hypothesis, each information arrival process has an effect on the aggregate latent volatility process. Assume that this combined effect may be represented by

$$V_t = \exp(\nu_t + \mu_\nu), \tag{4}$$

where $\nu_t \equiv \sum_{J=1}^{N} \nu_{j,t}$ and $\mu_\nu \equiv \sum_{J=1}^{N} \mu_j$. Note, the spectrum for the aggregate ν_t process at frequency ω is simply given by the sum of the spectra for the N underlying independent AR(1) processes, i.e.,

$$f_\nu(\omega) = (2\pi)^{-1} \cdot \sum_{j=1}^{N} \sigma_j^2 \cdot |1 - \alpha_j \cdot \exp(-i \cdot \omega)|^{-2}, \tag{5}$$

where $0 \leq \omega \leq \pi$. For small values of N, this spectral representation for ν_t can in principle be used to maximize Whittle's frequency domain approximation to the likelihood function for $\ln(R_t^2) = \mu_\nu + \nu_t + \ln(Z_t^2)$ as specified by equations (2), (3), and (4); see Breidt, Crato, and de Lima (1997) for an application of this frequency-domain based likelihood procedure in the estimation of a stochastic volatility model. Alternatively, the model may be estimated by any one of the Markov Chain Monte Carlo methods described in Jacquier, Palson, and Rossi (1994) and Shephard (1996), or by the Efficient Method of Moments developed by Gallant and Tauchen (1996). Yet, in the actual empirical implementation with high frequency data, a large number of heterogeneous information arrival processes is likely called for, rendering any of these direct estimation procedures for determining the α_js as well as the remaining model parameters intractable.

In light of this, suppose that the heterogeneity in the individual component processes, as dictated by the AR(1) parameters, may be approximated by the normalized beta distribution,

$$dF_{\alpha}(\alpha) = 2 \cdot B(p, q)^{-1} \cdot \alpha^{2p-1} \cdot (1 - \alpha^2)^{q-1} \, d\alpha, \tag{6}$$

where $0 \leq \alpha < 1$, $0 < p$, $1 < q < 2$, and the beta function is given by $B(p, q) \equiv \int_0^1 x^{p-1}(1 - x)^{q-1} dx = \Gamma(p) \cdot \Gamma(q) \cdot \Gamma(p + q)^{-1}$. This parametric density function allows for a wide variety of shapes in the bounded distribution of the α_js, and thus provides a flexible way of characterizing different forms for dynamic dependencies in the latent information arrival processes; see, e.g., Johnson and Kotz (1970) for a discussion of the beta distribution. Moreover, this particular distributional assumption regarding the heterogeneity in the underlying $v_{j,t}$ processes has a number of testable implications in regard to the dynamic dependencies in the observable process for the absolute returns.

Specifically, consider the situation in which the number of component processes is arbitrarily large; i.e., $N \to \infty$, so that the sum of the individual AR(1) spectra in equation (5) converges to the probability weighted integral over the distribution for the α_j coefficients. Following Granger (1980), the resulting spectrum for the v_t process may then be evaluated as

$$\begin{aligned} f_v(\omega) &= (2\pi)^{-1} \cdot \sigma_\varepsilon^2 \cdot \int_0^1 |1 - \alpha \cdot \exp(-i \cdot \omega)|^{-2} \, dF_\alpha(\alpha) \\ &= (2\pi)^{-1} \cdot \sigma_\varepsilon^2 \cdot 2 \cdot B(p, q)^{-1} \cdot \sum_{j=-\infty}^{\infty} \left[\int_0^1 \alpha^{2p+|j|-1} \cdot (1 - \alpha^2)^{q-2} \, dx \right] \\ &\quad \times \exp(-i \cdot \omega \cdot j) \\ &= (2\pi)^{-1} \cdot \sigma_\varepsilon^2 \cdot \Gamma(p + q) \cdot \Gamma(q - 1) \cdot \Gamma(p)^{-1} \cdot \Gamma(q)^{-1} \\ &\quad \times \sum_{j=-\infty}^{\infty} \Gamma(p + 1/2|j|) \cdot \Gamma(p + q - 1 + 1/2|j|)^{-1} \cdot \exp(-i \cdot \omega \cdot j), \end{aligned} \tag{7}$$

where $\sigma_\varepsilon^2 \equiv \lim_{N\to\infty} \sum_{J=1}^{N} \sigma_j^2$. Alternatively, the spectrum for the v_t process may be written as $f_v(\omega) \equiv \sigma_v^2 \cdot (2\pi)^{-1} \cdot \sum_{j=-\infty}^{\infty} \rho(v_t, j) \cdot \exp(-i \cdot \omega \cdot j)$, where σ_v^2 and $\rho(v_t, j)$ denote the variance and the jth order autocorrelation for v_t, respectively. Thus, by equating terms in the identical powers of j, it follows that the autocorrelations for v_t must be proportional to $\Gamma(p + ½|j| \cdot \Gamma(p + q - 1 + ½ \cdot |j|)^{-1}$. This implies that for large $|j|$, the autocorrelations for the aggregate latent logarithmic volatility process behaves like[12,13]

$$\rho(v_t, j) \sim j^{1-q} \tag{8}$$

The dependence in v_t will therefore dissipate at the slow hyperbolic rate of decay associated with the covariance stationary fractionally integrated, or I(d), class of models, with $d = 1 - ½ \cdot q$.[14]

---

[12]By Stirling's Formula $\Gamma(a + j) \cdot \Gamma(b + j)^{-1} \approx c \cdot j^{a-b}$ for large j, where c is a factor of proportionality.

[13]This same idea has recently been employed by Ding and Granger (1996) in imposing a slowly hyperbolically decaying structure on the parameters in a GARCH type model for daily stock returns.

[14]The process y_t is integrated of order d, or $I(d)$, if $(1 - L)^d y_t$ is stationary and ergodic with a positive and bounded spectrum across all frequencies, where the fractional differencing operator $(1 - L)^d$ is defined by the binomial expansion, $(1 - L)^d \equiv \sum_{J=0,\ldots,\infty} \Gamma(j - d) \cdot \Gamma(j + 1)^{-1} \cdot \Gamma(-d) \cdot L^j$. If $0 < d < ½$ the autocorrelations for y_t are all eventually positive, and decay at a hyperbolic rate. For recent surveys of the relevant literature see, e.g., Baillie (1996), Beran (1994), and Robinson (1994b).

Of course, the mixture-of-distributions hypothesis in equation (2) is phrased in terms of the latent volatility process, V_t, and not v_t. However, it is readily demonstrated that the long-run dependence induced in the autocorrelations for v_t, for $0 < d = 1 - \frac{1}{2} \cdot q < \frac{1}{2}$, carries over to any positive power transforms of the fundamental V_t process; say $V_t^\theta = \exp^\theta(v_t + \mu_v)$, where $\theta > 0$. First, note that $E(V_t^\theta \cdot V_{t-j}^\theta) = [E(V_t^\theta)]^2 \cdot \exp[\theta^2 \cdot \rho(v_t, j) \cdot \sigma_v^2]$; see Granger and Newbold (1976) for a general discussion regarding the autocorrelation functions of power transforms of normals, and Andersen (1994) for a more detailed analysis of the particular case analyzed here. Consequently, the jth order autocorrelation for V_t^θ may be written as

$$\rho(V_t^\theta, j) = [\exp(\theta^2 \cdot \sigma_v^2) - 1]^{-1} \cdot [\exp\{\theta^2 \cdot \sigma_v^2 \cdot \rho(v_t, j)\} - 1]. \tag{9}$$

However, $\rho(v_t, j) \sim J^{2d-1} \to 0$ for $j \to \infty$, so that by a first order Taylor series expansion $\exp[\theta^2 \cdot \sigma_v^2 \cdot \rho(v_t, j)] \approx 1 + \theta^2 \cdot \sigma_v^2 \cdot \rho(v_t, j)$. From this it follows immediately that, for large j,

$$\rho(V_t^\theta, j) \approx [\exp(\theta^2 \cdot \sigma_v^2) - 1]^{-1} \cdot \theta^2 \cdot \sigma_v^2 \cdot \rho(v_t, j) \sim j^{2d-1} \tag{10}$$

Thus, the V_t^θ and the v_t processes share the same long-run decay in their autocorrelation functions. More importantly, this long-run dependence in the V_t^θ process is propagated to the process for the absolute returns raised to an arbitrary power, $2 \cdot \theta$. To see this, note that from equation (2) any power transform of the absolute returns is directly related to the latent volatility process by $|R_t|^{2 \cdot \theta} = V_t^\theta \cdot |Z_t|^{2 \cdot \theta}$. Thus, because Z_t^2 is an i.i.d. process, it follows that $\rho(|R_t|^{2 \cdot \theta}, j)$ is proportional to $\rho(V_t^\theta, j)$. The return volatility will therefore exhibit the identical slow hyperbolic rate of decay whether measured in terms of the absolute returns, $|R_t|$, the squared returns, R_t^2, or any other power transform, $|R_t|^{2 \cdot \theta}$; i.e., for large j,

$$\rho(|R_t|^{2 \cdot \theta}, j) \sim j^{2d-1} \tag{11}$$

This result is important because it demonstrates how the long-memory features of volatility may arise naturally through the interaction of a large number of diverse information processes. From a conceptual perspective, it implies that the long-memory characteristics reflect inherent properties of the return-generating process, rather than external shocks that induce a structural shift in the volatility process, as, e.g., suggested by Lamoureux and Lastrapes (1990). In other words, the mechanism responsible for the fractional integration in volatility is generic to the returns process, and thus ever present, so that with high frequency data it may be feasible to identify the manifestation of the phenomenon even over relatively short spans of calendar time. We pursue this possibility in Section III.

For now, we simply note that the result in equation (11) is consistent with the empirical behavior of the autocorrelograms for the various power transforms of daily equity returns reported in Ding, Granger, and Engle (1993). Although Harvey and Streibel (1996) argue that it is impossible, by theoretical means, to ascertain which value of θ will uniformly maximize the autocorrelations for the simple stochastic volatility model, corresponding to $N = 1$ in the current setup, it is noteworthy that the sample autocorrelations for the daily returns analyzed in Ding, Granger, and Engle (1993) attain their maxima for θ very close to one-half.[15] Motivated by this observation, we concentrate on the correlation structure for the intradaily absolute returns in the empirical investigations below.[16]

---

[15]This phenomenon is referred to as the Taylor effect by Granger and Ding (1997).

[16]Varying the power of the absolute returns effectively amounts to varying the importance of extreme events. For the five-minute DM–$ returns analyzed here, the first order sample autocorrelations for $|R_t|$ and R_t^2 equal 0.309 and 0.201, respectively, consistent with the findings for other rates and time periods reported in Müller, Dacorogna, and Pictet (1996).

B. Temporal Aggregation of Volatility

The long memory characterization obtained in equation (11) may appear incomplete, because the mixture-of-distributions hypothesis is silent regarding the proper discrete time sampling interval for the intradaily return series. While the complex volatility structure entertained renders a full distributional characterization infeasible, it is possible to show that the autocorrelations for the temporally aggregated squared returns eventually exhibit the identical long-run hyperbolic rate of decay irrespective of the sampling frequency.[17] In particular, let $R_\tau^{(k)} \equiv R_{\tau \cdot k} + R_{\tau \cdot k-1} + \ldots + R_{\tau \cdot k-k+1} = V_{\tau \cdot k}^{1/2} \cdot Z_{\tau \cdot k} + V_{\tau \cdot k-1}^{1/2} \cdot Z_{\tau \cdot k-1} + \ldots + V_{\tau \cdot k-k+1}^{1/2} \cdot Z_{\tau \cdot k-k+1}$, where $\tau = 1, 2, \ldots$, and $k = 1, 2, \ldots$, denote the temporally aggregated returns.[18] Since the Z_ts are i.i.d., it follows that the jth order autocorrelation for $(R_\tau^{(k)})^2$ is proportional to the correlation between $V_{\tau \cdot k} \cdot Z_{\tau \cdot k}^2 + V_{\tau \cdot k-1} \cdot Z_{\tau \cdot k-1}^2 + \ldots + V_{\tau \cdot k-k+1} \cdot Z_{\tau \cdot k-k+1}^2$ and $V_{(\tau-j) \cdot k} \cdot Z_{(\tau-j) \cdot k}^2 + V_{(\tau-j) \cdot k-1} \cdot Z_{(\tau-j) \cdot k-1}^2 + \ldots + V_{(\tau-j) \cdot k-k+1} \cdot Z_{(\tau-j) \cdot k-k+1}^2$. Thus, by collecting terms corresponding to the same lag length, the latter correlation is, in turn, proportional to the sum of the autocorrelations between V_t^2 and $V_{t-j \cdot k-h}^2$, where the weights corresponding to $h = -k+1, -k+2, \ldots, k-1$ equal $(k - |h|)$, and zero otherwise. Consequently, for long lags, j,

$$\rho([R_\tau^{(k)}]^2, [R_{\tau-j}^{(k)}]^2) \sim k^{-2} \cdot \sum_{h=-k+1}^{k-1} (k - |h|) \cdot \rho(V_t^2, V_{t-j \cdot k-h}^2)$$

$$\sim k^{-2} \cdot \sum_{h=-k+1}^{k-1} (k - |h|) \cdot (j \cdot k + h)^{2d-1} \approx (j \cdot k)^{2d-1} \sim j^{2d-1}. \quad (12)$$

That is, the long-memory features of the squared returns are consistent with the characteristics of a self-similar process in the sense of Mandelbrot and van Ness (1968) and Mandelbrot and Wallis (1969). Moreover, by analogy to the $k = 1$ case detailed above, if the temporally aggregated latent volatility process is log-normally distributed, then the long-run autocorrelation structure for $|R_\tau^{(k)}|^{2 \cdot \theta}$ will be identical for all θ. Thus, in this case the autocorrelations for any power transform of the temporally aggregated absolute returns should again eventually decay at the identical hyperbolic rate of j^{2d-1} irrespective of the sampling frequency, k.[19]

C. Extensions

Before we describe the empirical findings pertaining to the propositions developed so far, we should emphasize that the theoretical model readily accommodates extensions in a number of directions that allow for added flexibility and realism in the portrayal of the volatility dynamics without affecting the salient long-run dependencies. First, the mixture-of-distributions hypothesis in equations (2), (3), and (4) obviously neglects the repetitive intradaily pattern in the volatility that is evident in the spectrum and the autocorrelogram for the 5-minute absolute DM-$ returns in Figures 1 and 2. To incorporate this periodicity, let $s(t)$ denote the stage of the periodic cycle at time t. A slight modification of

---

[17] In a related context, assuming a Wold type representation, Chambers (1995) has recently shown that the degree of fractional integration in the levels is preserved under temporal aggregation of both stock and flow variables.

[18] For the 74,880 five-minute returns analyzed here, an aggregation factor of $k = 2$ would correspond to the time series of 37,440 ten-minute returns, whereas $k = 3$ refers to the time series of 24,960 fifteen-minute returns, etc.

[19] Previous empirical work with much simpler dependency structures have found the log-normal distribution to work remarkably well at various return frequencies; see, e.g., Andersen (1996), Shephard (1996), and Taylor (1994).

the model in equation (2), that explicitly allows for the pronounced intradaily pattern, takes the form,

$$R_t = V_t^{1/2} \cdot S_{t,s(t)} \cdot Z_t, \tag{13}$$

where the spectrum for the independent seasonal component $S_{t,s(t)}$ has no mass at frequencies lower than one day.[20] Since $\ln(R_t^2) = \mu_v + v_t + \ln(S_{t,s(t)}^2) + \ln(Z_t^2)$, it follows that the long-run behavior, as dictated by the spectrum for v_t near frequency zero, is unaffected by this additional periodic component. Of course, the autocorrelation structure in the absolute returns may be severely influenced by the presence of the repetitive intradaily pattern. However, as demonstrated below, by explicitly filtering out the daily and higher frequency dynamics in the absolute returns process, it is possible to uncover the long-run hyperbolic rate of decay implied by the aggregation of the component processes.

Rather than being independent, the "news" arrivals might more realistically share a number of common factors related to the state of the overall economy, while still exhibiting their own separate influence on the valuation of the asset. To allow for such common effects, consider the following generalization of the simple logarithmic AR(1) processes in equation (3),

$$v_{j,t} = \alpha_j \cdot v_{j,t-1} + \sum_{k=1}^{K} \xi_{j,k} \cdot \kappa_{k,t} + \varepsilon_{j,t} \tag{14}$$

where $\kappa_{k,t}$ represents the de-meaned kth common factor, and the factor loading for the jth arrival process associated with common factor k is denoted by $\xi_{j,k}$.[21] Provided that each of the common factors is covariance stationary, so that their spectra are bounded across all frequencies, and that the heterogeneity in the individual persistence parameters, α_j, is determined by the beta distribution in equation (6), it follows immediately by analogy to the results in Granger (1980), that the hyperbolic decay in the autocorrelation function for v_t is preserved under this more general specification. The independence assumption in equation (3) merely serves to simplify the exposition. The implied degree of long-run dependence in the absolute returns remains intact under the more realistic assumptions in equation (14).

Finally, while the derivation above explicitly relies on the beta distribution in equation (6) for characterizing the heterogeneity in the individual component processes, it is obvious that the degree of fractional integration, $d = 1 - ½ \cdot q$, is independent of the p parameter in the beta distribution. Only the shape of the distribution for α close to unity, as dictated by q, is important. Intuitively, if a sufficient number of the individual information arrival processes have high persistence, albeit $\alpha_j < 1$, the aggregate information arrival process will display long-memory characteristics. This suggests that the aggregation argument behind the long-run dependence in v_t is somewhat more general than portrayed above. Indeed, Lin (1991) and Granger and Ding (1996) show that the so-called Generalized Integrated class of models, discussed by Granger (1987, 1988), may arise through the aggregation of a closely related component type structure.[22]

---

[20] A particularly simple representation that restricts $S_{t,s(t)}$ to depend only on the stage of the periodic cycle, *s(t)*, has been successfully employed by Andersen and Bollerslev (1997a) in modeling the periodicity in the DM–$ return series analyzed here. Note also that periodicities at, say, the weekly frequency may be accommodated analogously.

[21] This construction closely mirrors the spirit, if not the structure, of the arbitrage pricing theory of Ross (1976).

[22] A closely related method for simulating fractional Gaussian noise has been proposed by Mandelbrot and Wallis (1969) and Mandelbrot (1971).

TABLE I | Persistence Measures for Temporally Aggregated Absolute Intraday Returns

The percentage returns are based on interpolated five-minute logarithmic average bid-ask quotes for the Deutschemark–U.S. Dollar spot exchange rate from October 1, 1992 through September 29, 1993. Quotes from Friday 21:00 Greenwich Mean Time (GMT) through Sunday 21:00 GMT have been excluded, resulting in a total of 74,880 five-minute return observations. The length of the different intraday sampling intervals equal 5-k minutes. Each absolute return series consists of a total of 74,880/k nonoverlapping observations; i.e., $|R_{\tau}^{(k)}| \equiv |R_{\tau \cdot k} + R_{\tau \cdot k-1} + \ldots R_{\tau \cdot k-k+1}|$ where $\tau = 1, 2, \ldots, T/k$ and $T = 74{,}880$. The $\hat{\rho}^{(k)}$ column gives the first order autocorrelations for $|R_{\tau}^{(k)}|$. The Log-Periodogram estimates for d from equation (18) are denoted by $\hat{d}_{GH}^{(k)}$. The truncation and trimming parameters for $k = 2, 3, \ldots, 144$ are determined by $m = [(T/k)^{1/2}]$ and $\ell = [m^{1/4}]$, respectively, where $[\cdot]$ denotes the integer value. In order to avoid any confounding effects from frequencies corresponding to less than 1 day, the estimate for $\hat{d}_{GH}^{(1)}$ is based on $m = 255$ and $\ell = 3$. The $\hat{d}_{AP}^{(k)}$ column gives the average periodogram estimates for d defined in equation (21). The truncation parameters are determined by $m = [(T/k)^{1/2}]$ for $k = 2, 3, \ldots, 144$, while $\hat{d}_{AP}^{(1)}$ is based on $m = 255$. The scalar q is fixed at 1/4 across all sampling frequencies.

k	T/k	$\hat{\rho}^{(k)}$	$\hat{d}_{GH}^{(k)}$	$\hat{d}_{AP}^{(k)}$
1	74,880	0.309	0.321	0.385
2	37,440	0.313	0.367	0.375
3	24,960	0.307	0.337	0.376
4	18,720	0.287	0.339	0.364
6	12,480	0.268	0.288	0.351
8	9,360	0.272	0.281	0.340
9	8,320	0.251	0.214	0.333
12	6,240	0.229	0.309	0.317
16	4,680	0.246	0.269	0.303
18	4,160	0.193	0.457	0.310
24	3,120	0.164	0.220	0.291
32	2,340	0.171	0.221	0.302
36	2,080	0.097	0.178	0.275
48	1,560	0.075	0.236	0.311
72	1,040	0.007	0.214	0.270
96	780	−0.025	0.382	0.274
144	520	−0.033	0.382	0.286

III. Estimating Long-Memory in Volatility

The theoretical framework developed in the previous section builds on the idea that the aggregate market volatility represents the manifestation of numerous heterogeneous information arrival processes; some with short-run volatility dependencies, others possessing more highly persistent volatility patterns. As time passes the short-run processes decay significantly, while the more highly persistent processes remain influential. Hence, while sudden bursts of volatility typically will possess both short-run and long-run components, the short-run decay stands out most clearly over the intradaily frequencies, whereas the highly persistent processes only will be noticeable over longer horizons. However, traditional correlation based measures for the degree of volatility persistence, obtained from high frequency intradaily data, will tend to pick up only the effects of the complex interaction between the short-run decay associated with the less persistent processes and the strong intradaily periodicity, thus missing the importance of the long-run volatility components.

To illustrate, consider the third row in Table I, which reports the first order sample autocorrelation, $\hat{\rho}^{(k)}$, for the temporally aggregated absolute five-minute returns; i.e., $|R_{\tau}^{(k)}|$

for $\tau = 1, 2, \ldots, 74{,}880/k$. The first order sample autocorrelations for the highest intradaily frequencies all indicate very significant positive serial correlation in the absolute returns. However, there is a sharp dropoff in the value of the sample autocorrelations at the three-hour sampling frequency, i.e., $k = 36$. In fact, the first order autocorrelations for the eight and twelve hours absolute returns, i.e., $k = 96$ and 144, are both negative, suggestive of an anti-persistent volatility process.[23]

The latter conclusion is, of course, grossly misleading, being driven by the combined effects of the intradaily periodic pattern and the complex multiple volatility component structure, thus creating an overall system that conforms to the law of motion outlined in equation (13). In order to justify this interpretation, however, we must develop an alternative estimation approach. In particular, while strong intraday periodicity and pronounced volatility clustering have been extensively documented at the high frequency level, there is little direct evidence for the existence of longer-run volatility components that induce the type of long-memory behavior in the high frequency volatility process implied by our information aggregation rendition of the mixture-of-distributions hypothesis.

Specifically, from the model detailed in the previous section, the absolute returns should exhibit the identical long-run dependence for all sampling frequencies, say $I(d)$, where $0 < d < \frac{1}{2}$. Representing the process for the absolute returns as $(1 - L)^d\,|R_\tau^{(k)}| = \eta_\tau^{(k)}$, where $\eta_\tau^{(k)}$ is a stationary and ergodic process with a bounded spectrum, $f_{\eta,k}(\omega)$, for all frequencies, ω, the spectrum for $|R_\tau^{(k)}|$ may therefore be written as[24]

$$f_{|R|,k}(\omega) = |[1 - \exp(-i \cdot \omega)^{-d}|^2 \cdot f_{\eta,k}(\omega) = |2 \cdot \sin(1/2 \cdot \omega)|^{-2 \cdot d} \cdot f_{\eta,k}(\omega). \quad (15)$$

Since $\lim_{\omega \to 0} \omega^{-1} \cdot \sin(\frac{1}{2} \cdot \omega) = \frac{1}{2}$, it follows that for the frequencies close to zero, i.e., $\omega \approx 0$,

$$f_{|R|,k}(\omega) \approx f_{\eta,k}(0) \cdot |\omega|^{-2 \cdot d}, \quad (16)$$

or,

$$\text{In}[f_{|R|,k}(\omega)] \approx \text{In}[f_{\eta,k}(0)] - 2 \cdot d \cdot \text{In}(\omega). \quad (17)$$

Hence, the spectrum should be approximately log-linear for the long-run frequencies. Indeed, when viewed on the double logarithmic scale in Figure 1, the spectrum for the five-minute absolute returns, i.e., $k = 1$, is very close to a straight line over the interdaily frequencies, $0 < \omega < 2 \cdot \pi/288 \approx 0.0218$.

The Geweke and Porter-Hudak (1983) log-periodogram estimate for the fractional order of integration is based directly on this relationship. These estimates for the dependence in $|R_\tau^{(k)}|$, obtained across all of the intradaily frequencies, are reported in the column labeled $\hat{d}_{\text{GH}}^{(k)}$ in Table I. Formally,

$$\hat{d}_{\text{GH}}^{(k)} = -\frac{1}{2} \cdot \left\{ \sum_{j=\ell+1}^{m} [\text{In}(\omega_{k,j}) - \bar{\omega}_{k,\ell,m}] \cdot \text{In}(I_{|R|,k}(\omega_{j,k})) \right\} \cdot \left\{ \sum_{j=\ell+1}^{m} [\text{In}(\omega_{k,j}) - \bar{\omega}_{k,\ell,m}]^2 \right\}^{-1}, \quad (18)$$

[23]Müller et al. (1997) attribute this negative correlation for the half-day lag to a heterogeneous market with different groups of traders participating during their regular business hours.

[24] Formal conditions for the equivalence between this spectral definition of long-memory and the hyperbolic decay rate in the autocorrelation function are discussed in Beran (1994) and Robinson (1994b); see also Granger and Ding (1996).

where $\overline{\omega}_{k,\ell,m} \equiv (m - \ell)^{-1} \cdot \Sigma G_{j=\ell+1}^{m}\ \omega_{j,k}$, and $I_{|R|,k}(\omega_{j,k})$ denotes the sample periodogram for $|R_{\tau}^{(k)}|$ at the jth Fourier frequency, i.e., $\omega_{j,k} = 2 \cdot \pi \cdot j \cdot k/T$. Although this estimator for d has been fairly widely used in the literature, consistency for $0 < \mathrm{d} < ½$ has only recently been established by Robinson (1995) under regularity conditions that include the truncation and trimming parameters both tending to infinity, albeit at a slower rate than the sample size; i.e., $m \to \infty$, $\ell \to \infty$, $\ell/m \to 0$, and $m \cdot k/T \to 0$. However, the regularity conditions also require that $|R_{\tau}^{(k)}|$ be normally distributed, which in turn implies that the estimator itself, $\hat{d}_{\mathrm{GH}}^{(k)}$, is asymptotically normal with a variance of $m^{-1} \cdot (\pi^2/24)$, independent of the sample size, T/k.

For the results reported in Table I, we took $m = [(T/k)^{1/2}]$ and $\ell = [m^{1/4}]$, respectively, where [·] denotes the integer value. However, in order to avoid any confounding effects from frequencies corresponding to less than one day, the estimate for $\hat{d}_{\mathrm{GH}}^{(1)}$ is based on $m = 255$ and $\ell = 3$. Note that, in contrast to the sample autocorrelations reported in the $\hat{\rho}^{(k)}$ column, the $\hat{d}_{\mathrm{GH}}^{(k)}$ estimates for the degree of long-run volatility dependence are remarkably stable across the different intradaily return intervals. In fact, when judged by the asymptotic normal distributions, all of the estimates are within less than one asymptotic standard error of $d = 0.359$.[25] To illustrate, consider the estimate for $\hat{d}_{\mathrm{GH}}^{(k)} = 0.321$, corresponding to the average slope of the spectrum for the five-minute absolute returns in Figure 1 over the frequencies $0 < \omega \leq 255 \cdot 2 \cdot \pi/74{,}888 \approx 0.0214$.[26] The theoretical standard error for this estimate equals $\pi \cdot (24 \cdot 255)^{-1/2} \approx 0.040$. As such, the estimates for $k = 1, 2, \ldots, 144$ confirm the proposition that the degree of fractional integration in the absolute returns is invariant with respect to the sampling frequency.[27]

Unfortunately, the assumption of normality underlying the formal statistical justification for the $\hat{d}_{\mathrm{GH}}^{(k)}$ estimates is clearly violated in the present context. For instance, the sample skewness and kurtosis for the absolute five-minute returns equal 0.367 and 21.5, respectively. The last column in Table I therefore reports the results from a less restrictive semiparametric estimation procedure for determining d, based on the ratio of the periodogram for two frequencies close to zero.[28] To motivate this estimator, let

$$G_{m,k} = 2 \cdot \pi \cdot (T/k)^{-1} \cdot \sum_{j=1}^{m} I_{|R|,k}(\omega_{j,k}) \tag{19}$$

denote the average periodogram for the frequencies $j = 1, 2, \ldots, m$. Then, following Robinson (1994a), for $0 < \mathrm{d} < ½$ and $m \to \infty$, but $m \cdot k/T \to 0$,

$$\ln(G_{m,k}) - \ln(G_{[qm],k}) + (1 - 2 \cdot d) \cdot \ln(q) \approx 0, \tag{20}$$

where $0 < q < 1$. Thus, upon rearranging the terms in equation (20), the following estimator for d becomes apparent,

$$\hat{d}_{\mathrm{AP}}^{(k)} = 1/2 + 1/2 \cdot \ln(q)^{-1} \cdot [\ln(G_{m,k}) - \ln(G_{[qm],k})]. \tag{21}$$

[25] This value of d corresponds to the estimated hyperbolic decay rate in the low-pass filtered five-minute absolute returns described further in Section IV below.

[26] Including all of the frequencies up to $j = [74{,}880^{1/2}] = 273$, the estimate for $\hat{d}_{\mathrm{GH}}^{(k)}$ drops to a value of only 0.242, highlighting the importance of explicitly excluding the intradaily effects in the estimation.

[27] Similar estimates for d based on 10-minute absolute exchange rate returns, corresponding to $k = 2$, have been reported independently by Henry and Payne (1996). These results are also consistent with the notion of an intrinsic time scale in the foreign exchange market as discussed by Müller et al. (1993).

[28] The same log-periodogram and average periodogram estimators for d implemented here have previously been employed by Chambers (1995) and Delgado and Robinson (1994) in the analysis of various U.K. macroeconomic time series and monthly Spanish inflation rates, respectively.

Consistency of this frequency-domain estimator for d has been established by Robinson (1994a) under much weaker regularity conditions than those available for $\hat{d}^{(k)}_{\mathrm{GH}}$. Furthermore, given the assumption of normality underlying the existing consistency proof for the log-periodogram estimator, $\hat{d}^{(k)}_{\mathrm{GH}}$, Lobato and Robinson (1996) have recently shown that the alternative $\hat{d}^{(k)}_{\mathrm{AP}}$ estimator is asymptotically normal for $0 < d < 1/4$, but nonnormally distributed for $1/4 \leq d < 1/2$.

The estimates reported in the last column of Table I are based on a truncation parameter of $m = [(T/k)^{1/2}]$ for $k = 2, 3, \ldots, 144$, whereas $m = 255$ for $k = 1$ in order to avoid any confounding effects from the intradaily dependencies in the estimation of $\hat{d}^{(1)}_{\mathrm{AP}}$. The value for the scalar q was fixed at 0.25 across all the sampling frequencies. In line with the simulation evidence reported in Lobato and Robinson (1996), some informal sensitivity analysis revealed the results to be fairly robust with respect to this choice. Turning to the actual estimates, the similarities across the different values of k are even more striking than for the log-periodogram estimates. The average value of $\hat{d}^{(k)}_{\mathrm{AP}}$ equals 0.321, while ranging from a low of 0.270 for $k = 72$ to a high of only 0.385 for $k = 1$.[29]

Consistent with the notion of a heterogeneous component structure and the invariance under temporal aggregation, these estimates for d, based on a single year of intradaily returns, correspond very closely to the estimates reported in the extant literature with longer time-spans of daily data. For instance, the same log-periodogram regression and average periodogram estimates for d based on the 3,649 daily DM–$ absolute returns from March 14, 1979 through September 29,1993, equal 0.344 and 0.301, respectively.[30] Thus, the relatively simple semiparametric frequency-domain estimators in equations (18) and (21) are both capable of uncovering the inherent long-run volatility dependencies in the time series of high-frequency intradaily returns, without having to impose any specific structure on the short-run behavior of the system in order to accommodate the complex intradaily dynamics and repetitive periodic patterns that corrupt conventional correlation based measures.

To further appreciate the notion of long-memory volatility dynamics, consider the properties of the $(1 - L)^d$ filter designed to annihilate the long-run dependence in the absolute returns. Expressing the fractional differencing operator in terms of its binomial expansion, the gain of the filter may be written as

$$|[1 - \exp(-i \cdot \omega)]^d| = \left\{ \left[\sum_{j=0}^{\infty}, \ldots, _\infty \delta_j \cdot \cos(\omega \cdot j) \right]^2 + \left[\sum_{j=0}^{\infty}, \ldots, _\infty \delta_j \cdot \sin(\omega \cdot j) \right]^2 \right\}^{1/2}, \quad (22)$$

where $0 \leq \omega \leq \pi$, and $\delta_j \equiv \Gamma(j - d) \cdot \Gamma(j + 1)^{-1} \cdot \Gamma(-d)$ for $j = 0, 1, \ldots$. Intuitively, the gain at frequency ω represents the magnitude by which the filter multiplies the component of the time series with a repetitive cycle of $2 \cdot \pi/\omega$ periods. The enhanced flexibility provided by allowing for fractional orders of integration is evident from Figure 3, which plots the gains of $(1 - L)^d$ for $d = 0, 0.25, 0.359, 0.5$, and 1. Although the fractional differencing operators with $d > 0$ completely eliminate the zero frequency component, the filters differ greatly in terms of their gains over the finite frequencies, $0 < \omega \leq \pi$.[31]

[29] The estimate for $\hat{d}^{(1)}_{\mathrm{AP}}$, corrupted by the intradaily frequencies, $j = 256, 257, \ldots, 273$, equals 0.172.

[30] Both estimates are based on $m = 168$ corresponding to a period of $3{,}648/168 \approx 21.7$ trading days, or approximately one month, along with $\ell = 4$ and $q = 0.25$.

[31] Since the autocorrelations of a long-memory process with $d > 0$ is not summable, all of the $(1 - L)^d$ filters necessarily eliminate the zero frequency component in order to achieve a bounded spectrum for the fractionally differenced series.

FIGURE 3 | The Figure Graphs the Filter Gains for the Fractional Differencing Operators, $(1 - L)^d$, Corresponding to $d = 0, 0.25, 0.359, 0.5$, and 1.

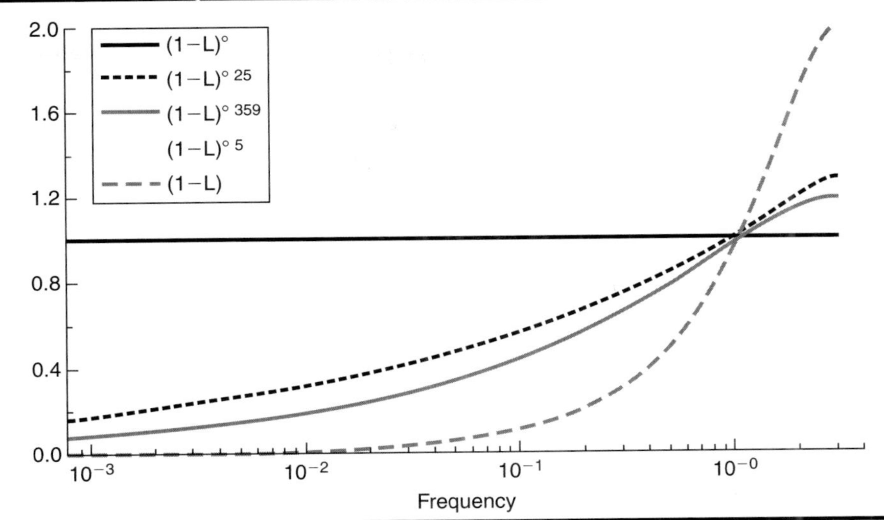

The filter gain of $[2 - 2 \cdot \cos(\omega)]^{1/2}$ for the first difference operator, $(1 - L)$, associated with the Integrated GARCH, or IGARCH, class of models for σ_t^2, implies a much greater down-weighting of the long-run dependencies than the fractional differencing filter with $d = 0.359$.

FIGURE 4 | The Figure Graphs the Spectrum for the Fractionally Differenced Five-Minute Absolute Returns on an Open Position in the Deutschemark–U.S. Dollar Spot Exchange Rate Market from October 1, 1992 Through September 29, 1993; i.e., $(1 - L)^{0.359} |R_t|$ where $t = 1, 2, \ldots, 74{,}880$.

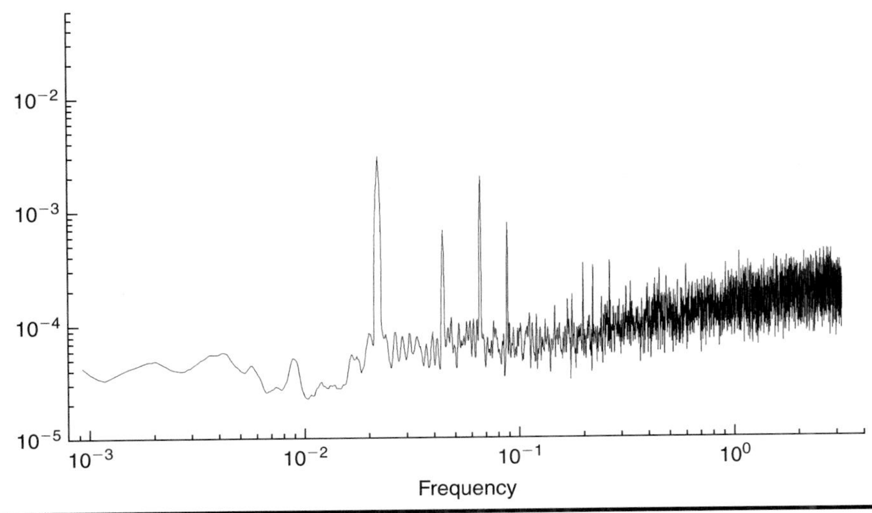

The spectrum is estimated as the smoothed sample periodogram using a triangular kernel with bandwidth of ten.

FIGURE 5 | The Figure Graphs the Sample Autocorrelogram for the Fractionally Differenced Five-Minute Absolute Returns on an Open Position in the Deutschemark–U.S. Dollar Spot Exchange Rate Market from October 1, 1992 Through September 29, 1993; i.e., $(1 - L)^{0.359} |R_t| \equiv |\ln(P_t) - \ln(P_{t-1})|$ where $t = 1, 2, \ldots, 74{,}880$.

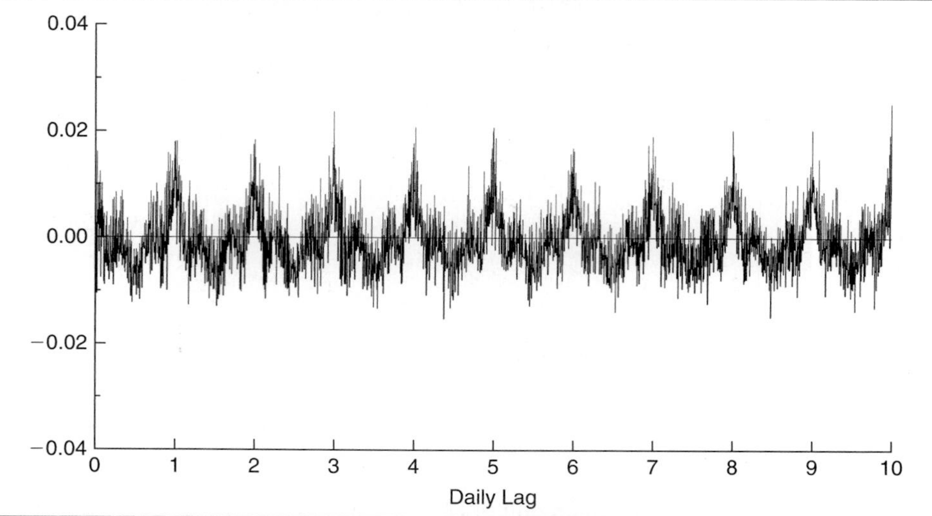

The justification of filtering the five-minute DM–$ absolute returns by $(1 - L)^{0.359}$ is also evident from the plot of the estimated spectrum for $(1 - L)^{0.359}|R_t|$ given in Figure 4.[32] The flat spectrum for $0 < \omega < 2 \cdot \pi/288 \approx 0.0218$ reveals that the fractional differencing operator is, indeed, successful in eliminating the longer-run dependencies. At the same time, the pronounced peaks associated with the daily periodicity remain very similar across Figures 1 and 4. These results are further underscored by the time-domain autocorrelogram for $(1 - L)^{0.359}|R_t|$ depicted in Figure 5. Although more noisy, the autocorrelations exhibit the same repetitive daily cycles as the autocorrelations for the raw absolute returns in Figure 2.[33] However, in contrast to the autocorrelogram for the raw absolute returns, which display an overall slow hyperbolic rate of decay, the daily periodic patterns in the autocorrelogram for the fractionally differenced five-minute absolute returns are centered on zero. The long-run dependence in the series has been eliminated.

IV. Low-Pass Filtering and Long-Run Volatility Dynamics

The frequency domain based estimators outlined in the previous section allow for the determination of the degree of long-run volatility dependence across the different sampling frequencies by explicitly focusing on the shape of the spectrum around the origin. Alternatively, a nonstructural time-domain estimation procedure could be based on the eventual

[32] The binomial expansion for $(1 - L)^{0.359}$ was truncated at a lag length of 1440, corresponding to one week. Also, following Baillie, Bollerslev, and Mikkelsen (1996) all of the presample values for $|R_t|$ were fixed at their unconditional sample analogues.

[33] Note that the scales for the autocorrelograms differ across Figures 2 and 5. In particular, the first order sample autocorrelation of -0.160 for $(1 - L)^{0.359} |R_t|$ does not fit on the scale in Figure 5.

hyperbolic decay of the autocorrelation function implied by the presence of long-memory. However, the implementation of this idea is obscured by the strong intradaily periodicity, as exemplified by the sample autocorrelogram for the five-minute absolute returns depicted in Figure 2. Various standardization procedures have previously been proposed for modeling the intradaily patterns in the volatility of high frequency foreign exchange rates, including the time-deformation approach advocated by Dacorogna *et al.* (1993) and Ghysels and Jasiak (1995), and the flexible Fourier functional form utilized by Andersen and Bollerslev (1997a, 1997b). These procedures are directly applicable in a forecasting context. In contrast, the low-pass filtering technique developed below is based on a two-sided weighted average of both past and future absolute returns. By explicitly annihilating the dependencies with a periodicity of less than one day, the in-sample low-pass filtered absolute returns are designed to be void of any short-run intradaily dynamics, and as such provide a framework for the ex-post analysis of the long-run volatility determinants based on conventional time-domain methods.

Restricting the attention to daily and longer run dynamics, the ideal low-pass filter would have a gain, or a frequency response function, of zero for all of the intradaily frequencies, and a gain of unity for the interdaily frequencies; i.e., $\beta(\omega) = 1$ for $0 \leq \omega < \omega_D$ and $\beta(\omega) = 0$ for $\omega_D \leq \omega \leq \pi$, where ω_D denotes the daily frequency. By standard filter theory the weights in the corresponding infinite two-sided time-domain filter, $b_\infty(L) = \Sigma_{j=-\infty}^{\infty} b_{\infty,j} L^j$, is readily found by the inverse Fourier transform; i.e., $b_{\infty,j} = \int_0^\pi \beta(\omega) \cdot \exp(i \cdot \omega \cdot j) d\omega = \sin(j \cdot \omega_D)/(j \cdot \pi)$ for $j \neq 0$ and $b_{\infty,0} = \int_0^\pi \beta(\omega) d\omega = \omega_D/\pi$. Of course, in practice, with a finite number of data points, this infinite filter is not applicable. However, the weights in the finite dimensional two-sided approximate filter,

$$b_p(L) = \sum_{j=-p}^{p} b_{p,j} L^j, \tag{23}$$

that achieves the minimum squared approximation error, subject to the constraint that the filter weights sum to unity, is given by $b_{p,j} = b_{\infty,j} - (b_{\infty,0} + 2 \cdot \Sigma_{h=1}^{p} b_{\infty,h} - 1)/(2 \cdot p + 1)$ for $j = -p, -p + 1, \ldots, p$; see, e.g., Baxter and King (1995).[34] Since the weights are symmetric, the gain of this approximate low-pass filter may be conveniently written as,[35]

$$|b_p[\exp(i \cdot \omega)]| = b_{p,0} + 2 \cdot \sum_{j=1}^{p} b_{p,j} \cdot \cos(j \cdot \omega). \tag{24}$$

The higher the value of p, the more accurate this gain approximates the ideal gain of $\beta(\omega)$. Of course, in practice a tradeoff is necessarily called for in terms of the shape of the gain given by equation (24) and the number of observations that have to be sacrificed at the beginning and end of the sample in the implementation of $b_p(L)$.

For the five-minute returns analyzed here, we took $\omega_D = 0.021$, corresponding to roughly 299 periods or close to 25 hours, along with $p = 1440$, or one week. The corresponding filter

[34]Formally, the weights minimize the squared approximation error, $\int_0^\pi [b_p(\exp(i \cdot \omega)) - \beta(\omega)]^2 d\omega$. The constraint that the weights sum to unity ensures that the long-run zero frequency behavior of the series is unaltered by the filtering.

[35]The symmetry of the filter also guarantees that the phase is equal to zero across all frequencies; i.e., $\phi(\omega) = \tan^{-1}\{\mathrm{Im}[b_p(\exp(i \cdot \omega))]/\mathrm{Re}[b_p(\exp(i \cdot \omega))]\} = 0$. Intuitively, $\phi(\omega)/\omega$ represents the amount by which the filter shifts the series back in time at frequency ω.

FIGURE 6 | The Figure Graphs the Filter Weights for the Approximate Two-Sided Low-Pass Filter; i.e., $b_{p,j} = b_{\infty j} - (b_{\infty,0} + 2 \cdot \sum_{j=1}^{P} b_{\infty' j} - 1)/(2 \cdot p + 1)$, Where $p = 1440$, $\omega_D = 0.021$, $b_{\infty,0} = \omega_D/\pi$, and $b_{\infty,j} = \sin(j \cdot \omega_D)/(j \cdot \pi)$ for $j = -1440, \ldots, -1, 0, 1, 2, \ldots, 1440$.

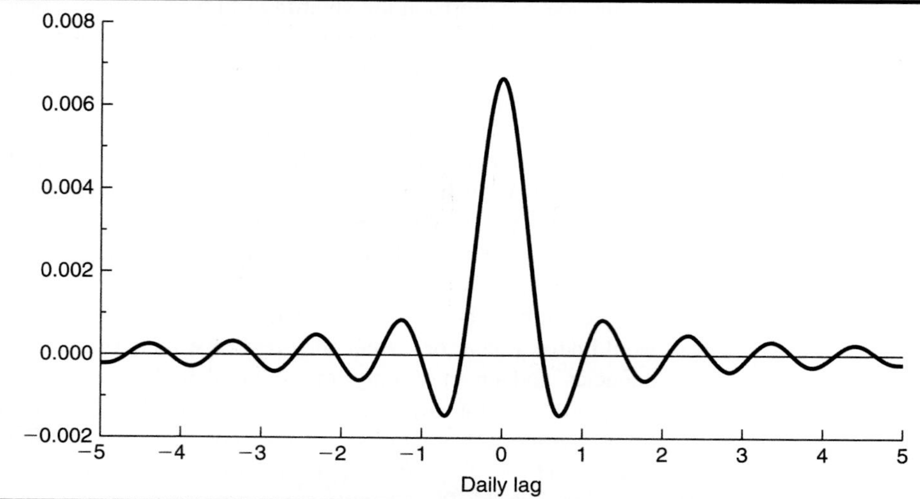

weights, $p_{-1440}, p_{-1439}, \ldots, p_{1440}$, are given in Figure 6. The accuracy afforded by this choice of p is illustrated in Figure 7, which graphs the gain of the ideal low-pass filter along with this two-sided approximation. The overall coherence between the gain of the two filters is generally very good. Only for the frequencies close to ω_D is there some evidence that the frequencies greater than ω_D do not receive a zero weight and that the frequency gains for $\omega < \omega_D$ are different from unity. Such "leakage" and "compression" is inevitable with a finite value of p.

FIGURE 7 | The Figure Graphs the Ideal and the Approximate Low-Pass Filter Gains for $\omega_D = 0.021$ and $p = 1440$.

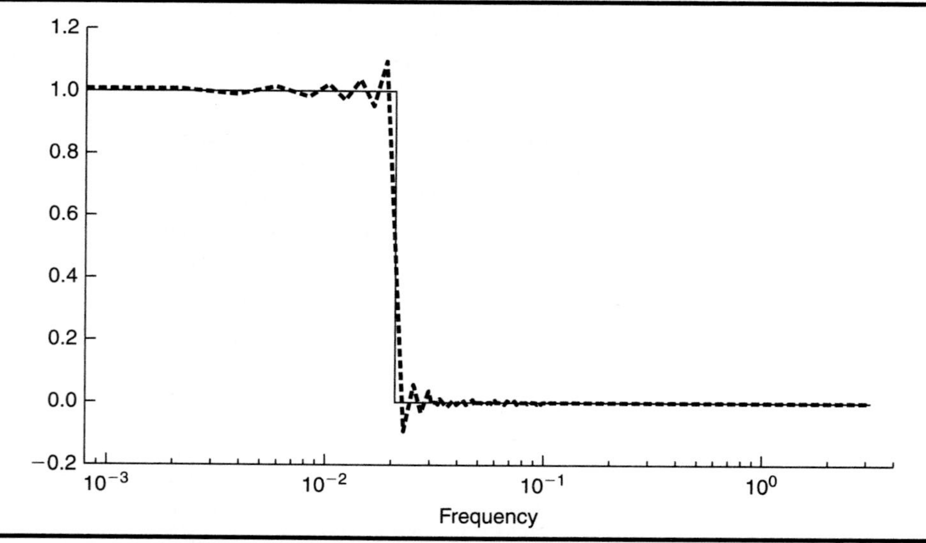

The gain for the approximate two-sided filter, $|b_{1440}[\exp(i \cdot \omega)]|$, is given by equation (24) in the text.

FIGURE 8 | The Figure Graphs the Spectrum for the Low-Pass Filtered Five-Minute Absolute Returns on an Open Position in the Deutschemark-U.S. Dollar Spot Exchange Rate Market from October 1, 1992 Through September 29, 1993; i.e., $b_{1440}(L)|R_t|$ Where $t = 1441, 1442, \ldots, 73440$, and the Coefficients in the Filter are Defined in the Text.

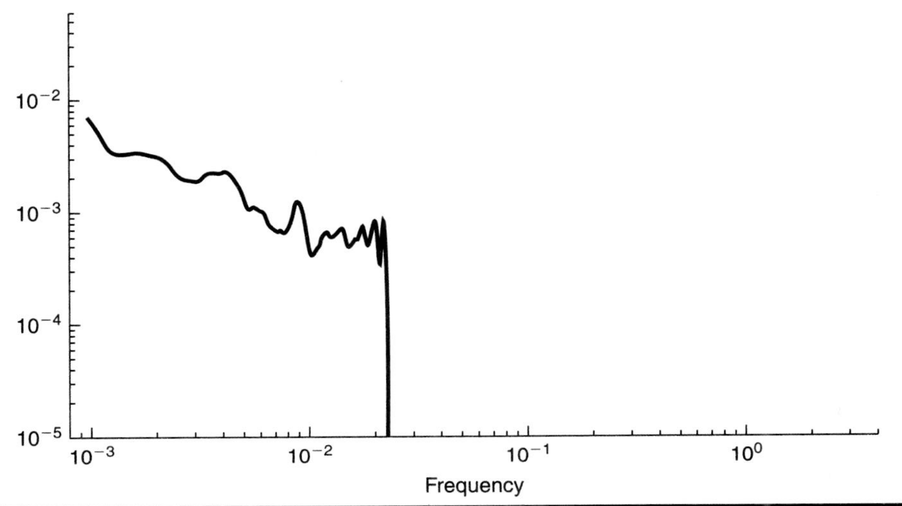

The spectrum is estimated as the smoothed sample periodogram using a triangular kernel with bandwidth of ten.

The effectiveness of this approximate low-pass filter in eliminating the/ short-run intradaily volatility components is clearly seen from Figure 8. The estimated spectrum for the filtered five-minute absolute returns, $b_{1440}(L)|R_t|$, where $t = 1441, 1442, \ldots, 73440$, has virtually no-mass at the frequencies higher than ω_D.[36] Of course, the log-linear relation for the interdaily frequencies, implied by the presence of long-memory, remains intact.

This long-run dependence is also evident in the autocorrelation function for the low-pass filtered absolute returns. In contrast to the overall decay of the autocorrelogram for the raw absolute returns in Figure 2, which is masked by the strong recurring daily pattern, the autocorrelation function for $b_{1440}(L)|R_t|$, depicted in Figure 9, display a distinct hyperbolic rate of decay.[37] The actual magnitude of the correlations have also increased substantially. Even out to lag 2,880, or ten days, the autocorrelations all remain above 0.2. Matching the sample autocorrelations for the low-pass filtered absolute returns with the hyperbolic decay implied by the presence of long-memory thus provides an alternative time-domain procedure for estimating d.

In general, since the autocorrelations of a long-memory process are eventually all positive, it follows that, for large j,

$$\ln(\rho_j) \approx \ln(c) + (2 \cdot d - 1) \cdot \ln(j), \tag{25}$$

[36] Due to the loss of one week of observations at the beginning and the end of the sample, the filtered time series consist of "only" $74{,}880 - 2 \cdot 1{,}440 = 72{,}000$ observations. Of course, the logarithmic scale in Figure 7 may be slightly misleading as the spectrum is not identically equal to zero for $\omega > \omega_D$.

[37] A similarly shaped autocorrelogram for twenty-minute absolute DM-$ returns standardized by a measure of the degree of market activity, or "theta-time," has been reported by Dacorogna et al. (1993).

FIGURE 9 | The figure graphs the Sample Autocorrelogram for the Low-Pass Filtered Five-Minute Absolute Returns on an Open Position in the Deutschemark–U.S. Dollar Spot Exchange Rate Market From October 1, 1992 Through September 29, 1993; i.e., $b_{1440}(L)|R_t|$ Where $t = 1441, 1442, \ldots, 73440$, and the Coefficients in the Filter Are Defined in the Text.

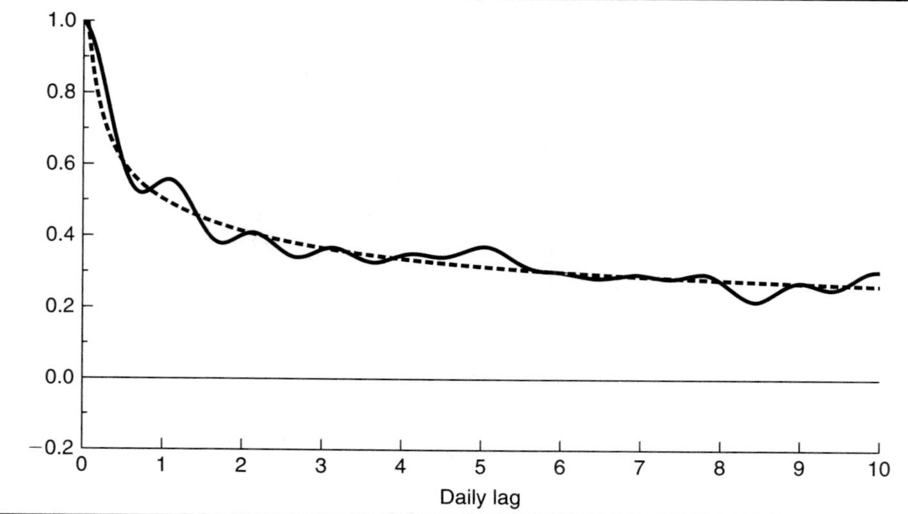

The dotted line gives the curve for the estimated hyperbolic decay rate; i.e., $j^{2 \cdot 0.359-1} = j^{-0.282}$.

where ρ_j denotes the jth order autocorrelation, and c is just a factor of proportionality. Replacing the autocorrelations by their sample analogues, $\hat{\rho}_j$ therefore suggests the following least squares estimator,

$$\hat{d}_{AC} = \frac{1}{2} + \frac{1}{2} \cdot \left\{ \sum_{j=r+1}^{r+n} [\text{In}(j) - \bar{j}_{r,n}] \cdot \text{In}(\hat{\rho}_j) \right\} \cdot \left\{ \sum_{j=r+1}^{r+n} [\text{In}(j) - \bar{j}_{r,n}]^2 \right\}^{-1} \tag{26}$$

where $\bar{j}_{r,n} \equiv n^{-1} \cdot \Sigma_{j=r+1}^{r+n} \text{In}(j)$, and $r \to \infty$, but $r/T \to 0$. This semi-parametric time-domain estimator for the fractional degree of integration, proposed by Robinson (1994b), is closely related to the minimum distance estimators recently analyzed by Tieslau, Schmidt, and Baillie (1996). No formal asymptotic distribution theory is yet available for the estimator in equation (26), although it seems likely that $\hat{d}_{AC}$ will be consistent under rather weak regularity conditions.

Applying this estimator to the sample autocorrelations for the low-pass filtered absolute returns, $\hat{\rho}(b_{1440}(L)|R_t|, j)$ for $j = 5, 6, \ldots, 2880$, yields $\hat{d}_{AC} = 0.359$. This estimate is thus fully consistent with the results from the frequency based procedures reported in the previous section. It is furthermore evident from the plot in Figure 9, that the implied hyperbolic rate of decay, $j^{2 \cdot 0.359-1} = j^{-0.282}$, is in close accordance with the actual shape of the autocorrelogram. It is worth stressing that, due to the strong intradaily volatility patterns and the associated recurring negative sample autocorrelations at the half-day lags, this estimation procedure for determining the fractional order of integration simply is not applicable with the raw absolute returns. Only by explicitly eliminating the intradaily dependencies do the sample autocorrelations all* become positive and the hyperbolic decay stand out clearly.

The low-pass filtered returns also set the stage for a more structural investigation of the determinants behind the important volatility components. A detailed analysis along these lines is beyond the scope of the present article. To simply illustrate the idea consider the announcement effects associated with the Employment report, the Bundesbank biweekly meeting, the Durable Goods figures, and the report on Business Inventories discussed in Section I above. On calculating the average increase in the absolute five-minute DM-$ returns in the two hours immediately following these announcements, the four effects, with robust standard errors in parentheses, are 0.0091 (0.0052), 0.0133 (0.0025), 0.0067 (0.0032), and 0.0143 (0.0023), respectively.[38] Thus, the increase in the volatility associated with the Employment report is apparently not significant at the usual five percent level, while the Durable Goods report is only marginally significant. Also, the figures on Business Inventories appear to be the most significant of the four "news" events. These estimates should be carefully interpreted, however, as the intradaily pattern is prone to obscure the fundamental relationships. In fact, on calculating the average two-hour increase in the volatility for the low-pass filtered returns, $b_{1440}(L)|R_t|$, the four effects are 0.0076 (0.0005), 0.0078 (0.0004), 0.0032 (0.0004), and −0.0005 (0.0005), respectively. The t-statistics for the three former announcements are now all overwhelmingly significant, while the release of the new figures for Business Inventories do not result in any increase in the volatility once the intradaily pattern in the absolute returns are filtered out.[39] As such, these results clearly demonstrate how the low-pass filtered absolute returns provide a valuable framework for the further study of the structural determinants behind financial market volatility clustering.

V. Conclusion

The temporal dependence in the volatility of speculative returns is of the utmost importance for the pricing and hedging of financial contracts. Yet, the empirical analysis of low frequency interdaily and high frequency intradaily returns have hitherto given rise to very different conclusions regarding the degree of volatility persistence for any particular asset. The mixture-of-distributions hypothesis developed here provides a justification for these conflicting empirical findings by interpreting the volatility as resulting from the aggregation of numerous constituent component processes; some with very short-run decay rates and others possessing much longer-run dependencies. When analyzing intradaily returns the short-run components will tend to dominate the estimates obtained with traditional time series models, whereas for daily or longer-run return intervals the estimates will be driven by the more persistent components. Nonetheless, under suitable conditions the aggregation of these multiple components implies, that the process for the volatility should exhibit the identical form of long-memory dependence irrespective of the sampling intervals. This proposition is confirmed by our empirical analysis, which also demonstrates that, by annihilating the intradaily dependencies in time series of intradaily returns, it is possible to uncover this inherent long-memory dependence in relatively short calendar time-spans of high frequency data using simple correlation based procedures. As such the techniques discussed here set the stage for the development of improved long-run interdaily volatility forecasts based on the large samples of intradaily prices that have recently become available for a wide variety of different instruments. Only future research will reveal the extent to which these techniques will support the development of new and improved empirical pricing relationships.

[38] In order to be compatible with the results for the low-pass filtered returns, the estimates are based on observations $t = 1441, 1442, \ldots, 73440$, only.

[39] These findings are directly in line with the evidence reported in Andersen and Bollerslev (1997b), who rely on a flexible Fourier functional form in explicitly modeling the periodicity in the intradaily volatility along with the imposition of a declining weight structure for the announcement effects.

References

Andersen, Torben G., 1994, Stochastic autoregressive volatility: A framework for volatility modeling, *Mathematical Finance* 4, 75–102.

Andersen, Torben G., 1996, Return volatility and trading volume: An information flow interpretation of stochastic volatility, *Journal of Finance* 51, 169–204.

Andersen, Torben G., and Tim Bollerslev, 1997a, Intraday periodicity and volatility persistence in financial markets, *Journal of Empirical Finance*, forthcoming.

Andersen, Torben G, and Tim Bollerslev, 1997b, DM–Dollar volatility: Intraday activity patterns, macroeconomic announcements, and longer run dependencies, *Journal of Finance*, forthcoming.

Baillie, Richard T., 1996, Long-memory processes and fractional integration in econometrics, *Journal of Econometrics* 73, 5–59.

Baillie, Richard T., and Tim Bollerslev, 1991, Intra-day and inter-market volatility in foreign exchange rates, *Review of Economic Studies* 58, 565–585.

Baillie, Richard T., Tim Bollerslev, and Hans-Ole Mikkelsen, 1996, Fractionally integrated generalized autoregressive conditional heteroskedasticity, *Journal of Econometrics* 74, 3–30.

Baxter, Marianne, and Robert G. King, 1995, Measuring business cycles: Approximate band-pass filters for economic time series, Working paper, University of Virginia.

Beran, Jan, 1994, *Statistics for Long-Memory Processes* (Chapman and Hall, New York).

Bollerslev, Tim, Ray Y. Chou, and Kenneth F. Kroner, 1992, ARCH modeling in finance, *Journal of Econometrics* 52, 5–59.

Bollerslev, Tim, and Ian Domowitz, 1993, Trading patterns and prices in the interbank foreign exchange market, *Journal of Finance* 48, 1421–1443.

Bollerslev, Tim, and Robert F. Engle, 1993, Common persistence in conditional variances, *Econometrica* 61, 166–187.

Bollerslev, Tim, and Hans-Ole Mikkelsen, 1996, Modeling and pricing long-memory in stock market volatility, *Journal of Econometrics* 73, 151–184.

Breidt, F. Jay, Nuno Crato, and Pedro J. F. de Lima, 1997, On the detection and estimation of long memory in stochastic volatility, *Journal of Econometrics*, forthcoming.

Chambers, Marcus J., 1995, Long memory and aggregation in macroeconomic time series, Working paper, University of Essex.

Clark, Peter K., 1973, A subordinated stochastic process model with finite variance for speculative prices, *Econometrica* 41, 135–155.

Dacorogna, Michel M., Ulrich A. Müller, Robert J. Nagler, Richard B. Olsen, and Olivier V. Pictet, 1993, A geographical model for the daily and weekly seasonal volatility in the foreign exchange market, *Journal of International Money and Finance* 12, 413–438.

Delgado, Miguel A., and Peter M. Robinson, 1994, New methods for the analysis of long memory time series: application to Spanish inflation, *Journal of Forecasting* 13, 97–107.

Ding, Zhuanxin, and Clive W. J. Granger, 1996, Modeling volatility persistence of speculative returns: A new approach, *Journal of Econometrics* 73, 185–215.

Ding, Zhuanxin, Clive W. J. Granger, and Robert F. Engle, 1993, A long memory property of stock market returns and a new model, *Journal of Empirical Finance* 1, 83–106.

Drost, Feike C., and Theo E. Nijman, 1993, Temporal aggregation of GARCH processes, *Econometrica* 61, 909–927.

Ederington, Louis H., and Jae Ha Lee, 1993, How markets process information: News releases and volatility, *Journal of Finance* 48, 1161–1191.

Epps, Thomas W., and Mary L. Epps, 1976, The stochastic dependence of security price changes and transaction volumes: Implications for the mixture-of-distributions hypothesis, *Econometrica* 44, 305–321.

Gallant, A. Ronald, and George E. Tauchen, 1996, Which moments to match, *Econometric Theory* 12, 657–681.

Geweke, John, and Susan Porter-Hudak, 1983, The estimation and application of long-memory time series models, *Journal of Time Series Analysis* 4, 221–238.

Ghose, Devajyoti, and Kenneth F. Kroner, 1996, Components of volatility in foreign exchange markets: An empirical analysis of high frequency data, Working paper, University of Arizona.

Ghysels, Eric, and Joanna Jasiak, 1995, Trading patterns, time deformation, and stochastic volatility in foreign exchange markets, Working paper, University of Montreal.

Goodhart, Charles A. E., S. G. Hall, S. G. B. Henry, and B. Pesaran, 1993, News effects in a high-frequency model of the sterling-dollar exchange rate, *Journal of Applied Econometrics* 8, 1–13.

Goodhart, Charles A. E., Takatoshi Ito, and Richard Payne, 1996, One day in June 1993: A study of the working of Reuters' Dealing 2000-2 electronic foreign exchange trading system, in Jeffrey A. Frankel, Giampaolo Galli, and Alberto Giovannini, Eds.: *The Microstructure of Foreign Exchange Markets* (University of Chicago Press, Chicago).

Goodhart, Charles A. E., and Maureen O'Hara (1997), High frequency data in financial markets: Issues and applications, *Journal of Empirical Finance*, forthcoming.

Granger, Clive W. J., 1980, Long memory relationships and the aggregation of dynamic models, *Journal of Econometrics* 14, 227–238.

Granger, Clive W. J., 1988, Models that generate trends, *Journal of Time Series Analysis* 9, 329–343.

Granger, Clive W. J., 1987, Generalized integrated processes, Working paper, University of California, San Diego.

Granger, Clive W. J., and Zhuanxin Ding, 1996, Varieties of long memory models, *Journal of Econometrics* 73, 61–77.

Granger, Clive W. J., and Zhuanxin Ding, 1997, Some properties of absolute returns: An alternative measure of risk, *Annales d'Economie et de Statistique*, forthcoming.

Granger, Clive W. J., and Paul Newbold, 1976, Forecasting transformed series, *Journal of the Royal Statistical Society, Series B* 38, 189–203.

Hamilton, James D., 1994, *Time Series Analysis* (Princeton University Press: Princeton, N.J.).

Harris, Lawrence, 1986, A transaction data study of weekly and intradaily patterns in stock returns, *Journal of Financial Economics* 16, 99–117.

Harris, Lawrence, 1987, Transaction data tests of the mixture-of-distributions hypothesis, *Journal of Financial and Quantitative Analysis* 22, 127–141.

Harvey, Andrew C., 1994, Long-memory in stochastic volatility, Working paper, London School of Economics.

Harvey, Andrew C., and Mariane Streibel, 1996, Testing for a slowly changing level with special reference to stochastic volatility, Working paper, London School of Economics.

Henry, Marc, and Richard Payne, 1996, An investigation of long range dependence in intra-day foreign exchange rate volatility, Working paper, London School of Economics.

Hogan, Kedreth C., Jr., and Michael T. Melvin, 1994, Sources of heat waves and meteor showers in the foreign exchange markets, *Journal of International Economics* 37, 239–247.

Ito, Takatoshi, and V. Vance Roley, 1987, News from the U.S. and Japan: Which moves the yen/dollar exchange rate?, *Journal of Monetary Economics* 19, 255–277.

Ito, Takatoshi, Richard K. Lyons, and Michael T. Melvin, 1996, Is there private information in the FX market? The Tokyo experiment, Working paper, University of California at Berkeley.

Jacquier, Eric, Nicholas G. Polson, and Peter E. Rossi, 1994, Bayesian analysis of stochastic volatility models, *Journal of Business and Economic Statistics* 12, 371–417.

Johnson, Norman L., and Samuel Kotz, 1970, *Continuous Univariate Distributions –2* (John Wiley and Sons, New York).

Lamoureux, Christopher G., and William D. Lastrapes, 1990, Persistence in variance, structural change, and the GARCH model, *Journal of Business and Economic Statistics* 8, 225–234.

Lin, Jin-Lung, 1991, Generalized integrated processes and the aggregation of dynamic time series, *Academia Economic Papers* 19, 207–226.

Lobato, Ignacio N., and Peter M. Robinson, 1996, Averaged periodogram estimation of long-memory, *Journal of Econometrics* 73, 303–324.

Mandelbrot, Benoit B., 1971, A fast fractional Gaussian noise generator, *Water Resources Research* 7, 543–553.

Mandelbrot, Benoit B., and J. R. Wallis, 1969, Computer experiments with fractional Gaussian noises, *Water Resources Research* 5, 321–340.

Mandelbrot, Benoit B., and J. W. van Ness, 1968, Fractional Brownian motions, fractional noises and applications, *SIAM Review* 10, 422–437.

Merton, Robert C., 1980, On estimating the expected return on the market, *Journal of Financial Economics* 8, 323–361.

Müller, Ulrich A., Michel M. Dacorogna, Rakhal D. Davé, Richard B. Olsen, Olivier V. Pictet, and Jakob E. von Weizsäcker, 1997, Volatilities of different time resolutions—-Analyzing the dynamics of market components, *Journal of Empirical Finance*, forthcoming.

Müller, Ulrich A., Michel M. Dacorogna, and Olivier V. Pictet, 1996, Heavy tails in high-frequency financial data, Working paper, Olsen & Associates, Research Institute for Applied Economics, Zürich, Switzerland.

Müller, Ulrich A., Michel M. Dacorogna, Rakhal D. Davé, Olivier V. Pictet, Richard B. Olsen, and Robert Ward, 1993, Fractals and intrinsic time—-A challenge to econometricians, Working paper, Olsen & Associates, Research Institute for Applied Economics, Zürich, Switzerland.

Nelson, Daniel B., 1990, ARCH models as diffusion approximations, *Journal of Econometrics* 45, 7–38.

Nelson, Daniel B., 1992, Filtering and forecasting with misspecified ARCH models: Getting the right variance with the wrong model, *Journal of Econometrics* 52, 61–90.

Perron, Pierre, 1989, The great crash, the oil price shock, and the unit root hypothesis, *Econometrica* 57, 1361–1401.

Priestley, Maurice B., 1981, *Spectral Analysis and Time Series* (Academic Press, London, UK).

Robinson, Peter M., 1994a, Semiparametric analysis of long-memory time series, *Annals of Statistics* 22, 515–539.

Robinson, Peter M., 1994b, Time series with strong dependence, in Christopher A. Sims, ed.: *Advances in Econometrics: Sixth World Congress* (Cambridge University Press, Cambridge, UK).

Robinson, Peter M., 1995, Log-periodogram regression of time series with long-range dependence, *Annals of Statistics* 23, 1048–1072.

Ross, Stephen A., 1976, The arbitrage theory of capital asset pricing, *Journal of Economic Theory* 13, 341–360.

Ross, Stephen A., 1989, Information and volatility: The no-arbitrage martingale approach to timing and resolution irrelevancy, *Journal of Finance* 44, 1–18.

Shephard, Neil, 1996, Statistical aspects of ARCH and stochastic volatility, in David R. Cox, David V. Hinkley, and Ole E. Barndorff-Nielsen, Eds.: *Likelihood, Time Series with Econometric and Other Applications* (Chapman and Hall, London, UK).

Shiller, Robert J., and Pierre Perron, 1985, Testing the random walk hypothesis: Power versus frequency of observations, *Economics Letters* 18, 381–386.

Tauchen, George E., and Mark Pitts, 1983, The price variability-volume relationship on speculative markets, *Econometrica* 51, 485–505.

Taylor, Stephen J., 1994, Modeling stochastic volatility, *Mathematical Finance* 4, 183–204.

Tieslau, Margie A., Peter Schmidt, and Richard T. Baillie, 1996, A minimum distance estimator for long-memory processes, *Journal of Econometrics* 71, 249–264.

Wood, Robert A., Thomas H. McInish, and J. Keith Ord, 1985, An investigation of transaction data for NYSE stocks, *Journal of Finance* 25, 723–739.

The Massachusetts Institute of Technology Generation

Twenty-Six

Leonid Kogan

Leonid Kogan received a Ph.D. from the Massachusetts Institute of Technology in 1999. He started out at the Wharton School, University of Pennsylvania, and now works at the Sloan School of Management, the Massachusetts Institute of Technology. •

When Steve Ross had joined MIT faculty, I was in my third year of graduate studies. His arrival was highly anticipated by faculty and students alike, after all his works accounted for a sizeable portion of the reading list for our first-year Ph.D. asset pricing class. The intimidation factor was, accordingly, substantial, and my initial interactions with Steve were mostly limited to observing him in seminars and auditing that first-year class which he was then teaching. Pretty quickly, I knew that in addition to his formidable intellect and encyclopedic knowledge of the field, Steve also possesses a certain je ne sais quoi, which I can best capture by paraphrasing a famous remark attributed to Stefan Banach: "Good minds see analogies. Great minds see analogies between analogies." It was clear that Steve's is one of these rare great minds.

Once I began discussing research with Steve, I discovered that despite the astonishing list of professional accomplishments, Steve is one of the most approachable, down-to-earth people I know. This is not to say that talking to Steve was always easy, because trying to keep up with turns and twists of his arguments is an exhilarating but a demanding task. However, I cannot remember him ever being discouraging in his feedback or trying to impose his own tastes. Instead, he was always willing to help, motivating by his own example to try harder and reach farther.

After graduation, I have been fortunate to interact with Steve as a fellow colleague. One recurrent theme in our conversations has been the growing influence of behavioral-finance ideas and their interaction with the neoclassical paradigm. Many fascinating discussions on this topic among Steve, Jiang Wang, Mark Westerfield and me have finally culminated in a paper, "The Price Impact and Survival of Irrational Traders." Quite a few people told me upon reading our results that they were surprised to see Steve, an outspoken proponent of neoclassical finance, endorse the message that irrational traders may have a sustained impact on prices, even in a frictionless financial market. My response to this has been that Steve does not object to behavioral finance as an area of research; he simply has little tolerance for what he sees as sloppy research, be it behavioral or neoclassical, empirical, or theoretical. To me, as to numerous collaborators and students of Steve's, his intellectual honesty and commitment to the highest standard of quality in any scientific pursuit have been a profound lesson and a source of constant inspiration.

Equilibrium Cross Section of Returns

Joao Gomes
University of Pennsylvania
Leonid Kogan
Massachusetts Institute of Technology
Lu Zhang
University of Rochester

We construct a dynamic general equilibrium production economy to explicitly link expected stock returns to firm characteristics such as firm size and the book-to-market ratio. Stock returns in the model are completely characterized by a conditional capital asset pricing model (CAPM). Size and book-to-market are correlated with the true conditional market beta and therefore appear to predict stock returns. The cross-sectional relations between firm characteristics and returns can subsist even after one controls for typical empirical estimates of beta. These findings suggest that the empirical success of size and book-to-market can be consistent with a single-factor conditional CAPM model. •

I. Introduction

The cross-sectional properties of stock returns have attracted considerable attention in recent empirical literature in financial economics. One of the best-known studies, by Fama and French (1992), uncovers the relations between firm characteristics such as book-to-market ratio and firm size and stock returns, which appear to be inconsistent with the standard capital asset pricing model (CAPM). Despite their empirical success, these simple statistical relations have proved very hard to rationalize, and their precise economic source remains a subject of debate.[1]

We construct a dynamic stochastic general equilibrium one-factor model in which firms differ in characteristics such as size, book value, investment, and productivity, among others. It establishes an explicit economic relation between firm-level characteristics and stock returns. The simple structure of our model provides a parsimonious description of the firm-level returns and makes it a natural benchmark for interpreting many empirical regularities.

---

[1]Campbell, Lo, and MacKinlay (1997), Cochrane (1999), and Campbell (2000) review the related literature. Various competing interpretations of observed empirical regularities include, among others, Lo and MacKinlay (1988), Fama and French (1993, 1995, 1996), Lakonishok, Shleifer, and Vishny (1994), Berk (1995), Kothari, Shanken, and Sloan (1995), MacKinlay (1995), Jagannathan and Wang (1996), Berk, Green, and Naik (1999), Liew and Vassalou (2000), and Lettau and Ludvigson (2001).

We gratefully acknowledge the helpful comments of Andy Abel, Jonathan Berk, Michael Brandt, John Cochrane, Kent Daniel, Gary Gorton, Shmuel Kandel, Craig MacKinlay, Robert Stambaugh, Jiang Wang, Amir Yaron, three anonymous referees, and seminar participants at the National Bureau of Economic Research Fall 2000 Asset Pricing meeting, the 2001 meeting of the Western Finance Association, the 2001 meeting of the Society of Economic Dynamics, Carnegie Mellon University, New York University, Stanford University, University of British Columbia, University of Chicago, University of Rochester, University of California at Los Angeles, and Wharton. All remaining errors are our own.

Reprinted with permission:
Gomes, Joao, Leonid Kogan, and Lu Zhang. "Equilibrium Cross Section of Returns." *Journal of Political Economy* 111 (2003): 693–732.

First, we show that our one-factor equilibrium model can still capture the ability of book-to-market and firm value to describe the cross section of stock returns. These relations can subsist after one controls for typical empirical estimates of conditional market beta. Second, we find that, in our model, the cross-sectional dispersion in individual stock returns is related to the aggregate stock market volatility and business cycle conditions. Third, we show that the size and book-to-market return premia are inherently conditional in their nature and likely countercyclical.

Our theoretical approach builds on the work of Berk et al. (1999), who construct a partial equilibrium model also based on the ideas of time-varying risks to explain cross-sectional variations of stock returns. However, our work differs along several important dimensions. First, ours is a single-factor model in which the conditional CAPM holds, whereas the model of Berk et al. introduces a second risk factor in addition to the market portfolio. The simple structure of our model allows us to derive an explicit link between the beta (and hence returns) and firm characteristics such as size and book-to-market. Instead of appealing to multiple sources of risk, we emphasize the role of beta mismeasurement in generating the observed cross-sectional relations between the Fama and French factors and stock returns. Second, by explicitly modeling the production and investment decisions of the firms, we are able to integrate our cross-sectional analysis into a general equilibrium model that allows us to present a self-consistent account of the business cycle properties of returns.

Our work belongs to a growing literature that explores the implications of production and investment on the cross section of returns. In addition to Berk et al. (1999), recent examples include Cochrane (1996), Gomes, Yaron, and Zhang (2002), and Zhang (2002). More broadly, this paper is also related to a variety of recent papers that focus on the asset pricing implications of production and investment in the time series. Examples of this line of research include Bossaerts and Green (1989), Cochrane (1991), Naik (1994), Rouwenhorst (1995), Coleman (1997), Jermann (1998), and Kogan (2000, 2001). To the best of our knowledge, however, this is the first work aiming directly at explaining the cross-sectional variations of stock returns from a structural general equilibrium perspective.

II. The Model

We develop a general equilibrium model with heterogeneous firms. There are two types of agents: a single representative household and a large number of competitive firms producing a single consumption good.

A. Production Sector

Production of the consumption good takes place in basic productive units, which we label *projects*. New projects are continuously arriving in the economy. Projects are owned by firms, and each firm operates a number of individual projects of different characteristics.

Existing Projects Let $\mathcal{I}_t$ denote the set of all projects existing at time t, and let i be the index of an individual project. Projects expire randomly according to an idiosyncratic Poisson process with common hazard rate δ (we define the arrival of new projects below). Existing projects have two individual features: productivity and scale.

Productivity is driven by a component common to all projects, x_t, and a project-specific element, ϵ_{it}. We assume that x_t follows the linear mean-reverting process,

$$dx_t = -\theta_x(x_t - \bar{x})dt + \sigma_x dB_{xt}, \tag{1}$$

and that ϵ_{it} is driven by a square root process,

$$d\epsilon_{it} = \theta_\epsilon(1 - \epsilon_{it})dt + \sigma_\epsilon\sqrt{\epsilon_{it}}\,dB_{it}, \tag{2}$$

where B_{xt} and B_{it} are standard Brownian motions.[2] We assume that the idiosyncratic productivity shocks are independent of the economywide productivity shock, that is, $dB_{xt}dB_{it} = 0$ for all i. We make a further assumption that if projects i and j are owned by the same firm (see below), $dB_{it}dB_{jt} = dt$; otherwise we set $dB_{it}dB_{jt} = 0$.

While the specific nature of processes (1) and (2) is merely convenient, mean reversion is important. At the aggregate level, it is necessary to ensure that the growth rate of output does not explode, a result consistent with standard findings in the growth literature (Kaldor 1961). At the firm level, mean reversion is required to obtain a stationary distribution of firms in equilibrium and is consistent with the evidence suggesting that growth rates decline with size and age (Evans 1987; Hall 1987).

The scale of a project, denoted k_i, is set at the time of creation, and it remains fixed throughout the life of the project. Given its scale and productivity, each project generates a flow of output (cash flows) at rate $\exp(x_t)\epsilon_{it}k_i$. We compute the net present value of the future stream of cash flows associated with the project, $P(x_t, \epsilon_{it}, k_i)$. Let $M_{t,t+s}$ denote the pricing kernel, which determines prices of all financial assets. If an asset pays a flow of dividends at rate Z_s, its time t price is given by

$$E_t\left[\int_0^\infty M_{t,t+s}Z_{t+s}\,ds\right].$$

Proposition 1. *Project valuation.*—The value of an existing project i is given by

$$\begin{aligned} P(x_t, \epsilon_{it}, k_i) &= E_t\left[\int_0^\infty e^{-\delta s}M_{t,t+s}(e^{x_{t+s}}\epsilon_{i,t+s}k_i)ds\right] \\ &= k_i[p(x_t) + \tilde{p}(x_t)(\epsilon_{it} - 1)], \end{aligned} \tag{3}$$

where $p(x_t)$ and $\tilde{p}(x_t)$ are defined as

$$p(x_t) = E_t\left[\int_0^\infty e^{-\delta s}M_{t,t+s}e^{x_{t+s}}ds\right] \tag{4}$$

and

$$\tilde{p}(x_t) = E_t\left[\int_0^\infty e^{-(\delta+\theta_\epsilon)s}M_{t,t+s}e^{x_{t+s}}ds\right]. \tag{5}$$

Proof See Appendix A

In (3), $e^{x_{t+s}}\epsilon_{i,t+s}k_i$ is the cash flow rate of project i, which is valued using the pricing kernel $M_{t,t+s}$. The factor $e^{-\delta s}$ captures the fact that existing projects expire randomly at rate δ. The present value $p(x)$ represents the component of the value of an existing project attributable to the level of aggregate productivity, and $\tilde{p}(x)$ captures the sensitivity of the value of the project to the idiosyncratic component of its productivity.

[2]The process in (1) is chosen to possess a stationary long-run distribution with constant instantaneous volatility. The advantage of (2) is that the conditional expectation of ϵ_{it} is an exponential function of time and a linear function of the initial value ϵ_{i0}, which facilitates computation of individual stock prices below. An additional advantage of this process is that its unconditional mean is independent of θ_ϵ and σ_ϵ, which simplifies the calibration.

Note that $p(x)$ and $\tilde{p}(x)$ differ only in the rate of discount, which implies that $\tilde{p}(x) < p(x)$, for all x. In addition, as $\theta_\epsilon \to 0$, we have that $\tilde{p}(x) \to p(x)$ and $P(x_t, \epsilon_{it}, k_i) = p(x_t)\epsilon_{it} k_i$.

New Projects At the aggregate level, new potential projects arrive continuously. These projects can be adopted at time t with an investment cost of $e_{it}k_i$, where e_{it} is the unit cost of adoption. If the project is not adopted, it disappears.

We assume that during any period $[t, t + dt]$, multiple projects arrive with various values of their unit cost e_{it}. For simplicity, we are assuming that the arrival rate of new projects is independent of project unit cost. The production scale of all new projects with unit cost between e and $e + de$ arriving during the time interval $[t, t + dt]$ adds up to $h_t dedt$, where h_t determines the instantaneous arrival rate of new projects.

We make two additional simplifying assumptions regarding the scale and productivity of these new projects. First, all projects of the same vintage have the same scale, k_i. This scale is chosen to ensure that the number of projects per firm has a stationary distribution (see App. B for details). Second, the initial productivity of a new project is drawn from the long-run distribution implied by (2), but only *after* the project is adopted. Given these assumptions, the value of a new project at time t immediately *before* the project is adopted is given by

$$E[P(x_t, \epsilon_{it}, k_i) \mid x_t] = k_i p(x_t)$$

since $E[\epsilon_{it} | x_t] = 1$.

Firms Projects are owned by infinitely lived firms. We assume that the set of firms $\mathcal{F}$ is exogenously fixed and let f be the index of an individual firm. Each firm owns a finite set of individual projects, $\mathcal{I}_{ft}$, which changes over time as new projects get adopted and existing projects expire.

Firms are financed entirely by equity, and outstanding equity of each firm is normalized to one share. We denote the firm's f stock price at time t by V_{ft}. Stocks represent claims on the dividends paid by firms to shareholders, and we assume that the dividend equals the firm's output net of investment costs. We assume that firms are competitive and their objective is to maximize the market value of their equity.

Regardless of its unit cost, each new project is allocated to a randomly chosen firm. Hence, all firms have an equal probability of receiving a new project at any point in time. Assuming that all firms are equally likely to receive new projects allows for tractability, but it is not crucial. Qualitatively, we need firm growth to be negatively related to size, a fact well documented in the data.

While firms do not control the scale or productivity of their projects, they make investment decisions by selecting which of these new projects to adopt. If the firm decides to invest in a new project, it must incur the required investment cost, which in turn entitles it to the permanent ownership of the project. These investment decisions are irreversible, and investment cost cannot be recovered at a later date.

For the firm, the arrival rate of new projects is independent of its own past investment decisions. Thus the decision to accept or reject a specific project has no effect on the individual firm's future investment opportunities and therefore can be made using a standard net present value rule. Given that the present value of future cash flows from a new project at time t equals $k_i p(x_t)$, it follows that new projects are adopted if and only if their unit investment cost is below $p(x_t)$:

$$e_{it} \leq p(x_t). \tag{6}$$

FIGURE 1 | Arrival of New Projects.
This figure illustrates the project arrival rate h_t as a function of its unit cost e. The function $p(x_t)$ denotes the component of the value of an existing project attributable to the level of aggregate productivity.

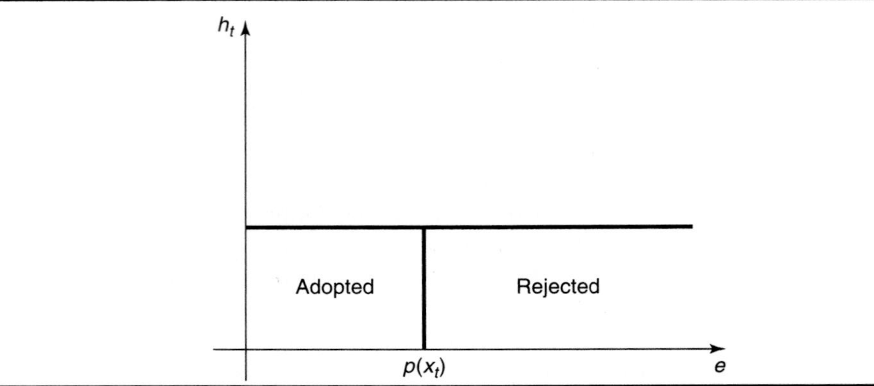

Hence, the decision to adopt new projects can be summarized by a function of aggregate productivity, x_t. Figure 1 illustrates this.

The value of the firm, V_{ft}, can be viewed as the sum of the present value of output from existing projects, V_{ft}^a, plus the present value of dividends (output net of investment) from future projects, V_{ft}^o. With the terminology from Berk et al. (1999), V_{ft}^a represents the value of *assets in place*, defined as

$$V_{ft}^a = \sum_{i \in \mathcal{I}_{ft}} P(x_t, \epsilon_{it}, k_i) = \sum_{i \in \mathcal{I}_{ft}} k_i [p(x_i) + \tilde{p}(x_t)(\epsilon_{it} - 1)], \tag{7}$$

whereas $V_{ft}^o = V_{ft} - V_{ft}^a$ can be interpreted as the value of *growth options*.

For future use we also define the book value of a firm as the sum of book values of the firm's (active) individual projects, $B_{ft} = \Sigma_{i \in \mathcal{I}_{ft}} e_i k_i$, and the book value of a project is defined as the associated investment cost $e_i k_i$.

Aggregation Let $\int_{\mathcal{I}_t} \cdot \, di$ denote the aggregation operator over projects, and define the aggregate scale of production in the economy, K_t, as

$$K_t \equiv \int_{\mathcal{I}_t} k_i di.$$

It follows that aggregate output, Y_t, is given by

$$Y_t = \int_{\mathcal{I}_t} \exp(x_t) k_i \epsilon_{it} di = \exp(x_t) K_t, \tag{8}$$

where the second equality follows from the fact that the project scale, k_i, is fixed at time of creation and is independent of idiosyncratic productivity, ϵ_{it}, and the law of large numbers applied to ϵ_{it}'s, which are independently and identically distributed with unit mean.[3] Equation (8) is then consistent with our interpretation of x_t as the aggregate productivity shock.

[3]Feldman and Gilles (1985) formalize the law of large numbers in economies with countably infinite numbers of agents by aggregating with respect to a finitely additive measure over the set of agents. Judd (1985) demonstrates that a measure and the corresponding law of large numbers can be meaningfully introduced for economies with a continuum of agents.

Since active projects expire at rate δ, whereas new projects are adopted only if their creation cost is below $p(x_t)$, the total scale of projects in the economy evolves according to

$$dK_t = -\delta K_t dt + \left[\int_0^{p(x_t)} h_t de\right] dt. \tag{9}$$

Balanced growth requires that the aggregate arrival rate, h_t, be proportional to the aggregate scale of existing projects, K_t. Formally, we assume that $h_t = zK_t$, where the parameter z governs the quality of the investment opportunity set.

Given our assumptions about h_t, (9) implies that the change in the total scale of production is given by

$$dK_t = -\delta K_t dt + zK_t p(x_t) dt \tag{10}$$

and the amount of resources used in the creation of new projects, I_t, equals

$$I_t = I(x_t) \equiv \int_0^{p(x_t)} ezK_t de = \tfrac{1}{2} zK_t [p(x_t)]^2. \tag{11}$$

The aggregate dividend of firms equals the aggregate output net of aggregate investment and is given by

$$D_t \equiv Y_t - I_t = \{e^{x_t} - \tfrac{1}{2} z\, [p(x_t)]^2\} K_t. \tag{12}$$

Note that since $p(x)$ is increasing in x, this implies that more expensive projects are adopted only in good times, when x_t is high. This rising cost of investment is then similar to the result obtained in a standard convex adjustment cost model. Together, our assumptions about productivity and costs guarantee that individual investment decisions can be aggregated into a linear stochastic growth model with adjustment costs. This provides a tractable setting for addressing the behavior of the cross section of returns.

The production environment in our model differs from that in Berk et al. (1999) in a number of critical aspects. First, Berk et al. simply assume that cash flows of existing projects are independently distributed over time and have a constant beta with respect to an exogenous stochastic pricing kernel that is driven by serially independent shocks. Second, in their model, exogenous fluctuations in real interest rates are driven by a separate first-order-stationary Markov process, creating an additional source of risk. As a consequence, the value of existing assets is exposed to two risk factors: while the capital gains component of returns is related to fluctuations in interest rates, cash flows from existing projects covary with the shocks to the pricing kernel. Moreover, the present value of future projects, that is, the value of growth options, depends only on the current level of the interest rate, since unexpected changes in the pricing kernel are independently and identically distributed. Thus, while the value of existing assets is exposed to both sources of risk, the value of growth options has a positive loading only on the level of the interest rate.

B. Households

The economy is populated by identical competitive households, which derive utility from the consumption flow of the single good, C_t. The entire population can then be modeled as a single representative household, and we assume that this household has standard time-separable iso-elastic preferences,

$$E_0\left[\frac{1}{1-\gamma}\int_0^{\infty} e^{-\lambda t} C_t^{1-\gamma} dt\right], \tag{13}$$

where λ is the subjective rate of discount and γ is the coefficient of relative risk aversion. Households do not work and derive income from accumulated wealth, W_t. We assume that there exists a complete set of financial markets and there are no frictions and no constraints on short sales or borrowing. The term $M_{t,t+s}$ is the unique equilibrium pricing kernel, which determines prices of all financial assets.

The representative household maximizes the expected utility of consumption (13), taking the prices of financial assets as given. In a complete financial market, the budget constraint is given by

$$E_t\left[\int_0^{\infty} M_{t,t+s}C_{t+s}ds\right] \leq W_t. \tag{14}$$

Optimality conditions imply a well-known relation between the consumption policy and the pricing kernel:

$$M_{t,t+s} = e^{-\lambda s}\left(\frac{C_t}{C_{t+s}}\right)^{\gamma}. \tag{15}$$

C. The Competitive Equilibrium

With the description of the economic environment complete, we are now in a position to state the definition of the competitive equilibrium.

Definition 1. *Competitive equilibrium.*—A competitive equilibrium is summarized by the pricing kernel $M_{t,t+s}$, the optimal household consumption policy C_t, and firm investment policy, described by $p(x_t)$, such that the following conditions hold: (*a*) Optimization: (i) With the equilibrium asset prices taken as given, households maximize their expected utility (13), subject to the budget constraint (14). (ii) With the equilibrium asset prices taken as given, firms select new projects according to (6) and (4). (*b*) Market clearing: Representative household consumption equals the aggregate dividend, given by (12):

$$C_t = D_t. \tag{16}$$

The competitive equilibrium has a very convenient structure. Since the cross-sectional distribution of firms has no impact on aggregate quantities, we characterize the optimal consumption and investment policies first and use them to compute the aggregate stock market value. Given the aggregate quantities, we then express explicitly the individual firm prices and returns.

Proposition 2 establishes that the optimal policies for consumption and investment can be characterized by a system of one differential equation and one algebraic equation.

Proposition 2. *Equilibrium allocations.*—The competitive equilibrium is characterized by the optimal investment policy, described by $p(x)$ in (6), and consumption policy, $C(x, K)$, which satisfy

$$C(x, K) = \{e^x - \tfrac{1}{2}z[p(x)]^2\}K \tag{17}$$

and

$$p(x) = \{e^x - \tfrac{1}{2}z[p(x)]^2\}^{\gamma}\phi(x), \tag{18}$$

where the function $\phi(x)$ satisfies

$$e^x\{e^x - \tfrac{1}{2}z[p(x)]^2\}^{-\gamma} = [\lambda + (1-\gamma)\delta + \gamma z p(x)]\phi(x) - \mathcal{A}[\phi(x)] \tag{19}$$

and $\mathcal{A}[\cdot]$ is the infinitesimal generator of the diffusion process x_t:

$$\mathcal{A}[g(x)] \equiv -\theta_x(x - \bar{x})g'(x) + \tfrac{1}{2}\sigma_x^2 g''(x). \tag{20}$$

Proof See Appendix A.

This concept of general equilibrium is also one of the key novelties in our analysis relative to that of Berk et al. (1999), who instead proceed by keeping the pricing kernel, $M_{t,t+s}$, entirely exogenous, thus separating the optimal investment decisions from the consumption allocation.

D. Asset Prices

With the optimal allocations computed, we now characterize the asset prices in the economy, including the risk-free interest rate and both the aggregate and firm-level stock prices.

Aggregate Prices The following proposition summarizes the results for the equilibrium values of the risk-free rate, r_t, and the aggregate stock market value, V_t.

Proposition 3. *Equilibrium asset prices.*—The instantaneous risk-free interest rate is determined by

$$r_t = -\frac{E_t[M_{t,t+dt} - 1]}{dt} = \lambda + \gamma[zp(x_t) - \delta] + \gamma\frac{\mathcal{A}[C(x_t, K_t)]}{C_t} - \tfrac{1}{2}\gamma(\gamma + 1)\sigma_x^2\left[\frac{\partial \ln C(x_t, K_t)}{\partial x_t}\right]^2. \tag{21}$$

The aggregate stock market value, V_t, can be computed as

$$\begin{aligned} V_t &= E_t\left[\int_0^\infty M_{t,t+s}D_{t+s}ds\right] \\ &= E_t\left[\int_0^\infty e^{-\lambda s}\left(\frac{C_t}{C_{t+s}}\right)^\gamma C_{t+s}ds\right] \\ &= \{e^{x_t} - \tfrac{1}{2}z[p(x_t)]^2\}^\gamma \psi(x_t)K_t, \end{aligned} \tag{22}$$

where the function $\psi(x)$ satisfies the differential equation

$$\lambda\psi(x) = \{e^x - \tfrac{1}{2}z[p(x)]^2\}^{1-\gamma} + (1 - \gamma)[zp(x) - \delta]\psi(x) + \mathcal{A}[\psi(x)],$$

and $\mathcal{A}[\cdot]$ is defined as in (20).

Proof See Appendix A.

While these exact conditions are somewhat technical, the intuition behind them is quite simple. The instantaneous risk-free interest rate is completely determined by the equilibrium consumption process of the representative household and its implied properties for the pricing kernel. The aggregate stock market value represents a claim on the future stream of aggregate dividends, D_t, paid out by firms, which in equilibrium must equal aggregate consumption, C_t.

Finally, given (22), we can also define the process for cumulative aggregate stock returns as

$$\frac{dR_t}{R_t} = \frac{dV_t + D_t dt}{V_t}. \tag{23}$$

In addition to the definition above, the value of the stock market can also be viewed as a sum of two components. The first is the value of assets in place: the present value of output from existing projects. It is given by the expression

$$\begin{aligned} V_t^a &= \int_{\mathcal{F}} V_{ft}^a \, df \\ &= \int_{\mathcal{F}} \left\{ \sum_{i \in \mathcal{I}_{ft}} k_i [p(x_t) + \widetilde{p}(x_t)(\epsilon_{it} - 1)] \right\} df \\ &= p(x_t) \int_{\mathcal{I}_t} k_i di + \widetilde{p}(x_t) \int_{\mathcal{I}_t} k_i(\epsilon_{it} - 1) di \\ &= p(x_t) K_t, \end{aligned} \tag{24}$$

where the last equality follows from applying the law of large numbers to ϵ_{it}. The difference between the aggregate market value and the value of assets in place is the value of aggregate growth options, defined as the present value of dividends from all projects to be adopted in the future. By definition, the value of aggregate growth options equals

$$V_t^o = V_t - V_t^a. \tag{25}$$

Firm-Level Stock Prices Valuation of individual stocks is straightforward once the aggregate market value is computed. First, the value of a firm's stock is the sum of the value of assets in place for the firm, (7), and the value of growth options. Given our assumption that new projects are distributed randomly across all firms with equal probabilities, all firms will derive the same value from growth options. Hence, the value of growth options for each firm, V_{ft}^o, equals

$$V_{ft}^o = \bar{V}_t^o = \frac{1}{\int_{\mathcal{F}} 1 df} V_t^o. \tag{26}$$

We obtain the total value of the firm, V_{ft}, as

$$V_{ft} = \sum_{i \in \mathcal{I}_{ft}} k_i [\widetilde{p}(x_t)(\epsilon_{it} - 1) + p(x_t)] + \bar{V}_t^o. \tag{27}$$

By relating individual firm value to market aggregates, the decomposition (27) implies that the instantaneous market betas of individual stock returns can also be expressed as a weighted average of market betas of three *economywide* variables, p, $\widetilde{p}$, and $\bar{V}_t^o$. Proposition 4 formally establishes this property.

Proposition 4. *Market betas of individual stocks.*—Firm market betas are described by

$$\beta_{ft} = \widetilde{\beta}_t^a + \frac{\bar{V}_t^o}{V_{ft}} (\beta_t^o - \widetilde{\beta}_t^a) + p(x_t) \frac{K_{ft}}{V_{ft}} (\beta_t^a - \widetilde{\beta}_t^a), \tag{28}$$

where

$$K_{ft} = \sum_{i \in \mathcal{I}_{ft}} k_i$$

and

$$\beta_t^a = \frac{\partial \log p_t / \partial x}{\partial \log V_t / \partial x}, \qquad \widetilde{\beta}_t^a = \frac{\partial \log \widetilde{p}_t / \partial x}{\partial \log V_t / \partial x}, \qquad \beta_t^o = \frac{\partial \log V_t^o / \partial x}{\partial \log V_t / \partial x}. \tag{29}$$

Proof Since the market beta of a portfolio of assets is a value-weighted average of betas of its individual components, the expression for the value of the firm (27) implies that

$$\beta_{ft} = \left(1 - \frac{V_{ft}^o}{V_{ft}}\right)\beta_{ft}^a + \frac{V_{ft}^o}{V_{ft}}\beta_t^o$$
$$= \left(1 - \frac{V_{ft}^o}{V_{ft}}\right)[(1 - \pi_{ft})\,\widetilde{\beta}_t^a + \pi_{ft}\beta_t^a] + \frac{V_{ft}^o}{V_{ft}}\beta_t^o,$$

where

$$\pi_{ft} = \frac{K_{ft}}{V_{ft}^a}\left(\frac{K_t}{V_t^a}\right)^{-1} = \frac{K_{ft}}{V_{ft}^a}p(x_t).$$

Simple manipulation then yields (28). Q.E.D.

Stock Returns and Firm Characteristics By definition, β^a is the market risk of aggregate assets in place, (24), and β^o is the market risk of aggregate growth options, (25). Potential future projects are valued as growth options because they have a positive net present value; that is, new potential projects are adopted only if $p(x) - e > 0$. Since the volatility of $p(x) - e$ exceeds the volatility of $p(x)$, this leverage effect will likely imply that $\beta^o > \beta^a$. In this respect, our model differs from that of Berk et al. (1999) in that the risk of growth options in their model is relatively low, being entirely determined by the exogenous process for the interest rate.[4]

At the level of individual projects, according to the interpretation of the present values $p(x_t)$ and $\widetilde{p}(x_t)$, β^a describes the component of systematic risk that is common to all existing projects, and $\widetilde{\beta}^a$ captures the cross-sectional differences between projects due to the idiosyncratic component of their productivity. The relation between these two aggregates is less immediate. By definition, $p(x_t)$ and $\widetilde{p}(x_t)$ differ only with respect to the discount rate in the present value relations (4) and (5). Since the "effective duration" of the cash flows defining $p(x_t)$ exceeds that of $\widetilde{p}(x_t)$, the relation between β^a and $\widetilde{\beta}^a$ depends on the equilibrium term premium; specifically, a positive term premium will tend to raise β^a relative to $\widetilde{\beta}^a$. In the calibrated version of our model, β^a actually exceeds $\widetilde{\beta}^a$, as shown in figure 2. This implies that more productive projects, that is, those with higher values of ϵ_{it}, have lower systematic risk in our model.

Proposition 4 shows that the weights on the "aggregate" betas, β_t^a, $\widetilde{\beta}_t^a$ and β_t^o, depend on the economywide variables $p(x_t)$ and V_t^o and, more important, on firm-specific characteristics such as the size, or value, of the firm, V_{ft}, and the ratio of the firm's production scale to its market value, K_{ft}/V_{ft}.

The second term in (28) creates an inverse relation between size and beta, as the weight on the beta of growth options, β_t^o, depends on the value of the firm's growth options relative to its total market value. Firms with a small production scale, K_{ft}, derive most of their value from growth options, and their betas are close to β_t^o. Since all firms in our economy have identical growth options, the cross-sectional dispersion of betas due to the loading on β_t^o is captured entirely by the size variable V_{ft}. Large firms, on the other hand, derive a larger proportion of their value from assets in place; therefore, their betas are close to a weighted average of β_t^a and $\widetilde{\beta}_t^a$. While this "size effect" is a result of our assumption about the distribution of growth options across firms, the effect will survive as long as V_{ft}^o/V_{ft} differs across firms, which requires only that growth options are less than proportional to size. Given the observed negative relation between firm size and growth (Evans 1987; Hall 1987), this seems quite plausible.

[4]See Berk et al. (1999, n. 7) for a detailed discussion of this issue.

FIGURE 2 | Some Key-Aggregate Variables in Competitive Equilibrium.
This figure plots some key aggregate variables in competitive equilibrium. *a*, Market Sharpe ratio. *b*, Volatility of consumption growth. *c*, The function *p(x)* or, equivalently, V^a/K in (24). *d*, The ratio of total market value to aggregate capital stock, V/K. *e*, The ratio of aggregate value of assets in place to total market value, V^a/V. *f*, Three aggregate-level betas: β^a (solid line), $\tilde{\beta}^a$ (dashed-dotted line), and β^o (dashed line), defined in (29).

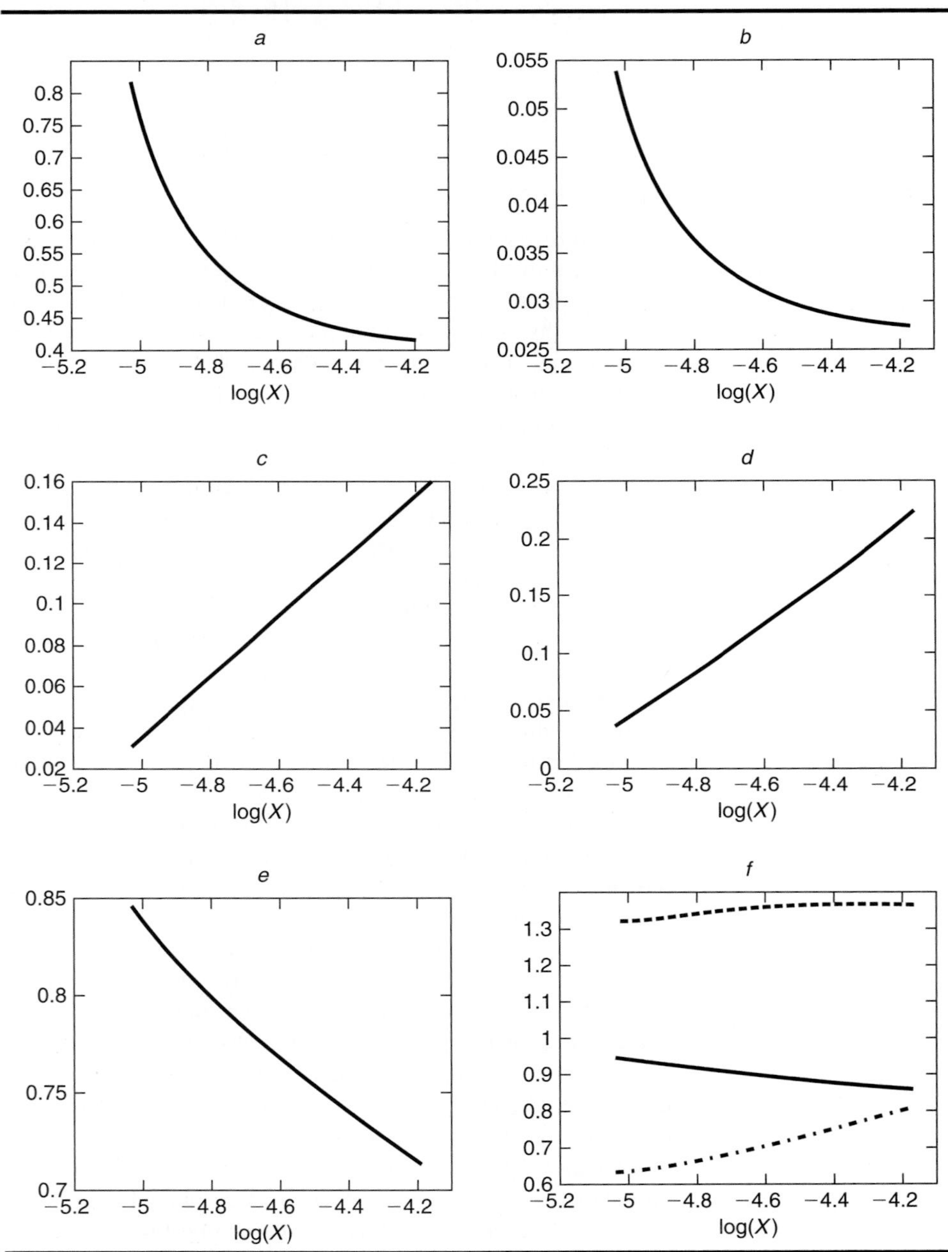

The last term in (28) shows that a part of the cross-sectional dispersion of market betas is also related to the firm-specific ratio of the scale of production to the market value, K_{ft}/V_{ft}, to a certain extent similar to the empirical measure of the firm's book-to-market ratio.[5] To see the intuition behind this result, consider two firms, 1 and 2, with the same market value. Since the value of growth options of these two firms is also identical, differences in their market risk are due only to the distribution of cash flows from the firms' existing projects. For simplicity, assume that each firm has a single active project. Let firm 1's project have a larger scale, so that firm 1 has a higher ratio K_{ft}/V_{ft}. Because the market value of a project is increasing in its idiosyncratic productivity, firm l's project must have lower productivity than firm 2's project. As we have discussed above, more productive projects in our model have lower systematic risk; hence firm 2 should have a lower market beta than firm 1. This argument shows that in our model the book-to-market ratio measures the systematic risk of a firm's returns because of its relation to the productivity and systematic risk of a firm's existing projects.

In the argument above, we considered single-project firms. We show below that, more generally, the book-to-market ratio in our model is negatively related to firm profitability, defined as the ratio of a firm's output to its book value. See Section IV*C* below for more discussion on this relation.

Although the book-to-market ratio is commonly interpreted as an empirical proxy for the firm's growth options, the preceding discussion shows that this need not be the case. In our model, size serves as a measure of a firm's growth options relative to its total market value, and the book-to-market ratio captures the risk of the firm's assets in place. Berk et al. (1999) point out a similar effect in the context of their model, even though the structure of their economy is substantially different from ours.

Because of the single-factor nature of our model, the cross-sectional distribution of expected returns is determined entirely by the distribution of market betas, since returns on the aggregate stock market are instantaneously perfectly correlated with the consumption process of the representative household (and hence the pricing kernel; e.g., Breeden [1979]). Thus, if conditional market betas were measured with perfect precision, no other variable would contain additional information about the cross section of returns. However, equation (28) implies that if for any reason market betas were mismeasured (e.g., because the market portfolio is not correctly specified), then firm-specific variables such as firm size and book-to-market ratios could appear to predict the cross-sectional distribution of expected stock returns simply because they are related to the true conditional betas. In Section IV we generate an example within our artificial economy of how mismeasurement of betas can lead to a significant role of firm characteristics as predictors of returns.

III. Aggregate Stock Returns

In this section we evaluate our model's ability to reproduce a few key features of aggregate data on returns. While this is not our main objective, it seems appropriate to ensure that the model's implications for the time series of stock returns are reasonable before examining its cross-sectional properties. To guarantee this, we restrict the values of the seven aggregate-level parameters, γ, λ, δ, $\bar{x}$, θ_x, σ_x, and z, to approximately match seven key unconditional moments: the first two unconditional moments of stock returns, the risk-free rate and aggregate consumption growth, and the average level of the investment-to-output ratio. We then examine the implications of these choices for a number of conditional moments of asset returns.

[5]The ratio K_{ft}/V_{ft} can also be approximated by other accounting variables, e.g., by the earnings-to-price ratio.

TABLE 1 | Moments of Key Aggregate Variables

	Data		Population		Sample	
	Mean (1)	Standard Deviation (2)	Mean (3)	Standard Deviation (4)	Mean (5)	Standard Deviation (6)
$(C_{t+1}/C_t) - 1$	1.72	3.28	.85	3.22	.84	3.06
					(.28)	(.26)
					[.22 1.33]	[2.56 3.50]
r_t	1.80	3.00	1.30	4.33	1.34	3.98
					(1.30)	(.85)
					[−.63 4.23]	[2.55 5.73]
$\log R_t - \log r_t$	6.00	18.0	6.00	14.34	5.89	15.28
					(1.32)	(1.73)
					[2.97 8.13]	[11.80 18.58]
I_t/Y_t	.19		.23		.23	
					(.02)	
					[.19 .26]	

NOTE.—This table reports unconditional means and standard deviations of consumption growth ($[C_{t+1}/C_t] - 1$), real interest rate (r_t), equity premium ($\log R_t - \log r_t$), and the mean of the investment-to-output ratio (I_t/Y_t). The numbers reported in cols. 1 and 2 are taken from Campbell, Lo, and MacKinlay (1997), except for the mean of the investment-to-output ratio, which equals the postwar average for the U.S. economy. The numbers reported in cols. 3 and 4 are population moments. These statistics are computed on the basis of 300,000 months of simulated data. Cols. 5 and 6 report the finite-sample properties of the corresponding statistics. We simulate 70-year-long monthly data sets, a length comparable to the sample length typically used in empirical research. Simulation is repeated 200 times, and the relevant statistics are computed for every simulation. Then we report the averages across the 200 replications. The numbers in parentheses are standard deviations across these 200 simulations, and the two numbers in brackets are 2.5th and 97.5th percentiles of the resulting empirical distribution, respectively. All numbers except those in the last row are in percentages.

A. Unconditional Moments

The values of the model parameters used in the simulation are as follows: the risk aversion coefficient, γ, 15; the time preference parameter, λ, 0.01; the rate of project expiration, δ, 0.04; the long-run mean of the aggregate productivity variable, $\bar{x}$, log(0.01); the quality of investment opportunities, z, 0.50; the volatility of the productivity variable, σ_x, 0.08; the rate of mean reversion of the productivity variable, θ_x, 0.275; the rate of mean reversion of the idiosyncratic productivity component, θ_ϵ, 0.50; and the volatility of the idiosyncratic productivity component, σ_ϵ, 2.00. Table 1 compares the implied moments of the key aggregate variables in the model with corresponding empirical estimates. We report both population moments, estimated by simulating a 300,000-month time series, and sample moments based on 200 simulations each with 70 years of monthly data. For the sample moments, in addition to point estimates and standard errors, we also report 95 percent confidence intervals based on empirical distribution functions from 200 simulations.

Essentially, our model captures the historical level and the volatility of the equity premium, while maintaining plausible values for the first two moments of the risk-free rate. Given the simple time-separable constant relative risk aversion utility and volatility in consumption growth of about 3 percent, this is possible only with a sizable degree of risk aversion (15). Since instantaneous consumption growth and aggregate stock returns are perfectly correlated in our single-factor model, this implies that the instantaneous Sharpe ratio of returns is approximately equal to $15 \times 0.03 = 0.45$, which is close to its historical average. Figure 2 shows that the Sharpe ratio of the aggregate stock market returns in our model is also countercyclical, which is consistent with empirical facts.

A. Calibration

To examine the cross-sectional implications of the model, we need to choose parameters for the stochastic process of the firm-specific productivity shocks, θ_ϵ and σ_ϵ. They are restricted by two considerations. First, we must generate empirically plausible levels of volatility of individual stock returns, which directly affects statistical inference about the relations between returns and firm characteristics. Second, we also want to match the observed cross-sectional correlation between (the logarithms of) firm value and the book-to-market ratio since, as we shall see below, this correlation is critical in determining the *univariate* relations between firm characteristics and returns.

Our goals are accomplished by setting $\theta_\epsilon = 0.50$ and $\sigma_\epsilon = 2.00$. These values imply an average annualized volatility of individual stock returns of approximately 27 percent (a number between the 25 percent reported by Campbell et al. [2001] and 32 percent reported by Vuolteenaho [2002]), while exactly matching the observed correlation between size and book-to-market (−.26) reported by Fama and French (1992).

The sign of the cross-sectional relation between the conditional market betas and firm characteristics depends on the aggregate-level variables $\beta_t^o - \widetilde{\beta}_t^a$ and $\beta_t^a - \widetilde{\beta}_t^a$ in (28). Given our parameter choices, the long-run average values of $\beta_t^o - \widetilde{\beta}_t^a$ and $\beta_t^a - \widetilde{\beta}_t^a$ are 0.67 and 0.21, respectively, thus guaranteeing a negative relation between the conditional market beta and firm size and a positive one between the conditional beta and book-to-market. Given the negative correlation between size and book-to-market, the signs of these partial regression coefficients will be preserved in univariate regressions, despite the omitted variable bias.

B. Simulation and Estimation

Our artificial panel is carefully constructed to replicate the procedures in Fama and French (1992). We start by constructing an artificial panel consisting of 360 months of observations for 2,000 firms. This is comparable to the panel of 2,267 firms for 318 months used in Fama and French's study. We adhere to Fama and French's timing conventions by matching accounting variables at the end of the calendar year $t - 1$ with returns from July of year t to June of year $t + 1$. Moreover, we also use the values of the firm's equity at the end of calendar year $t - 1$ to compute its book-to-market ratios for year $t - 1$ and use its market capitalization for June of year t as a measure of its size.[7] In all cases we repeat the entire simulations 100 times and average our results across the simulations. Further details of our simulation procedure are summarized in Appendix B.

Some of our tests use estimates of market betas of stock returns, which are obtained using the empirical procedure detailed in Fama and French (1992). Essentially, their procedure consists of two steps. First, *preranking* betas for each firm and period are estimated on the basis of the previous 60 monthly returns. Second, for each month, stocks are grouped into 10 portfolios sorted by market value. Each portfolio is then further divided into 10 subportfolios by sorting stocks according to their preranking beta.[8] *Post-ranking* betas are then estimated for each portfolio, and these betas are then allocated to *each* of the stocks within the portfolio. We shall refer to these betas as the Fama-French betas.

---

[7]Berk et al. (1999) use only a straightforward timing convention (one-period-lag values of explanatory variables) that does not agree with the definitions in Fama and French (1992).

[8]Sometimes the top and bottom deciles are also divided in half.

TABLE 3 | Properties of Portfolios Formed on Size

	Portfolio											
	1A	IB	2	3	4	5	6	7	8	9	10A	10B
	A. Historical Data											
Return	1.64	1.16	1.29	1.24	1.25	1.29	1.17	1.07	1.10	.95	.88	.90
β	1.44	1.44	1.39	1.34	1.33	1.24	1.22	1.16	1.08	1.02	.95	.90
$\log(V_f)$	1.98	3.18	3.63	4.10	4.50	4.89	5.30	5.73	6.24	6.82	7.39	8.44
$\log(B_f/V_f)$	−.01	−.21	−.23	−.26	−.32	−.36	−.36	−.44	−.40	−.42	−.51	−.65
	B. Simulated Panel											
Return	.73	.72	.71	.70	.69	.70	.68	.67	.66	.64	.61	.55
β	1.05	1.05	1.03	1.02	1.01	1.01	1.00	.99	.97	.95	.89	.89
$\log(V_f)$	4.86	5.04	5.12	5.16	5.20	5.24	5.27	5.32	5.37	5.46	5.58	5.84
$\log(B_f/V_f)$	−.93	−.86	−.85	−.84	−.85	−.86	−.87	−.90	−.97	−1.09	−1.24	−1.49

NOTE.—At the end of June of each year t, 12 portfolios are formed on the basis of ranked values of size. Portfolios 2–9 cover corresponding deciles of the ranking variables. The bottom and top two portfolios (1A, IB, 10A, and 10B) split the bottom and top deciles in half. The break points for the size portfolios are based on ranked values of size. Panel A is taken from Fama and French (1992, table 2, panel A). Panel B is constructed from the simulated panel. The average returns are the time-series averages of the monthly equal-weighted portfolio returns, in percentages. The terms $\log(V_f)$ and $\log(B_f/V_f)$ are the time-series averages of the monthly average values of these variables in each portfolio, and β is the time-series average of the monthly portfolio postranking betas.

C. Size and Book-to-Market Effects

Tables 3 and 4 compare the summary statistics of our model with those reported by Fama and French (1992). We report the postranking average returns for portfolios formed by a one-dimensional sort of stocks on firm size and book-to-market. Panel A is taken from Fama and French (1992) and panel B is computed on the basis of the simulated panels.

Since our model abstracts from inflation, the level of stock returns is naturally higher in panel A. In both cases, however, the pattern of stock returns in the model seems to match the evidence well. Similarly to the historical data, our simulated panels show a negative relation between average returns and firm value (table 3) and a positive relation with the book-to-market ratio (table 4).

Table 5 shows the results from the Fama and MacBeth (1973) regressions of stock returns on size, book-to-market, and the conditional market betas implied by our theoretical model. For each simulation, the slope coefficients are the time-series averages of the cross-sectional regression coefficients, and the t-statistics are these averages divided by the time-series standard deviations. We also report empirical findings of Fama and French (1992) and simulation results of Berk et al. (1999) in columns 1 and 2 of the same table. For completeness, figure 3 shows the histogram of the realized t-statistics across simulations.

Our first univariate regression shows that the logarithm of firm market value appears to contain useful information about the cross section of stock returns in our model. The relation between returns and size is significantly negative. Moreover, the average slope coefficient as well as the corresponding t-statistic are close to their empirical values reported by Fama and French (1992). Figure 3*a* also shows that the empirical value of the t-statistic is well within the body of realizations produced by the model.

The second univariate regression confirms the importance of the book-to-market ratio in explaining the cross-sectional properties of stock returns. While both our slope coefficient and t-statistic are smaller than the values obtained by Fama and French (1992), our estimates are positive and, as figure 3*a* shows, the coefficient of book-to-market is often quite significant at traditional levels. In Section II*C*, we argued that the book-to-market

TABLE 4 | Properties of Portfolios Formed on Book-to-Market

	Portfolio											
	1A	1B	2	3	4	5	6	7	8	9	10A	10B
	A. Historical Data											
Return	.30	.67	.87	.97	1.04	1.17	1.30	1.44	1.50	1.59	1.92	1.83
β	1.36	1.34	1.32	1.30	1.28	1.27	1.27	1.27	1.27	1.29	1.33	1.35
$\log(V_f)$	4.53	4.67	4.69	4.56	4.47	4.38	4.23	4.06	3.85	3.51	3.06	2.65
$\log(B_f/V_f)$	−2.22	−1.51	−1.09	−.75	−.51	−.32	−.14	.03	.21	.42	.66	1.02
	B. Simulated Panel											
Return	.61	.65	.67	.70	.70	.71	.71	.71	.71	.70	.71	.71
β	.95	.98	1.01	1.02	1.02	1.02	1.03	1.02	1.02	1.02	1.02	1.02
$\log(V_f)$	5.54	5.30	5.18	5.11	5.10	5.09	5.10	5.10	5.12	5.13	5.14	5.16
$\log(B_f/V_f)$	−1.54	−1.29	−1.15	−1.05	−.98	−.92	−.87	−.83	−.78	−.72	−.66	−.59

NOTE. —At the end of June of each year t, 12 portfolios are formed on the basis of ranked values of book-to-market, measured by $\log(B_f/V_f)$. The preranking betas use five years of monthly returns ending in June of t. Portfolios 2–9 cover deciles of the ranking variables. The bottom and top two portfolios (1A, IB, 10A, and 10B) split the bottom and top deciles in half. The break points for the book-to-market portfolios are based on ranked values of book-to-market equity. Panel A is taken from Fama and French (1992, table 4, panel A). Panel B is taken from the simulated panel. The average returns are the time-series averages of the monthly equal-weighted portfolio returns, in percentages. The terms $\log(V_f)$ and $\log(B_f/V_f)$ are the time-series averages of the monthly average values of these variables in each portfolio, and β is the time-series average of the monthly portfolio postranking betas.

TABLE 5 | Exact Regressions

	Fama-French (1)	Berk et al. (2)	Benchmark (3)	High Variance (4)	Low Persistence (5)
$\log(V_t)$	−.15	−.035	−.139	−.172	−.141
	(−2.58)	(−.956)	(−2.629)	(−3.016)	(−2.729)
$\log(B_t/V_t)$	.50	...	.082	.107	.103
	(5.71)		(1.955)	(2.274)	(2.341)
$\log(V_t)$	−.11	−.093	−.127	−.156	−.121
	(−1.99)	(−2.237)	(−2.516)	(−2.875)	(-2.446)
$\log(B_t/V_t)$	.35	.393	.045	.053	.052
	(4.44)	(2.641)	(1.225)	(1.261)	(1.340)
β	−.37	.642	1.048	1.193	1.050
	(−1.21)	(2.273)	(2.629)	(2.634)	(2.454)
$\log(V_t)$	−.17	.053	.033	.022	.035
	(−3.41)	(1.001)	(.518)	(.323)	(.524)
β	...	...	.892	1.085	.859
			(2.933)	(3.337)	(2.893)
$\log(B_t/V_t)$	...	...	.014	.020	.024
			(.385)	(.452)	(.604)
β	.15	.377	.916	1.115	.914
	(.46)	(1.542)	(3.079)	(3.432)	(3.106)

NOTE.—This table lists summary statistics for the coefficients and the t-statistics of Fama-MacBeth regressions using exact conditional β on the simulated panel sets. The dependent variable is the realized stock return, and independent variables are market beta, the logarithm of the market value, $\log(V_t)$, and the logarithm of the book-to-market ratio, $\log(B_t/V_t)$. Col. 1 gives the empirical results obtained by Fama and French (1992, table 3), using the historical returns of 2,267 firms over 318 months. Col. 2 gives the results obtained by Berk et al. (1999). Col. 3 reports the regression results for our model under benchmark parameterization in Sec. III*A*. Col. 4 reports the results from the model with the calibrated parameter values $\theta_\epsilon = 0.50$ and $\sigma_\epsilon = 2.50$ such that the average individual volatility is 30 percent, which is higher than the benchmark case of 27 percent. Col. 5 reports the results from the model with the calibrated parameter value $\theta_\epsilon = 0.40$ such that the persistence level is now lower. The regression coefficients are in percentage terms. The numbers in parentheses are t-statistics. The coefficients in the columns are in percentage terms. The numbers in parentheses are their corresponding t-statistics. Both coefficients and t-statistics are averaged across 100 simulations.

FIGURE 3 | Size and Book-to-Market in Cross-Sectional Regressions.
a, The histogram of *t*-statistics of univariate regressions of returns on size. *b*, The histogram of *t*-statistics of univariate regressions of returns on book-to-market across 100 simulations. *c*, The scatter plot of *t*-statistics on size and book-to-market. *d*, The scatter plot of *t*-statistics on size and Fama-French (FF) beta in a joint regression of returns.

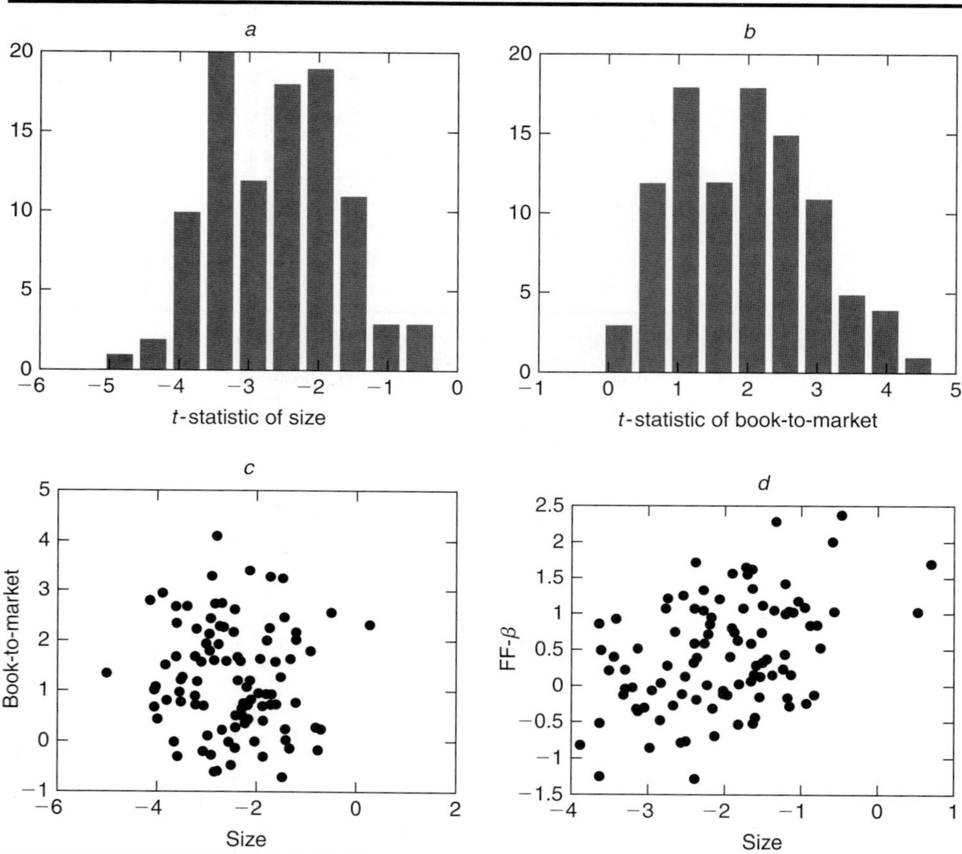

ratio in our model is related to expected returns because it is a proxy for firm productivity; that is, firms with a higher book-to-market ratio tend to be less productive and therefore have higher systematic risk. Figure 4 shows that, in our model, a negative relation also exists between the book-to-market ratio and firm profitability, defined as the ratio of profits (output) to book value. Firms with a low book-to-market are more productive than firms with a high book-to-market both before and after the portfolio formation date, with the difference in productivity declining over time. This pattern is also qualitatively consistent with the empirical results reported in Fama and French (1995, fig. 2).

Regressing returns on size and book-to-market jointly, we find that, on average, our coefficients have the same signs as in Fama and French (1992) and Berk et al. (1999). While our average size slope and the corresponding *t*-statistic are close to the empirical values, the average slope on book-to-market is again smaller than in Fama and French (1992). Figure 3*c* illustrates the range of *t*-statistics in a joint regression of returns on size and book-to-market. Each point corresponds to a realization of two *t*-statistics obtained in a single simulation. It is clear that, while the observed *t*-statistic on the size variable is

FIGURE 4 | Value Factor in Earnings.
This figure illustrates the relation between the book-to-market ratio and firm profitability in the simulated data. It shows the 11-year evolution of profitability for book-to-market portfolios. Growth (value) indicates the portfolio containing firms in the bottom (top) 30 percent of the values of book-to-market ratios. Profitability (or return on book equity) is measured by $(\triangle B_{ft} + D_{ft})/B_{ft-1}$, where B_{ft} denotes the book value of equity and D is the dividend payout. Thus profitability equals the ratio of common equity income for the fiscal year ending in calendar year t to the book value of equity for year $t-1$. The profitability of a portfolio is defined as the sum of $\triangle B_{jt} + D_{jt}$ for all firms j in a portfolio divided by the sum of B_{jt-1}; thus it is the return on book equity by merging all firms in the portfolio. For each portfolio formation year t, the ratios of $(\triangle B_{t+i} + D_{t+i})/B_{t+i-1}$ are calculated for year $t+i$, $i = -5, \ldots, 5$. The ratio for year $t+i$ is then averaged across portfolio formation years. Time 0 in the horizontal axis is the portfolio formation year.

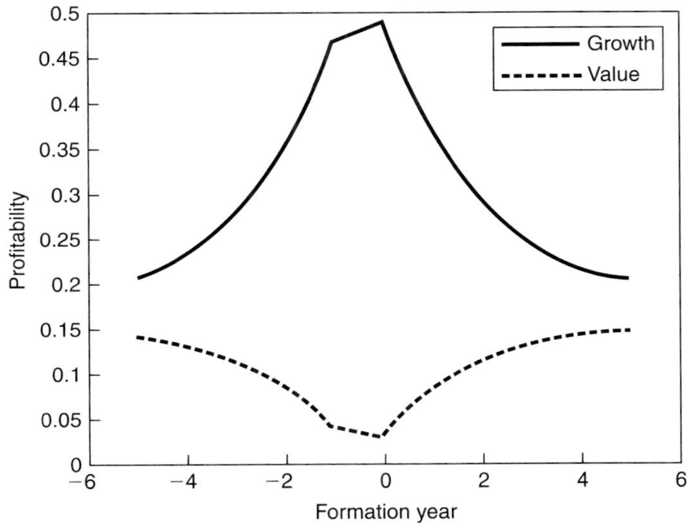

comparable to typical realizations produced by the model, the t-statistic on book-to-market is usually lower than that in Fama and French (1992).

These first three regressions in table 5 conform to the intuition that size and book-to-market are related to systematic risks of stock returns and therefore have explanatory power in the cross section. The fourth row of table 5 shows, however, that when we control for market beta, both the average coefficient on size and the corresponding t-statistic are close to zero. Within our theoretical framework, firm characteristics add no explanatory power to the conditional market betas of stock returns. This is not surprising since the market betas are sufficient statistics for instantaneous expected returns in our model. As shown in Section III, even at monthly frequency, the market portfolio is almost perfectly correlated with the pricing kernel.

To reconcile our results with the poor empirical performance of beta, one must take into account the fact that we have been using exact conditional betas, which are not observable in practice. Instead, betas must be estimated, which leaves room for measurement error.[9] Given the relation between beta and firm characteristics in (28), this measurement error in beta will also have an effect of creating a role for size and book-to-market as predictors of expected returns.

[9]Potential sources of errors are, among others, the fact that the market proxy used in estimation is not the mean-variance efficient portfolio (Roll 1977) or the econometric methods employed in estimation do not adequately capture the *conditional* nature of the pricing model (e.g., Ferson, Kandel, and Stambaugh 1987; Jagannathan and Wang 1996; Ferson and Harvey 1999; Campbell and Cochrane 2000; Lettau and Ludvigson 2001).

TABLE 6 | Average Returns for Portfolios Formed on Size (Down) and Then Beta (Across)

	All	Low-β	β-2	β-3	β-4	β-5	β-6	β-7	β-8	β-9	High-β
	A. Average Monthly Returns (Percent) from Fama and French (1992)										
All	1.25	1.34	1.29	1.36	1.31	1.33	1.28	1.24	1.21	1.25	1.14
Small market equity	1.52	1.71	1.57	1.79	1.61	1.50	1.50	1.37	1.63	1.50	1.42
Market equity 2	1.29	1.25	1.42	1.36	1.39	1.65	1.61	1.37	1.31	1.34	1.11
Market equity 3	1.24	1.12	1.31	1.17	1.70	1.29	1.10	1.31	1.36	1.26	.76
Market equity 4	1.25	1.27	1.13	1.54	1.06	1.34	1.06	1.41	1.17	1.35	.98
Market equity 5	1.29	1.34	1.42	1.39	1.48	1.42	1.18	1.13	1.27	1.18	1.08
Market equity 6	1.17	1.08	1.53	1.27	1.15	1.20	1.21	1.18	1.04	1.07	1.02
Market equity 7	1.07	.95	1.21	1.26	1.09	1.18	1.11	1.24	.62	1.32	.76
Market equity 8	1.10	1.09	1.05	1.37	1.20	1.27	.98	1.18	1.02	1.01	.94
Market equity 9	.95	.98	.88	1.02	1.14	1.07	1.23	.94	.82	.88	.59
Large market equity	.89	1.01	.93	1.10	.94	.94	.89	1.03	.71	.74	.56
	B. Average Monthly Returns (Percent) from Simulated Panel										
All	.67	.67	.68	.67	.68	.68	.68	.67	.68	.68	.67
Small market equity	.72	.72	.72	.72	.72	.73	.72	.72	.73	.72	.72
Market equity 2	.71	.70	.71	.71	.71	.70	.72	.71	.70	.71	.70
Market equity 3	.70	.70	.70	.70	.71	.69	.70	.70	.69	.71	.70
Market equity 4	.69	.69	.69	.69	.71	.70	.70	.67	.70	.69	.68
Market equity 5	.70	.70	.72	.70	.70	.71	.71	.69	.70	.69	.68
Market equity 6	.68	.64	.68	.68	.67	.70	.69	.68	.69	.69	.70
Market equity 7	.67	.65	.66	.65	.68	.68	.68	.67	.65	.69	.65
Market equity 8	.66	.64	.67	.65	.67	.68	.66	.66	.64	.67	.65
Market equity 9	.64	.61	.65	.61	.65	.63	.63	.64	.66	.64	.65
Large market equity	.58	.61	.56	.55	.57	.55	.63	.58	.61	.59	.56

NOTE.—Panel A is identical to panel A of table 1 in Fama and French (1992), in which the authors report average returns for 100 size-β portfolios using all New York Stock Exchange, American Stock Exchange, and NASDAQ stocks from July 1963 to December 1990 that meet certain Center for Research in Security Prices-Compustat data requirements. Panel B is produced using our simulated panel data set. The portfolio-sorting procedure is identical to that used in Fama and French's study. In particular, portfolios are formed yearly. The break points for the size deciles are determined in June of year t using all the stocks in the panel. All the stocks are then allocated to the 10 size portfolios using the break points. Each size decile is further subdivided into 10 beta portfolios using preranking betas of individual stocks, estimated with five years of monthly returns ending in June of year t. The equal-weighted monthly returns on the resulting 100 portfolios are then calculated for July of year t to June of year $t + 1$. The preranking betas are the sum of the slopes from a regression of monthly returns on the current and prior month's market returns. The average return is the time-series average of the monthly equal-weighted portfolio returns (percent). The All column shows statistics for equal-weighted size-decile (market equity) portfolios and the All rows show statistics for equal-weighted portfolios of the stocks in each beta group.

To illustrate the impact of beta mismeasurement, we now apply the Fama and French (1992) estimation procedure to our simulated data. Table 6 provides preliminary evidence on the relation between the Fama and French beta and average returns. As in the data, we find that after stocks have been sorted by size, variation in beta sort produces very little variation in average returns.

TABLE 7 | Fama-French Regressions

	Fama-French (1)	Berk et al. (2)	Benchmark (3)	High Variance (4)	Low Persistence (5)
log (V_t)	−.15	−.035	−.139	−.172	−.141
	(−2.58)	(−.956)	(−2.629)	(−3.016)	(−2.729)
log(B_t/V_t)	.50	...	.082	.107	.103
	(5.71)		(1.955)	(2.274)	(2.341)
log (V_t)	−.11	−.093	−.127	−.156	−.121
	(−1.99)	(−2.237)	(−2.516)	(−2.875)	(−2.446)
log(B_t/V_t)	.35	.393	.045	.053	.052
	(4.44)	(2.641)	(1.225)	(1.261)	(1.340)
β	−.37	.642	.133	.178	.214
	(−1.21)	(2.273)	(.429)	(.590)	(.727)
log(V_t)	−.17	.053	−.121	−.151	−.108
	(−3.41)	(1.001)	(−2.057)	(−2.298)	(−1.821)
β	.15	.377	.590	.721	.605
	(.46)	(1.542)	(2.158)	(2.472)	(2.367)

NOTE.—This table lists summary statistics for the coefficients and the t-statistics of Fama-MacBeth regressions using: the estimated Fama-French β on the simulated panel sets. See also the note to table 5.

As table 7 shows, using the Fama-French beta significantly changes our results. Now, beta is, on average, statistically insignificant whereas size remains both negative and significant even in a joint regression with beta. The scatter plot in figure 3d shows that the t-statistic on the Fama-French beta is usually far below 1.96, whereas the coefficient on size often appears significant.

Table 8 presents a measure of the noise in the construction of the Fama-French beta. It shows the average correlation matrix (standard errors included) between the true conditional betas, Fama-French betas, size, and book-to-market. It is easy to see that while the exact conditional beta is highly negatively correlated with size, the correlation with the Fama-French beta is much lower. Not surprisingly then, size serves as a more accurate

TABLE 8 | Cross-Sectional Correlations

	True β	Fama-French β	log(B_t/V_t)	log (V_t)
True β	1	.598	.324	−.764
		(.028)	(.022)	(.012)
Fama-French β		1	.270	−.758
			(.031)	(.036)
log (B_t/V_t)			1	−.262
				(.019)
log (V_t)				1

NOTE.—We calculate the cross-sectional correlations of exact conditional beta, Fama-French beta, book-to-market, and size for every simulated panel every month and then report the average correlations across 100 simulations. The numbers in parentheses are cross-simulation standard deviations.

measure of systematic risk than Fama-French beta and hence outperforms it in a cross-sectional regression.

The relation between expected returns, firm size, and market beta in our model is drastically different from that in the partial equilibrium model of Berk et al. (1999), who report that in a joint regression, firm size enters with a positive coefficient, on average; the loading on the Fama-French beta is positive and significant. Both in our model and in the Berk et al. model, the firm size proxies for the relative value of the firm's growth options. However, while in our model growth options are driven by the same risk factor as the assets in place and are relatively more risky, in the model of Berk et al., the growth options load only on the interest rates and therefore have a relatively low risk premium. Such a difference in the properties of growth options could explain why the two models have very different implications for the joint behavior of returns, firm size, and the market beta.

Sensitivity Analysis Columns 4 and 5 of tables 5 and 7 report the effects of alternative choices for the parameters, θ_ϵ and σ_ϵ, governing the cross-sectional properties of stock returns. Column 4 in these tables looks at the effects of increasing the cross-sectional dispersion of stock returns to 30 percent, which corresponds to a value for σ_ϵ of 2.50. Column 5 studies the effects of changing the persistence of the idiosyncratic productivity shocks by raising the value of θ_ϵ to 0.4. In both cases it is easy to see that our main results appear to be robust. In all cases, both the signs and significance of all the coefficients are preserved.

D. Business Cycle Properties

The theoretical characterization of stock prices and systematic risk, as given by (27) and (28), highlights the fact that the properties of the cross section of stock prices and stock returns depend on the current state of the economy. This dependence is captured by the economywide variables $p(x_t)$, $\widetilde{p}(x_t)$, and V_t^o and their market betas. Thus our model also gives rise to a number of predictions about the variation of the cross section of stock prices and returns over the business cycle. These properties of the cross section of stock returns may have important implications for optimal dynamic portfolio choice.

Firm Characteristics To help understand the relation between the cross section of firm characteristics and the business cycle, we first characterize the cross-sectional dispersion of firm market values. To this end, let Var (h) denote the variance of the cross-sectional distribution of a firm-specific variable h. According to our characterization of firm market value (27), it follows immediately that

$$\mathrm{Var}\left(\frac{V_{ft}}{V_t}\right) = \left[\frac{\widetilde{p}(x_t)K_t}{V_t}\right]^2 \mathrm{Var}\left[\sum_{i\in\mathcal{I}_{ft}} (\epsilon_{it} - 1)\frac{k_i}{K_t}\right] + \left[\frac{p(x_t)K_t}{V_t}\right]^2 \mathrm{Var}\left[\sum_{i\in\mathcal{I}_{ft}} \frac{k_i}{K_t}\right]. \tag{30}$$

The right-hand side of (30) captures the cross-sectional dispersion of relative firm size. This dispersion can be attributed to (i) the cross-sectional variation of project-specific productivity shocks ϵ_{it} as well as project-specific and firm-specific production scale and (ii) economywide variables $p(x_t)$, $\widetilde{p}(x_t)$, and K_t/V_t.

The contribution of the firm heterogeneity, captured by

$$\mathrm{Var}\left[\sum_{i\in\mathcal{I}_{ft}} \frac{k_i}{K_t}\right]$$

FIGURE 5 | Business Cycle Properties (I).
This figure illustrates the business cycle properties of some aggregate and cross-sectional variables. *a*, $p(x)K/V$ (the solid line) and $\tilde{p}(x)K/V$ (the dashed line) plotted as functions of x. *b*, Log of the price-dividend ratio, $\log(V/D)$, as a function of $\log(X)$. *c*, Size ($\log[V_f]$) dispersion as a function of $\log(V/D)$. *d*, Dispersion of book-to-market ($\log[B_f/V_f]$) as a function of $\log(V/D)$.

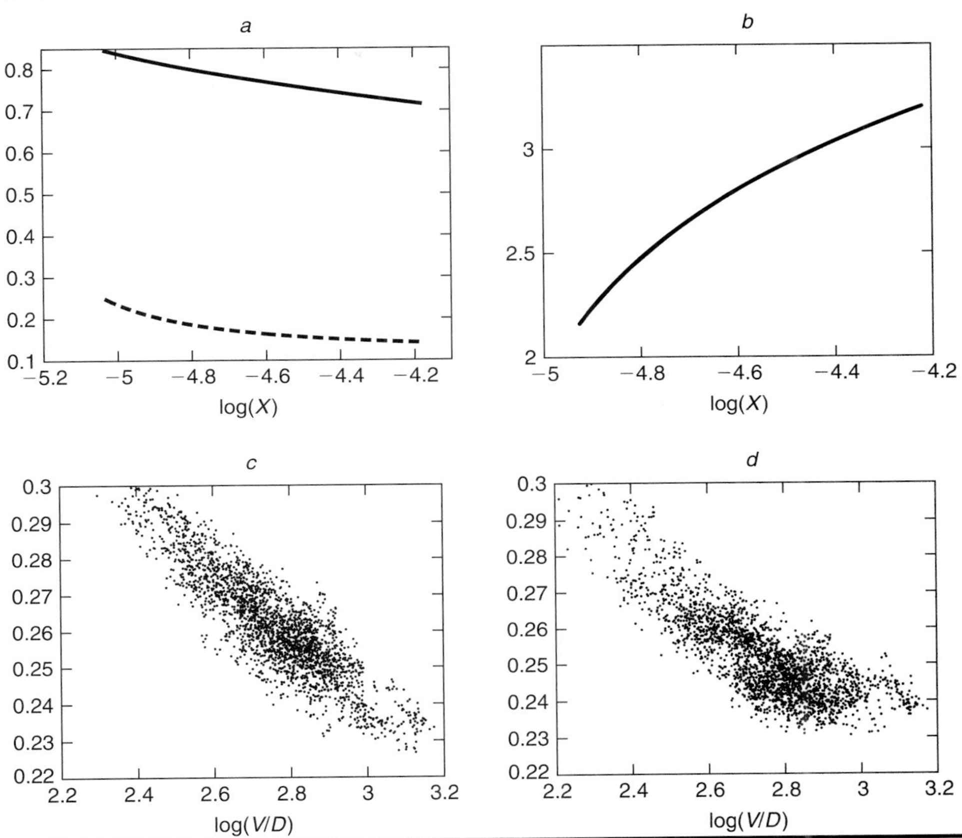

and

$$\mathrm{Var}\left[\sum_{i\in\mathcal{I}_{ft}}(\epsilon_{it}-1)\frac{k_i}{K_t}\right],$$

is clearly path-dependent in theory, since the scale of new projects depends on the current aggregate scale of production K_t. Intuitively, however, this dependence is fairly low when the average lifetime of individual projects is much longer than the average length of a typical business cycle.[10]

It falls then on the aggregate components to determine the cross-sectional variance in market value. Given the properties of our environment, it is easy to see that this implies that the cross-sectional dispersion of firm size is countercyclical; that is, it expands in recessions and becomes compressed in expansions. We can see this by looking at figure *2d*. Since the market betas of $p(x_t)$ and $\tilde{p}(x_t)$ are less than one, the ratios $p(x_t)K_t/V_t$ and $\tilde{p}(x_t)K_t/V_t$ should be negatively related to the state variable x_t. Figure 5 confirms this finding.

[10]Note that the average project life is about $1/\delta = 25$ years, given our calibration.

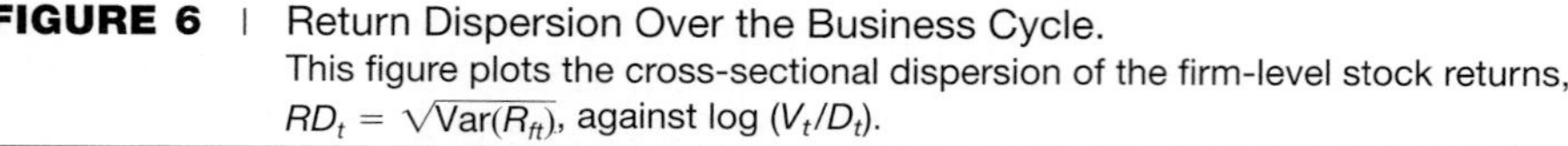

FIGURE 6 | Return Dispersion Over the Business Cycle.
This figure plots the cross-sectional dispersion of the firm-level stock returns, $RD_t = \sqrt{\text{Var}(R_{ft})}$, against log (V_t/D_t).

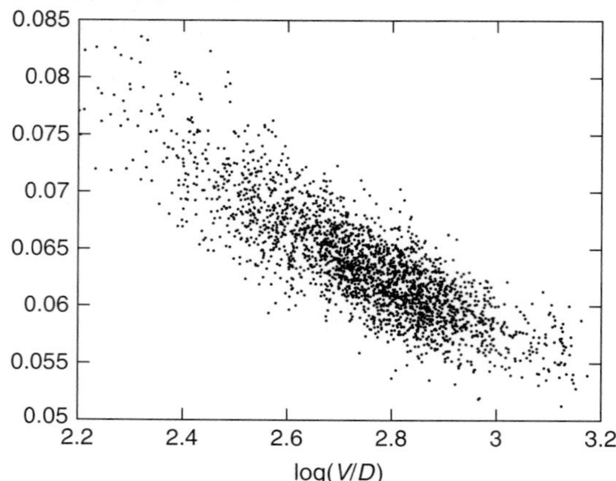

To quantify this relation, we simulate our artificial economy over a 200-year period and compute the cross-sectional standard deviation of the logarithm of firm values and book-to-market ratios on a monthly basis. Since the state variable x_t is not observable empirically, we choose to capture the current state of the economy by the price-to-dividend ratio of the aggregate stock market.[11]

Figure 5 presents scatter plots of the cross-sectional dispersion of firm characteristics against the logarithm of the aggregate price-dividend ratio. In both cases the relation is clearly negative. Note that cross-sectional dispersion is not a simple function of the state variable partially because we are using a finite number of firms and projects in our simulation; therefore, our theoretical relations hold only approximately. Moreover, as suggested by the theoretical argument above, such relations are inherently history-dependent.

Stock Returns Next we study how the cross-sectional distribution of actual stock returns depends on the state of the aggregate economy. First, we analyze the degree of dispersion of returns, $RD_t = \sqrt{\text{Var}(R_{ft})}$, where R_{ft} denotes monthly returns on individual stocks. We construct a scatter plot of RD_t versus contemporaneous values of the logarithm of the aggregate price-dividend ratio.

According to figure 6, our model predicts a negative contemporaneous relation between return dispersion and the price-dividend ratio. This can be attributed to die countercyclical nature of both aggregate return volatility, as shown in figure 7*a*, and the dispersion in conditional market beta, as shown in figure 7*b*.

Since investment in our model is endogenously procyclical, an increase in aggregate productivity shock is accompanied by an increase in the rate of investment and hence a higher growth rate of the scale of production, as well as an increase in stock prices. On the other hand, since investment is irreversible, the scale of production cannot be easily reduced during periods of low aggregate productivity, increasing volatility of stock prices.[12]

[11] In the model, the unconditional correlation between x_t and log (V_t/D_t) is 98.8 percent.

[12] Qualitatively, the impact of the irreversibility on conditional volatility of stock returns in our model is similar to that in Kogan (2000, 2001).

FIGURE 7 | Business Cycle Properties (II).
This figure illustrates the business cycle properties of some aggregate and cross-sectional variables. *a*, Conditional stock market return volatility plotted as a function of the log price-dividend ratio, log (V/D). *b*, Cross-sectional dispersion of the firm-level market betas, $\sqrt{\mathrm{Var}(\beta_{ft})}$, plotted against log ($V_t/D_t$).

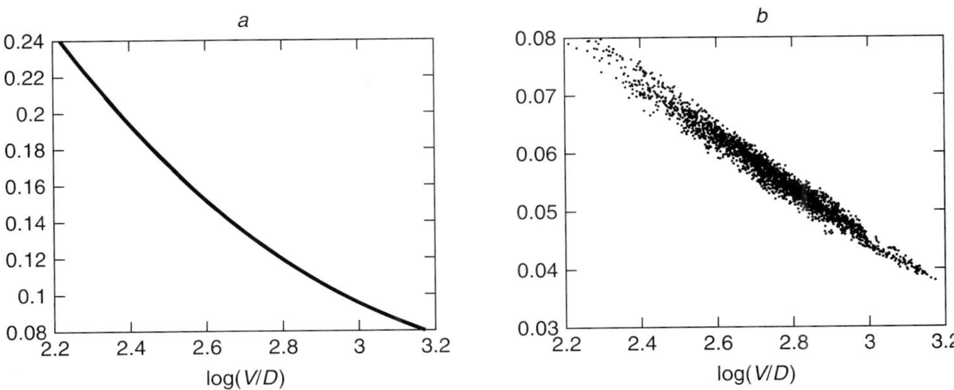

The countercyclical dispersion of conditional betas follows from the characterization of the systematic risk of stock returns (28) and the pattern observed in figure 2*d*. During business cycle peaks, the dispersion of aggregate betas, that is, β_t^a, $\tilde{\beta}_t^a$, and β_t^o, is relatively low, contributing to lower dispersion of firm-level market betas. This effect is then reinforced by the countercyclical behavior of dispersion of firm characteristics. In this respect our model matches the empirical regularity pointed out by Chan and Chen (1988, n. 6), that the cross-sectional spectrum of conditional market betas of size-sorted portfolios contracts during business cycle booms and expands during business cycle troughs.

An interesting empirical finding by Stivers (2001) is the ability of return dispersion to forecast future aggregate return volatility, even after one controls for the lagged values of market returns. We conduct a similar experiment within our model by simulating monthly stock returns and regressing absolute values of aggregate market returns on lagged values of return dispersion and market returns. As in Stivers' study, we allow for different slope coefficients depending on the sign of lagged market returns. As shown in table 9, return dispersion retains significant explanatory power even after we control for market returns in the regression. The reason is that lagged market returns provide only a noisy proxy for the current state of die economy. At the same time, return dispersion contains independent information about the current state of the economy and hence the conditional stock market volatility, as shown in figure 6.

Conditional Size and Book-to-Market Effects The fact that dispersion of returns on individual stocks in our model changes countercyclically suggests that the size and book-to-market effects analyzed in subsection *C* are also conditional in nature. To capture this cyclical behavior of cross-sectional patterns in returns and its implications for dynamic portfolio allocation, we analyze the conditional performance of alternative size- and value-based strategies. Specifically, we simulate 1,000 years of monthly individual stock returns and then form zero-investment portfolios by taking a long position in bottom-size-decile stocks and a short position in top-size-decile stocks, as sorted by size, with monthly rebalancing. We also construct alternative portfolios by doing the opposite for book-to-market

TABLE 9 | Cross-Sectional Return Dispersion as a Predictor of Market Volatility

	Coefficient				JOINT $b_1 = 0$ $b_2 = 0$	JOINT $c_1 = 0$ $c_2 = 0$	R^2 (%)
	b_1	b_2	c_1	c_2			
	A. Results from Stivers (2001)						
Full model	.365	.111	−.157	.221	10.08	2.69	10.45
	(3.61)	(1.40)	(−2.94)	(1.84)	(.000)	(.069)	
	B. Simulation Results						
Full model	.918	.016	.019	.008	8.467	.949	3.72
	(3.408)	(.233)	(.285)	(.059)	(.035)	(.534)	

NOTE.—This table illustrates the intertemporal relation between market volatility and the lagged cross-sectional return dispersion (*RD*). The volatility is measured by the absolute value of the market excess return. Variations of the following model are estimated as follows:

$$|R_t^e| = a + b_1 RD_{t-1} + b_2 1_{(R_{t-1}^a < 0)} RD_{t-1} + c_1 |R_{t-1}^e < 0| + c_2 1_{(R_{t-1}^a < 0)} (R_{t-1}^e < 0) + \in_t,$$

where $|R_t^a|$ is the absolute value of the market excess return, *RD*, is the cross-sectional standard deviation of the individual stock returns, $1_{(R_{t-1}^a < 0)}$ is a dummy variable that equals one when the market excess return is negative and zero otherwise, and ϵ_t, is the residual. All *t*-statistics are adjusted with respect to heteroscedasticity and autocorrelation using the Newey-West procedure. For die *F*-test on joint restrictions, the *p*-values are in parentheses. Panel A is taken from Stivers (2001), which uses 400 firm returns from July 1962 to December 1995. Panel B is generated as the average coefficients and statistics across repeated simulations.

deciles. We then regress portfolio returns on the logarithm of the aggregate price-dividend ratio.

Our model predicts an average annualized value (book-to-market) premium of 1.47 percent and an average annualized size premium of 1.62 percent. Moreover, both strategies exhibit significant countercyclical patterns in their expected returns. In particular, we find that a 10 percent decline in the log price-dividend ratio below its long-run mean implies approximately a 25 percent and 6 percent increase in expected returns on the size and book-to-market strategies, respectively, measured as a fraction of their long-run average returns.

V. Conclusion

This paper analyzes a general equilibrium production economy with heterogeneous firms. In the model, the cross section of stock returns is explicitly related to firm characteristics such as size and book-to-market. Firms differ in the share of their total market value derived from their assets, as opposed to future growth opportunities, which is captured by their characteristics. Since these two components of firm value have different market risk, firm characteristics are closely related to market beta.

To the best of our knowledge, our paper is the first to explain the cross section of stock returns from a general equilibrium perspective. Our model demonstrates that size and book-to-market can explain the cross section of stock returns because they are correlated with the true conditional beta. We also provide an example of how empirically estimated beta can perform poorly relative to firm characteristics because of measurement errors.

Our model also gives rise to a number of additional implications for the cross section of returns. In this paper, we focus on the business cycle properties of returns and firm characteristics. Our results appear consistent with the limited existing evidence and provide a natural benchmark for future empirical studies.

Appendix A Proofs and Technical Results

A. Proof of Proposition 1

The value of an ongoing project i is the present value of the future stream of cash flows, $e^{x_{t+s}}\epsilon_{i,t+s}k_i$, taking into account that the project can expire at the random rate δ. Hence

$$P(x_t, \epsilon_{it}, k_i) = E_t\left[\int_0^\infty e^{-\delta s} M_{t,t+s}(e^{x_{t+s}}\epsilon_{i,t+s}k_i)ds\right]$$

$$= k_i\left[\int_0^\infty e^{-\delta s} E_t[M_{t,t+s}e^{x_{t+s}}]E_t[\epsilon_{i,t+s}]ds\right],$$

where the equality follows from mutual independence of X_t and ϵ_{it}. Given (2), it follows that

$$E_t[\epsilon_{i,t+s}] = \epsilon_{it}e^{-\theta_\epsilon s} + (1 - e^{-\theta_\epsilon s}),$$

which implies that

$$P(x_t, \epsilon_{it}, k_i) = k_i\left\{\int_0^\infty e^{-\delta s}E_t[M_{t,t+s}e^{x_{t+s}}][\epsilon_{it}e^{-\theta_\epsilon s} + (1 - e^{-\theta_\epsilon s})]ds\right\}$$

$$= k_i\left\{\int_0^\infty e^{-\delta s}E_t[M_{t,t+s}e^{x_{t+s}}]ds + \int_0^\infty e^{-(\delta+\theta_\epsilon)s}E_t[M_{t,t+s}e^{x_{t+s}}](\epsilon_{it} - 1)ds\right\}$$

$$= k_i[p(x_t) + \tilde{p}(x_t)(\epsilon_{it} - 1)],$$

where $p(x)$ and $\tilde{p}(x_t)$ depend only on x_t since $M_{t,t+s}$ is a function of x_t and x_{t+s} and x_t is a univariate Markov process.

B. Proof of Proposition 2

Equation (17) is the resource constraint (16). As we have seen in Section IIA, the optimal firm investment policy $p(x)$ is defined by

$$p(x_t) = E_t\left[\int_0^\infty e^{-\lambda s}\left(\frac{C_t}{C_{t+s}}\right)^\gamma (e^{-\delta s}e^{x_{t+s}})ds\right] \tag{A1}$$

where we now impose that optimal consumption decisions are used in determining the pricing kernel in equilibrium. When we use the resource constraint (16) and the accumulation equation (9), it follows that

$$p(x_t) = (C_t)^\gamma E_t\left[\int_0^\infty e^{-(\lambda+\delta)s}\frac{e^{x_{t+s}}}{(C_{t+s}/K_{t+s})^\gamma K_{t+s}^\gamma}ds\right]$$

$$= (C_t)^\gamma E_t\left[\int_0^\infty e^{-(\lambda+\delta)s}\frac{e^{x_{t+s}}}{\{e^{x_{t+s}} - \frac{1}{2}z[p(x_{t+s})]^2\}K_t^\gamma \exp[\int_0^s - \gamma\delta + \gamma z p(x_t - \tau)d\tau]}\right]$$

$$= \{e^{x_t} - \tfrac{1}{2}z[p(x_t)]^2\}^\gamma \phi(x_t),$$

where the Feynman-Kac theorem implies then that $\phi(x)$ satisfies the differential equation (see, e.g., Duffie 1996, app. E):

$$[\lambda + (1-\gamma)\delta + \gamma z p(x)]\phi(x) - \mathcal{A}[\phi(x)] - \frac{\exp(x)}{\{e^x - \frac{1}{2}z[p(x)]^2\}^\gamma} = 0.$$

C. Proof of Proposition 3

Let $m_t = (C_t)^{-\gamma}$ and $M_{t,t+s} = e^{-\lambda s} m_{t+s}/m_t$, and by Ito's lemma,

$$E_t[M_{t,t+dt} - 1] = E_t\left[\left.\frac{\partial M}{\partial s}\right|_{s=0} dt + \frac{\partial m_t}{m_t \partial C_t} dC_t + \frac{1}{2}\frac{\partial^2 m_t}{m_t \partial (C_t)^2}(dC_t)^2\right]$$

$$= -\lambda m_t dt - \frac{\gamma}{C_t} m_t E_t[dC_t] + \frac{1}{2}\frac{\gamma(\gamma+1)}{(C_t)^2} m_t E_t[dC_t]^2.$$

Another application of Ito's lemma yields

$$E_t[dC_t] = \frac{C(x_t, K_t)}{K_t} dK_t + K_t E_t\left[d\frac{C(x_t, K_t)}{K_t}\right]$$

$$= C(x_t, K_t)[zp(x_t) - \delta]dt + \mathcal{A}[C(x_t, K_t)]dt,$$

$$(dC_t)^2 = \left[\frac{\partial^2 C(x_t, K_t)}{\partial x_t^2}\right]^2 \sigma_x^2,$$

where

$$\mathcal{A}[C(x,K)] \equiv \theta_x(x - \bar{x})\frac{\partial C(x,K)}{\partial x} + \frac{1}{2}\frac{\partial^2 C(x,K)}{\partial x^2}\sigma_x^2.$$

As a result,

$$r_t = \lambda + \gamma[zp(x_t) - \delta] + \gamma\frac{\mathcal{A}[C(x_t, K_t)]}{C(x_t, K_t)} - \frac{1}{2}\gamma(\gamma+1)\sigma_x^2\left[\frac{\partial \operatorname{Rn} C(x_t, K_t)}{\partial x_t}\right]^2.$$

Now, the value of the aggregate stock market, V_t, can be computed as

$$V_t = E_t\left[\int_0^\infty M_{t,t+s} D_{t+s} ds\right]$$

$$= E_t\left[\int_0^\infty e^{-\lambda s}\left(\frac{C_t}{C_{t+s}}\right)^\gamma C_{t+s} ds\right]$$

$$= (C_t)^\gamma E_t\left[\int_0^\infty e^{-\lambda s}\left(\frac{C_{t+s}}{K_{t+s}}\right)^{1-\gamma} K_{t+s}^{1-\gamma} ds\right]$$

$$= \left(\frac{C_t}{K_t}\right)^\gamma K_t E_t\left[\int_0^\infty e^{-\lambda s}\left(\frac{C_{t+s}}{K_{t+s}}\right)^{1-\gamma} \exp\left[\int_0^s -(1-\gamma)\delta + (1-\gamma)zp(x_t + \tau)d\tau\right] ds\right]$$

$$= \{e^{x_t} - \tfrac{1}{2}z[p(x_t)]^2\}^\gamma \psi(x_t) K_t,$$

where $\Psi(x)$ satisfies the following differential equation:

$$\lambda\psi(x) = \{e^{x_t} - \tfrac{1}{2}z[p(x)]^2\}^{1-\gamma} + (1-\gamma)[zp(x) - \delta]\psi(x)$$

$$-\theta_x(x - \bar{x})\psi'(x) + \tfrac{1}{2}\sigma_x^2\psi''(x).$$

Appendix B Some Details of Computation

We use a finite, large number of firms in the numerical implementation. While the number of firms is fixed, the total number of projects in the economy is time-varying and stationary. We let the scale of new projects be proportional to the aggregate production scale in the economy, which ensures stationarity of the cross-sectional distribution of the number of projects per firm. Thus $k_i = K_t/\varphi$, where the constant φ controls the long-run average number of projects in the economy, N.* On average, projects expire at the total rate δN^*. The arrival rate of new projects is $zp(x_t)\varphi$. Therefore, φ is defined from the equation $zE[p(x_t)]\varphi = \delta N^*$.

In the simulation, time increment is discrete. The unit costs of new projects are spaced out evenly over the interval $(0, p(x_t)]$. The investment of an individual firm at time t is computed as the total amount the firm spends on its new projects at time t. The dividend paid out by a given firm during period t is defined as the difference between the cash flows generated by the firm's existing projects and its investment. Finally, the individual firm's book value is measured as the cumulative investment cost of the firm's projects that remain active at time t.

In our simulation, we first generate 200 years' worth of monthly data to allow the economy to reach steady state. After that, we repeatedly simulate a 420-month panel data set consisting of the cross-sectional variables (360 months of data constitute the main panel, and 60 extra months are used for preranking β estimation).

References

Berk, Jonathan B. "A Critique of Size-Related Anomalies." *Rev. Financial Studies* 8 (Summer 1995): 275–86.

Berk, Jonathan B.; Green, Richard C. and Naik, Vasant. "Optimal Investment, Growth Options, and Security Returns." *J. Finance* 54 (October 1999): 1553–1607.

Bossaerts, Peter, and Green, Richard C. "A General Equilibrium Model of Changing Risk Premia: Theory and Tests." *Rev. Financial Studies* 2 (Winter 1989): 467–93.

Breeden, Douglas T. "An Intertemporal Asset Pricing Model with Stochastic Consumption and Investment Opportunities." *J. Financial Econ.* 7 (September 1979): 265–96.

Campbell, John Y. "Asset Pricing at the Millennium." *J. Finance* 55 (August 2000): 1515–67.

———. "Consumption-Based Asset Pricing." In *Handbook of the Economics of Finance*, vol. 1B, edited by George M. Constantinides, Milton Harris, and Rene M. Stulz. Amsterdam: North-Holland, 2003.

Campbell, John Y., and Cochrane, John H. "Explaining the Poor Performance of Consumption-Based Asset Pricing Models." *J. Finance* 55 (December 2000): 2863–78.

Campbell, John Y.; Lettau, Martin; Malkiel, Burton G.; and Xu, Yexiao. "Have Individual Stocks Become More Volatile? An Empirical Exploration of Idiosyncratic Risk." *J. Finance* 56 (February 2001): 1–43.

Campbell, John Y.; Lo, Andrew W.; and MacKinlay, A. Craig. *The Econometrics of Financial Markets.* Princeton, N.J.: Princeton Univ. Press, 1997.

Chan, K. C., and Chen, Nai-Fu. "An Unconditional Asset-Pricing Test and the Role of Firm Size as an Instrumental Variable for Risk." *J. Finance* 43 (June 1988): 309–25.

Cochrane, John H. "Production-Based Asset Pricing and the Link between Stock Returns and Economic Fluctuations." *J. Finance* 46 (March 1991): 209–37.

———. "A Cross-Sectional Test of an Investment-Based Asset Pricing Model." *J.P.E.* 104 (June 1996): 572–621.

———. "New Facts in Finance." *Fed. Reserve Bank Chicago Econ. Perspectives* 23 (3d quarter 1999): 36–58.

Coleman, Wilbur J., II. "Behavior of Interest Rates in a General Equilibrium Multisector Model with Irreversible Investment." *Macroeconomic Dynamics* 1, no. 1 (1997): 206–27.

Duffie, Darrell. *Dynamic Asset Pricing Theory.* 2d ed. Princeton, N.J.: Princeton Univ. Press, 1996.

Evans, David S. "The Relationship between Firm Growth, Size, and Age: Estimates for 100 Manufacturing Industries." *J. Indus. Econ.* 35 (June 1987): 567–81.

Fama, Eugene F., and French, Kenneth R. "The Cross-Section of Expected Stock Returns." *J. Finance* 47 (June 1992): 427–65.

———. "Common Risk Factors in the Returns on Stocks and Bonds." *J. Financial Econ.* 33 (February 1993): 3–56.

———. "Size and Book-to-Market Factors in Earnings and Returns." *J. Finance* 50 (March 1995): 131–55.

———. "Multifactor Explanations of Asset Pricing Anomalies." *J. Finance* 51 (March 1996): 55–84.

Fama, Eugene F., and MacBeth, James D. "Risk, Return, and Equilibrium: Empirical Tests." *J.P.E.* 81 (May/June 1973): 607–36.

Feldman, Mark, and Gilles, Christian. "An Expository Note on Individual Risk without Aggregate Uncertainty." *J. Econ. Theory* 35 (February 1985): 26–32.

Ferson Wayne E., and Harvey, Campbell R. "Conditional Variables and the Cross Section of Stock Returns." *J. Finance* 54 (August 1999): 1325–60.

Ferson, Wayne E.; Kandel, Shmuel; and Stambaugh, Robert F. "Tests of Asset Pricing with Time-Varying Expected Risk Premiums and Market Betas." *J. Finance* 42 (June 1987): 201–20.

Gomes, Joao; Yaron, Amir; and Zhang, Lu. "Asset Pricing Implications for Firms' Financing Constraints." Manuscript. Philadelphia: Univ. Pennsylvania, Wharton School, Finance Dept., 2002.

Hall, Bronwyn H. "The Relationship between Firm Size and Firm Growth in the U.S. Manufacturing Sector." *J. Indus. Econ.* 35 (June 1987): 583–606.

Jagannathan, Ravi, and Wang, Zhenyu. "The Conditional CAPM and the Cross-Section of Expected Returns." *J. Finance* 51 (March 1996): 3–53.

Jermann, Urban J. "Asset Pricing in Production Economies." *J. Monetary Econ.* 41 (April 1998): 257–75.

Judd, Kenneth L. "The Law of Large Numbers with a Continuum of IID Random Variables." *J. Econ. Theory* 35 (February 1985): 19–25.

Kaldor, Nicholas. "Capital Accumulation and Economic Growth." In *The Theory of Capital: Proceedings of a Conference Held by the International Economic Association*, edited by Friedrich A. Lutz and Douglas C. Hague. London: Macmillan, 1961.

Kogan, Leonid. "Asset Prices and Irreversible Real Investment." Manuscript. Cambridge: Massachusetts Inst. Tech., Sloan School Management, 2000.

———. "An Equilibrium Model of Irreversible Investment." *J. Financial Econ.* 62 (November 2001): 201–45.

Kothari, S. P.; Shanken, Jay; and Sloan, Richard G. "Another Look at the Cross-Section of Expected Stock Returns." *J. Finance* 50 (March 1995): 185–224.

Lakonishok, Josef; Shleifer, Andrei; and Vishny, Robert W. "Contrarian Investment, Extrapolation, and Risk." *J. Finance* 49 (December 1994): 1541–78.

Lettau, Martin, and Ludvigson, Sydney. "Resurrecting the (C)CAPM: A Cross-Sectional Test When Risk Premia Are Time-Varying." *J.P.E.* 109 (December 2001): 1238–87.

Liew, Jimmy, and Vassalou, Maria. "Can Book-to-Market, Size and Momentum Be Risk Factors That Predict Economic Growth?" *J. Financial Econ.* 57 (August 2000): 221–45.

Lo, Andrew W., and MacKinlay, A. Craig. "Stock Market Prices Do Not Follow Random Walks: Evidence from a Simple Specification Test." *Rev. Financial Studies* 1 (Spring 1988): 41–66.

MacKinlay, A. Craig. "Multifactor Models Do Not Explain Deviations from the CAPM." *J. Financial Econ.* 38 (May 1995): 3–28.

Naik, Vasanttilak. "Asset Prices in Dynamic Production Economies with Time-Varying Risk." *Rev. Financial Studies* 7 (Winter 1994): 781–801.

Pontiff, Jeffrey, and Schall, Lawrence D. "Book-to-Market Ratios as Predictors of Market Returns." *J. Financial Econ.* 49 (August 1998): 141–60.

Roll, Richard. "A Critique of Asset Pricing Theory's Test: Part I: On Past and Potential Testability of the Theory." *J. Financial Econ.* 4 (March 1977): 129–76.

Rouwenhorst, K. Geert. "Asset Pricing Implications of Equilibrium Business Cycle Models." In *Frontiers of Business Cycle Research*, edited by Thomas F. Cooley. Princeton, N.J.: Princeton Univ. Press, 1995.

Stivers, Christopher T. "Firm-Level Return Dispersion and the Future Volatility of Aggregate Stock Market Returns." Manuscript. Athens: Univ. Georgia, Terry Coll. Bus., 2001.

Vuolteenaho, Tuomo. "What Drives Firm-Level Stock Returns?" *J. Finance* 57 (February 2002): 233–64.

Zhang, Lu. "The Value Premium." Manuscript. Rochester, N.Y.: Univ. Rochester, Simon Grad. School Bus. Admin., 2002.

Twenty-Seven

Jennifer Huang

Jennifer Huang received a Ph.D. from the Massachusetts Institute of Technology in 2003. She has been working at the University of Texas at Austin since graduation.

Steve Ross is one of the greatest mentors in finance. One reason, I believe, is that he coaches students at their own paces. The most humbling experience for most first- and second-year Ph.D. students at MIT is to attend the weekly seminar and listen to the faculty members—quite often Steve Ross—telling the speakers the intuition behind their papers after five minutes of the presentation. When the students wonder whether they will ever have this kind of intuition, Steve encourages, "You learn the mechanics first; the intuition comes later." For third-year students who are eager to mimic the masters by conjuring the results instead of actually deriving them, he holds them in place, "Show me the model." Finally, for fourth- and fifth-year students who manage to put together a model, he pushes the limit, "What is the intuition behind this result? Why is it interesting? Is it empirically testable?"

I was one of the first few MIT students who were fortunate enough to have Steve Ross as an advisor. Having received a mathematics degree before entering the finance program, I have always appreciated the importance of models. Steve, however, has given me an entirely new perspective on their role. From him, I learned that a model is a language to express an idea. It is a platform to lay down all assumptions, to develop the links between various ideas, and finally, to derive new testable predictions.

Steve's emphasis on the importance of models is evident in the paper included in this volume, "Participation Costs and the Sensitivity of Fund Flows to Past Performance," which I wrote with my colleagues Hong Yan and Kelsey Wei. We started with the well-documented fact that funds with superior recent performance enjoy disproportionately large new money inflows, while funds with poor performance suffer smaller outflows. The literature had largely attributed the result to investors' irrational star-chasing behavior. Our idea was that, instead of each investor placing an excessive amount of money at the star fund, the extra inflow may have come from rational new investors who are attracted into the fund by its stellar recent performance. The idea is extremely simple, yet hard to distinguish from other theories. Rather than trying to think of empirical tests directly, we started with what Steve would have recommended—formalizing the intuition in a simple model. Once the model was in place, it was obvious that the cost for new investors to participate in a fund is pivotal in distinguishing our theory from others, and all the empirical tests followed naturally.

This is just one example of Steve Ross's influence on my research. I owe a debt of gratitude for his guidance and encouragement throughout the years. Thank you, Steve.

Participation Costs and the Sensitivity of Fund Flows to Past Performance

*Jennifer Huang, Kelsey D. Wei, and Hong Yan**

Abstract

We present a simple rational model to highlight the effect of investors' participation costs on the response of mutual fund flows to past fund performance. By incorporating participation costs into a model in which investors learn about managers' ability from past returns, we show that mutual funds with lower participation costs have a higher flow sensitivity to medium performance and a lower flow sensitivity to high performance than their higher-cost peers. Using various fund characteristics as proxies for the reduction in participation costs, we provide empirical evidence supporting the model's implications for the asymmetric flow-performance relationship. •

Many researchers document an asymmetric relationship between mutual fund flows and past performance: Funds with superior recent performance enjoy disproportionately large new money inflows, while funds with poor performance suffer smaller outflows.[1] Moreover, fund characteristics such as age, volatility of past performance, affiliation with a large or "star"-producing fund complex, and marketing expenditures affect both the level of fund flows and the sensitivity of flows to past performance.[2] In this paper, we develop a rational model to explain simultaneously the asymmetric response of fund flows to past performance and the impact of various fund characteristics on the flow-performance relationship. We then conduct an empirical analysis to test the model predictions.

Our model relies on two main assumptions regarding investor behavior. First, investors learn about unobservable managerial ability from realized fund performance. This assumption, common to most existing models of mutual fund flows, implies that fund flows chase

---

[1]See, for example, Ippolito (1992), Gruber (1996), Chevalier and Ellison (1997), and Sirri and Tufano (1998).

[2]See, for example, Chevalier and Ellison (1997) for the impact of fund age; Sirri and Tufano (1998), Jain and Wu (2000), and Gallaher, Kaniel, and Starks (2005) for the effect of marketing and advertising expenses; Sirri and Tufano (1998) and Huang, Wei, and Yan (2004) for the importance of performance volatility; and Sirri and Tufano (1998), Massa (2003), Khorana and Servaes (2004), and Nanda, Wang, and Zheng (2004b) for the significance of the affiliation with large or star-producing fund families.

*Huang is at the McCombs School of Business, University of Texas at Austin. Wei is at the School of Management, University of Texas at Dallas. Yan is at the Moore School of Business, University of South Carolina. We thank Jonathan Berk, Keith Brown, Wayne Ferson, Alexei Goriaev, Anthony Lynch, David Musto, Lubos Pastor, Lukasz Pomorski, Brian Reid, Mark Seasholes, Clemens Sialm, Erik Sirri, Laura Starks, Sheridan Titman, Jay Wellman, Tong Yao, Lu Zheng, and an anonymous referee for insightful suggestions, and presentation participants at Australian Graduate School of Management, Boston University, Cheung Kong Graduate School of Business, the U.S. Securities & Exchange Commission, the University of Texas at Austin, the 2004 European Finance Association meeting, the 2005 China International Conference in Finance, the 2005 Michigan Mitsui Life Symposium, the 2005 Texas Finance Festival, and the 2005 Western Finance Association meeting for useful comments. All remaining errors are our own.

Reprinted with permission:
Huang, Jennifer, Kelsey D. Wei, and Hong Yan. "Participation Costs and the Sensitivity of Fund Flows to Past Performance." *The Journal of Finance* LXII (2007): 1271–1309.

after past performance due to investors' Bayesian updating process. Second, investors face participation costs when investing in mutual funds. We show that participation costs can lead to different flow responses at different performance levels and can cause cross-sectional variations in the flow-performance relationship.

The consideration of participation costs is plausible given the naivety of average investors and the dizzying array of funds from which they can choose, as Capon, Fitzsimons, and Prince (1996) and Goetzmann and Peles (1997) demonstrate.[3] We examine two types of participation costs in this paper. The first type of cost is related to the *information cost* of collecting and analyzing information about a new fund before investing in it.[4] We model the information cost as a fixed cost faced by new investors. Although investors can freely observe past performance of all funds, they have varied degrees of familiarity with different funds. To make an informed choice, investors can either *actively* seek out the relevant information about the fund or *passively* accumulate knowledge as it comes to them through advertising or broker recommendations. These two types of information gathering are complementary to each other: The more funds expend in resources to lower information barriers, the less investors have to bear the active cost. The second type of cost is related to the *transaction cost* of purchasing or redeeming fund shares. We model the transaction cost as a proportional cost that applies to both existing and new investors.

Participation costs affect fund flows through three channels. First, for a given fund, there are cross-sectional differences in participation costs due to investors' various levels of financial sophistication. Because past performance has to exceed a threshold value for an individual investor to realize a utility gain from investigating and potentially investing in the fund, better past performance attracts investors with higher costs to overcome their participation barriers. Hence, fund flows are increasingly more sensitive to higher past performance. We use the term *participation effect* to account for this differential participation of new investors. Second, for an individual investor, the cost of active information collection limits the number of funds he investigates. Since past performance provides a signal of managerial ability, the investor considers both the ranking of past performance and his participation costs in each fund when deciding which funds to learn more about. The higher his participation costs, the fewer funds he investigates, and the more likely he concentrates his investment in a few funds with superior past performance. We denote this reliance on relative performance the *individual winner-picking effect.* Third, transaction costs make it more costly for investors to trade in mutual funds. As a result, investors do not purchase (sell) funds unless their past performance is sufficiently good (bad). This *no-trading effect* makes flows less sensitive to medium levels of performance for higher transaction-costs funds.

Our theory suggests that funds with different participation costs should have different sensitivities of flows to past performance. First, the participation effect is driven by the differential costs of individual investors, and the range of these costs varies across funds. For example, the high profile of the Fidelity Magellan Fund lowers its information barrier so that most investors can overcome their participation hurdles even if the fund has only mediocre performance; therefore, its participation effect is stronger in the medium

[3]According to the Investment Company Institute data, the number of stock mutual funds in the United States increased from 399 in January 1984 to 4,601 in December 2003. Meanwhile, in 2001, 52% of households held assets in mutual funds, up from a mere 6% in 1980 (see, e.g, Hortaçsu and Syverson (2004)).

[4]The type of information we are concerned about may be regarded as "soft" information. It is related to the familiarity of an investor with a fund, and is crucial for investors in making their allocation decisions as it helps narrow the variance of their expectation of future fund returns. In contrast, the cost of acquiring "hard" information, such as funds' past performance, is minimal given the vast amount of financial data publicly available.

performance range. In contrast, a small no-name fund's information barrier is very high, especially for unsophisticated investors; a superior past performance is required before these investors will find it worthwhile to learn more about the fund, and thus the participation effect for this fund is more significant in the high performance range.

Second, the individual winner-picking effect is more pronounced for funds with higher participation costs, since investors will only investigate and eventually invest in a few funds with superior performance within this group. For lower-cost funds, investors can afford to study more of them and may discover good investments even if the recent performance of these funds has not been stellar. Therefore, their flows are more sensitive to medium performance. Finally, proportional transaction costs reduce trade in funds with medium performance and in turn the flow sensitivity. This no-trading effect is stronger for funds with larger transaction costs.

We carry out an empirical analysis to test these predictions. Although the information costs for individual investors are not directly observable, we can proxy for them using various fund characteristics that relate to fund visibility. Specifically, we use marketing expenses and the affiliation with fund families that have produced "star" funds to proxy for the variation in investors' information costs across funds, as these variables relate to the level of visibility that funds enjoy. We also use the parent family size, measured by either the value of assets under management or the diversity of fund categories offered, to capture participation costs related to the economy of scale in distribution and services that helps reduce participation barriers. Given that the overall level of information costs has declined over time due to the maturing of the mutual fund industry, we examine different time periods to investigate the effect of the change in the overall cost level. Finally, to isolate the effect of transaction costs, we compare flows to different share classes of the same fund because they are associated with the same underlying portfolios and differ mainly in their transaction costs.

Using these various proxies, we find that participation costs contribute significantly to the previously documented nonlinear flow-performance relationship. Specifically, in the medium performance range, funds with lower participation costs have higher flow sensitivities than their higher-cost counterparts, while in the high performance range, this relationship may be reversed. This finding demonstrates the significant effect of participation costs on investors' choice of mutual funds and is consistent with the predictions of our model.

Our paper is closely related to that of Sirri and Tufano (1998). They conjecture that reducing search costs should lead to an increased sensitivity of fund flows to past performance. Our main contribution is to carry this intuition further by constructing a rational model to examine how participation costs affect investors' allocation decisions among funds. Our model delineates the effect of investor participation across different performance ranges and illustrates how participation costs affect the flow-performance relationship in a structural framework. Our empirical analysis provides supporting evidence for this theoretical insight.

Several previous theoretical studies examine the asymmetric flow-performance relationship. Berk and Green (2004) assume a perfectly competitive capital market in which the return to an actively managed fund decreases with its portfolio size. Using variable cost functions for managers, they show that a convex relationship between new investments and past performance exists even in the absence of performance persistence. Lynch and Musto (2003) argue that investment companies can exercise an option to abandon poorly performing strategies and/or fire bad managers. Since poor returns are not likely to be informative about future performance, investors will respond less strongly to bad performance, leading to the convexity in the flow-performance relationship.

Our model departs from these studies by recognizing the frictions investors encounter in allocating their wealth among actively managed mutual funds. We propose a new mechanism for explaining the documented nonlinear flow-performance relationship and its cross-sectional variation. The impact of participation costs on the flow-performance relationship underscores the idea that funds without superior performance can still attract new investors by reducing their participation barriers through non-performance-related means. Moreover, our model provides a fresh perspective on the flow-performance relationship by emphasizing the role of new investors to a mutual fund. This is particularly relevant given the tremendous growth of the mutual fund industry over the past two decades.

The rest of the paper is organized as follows: In Section I we present our theoretical model and outline its empirical implications. The data and the empirical methodology are described in Section II. We discuss our empirical results in Section III, and Section IV concludes. Appendix A contains proofs for the model and Appendix B presents the simulation procedure.

I. The Model

A. Model Setup

We consider a partial equilibrium model with a finite horizon of three dates, $t = 0, 1, 2$. Investors allocate wealth between a risk-free bond and an array of actively managed mutual funds. The return on the risk-free bond is normalized to $r_f = 0$ each period, and mutual fund i produces a risky return of r_{it} at time $t = 1, 2$ according to the process

$$r_{it} = \alpha_i + \epsilon_{it}. \tag{1}$$

The term α_i, which represents the unobservable ability of the manager of fund i to deliver positive excess returns, is assumed to be constant over time for each fund and independently and identically distributed (i.i.d.) across funds; ϵ_{it}, which represents the idiosyncratic noise in the return of fund i, is i.i.d. both over time and across funds with a normal distribution, that is,

$$\epsilon_{it} \sim N(0, \sigma_\epsilon^2). \tag{2}$$

The return r_{it} should be interpreted as the fund return in excess of a benchmark. Therefore, the assumption that both α_i and ϵ_{it} are i.i.d. across funds should be reasonable. This modeling technique, following both Berk and Green (2004) and Lynch and Musto (2003), allows us to abstract away the common component in fund returns and thereby focus on the differential ability across fund managers.[5]

For each fund i, there are two types of investors, each with a different information set regarding the distribution of α_i. *Existing investors*, indexed by e, invest in fund i at time 0 and have a prior belief that managerial ability a_i is also normally distributed,

$$\alpha_i \sim N(\alpha_{i0}, \sigma_0^2). \tag{3}$$

At time 1, the existing investors observe the first-period return (r_{i1}) of fund i, and then use Bayesian updating to derive the following posterior distribution regarding managerial ability:

$$\alpha_i | r_{i1} \sim N(\alpha_{i1}, \sigma_1^2), \tag{4}$$

[5]As Lynch and Musto (2003) argue, investors may use index funds or index futures contracts to hedge out their market exposure and isolate the return component attributable to the manager's ability.

where

$$\alpha_{i1} = \alpha_{i0} + \frac{\sigma_0^2}{\sigma_0^2 + \sigma_\epsilon^2}(r_{i1} - \alpha_{i0}), \quad \sigma_1^2 = \frac{\sigma_0^2 \sigma_\epsilon^2}{\sigma_0^2 + \sigma_\epsilon^2}. \tag{5}$$

New investors, indexed by n, initially have coarser information about fund i than existing investors. Specifically, although both types of investors believe that the ability α_i is normally distributed, existing investors know with certainty the expected ability level α_{i0} while new investors know only that α_{i0} is drawn from a normal distribution,

$$\alpha_{i0} \sim N(\mu_0, \sigma_\mu^2). \tag{6}$$

New investors can improve their information set by paying participation costs, however. For simplicity, we assume that once new investors have incurred a fixed participation cost, they acquire all the relevant information that existing investors have and, in particular, they know α_{i0} for certain.

It is conceivable that the participation cost will vary both across investors and across funds. We assume that it takes the form $c_{ki} = \delta_k \bar{c}_i$ for investor k and fund i, where $\delta_k \sim$ Unif[0, 1] captures the level of financial sophistication across new investors,[6] and $\bar{c}_i$ reflects the variation across funds in the difficulty with which investors narrow down the uninformative prior for α_{i0}. Since the uninformative prior is assumed to be identical across funds, the overall cost of narrowing down a prior should be similar across all funds. However, this overall cost can be shared by individual investors through active information acquisition, and by the mutual fund through the improvement of its visibility and the reduction of other information barriers for investors. Given the complementarity between the costs borne by the mutual fund and those incurred by investors, the participation cost $\bar{c}_i$, which measures the maximum cost incurred by investors for active information acquisition, is lower for funds with a higher level of visibility and familiarity.

The investors' costs correspond to any active information collection costs that may help investors form an opinion about a particular fund. These may include the cost of studying the fund prospectus, determining its Morningstar rating, understanding its investment strategies, and seeking advice from friends and financial advisors. This type of information is of the "soft" variety that helps investors narrow the variance of their expectations. Although the costs of these individual activities may not be significantly different across funds, the amount of work that investors need to do before they can comfortably form an opinion varies across funds. For example, given the high profile of the Fidelity Magellan fund, investors need little additional information before they feel comfortable investing in the fund. On the other hand, investors are generally much more skeptical about a no-name fund, in which case they may require a lot more additional information before they decide whether it is a good investment. We note, however, that arriving at an informed expectation (reduction in σ_μ) is different from forming a favorable opinion (higher α_{i0}). Therefore, investors will not automatically choose more familiar funds.

The population mass is normalized to one for existing investors and λ_i for new investors. All investors are assumed to have constant absolute risk aversion (CARA) utility over their terminal wealth W_{j2} at date $t = 2$:

$$E[-e^{-\gamma W_{j2}}], \quad j = e, n.$$

They have the same risk aversion coefficient γ and the same initial wealth W_0 at time 0. Each investor is endowed with a stake X_{i0} in fund i at time 0, where $X_{i0} > 0$ for an existing

[6]This distributional assumption is made for tractability. Other continuous distributions can also be used without qualitatively affecting our results.

investor in fund i and $X_{i0} = 0$ for a new investor to the fund. At time 1, investors optimally allocate their wealth between the risk-free asset and the mutual funds to maximize their terminal utility. Since our study focuses on open-end mutual funds, we assume that investors are not allowed to sell funds short.

In the following subsections, we first discuss the results from a setting in which investors have no portfolio constraints, that is, they can freely borrow to finance their purchases in as many funds as they wish. Then we introduce portfolio constraints in a reduced-form specification to examine the role of participation costs in the presence of competition for flows among funds.

B. The Benchmark Case: No Portfolio Constraints

Each investor has two decisions to make at $t = 1$. First, after observing the first-period returns of all funds, he decides for each fund i that he does not own whether or not to pay the participation cost c_{ki} to acquire full information about α_{i0}. Second, for all the funds he owns or for which he chooses to pay the cost, he decides if and how much he will allocate to each one. If he chooses not to pay the cost for a new fund, he makes no investment in it.

We solve for the optimal decisions backwards by first deriving the optimal portfolio allocation given the participating decision, and then solving for the participation decision itself. The following lemma indicates that the allocation to fund i is identical between the existing and new investors.

Lemma 1 *At time $t = 1$, the optimal holdings of both existing investors and participating new investors in fund i are*

$$X^e_{i1} = X^n_{i1} \equiv X_{i1}(r_{i1}) = \begin{cases} \dfrac{\alpha_{i0}}{\gamma(2\sigma_0^2 + \sigma_\epsilon^2)} + \dfrac{\sigma_0^2}{\gamma\sigma_\epsilon^2(2\sigma_0^2 + \sigma_\epsilon^2)} r_{i1}, & r_{i1} \geq \underline{r_i} \\ 0, & \textit{otherwise}, \end{cases} \tag{7}$$

where $\underline{r_i} = -\alpha_{i0}\sigma_\epsilon^2/\sigma_0^2$.

The allocation to fund i depends only on the information related to fund i, that is, it is independent of other funds. This independence result and the fact that holdings are linear and increasing in past performance are common to CAEA-normal models with learning about managerial ability; see, for example, Berk and Green (2004) and Lynch and Musto (2003). Investors increase their holdings of the fund because a higher realized return leads to a higher posterior expected ability of the fund manager. If $r_{i1} < \underline{r_i}$, the unconstrained optimal holding is negative, so the short-sale constraint bounds the holdings from below at zero. Because all participating new investors share the same information set as existing investors, they have identical holdings when there are no additional frictions.

After deriving the optimal individual allocation for participating new investors, we compute their certainty-equivalent wealth gain from investing in new funds and solve for the optimal participation decision, whereby new investors choose to participate if and only if doing so leads to a net gain in their expected utility.

Lemma 2 *The certainty-equivalent wealth gain from investing in fund i is*

$$g(r_{i1}) \equiv -\frac{1}{\gamma}\ln\left(\frac{1 - \operatorname{erf}(B)}{2} + \frac{1 + \operatorname{erf}\left(\dfrac{B}{A}\right)}{2A} e^{-(1-\frac{1}{A^2})B^2}\right), \tag{8}$$

where $\operatorname{erf}(x) = \frac{2}{\sqrt{\pi}}\int_0^x e^{-t^2}\,dt$ *is the error function, and*

$$A \equiv \sqrt{1 + \frac{\sigma_\epsilon^2\sigma_\mu^2}{(\sigma_\epsilon^2 + \sigma_0^2)(\sigma_\epsilon^2 + 2\sigma_0^2)}}, \qquad B \equiv \frac{\sigma_\epsilon^2\mu_0 + \sigma_0^2 r_{i1}}{\sqrt{2}\sigma_\epsilon^2\sigma_\mu}. \tag{9}$$

A new investor k chooses to pay the cost c_{ki} *to investigate fund i if and only if the cost is lower than the certainty-equivalent wealth gain,* $c_{ki} \leq g(r_{i1})$.

The certainty-equivalent wealth gain $g(r_{i1})$ is a function of the uninformative prior μ_0. It does not depend on existing investors' knowledge of α_{i0}, because new investors do not have that information before they incur the cost. The gain is monotonically increasing in r_{i1} and is independent of other funds. Hence, investors base their participation decision in each fund only on its own past performance.

Corollary 1 *For a new investor with participation* cost c_{ki} *for fund i, there exists a unique cutoff return level* $\hat{r}(c_{ki})$ *such that the investor chooses to participate if and only if the first-period return of the fund* $r_{i1} \geq \hat{r}(c_{ki})$, *where* $\hat{r}(c_{ki})$ *is the solution of* r_{i1} *for* $g(r_{i1}) = c_{ki}$. *Moreover, the cutoff return* $\hat{r}(c_{ki})$ *increases with the cost level* c_{ki}.

Our model recognizes the sunk nature of information costs, that is, new investors may choose not to invest in a fund after expending resources to investigate it. This situation can arise, for example, if a fund has a good realized return, r_{i1}, but a low ex ante expected ability level, α_{i0}, such that $\hat{r}(c_{ki}) < r_{i1} < \underline{r}_i(\alpha_{i0})$. Without knowing a_{i0} a priori, new investors would optimally decide that it is worthwhile to pay the cost to study the fund, only to find out later that the fund manager was just lucky.

To facilitate discussion of empirical implications, we define the flow, f_i, as the new money invested in the fund from time 0 to time 1. We express f_i in terms of a fraction of the initial asset in the fund, X_{i0}. The following proposition combines the previous results regarding participation and optimal allocation decisions to characterize the net flow into the fund at time 1.

Proposition 1 *The net flow into fund i on date 1 is given by*

$$f_i(r_{i1}) = \frac{X_{i1}^e - X_{i0}(1 + r_{i1})}{X_{i0}} + \lambda_i \min\left[1, \frac{g(r_{i1})}{\overline{c}_i}\right]\frac{X_{i1}^n}{X_{i0}}, \tag{10}$$

where X_{i1}^e *and* X_{i1}^n *are given in equation (7), and* $g(r_{i1})$ *is the certainty-equivalent wealth gain in equation (8).*

The first term of equation (10) describes the new money flow from existing investors, whereas the second term corresponds to the flow from participating new investors. Past performance has two effects on the current-period fund flows. The first is the *learning effect*, in which both existing investors and participating new investors allocate more wealth to the fund given a higher realized return, r_{i1}, since their allocations, (X_{i1}^e, X_{i1}^n), are increasing in r_{i1}. The second effect is the *participation effect*, in which higher past returns attract more new investors into the fund. This is because better past performance implies a higher certainty-equivalent wealth gain ($g(r_{i1})$) for new investors and enables investors with higher costs to overcome their participation hurdles.

In Figure 1, we plot fund flows in equation (10) as a function of past performance. Given the independence of flows across funds, we can interpret the comparative static analysis in this figure as the cross-sectional flow-performance relationship for funds with similar characteristics but different past performance. When costs are low (solid line, $\overline{c} = 0.1$), the fund

FIGURE 1 | Theoretical Flow-Performance Relationship for Different Levels of Information Costs.

The solid line corresponds to a low information cost, where the maximum cost is $\bar{c} = 0.1$, and the other two lines correspond to higher information costs, where the dot-dashed line has maximum cost $\bar{c} = 0.2$ and the dashed line has $\bar{c} = 0.3$. Other parameters are $\gamma = 1$, $\lambda = 0.5$, $\sigma_\epsilon = 16\%$, $\alpha_{i0} = 3\%$, $\sigma_0 = 8\%$, $\mu_0 = 3\%$, and $\sigma_\mu = 3\%$, where γ is the risk aversion of the CARA investor, and λ is the relative population weight of new investors. Fund return is $r_{it} = \alpha_i + \epsilon_{it}$, where $\alpha_i \sim N(\alpha_{i0}, \sigma_0^2)$ is the prior about the managerial ability and $\epsilon_{it} \sim N(0, \sigma_\epsilon^2)$ is the i.i.d. noise over time and across funds. While the existing investors know the expected ability α_{i0} for sure, the new investors only have an uninformative prior about it, $\alpha_{i0} \sim N(\mu_0, \sigma_\mu^2)$.

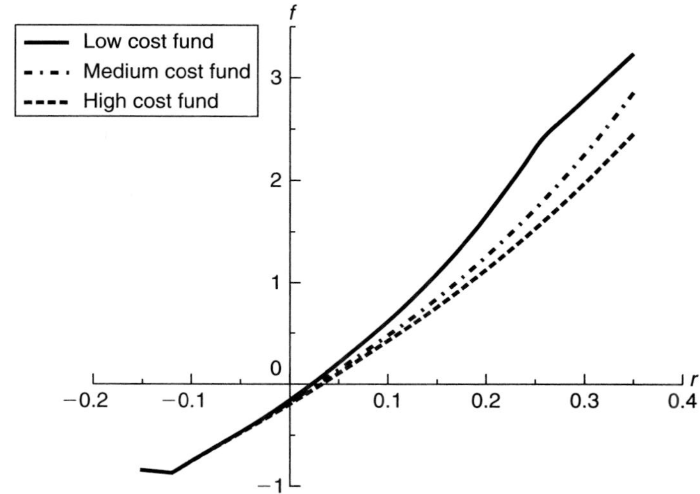

flow is an increasing and convex function of the past performance in the low-to-medium performance range (approximately $r_{i1} < 0.25$ in the figure), and it becomes linear in the high performance range ($r_{i1} > 0.25$).[7] For these funds, even high-cost (δ high) investors have low levels of costs ($\delta\bar{c}$ low). Medium performance is sufficient to attract most investors to these funds. Hence, fund flows respond more strongly to past performance and the participation effect is more pronounced in the medium performance range. On the other hand, if these funds achieve high levels of performance, all potential new investors participate in the funds. Beyond the saturation point (around $r_{i1} \sim 0.25$), the participation effect dissipates and the fund flow is a linear function of performance as it is driven only by the learning effect.

For high-cost funds (dot-dashed and dashed lines), however, a large fraction of potential investors face high levels of information costs. So, while low-cost investors (with low δ) may participate in the low-to-medium performance ranges, the rest are only drawn to the funds at high levels of performance. As a result, these funds have a flatter flow response to past medium performance than do their lower-cost peers (solid line), while the response is steeper in the range of superior performance, as demonstrated in the figure.[8]

[7]In the very low performance range ($r_{i1} < -0.07$), the flow should be constant at -100%, yet the plotted line appears to be decreasing in performance. This feature is an artifact of the definition of the fund flow, as equation (10) reduces to $f = -(1 + r_1)$ when $X_1 = 0$. See also Berk and Green (2004) for further discussion.

[8]The critical level of performance at which all potential investors will participate is much higher for these funds. In reality, it may be the case that the distribution of participation costs has an infinite support, and funds never totally exhaust the pool of potential investors. However, the intuition that funds with different participation costs have different intensities in attracting new investors is robust. We numerically solve a case in which the participation cost is normally distributed and reach similar conclusions.

For these high-cost funds, the saturation point may not be reached at any realistic performance level. A comparison between the two high-cost funds implies that, in the empirically relevant performance range, the lower-cost fund of the two will always have higher flow sensitivities to performance than the higher-cost fund. Combined with the behavior of the low-cost fund (solid line), this observation illustrates that whether higher-costs funds have higher (solid vs. dashed lines) or lower (dot-dashed vs. dashed lines) sensitivities in the empirically feasible high-performance range is an empirical question to be answered by the data.

C. With Portfolio Constraints

In our benchmark model there is no interaction among funds. Individual investors rely solely on the *absolute* performance of each fund when they allocate wealth across funds. Interestingly, even in this setting, we show that the predicted flow-performance relationship is consistent with the "winner-take-all" phenomenon in which winner funds have much higher flow sensitivity to performance than loser funds.

In reality, investors face various constraints that may lead to the consideration of funds' *relative* performance in wealth allocation. For instance, given the minimum investment levels required by most mutual funds and the existence of reasonable fixed costs for keeping track of their portfolios, investors are likely to concentrate their investment in a few funds with superior past performance. It is sensible to conjecture that this individual-level winner-picking behavior will lead to a more convex overall flow-performance relationship. What is less obvious, however, is whether the previously predicted impact of participation costs on the flow-performance relationship carries through in this case. To answer this question, we explicitly incorporate this individual winner-picking behavior into the existing model and reexamine the impact of participation costs.

To focus on the combined effect of participation costs and the winner-picking behavior on fund flows, we take a reduced-form approach to capture the reliance on relative fund performance in wealth allocation. Specifically, instead of trying to distinguish among different frictions that may lead to winner-picking by individual investors, we directly impose the portfolio constraint that each investor can invest in at most one new fund at time 1. Since the investor is still allowed to investigate as many funds as he chooses, this constraint naturally leads to the winner-picking behavior.

With the portfolio constraint, an investor takes a sequential approach in making participation and investment decisions, that is, he chooses whether to invest in the best fund that provides the highest utility gain among the ones that he has studied so far, or to incur additional costs to investigate another fund in the hope of identifying a better one. The following lemma establishes the criteria for such a decision based on the certainty-equivalent wealth gain.

Lemma 3 *Assume that an investor can invest in at most one new fund at time 1. Let $\hat{\alpha}_1$ be the maximum posterior ability for all the funds that he has studied so far and $\mathcal{I}$ be the remaining set of funds available to him. Then,*

(i) The certainty-equivalent gain of studying a new fund with past performance r_{i1} is

$$G(r_{i1}, \hat{\alpha}_1) \equiv -\frac{(A^2-1)B_1^2}{\gamma} - \frac{1}{\gamma}\ln\left(\Phi_1 e^{-(A^2-1)B_1^2} + \Phi_2 e^{-(A^2-1)\frac{B^2}{A^2}}\right), \tag{11}$$

where A and B are as defined in Lemma 2,

$$B_1 \equiv \frac{(\sigma_\epsilon^2+\sigma_0^2)\hat{\alpha}_1}{\sqrt{2\sigma_\epsilon^2}\sigma_\mu}, \quad \Phi_1 \equiv \frac{1-\operatorname{erf}(B-B_1)}{2}, \textit{ and } \Phi_2 \equiv \frac{1+\operatorname{erf}\left(\frac{B}{A}-AB_1\right)}{2A}.$$

Moreover, $G(r_{i1}, \hat{\alpha}_1)$ *is increasing in* r_{i1} *and is decreasing in* $\hat{\alpha}_1$.

(ii) Investor k with cost level c_{ki} *chooses to investigate a new fund* $i_{\max}$ *if and only if*

$$\max_{i \in \mathcal{I}} G(r_{i1}, \hat{\alpha}_1) - c_{ki} > 0 \quad \textit{and} \quad i_{\max} \equiv \arg\max_{i \in \mathcal{I}} G(r_{i1}, \hat{\alpha}_1) - c_{ki},$$

and he invests in the fund with ability level $\hat{\alpha}_1$ *when he stops investigating.*

In general, an investor trades off the gain and the cost of investigating another fund in order to maximize his net utility gain. Given the portfolio constraints, whether or not an investor decides to investigate a fund depends not only on the fund's past performance (r_{i1}) and his participation costs (c_{ki}), but also on the performance of other funds. In particular, the certainty-equivalent wealth gain $G(r_{i1}, \hat{\alpha}_1)$ is decreasing in $\hat{\alpha}_1$, indicating that an investor is less inclined to investigate more funds if he has identified one with high posterior ability. Similar to the unconstrained case, $G(r_{i1}, \hat{\alpha}_1)$ is increasing in r_{i1}. Among mutual funds with the same level of participation costs, an investor always starts with the one with the highest rank of past performance.

To understand the impact of participation costs on fund flows in the presence of portfolio constraints, we consider the case in which all funds have the same participation cost $\bar{c}$. If $\bar{c} = 0$, all investors optimally choose to investigate all available funds. With homogeneous expectations, they all choose to invest in the same fund. It is important to point out that the best fund may not be the one with the highest past performance. Rather, it is the one with the highest posterior managerial ability, which also depends on the prior α_{i0}. If $\bar{c} > 0$, for an investor with a very low individual cost (δ_k close to zero), the decision is similar to that in the zero-cost case. Specifically, he studies all funds and invests in the best fund with the highest posterior ability. On the other hand, an investor with a high level of individual costs (large δ_k) would optimally investigate funds with higher past returns first. He is likely to stop investigating more funds once he has identified a reasonably good one, potentially missing the best fund which may not have a stellar recent performance. Contrasting these two cases, we conclude that flows to mutual funds with higher participation costs are more concentrated in funds with superior performance relative to their lower-cost counterparts.

This setting also implies that flows are likely to be concentrated in just a few funds. In reality, however, a large number of mutual funds receive inflows. This discrepancy may be accounted for by realizing that there are a lot of investor heterogeneities that we have not considered in the model. Most investors settle on a subset of funds in which they will potentially invest in a rather arbitrary way. For example, they may heed the recommendations of friends or brokers, or may simply be constrained by the limited offerings in their 401(K) plans. To account for these heterogeneities, we assume that each individual investor has access to only a random subset of n mutual funds. They are either unaware of or, for exogenous reasons, unwilling to invest in other funds. We further assume that the investment opportunity sets are independent across investors, and that the probability of a fund being included in an investment opportunity set is independent of its past performance.[9]

While a closed-form solution is not attainable, we can obtain the flow-performance relationship using numerical simulations, which we describe in Appendix B. The results are illustrated in Figure 2. Since fund flows for existing investors are not affected by participation costs and are exactly the same as those in the unconstrained case, we plot only the flows for new investors to focus on the impact of participation costs. To be consistent with our empirical tests later, we use the relative performance rank in percentiles.

[9]Although a fund's past superior performance generally helps improve its visibility, our assumption is conservative in that it biases against finding the result that high-cost funds have higher flow-performance sensitivity in the high performance range.

FIGURE 2 | Theoretical Flow-Performance Relationship for Different Levels of Information Costs, Under Portfolio Constraints.

We report only the flow from new investors. Panel A (B) reports fund flows in the absence (presence) of individual winner-picking by assuming that investors have access to a randomly selected subset of $n = 1 (n = 10)$ fund(s). The solid line in each panel corresponds to no participation costs ($\bar{c} = 0$), and the dashed line to high participation costs ($\bar{c} = 0.2$). Other parameters are $\gamma = 1$, $\sigma_\epsilon = 16\%$, $\alpha_{i0} = 3\%$, $\sigma_0 = 8\%$, $\mu_0 = 3\%$, and $\sigma_\mu = 3\%$, where γ is the risk aversion of the CARA investor. Fund return is $r_{it} = \alpha_i + \epsilon_{it}$, where $\alpha_i \sim N(\alpha_{i0}, \sigma_0^2)$ is the prior about the managerial ability and $\epsilon_{it} \sim N(0, \sigma_\epsilon^2)$ is the i.i.d. noise over time and across funds. While the existing investors know the expected ability α_{i0} for sure, the new investors only have an uninformative prior about it, $\alpha_{i0} \sim N(\mu_0, \sigma_\mu^2)$.

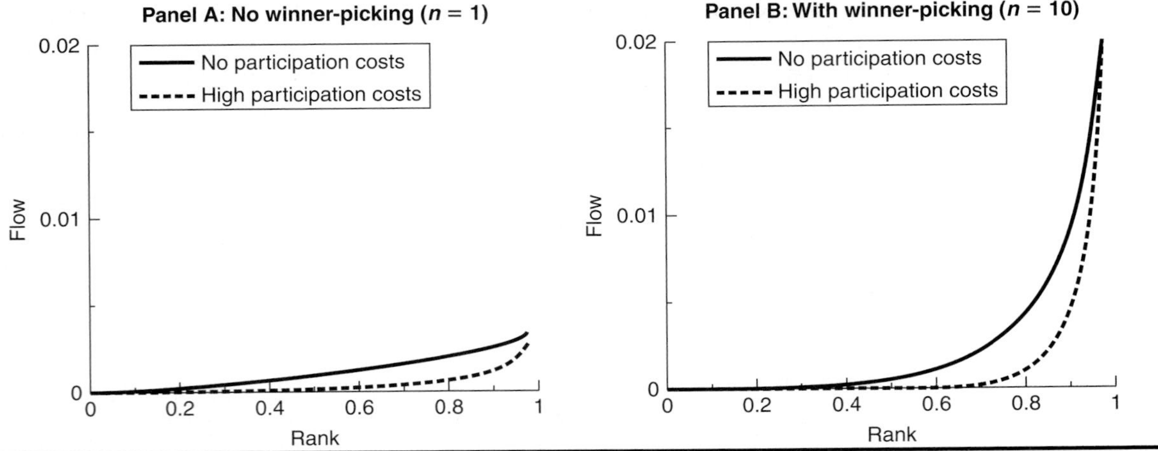

In Panel A, we plot fund flows for the case of each investor having only one randomly selected fund in his opportunity set. There is no winner-picking at the individual level, and the resulting fund flows are driven by the gradual participation of new investors identified in the unconstrained case. Our previous result on the participation effect is confirmed by comparing the dashed (high-cost funds) and the solid lines (zero-cost funds). In Panel B, there is individual winner-picking since each investor is restricted to investing in only one fund out of the 10 randomly selected funds in his opportunity set ($n = 10$). The graph clearly demonstrates that investment from new investors in funds with lower participation costs is more sensitive to past performance in the medium performance range and that this relationship is reversed in the high performance range.

Comparing the solid lines (or the dashed lines) across Panels A and B, we observe that, for a given level of participation costs, the individual winner-picking effect leads to a more convex flow-performance relationship. Moreover, the contrast between the solid and the dashed lines in Panel B indicates that the participation and the individual winner-picking effects reinforce each other and produce the same prediction regarding the impact of participation costs on fund flows.

D. Transaction Costs

In addition to a fixed information cost for investing in a new fund, both existing and new investors may also face a proportional transaction cost for purchasing (or redeeming) shares of a mutual fund, corresponding to front (or back)-end loads. For simplicity, we consider fund flows in the absence of portfolio constraints in this part.

Lemma 4 *Let ρ_+ (or ρ_-) be the proportional transaction cost for purchasing (or redeeming) shares of the mutual fund. At time $t = 1$, the existing investor allocates X_{i1}^e dollars to the mutual fund, where*

$$X_{i1}^{e}\,(X_{i0},r_{i1}) = \begin{cases} \dfrac{1}{\gamma(2\sigma_0^2+\sigma_\epsilon^2)}(\alpha_{i0}-\rho_+) + \dfrac{\sigma_0^2}{\gamma\sigma_\epsilon^2(2\sigma_0^2+\sigma_\epsilon^2)}(r_{i1}-\rho_+), & \text{if } r_{i1} \geq \bar{r}_{i+} \\ X_{i0}(1+r_{i1}), & \text{if } \bar{r}_{i-} \leq r_{i1} < \bar{r}_{i+} \\ \dfrac{1}{\gamma(2\sigma_0^2+\sigma_\epsilon^2)}(\alpha_{i0}+\rho_-) + \dfrac{\sigma_0^2}{\gamma\sigma_\epsilon^2(2\sigma_0^2+\sigma_\epsilon^2)}(r_{i1}+\rho_-), & \text{if } \underline{r_i} \leq r_{i1} < \bar{r}_{i-} \\ 0, & \text{otherwise,} \end{cases} \quad (12)$$

and $\bar{r}_{i+}, \bar{r}_{i-}$, and $\underline{r_i}$ are defined in Appendix A. The dollar holding for participating new investors is $X_{i1}^{n}\,(r_{i1}) = X_{i1}^{e}\,(0, r_{i1})$.

The desired holding of the mutual fund is piecewise linear in past performance r_{i1} When $r_{i1} > \bar{r}_{i+}$, the past performance is sufficiently good that investors choose to purchase additional shares of the fund. Proportional transaction costs effectively reduce the posterior expected return in equation (5) by ρ_+ for the next period. In contrast, when $r_{i1} < \bar{r}_{i-}$, the past performance is so bad that investors choose to sell some of their existing holdings. Since investors save the transaction cost ρ_- on each dollar they do not sell, their holding level is determined as if the expected posterior return were increased by ρ_-. Between the two cutoff return levels is a no-trade region where the past performance is not sufficient to induce new purchases but still high enough to discourage redemptions. Investors do not trade and the dollar holdings change only due to the realized return on existing positions. Holdings have a lower bound of zero since investors are not allowed to sell short the fund. Finally, since a participating new investor has the same information as an existing investor, the holding of the former is the same as that of the latter with zero initial holding of the fund.

Figure 3 plots the flow-performance relationship in equation (10) with the optimal holdings X_{i1}^{n} and X_{i1}^{e} given in Lemma 4. Comparing the cases with (the dotted line) or without (the solid line) transaction costs, we observe that fund flows are less sensitive to medium performance for funds with higher transaction costs. The driving force for this result is the presence of the no-trade region. Although the mechanisms are entirely different, the predicted impact of proportional transaction costs on the flow-performance relationship is similar to that of information costs in the medium performance range.

E. Empirical Implications

Our theory highlights the effect of participation costs on the flow-performance relationship. While in the model the participation cost refers mainly to the individual investors' costs of actively seeking out information about funds, it is complemented by the cost borne by funds to increase their visibility and reduce information barriers for investors. The more a fund expends resources in this effort, the less cost an investor needs to incur in actively collecting information. This leads to cross-sectional implications of our model that may be tested using fund characteristics that proxy for differences in visibility and information barriers across funds. For expositional convenience, we describe funds with high information barriers or low visibility as having high information costs.

In our model, we outline three channels through which participation costs can influence fund flows, namely, the participation and individual winner-picking effects due to information costs, and the no-trade effect due to transaction costs. All three effects lead to a stronger response of flows to performance in the medium performance range for funds

FIGURE 3 | Theoretical Flow-Performance Relationship for Different Levels of Transaction Costs.

The solid line corresponds to zero transaction costs when $\rho_+ = \rho_- = 0$, and the dotted line corresponds to positive transaction costs when $\rho_+ = 1\%$ and $\rho_- = 0.5\%$. Other parameters are $\bar{c} = 0.1$, $\gamma = 1$, $\lambda = 0.5$, $\sigma_\epsilon = 16\%$, $\alpha_{i0} = 3\%$, $\sigma_0 = 8\%$, $\mu_0 = 3\%$, and $\sigma_\mu = 3\%$, where $\bar{c}$ is the maximum participation cost, γ is the risk aversion of the CARA investor, and λ is the relative population weight of new investors. Fund return is $r_{it} = \alpha_i + \epsilon_{it}$, where $\alpha_i \sim N(\alpha_{i0}, \sigma_0^2)$ is the prior about the managerial ability and $\epsilon_{it} \sim N(0, \sigma_\epsilon^2)$ is the i.i.d. noise over time and across funds. While the existing investors know the expected ability α_{i0} for sure, the new investors only have an uninformative prior about it, $\alpha_{i0} \sim N(\mu_0, \sigma_\mu^2)$.

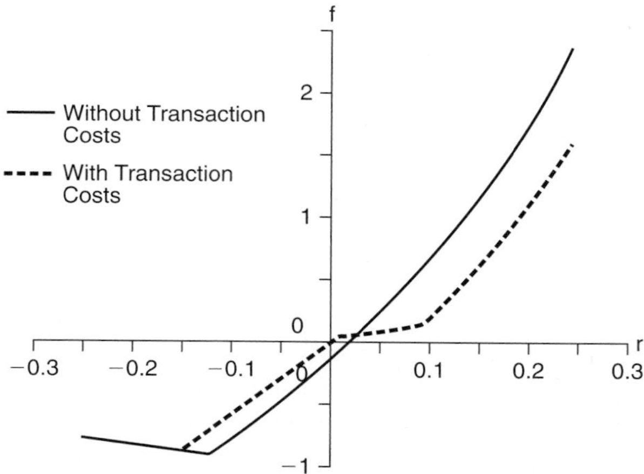

with lower participation costs. In the high performance range, although the individual winner-picking effect predicts a stronger response of flows to performance for funds with higher participation costs, the implication of the participation effect may depend on the overall level of participation costs among the funds, as we discussed earlier in connection with Figure 1. Finally, the effect of transaction costs alone does not predict a difference in the high performance range.

Therefore, our main empirical prediction is that, in the medium performance range, both information costs and transaction costs will lead lower-cost funds to have a higher flow sensitivity to performance than their higher-cost counterparts. In the high performance range, information costs may cause this relationship to reverse.[10] In the following sections, we identify different proxies for both information costs and transaction costs and empirically verify this prediction.

II. Data and Empirical Methodology

A. Data

Our main data source is the Center for Research in Security Prices (CRSP) Survivorship Bias Free Mutual Fund Database, from which we obtain information about fund net asset value, return, and characteristics. Since CRSP does not provide consistent fund investment objectives and fund family names for the years prior to 1992, we classify funds into different types and identify their family affiliation based upon the CDA-Spectrum mutual fund data from Thomson Financial, Inc. Because we focus on flows into actively managed funds, we exclude

[10] Participation costs also have an effect on the level of fund flows, as Figure 1 illustrates. This is consistent with the earlier empirical evidence in Sirri and Tufano (1998), Jain and Wu (2000), Massa (2003), and Nanda et al. (2004b). In this paper, we focus instead on the implications of our model for the sensitivity of flows to past performance.

index funds from our sample. To facilitate comparison with the prior literature, we also exclude sector funds, international funds, bond funds, and balanced funds from our study. Consequently, our data set mainly consists of actively managed equity funds in the following investment objective categories: aggressive growth, growth, and growth and income.

Our sample period spans the years from 1981 to 2001, when complete information about fund managers and investment objectives is available.[11] Since CRSP does not report end-of-month total net asset values until after 1991, we examine fund flows at the quarterly level for our entire sample period. To control for fund growth that is driven by fund characteristics such as total expense ratios, age, and total net assets, we extract these data from the CRSP mutual fund database.

Using quarterly total net asset values from CRSP, we define the quarterly net flow into a fund as

$$Flow_{i,t} = \frac{TNA_{i,t} - TNA_{i,t-1}(1 + R_{i,t})}{TNA_{i,t-1}},$$

where $R_{i,t}$ is the return of fund i during quarter t, and $TNA_{i,t}$ is fund i's total net asset value at the end of quarter t. Hence, our definition of the fund flow reflects the percentage growth of a fund that is due to new investments. By adopting this definition, we are assuming that new money comes in at the end of each quarter since we have no information regarding the timing of new investment. As Elton, Gruber, and Blake (2001) indicate, there exists a large number of errors associated with mutual fund mergers and splits in the CRSP mutual fund database, which leads to extreme values of flows. To prevent a potential impact from these outliers, we filter out the top and bottom 2.5% tails of the net flow data.

Table I shows the number of funds included in this study at the end of each year. Over time, the number of actively managed funds has grown tremendously. We utilize 217 funds in 1981 and 3,265 funds in 2001 for our empirical analysis.[12] During our sample period, the average number of funds managed by each fund family has increased from about 4 in 1981 to 14 in 2001. At the same time, the average age of funds has decreased due to the mushrooming of new funds in recent boom markets. The total fees, defined as the total expense ratio plus one-seventh of the up-front load,[13] have remained rather stable. Table I also reports that the cross-sectionally averaged year-end quarterly fund flow has varied between −4.03% and 4.41%. Volatility of fund returns, measured as the standard deviation of monthly returns in the 12-month period prior to each quarter, has fluctuated between the mid-1990 low of 2.63% and the post-1987 high of 8.29%.

B. Empirical Methodology

To examine the flow-performance sensitivity, in each quarter we run cross-sectional regressions to estimate the sensitivity of flows to performance, controlling for other factors that could potentially affect the level of flows. We report the means and t-statistics from the time

[11]Although the CRSP-CDA merged data set begins in 1980, our empirical analysis begins in 1981 because lagged information is required to calculate fund flow, performance, and other variables.

[12]During the 1990s, mutual funds started to offer different share classes that represent claims to the same underlying portfolios but with different fee structures. As noted in the CRSP mutual fund manual, CRSP treats each share class as a stand-alone fund and assigns it a separate fund identification number. Since our main purpose is to study fund flows, listing each share class separately does not lead to the double-counting problem. Nonetheless, we have also conducted all analysis at the fund level by combining multiple share classes of the same fund. Our results regarding the effect of information costs are not affected by the treatment of share classes.

[13]Sirri and Tufano (1998) estimate that the TNA-weighted redemption rate of equity funds was 14% in 1990. This implies an average holding period of 7 years.

TABLE I | Summary Statistics

This table reports summary statistics of our full sample from 1981 to 2001. At the end of each year, we calculate the cross-sectional mean value of the following fund characteristics: total net asset value, fund age, total fees, average number of funds per family (we count multiple share classes of the same fund only once), average quarterly flow per fund, four-factor model-adjusted return (alpha), and standard deviation of monthly fund returns in the 12 months prior to each quarter (volatility).

	N	TNA (in millions)	Age	Total Fees (%)	Number of Funds per Family	Quarterly Flow (%)	Four-Factor Alpha (%)	Volatility (%)
1981	217	148.93	21.05	1.68	3.84	−0.36	−0.05	4.89
1982	231	157.08	21.24	1.60	3.82	0.10	0.06	4.76
1983	239	242.53	21.36	1.65	3.86	0.72	−0.02	4.50
1984	262	236.73	21.12	1.56	4.43	−1.59	−0.02	4.78
1985	287	277.60	20.10	1.59	5.11	1.11	−0.06	3.73
1986	329	331.92	20.12	1.58	5.56	0.20	−0.05	5.02
1987	404	445.30	18.23	1.48	7.26	−4.03	0.02	4.29
1988	466	326.37	17.36	1.49	9.21	−3.58	0.07	8.29
1989	515	372.61	16.65	1.67	10.28	−0.23	0.09	3.21
1990	544	305.81	16.36	1.70	9.72	0.93	0.07	5.13
1991	604	406.56	15.82	1.74	9.61	3.47	−0.01	4.20
1992	718	450.79	14.05	1.40	9.20	4.27	0.01	4.33
1993	891	533.47	12.29	1.66	9.29	2.51	0.04	2.65
1994	1339	415.63	9.22	1.61	12.59	0.69	−0.04	3.11
1995	1793	452.10	7.84	1.62	14.58	4.00	−0.07	2.63
1996	2131	539.68	7.59	1.71	12.05	3.88	−0.10	3.46
1997	2629	615.88	6.95	1.73	14.38	4.41	−0.09	4.45
1998	3213	540.31	6.64	1.72	14.80	1.07	−0.19	6.38
1999	3434	662.38	7.12	1.71	10.61	0.60	−0.19	4.75
2000	3446	805.06	7.67	1.72	14.43	1.65	0.14	6.91
2001	3265	578.60	8.63	1.68	14.16	1.49	0.11	6.53

series of coefficient estimates following Fama and MacBeth (1973).[14] Because we relate quarterly flows to past performance measured over the preceding 12 or 36 months, the cross-sectional flow-performance sensitivity estimated in each quarter is likely to be autocorrelated. To account for this problem, we calculate the Fama–MacBeth *t*-statistics using the Newey and West (1987) autocorrelation and heteroskedasticity consistent standard errors.

We use two measures of fund performance. The first measure is the ranking of funds' preceding 12-month returns within their respective investment objective categories. The second measure is the ranked risk-adjusted returns in the preceding 36 months according to the four-factor model of Carhart (1997):

$$R_{i,t} - R_{f,t} = \alpha_i + \beta_i^{MKT} MKT_t + \beta_i^{SMB} SMB_t + \beta_i^{HML} HML_t + \beta_i^{MOM} MOM_t + \epsilon_{i,t}, \tag{13}$$

[14] We also repeat all analysis using unbalanced panel regressions with time effects and panel-corrected standard errors that adjust for autocorrelations for each fund and heteroskedasticity across funds. The results are not materially different from those reported later in this paper.

where $R_{i,t}$ and $R_{f,t}$ are the return for fund i and the one-month T-bill rate in month t, respectively, and MKT_t, SMB_t, HML_t, and MOM_t are the month-t returns of the three Fama and French (1993) factors and the momentum factor.[15] To ensure the accuracy of estimation, we include only funds that exist for at least 20 months during the estimation period.

Previous studies document that other non-performance-related variables also affect flows and their sensitivity to performance. Therefore, we include as control variables the total risk of a fund measured by the standard deviation of returns over the performance estimation period, fund age measured by the natural logarithm of $(1 + age)$ and its interaction with performance, fund size measured by the natural logarithm of fund TNA in the previous quarter, and the lagged total fee ratio. Finally, we include the aggregate flow into each fund category in quarter t to control for other unobserved factors, such as sentiment shifts, that can potentially influence fund flows.

Because our main interest is in the asymmetric flow-performance relationship, we estimate flows using a piecewise linear regression that allows for different flow-performance sensitivities at different levels of performance. Each quarter we rank all funds according to their past relative performance within their respective investment objective categories or their Carhart four-factor alphas, and assign them a continuous rank ranging from zero (worst) to one (best), with the rankings corresponding to their performance percentiles. Funds are then classified into low, medium, and high performance groups. Funds ranked in the lowest (highest) performance quintile are in the low (high) group. The medium group includes funds with performance ranked in the middle three quintiles. To examine the impact of participation costs on the flow-performance sensitivity at different performance levels, we interact performance rank with a proxy for lower participation costs ($LPC_{i,t-1}$) in the following regression:

$$\begin{aligned} Flow_{i,t} &= a + b_1 * Low_{i,t-1} + \beta_1 * Low_{i,t-1} \times LPC_{i,t-1} \\ &+ b_2 * Mid_{i,t-1} + \beta_2 * Mid_{i,t-1} \times LPC_{i,t-1} \\ &+ b_3 * High_{i,t-1} + \beta_3 * High_{i,t-1} \times LPC_{i,t-1} \\ &+ Controls + \epsilon_{i,t}, \end{aligned} \tag{14}$$

where $Low_{i,t-1}$ represents the performance rank in the lowest quintile, $Mid_{i,t-1}$ represents the performance rank in quintiles 2–4, and $High_{i,t-1}$ represents the performance rank in the highest quintile.[16]

III. Empirical Results

Our theory highlights investors' participation costs as an important determinant of the asymmetric flow-performance relationship. In this section, we empirically test this prediction using several proxies for variations in funds' participation costs.

A. The Effects of Information Costs

Since funds' marketing efforts can potentially lower investors' information costs, we use marketing expenses as one proxy for the reduction in fund-level participation costs. Due to

[15] All of these factor returns are obtained through Ken French's Web site. We thank Ken French for making the data available to the public.

[16] Specifically, the fractional rank for fund i is defined as: $Low_{i,t-1} = Min(Rank_{i,t-1}, 0.2)$, $Mid_{i,t-1} = Min(0.6, Rank_{i,t-1} - Low_{i,t-1})$, and $High_{i,t-1} = Rank_{i,t-1} - Low_{i,t-1} - Mid_{i,t-1}$, where $Rank_{i,t-1}$ is fund i's performance percentile. We also form three groups consisting of an equal number of funds based on their performance ranking and find similar results.

data limitations, we follow Sirri and Tufano (1998) and measure marketing expenses using a fund's total fee ratio, defined as the annual expense ratio plus one-seventh of the up-front load fees. Although this measure includes components other than marketing expenses, Sirri and Tufano point out that funds spend close to half of their expenses on marketing. Therefore, it is reasonable to conjecture that funds with higher total fees spend more on advertising and distribution efforts on average.[17]

Del Guercio and Tkac (2002b), Khorana and Servaes (2004), and Nanda et al. (2004b) provide evidence indicating that the presence of a "star" fund can have a positive spillover effect, whereby other funds in the same family also enjoy increased fund flows. Since investors who are attracted to a star fund can potentially become aware of other offerings of the family, the information costs for those star-affiliated funds may be reduced. Therefore, we use a fund's affiliation with a family that has produced star funds as a second proxy for the reduced participation costs.[18]

A fund's affiliation with a large family can proxy for lower participation costs due to brand recognition, since it is easier for new investors to pay attention to large and established families such as Fidelity or Vanguard (see Capon et al. (1996) and Goetzmann and Peles (1997)). Affiliated funds are also able to tap into the investor base of the whole family by increasing investors' recognition of the fund and reducing the transaction costs associated with switching from one fund to another. Therefore, our third and fourth proxies capture the effect of family affiliation, which leads to reduction of information barriers and the economy of scale in services provided. Specifically, the third proxy is family size, measured by the total net assets under management in the affiliated family, which reflects the brand recognition and resources of the family; the fourth proxy is the number of fund categories offered by the affiliated family, which measures the breadth of offerings.

To get an overview of the impact of participation costs, we first compare the flow-performance relationship for funds with different levels of participation costs. In each quarter of our sample period, we separate all funds into two groups according to their respective levels of the aforementioned characteristics. For the star-affiliation measure, the groups are defined as whether or not the fund is affiliated with a family that has produced other star funds. For all other measures, we use the median level of the particular characteristic as the break point for the two groups. Within each group, we rank fund returns into ten bins based on their Carhart four-factor alphas estimated from equation (13). We average the flows for all funds in each performance bin to obtain a flow performance relationship. The results are presented in Figure 4.

The first impression one obtains from the figure is that, for all four proxies, funds with low participation costs (solid lines) attract more flows than funds with high participation costs across the entire performance spectrum. This effect of participation costs on the level of flows is consistent with both our model prediction and earlier empirical evidence, as documented in Sirri and Tufano (1998), Jain and Wu (2000), Del Guercio and Tkac (2002b), Massa (2003), and Nanda et al. (2004b). The only exception is that the non-star-affiliated funds do not seem to attract lower flows when they achieve superior past performance than do the star-affiliated funds. This is mainly because funds achieving this level of performance are more likely to be stars than star-affiliated, and hence attract more inflows by themselves.

Close inspection of Figure 4 reveals that, in Panel A, funds with high-marketing expenses have a stronger flow-performance sensitivity in the medium performance range

[17]We also use the 12b-1 fees plus one-seventh of front-end loads as an alternative measure of marketing expenses.

[18]Details of the identification of a star fund are discussed later.

FIGURE 4 | The Flow-Performance Relationship for Different Levels of Information Costs Proxied by Fund Characteristics During 1981–2001.

Panel A reports the result for marketing expenses, measured by the total fee ratio. Panel B reports the result for the affiliation with a star-producing family. Panel C reports the result for the affiliated-family size, measured by the total net assets under management within the fund family. Panel D reports the result for the diversity of the affiliated-family offering, measured by the number of fund categories offered by the fund family.

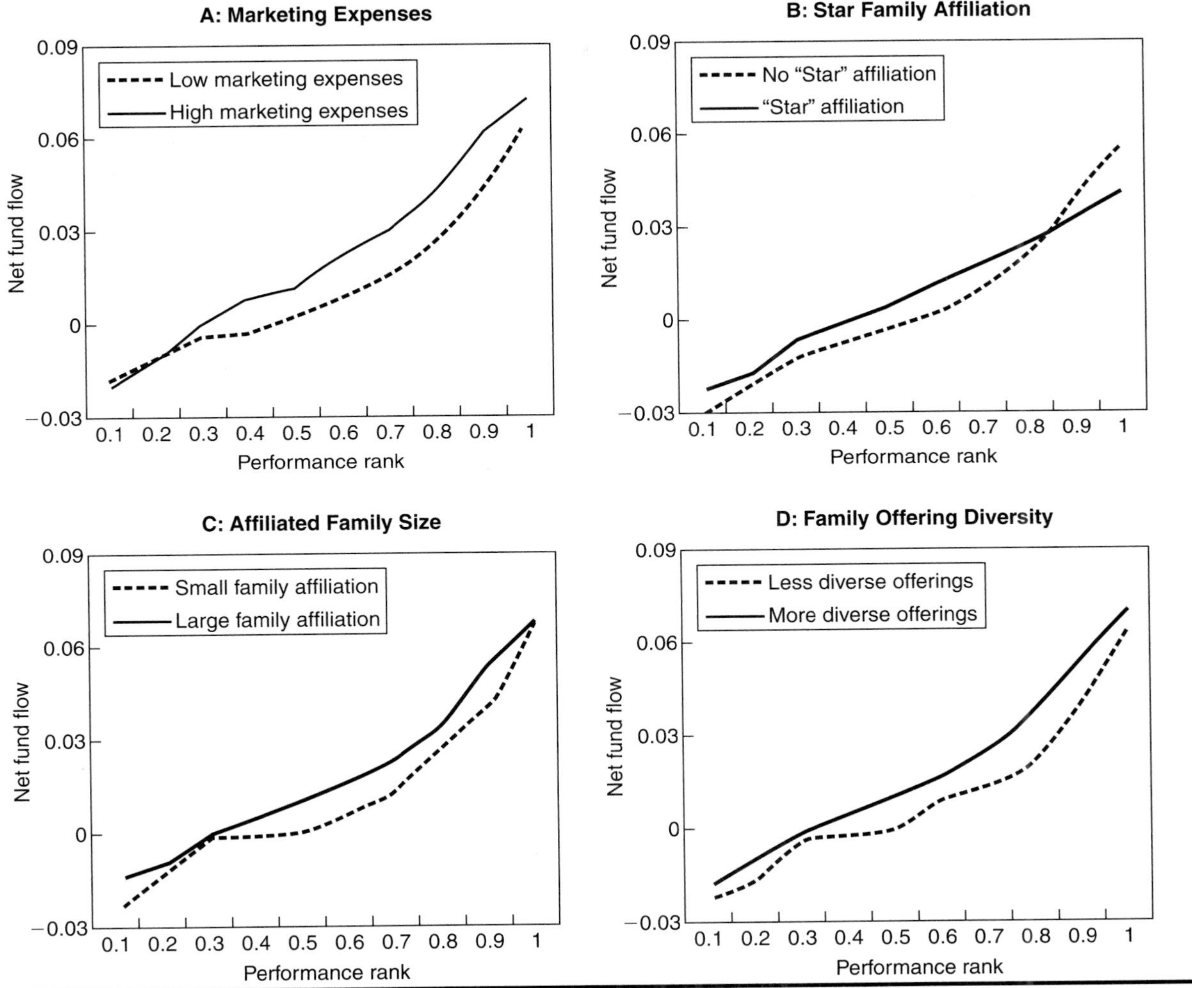

than do their low-marketing-expenses counterparts, while in the high performance ranges, the slope for the low-marketing-expenses funds is higher. Similar patterns obtain in all other panels as well.

Although the flow-performance relationships presented in Figure 4 are consistent with our predictions, we need to interpret these observations with caution, as we have not controlled for other fund characteristics that also have effects on fund flows. To provide more rigorous statistical evidence for our predictions, we carry out regression analyses in the following subsections using the four proxies discussed above. Specifically, after controlling for other characteristics known to affect fund flows, we expect to find a positive coefficient β_2 and a negative coefficient β_3 in the regression (14).

A.1. Marketing Expenses Using the total fee ratios in place of $LPC_{i,t-1}$ in regression (14), we study the effect of marketing expenses on flow sensitivity to performance in a multivariate regression analysis. The results are presented in Table II. Consistent with the model prediction, the coefficient for the interaction term between performance and the total fee ratio is significantly positive in the medium performance range and significantly negative in the high performance range. In particular, if we focus on the first column, where the ranking of raw returns is used as a measure of performance, the result shows that a 1% increase in the total fee ratio will increase the sensitivity of flows to the mid-range performance from 0.104 to 0.122, an 18% increase, while reducing flow sensitivity to the top-quintile performance from 0.428 to 0.380, an 11% decrease. This leads to an overall less convex flow-performance relationship for funds that have high marketing expenditures. Moreover, this result is robust if we use a performance ranking based on risk-adjusted returns measured by the four-factor alphas (Carhart 1997), as shown in the second column of Table II.

The effects of other determinants of flows shown in Table II are consistent with those demonstrated in previous studies. For example, we find a negative relationship between fund flows and the standard deviation. This finding holds for regressions with both performance measures, although the effect of risk on fund flows is weaker when performance is measured using the four-factor alphas. Consistent with the results of Chevalier and Ellison (1997), we find that both the level of flows and the sensitivity of flows to past performance are lower for older funds. In addition to the interaction between total fees and performance, we control for the total expense ratio itself in the regression. As the table shows, after controlling for the effect of the expense ratio on reducing information costs, a higher expense ratio lowers the level of fund flows.

Barber, Odean, and Zheng (2005) document that flows are more sensitive to 12b-1 fees than other components of the costs incurred by fund investors. Therefore, we use distribution expenses, which is the sum of the 12b-1 fees plus one-seventh of the front-end loads, as an alternative measure of marketing expenses.[19] The results, also presented in Table II, are qualitatively similar to the ones using total fee ratios.

In summary, funds with greater marketing and distribution efforts enjoy greater investor recognition and a lower performance threshold for attracting new investors. A moderate level of performance is sufficient to attract most investors into these funds, leading to higher flow sensitivity in the medium performance range. On the other hand, funds with lower marketing expenses will start to attract more new investors only as performance improves further, and flows become more sensitive to performance only in the superior performance range.

A.2. "Star" Family Affiliation As a prominent gauge of fund quality followed by many investors, Morningstar five-star ratings can bring the designated funds elevated visibility. Del Guercio and Tkac (2002b) show that Morningstar ratings can significantly affect fund flows. An upgrade or downgrade by Morningstar is usually followed by abnormal cash flows, in addition to those induced by performance changes. Following Nanda et al. (2004b), we use a procedure to mimic the Morningstar ratings by ranking funds according to their risk-adjusted performance.

[19]The 12b-1 fees were not explicitly recognized until 1992. Our results are robust to using either the post-1992 sample period or the entire sample period with the 12b-1 fees in the pre-1992 period set to be zero. The results presented here are from the entire sample period. We also use 12b-1 fees only as a proxy for the post-1992 period and find consistent results.

TABLE II | The Effect of Marketing Expenses on the Flow-Performance Relationship

This table examines the effect of marketing expenses on the sensitivity of flow to past performance. Each quarter, fractional performance ranks ranging from zero to one are assigned to funds according to their returns in the past 12 months relative to other funds with similar investment objectives, or according to their four-factor model alphas during the past 36 months. The fractional rank for funds in the bottom performance quintile (Low) is defined as Min ($Rank_{t-1}$, 0.2). Funds in the three medium performance quintiles (Mid) are grouped together and receive ranks that are defined as Min (0.6, Rank_{t-1} − Low). The rank for the top performance quintile (High) is defined as Rank_{t-1} − Mid − Low. Each quarter a piecewise linear regression is performed by regressing quarterly flows on funds' fractional performance rankings over the low, medium, and high performance ranges, their interaction terms with total fees, or distribution expenses (measured as 12b-1 fees plus one-seventh front-end loads). The control variables include aggregate flow into the fund objective category, volatility of monthly returns during the performance measurement period, the logarithm of one plus fund age and its interaction with performance, the logarithm of fund size as proxied by lagged total net asset value, and lagged total fees (or lagged distribution expenses). Time-series average coefficients and the Fama–MacBeth *t*-statistics (in parentheses) calculated with Newey–West robust standard errors are reported. *, **, and *** denote significance at the 10%, 5%, and 1% level, respectively.

Marketing Expense Proxy	**Expense Ratio + 1/7 Front-End Loads**		**12b-1 Fees + 1/7 Front-End Loads**	
Performance Measured by	**Raw Return**	**Four-Factor Alpha**	**Raw Return**	**Four-Factor Alpha**
Intercept	0.015*	0.020**	0.008	0.012
	(1.78)	(2.54)	(1.09)	(1.51)
Category Flow	0.671***	0.362***	0.652***	0.327***
	(7.57)	(5.05)	(7.58)	(3.76)
Low	0.117***	0.064**	0.009***	0.057***
	(3.32)	(2.44)	(4.39)	(3.26)
Low * Marketing Expense	1.645	1.434	9.583***	8.468***
	(0.98)	(1.22)	(3.78)	(3.99)
Mid	0.104***	0.064***	0.123***	0.072***
	(9.52)	(6.12)	(14.17)	(9.75)
Mid * Marketing Expense	1.802***	1.023***	1.747**	1.136**
	(3.79)	(2.70)	(2.48)	(2.09)
High	0.428***	0.291***	0.380***	0.227***
	(10.06)	(8.87)	(13.90)	(10.20)
High * Marketing Expense	−4.810**	−5.256***	−5.536*	−5.273**
	(−2.26)	(−3.05)	(−1.96)	(−2.05)
Volatility	−0.271***	−0.164*	−0.257***	−0.156*
	(−3.15)	(−1.90)	(−3.02)	(−1.77)
Age	−0.011***	−0.012***	−0.010***	−0.012***
	(−6.93)	(−9.33)	(−7.21)	(−9.83)
Age * Performance	−0.022***	−0.006***	−0.022***	−0.005***
	(−9.76)	(−2.97)	(−9.97)	(−2.72)
Size	−0.002***	−0.001**	−0.001	0.000
	(−3.70)	(−2.44)	(−1.59)	(−0.33)
Expense Ratio			0.141	0.353**
			(0.93)	(2.50)
Distribution Expenses			−1.965***	−1.667***
			(−5.30)	(−4.80)
Total Fees	−0.723***	−0.345*		
	(−3.14)	(−1.91)		

According to this procedure,[20] in each period a fund is assigned a score based upon the difference between a load-adjusted return and a risk measure during the past three years. Within each fund category, funds are then ranked according to their three-year scores relative to their peers. Funds that are ranked in the top 10% of each category are assigned five-star ratings. Morningstar also provides five-year and ten-year star ratings and computes the overall rating as a weighted average of ratings over different horizons. Although the overall star rating is widely cited in business publications, it is highly correlated with the three-year ratings, as Sharpe (1997) points out. Therefore, we focus on the three-year ratings to designate star funds. Their parent companies are hence designated as star families.

Table III presents an analysis based on this star-identifying scheme. We proxy for participation costs with a dummy variable that is equal to one if a fund is affiliated with a star family but is not a star itself, and zero otherwise. To control for the effect of the publicity surrounding star status, we also include a dummy variable indicating star funds.

As Table III shows, the interaction term between mid-range performance and the star family affiliation dummy is significantly positive, indicating that being in a star family helps a fund attract more potential investors by raising their awareness of the fund, even if the fund itself is not a star. Meanwhile, the interaction term for the high performance range is not significant. This shows that being affiliated with a star-producing family does not help a fund that has already achieved superior performance. This can be seen in that the star dummy itself is significantly positive, which is also an indication that our star rating scheme well captures the name recognition and media attention received by funds with outstanding performance. Based on point estimates, being affiliated with a star family changes the flow sensitivity to different levels of performance from (0.16, 0.11, 0.24) to (0.13, 0.13, 0.21), for (low, medium, high) performance ranges.

A.3. Affiliation with Large Families In this subsection, we examine the effect of affiliation with large fund families to account for the economy of scale in raising fund visibility, providing services, and reducing investment barriers. We measure the effect of family affiliation in two different ways. The first measure is the logarithm of total net assets under management for the fund complex at the beginning of each quarter. The second measure is the number of fund categories offered by the affiliated family.

Sirri and Tufano (1998) posit that funds affiliated with larger families will receive greater inflows, and that the flow-performance relationship will be stronger for larger complexes. Our results in Table IV reveal a more specific mechanism by which parent complex size affects the flow-performance relationship: Affiliation with a large family makes it easier for funds with moderately good performance to attract new investors, resulting in a higher flow sensitivity to medium performance. This affiliation also leads to a reduction in the sensitivity of flows to superior performance.

Another benefit of being affiliated with a large family is that investors can obtain access to a wide range of products. Accordingly, we use the number of fund types available to measure the breadth of offerings by the family. While this measure may be correlated with family size, it captures the effort by fund families to accommodate investors' desire to diversify within the same family, as well as to target investor heterogeneity and increase

[20] Details of the procedure that mimics the Morningstar ratings system may be found in the appendix of Nanda et al. (2004b). They find that 88% of the five-star funds determined by this mimicking procedure overlap five-star funds from the Morningstar publications for a randomly selected date in May 1995.

TABLE III | The Effect of Affiliation with a Star Family on the Flow-Performance Relationship

This table examines the effect of affiliation with a star-producing family on the sensitivity of flow to past performance. Each quarter, funds are ranked according to their performance during the past 36 months by a procedure that mimics the Morningstar rating system. A dummy variable is assigned one for funds that are affiliated with star families but are not stars themselves, and zero otherwise. A piecewise linear regression is performed by regressing quarterly flows on funds' fractional performance rankings over the low, medium, and high performance ranges, a dummy variable indicating star family affiliation, and their interaction terms. The control variables include a dummy variable indicating funds' own star status, aggregate flow into the fund objective category, volatility of monthly returns during the performance measurement period, the logarithm of one plus fund age and its interaction with performance, the logarithm of lagged fund size, and lagged total fee ratio. Time-series average coefficients and the Fama–MacBeth *t*-statistics (in parentheses) calculated with Newey–West robust standard errors are reported. *, **, and *** denote significance at the 10%, 5%, and 1% level, respectively.

Performance Measured by	Raw Return	Four-Factor Alpha
Intercept	−0.035***	−0.020***
	(−6.58)	(−3.40)
Category Flow	0.567***	0.331***
	(7.99)	(5.32)
Low	0.160***	0.126***
	(11.32)	(9.50)
Low * Star Affiliation	−0.030	0.008
	(−0.82)	(0.09)
Mid	0.113***	0.084***
	(14.61)	(11.86)
Mid * Star Affiliation	0.020***	0.018***
	(3.21)	(3.15)
High	0.242***	0.127***
	(14.74)	(7.70)
High * Star Affiliation	−0.031	−0.012
	(−0.67)	(−0.41)
Star Affiliation	0.006	−0.001
	(0.97)	(−0.06)
Star	0.038***	0.040***
	(15.49)	(14.58)
Volatility	−0.158**	−0.031
	(−2.31)	(−0.41)
Age	−0.002	−0.005***
	(−1.46)	(−4.08)
Age * Performance	−0.022***	−0.013***
	(−10.48)	(−6.16)
Size	−0.000	−0.000
	(−0.07)	(−1.08)
Total Fees	0.030	0.132*
	(0.42)	(1.94)

market share. Elton, Gruber, and Busse (2004) find that, among funds that offer an essentially homogeneous product (an S& P 500 index fund), those that are part of a family that offers a variety of other types of funds attract significantly more cash flows. To examine the effect of this type of reduction in participation costs for investors, we use the number of CDA investment objectives offered by the parent family as our second measure of family

TABLE IV | The Effects of Family Size on the Flow-Performance Relationship

This table examines the effect of family size, as measured by total assets or total number of investment categories under the management of the fund family, on the sensitivity of flow to past performance. Each quarter a piecewise linear regression is performed by regressing quarterly flows on funds' fractional performance rankings over the low, medium, and high performance ranges, a measure of the size of their parent families, and their interaction terms. The control variables include aggregate flow into the fund objective category, volatility of monthly returns during the performance measurement period, the logarithm of one plus fund age and its interaction with performance, the logarithm of lagged fund size, and lagged total fee ratio. Time-series average coefficients and the Fama–MacBeth *t*-statistics (in parentheses) calculated with Newey–West robust standard errors are reported. *, **, and *** denote significance at the 10%, 5%, and 1% level, respectively.

Family Size Proxy	Log [Family Assets]		Diversity Dummy	
Performance Measured by	Raw Return	Four-Factor Alpha	Raw Return	Four-Factor Alpha
Intercept	−0.020**	−0.001	0.002	0.009
	(−2.32)	(−0.07)	(0.24)	(1.27)
Category Flow	0.605***	0.272***	0.667***	0.358***
	(6.76)	(3.35)	(7.79)	(5.09)
Low	0.240***	0.121***	0.161***	0.103***
	(6.23)	(4.27)	(8.76)	(5.78)
Low * Family Size	−0.013*	−0.005	−0.011	−0.017
	(−1.91)	(−0.93)	(−0.43)	(−0.79)
Mid	0.105***	0.056***	0.123***	0.072***
	(9.41)	(5.85)	(14.11)	(10.27)
Mid * Family Size	0.004***	0.004***	0.013**	0.017***
	(3.94)	(3.49)	(2.13)	(3.63)
High	0.394***	0.368***	0.380***	0.265***
	(9.01)	(8.28)	(15.47)	(12.76)
High * Family Size	−0.006	−0.023***	−0.054*	−0.083***
	(−0.85)	(−3.54)	(−1.80)	(−3.69)
Family Size	0.004***	0.002**	0.004	0.004
	(3.33)	(2.63)	(0.96)	(1.12)
Volatility	−0.260***	−0.108	−0.295***	−0.166*
	(−2.97)	(−1.21)	(−3.35)	(−1.93)
Age	−0.009***	−0.011***	−0.010***	−0.011***
	(−5.63)	(−9.06)	(−6.68)	(−8.80)
Age * Performance	−0.025***	−0.006***	−0.023***	−0.007***
	(−10.68)	(−3.07)	(−10.11)	(−3.53)
Size	−0.003***	−0.003***	−0.002***	−0.001***
	(−5.47)	(−4.66)	(−4.30)	(−2.91)
Total Fees	−0.063	0.039	−0.076	0.043
	(−0.74)	(0.56)	(−0.86)	(0.60)

affiliation.[21] Because of the clustering nature of such a measure, we employ a binary dummy that takes the value of one if the measure is above the median among all families, and zero otherwise.

These results are also reported in Table IV. On average, funds in families with diverse offerings see their flow sensitivities to mid-range performance increase by about 10%, from 0.123 to 0.136, when the performance is measured by the rank of returns (or

[21]When constructing this measure, we examine all types of funds managed by a fund family rather than restricting the analysis to the sample of equity funds.

TABLE V | Correlation Matrix among Proxies for Information Costs

This table presents the correlation matrix among proxies for information costs, flow, and performance. "Performance" is measured as the Carhart four-factor alphas during the previous 36 months; "Total Fees" is the expense ratio plus one-seventh front-end loads; "Distribution Expenses" is measured as 12b-1 fees plus one-seventh front-end loads; "Star Affiliation" is a dummy variable that is one if the fund is affiliated with a star-producing family, where a star fund is designated by mimicking the Morningstar classification; "Family Assets" measures the logarithm of total net assets managed by the affiliated family; and "Diversity" is a dummy variable that is one if the number of different fund categories offered by the affiliated family is larger than the medium number for all families, and zero otherwise. The correlations reported are time-series averages of the Pearson correlations calculated each quarter.

	Performance	Flow	Total Fees	Distribution Expenses	Star Affiliation	Family Assets	Diversity
Performance	1.00						
Flow	0.22	1.00					
Total Fees	−0.12	0.00	1.00				
Distribution Expenses	−0.01	−0.01	0.59	1.00			
Star Affiliation	−0.01	0.00	−0.04	0.06	1.00		
Family Assets	0.15	0.05	−0.17	0.17	0.39	1.00	
Diversity	0.03	0.01	0.01	0.21	0.28	0.59	1.00

by about 25%, from 0.072 to 0.089, when the performance is measured on a risk-adjusted basis). The sensitivity of flows to top-tier performance tends to be lower for these funds. This is consistent with the hypothesis that diversity of offerings helps reduce participation costs.

A.4. The Combination of Various Proxies The analysis so far focuses on individual variables that proxy for different aspects of information costs. It is possible that some of these variables may be correlated with each other and hence affect our interpretation of their respective effects. In Table V, we report the time-series averages of the cross-sectional correlation coefficients of these proxies, flow, and performance. The table shows that larger fund families tend to charge lower fees, produce more star funds, and offer a wider range of funds. It is, therefore, useful to examine the joint effect of these variables in a multiproxy regression analysis. The results of this analysis are presented in Table VI, where, due to space limitations, we only report the slope coefficients for different levels of performance, measured by the Carhart four-factor alpha, and their interaction terms with proxies for participation costs.

Column 1 of Table VI reports the results with both marketing expenses and star family affiliation. The patterns that we observe with these variables individually in Tables II and III are preserved. This is not surprising, given the low correlation between these two variables. In particular, the interaction terms between medium performance and these two variables are both very significant, implying that these two variables capture complementary ways of reducing a fund's information barriers to investors, one through spotlighting the fund itself and the other through the spillover effect from the attention paid to a star fund in the same family.

When we add an additional variable, family assets, to column 2 of our regression model, we observe that the variable total fees maintains its own effect as expected. The individual effects of star affiliation and family size are also statistically significant, although their magnitudes are weakened somewhat due to the positive correlation between them. The same pattern persists when we replace the family assets variable with the diversity of offerings variable, as shown in column 3. Because of the relatively high correlation between these two variables, their joint presence in the regression diminishes their statistical significance, as demonstrated in column 4, although both have the correct sign. Overall, these results are consistent with our earlier findings with individual proxies.

TABLE VI | The Joint Effect of Proxies for Information Costs on the Flow-Performance Relationship

This table examines the combined effect of all proxies for lower information costs, as measured by total fee ratio, star family dummy, logarithm of total net assets managed by the affiliated family, and the diversity of its fund offerings dummy. Each quarter a piecewise linear regression is performed by regressing flows on funds' fractional performance rankings over the low, medium, and high performance ranges, proxies of information costs, and their interaction terms. The control variables include aggregate flow into the fund objective category, volatility of performance, the logarithm of one plus fund age and its interaction with performance, the logarithm of lagged fund size, and lagged total fee ratio. To save space, only the time-series average coefficients on performance rankings and their interaction terms with proxies of information costs and their corresponding Fama–MacBeth *t*-statistics (in parentheses) calculated with Newey–West robust standard errors are reported. *, **, and *** denote significance at the 10%, 5%, and 1% level, respectively.

Proxy for Lower Information Costs	(1)	(2)	(3)	(4)
Low	0.135***	0.150***	0.135***	0.138***
	(5.66)	(3.13)	(4.82)	(2.83)
Low * Total Fees	−0.756	−0.859	−0.732	−0.723
	(−0.69)	(−0.75)	(−0.64)	(−0.60)
Low * Star Affiliation	0.048	0.033	0.045	0.020
	(0.41)	(0.30)	(0.37)	(0.19)
Low * Family Assets		0.000		0.001
		(−0.03)		(0.07)
Low * Diversity			0.005	0.011
			(0.22)	(0.43)
Mid	0.059***	0.045***	0.055***	0.047***
	(5.51)	(3.81)	(5.07)	(3.76)
Mid * Total Fees	1.261***	1.259***	1.188***	1.225***
	(3.54)	(3.52)	(3.35)	(3.46)
Mid * Star Affiliation	0.017***	0.013*	0.013**	0.014**
	(2.84)	(1.93)	(2.17)	(2.06)
Mid * Family Assets		0.003**		0.002
		(2.07)		(1.23)
Mid * Diversity			0.011**	0.006
			(2.62)	(1.12)
High	0.197***	0.336***	0.241***	0.300***
	(4.97)	(5.93)	(5.97)	(4.81)
High * Total Fees	−4.883**	−4.840**	−4.001**	−3.860*
	(−2.51)	(−2.49)	(−2.00)	(−1.99)
High * Star Affiliation	0.014	0.051	0.045	0.052
	(0.41)	(1.48)	(1.28)	(1.49)
High * Family Assets		−0.019***		−0.009
		(−2.77)		(−0.91)
High * Diversity			−0.094***	−0.062*
			(−4.41)	(−1.95)

TABLE VII | The Flow-Performance Sensitivity Over Time

This table compares the sensitivity of flow to past performance in the two subperiods: 1981–1989 and 1990–2001. Each quarter a piecewise linear regression is performed by regressing quarterly flows on funds' fractional performance rankings over the low, medium, and high performance ranges, aggregate flow into the fund objective category, volatility of performance, the logarithm of one plus fund age and its interaction with performance, the logarithm of lagged fund size, and lagged total fees. Time-series average coefficients and the Fama–MacBeth *t*-statistics (in parentheses) calculated with Newey–West robust standard errors are reported. The differences of the coefficients on the low, medium, and high performance rankings between the two subperiods and their corresponding F-test statistics are presented in the last column. *, **, and *** denote significance at the 10%, 5%, and 1% level, respectively.

Sub-Period	1981–1989	1990–2001	Difference
Intercept	0.028**	0.018**	
	(2.30)	(2.16)	
Category Flow	0.420**	0.219**	
	(2.40)	(2.53)	
Low	0.037	0.118***	−0.080***
	(1.60)	(8.20)	(8.63)
Mid	0.058***	0.093***	−0.035**
	(4.73)	(12.10)	(5.69)
High	0.220***	0.255***	−0.036
	(5.47)	(11.04)	(0.60)
Volatility	−0.455***	−0.191	
	(−3.67)	(−1.65)	
Age	−0.007***	−0.018***	
	(−3.66)	(−14.11)	
Age * Performance	−0.006	−0.002	
	(−1.64)	(−1.24)	
Size	−0.0005	−0.002***	
	(−0.77)	(−4.63)	
Total Fees	0.055	0.083	
	(0.49)	(0.83)	

B. The Effect of Time-Varying Information Costs

Another way to examine the effect of participation costs is to compare the flow-performance relationship over time. It can be argued that the overall level of participation costs for investors has declined over time, due either to the effort of mutual funds to reduce information barriers in the face of increasing competition by educating investors and raising their own visibility, or to the increasingly easy access to financial information provided by technological advances. Therefore, we should expect a different shape of the flow-performance relationship in the 1980s versus the 1990s. The results of such an analysis, illustrated in Table VII, show that in the 1990s, flows become significantly more sensitive in the low and medium performance ranges than they were in the 1980s, while there is no notable difference in the sensitivity of flows to high performance levels across these two periods. This finding is in accordance with our expectation that fund flows should be more responsive to performance in the medium performance range when the general level of participation costs is lower (as in the 1990s) than when the general cost level is high (as in the 1980s), leading to an overall less convex flow-performance relationship.

This difference across time periods may also explain the discrepancy between our results and those of Sirri and Tufano (1998). Using data from 1971 to 1990, they assert that only the interaction term between marketing expenses and top-tier performance is significantly positive. As we illustrate in the discussion following Figure 1, if both the higher- and lower-cost groups of funds all have high absolute levels of costs (which was likely true in the 1970s), the higher-cost funds will have lower flow sensitivities in the high performance range, resembling the comparison between the dot-dashed and dashed lines in Figure 1. Therefore, the empirical finding of Sirri and Tufano (1998) is in fact consistent with our model prediction. On the other hand, in our sample period, especially in the 1990s, lower-cost funds such as the Fidelity Magellan Fund may have had very low absolute levels of costs. Therefore, our empirical results likely correspond to the comparison between the solid and dot-dashed lines in the figure.

C. The Effect of Transaction Costs

Although the proxies for participation costs that we have discussed so far pertain mainly to information costs for investors, loads and family affiliation are also related to transaction costs. In order to investigate the separate effect of transaction costs on the asymmetry of the flow-performance relationship, in this subsection we examine a subsample of funds that offer multiple share classes.

By construction, different share classes of the same fund are associated with the same underlying portfolio. They only differ in terms of distribution strategies and the means by which investors pay for advice and services. This sample of funds provides an ideal setup for our study because different share classes of the same fund serve as control samples for each other in terms of other fund-level factors that can also affect flows. While Nanda et al. (2004a) consider how the existence of multiple share classes affects the level and volatility of fund flows as well as fund performance, our focus is on the effect of transaction costs on the flow-performance sensitivity.

Among these different share classes, class A shares generally charge a front-end load. Class B shares charge a back-end load that is triggered on redemption and usually decreases by 1% each year. In addition, after 6 to 8 years, B shares can be converted to A shares that carry lower 12b-1 fees. Like B shares, C shares charge a back-end load of 1%, but only for the first year (see Reid and Rea 2003). Therefore, class C shares are considered most attractive by investors who prefer flexibility in switching across different fund families with a relatively short investment horizon.

Class B shares feature a contingent deferred sales load whose impact on investors depends on their investment horizons. Moreover, back-end loads should affect fund flows mostly in the low performance range. Since our main focus is on the response of flows to high performance, we limit our comparison to respective flows into class A and class C shares.[22] When identifying the two share classes, we mainly rely on checking fund names, though we supplement this with information on loads and 12b-1 fees. To create a sample with a perfect control of performance, we include only funds that offer both A and C classes. Since most funds did not introduce multiple share classes until the early 1990s, we focus on the post-1993 period in order to have sufficient observations for each year.

In Table VIII, we include in the flow estimation the interaction terms between a dummy indicating C shares and performance rankings in low, medium, and high ranges. We expect that, compared with flows into A shares, flows into C shares should be more responsive to medium performance because of the lower transaction costs for investors in buying C shares.

[22] In addition to classes A, B, and C, in recent years many funds have also created share classes targeted to specific investor groups, such as institutional share classes and retirement and 529 plan classes. Since investors in these classes may have very different investment objectives, in this study we do not consider these other classes.

TABLE VIII | Comparing the Flow-Performance Sensitivity Between Different Share Classes

This table presents results on the difference in the flow-performance sensitivity between A shares and C shares of the same fund. Each quarter during 1994 to 2001, we identify funds that offer both A and C shares. Among these funds, a piecewise linear regression is performed by regressing quarterly flows on funds' fractional performance rankings over the low, medium, and high performance ranges, a dummy variable indicating C shares, and their interaction terms. The control variables include aggregate flow into the fund objective category, volatility of monthly returns during the performance measurement period, the logarithm of one plus fund age and its interaction with performance, the logarithm of lagged fund size, and lagged total fees. Time-series average coefficients and the Fama–MacBeth *t*-statistics (in parentheses) calculated with Newey–West robust standard errors are reported. *, **, and *** denote significance at the 10%, 5%, and 1% level, respectively.

Performance Measured by	Raw Return	Four-Factor Alpha
Intercept	0.007	0.008
	(0.60)	(0.55)
Category Flow	0.977***	0.337
	(2.93)	(1.62)
Low	0.219***	0.123***
	(6.88)	(3.88)
Low * C Class Dummy	−0.061	0.007
	(−1.22)	(0.12)
Mid	0.186***	0.112***
	(10.06)	(8.92)
Mid * C Class Dummy	0.069***	0.043**
	(4.76)	(2.30)
High	0.419***	0.311***
	(7.84)	(6.51)
High * C Class Dummy	0.081	−0.167*
	(0.70)	(−2.01)
C Class Dummy	0.010	0.004
	(1.12)	(0.37)
Volatility	−0.259	0.081
	(−1.54)	(0.40)
Age	−0.014***	−0.013***
	(−4.28)	(−5.37)
Age * Performance	−0.031***	−0.006
	(−5.69)	(−1.69)
Size	−0.006***	−0.006***
	(−6.21)	(−4.39)
Total Fees	−0.187	−0.011
	(−0.90)	(−0.04)

Indeed, Table VIII shows that the interaction term between the C-share dummy and performance is significantly positive in medium performance ranges. Based on point estimates, the flow sensitivity in the medium performance range varies from 0.186 for A shares to 0.255 for C shares, when performance is measured by the rank of fund returns within respective objective categories. When performance is measured by four-factor adjusted returns, the change is from 0.112 for A shares to 0.155 for C shares. Therefore, the lower transaction costs for C shares lead to an enhanced flow sensitivity to the medium level of performance.

IV. Concluding Remarks

We present a simple rational model that highlights the effect of new investors' participation costs on the flow-performance relationship. Given fund-level participation barriers, more new investors are able to overcome their participation costs to invest in a fund only as its performance improves. Hence, flows are increasingly more sensitive to performance. Moreover, different levels of participation costs across funds affect flows in various performance ranges differently. For example, at medium levels of performance, funds with low participation costs may attract more investors and enjoy a more sensitive flow-performance relationship than their high-cost peers. High-participation-cost funds, on the other hand, have a more sensitive flow response to their performance than their low-cost counterparts in the high performance range. We show that this result is robust even with portfolio constraints that lead investors to exhibit winner-picking behavior. Using fund characteristics as proxies for participation costs, our empirical analysis supports the model predictions.

The results add to our understanding of the behavior of investors when investing in mutual funds and show that the asymmetric response of fund flows to past performance is consistent with individual optimization. Our findings also have important implications for the literature regarding fund managers' risk-taking incentives, because, given mutual funds' compensation structure, the asymmetric sensitivity of flows to performance yields an implicit call-option-like payoff for fund managers.[23] Our paper suggests a new vantage point for examining this issue by highlighting the effect of participation costs on the flow-performance relationship.

Appendix A: Proofs

Proof of Lemmas 1 and 4 Let $\mathcal{P}$ be the set of funds that an investor chooses to participate in and X_{i0} be his initial holdings. The investor maximizes the following utility function at time $t = 1$:

$$J_{\mathcal{P}} \equiv \max_{\{X_{i1}\geq 0,\, i\in\mathcal{P}\}} \mathrm{E}[-e^{-\gamma W_2}] \tag{A1}$$

$$\text{s.t.} \quad W_2(X_{i0}, X_{i1}) = W_1 + \sum_{i\in\mathcal{P}} [X_{i1}r_{i2} - (X_{i1} - (1 + r_{i1})X_{i0})\rho_i(X_{i1})],$$

where

$$r_{i2} = \alpha_{i1} + \epsilon_{i2}, \quad \rho_i(X_{i1}) = \begin{cases} \rho_+, & \text{if } X_{i1} > (1 + r_{i1})X_{i0}; \\ 0, & \text{if } X_{i1} = (1 + r_{i1})X_{i0}; \\ -\rho_-, & \text{if } X_{i1} < (1 + r_{i1})X_{i0}. \end{cases}$$

Solving the first-order conditions yields the optimal holding X_{i1} in fund i:

$$X_{i1}(r_{i1}) = \begin{cases} X_{i1,+}(r_{i1}) \equiv \dfrac{\alpha_{i1}(r_{i1}) - \rho_+}{\gamma(\sigma_1^2 + \sigma_\epsilon^2)}, & \text{if } X_{i1} > (1 + r_{i1})X_{i0}; \\ (1 + r_{i1})X_{i0}, & \text{if } X_{i1} = (1 + r_{i1})X_{i0}; \\ X_{i1,-}(r_{i1}) \equiv \dfrac{\alpha_{i1}(r_{i1}) + \rho_-}{\gamma(\sigma_1^2 + \sigma_\epsilon^2)}, & \text{if } X_{i1} < (1 + r_{i1})X_{i0}. \end{cases}$$

[23] The theoretical papers on managers' incentives include Carpenter (2000), Dybvig, Farnsworth, and Carpenter (2003), Grinblatt and Titman (1989), Ross (2004), and Starks (1987). The empirical literature includes Brown, Harlow, and Starks (1996), Busse (2001), Chen and Pennacchi (2002), Chevalier and Ellison (1997), Del Guercio and Tkac (2002a), and Golec and Starks (2004).

Let $\bar{r}_{i+}$, $\bar{r}_{i-}$, and $\underline{r}_i$ solve the boundary conditions

$$\begin{cases} X_{i1,+}(\bar{r}_{i+}) = (1 + \bar{r}_{i+})X_{i0}, \\ X_{i1,-}(\bar{r}_{i-}) = (1 + \bar{r}_{i-})X_{i0}, \\ X_{i1,-}(\underline{r}_i) = 0. \end{cases}$$

The first two boundary conditions separate the purchasing, no trade, and redemption regions in the return space. The last condition is the short-selling constraint. Plugging in the definitions of $\alpha_{i1}(r_{i1})$ and σ_1 from equation (5), we can derive the optimal holding in Lemma 4 with the following bounds that separate all the cases:

$$\begin{aligned} \bar{r}_{i+} &\equiv \frac{\rho_+(\sigma_0^2 + \sigma_\epsilon^2)}{\sigma_0^2 - \gamma X_{i0}\sigma_\epsilon^2(2\sigma_0^2 + \sigma_\epsilon^2)} - \frac{\sigma_\epsilon^2(\alpha_{i0} - \gamma X_{i0}(2\sigma_0^2 + \sigma_\epsilon^2))}{\sigma_0^2 - \gamma X_{i0}\sigma_\epsilon^2(2\sigma_0^2 + \sigma_\epsilon^2)}, \\ \bar{r}_{i-} &\equiv -\frac{\rho_-(\sigma_0^2 + \sigma_\epsilon^2)}{\sigma_0^2 - \gamma X_{i0}\sigma_\epsilon^2(2\sigma_0^2 + \sigma_\epsilon^2)} - \frac{\sigma_\epsilon^2(\alpha_{i0} - \gamma X_{i0}(2\sigma_0^2 + \sigma_\epsilon^2))}{\sigma_0^2 - \gamma X_{i0}\sigma_\epsilon^2(2\sigma_0^2 + \sigma_\epsilon^2)}, \\ \underline{r}_i &\equiv -\frac{\rho_-(\sigma_0^2 + \sigma_\epsilon^2)}{\sigma_0^2} - \frac{\alpha_{i0}\sigma_\epsilon^2}{\sigma_0^2}. \end{aligned}$$

Since a new investor in a fund has an initial holding of $X_{i0} = 0$, and his information set is identical to that of an existing investor, the optimal holding for a new investor is a simple application of the general result. This concludes the proof for Lemma 4.

Lemma 1 is a special case of Lemma 4 in which $\rho_+ = \rho_- = 0$. In particular, the top three cases collapse to one case since $\bar{r}_{i+} = \bar{r}_{i-}$, $X_{i1,+} = X_{i1,-}$. The condition for the short-selling constraint reduces to $\underline{r}_i = -\frac{\alpha_{i0}\sigma_0^2}{\sigma_0^2}$. Q.E.D.

Proof of Lemma 2 We solve for the optimal participation in two steps: (i) We start with no participation in any fund and consider the sequential participation decision one fund at a time, and (ii) we show that the participation decision for each fund is independent of the rest of the funds and hence the sequential solution is equivalent to the optimal solution.

Let $\mathcal{P}$ be the set of all funds that the investor has chosen to participate in, and $J_\mathcal{P}$ be the value function in equation (A1). Consider the decision to participate in a new fund $j \not\in \mathcal{P}$. If the investor chooses to pay the cost c_{kj} to learn the posterior ability α_{j1}, his value function conditional on α_{j1} can be written as

$$\begin{aligned} J_{\mathcal{P}\cup\{j\}}|_{\alpha j1} &= \max_{\{X_{i1}\ge 0, i\in\mathcal{P}\cup\{j\}\}} \mathrm{E}[-e^{-\gamma W_2}|_{\alpha j1}] \\ &\equiv \left(\max_{\{X_{i1}\ge 0, i\in\mathcal{P}\}} \mathrm{E}[-e^{-\gamma W_2}]\right) \times \left(\max_{X_{j1}\ge 0} \mathrm{E}[e^{-\gamma[-c_{kj} + X_{j1}r_{j2}]}|_{\alpha j1}]\right) \\ &= J_\mathcal{P} \times e^{-\gamma(\hat{g}(\alpha_{j1}) - c_{kj})}, \end{aligned}$$

where $\hat{g}(\alpha_{j1})$ is the certainty-equivalent wealth gain for investing in fund j,

$$\hat{g}(\alpha_{j1}) = \begin{cases} \dfrac{\alpha_{j1}^2}{2\gamma(\sigma_1^2 + \sigma_\epsilon^2)}, & \text{if } \alpha_{j1} > 0 \\ 0, & \text{otherwise.} \end{cases} \tag{A2}$$

Substituting in the definition of α_{j1} and σ_1 from equation (5) and integrating over the prior regarding the distribution of α_{j0}, we obtain the expected utility

$$J_{\mathcal{P}\cup\{j\}} = J_\mathcal{P} \times e^{-\gamma(g(r_{j1}) - c_{kj})},$$

where $g(\cdot)$ is defined in equation (8). Investors choose to participate in fund j if and only if $J_{\mathcal{P}\cup\{j\}} > J_{\mathcal{P}}$, which is achieved if and only if $g(r_{j1}) > c_{kj}$ (since $J_{\mathcal{P}} < 0$). Clearly, the participation decision for fund j is independent of all other funds, completing the proof. Q.E.D.

Proof of Proposition 1 The proposition follows directly from Lemmas 1 and 2 and the definition of fund flows. Corollary 1 shows that all new investors with $c_{ki} < g(r_{i1})$ choose to participate. Hence the fraction of new investors who participate is simply min $[1, \frac{g(r_{i1})}{e}]$. Q.E.D.

Proof of Lemma 3 If an investor participates in only one fund with posterior ability α_{i1}, then the certainty-equivalent gain from investing in the fund is given by (A2). Since $\hat{g}(\alpha_{i1})$ increases in α_{i1}, investors optimally invest in the fund with the highest α_{i1} within his information set.

Assume that the investor has investigated some funds and the best fund has a posterior ability level $\hat{\alpha}_1$. If he decides to stop investigating, he can invest in this fund and obtain certainty-equivalent wealth gain $\hat{g}(\hat{\alpha}_1)$. If he chooses to investigate another fund with past return r_{i1}, then his certainty-equivalent wealth gain, conditional on his updated information α_{i1}, can be expressed as

$$G^p(\alpha_{i1}, \hat{\alpha}_1) = \begin{cases} \hat{g}(\alpha_{i1}), & \text{if } \alpha_{i1} > \hat{\alpha}_1 \\ \hat{g}(\alpha_1), & \text{otherwise.} \end{cases}$$

Therefore, the expected wealth gain from paying the cost c_{ki} can be calculated by integrating $G^p(\alpha_{i1}, \hat{\alpha}_1)$ over the distribution of α_{i0}:

$$\begin{aligned} G(r_{i1}, \hat{\alpha}_1) &= \int_{\{\alpha_{i0}\}} G^p(\alpha_{i1}(\alpha_{i0}), \hat{\alpha}_1) f(\alpha_{i0})\, d\alpha_{i0} \\ &= \int_{\{\alpha_{i1}(\alpha_{i0}) > \max\{0, \hat{\alpha}_1\}\}} \frac{\alpha_{i1}^2(\alpha_{i0})}{2\gamma(\sigma_1^2 + \sigma_\epsilon^2)} f(\alpha_{i0}) d\alpha_{i0} \\ &\quad + \int_{\{\alpha_{i1}(\alpha_{i0}) \leq \hat{\alpha}_1, \hat{\alpha}_1 > 0\}} \frac{\hat{\alpha}_1^2}{2\gamma(\sigma_1^2 + \sigma_\epsilon^2)} f(\alpha_{i0}) d\alpha_{i0}, \end{aligned}$$

where α_{i1} and σ_1 are defined in equation (5). Simplifying the expression for $G(r_{i1,}\hat{\alpha}_1)$ yields the results in Lemma 3.

Appendix B: The Simulation Procedure

The following is the simulation procedure to derive fund flows when each investor has access to a random subset of n funds. For simplicity, we assume that all the N funds in the universe have identical maximum cost level $\bar{c}_i = \bar{c}$.

Step 1: For N funds, simulate (i) prior ability level, $\alpha_{i0} \sim N(\mu, \sigma_\mu^2)$, and (ii) true ability level, $\alpha_i \sim N(\alpha_{i0}, \sigma_0^2)$.

Step 2: Simulate the past return through $r_{i1} = \sigma_i^2 + \epsilon_{i1}$ for each fund i and then rank all the funds by their past returns. Index the rank by $i = 1, \ldots, N$; that is, fund 1 has the highest past return, and fund N the lowest. Let F_i be the dollar flow of new investors to fund i and initialize it to zero.

Step 3: Apply equation (5) to calculate the posterior ability level of all funds, α_{i1}.

Step 4: Randomly select a subset of n funds out of the total N funds. Let $s_1 < s_2 < \ldots < s_n$ be the overall index of these n funds (which correspond to their return ranks in Step 2). Then fund s_1 has the highest past return among the n funds in the subset, and investors optimally follow the sequence of $s_1, \ldots, s_n$ in choosing funds to investigate. Use set $\mathcal{S} = \{s_1, \ldots, s_n\}$ to denote this subset of funds.

Step 5: Assume there is a continuum of investors (with total population mass normalized to one), with different individual costs $\delta_k \in \text{Unif}[0, 1]$, who observe the same subset of funds. Calculate the fraction β_{s_j} of those investors who choose to invest in fund $s_j, j = 1, \ldots, n$.

- Step 5a: Initialize $\beta_{s_j} = 0$ for all, j. Let α_{s_j1} be the posterior ability of fund $s_j, j = 1, \ldots, n$ calculated in Step 3.
- Step 5b: Let m_j be the index of the fund with the maximum posterior ability among funds $\{s_1, \ldots, s_j\}$. That is, $m_j = m_{j-1}$ if $\alpha_{m_{j-1}1} > \alpha_{s_j1}$ and $m_j = s_j$ otherwise. Clearly, $m_1 = s_1$. We also set $m_0 = 0$, since $G(r_{i1}, 0) = g(r_{i1})$, that is, for an investor who has not studied any fund, the utility gain from studying a new fund is the same as that for an investor whose best fund has ability $\hat{\alpha}_1 = 0$. Thus, investors who have investigated j funds within the subset would optimally invest in fund m_j. Moreover, only funds with $m_j = s_j$ could potentially receive inflows.
- Step 5c: Find the largest $s_j \in \mathcal{S}$ such that $m_j = s_j$. This is the best fund within the set $\mathcal{S}$. Use index $j^* = j$ to denote the j-index of this fund. Since m_{j^*-1} is the best fund for any investor who has not investigated fund m_{j^*}, an investor would optimally choose to investigate fund m_{j^*} if and only if his cost is lower than the expected utility gain, or $\delta_k \bar{c} < G(r_{m_{j^*}}, \alpha_{m_{j^*-1}1})$ (where $G(\cdot)$ is defined in Lemma 3. Once having investigated this fund, investors would only invest in funds $s_j \geq m_{j^*}$ since m_{j^*} is better than any fund $s_j < m_{j^*}$. Given the uniform distribution of δ_k, we can update the fraction of investors who invest in fund m_{j^*} as follows:

  $$\beta_{m_{j^*}} = \frac{\min\{G(r_{m_{j^*}}, \alpha_{m_{j^*-1}1}), \bar{c}\}}{\bar{c}} - \left(\sum_{j=j^*+1}^{n} \beta_{s_j}\right).$$

  The second term in the expression represents the fraction of investors investing in funds better than j^*.
- Step 5d: If $j^* = 1$, go to Step 6. Otherwise, reset $\mathcal{S} = \{s_1, \ldots, s_{j^*-1}\}$ and repeat Step 5c.

Step 6: Update the fund flows from new investors:

$$F_{s_j} = F_{s_j} + \beta_{s_j} X^n_{s_j1}, \quad j = 1, \ldots, n,$$

where $X^n_{s_j1}$ is defined in equation (7) for fund s_j as a function of α_{s_j0} and r_{s_j1}.

Step 7: Repeat Steps 4–6 for desired number of simulations, say 1,000 times, to yield realistic flows for a given fund return realization.

Step 8: Repeat Steps 2–7 for desired number of simulations, say 100 times, to yield flow-performance rank relationship for different return realizations. Average fund flows for the same performance rank over different simulations.

References

Barber, Brad M., Terrance Odean, and Lu Zheng, 2005, Out of sight, out of mind: The effects of expenses on mutual fund flows, *Journal of Business* 78, 2095–2120.

Berk, J. B., and Richard C. Green, 2004, Mutual fund flows and performance in rational markets, *Journal of Political Economy* 112, 1269–1295.

Brown, Keith C., W. V. Harlow, and Laura T. Starks, 1996, Of tournaments and temptations: An analysis of managerial incentives in the mutual fund industry, *Journal of Finance* 51, 85–110.

Busse, Jeffrey A., 2001, Another look at mutual fund tournaments, *Journal of Financial and Quantitative Analysis* 36, 53–73.

Capon, Noel, Gavan J. Fitzsimons, and Russ A. Prince, 1996, An individual level analysis of the mutual fund investment decisions, *Journal of Financial Services Research* 10, 59–82.

Carhart, Mark M., 1997, On persistence in mutual fund performance, *Journal of Finance* 52, 57–82.

Carpenter, Jennifer N., 2000, Does option compensation increase managerial risk appetite? *Journal of Finance* 55, 2311–2331.

Chen, Hsiu-lang, and George G. Pennacchi, 2002, Does prior performance affect a mutual fund's choice of risk? Theory and further empirical evidence, Working paper, University of Illinois at Urbana-Champaign.

Chevalier, Judith A., and Glenn Ellison, 1997, Risk taking by mutual funds as a response to incentives, *Journal of Political Economy* 105, 1167–1200.

Del Guercio, Diane, and Paula A. Tkac, 2002a, The determinants of the flow of funds of managed portfolios: Mutual funds vs. pension funds, *Journal of Financial and Quantitative Analysis* 37, 523–557.

Del Guercio, Diane, and Paula A. Tkac, 2002b, Star power: The effect of Morningstar ratings on mutual fund flows, Working paper, University of Oregon.

Dybvig, Philip H., Heber K. Farnsworth, and Jennifer N. Carpenter, 2003, Portfolio performance and agency, Working paper, New York University.

Elton, Edwin J., Martin J. Gruber, and Christopher R. Blake, 2001, A first look at the accuracy of CRSP mutual fund database and a comparison of the CRSP and Morningstar mutual fund database, *Journal of Finance* 56, 2415–2430.

Elton, Edwin J., Martin J. Gruber, and Jeffrey A. Busse, 2004, Are investors rational? Choices among index funds, *Journal of Finance* 59, 261–288.

Fama, Eugene F., and Kenneth R. French, 1993, Common risk factors in the returns on stocks and bonds, *Journal of Financial Economics* 33, 3–56.

Fama, Eugene F., and James D. MacBeth, 1973, Risk, return and equilibrium: Empirical tests, *Journal of Political Economy* 81, 607–636.

Gallaher, Steven, Ron Kaniel, and Laura T. Starks, 2005, Madison Avenue meets Wall Street: Mutual fund families, competition and advertising, Working paper, University of Texas at Austin.

Goetzmann, William N., and Nadav Peles, 1997, Cognitive dissonance and mutual fund investors, *Journal of Financial Research* 20, 145–158.

Golec, Joseph, and Laura T. Starks, 2004, Performance fee contract change and mutual fund risk, *Journal of Financial Economics* 73, 93–118.

Grinblatt, Mark, and Sheridan Titman, 1989, Adverse risk incentives and the design of performance-based contracts, *Management Science* 35, 807–822.

Gruber, Martin J., 1996, Another puzzle: The growth in actively managed mutual funds, *Journal of Finance* 51, 783–810.

Hortaçsu, Ali, and Chad Syverson, 2004, Product differentiation, search costs, and competition in the mutual fund industry: A case study of S&P 500 index funds, *Quarterly Journal of Economics* 119, 403–456.

Huang, Jennifer, Kelsey D. Wei, and Hong Yan, 2004, Volatility of performance and mutual fund flows, Working paper, University of Texas at Austin.

Ippolito, Richard A., 1992, Consumer reaction to measures of poor quality: Evidence from the mutual fund industry, *Journal of Law and Economics* 35, 45–70.

Jain, Prem C., and Joanna S. Wu, 2000, Truth in mutual fund advertising: Evidence on future performance and fund flows, *Journal of Finance* 55, 937–958.

Khorana, Ajay, and Henri Servaes, 2004, Conflicts of interest and competition in the mutual fund industry, Working paper, London Business School.

Lynch, Anthony W., and David K. Musto, 2003, How investors interpret past fund returns, *Journal of Finance* 58, 2033–2058.

Massa, Massimo, 2003, How do family strategies affect fund performance? When performance-maximization is not the only game in town, *Journal of Financial Economics* 67, 249–304.

Nanda, Vikram, Zhi Wang, and Lu Zheng, 2004a, The ABCs of mutual funds: On the introduction of multiple share classes. Working paper, University of Michigan.

Nanda, Vikram, Zhi Wang, and Lu Zheng, 2004b, Family values and the star phenomenon: *Review of Financial Studies* 17, 667–698.

Newey, Whitney K., and Kenneth D. West, 1987, A simple, positive semi-definite heteroskedasticity and autocorrelation consistent covariance matrix, *Econometrica* 55, 703–708.

Reid, Brian K., and John D. Rea, 2003, Mutual fund distribution channels and distribution costs, *Perspectives* 9, Investment Company Institute.

Ross, Stephen A., 2004, Compensation, incentives, and the duality of risk aversion and riskiness, *Journal of Finance* 59, 207–225.

Sharpe, William, 1997, Morningstar's performance measures, Working paper, Stanford University.

Sirri, Erik R., and Peter Tufano, 1998, Costly search and mutual fund flows, *Journal of Finance* 53, 1589–1622.

Starks, Laura T., 1987, Performance incentive fees: An agency theoretic approach, *Journal of Financial and Quantitative Analysis* 22, 17–32.